Prelude to Berlin: The Red Army's Offensive Operations in Poland and Eastern Germany 1945 offers a panoramic view of the Soviet strategic offensives north of the Carpathians in the winter of 1945. During the course of this offensive the Red Army broke through the German defences in Poland and East Prussia and eventually occupied all of Germany east of the Oder River.

The book consists primarily of articles that appeared in various military journals during the first decade after the war. The General Staff's directorate charged with studying the war experience published these studies, although there are other sources as well. A particular highlight of these is a personal memoir that offers a rare insight into Soviet strategic planning for the winter–spring 1945 campaign. Also featured are documents relating to the operational-strategic conduct of the various operations, which were compiled and published after the fall of the Soviet Union.

The book is divided into several parts, corresponding to the operations conducted. These include the Vistula–Oder operation by the First Belorussian and First Ukrainian Fronts out of their respective Vistula bridgeheads. This gigantic operation, involving over a million men and several thousand tanks, artillery and other weapons sliced through the German defences and, in a single leap, advanced the front to the Oder River, less than 100 kilometres from Berlin, from which they launched their final assault on the Reich in April. Equally impressive was the Second and Third Belorussian Fronts' offensive into Germany's East Prussian citadel. This operation helped to clear the flank to the north and exacted a long-awaited revenge for the Russian Army's defeat here in 1914. This effort cut off the German forces in East Prussia and concluded with an effort to clear the flanks in Pomerania and the storming of the East Prussian capital of Königsberg in April. The study also examines in considerable detail the First Ukrainian Front's Upper and Lower Silesian operations of February–March 1945. These operations cleared the army's flanks in the south and deprived Germany of one of its last major industrial and agricultural areas.

Richard W. Harrison earned his undergraduate and master's degrees from Georgetown University, where he specialized in Russian area studies. In 1994 he earned his doctorate in War Studies from King's College London. He also was an exchange student in the former Soviet Union and spent several years living and working in post-communist Russia.

Dr. Harrison has worked for the US Department of Defense as an investigator in Russia, dealing with cases involving POWs and MIAs. He has also taught Russian history and military history at college and university level, most recently at the US Military Academy at West Point.

Harrison is the author of two books dealing with the Red Army's theoretical development during the interwar period: *The Russian Way of War: Operational Art, 1904–1940* (2001), and *Architect of Soviet Victory in World War II: The Life and Theories of G.S. Isserson* (2010). He has also authored a number of articles on topics in Soviet military history. He is currently working on a history of the Red Army's high commands during World War II and afterwards.

Dr. Harrison currently lives with his family near Carlisle, Pennsylvania.

PRELUDE TO BERLIN

THE RED ARMY'S OFFENSIVE OPERATIONS IN POLAND AND EASTERN GERMANY, 1945

PRELUDE TO BERLIN

The Red Army's Offensive Operations in Poland and Eastern Germany, 1945

Soviet General Staff

Edited and translated by Richard W. Harrison

Helion & Company

Published in cooperation with the Association of the United States Army

Helion & Company Limited
26 Willow Road
Solihull
West Midlands
B91 1UE
England
Tel. 0121 705 3393
Fax 0121 711 4075
Email: info@helion.co.uk
Website: www.helion.co.uk
Twitter: @helionbooks
Visit our blog http://blog.helion.co.uk/

Published by Helion & Company 2016, in cooperation with the Association of the United
States Army

Designed and typeset by Mach 3 Solutions Ltd, Bussage, Gloucestershire
Cover designed by Paul Hewitt, Battlefield Design (www.battlefield-design.co.uk)
Printed by Lightning Source Limited, Milton Keynes, Buckinghamshire

Text and maps © Association of the United States Army. English edition translated and
edited by Richard W. Harrison. Maps drawn by David Rennie.

ISBN 978-1-910777-16-9

British Library Cataloguing-in-Publication Data.
A catalogue record for this book is available from the British Library.

For details of other military history titles published by Helion & Company Limited contact
the above address, or visit our website: http://www.helion.co.uk.

We always welcome receiving book proposals from prospective authors.

Contents

List of Maps

List of Tables

Preface to the English-language edition

Unlike other works in this series, which contain translations of a single major work, this study is a composite one, consisting of seven parts, each drawn from a different source. Given the large scope of the operations depicted here, it would have admittedly been more helpful to present separate, full-scale studies of the Vistula-Oder and East Prussian offensive operations, as well as the operations in upper and lower Silesia, as separate works. Unfortunately, such studies, and they must surely exist, have not yet been released for public consumption, leaving us with the expedient at hand.

The first part of this book, "How the Last Campaign for Defeating Hitler's Germany was Planned," is from a 1965 article in the *Voenno-Istoricheskii Zhurnal* by Colonel General Sergei Matveevich Shtemenko, a wartime deputy chief of the General Staff. This article provides an illuminating insight into the strategic planning for the 1945 campaign and lays out in intriguing detail how the Red Army arrived at its strategic objectives. The second part is taken from an internal work entitled *The Vistula-Oder Operation. The Defeat of the German-Fascist forces in Poland by Soviet Forces in January 1945*, by Colonel A.D. Bagreev, and issued by the Voroshilov General Staff Academy in 1957.

The third part is drawn from a detailed study of the East Prussian operation, conducted by the Second and Third Belorussian front which appeared in the *Sbornik Materialov po Izucheniyu Opyta Voiny* (No. 24), in 1947. The fourth section is a study of the East Pomeranian operation of February-March 1945, involving the First and Second Belorussian fronts in clearing the right flank of the Soviet offensive in Poland and eastern Germany. This material appeared in the *Sbornik Materialov* (No. 1), in 1949.

The fifth section covers the Lower Silesian offensive operation of February 1945, which represented a continuation of the First Ukrainian Front's Vistula-Oder operation along its southern flank. The study appeared in the *Sbornik Voenno-Istoricheskikh Materialov Velikoi Otechestvennoi Voiny* (nos. 10-11), in 1953. The sixth section covers the Upper Silesian offensive operation of March 1945, which was the First Ukrainian Front's final offensive effort before the start of the offensive on Berlin. This work appeared in the *Sbornik Voenno-Istoricheskikh Materialov Velikoi Otechestvennoi Voiny* (No. 8), in 1952.

The seventh part is drawn from two sources taken from a post-Soviet publication: *Velikaya Otechestvennaya Voina*, a multi-volume compilation of documents from that period. This section includes numerous documents generated by the *Stavka* of the Supreme High Command and the General Staff during 1944-45.

The book contains a number of terms that may not be readily understandable to the casual reader in military history. Therefore, I have adopted a number of conventions designed to ease this task. For example, a *front* is a Soviet wartime military organization roughly corresponding to an American army group. Throughout the narrative the reader will encounter such names as the First Belorussian Front, the Second Belorussian Front, and the First Ukrainian Front, etc. To avoid confusion with the more commonly understood meaning of the term front (i.e., the front line); italics will be used to denote an unnamed *front*. Similar German formations (i.e., Army Group Center) are also spelled out in full.

I have chosen to designate Soviet armies using the shortened form (i.e., 6th Army). Axis armies, on the other hand, are spelled out in full (i.e., Seventeenth Army). In the same vein, Soviet corps are designated by Arabic numerals (5th Guards Corps), while German and Axis corps are denoted by Roman numerals (e.g., XXVI Corps). Smaller units (divisions, brigades, etc.) on both sides are denoted by Arabic numerals only (124th Rifle Division, 61st Infantry Division, etc.).

Given the large number of units involved in the operation, I have adopted certain other conventions in order to better distinguish them. For example, Soviet armored units are called tank corps, brigades, etc., while the corresponding Axis units are denoted by the popular term *panzer*. Likewise, Soviet infantry units are designated by the term rifle or motorized rifle, while the corresponding Axis units are simply referred to as infantry or panzergrenadier.

The work subscribes to no particular transliteration scheme, because no entirely satisfactory one exists. I have adopted a mixed system that uses the Latin letters ya and yu to denote their Cyrillic counterparts, as opposed to the ia and iu employed by the Library of Congress, which tends to distort proper pronunciation. Conversely, I have retained the Library of Congress's ii ending (i.e., Rokossovskii), as opposed to the commonly-used y ending. I have also retained the apostrophe to denote the Cyrillic soft sign.

The original work contains a number of footnotes inserted by the authors, in order to explain this or that technical question. These have been retained as footnotes and have been supplemented by a number of appropriately identified editorial notes, which have been inserted as an explanatory guide to a number of terms that might not be readily understandable to the foreign reader.

Given the numerous territorial changes that have transpired in this area since the end of the first World War and the renaming of a number of cities and towns in the territories east of the Oder and Neisse rivers, I have chosen to use the spelling of this or that place name as was the case before 1945, when these areas were transferred to the Soviet Union and Poland. For example, the present-day Polish city of Wroclaw will be designated by its prewar German name of Breslau. On the other hand, the pre-First World War German city of Posen is referred to here by its Polish interwar and postwar name of Poznan. Rivers present a particular problem which I sought to resolve by referring to, for example, the Warthe River, where it flows in Germany and the Warta River when it is located in Poland.

Spelling represents a particular problem, particularly regarding Polish place names. For example, I adhered throughout to the Anglicized spelling of Warsaw, instead of the Polish Warszawa, which might only serve to mislead the casual reader. On the other hand, I adhered to the Polish spelling of Krakow, instead of the Cracow commonly found in the English-speaking world.

The studies also present other problems for the translator in this regard. A number of the smaller towns and villages may have disappeared since the events described here, or they may have been renamed in a way making it impossible to trace them. Despite my best efforts, I was not always able to find those smaller locales mentioned in the text. I apologize beforehand for any mistakes committed here.

Elsewhere, I have taken some small liberties as regards the book's overall organization, although there is nothing here that deviates in a major way from the original works. These liberties primarily involve leaving out some maps, copies of orders and tables, the inclusion of which would have made the final product too long. On the other hand, I do not take issue with some of the claims made in the text, and any errors or interpretations should be disputed after examining the relevant documents in the military archives. Neither have I attempted to make the language more "literary," and have striven throughout to preserve the military-bureaucratic flavor of the original.

Part I

How the Last Campaign for Defeating Hitler's Germany Was Planned

Colonel General S.M. Shtemenko[1]

---

1   Sergei Matveevich Shtemenko (1907-76) joined the Red Army in 1926. Editor's note. During the Great Patriotic War he served in the General Staff apparatus as a deputy chief and later chief of the General Staff's operational directorate, while also serving as a *Stavka* representative with various *fronts*. Following the war, Shtemenko served as chief of the General Staff and chief of staff of the Warsaw Pact forces.

1

How the Last Campaign for Defeating Hitler's Germany Was Planned

Despite the fact that 20 years have passed since the end of the Great Patriotic War, the work of the General Staff has almost never been illuminated in our military-historical literature. Nevertheless, the General Staff, being the *Stavka's*[1] working organ, carried out important and complex functions, connected with the planning and control of the armed struggle. On the basis of existing documents and personal reminiscences, I would like to relate in this article how the planning of operations was carried out in the General Staff at the concluding stage of the war, and how these problems were resolved in the *Stavka*.

The first thing we should examine is the General Staff's evaluation of the situation that had arisen by the fall of 1944, and the planning of the initial operations of the 1945 campaign.

The work in planning the concluding stage of the armed struggle on the Soviet-German front began as early as the summer-fall campaign of 1944. The evaluation of the strategic situation and the conclusions drawn from it did not arise immediately in the General Staff and *Stavka*, nor as the result of some kind of single act; but rather gradually developed in the process of ongoing work, as part of the study of the totality of facts and foreseeing the development of combat activities along the various *fronts*.

The results of the Soviet army's unprecedented offensive along all the directions, without exception, were more than promising. As is known, during the offensive in the summer and fall of 1944 the Soviet army destroyed or captured 96 divisions and 24 brigades and defeated 219 divisions and 22 brigades. Overall, the enemy lost 1,600,000 men, 6,700 tanks, 28,000 guns and mortars, and 12,000 aircraft. Fascist Germany was no longer capable of restoring these losses. Also great was the force of the morale loss the enemy suffered.

At the end of October 1944 Soviet troops stood along the border with Finland and were successfully attacking in northern Norway and had cleared out the Baltic States, except for the Sorve Peninsula and Courland, where they had isolated 34 enemy divisions, and had broken into East Prussia along the line Goldap—Augustow. To the south of East Prussia the Narew and Vistula rivers had been forced along a number of sectors and important bridgeheads had been seized in the areas of Rozan, Serock, Magnuszew, Pulawy, and Sandomierz. The troops were aimed along the Berlin strategic direction. Major achievements had been accomplished in eastern Hungary, where the Second Ukrainian Front was approaching Budapest. In the Third Ukrainian Front's zone, the capital of Yugoslavia, Belgrade, was liberated on 2 October.

---

1   Editor's note. The *Stavka* of the Supreme Commander-in-Chief (*Stavka Verkhovnogo Glavnokomanduyush-chego*) was the highest Soviet military body during the Second World War. It was formed on 23 June 1941.

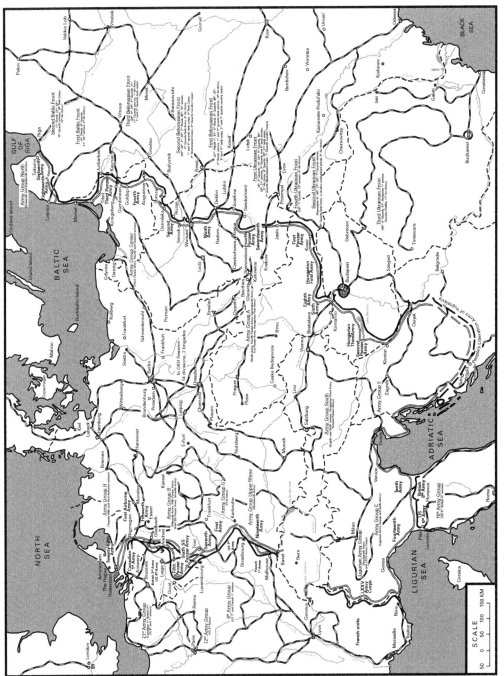

Map 1 Overall Situation by the Start of the 1945 Campaign in Europe.

These successes had been achieved by the Soviet armed forces under the leadership of the Communist Party. The commanders, raised by the party and relying on their staffs and political organs, were leading their troops from victory to victory.

Our victories, however, had not been won easily. Our divisions had been reduced in strength. The advance of the Soviet forces, which had been attacking for several months, without operational pauses, had declined noticeably. The Hitlerites, by moving forces from some sectors of the front in Western Europe, as well as by employing their reserves, had managed to carry out a maneuver with a portion of their forces to the east and here create a continuous and firm front, the breakthrough of which would require serious preparation.

In evaluating the situation, the General Staff understood the complexity of subsequently developing the success achieved. The conditions and prospects for an offensive were not the same everywhere. The enemy's defense in Courland was distinguished by its particular firmness. To break through and completely rout the troops entrenched there might cost us very dearly.

The situation in East Prussia seemed more favorable. There the forces of the Third Belorussian Front enjoyed a certain superiority in forces.[2] On this basis, in the latter third of October 1944 the General Staff considered it possible, given a certain reinforcement of the *front* with forces from the High Command Reserve, to launch a powerful blow throughout all of East Prussia to the mouth of the Vistula to a depth of 220-250 kilometers. However, a further analysis of the situation revealed the necessity of limiting ourselves, at least at first, to more modest tasks.

As regards the Warsaw, Poznan, Lodz, and Kalisz axes, as well as Silesia, where the fate of Berlin would essentially be decided, particularly powerful resistance was expected, which, as we then calculated, would not allow us to carry out offensive operations by the First Belorussian and First Ukrainian fronts to a depth of more than 140-150 kilometers, even given a maximum exertion of force.

On the other hand, the General Staff, based chiefly on political considerations, was counting on significant success along the Fourth, Second and Third Ukrainian fronts' sectors. We could foresee the possibility of a headlong leap to the Moravska Ostrava—Brno line, to the approaches to Vienna, the capture of Budapest, and the forcing of the Danube River. A significant part of the enemy's infantry here consisted of Hungarian divisions, the reliability of which, according to our assumptions, could be radically undermined by the growing antiwar attitudes and the fascists' atrocities in connection with their efforts to keep Hungary allied to Hitler's Reich. The fall of the Salaszi[3] regime would lead to Hungary's leaving the war and put the German forces in a difficult situation. Unfortunately, these calculations proved to be mistaken. The fascist dictatorship, supported by the Germans, was able to tie Hungary to Germany's military chariot for some time. Extremely heavy and bloody fighting broke out along the Budapest axis from the end of October. Facing the Second Ukrainian Front[4] were 39 formations, according to our data at the time. The core of this powerful group of forces consisted of seven panzer (five German and two Hungarian) divisions. Our troops advanced slowly. Difficulties in troop command and control and supply

---

2   The Germans had facing the *front* 11 infantry divisions, two panzer divisions, two panzer brigades, and two cavalry brigades. Altogether, this amounted to 17 formations. The Third Belorussian Front numbered 40 rifle divisions, two tank corps and five tank brigades. In all, this amounted to 47 formations. However, the strength of the enemy's infantry divisions significantly exceeded the number of men in our rifle divisions. The combat capabilities of the Soviet tank corps and the Germans' panzer divisions were approximately the same.

3   Editor's note. Ferenc Salaszi (1897-1946) was the leader of the Iron Cross Party in Hungary, whom the Germans placed in power in late 1944, following the overthrow of Admiral Miklos Horthy's government, which was trying to arrange a separate peace with the Allied powers. Salaszi's reign was brief, however, and following the war he was turned over to the new Hungarian authorities and executed.

4   This *front* contained 43 rifle divisions, three tank corps, three mechanized corps, and three cavalry corps.

arose as the result of bad weather. The enemy was relying on a broad-based system of well-prepared fortifications and was putting up fierce resistance. Although the Hungarian capital was blockaded, its capture dragged on until 13 February 1945. Such was the situation in which the General Staff drew up a plan in October 1944 for the final campaign in Europe.

The extremely limited successes achieved by us in October indicated that it was necessary to reinforce the troops attacking in the south, to rest those divisions that had not been relieved for some time, to regroup, bring up our rear services, and to create the materiel supplies necessary for a breakthrough and the subsequent development of operations. Finally, it was necessary, based on an evaluation of the situation, to choose the most favorable directions and draw up a plan for the most rapid and final defeat of German fascism in the coming year. Time and resources were required for all of this.

At the very beginning of November 1944 the situation along the Second and First Belorussian and First Ukrainian fronts' sectors was reviewed in the *Stavka*. These *fronts* were opposed by a large part of the forces of army groups Center and A—the enemy's main strategic group of forces—and did not have the necessary superiority of force for an offensive. From this it followed that it was not expedient to continue attacking along the Berlin strategic direction and that we must temporarily go over to the defensive.

In his latest report to the Supreme Commander-in-Chief, General A.I. Antonov,[5] the deputy chief of the General Staff, recommended going over to the defensive along the western direction and requested permission to prepare the necessary directives on this matter. We received Stalin's[6] permission and on the night of 4-5 November 1944 a directive was issued to the Third and Second Belorussian fronts to assume the defensive. An analogous order to the forces along the First Belorussian Front's right wing followed a few days later.

Along with this, work continued in the General Staff on a plan for forthcoming operations. It was planned from the very beginning to carry out the task of defeating Hitler's Germany by means of two consecutive efforts, which comprised the campaign's stages. During the first stage active operations were to continue primarily along the old, if one may use the term, direction—along the southern flank of the Soviet-German front in the Budapest area. It was planned to bring about a turning point in the situation by means of withdrawing the Third Ukrainian Front's main forces between the Tisza and Danube rivers to the area south of Kecskemet, from where they could assist the forces of the Second Ukrainian Front by attacking to the northwest and west. It was believed that the two *fronts'* forces would have the opportunity to advance at a high rate of speed and by 30 November reach the line Banska Bystrica—Komarno—Nagykanizsa, and by 30 December reach the approaches to Vienna.

The threat of having its southern flank routed would undoubtedly force the German command to shift additional forces to this area at the expense of the western direction, which in turn would create favorable conditions for our forces' advance along the Berlin direction—those *fronts* located to the north of the Carpathian Mountains. The General Staff planned that in the beginning of

---

5   Editor's note. Aleksei Innokent'evich Antonov (1896-1962) served as a junior officer in the Russian imperial army during the First World War. He joined the Red Army in 1918 and took part in the civil war. During the Great Patriotic War he served in various front-line staff assignments, before being appointed chief of the General Staff's operational directorate in 1942 and deputy chief of staff the following year. Antonov was appointed chief of the General Staff in 1945, although he held that post for less than a year. Following the war, Antonov commanded a military district and served as chief of staff of the Warsaw Pact forces.

6   Editor's note. Iosif Vissarionovich Stalin (Dzhugashvili) (1879-1953) was the unchallenged dictator of the Soviet Union for a quarter century, during which time he established a totalitarian regime equal in its ferocity to Hitler's, if not worse. During the Great Patriotic War he served as general secretary of the Communist Party, chairman of the Council of People's Commissars, defense commissar, supreme commander-in-chief of the armed forces, and chairman of the State Defense Committee (GKO).

1945 the Soviet army's forces would reach the lower course of the Vistula as far as Bromberg,[7] capture Poznan, and reach the line Breslau—Pardubice—Jihlava—Vienna; that is, advance 120-350 kilometers along all axes from the line they occupied on 28 October. The defeat of the enemy's main forces and the arrival at the aforementioned line would create conditions for the conduct of the campaign's second stage, as a result of which Germany would have to capitulate.

Thus in the plan's first rough draft, which dated to the end of October 1944, only the general content of the war's concluding campaign was planned, as was its division into two stages. The axis of the main attack had not yet been determined and the idea of splintering the enemy's strategic front and breaking up his groups of forces in the east had not yet been expressed.

In the beginning of November the General Staff, in the interests of a more exact rendering of the operational plan for 1945, toted up the chief results of the recently completed stage of the war by our army and tightly formulated its evaluation of the sides' strategic situation. The Soviet army had won victories that had decided the outcome of the war. The conclusion of the struggle along the Soviet-German front had now been decided in our favor and the hour of the enemy's final defeat had been advanced. At the present time we were superior to the enemy not only in numbers of men, but in combat skill and military equipment. The struggle along the front was fully supported by the smooth working of the rear, which rendered growing assistance to the front.

The strategic situation of the Soviet army and the forces of the anti-Hitler coalition were evaluated by us as being close to surrounding Germany. The attacks by our forces were well coordinated with the actions of the Allies in Western Europe. Essentially, the Soviet army and the Anglo-American forces occupied jumping-off positions for a decisive offensive against the vital centers of Germany. It now remained to accomplish a final rapid effort and quickly crush the enemy. On the whole, we stood on the eve of complete victory. The given evaluation of the sides' strategic situation which, as subsequent events confirmed, was correct and served as the basis for a detailed drawing up of an operational plan for the 1945 campaign in Europe.

Aside from General A.I. Antonov, the chief of the operational directorate, his deputies A.A. Gryzlov[8] and N.A. Lomov,[9] and the chiefs of the corresponding directions, as a rule, took part in the preliminary discussions of the plan in General Antonov's office. Guided by Antonov's map, the operational directorate refined the notations made, calculated the forces and equipment and other elements of the operation. Finally, the graphic plan of the operations, with all the calculations and justifications was laid out on a special map, after which it once again was attentively, one might say nit-picked, discussed by General Antonov together with the operations officers. As in preceding years, the opening operations were planned out in greatest detail. The *fronts'* subsequent operations were noted only in general terms.

In the course of these creative searches the main general idea, which touched upon the conditions for the success of our operations along the main direction, first arose and was then fully worked out. The idea consisted of drawing off enemy forces from the central sector by means of active operations along the flanks of the strategic front. It was proposed to do this not only

---

7   Editor's note. Here, Shtemenko refers to the Polish city of Bydgoszcz by its pre-First World War name of Bromberg.
8   Editor's note. Anatolii Alekseevich Gryzlov (1904-74) joined the Red Army in 1923 and completed the General Staff Academy in 1940. During the Great Patriotic War he served in various staff assignments and was later first deputy chief of its operational directorate. Following the war, Gryzlov occupied various staff positions with the troops and within the General Staff apparatus.
9   Editor's note. Nikolai Andreevich Lomov (1899-1990) joined the Red Army in 1919 and fought in the civil war. During the Great Patriotic War he served in various staff positions and was deputy chief of the General Staff's operational directorate. Following the war, Lomov served in various staff positions and in the General Staff Academy.

in Hungary and Austria, further from the main direction of our future offensive, but in East Prussia as well. For this it was necessary to energetically develop the offensive around Budapest and conduct offensive operations in the Königsberg area.

We were aware that the enemy was especially sensitive about East Prussia and Hungary. This meant that if we were to press him hard here he would certainly shift his reserves and forces from the non-active sectors here. The upshot of this was that the western direction, which was important for the achievement of a decisive success by the Soviet army, would be seriously weakened.

Our expectations were justified. As a result of our forces' offensive operations in East Prussia and around Budapest in November and December, the enemy concentrated, according to our calculations, 26 divisions (including seven panzer) in East Prussia and 55 divisions (including nine panzer) in the area of the Hungarian capital. As we later learned, Hitler nonetheless believed that the Soviet army would not launch its main attack in 1945 along the Berlin direction, but through Hungary and western Czechoslovakia, to where the main attention of the German command and its forces was therefore directed.[10] This time the Germans, just as in 1944, committed a very crude strategic miscalculation and left only 49 divisions along the sector of the front that was most important for us. This figure included only five panzer divisions. Thus the General Staff's calculations proved to be correct.

The fact that the enemy front had taken on a peculiar and dangerous form for him, when along the flanks there sat powerful defending groups of forces, with a weak center, unsupported by major reserves, forced us to think about the most expedient forms for operations along the main direction. In this case, did it not then follow that we should abandon the idea of a general advance along the entire front, which would lead to pushing the enemy back, or break through the weak center with a direct attack, split the German strategic front and, without losing time, develop the attack directly on Berlin? In such a case, it would be significantly easier to completely eliminate the disjointed enemy forces and in this way significantly ease our task of achieving the final goal of the war. The General Staff decided on this method of operations, which later justified itself.

Thus from the beginning of the planning for the final campaign, the General Staff believed that an attack on Berlin should be begun and conducted as quickly as possible, without stopping. Thus the opinion of those comrades, who maintain that the General Staff put off the question of taking Berlin to an indefinite time, is mistaken. To be sure, the situation introduced some changes into this plan.

In evaluating the operational situation, the likely missions and operational means, each *front* had its peculiar difficulties. This was particularly the case with the Third Belorussian Front. The group of German forces in East Prussia was quite powerful and deeply echeloned. This group of forces relied on powerful permanent fortifications, natural obstacles and inhabited locales, which had been configured for defense and reinforced with engineering structures and obstacles, and which could strike at the flank of our front attacking directly along the Berlin direction. Such flank attacks were also dangerous because the German forces in this area had increased considerably.

It followed that the East Prussian group of forces must not only be tied down, but isolated from the other sectors of the strategic front and, insofar as this was possible, to be broken up, so as to prevent the German command from employing its forces in a concentrated form along a single direction.

Such a multifaceted operational task—to tie down, isolate and break up—meant that we should plan to employ at least two *fronts* for the offensive into East Prussia: one to strike toward Königsberg from the east, and the second to isolate the East Prussian group of forces from Army Group A and the rear by outflanking it from the south and southwest. This *front* would simultaneously secure

---

10 Tippelskirch, K. *Istoriia Vtoroi Mirovoi Voiny.* Moscow: Voennoe Izdatel'stvo, 1956, p. 542.

our forces attacking along the Warsaw—Poznan—Berlin direction. According to the location of the *fronts*, which had arisen as a result of the 1944 operations, the Third Belorussian Front could attack East Prussia from the east, while the Second Belorussian Front could outflank the German forces.

In order to resolve the main task—the creation of breaches in the enemy's strategic front and the conduct of a vigorous offensive to the west, the First Belorussian and First Ukrainian fronts, which were already along this direction and had bridgeheads along the Vistula, could be employed. Insofar as they had to break through the defense and develop the success at a high rate of speed, these *fronts* would have to be heavily reinforced with tanks, particularly tank armies and corps.

During the last three days of October and the beginning of November 1944, General Antonov and the General Staff's operational officers worked on the operational portion of the forthcoming activities. At this time the general idea took on a concrete form in the sense of exactly defining the axes of the *fronts'* and armies' attacks, the attack sectors, the depth of the immediate and subsequent missions, and the timetables for carrying them out. The sides' capabilities were analyzed several times and the numerous operational variations were weighed.

The minimal deadline necessary for defeating Germany was approximately calculated at this stage of our work. It was planned to achieve this in the course of 45 days of offensive activities to a depth of 600-700 kilometers, in the course of two consecutive efforts (stages), without operational pauses between them. It was planned that the first stage, which had the goal of defeating the opposing forces and arriving at the line Bromberg—Poznan—Breslau—Vienna to a depth of 250-300 kilometers, would last 15 days. The second stage—the completion of the defeat of Germany and the capture of Berlin—was planned to last 30 days. The pace was not high, insofar as fierce resistance was expected in the final battles to eliminate fascist Germany's main forces. In reality, the heroic Soviet forces exceeded all the plans in this regard.

The depth of the *fronts'* missions was significantly refined in connection with the concrete conditions of the situation, particularly the terrain features. For example, the depth of the Third Belorussian Front's immediate mission was only 50-60 kilometers, insofar as the area of combat activities was very difficult and the enemy strong. In the Second Belorussian Front's sector the opportunities for the troops' advance were better, which enabled us to plan the *front's* immediate mission as far as the line Mlawa—Drobin, that is, to a depth of 60-80 kilometers. The depth of the First Belorussian and First Ukrainian fronts' immediate mission, and partly that of the Fourth Ukrainian Front, could reach 120-160 kilometers.

In the conditions of the level terrain of western Poland, the depth of the First Belorussian and First Ukrainian fronts' subsequent missions along the main directions was calculated at 130-180 kilometers.

At first it was not planned to launch the first attack in some areas of the enemy's territory. This was the case, for example, with Silesia. The relatively weak Fourth Ukrainian Front, which it was planned to include in the overall offensive, would not have been able to overcome the firm defense here. The *front's* 38th and 1st Guards armies, which were designated for attacking along the boundary with its northern neighbor, were to operate at first in difficult and mountainous terrain, and then were to attack in the industrial area.

As concerns the directions of the *fronts'* attacks, we confidently mapped out the Second Belorussian Front's offensive axes toward Marienburg, thus cutting off the East Prussian group of forces from Germany and the other armies, and toward Allenstein, in order to split up this group of forces. Also determined were the axes of part of the First Belorussian Front's forces around Warsaw and the attacks to meet the First Ukrainian Front's forces while defeating the Germans' Kielce—Radom group of forces. Finally, we determined the operational sectors of the First and Fourth Ukrainian fronts' neighboring groups of forces in the Krakow area. As before, the final goal for the two southern Second and Third Ukrainian fronts remained Vienna.

In our daily reports to the *Stavka*, we to one degree or another raised questions of the Soviet armed forces' activities in the concluding campaign. Thus many of these questions had already been coordinated with the supreme commander-in-chief before being broadly discussed with the *front* commanders. A number of corrections were made to the plan during November. This was connected with the already well-established procedure for operational planning, during which the General Staff's initial ideas served only as the point of departure for the drawing up of the future plan for the *fronts'* operations.

In preparing the idea of the 1945 campaign, the *Stavka* did not gather the *front* commanders for a special meeting, which had been the case in the past; for example, according to the plan for "Bagration"[11] and the conduct of the summer offensive in Belorussia. This time, we limited ourselves to summoning the *front* commanders separately to the General Staff and a discussion of everything that related to their *fronts'* operation; then we reported these already-coordinated ideas to the *Stavka*.

Marshals of the Soviet Union F.I. Tolbukhin,[12] K.K. Rokossovskii[13] and I.S. Konev,[14] General I.D. Chernyakhovskii,[15] and the *Stavka* representatives[16] with the *fronts* worked until 7 November during the celebratory days of the October Revolution. The variant of the overall idea for combat operations against Germany in 1945 was studiously analyzed in the General Staff. After this, the *front* commanders, A.I. Antonov and I set out for the *Stavka*, where, following a short report by Antonov, an all-round discussion of the plan took place. No significant amendments were made to the plan. It was planned to begin the offensive along the main direction on 20 January 1945, although the operational plans had not yet been confirmed and no directives to the *fronts* had been issued.

Within a few days of the discussion of the plan for the initial operations of 1945, in the *Stavka* the supreme commander-in-chief determined that the forces that would take the German capital of Berlin would be commanded by his first deputy, Marshal of the Soviet Union G.K. Zhukov,[17]

---

11 Editor's note. Operation Bagration was the code name for the Red Army's multi-*front* offensive operation in Belorussia in the summer of 1944.

12 Editor's note. Fedor Ivanovich Tolbukhin (1894-1949) served in the Russian imperial army and joined the Red Army in 1918. During the Great Patriotic War he served as chief of staff with various *fronts* and commanded a number of armies and *fronts*, including the Third Ukrainian Front (1944) to the end of the war. Following the war, Tolbukhin commanded the southern group of forces and a military district.

13 Editor's note. Konstantin Konstantinovich Rokossovski (1896-1968) served in the Russian imperial army and joined the Red Army in 1918. Rokossovskii was arrested in 1937, but managed to survive and return to the army in 1940. During the Great Patriotic War he commanded a mechanized corps and an army, as well as several *fronts*, including the Second Belorussian Front from late 1944. Following the war, Rokossovskii commanded the northern group of Soviet forces and served several years a Polish defense minister. Upon his return to the USSR, he commanded a military district and held posts in the central military apparatus.

14 Editor's note. Ivan Stepanovich Konev (1897-1973) served in the Russian imperial army and joined the Red Army in 1918, where he originally served as a political commissar, before switching to command responsibilities. During the Great Patriotic War he commanded an army and several *fronts*, the last being the First Ukrainian Front, from 1944. Following the war, he commanded Soviet occupation forces in Czechoslovakia and Austria and served as commander-in-chief of the Soviet Ground Forces. He later commanded the Warsaw Pact forces and the Group of Soviet Forces in Germany.

15 Editor's note. Ivan Danilovich Chernyakhovskii (1906-45) joined the Red Army in 1924 and served in various command capacities before the war. During the Great Patriotic War he advanced from the command of a division to that of a corps and army, and in 1944 was appointed to command the Third Belorussian Front. He was killed during the East Prussian operation in February 1945.

16 Editor's note. The *Stavka* representatives were high-ranking officers who were dispatched to the various *fronts*, to insure more efficient control from the center. As the war progressed, a number of representatives, such as G.K. Zhukov, A.M. Vasilevskii and others coordinated the operations of two or more *fronts*.

17 Editor's note. Georgii Konstantinovich Zhukov (1896-1974) served in the Russian imperial army and joined

who on 16 November 1944 was appointed to the post of commander of the First Belorussian Front. Marshal of the Soviet Union K.K. Rokossovskii replaced the commander of the Second Belorussian Front, General G.F. Zakharov.[18] Stalin personally informed the above-named commanders of his decision by telephone.

Stalin took upon himself the coordination of the activities of four *fronts* along the Berlin direction in the concluding campaign of the war with Germany. As a result, there was no longer any need for the work of the chief of the General Staff, A.M. Vasilevskii,[19] on the Third Belorussian Front. He remained, as a *Stavka* representative, in charge of the First and Second Baltic fronts' operations, and on 20 February 1945, following the death of General I.D. Chernyakhovskii, he became commander of the Third Belorussian Front.

Thus the 1945 campaign, , which had been drawn up together with the *front* commanders in accordance with the General Staff's plan, was to begin with simultaneous powerful attacks by the *fronts* deployed along the Berlin strategic direction. These attacks had as their goal the breaking through and splitting up of the front into parts, disrupting communications and disorganizing the coordination of the enemy groups of forces and, as early as the first stage, of destroying the main forces of the opposing German-Fascist troops. In this way, the campaign's first-stage operations were to create favorable conditions for concluding the war.

A great deal of attention during this time was devoted to how best to secure the rapid breakthrough of the enemy's defense and to develop the First Belorussian Front's success. The *front's* forces had to attack from the Magnuszew and Pulawy bridgeheads, which predetermined the axes of the attacks and thus made the enemy's job easier. Connected with this, in a way, was the neighboring First Ukrainian Front on the left, which was to develop its offensive not along the shortest route to the German border, but on Kalisz, which lay considerably to the north. The General Staff believed that the First Ukrainian Front's shortest route was not justified in this case, due to a series of purely military and economic considerations. Its route along Polish territory would pass through the Upper Silesian industrial area and come up against German Silesia, where the Hitlerites, by organizing a stubborn defense, could halt the offensive. We could foresee extended fighting, the loss of speed in the operation's development and numerous unjustified losses. Therefore, following numerous discussions and talks with Marshal of the Soviet Union Konev, we fixed upon an offensive variation that would bypass Silesia from the northeast and north. The *Stavka* agreed with this plan, insofar as the attack would create an immediate threat to the rear of the enemy arrayed

---

the Red Army in 1918. The forces under his command defeated the Japanese along the Khalkhin-Gol River in Mongolia in 1939. During the Great Patriotic War he served as chief of the General Staff and commanded a number of *fronts*. In 1942 he was appointed deputy supreme commander-in-chief and also served as a *Stavka* representative to various *fronts*. From late 1944 he commanded the First Belorussian Front. Following the war, Zhukov fell afoul of Stalin and was relegated to the command of a number of secondary military districts. Following Stalin's death, he served as defense minister until his removal in 1957 by party leader Nikita Sergeevich Khrushchev.

18   Editor's note. Georgii Fedorovich Zakharov (1897-1957) served in the Russian imperial army and joined the Red Army in 1919. During the Great Patriotic War he served as a commander, deputy commander and chief of staff of a number of *fronts*, and also commanded several armies. In 1945 he was appointed deputy commander of the Fourth Ukrainian Front. Following the Great Patriotic War, Zakharov commanded a number of military districts, among other positions.

19   Editor's note. Aleksandr Mikhailovich Vasilevskii (1895-1977) served in the Russian imperial army and joined the Red Army in 1919. During the Great Patriotic War Vasilevskii served in the General Staff apparatus and was appointed chief of staff in 1942, and in 1945 was made a member of the *Stavka* of the Supreme High Command. Vasilevskii also served as the *Stavka* representative to a number of *fronts*, charged with coordinating their activities. In 1945 he commanded the Third Belorussian Front and was commander-in-chief of Soviet Forces in the Far East, where he supervised the Soviet invasion of Manchuria and Korea. Following the war, Vasilevskii again served as chief of staff and minister of the armed forces.

against the First Belorussian Front and would significantly ease the advance of our forces on Poznan. Aside from these considerations, in this case all the structures in the industrial region would remain untouched by the main attack and could be preserved, in the main, unharmed, which would enable us subsequently to make use of their output without major expenditures for reconstruction.

On 27 November, during the visit by the commander of the First Belorussian Front, who had been summoned to Moscow by the *Stavka*, the operational aspect of the First Belorussian Front's initial operation was changed somewhat. According to data received by *front* intelligence, an attack due west had been made more difficult, due to the presence of the enemy's numerous defensive lines, which had been occupied by troops. In the *front* commander's opinion, a success was more likely to be gained through operations of the *front's* main forces towards Lodz, with their subsequent arrival at Poznan. The supreme commander-in-chief agreed with this refinement.

This circumstance altered matters as to the direction of the attack by the *front's* neighbor to the left: the First Belorussian Front's arrival at Kalisz would lose its significance. Thus Marshal Konev was assigned Breslau as his main axis of attack.

Taking into account all of these amendments, the *front* commanders and their staffs worked out operational plans for each *front*, which were examined by the General Staff and confirmed by the *Stavka*.

About two and a half months were spent on all these planning measures at the *Stavka-front* level. It stands to reason, of course, that during this entire time the preparation for the operations proceeded at full speed and activities for concentrating reserves and equipment necessary for the *fronts* took place. After the fundamentals of the future operations had been worked out with the *front* commanders, the accumulation of the necessary supplies began at the front.

Thus in November 1944 the picture of the Soviet army's forthcoming winter offensive was fully defined, although the operational plans were confirmed by the *Stavka* only at the end of December. Only small changes were subsequently introduced into the plan for the campaign and the initial operations.

Let us now examine how there gradually arose and how, finally, the plan for the concluding Berlin operation took form.

The Soviet forces' offensive in East Prussia, along the Vistula and in Silesia was so decisive and rapid that within two weeks the armies of the First Belorussian and First Ukrainian fronts had carried out their assigned tasks, having reached the line Poznan—Breslau.

In connection with the achievement of the campaign's first-stage goal, it was necessary, without losing time, to determine what to do next, insofar as an attack on Berlin was on the agenda and was now, so to say, the immediate objective.

On 26 January 1945 the General Staff received the decision by the commander of the First Belorussian Front to conduct what was essentially a non-stop offensive by the *front* up to and including the capture the German capital. It was planned to bring up forces, particularly artillery, the rear organs, replenish supplies, put the combat vehicles in order, and to put the 3rd Shock Army and the Polish 1st Army into the first echelon in four days, and beginning on 1-2 February to continue the offensive with all the *front's* forces. The immediate objective was to force the Oder River from the march and to subsequently develop a rapid attack toward Berlin, directing the main forces toward bypassing the German capital from the northeast, north and northwest. During this time the 2nd Guards Tank Army would outflank Berlin from the northwest, while the 1st Guards Tank Army did the same from the northeast.

Within a day the General Staff received the decision by the commander of the First Ukrainian Front, according to which his *front* was also to operate without a noticeable pause, beginning its offensive on 5-6 February, so as to reach the Elbe River by 25-28 February, while its right flank, in conjunction with the First Belorussian Front, would take Berlin.

Thus the forces of both *fronts* were to be directed at capturing Berlin without any kind of pause. But how could Marshal Konev's decision be squared with Stalin's instructions that only the First Belorussian Front would take Berlin? Following heated debates in General Antonov's office, the General Staff suggested confirming both decisions, to which the *Stavka* agreed. However, they established the same boundary line between the *fronts* as that recommended by Marshal Zhukov: as far as Smigiel, as before, then Unruhstadt—the Faule Obra River—Oder River—Ratzdorf—Friedland—Gross Keris—Michendorf. Such a boundary line would effectively push the First Ukrainian Front to the south of Berlin, without leaving it any sort of window for a direct attack from the south or southwest, forcing it to attack toward Guben and Brandenburg.

The General Staff understood the absurdity of the situation: on the one hand, they had confirmed Marshal Konev's decision to attack with his right flank toward Berlin, while at the same time they had established a boundary line that prevented him from doing that.

It was necessary to search for some sort of way out of the existing situation. We calculated that either the situation would make the necessary changes, or that we would be able to rectify this nonsense during the course of the operation, all the more so that it was still a long way to Berlin. However, as subsequent events showed, we were unable to carry out the planned offensive on Berlin in a short period of time.

By the end of January it became clear that the enemy in Pomerania was creating a powerful group of forces. The General Staff interpreted this as a threat to the right flank and rear of our forces attacking toward Berlin. Besides, a gap of more than 100 kilometers had developed between the First and Second Belorussian fronts, which was being covered only by cavalry, while the troops were suffering from a serious shortage of ammunition and fuel, because their supplies remained along the Vistula. Such a situation forced the *Stavka* and General Staff to review their initial decision: it would be wrong, while ignoring the enemy's powerful forces along the flank and not worrying about the rear organs and supply, to rush onto Berlin. And now, 20 years later, when all the maps are available and one is no longer responsible for making a decision, certain comrades in their memoirs make deeply thought-out conclusions as to the possibility of taking Berlin in February 1945.[20]

In the middle of February the enemy's Pomeranian group of forces attacked. Stubborn fighting broke out. The Soviet command did not doubt that the Germans would fail to push back our attacking forces. At the same time, without defeating the enemy group of forces we could not consider the idea of a non-stop offensive on Berlin by all the First Belorussian Front's forces. We had to throw a large part of these against this Pomeranian splinter. Only later, when the Second Belorussian Front's main forces turned toward Pomerania, could one consider the First Belorussian Front's rear secured.

Matters stood more favorably in the First Ukrainian Front's zone, where its right flank was approaching the Neisse River and reached it on 24 February, after which it successfully defeated the enemy in Upper Silesia (the Oppeln area). However, the *front* would still require a significant amount of time to completely defeat the enemy.

A promising situation had developed along the Fourth, Second and Third Ukrainian fronts' sectors. On 13 February the Hitlerites' resistance in Budapest was finally broken. This, in the General Staff's opinion, would open up a favorable opportunity for developing the offensive in the directions of Olomouc and Prague; Vienna and Plzen—the soft underbelly of Fascist Germany—and enable us to attract as many enemy forces as possible here, including from the extremely

---

20 Editor's note. This remark may be a reference to a recent article by Marshal Vasilii Ivanovich Chuikov (1900-1982). During this time Chuikov served as commander of the 8th Guards Army on the First Belorussian Front. See his "Kapitulyatsiya Gitlerovskoi Germanii," *Novaya i Noveishaya Istoriya*, No. 2 (1965):3-25.

important central direction. We didn't know at the time that the enemy viewed these directions as constituting the greatest threat and he was already dispatching pick forces here, hoping to change the situation in his favor.

The General Staff continued to draw up a plan for operations in Austria and Czechoslovakia, intending on the offensive's fifteenth-twentieth day to reach the line Pardubice—Brno—Vienna, and on the fortieth-forty fifth day force the Vltava River and liberate Prague. The Soviet forces' advance along these directions would simultaneously deprive Germany of important coal mining areas (Moravska Ostrava), oil extraction (western Hungary) and iron (Linz), which, taken with the loss of the Silesian industrial area and the agricultural regions of East Prussia, would mean the significant undermining of the economic foundations of the enemy's military potential.

As concerns the further course of the war, our calculations were carried out by taking into account the most unfavorable circumstances, namely that the Allies would not be able to overcome the German forces' defense. In such a case, it was considered possible that the enemy would seek to remove a significant portion of his troops from the western front and throw them to the east to defend the capital of the fascist state. The significance of the outcome of the battle for Berlin was too important for the fate of the Hitlerite clique and, on the whole, for the German-Fascist state.

The General Staff's work in planning the final attacks was complicated in the extreme by Stalin's subjective and categorical decision as to the First Belorussian Front's special role. This was particularly felt by General Antonov, who on 19 February entered into the difficult and responsible duties of chief of the General Staff.

To capture such a major city as Berlin, which had been vigorously prepared for defense, would be extremely difficult for a single *front*, even such a powerful one as the First Belorussian Front. The situation insistently demanded that we direct at least the First Belorussian and First Ukrainian fronts on Berlin, just as it was of course also necessary to somehow avoid an ineffective frontal attack by our main forces. Thus General Antonov's map reflected the General Staff's and *front* commanders' January idea of taking Berlin by the First Belorussian Front's flanking attack from the north and northwest and the double flanking attack by the First Ukrainian Front from the southwest and west. It was planned to link up the *fronts'* forces in the Brandenburg—Potsdam area. In this way not only would an internal encirclement front be created around the enemy in the capital, but also an external one, which would enable us to repel possible counterattacks by German forces from the west and southwest. If the Hitlerites were to somehow manage to restore the front to the west of Berlin, we would, of course have to continue the offensive to their complete defeat.

Subsequent events eliminated the question as regards our allies' actions. They moved slowly and carefully forward. During February-March 1945 the Allied armies threw the Germans back to the Rhine River, and in certain areas they seized bridgeheads and began preparing for operations to the east of the river.

The ferocity of the fighting on the Soviet-German front did not slacken; quite the contrary, it increased. In February-March a number of important events took place. In eastern Pomerania the forces of the Second Belorussian and part of the First Belorussian fronts routed the enemy and removed the threat of a flank attack from the north into the rear of the armies aimed at Berlin. At the same time bloody fighting went on to expand the bridgehead over the Oder west of Küstrin, which ended successfully for us. Soviet forces stood 60 kilometers from the German capital.

The First Ukrainian Front's right-wing armies had encircled and destroyed more than five German divisions in Upper Silesia and, having thrown back the remainder into the Sudeten Mountains, had occupied a favorable position for attacks on Dresden and Prague. The forces of the Fourth Ukrainian Front had achieved notable successes in the Carpathian Mountains.

Combat operations in western Hungary along the Vienna axis had extremely important consequences. Despite the overall unfavorable situation for him, the enemy here attempted to bring about a change in the situation along the front in his favor, for which he concentrated here all possible reserves and undertook a counteroffensive against the Third Ukrainian Front in the area of Lake Balaton. The extremely heavy Balaton battle lasted ten days. The enemy's attempt to seize the initiative was repulsed. Literally on the day following the end of the fighting in the Lake Balaton area, our offensive on Vienna unfolded. The *Stavka* warned the commander of the Third Ukrainian Front beforehand about the necessity of keeping the 9th Guards Army, which had been designated for the offensive on the Austrian capital, free from defensive operations. This enabled not only the troops of the Second Ukrainian Front, but of the Third Ukrainian Front, to immediately lunge forward. On 13 April Vienna was liberated and our forces moved further to the west.

The end of March was employed by our allies to force the Rhine and to simultaneously develop the offensive into the depth of central Germany and Bavaria. It was subsequently planned to split the German forces by linking up with the Soviet army. The Soviet supreme high command was informed of this plan, which flowed from the decisions of the Yalta conference of the leaders of the three major allied powers, in a 28 March letter from the supreme commander-in-chief of the combined Anglo-American forces, General Eisenhower.

Now the Allies were advancing at a higher rate of speed than before. In the Ruhr they had encircled a significant enemy group of forces, which was then split up and before long ceased its resistance. The Anglo-American troops' main forces, while encountering weak resistance, advanced to the east toward the Elbe River and the shore of the Baltic Sea in the Lubeck area.

There was no doubt remaining that the Allies were determined to seize Berlin before us, although according to the Yalta agreements the city was to be inside the Soviet occupation zone. As it later became known from the memoirs of the late Winston Churchill, he goaded in every way possible Roosevelt and Eisenhower to seize the German capital. In a message to the American president, he wrote:

> Nothing will exert a psychological effect of despair upon all German forces of resistance equal to that of the fall of Berlin. It will be the supreme signal of defeat to the German people. On the other hand, if left to itself to maintain a siege by the Russians among its ruins, and as long as the German flag flies there, it will animate the resistance of all Germans under arms.
>
> There is moreover another aspect which it is proper for you and me to consider. The Russian armies will no doubt overrun all Austria and enter Vienna. If they also take Berlin will not their impression that they have been the overwhelming contributor to our common victory be unduly imprinted in their minds, and may this not lead them into a mood which will raise grave and formidable difficulties in the future? I therefore consider that from a political standpoint we should march as far east into Germany as possible, and that should Berlin be in our grasp we should certainly take it. This also appears sound on military grounds.[21]

At the end of March all the main ideas for the Berlin operation had been worked out in the General Staff. During this work the General Staff was constantly consulting with the commanders of the Second and First Belorussian and First Ukrainian fronts, as well their chiefs of staff, General

---

21 Editor's note. The full text of this message may be found in W.S. Churchill, *The Second World War* (Boston, 1948-1953), vol. 6:464-466.

A.N. Bogolyubov,[22] General M.S. Malinin[23] and General V.D. Sokolovskii,[24] and later with General I.Ye. Petrov,[25] as to the content of our forces' activities in the forthcoming offensive. Thus as soon as it became clear that the allies were striving to take Berlin first, the commanders of the First Belorussian and First Ukrainian fronts were immediately summoned to Moscow.

On 31 March the General Staff reviewed together with the *front* commanders the plan for the *fronts'* actions and coordinated all its details. Marshal Konev was very agitated about the boundary line with his neighbor on the right, which gave him no opportunity for an attack on Berlin. However, no one in the General Staff could remove this impediment.

The following day, 1 April 1945, the plan for the Berlin operation was discussed in the General Staff. The situation at the front and the actions of our allies and their plans were reported in detail. Stalin concluded that Berlin should be taken as quickly as possible, and thus the timetable for preparing the operation was extremely limited. It was necessary to begin no later than 16 April and to finish within no more than 12-15 days.

The *front* commanders agreed with these conclusions and assured the *Stavka* that their forces would be ready in time. After this the plan, which had been coordinated with them, was reviewed. The chief of the General Staff reported on the plan and noted that the boundary line between the *fronts* excluded the immediate participation by the forces of the First Ukrainian Front in the fighting for the city, which could negatively affect the timetable for carrying out the missions. Marshal Konev expressed himself against such a boundary line and emphasized the expediency of directing part of the First Ukrainian Front's forces, particularly the tank armies, against the southwestern outskirts of Berlin.

Stalin, evidently understanding the lack of foundation for the existing boundary line between the *fronts*, and desiring to take Berlin as quickly as possible, resolved the problem in his own way: he did not completely abandon his idea, but agreed neither with the General Staff or the commander of the First Ukrainian Front. On the planning map he silently crossed out that part of the boundary line that cut off the First Ukrainian Front from Berlin and traced it as far as Lubben, 60 kilometers to the southeast of the city, where he broke it off. He later told us, "Whoever breaks in first, let him take Berlin."

Such was the origin of the specific boundary line in the Berlin operation between the First Belorussian and First Ukrainian fronts, which was not continued throughout the entire depth of the offensive, but ended along the southeastern approaches to the city.

---

22 Editor's note. Aleksandr Nikolaevich Bogolyubov (1900-56) joined the Red Army in 1918. During the Great Patriotic War he occupied several staff positions at the army and *front* level and served as chief of staff of the Second Belorussian Front until the end of the war. Following the war, Bogolyubov served in various capacities within the central military apparatus.

23 Editor's note. Mikhail Sergeevich Malinin (1899-1960) joined the Red Army in 1919. During the Great Patriotic War he served in a variety of staff assignments, including chief of staff of an army and several *fronts*, including g the First Belorussian Front to the end of the war. Following the war, Malinin continued to serve in staff assignments in the field and the central military apparatus.

24 Editor's note. Vasilii Danilovich Sokolovskii (1897-1968) joined the Red Army in 1918. During the Great Patriotic War he served in a variety of *front* staff positions and also commanded a *front*. During this period he served as chief of staff of the First Ukrainian Front. Following the war, Sokolovskii served as deputy commander and commander of the group of Soviet forces in Germany and the Soviet military administration in that country. He later served as chief of the General Staff.

25 Editor's note. Ivan Yefimovich Petrov (1896-1958) joined the Red Army in 1918. During the Great Patriotic War he commanded a division and a corps, as well as a number of armies and *fronts*. He was appointed commander of the Fourth Ukrainian Front in 1944, but was relegated to the position of chief of staff the following year. Following the war, Petrov held a number of field and central administrative assignments.

The General Staff was satisfied with such a turn of events, because this accursed boundary line had given us no peace for more than two months. Nor did Marshal Konev object. The new line suited him as well. Events actually unfolded later so that both *fronts* took Berlin.

The beginning of the offensive was set for 16 April. Only by that date could the *fronts*, especially the First Ukrainian, accumulate the necessary materiel stores.

On that day the commander of the First Belorussian Front was issued a directive on the preparation and conduct of the operation for the purpose of taking Berlin and, no later than the twelfth-fifteenth day of the operation, of reaching the Elbe. It was ordered to launch the main attack from the Küstrin bridgehead with the forces of four combined-arms and two tank armies, with the latter two to be committed into the breach in the enemy's defenses for developing the success to outflank Berlin from the north and northeast. The *front's* second echelon would be employed along the main direction. This was the 3rd Army, under the command of Colonel General A.V. Gorbatov.[26]

On 2 April a directive was issued to the commander of the First Ukrainian Front. He was ordered to defeat the enemy group of forces in the Cottbus area and south of Berlin and no later than the tenth-twelfth day of the operation to reach the line Beelitz—Wittenberg, and then along the Elbe as far as Dresden. The *front's* main attack was planned along the Spremberg—Beelitz axis, that is, 50 kilometers south of Berlin. It was planned to commit the tank armies (3rd and 4th guards) after the breakthrough of the enemy's defense, in order to develop the success along the main direction.

Besides this, the *Stavka* foresaw as a possible variation the turning of the First Ukrainian Front's armies directly on Berlin, after which they would bypass Lubben. It was undoubtedly in this variant that the above-listed debates at the *Stavka* meeting were reflected.

On 6 April a directive was issued to the Second Belorussian Front, which was not to take a direct part in the capture of Berlin, but which had a very responsible mission—to attack to the west north of the German capital and, upon defeating the enemy's powerful Stettin group of forces, to secure the entire operation from this direction.

Thus the idea and plan of the Berlin operation, which was to bring fascist Germany's armed forces to the point of capitulation, called for the splitting and encirclement of the enemy east of the German capital, along with the simultaneous destruction of the surrounded enemy forces in detail. The Soviet army's vigorous advance to the west also had as its goal the prevention of any possibility of the Hitlerites creating a new organized front.

The commanders' decisions, which were adopted in accordance with the *Stavka* directives, ensured the fulfillment of these responsible tasks. Powerful groups of forces, with an enormous amount, for the time, of artillery, tanks and aviation, were concentrated along the axes of our attacks. The offensive began on time, and with the forces of three cooperating *fronts* the final defeat of the enemy along the critically important Berlin direction was accomplished. On 2 May Berlin ceased its resistance. Within six days fascist Germany capitulated unconditionally.

This, in brief, is the story of the General Staff's work on the idea of the concluding operations of the war's final campaign. This represented the intense and creative activity of a large group of officers, generals and marshals of the General Staff and the army. During the course of this work it was determined how to better, more quickly and more completely employ the energy and might of the Soviet armed forces and the entire people in the interests of victory over fascism. Now no one doubts that our armed forces were superior to Hitlerite Germany's army as to the level of its

---

26   Editor's note. Aleksandr Vasil'evich Gorbatov (1891-1973) joined the Red Army in 1919. He was arrested in 1937 during Stalin's military purge, but survived and returned to active duty shortly before the war. During the Great Patriotic War he commanded a number of formations and was appointed commander of the 3rd Army in 1943 and served there until the end of the war. Following the war, Gorbatov served as commander of a number of higher formations.

military art. In this there is a portion of the services of those staff officers who spent day and night over maps in the difficult and heroic time of the Great Patriotic War.

The concluding stage of the war in Europe was typified by the realism of the strategic goals assigned at that time to the Soviet armed forces. The direction of our main attack in 1945, which was conditioned by well-calculated political and political considerations and estimates, led directly to Berlin. Here were concentrated the Soviet army's main forces. The employment of our forces was scrupulously and thoroughly prepared. Moreover, the offensive operational plans called for our forces' significant superiority over the enemy in men and materiel throughout the entire offensive, increasing especially at the concluding stage of military operations.

A sufficiently exact knowledge of the opportunities and foreseeing the character of enemy resistance enabled the Soviet command to eliminate all the enemy's attempts to reclaim the initiative and change the course of the war.

In its work, the Soviet strategic leadership skillfully and widely relied on the experience achieved in the course of preceding campaigns, was highly skilled in the art of controlling the armed forces' operations, and fully employed the brilliant military gifts of major and minor commanders—the *front* and army commanders and the commanders of formations, units and subunits. Its worthy assistants were the troop staffs at all levels, which by this time had achieved a high level of troop control.

Part II

The Vistula-Oder Operation. The Defeat by Soviet Forces of the German-Fascist Troops in Poland in January 1945

Colonel A.D. Bagreev, Candidate of Military Sciences
A Textbook
1957

This textbook is intended for Academy students.

The textbook's sections on questions of aviation (the air situation, the aviation support of the operation, etc.) were written by Lieutenant Colonel V.F. Yudin.

The editor is assistant professor and candidate of military sciences Major General A.V. Vasil'ev.

1

Introduction

The Vistula-Oder operation is one of the largest offensive operations by the Soviet army during the fourth and concluding period of the Great Patriotic War, which was conducted by the forces of the First Belorussian and First Ukrainian fronts, with the assistance of the Fourth Ukrainian Front and formations of the 18th Air Army (Long-Range Aviataion), from 12 January through 3 February 1945 along the Warsaw—Berlin direction. The operation was a component part of the strategic offensive by the Soviet Armed Forces in Europe in 1945.

The multi-*front* Vistula-Oder offensive operation includes the following *front* offensive operations: Vistula-Oder (Warsaw—Poznan) by the First Belorussian Front, and the Sandomierz—Silesian operation by the First Ukrainian Front. The Western Carpathian operation was simultaneously conducted by the Fourth Ukrainian Front. These operations played a major role in the Soviet army's strategic offensive in the winter of 1945 for the defeat of the German-Fascist forces in Poland. The Soviet forces completed the liberation of our Polish ally and her major industrial areas, as a result of which a very powerful blow was dealt to the military-political prestige of fascist Germany and her economy. Besides this, as a result of the successful completion of the multi-*front* Vistula-Oder operation the calculations of international reactionary forces for maintaining a fascist regime in the countries of eastern and southeastern Europe collapsed.

In its scope, the Vistula-Oder operation surpassed many other large operations of the Great Patriotic War. The First Belorussian and First Ukrainian fronts attacked from the line of the Vistula River along an overall front of 490 kilometers, and in the course of 18 days advanced to a depth of 570 kilometers and reached the Oder River.

In this operation Soviet military art fully resolved the mission (applicable to the conditions of the time) of vigorously breaking through the enemy's prepared defense and pursuing him to a great operational depth.

As a result of this operation, the main group of Soviet forces occupied new and favorable strategic lines for resolving the last objective—the final defeat of fascist Germany.

The goal of this textbook is to present a brief overview of the Vistula-Oder operation and to show the state of Soviet military art in the given operation, chiefly its operational art, and particularly in that part that retains practical significance for modern military theory.

2

The Military–Political Situation by the Start of the Vistula-Oder Operation. The Sides' Situation and Plans[1]

The Military-Political Situation

By the start of the operation in the middle of January 1945, the military-political situation was favorable for the Soviet Union and its armed forces.

As a result of the outstanding victories won by the Soviet army in 1944, by the start of 1945 our forces had entered East Prussia, liberated the eastern part of our Polish ally, having reached the Vistula River and seized bridgeheads on its western bank; had entered the eastern areas of Czechoslovakia, Hungary and Yugoslavia, bringing liberation to their peoples, and; in Courland we had pressed the formations of the Sixteenth and Eighteenth German-Fascist armies to the sea between Tukums and Libava.

Under the influence of the Soviet army's historic victories, the peoples of Europe had strengthened the struggle for their liberation from imperialist and fascist oppression.

The successes of the Soviet armed forces inspired the peoples of the colonial and semi-colonial countries of Asia and, first of all, the great Chinese people, to increase the struggle against the imperialist aggressors.

Finland, Romania, Bulgaria, and Hungary[2] had been taken out of the war on the side of fascist Germany. The peoples of these countries, under the leadership of their communist and workers' parties, having taken the fate of their states in their own hands, declared war on fascist Germany.

By the beginning of 1945 fascist Germany had already been significantly weakened, having suffered enormous losses on the Soviet-German front and the other fronts of the Second World War. It had been deprived of its satellites and a significant part of its sources of natural resources. From the summer of 1944 the German-Fascist forces had been forced to wage the war in Europe on two fronts. However, the armies of fascist Germany still represented a significant force. Of the 313 divisions at the disposal of the German-Fascist command by the beginning of 1945, up to 210

---

1   The following sources were used for this section: the combat journals and other documents for the First Belorussian, First and Fourth Ukrainian fronts for January 1945; the *fonds* for the First Belorussian, First and Fourth Ukrainian fronts in the Central Ministry of Defense Archives; *Sbornik Materialov po Izucheniyu Opyta Voiny*, no. 25; Directorate for the Study of the History of the Great Patriotic War, General Staff of the USSR Armed Forces, inventory no. 7235; *Sandomirsko-Silezskaya Operation*, inventory no. 8201, by the Military-Historical Directorate of the General Staff of the USSR Armed Forces, and; other materials.

2   A number of Hungarian formations, which were being controlled by fascist elements, still continued to wage combat operations on the side of the German-Fascist forces.

(of these, 30 were panzer and panzergrenadier) were operating against Soviet forces and only 72 divisions (23 percent) against the Anglo-American forces.

The German-Fascist command continued its resistance, while counting on drawing out the war, the exacerbation of contradictions within the anti-fascist coalition, and the conclusion of a separate peace with the USA and England.

In Western Europe by this time the American and English forces, following their successful landing in northern and then southern France had reached the borders of Germany proper. During the 16 December-5 January 1945 time period they were thrown back 80-90 kilometers by the attacking German-Fascist forces along the Ardennes sector of the front and were waging an intense defensive battle.

On 6 January 1945 Prime Minister Churchill of Great Britain addressed an appeal to the Soviet government to speed up the offensive by Soviet forces, in order to ease the American-English forces' difficult situation along the Ardennes sector of the Western European front.

True to its allied duty, the Soviet government changed the beginning of the Soviet forces' winter offensive from 20 January to 12-14 January 1945.

The attacks were to be launched along a 1,200-kilometer front from the Baltic Sea to the Carpathian Mountains against the most powerful German-Fascist group of forces, which included army groups Center and A, which numbered 83 divisions, of which 12 were panzer and panzer-grenadier (up to 40 percent of all forces), and which were defending East Prussia, the extremely important Warsaw—Berlin strategic direction, and the Silesian industrial area.

The enemy was stubbornly defending along the entire Soviet-German front.

The German-Fascist Forces' Situation

Along the Warsaw—Berlin direction the enemy's front line ran from Modlin along the western bank of the Vistula River through Warsaw, the Magnuszew, Pulawy and Sandomierz bridge-heads, and then to Jaslo. Here were deployed the forces of Army Group A,[3] consisting of the Ninth, Seventeenth and First (Hungarian) field armies, and the Fourth and First panzer armies, numbering 43 divisions (of which six were panzer).

The German-Fascist forces defending in Poland, through a stubborn defense, were to prevent the advance of the Soviet army toward Berlin and the most important industrial areas of Germany.

For this purpose, seven defensive lines, which included field engineering structures, permanent fortified areas, fortresses and inhabited locales configured for defense, had been prepared in the First Belorussian Front's sector between the Vistula and Oder rivers to a depth of 570 kilometers.

The most powerful of these was the first (Vistula) line, which had been occupied beforehand by the enemy forces, and which consisted of four defensive zones with a depth of 30-70 kilometers.

The second defensive line had been prepared 60-125 kilometers from the forward edge of the first line along the Bzura, Pilica, Szreniawa, and Raba rivers. This line had not been completed and consisted of two positions with a depth of 3-5 kilometers.

The third, or Warta, defensive line ran along the line Thorn (Torun)—Konin—Warta River to Kaluze (east of Wozniki)—Pszemta River (west of Krakow) and covered the Silesian industrial area from the east.

The fourth, or Poznan, defensive line ran along the line east of Schneidemühl, Poznan, Ostrow, and Kreuzburg. The line consisted of a series of powerful strong points, connected with each other by trenches.

---

3   The commander of Army Group A was Colonel General Harpe until 17 January 1945, and afterwards Colonel General Schörner.

The third and fourth lines were connected by a switch position running along the line excluding Thorn (Torun)—Bromberg (Bydgoszcz)—excluding Schneidemühl. Along with the Warta position, this zone was named "Line C" by the Germans.

The fifth line ran along the former German-Polish border along the line Neustettin—Schloppe—Schwerin—Grunberg. In the north the line covered the border fortified areas.

The sixth line ran in the First Belorussian Front's sector and consisted of the Pomeranian and Mesertiz fortified areas. The density of the reinforced concrete structures along this line was the highest and reached seven and more permanent firing points per kilometer of front, which were echeloned to a depth of 4-6 kilometers.

The seventh, or Oder, defensive line ran along the western bank of the Oder River, from the shore of the Baltic Sea to Grunberg and then to the southeast. This line also had permanent firing points. Insofar as the line covered the immediate approaches to Berlin, great significance was attached to its defense.

Thus the first (Vistula)and sixth lines were the most highly developed, in the engineering sense, as well as such centers of resistance as Warsaw, Modlin, Thorn (Torun), Poznan, Glogau, Küstrin, and others.

By the beginning of the offensive by our armed forces, the German-Fascist forces occupied only the first (Vistula) line of defense

The enemy facing the First Ukrainian Front had created four defensive lines at a depth of up to 120 kilometers. The defense was built on the combination of hard-to-overcome natural conditions (mountains) and engineering-field fortifications. The first defense line, the best prepared in the engineering sense and occupied by the enemy's forces, consisted of two defensive zones—a main one (the "main battlefield") and a second one (the "position of corps reserves"), as well as individual centers of resistance in inhabited locales in difficult-to-overcome mountain defiles. The succeeding defensive lines usually included non-contiguous positions located along the most accessible mountainous sectors; these positions were not occupied by the troops beforehand. The basic difficulty in overcoming such a defense was due to the fact that the mountainous and wooded character of the terrain made outflanking movements by large forces with a lot of equipment, difficult.

The idea of the enemy's defense along the Warsaw—Berlin direction was to employ the forces of Army Group A to prevent the breakthrough of the main Vistula defensive line by Soviet forces and, in the event of the latter's success, to slow down their offensive along the succeeding lines and through flank attacks by their forces restore the situation.

The enemy forces occupied, as a rule, only the main defensive zone, with their operational formation in a single echelon. There were no troops along the remaining defensive zones and lines, with the exception of individual centers of resistance. Reserves were comparatively few in number. The defense basically relied on the first-echelon forces, which in the case of necessity were to successively fall back and occupy defensive positions that had been prepared in depth, as well as reserves, which it was planned to throw into the battle during the course of the battle from other sectors of the front and from the depths of Germany (the German-Fascist command transferred to the Warsaw—Berlin direction 23 divisions during the course of the Vistula-Oder offensive operation, not counting a large number of various independent units and elements).

In all, the enemy had 35 divisions (including four panzer and two panzergrenadier), two combat groups, ten independent regiments, more than 50 independent battalions, and one screening and six sapper brigades) facing our two *fronts* (First Belorussian and First Ukrainian). All of these forces formed part of the German-Fascist Ninth and Seventeenth field and Fourth Panzer armies.[4]

---

4   This information is taken from captured situation maps of the German General Staff for January 1945. Archives of the Main Military-Scientific Directorate, USSR General Staff.

The average operational density along the entire front reached up to one division for 18-20 kilometers, and 12-15 guns and mortars, and 1-2 tanks per kilometer of front. Opposite the bridgeheads seized by our forces this density was a little higher and reached one division per 12-16 kilometers, up to 43 guns and mortars, and up to 23 tanks and assault guns per kilometer of front.

The Soviet Forces' Situation

As a result of the Lublin–Brest operation of 1944, the forces of the First Belorussian Front reached the Vistula River from Jablonna to Jozefow, forced this important river barrier along individual sectors, and seized bridgeheads in the areas of Magnuszew (45 kilometers wide and up to 10-18 kilometers deep) and Pulawy (up to 30 kilometers wide and up to ten kilometers deep). By the start of the operation the *front* occupied a line up to 230 kilometers in width. The *front* contained eight combined-arms armies (47th, Polish 1st, 8th Guards, 69th, 5th Shock, 3rd Shock, 33rd, and 61st), two tank armies (1st and 2nd guards), two air armies (16th and 6th), two tank (9th and 11th), two cavalry (2nd and 7th guards) corps, two fortified areas (115th and 119th), and other reinforcement units and formations. Of this number, four combined-arms (3rd and 5th shock, 33rd and 61st) and two tank (1st and 2nd guards) armies had arrived from the *Stavka* of the Supreme High Command Reserve.

The *front's* forces were opposed by ten divisions of the German Ninth Army (seven infantry, two panzer and one panzergrenadier) and a significant number of independent units (one independent screening brigade, one independent infantry regiment and 14 independent battalions). The army had three corps—XLVI Panzer (73rd and 337th infantry divisions), VIII Army (251st, 6th and 45th infantry divisions) and LVI Panzer (17th and 214th infantry divisions) corps—in its first echelon, for a total of seven infantry divisions. The Ninth Army's operational reserve was the XL Panzer Corps (25th and 19th panzer and the 174th Panzergrenadier divisions), which was located in the Radom area.[5] Besides this, the enemy could also employ up to five divisions from neighboring axes to resist the *front's* forces.

The overall correlation of forces along the First Belorussian Front's sector was in the *front's* favor in the following way: 6-7:1 in infantry, 8-9:1 in artillery and mortars, 4-5:1 in tanks and self-propelled guns, and 7-8:1 in aviation.

During September-December 1944 and the first half of January 1945, the two sides' forces received personnel and equipment reinforcements and were brought up to 80-90 percent of their authorized strength. However, in qualitative terms the reinforcements being received by the German-Fascist forces were more and more inferior to those of the Soviet forces, because fascist Germany's mobilization possibilities were at their limit and most of the German-Fascist armed forces were being reinforced with cohorts that had been excused from military service during the call-ups of the early war years. In quantitative terms a German-Fascist infantry division contained approximately 1/3 more men and materiel than our rifle division. The qualitative state of the Soviet forces' equipment was no lower, and in many cases higher, than that of the enemy. The state of the Soviet armed forces' morale was higher than that of the enemy.

The German-Fascist Ninth Army, which was covering the extremely important Warsaw—Berlin direction, had as its main task preventing the Soviet troops' arrival at the borders of Germany and the approaches to her capital of Berlin through the stubborn defense of the previously-occupied Vistula defensive line and the launching of flank attacks by operational reserves from the Radom

---

5   This information is taken from captured German General Staff maps for January 1945. Archives of the Main Military-Scientific Directorate of the USSR General Staff.

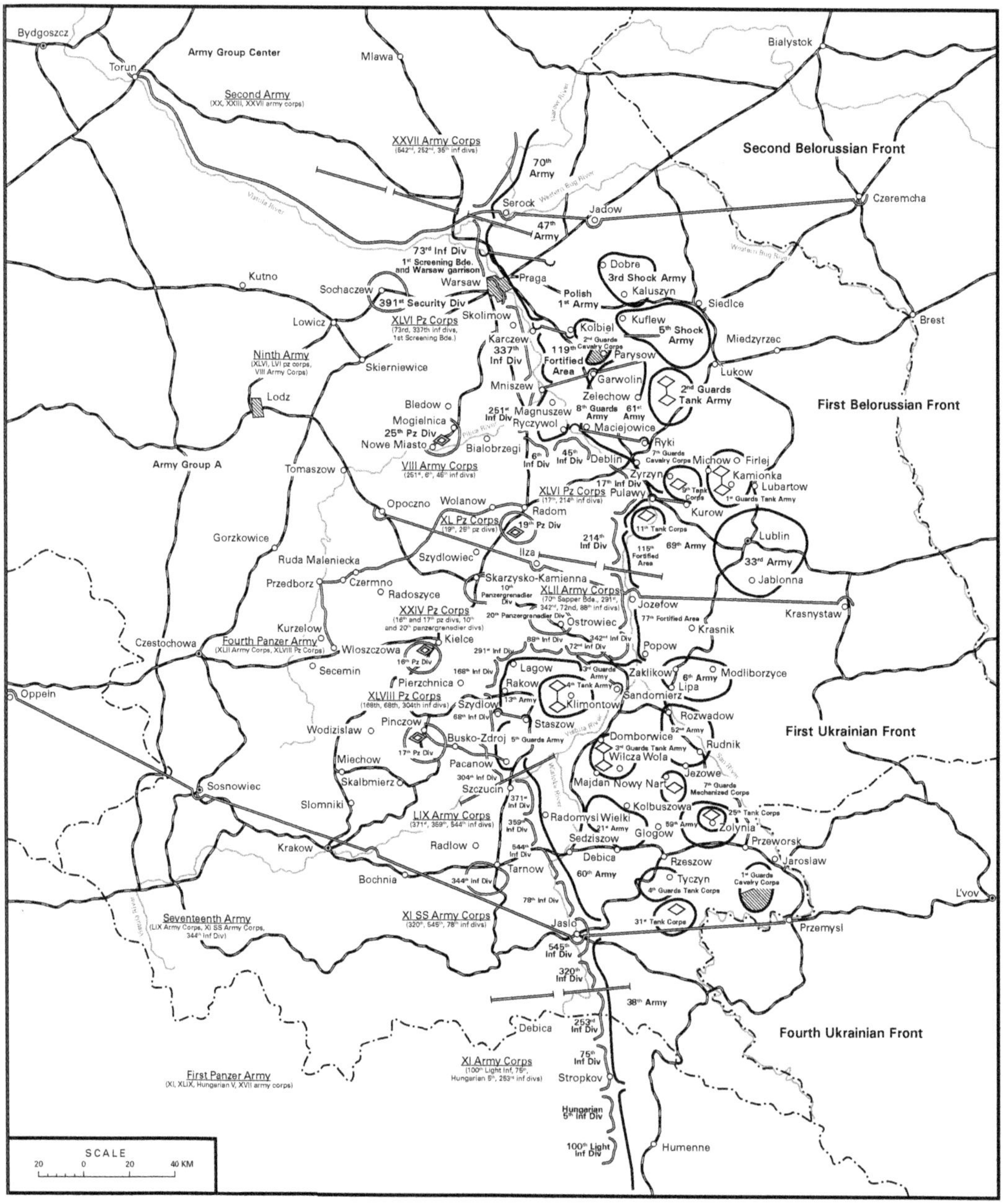

Bydgoszcz

Army Group Center

Torun

Second Army
(XX, XXIII, XXVII army corps)

Mlawa

Bialystok

Second Belorussian Front

XXVII Army Corps
(542nd, 252nd, 35th inf divs)

70th Army

Czeremcha

Serock

Jadow

47th Army

73rd Inf Div
1st Screening Bde.
and Warsaw garrison

Warsaw — Praga

Kutno

Sochaczew

Dobre
3rd Shock Army
Kaluszyn

391st Security Div

Polish 1st Army

Siedlce

Lowicz

Skolimow

Kolbiel

Kuflew
6th Shock Army

Brest

XLVI Pz Corps
(73rd, 337th inf divs,
1st Screening Bde.)

Karczew

2nd Guards
Cavalry Corps

Farysow

Miedzyrzec

Skierniewice

337th
Inf Div

119th
Fortified
Area

Ninth Army
(XLVI, LVI pz corps,
VIII Army Corps)

Mniszew

Garwolin

Lukow

First Belorussian Front

Lodz

Bledow

Mogielnica
25th Pz Div
Nowe Miasto

251st
Inf Div

Magnuszew
Ryczywol

Zelechow

8th Guards
Army

61st
Army

2nd Guards
Tank Army

Bialobrzegi

Maciejowice

Ryki

Army Group A

Tomaszow

45th
Inf Div

Deblin

7th Guards
Cavalry Corps

Michow

Firlej

VIII Army Corps
(251st, 6th, 45th divs)

Wolanow

17th Inf Div

Zyrzyn

Pulawy

Kamionka

Lubartow

1st Guards Tank Army

Opoczno

XLVI Pz Corps
(17th, 214th inf divs)

Kurow

XL Pz Corps
(19th, 25th pz divs)

Radom

19th Pz Div

214th
Inf Div

11th Tank Corps

69th Army

Lublin

Gorzkowice

Ruda Maleniecka

Szydlowiec

Ilza

118th
Fortified
Area

33rd Army

Jablonna

Przedborz

Czermno

Skarzysko-Kamienna

Radoszyce

10th
Panzergrenadier
Div

XLII Army Corps
(70th Sapper Bde., 291st,
342nd, 72nd, 88th inf divs)

Jozefow

77th Fortified Area

Krasnystaw

Kurzelow

XXIV Pz Corps
(16th and 17th pz divs, 10th
and 20th panzergrenadier divs)

20th Panzergrenadier Div

Ostrowiec

Krasnik

Fourth Panzer Army
(XLII Army Corps, XLVIII Pz Corps)

Kielce

88th Inf Div

342nd Inf Div

72nd Inf Div

Popow

Czestochowa

Wloszczowa

16th Pz Div

291st Inf Div

Oppeln

Pierzchnica

168th Inf Div

Lagow

3rd Guards
Army

Zaklikow

Lipa

6th
Army

Modliborzyce

Secemin

XLVIII Pz Corps
(168th, 68th, 304th inf divs)

Szydlow

Rakow

4th Tank Army

Klimontow

Sandomierz

Wodzislaw

Pinczow

68th Inf Div

Staszow

5th Guards Army

Rozwadow

52nd Army

First Ukrainian Front

Miechow

17th Pz Div

Busko-Zdroj

Domborwice

3rd Guards Tank Army
Wilcza Wola

Rudnik

Skalbmierz

Pacanow

Jezowe

Sosnowiec

Szczucin

304th Inf Div

Majdan Nowy Nart

7th Guards
Mechanized Corps

Slomniki

LIX Army Corps
(371st, 359th, 544th inf divs)

371st
Inf Div

Radomysl Wielki

21st Army

Kolbuszowa

59th Army

25th Tank Corps

Zolynia

Krakow

Radlow

359th
Inf Div

Sedziszow

Glogow

Przeworsk

544th
Inf Div

Debica

Rzeszow

Jaroslaw

Bochnia

344th Inf Div

Tarnow

60th Army

Tyczyn

4th Guards Tank Corps

1st Guards
Cavalry Corps

L'vov

78th Inf Div

Seventeenth Army
(LIX Army Corps, XI SS Army Corps,
344th Inf Div)

XI SS Army Corps
(320th, 545th, 78th divs)

Jaslo

31st Tank Corps

Przemysl

545th
Inf Div

320th
Inf Div

38th Army

Debica

252nd
Inf Div

Fourth Ukrainian Front

First Panzer Army
(XI, XLIX, Hungarian X, XVII army corps)

XI Army Corps
(100th Light Inf, 75th,
Hungarian 5th, 253rd inf divs)

75th
Inf Div

Stropkov

Hungarian
5th Inf Div

Humenne

100th Light
Inf Div

SCALE
20 0 20 40 KM

Map 2 The Situation along the First Belorussian and First Ukrainian Fronts' Sectors by the Beginning of January 1945.

area against the First Belorussian Front's forces, in the event of their offensive from the Magnuszew and Pulawy bridgeheads.

As a result of the L'vov—Sandomierz operation of 1944, the forces of the First Ukrainian Front reached the Vistula River and seized the broad Sandomierz bridgehead (up to 70 kilometers in width and up to 50 kilometers deep). By the start of the operation the *front* occupied a 250-kilometer line from Jozefow to Jaslo. The *front* contained eight combined-arms (3rd and 5th guards, 13th, 60th, 6th, 52nd,[6] 21st, and 59th) armies, two tank (3rd Guards and 4th) armies and one air (2nd) army, three tank (4th Guards, 25th and 31st), a mechanized (7th Guards) and one cavalry (1st Guards) corps. Of this number, four combined-arms (6th, 21st, 52nd, and 59th) and two tank (3rd Guards and 4th) armies had arrived from the *Stavka* of the Supreme High Command Reserve.

Defending against the *front* were the German Fourth Panzer and Seventeenth armies, which numbered overall 13 infantry divisions and two combat groups. The Fourth Panzer Army's first echelon contained two corps—XLII Army (342nd, 72nd, 88th, and 291st infantry divisions) and XLVIII Panzer (168th, 68th and 304th infantry divisions). In reserve were two combat groups (up to 10,000 men in Sochaczew, and up to 3,000 officers and men in the Opatow area). The Seventeenth Army had in its first echelon two corps—LIX Army (371st, 359th and 544th infantry divisions) and the XI Army SS (78th, 545th and 344th infantry divisions) corps.

The overall correlation of forces in the First Ukrainian Front's sector was in the *front's* favor: 3:1 in infantry, 4-5:1 in guns and mortars, more than 6:1 in tanks and self-propelled artillery, and 7-8:1 in aviation.

The sides' qualitative situation was approximately the same as that in the First Belorussian Front's zone.

The German-Fascist Fourth Panzer and Seventeenth armies had as their chief task covering the Sandomierz—Czestochowa and Krakow axes by means of a stubborn defense of previously constructed defensive zones.

The commander of Army Group A had the following reserve: XXIV Panzer Corps (16th and 17th panzer and the 20th panzergrenadier divisions) in the Kielce—Chmielnik area, the 391st Security Division in the Sochaczew area, the 431st and 432nd reserve divisions in the Lodz and Plock areas, the 27th Panzer Division in the area south of Krakow, the 620th Grenadier Division in the Zdunska Wola area, and the 601st, 602nd, 603rd, and 608th special designation divisions were in the Krakow—Michalow—Koniecpol area.[7]

Assuming that the First Belorussian Front's main attack would be launched to the southwest, and that of the First Ukrainian Front to the northwest (toward Kielce), the German-Fascist command calculated, while relying on the constructed defensive lines, on halting the Soviet forces' advance through a stubborn defense and, subsequently, through attacks by two panzer groups of forces (from the area south of Kielce and north of Krakow), to restore the situation. In the event of a breakthrough of the Vistula defensive line by Soviet forces, it was planned to wear out the Soviet units by means of stubborn defensive fighting along the succeeding lines.

In all, the First Belorussian and First Ukrainian fronts contained 16 combined-arms, four tank and three air armies, and five independent tank, one mechanized and three cavalry corps. These forces numbered 137 divisions, 26,276 guns and mortars (76mm and higher), 7,049 tanks and self-propelled guns, and 4,872 planes.

The enemy's forces defending against the two *fronts* numbered two field and one panzer armies and one air fleet, for a total of 35 divisions (of these, four panzer and two panzergrenadier), two

---

6   Editor's note. This army is mistakenly designated the 62nd in the text.

7   This information is taken from captured German General Staff maps. Archives of the Main Military-Scientific Directorate.

combat groups, one covering and six sapper brigades, ten independent regiments, and more than 50 independent battalions. In all, they numbered 4,261 guns and mortars, 1,272 tanks and assault guns, and up to 700 aircraft.

The overall superiority of our forces over the enemy was 6.1:1 in divisions, artillery and mortars, 5.5:1 in tanks and self-propelled guns, and 7:1 in aircraft.

Thus the Soviet forces' offensive along the Warsaw—Berlin direction in January 1945 began in a favorable situation for the Soviet forces. The *fronts'* forces occupied a favorable position along the most direct routes leading to the capital of fascist Germany, Berlin, and to the Silesian industrial area.

The bridgeheads over the Vistula River in the First Belorussian and First Ukrainian fronts' sectors were extremely important, as their presence made it possible to begin an offensive operation without having to force a major water barrier such as the Vistula, which facilitated the achievement of high rates of attack.

The Fourth Ukrainian Front, consisting of four combined-arms (38th, 1st Guards, 18th, and 40th) armies, a Czechoslovak army corps and an air army (8th), was faced by the enemy in the Western Carpathians with up to nine divisions from the German Seventeenth and First Panzer armies and the Hungarian First Army.

The Air Situation[8]

During the course of the Soviet army's successful offensive operations in 1944, German-Fascist aviation suffered major losses. As a result, the overall number of the enemy's combat aircraft operating on the Soviet-German front (also counting Hungarian planes), which included the First, Fourth and Sixth air fleets, fell to 1,800 aircraft. However, as the Soviet forces advanced further to the west, the German-Fascist command had the opportunity to bring in aviation based in Germany and operating on the Western Front. At the same time, with the loss of Romanian oil, the reserves of aviation fuel in fascist Germany sharply fell.

Army Group Center (in East Prussia) and Army Group A (in Poland) were supported by the Sixth Air Fleet, which numbered about 700 aircraft, of which there were up to 500 fighters (Me-109s[9] and Fw-190s[10]), up to 90 bombers (Ju-88s,[11] Ju-87s[12] and He-111s[13]), and up to 90 reconnaissance aircraft of various types. Of this number, about 400 aircraft were based in East Prussia and only about 300 in Poland (of these, there were 200 fighters, 40 bombers and 40 reconnaissance aircraft, while the remainder consisted of transport and other aircraft). The Sixth Air Fleet's planes were dispersed among many airfields in East Prussia and in Poland and maneuvered widely along the front, depending upon the ground situation, weather conditions and the availability of aviation

---

8   Based on reports by the 16th and 2nd air armies for January 1945. Archive of the Main Air Force Staff.

9   Editor's note. The Me-109 first appeared in 1937 and was the most popular German fighter of World War II. It had a speed of 640 kilometer per hour and mounted two 13mm machine guns and three 20mm cannons. The Me-109 could also carry a single 250-kilogram bomb.

10   Editor's note. The Fw-190 was a single-seat fighter that appeared in 1941. One model had a top speed of 656 kilometers per hour and could carry two 13mm machine guns and four 20mm cannon.

11   Editor's note. The Ju-88 was a twin-engine bomber that appeared in 1939. It carried a crew of four and had a top speed of 510 kilometers per hour. It carried five 7.92mm machine guns and could deliver up to 1,400 kilograms of bombs.

12   Editor's note. The Ju-87 ("Stuka") was a two-man dive bomber with a top speed of 390 kilometers per hour. It carried three 7.92mm machine guns and could carry up to 250 kilograms of bombs.

13   Editor's note. The He-111 was used as a transport plane and a bomber. It had a five-man crew and a top speed of 440 kilometers per hour. It carried up to seven 7.92mm machine guns, a 20mm cannon, one 13mm machine gun, and had a bomb load of 2,000 kilograms.

fuel at the airfields, for the purpose of maximally concentrating air strength along this or that axis. This maneuver enabled them to create a false impression of a large number of enemy aircraft. For example, according to the data from the air armies' headquarters, it worked out that the enemy had more than 1,000 planes in East Prussia and about 1,000 in Poland.

As a result of Soviet aviation's air superiority and the small number of enemy planes (in all, about 700 aircraft), a shortage of aviation fuel, and the difficult meteorological conditions, the enemy's air activity along the Warsaw—Berlin direction was insignificant and its activity was basically limited to carrying out air reconnaissance. For example, in the First Belorussian Front's sector only 112 enemy flyovers were noted in the first half of January.

The greatest resistance to Soviet aviation was put up by the enemy's anti-aircraft artillery, which numbered up to 200 batteries, or about 900 guns. The anti-aircraft artillery was mainly grouped in the areas with important rear targets, communications centers, depots, and main groups of forces. In particular, up to 40 batteries were noted in the area of the Magnuszew bridgehead and up to 25 batteries in the Warsaw area.

The First Belorussian Front included the 16th Air Army, which consisted of the 6th and 13th fighter corps, the 6th Assault Air Corps, the 1st Guards, 282nd and 286th fighter divisions, the 2nd and 11th guards assault air divisions, the 221st and 183rd bomber divisions, the 9th Guards Night Bomber Division, the 16th Independent Reconnaissance Regiment, and the 980th Independent Fire-Adjustment Reconnaissance Regiment.

Aside from this, the *front* also included formations of the 6th Air Army, which were supporting the Polish 1st Army and which had arrived as reinforcements from the *Stavka* reserve—the 5th Guards Fighter Corps, 9th Assault Air Corps, the 183rd Bomber Division, the 242nd Night Bomber Division, the 1st Guards Fighter Division, and the 72nd Independent Fire-Adjustment Reconnaissance Regiment.

The First Ukrainian Front included the 2nd Air Army, consisting of the 6th Guards, 2nd and 5th fighter corps, the 5th and 2nd guards and 3rd assault air corps, the 2nd Guards and 4th bomber corps, the 208th Night Bomber Division, the 98th and 193th independent reconnaissance regiments, and the 118th Independent Fire-Adjustment Reconnaissance Regiment.

The Fourth Ukrainian Front included the 8th Air Army, which consisted of the 10th Fighter Corps, 8th Assault Air Corps, the 321st Bomber Division, the 3rd Fighter Regiment, the 208th Assault Air Regiment, and the 8th Independent Reconnaissance Regiment.

In all, the 16th, 2nd and 8th air armies included the following number of combat aircraft:

Air Army Combat Aircraft

Air Army	Total Aircraft	Of these	
		Fighters	Assault
16th Air Army	1,275	637	300
Reinforcements for the 16th Air Army	1,015	361	395
Total for 16th Air Army	2,290	998	695
2nd Air Army	2,582	1,172	775
8th Air Army	560	211	209
Total	5,432	2,381	1,679

Air Army		Of these	
	Long-Range Bombers	Night Bombers	Reconnaissance and Fire-Adjustment
16th Air Army	192	83	63
Reinforcements for the 16th Air Army*	137	91	31
Total for 16th Air Army	329	174	94
2nd Air Army	417	114	104
8th Air Army	81	–	59
Total	827	288	257

* Including the 6th Air Army and formations from the Supreme High Command Reserve.

It follows that Soviet aviation, in the person of the 16th, 2nd and 8th air armies, enjoyed a nearly eight-fold superiority in air power over the German Sixth Air Fleet. Actually, this superiority was even greater, if one takes into account the fact that a significant part of the Sixth Air Fleet's aircraft was tied down by Soviet air operations in East Prussia, where the Third and Second Belorussian fronts' operation was simultaneously unfolding.

Aside from *front* aviation along the Warsaw—Berlin direction, it was also planned to employ the 18th Air Army of long-range bombers, under the command of Chief Air Marshal A.Ye. Golovanov.[14]

Thus the air situation was also favorable for the Soviet forces.

A Brief Military-Geographical Description of the Operational Area

Military operations in the Vistula-Oder operation unfolded along the Berlin strategic direction, on Polish territory between the Vistula and Oder rivers.

The operational area was delimited as follows: the Vistula River from the east and the Oder River from the west; the Vistula and Warta rivers from the north and the Carpathian Mountains from the south.

The terrain in the First Belorussian Front's offensive zone is a slightly hilly plain.

A large part of the area in the First Ukrainian Front's sector is made up of the hilly Little Polish Uplands, the Kielce—Sadomierz Uplands, which contains more difficult terrain, and the Krakow Uplands, which is a continuation of the northern spurs of the Carpathian Mountains. Up to half of the area is covered in forests.

The Fourth Ukrainian Front's operational area represents, particularly in the southern part, a mountainous and wooded section of the Carpathians, which is particularly difficult for the conduct of military operations.

The operational area had important economic significance for fascist Germany. Here were located the Kielce—Radom center of military industry, the Silesian coal and metallurgical area, and the Warsaw and Lodz industrial areas.

The entire terrain sector between the Vistula and Oder is cut by several rivers. The Vistula, Warta, Pilica, and Oder rivers are natural barriers along the path of attacking forces. The largest of them, the Vistula, is 400-1,900 meters wide and 1.5-8 meters deep; the Oder River is correspondingly

---

14 Editor's note. Aleksandr Yevgen'evich Golovanov (1904-75) joined the Red Army in 1919 and spent several years in the secret police before transferring to the aviation branch. During the Great Patriotic War he served as an air division commander and in 1942 was appointed chief of Long-Range Aviation. Following the war, Golovanov's star faded and he was retired following Stalin's death.

200-400 meters wide and 2.5-10 meters deep; the Warta River is correspondingly 40-100 meters wide and 0.6-4 meters deep; the remaining rivers have a smaller width and depth. The majority of rivers flow from south to north, cutting across the path of troops moving from east to west. During the operation the rivers were covered with ice to a thickness of 12-15 centimeters, and in places up to 40 centimeters. Bridges had to be laid down in order to ferry tanks and heavy artillery. The water barriers made both the breakthrough of the defense and the development of the operation considerably more difficult.

The railroad density in the area was from four to 18 kilometers per 100 square kilometers and 30-39 kilometers of auto and animal-drawn transport roads per 100 square kilometers, which made possible the free maneuver of men and materiel along all axes. However, our forces' exploitation of the railroads was made difficult by the fact that these railroads used the Western European gauge, and were moreover significantly damaged by the enemy during his withdrawal.

The strategic significance of the operational area was also determined by the fact that the capital of our Polish ally, Warsaw, was in our forces' offensive zone, and upon their arrival at the Oder River our forces were at a distance of 60-70 kilometers from the capital of Germany, Berlin.

On the whole, the terrain allowed for the deployment of major forces in an offensive operation, with the employment of all combat arms, and the conduct of broad maneuver along the front and in depth. Simultaneously, it afforded the enemy the opportunity to employ natural lines and inhabited locales for defensive purposes.

3

The Operation's Preparation

The *Stavka* of the VGK's Plan for the Operation

The *Stavka* defined the goal of the Vistula-Oder offensive operation as the defeat of the German-Fascist Army Group A on Polish territory, the completion of the liberation of her territory and population from the power of the fascists, and the transfer of military operations to German territory along the Berlin direction in the interests of creating conditions for the subsequent launching of concluding attacks against the fascist armed forces in Europe.

The *Stavka* of the Supreme High Command's operational plan[1] was that the forces of two *fronts* (First Belorussian and First Ukrainian), with the assistance of a third *front* (Fourth Ukrainian), were to break through the enemy's defense along the line of the Vistula River along several axes; while launching deep frontal attacks from the Magnuszew, Pulawy and Sandomierz bridgehead, in conjunction with attacks along intersecting axes, they were to split up the enemy's Army Group A into a series of isolated groups of forces and then, while developing the offensive at high speed to the west in the area between the Vistula and Oder rivers, destroy the bulk of the enemy group of forces during the course of the pursuit.

The enemy's defense was to be pierced simultaneously along four sectors, each 50-100 kilometers from each other and totaling 62-64 kilometers in width.

According to the *Stavka* plan, the main attack would be launched by the forces of the First Belorussian Front south of Warsaw, from the Magnuszew and Pulawy bridgeheads, in the general direction of Poznan, with a second attack by the forces of the First Ukrainian Front from the Sandomierz bridgehead toward Radomsko and Breslau. The overall front of the First Belorussian and First Ukrainian fronts would be 480 kilometers. The Fourth Ukrainian Front would simultaneously launch an attack with part of its forces toward Krakow.

The basic idea of the *Stavka* plan involved the very rapid defeat of the enemy's first operational echelon and his operational reserves, followed by the vigorous development of the operation in depth.

The *Stavka* plan called for the Soviet forces' high rate of advance, so that the enemy could not succeed in occupying beforehand the prepared rear defensive lines, either with his retreating forces, or by his reserves from the depth.

The offensive by the First Belorussian and First Ukrainian fronts was to be supported from the north with the simultaneous conduct of the East Prussian offensive operation by the forces of the Third and Second Belorussian fronts, supported by the First Baltic Front.

On the basis of this plan, the *Stavka* of the Supreme High Command assigned the *fronts* and long-range aviation the following objectives:

---

1   See *Stavka* directives no. 22070 of 25.11 1944, no. 220275 of 28.11 1944. Ministry of Defense Archives. First Belorussian and First Ukrainian front *fonds*, and other materials.

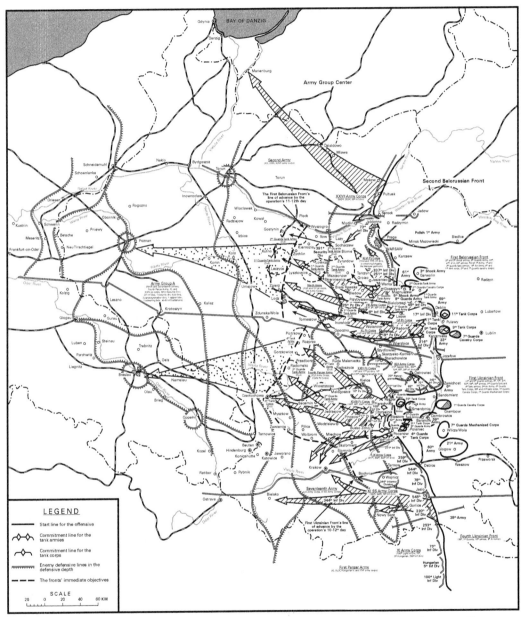

Map 3 The Decision by the Commanders of the First Belorussian and First Ukrainian Fronts on the Conduct of the Operation along the Poznan and Breslau Directions.

The forces of the First Belorussian Front (Marshal of the Soviet Union G.K. Zhukov, commanding) were to launch their attacks from two bridgeheads south of Warsaw in the general direction of Poznan. The breadth of the attack front was 230 kilometers.

The *front* was given the immediate objective of defeating, in conjunction with the forces of the Second Belorussian Front and together with the First Ukrainian Front, the Warsaw—Radom enemy group of forces, liberate Warsaw and to arrive with its main forces at the line Piotrkowek—Zychlin—Lodz by the eleventh or twelfth day of the operation.[2]

The *front* was assigned the subsequent objective of developing the offensive in the general direction of Poznan.

It was ordered to launch the main attack with the forces of four combined-arms armies, two tank armies and a single cavalry corps from the Magnuszew bridgehead in the general direction of Kutno, while part of its forces would attack to the northwest and, in conjunction with the *front's* right wing attacking north of Warsaw, defeat the enemy's Warsaw group of forces and capture Warsaw.

The defense along the main axis was to be pierced by three armies along a 16-17-kilometer front. One combined-arms army was detailed to the *front's* second echelon. It was planned to commit it for the development of the success along the main axis in the general direction of Kutno and then to Poznan.

The *front* was ordered to create an artillery density along the main axis of up to 240 guns and mortars per kilometer of breakthrough front.

The *front's* mobile group — 1st and 2nd guards tank armies—was to attack from the Magnuszew bridgehead for the development of the success in depth and to outflank Warsaw from the south-west. An additional *Stavka* directive instructed that "… it is not necessary to carry out the commitment of the tank armies into the breach on the offensive's first day, but after the tactical depth of the enemy's defense is pierced, having received the *Stavka's* preliminary permission for the commitment of the armies into the breach."[3]

The Polish 1st Army, which was operating as part of the First Belorussian Front, was deployed in the first operational echelon opposite the city of Warsaw. It was planned to employ the army for capturing the capital of Poland, following the breakthrough of the enemy's defense along the main axis.

Support for the main group of forces' offensive would be carried out from the north by the offensive of part of the Second Belorussian Front's forces, according to the plan for the East Prussian operation along the northern bank of the Vistula River, through an offensive by the First Belorussian Front's auxiliary group of forces, and by the attack by part of the main group of forces' troops from the Magnuszew bridgehead to the northwest, and from the south by part of the forces of the *front's* Pulawy group of forces attacking to the southwest.

It was planned to launch a second *front* attack with the forces of two combined-arms armies, two tank corps and a cavalry corps from the Pulawy bridgehead in the general direction of Radom and Lodz, along a 12-13-kilometer front.

The *front* was to launch an attack with part of this group's forces in the direction of Szydlowiec toward the forces of the First Ukrainian Front, for the purpose of defeating the enemy's Kielce—Radom group of forces.

---

2   *Stavka* of the Supreme High Command directive no. 220275 of 28 November 1944. Ministry of Defense Archives. First Belorussian Front *fond*.

3   *Stavka* of the Supreme High Command directive no. 220290 of 29 December 1944. Ministry of Defense Archives. First Belorussian Front *fond*.

The *front* was ordered to launch a supporting attack north of Warsaw with the forces of the 47th Army, along a 4-kilometer front, for the purpose of clearing the enemy's forces out of the area between the Vistula and Western Bug rivers (in conjunction with the Second Belorussian Front's left-wing formations).

It was subsequently planned to employ this army for developing the success along the main direction or for launching an attack to outflank Warsaw from the northwest.

The forces of the First Ukrainian Front (Marshal of the Soviet Union I.S. Konev, commanding) were to launch an attack from the Sandomierz bridgehead in the general direction of Breslau, and with part of its forces toward Krakow.

The *front* was given the immediate objective of defeating, in conjunction with the First Belorussian Front, the enemy's Kielce—Radom group of forces and no later than the operation's tenth or eleventh day the line Piotrkow—Radomsko—Czestochowa—Zawiercie—Miechow—Bochnia.[4]

The *front* had the subsequent objective of developing the offensive in the general direction of Breslau.

The *front* was ordered to launch its main attack with the forces of five combined-arms armies and two tank armies, three tank corps and one mechanized corps from the Sandomierz bridgehead in the general direction of Radomsko. It was planned to break through the enemy's defense with the forces of three armies along a single 34-kilometer sector. The *front's* operational formation was to be in two echelons, with powerful mobile groups. It was ordered to raise the artillery density to 220 guns and mortars per kilometer along the breakthrough front.

It was planned to support the offensive by the *front's* main group of forces from the north, from the Ostrowiec area by the defense of one army and a fortified area; from the south by an offensive by two armies in the general direction of Krakow (with the latter's capture, under favorable conditions), as well as through a defense by part of the forces of one of the left wing's armies.

The forces of the Fourth Ukrainian Front (General I.Ye. Petrov, commanding) were given the objective of launching an offensive in the western Carpathian Mountains. Part of the *front's* forces was to attack toward the Silesian industrial area and, in conjunction with the First Ukrainian Front, to capture Krakow.[5]

The 18th Long-Range Aviation Air Army received the objective in the beginning of 1945 of primarily assisting the forces of the Third and Second Belorussian fronts in defeating the German-Fascist East Prussian group of forces by launching bombing raids against major railroad junctions and against ports in the southern part of the Baltic Sea, for the purpose of disrupting the enemy force's operational shipments. Simultaneously, the 18th Air Army was to be ready to support the offensive by the forces of the First Belorussian and First and Fourth Ukrainian fronts.

Thus, according to the *Stavka* plan, powerful shock groups of forces were to be created within the *fronts*, which were to ensure the rapid smashing of the enemy's defense and then the successful development of the offensive in depth, with the employment of mobile forces for this. The *fronts'* forces were to ensure the augmentation of efforts during the operation.

The forces of the Soviet air force were to be distributed in accordance with the plan for the overall strategic offensive by the Soviet army in 1945. Of the ten *front* air armies operating along the Soviet-German front, six armies (3rd, 1st, 4th, 16th, 6th, and 2nd), numbering more than 10,000 aircraft, and the main forces of the 18th Air Army's long-range heavy bombers, were concentrated for operations against the forces of the enemy's army groups Center and A. Moreover,

---

4   *Stavka* of the Supreme High Command directive no. 220271 of 25 November 1944. Ministry of Defense Archives. First Ukrainian Front *fond*.

5   Ministry of Defense Archives. Fourth Ukrainian Front *fond*. Excerpt from a brief report no. 1 from the generalized experience of the Fourth Ukrainian Front for January 1945 (inventory no. 4738) and other materials.

the combat strength of the 16th, 6th and 2nd air armies supporting the offensive by Soviet forces along the Warsaw—Berlin direction, had been raised to 4,872 planes; these included six fighter, five assault air and two bomber corps, as well as several independent aviation divisions.

The launching of frontal attacks by our forces simultaneously along several directions was supposed to result in the splitting of the main forces of the German-Fascist Army Group A into separate Warsaw, Kielce—Radom and Krakow groups of forces and create conditions for their defeat in detail.

Thus the form of conducting the multi-*front* Vistula-Oder offensive operation was the launching of several deep frontal attacks, with the development of the success into the depth and toward the flanks, for the purpose of splitting up the enemy's major group of forces and its subsequent defeat during the pursuit. The expediency of such a form was determined by the necessity of rapidly breaking through a deep (more than 500 kilometers) and well prepared, in the engineering sense, enemy defense, the location of his main forces along the Vistula defensive line, and the absence of his sufficient reserves in depth. Such a form for conducting the operation ensured, in the given operation, a high rate of offensive advance and enabled us to preempt the enemy in creating a defense along the rear lines.

The plan also called for measures for supporting the main groups of forces and a secure basis for close cooperation was laid down, both between the *fronts* taking part in the given operation, as well as with the Third and Second Belorussian fronts operating along the East Prussian direction.

As can be seen from the plan, the *Stavka* oriented the *fronts* toward the defeat, particularly of the enemy's Kielce—Radom group of forces, which was concentrated along the boundary of two *fronts*; this was to secure the timely arrival of our forces at this line on the eleventh or twelfth day of the operation and the subsequent successful development of the offensive in depth.

The *fronts'* immediate objective in depth was defined as 140-150 kilometers, and the offensive's daily advance at 12-14 kilometers. The overall depth of the *front* operations up to the arrival of our forces at the line Bromberg (Bydgoszcz)—Poznan—Breslau (Wroclaw) was 350 kilometers.

On the whole, the plan of the *Stavka* of the Supreme High Command directed the *fronts'* forces toward conducting large-scale operations and with decisive goals, which corresponded to the actual situation and correlation of forces.

The Decisions by the Front Commanders

First Belorussian Front. The plan by the commander of the First Belorussian Front, Marshal of the Soviet Union G.K. Zhukov, for the Vistula-Oder offensive operation consisted of launching powerful frontal attacks from the Magnuszew and Pulawy bridgeheads, and a supporting attack from the area north of Warsaw, breaking through the enemy's defense along three sectors and splitting the enemy group of forces into several parts and, developing the frontal attack in the general direction of Kutno and Poznan, defeating, in conjunction with the First Ukrainian Front, the enemy's opposing forces, and subsequently reaching the line Bromberg (Bydgoszcz)—Poznan.[6]

Three groups of forces were created to carry out the operation: Magnuszew, Pulawy and Warsaw.

The main attack, with the forces of four combined-arms (61st, 5th Shock, 8th Guards, and 3rd Shock) armies, two tank (1st and 2nd guards) and one cavalry corps (2nd Guards) was to be made from the Magnuszew bridgehead in the general direction of Kutno, and then toward Poznan. The piercing of the enemy defense would be carried out by the 61st, 5th Shock and 8th Guards armies

---

6   The First Belorussian Front's combat journal and other documents. Ministry of Defense Archives. First Belorussian Front *fond. Sbornik Materialov po Izucheniyu Opyta Voiny*, no. 25. Directorate for the Study of War Experience, the USSR Armed Forces General Staff, inventory no. 7235, and other materials.

along a 17-kilometer front between Mniszew and Szmielnik (west and southwest of Magnuszew), while the 3rd Shock Army would be moved to the *front's* second echelon).[7] It was planned to commit the army behind the first echelon's main forces, in readiness to develop the offensive toward Poznan. Part of the 8th Guards Army's forces was to attack toward Urbanow (northwest of Radom), in order to outflank the enemy's Radom group of forces from the northwest.

54 rifle divisions (80 percent of all the *front's* divisions), 10,032 guns and mortars (73 percent of all the artillery) and 3,000 tanks and self-propelled guns (87 percent of the *front's* entire tank park) formed the *front's* Magnuszew group of forces along the axis of the main attack.

The concentration of the *front's* main forces along the axis of the main attack enabled us to achieve the following correlation of forces along this axis in favor of the *front*: 8.7:1 in infantry; 11.1: 1 in guns; 12.2:1 in mortars, and; 12.5:1 in tanks and self-propelled guns. The density of guns and mortars was 183-282 tubes, and the density of infantry-support tanks from 15 to 29 armored vehicles per kilometer of breakthrough front.[8] In all, there were 75-116 tanks and self-propelled guns per kilometer of breakthrough front, counting the tank armies.

The second attack, by the forces of the 69th and 33rd armies and the 11th and 9th tank and 7th Cavalry corps, was to be launched by the *front* from the Pulawy bridgehead along a 13-kilometer sector in the general direction of Radom, and then toward Lodz. Part of the 33rd Army's forces would attack toward Szydlowiec, toward the First Ukrainian Front's forces, for the purpose of defeating the enemy's Ostrowiec group of forces. The densities to be created along the given axis were also large, rising to 213-252 guns and mortar and 23-27 tanks and self-propelled guns per kilometer of front.[9]

The following correlation of forces in favor of the *front* achieved along this axis was: 12:1 in infantry; 10-11:1 in guns and mortars, and; 10:1 in tanks and self-propelled guns.

A supporting attack, in conjunction with the *front's* main forces, for the purpose of defeating the enemy's Warsaw group of forces and capturing Warsaw, was to be launched by a group of forces consisting of the 47th and Polish 1st armies and part of the 61st Army. The breakthrough front of the 47th Army, which was to make the main attack north of Warsaw, was four kilometers.

The forces of the armies making up the Magnuszew group of forces were to break through the enemy's defense in the first two days to a depth of 25-30 kilometers, with a daily rate of advance of 12-15 kilometers, defeat the first echelon of the enemy forces and his immediate operational reserves, and on the operation's tenth or twelfth day reach the front Piotrkowek—Zychlin—Piontek—excluding Lodz, and to then continue the offensive in the general direction of Poznan.

The forces of the armies making up the Pulawy group of forces were also to break through the enemy's defense in the first two days to a depth of 25-30 kilometers, and on the tenth or twelfth day of the operation reach the front Lodz—Pabianice, and to then continue the offensive to the west.

The forces of the Warsaw group of forces were to launch attacks along converging axes. The 47th Army was to go over to the attack on the operation's second day, with the objective of eliminating the enemy's bridgeheads in the area between the rivers and developing the success toward Leszno (northwest of Warsaw), for the purpose of outflanking the enemy's Warsaw group of forces from the northwest. The Polish 1st Army was to go over to the offensive on the operation's fourth day, with the objective of rolling up the enemy's defense along the western bank of the Vistula River,

---

7   In the *front's* planning documents this was called the reserve.
8   For example, in the 5th Guards Army, which was to break through the defense along a 6-kilometer front, 282 guns and mortars and 23 tanks and self-propelled guns were concentrated along one kilometer of break-through front.
9   For example, the density along the 69th Army's 7-kilometer breakthrough sector was 252 guns and mortars and 27 tanks and self-propelled guns per kilometer of front.

south and north of Warsaw, and, in conjunction with the 47th Army and part of the 61st Army's forces attacking from the southeast in the direction of Blonie (southwest of Warsaw), to liberate the Polish capital of Warsaw.

The *front* had a two-echelon operational formation. The first operational echelon contained seven combined-arms armies and two tank corps. The second echelon contained one army (3rd Shock). Besides this, a *front* mobile group of two tank armies (1st and 2nd guards) and two cavalry corps (2nd and 7th guards) was to be formed. The armies were deployed in a single echelon, having no less than a rifle division in reserve. The corps' and divisions' combat formations consisted of two echelons.

The overall depth of the *front* operation was planned at up to 300-350 kilometers. It was planned to carry out the immediate objective to a depth of 120-150 kilometers, with an average daily rate of advance of 12-15 kilometers for the infantry, and up to 30 kilometers for the mobile forces. The depth of the army operations was planned at 125-180 kilometers.

The combined-arms armies were to break through the enemy's defensive front along 4-7 kilometer sectors, corps along 2.5-4 kilometer sectors, and divisions along 1.3-2.5 kilometers sectors. The depth of the army operations was planned at 125-180 kilometers. Corps were assigned immediate objectives to a depth of 8-12 kilometers, and divisions to a depth of 4-8 kilometers.

The *front's* mobile group was to operate in the following manner.

It was planned to commit the 2nd Guards Tank Army (824 tanks and self-propelled guns) into the breach on the operation's third day, depending upon the situation in the sector of the 5th Shock or 61st armies (after the infantry's arrival at the northern bank of the Pilica River), with the objective of launching an attack in the rear of the enemy's Warsaw group of forces in the general direction of Sochaczew and, by the close of the operation's fifth day, capture the Gostynin area (at a depth of 150 kilometers), and to then develop the offensive toward Inowroclaw. The commitment line was Gnewice—Goszczyn (20-30 kilometers west of Magnuszew). The army was to be committed into the breach along a 9-kilometer zone in a two-echelon formation, having two tank corps in the first echelon and a mechanized corps in the second.

It was also planned to commit the 1st Guards Tank Army (717 tanks and self-propelled guns) on the operation's third day along the 8th Guards Army's sector from the line Urbanow—Lesow (northwest of Radom), with the objective of developing the offensive on Poznan and, on the operation's fifth or sixth day (the third or fourth day following its commitment), to capture the Kutno area (at a depth of 180 kilometers). The army was to be committed into the breach in a single-echelon formation.

According to the operational plan, the 2nd Guards Cavalry Corps would be committed into the breach behind the 2nd Guards Tank Army and was to attack in close coordination with it.

On the whole, the 1st and 2nd guards tank armies and the 2nd Guards Cavalry Corps were to be committed after the breakthrough of the tactical defense zone to a depth of 20-30 kilometers and by the close of the offensive's fifth or sixth day reach the Gostynin—Kutno—Piontek area; they were to subsequently develop the offensive in the general direction of Poznan.

It was planned to employ the 7th Guards Cavalry Corps to develop the success of the *front's* shock group attacking from the Pulawy bridgehead.

According to the plan, the tank corps were to operate as the armies' mobile groups: the 11th Tank Corps with the 69th Army and the 9th Tank Corps with the 33rd Army, and were to be committed following the breakthrough of the main defensive zone, with the objective of seizing the second defensive zone on the march and developing the offensive on Lodz.

The 3rd Shock Army was designated for operating from the Magnuszew bridgehead for the purpose of augmenting our efforts along the main axis.

The beginning of the *front's* offensive was set for 20 January 1945 and was then shifted to 14 January, in connection with the difficult condition in which the Anglo-American forces found themselves as a result of the German-Fascist forces breaking through their front in the Ardennes.

First Ukrainian Front. The plan of the *front* commander, Marshal of the Soviet Union I.S. Konev, for the Sandomierz—Silesian offensive operation consisted of launching a single powerful frontal attack from the Sandomierz bridgehead, with its subsequent development in depth with the goal of defeating the opposing enemy and operating toward the flanks for the purpose of encircling and destroying, in conjunction with the First Belorussian Front, the Ostrowiec—Opatow and Kielce—Radom enemy groups of forces.

The main attack would be launched with the forces of three combined-arms (13th, 52nd and 5th Guards) and two tank (3rd Guards and 4th) armies and two tank corps (4th and 31st) from the Sandomierz bridgehead in the general direction of Radomsko and then toward Breslau.[10]

The breakthrough of the enemy's defense was to be carried out along a single 39-kilometer sector, which comprised 15.6 percent of the *front's* entire 250-kilometer front. A density of 223-296 guns and mortars and 18-25 tanks and self-propelled guns per kilometer of front was to be created.[11] In this manner the *front* was ensured the following favorable correlation of forces: 9.6:1 in infantry; 9.7:1 in artillery and mortars, and; 10.2:1 in tanks and self-propelled guns. When taking into account the tank armies and formations, the density of tanks along the breakthrough sector could be raised to 98-122 armored vehicles.

The *front's* shock group would be secured from the north from the Ostrowiec direction by the 6th Army's defense and by an attack by the 3rd Guards Army's main forces, along with the 25th Tank Corps, in the direction of Skarzysko-Kamienna and Szydlowiec (a 3-kilometer breakthrough front) and bypassing Ostrowiec from the west; from the south, from the direction of Krakow, the *front* would be secured by an attack by the 60th Army in the direction of Krakow (a 2-kilometer breakthrough front), in order to capture Krakow in conjunction with the Fourth Ukrainian Front.

The combined-arms armies comprising the *front's* shock group, while attacking in the direction of Radomsko, were to break through the enemy's defense through the entire tactical depth on the operation's first day and create the conditions for the tank armies' commitment into the breach. During the next two days they were to defeat the enemy's immediate operational reserves and on the operation's tenth or eleventh day reach the line of the *front's* immediate objective—Piotrkow—Czestochowa—Miechow—Bochnia (130-140 kilometers deep), from which they would develop the offensive toward Breslau (Wroclaw). The armies would break through the enemy's defense along sectors ten to 13 kilometers wide.

The *front* operation was planned to an overall depth of up to 290 kilometers (from the Sandomierz bridgehead to Breslau). It was planned to achieve the *front's* immediate objective to a depth of 130-140 kilometers in two stages. The planned daily rate of advance for the infantry was 12-13 kilometers, and 23-30 kilometers for the mobile formations.

The *front* had two-echelon operational formation. The first operational echelon contained six combined-arms armies, and the second two armies—21st and 59th.

The *front's* second-echelon armies had the following objectives: 21st Army—to augment efforts along the main direction, and the 59th Army—to secure the main group of forces from the southwest and simultaneously capture Krakow with part of its forces (one rifle corps and the 4th Guards Tank Corps), in conjunction with the 60th Army.

---

10 First Ukrainian Front operational directive no. 001472/490/op of 23 December 1944. Ministry of Defense Archives, fond 334, opis' 125959, delo 5, p. 1. *Sandomirsko-Silezskaya Operatsiya*, inventory no. 8201. Military-Historical Directorate, USSR Armed Forces, and others.

11 For example, along the 52nd Army's 10-kilometer sector the density was 296 guns and mortars and 25 tanks and self-propelled guns per kilometer of front.

The 7th Guards Mechanized and the 1st Guards Cavalry corps were to be delegated to the *front* reserve.

The armies along the main axis would be organized in two echelons. The corps' and divisions' combat formations would consist of two echelons, and sometimes of three.

The rifle corps and divisions were to break through the enemy's defense along wider sectors and had deeper objectives than did the First Belorussian Front's formations. For example, the corps' breakthrough sectors were 3-6 kilometers wide, with 2-3 kilometers for the divisions; the rifle corps' objectives were as follows: an immediate objective of 9-12 kilometers (the breakthrough of the main zone) and the day's objective of 18-21 kilometers (the breakthrough of the second zone); the rifle divisions' objectives were correspondingly an immediate one of 6-10 kilometers, a subsequent one of 10-12 kilometers, and the day's objective of 18-21 kilometers.

The tank armies constituted the success development echelon (the *front's* mobile group).[12] Two variations for employing the tank armies were foreseen: the first was for developing the success following the breakthrough of the enemy's tactical defense zone, and the second for completing the breakthrough of the main defensive zone in the event of the combined-arms armies' slow advance on the operation's first day.

The tank armies received the following objectives:

The 4th Tank Army was to enter the breach in the 13th Army's sector and develop the offensive to the northwest in the direction of Piotrkow, with the objective of cutting the line of retreat of the enemy's Kielce—Radom group of forces, and assisting the 13th Army in capturing Kielce; by the close of the operation's third day the army was to capture the crossings over the Pilica River east of Piotrkow. The depth of the objective was 135 kilometers.

The 3rd Guards Tank Army was to enter the breach in the 52nd Army's sector and develop the offensive in the general direction of Radomsko, and on the operation's third day to capture the crossings over the Pilica River and subsequently to reach the Radomsko area and capture Czestochowa with a powerful flank detachment. The depth of the objective was 150 kilometers.

The tank corps were designated for commitment into the breach and to develop the success: 25th Tank Corps in the 3rd Guards Army's sector; 31st and 4th Guards tank corps in the 5th Guards Army's sector. It was planned to commit the tank corps into the breach on the operation's first day in order to complete the breakthrough of the main defensive zone. They were to subsequently develop the offensive along the flanks of the *front's* shock group.

The beginning of the *front's* offensive was set for 20 January 1945, but was then moved to 12 January in connection with the difficult condition in which the Anglo-American forces found themselves in the Ardennes.

Fourth Ukrainian Front. The *front* commander's plan called for an offensive by part of his forces to the northwest toward Krakow, for the purpose of assisting the forces of the First Ukrainian Front in capturing this locale. The right-flank 38th Army was to break through the defense south of Jaslo along a 6-kilometer sector and launch an attack in the general direction of Nowy Sacz and Krakow.

The rifle corps', rifle divisions' and rifle regiments' formations were organized into two echelons.[13] The gun and mortar density was to be raised to 180-190 tubes per kilometer of breakthrough front. The start of the offensive was set for 15 January.

---

12 This is according to the First Ukrainian Front's terminology.

13 An excerpt from a brief report on the generalized experience of the Fourth Ukrainian Front for January 1945, inventory no. 4738, pp. 6-8.

Thus in their decisions the *front* commanders fully realized the *Stavka's* idea of the necessity of defeating the enemy's first operational echelon as quickly as possible, as well as his operational reserves, and the subsequent vigorous development of the offensive into the depth.

The realization of these assigned tasks would be achieved by creating powerful and fully supported shock groups of forces, which were to, as was instructed, by means of powerful frontal attacks in conjunction with attacks along converging axes, break through the enemy's tactical defense zone and develop the offensive at a high rate of advance, in order to preempt the enemy in occupying intermediate lines in the depth.

Worthy of note are the great massing of men and materiel and the creation of powerful shock groups along the axes of the main attacks, with the several-fold superiority in force over the enemy, and the deep formation of the *fronts'* forces.

In the *front* commanders' decisions an important role was assigned to the tank armies. It should be noted that in the First Belorussian Front the defeat of the immediate operational reserves was to be carried out by the combined-arms armies, and in the First Ukrainian Front this objective was to be carried out by the tank armies, which were to be committed into the breach on the operation's first day. However, the possibility of employing them for the purpose of completing the breakthrough of the enemy's tactical defense zone was not excluded.

The forces' operational formation and combat orders were deep, which was to secure the unbroken augmentation of efforts during the course of the operation and battle, and thus an increase in the pace of the offensive.

The main mass of tank and mechanized units and formations were to be included within shock groups. This aside, independent tank brigades and regiments and self-propelled artillery brigades, regiments and battalions were to be included as part of the armies' first operational echelon for immediate infantry support, while the tank corps and armies were designated for developing the success in the operational depth of the enemy's defense.

The presence of a large number of tanks in the First Belorussian and First Ukrainian fronts enabled us, aside from creating powerful mobile groups, to set aside from 24 percent (in the First Ukrainian Front) to 42 percent (in the First Belorussian Front) of their overall number for direct infantry support. The average density of direct infantry support tanks per kilometer along the breakthrough sectors was 21.4 (First Ukrainian Front) and 24.6 (First Belorussian Front) vehicles.

In the First Belorussian Front the tank units designated for infantry support were broken down to companies, which were attached to the rifle battalions and were to operate along their axes throughout the entire depth of the breakthrough. Heavy tank and self-propelled artillery regiments were broken down by platoons (by batteries) and were to follow behind the first line's infantry support tanks. In the 5th Shock Army the tank units and subunits of the direct infantry support groups, following the breakthrough of the enemy's main defensive zone, were to unite in an army mobile detachment for seizing the second defensive zone from the march. In the 8th Guards Army the tank groups designated for this purpose were to be created from tank regiments not assigned to break through the main zone. The composition of such tank groups varied; for example, a tank brigade with a self-propelled artillery regiment and a regiment of tank trawlers (in the 5th Shock Army), or three tank regiments (in the 8th Guards Army). In the First Ukrainian Front's 52nd and 13th armies such tank groups consisted of a tank brigade each. The creation of such groups expressed the desire to quickly complete the breakthrough of the entire tactical zone of the enemy's defense. However, it should be noted that the creation of army mobile groups weakened the direct infantry support tank echelon, which could not but negatively tell on the pace of the breakthrough of the main defensive zone.

Artillery Support for the Operation[14]

The artillery support for the Vistula-Oder operation[15] had as its goal supporting the uninterrupted advance by the *fronts'* forces at a high speed and to a great depth.

The First Belorussian and First Ukrainian fronts' groups of forces were to be supported and accompanied by fire from a large number of guns and mortars from the bridgeheads and from the eastern bank of the Vistula River.

According to the decision by the *front* commanders, a large-scale regrouping of artillery equipment was undertaken before the start of the operation. In the First Belorussian Front's two bridgeheads, which included the 61st, 5th Shock and 8th Guards armies, 8,672 guns and mortars were concentrated. The First Ukrainian Front's 5th Guards, 13th and 52nd armies included 7,673 guns and mortars, and up to 9,500 guns and mortars (counting the neighboring armies' artillery and that of the second echelons) were brought in for the artillery preparation.

During the breakthrough period the artillery and mortars of the tank armies, independent tank, mechanized and cavalry corps were to be brought in, as well as that of the *fronts'* second-echelon armies.

Powerful artillery groups were to be created in the *fronts*, from regiment to army inclusively (PAG, DAG, KAG, and AAG).[16] The corps artillery groups (KAG) usually included two artillery and one anti-tank artillery brigades, and an artillery regiment from the corps' second-echelon division, for a total of 80-240 guns and mortars. The divisional artillery groups (DAG) included 2-3 howitzer brigades (up to 200 guns and mortars). The regimental artillery groups (PAG) included 2-5 artillery regiments (72-114 guns and mortars). It should be noted that in the First Ukrainian Front there were no corps artillery groups in the majority of corps and their role was carried out by army subgroups, while counter mortar groups were created in the divisions.

20-30 guns per kilometer of front were set aside for firing over open sights along the axes of the armies' main attacks.

The artillery preparation in the *fronts* was planned in such a way that from the beginning the activities of the forward battalions, and then the main forces, would be supported by fire onslaughts of 7-25 minutes duration.

The conduct of the artillery preparation in the First Belorussian Front was planned according to two variations, depending upon the success of the forward battalions' battle. According to the first variation, the artillery preparation of the forward battalions' attack was to be conducted as follows—a fire onslaught lasting 25 minutes by the *front's* entire artillery against the forward edge of the enemy's defense, along with its simultaneous suppression to a depth of 6-7 kilometers. There would then follow the support of their attack to a depth of 1.5-2 kilometers by single rolling barrage[17] for 60 minutes. According to this variation, the artillery preparation of the attack was not called for. In the event of the forward battalions' successful activities, the main forces of the first-echelon divisions would be committed into the battle, the attack of which would be supported by a double rolling barrage. A second variation was planned in the event of the forward battalions' failure in the battle. In this instance, an artillery preparation of the main forces' attack, lasting 70

---

14 The "artillery offensive," according to the terminology of the time. In this section problems of preparing the artillery offensive are examined.

15 "Artillery Support of a *Front* Offensive Operation, According to the Experience of the First Belorussian Front." *Artillery Information Collection*, no.1/18. "Instructions for the Organization of the Artillery Support of an Offensive." *Sbornik Boevykh Dokumentov Velikoi Otechestvennoi Voiny*. Vypusk 11, Main Military-Historical Directorate of the General Staff, pp.69-74, inventory no. 13270, and other materials.

16 Editor's note. These abbreviations stand for, respectively, regimental artillery group, divisional artillery group, corps artillery group, and army artillery group.

17 According to the terminology of the time.

minutes (a 20-minute fire onslaught, 30 minutes of destructive fire, and a repeat 20-minute fire onslaught) would be conducted. In this case the attack would be supported by a double rolling barrage to a depth of 2.5-3 kilometers. It was planned to carry out the accompaniment of the infantry and tanks in the battle for the depth of the enemy's defense by means of a consecutive concentration of fire.

In the First Ukrainian Front the activities of the forward battalions would be preceded by an artillery preparation, conducted by part of the *front* shock group's artillery, which had been specially set aside for this purpose. It was planned to conduct the main artillery preparation for 107 minutes. The artillery preparation would begin with 15-20 minute fire onslaughts against the enemy's trenches to a depth of 6-7 kilometers. A destruction and suppression period would then follow for 40 minutes. A 7-minute fire onslaught, repeat destructive and suppression fire for 30 minutes, and, finally, a concluding 15-minute fire onslaught.

It was planned to support the attack by the main forces in both *fronts* by means of a double rolling barrage to a depth of 2.5-3 kilometers. The accompaniment of the troops' attack was to be carried out by the consecutive concentration of fire to a depth of 5-7 kilometers.

In both *fronts* instructions for the artillery support of the mobile formations' commitment into the breach were drawn up. This task was to be carried out by the artillery of those armies, in the sector of which the mobile groups would be committed into the breach. 2-3 artillery brigades for each of the first echelon's tank or mechanized corps were set aside for accompanying the mobile forces, which were to support the advance by the method of consecutively concentrating their fire to a depth of up to 15-16 kilometers (along six lines).

In the Fourth Ukrainian Front artillery groups were created in the rifle regiments, rifle divisions and the armies. The duration of the artillery preparation was to be 65 minutes. It was planned to support the attack by means of a consecutive concentration of fire.

Air Support for the Operation[18]

Our aviation in the Vistula-Oder operation[19] had as its goal the support of the uninterrupted advance by the *fronts'* forces at a high rate of speed and to a great depth.

The command of the First Belorussian and First Ukrainian fronts assigned the 16th and 2nd air armies the following basic objectives:

A. For the period of preparing the operation:
    1. To cover the regrouping and concentration of the shock groups against enemy air attack and the appearance of his aerial reconnaissance.
    2. To destroy the enemy's aviation in the air in air battles, and on his airfields.
    3. To carry out uninterrupted air reconnaissance.
    4. To demoralize the enemy forces through dropping leaflets.

B. From the beginning of the operation:
    1. To assist the *front's* shock groups in breaking through the enemy defense through massed strikes by assault and bomber aviation against the enemy's men and materiel, as well as the commitment into the breach and the mobile formation's operations in depth.

---

18 This was called the aviation offensive, according to the terminology of the time. In this section problems of preparing the aviation offensive are examined.
19 From headquarters reports of the 16th and 2nd air armies for January-February 1945. Archives of the Main Air Force Staff, and other materials.

2.   To pursue the enemy's retreating forces through continuous strikes, while destroying them along the roads and concentration areas, and also to disrupt the work of his railroads. To assist the mobile forces in developing the success.
3.   To prevent the arrival of the enemy's reserves and his occupation of intermediate defensive lines.
4.   To destroy the enemy's aviation in the air in air battles and on his airfields.
5.   To carry out continuous air reconnaissance.

In accordance with the plan for the *front's* offensive operation and for carrying out their assignments, the commanders of the air armies made the decision on the combat employment of their aviation, while their staffs planned the aviation offensive.

During the preparatory stage in the 16th and 2nd air armies the main attention was devoted to the conduct of air reconnaissance to a depth of up to 300 kilometers, of which up to an average of 75 sorties were planned per day in the 16th Air Army, and up to 150 sorties in the 2nd Air Army. All available air reconnaissance regiments were brought in for carrying out aerial reconnaissance, as well as all air formations in the 2nd Air Army, and the 6th Fighter Corps, 286th Fighter Division and the 9th Guards Night Bomber Division in the 16th Air Army, for which reconnaissance areas were set aside and a plan for conducting reconnaissance was drawn up. Aside from reconnaissance, strikes against the enemy's airfields were planned, involving the 18th Air Army's heavy bombers.[20]

According to the decisions by the air army commanders, the following measures were called for to assist the *front's* forces in breaking through.

In the 16th Air Army.[21]

According to the decision by the commander of the 16th Air Army for supporting the *front's* shock group attacking from the Magnuszew bridgehead, the 2nd Guards Assault Air Division and the 282nd Fighter Division were detailed for supporting the 61st Army; the 6th Assault Air Corps and the 6th Fighter Corps for supporting the 5th Shock Army; the 11th Guards Assault Air Division and the 286th Fighter Division for supporting the 8th Guards Army; the 3rd Bomber Corps, with the operationally subordinated 1st Guards Fighter Division, the 183rd and 221st bomber divisions, as well as the 9th Guards Night Bomber Division were designated for operating in all three armies' interests, while the 183rd Bomber Division was designated for operations north of the Pilica River and the 221st Bomber Division for operations south of the Pilica River. Thus 14 (64 percent) of the available 22 air divisions were set aside.

For supporting the armies attacking from the Pulawy bridgehead, the 3rd Guards Assault Air Division (9th Assault Air Corps) and the 193rd Fighter Division (13th Fighter Corps) were assigned to support the 69th Army; the 300th Assault Air Division (9th Assault Air Corps) and the 193rd Fighter Division (13th Fighter Corps) were to support the 33rd Army, and; the 242nd Night Bomber Division was to operate in both armies' interests. In all, five (23 percent) of the available 22 air divisions were set aside for this purpose.

In order to support the 47th Army, which was to launch a supporting attack, the 4th Composite Air Division of the Polish Air Force (6th Air Army) and a single air regiment each from the 2nd Guards Assault Air Division and the 282nd Fighter Division.

The 3rd Fighter Corps (two fighter divisions) was slated specially for fighting the enemy's aviation and cover the *front's* forces operating along the Magnuszew bridgehead, from the air, and for the *front's* forces operating along the Pulawy bridgehead the 283rd Fighter Division (13th Fighter

---

20   Editor's note. The 18th Air Army comprised Long-Range Aviation.
21   Report by the headquarters of the 16th Air Army for January 1945. Main Air Force Staff Archives.

Corps); that is, a total of three air divisions out of eight available, which were to begin patrolling in the air two hours before the start of the attack, simultaneously blocking the enemy's nearest airfields.

Taking into account the several-fold superiority in firepower over the enemy and the power of the artillery preparation, the *front* command decided not to conduct an air preparation, but limit itself to a strike by the 9th and 242nd night bomber divisions against the enemy's headquarters, for the purpose of disrupting the enemy's troop control, which would be launched five minutes before the artillery preparation.

It was planned to begin the *front* aviation's main operations with the beginning of the shock groups' attack. At the same time, in the course of three hours assault air was to uninterruptedly accompany the attacking troops in groups of 10-12 aircraft, launching strikes, most importantly against the enemy's weapons. Bomber aviation was to carry out one sortie for supporting the *front's* attacking forces.

In striving to ensure our aviation's closer cooperation with the *front's* attacking forces, it was decided to operationally subordinate to the commanders of the combined-arms armies the assault air and fighter formations supporting the combined-arms armies within three hours following the beginning of the troops' attack. It was planned to leave in the air army commander's hands the bombers slated for fighting the enemy's reserves, and the fighters slated for battling the enemy's aviation.

With the commitment of the mobile formations into the breach, the assault air and fighter aviation supporting the combined-arms armies was to be operationally subordinated to the commanders of the mobile formations and shifted to support them. The 6th Assault Air Corps was to support the 2nd Guards Tank Army; the 2nd and 11th guards assault air divisions and the 282nd and 286th fighter divisions were to support the 1st Guards Tank Army; the 3rd Guards Assault Air Division (9th Assault Air Corps) and the 193rd Fighter Division (13th Fighter Corps) were to support the 7th Guards Cavalry Corps. The covering fighters were to be simultaneously switched to covering the mobile formations.

The air offensive was planned in detail for the first four days of the offensive, that is, for the first stage of the *front* operation. In all, 13,374 sorties were planned, of which 7,945 (59 percent) were to be conducted on the first two days. It was planned to concentrate *front* aviation's main efforts during the first days on supporting the combined-arms armies that were part of the shock groups, and then later in the interests of the mobile formations.

In the 2nd Air Army.[22]

According to the decision by the commander of the 2nd Air Army, all of the *front's* aviation forces were to be thrown into supporting, first of all, the combined-arms armies launching the main attack: the 2nd Guards Assault Air Corps and the 2nd Fighter Corps were assigned to support the 13th Army; the 1st Guards Assault Air Corps and the 6th Guards Fighter Corps were to support the 52nd Army, and; the 3rd Assault Air Corps and the 5th Fighter Corps were to support the 5th Guards Army. The fighter corps were also to be entrusted with the task of combating the enemy's aviation in the sector of the army being supported; that is, covering the troops and securing the operations of assault and bomber aviation. It was simultaneously planned to have ready the 2nd Guards and 3rd assault air corps and the 2nd and 5th fighter corps for supporting the 3rd Guards and 59th armies, and a permanent reserve in the form of two of the 3rd Assault Air Corps' assault air regiments and one of the 6th Fighter Corps' fighter divisions, to which a number of sorties were assigned.

---

22 Report by the headquarters of the 2nd Air Army for January 1945. Main Air Force Staff Archives.

The 2nd Guards and 4th bomber corps and the 208th Night Bomber Division were to be employed in the beginning of the offensive for supporting the offensive by the *front's* shock group for launching strikes against the enemy's artillery positions, headquarters and airfields, and then were to be placed in the commander of the 2nd Air Army's reserve for combating the enemy's reserves.

No preliminary air preparation was planned, in order to guarantee the surprise of the offensive, and only a strike by the 208th Night Bomber Division was planned on the night before the offensive along the Skarzysko-Kamienna and Ostrowiec railway stations. Besides this, it was planned to launch a strike with the forces of the 1st Guards Assault Corps, the 2nd Guards and 4th bomber corps, and the 6th Guards, 2nd and 5th fighter corps against the enemy's airfields in the Krakow area ten minutes before the start of the artillery preparation, in order to block the remaining airfields in the Jedrzejow And Krakow air centers.

The decision called for a direct air preparation for 15 minutes at the end of the artillery preparation along the front of the 13th, 52nd and 5th armies, by the forces of the assault air corps for suppressing the enemy's artillery. Operations by the fighter corps for chasing the enemy's aviation from the battlefield were to precede the direct air preparation.

It was planned to carry out the support of the 13th, 52nd and 5th Guards armies' attack through echeloned strikes by groups of assault aircraft in groups of 8-24 planes, and including bomber aviation. Within an hour and a half after the beginning of the attack, assault aviation was to be ready for operations against the enemy's reserves.

With the commitment of the mobile formations into the breach, the aviation set aside for supporting the combined-arms armies was to be switched to supporting the mobile formations.

The aviation offensive was planned fully and in a detailed manner for the first three days of the offensive. It was planned to carry out 4,700 sorties on the first day, 3,950 on the second, and 3,370 on the third, for a total of 12,080 sorties; the intensity was 2.5 sorties for the fighters, two for assault aircraft; 1.5 for day bombers, and; 3 sorties for night bombers. 249 sorties were planned for strikes against three airfields.

The centralized control of the *front's* entire aviation was planned for the duration of the entire operation; a certain decentralization was to be allowed for controlling the aviation resources slated for supporting the mobile formations.

In the 8th Air Army.[23]

According to the decision by the commander of the 8th Air Army, the army's efforts were to be concentrated on supporting the 38th Army, which was to launch the main attack, and only one assault air and one fighter regiments were to be designated for supporting the 18th Army. A plan for the 8th Air Army's combat operations was drawn up for the offensive's first day, according to which operations by *front* aviation would begin by driving the enemy's air assets from the battlefield 20 minutes before the attack. A direct air preparation was prepared ten minutes before the attack and then the support for the offensive through echeloned strikes by groups of assault aviation. In all, more than 800 sorties were planned for the first day of the offensive.

Plans for airfield maneuver, in order to prevent our aviation from falling behind the ground forces, were drawn up in the headquarters of the air armies alongside the plan for the combat employment of our aviation.

This was organized most successfully in the 16th Air Army; where as a result of the scrupulous study of the offensive area, an orientation plan was drawn up for the aviation's planned basing as the *front's* forces moved forward. According to this plan, the fighter and assault air formations were to begin rebasing first, upon receiving strictly determined basing areas in the sectors of those

---

23 From materials in the Air Force Staff Archives.

armies or mobile formations they were supporting. Engineer-airfield battalions and the forward teams of airfield service battalions were designated to advance with the mobile forces for building airfields. The commanders of the mobile formations were obliged to set aside forces and equipment for aiding in the preparation of new airfields, as well as special tank elements for seizing and defending airfields in their movement zone, for securing the rebasing of their aviation there, and for carrying out combat activities from these airfields until the arrival of the rifle formations.

In studying the plans for the aviation offensive by the 16th and 2nd air armies, it should be mentioned that they corresponded to the plan for the *fronts'* offensive operations at a high offensive pace and to a great depth and had a lot in common in their planning. *Front* aviation's efforts were to be concentrated along the direction of the *front's* main attack. Moreover, if in the first days they were to mainly operate to support the breakthrough in the interests of the combined-arms armies, they were to subsequently be switched to the support and accompaniment of the mobile formations, with assault air and fighter aviation subordinated to them, in order to ensure the development of the success in the depth at a high rate of attack.

Our aviation's combat activities were planned in detailed by day and for the first stage of the *front* offensive operation, foreseeing not only the aviation's actions during the breakthrough, but also during the pursuit.

However, the plans for the aviation offensive were also somewhat different.

In the 16th Army the control of assault air and, partially, that of fighter aviation, was decentralized, while it was centralized in the 2nd Air Army, which more corresponded to the character of the planned operation. At the same time in the 2nd Air Army the forces of assault and fighter aviation were to be distributed equally among the combined-arms armies, while in the 16th Air Army this was done in accordance with the army's role in the offensive, which was more in tune with the character of the planned operation. In the 16th Air Army, by renouncing the air preparation, the strength of the air support during the first hours of the offensive would be increased, while in the 2nd Air Army a larger number of planes enabled us to carry out direct aviation preparation at the end of the artillery preparation. Later, in the 16th Air Army there were fighter formations that had been specially delegated for combating the enemy's aviation and which were not involved in carrying out other assignments, while this was not the case in the 2nd Air Army. At the same time, in the 16th Air Army it was planned to destroy the enemy's air assets primarily in air battles, while in the 2nd Air Army this was to be done in conjunction with organized strikes against the enemy's airfields, which imparted a more decisive aspect to the fight for maintaining air superiority; besides this, in the 2nd Air Army more attention was devoted to reserving air assets and efforts.

The employment of long-range aviation directly in the interests of the *fronts* on the battlefield was not planned, because these planes were to carry out tasks for assisting in the defeat of the enemy's East Prussian group of forces.

Operational Support for the Operation

Intelligence.[24] A great deal of attention in operational support was devoted to intelligence gathering of all types: troop, aerial, agent, and radio intelligence.

Our intelligence was given the following tasks: to determine the composition and disposition of the enemy's forces, the system of his defensive structures, obstacles and obstructions, and his fire system; to uncover the concentration areas of the enemy's men and materiel in the rear, the

---

24 "Operational Intelligence in the Vistula-Oder Operation." Main Intelligence Directorate of the USSR Armed Forces General Staff, inventory no. 7235, and other materials.

presence of intermediate defensive lines, their character and degree of readiness, and; to follow the arrival of the enemy's new formations and his troop regroupings.

The reconnaissance of the tactical defensive zone was mainly entrusted to troop intelligence. The reconnaissance of the operational zone was primarily carried out with the aid of aircraft, agent intelligence and radio intelligence.

A great deal of attention was devoted to the organization of observation by our troops. For example, by the start of the offensive up to 750 combined-arms and up to 520 artillery observation posts had been deployed along a 15-kilometer front in the 69th Army, which comprised on the average up to 85 observation posts per kilometer of front. Observation was carried out around the clock. A significant amount of intelligence information was received from engineer reconnaissance, tank reconnaissance, and artillery instrumental reconnaissance.

Reconnaissance in force was broadly practiced. According to the decision by the *front* commanders, a reconnaissance in force by the forward battalions was to precede the attack by the main forces. In the First Belorussian Front it was planned to conduct the reconnaissance in force immediately before the attack by the main forces, and in the First Ukrainian Front five hours before the start of the artillery preparation.

Aerial reconnaissance was carried out as follows: tactical reconnaissance to a depth of 80-100 kilometers, and operational reconnaissance to a depth of 300-500 kilometers. During the first half of January the 16th and 2nd air armies devoted up to 600 sorties to aerial reconnaissance. Aerial photography of the enemy's defense to a depth of 20-40 kilometers was carried out in the forthcoming offensive zone. All commanders down to the battalion level inclusively were supplied with reconnaissance maps.

Radio intelligence was broadly employed, with the aid of which a number of the German-Fascist forces' major headquarters were unearthed.

As a result of this reconnaissance, the enemy's forces and disposition were uncovered, the character of his defense and fire system was made more precise, and the concentration areas of the enemy's reserves were defined. On the whole, the *fronts'* intelligence successfully coped with their assignments.

Operational concealment.[25] The basic goal of the concealment of the operation was to disguise the plan, the attacks being prepared, and the troop regroupings. In the First Belorussian Front the basis of the plan was the requirement to imitate the withdrawal of men and combat materiel from the bridgeheads and to disguise the arrival of a large number of military trains at the Brest and Kovel' stations. In the First Ukrainian Front the concealment maneuver consisted of carrying out the false concentration of two tank armies along the *front's* left flank in the 60th Army's zone, in order to disorient the enemy as to the operational plan and the true disposition of our forces. The measures carried out for this purpose yielded their results. For example, the enemy did not immediately make the decision to weaken his group of forces opposite the our forces' false concentration area; the enemy's aviation carried out 250 sorties in the false concentration area; 220 artillery onslaughts were carried out against the areas of our artillery positions where dummy guns had been set up; a German panzer division was concentrated in the Tarnow area; the main forces of the enemy's Seventeenth Army were also grouped along this direction. All of this enables us to reach the conclusion that the First Ukrainian Front's concealment maneuver played a certain positive role.

---

25 "Collection of Materials for the Study of the War's Experience," no. 25, inventory no. 7235. *Sandomirsko-Silezskaya Operatsiya*, inventory no. 8201, and other sources.

False airfields with fake work crews and dummy planes (the 16th Air Army had 55 such airfields) were created in the air armies for the purpose of misleading the enemy as to the disposition of our air assets.

In order to maintain the secrecy of our operational preparations, only a limited number of people were given access to its compilation in the *fronts* and armies. Aside from the army commander, only the chief of staff and the chief of the operational section were acquainted with the *front's* operational directive. Only that part of the directive that concerned them reached the commanders of the combat arms. Written assignments to the corps were issued five days before the start of the offensive, and 2-3 days beforehand to the divisions, while objectives were only conveyed to the regiments orally.

Anti-tank defense. In the *fronts* the anti-tank artillery weapons were distributed among the troops. The army commanders had artillery anti-tank reserves (anti-tank artillery brigades). In the First Belorussian Front the density of anti-tank artillery in the armies along the most important axes reached 38 guns per kilometer of front. Mobile obstacle detachments were to play a significant role in the fight against the enemy's tanks. For example, in the First Belorussian Front 57 divisional (21,000 anti-tank and 12,000 anti-personnel mines) and 45 army (32,700 anti-tank and 18,400 anti-personnel mines) detachments were operating. These mobile obstacle detachments were designated for moving along those axes and sectors where the enemy was supposed to employ tanks for counterattacks, or when launching counterblows with them against our attacking forces. Particular attention was devoted to the anti-tank support of flanks and boundaries.

Anti-aircraft defense. Fighter aviation, troop anti-aircraft artillery, anti-aircraft artillery from the High Command Reserve, and smoke equipment were employed for organizing anti-aircraft defense in the *fronts*.

The air armies' fighter aviation was designated for actively fighting the enemy air force by carrying out tasks for covering our troops, escorting bombers and assault aircraft, and for strikes against airfields. The percentage of fighter aircraft in the air armies ranged from 45 percent (2nd Air Army) to 48 percent (16th Air Army).

The supply of anti-aircraft artillery to the *fronts'* forces was to guarantee the successful fight against the enemy's aviation. For example, by the start of the operation in the First Belorussian Front the density of medium-caliber and small-caliber anti-aircraft artillery was 22.5 guns per kilometer of front and 3.3 guns per square kilometer of covered territory, which was an increase of 1.3 guns compared with the density in 1944.

National air defense weapons were deployed in the *fronts'* rear.

Smoke equipment was primarily employed for covering the crossings over the Vistula River. During 22 January crossings were covered over the Vistula. There were only three cases of these crossings being damaged by the enemy, which confirms the effectiveness of employing smoke equipment in the given situation.

Engineer Support for the Operation

Engineer support had a number of features in connection with the fact that the *front* operations began from bridgeheads restricted in size, upon which it was necessary to concentrate major shock groups of forces, while during the course of the operation we had to overcome several defensive lines.

The engineering troops had to prepare the bridgeheads for the offensive, construct command and observation posts, render engineer support to the regrouping and concentration of forces, carry out engineering reconnaissance of the enemy, conduct the necessary preparation for accompanying the infantry, artillery and tanks, and also to support the troops with the necessary engineering equipment.

A particularly large amount of work was carried out to prepare the bridgeheads for the offensive. The following figures speak to the scale of this work. By the start of the offensive along the First Belorussian Front up to 10,000 guns had been hidden in the earth, as were up to 5,000 train cars of munitions and up to 15,000 motor vehicles and tows, while more than 20,000 overhead covers, observation and command posts, and dugouts were outfitted. Worthy of attention is the widespread use of vertical drapes for concealment.

In connection with the planned great intensity of the movement of troops and supplies on the bridgeheads, 113 kilometers of roads were built along the Magnuszew bridgehead, 16 kilometers along the Pulawy bridgehead, and 232 kilometers along the Sandomierz bridgehead. Beside this, many roads underwent major repairs. On the average, 2-3 bridges over the Vistula River were built for each combined-arms army for concentrating forces along the bridgeheads, with a capacity of 16, 30 and 60 tons. For example, eight bridges, with an overall length of 6,437 meters were constructed for crossing troops over the Vistula River in the area of the Magnuszew bridgehead; five bridges, with an overall length of 2,872 meters, were built in the area of the Pulawy bridgehead, and; 13 bridges in the area of the Sandomierz bridgehead.

While preparing for the operation, all of the minefields in the rear of our forces were cleared. 1-3 nights before our offensive, passages in both our and the enemy's minefields in front of the forward edge were cleared, based on a calculation of 9-12 passages of no less than 30 meters for each first-echelon rifle division.

Powerful mobile obstacle detachments were created in the corps, divisions and regiments.

For the purposes of engineer support for the breakthrough of a large number of the enemy's defensive zones, the First Belorussian Front's engineer troops were echeloned in the following manner: the first echelon was to operate with the forward battalions ("with the special echelon"), the second would support the main group of forces, the third would follow behind the main forces, and the fourth echelon would operate according to the plans of the *front's* and armies' engineering chiefs, while the fifth echelon would constitute the *front* and armies' reserve. The density along the breakthrough sectors was raised to 5-6 sapper companies per kilometer of front.

Up to 100 airfields were prepared in the air armies, at a remove of 10-80 kilometers from the front line, which enabled us to maneuver our air assets along the front and in depth.

Political Support for the Operation

Political support for the operation was conducted, based upon the concrete situation that had arisen by the beginning of the operation. The losses suffered by the German-Fascist armies strongly influenced the enemy's state of morale, and that of the *fronts* opposite him.

Our forces' morale was high. There was firm communication between the front and rear. The main means of raising the level of the troops' morale and combat-readiness was the propagation of the idea of defending the socialist motherland, the organizing and inspiring role of the CPSU,[26] the heroic work of the rear, and the inculcation of a boundless love for the socialist fatherland and a burning hatred of the enemy.

All of our party-political work was directed at preparing the troops for combat operations on the territory of allied Poland for the purpose of freeing her from the fascist occupiers. The necessity of observing proper relations with the Polish population was explained to the rank and file.

Meetings, gatherings, conversations, written propaganda, and others were the chief forms of party-political work.

---

26   Editor's note. Communist Party of the Soviet Union.

Great importance was attached to supporting the vanguard role of communists and Komsomol[27] members. The party's ranks grew continuously. For example, in the First Belorussian Front's 47th Army alone 604 men were accepted as candidates or promoted to members of the Communist Party of the Soviet Union between 15 December 1944 and 15 January 1945. By the start of the operation full-blooded party organizations had been created in the *fronts*. In many companies the party-Komsomol element reached 25-30 percent.

On the whole, the party-political organs coped with their work of supporting the troops' preparation for the operation. Raised in a spirit of devotion to the Communist Party and to the Soviet fatherland, the troops of the Soviet army were ready to go over to a decisive offensive and carry out their assigned tasks.

Materiel and Technical Support

A great deal of attention was devoted to materiel and technical support in the *fronts*.[28] The field army bases in their jumping-off positions were moved significantly closer to the troops. On the whole, these bases were located along the Praga—Deblin lateral railroad. The *front* forward depots were also located at a comparatively short distance from the front line.

The Organization of Troop Control

After drawing up and relaying the *front* commanders' decisions to their subordinates, attention was chiefly devoted to checking that they were carried out. The commanders of the *fronts* and armies and their staffs looked into all details of their subordinate forces' and headquarters' preparations for the operation. Instructions were issued on raising the role of the staffs as the main organizers of troop control. The armies' command posts were moved closer to the front line and deployed on the bridgeheads at a distance of 4-8 kilometers from the forward edge.

In breaking through the Vistula defensive line, the armies' command posts were located at a distance of 8-12 kilometers from the forward edge. The corps commanders' command posts were located at 3-6 kilometers from the forward edge, and those of the division commanders 1-4.5 kilometers. Air formation commanders were located at the command posts of the commanders of the rifle formations, whose units they were supporting.

The distance of the observation posts was determined by the requirement of the possibility of physically viewing our forces' operations along the axis of the main attack. Thus the observation posts were located 2.5-3 kilometers from the line of the forward units in the armies, 1.5-2 kilometers in the corps, and 1-1.5 kilometers in the divisions.

The echeloning of the command and control organs was foreseen during the development of the breakthrough and the pursuit of the enemy, in particular the creation and dispatching ahead of operational groups, which usually moved together with the army or formation commander. It was planned to relocate the operational groups and headquarters in leaps: 40-50 kilometers for the armies, 15-20 kilometers for the corps, and 8-10 kilometers for the divisions.

The reliability of our communications was guaranteed by the scrupulous preparation of the communications troops for the operation, the skillful employment of all types of communications, and the correct planning of maneuvering communications forces and equipment. A system of wire communications was widely deployed in the jumping-off position. During the operation,

---

27   Editor's note. The Komsomol (*Kommunisticheskii Soyuz Molodezhi*) was the Communist Party's youth wing.
28   Questions of materiel and technical support are not examined in detail in this study.

particularly in the switch to the pursuit, radio communications was to become the chief type of communications.

The organization of the troops' coordination at all levels was conducted in a strictly centralized manner, according to a single plan, which was drawn up by the *fronts'* headquarters. For example, in the First Belorussian Front coordination was organized according to the following schedules: 22-25 December at the army-corps level; 26-27 December at the corps-division level; 29-30 December at the division level; 31 December at the regimental level; 3-4 January at the battalion level, and; 8-9 January at the company level. Questions of coordination were worked out at command-staff games and in practical exercises with the troops.

Regrouping of Forces and the Occupation of Jumping-Off Positions

The regrouping of our forces and their occupation of their jumping-off positions for the offensive was to be carried out in short a rigorously defined time periods and conducted when it was dark. The troops were to reach the crossing areas and the bridgeheads 4-5 days before the start of the offensive. Artillery units were to be moved to the bridgeheads beginning on 25 December. The relief of the troops at the jumping-off positions was to be carried out 1-2 days before the start of the offensive. On the whole, all of this supported the troops' timely readiness for going over to the offensive.

Troop and Staff Training

During the preparatory phase the all-round work of training the troops and staffs for the forthcoming operation went on. Command-staff exercises and tactical exercise were carried out according to plans drawn up by the *fronts.*

As experience showed, such training imparted to the troops and their commanders confidence in their actions and significantly contributed to the overall success of the operation.

The *fronts'* forces actually began preparing for the offensive in August-September 1944. The immediate preparation for the operation began at the end of November 1944, after receiving operational directives from the *Stavka.* By 12-14 January the focused and all-round preparation for the operation had been conducted by the *fronts,* which contributed subsequently to its successful conduct and completion.

4

The Conduct of the Operation[1]

Operational Stages

One may divide the Vistula-Oder multi-*front* operation into two stages, according to the actual course of events.

The first stage, lasting from 12-24 January, includes the breakthrough of the enemy's defense along the Vistula line, the defeat of Army Group A's main forces (the Warsaw and Radom groups of forces and operational reserves), the liberation of Warsaw, the shift to the pursuit of the enemy, and the arrival of the First Belorussian Front's forces at the Poznan defensive line, and the First Ukrainian Front's forces at the Oder River.

The second stage, lasting from 25 January to 3 February, includes the development of the Soviet forces' offensive along the Poznan and Breslau axes, the breakthrough of the Germans' border fortified areas by the forces of the First Belorussian Front, the arrival of the *fronts'* forces on German territory, the forcing of the Oder River in the Küstrin area, the capture by the First Ukrainian Front's forces of the Silesian industrial area, and their forcing of the Oder River along a broad front.

THE FIRST STAGE OF THE OPERATION (12-14 JANUARY)

Military Operations, 12-17 January 1945. The Breakthrough of the Enemy's Defense

The Vistula-Oder operation began with an offensive by the forces of the First Ukrainian Front[2] at 0500 on 12 January with an attack by forward battalions,[3] which, following a 15-minute fire onslaught by the *front's* artillery, attacked the enemy and before long captured his first trench. Then the battalions reached the second trench, which was basically the forward edge, in fighting.

At 1000 the artillery preparation for the main forces' attack began and continued to 1147. A half hour before its completion the rifle platoons, which had been detailed from each battalion of the main forces' first echelon, went over to the attack from the line achieved by the forward battalions. The enemy took this for the beginning of our main forces' attack and brought out his guns from their shelters in order to repel it. It was on these weapons that our artillery inflicted a final 15-minute artillery onslaught. After this the offensive by the *front's* main forces began with an attack of the second trench of the enemy's first position.

---

1   Taken from combat journals and others documents generated by the major field forces and formations of the First Belorussian and the First and Fourth Ukrainian fronts during January-February 1945. Ministry of Defense Archives, *fonds* of the First Belorussian and the First and Fourth Ukrainian fronts, and other materials.

2   *Sandomirsko-Silszskaya Operatsiya*, inventory no. 8201, Military-Historical Directorate of the USSR Armed Forces General Staff. Voennoe Izdatel'stvo, 1948, and other materials.

3   The approximate composition of a forward battalion included a rifle battalion, a platoon of automatic riflemen and a battery of regimental artillery, an anti-tank artillery battalion, a sapper company, and a punishment company.

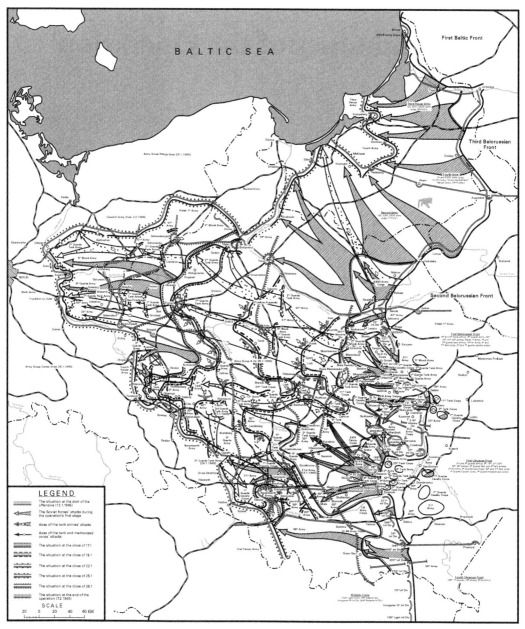

Map 4 The Course of Operations (January 12-February 7, 1945).

An air preparation was not carried out because of the unfavorable weather. Our aviation could only begin carrying out the plan for the aviation offensive from the beginning of the attack by the main ground forces of the *front*; but due to the poor meteorological conditions it at first operated only in small groups.

The attack by the main forces of the *front's* shock group began at 1147 and was accompanied by a rolling barrage to a depth of 2.5-3 kilometers. Simultaneously the 3rd Guards Army and the 60th Army's right-flank formations began their attack along the auxiliary axes.

Along the axis of the main attack our forces' combat activities developed successfully. Attacking vigorously, the first-echelon forces overcame the first enemy position in the first 2-3 hours, and the second position along some sectors, and advanced 6-8 kilometers into the depth of his defense. The tank armies' forward brigades moved out behind the first-echelon battalions. The enemy was unable to hold the main defensive zone and his forces began to fall back. The German-Fascist command began to hurriedly organize a defense along the second line, toward which formations of the XXIV Panzer Corps were moving up from the depth.

The *front* commander evaluated the situation that had arisen by the second half of the day in the following manner: the first echelon of the enemy's group of forces and his anti-tank defensive system had been defeated and the next task was the battle with the enemy's operational reserves, mainly armored. Should this task be entrusted only to the combined-arms armies, then the battle might be drawn out and thus the offensive pace would be reduced. The enemy, having won time, would be able to organize his defense along the next line. In order to prevent this, at 1400 on the operation's first day, the *front* commander issued an order to commit both tank armies for completing the breakthrough of the main zone and the enemy's entire tactical defensive zone.

During the latter half of 12 January the 4th Guards Tank Army[4] was committed along the 13th Army's sector at a depth of 4-5 kilometers from the forward edge; the 3rd Guards Tank Army was committed along the 52nd Army's sector at a depth of 6-8 kilometers, while the 31st and 4th Guards tank corps were committed along the 5th Guards Army's sector. Their forward detachments bypassed the infantry and completed the breakthrough of the main defensive zone.

The 2nd Air Army's aviation began to operate with the attack by the main forces and during the first day, according to weather conditions, operated in a limited fashion, mainly in groups of 2-4 aircraft. Our aviation directed all its efforts at supporting the *front's* shock group, by destroying the enemy's retreating troops and disrupting his communications with the reserve XXIV Panzer Corps. During this time the assault aircraft and fighters attacked the enemy's retreating troops along the roads to Opoczno and Chmielnik, while the 4th Bomber Corps supported the offensive by the 52nd and 5th Guards armies with strikes against the enemy's surviving artillery positions. The 2nd Guards Bomber Corps was destroying the enemy's communications along the roads to Kielce and blocking the enemy's aviation at its airfields around the Jedrzejow air center. In all, on the first day the 2nd Air Army carried out only 468 sorties, of which 271 (58 percent) were directly against the enemy's forces, thus increasing their demoralization, and 87 reconnaissance flights.

The enemy air force was not very active, limiting itself only to reconnoitering the *front's* attacking forces; only four enemy flights were noted on the first day. The enemy air force attempted to resist the Soviet aviation over its own territory, losing one plane in four air battles. Soviet aviation suffered no losses.

On the *front's* right wing the 3rd Guards Army, while operating in conditions of highly broken and wooded terrain and a lack of roads, rolled up the enemy's defense toward the north, and by the

---

4   Editor's note. This is a mistake, as the 4th Tank Army had not yet been elevated to guards status.

end of the day, despite the commitment of the 25th Tank Corps along this axis, advanced only six kilometers and was not able to completely break through the enemy's main defensive zone.

On the *front's* left wing the 60th Army, misleading the enemy with a smoke screen, broke through his defense along a 5-kilometer front and advanced 6-12 kilometers during the day.

The commitment of the tank armies secured the piercing of the enemy's defense by the end of the first day to a depth of 15-20 kilometers along a 35-kilometer front. Formations from the 13th, 52nd and 5th Guards armies also reached the second defensive zone behind the mobile forces. During the night of January 12-13 the mobile forces began fighting in the area east of Chmielnik with the forward units of the enemy's XXIV Panzer Corps. Employing surprise, the 3rd Guards Tank Army's forward detachments, under the cover of night, overcame the enemy's second defensive zone along some sectors.

During 13-18 January the main fighting unfolded along the Czestochowa axis and in the Kielce area with the enemy's operational reserves, and to defeat his Opatow—Ostrowiec group of forces, in conjunction with the First Belorussian Front's forces.

On 13 January the commander of Army Group A, as was expected, committed his reserve— the XXIV Panzer Corps—into the fighting. His 16th Panzer and 20th Panzergrenadier divisions attacked southward from the Kielce area and the 17th Panzer Division attacked north from Chmielnik, with the intention of first defeating our mobile formations, and then by attacking our infantry, to restore the situation along the second defensive zone. However, the enemy was not able to carry out his plan. The enemy's 17th Panzer Division was attacked by the 3rd Guards Tank Army's formations in the Chmielnik area and suffered a defeat. The 16th Panzer and 20th Panzergrenadier divisions moved up from the Kielce area to help it, but they were routed in a meeting battle by the 4th Tank Army's forces and halted. In this fashion the enemy's counterstroke was foiled and the XXIV Panzer Corps, having suffered heavy losses, was thrown back to the Kielce area.

By the close of the day Chmielnik was taken. In this way the second defensive zone, and thus the enemy's entire tactical defensive zone along the Czestochowa axis, were broken through and the way west was opened to our forces. The enemy had no major operational reserves in depth. Our forces' subsequent objective along this direction was to preempt the retreating enemy in occupying in an organized fashion the succeeding defensive lines. In carrying out this assignment, on the morning of 14 January our troops embarked on a vigorous pursuit of the remnants of the enemy's defeated units.

It was necessary to defeat the enemy's groups of forces in the Kielce, Ostrowiec and Opatow areas for the more successful development of the operation. By holding Kielce, the enemy secured the stability of the Ostrowiec—Opatow group of forces and restricted the freedom of maneuver of the *front's* main group of forces.

Combat operations for eliminating the enemy in Kielce were bitter. By the close of 14 January Soviet forces broke through the outer perimeter of the Kielce fortifications and outflanked the city from three sides. The defeat of the enemy group of forces in the Kielce area (the remnants of the XXIV Panzer Corps and units of the newly-committed 72nd Infantry Division) was realized by the forces of the 3rd Guards and 13th armies, in conjunction with the 4th Tank Army. The defeat of this group of forces would ensure conditions for widening the pursuit front along the axis of the main attack and the arrival of the 3rd Guards Army at the communications of the enemy's Ostrowiec—Opatow group of forces.

On 15 January the enemy's Kielce group of forces was defeated by joint attacks by the 3rd Guards Army and the 25th Tank Corps from the northeast, the 13th Army from the south, and the 4th Tank Army from the west, and Kielce was captured. Our forces began to pursue along the Piotrkow axis. On 17 January they forced the Warta River and captured the city of Czestochowa on the march, and on 18 January they captured the town of Piotrkow.

The defeat of the Opatow—Ostrowiece group of forces (XLII Army Corps) was carried out simultaneously with the defeat of the enemy's group of forces in the Kielce area, which was supposed to secure its withdrawal from the line of the Vistula River. Forces of the 3rd Guards and 6th armies took part in defeating the above-named group of forces. The 3rd Guards Army received instructions to widen the breach to the north in the direction of Skarzysko-Kamienna. Simultaneously, the 6th Army was to regroup its forces to the left flank and break through the enemy's defense southwest of Opatow.

The arrival of the First Ukrainian Front's forces in the Kielce area and the simultaneous offensive by the First Belorussian Front's forces from the Pulawy bridgehead to the southwest created the threat of surrounding the enemy group of forces defending along the boundary between the two *fronts*. Under the threat of encirclement, the enemy on 15 January began to hurriedly withdraw this group of forces. In order to prevent the enemy from withdrawing his forces, at 1600 on 15 January the 6th Army attacked, broke through the enemy's defense and began to pursue him. Simultaneously, the 3rd Guards Army attacked to the north.

The attacks by the two armies flowed into a single one, which was directed at cutting the communications of the entire Ostrowiec—Opatow group of forces. The enemy's command and control was disrupted. During 16-17 January the 3rd Guards Army's forces fought on the approaches to Skarzysko-Kammienna. On 18 January they linked up with the forces of the First Belorussian Front in this area and turned their front to the west. The 6th Army remained to complete the enemy's defeat in the Ostrowiec salient and was subsequently pulled back into the *front's* reserve.

The offensive was also developing successfully along the Krakow axis. During 13 January the forces of the 60th Army advanced 15 kilometers. Insofar as the front between the 5th Guards and 60th armies was broadening, the 59th Army (the *front's* second echelon), with the attached 4th Guards Tank Corps, was committed into the boundary between them on the morning of 14 January, with the objective of supporting the main group of forces from the southwest and attacking toward Krakow with part of its forces. The forces of the 59th and 60th armies, while developing the offensive, advanced up to 45 kilometers on 14-16 January.

On 15 January the Fourth Ukrainian Front's 38th Army[5] attacked in the general direction of Nowy Sacz and then toward Krakow, creating the threat of encircling the enemy's Tarnow group of forces (Seventeenth Army), as a result of which the enemy on 16 January began to pull back his forces toward Krakow. The 38th Army's offensive was supported by the 8th Air Army, which during 15-18 January carried out 1,756 sorties, of which 1,254 (71 percent) were directly against the enemy's forces. By the close of 18 January the 38th Army had advanced 50-60 kilometers. The First Ukrainian Front's 60th Army, taking advantage of the success of its neighbor to the left (38th Army), began to pursue with all its forces and by the close of 18 January had advanced 30 kilometers. On 17 January the 4th Guards Tank Corps broke through to the outer ring of the Krakow fortified area; on 18 January the 59th and 60th armies, pursuing the enemy, reached this area. Thus the *front's* forces successfully advanced along all axes.

The 2nd Air Army's combat operations were limited by the unfavorable weather. On 13 January 698 sorties were carried out, of which 339 (57 percent) were directly against the enemy's forces, and 124 (18 percent) for reconnaissance purposes. As early as the night 11-12 January the air army's main forces were directed at the Kielce area and against the roads leading there, in order to interfere with the arrival of the enemy's XXIV Panzer Corps. Simultaneously the 2nd Air Army's planes were blocking the enemy's Jedrzejow and Krakow air centers. As a result, the enemy air force was forced to limit itself to reconnaissance (five flights were noted) over our territory.

---

5   Excerpts from brief reports nos. 1 and 2 of the generalized experience of the Fourth Ukrainian Front's forces for January-March 1945, inventory no. 4738 and no. 4824, and other materials.

However, the enemy air force sought to resist our aviation over its territory and lost five aircraft in eight air battles.

During 14-17 January the 2nd Air Army, in connection with the improving weather, increased its activity: on 14-15 January it carried out 372 and 510 sorties, respectively; 1,711 on 16 January and 2,441 on 17 January, going over to operations in groups of 6-30 aircraft. The assault air's efforts were directed at destroying the enemy's retreating forces along the roads and concentration areas, particularly opposite the 3rd Guards and 6th armies, and assisting them in encircling the enemy's Ostrowiec group of forces. On 14-16 January bomber aviation launched strikes against the enemy's troop concentrations opposite the 3rd Guards and 6th armies, and on 17 January opposite the 59th and 60th armies, assisting their offensive on Krakow. The bomber strikes were first of all directed against road junctions and inhabited locales, as well as railroad stations and the Skarzysko-Kamienna junction, and against railroad stations west of Krakow, in order to disrupt the enemy's organized withdrawal and to prevent his forces from combining to launch coun- terattacks. Besides this on 16-17 January the day bombers launched strikes against the enemy's airfields in the areas of Czestochowa and Krakow, as a result of which up to 20 enemy aircraft were destroyed. During 14-17 January the 2nd Air Army carried out 5,663 sorties, of which 2,849 (52 percent) were against enemy forces and 618 (11 percent) were for reconnaissance.

Simultaneous with the completion of its combat tasks, *front* aviation continued to concentrate at airfields closer to the front line, having occupied all the airfields on the bridgehead, from which it flew to support the *front's* attacking forces. However, as early as 14 January the threat arose of the aviation falling behind, because of the difficulties in preparing and restoring the airfields on moist soil (the enemy ruined his airfields during the withdrawal) and the shortage of auto transport, while up until 18 January we were able to rebase only part of the fighters from the 6th Guards Fighter Corps and the 1st Guards Assault Air Corps to the Jedrzejow area behind the troops; the remaining air formations were operating from airfields east of the Vistula and from the bridge- head, gradually falling behind the *front's* forces.

This enabled the enemy's aviation to increase its activity against the *front's* forces. During these days an average of 40-50 enemy flights were noted. Besides carrying out reconnaissance, the enemy's aviation sometimes tried to attack Soviet forces, chiefly with Fw-190 planes. It also sought to oppose our aviation, losing 23 planes in 27 air battles.

As a result of its 6-day offensive, the First Ukrainian Front's forces broke through the enemy's tactical defensive zone and, upon defeating his operational reserves, advanced 120-160 kilometers and widened the breakthrough front to 250 kilometers and carried out the *front's* immediate objective 5-6 days ahead of schedule. During this time the 2nd Air Army, although the weather limited its activities for a few days, carried out 6,829 sorties, of which 3,519 (52 percent) were against the enemy's forces, while concentrating its main efforts along the decisive axes and thus disrupting the organized withdrawal of the enemy's forces. While retaining air superiority, our aviation sharply restricted the activity of the enemy's air force against the *front's* attacking forces and forced it to limit itself primarily to aerial reconnaissance. The 2nd Air Army's combat opera- tions were limited by difficult meteorological conditions and the growing difficulties of rebasing, in spite of the timely preparation for airfield maneuver.

The offensive by the forces of the First Belorussian Front. On 14 January the forces of the First Belorussian Front[6] attacked from the Magnuszew and Pulawy bridgeheads. At 0855, following a 25-minute fire onslaught by all of the *front's* artillery, the forward battalions ("special echelons")

---

6   *Sbornik Materialov po Izucheniyu Opyta Voiny*, no. 25, 1947. Directorate for the Study of the War Experience, USSR General Staff, inventory no. 7235, and other materials.

went over to the attack. 22 reinforced battalions and 25 rifle companies took part in the reconnaissance in force along a front more than 100 kilometers wide.

The group of forces that had forward battalions in all its armies (except the 61st), while attacking from the Magnuszew bridgehead, quickly captured 3-4 lines of enemy trenches. In the 61st Army the forward battalions were halted by enemy fire in front of the switch position along the line of the Pilica River and could not force the river. A two-hour artillery preparation and the commitment of the army's main forces into the battle at 1100 were required to overcome the enemy's resistance. On the operation's first day the forces of the 61st Army advanced only 2-4 kilometers. Along the remainder of the front, the main forces of the 5th Shock and 8th Guards armies' first-echelon rifle divisions, by taking advantage of the forward battalions' success and attacking without an artillery preparation, but supported by a double rolling barrage, broke through the enemy's main defensive zone along two sectors and advanced 12-13 kilometers.

The group of forces operating from the Pulawy bridgehead, upon going over to the offensive with its forward battalions and then the main forces of the 69th and 33rd armies' first-echelon divisions, committed the 9th and 11th tank corps to complete the breakthrough of the tactical defense zone. By the close of the day the troops along this axis had advanced 18 kilometers.

Because of the worsening of the weather (fog), the 16th Air Army's air preparation was not carried out. During the night of 13-14 January the army managed to carry out 42 sorties for aerial reconnaissance and dropping leaflets. During the daylight hours of 14 January 33 sorties were carried out, but only two assault aircraft and two reconnaissance planes managed to carry out their combat assignment in Po-2[7] aircraft, due to the weather conditions. Two reconnaissance sorties by the enemy's aviation were noted.

Thus, as early as the first day of the First Belorussian Front's offensive, conditions had been created for the defeat of the enemy's Warsaw and Radom groups of forces and the successful development of the operation in depth.

On the night of 14-15 January and all of 15 January the offensive by both groups of forces (Magnuszew and Pulawy) developed successfully, despite the fact that the enemy began to commit in detail his operational reserves (the XL Panzer Corps' 25th and 9th panzer and 117th Panzergrenadier divisions) into the fighting. During the middle of the day the 1st Guards Tank Army was committed into the breach along the 8th Guards Army's sector at a depth of 12-15 kilometers, and proceeded to develop the success in the general direction of Nowe Miasto and Lodz; simultaneously, the tank corps of the 69th and 33rd armies' mobile groups broke through toward Radom. The main forces of the enemy's XL Panzer Corps were defeated and thrown back to the west and southwest.

On the whole, as a result of the two days of fighting, the defense of the Magnuszew and Pulawy enemy groups of forces had been pierced along a 120-kilometer front to a depth of 30-50 kilometers. The enemy suffered heavy losses and began to fall back to the west. The *front's* forces during the latter half of 15 January went over to the pursuit. The attacks from two bridgeheads merged into a single powerful blow.

Due to the weather conditions, the 16th Air Army began to operate only from the latter half of 15 January and carried out 181 sorties, of which 102 were against enemy forces operating, for the most part, opposite the 61st Army, which, having encountered the enemy's stubborn resistance could not break through his main defensive zone. In all, four reconnaissance flights by the enemy's air force were noted.

---

7   Editor's note. Also known as the U-2, this aircraft first appeared in 1929. The aircraft had a one-man crew and a tops speed of 152 kilometers per hour. It carried one 7.62mm machine gun and a bomb load of six 50-kilogram bombs.

The defeat of the enemy's Warsaw group of forces was accomplished by the forces of the 47th, Polish 1st, 61st, and 2nd Guards Tank armies.

On 15 January, following a 55-minute artillery preparation, the 47th Army attacked north of Warsaw and by the close of the day had cleared the enemy of the area between the Western Bug and Vistula rivers east of Modlin. During the night of 15-16 January the Vistula River was forced over the ice by employing materials at hand for reinforcing by the army's 129th Rifle Corps. The army's success was aided by our forces' vigorous offensive from the Magnuszew bridgehead, where on 16 January the 2nd Guards Tank Army, which had entered the breach along the 5th Shock Army's sector, attacked to the northwest. The 2nd Guards Tank Army, having completed a leap of 80 kilometers on that day, had by the end of the day arrived at the Warsaw group of forces' path of retreat to the west. On this day the 61st Army, taking advantage of the 2nd Guards Tank Army's success, also defeated the opposing enemy and began to roll up his defense along the western bank of the Vistula River to the northwest. In the meantime, units of the Polish 1st Army forced the Vistula River north and south of Warsaw.

On 17 January the main forces of the Polish 1st Army began the fight for Warsaw. The enemy, faced with the threat of encirclement, abandoned the Warsaw fortified area, and the group of forces immediately defending the city was destroyed. The capital of Poland—Warsaw—had been liberated.

On the occasion of Warsaw's liberation by Soviet forces, the people's government of the Polish Republic, in the name of the Polish people, sent a telegram to the Soviet government expressing to the Soviet people and the Soviet army its profound thanks: "The Polish people will never forget that it received freedom and the opportunity to reestablish an independent state existence thanks to the brilliant victories of Soviet arms and thanks to the profusely spilled blood of the heroic Soviet soldiers."[8]

The defeat of the enemy's Radom group of forces and the capture of the city of Radom was accomplished by the forces of the 69th Army, along with the 11th Tank Corps. The city of Radom had been bypassed from the north and south, and then the army stormed and captured it on 16 January. The enemy's main operational reserves, which had been along the *front's* sector since the start of the operation, were defeated in the Radom area.

On 16-17 January the 16th Air Army, in connection with the improvement in the weather, was able to carry out up to 3,000 and more sorties per day. At the same time, formations of assault and night light-bomber aircraft, having been assigned specific sectors of dirt roads, destroyed the retreating enemy forces over two days, both day and night, along all roads in the *front's* sector, particularly along roads leading to the west, northwest and southwest from Warsaw and from the areas of Nowe Miasto, Opoczno, Piotrkow, and Lodz. On 16 January the day bombers concentrated their strikes against the railroad stations and stages leading from Warsaw to the southwest, especially in the Sochaczew area, while striving to foil the enemy's rail shipments. On 17 January the bombers' strikes were directed at destroying the railroad bridges in the Kutno and Sieradz areas, and the Lodz railroad junction, the work of which was disrupted for several days. The bridges were dive bombed, as well as horizontally. The most effective method was dive bombing, as was the case of the railroad bridge over the Warta River near Sieradz, which required five sorties. The enemy's airfields were also subjected to bombing.

During 14-17 January the 16th Air Army carried out 6,481 sorties, of which 3,638 (56 percent) were against enemy forces and 687 (11 percent) were for reconnaissance.

---

8   *Krasnaya Zvezda*, 20 January 1945.

Up to 30 sorties a day by enemy aircraft were noted, attempting to attack the *front's* forces. On 16 January 24 air battles took place, in which the enemy lost 19 aircraft, while our aviation had no losses.

The situation from the first days of the offensive showed the inexpediency of the decentralized command and control of aviation and this method was soon abandoned. The rebasing of our aviation behind the attacking forces was also difficult. The enemy destroyed the existing airfields during his withdrawal, and it was difficult to prepare new ones in a short time, because of the muddy soil and the shortage of technical equipment. As a result, up to 18 January units of the 16th Air Army continued to operate from airfields east of the Vistula, having fallen behind the *front's* attacking forces by up to 100 kilometers. Only to the airfield in the Sochaczew area, which had been seized by tank troops and was being guarded by them, did we manage to rebase a regiment from the 3rd Guards Fighter Corps, and from which it covered the troops. However, these forces were insufficient.

As a result of the *front's* operations during 14-17 January the enemy's tactical defensive zone had been completely broken through and his immediate operational reserves defeated. By the close of 17 January the *front's* forces had advanced 70-100 kilometers to the west, having created a break-through front up to 110 kilometers in width.

The Fourth Ukrainian Front's[9] right flank, due to the difficult mountainous and forested area of the Carpathians, began to lag behind the First Ukrainian Front's left-flank armies.

Thus by the close of 17 January the forces of the First Belorussian and First Ukrainian fronts had broken through the enemy's first Vistula defensive line, defeated his Warsaw—Radom and Kielce—Radom groups of forces and liberated the capital of Poland, Warsaw, from the fascist aggressors. In all, the troops advanced to a depth of 100-160 kilometers at a rate of 17-25 kilometers per day. The enemy's operational reserves had been defeated and the remnants of his defeated formations were fighting in small groups or hurriedly falling back to the west under the attacks by our forces.

The forces of the Fourth Ukrainian Front were slowly advancing in the Carpathian mountainous and forested area.

Combat Operations from 18-24 January 1945. The Development of the Success in the Depth of the Enemy's Defense

The *Stavka* of the Supreme High Command, in its directives of 17 January, demanded of the *front* commanders that they advance their forces to the Oder (Odra) River, while overcoming the intermediate defense lines from the march.

The First Belorussian Front was ordered to speed up its arrival at the line Bromberg (Bydgoszcz)— Poznan, and then to the Oder River. The First Ukrainian Front was ordered to continue the offensive with its main forces toward Breslau (Wroclaw), and no later than 30 January reach the line of the Oder River to the south of Lissa (Leszno), seizing bridgeheads along its western bank. The *front's* left-wing armies were ordered to capture the city of Krakow and the Silesian industrial area.

On the basis of the *Stavka's* instructions and an evaluation of the difficult situation, the *front* commanders assigned their armies subsequent objectives, while demanding that they increase the pace of the offensive. For this, the mobile forces were ordered to bypass powerful centers of resistance and to strive to preempt the enemy in occupying rear defensive lines. The rifle formations were ordered to follow behind the mobile forces at a pace of no less than 25 kilometers per day.

---

9   Excerpt from brief reports nos. 1 and 2 of the generalized experience of the Fourth Ukrainian Front for January-March 1945, inventory nos. 4738 and 4824, and other materials.

The German-Fascist command was hurriedly bringing up new forces and equipment from the interior of Germany and partially from the Western European front, while striving to halt our forces' advance. In the period from 19 January through 3 February alone more than 30 new German-Fascist divisions and up to 350 independent battalions were transferred to the First Belorussian and First Ukrainian fronts' offensive sectors.

The Soviet forces, while repelling the enemy's attempts to halt the offensive, continued to launch attacks along all axes.

The forces of the First Belorussian Front vigorously pursued the retreating enemy. The mobile formations and powerful forward detachments played the main role in the pursuit. The main forces moved by forced marches in columns and deployed as necessary for eliminating major centers of resistance or significant enemy groups of forces remaining in the rear.

The tank armies, while operating ahead of the combined-arms armies, detached forward detachments from each tank or mechanized corps of the army's first echelon. A forward detachment consisted of a tank brigade, a self-propelled artillery regiment, a battalion of rocket-propelled artillery, 2-3 anti-aircraft artillery brigades, a pontoon battalion, and 1-2 sapper companies. These forward detachments' task was to seize and retain important lines and targets until the arrival of the tank army's main forces.

Behind the tank armies, or along independent axes, moved the mobile detachments of the combined-arms armies, which included a tank brigade or tank regiment, a rifle regiment mounted on motor vehicles, a battalion of self-propelled artillery, and an anti-tank artillery regiment, a battalion of rocket-propelled artillery, an anti-aircraft artillery regiment, and a sapper company. The gap between the army forward detachments from the army's main forces reached 25-50 kilometers and more.

During 18-19 January the First Belorussian Front's mobile forces covered more than 100 kilometers and by the close of 19 January reached the third Warsaw defensive line. During this time the combined-arms armies advanced 50-55 kilometers and overcame the enemy's second defensive line. The 8th Guards Army, with the support of the 11th and 9th tank corps, captured the major Polish industrial center of Lodz.

On the operation's sixth day (19 January) the *front's* combined-arms armies reached the line which it had been planned to reach only on the operation's twelfth day (25 January).

The German-Fascist command, in order to delay the attacking forces along the third Warsaw defensive line, was bringing up for its defense its reserves (three infantry and one panzer division, as well as several battalions). However, the vigor of the pursuit of the enemy's retreating forces prevented him from organizing a defense and during 20-22 January the third line was broken through and the *front's* forces, having advanced 120-140 kilometers in three days, reached the Poznan defensive line.

From 23 January fighting by the *front's* mobile forces began for the Poznan defensive line. This objective was accomplished by the 2nd Guards Tank Army along with the 2nd Guards Cavalry Corps, units of which during 22-23 January captured the city of Bromberg (Bydgoszcz). On 24 January the forces of the 1st Guards Tank Army blockaded the city of Poznan.

During the advance to Poznan and the fighting for the Poznan defensive line, the mobile forces operated ahead of and apart from the infantry by a distance of 50-100 kilometers, and up to 350 kilometers from their bases of supply. In view of the mobile forces' rapid advance a shortage of fuel and munitions began to be felt in the tank armies and the *front* command was forced to employ transport aviation to deliver these articles.

By this time, in connection with the concentration of a major group of forces in East Pomerania by the German-Fascist command, as well as due to the lagging behind of its neighbor to the right, the Second Belorussian Front, the enemy's resistance began to grow along the right flank, while the gap between the *fronts'* flanks had reached 40 kilometers by 19 January, and by 24-25 January it had grown to 110-120 kilometers. The danger arose of a powerful enemy counterblow against the *front's* right flank. Thus, in order to secure this flank, the *front* command brought up the forces of the 47th, Polish 1st and 3rd Shock armies, and the 2nd Guards Cavalry Corps. This was a timely measure and enabled the *front's* remaining forces to continue to develop the offensive to the west.

Thus during 18-24 January the enemy's Ninth Army was completely defeated, the Warta line was broken through, and the *front's* forces penetrated into the Poznan defensive line. The enemy group of forces in Poznan was simultaneously encircled and conditions were created for the subsequent development of the *front's* offensive for the purpose of reaching the German frontier fortifications and the line of the Oder.

From 18 January the 16th Air Army's combat operations were once again significantly limited by the difficult meteorological conditions, the soaked earth of the field airstrips, and breakdowns in supply due to difficulties in rebasing, which led to the aviation's lagging behind. During the 18-20 January period the 16th Air Army carried out 730-940 sorties per day. At the same time, the main efforts of our assault air aviation, which was operating in small groups of 2-4 planes, were directed at destroying the enemy's retreating forces along the roads, especially from the Kutno and Lodz areas, as well as against concentrations of his forces along the western bank of the Warta River, in the Sieradz area, while preventing the enemy from consolidating along the Warta defensive line.

The efforts of our bomber aviation were directed, first of all, at halting the movement of troops and cargoes through the Lodz railroad junction by destroying the stations to the west of Lodz and the railroad bridges over the Vistula River at Plock, Wloclawek and Thorn (Torun). The destruction of the bridges was conducted in groups of 5-7 Pe-2[10] planes by dive bombing at a 15-20 degree angle from a height of 1,500-2,000 meters. However, the poor weather did not allow our aviation to fully carry out its assigned objectives.

During the remaining days, that is during 21-24 January, the 16th Air Army was limited to just conducting reconnaissance, while carrying out nine to 70 sorties per day.

By 22 January the first stage of rebasing *front* aviation to airfields west of the Vistula River had been completed. The main forces of our assault air and fighter aviation were concentrated on airfields in the Sochaczew area and to the south; that is, at a 75-100 kilometer remove from our forces. So as to prevent the aviation from lagging behind the troops and to make more exact the order of rebasing, on 21 January new instructions were issued by the commander of the 16th Air Army on rebasing, in which the aviation formations were assigned sectors for reconnoitering airfields and tentative basing areas, and the schedules and order for rebasing to new airfields. At the same time, the 3rd Fighter Corps was to be rebased first, so as not to lag behind the mobile formations.

However, despite the measures adopted, the lagging behind of the 16th Air Army's main forces ranged from 150-200 kilometers on 24 January. Only part of the 3rd Guards Fighter Corps' and the 9th Guards Night bomber Division's planes managed to rebase to less removed airfields (they lagged 100 kilometers behind the troops).

During 18-24 January the 16th Air Army carried out 2,484 sorties, of which 702 (28 percent) were against the enemy's forces and 649 (26 percent) were for reconnaissance, while it securely maintained air superiority and rendered the greatest possible assistance to the *front's* forces.

As before, the enemy's aviation was not very active in operating against the *front's* forces, limiting itself to carrying out reconnaissance. In all, 32 enemy flights were noted during these

---

10 Editor's note. The Pe-2 was a twin-engine bomber that appeared in 1936. It had a three-man crew and a maximum speed of 450 kilometers per hour. Its armament consisted of four 7.62mm machine guns, while it could carry six 100 kilogram bombs in its bomb bay and two 250 kilogram bombs on its wings.

days. However, the enemy's air resistance over enemy territory began to increase, due to the arrival of new air units.

The First Ukrainian Front's forces also continued their successful offensive in the general direction of Breslau, having as their objective reaching the Oder River to the south of Lissa (Leszno), forcing the river and seizing bridgeheads on its western bank. The left-wing armies were ordered to take the city of Krakow.

The pursuit of the retreating enemy[11] was conducted along a broad front and along all the roads in the attacking armies' zones, and column routes of march. The situation of the *front's* armies operating along the Breslau axis took on the form of a wedge, the tip of which was formed by the 3rd Guards Tank and 52nd armies. The armies attacked with a deep operational formation, which enabled them to parry the enemy's attacks against the flank and rear of the forward units and formations.

While continuing the pursuit of the enemy, the forces of the *front's* main group of forces (3rd Guards, 13th, 52nd, and 5th Guards combined-arms armies, and the 4th and 3rd guards tank armies), forced the Warta River on the march across the ice, by using the materials at hand to strengthen it, and by the close of 19 January broke into the territory of fascist Germany. Beginning on 22 January, the *front's* forces began to arrive at the Oder River along a broad front.

If the enemy was waging rearguard actions along the Breslau axis, while trying to withdraw his main forces behind the Oder, then along the Krakow axis he decided to put up a serious fight in order to retain the Silesian industrial area. For this purpose, the enemy planned to launch a powerful counterblow with the formations of his Seventeenth Army against the flank and rear of the First Ukrainian Front's main group of forces. This was facilitated by the lagging behind of the Fourth Ukrainian Front's forces, which in places reached up to 80 kilometers.

Following three days of intense fighting along the outer ring of the Krakow fortified area, units of the 59th Army, along with the 4th Guards Tank Corps, supported by the 60th Army's right-wing units and also air support, captured the city of Krakow in a combined attack from the west, north and east and continued to attack toward the Silesian industrial area.

Having lost Krakow, the enemy hurriedly abandoned the areas situated to the southeast, because maintaining them threatened several divisions with encirclement and defeat.

In order to cover the Silesian industrial area, the German-Fascist command concentrated a large group of forces, consisting of nine divisions, up to five various combat groups, up to six independent regiments, and up to 20 independent battalions from the German-Fascist Seventeenth Army.

During the offensive toward Breslau, the 5th Guards Army, which was the connecting link between the *front's* shock group and its left wing, by 21 January, was lagging 20 kilometers behind its neighbors. In this way a threat arose to the left flank of the *front's* main group of forces. In these conditions, the *front* commander, on the basis of the *Stavka's* instructions, decided to turn the 3rd Guards Army sharply toward the Oppeln axis and thus create the conditions for the 5th Guards Army's most rapid advance to the Oder River in the area northwest of Oppeln. The maneuver by the tank army from the Namslau area to Oppeln was an unexpected one for the enemy. By the close of 22 January the army's tank formations, having advanced more than 50 kilometers in a day in the enemy's rear, reached the town of Oppeln. As a result of this maneuver, the 5th Guards Army sped up its rate of advance and by the close of 22 January had reached the Oder River in the

---

11 Documents on the pursuit of the retreating enemy during the Sandomierz-Silesian offensive operation in January 1945 are contained in the *Sbornik Boevykh Dokumentov Velikoi Otechestvennoi Voiny.* Vypusk 28. Main Military-Scientific Directorate of the General Staff, 1956, pp. 169-88, inventory no. 39864, and other materials.

area northwest of Oppeln. On 23 January the 3rd Guards Tank Army, in conjunction with the 5th Guards Army's formations and part of the 21st Army's forces, completely captured Oppeln.

By this time the *front's* remaining armies were also successfully developing the offensive. The 3rd Guards Army, by means of a skillful maneuver, surrounded an enemy group of forces numbering up to 17,000 men in the woods south of Opoczno and then destroyed it. On 22 January this army's forces encircled and defeated a second enemy group of forces numbering up to 12,000 men and 100 tanks, northeast of Widawa. On the night of 22-23 January the army crossed the Warta River over the ice, using materials at hand to strengthen it, and by 24 January had completely crossed over to its western bank.

In order to more quickly outflank the Silesian industrial area from the north, on 19 January the 21st Army, along with the 31st Tank Corps, was committed into the battle. The army's right-flank formations on 23 January reached the Oder River south of Oppeln and began fighting for the town of Tarnowiec, while hanging over the industrial area from the north.

On the night of 23-24 January the 3rd Guards Tank Army began an attack from the Oppeln area into the rear of the enemy's Silesian group of forces.

At this time the 59th and 60th armies were fighting with little success, while encountering fierce resistance on the part of the enemy's Silesian group of forces.

During the 18-24 January period the 2nd Air Army's combat activities were limited by the difficult meteorological conditions. Only on certain days (19-20 and 24 January) did the army manage to carry out 900-1,000 sorties per day. None the less, the efforts of two assault air and two fighter corps were directed at supporting the *front's* shock group, while the remaining air formations supported the offensive by the 21st, 59th and 60th armies to take Krakow and the Silesian industrial area. On 19 January all of the 2nd Air Army's efforts were concentrated on supporting the 59th and 60th armies in taking Krakow. At the same time, our assault air and bomber aviation, operating in groups of 60-80 planes, launched strikes against the enemy's fortifications, his troop concentrations and railroad stations southwest of Krakow. On the other days, assault air and bomber aviation, operating in small groups, supported the offensive by the *front's* forces, while devoting the greatest attention to destroying the enemy's fortifications and launching strikes against the enemy's troop concentrations in groups of 50-70 planes. At the same time, the 2nd Air Army was assisting the *front's* forces in holding and expanding the captured bridgeheads over the Oder River.

In all, during the 18-24 January period the 2nd Air Army carried out 3,269 sorties, of which 1,115 (24 percent) were against the enemy's forces, 292 (9 percent) were for reconnaissance, 529 (16 percent) were against rail targets, and 1,329 (41 percent) for against the enemy's aviation.[12] A great deal of attention was devoted to foiling the enemy's rail shipments, in order to prevent him from evacuating equipment.

The enemy air force increased its activity, particularly in repelling the *front's* air attacks. Only 187 sorties were noted during these days against Soviet troops. The enemy lost 52 planes in 29 air battles.

Simultaneous with the conduct of combat activities, the 2nd Air Army carried out the rebasing of its air units to new airfields behind the *front's* attacking troops. Due to the lengthening of the communications of the rear units, which were short of auto transport, and due to the moistness of the soil, which made it difficult to prepare airfields, the rebasing proceeded in echelon fashion by regiments, and even by squadrons. As a result, the main forces of *front* aviation fell behind the troops, especially in supporting the right-flank armies. By 24 January the air units were lagging 100-150 kilometers behind. All of this limited aviation's capabilities for supporting the *front's*

---

12 Editor's note. There is no explanation for the author's bad math.

forces. The enemy's captured airfields that did not require a great deal of work to restore them were usually occupied by our air units on the second or third day following their liberation. The 2nd Guards Assault Air and 2nd Fighter corps were rebased most slowly, due to the poor airfield reconnaissance in their sector, as well as uncoordinated work with the rear units, which prepared the airfields slowly.

As a result of the *front's* operations during 18-24 January, the enemy's Fourth Panzer Army and its operational reserves were completely defeated. All the conditions had been created for forcing the Oder River along a broad front and the capture of the Silesian industrial area.

On 20 January the forces of the Fourth Ukrainian Front captured Presov and Kosic. The 38th Army, attacking in difficult mountainous and forested terrain, reached the Brzeznica—Makov line. The 8th Air Army was limited in its operations by the poor weather; during 19-24 January the air army carried out only 623 sorties for supporting the *front's* forces, of which 364 (58 percent) was directed against the enemy's retreating forces.

The Results of the Vistula-Oder Operation's First Stage

During the operation's first stage, during 12-24 January, the forces of the First Belorussian and First Ukrainian fronts achieved major operational results.

On the whole, during the first stage of the multi-*front* operation the main forces of the enemy's Army Group A were defeated and conditions created for further offensive operations. The lagging behind of the neighboring *fronts* (the Second Belorussian Front on the right and the Fourth Ukrainian Front on the left) forced us to adopt special measures for securing the flanks.

During the period 12-14 January through 17 January; that is, during 4-6 days, the *fronts'* forces completely broke through the enemy's tactical defensive zone, defeated his first operational echelon and his immediate operational reserves, and went over to a vigorous pursuit. During these days the First Belorussian and First Ukrainian fronts' combined-arms armies advanced at a rate of 12-35 kilometers per day, while the mobile formations advance from 15 to 45 kilometers per day.

During 18-24 January both *fronts'* forces pursued the enemy, with the active support of our aviation, while preventing him from occupying an organized defense along the intermediate lines. The rates of pursuit were high and reached on both *fronts* an average of 21-37 kilometers per day for the combined-arms armies, and 26-45 kilometers for the mobile formations.

Characteristic features of the troops' activities during the operation's first stage were as follows: a) the wide-ranging and skillful employment of forward battalions; b) the rapid breakthrough of the enemy's tactical defense zone by the combined-arms armies, with the employment of the tank armies (the First Ukrainian Front) and with the forces of the combined-arms armies alone (First Belorussian Front); c) the defeat of the enemy's operational reserves by the two *fronts'* adjoining flanks; d) the skillful organization of the pursuit of the enemy; e) the breakthrough of the intermediate lines from the march; f) the encirclement and destruction of individual enemy groups of forces during the pursuit, and; g) the skillful maneuver by the First Ukrainian Front's 3rd Guards Tank Army along the Oppeln axis.

The shortcomings in the *fronts'* activities during the operation's first stage are as follows: a) the insufficiently completely reconnaissance of the enemy's equipment along certain parts of the front, which forced the First Belorussian Front's 61st Army to conduct an additional artillery preparation for two hours in order to secure the crossing of the Pilica River; b) the insufficiently complete employment by the 61st Army of the 2nd Guards Tank Army's success, which enabled a significant part of the enemy's Warsaw group of forces to escape in time from the planned encirclement.

During the operation's first stage the 16th and 2nd air armies carried out 19,292 sorties, of which 9,562 (50 percent) were against enemy forces and railroad targets, 7,041 (36 percent) were against the enemy's air force, and 2,430 (13 percent) were for reconnaissance. The 8th Air Army carried out 2,379 sorties, of which 69 percent were against enemy forces. As a result of difficult meteorological conditions and the untimely rebasing of their air units, the air armies did not fully take advantage of their capabilities for assisting the *fronts'* forces in breaking through the enemy's defense and pursuing his forces.

The breakthrough of the enemy's defense occurred almost without the participation of *front* aviation, which began to actively operate against the enemy's forces only from the beginning of the pursuit. At the same time, *front* aviation's limited efforts were not dispersed along the entire front, but were concentrated along the decisive axes and the most important targets.

Despite the preparation carried out for airfield maneuver, during the pursuit the airfields were not prepared in time; the rebasing took place slowly by regiments and even by squadrons, and the air armies' main forces lagged behind the *front's* forces, which, along with the worsening of the weather after 17 January, sharply reduced the intensity of *front* aviation's activities against the retreating enemy forces.

The enemy air force, in view of the Soviet air force's air superiority, was not particularly active, limiting itself to carrying out reconnaissance. In both *fronts* 429 enemy flights were recorded, of which 340 (80 percent) were in the First Ukrainian Front's sector. However, the enemy's air force actively opposed Soviet air strikes by bringing in Germany's national air defense fighter aviation.

THE SECOND STAGE OF THE OPERATION (25 JANUARY-3 FEBRUARY)

The Development of The Offensive Along the Poznan and Breslau Axes

The second stage of the Vistula-Oder multi-*front* operation was characterized by the further unrelenting pursuit of the enemy's forces in the direction of Poznan and Breslau, the completion of the defeat of the entire opposing enemy group of forces, and the arrival of our forces at the near approaches to the German capital of Berlin.

With the arrival of the First Belorussian Front's forces at the Poznan defensive line and the beginning of the tank armies' piercing of it, the *Stavka* of the Supreme High Command demanded that the *fronts* continue the offensive for the purpose of shifting combat operations to German territory and reaching the line of the Oder River no later than 30 January, and seizing bridgeheads on its western bank.

The necessity of securely covering the *front's* right flank from the direction of East Pomerania was simultaneously pointed out.

The German-Fascist command, while trying to prevent the invasion of German territory by Soviet forces, threw five fresh divisions and a number of independent units and subunits to the Poznan line. Simultaneously reserves for occupying Germany's frontier fortifications were thrown in.

During the operation's second stage the First Belorussian Front's forces carried out tasks for completing the overcoming of the Poznan line, the breakthrough of the frontier fortified areas, the forcing of the Oder River, and the seizure of bridgeheads on its western bank. The *front's* offensive developed in the following manner.

The tank armies were given a somewhat unusual objective for mobile forces—to complete the breakthrough of the Poznan line and, while developing the offensive, to break through the German frontier fortifications from the march. The first task was accomplished by them on 25 January after three days of fierce fighting, with the assistance of the arriving combined-arms formations.

The tank forces rushed toward the frontiers of fascist Germany, concentrating their main efforts along the Poznan axis. The city and fortress of Poznan, with its 60,000-man garrison of German-Fascist troops, had by the close of 25 January been completely surrounded by the forces of the 8th Guards Army and part of the 1st Guards Tank Army's forces.

On 26 January the mobile forces began operations to break through the frontier fortified areas. By the close of 28 January they had reached the German border along the Berlin axis and the First Belorussian Front's combined-arms armies covered more than 100 kilometers in three days and caught up with the mobile forces. On that day formations of the 2nd Guards Tank and 5th Guards armies broke through the Pomeranian fortified area from the march. The fortifications of the Meseritz fortified area were bypassed from the north. At the end of January the forces of the 2nd Guards Tank and 5th Shock armies reached the Oder River north of Küstrin.

During 26 January-3 February the German frontier fortifications along the Berlin axis were broken through. By 1 February the fortifications of the Meseritz fortified area had been overcome.

By the close of 3 February the forces of the First Belorussian Front's center and left wing had almost completely cleared the enemy from the right bank of the Oder River from Zeden to Lochwitz, while the 8th Guards Army forced the Oder River south of Küstrin and seized a bridge-head 12 kilometers in width and up to three kilometers deep.

The enemy, in trying to delay the Soviet forces' offensive, threw four fresh divisions to the Oder River line from the depth, which undertook a series of counterattacks. Besides this, in the latter half of January the German-Fascist command hurriedly began to concentrate Army Group Vistula in Eastern Pomerania, for attacking the right flank and rear of the forces of the First Belorussian Front's forces that had reached the Oder River.

By this time the gap between the First Belorussian Front's right flank and the Second Belorussian Front's left flank had increased even further and by the time the our forces arrived at the Oder River it had reached 300 kilometers. Covering this gap demanded the deployment here of a signifi-cant part of the *front's* forces.

By the start of February the *front* command had moved up the *front's* second echelon—the 3rd Shock and Polish 1st armies—opposite the above-cited enemy group of forces, and had also turned the 47th and 61st armies to the north. Simultaneous with the arrival of the *front's* mobile forces at the Oder River, the 2nd and 1st guards tank armies were thrown to the north, followed by the 2nd and 7th guards cavalry corps.

Thus by the end of January and the beginning of February 1945, the efforts of the First Belorussian Front's forces were divided. Approximately half of these forces had been forced to turn their front north against the German-Fascist group of forces in Pomerania, while the remaining forces continued to engage in active operations along the Berlin axis against a new enemy group of forces that had been created here, which was supported by aircraft from the Berlin air defense zone.

With the arrival of the First Belorussian Front's forces at the Oder River the degree of enemy air resistance, which was based on the permanent airfields of the Berlin air center, sharply increased. On some days the enemy carried out 2,000-3,000 sorties, while actively attacking the *front's* forces and seizing operational superiority in the air along some axes. Simultaneously, the enemy air force supplied by air its surrounded forces in Poznan.

All of this was a result of the fact that the basing of the 16th Air Army sharply worsened in view of the moist soil of the field airstrips, while the permanent airfields were located 100-150 kilom-eters and more from the front line, which alongside the worsening weather sharply reduced the combat operations of the 16th Air Army, which carried out on the average about 180 sorties per day, mainly by carrying out reconnaissance of enemy forces west of the Oder and in Pomerania, while covering friendly forces. Several sorties were carried out during 29-31 January for destroying the enemy's surrounded forces in Poznan.

In all, during 25 January-3 February the 16th Air Army carried out 2,350 sorties, of which 1,370 (58 percent) were directed against enemy forces, 381 (16 percent) against enemy aircraft, and 599 (26 percent) for reconnaissance. Over 4,000 flights by enemy aircraft were noted. The latter lost 38 planes in 40 air battles.

As a result of the operation's second stage, the forces of the First Belorussian Front completed the breakthrough of the Poznan defensive line, broke through the frontier fortified areas, forced the Oder River and seized two bridgeheads on its western bank, and reached a line located 60 kilometers from Berlin.

The First Ukrainian Front's offensive. The *front's* forces had the objective of reaching the Oder River, forcing it and defeating the last enemy group of forces defending the Silesian industrial area.

Operations by the *front's* forces developed as follows:

Many enemy units, which had earlier been operating along the First Belorussian Front's sector, appeared opposite the 3rd Guards Army upon its arrival at the Oder. Overall, units of 17 divisions were putting up resistance, including seven panzer and panzergrenadier divisions.

By the close of 28 January the army's 76th Rifle Corps skillful bypassed the enemy's group of forces in the Gurau area and forced the Oder River. The enemy, for the purpose of securing his forces' withdrawal behind the Oder River, concentrated in the Lisso and Gurau areas a group of forces with which he intended to launch an attack so the south from the Gurau area to cut off the 76th Rifle Corps from the 3rd Guards Army's remaining forces. On 29 January the enemy launched his counterblow.

At first the attacks by the above-listed groups of forces enjoyed success. However, the commander of the 3rd Guards Army, by means of skillful maneuver of his formations and the commitment of his second echelon (21st Rifle Corps) into the battle, was able in the course of three days to defeat the enemy, who numbered 15,000 men. At the same time the 76th Rifle Corps, despite the threat from the rear, stubbornly fought to hold and widen the bridgehead.

As a result of the advance by the 3rd Guards Tank and 21st armies, along with the 1st Guards Cavalry Corps, against the flank and rear of the enemy's Silesian group of forces, the latter ended up in a very difficult situation. The further offensive by the 3rd Guards Tank Army from the Gleiwitz area to the east, and that of the 59th Army and the 4th Guards Tank Corps from the Jaworzno area to the west would have led to the complete encirclement of this group of forces. However, the *front* commander, guided by instructions from the *Stavka* of the Supreme High Command, made the decision not to encircle the enemy, but to leave him an opening 4-6 kilometers wide between the forces of the 3rd Guards Tank and the 59th armies. This was done so as to preserve the factories and enterprises of the industrial area from destruction. The fact is that the Silesian industrial area represented a huge city, consisting of industrial enterprises. Combat operations to encircle and destroy the German-Fascist group of forces inside this area would have led to the major destruction of very valuable factories, pits and mines. It was important to preserve this area whole. This is why the Soviet command in this case found it possible to purposely let the enemy escape from the inevitable "bag."

The enemy hurriedly abandoned the industrial cities of Polish Silesia and fell back through the proffered opening to the southwest. The enemy groups of forces that retreated were later destroyed in the forests beyond the bounds of the industrial area.

During 25 January-3 February the 2nd Air Army continued to operate in a limited fashion, due to the weather conditions and the worsening of the basing situation (the soil of the field airfields was moist), carrying out on the average about 397 sorties per day. During the first days *front* aviation's main efforts were directed at assisting the 21st, 59th and 60th armies in defeating the enemy's Silesian group of forces, and later at assisting the *front's* forces in holding the bridgeheads across the Oder River.

In all, during these days the 2nd Air Army carried out 3,977 sorties, of which 903 (23 percent) were against the enemy's forces, 560 (14 percent) against rail targets, and 419 (10 percent) for reconnaissance. The enemy air force sharply increased its activity and 740 sorties were noted. The enemy lost 58 planes in 56 air battles.

As a result of the *front's* activities during the operation's second stage, the main forces of the enemy's Fourth Panzer and Seventeenth armies were defeated. The *front's* forces reached the Oder River and forced it along six sectors, with an overall frontage of about 150 kilometers in width.

With the arrival of the First Ukrainian Front's forces at the Oder River on 30 January and the seizure of bridgeheads along its western bank, the First Ukrainian Front's Sandomierz-Silesian operation came to a close.

The offensive by the Fourth Ukrainian Front's forces. During January the Fourth Ukrainian Front's forces, in close coordination with the forces of the First Ukrainian Front, attacked in the Western Carpathians. By the close of January they had advanced 100-200 kilometers. As a result of this offensive, heavy losses were inflicted on the formations of the enemy's Seventeenth and First Panzer armies. The Czechoslovak Corps fought alongside the forces of the Fourth Ukrainian Front on Czechoslovak territory.

Operations of the 18th Long-Range Aviation Air Army. During the conduct of the Vistula-Oder operation the 18th Air Army operated mostly in the interests of the forces of the Third and Second Belorussian fronts in defeating the enemy's East Prussian group of forces.

The 18th Air Army operated in an extremely limited manner in the immediate interests of the conduct of the Vistula-Oder operation: in January it carried out 159 sorties against the Lodz railroad junction, dropping 157 tons of aviation bombs on it for the purpose of disrupting the junction's work. Besides this, the 18th Air Army's formations assisted the offensive by the forces of the Fourth Ukrainian Front, while carrying out 240 sorties aimed at destroying the Katowice and Moravska Ostrava railroad junctions.

The 18th Air Army's greatest efforts were aimed at destroying the enemy's encircled troops in the Breslau area. While these units were being destroyed, the 18th Air Army's formations and units carried out 34 strikes in the Breslau area, of which 20 were launched in the daytime and 14 at night. In all, 1,980 sorties were carried out and 2,500 tons of bombs were dropped. As a result, a great deal of damage was caused to military targets and losses inflicted on the encircled enemy forces in the Breslau area.

Results of the Operation's Second Stage

During the second stage of the Vistula-Oder operation (25 January-3 February 1945) the forces of the First Belorussian and First Ukrainian fronts achieved a major operational success by completing the defeat of the forces of the German-Fascist Army Group A, reaching the enemy's last major defensive line along the Oder River, which they forced in places, and seizing important bridgeheads. At the same time enemy forces were cleared out of the Silesian industrial area and a major regrouping of forces accomplished along the Pomeranian axis.

The forces of the First Belorussian Front, while vigorously pursuing the enemy, successfully broke through the enemy's intermediate lines, arrived with their center and left wing at the Oder River and seized two bridgeheads along its western bank. The threat of a counterblow along the flank forced the *front* commander to detach 50 percent of his forces for securing his open right wing. During 25 January-3 February the *front's* forces covered 260 kilometers in fighting, at an average pace of 26 kilometers per day.

During the second stage the forces of the First Ukrainian Front captured the important Silesian industrial area, preserving its industry intact. By the close of this stage the *front's* forces had seized important bridgeheads along the western bank of the Oder River, which guaranteed conditions for a subsequent offensive.

As a result of the arrival of wet weather, which made the preparation of new airfields more difficult and which limited airfield maneuver, as well as the difficult meteorological conditions, the 16th and 2nd air armies operated in a very limited fashion, carrying out 5,946 sorties in all, of which 1,833 (31 percent) were against enemy forces and railroad targets, 2,924 (50 percent) against the enemy air force, and 1,018 (17 percent) for reconnaissance. The 8th Air Army carried out about 1,000 sorties, of which more than 50 percent were directed against the enemy's troops. At the same time the enemy, drawing on aviation from the Berlin air center, sharply increased his resistance to our aviation, especially along the line of the Oder River, temporarily winning air superiority along some sectors. 5,000 enemy air sorties, mainly by fighter aviation, were noted along both *fronts*.

The following were features of our forces' operations during the operation's second stage: a) the organization of the rapid breakthrough of the enemy's intermediate defensive lines in depth; b) the skillful securing of the *front's* flank during the operation, and; c) the skillful conduct of a maneuver to encircle the enemy's Silesian group of forces.

5

The Results of the Vistula-Oder Operation and Conclusions on Military Art

The Results of the Operation

The operation's political results. The Soviet forces completed the liberation of our Polish ally and shifted combat operations immediately to the confines of fascist Germany along the very important Berlin axis. At the same time, the Fourth Ukrainian Front's armies liberated a significant part of Czechoslovakia. Fascist Germany was deprived of the capability of employing important industrial areas of Poland (Warsaw, Silesia, Lodz, and others).

In the greetings by the Central Committee of the Polish United Workers' Party to the XIX Congress of the Communist Party of the Soviet Union, we read:

> The Polish toilers are obliged for many, immeasurably many things, to the VPK(b),[1] its policy, its struggle, its victories and achievements. They are obliged to it for everything that was and is most important for them: the liberation from fascist slavery, the confirmation of national independence, the rapid development of the national economy and culture, and the growth in the internal forces of its popular government.[2]

The Polish people actively joined the joint struggle with the Red Army against the German-Fascist forces, embarked upon the democratic path of development, became the master of its own fate, and embarked on the construction of a new life. In this fashion the calculations of international reaction on maintaining a reactionary anti-Soviet regime in Poland were foiled.

The operation's military results. The forces of the First Belorussian and First Ukrainian Fronts, with the assistance of the Fourth Ukrainian Front, completely carried out the tasks which had been assigned to them by the *Stavka* of the Supreme High Command. As a result of a vigorous offensive, in the short period of 21-23 days the German-Fascist forces' deeply-echeloned defense between the Vistula and Oder was broken through and Soviet forces occupied favorable lines for launching the final attack against fascist Germany. A major enemy group of forces, Army Group A, consisting of the Fourth Panzer Army and the Ninth and Seventeenth field armies was defeated. During the operation more than 70 German-Fascist divisions[3] and about 350 independent units and subunits were defeated or suffered serious losses. The enemy's losses amounted to 416,000

---

1   Editor's note. This abbreviation stands for the All-Union Communist Party (Bolsheviks) *Vsesoyuznaya Kommunisticheskaya Partiya (Bol'shevikov)*, the official party name until 1952.
2   *Privetstviya XIX S"ezdu KPSS Kommunisticheskikh Rabochikh Partii.* Izdatel'stvo "Pravda," 1953, p. 3.
3   Including up to 30-35 divisions transferred to reinforce Army Group A during the operation.

officers and men killed and about 105,000 captured. More than 1,000 planes[4] (879 destroyed and 266 captured), about 1,500 tanks and assault guns, and more than 1,500 guns and mortars were destroyed or captured. At the same time, the forces of the First Belorussian and First Ukrainian fronts liberated a territory exceeding 100,000 square kilometers.

Soviet forces advanced 480-570 kilometers to the west.

The unprecedentedly powerful attack by the Soviet armed forces, which was launched against the enemy in January 1945, led, first of all, to the result that the German-Fascist forces along the Western Front, particularly in the Ardennes, completely renounced their offensive plans. The Sixth SS Panzer Army was hurriedly transferred from the Ardennes, along with a number of formations from other armies, to the Soviet-German front. In this way the situation of the Anglo-American forces was eased.

The calculations by the German-Fascist command on bleeding the Soviet forces dry and exhausting them by organizing a defense along a series of successively occupied lines between the Vistula and Oder rivers proved groundless.

With our forces' arrival at the Oder River and the seizure of bridgeheads along its western bank, conditions were created for the launching of the final and concluding attack against fascist Germany.

The *fronts'* 16th, 2nd, 6th, and 8th air armies and the 18th Long-Range Air Army took part In the multi-*front* offensive operation. During the Soviet forces' offensive the 16th and 2nd air armies alone carried out 25,238 sorties, of which 11,395 (45 percent) were directed at the enemy's forces and his railroad targets, 9,965 (39 percent) against his aviation, and 3,448 (14 percent) for air reconnaissance. *Front* aviation, while maintaining operational superiority in the air, created favorable conditions for the offensive by the First Belorussian and First Ukrainian fronts and, in spite of the unfavorable meteorological conditions, rendered assistance to the *fronts'* forces in the pursuit of the enemy.

CONCLUSIONS ON MILITARY ART

Questions of Strategy

1. The Vistula-Oder multi-*front* offensive operation should be rated among the most important strategic operations of the Great Patriotic War and of the Second World War as a whole, in terms of its significance and place in the Soviet armed forces' 1945 campaign in Europe, as well as in terms of the objectives assigned and achieved.

2. The multi-*front* Vistula-Oder offensive operation, which was conducted along the Warsaw—Berlin direction, was organized and accomplished under the leadership of the *Stavka* of the Supreme High Command and was a component part of the overall winter strategic offensive by the Soviet armed forces in the 1945 campaign in Europe.

In drawing up the operational plan, there was fully taken into account the major political and strategic significance of the Warsaw—Berlin direction, which was the direction of the Soviet forces' main attack in this offensive. This may be explained by the fact that, first of all, this direction was the shortest route to Berlin; second, the enemy's most powerful group of forces was concentrated along this direction; third, this direction ran through Polish territory, where the Soviet forces could get support from the majority of the population, and; fourth, this direction could support the offensive by a major group of forces.

---

4   Including more than 700 transferred to Army Group A's sector during the operation.

Thus, the operation in question played a major role in the overall strategic offensive in the 1945 campaign in Europe.

The plan by the *Stavka* of the Supreme High Command was distinguished by the exceptional importance of the assigned objectives and called for decisive operations by our forces and the complete rout of the enemy's group of forces along the Berlin axis. The launching of powerful attacks by the forces of the First Belorussian and First Ukrainian fronts was to result in and did result in the splintering of the main forces of Army Group A into the Warsaw, Kielce—Radom and Krakow groups of forces and their destruction in detail, which secured the rapid arrival of the Soviet forces at the Oder River.

The *Stavka* of the Supreme High Command detached for the offensive along this direction major forces of men and materiel, which were to secure the successful fulfillment of the assigned objectives. Of the overall number of 46 combined-arms, six tank and nine air armies along the Soviet-German front at the beginning of January, 16 combined-arms (34.5 percent), four tank (66 percent) and three air (33 percent) armies were concentrated along the Warsaw—Berlin direction. 1,500,000 officers and men, more than 7,000 tanks, more than 26,000 guns and mortars, and up to 5,000 planes were assembled for the operation.

All of this testifies to the major strategic significance of the operation under study.

3. The Soviet forces' offensive in the winter of 1945 began simultaneously along the East Prussian and Warsaw—Berlin directions. Besides this, our forces were conducting offensive operations along the southern wing of the Soviet-German front, in Hungary. Thus the operations of three groups of *fronts* were conducted in close strategic coordination: in East Prussia (Third and Second Belorussian fronts), in Poland (First Belorussian and First Ukrainian fronts, with the assistance of the Fourth Ukrainian Front), and in Hungary (Second and Third Ukrainian fronts). In the final analysis, these operations led to: a) the foiling of the enemy's defensive plan along the main strategic direction, and; b) the foiling of the enemy's maneuver of operational and strategic reserves for the purpose of reinforcing his group of forces along the Warsaw—Berlin direction. From this it follows that the *Stavka* of the Supreme High Command, in organizing strategic coordination, correctly coordinated the efforts of several *fronts* operating along a number of directions, according to goals, time and lines of advance.

4. In evaluating the given operation, one should also take into account the fact that it was conducted against a significantly weakened enemy, but one still capable of stubborn resistance; by this time the ongoing exhaustion of the German-Fascist army was beginning to tell to a significant degree, as well as its decline in morale. On the other hand, the Soviet army's superiority in men and materiel still continued to increase, while its morale was quite high.

The relationship of the Vistula-Oder operation to strategic operations, according to its place in the 1945 campaign and the goals that were achieved, does not exclude the examination of the forms and methods of the Soviet operational major field forces in the multi-*front* operation in the section on operational art.

Questions of Operational Art

1. The preparation of the multi-*front* Vistula-Oder offensive operation, and the *front* and army operations that made it up, was distinguished by its thoroughness and began, basically, as early as August-September 1944, following our forces' consolidation along the lines reached and the seizure of bridgeheads along the Vistula River. The immediate preparation for the operation began

from the end of November 1944, following the reception of the *Stavka's* operational directives,[5] and continued for a month and a half.

Characteristic of the operation was the decisive massing of men and materiel along the axes of the *fronts'* main attacks. Powerful shock groups of forces were created for breaking through the enemy's defense along the axes of the *fronts'* main attacks, which included up to 78 percent of the combined-arms formations, up to 90 percent of the tanks and self-propelled guns, 75-89 percent of the artillery and mortars, and 100 percent of our aviation strength, which enabled us to achieve a tenfold superiority over the enemy and to concentrate up to 232-250 guns and mortars, and 77-122 tanks and self-propelled guns per kilometer along the breakthrough front. For example, the First Belorussian Front, while occupying a line 230 kilometers wide, was to break through the enemy's defense along the main axis (the Magnuszew bridgehead) along a 17-kilometer sector, which comprised 7.4 percent of the overall offensive sector. 78 percent of the rifle formations, 90 percent of the armored forces and more than 75 percent of artillery and mortars were concentrated along this axis. The First Ukrainian Front occupied a 250-kilometer front and was to break through the enemy's defense along a 34-kilometer front, which comprised 13.6 percent of the *front's* overall offensive sector. 78 percent of the rifle formations, up to 90 percent of the tanks and self-propelled guns, and 89 percent of all the artillery were concentrated along this sector.

The skillful massing of men and materiel along the decisive axes enabled us to quickly break through the powerful Vistula defensive line simultaneously along several axes. The experience of massing men and materiel along these axes justified itself in the context of the Great Patriotic War. In modern conditions, taking into account the capabilities of the new weaponry,[6] we need to disperse our men and materiel along a significantly greater territory than was the case in the operation under study, because the piling up of troops on comparatively small bridgeheads can result in large, unjustified losses.

The breakthrough of the enemy's defense in the First Belorussian Front's operation was accomplished along three axes. The overall width of the breakthrough sectors was 34 kilometers. Each army was to break through along one sector 4-8 kilometers in width (except for the 61st Army, which had two breakthrough sectors). In the First Ukrainian Front's operation the breakthrough of the defense was to be accomplished along a 39-kilometer sector. The armies of the *front's* main group of forces were to break through the defense along their entire offensive sector (10-12 kilometers).

The breakthrough of the enemy's defense along several axes, as was the case with the First Belorussian Front, may be recognized as expedient in modern conditions, given the presence of sufficient men and materiel for carrying out the given method.

2. According to the plan for the Vistula-Oder operation, it was necessary to overcome from the march all the defensive lines created by the enemy in the operational depth. This could be accomplished only by the vigorous breakthrough of the tactical defense zone and a high offensive pace by our forces during the operation and shaped the necessity of launching the *fronts'* main attacks from the Vistula bridgeheads. The launching of the main attack by the First Belorussian Front from the Vistula bridgeheads guaranteed the *front's* rapid offensive pace and the arrival of the *front's* forces as quickly as possible (on the operation's third day) in the rear of the enemy's Warsaw group of forces. Thus the rapid defeat of the enemy's entire Warsaw—Radom group of forces and the liberation of the Polish capital of Warsaw were assured. The launching of the main attack by

---

5   Directives of the *Stavka* VGK nos. 220271 and 220275 of 25 and 28 November 1944. USSR Ministry of Defense Archives, Podol'sk. *Fonds* of the First Belorussian and First Ukrainian fronts, 1945.

6   Editor's note. Here, the author evidently has in mind the appearance of nuclear weapons.

the First Ukrainian Front from the Sandomierz bridgehead enabled the *front* to rapidly split the Fourth Panzer Army's main forces and to quickly (on the operation's eleventh day) bring the *front's* main group of forces to the Oder River.

3. The Vistula-Oder offensive operation is characterized by the organization of the close cooperation of the two *fronts*, which carried out the same task of defeating the German-Fascist forces in Poland. Their actions were closely tied together in time and place. Both *fronts* began their combat operations from the same line of the Vistula River and were to conclude them simultaneously along the line of the Oder River. During the *front* operations a number of operational lines were indicated, which the forces of both *fronts* were to reach at an exactly appointed time and thus securely guard their internal flanks. Particular attention was devoted to the organization of coordination while eliminating the enemy's flank groups of forces. For example, in order to eliminate the enemy's Kielce—Radom group of forces, the actions of the First Belorussian Front's 33rd Army and the First Ukrainian Front's 3rd Guards and 6th armies were scrupulously planned and coordinated according to place and time in their overall offensive toward Szidlowiec. Only such an organization of cooperation between the *front's* forces could secure and did secure the successful realization of their assigned tasks.

4. The multi-*front* Vistula-Oder offensive operation was distinguished by its great scope. It was carried out by the forces of two *fronts*, with the assistance of a third *front* and Long-Range Aviation. The operation lasted 23 days. The enemy's defensive front along the Vistula, opposite the two *fronts'* sectors, about 490 kilometers in width, was broken through in the course of 2-4 days. The troops' advance in depth was equal to 570 kilometers, at an offensive pace of up to 24-25 kilometers per day. On some days the combined-arms formations' offensive pace reached up to 40-45 kilometers per day, and that of the mobile forces up to 70-80 kilometers.

All of these operational indices characterize it as a major multi-*front* offensive operation, carried out on the basis of the USSR's increased materiel-technical capabilities and the troops' accumulation of combat experience and deserve to be carefully studied, because they approach the indices of modern offensive operations. Only in modern conditions may the enemy's resistance be smashed by the employment of new weaponry, while in the operation under study it was overcome thanks to the overwhelming superiority of the Soviet forces in men and materiel over the enemy.

5. The achievement of decisive results was due to a significant degree to the skillful choice of the form of conducting the operation, the essence of which was in launching deep frontal attacks along several axes for the purpose of splitting the enemy's front throughout the entire depth of the operation from the Vistula to the Oder, with the subsequent defeat of the enemy in detail during the pursuit.

The choice of such a form of conducting the given offensive operation was conditioned by the disposition of the main forces of the enemy's group of forces in the first operational echelon, the comparative remove of his operational reserves from the tactical defensive zone, and the presence of a significant number of prepared defensive lines along the entire territory from the Vistula to the Oder, inclusively, which had not been occupied by the enemy beforehand, and thus the necessity that our forces preempt the enemy in the organized occupation of these lines. On the whole, such a form of operational conduct under these concrete conditions justified itself and once again showed that a decisive success in defeating the enemy may be achieved not only through encirclement operations, despite their effectiveness, but by the employment of other forms of conducting operations depending upon the concrete situation.

Part of the *fronts'* forces in the operation in question were to, by vigorously developing the breakthrough toward the flanks, encircle and defeat the enemy's flank groups of forces, which was to secure the main forces in their westward advance. Such a method should also be recognized as expedient.

The armies' basic form of operational maneuver, especially in breaking through the enemy's tactical defense zone, was the frontal attack for the purpose of breaking through. This was conditioned by the presence of a continuous and previously prepared (by engineers) front, already occupied by enemy forces. Subsequently, during the development of the success in the operational depth, alongside with the frontal attack, different forms of operational maneuver were employed, depending on the situation. For example, the 47th Army carried out the operational envelopment of the enemy's entire Warsaw group of forces; the 60th Army carried out the operational outflanking of the enemy's Seventeenth Army in the Tarnow area. A brilliant example of the achievement of a deep operational turning is the maneuver by the 3rd Guards Tank Army for encircling the enemy's group of forces in Polish Silesia. Such broad maneuvering guaranteed our forces the initiative and a vigorous pursuit.

6. The breakthrough of the tactical defense zone and the vigorous development of the success throughout the entire operational depth, along with overcoming intermediate lines from the march, were achieved through the skillful choice of the main attack's axes, the creation of powerful groups of forces along these axes, the deep operational disposition of the *fronts'* forces and armies, the conduct of the entire operation at a high tempo, and the manifestation of military skill in controlling the troops' activities on the part of the commanders of the *fronts* and armies and their staffs. The secure and constant protection of the flanks of the *fronts'* shock groups enabled us to fully employ their forces for launching a powerful attack to a great depth.

The breakthrough of the enemy's defense was to be carried out almost simultaneously along several axes, which was to be secured by a realistic correlation of forces and was to deny the enemy the opportunity of maneuvering his men and materiel along the front. The breakthrough was to be accomplished as follows: a) by systematic preparation, in those cases in which the defense was prepared beforehand by the enemy and occupied by his forces (for example, along the first, Vistula, line), and; b) from the march—while breaking through the intermediate defensive zones in the operational depth, which had been hurriedly occupied by the enemy's forces, with insufficient density.

Direct aviation preparation was planned for securing the breakthrough of the enemy's tactical defense zone, although it was not conducted due to the unfavorable meteorological conditions, and thus one cannot come to any conclusions about the most expedient methods of its conduct. An artillery preparation was planned to last for 95-107 minutes, while its actual duration depended upon the actions of the forward battalions—in the event of their successful actions, the main forces developed the success of the forward battalions without an extended artillery preparation, following short fire onslaughts; support for the infantry-tank attack was carried out by means of a double rolling barrage to a depth of 2.5-3 kilometers; accompaniment by the method of consecutively concentrating fire to a depth of 5-7 kilometers and launching concentrated strikes by large bomber forces in conjunction with echeloned strikes by small groups of assault air. The armies' first-operational-echelon rifle formations played the main role in breaking through the tactical defense zone; the tank armies (in the First Ukrainian Front) were employed to complete the breakthrough of the main defensive zone and overcoming the second zone from the march.

On the whole, such methods while breaking through the defense justified themselves. The breakthrough of the enemy's tactical defense zone by the forces of the First Ukrainian Front was completed during the night before the operation's second day, and by the forces of the First Belorussian Front attacking from the Pulawy bridgehead on the first day, and from the Magnuszew bridgehead on the second day of the *front* operation, which corresponded to the level of the development of military art at that time.

7. The development of the tactical success into an operational one was carried out at sufficiently high speeds for the time. The *fronts'* forces advanced 110-130 kilometers in four days and then took up a vigorous pursuit and reached a depth of up to 570 kilometers, depriving the enemy of the opportunity of consolidating along his prepared intermediate defense lines and system of fortified areas.

The *fronts'* and armies' mobile groups were the chief means of vigorously developing the success to a great depth. Through their maneuver actions, they made it possible for our forces to overcome from the march previously prepared defensive lines and numerous water obstacles in the depth of the enemy's defense.

The *fronts'* and armies' deep operational formation enabled us to uninterruptedly augment our efforts along the main axes, which made possible our vigorous advance in depth. The presence of two combined-arms armies in the First Ukrainian Front's second echelon was conditioned by the necessity of carrying out simultaneously two important tasks during the operation—the development of the operation along the main axis, as well as the defeat of the Krakow group of forces and the capture of the Silesian industrial area. The depth of the *fronts'* operational formation reached 100 kilometers, and that of the armies 50 kilometers. The troops' were echeloned particularly deeply during the operational pursuit of the enemy, which enabled us to carry out broad-ranging maneuver for seizing intermediate defensive zones.

The high rates of the offensive's advance characterize the vigor of the breakthrough of the enemy's defense to a great depth and the overcoming of his intermediate lines from the march.

All of this testified to the Soviet forces' possession of the art of breaking through the enemy's prepared defense and the development of the success throughout the entire operational depth, and also indicated the further growth in the Soviet armed forces' offensive capabilities.

8. Operational pursuit in both *fronts* was parallel and frontal and was conducted along a broad front at extremely high speeds. The overall depth of the pursuit reached 230 kilometers and more.

First of all, mobile formations, operating at a distance of 30-50 kilometers and more from the combined-arms armies, conducted the pursuit. Of great importance were the powerful forward detachments, detached by the mobile formations and operating 30-40 kilometers ahead of the main forces, which seized crossings, strong points and important lines in the enemy's depth, and carried out reconnaissance. For pursuit purposes, the combined-arms armies also created powerful mobile forward detachments, which included, depending upon the situation, a tank brigade or a rifle regiment, reinforced with self-propelled and anti-tank artillery, guards mortar units, and sappers. The mobile detachments operated ahead of the main forces at a remove sometime reaching 30-60 kilometers, preempting the enemy in occupying important lines.

Our aviation played an important role in supporting the pursuit of the enemy. The main efforts of the *fronts'* aviation were directed at supporting the tank armies operating ahead of the *front's* forces. Our aviation launched strikes against the retreating enemy, preventing him from occupying the intermediate lines in an organized fashion, and destroyed bridges and crossings along the path of the enemy's likely path of retreat, complicating his systematic retreat to the west.

The artillery was echeloned throughout the entire depth of the army's formation, which enabled us to more rapidly support the activities of the armies' formations upon encountering individual enemy groups of forces.

While pursuing the enemy, the tank armies' first-echelon forces seized important lines and held them until the arrival of the combined-arms formations. The second echelons were employed for fighting for the subsequent lines and strong points. Through this the uninterrupted pursuit was achieved.

During the pursuit there were instances of the encirclement and destruction of the enemy's groups of forces in the operational depth of his defense. For example, the Ostrowiec—Opatow group of forces was encircled at a depth of 100-120 kilometers, while the Poznan and Schneidemühl groups of forces were encircled at a depth of 300-350 kilometers from the jumping-off position before the start of the offensive.

All of this testifies to the fact that the given operation offers many instructive examples in questions of pursuit.

9. The fight against the enemy's operational reserves was conducted throughout the operation. The tank armies, which were boldly moved forward to develop the success in the operational depth, played a particularly large role in this struggle. Our aviation, which was supporting the tank armies, also played an active part.

During the operation the German-Fascist command transferred a significant number of new reserves to the two *fronts'* sectors. For example, the number of new divisions and units thrown against the First Belorussian Front exceeded the initial strength of the enemy's Ninth Army by a factor of two.

The enemy's operational reserves had as their chief task holding our forces along any line and thus winning time for the organization of a solid defense along the following line. However, the vigorous pursuit of the retreating enemy and the bold actions of the tank armies led to a situation in which the enemy's reserves would suffer a defeat on the march, or while deploying for a counterattack or while repelling counterattacks.

Thus the complete defeat of the enemy's operational reserves was achieved by the rapid piercing of the enemy's tactical defense zone, the high rates of the *fronts'* offensive in the operational depth, and by the skillful employment of the *fronts'* mobile forces and aviation.

10. The timely securing of the flanks of the *fronts'* shock groups played a major role in the operation's successful realization. Particularly instructive in this case is the securing of the First Belorussian Front's right flank from the north against the enemy's Pomeranian group of forces. By the close of the operation four combined-arms (Polish 1st, 3rd Shock, 61st, and 47th) and two tank (1st and 2nd guards) tank armies and a cavalry corps (2nd Guards) had been employed for operationally securing the *front's* right flank and had formed a 300-kilometer front facing north, which was a characteristic feature of the given operation.

The operational securing of the flank of the First Ukrainian Front's main group of forces in the beginning of the operation was realized by the attack by two armies (60th and 59th) in the general direction of Krakow, and during the operation by the 3rd Guards Tank Army's maneuver along the eastern bank of the Oder River into the rear of the enemy's Silesian group of forces, as well as the attack by the *front's* second-echelon army (21st), along with the 1st Guards Cavalry Corps, along this axis.

The internal flanks of the shock groups and the *fronts'* boundary were secured by the attacks of the 33rd Army and the 9th Tank Corps, and the 3rd Guards Army and the 25th Tank Corps toward Szidlowiec, for the purpose of defeating the enemy's Ostrowiec—Opatow group of forces in conjunction with the 6th Army.

During the pursuit, the internal flanks were secured by detaching a part of the *fronts'* forces. For example, for this purpose the First Belorussian Front detached the 33rd Army's 38th Rifle Corps, which was following echeloned back and to the left, as well as the 7th Guards Cavalry Corps and the 9th Tank Corps.

All these methods for securing the flanks essentially justified themselves.

11. The correct employment of the *fronts'* and combined-arms armies' second echelons enabled the *front* commands to influence the development of the operation.

The Vistula-Oder offensive operation is an example not of a hackneyed, but of a diverse employment of second echelons, depending upon the concrete situation. A *front's* second-echelon armies were employed not only for developing the operation in depth along the main axis, but also for carrying out the following tasks: a) for securing the flank during the operation (the First Belorussian Front's 3rd Shock Army); b) for augmenting efforts along one of the axes (the First Ukrainian Front's 59th Army); c) for defeating the enemy's group of forces by carrying out an enveloping maneuver (the First Ukrainian Front's 21st Army); d) for clearing the rear area of the remains of the enemy's forces (the First Ukrainian Front's 6th Army, which was moved to the *front's* second echelon during the operation), and; e) for seizing and holding bridgeheads (the armies' second echelons in the First Ukrainian Front). The deadlines and depth of the second echelons' commitment also varied; for example, the 59th Army was committed on the third day, and the 21st Army on the operation's eighth day, at a corresponding distance of 25-30 and 100-120 kilometers from the jumping-off position.

12. The combat employment of the tank armies also varied. Operating as mobile groups (the success development echelon), they were committed into the breach, depending on the situation on the operation's first day (3rd Guards and 4th tank armies), on the second day (1st Guards Tank Army), and on the third day (2nd Guards Tank Army), both for completing the breakthrough of the enemy's tactical defense zone, and for developing the success in the operational depth following the breakthrough of the tactical defense zone by the rifle formations (First Belorussian Front).

In the present operation the actions of the mobile forces were characterized by high rates of advance, which reached up to 40-50 kilometers per day, and on certain days up to 80 kilometers. Besides this, regroupings of mobile formations to new axes for the resolution of new tasks were successfully realized during the course of the operation.

The basic assignment of the mobile forces during the operation was the development of the success in the operational depth, and the seizure of the enemy's defensive zones in depth from the march.

The tank armies carried out tasks for breaking through from the march not only previously prepared defensive zones, but also of fortified areas, while they persistently and tirelessly pursued the enemy and skillfully forced rivers.

Of interest is the example of a tank army's flank maneuver in the operational depth of the enemy's defense for assisting a combined-arms army's offensive, and then for the purpose of getting into the rear of the opposing enemy group of forces (3rd Guards Tank Army).

The tank armies, while operating along the most important axes, cooperated not only with each other, but with the independent tank corps, which usually attacked along the flanks of the *fronts'* shock groups.

The tank corps operated as the armies' mobile groups (success development echelons).

These actions by the mobile forces enriched Soviet military art with diverse examples of employing tank armies and formations.

13. One should note as a positive quality in the employment of *front* aviation the fact that its efforts were not dispersed along the front, but were concentrated along the decisive axes through centralized control from the air army commander's command post. However, due to the inclement weather, the tactical breakthrough of the enemy's tactical defense zone was accomplished almost without the participation of *front* aviation, which began to more actively operate only with the beginning of the pursuit of the enemy's forces. However, even during the pursuit our aviation's efforts and capabilities were sharply reduced by the inclement weather and our aviation most often operated in small groups, single planes, and in pairs. Our aviation's main task was the destruction of the retreating enemy forces along the roads and in concentration areas. Moreover, if the weather

allowed, our aviation operated against the enemy's concentration areas in groups of 50-80 planes. Bomber aviation's efforts were directed at foiling railroad shipments through strikes against railroad stations and junctions. All of this was typical of the methods of employing aviation in the Great Patriotic War in 1945.

14. Also worthy of attention is the fact that in the present operation airfield maneuver was prepared and planned and men and materiel for preparing airfields during the operation were detached, with the participation of the combined-arms and tank armies. The mobile formations had the task of seizing the enemy's airfields and holding them until the infantry's arrival. Aviation formations were assigned zones for reconnoitering possible airfields, approximate basing areas and deadlines for rebasing. The fighters would begin rebasing first, followed by assault aircraft and then by bombers.

The onset of the thaw and the limited equipment in the rear units, and sometimes the inefficiency of the rear area aviation units' commanders made the preparation of new airfields extremely difficult. As a result, the rebasing of our aviation formations would take place in an untimely manner, as well as in small groups, which lowered the intensity of air flights. As a rule, fighter and assault air's main forces lagged behind the ground forces.

15. The offensive in the Vistula-Oder operation began and developed in a situation of Soviet aviation's quantitative and qualitative superiority and our operational superiority in the air. Thus the fighting was conducted only for maintaining air superiority through destroying the enemy's aviation in air battles and on their airfields. However, as a result of *front* aviation's lagging behind, especially during the operation's conclusion along the Oder River, and the enemy's movement of his aviation there from the center of Germany, by the end of the operation operational air superiority along certain axes was sometimes held by the enemy. This experience indicates that aviation, without airfield maneuver, even given a quantitative superiority over the enemy in planes, cannot be fully employed during the operation.

16. Troop command and control in the Vistula-Oder offensive operation was distinguished by its centralization (especially during the first stage) and the close proximity of command posts to the troops.

During the operation operational groups, with communications equipment, were dispatched from headquarters at all levels. Troop tasks, particularly during the pursuit, were assigned and refined daily.

Radio was the chief communications means. Mobile communications means, including aircraft, were broadly employed.

The *front* and army commanders carried out command and control functions from forward command posts, which had been moved forward along the decisive axis.

During the operation a high degree of mobility, the maximum proximity to the troops and the frequent shifting of command and observation posts were required of commanders and their staffs at all levels.

Questions of Tactics

1. The Soviet forces' tactics in the Vistula-Oder offensive operation were further perfected, particularly in the area of preparing for and conducting the vigorous and uninterrupted breakthrough of the enemy's main defensive zone in difficult meteorological conditions, as well as in organizing the cooperation of all combat arms, the overcoming of intermediate zones from the march by Soviet units, and the organization of maneuver on the battlefield.

The operation's experience showed the utility of organizing, in this concrete instance, the rifle corps' and divisions' combat formations in two echelons, along with artillery groups and reserves. The rifle corps' breakthrough sectors were 2.5-5 kilometers in width and 1.2-2.5 kilometers for the divisions. The depth of a rifle corps' immediate objective reached 8-10 kilometers (the breakthrough of the enemy's main defensive zone), while the depth of the task for the day was 15-17 kilometers (reaching the second zone). The depth of a rifle division's immediate objective was 3.5-7 kilometers, 8-10 kilometers for the subsequent objective, and the task for the day 12-15 kilometers. On the whole, all of this corresponded to the level achieved by Soviet military art at the time under consideration.

A corps was given 6-7 days to organize for the battle in the jumping-off position, which enabled us to organize coordination and the conduct of all measures for preparing for the offensive.

2. The employment of forward battalions on the operation's first day, 3-5 hours before the general offensive, fully justified itself. The forward battalions, in successfully conducting the battle, deprived the enemy of the capability of withdrawing his forces and created favorable conditions for committing the rifle formation's main forces into the battle and for the vigorous and unremitting breakthrough of the enemy's tactical defense zone. Characteristic of the present operation is that all the artillery of the *front's* (First Belorussian Front) shock groups prepared the attack by the forward battalions, and not only the artillery specially detached for this purpose, as had been the case in the majority of operations. The forward battalions' attack was supported by a rolling barrage.

The forward battalions' successful actions were immediately developed by the main forces' attack. At the same time, in one case the forward battalions' attack grew immediately into a general offensive by the main forces, without an artillery preparation (First Belorussian Front), and in another case it enabled us to reveal the true shape of the forward edge of the enemy's defense.

3. The rapid breakthrough of the enemy's main defensive zone and the entire tactical zone by the forces of both *fronts* guaranteed the rapid development of the operation's success as a whole.

The decisive conditions aiding the rapid breakthrough of the enemy's main defensive zone in the present operation were the high concentration of forces along the decisive axes, the deep echeloning of our combat formations, the high density of fire during the artillery preparation, which was carried out throughout the entire tactical depth, the forward battalions' skillful actions, the artillery and aviation preparation and accompaniment by the infantry's and tanks' offensive, and the close cooperation by the combat arms.

The troops' broad ranging maneuver on the battlefield for the purpose of encircling and destroying the enemy in the present operation was highly developed. During the breakthrough of the enemy's main defensive zone our formations and units boldly outflanked the enemy's groups of forces and destroyed them.

4. Maneuver on the battlefield and during the pursuit of the enemy was widely practiced. The troops outflanked the enemy from the flanks, got into the rear of individual enemy groups, slipped into the gaps between the enemy's forces, defeated his formations and units, or preempted them in occupying defensive positions.

The mobile forces' forward detachments and the corps' and divisions' mobile detachments, while maneuvering and destroying the enemy, boldly and decisively advanced.

The broad maneuver of the troops on the battlefield was carried out in close cooperation between all the combat arms and with the active support of aviation.

The operation's experience showed that the most expedient method of breaking through the fortified areas in the enemy's operational depth was their breakthrough from the march.

The forcing of rivers from the march in winter conditions was aided by the skillful and vigorous actions of the forward detachments, which preempted the enemy in organizing a defense along the rivers, seized bridgeheads and thus created favorable conditions for crossing the attacking troops' main forces. The crossing of the infantry and light artillery was carried out over ice, the thickness of which reached 15-20 centimeters. Tanks, mechanically-towed artillery and auto transport crossed on ferries and over bridges, or over the ice, supporting it with planking from materials at hand. Such methods justified themselves in these conditions.

5. The tactics of employing aviation combat arms was further perfected. In particular, the employment of bomber aviation for attacking small targets (for example, bridges) and dive bombing was more widely employed than in the Soviet forces' preceding operations.

Annex 1

List of Front and Army Commanders for the First Belorussian and First Ukrainian Fronts During the Vistula-Oder Operation

First Belorussian Front—Marshal of the Soviet Union G.K. Zhukov
47th Army—Major General F.I. Perkhorovich
Polish 1st Army—Lieutenant General S.G. Poplawski
61st Army—Colonel General P.A. Belov
5th Shock Army—Lieutenant General N.E. Berzarin
8th Guards Army—Colonel General V.I. Chuikov
3rd Shock Army—Lieutenant General N.P. Simonyan
69th Army—Colonel General V.Ya. Kolpakchi
33rd Army—Colonel General V.D. Tsvetaev
1st Guards Tank Army—Colonel General of Tank Troops M.E. Katukov
2nd Guards Tank Army—Colonel General of Tank Troops S.N. Bogdanov
16th Air Army—Colonel General of Aviation S.I. Rudenko
6th Air Army—Colonel General of Aviation—F.G. Polynin

First Ukrainian Front—Marshal of the Soviet Union I.S. Konev
13th Army—Colonel General N.P. Pukhov
52nd Army—Colonel General K.A. Koroteev
5th Guards Army—Colonel General A.S. Zhadov
3rd Guards Army—Colonel General V.N. Gordov
60th Army—Colonel General P.A. Kurochkin
21st Army—Colonel General D.N. Gusev
59th Army—Lieutenant General I.T. Korovnikov
3rd Guards Tank Army—Colonel General of Tank Troops P.S. Rybalko
4th Tank Army—Colonel General of Tank Troops D.D. Lelyushenko
2nd Air Army—Colonel General of Aviation S.A. Krasovskii

Part III

The Second and Third Belorussian Fronts' East Prussian Operation

The present collection is dedicated to a description of the East Prussian operation of 1945, conducted by the Second and Third Belorussian fronts.

The operational-strategic sketch of the operation was written by a group of generals and officers under the overall leadership of Lieutenant General, professor and doctor of military sciences Ye.A. Shilovskii.

The sections relating to the Second Belorussian Front were put together by a group of officers under the overall leadership of professor and Lieutenant General F.P. Shafalovich.

The following took part in drawing up materials for the collection: Lieutenant General Ye.A. Shilovskii, Lieutenant General F.P. Shafalovich, colonels P.F. Boldyrev, A.Ya. Brod, A.V. Vasil'ev, K.V. Vavilov, N.S. Klimov, S.Ye. Solov'ev, N.V. Sokolovskii, and Lieutenant Colonel A.F. Zhuchkov.

The following took part in the final writeup and preparation of the materials for the collection for publication: Colonel N.G. Pavlenko and Lieutenant Colonel P.M. Isakov.

Editor-in-chief, Major General V.A. Nebuchinov.

Introduction

The overall situation that preceded the East Prussian operation came about as the result of the Red Army's offensive operations in the summer and fall of 1944. As a result of the Red Army's summer offensive in Belorussia, our forces forced completely liberated the Belorussian Soviet Republic, then forced the Neman River, reached the Vistula River, liberated the greater part of the Lithuanian Soviet Republic, a significant portion of allied Polish territory, and reached the borders of East Prussia. To the north, in September 1944 the Red Army's forces developed the offensive along the Memel and Libava axes and reached the shore of the Baltic Sea. More than 30 German divisions were cut off in the area between Tukums and Libava.

At the beginning of October 1944 the Soviet forces' front line ran generally from north to south, from the Baltic shore east of Memel and Tilsit to Jurborg (on the Neman River), then to Shirwindt, east of Suwalki to Augustow and then along the Augustow Canal, the Biebrza and Narew rivers (through Lomza and Ostroleka) to Pultusk and Praga (a suburb of Warsaw).

Active operations continued during the fall of 1944, sometimes reaching great intensity. The First Baltic Front, with its main forces along the Libava axis, was engaged in heavy fighting there with the isolated German group of forces. The *front's* forces advanced up to 15 kilometers along the left flank along the Tilsit axis and reached the Neman River here. The Third Belorussian Front had entered East Prussia. During 16-28 October the *front's* forces overcame powerful field and permanent fortifications in the frontier zone, inflicted heavy losses (more than 40,000 men, 665 tanks and assault guns, 690 guns, etc.) on the enemy and advanced 20-45 kilometers along the Gumbinnen and Goldap axes, forming a salient here that jutted into German territory. To the south, the forces of the Second Belorussian Front and the right wing of the First Belorussian Front were engaged in stubborn fighting to broaden the bridgeheads seized earlier along the western bank of the Narew and Western Bug rivers in the Rozan, Pultusk and Serock areas (the so-called Rozan and Serock bridgeheads). As a result of heavy fighting, our forces managed to widen both of these bridgeheads.

At the end of October and beginning of November our forces' front line had stabilized for the most part until the beginning of the Red Army's January offensive. This was how the jumping-off position, from which the Red Army's forces moved to storm the lair of the fascist beast in the winter of 1945, was formed.

The Soviet forces' offensive in East Prussia, which began in January 1945, was a component part of the Red Army's overall offensive between the Baltic Sea and the Carpathian Mountains. The Third and Second Belorussian fronts had the important objective of cutting off East Prussia and the German troops occupying it from central Germany and defeating and destroying the northern strategic wing of the German front. Combat operations of great force and intensity unfolded in a specialized area, with its characteristic political and military features. The conditions for conducting operations, their forms and methods, also had their peculiar features, which will be noted later on.

East Prussia was historically a seat and springboard for German imperialism in the East, a nest of Prussian junkers and militarists, who long occupied leading posts in the government and army. In the military-geographical sense, East Prussia is a broad springboard, thrust forward and favorable for attacking the USSR. This springboard has repeatedly been used by German imperialists for aggressive purposes in the east (for example, in 1914-15 and 1941). It was heavily fortified and useful both for stubborn defense and for flank attacks against enemy forces attacking toward Warsaw and Berlin. German military specialists at the end of the nineteenth and first half of the twentieth centuries carefully studied the conditions of conducting military operations in East Prussia and drew up different variations of operational plans (for example, the works of Moltke,[1] Schlieffen[2] and others).

The East Prussian operation of 1945, in terms of its planning and conduct, represents an extremely instructive offensive operation of strategic significance, which was conducted by the *Stavka* of the Supreme High Command, involving the coordination of two *fronts* (with the involvement of part of a third *front's* forces). In it we see the further development of the Soviet armed forces' military art, corresponding to the concluding phase of the Great Patriotic War.

---

1   Editor's note. Karl Bernhard Graf von Moltke (1800-91) joined the Prussian army in 1822 and was appointed chief of the General Staff in 1857. He commanded the army in the German Wars of Liberation (1864, 1866, 1870-71) and continued as chief of staff in the new German imperial army. He retired in 1888.
2   Editor's note. Alfred Graf von Schlieffen (1833-1913) joined the Prussian army in 1853 and took part in the Austro-Prussian and Franco-Prussian wars. He became chief of the German General Staff in 1891. He retired in 1906.

1

A Military-Geographical Description of the Operational Area

A Geographical and Political-Economic Survey

The area in which the offensive by our forces unfolded in the East Prussian operation had the following boundaries.

In the northeast, east and southeast, the border (taking into account the front line by the start of the January offensive) ran along the Neman River from its mouth to Sudargas, then to Schillenen (80 kilometers west of Kaunas), and then Goldap, Augustow, the Biebrza, Narew and Western Bug rivers. The Vistula River from Modlin to its mouth served as the area's boundaries to the south and west. To the north the boundary ran along the shore of the Baltic Sea from the mouth of the Vistula River to the mouth of the Neman River. Thus the operational area included the territory of East Prussia and part of northern Poland.

The overall area of military operations within these bounds was about 60,000 square kilometers. The width of the area, when measured from the northeast to the southwest, along the Tilsit—Torun line, reached 330 kilometers, while its depth along the line Lomza—Königsberg was about 200 kilometers. Thus this area was favorable for conducting wide-ranging offensive operations by major combat forces.

East Prussia has historically been a springboard for German imperialism in the East, a nest of Prussian Junkers and militarists, and a stronghold of political reaction. In the military sense, it represented a broad and heavily fortified bridgehead, thrust forward, serving to concentrate forces designed for invading the USSR, or attacking our forces advancing on Warsaw and Berlin in the flank. The strategic significance of the East Prussian area was also conditioned by the fact that the shortest routes to the lower Vistula ran through here, as well as onward to the lower Oder River, around the Berlin area, from the north. The highly developed fortifications facilitated the Germans' stubborn defense of East Prussia, even against superior enemy forces.

The surface of East Prussia represents a slightly hilly plain, which is part of the broad Baltic lowland. The area is most elevated in the south. Here runs a ridge of hills, which begins south of Goldap and, under the name of the East Prussian Highland, stretches, with breaks, through Sensburg (50 kilometers east of Allenstein) to Lidzbark (70 kilometers southwest of Allenstein). The average height of these hills is 150 meters. The highest points are the Zeeskerhoehe—309 meters (seven kilometers south of Goldap) and the Kernsdorferhoehe—312 meters (15 kilometers south of Osterode).

The following three main groups of uplands make up the East Prussian Ridge.

a) The Suwalki Upland in the Pillupenen (35 kilometers southeast of Gumbinnen)—Goldap—Marggrabowa—Suwalki area. This is the most elevated part of the East Prussian uplands, with an average height of 200 meters.
b) The Bischofsburg Upland in the Lötzen—Seeburg (30 kilometers northeast of Allenstein)—Ortelsburg area. This upland represents individual ridges of hills, which stretch predominantly

from south to north and are divided by lakes and streams. The average height of the hills here is about 150 meters.

c)   The Gilgenburg Upland in the Osterode—Lidzbark—Przasnysz area. This upland also consists of several ridges of hills, divided among themselves by rivers and a chain of lakes. The average height of the hills does not exceed 150 meters.

Two ridges of uplands peel off from the main East Prussian Highland. The first ridge begins south of Heilsberg (60 kilometers south of Königsberg) and stretches, with breaks, to the north-west and ends southwest of Preussisch Eylau in the so-called Stablack Hills (with an average height of about 150 meters). The second ridge begins northwest of Allenstein, stretches to the northwest and consists of three groups of uplands: a) northwest of Allenstein; b) northwest of Morungen, and; c) northeast of Elbing. The average height of this ridge is about 150 meters.

The most characteristic feature of the East Prussian terrain is the individual hills and short ridges of hills, divided between themselves by lakes and streams. The uplands and lakes, along with their tributaries, form a series of defiles making defense easier. This terrain feature is particularly sharply displayed in the zone of the Masurian Lakes.

A large number of individual farms with strong stone structures served as natural strong points and facilitated the organization of a durable defense.

Lowlands are encountered throughout the entire area, the majority of which are well cultivated, inhabited and have a well developed road net. An exception is the swampy valley of the Biebrza River, from 2-11 kilometers wide.

Swamps are also located between the Pisa and Orzyc rivers. These swamps are mostly peat and difficult of access even in the dry season.

Finally, there are also large swamps in the delta of the Neman River, where they cover the shore of the Kurisches Haff and reach as far inland as Tilsit.

Overall, the majority of the East Prussian lowlands fully allow for the waging of operations by major combat forces and the conduct of wide-ranging offensive operations.

Forests cover 15-17 percent of the entire area. The most significant forest tracts are found in the northeastern and central parts of the area, where woods intersect the routes leading to East Prussia and increase the area's inaccessibility, particularly in the Johannisburg (45 kilometers south of Lötzen)—Ortelsburg sector.

According to the direction of their flow, the majority of East Prussia's river intersect routes running from the northeast to the southwest and create a series of boundaries along these routes, which are convenient for defense and which make it difficult to develop our forces' offensive operations to the southwest and west.

Thus in this instance the most favorable route for our forces' offensive is from the southeast to the northwest, because such a direction of attack runs predominantly along the river valleys and the riverine defensive lines can be taken in the flank.

The majority of the area's rivers do not represent serious obstacles. The exceptions are the Neman, Biebrza, Narew Western Bug, and Vistula rivers, as well as the Augustow Canal.

The Neman River, along the Sudargas (50 kilometers east of Tilsit) sector to its mouth ran along the front line and divided our forces from those of the enemy. The width of the uncontrolled river channel is 180-380 meters, which shrinks to 170-185 meters along the controlled sectors. The river's depth varies from 1-5 meters. The speed of the current is 0.5-1.2 meters per second. Thus, along its lower course the Neman River represented a serious obstacle and secured the northern wing of the German forces defending against our forces' offensive along the Insterburg axis.

The Biebrza River along the sector from the Augustow Canal to its mouth ran along the front line and divided the sides' forces. The river is 30-60 meters wide and 2-5 meters deep, while in many places it is only 0.5 meters deep. The river has a silted bottom. Due to its size, the Biebrza

River cannot serve as a serious obstacle. However, the river's wide and swampy valley presented significant difficulties for the offensive, and thus, on the whole the Biebrza River was a strong defensive line and made it easier for the enemy to defend the southeastern approaches to East Prussia.

The Narew River varies from 65-300 meters in width along the sector from the Biebrza River to its mouth. The river is 2-6 meters deep. The bottom is predominantly sandy. The valley is wide (2-4 kilometers) for a long way; its banks are steep and in places reach a height of 40 meters. Overall, the valley is accessible, with the exceptions being the broad swamps near Wizna, below Lomza and south of Rozan. Therefore, the Narew River represented a serious obstacle, which is why the bridgeheads we seized near Rozan and Serock along the western bank were so important for the Soviet forces' offensive. Aside from these two bridgeheads, the Narew River divided our forces from those of the enemy along the remainder of its course.

The Western Bug River is 120-180 meters wide and 2-2.5 meters deep along the sector from the Narew River to its mouth. The valley is swampy in places, with a width of 2-6 kilometers. The Western Bug represented a powerful defensive line against our offensive along the right bank of the Vistula River. However, the importance of this line was lessened by the fact of our Serock bridgehead.

The Vistula River represented the greatest water barrier in this operational area and, depending on the direction of its flow, had a varying significance during the conduct of the East Prussian operation of 1945.

Along the sector from the Western Bug River to Bydgoszcz the river is 300-400 meters wide and 1-6 meters deep. The speed of the current is about 0.5 meters per second. The river valley is wide (up to ten kilometers), with steep banks. Only near Wyszogrod and Torun does the valley narrow to 1-2 kilometers. Along this sector, where the Vistula River flows in a northwesterly direction, the Second Belorussian Front's forces operating along the right bank, were divided from the forces of the First Belorussian Front, which were attacking along the river's left bank.

The river is 250-400 meters wide along the sector from Bydgoszcz to the mouth; the depth is 2-5 meters. The speed of the current is about 0.7 meters per second. The river bottom is sandy and silted in places. The river valley is 5-8 kilometers wide and only near Fordon does the valley narrow to three kilometers. The Vistula River flows in a northerly direction along this sector and during the East Prussian operation of 1945 it had a double significance. First of all, the Vistula River along this sector was a serious water obstacle for our further offensive from East Prussia to the west. Secondly, it could also be used by us as a powerful defensive line for securing our operations against the enemy's East Prussian group of forces, in the case of the arrival here of major reserves from Pomerania.

Besides this, the Dieme, Pregel and Alle rivers were important in the depth of the enemy's defense and had been prepared for stubborn defense.

The Augustow Canal is 10-20 meters wide and 1-5 meters deep along the Netta River (a tributary of the Biebrza River)—Augustow sector. For the most part, the canal runs along swampy terrain. The Netta River is 20-30 meters wide and 1.5-3.5 meters deep; the river valley is swampy. In general, the Augustow Canal and the Netta River, along with the surrounding swamps, presented a serious obstacle. We had bridgeheads along the northwestern bank of the canal in the Augustow area. The Augustow Canal and the Netta River divided our forces from those of the enemy along the rest of their course.

Lakes. There are a lot of lakes in East Prussia, but the majority of them are scattered along the entire territory and do not form favorable defensive lines. The exception is the line of the Masurian Lakes in the central part of the area. This strip of lakes begins near Angerburg with the broad Lake Mauer and stretches through Lötzen, where it ends with the horseshoe-shaped Lake Nieder. The overall north-south length of the Masurian Lakes is 80 kilometers, while this lake zone is passable from east to west only along a small number of narrow defiles between the lakes. In general, the zone of the Masurian Lakes, according to its natural features, represented a powerful defensive line and enabled the Germans to organize a strong defense facing east and southeast.

Forces attacking into East Prussia are divided by the Masurian Lakes into two independent groups: one attacking to the north of the Masurian Lakes, and the other to the south.

Baltic Seacoast. A large part of the Baltic seacoast consists of broad lowlands formed by the lower reaches of the Neman, Pregel and Vistula rivers. It is only on the Samland peninsula, located between the Kurisches Haff and Frisches Haff that cliffs reach 30-60 meters in height.

The 10-meter depth necessary for large military vessels and military transports runs 400-1,000 meters from the shore. The most convenient place for large landing operations is the northern shore of the Samland peninsula (in the area of Kranz), where the necessary depth is 300 meters from the shore.

The largest port on the seacoast was Königsberg. This port could handle up to 3.7 million tons of freight per year; that is, about 17 pairs of trains per day, while the length of the mooring line supported the landing of up to an infantry division per day. Large ocean-going vessels often stopped at the town of Pillau, which is located on the spit along the exit into the bay and which served as Königsberg's preliminary port.

Climate. The area of East Prussia is under the influence of the Baltic Sea and is distinguished by a mild and moist climate. The average year-round temperature varies from 6.3-8.4 degrees Celsius. The average year-round precipitation is 700 mm.

During the first stage, when the East Prussian operation was being prepared and conducted— that is, December 1944-January 1945—the winter was not very snowy and the snow cover did not exceed 5-6 centimeters. Along with this, the frosts hardened the swampy sectors and made them passable for infantry. The thickness of the ice along the Narew and Western Bug rivers reached 30-40 centimeters, which made it possible to cross troops over the ice. Therefore, the forcing of rivers and lakes did not present major difficulties in the beginning of the offensive.

Subsequently, at the end of January 1945, when our forces reached the approaches to Königsberg and had advanced to the Elbing area along the Mlawa axis and cut off the Germans' East Prussian group of forces from the rest of Germany, the weather changed. Heavy snowfalls and snowstorms began. The temperature fell to minus 15-20 degrees and the snow cover reached an average thickness of 20 centimeters, and 60 centimeters for the drifts. The passability of the roads sharply worsened and much effort was required to clear them. Such weather made particularly difficult the work of tanks and auto transport and reflected unfavorably on the speed of the advance. A significant warming later set in.

The spring of 1945 arrived in the beginning of March and the breakup of the ice on the rivers began in the middle of March. The spring breakdown of the roads, along with prolonged freezing rains and a great deal of mud complicated combat operations significantly and slowed down the pace of the offensive.

Finally, it should be noted that during our offensive overcast weather and fogs predominated, and this made much more difficult the activities of our aviation and restricted the employment of artillery. For example, during the first three days of the offensive (13-15 January) there was overcast weather and fog, which reduced visibility to 150-200 meters, as a result of which the infantry's offensive, was often conducted with weak artillery support and without participation by aviation. Thick fogs were a common phenomenon during the elimination of the Germans' isolated East Prussian group of forces (February-March 1945).

In general, during the East Prussian operation of 1945 the meteorological conditions were unfavorable for the conduct of major offensive operations.

A political-economic survey of East Prussia. First of all, it should be borne in mind that an economic survey of East Prussia is based on prewar statistical materials and therefore does not reveal the actual political-economic situation of East Prussia at the time of our invasion of this province and does not reflect, of course, those profound changes that took place in the national economy and the economy of the areas under study in connection with the war. However, the prewar data enable us to more fully reveal the German command's plans for defending East Prussia and thus more deeply to understand the significance of the East Prussian operation of 1945, which is why the prewar data are presented here for general guidance.

East Prussia was one of Germany's agricultural regions and characterized by the predominance of large landlord ownership and was one of the country's main food bases. Here our forces found large supplies of bread, potatoes and forage, and large amounts of livestock, and were able to live off local resources.

Industry in East Prussia was poorly developed. The majority of enterprises were small handicraft affairs, which mainly processed agricultural and forest produce. There were machine construction and timber processing enterprises in Königsberg, Tilsit and Elbing, as well as military factories. During the war the Hitlerites secretly outfitted and established a number of major military enterprises.

According to the 1939 census there were up to 2,488,000 inhabitants in East Prussia, which yielded a sufficiently high average density of 63 persons per square kilometer. The province's population was homogenous according to nationality and religion, because the chief group consisted of Germans (95 percent of the entire population), of which the overwhelming majority were Lutherans. The German population of East Prussia, which had been raised in the spirit of the bestial Nazi ideology, was hostile to our forces.

Even before the First World War the German ruling classes devoted particular attention to East Prussia. In this province, with its poorly developed large industry, industrial workers were scattered among small enterprises and constituted only an insignificant part of the proletariat. The main mass of workers was agricultural workers, poorly organized and scattered all over the country.

Alongside this, up to 90 percent of all the land in the Prussian countryside was concentrated in the hands of rich farmers and landowners. Of the landowners, particularly noteworthy were the landowning gentry (Junkers), who owned 45 percent of all the land. Their large estates represented large capitalist enterprises and were the basis of that influence that the Prussian Junkers had long enjoyed in Germany, especially after the fascists came to power. The representatives of the Junker class had long occupied the leading posts in the German army and the central state apparatus. Therefore, East Prussia was considered one of the main political bases of the German ruling classes, a nest of Prussian militarism and a stronghold of German reactionary forces.

Moreover, as was noted earlier, East Prussia was the most eastern German province and thus had major strategic significance for imperial and Hitlerite Germany as a springboard for aggression to the east. The German imperialists called East Prussia the "German outpost in the East" and declared that it "must remain German forever."

Therefore, great significance was attached to East Prussia and it was accorded one of the first places in plans for aggressive wars in the East, which were drawn up by the German General Staff. However, during the last two wars the German command, under the influence of the reasons stated above, was inclined to somewhat overestimate the significance of East Prussia and was not able to correctly comprehend those changes which were taking place during in the strategic situation during the course of the war.[1]

---

1   It is a well known fact that in 1914, before the start of the Battle of the Marne, which was the center of combat operations, the German command did not think twice about transferring two army corps and a cavalry division from the French front to East Prussia, in order to save the holdings of the East Prussian landowners

Communications routes. In East Prussia there are ten kilometers of railroads for every 100 square kilometers, while at the same time for every 100 square kilometers there are: two kilometers in Lithuania, 3.7 kilometers in western Belorussia, and four kilometers in Poland.

From east to west there run five railroad lines over the Vistula River bridges at Tczew (Dirschau), Marienwerder, Graudenz, Fordon, and Torun, with an overall capacity, according to data from 1938, of up to 300 pairs of trains per day. Besides this, the port of Königsberg could handle more than 10,000 tons of freight daily. All of this amounted to 317 pairs of trains overall.

Therefore, East Prussia was securely linked with the rest of Germany, while the highly developed rail net in East Prussia itself enabled the German army to maneuver widely by rail and to quickly concentrate its forces. However, in reality, at the start of 1945; that is at the time of our winter offensive, the capacity of the East Prussian railroads was significantly lower—300 pairs of trains per day, which is explained by the sharp shrinkage of the engine and wagon park and the poor technical condition of the railroad lines, which were being systematically attacked by our aviation.

However, it is necessary to note that the existing rail network was perfectly adequate to assist the Germans' stout defense of East Prussia.

There were about 37 kilometers of surfaced roads per 100 square kilometers in East Prussia. Such a thick network of surfaced roads created favorable conditions for carrying out major auto and march transfers of forces and completely supported the conduct of major operations.

East Prussia's Engineering Preparation

During the course of several years the Germans had created a prepared system of field and permanent fortifications, which had been strengthened by natural and artificial anti-tank and anti-personnel obstacles. Before the beginning of the Second World War the Germans had created in East Prussia fortified areas No. 13 (Elmenhorst—Lötzen) and No. 11 (Allenstein—Heilsberg), and also took advantage of the permanent structures in the Mlawa and Torun fortified areas.

Besides this, the Germans attached great significance to modernizing the fortress of Königsberg.

For the purpose of strengthening the defense of East Prussia and northern Poland, the Germans created between the frontier defensive zone and the fortress of Königsberg a number of field lines, which were supplemented by a permanent defensive system. During the war the forces of the field troops, special organizations, prisoners of war, and the local population dug tens of thousands of kilometers of trenches and anti-tank ditches, set up barbed wire obstacles and powerful explosive obstacles.

Therefore, the forces of the Third and Second Belorussian fronts had to overcome a deeply echeloned and powerful defense, which represented a system of fortified areas and positions. At the same time, the Germans employed and configured for defense, having included them in the overall defensive system, nearly every farm, major inhabited locale and city, as well as the remaining fortress structures and fortresses built at the end of the nineteenth and beginning of the twentieth centuries (Lötzen, Modlin, Mlawa, Königsberg, Pillau, Graudenz, Kulm, and Torun). The Germans, by employing natural conditions and, most of all, the many lakes, rivers and swamps, created a network of canals and hydrotechnical structures and prepared areas for flooding.

By the time of the start of our offensive in the middle of January 1945, the defensive system in East Prussia and the adjoining part of northern Poland was as follows.

---

from a Russian invasion. The absence of these forces during the decisive days of the Battle of the Marne told on the course of combat operations and facilitated the collapse of the Germans' military plans.

The same thing happened in 1945, when at the concluding stage of the Great Patriotic War, the German command assigned major forces (up to 38 divisions) to retain East Prussia, despite the fact that the strategic situation demanded the concentration of the maximum number of forces along the decisive Berlin direction.

A. In the Third Belorussian Front's Offensive Sector[2]

The enemy had the following fortifications in the Third Belorussian Front's offensive sector.

a)   A main defensive sector, with the forward edge along the following line: west of Sudargas—Pilkallen—Walterkemen—Goldap—west of Augustow. The depth and degree of the engineering outfitting of the defense was not the same and along the most important axes its depth reached ten kilometers. Along the axis of our forces' main attack the enemy's defense consisted of two positions, and one along the secondary axes. Both positions were of the field type, having 3-5 trenches.

b)   An intermediate fortified zone along two sectors: the first ran along the line Hartigsberg (along the southern bank of the Neman River)—the heights five kilometers west of Pilkallen—Jodzunen (eight kilometers southeast of Gumbinnen), and a second along the line Regellen (eight kilometers southeast of Goldap)—Zawadden—Treuburg—Lyck. These intermediate positions had a single trench each and 2-3 trenches along certain sectors.

c)   Fortified area no. 13, which covered the far approaches to the fortress of Königsberg from the east and had a forward edge that ran along the line Tilsit—Gumbinnen—Lissen, with a rear-area position in Welau.
This fortified area consisted of three field defensive zones.
1.   The first zone ran along the line Bambe—Gumbinnen—Lissen.
2.   The second zone ran along the line Heinrichswalde (12 kilometers southwest of Tilsit)—Zillen—Mulinen—Ischdaggen—Kunigelen.
3.   An intermediate line, Gross Skeisgirren—Kuhreiten.
4.   A third zone, Welau—Nordenburg, which ran through a flooded area. This zone covered the space between the Heilsberg and Lötzen fortified areas.

d)   The Lötzen fortified area, which covered the far approaches to the fortress of Königsberg from the southeast, included the following:
1.   A field-type forward position along the line Lissen—Neu Jucha (1-2 fully-outfitted trenches).
2.   A first fortified zone (eastern wall) along the line of the Strengelnsee—the Goldapersee—Gross Konopken—the northern bank of the Spirdingsee (1-2 fully-outfitted trenches and an average of 3-5 pillboxes per kilometer of front).
3.   A second fortified zone along the western bank of the Lewentinsee—Taltowiskosee, which had field fortifications.
4.   Two fortified zones (western wall) facing west; the first along the line of the Dobensee—Steinwalde—Nikolaiken, and a second along the line Drengfurt—Rastenburg—Steinwalde. The first zone had 2-3 trenches, and the second two trenches, although the fortification of the northern sector had only begun.
5.   The old fashioned Lötzen fort-outpost, which was used by the Germans as a depot.
In general, the Lötzen fortified area relied on the system of the Masurian Lakes (from the Mauersee to the Spirdingsee) and securely covered East Prussia from an invasion by our troops from the southeast.

---

2   The boundary line between the Third and Second Belorussian fronts was as follows: Augustow—Stradaunen—Rhein—Heilsberg (all locales, except Augustow, were for the Third Belorussian Front).

e)   The Heilsberg fortified area, which covered the near approaches to the fortress of Königsberg from the south and was one of the most powerful fortified areas in East Prussia. It was calculated that this area could hold nine infantry divisions, with reinforcements.

The Heilsberg fortified area included the following:

1.   A permanent fortified position (Heilsberg—Deime), which had been prepared along the line Tapiau—Friedland—Workeim—Baude Hacken (two kilometers northeast of Frauenburg). There were up to 911 pillboxes along this position, which meant an average of up to five pillboxes per kilometer of front, and 10-11 pillboxes along certain axes. It should be noted that in withdrawing the Germans employed only an insignificant part of their permanent structures and that the majority of pillboxes were not used, and some were even locked up.

This position reinforced the field defensive line that ran along the line Friedland—Schippenbeil—Bartenstein—Heilsberg—Wormditt—Frauenburg. By the start of the operation this line had not been completed and there were trenches only in the areas of the strong points.

2.   A field position that ran along the line Postnikken—Uderwangen—Brandenburg and which consisted of two trenches.

3.   A field position located in the Brandenburg—Baude Hacken—Braunsberg area.

4.   A fortified zone, which ran along the line Gross Heidekrug (14 kilometers west of Königsberg)—Fuchsberg (eight kilometers northwest of Königsberg)—Neuhausen—Arnau—Bergau—Heide Maulen (along the seacoast six kilometers southwest of Königsberg). This zone consisted of 2-3 trenches. According to German documents, this was the external line of the Königsberg fortress.

5.   The fortress of Königsberg, which had two lines of forts. There were 15 old-fashioned forts along the outer belt, which were located 6-7 kilometers from the center of town. A heavily fortified zone had been prepared in front of the outer line of forts and in front of the circular paved road, which consisted of 2-4 trenches, and in some places of seven trenches.

An internal line of forts ran within the city (along the line of the old city limits). The forts were old fashioned, with an earthen wall and open moat, which was usually filled with water.

6.   Finally, a fortified zone, facing east, had been prepared along the line Darinen (18 kilometers north of Königsberg)—Neuhausen—Fuchsberg and whose flanks were anchored on the Kurisches Haff and the Königsberg fortress, thus transforming the Samland peninsula into a broad beachhead.

This zone consisted of 2-3 fully-outfitted trenches, eight earth and timber pillboxes and 25 permanent concrete shelters built before 1914.

From the preceding description it is clear that the fortress of Königsberg, along with the Heilsberg fortified area, comprised the core of the entire defense of East Prussia.

B. In the Second Belorussian Front's Offensive Sector

The enemy had the following fortifications in the Second Belorussian Front's offensive sector:

a)   The frontier fortifications along the Lyck—Bialla—Johannisburg sector consisted of several individual strong points along the main road and railroad junctions.

A field position, counting 1-2 trenches had been built behind this line of strong points along the line Neu Jucha—Johannisburg.

b)   The main defense zone ran along the line of the height 4-6 kilometers west of Augustow—Netta River—Augustow Canal—Biebrza River—Narew River as far as Mlynarz, Makow, Pultusk, and Dembe. These were field fortifications with 2-3 fully-outfitted trenches; only in the Dembe area were there four machine gun pillboxes.

c)   The second defensive zone ran along the line Rachki—Prostken—Kadzidlo—the heights west of Makow—Strzegocin—the heights west of Dembe and had two trench lines along its entire length. 3-6 kilometers in front of the second defensive zone a field position had been prepared, with Graewo as its major strong point, along the line Graewo—the heights north of Kumelsk. All of this fortification system covered the approaches to the Lötzen fortified area from the southeast.

d)   The third defensive zone ran along the line Ortelsburg—Przasnysz—Nowe Miasto (20 kilometers north of Modlin)—Dzialdowka River and consisted of 2-4 fully-outfitted trenches.

e)   The following switch positions had been constructed between the first three defensive zones:
  • a switch position along the western bank of the Pisa River along the Johannisburg—Nowogrod sector, facing to the east; this position was part of the Lötzen fortified area and consisted of one, and in places two, trenches; besides this, two trenches had been prepared along the eastern bank of the Pisa River along the Johannisburg—Hessen sector.
  • a switch position along the line Wronowo (18 kilometers northwest of Pultusk)—Golotczizna—Rakowo (six kilometers west of Plonsk), facing southeast and south; this was a field position and consisted of two trenches.

f)   Fortified area no. 11, which covered the fortress of Königsberg from the south and included a permanent zone running along the line Grunwalde—Ortelsburg—Waplitz as far as the Schillingsee. This zone consisted of fully-outfitted trenches and had 1-2 pillboxes per 4-6 kilometers of front. By the start of the operation the construction of this zone had not been completed.

g)   The Mlawa fortified area had the following engineer preparation:
  1.   The main defensive line ran along the line Naperken—Wola Szydlowska—Pnewo Wielkie (18 kilometers southeast of Mlawa) and consisted of two trenches.
  2.   Two forward positions: one along the line Kreky—the heights four kilometers east of Grudusk—Wola Szydlowska and the other along the line of the heights four kilometers southeast of Kreky—the heights west of Grudusk—Wola Szydlowska. Both forward positions were of the field type and contained a trench each.
  3.   The Mlawa strong point, which consisted of two enclosures: an internal one with a radius of 1-1.5 kilometers, and an external one with a radius of 2-3 kilometers. Each enclosure had a trench each. Besides this, 53 pillboxes had been included in the external enclosure, which had been built by the Poles. There were about three pillboxes per kilometer of front.
  In general, the Mlawa fortified area was located along an important operational direction and solidly covered the town of Mlawa, which was the junction of two railroads and eight survaced roads.

h)   The fortress of Modlin was an old Russian fortress (Novogeorgievsk) and had an external and internal line of forts. The forts along the internal line were old and made of brick and had been strengthened by several concrete casemates. The construction of the external line of concrete forts had not been completed; eight forts had been built along the northern bank of the Vistula River, and three along the southern bank.

The fortress of Modlin covered the crossings over the Vistula River and enabled the Germans to maneuver on both sides of the river.

i)   The fourth fortified zone ran along the line Waplitz (five kilometers southeast of Hohenstein)— Nowe Miasto—Drewenz River and in the Waplitz area it intersected with fortified area no. 11 and, together with the latter, formed a single defensive zone covering East Prussia against our invasion from the southeast. This defensive zone had three fully-outfitted trenches along almost its entire length.

The Torun fortified area (bridgehead) consisted of the fortress of Torun, the bridgehead fortifications of Graudenz and Kulm and the Graudenz—Torun fortified position.

The fortress of Torun had 15 old brick forts, which formed the fort belt with a diameter of seven kilometers. The Germans had configured the fortress for modern defense.

The Graudenz bridgehead fortifications consisted of: 1) a group of small forts near the northern outskirts of the town, which had been strengthened with trenches, and; 2) field fortified positions, built along a line 5-8 kilometers east of town and whose flanks rested on the Vistula River.

The Kulm bridgehead fortifications had been built in the shape of a half enclosure along the right bank of the Vistula River, 5-6 kilometers from the town and consisting of two trench lines.

The Graudenz—Torun fortified position consisted of two fully-outfitted trenches and had 28 pillboxes, the construction of which had not been completed.

In general, the fortress of Torun and the Graudenz and Kulm bridgehead fortifications were located 15-40 kilometers from each other and, together with the Graudenz—Torun fortified position, formed a spacious bridgehead along the right bank of the Vistula River, relying on which the Germans could put up an active defense of the lower Vistula and launch flank attacks against our forces operating north and south of this triangle of fortifications. Therefore, the Torun fortified bridgehead was of great significance for the Germans' defense of the lower Vistula.

The fortifications along the Deutsch Eylau—Freistadt sector. Along this sector, along the more important axes, there were individual pillboxes, which did not constitute a continuous fortified zone and which were not used by the enemy during our January offensive.

The fortifications at Elbing and Marienburg. The area of the town of Marienburg had been outfitted by the Germans as a powerful center of resistance, involving the use of permanent fortifications that had been built even before the 1914-1918 war. This center of resistance had been prepared in the shape of a half enclosure around the town, with a radius of 4-5 kilometers and whose flanks rested on the Nogat River. The half enclosure consisted of two lines of trenches.

In the Elbing area the Germans had configured for defense the embankment of the Elbing—Königsberg highway, which covered the approaches to the town from the south. The embankment's great height and its steep slopes served as a good anti-tank obstacle.

The system of German fortifications described above reflects the actual condition of East Prussia's engineering preparation at the moment of our resumption of the offensive, and it is distinguished somewhat from those data that we had before the beginning of the operation as to the outline and character of the East Prussian fortifications.

The fortified zones' density of permanent structures was actually lower than assumed due to intelligence data. The approximate number of fortified concrete pillboxes per kilometer is shown in the following table.

Table III/1.1 Approximate Number of Fortified Concrete Pillboxes in the Second Belorussian Front's Offensive Sector

	Number of Pillboxes	
	Per Kilometer of Front	Along Individual Sectors and in Lake Defiles
Heilsberg Fortified Area:		
a) along the Deime River	2	–
b) the front Tannis— Workein—Blaude-Hacken	5	10-12
Lötzen fortified area	3	8
Rudczanny—the Schillingsee	0.2-0.3	–

The majority of the permanent fortifications were of the machine gun pillbox type, with a thickness of no more than one meter for the walls and cover. Large artillery reinforced concrete firing positions and mixed pillboxes were rarely encountered.

The majority of the fortified zones were only of the field type and consisted of one or several trenches, with machine gun platforms and light shelters. Standard reinforced concrete wells for building machine gun nests and observation posts were widely used in fortifying the lines. Inhabited locales (towns, farms with solid stone structures), as a rule, were employed by the Germans for creating strong points and centers of resistance.

Conclusions on the system of defensive lines in East Prussia:

1. In East Prussia the Germans had created a deeply-echeloned and developed system of field and permanent fortified zones, reinforced with natural and artificial obstacles and located at a comparatively close distance from each other.
2. Field-type structures (trenches, communications trenches) were widely developed, which were reinforced with small reinforced concrete firing points – so-called – wells. These field structures were the basis of the engineering preparation in East Prussia.
3. The most refined engineering preparation of the enemy's defense was in the Third Belorussian Front's offensive sector, where the fortress of Königsberg and the Heilsberg and Lötzen fortified areas were located.
   On the other hand, the enemy had comparatively more weakly prepared the defense in the Second Belorussian Front's offensive zone, where the stronger fortifications were along the Mlawa axis.
4. Therefore, the forces operating in the zone to the south of the Masurian Lakes, going around the powerfully fortified Heilsberg and Lötzen fortified areas, were in more favorable conditions for an offensive. The forces attacking north of the Masurian Lakes were in a less favorable condition.

Operational Axes

Given the shape of the front that had been established along the East Prussian strategic direction at the end of 1944, the following operational axes could be employed for our invasion into East Prussia:

1. The Tilsit axis ran from Tilsit to Königsberg; the boundary on the left ran through Sudargas (on the Neman River) and Aulowenen (30 kilometers north of Insterburg).
2. The Insterburg axis ran from Stallupönen to Insterburg and then to Königsberg, or in the space between the Königsberg fortified area and the Masurian Lakes toward Gerdauen; the boundary on the left ran along the line Suwalki—Angerburg (50 kilometers south of Insterburg).

3. The Masurian axis ran from the front Suwalki—Osowiec, through the Masurian Lakes and then to Rastenburg; the boundary on the left was Jedwabno (20 kilometers northeast of Lomza)—Bischofsburg (30 kilometers northeast of Allenstein).

4. The Allenstein axis ran from Ostroleka (on the Narew River) through Ortelsburg toward Allenstein; the boundary on the left was Ostrow Mazowiecka (40 kilometers southwest of Lomza)—Hohenstein (25 kilometers southwest of Allenstein).

5. The Mlawa axis ran from Makow through Mlawa toward Deutsch Eylau; the boundary on the left was Pultusk—Rypin (20 kilometers south of Brodnica).

6. The Torun axis ran from Serock through Sierpc to Torun; the boundary on the left was the Vistula River.

The Tilsit operational axis included the shortest paths to Königsberg. Besides this, the area between the Neman and Deime rivers was less fortified than along the Insterbrug direction. However, the wooded and swampy terrain in the maritime zone and the less developed road network made an offensive by large numbers of troops more difficult. Alongside this, an offensive along this axis would result in the necessity of subsequently forcing the Deime River and launching a frontal attack for the purpose of breaking through the powerfully fortified Königsberg area. The undesirability of the Tilsit axis was also conditioned by the presence of the Neman River and fortifications in the area of Tilsit and Ragnit, which needed to be forced during an attack against the forward edge. And, finally, the undesirability of the Tilsit axis for an offensive also consisted in the fact that our forces would have been forced to carry out major regroupings and to organize their rear correspondingly. The Tilsit axis was a secondary one, but its significance increased in connection with the fact that the important Insterburg axis was solidly blocked by the enemy and that the Tilsit direction made it possible to carry out carry out a flanking maneuver in relation to the Germans' Insterburg group of forces.

An offensive along the Insterburg operational axis would lead us around the line of the Masurian Lakes from the north. According to terrain conditions, the most favorable area for an offensive was the 60-70 kilometer-wide zone along both sides of the Stallupönen—Insterburg railroad. Here were a large number of good roads and this direction had served for a long time as the main axis along which forces invading East Prussia had advanced, and along which, in turn, invasions from East Prussia into Lithuania had been launched.[3]

Alongside this, the Germans' engineering preparation along the Insterburg axis was more powerfully developed, and during an offensive here our forces would have to break through a series of fortified and zones, heavily occupied by the enemy. Our offensive along this axis would result in a frontal attack and to the splitting up of the Germans' East Prussian group of forces into parts.

The Masurian axis was the central one of the other axes to the north and south and was the link between them. Along this direction the Augustow Canal and the Biebrza River divided our forces from the German positions along almost the entire length, and it was only in the Augustow area that we had a small bridgehead. In assuming the offensive, our forces had at first to force a water line and then overcome the Masurian Lakes system, which represented a favorable natural defensive line, and which had been scrupulously fortified and was covered from the south by a wooded and swampy zone.

---

3   For example, in 1757, during the Seven Year's War, Saltykov's Russian army invaded East Prussia through Virbalis (Wierzbolow) toward Gumbinnen. In 1812, during Napoleon's invasion of Russia, the French army's main forces attacked along this route and crossed the Neman River near Kaunas. In 1914, at the start of the First World War, the 1st Russian Army operated along this direction and attacked in the general direction of Wierzbolow and Gumbinnen. Finally, in June 1941 this axis (among others) was used by the Germans for their perfidious attack on the USSR.

Therefore, as regards both the terrain conditions and the degree of engineering preparation, the unfolding of major operations along the Masurian axis was linked with great difficulties and was unpromising in the operational sense. Limited forces were left along the Masurian axis during the East Prussian operation, while combat operations here were of secondary importance and for tying down the enemy, while the boundary line between the Third and Second Belorussian fronts ran through the Masurian Lakes.

The terrain along the Allenstein operational axis is closed and broken. The largest wooded areas are in the Ortelsberg area and south of Allenstein. Furthermore, adjoining these wooded areas from the south is a wooded-swampy area, which is located between the Szkwa and Orzyc rivers. Finally, the enemy disposed of four fortified zones along this direction. In general, as regards the terrain conditions and the enemy's engineering preparation, the Allenstein axis did not offer great advantages for our offensive.

The terrain between the Rozoga and Omulew rivers, in the general direction of Myszyniec, was more favorable for an offensive.

According to exaggerated intelligence data, the enemy disposed along the Mlawa axis five fortified zones and the powerful Mlawa fortified area.

The terrain along the Mlawa axis was fully favorable to our offensive and allowed for the employment of major mechanized formations. Aside from this, our offensive here was favorable in the operational sense, because it would lead to the deep outflanking of the Germans' East Prussian group of forces from the south and its isolation from the rest of Germany.

The terrain along the Torun operational axis fully favored the conduct of broad offensive operations, while an offensive here would also enable us to more deeply outflank from the south the Germans' East Prussian group of forces. However, when launching the main attack along the Torun direction, the operation would take on a broader scope and would require more powerful forces than if the main attack were launched along the Mlawa direction. Besides this, an offensive along the Torun axis would be threatened by flank attacks from beyond the Vistula, the significance of which, as a covering defensive line, would decrease in the event of ice cover. To be sure, the First Belorussian Front's vigorous offensive along the Warsaw—Poznan direction in January 1945 actually eliminated this danger.

Finally, our forces' offensive along the Torun axis was linked to the capture of the fortresses of Modlin and Torun, as well as with the breakthrough of four of the enemy's fortified zones.

Conclusions

1. East Prussia was one of Hitlerite Germany's main political, military and food bases. Even before the war it had been transformed into a broad and powerfully fortified jumping-off base. The province's salient position was favorable both for the conduct of aggressive wars in the East (for attacking, first of all, the Soviet Union) and for flank attacks against forces attacking along the Warsaw—Berlin direction.

However, alongside the advantages that East Prussia offered to the Germans as a jumping-off position for an attack, given the other side's superiority in forces, its exposed position had a negative side. It was unfavorable for defensive operations, especially given a shortage of forces, because the German forces defending this jumping-off position could be deeply turned from the south and cut off from the remainder of Germany. Thus the retention by German forces of part of the territory of northern Poland (to the north of the Warsaw—Torun line) was very important for the success of their defense of East Prussia.

The Hitlerite command failed to take into account the sharp shift in the strategic situation and decided to stubbornly defend East Prussia, despite the fact that it did not dispose of sufficient forces and that the forces defending the East Prussian bridgehead were in an unfavorable situation.

2. The Mlawa operational axis was the most favorable for our offensive by major forces, both in terms of terrain conditions and in the degree of engineering preparation. Moreover, the launching of a powerful attack here was also favorable from the operational point of view, in that it would lead to the deep outflanking of the Germans' East Prussian group of forces from the south and to its isolation from the rest of Germany.

The Insterburg axis ought to be recognized as the second most important; where on both sides of the Stalluponen—Insterburg railroad there was a strip of terrain 60-70 kilometers wide, which was quite favorable for an offensive by large forces. However, the engineering preparation along the Insterburg axis was significantly stronger than along the Mlawa axis and was more complete. The opportunities for operational maneuver here were limited and an offensive would turn into a frontal attack and the splitting of the enemy into parts.

As concerns the Masurian and Allenstein operational axes, the conduct here of major offensive operations would encounter serious difficulties, as the result of the unfavorable terrain conditions and the presence of the powerfully fortified zone of the Masurian Lakes.

Launching the main attack along the Torun axis would enable us to even more deeply outflank the Germans' East Prussian group of forces. However, it would require even larger forces than for an attack on Mlawa in order to carry out such a broad outflanking maneuver, and besides, an offensive along this axis was linked to the necessity of capturing the fortresses of Modlin and Torun and forcing the Vistula River along its lower course. Therefore, our forces operating along the Torun axis could be assigned a more limited objective: to reach the Vistula River for the purpose of securing our main attack along the Mlawa axis and preventing the arrival of large enemy reserves from the west and southwest to aid the German forces cut off by us in East Prussia. Subsequently, given the favorable development of events, this objective could be enlarged.

2

The General Situation and the Operational Plan

The General Situation at the Beginning of 1945

As a result of the offensive operations brilliantly realized by the Soviet supreme high command in the summer and fall of 1944, the enemy, having suffered huge losses in men and materiel, had been thrown back to the west along the entire length of the Soviet-German front, from the Gulf of Finland to the Black Sea. By the close of 1944 the front ran along the line Tukums—east of Memel and Gumbinnen—Augustow—west of Grodno—Warsaw—west of Sandomierz and Uzhgorod—northwest of Lake Balaton.

In January 1945 the following forces were deployed along the East Prussian strategic direction: part of the forces of the First Baltic Front, which were located along the Neman River from its mouth to Sudargas (southwest of Jurburg). To the south, the Third Belorussian Front was thrust forward into German territory along a broad salient, occupying a curved line that ran east of Stallupönen, east of Goldap, and then toward Augustow. From Augustow to the south and south-west were deployed the forces of the Second Belorussian Front along the Augustow Canal and the Biebrza and Narew rivers, with bridgeheads along the western bank near Rozan and Serock. Along the Warsaw axis and to the south the front was occupied by the First Belorussian and First Ukrainian fronts.

In the operational area, along the terrain between the lower course of the Neman and the Vistula, including the territory of East Prussia and the frontier area of northern Poland, were the following German forces.

The Königsberg axis was covered from the northeast and east by the forces of General Raus's[1] Third Panzer Army, consisting of the IX, XXVI and XXVIII army corps. Along the Insterburg, Masurian and Allenstein axes were deployed the forces of General Hossbach's[2] Fourth Army, consisting of the VI and LV army corps and the XLI Panzer Corps, as well as units of the "Hermann Goring" Parachute-Panzer Corps. Along the Mlawa axis, and then south to the Vistula River were the XX, XXIII and XXVII army corps, belonging to Colonel General Weiss'[3] Second Army.

---

1   Editor's note. Erhard Raus (1889-1956) joined the Austro-Hungarian army in 1905 and fougth in the First World War. During the Second World War he commanded a regiment and a brigade, a panzer division and a panzer corps. He was appointed commander of the Third Panzer Army in 1944.

2   Editor's note. Friedrich Wilhelm Ludwig Hossbach (1894-1980) joined the army in 1913 and fought in the First World War. He briefly served as Hitler's adjutant and in the Second World War commanded a division and a corps. He was appointed to command the Fourth Army in 1944. He was dismissed by Hitler the following year.

3   Editor's note. Walter-Otto Weiss (1890-1967) joined the army in 1908 and fought in the First World War. During the Second World War he commanded an infantry division and was appointed commander of the Second Army in 1943. He later commanded Army Group North.

All of these forces were subordinated to Army Group Center under Colonel General Reinhardt.[4] Before the start of the operation there were reports of seven enemy panzer divisions in East Prussia. However, during the course of the fighting the presence of some of these was either not confirmed, or they were transferred to other parts of the front before the beginning of active operations. Of the enemy's panzer divisions that were earlier identified, only the 5th and 7th panzer divisions and the *Grossdeutschland* Panzer Division actually took part in the operation's first stage.

In all, the enemy had 36-38 field divisions in the area of operations, which had been reinforced by a large amount of equipment. Besides this, in East Prussia, which was one of Hitlerite Germany's military-political centers, there were deployed a large number of various specialized and auxiliary units and establishments (fortress, training, reserve, police, rear, etc.). They also participated in the fighting that unfolded and their men and materiel should also be taken into account.

On the basis of material we now have as regards the enemy's intentions and the actual course of events, one can assume that the main objective of the German forces in East Prussia was to stubbornly defend the province with all means at their disposal. By taking into account the presence of a large number of forces and current intelligence on the disposition of the enemy's panzer divisions, one may also assume that that the Hitlerite command at one time considered an active variant: the launching from East Prussia of a counterblow in the flank and rear of our forces operating along the Warsaw—Berlin direction. However, our powerful offensive, which began along an enormous front from the Baltic Sea to the Carpathians, foiled the enemy's active intentions and forced him to limit himself to the stubborn defense of East Prussia.

The General Plan of the Red Army's January Offensive

The Soviet forces' offensive in East Prussia, which began in January 1945, was a component part of the Red Army's general offensive along an enormous front, from the Baltic Sea to the Carpathians.

The First Baltic Front, with its main forces along the Libava axis, had its left wing (43rd Army) deployed along the Neman River along the Tilsit direction. Subsequently, with the development of active operations, the 43rd Army was transferred to the Third Belorussian Front and took part in the attack on Königsberg.

The Third and Second Belorussian fronts were entrusted with the important objective of cutting off East Prussia and the German forces occupying it from the central areas of Germany, followed by the subsequent defeat and destruction of the entire northern strategic wing of the German front. Upon our occupation of East Prussia, the enemy would be deprived of one of the most important political and economic centers of fascist Germany. We would win a strategically favorable flanking position in relation to the most important Warsaw—Poznan direction, leading to Berlin. We would reach the shortest routes leading to the outflanking of Berlin from the north. Along with this, the defeat of the Germans' East Prussian group of forces and the occupation of East Prussia by Soviet forces would secure from the north the offensive by our forces along the highly important Warsaw—Poznan direction, leading to the approaches to Berlin.

The First Belorussian Front, which was located immediately south of the Second Belorussian Front, was to launch a powerful destructive attack along the Warsaw—Poznan axis and develop the offensive toward Berlin. The main attack was to be launched from the bridgeheads along the

---

4   Editor's note. Georg Hans Reinhardt (1887-1963) joined the army in 1908 and fought in the First World War. During the Second World War he commanded a panzer division, corps and panzer army, before being appointed to command Army Group Center in 1944. Reinhardt was imprisoned for war crimes after the war, but released in 1952.

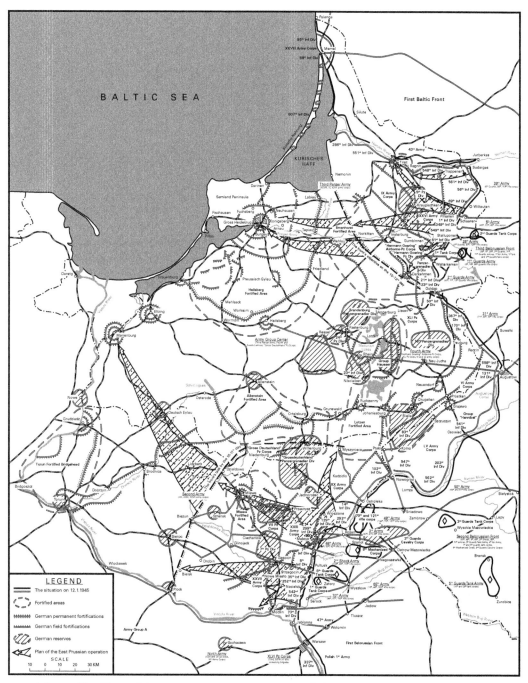

Map 5 The Plan of the East Prussian Operation and the Overall Situation by its Start.

western bank of the Vistula south of Warsaw. Still further to the south, the First Ukrainian Front was to conduct a major offensive in the general direction of Breslau (into Silesia).

The operational plan of the Red Army's *Stavka* of the Supreme High Command along the East Prussian direction called for the conduct of a major strategic operation involving the coordination of two *fronts* for the purpose of:

- cutting off East Prussia and the German forces there from the rest of Germany through the simultaneous launching of a deep frontal attack on Königsberg;
- splitting the East Prussian group of forces into parts, surrounding them and consecutively destroying them.

The following main attacks were planned:

The Third Belorussian Front would launch a frontal attack on Königsberg in the area north of the Masurian Lakes;

The Second Belorussian Front would launch an attack along the southern frontier of East Prussia to outflank the Masurian Lakes and the most important fortifications of East Prussia from the south.

The Third Belorussian Front had to defeat the enemy's Tilsit—Insterburg group of forces and no later than the tenth-twelfth day of the operation reach the line Nemonin—Zargillen—Norkitten—Darkemen—Goldap. The *front* would subsequently attack toward Königsberg along both banks of the Pregel River, with its main forces along the south bank. The main attack, with the forces of four combined-arms armies and two tank corps, would be launched along the Malwischken—Aulowenen—Welau axis. Supporting attacks would be launched toward Tilsit and Darkemen. The left-flank 31st Army would securely defend the front south of Goldap.

The Second Belorussian Front was to defeat the enemy's Przasnysz—Mlawa group of forces and not later than the offensive's tenth-eleventh day reach the line Myszyniec—Neidenburg—Dzialdowo—Plock. The *front* would subsequently attack in the direction of Nowe Miasto and Marienburg. The main attack would be launched by four combined-arms armies, a tank army and a tank corps from the Rozan bridgehead toward Mlawa. A second attack by two combined-arms armies and a tank corps would be launched from the Serock bridgehead toward Plonsk and Bielsk. Supporting attacks would be launched to the north toward Myszyniec, and to the southwest in order to outflank Modlin from the west and assist the First Belorussian Front. The right-flank 50th Army was to securely defend the front Augustow—Lomza—Ostroleka.

In this plan by the *Stavka* of the Supreme High Command we see the precisely aimed and coordinated attacks by two *fronts* for the achievement of the overall goal of defeating the Germans' East Prussian group of forces. The plan for a future major operation of strategic significance was based upon a profound analysis of the existing situation and a complete consideration of the concrete conditions and features in which this or that *front* had to operate in. The character of the forthcoming objectives and conditions of carrying them out were not the same for the Third and Second Belorussian fronts.

For example, the Third Belorussian Front was to launch a deep frontal attack along the Königsberg axis, defeat the German's Tilsit—Insterburg group of forces, prevent the enemy from maneuvering to oppose the Second Belorussian Front, and to subsequently attack and cut off the enemy's Tilsit group of forces. The Third Belorussian Front's forces had to overcome the most powerful fortifications, defended by a compact group of enemy forces. The opportunities for operational maneuver here were quite limited. Upon taking into consideration all of these concrete conditions, it was planned to launch a single powerful attack by the *front*, a breakthrough along a single overall sector, supported by the forces' deep formation.

On the Second Belorussian Front the conditions for the accomplishment of the breakthrough and the operational development of the success were more favorable. The Second Belorussian Front had the opportunity to carry out a broad outflanking maneuver for the purpose of cutting off the enemy's East Prussian group of forces from the rest of Germany. The *front* disposed of large forces; it had more mobile formations than the Third Belorussian Front (including a tank army), in accordance with the character of the forthcoming task. Taking into account this information, as well as the presence of two bridgeheads on the western bank of the Narew and Western Bug rivers, the Second Belorussian Front was to launch two coordinated attacks and to carry out breakthroughs simultaneously along two directions.

The Third Belorussian Front

The sides' situation. In the beginning of January 1945 the forces of the Third Belorussian Front, which consisted of five armies (39th, 5th, 28th, 2nd Guards, and 31st), occupied defensive positions from the Neman River to Augustow along a 170-kilometer front. The defense's forward edge ran along the line Sudargas—Pilkallen—Kischen—Walterkemen—Goldap, and then along the Rospud River as far as Augustow. The 11th Guards Army and two tank corps (1st and 2nd guards) were in the *front* reserve between Kybartai and Wischtinetz.

Facing the Third Belorussian Front were the German Third Panzer and Fourth armies, which were part of Army Group Center.

The XXVI and VI army and XLI Panzer corps, which comprised 14 divisions (561st, 56th, 69th, 1st, 349th, 549th, and 61st infantry divisions, the "Hermann Goring" 2nd Panzergrenadier Division, the 21st Infantry Division, 28th Light[5] Infantry Division, the 50th, 367th, 170th, and 558th infantry divisions, and the "Hermann Goring" 1st Panzer Division[6]) occupied the main defensive zone.

All of the infantry divisions were located in a line and only the 5th Panzer Division, which comprised the army group commander's reserve, was moving toward Gumbinnen. Units of the LV Army Corps were arriving in this area, as well as specialized units at the disposal of Army Group Center's headquarters.

According to intelligence data, there was also a large amount of enemy reinforcement units, training formations, security troops, and worker's battalions in the Third Belorussian Front's operational sector, which during the operation were employed by the German command for resisting our forces' offensive. Among these were the Fourth Army's 1st and 2nd fortress regiments, an air communications regiment from the Air Force High Command, the 5th Police, 33rd Transport, 107th Worker's, 589th, 597th and 489th independent communications regiments, the 704th Auto Transport Regiment, the 999th Sapper-Construction Regiment, the "Dresden" Police Regiment, the 45th, 60th, 75th, and 611th security regiments, the 54th Officer's Regiment, the 206th Security Regiment for guarding prisoners of war, and the 260th Airfield Service Regiment, two mortar brigades, two artillery brigades, 21 artillery regiments, ten anti-aircraft regiments, 15 assault gun brigades, three anti-tank brigades, and four panzer battalions, as well as a large number of sapper-construction, searchlight, naval, and machine gun battalions and other units and elements. The overall number of soldiers and officers in these units numbered more than 200,000 men.

---

5   What the Soviets call "light divisions" are possibly fusilier regiments or battle groups.
6   When counting the 551st and 548th infantry divisions and the 286th Security Division, which subsequently operated in the Third Belorussian Front's offensive zone, this yields 17 divisions. If one counts the various units and formations located within the Third Belorussian Front's operational sector, then the overall number of enemy units rises to 25 calculated divisions.

The enemy's infantry divisions were outfitted according to new tables, but had varying personnel strength. For example, the 61st Infantry Division numbered 6,700 men, at the same time that the "Hermann Goring" 2nd Panzergrenadier Division had 10,000 men. The remaining divisions numbered from 6-9,000 men and officers. All the divisions were fully equipped with weapons and transportation.

Residents of East Prussia made up the overwhelming majority of the German forces, while a significant percentage of these were volunteers. Discipline in the enemy units was at a sufficiently high level; a significant portion of the troops, especially the younger ones, was firmly committed to resisting to the last bullet. However, following our crushing attacks in East Prussia, the combat capabilities of the enemy's forces began to decline.

The Germans had built along this direction two very powerful fortified centers—Gumbinnen and Insterburg—which covered the approaches to Königsberg from the east. To handle coordination between them, the German command had prepared two more major centers of resistance—Tilsit and Darkemen, which together with the Gumbinnen and Insterburg centers served as the basis for the defense in the central and northern parts of East Prussia. The defense along the Gumbinnen—Insterburg axis was distinguished by its great depth and the presence of powerful engineering and all kinds of explosive obstacles. It was here that the enemy kept his densest group of forces. According to air reconnaissance, there were up to 670 planes along the *front's* sector. Aside from this, there were up to 600 planes at airfields of the neighboring fronts' sectors. In all, the enemy could employ up to 800 planes, of which about half were bombers.

The operational density of the Germans' defense was an average of 12 kilometers per division. This density rose to 8-9 kilometers along the Gumbinnen—Insterburg axis.

In organizing its defense, the German command devoted its main attention to the Gumbinnen—Königsberg axis, which constituted the shortest and most convenient route for the attacker.

The directive of the *Stavka* of the Supreme High Command. On 3 December 1944, in its directive no. 220277, the *Stavka* of the Supreme High Command ordered the Third Belorussian Front to prepare and carry out an offensive operation for the purpose of defeating the enemy's Tilsit—Insterburg group of forces and no later than the tenth-eleventh day of the operation to seize the line Nemonin—Zargillen—Norkitten—Darkemen—Goldap.

Subsequently, while securely covering the *front's* main group of forces from the south, it was to develop the offensive toward Königsberg, along both banks of the Pregel River, with its main forces on the southern bank of the Pregel River. The *front* was to launch its main attack with the forces of four combined-arms armies and two tank corps from the area north of Stallupönen and Gumbinnen, in the general direction of Mallwischken, Aulowenen and Welau. The enemy's defense was to be pierced by the forces of three armies (39th, 5th and 11th Guards) along a single 18-19 kilometer sector. Three artillery breakthrough divisions were to be concentrated along the breakthrough sector, in order to create an artillery and mortar (76mm and higher) density of no less than 200 tubes per kilometer of breakthrough front.

The *front* was to have one army and a tank corps in its second echelon and employ it for augmenting the attack along the main axis.

The operations of the main group of forces would be secured as follows: from the north, in the direction of the Neman River—through the defense by one of the 39th Army's rifle corps, while its main forces attacked toward Tilsit; from the south, by the 28th Army's defense south of Walterkemen and an attack by part of its forces from behind the left flank of the breakthrough sector in the general direction of Darkemen.

In any event, the 31st Army was to securely defend its front to the south of Goldap.

The tank corps were to be employed for developing the success following the breakthrough along the main axis.

The Third Belorussian Front's operational plan. In carrying out the order by the *Stavka* of the Supreme High Command, the commander of the Third Belorussian Front, General Chernyakhovskii, decided to break through the enemy's defense by a powerful attack in the center of the front along the Pilkallen—Stallupönen sector and, while vigorously attacking to the west, to defeat his Tilsit—Insterburg group of forces. Subsquently, while developing the success in the general direction of Welau, the *front* was to reach the line Nemonin—Norkitten—Darkemen.

The offensive operation was planned in two stages: the first involved the breakthrough of the enemy's defense and the arrival of the *front's* forces at the line Tilsit—Insterburg, at a depth of 45-50 kilometers; this stage was to last five days; the second stage involved the completion of the total defeat of the Tilsit—Insterburg group of forces and our troops' arrival at the line Nemonin—Norkitten—Darkemen, at a depth of 20-30 kilometers; this stage was to last two days. The operation's overall depth was to be 70-80 kilometers. The average daily rate of advance was to be 10-12 kilometers per day.

The shock group would be organized into two echelons: the 39th, 5th and 28th armies would be in the first echelon, with the more powerful 11th Guards Army and two tank corps in the second.

From the moment of the commitment of the 11th Guards Army into the first line, the main group's center of gravity was to shift to that axis.

It was first planned to regroup the 39th Army to the Darkemen axis by the operation's tenth day and to entrust the clearing of the lower reaches of the Neman River to the neighboring First Baltic Front's 43rd Army, in order to better secure the left flank. At the same time, it was considered expedient for better coordination by the Third Belorussian Front to resubordinate the 43rd Army to the Third Belorussian Front.

Based on the overall idea and plan for the operation, the armies were assigned the following tasks.

The 39th Army, consisting of three rifle corps (5th Guards Rifle Corps—17th, 19th and 91st Guards rifle divisions; 94th Rifle Corps—124th, 221st and 358th rifle divisions; 113th Rifle Corps—192nd, 262nd and 338th rifle divisions), along with reinforcements, having its main forces along its left flank, was to launch a vigorous attack in the general direction of Pilkallen and Tilsit, with the task of defeating the enemy's Tilsit group of forces in conjunction with the forces of the 5th Army. The army's immediate task was as follows: the 5th Guards and 94th rifle corps were to break through the enemy's defense along an 8-kilometer sector excluding Wiltauten—excluding Schaaren and to destroy the enemy operating in the Sudargas—Ragnit—Pilkallen area. Developing the success along the southern bank of the Neman River, our forces were to capture Tilsit by the close of the fifth day.

The forces of the 113th Rifle Corps were to launch an attack from behind the right flank of the army's shock group in the direction of Lazdenen, with the task of energetically rolling up the enemy's defense to the north.

The 5th Army, consisting of three rifle corps (72nd Rifle Corps—277th, 215th and 63rd rifle divisions; 45th Rifle Corps—159th, 157th and 184th rifle divisions; 65th Rifle Corps—97th, 144th and 371st rifle divisions), along with reinforcements, was to launch a vigorous attack in the general direction of Mallwischken and Gross Skeisgirren. The army's immediate task was to break through the enemy's defense along the 9-kilometer Schaaren—Schwentakemen sector and encircle and destroy the enemy's Tilsit group of forces in conjunction with the 39th Army. The army was to subsequently develop the success toward the Deime River. On the morning of the operation's second day, it was to secure the commitment into the breach of the 2nd Guards Tatsinskaya Tank Corps, which was to operate in the direction of Radschen, Kraupischken and Gross Skeisgirren. On the morning of the operation's fourth day the left-flank units were to support the deployment of the 11th Guards Army along the Inster River.

The 28th Army, consisting of three rifle corps (3rd Guards Rifle Corps—50th, 54th and 96th Guards rifle divisions; 20th Rifle Corps—48th, 55th Guards and 20th rifle divisions; 128th Rifle Corps—61st, 130th and 152nd rifle divisions), along with reinforcements, having its main forces along the right flank, was to launch a vigorous attack north of the Stallupönen—Gumbinnen surfaced road in the general direction of Insterburg. The army's immediate objective was as follows: to break through the enemy's defense along the 7-kilometer front Schwentakemen—Kalpakin and, in conjunction with the 5th Army, defeat the enemy's Gumbinnen group of forces. Subsequently, in conjunction with the 11th Guards Army, the army was to capture Insterburg and develop the offensive in the direction of Gerdauen. On the morning of the operation's fourth day, the army's right-flank units were to assist the deployment of the 11th Guards Army along the line of the Inster River.

The 11th Guards Army, consisting of three rifle corps (8th Guards Rifle Corps—1st, 5th and 26th Guards rifle divisions; 16th Guards Rifle Corps—11th, 31st and 83rd Guards rifle divisions; 36th Guards Rifle Corps—16th, 18th and 84th Guards rifle divisions), was to attack in the second echelon, behind the 5th and 28th armies' units, along the sector (from the right) Kybartai—Kussen—Kaukern and (from the left) Millunen—excluding Gumbinnen—Georgenburg. By the close of the operation's fourth day the army was to deploy along the line Gaidzen—Rossthal, and from the morning of the fifth day, in conjunction with the 1st Tank Corps, was to launch a vigorous attack in the direction of Ponnau and Welau. Part of the army's forces, in conjunction with the 28th Army, was to capture Insterburg by the close of the fifth day.

Two of the 2nd Guards Army's rifle corps (11th Guards Rifle Corps—2nd, 32nd and 33rd Guards rifle divisions; 13th Guards Rifle Corps—3rd, 24th and 87th Guards rifle divisions), taking advantage of the 28th Army's breakthrough, were to begin the consecutive rolling up of the enemy's defense to the south on the morning of the operation's third day. The attack was to be launched in the direction of Darkemen, having as its main objective the support of the 28th Army's offensive through its energetic actions and repelling all of the enemy's possible counterattacks from the direction of Goldap and Darkemen. The army's 60th Rifle Corps (154th, 251st and 334th rifle divisions) was to defend along a broad front to the north of Goldap.

From the morning of the operation's second day the 2nd Guards Tatsinskaya Tank Corps, upon the arrival of the 5th Army's infantry at the line Kussen—Brackupenen, was to be ready to be committed along the front Kussen—Radschen. The corps was not to get involved in extended fighting with the enemy and, while bypassing his centers of resistance, was to develop the offensive with vigorous actions in the direction of Kraupischken and Melauken. By the close of the operation's fourth day, the corps' main forces were to capture the major road junctions of Gross Skeisgirren and Milawischken.

The 1st Guards Tank Corps, located in the *front* reserve, was to advance behind the 11th Guards Army's units and by the close of the operation's fourth day was to concentrate in the Rohrfeld area. It was to subsequently be in readiness, in conjunction with the 11th Guards Army, to vigorously develop the offensive in the direction of Neunischken, Berschkallen and Taplakken.

The 31st Army, consisting of three rifle corps (71st Rifle Corps—220th, 88th and 331st rifle divisions; 44th Rifle Corps—62nd, 54th and 176th rifle divisions; 36th Rifle Corps—325th, 173rd and 174th rifle divisions) was to stubbornly defend its position.

The length of the artillery preparation was planned at one hour and 45 minutes, of which there would be a 5-minute onslaught, 60 minutes of destructive fire, and 40 minutes of suppression fire. The infantry was to be accompanied for one hour. It was planned to raise the average artillery and mortar density to 200 tubes per kilometer of front.

The 1st Air Army's main forces were to support the 5th Army's offensive. One of its assault air divisions was to assist the 28th Army's right-flank corps.

Simultaneously, the *front* commander raised before the *Stavka* of the Supreme High Command the question of subordinating the First Baltic Front's 43rd Army to him. According to the operational plan, this army was supposed to regroup its main forces to the left flank and launch an attack with the 39th Army along the southern bank of the Neman River. Upon capturing the towns of Ragnit and Tilsit, the 43rd Army's shock group would be entrusted with the task of destroying the remnants of the enemy along the shore of the Baltic Sea and to take up defensive positions from the Neman River to the mouth of the Deime River.

The *front's* forces were to be ready to attack on 8 January 1945.

Conclusions

1. Thus the idea of the offensive operation called for the breakthrough of the enemy's defense by three armies, which had concentrated their main forces along a 24-kilometer sector. Of these three armies, the 5th Army would launch the main attack. The army was not only to carry out the breakthrough, but also to support the commitment of the *front's* powerful second echelon, in conjunction with the 28th Army.

2. Simultaneously with the breakthrough of the defense, it was planned to immediately and energetically expand it toward the flanks. In conditions of a powerfully fortified and deeply echeloned defense, this measure would acquire decisive significance for the operation's success.

3. In the operation's first stage, the commander would strive to destroy the Tilsit group of forces and reach the line Tilsit—Insterburg. The successful resolution of this task would provide the right wing and center of the *front's* shock group with freedom of maneuver and the readiness to move into the second stage—the completion of the defeat of the Tilsit—Insterburg group of forces and the arrival at the line Nemonin—Norkitten—Darkemen.

The achievement of success in the first stage was considered possible given the solid situation along the *front's* left wing—the 28th and 2nd Guards armies—which were to not only repel all possible enemy counterattacks, but to capture the major centers of resistance of Gumbinnen and Darkemen, while developing an energetic offensive toward Insterburg from the east.

4. In order to overcome the entire depth of the enemy's defense, the *front's* forces would be deeply echeloned. The shock group was organized into two operational echelons: the 39th, 5th and 28th armies would operate in the first echelon; the more powerful 11th Guards Army and two tank corps would operate in the second. These formations were to augment the power of the first echelon's attack (first the 2nd Guards Tank Corps from the line Kussen—Radschen, and then the 11th Guards Army and the 1st Tank Corps from the line of the Inster River.

5. The main attack by the *front's* forces was to be directed at the boundary between the enemy's powerfully fortified defensive centers, which would achieve not only the splitting of the enemy at the start of the operation, but also the outflanking from the north of the main Insterburg center of resistance and the encirclement of the German forces operating along this axis.

6. The operational-battle organization of the armies and the *front* corresponded to the idea of the forthcoming operation and created the conditions for the breakthrough of a powerful and deeply echeloned defense and for the successful development of the offensive in depth.

The Second Belorussian Front

The sides' situation. As a result of the local offensive operations conducted in October 1944, the *front's* forces improved their positions and by the beginning of November the front had stabilized along the line of the Augustow Canal, then along the Biebrza and Narew rivers to Pultusk. During this time the *front's* forces repelled all the enemy's infantry and tank attacks and securely held their bridgeheads: a) along the western bank of the Augustow Canal in the Augustow area, with an overall area of 60 square kilometers, and; b) along the western bank of the Narew River in the Rozan area, with an area of 400 square kilometers, which enabled us to concentrate large forces for assuming the offensive.

Immediately to the south the forces of the First Belorussian Front occupied a bridgehead near Serock.

In the middle of November the *front* was included the 50th, 49th, 3rd, 48th, and 2nd Shock armies, as well as the 4th Air Army.

The *front's* forces remained in this situation throughout November and continued to defend the occupied lines.

On 19 November 1944, in connection with the forthcoming offensive, the Serock bridgehead was transferred to the Second Belorussian Front, while the *front* was reinforced with the following armies:

a) 65th Army, which was holding the Serock bridgehead, while defending the line, excluding Poplawy—Izbica (on the Western Bug River).
b) 70th Army, which was deployed in the Tluszcz area (25-45 kilometers northeast of Warsaw) and constituted the *front* reserve.

For going over to the offensive, the Second Belorussian Front was reinforced with, besides the 65th and 70th armies, major rifle, tank, artillery, and other formations

Finally, in drawing up a plan for the operation, the *front* command knew that the *Stavka* would transfer to it the 5th Guards Tank Army, consisting of the 10th and 29th tank corps, the 47th Independent Mechanized Brigade, and other reinforcements, which was to complete its concentration in the Bransk area (50 kilometers southwest of Bialystok) by 9 January 1945.

In general, by the beginning of the offensive the combat strength of the Second Belorussian Front was as follows: seven combined-arms armies, a tank army, three tank corps, a mechanized corps, a cavalry corps, two artillery corps, an air army, and other specialized and technical units.

Information about the enemy. At the end of November 1944, that is, while drawing up the plan for the East Prussian operation, the forces of the Second Belorussian Front were opposed by formations from Army Group Center, belonging to the Second and Fourth armies. According to intelligence data, the enemy held in the first line, as well as in his corps and army reserves, a total of 16 infantry division and one divisional group (Danz), two cavalry brigades, five panzer divisions (3rd Panzer and 5th SS Panzer, and the 6th, 19th and 25th panzer), a panzer brigade, and four panzer battalions; all five panzer divisions were grouped opposite the *front's* left wing. Besides this, up to six infantry divisions were in the army group reserve, of which two were still undergoing formation.

Therefore, the enemy was taking into account the significance that our offensive might have along the Mlawa and Torun axes, and maintained a major group of forces here.

During the 1 December 1944-14 January 1945 period the German command was forced, as the result of the worsening of the overall strategic situation along the entire broad Soviet-German front, to weaken his defense opposite the Second Belorussian Front and remove from there one infantry division, all the panzer divisions, and two cavalry brigades. It thus follows that upon assuming the offensive the forces of the Second Belorussian Front encountered a significantly weaker enemy than was assumed during the operational planning and preparation periods.

In general, by the close of 13 January 1945, that is, on the eve of our offensive, the Second Belorussian continued to be faced by units of the Fourth Army's (General Hossbach) LV Army Corps and the Second Army's (Colonel General Weiss) XXIII, XX and XXVII army corps, while the first-echelon disposition of the enemy's group of forces was as follows:

a)   The 131st Infantry Division, Colonel Hannibal's police group (three infantry and one artillery regiments, formerly commanded by Colonel Danz), and the 541st, 203rd, 562nd, and 547th infantry divisions, were grouped along the Augustow—Nowogrod sector (150 kilometers), for a total of six infantry divisions.

b)   The 102nd and 14th infantry divisions were defending along the Nowogrud—Nozewo sector (40 kilometers).

c)   The 292nd, 129th, 299th, and 7th infantry divisions were defending between Nozewo and the height three kilometers south of Dzierzanowo (45 kilometers).

d)   The 5th Light Infantry Division was defending the Pultusk sector (15 kilometers).

e)   The 35th, 252nd and 542nd infantry divisions were deployed opposite the Serock bridgehead (24 kilometers). Besides this, ten kilometers southwest of Myszyniec a fusilier battalion from the *Grossdeutschland* Panzer Division was noted, and thus we could expect the appearance of the entire *Grossdeutschland* Panzer Division in the Second Belorussian Front's combat sector. Moreover, at a later point during our offensive, the presence of the Germans' 7th Panzer Division was established.

The enemy's reserves were deployed as follows: up to 8,000 men in the Szrensk area (20 kilometers southwest of Mlawa); up to 4,000 men in the Skrwilno area (50 kilometers southwest of Mlawa); up to 10,000 men in the Sierpc area; the 432nd Special Designation Division in Plock; up to 10,000 men in the Rypin area (50 kilometers northeast of Torun); the 461st Reserve Division in Deutsch Eylau; a *volksgrenadier*[7] division in Torun, and; an infantry division of unknown number in Nowe (40 kilometers north of Graudenz), as well as our units of various types. Overall, the enemy had in his operational reserve up to 6-8 divisions, of which part was undergoing formation.

In the *front's* sector, according to air reconnaissance data, the enemy had up to 350 aircraft based on 16 airfields. Besides this, the following aircraft were noted on airfields within the neighboring *fronts'* sectors: 670 aircraft opposite the *front* to the right, and 440 aircraft opposite the *front* to the left. In all, the enemy facing the Second Belorussian Front could employ 600-700 planes, of which about 180 bombers and up to 300 fighters were noted.

Therefore, by the beginning of our offensive, the enemy opposite the Second Belorussian Front disposed of the following forces: up to 16 infantry divisions, a panzer brigade and four panzer battalions were in the first echelon along a 285-kilometer front. The average operational density was equivalent to one infantry division per 13-15 kilometers of front. Taking into account all the forces located in the rear, which could be employed as reserves, one arrives at a total of 22 divisions, of which two were panzer.

The numerical and combat strength of the enemy's first-echelon forces was calculated at 140 infantry battalions, 28 specialized battalions, 241,000 men, 9,166 automatic rifles, 1,523 heavy

---

7   Editor's note. The *volksgrenadier* divisions were emergency units formed to meet the manpower crisis in the German army from the autumn of 1944. These divisions generally consisted of six battalions, instead of the standard nine. They also lacked much of the regular divisions' heavy equipment and were generally more configured for defensive fighting than attacking.

machine guns, 8,076 light machine guns, 2,245 guns, 1,347 mortars, and 400 tanks and assault guns.

The greatest density of enemy forces was along the front Nozewo (seven kilometers southwest of Ostroleka)—Dzierzanowo, where an infantry division occupied an average front of about 11 kilometers, and also facing the Serock bridgehead, where a single infantry division occupied an average of eight kilometers of front. The enemy's smallest density was along the Augustow—Nozewo sector, where the operational density was equivalent to one infantry division per 21 kilometers of front.

One should add that the enemy's reserves were deeply echeloned (as far back as the Vistula River) and, with the exception of the Allenstein group, were deployed opposite the *front's* left wing.

In general, the enemy's densest defense was along the Mlawa and Torun directions; the enemy evidently considered our offensive here the most threatening and the most likely, both according to the terrain conditions, as well as a result of the presence of our Rozan and Serock bridgeheads.

The Second Belorussian Front's operational plan. The main instructions to the Second Belorussian Front were laid out in a directive by the *Stavka* of the Supreme High Command, No. 220274, of 28 November 1944. On the basis of these instructions, a plan for the *front's* operation was drawn up.

The main attack would be launched from the Rozan bridgehead with the forces of four combined-arms armies, a tank army, a tank corps, and a mechanized corps in the general direction of Przasnysz, Mlawa and Lidzbark, for the purpose of isolating and, together with the Third Belorussian Front, to destroy the enemy's East Prussian group of forces. At the same time, the enemy's defense would be penetrated by three armies, while the fourth army remained in the *front's* second echelon.

A second attack would be launched from the Serock bridgehead with the forces of two combined-arms armies and a tank corps in the general direction of Nasielsk, Plonsk and Bielsk, for the purpose of developing the offensive to the west and securing the *front's* main group of forces against the enemy's flank attacks from the southwest.

It was planned to break through along a 26-28 kilometer front. Thus, given an overall length of front of 285 kilometers, the enemy's defense was to be broken along a sector whose width amounted to 9-10 percent of the front's overall length, which enabled us to achieve a high density of suppression weapons along the breakthrough sectors.

The tank army was to be committed into the breach along the main attack's axis through Mlawa toward Lidzbark, for the purpose of cutting the German's East Prussian group of forces' path of retreat to the west and to cut off this group of forces from the rest of Germany.

The *front's* second-echelon army was to be committed into the breach on the Rozan bridgehead in the general direction of Myszyniec, with the objective of rolling up the enemy's defense opposite the *front's* right wing, so as to secure the main group of forces against enemy attacks from the north. Besides this, the cavalry corps would be committed into the breach in the general direction of Chorzele and Allenstein, for the purpose of cutting the enemy's most important routes of retreat and preventing his reserves from launching attacks from the north. Finally, the operations of the *front's* main forces would be secured against enemy attacks from the north by the defense of one army along the line of the Narew River, along the Augustow—Lomza sector.

By the close of the operation's first day, the first-echelon armies were to reach the front Rafaly-Glinki (15 kilometers northwest of Rozan)—Jacionzek—Karniewo (15 kilometers northwest of Pultusk)—Gasiorowo—Nasielsk—Brody (five kilometers northeast of Modlin), and by the close of the operation's third day reach the front Aleksandrowo (15 kilometers northwest of Ostroleka)—Jednorozec (17 kilometers northeast of Przasnysz)—Przasnysz—Ciechanow—Plonsk. Thus is was planned to carry out the breakthrough of the enemy's tactical defense at a pace of 10-12 kilometers per day, and to develop the breakthrough at a pace of up to 15 kilometers per day. The overall depth of the *front's* operation (as far as Marienburg) was equivalent to 200 kilometers.

The operational plan foresaw four stages, aside from the preparatory stage.

The first stage involved the breakthrough of the enemy's tactical defense and our arrival at the line Rafaly-Glinki—Jacionzek—Gasiorowo—Brody. This was to take one day.

The second stage involved the development of the breakthrough and the commitment of the mobile forces into the breach and the arrival at the line Jednorozec—Przasnysz—Ciechanow—Plonsk. This was to take two days.

The third stage involved the defeat of the enemy's Mlawa group of forces and our arrival at the line Myszyniec—Willenberg—Neidenberg—Biezun—Bielsk—Plock. This was to take 7-8 days, with a daily rate of advance of seven kilometers.

The fourth stage involved the pursuit of the enemy in the general direction of Marienburg.

In accordance with the operational plan, the *front's* forces were deployed as follows:

The 3rd Army, consisting of three rifle corps (40th Rifle Corps—169th, 129th and 5th rifle divisions; 41st Rifle Corps—269th, 120th Guards and 283rd rifle divisions; 35th Corps—250th, 348th and 290th rifle divisions), was deployed along the line Mlynarz—the height southeast of Dombrowka. The army's task was to launch an attack along its left flank (on a 6-kilometer front) in the direction of Krasnosielc and Janowo, and a supporting attack with the forces of no less than a rifle corps in the direction of Aleksandrowo, and by the close of the operation's first day reach the line Rafaly—Glinki—excluding Jacionzek; by the close of the operation's third day the army was to reach the line Jednorozec—Przasnysz, and along the axis of the supporting attack the Omulew River in the Aleksandrowo area. By subsequently attacking in the direction of Janowo and Allenstein, by the close of the offensive's tenth day the army was to reach the front Klein Dankheim (ten kilometers northeast of Janowo)—Neidenburg.

The army was to keep in mind that approximately from the line Jednorozec—Przasnysz, the 3rd Guards Cavalry Corps was to be committed into the breach in the general direction of Chorzele and Allenstein.

In breaking through the defense along the main axis, the army should have no less than 220 tubes[8] (76mm and higher) per kilometer of front.

Upon the 49th Army's commitment into the battle, the army was to have no less than a rifle corps in reserve.

The 48th Army, consisting of three rifle corps (29th Rifle Corps—73rd, 217th and 102nd rifle divisions; 53rd Rifle Corps—96th, 194th and 17th rifle divisions; 42nd Rifle Corps—170th, 399th and 137th rifle divisions) was deployed along the line excluding the heights southeast of Dombrowka—the heights east of Dzierzanowo. The army's task was to launch its main attack, in conjunction with the 2nd Shock Army, along its left flank (on a 6-kilometer front) in the direction of Karniewo, Dzbonie and Mlawa, and by the close of the operation's first day reach the line Jacionzek—Karniewo; by the close of the offensive's third day the army was to take the line excluding Przasnysz—excluding Ciechanow.

By subsequently attacking toward Dzialdowo and Lubawa, the army was to take the line excluding Neidenburg—Dzialdowo no later than the offensive's tenth day.

The army should have no few than 220 tubes (76mm and higher) per kilometer of front along the breakthrough sector.

The army should have no fewer than two rifle divisions in reserve.

---

8   The artillery's actual density per kilometer of front by the beginning of the breakthrough was different. Along the Rozan bridgehead the artillery density among the armies varied from 220 to 300 tubes per kilometer of front, and along the Serock bridgehead, 180-200 tubes.

The army was to be reinforced with the 8th Mechanized Corps for developing the success in the direction of Mlawa and Dzialdowo.

The 2nd Shock Army, consisting of three rifle corps (108th Rifle Corps—90th, 46th and 372nd rifle divisions; 98th Rifle Corps—142nd, 381st and 281st rifle divisions; 116th Rifle Corps—86th, 321st and 326th rifle divisions) was deployed along the line excluding the heights east of Dzierzanowo—Borsuki. The army's task was to launch its main attack, in conjunction with the 48th Army, along its right flank (along a 6-kilometer front) in the direction of Golmin Stary, Ciechanow, Szrensk, and Zielun, and by the close of the operation's first day reach the line excluding Karniewo—Gasiorowo. Part of the army's forces (no less than two rifle divisions), in conjunction with the 65th Army's right flank, were to eliminate the enemy in the Pultusk area during the operation's first day; by the close of the offensive's third day, the army was to capture Ciechanow and reach they line Ciechanow—Mlock.

By subsequently attacking in the direction of Szrensk, Zielun and Brodnica, the army was to reach the line Nowa Wies (20 kilometers west of Mlawa)—Biezun.

The army was to have no less than 220 tubes (76mm and higher) per kilometer of front along the breakthrough sector.

The army was to keep one rifle corps in reserve.

In order to develop the success in the direction of Ciechanow, Szrensk and Zielun, the army was to be reinforced, following the breakthrough of the enemy defense, by the 8th Guards Tank Corps.

The 49th Army, consisting of three rifle corps (124th Rifle Corps—51st, 208th and 216th rifle divisions; 70th Rifle Corps—385th, 238th and 139th rifle divisions; 121st Rifle Corps—199th and 380th rifle divisions) was to securely defend with one rifle corps the line along the eastern bank of the Narew River from Nowogrod to Chelsty (five kilometers northeast of Rozan), while its main forces, taking advantage of the breakthrough of the front along the 3rd Army's sector and, with the latter army's arrival approximately at the line Rafaly—Glinki—excluding Jacionzek, was to go over to the attack in the direction of Myszyniec.

The army's immediate objective was, while rolling up the enemy's defense along the western bank of the Narew River, to capture the line Kurpiewski Gury—Aleksandrowo—excluding Jednorozec. The army is to plan an attack by two rifle divisions from the Ostroleka area in the direction of Kadzidlo.

Subsequently, the army was to reach the front Nowogrod—Myszyniec—Klein Dankheim no later than the offensive's tenth day, while securely defending the *front's* main group of forces against the enemy's attacks from the north.

The 65th Army, consisting of three rifle corps (18th Rifle Corps—69th, 15th and 37th Guards rifle divisions; 46th Rifle Corps—413th, 108th and 186th rifle divisions; 105th Rifle Corps— 354th, 44th Guards and 193rd rifle divisions), was deployed along the line Borsuki—Ceppelin. The army's task was to launch its main attack along the left flank (a 7-kilometer front) in the direction of Jackowo, Sochocin and Drobin (25 kilometers southeast of Sierpc) and by the close of the offensive's first day reach the line excluding Gasiorowo—Nasielsk. Part of the army's right-flank forces (no less than two rifle divisions), in conjunction with the 2nd Shock Army, was to eliminate the enemy in the Pultusk area. By the close of the offensive's third day, the army was to capture the line excluding Plock—Plonsk.

Subsequently, by cooperating with the 70th Army and developing the offensive in the direction of Drobin, the army was to capture the line excluding Biezun—Bielsk no later than the offensive's tenth day. The army was to keep in mind the turning of part of the army's forces from the Racionz—Drobin area in the direction of Plock.

The army was to have no less than 210 tubes (76mm and higher) per kilometer of front along the breakthrough sector.

The army is to maintain a reserve of no less than two rifle divisions.

In order to develop the success in the direction of Plonsk following the breakthrough of the enemy's defense, the army was to be reinforced with the 1st Guards Tank Corps.

The 70th Army, consisting of three rifle corps (96th Rifle Corps—1st, 38th Guards and 165th rifle divisions; 47th Rifle Corps—136th, 162nd and 71st rifle divisions; 114th Rifle Corps—160th, 76th Guards and 200th rifle divisions) was deployed along the line excluding Ceppelin—the heights southeast of Dembe. The army's task was to launch its main attack along its center (along a 3-kilometer front) in the direction of Nasielsk, and by the close of the offensive's first day capture the line excluding Nasielsk—Brody. Afterwards, while outflanking Modlin from the north and attacking to the west, the army was to prevent the withdrawal of the enemy's Warsaw group of forces behind the Vistula River and be ready to force the Vistula River west of Modlin.

In breaking through the enemy's defense, the army was to have no less than 210 tubes (76mm and higher) per kilometer of front.

The army was to maintain a reserve of no less than one rifle corps.

The right-flank 50th Army, consisting of nine rifle divisions and three fortified areas (153rd, 110th, 324th, 307th, 343rd, 369th, 2nd, 330th, and 191st rifle divisions, and the 91st, 161st and 153rd fortified areas), was to securely defend its sector along the forward edge Augustow—Osowiec—excluding Nowogrod. The army was to pay special attention to defending the bridge-head west of Augustow and the following axes: a) Augustow—Grodno; b) Wizna—Bialystok, and; c) Lomza—Zambrow.

According to *front* directive No. 00110/op of 29 December 1944, the 50th Army was to originally have five rifle divisions and three fortified areas (UR) in the first line, with two rifle divisions in reserve. Besides this, the 50th Army was to dispatch two rifle divisions—the 369th to Zambrow and the 330th to Sniadowo—to the *front* reserve. However, in accordance with later orders, the 50th Army did not dispatch a single rifle division to the *front* reserve, and was to keep three rifle divisions in the army reserve.

The 5th Guards Tank Army, consisting of the 10th and 29th tank corps, was in the *front* reserve in the area north and south of Bransk. The army was to be ready for combat by 10 January 1945. The army was to keep in mind entering the breach in the general direction of Mlawa and Lidzbark.

The 3rd Guards Cavalry Corps was in the Suchczice (16 kilometers southeast of Rozan)—Przedswit—Jartuzy (16 kilometers northeast of Ostrow Mazowiecka) area. The corps was to be in readiness to operate in the 3rd Army's sector in the general direction of Chorzele and Allenstein, for the purpose of cutting the enemy's most important avenues of retreat and to prevent an attack by his reserves from the north.

The 8th Mechanized Corps was in the area between the Narew River and Ostrow Mazowiecka. The corps was to be in readiness to operate in the 48th Army's sector in the direction of Mlawa and Dzialdowo.

The 8th Guards Tank Corps was in the area northwest of Wyszkow. The corps was to be in readiness for operating in the 2nd Shock Army's sector, in the direction of Golmin Stary, Ciechanow, Szrensk, and Zielun.

The 1st Guards Tank Corps was in the area 12-20 kilometers west of Wyszkow. The corps was to be in readiness to operate in the 65th Army's sector, in the direction of Jackowo, Sochocin and Drobin.

The 3rd Guards Tank Corps was in the area 8-16 kilometers east of Zambrow. The corps was not fully fitted out and did not take part in the East Prussian operation.

The 4th Air Army:

a) On the night before the offensive, the air army was to carry out no less than 1,000 sorties with Po-2s, for the purpose of wearing out the enemy's personnel, destroying his firing points along the forward edge, disrupting the work of his headquarters, blocking the main dirt roads and railroads, depots, bases, and airfield centers.

b) On the operation's first day, the air army was to launch its main attack with assault aviation along the 48th and 2nd Shock armies' sectors with the forces of no less than four air divisions and to assist the 65th and 70th armies with the forces of no less than an aviation division, and the 3rd Army with the forces of no less than an aviation division. Bomber aviation would operate against the movements and concentrations of troops, and against headquarters and communications centers in the depth.

c) The commander of the 4th Air Army was to deploy at the army commanders' command posts the commanders of the aviation formations supporting those armies.

d) On the operation's second day, the air army was to plan for the operational subordination of one assault air division apiece to the 48th, 2nd Shock, 65th, 70th, and 3rd armies. With the commitment of the mobile formations into the breach, assault air was to be assigned to accompany these formations.

e) The air army was to cover the troops with fighter aviation in their jumping-off positions and throughout the entire depth of the operation.

The initial plan for the operation was presented by the Second Belorussian Front command to the *Stavka* of the Supreme High Command on 17 December 1944, along with memorandum No. 00650/op, from which it is obvious that:
1. The gap between the 3rd and 48th armies' shock groups along the Dombrowka—Orzyc River sector was brought about by the closed and broken terrain along this sector, the presence of the enemy's powerful fortified defensive zone, and the necessity of forcing the Orzyc River in the further development of the breakthrough.
2. The gap between the 65th and 70th armies' shock groups was explained by the presence of the enemy's powerfully fortified defensive center along this sector in the Powelin area (ten kilometers west of Serock).
3. Finally, the 50th Army was assigned a defensive sector only as far as Nowogrod, because the stretching of the 50th Army's left flank as far as Ostroleka was seen as unfavorable. The *front* command considered it more expedient to leave the sector from Nowogrod to Ostroleka for the 49th Army, which, while attacking toward Myszyniec, was to roll up the enemy's defense along the western bank of the Narew River and by the close of the tenth-eleventh day of the offensive reach the area west of Nowogrod with its right flank.

The operational plan presented by the Second Belorussian Front was confirmed by the *Stavka* of the Supreme High Command, which added the following instructions:

To the Commander of the Second Belorussian Front
The *Stavka* of the Supreme High Command confirms the operational plan presented by you and orders:
1. The gap between the infantry and the cavalry and tank formations operating ahead of it should not be allowed to exceed 25-30 kilometers.
2. The employment of a mechanized corps or a tank corps alongside the cavalry is not required and should be allowed only in cases of particular necessity.

3. Keep in mind, that Popov's 8th Guards Tank Corps and Vol'skii's[9] 5th Guards Tank Army, consisting of Sakhno's 10th Tank Corps and Malakhov's 29th Tank Corps, should be completely up to strength by the start of the offensive.

Panov's 1st Guards Tank Corps is to receive heavy tanks and heavy self-propelled guns up to 100 vehicles, which will make it more combat-capable.

Panfilov's 3rd Guards Tank Corps is assigned to the front, in order to bring it up to strength during the second half of January. In connection with this, it is recommended to strengthen the front's left wing with Panov's 1st Guards Tank Corps.

4. Don't count on the *Stavka* reserve in the Bialystok area.

Stavka of the Supreme High Command

I. Stalin

A. Antonov

22 December 1944

No. 220284

Conclusions

1. The launching of the main attack along the Mlawa axis fully conformed to the situation that had arisen along the East Prussian strategic direction at the end of 1944. First of all, the main attack through Mlawa on Marienburg would isolate the enemy's East Prussian group of forces from the rest of Germany and would lead to its encirclement and destruction. Also, the terrain conditions along the Mlawa direction were more favorable for an offensive by large bodies of troops, supplied with all kinds of modern equipment. Finally, the main attack along the Mlawa axis was to be launched from the south, bypassing East Prussia's most powerful fortifications.

2. One of the operation's features was the launching of the attack not along a single front, but along a series of separate sectors, divided from each other by unattacked spaces. In the *front's* explanatory note No. 00650/op of 17 December 1944, it was stated that such a breakthrough form was conditioned by the peculiarities of the terrain and the presence of the enemy's powerfully fortified defensive centers. To this it should be added that we could adopt such an operational method, given the decisive superiority in men and materiel that we enjoyed over the enemy along the Second Belorussian Front's offensive sector.

3. Another characteristic feature of the operational plan is the maximum employment of the Rozan and Serock bridgeheads for launching the main and supporting attacks. This employment made its mark on the combat formation of the *front's* shock groups and on the course of combat operations. We see three armies deployed along the Rozan bridgehead, while a fourth (49th) is committed here for the subsequent development of the breakthrough toward the flank.

The absence of sufficient free space for deploying the shock groups made the organization of the combat formations and the development of the offensive more difficult.

4. On the whole, the operational-combat organization of the armies and *front* corresponded to the operational plan.

---

9 Editor's note. Vasilii Timofeevich Vol'skii (1897-1946) joined the Red Army in 1919 and fought in the civil war. During the Great Patriotic War he commanded a combined-arms army and a tank corps. From 1944 he commanded the 5th Guards Tank Army.

3

The Preparation of the Offensive Operation

Throughout December and the first half of January intense work proceeded along the Second and Third Belorussian fronts in preparing for the offensive. This work included training the troops and staffs, the organization of the artillery and air offensives, the employment of tank troops, and the engineering support for the operation. Serious attention was also devoted to the further study of the enemy, preparing the operational area, the organization of regrouping and relieving the troops in order to create shock groups, and organizing uninterrupted command and control during the course of the operation. Assuring the high political-morale condition of the troops was an important and responsible task of the command and political organs. Finally, problems of rear-area organization and the materiel-technical support for the operation also required the most serious elaboration.

Along with this, a great deal of work on the organizational strengthening and reinforcement of the troops was carried out. The main mass of troops assigned for the main blow was pulled back from the forward edge to the rear, for the purpose of creating the best conditions for their combat training and rest.

The Third Belorussian Front

The preparation for the offensive by the troops of the Third Belorussian Front began immediately after the reception of the directive by the *Stavka* of the Supreme High Command and had fully unfolded by the middle of December 1944. The chief task of this preparation was to teach the troops to operate in conditions of a powerfully fortified and deeply echeloned defense, to organize close cooperation between them and to establish uninterrupted command and control.

Intelligence on the enemy. The successful resolution of tasks in the forthcoming operation was unthinkable without the organization and conduct of careful and uninterrupted intelligence. Thus chief attention in preparing the troops for the offensive was given, first of all, to the all-round study of the enemy's defense.

First of all, the entire depth of the defense as far as Königsberg, inclusively, was photographed by our aviation. Assembled charts with coded defensive structures were issued to the troops down to battalion commander, inclusively. The main defensive zone, as well as a number of other lines was photographed (in the beginning of the preparation for the offensive, in the middle, and the last time two days before the start of the attack). Besides photography, reconnaissance planes continually observed the enemy's activities. While investigating the zones assigned to them, the pilots checked daily the movement of enemy forces along the railroads and paved roads, uncovered areas of tank and infantry concentration, and the construction of new defensive structures, etc. As of 5 January 1945 the 1st Air Army's aerial photography and observation had uncovered up to 500 permanent reinforced concrete and wood and earth structures, more than 850 machine gun nests, 350 artillery and mortar batteries, 26 areas for concentrating the enemy's tanks and infantry, 140 depots and 450 dugouts, as well as a large number of trenches, switch positions, communications trenches, and other defensive structures.

Alongside this it was necessary long before the beginning of the offensive to study the enemy's fire system along the forward edge, to uncover his permanent structures, to determine their durability, to find vulnerable places in each structure, to determine the possible approaches to them, to reconnoiter the outline of the enemy's trenches, and to determine their fire coordination with the garrison of each permanent structure, etc. In order to resolve these tasks, our troops broadly employed reconnaissance in force. The reconnaissance in force was carried out in front of each rifle division by independent detachments, consisting of a rifle company or a rifle battalion reinforced with tanks and self-propelled guns. In order to keep the selected breakthrough sector a secret, reconnaissance in force was carried out along the entire front, according to the plan by army and *front* headquarters.

Night searches were widely employed to study the German defense. By these means we carried out follow-up reconnaissance of enemy structures that had been uncovered by observation, their destruction, and passages were made in the engineering obstacles in front of our lines, etc. However, the chief objective of these searches was the seizure of prisoners. The search groups resolved these tasks very successfully. In the 39th Army, for example, more than 30 German soldiers and officers were captured during the preparatory period, which yielded valuable information during questioning.

Besides this, in the sector of the forthcoming offensive a broad network of observation posts was deployed. Here, aside from the combined-arms commanders, artillery commanders and the commanders of engineering troops, tank commanders, air force representatives and second-echelon formations systematically carried out observation, while officers from *front* headquarters had their own observation posts. The observation posts were everywhere moved as close to the troops as possible, while many of them were located among the forward units and subunits. Observation was in full swing from 1 January 1945, that is, nearly two weeks before the start of the operation.

Radio intelligence, which enabled us to uncover the work of a number of major German radio stations, was widely organized. These included, in particular, the Third Panzer Army's radio station in Krakau, the Fourth Army's in Kruglanken, the XXVI Army Corps' station in Mallwischken, and others.

Incoming radio data was studied in the headquarters and entered on a general intelligence map. The intelligence maps were systematically refined, reproduced and regularly sent to the troops.

The important work of the Third Belorussian Front's intelligence organs helped the command to fully uncover the enemy's defense system in a timely manner and to correctly direct our forces at carrying out tasks, which made the conduct of the offensive operation easier.

Masking the operation. Simultaneous with intelligence gathering on the enemy, our troops carried out a great deal of work in masking the operation and ensuring surprise for the forthcoming offensive. Combat documents concerning the preparations for the offensive were drawn up, as a rule, by hand, in one copy, and were known to a limited number of people. Formation commanders and chiefs of the combat arms were summoned to the next higher headquarters in order to familiarize themselves with the operational plan and to receive the necessary instructions. They were allowed to take notes of the combat documents only of those sections that concerned the activities of their formations.

Reconnaissance groups, as a rule, operated along the entire front. All officers participating in reconnaissance put on an enlisted man's uniform. So as to avoid revealing the secret of the forthcoming offensive beforehand, reconnaissance was conducted under the guise of checking the condition of our defense and the elements' duties along the forward edge, etc.

The number of duty elements was increased in the first trenches for combating the enemy's search groups, while observation was also strengthened. The concentration of troops toward the front, regroupings and the preparation of the jumping-off positions for the offensive were carried out only at night or in overcast weather.

In order to hide from the enemy the offensive's true intentions and to confuse him as to the direction of the main attack, the *front* command during 1-10 January carried out a great deal of work to misinform the enemy. Its goal consisted in showing the preparations for our offensive along a secondary axis and to thus make the German command pull part of his forces from the Gumbinnen area. To achieve this, the false preparation of a major offensive in the 31st Army's sector along the Treuburg axis was organized. From 1 January a false concentration of a large number of infantry, tanks, motor vehicles, and artillery was carried out in the Suwalki area. The troops set aside for the demonstration passed through inhabited locales, including Suwalki, at night on a daily basis to create the impression of their concentration toward the forward edge. Dummy guns and tanks were set up in the concentration area; artillery fire was increased (including that of heavy-caliber guns), and new observation towers built, etc. Our fighters patrolled the area over our false concentration. Motor vehicles with specially trained drivers were authorized to travel at night, while periodically switching on their lights. The arrival and work of a major headquarters was shown in the town of Suwalki. For this purpose, the local population was removed from several blocks, while our generals and large groups of officers, staff cars and radio stations would arrive, and communications lines were laid down. All kinds of reconnaissance and observation were strengthened along the forward edge, while snipers became more active, and in many places false crossings were prepared. The 31st Army's headquarters carried out a lot of work in elaborating the offensive operation. Groups of the army's commanders carried out reconnaissance along the forward edge.

The measures conducted facilitated the distraction of the enemy's attention to the south and somewhat eased the preparation of the offensive along the main axis.

The operation's artillery support. The troops of the Third Belorussian Front had to break through and overcome a powerful and deeply echeloned positional defense. Naturally, the inclusion of a large mass of artillery of various calibers was required for the artillery support of the breakthrough.

Thus the organization of concentrating large masses of artillery in the breakthrough area, while observing masking and secrecy measures, had extremely great significance.

The concentration of the *front's* artillery to the site of the breakthrough was also made more difficult by the circumstance that along with the preparation for the offensive, one could not allow the defense to be weakened, because the possibility of the enemy's active operations could not be excluded.

In order to support the breakthrough of the enemy's defense, the *front* command concentrated a powerful artillery grouping in the zone of those armies operating along the main axis.

Suffice it to say, for example, that in the 5th Army's attack sector (a 9-kilometer front), 1,994 artillery tubes of all calibers and 432 guards mortar platforms were concentrated, which yielded an artillery density (not counting 45mm and 57mm guns and guards mortar vehicles) of 221.5 tubes per kilometer of front. Along the 28th Army's 7-kilometer breakthrough front there were 1,527 tubes (of these, there were 442 76mm, 231 122mm, 144 152mm, and 24 203mm guns, and 686 82mm and 120mm mortars), while along the sector of the 3rd Guards Rifle Corps, which was to launch the main attack, an artillery density of 205 tubes per kilometer of front was achieved. Along the 39th Army's 8-kilometer front there were 1,284 tubes.

Artillery groups were created in each army and were slated for carrying out the following tasks:

1) Corps groups for destroying the enemy's earth and timber pillboxes, dugouts and observation posts, as well as stone structures that had been configured for defense;
2) Corps groups for counterbattery work;
3) Division and regimental artillery groups;

4) Mortar groups for destroying trenches and personnel (these groups operated only during the period of the artillery preparation and while supporting the infantry and tank attack and were not part of the artillery groups);

5) Guns for firing over open sights to destroy the enemy's individual firing points along the forward edge and while accompanying the infantry during the attack;

6) Corps groups of guards mortars, which were slated for suppressing weapons and personnel in the enemy's strong points and centers of resistance.

It was planned to move up the artillery units into their positional areas between 23-28 December 1944, on the condition that the beginning of the operation was slated for 1 January 1945; that is, the artillery would be moved up two days before the artillery offensive. However, given the fact that the date for the offensive was delayed until 13 January 1945, the movement of the artillery to its positional areas was drawn out to 11 January 1945. Guns for firing over open sights were moved up during the night of 10-11 January.

Work for the engineering outfitting of the artillery was carried out exclusively at night by special teams from the artillery units and the crews of registry guns. With the arrival of the dawn these structures were carefully disguised and the rank and file pulled back into their corresponding shelters. The noise from motor vehicles' and tractors' motors was covered up by the fire of specially designated batteries, which had been specially set aside for this purpose and which fired on the enemy's forward edge from temporary firing positions.

At the basis of the planning for the artillery offensive in the armies were the firing schedule and a number of additional instructions by the commander of the Third Belorussian Front.

On the basis of this document, the armies' artillery headquarters had essentially completed their planning by 14 December 1944, while the following documents had been drawn up:

1. A plan for the artillery offensive and instructions for planning it.
2. A firing chart by periods.
3. A chart and a table for the period of infantry accompaniment.
4. A plan for adjustment of fire.
5. An ammunition expenditure table by days.
6. A regrouping plan and charts for moving up units to their positional areas.
7. Instructions for organizing headquarters commandants' service.

On the basis of these documents, by 17 December 1944 planning had been basically completed in the rifle corps' and divisions' artillery headquarters, but as new data about the enemy was accumulated, the planning was augmented and corrected up to 5 January 1945.

All the planning for the artillery offensive in the higher headquarters was accumulated from the bottom upwards. The battery commanders took account of the uncovered targets, compiled charts of the targets and presented them to the battalions' headquarters, then the latter passed them on to the headquarters of the artillery regiments and higher. Thus during the preparatory period detailed charts of targets were compiled in the artillery headquarters, along with their description and instructions as to which batteries were responsible for suppressing these targets. The division and corps artillery commanders visited the batteries' observation posts, became acquainted with the uncovered targets and assigned them to the commander of this or that battery.

According to the plan for the artillery offensive, the employment of artillery and mortars according to periods was planned in the following manner.

The first period—a 5-minute fire onslaught against the most important targets in the enemy defense.

Guns for firing over open sights were to fire on targets located along the forward edge of the defense, suppress and destroy permanent firing positions, dugouts, overhead covers, observation posts, and anti-tank guns, etc.

Mortars (82mm and 120mm) were to suppress and destroy the enemy's personnel in the first and second trenches and in the communications trenches.

The regimental groups' artillery was to suppress and destroy personnel in the trenches, communications trenches, suppress observation posts, communications centers, and mortar batteries to a depth of up to six kilometers.

The artillery groups of the rifle divisions and rifle corps were to suppress and destroy the enemy's personnel and weapons in the second trench, dugouts and overhead covers. They were to suppress observation posts, communications centers, headquarters, concentration areas for the enemy's personnel and equipment, and mortar batteries to a depth of up to six kilometers.

ADD (long-range artillery) groups were to carry out a fire onslaught against the enemy's batteries.

The AR (destruction artillery) group was to fire on the enemy's defensive centers and destroys individual targets in his engineering structures.

A group of M-31[1] RS (guards mortars) was to carry out brigade salvos against the main centers of the enemy's defense in the area of the forward edge.

While employing the experience of preceding offensive operations, the fire from small-caliber anti-aircraft regiments was to be employed for "combing" individual targets, which had a powerful morale effect on the enemy's personnel located outside their shelters.

Thus the fire from artillery and mortars during the first period of the artillery offensive had the purpose of inflicting the greatest damage to the enemy's personnel and equipment, to disrupt his command and control and to disorganize his defensive fire system to a depth of up to six kilometers.

The second period would last 60 minutes and include the destruction of targets along the forward edge and within the depth of the enemy's defense.

Guns firing over open sights were to begin firing only 15 minutes before the end of this period. Throughout the final 15 minutes they would attempt to destroy firing points, dugouts, overhead covers, timber and earth pillboxes, observation posts, and anti-tank defense guns to a depth of up to 500 meters from the forward edge, and attempt to create passages through the enemy's wire.

Individual 120mm mortar batteries were to carry out the destruction of their planned targets.

The artillery from the regimental groups was to destroy, with specially detached howitzer batteries, individual trench sectors and communications trenches and stone structures configured for defense. During the second period's last 15 minutes they were to suppress the enemy's observation posts and active mortar batteries.

Artillery from the rifle divisions' and rifle corps' groups, employing specially detached batteries, was to destroy observation posts, timber and earth pillboxes, and trench and communications trench intersections. During the second period's final 15 minutes, this artillery would cover the guns firing over open sights with its own fire, suppressing the enemy's observation posts and mortar batteries.

The ADD (long-range artillery) group was to carry out a repeat fire onslaught against the enemy's batteries.

The AR (destruction artillery) group would destroy concrete and timber and earth pillboxes, durable observation posts, overhead covers, and the intersections of trenches and communications trenches.

---

1   Editor's note. The M-31 was a 300 caliber variant of the Red Army's multiple rocket launcher, popularly known as the "Katyusha."

Thus throughout 45 minutes during the second period, excluding a 15-minute pause following the first period, fire by heavy artillery was to be directed at destroying the most important targets. Special attention was to be devoted to destroying stone structures that had been configured for sheltering firing points, the intersections of trenches and communications trenches, and observation posts, etc.

A 40-minute third period involved the suppression of the enemy's personnel along the forward edge and in the immediate depth of the defense by deliberate fire.

During this period a zone to a depth of 1.5 kilometers was to be worked over with a double density in comparison with the remaining depth of the defense (six kilometers). Considering that the enemy attempts to pull back his personnel from the first trench to the second during the artillery preparation, 3/5 of all the artillery's fire was planned for the second trench and 2/5 for the first.

During this period guns firing over open sights would continue to fire on targets along the forward edge, while the 82mm and 120mm mortars would suppress the enemy's personnel in the first and second trenches and communications trenches.

The regimental groups' artillery was to suppress and destroy the enemy's personnel and weapons in the trenches, communications trenches, dugouts, and overhead covers; it was to suppress observation posts, communications centers, headquarters, and mortar batteries.

The rifle divisions' and rifle corps' artillery groups were to suppress and destroy personnel and weapons in the second trench, communications trenches, communications centers, headquarters, and mortar batteries.

ADD (long-range artillery) groups were to carry out volley fire and deliberate fire against the enemy's batteries, suppress target sectors, and concentration areas for the enemy's personnel and equipment in the depth of the defense.

The AR (destruction artillery) group was to continue firing against the second period's targets.

Guards mortar groups were to carry out a repeat salvo to suppress and destroy the enemy's personnel and equipment in their areas of concentration in the main defensive centers and in the zone of the forward edge.

During the third period the fire from the main mass of artillery and mortars would be directed at suppressing personnel and equipment along the forward edge of the enemy's defense.

The period of accompanying the infantry and tank attack. During this period, the artillery was to be primarily employed for supporting the infantry's advance following its breakthrough of the forward edge into the immediate depth of the enemy's defense.

The accompaniment of the infantry's attack by artillery fire was to be carried out to a depth of 1,500-1,800 meters, counting from the forward edge of the defense. During this period the second and third trench lines, firing points, observation posts, headquarters, and communications centers would be subjected to fire. For this purpose, from five to six artillery battalions would be concentrated per kilometer of front. The entire artillery detached for accompanying the infantry attack was to fire only on targets within these zones, moving it to the depth according to time. This variant was organized as follows along the 28th Army's breakthrough zone: artillery fire was planned along five main lines, each 300-500 meters from each other. Each battery and battalion was assigned concrete targets for suppression, gleaned from aerial reconnaissance or obtained by other means. Thus the planned targets and target sectors comprised a broken system of narrow zones, which would be subject to fire during the accompaniment period.

From the start of the attack the artillery's fire would be switched to targets located in the first zone, at a distance of no closer than 250-300 meters from the forward edge. Accompanying fire would be waged against targets along the first line of the first zone, at a slightly higher density than the density of fire of the final, third period of the artillery preparation. At the same time, deliberate fire would be waged against targets along the second line of the first zone. With the infantry's approach to within 100-150 meters of the explosions, fire would once again be shifted from the targets along the second line of the first zone's second line to targets in the second zone's first line, against which deliberate fire would be waged. At that moment the fire regime against targets in the first zone's second line would be changed from deliberate fire to a fire onslaught. In its turn, fire against these targets would be lifted at the infantry's approach to 100-150 meters and would be shifted to targets in the second zone's second line; the fire regime would simultaneously be changed against targets in the second zone's first line from deliberate fire to a fire onslaught. Such an order of shifting fire and the change of the firing regimen was to be conducted up to the final line for accompanying the infantry attack to a depth of 1,500-1,800 meters. The shifting of fire to the following target or target sector would be carried out only according to time, and the attacking rifle elements were to follow behind the explosions and not lag behind them. In order to hide the end of the artillery preparation from the enemy, the density of fire against targets in the first zone, with the start of the period for accompanying the infantry attack, was to increase in comparison with the density of fire at the end of the artillery preparation. In its turn, the density of fire in the first, second and third accompaniment zones was also to gradually increase.

The distribution of shells by targets would be conducted on the basis of norms assigned for the accompaniment period; at the same time, shells were assigned for each target, depending on the concrete conditions.

In analyzing all the measures for the artillery support of the operation, one may make the following conclusions:

1. The artillery groups created in the armies fully corresponded to the decisions adopted; the artillery density achieved supported the fulfillment of the *front's* troops' task for breaking through the defense.

2. A sufficient deadline for the preparatory work and the significant experience of the officers of the artillery units and formations, acquired in preceding operations, enabled us to plan and organize the concentration of artillery masses and to ensure their timely arrival at their new positional areas. The thoroughness of drawing up movement routes, good march discipline, the developed system of headquarters commandant's service, and headquarters control supported the concentration of large masses of artillery and mortars in immediate proximity to the forward edge of the enemy's defense.

3. However, despite all of the measures adopted to ensure secret regrouping, the beginning of the offensive was not a surprise for the enemy.
    The reasons for this, evidently, were:
    • the extended period for moving the artillery to its positional areas, due to the change in the start of the operation (from 1 January to 13 January 1945) and related circumstances that revealed our intentions;
    • on the basis of firing for adjustment, which was conducted by our artillery during the preparatory period, the enemy was able to establish through signals reconnaissance the presence of a large amount of artillery along the axis of the main attack;
    • the enemy's aerial reconnaissance could not but note the significant terrain changes along the axis of the main attack, which once again could confirm the supposition that we were preparing an attack;
    • during the night preceding the offensive, the troops that were being moved up to the forward edge, made noise, which also gave the enemy the opportunity to determine the time for the offensive.

This is also confirmed by the fact that along the 39th Army's front the enemy carried out an artillery conterprepration two hours before the start of our artillery offensive (at 0700 on 13 January 1945).

Air support. Included in the Third Belorussian Front was the 1st Air Army, which by the start of the operation had 1,333 serviceable aircraft. The number of formations and their combat strength is shown in Table III/3.1.

Table III/3.1 1st Air Army Strength, January 1945

Name of Formation	Number of Air Regiments	Number of Aircraft
303rd Fighter Division	3	140
240th Fighter Division	3	135
129th Fighter Division	3	75
130th Fighter Division	3	110
330th Fighter Division	3	42
9th Fighter Regiment	1	34
TOTAL	16	536
6th Bomber Division	3	111
276th Bomber Division	3	101
213th Night Bomber Division	3	86
TOTAL	9	298
311th Assault Air Division	3	97
217th Assault Air Division	3	103
1st Guards Assault Air Division	4	151
282nd Assault Air Division	3	102
TOTAL	13	453
10th Air Reconnaissance Regiment	1	17
117th Fire Correction Reconnaissance Regiment	1	15
151st Fire Correction Reconnaissance Regiment	1	14
TOTAL	3	46
GRAND TOTAL	41	1,333

Note: In the Third Belorussian Front's operational zone the enemy had 670 aircraft by the start of the operation.

Table III/3.2 Correlation of Aviation Forces in the Third Belorussian Front's Operational Zone

Type of Aircraft	Number of Aircraft		Approximate Correlation
	1st Air Army	Enemy	
Fighters	536	280	2:1
Bombers	298	165	2:1
Assault Aircraft	453	160	3:1
Reconnaissance Aircraft	46	65	1:1.5
TOTAL	1,333	670	2:1

Thus the overall superiority of force was 2:1 in favor of the 1st Air Army. However, this correlation should not be considered correct, because the enemy had the opportunity to bring in aviation from other axes, just as the Soviet command could bring in part of the 18th Air Army (Long-Range Aviation) for operations in the Third Belorussian Front's area, as well as the First Baltic Front's 3rd Air Army.

It should be noted that the *front's* aviation, aside from the overall superiority in forces, had a great advantage in assault aircraft, which represented a significant strike force capable of rendering uninterrupted support to the infantry and tanks both in breaking through the enemy's defense, as well as the troops' operations in depth. Fighters accounted for 40 percent of all the army's combat aircraft, which would undoubtedly make possible the secure cover of the ground forces along the main axis of the breakthrough and to support our bomber and assault aviation in carrying out their combat tasks.

Planning combat activities. Proceeding from the overall operational decision, the *front* commander assigned the 1st Air Army the following tasks:

- the main forces were to support the *front's* shock group in breaking through the main defensive zone;
- to destroy the enemy's reserves arriving at the breakthrough sector and prevent them from occupying intermediate lines; be ready to render assistance in repelling the enemy's tank counterattacks;
- to assist the commitment of the 2nd Guards Tank Corps into the breach (the operation's second day) and then to assist the activities of the success development echelon, consisting of the 11th Guards Army and 1st Guards Tank Corps (the operation's fourth day);
- to securely cover the *front's* main group against the aerial enemy, both during the concentration period and during the offensive, destroying the enemy's aviation on the ground and in the air;
- to try to destroy the enemy's headquarters and command and control system;
- to carry out uninterrupted reconnaissance (day and night) of the enemy's forces, with the main task the timely uncovering of the preparations for enemy counterattacks.

On the basis of the tasks assigned, the *front* commander drew up a plan for employing our aviation, in which our aviation's combat activities were planned in detail for the first four days of the operation. This period was to embrace the breakthrough of the enemy's main defensive zone, the commitment of the mobile formations into the breach and their support in depth.

The following combat schedule was planned for the bombers for the operation's first day: day bombers were to carry out 1.5-2 sorties per plane and night bombers 5-7 sorties; assault and fighter aircraft were to carry out 2-3 sorties per plane, while reconnaissance and artillery correction planes would carry out two sorties per plane.

According to the plan, our aviation was to carry out 12,565 sorties over the first four days of the operation, which yielded an average of two sorties per day for each combat-ready plane. Such intensity during the winter, when there is a limited amount of daylight, is the maximum and may be planned only for the operation's first day.

On the night before the offensive our aviation was to launch uninterrupted strikes with Po-2 or Il-4[2] night aircraft (the latter from the 18th Air Army) against the enemy's fortified points of Gumbinnen, Jentkutkampen, Kattenau, Neu Trakenen, Walenkemen, and Berzbruchen. Thus

---

2   Editor's note. The Il-4 was a twin-engine medium bomber that appeared toward the end of the 1930s. The aircraft carried a four man crew and was armed with two 7.62mm and one 12.7mm machine guns, and carried a maximum bomb load of 2,700 kilograms.

our planes were to carry out about 1,300 sorties during the night against the main strong points of the enemy's defense.

On the operation's first day our aviation was to begin the preparation for the attack at H minus one hour and 45 minutes, mainly launching raids in the 5th Army's operational zone. For one hour and 45 minutes our bombers and assault aircraft were to carry out 536 sorties, with the greater part of them in the final 30 minutes before the start of the infantry's attack along the 5th Army's sector. Within 20 minutes following the start of the infantry attack, a concentrated attack against the Jentkutkampen strong point (located two kilometers from the forward edge of the enemy's defense) was planned, in which 100 bombers were to take part.

During the preparation period for the attack, the plan called for our aviation's main efforts to be concentrated in the 5th Army's sector; here our aviation was to carry out 80 percent of all sorties planned for the first day for supporting the ground forces.

During this period the main targets were chiefly the enemy's heavily fortified strong points of Uzdegen, Katenau, Eimenischken, Strelkemen, Brudzen, Jentkutkampen, Dergemmen, Gumbinnen, Pilkallen, and others.

It was planned to carry out 2,575 sorties on the operation's first day.

On the operation's second day our aviation was to support the ground forces' offensive, while our aviation's activities were planned in the following manner: night aviation was to launch raids against the enemy's headquarters in the 5th Army's sector for the purpose of disrupting the enemy's command and control;

–day aviation was to support the forces of the 5th, 28th and 39th armies in widening the breakthrough and supporting the commitment of the 2nd Guards Tank Corps into the breach, for which the 6th and 276th bomber divisions were designated, as were the 1st, 217th and 282nd assault air divisions.

Besides this, the 130th Fighter Division was detailed for launching strikes against the enemy's airfields. According to the plan, the overall number of sorties during the operation's second day was to be 2,335.

The following units were designated for accompanying the ground forces: for the 5th Army— the 217th Assault Air Division; for the 39th Army—the 282nd Assault Air Division; for the 28th Army—the 311th Assault Air Division, and; for the 2nd Tank Corps—the 1st Guards Assault Air Division. Bomber aviation was to remain in the army commander's reserve and was slated for combating the enemy's railroad shipments. Our fighter aviation was to cover the ground forces and escort assault aviation and the bombers. Besides this, the 130th Fighter Division had the task of operating against enemy reserves arriving at the line Insterburg—Gumbinnen.

In accordance with such a distribution, plans were drawn up for the aviation's cooperation with the ground forces for the entire operation. These plans called for the support of this or that combined-arms army by not only a single air division, but also by units in the army commander's reserve, which, depending on the course of combat activities, could be employed to augment the aviation's forces along any axis.

The fight against the enemy's aviation over the battlefield and on his airfields was entrusted to the 303rd Fighter Division, which was to carry out this task throughout the entire operation.

The aviation's cooperation with the ground forces was to be accomplished on the support principle and the air formations were not to be operationally subordinated to the combined-arms commanders. This was dictated by the fact that the breakthrough of the heavily fortified enemy defense required massed air activities along definite axes. Having the entire air strength in his hands, the commander of the air army could at any moment concentrate its efforts along that axis where the main task was being resolved by the combined-arms armies.

Aviation basing. The air army's airfield network within the bounds of the Third Belorussian Front included 120 airfields. Besides these, by the start of the operation new forward airfields were being built. As a result of this work, the number of airfields was raised to 146. The airfield network was not uniform in quality and represented the following picture:

- airfields with a concrete surface—1;
- airfields with a metal surfaces—2;
- airfields with a gravel surface—1;
- airfields with a sand surface—55;
- airfields with a loam surface—87.

The airfields were located at the following distances from the front line:

- up to 25 kilometers—26 airfields;
- up to 50 kilometers[3]–47 airfields;
- up to 75 kilometers—73 airfields;
- up to 100 kilometers—115 airfields.

An average of 50 airfields, out of the overall number of airfields, was in use; it should be taken into account that the army had 46 air regiments, which included communications, transportation and medical regiments. Thus the number of airfields enabled us to base our entire aviation quite freely by the start of the operation, based on the calculation that each air regiment would have its own airfield.

Special groups were created for locating and outfitting new airfields to support our aviation units and formations during the *front's* advance. These groups noted 53 areas on enemy territory, which could be occupied and outfitted for our planes' combat activities.

The 1st Air Army disposed of 36 airfield service battalions and six engineer-airfield battalions for the purpose of uninterrupted materiel supply during the operation, as well as 36 airfield-technical companies. Such an amount of rear units was able to support the air army with the necessary materiel supplies during the operation.

Up to 40 combat loads of bombs and bullets and 10-12 refuelings were concentrated at depots and airfields.

Aviation command and control. The organization of aviation command and control was based on centralization. This was necessary so that the aviation's efforts would not be dispersed along individual axes, but rather concentrated on supporting the *front's* shock group.

Aviation representatives were dispatched to the rifle and tank corps with the task of supporting communications with the army headquarters and transmitting requests from the ground forces' commanders. Besides this, the aviation representatives were to inform the air army headquarters of the ground situation along their sector, which would keep the army commander on top of things.

The command and control of groups of planes in the air was to be exercised by the commanders of the air divisions from their command posts, while air controllers, located among the ground forces' forward units, would guide them to their targets.

Engineer support. The engineering preparation of the breakthrough in the Third Belorussian Front's zone began on 10 December 1944. Its chief task consisted of supporting our forces' concentration and regrouping and preparing the necessary jumping-off position for the offensive, as well as supplying the formations and units with engineering equipment necessary for breaking through the enemy's defense and developing the success in depth.

The careful observation of the enemy and engineering searches were organized from the first days of the preparatory period in the planned breakthrough zone. Observation was carried out

---

3   The airfields from the preceding zones are part of the next zone.

uninterruptedly by sappers from fixed observation posts (NP). An average of 2-3 such posts was set up per kilometer of front. For example, along the 5th Army's 9-kilomter breakthrough sector there were 28 NPs, with 26 NPs in the 28th Army's zone, etc.

The engineering observation posts had as their task the uncovering of the engineering system in the enemy's main defensive zone, individual fortified structures and their characteristics, and their depth, etc. Alongside fixed observation, our engineering units widely employed reconnaissance searches, which usually carried out the reconnaissance of the forward edge of the enemy's defense, penetrating into his lines up to the second trench inclusively. These searches had the objective of firming up data on the German fortifications derived from observers at the permanent observation posts, divining the character of the engineering defense in the main zone, and planning the necessary measures for getting rid of obstacles, etc.

The dispatch of engineering reconnaissance groups into the enemy's immediate rear was also practiced, with the task of uncovering the enemy's defensive system in the depth, determining the types, locations, boundaries and character of the natural and artificial barriers here, as well as mine obstacles. During the preparatory period we managed to gather all the necessary information about the enemy's fortifications through engineering searches and observation and to supply the command with data for making the most correct decisions regarding the breakthrough.

Preparing the jumping-off position included work on the further development of trenches, the construction, repair, restoration and strengthening of roads and bridges, as well as the thorough clearing of mines in the depth of one's defense and the construction of passages in the enemy's obstacles. Following the October offensive, all defensive work was carried out with the idea of preparing a jumping-off position. The *front's* engineer units, along with the troops, built a large number of trenches, communications trenches, commander's observation posts, and dugouts, etc.

Following the decision to break through, the *front's* forces set about finishing a jumping-off position for the purpose of bringing it closer to the forward edge of the enemy's defense at a distance supporting a rapid attack (150-200 meters). This closing was carried out by the successive movement forward of separate trench sectors and their unification by communications trenches, as well as by sapping, in which "mustaches" (three per rifle company) would be moved forward from the main trench and which would then be connected by short trench sectors. The advanced trenches and communications trenches would then be immediately configured for defense and outfitted with shelters for the troops, ammunition niches and fixtures for jumping out of the trenches. The communications trench system was developed in depth, so that by the start of the operation the battalion and regimental commanders' command posts were connected between themselves by fully-outfitted communications trenches. The system of command and observation posts was augmented by the preparation of 1-2 reserve observation posts for commanders of all levels. Firing positions and shelters for the rank and file and equipment were prepared. In the tanks' jumping-off positions, shelters for the rank and file (slit trenches) and equipment (ramps) were prepared. All engineering work for preparing the jumping-off position at a distance of 1.5-2 kilometers from the enemy was carried out only at night.

The amount of work carried out during the preparatory period is shown in Table III/2.3.

In order to support the movement of the infantry and tanks to the jumping-off position and the troops' maneuver by 5 January, that is, seven days before the start of the offensive, all mine fields that had been laid in the depth of our defense (from the second trench and deeper) along the main axis had been completely cleared. Passages in the obstacles in front of the front line, both in our minefields and in the enemy's, began to be made on the night of 9-10 January; that is, four days before the start of the attack. Passages for the infantry were made 15-25 meters wide and 30-50 meters for tanks. On the eve of the breakthrough a control testing was carried out in the passages through the minefields and they were signed over to the commanders of the rifle subunits and the commanders of the lead tanks and self-propelled guns.

Table III/3.3 Preparatory Work in the Third Belorussian Front's Zone

Type of Work	39th Army	5th Army	28th Army	2nd Guards Army	31st Army	*Front*
Trenches dug along all lines (in km)	253	300	318	193	703	1,767
Communications trenches dug (in km)	64	65	116	37	122	404
Total trenches and communications trenches dug (in km)	317	365	434	230	825	2,171
Commander's observation posts built	289	60	937	327	445	2,058
Overhead covers and dugouts built	1,316	1,107	4,019	1,292	2,695	10,429
Wire obstacles constructed (in km)	56	25	66	20	116	283

By the start of the offensive the following number of passages had been completely prepared: in our minefields and in the enemy's: in the 39th Army—118; in the 5th Army—71; in the 28th Army—80, that is, an average of 12 passages per rifle division.

In January, in order to support delivery and evacuation in the *front's* sector, new roads to the tune of one per rifle division were built, 122.5 kilometers of old roads were repaired, 37 kilometers of routes of march laid down, 2,145 linear meters of pole flooring laid down, 19 bridges with a capacity of 70 tons built for passing artillery and tanks through the trenches, anti-tank ditches and communications trenches, and four bridges with an overall length of 350 linear meters, etc. All the roads were completed up to the jumping-off position. Special road-bridge detachments were created in each corps and army for repairing and restoring roads and bridges in the depth of the enemy's defense.

Besides this, mine clearing groups from the rifle elements and troop sapper elements and units trained in engineering skills, were created within the first-echelon divisions, to move with the infantry and make passages in the enemy's minefields. For example, in the 5th Army there were more than 70 such groups, and 197 in the 28th Army. In the armies operating along the axis of the main attack there were also engineer-tank regiments of trawler tanks for this purpose.

In order to counteract major enemy tank counterattacks, special mobile obstacle detachments (POZ) were created in the rifle regiments, divisions, corps, and armies, which had the following tasks:

• to cover our open flanks and gaps along the boundaries with neighboring units and formations;
• to consolidate the success achieved by the units and formations;
• to blockade the encircled enemy;
• to block the arrival of enemy reserves;
• to counteract enemy tank and infantry counterattacks.

The composition of the mobile obstacle detachments was not uniform:

• in a rifle regiment, for example, a detachment consisted of a section of sappers, with three two-horse wagons or a single ZIS-5[4] vehicle; the detachment's equipment consisted of 100 anti-tank and 100 anti-personnel mines and 25 kilograms of explosives;

---

4   Editor's note. The ZIS-5 was a popular Soviet truck model produced at the Stalin Factory (Zavod imeni

- in a rifle division a detachment consisted of 1-2 platoons of sappers with two motor vehicles, up to 300 anti-tank and 150 anti-personnel mines and 50 kilograms of explosives;
- in a rifle corps a detachment consisted of a company of sappers with three motor vehicles, 500 anti-tank and 250 anti-personnel mines and 100 kilograms of explosives;
- in an army a detachment consisted of an engineer battalion with nine motor vehicles, 1,500 anti-tank and 750 anti-personnel mines and 300 kilograms of explosives.

At the *front* level the 13th Motorized Engineer Brigade had been prepared for this purpose.

During the preparatory period a great deal of attention was devoted to training the infantry, artillery troops and tank troops in engineering matters. The training was carried out on training grounds specially prepared by engineering units and constructed to resemble the German defenses. Besides this, non-organic sapper sections were trained in every rifle company and battery.

In light of the fact that there were a large number of various hydrotechnical structures in East Prussia, with the aid of which the enemy could raise the water level in the rivers (Angerapp, Inster, Pregel, Deime, Alle, and others) and flood the area and make it swampy, the headquarters for engineering troops prepared eight special sapper companies for hydrotechnical work during the offensive, supplied with the necessary equipment and transport.

By the start of the operation, all units and troop formations had been completely supplied with the necessary engineering equipment. They had all the equipment for building bridges and constructing crossings, as well as for consolidating captured territory—anti-tank and anti-personnel mines, hard-to-see obstacles, spiral barbed wire, and explosives.

The infantry prepared fascines, mats, ladders, and treadway bridges for overcoming trenches, communications trenches, anti-tank ditches, and other obstacles; the artillery and tank troops prepared collapsible treadway bridges 10-12 linear meters long (one bridge per company or battery). All of this equipment had been concentrated at the *front* and army depots and mobile installations and were also in companies, batteries, on tanks, and in mobile obstacle detachments, etc. Each army operating along the main axis (39th, 5th and 28th armies) had assault and engineer-sapper brigades attached to them.

There was a permanent reserve—13th Motorized Engineer Brigade, and the 4th and 8th pontoon-bridge brigades—at the disposal of the chief of the *front's* engineering troops. The 13th Motorized Engineer Brigade was chiefly designated for clearing mines from major towns (Gumbinnen, Insterburg, Tilsit, etc.); the pontoon-bridge brigades, which consisted of four battalions each with N2P (five sets), DMP-41 and DMP-42 (2 ½ sets) park equipment, was slated for supporting the forcing of the Angerapp, Alle, Pregel, and other rivers. They were to advance behind the 5th and 28th armies' units.

The engineer units were echeloned in depth in the following manner.

The first echelon consisted of specially trained riflemen, regimental and divisional sappers, and part of the engineering units attached as reinforcements, which were organized into reconnaissance, obstacle removal and storming groups; that is, sappers for escorting the first-echelon infantry and tanks.

The second echelon consisted of engineering units, designated for the constructions of routes of march and roads, the organization of crossings, escorting tanks, artillery and mortars; that is, sappers for supporting regrouping, movement, delivery, and evacuation (road-bridge detachments).

The third echelon was designated for organizing the maneuver of obstacles for securing flanks and consolidating terrain.

Stalina) in Moscow between 1932 and 1958.

The fourth echelon was the reserve of the chief of the *front* and army engineering troops.

Carefully organized engineering reconnaissance aided the command in determining in a timely manner the type of enemy fortifications, the weak and strong aspects of his defense, the boundaries of permanent lines and fortified areas, flooded sectors and, in connection with this, to determine the direction of the main attack.

The complete removal of our minefields and putting roads and bridges in excellent order aided the troops' timely concentration and regrouping, their occupation of the jumping-off position for the offensive and attack, as well as timely delivery and evacuation.

The organization of command and control and communications. The headquarters of the Third Belorussian Front was located in a woods ten kilometers southeast of Vilkaviskis. A forward command post for the *front* commander was outfitted in Stallupönen. The *front* command was here along with an operational group. The operational group included the chief of the *front* staff's operational directorate, the chief of the intelligence section, the artillery commander, the commander of the *front's* armored and mechanized troops, a group of communications officers, a coding section, and others. As the offensive developed, it was planned to shift the *front* headquarters to Stallupönen and the forward command post to Gumbinnen.

The *front* commander personally assigned objectives to the army commanders, which were then drawn up in fragmentary field orders. Communications with the armies was organized from both the main and forward command posts. Communications with neighboring *fronts* was conducted through the *front* headquarters: with the First Baltic Front through Baudet code and with the Second Belorussian Front through Baudet apparatus and Morse code. It was from here that the *front* maintained communications over high frequency radio with the armies' headquarters.

In order to ensure uninterrupted command and control, the *front's* communications troops carried out a great deal of work during the preparatory period. During 1-15 January 1945 alone 44.5 kilometers of permanent telephone-telegraph lines were constructed, 436 kilometers of wire were hung on existing telephone-telegraph lines and 264 kilometers of wire were repaired. 1,030 telephone poles, a large number of wire, telephone and telegraph apparatus, and the necessary horse-drawn and auto transport were prepared for developing the communications network during the offensive.

Training the troops and staffs. The training of troops and staffs for the offensive was carried out according to a plan drawn up by the *front* headquarters. The plan indicated the training themes, the order in which they should be carried out and schedules, and also the names of those responsible for conducting the training. At the same time, measures were adopted for organizationally strengthening and reinforcing the troops, in order to bring up the main group's rifle divisions to 6,000-7,000 men.

The chief attention in preparing for the offensive was directed toward seeing that the troops had fully mastered the techniques of the offensive battle in conditions of a deeply-echeloned trench defense. Each training theme was worked out beforehand with officers and then with the subunits and units. Besides this, officers studied the character of the enemy defense and the approaches to his forward edge by relief maps and personal observation; under the leadership of a representative from higher headquarters, they researched the troop concentration areas and the jumping-off positions for the offensive. Gatherings of the commanders of rifle corps, divisions and regiments and their staffs, and commanders of reinforcements, which were conducted at army headquarters, as well as gatherings of commanders of rifle battalions and companies and artillery batteries at corps headquarters were very important to the operation's success. A number of lectures on problems of organizing the breakthrough of a deeply-echeloned defense were read at gatherings of formation commanders, while war games on maps and on the spot were conducted. Among the war game themes were: "The Breakthrough of the Enemy's Heavily Fortified Defense," "The Development of the Breakthrough and the Commitment of Large Tank Formations into the Battle," "The

Elimination of Major Centers of Resistance," and "The Organization of Command and Control in the Offensive," etc. War games were played out on the basis of the actual situation at the front. The gatherings conducted aided the commanders and their staffs to scrupulously study the enemy's defense, to tighten up offensive plans, to organize cooperation between the combat arms, to draw up the necessary planning documents, and to establish uninterrupted troop command and control.

Troop training was carried out on training grounds, outfitted to resemble the German defense. Here exercises were conducted on individual troop training and in knocking units together, practice firing, and demonstration training of the combat arms, etc. During this time attention was chiefly devoted to teaching the infantry to fight in trenches, to skillfully cooperate with tanks and escorting guns while eliminating the enemy's individual permanent structures and his strong points, to employ heavy weapons fire in battle, the repelling of enemy counterattacks, and also to consolidate captured lines. 50 percent of all exercises were conducted at night and in poor visibility. Officers from tank, artillery and aviation units, which had been detached for supporting the attack by the given unit or formation, had to take part in all exercises. In the process of training they coordinated their activities with the infantry officers, exchanged experience from preceding offensive battles with them, and established the most convenient coordination signals, etc. The elaboration of the exercise would conclude with practice firing by tanks and part of the air force slated for supporting the offensive. All exercises were conducted, as a rule, with a designated enemy. Aside from tactical training, gatherings of snipers, machine gunners, mortar operators, signals troops, and tank destroyers, as well as of the deputy commanders of sections and platoons, were conducted in every rifle division. The course of combat training was uninterruptedly controlled by representatives of the *front* headquarters.

Simultaneous with troop training, a great deal of materiel preparation for the offensive was carried out. By 10 January all subunits and units had been brought up to authorized strength in weapons, ammunition and visual and sound signaling. The troops had new camouflage uniforms. In all subunits mats for overcoming wire obstacles, throw bridges for crossing the artillery over trenches, ladders, fascines and trestles for helping tanks overcome anti-tank ditches had been gathered. There were rope ladders, which made it easier for the troops to jump up during the attack, in the jumping-off trench, and in many places exits from the trenches had been dug for the machine gun and mortar crews.

The great deal of work carried out to train the troops and staffs for the offensive made it significantly easier for them to carry out their assigned task of breaking through the enemy's defense.

Political support for the operation. Political support for the operation was built around three main questions:

a) the propagandizing and practical realization of comrade Stalin's instructions, laid out by him in the report and order on the twenty-seventh anniversary of the Great October Socialist Revolution; the inculcation of great offensive élan, burning hatred for the enemy and confidence in our near and final victory;
b) the ideological-political education of communists;
c) the strengthening of the political-morale condition in units and formations, the strengthening of discipline and the raising of vigilance.

In order to successfully resolve these tasks, meetings of the political section chiefs of corps, divisions and brigades were carried out in January on the question "Tasks of Party-Political Work during the Preparation and Conduct of Offensive Battles," under the leadership of representatives of the *front's* political directorate. Gatherings of assistant regimental commanders for political affairs and regimental and battalion party organizers were conducted on this question, as well as two-day seminars for senior instructors for organizational and party work, agitators from the formations' and units' political sections, and editors of division newspapers. Aside from discussing the tasks of party-political work in the offensive at these meetings, representatives of the *front's* political directorate delivered a number of reports on the theme of "Comrade Stalin's November Report and Order no. 220 of 7 November 1944—the Combat Program of the Red Army and Soviet people in the Struggle for the Final Defeat of Hitlerite Germany" and "The Experience and Practice of Agitation and Propaganda Work in Offensive Battles," and others.

Methodological works were printed to assist the group leaders of political studies and discussions on the following themes: "The Party of Lenin and Stalin is Leading us to Final Victory over the Enemy," "The Soldier's Order of 'Glory' and the 'Combat Banner' are the Sacred Object of the Unit," "A High Level of Vigilance is a Necessary Condition of Victory," and "The Great Liberation Mission of the Red Army." Besides this, a large number of leaflets and brochures were published for the *front* rank and file, in which the soldier's tasks in the offensive were laid out and which told about the methods of combating German tanks and assault guns, on the superiority in force of the Red Army and the Allies over the forces of fascist Germany. Five radio broadcasts were prepared on the following themes: "On the Soviet Army's Victories," "On the Hopelessness of the German Forces' Resistance," and "On the Superiority of Soviet Arms," etc. The best communists and Komsomol members were sent from the reserve to strengthen the party and Komsomol organizations in the rifle and machine guns companies before the battle. Corps and divisional political sections prepared before the battle the necessary amount of red flags, slogans, posters, and portraits for the front-line roads. The editorial offices of the divisional papers were provided with a two-month supply of paper and colors, and the divisional clubs with agitation posters, portraits, literature, and cultural supplies.

The result of the broadly employed party-political work among the troops and officers was a great offensive élan and the desire to more quickly get into the fight against the hated enemy. The best soldiers and officers, burning with the desire to enter the fighting as communists, put in applications to join the party. Guards Sgt. Ivchenko wrote in his application: "I request the battalion party organization to accept me as a member of the VKP(b),[5] because I want to go into the battle as a communist. I will ruthlessly avenge, not sparing any efforts for achieving victory over the enemy. If necessary, I will give my life for our Motherland." Sgt. Ivchenko died the death of the brave while carrying out his combat assignment, but justified the title of communist.

The organization and work of the Third Belorussian Front's rear services in the East Prussian operation. The characteristic features that influenced the organization and work of the Third Belorussian Front's rear in the East Prussian operation were as follows:

a) The *front's* operation was to develop along German territory, in East Prussia, which was the springboard for the Germans' invasion of the Baltic area. Preparatory work for outfitting this springboard (the erection of defensive structures and road construction) had begun long before the Great Patriotic War. There was information to the effect that while retreating, the enemy would destroy all crossings and bridges over streams and rivers, which East Prussia is full of.

These circumstances demanded that the rear deliver a large amount of ammunition and correctly employ the road and bridge construction units for restoring bridges and crossings.

b) The presence in the *front's* rear area of the great river barrier of the Neman River, and crossing it the single rail line on which the *front* received supplies, made it necessary for the *front's* rear

---

5   This stands for *Vsesoyuznaya Kommunisticheskaya Partiya (Bol'shevikov)* , or All-Union Communist Party (Bolsheviks), the pre-1952 name of the Communist Party of the Soviet Union

services to create large supplies of all kinds of military equipment to the west of the Neman River and to securely cover the railroad bridge over the river at Kaunas.

c) Winter in the Baltic area is usually unstable (frequent thaws alternating with snowfalls and black ice), which creates additional difficulties for the attacking forces' communications. This forced the workers in the *front* and army rear services to also be concerned over their communications.

Rear area tasks. The *front* rear services faced the following tasks:

1) To provide the troops with a sufficient amount of ammunition for breaking through the enemy's defensive zone and for the development of the entire operation.

2) Through all road and bridge restoration measures, to provide for the troops' planned offensive pace (10-12 kilometers per day) and to prevent breakdowns in the supply of fuel and food.

3) To organize the reliable guarding of bases and communications against saboteurs and the remnants of the enemy's defeated units, as well as against enemy air raids.

4) Taking into account the difficulties arising in winter and the possibility of significant losses while breaking through the enemy's permanent fortifications, to maximally move forward all the medical-evacuation means.

The basing of the *front* and armies. During the East Prussian operation the Third Belorussian Front was based on two railroad sections: 1) Vilnius—Kaunas—Kozlova-Ruda—Stallupönen; 2) Kozlova- Ruda—Kalwaria—Suwalki. Beginning on 1 February 1945 the *front* began to be based on the following railroad sections: 1) Kaunas—Kozlova-Ruda—Eydtkunen—Stallupönen—Gumbinnen—Insterburg—Tapiau; 2) Stallupönen—Tollmingkemen—Makunischken—Gross Rominten.

The *front* regulating station during the preparatory phase was located in Vilnius. There was a branch of the *front* regulating station in Palemonas. On 21 January 1945 the *front* regulating station was shifted to Palemonas and Kaunas, while the branch of the *front* regulating station shifted to Virbalis station. These *front* basing locales remained until the end of the operation.

The basing of the 39th, 5th and 28th armies was conducted along the Kaunas—Eydtkunen railroad section; the 2nd Guards and 31st armies were based on the following railroad sections: a) Kozlova-Ruda—Suwalki; b) Stallupönen—Schittkehmen. The 11th Guards Army's supply station was in Mariampole and its unloading station in Virbalis. During the operation (from 1 February 1945) the basing of the armies shifted: the 43rd, 39th, 11th Guards, 5th, and 28th armies to the Stallupönen—Insterburg—Tapiau railroad section and that of the 2nd Guards and 31st armies to the Stallupönen—Tollmingkemen—Gross Rominten railroad section.

The armies' supply and unloading stations were established as follows.

During the Preparatory Period

Army	Supply Station	Unloading Station
39th	Kozlova-Ruda	Vilkaviskis
5th	Pilwischki	Eydtkunen
28th	Mawruce	Olwita and Pillupenen
11th Guards	Mariampole	Virbalis
2nd Guards	Kalwaria	Nassawen
31st	Szestakow	Schittkehmen and Suwalki

During the Offensive Operation

Army	21-31.01.1945		From 01.02.1945	
	Supply Station	**Unloading Station**	**Supply Station**	**Unloading Station**
43rd	Stallupönen	–	Pogegen	Welau
39th	Vilkaviskis	Trakenen	Trakenen	Tapiau
11th Guards	Virbalis	Gross Beitchen	Gross Beitchen	Puschdorf
5th	Eydtkunen	Gumbinnen	Gubinnen	Waldhausen
28th	Olwita	Geritten	Jutschen	Norkitten
2nd Guards	Kalwaria	Tollmingkemen	Tollmingkemen	Insterburg
31st	No change	–	Makunischken	Insterburg

In light of the fact that all of the rear units and installations of the 43rd Army, which had arrived from the First Baltic Front, were echeloned to the northeast of Tilsit and that rebasing the army to Stallupönen station would create many difficulties, General Staff directive no. 117273 of 25 January 1945 shifted the 43rd Army's basing, as of 26 January 1945, to the Taurage—Pogegen (northeast of Tilsit) railroad section, with a capacity of 2-3 supply trains for this army along the Kedainiai (45 kilometers north of Kaunas)—Radviliskis—Taurage railroad section.

Railroad restoration. In order to more quickly exploit East Prussia's railroads following their liberation from the enemy, the Vilkaviskis—Stallupönen railroad section was to be developed as a transshipping base for transferring freight from the Soviet to the Western European gauge.

It was planned to complete all the work by 12 January 1945; that is, by the start of the operation. At this transshipping base it was planned to open on 15 January 1945 branches of the *front* depots: artillery, food and fuels and lubricants. Besides this, the chief of the *front's* military communications was given the task of organizing the restoration of the railroad from Stallupönen to Insterburg. The planned pace of restoration was to be seven kilometers per day. The *front* disposed of two railroad brigades (1st and 26th) for this task. In reality, the restoration of the railroads during the operation lagged considerably behind the pace of the attacking troops' advance, and the delivery of combat equipment to the troops was mainly carried out by auto transport from the supply stations and the unloading stations that had been set up by the start of the operation. The rebasing of the armies to the railroad stations indicated in the *front* directive of 21 January was accomplished only during 29 January-2 February 1945.

The Kaunas—Insterburg railroad sector was configured for the USSR gauge by 2 February 1945, while in Insterburg a transshipping based was outfitted for the conveyance of freight, traveling toward Allenstein, to European-gauge transport, which was being restored along the Insterburg—Bischdorf section since 4 February 1945.

In the Third Belorussian Front's rear area directive no. 002 of 1 February 1945, the chief of the *front's* military communications was assigned the task of organizing the alteration of the railroad gauge to the Soviet one along the Gumbinnen—Tapiau sector at a rate of 20-25 kilometers per day. By 3 February 1945 the railroad stations of Makunischken, Jutschen, Waldhausen, Norkitten, and Puschdorf were to be restored and developed, and the stations of Welau and Tapiau by 9 February 1945. All the indicated work was not completed according to schedule by the military communications service, because the alteration of the permanent way to metal railroad ties was very slow—four kilometers per day.

The capacity of the railroad sectors on which the Third Belorussian Front was based is shown in Table III/2.4.

Table III/3.4 Railroad Capacity in the Third Belorussian Front Zone

Railroad Sectors	Pairs of Trains Per Day
Vilnius—Kaunas	45
Kaunas—Kozlova-Ruda	37
Kozlova-Ruda—Virbalis	27
Virbalis—Stallupönen	24
Kozlova-Ruda—Suwalki	14
Stallupönen—Schittkemen	19

The capacity of the railroad sectors did not fall over the operation's 23 days and even rose by a few pairs of trains.

Such a capacity by the rail network enabled the *front* to accumulate the assigned supplies beforehand and to uninterruptedly feed the *front* with combat equipment throughout the operation.

By the start of the operation the 11th Guards Army's rear area was located in the 28th Army's rear areas, and partially in that of the 5th Army. With the beginning of the offensive, the 11th Guards Army was to move in the *front's* second echelon, behind the 5th and 28th armies, in the following zone: from the right, Kybartai—Kussen—Kaukern; from the left, Millunen—excluding Gumbinnen—Georgenburg.

The depth of the rear areas of the army and troop rear and the lengthening of the supply links was insignificant during the preparatory period. For example, from the rear boundaries of the army rear areas to the rear boundaries of the troop rear was 50-80 kilometers; from the unloading stations to the division depots (DOP) was 10-25 kilometers; from the forward branches of the army depots in the open air to the division depots (DOP) was 10-20 kilometers.

The boundary of the *front* rear area with the army rear areas was established on 21 January 1945 along the line Jurbarkas (Jurburg)—Schirwindt—Vilkaviskis—Kalwaria—Lazdijai—Sonichi. From 1 February 1945 this boundary was shifted to the west and ran along the line Ragnit—Gross Trakenen—Tollmingkemen—Treuburg—Gollubin. The latter boundary remained without change until the end of operations.

Boundary lines between the armies changed from 21 January 1945, when the 11th Guards Army was committed into the first line (19 January 1945) and the 43rd Army was subordinated to the Third Belorussian Front.

According to the Third Belorussian Front's rear area directive no. 002 of 1 February 1945, the boundary lines between the armies were reestablished.

In this situation, the depth of the *front* rear area reached 200 kilometers. The depth of the army rear (from the army rear boundaries to the rear boundaries of the troop rear) reached 100-120 kilometers; from the unloading stations to the division depots—100-140 kilometers; from the advance branches of the army depots (artillery, fuels and lubricants, food) in the open air to the division depots (DOP)—15-25 kilometers.

Thus the *front* and army rear areas during the preparatory period were moved significantly closer to the troops and could provide for the attacking troops without changing their base stations before the end of the operation's first stage. During the operation the lengthening of the army rear along the *front's* right wing reached 150 kilometers, although this did not lead to breaks in the supply of the attacking troops.

Automobile roads. A developed network of paved and dirt roads in the area of combat operations fully met the requirements of the armies. Each army operating along the shock axis had two roads (one from the supply station and the other from the unloading station).

Besides this, the chief of the *front's* road directorate's forces outfitted and maintained the following automobile roads: 1) Vilnius—Kaunas—Mariampole—Vilkaviskis—Stallupönen; 2) Mariampole—Suwalki; 3) Oskiski—Pilviskiai; 4) Turgalaukis—Keturvloki—Potiche—Kunigiskes—Vistytis; 5) Kalwaria—Vistytis. Heating stations and technical assistance posts were set up along these roads. The outfitting of these routes with road signs and indicators was completed by 31 December 1944. By this date all of the roads had been restored to service. All equipment for clearing the roads of snow had been put in order—repaired and distributed along the most important routes. The quality of the army and *front* roads enabled us to move our auto transport at speeds of 20-40 kilometers per hour.

There were 24 road construction and bridge construction battalions for repairing roads and restoring bridges within the *front*, which completely met the requirements of the *front* and armies during the Third Belorussian Front's advance to the west.

The restoration of normal traffic along all the dirt roads was chiefly delayed by the restoration of high-water bridges with a capacity of 60 tons over the Auksine (Juenischken, 11 kilometers southwest of Insterburg) River; the Ilme River (near Obelisken), the Svin River (near Pentlak and Nordenburg), as well as over streams and canals. In all, during the operation it was necessary to restore about 16 bridges. Upon the restoration of the above-named bridges, the delivery routes shortened significantly, as we no longer had to make long detours.

Auto transport. By the start of the operation, the Third Belorussian Front contained one auto brigade, 15 independent auto transport battalions and three independent fuel delivery companies.

The auto transport's capacity by armies is as follows: 551 tons in the 39th Army; 530 tons in the 5th Army; 712 tons in the 28th Army; 618 tons in the 11th Guards Army; 347 tons in the 2nd Guards Army, and; 491 tons in the 31st Army.

The overall number of motor vehicles in the army and *front* auto units was 3,862, of which 395 were undergoing repairs. Besides this, the 23rd Auto Regiment, numbering 587 vehicles, from the High Command Reserve had been attached to the *front*. Thus in all 4,054 vehicles were at the disposal of our larger units, with an overall capacity of 9,975 tons. Given the length of our communications during the preparatory period, this enabled us to deliver 19,950 tons daily in two trips, which amounted to:

One day's ration of food and forage—2,658 tons;
0.5 of a fuel refill—1,556 tons;
0.5 combat loads of munitions—10,105 tons;
Other freight—5,631 tons

The technical readiness of the *front* and army auto transport by the start of the operation stood at 90 percent, while army transport stood at 85 percent readiness. During the Third Belorussian Front's offensive operation the army and *front* auto transport played an exclusive role in delivering combat equipment and food to the troops, as well as in evacuating the sick and wounded, because the pace of restoring the railroads lagged significantly behind the attacking troops' pace of advance and the armies' rebasing was delayed until 29 January.

Despite the intensive work over the course of nearly a month, the *front* and army auto park did not shrink, but grew by 267 motor vehicles, mainly captured ones. The technical state of the *front* auto park during this period worsened somewhat, while it actually rose in army transport and was at 88 percent readiness for the entire auto park. This may be explained by the presence of good roads in the *front's* zone and the raising of the drivers' qualifications.

Front supplies. The plan called for the creation of the following materiel reserves by 31 December 1944.

Ammunition

(Among the troops and in army and *front* depots; in combat loads for the chief calibers)

82mm mortars—4
120mm mortars—5
76mm PA-27 regimental artillery rounds—4
76mm PA-43 regimental artillery rounds—4
76mm divisional artillery rounds—4
122mm howitzer rounds—4
122mm artillery rounds—4.5
152mm rounds—4.5
203mm howitzer rounds—3

Fuels and Lubricants

In rifle units—2 refills
In tank units—4 refills
At army depots—2 refills
At *front* depots—1 refill

Food and Forage

With the troops—7 days' rations
At army depots—8-10 days' rations of food and forage
At *front* depots—15 days' rations of food and forage

Thus, on the whole the *front* was supposed to have 4-5 combat loads of munitions, 5-7 refills of fuel, 30 days' rations of food and forage by the start of the operation.

The actual provision of the Third Belorussian Front's forces by the start of the operation (13 January 1945) is shown in Table III/3.5.

Table III/3.5 Provision of Supplies for the Third Belorussian Front, 13 January 1945

Item	Front Depots	In the Armies Operating Along the Main Axis					
		39th Army		5th Army		28th Army	
		Among Troops	In Depots	Among Troops	In Depots	Among Troops	In Depots
A. Ammunition (in Combat Loads)							
82mm mortar	1.5	2.0	0.8	2.0	1.9	2.0	1.5
120mm mortar	2.5	2.2	1.4	1.9	1.8	2.0	1.8
76mm regimental artillery	1.5	2.2	0.9	2.5	1.0	2.2	0.8
76mm division artillery	0.7	1.9	0.7	1.9	0.6	2.1	0.7
122mm howitzer	0.6	2.2	1.6	2.0	0.5	1.9	1.0
122mm artillery	1.6	2.0	1.3	2.0	2.3	2.0	2.0
152mm artillery	1.4	2.2	1.5	1.9	2.1	2.0	2.0
203mm artillery	3.8	–	–	2.0	0.7	2.2	–

Item	In the Armies Operating Along the Main Axis		In the Armies Operating Along a Secondary Axis			
	11th Guards Army		2nd Guards Army		31st Army	
	Among Troops	In Depots	Among Troops	In Depots	Among Troops	In Depots
A. Ammunition (in combat loads)						
82mm mortar	1.1	2.2	1.6	1.5	1.3	0.9
120mm mortar	2.4	0.7	0.6	2.8	1.5	1.8
76mm regimental artillery	1.1	0.9	1.7	0.3	1.0	0.4
76mm division artillery	2.0	0.5	1.3	0.3	1.5	0.3
122mm howitzer	2.4	0.1	1.0	0.3	1.0	0.5
122mm artillery	1.9	1.4	1.5	1.4	2.0	0.3
152mm artillery	2.4	0.8	1.5	1.5	1.8	0.2
203mm artillery	1.6	0.9	–	–	–	–

Item	Front Depots	In the Armies Operating Along the Main Axis					
		39th Army		5th Army		28th Army	
		Among Troops	In Depots	Among Troops	In Depots	Among Troops	In Depots
B. Fuel (in refills)							
Auto Fuel	0.6	2.6	0.6	2.3	0.7	2.5	0.4
Diesel Fuel	2.1	1.5	0.8	1.1	0.9	1.0	0.4
KB-70 Aviation Fuel	3.2	1.7	2.0	2.8	1.8	1.6	1.3
B-70 Aviation Fuel	8.1	2.9 refills in the air units. In all, 11 refills					

Item	In the Armies Operating Along the Main Axis		In the Armies Operating Along a Secondary Axis			
	11th Guards Army		2nd Guards Army		31st Army	
	Among Troops	In Depots	Among Troops	In Depots	Among Troops	In Depots
B. Fuel (in Refills)						
Auto Fuel	2.9	0.7	3.0	0.2	3.4	1.2
Diesel Fuel	2.0	1.7	1.7	0.8	3.5	3.0
KB-70 Aviation Fuel	3.0	0.9	1.7	2.8	3.4	2.4
B-70 Aviation Fuel	2.9 refills in the air units. In all, 11 refills					

Item	Front Depots	In the Armies Operating Along the Main Axis					
		39th Army		5th Army		28th Army	
		Among Troops	In Depots	Among Troops	In Depots	Among Troops	In Depots
C. Food and Forage (in Daily Rations)							
Flour and Rusks	17.2	6.5	6.5	12.6	11.8	8.0	12.2
Groats and Macaroni	9.9	8.7	0.2	12.2	6.7	12.5	2.4
Meat Products	2.1	10.0	6.6	6.5	2.2	7.5	0.8
Fats	6.9	9.3	3.8	8.5	5.4	10.9	8.2
Sugar	43.8	12.5	5.4	12.0	5.7	12.3	3.0
Tobacco	1.3	1.3	3.8	3.5	1.0	5.2	0.5
Oats and Mixed Fodder	4.8	5.7	2.5	2.8	1.4	5.0	1.1
Hay	–	6.1	1.8	12.2	6.4	14.6	16.9

Item	In the Armies Operating Along the Main Axis		In the Armies Operating Along a Secondary Axis			
	11th Guards Army		2nd Guards Army		31st Army	
	Among Troops	In Depots	Among Troops	In Depots	Among Troops	In Depots
C. Food and Forage (in Daily Rations)						
Flour and Rusks	5.6	7.7	12.6	4.1	8.4	9.8
Groats and Macaroni	4.8	7.9	10.1	8.3	7.1	3.0
Meat Products	4.2	4.6	5.0	7.3	3.6	2.1
Fats	8.0	6.2	6.6	11.1	12.6	6.0
Sugar	9.4	15.1	8.2	5.5	9.3	14.0
Tobacco	0.8	1.1	0.9	4.0	4.5	2.0
Oats and Mixed Fodder	2.4	0.8	4.4	3.6	3.9	–
Hay	9.9	19.8	4.7	17.8	13.6	23.6

Thus by the start of the operation the *front* disposed of reserves within the limits of established norms for the main types of combat means.

The provisioning of the troops during the operation with all the necessary means for fighting unfolded uninterruptedly, which is chiefly explained by the auto transport's good work and the comparatively rapid restoration of the dirt and paved roads, as well as the systematic arrival of freight from the interior and the comparatively normal expenditure of all kinds of means during the operation.

Data on the expenditure and renewal of supplies during the operation is shown in tables III/3.6 and III/3.7.

Table III/3.6 Expenditure of Supplies by the Third Belorussian Front

Rounds	By 13.01. 1945	Arrived During Operation	Expended			Total	By the Close of the Operation
			13-20.01. 1945	20/01- 01/02.1945	01-15.02. 1945		
A. Ammunition (in Combat Loads)							
82mm mortar	3.7	0.27	1.17	0.75	1.12	3.04	1.3
120mm mortar	5.2	1.0	1.75	0.77	1.36	3.88	2.8
76mm regimental artillery (1927)	2.5	0.85	0.61	0.53	0.65	1.79	2.8
76mm regimental artillery(1943)	2.4	0.87	0.4	0.31	0.54	1.25	1.2
76mm division artillery	2.5	1.05	1.0	0.51	0.73	2.24	1.3
122mm howitzer	2.3	1.01	1.73	0.78	1.1	3.61	0.6
122mm artillery	4.0	0.9	1.49	0.51	0.94	2.94	2.5
152mm howitzer	6.2	–	2.0	0.74	1.08	3.82	4.1
152mm artillery (1937)	4.1	0.98	2.32	0.93	1.11	4.36	1.5
203mm howitzer (1931)	5.7	–	2.34	0.3	0.37	3.01	2.9

Type	By 13.01. 1945	Arrived During Operation	Expended			Total	By the Close of the Operation
			13-20.01. 1945	20.01- 01.02.1945	01-15.02. 1945		
B. Fuel (Numerator—*front* refills; Denominator–tons)							
High Octane	12.3	10.4	4.8	3.2	3.4	11.4	8.4
	7,046	6,929	3,215	2,121	2,274	7,610	6,365
B-70 and KB-70	7.8	4.0	0.9	2.2	2.0	5.1	6.5
Aviation Fuel	2,291	1,144	265	639	569	1,473	1,962
Gasoline	3.8	7.1	1.2	3.8	2.8	7.8	2.8
	10,645	21,369	3,488	11,185	8,430	23,103	8,411
Diesel Fuel	4.4	2.3	0.5	1.7	1.0	3.2	3.4
	5,031	2,734	529	1,975	1,202	3,706	4,059

Note. In the section "By the end of the operation" the *front* combat load and the *front* refill are calculated according to the *front's* new makeup, which had changed significantly by the close of the operation.

Table III/3.7 Provision of Food and Forage (in Daily Rations) for the Third Belorussian Front

Products	Size of Daily Ration on 10.01.1945(in tons)	Daily Rations in the Front, 10.01.1945	Size of Daily Ration on 15.02.1945 (in tons)	Daily Rations in the Front, 15.02.1945
Bread, Flour, Rusks	425	35.7	475	27.6
Groats and Macaroni	142	30.8	146	15
Meat	147	13	154	38.5
Fats	35.7	29.6	35.2	19.3
Sugar	29.6	67.5	31.8	63.6
Tobacco	20.1	9	21.4	8
Oats	364	15	390	18.5
Hay	476	26	547	23

Products	During the Operation	
	Delivered from the Center	Prepared on Site
Bread, Flour, Rusks	21	9
Groats and Macaroni	12	10
Meat	42	20
Fats	18	9
Sugar	20	13
Tobacco	36	–
Oats	34	6
Hay	–	34

The table (no. III/3.7) dealing with the provisioning of food and forage shows that despite the enemy's driving away of the local population from East Prussia and the removal of significant reserves of food, nevertheless the *front* managed during the operation to prepare and employ from captured stocks the following: nine daily rations of flour and fats, ten daily rations of groats, 20 daily rations of meat, 35 daily rations of vegetables, 13 daily rations of sugar, six daily rations of oats, and 34 daily rations of hay, which significantly eased the troops' provisioning, particularly with vegetables, hay, meat, and partially with oats.

Medical support for the operation. In order that the units not be burdened with rebasing the *front* medical-evacuation establishments during the operation, the *front's* and the armies' medical-evacuation establishments were moved as close as possible to the front line. For example, by 31 December 1944 a forward hospital base (10,000-12,000 beds) had been deployed in Eydtkunen. An auxiliary *front* hospital base (8,000 beds) had been deployed by this time in Mariampole. The 39th Army's hospital base (6,000 beds) was to be deployed by 31 December 1944 in Vilkaviskis. It was planned to evacuate the wounded from the 5th and 28th armies, as well as the 11th Guards Army to the forward hospital base in Eydtkunen and Kybartai. At the same time, the movement of wounded was to be carried out with army transport. The 2nd Guards, 39th and 31st armies were to evacuate their wounded to their own hospital bases.

The main *front* hospital base of 42,785 beds was deployed in Kaunas and Vilnius. The evacuation of wounded to the main hospital base was to be carried out with *front* transportation.

The *front* medical directorate disposed of 19 railroad mobile installations, with a capacity of 6,650 men, and seven military-medical trains for 4,186 men for evacuating the sick and wounded from army hospitals.

The bed network in the *front's* and armies' hospital bases grew systematically during the operation. While on 13 January 1945 the *front* disposed of 105,985 authorized beds (of these 43,200 were subordinated to the armies and 62,785 to the *front*), on 1 February 1945 there were 50,200 army beds and 63,785 *front* beds, for a total of 113,985 authorized beds.

All of the beds in the *front* were not fully employed, which meant that the armies and the *front* always had a reserve of hospitals to move forward, closer to the troops, because the pace of the advance was significant, particularly in the 39th, 11th Guards and 5th armies. The capacity of the hospitals to admit the wounded and sick did not exceed the hospital bases' capacity throughout the operation.

Veterinary evacuation. In order to admit wounded and sick horses from the armies, the *front* deployed two *front* veterinary hospitals: *front* veterinary hospital no. 397 in Pilni (three kilometers southeast of Pilviskiai) for the 39th, 11th Guards and 5th armies; *front* veterinary hospital no. 309 in Kusliski (one kilometer west of Kalwaria) for the 28th, 2nd Guards and 31st armies.

The *front's* remaining two veterinary hospitals—no. 258 in Saltupe and no. 402 in Koshedori—completed the treatment of the horses remaining there, after which they were to move forward behind the attacking troops. The overall capacity of the *front* veterinary hospitals was 1,200 stalls. 2,500 stalls had been deployed by the start of the operation. During the operation the deployed stalls in the *front's* veterinary hospitals were not fully occupied, thanks to which they were able to move forward behind the attacking armies.

Evacuation of prisoners. The evacuation of prisoners from the army reception posts was to be carried out to *front* reception posts (SPV) as follows: the 39th and 5th armies were to evacuate their prisoners to SPV no. 2 in Naumiestis, and the 11th and 2nd guards and 28th armies to SPV no. 4 in Kybartai. The 31st Army was to evacuate its prisoners to Suwalki to *front* prisoner gathering post no. 1. From 24 January 1945 the prisoner gathering posts were shifted to the west. SPV no. 2 was deployed in Zillen for the 43rd, 11th Guards and 39th armies; SPV no. 4 was shifted to Stallupönen for the 2nd Guards, 5th and 28th armies, while SPV no. 1, to which the 31st Army's prisoners were being evacuated, remained in place, in Suwalki. *Front* POW camp no. 24 was moved from the Kaunas area to Kybartai.

From 3 February 1945 this camp began to receive prisoners in Insterburg, where it remained until the end of the operation. By 3 February 1945 prisoner collection posts had also shifted to the west and had deployed as follows: SPV no. 2, for the 43rd and 39th armies, in Goldbach; SPV no. 1, for the 11th Guards, 5th, 28th, 2nd Guards, and 31st armies, in Allenburg.

Thus the frequent movements of the *front's* prisoner collection posts enabled the armies to quickly unload their prisoners and move their prisoner gathering-delivering posts to the area of the division distributing posts.

Conclusions

1. The Third Belorussian Front's rear services in the East Prussian operation successfully coped with their task. The provisioning of the operation with ammunition, fuel and food unfolded without breaks.

Despite the significant expenditure of ammunition, especially that of heavy shells—3-4 combat loads for 30 days of the operation—the *front* nevertheless ensured that the supply of ammunition among the troops remained at the level of 1.5-2 combat loads.

The expenditure of fuel slightly exceeded the delivery of fuels and lubricants from the center; for example: by 1-1.5 refills of aviation fuel, 0.6 refills of gasoline, and 0.9 refills of diesel fuel.

2. The correct distribution of road construction and bridge construction units along routes, as well as the good work of these units during the operation, enabled the *front* to shift its rear establishments to new communications in a timely manner and thus move all food depots and hospital bases closer to the troops. The construction of bridges, chiefly high-water ones with a capacity of 60 tons, somewhat delayed the overall pace of restoring communications for 6-9 days, although this did not affect the delivery of supplies, because the road network enabled us to us detours.

3. The organization of the rear and the delivery system that formed the basis of the Third Belorussian Front's rear organization in the East Prussian operation corresponded to the *front* command's plan.

The network of paved and dirt roads along the axis of the main attack enabled us to deliver supplies by auto transport, with a gap of more than 150 kilometers from the supply stations.

4. Despite the low pace of railroad restoration, the high capacity of railroad sections restored earlier enabled the *front* to successfully cope with the task of delivery and evacuation throughout the entire operation.

5. Our auto transport's good technical condition, the developed road network in the *front's* offensive sector and the drivers' level of training enabled the *front* to conduct the operation at a significant remove of the *front's* right-wing forces from the railroads upon which they were based, as well as along the remaining armies' sectors, given the lag in the pace of restoring the railroads from the pace of the *front's* advance.

6. The correct distribution of medical-evacuation units and establishments enabled the *front* to carry out the rapid evacuation of wounded and sick soldiers to the rear in winter, while managing to avoid personnel losses along the evacuation routes.

The regrouping and concentration of forces. For a certain time the disposition of the *front's* forces following the autumn fighting of 1944 remained pretty much the same.

At the end of December 1944 and at the beginning of January 1945, according to the operational plan, the Third Belorussian Front's headquarters strengthened the center, primarily by contracting the armies' boundaries, bringing in reinforcements, and also by creating a powerful *front* breakthrough development echelon. On 2 January 1945 the 11th Guards Army was shifted from the *front's* first echelon to the second and concentrated in the area east of the area Stallupönen—Pillupenen—Kybartai and the 2nd Guards Army moved into its sector. The 11th Guards Army received was reinforced with men and materiel. The 1st and 2nd guards tank corps were moved up to this area.

In order to reduce the front of the 5th Army, which was to launch the main attack, the 39th Army's front was extended from Pilkallen to Schaaren. The 94th Rifle Corps, which had earlier been part of the 31st Army, was moved into this area. The other armies' boundaries did not change.

The correlation of the sides' forces. By the start of the operation, following the regrouping of our forces and the concentration of our reserves, the overall correlation of forces within the confines of the *front* was as shown in Table III/3.8.

Table III/3.8 Correlation of Forces in the Third Belorussian Front's Zone

Men and Materiel	The Enemy		Our Forces		Correlation
	Total	Per km of Front	Total	Per km of Front	
Infantry (rifle) Divisions	14	1 per 12 km	54	one per 3 km	3.7:1
Men	135,480	797	479,331	2,819	3.5:1
Machine Guns	8,174	48	16,479	97	2:1
Mortars	1,605	9.4**	5,078	30	3.2:1
Anti-Tank Guns	1,060	6	2,080	12.2	2:1
Artillery	1,432	8.4***	4,496	26.4	3.1:1
Tanks and Self-Propelled Guns	367	2.1	1,544	9	4.3:1
Aircraft	670	–	1,350****	–	2:1

* This calculation of the correlation of forces excludes various enemy special units and subunits (fortress, naval, security, anti-aircraft and searchlight, sapper-construction, worker's units, etc.), which were employed by the German command during combat operations in defending East Prussia. Taking these into account, the overall number of enemy men and materiel facing the Third Belorussian Front was as follows: up to 25 divisions, 340,000 men, 12,000 machine guns, 2,100 anti-tank guns, and 1,800 field artillery pieces.

** Including six-barreled mortars.

*** Not counting regimental artillery.

**** The correlation of forces does not include aircraft from the 3rd and 18th air armies, which it was planned to employ in the Third Belorussian Front's operation.

Table III/3.9 Correlation of Forces Along the Axis of the Main Attack of the Third Belorussian Front

Men and Materiel	The Enemy		Our Forces		Corrleation
	Total	Per km of Front	Total	Per km of Front	
Infantry (rifle) Divisions	3	1 per 8 km	18	1 per 1.3 km	6:1
Men	31,440	1,310	159,542	6,648	5:1
Machine Guns	864	36	5,522	230	6.4:1
Mortars	168	7	1,400	58	8.3:1
Anti-Tank Guns	310	13	958	39	3:1
Artillery	298	12.4	3,470	145	11.7:1
Tanks and Self-Propelled Guns	177	7.4	1,238	51*	7:1

* 30 tanks and self-propelled guns per kilometer without the tank corps.

The correlation of forces along the axis of the main attack (the 24-kilometer sector Wiltauten—the railroad north of Kalpakin) is shown in Table III/2.9.

Thus, out of the 170 kilometers of the overall front, it was planned to break through along a 24-kilometer sector. Along the axis of the main attack; that is, the sector Wiltauten—Kalpakin, there were concentrated 27 rifle divisions,[6] or 50 percent of the total, 1,238 tanks and self-propelled guns, or 80 percent, 3,470 field guns (division and corps artillery and high command reserve artillery), or 77 percent.

---

6   Including those of the 11th Guards Army; 18 without them.

The superiority in force achieved over the enemy enabled the *front* to successfully resolve its assigned tasks.

The *front's* operational-combat formation. Of six combined-arms armies, five were in the *front's* first operational echelon. The *front's* second echelon consisted of the 11th Guards Army and two tank corps, slated for developing the breakthrough.

The corps were located side by side in the armies. Each army commander had a rifle division apiece in his reserve. The rifle corps organized their combat formation, as a rule, in two echelons. The rifle divisions and rifle regiments, for the most part, also organized their combat formations in two echelons.

The *front's* tank brigades and regiments, as well as self-propelled artillery, attacked within the infantry's first-echelon combat formations and only partially (mostly reserves) were they employed to support the second echelons.

The presence of powerful second echelons in our troops' combat formations was to support the development of the success achieved in breaking through and in transforming the tactical breakthrough into an operational one.

The troops' occupation of their jumping-off positions. On 12 January the formations and units of the *front's* shock group began to occupy their jumping-off positions for the offensive. The day before, on January 11, the artillery had completed its deployment and the tanks had occupied their intermediate positions. Simultaneous with the troops' occupation of their jumping-off positions, the army commanders and the *front* commander left for their observation posts.

During the night of 12-13 January the forces of the Third Belorussian Front were ready for the offensive and awaited the order for the start of the artillery preparation.

The Second Belorussian Front

Studying the enemy. The *front* commander laid down the following tasks regarding intelligence work.

Troop reconnaissance and reconnaissance by the combat arms and services was to illuminate the outline of the forward edge of the enemy's defense, the disposition of his forces and weaponry, the organization of his fire system, as well as the degree of engineering preparation of the enemy's defensive zone.

Air reconnaissance was to be employed to uncover the main zone of the enemy's defensive system and in the depth as far as the Vistula River, as well as to uninterruptedly observe the concentration areas of the enemy's tanks, artillery and troops.

Radio reconnaissance was to observe the headquarters of the enemy's units and formations facing the *front* and the arrival of the enemy's new combat formations to the front from the depth.

Agent reconnaissance was to be conducted to a depth of up to 500 kilometers and to take in all of the more important rail and dirt road junctions, the most important concentration areas for the enemy's reserves, possible lines along which the enemy might try to organize a defense, with the help of units retreating from the front and those reserves arriving from the depth.

As a result of a prolonged and comprehensive study of the enemy during the preparatory stage of the operation, our intelligence managed to sufficiently accurately uncover the disposition of the enemy's forces, both in the tactical defensive zone and in the operational depth as far as the Vistula River, and to also determine his fire system and the degree of engineering preparation of the first defensive line.

However, our intelligence, mainly human, yielded exaggerated information as to the system, strength and character of the engineering preparation in the area to the west and northwest of Mlawa and as far as the Vistula River. In the meantime, this exaggerated data served as the justification for our artillery maneuver (the concentration of up to three artillery divisions in the 2nd

Shock Army's sector by the army's arrival at the frontier fortified zone). Such an artillery regrouping proved excessive, because the frontier fortified zone was actually shallow, was poorly outfitted with permanent structures, and its construction had not yet been completed.

Along with this, our intelligence yielded incorrect information as to the absence of food and forage in the territory occupied by the enemy. Therefore, the decision was made to create 30-day stores of food and forage, which was linked to the excessive overloading of the railroad and automobile transport system, which was intensively enough engaged without that.

During the course of the offensive itself, our intelligence repeatedly relayed precise information on the enemy's activities. For example, the 50th Army's intelligence uncovered in a timely manner the time and direction of the enemy's withdrawal in front of the army. Air reconnaissance and human intelligence established in the beginning of January the concentration of the *Grossdeutschland* Panzer Division, which had been transferred there from Königsberg, in the Myszyniec area.

Artillery support for the operation. The artillery's tasks. In *front* directive No. 00110/op of 29 December 1944, the *front's* artillery was assigned the following objectives:

a)   to create an artillery group of forces along the shock axes in accordance with the *front* directive's instructions;
b)   to carry out the artillery's concentration and deployment into its combat formations, while observing all concealment measures;
c)   the artillery's main task was to support the breakthrough of the enemy's entire tactical defense zone and the subsequent accompaniment of the infantry and the breakthrough development echelon throughout the entire depth of the operation;
d)   during the pursuit, the heavy artillery was to be kept in the armies' reserve, in readiness to deploy for breaking through the subsequent lines of the enemy's defense;
e)   the armies' plans should call for the reliable cover of the troops in their jumping-off positions for the offensive and the uninterrupted accompaniment of the troops with anti-aircraft reinforcements;
f)   planning the artillery offensive in the 48th, 2nd Shock, 65th, and 70th armies should be carried out in accordance with the instructions of the *front* artillery commander, while the planning of the artillery offensive in the 3rd Army according to the plan of the army commander, followed by its confirmation by the *front* commander.

It is necessary to note that the 3rd Army was to be reinforced during the breakthrough of the enemy's main defensive zone by the 49th Army's artillery, because, according to the operational plan, two of the 49th Army's corps were to be located in the second echelon and committed into the breach that the 3rd Army was supposed to create along its right flank. In accordance with this, the 49th Army temporarily transferred the following artillery units to the 3rd Army: the 143rd Artillery Brigade and the rifle divisions' 354th, 500th, 693rd, 945th, and 948th artillery regiments. Then, as can be seen from the artillery distribution among the armies, the 317th Heavy Caliber Artillery Battalion (six 280mm guns) was attached to the 70th Army, along the front of which were noted up to four pillboxes.

In general, the artillery's distribution among the armies was carried out in complete accord with the operational plan and took into account the situation in which the armies had to operate.

The disposition of the artillery. The artillery's disposition in the armies along the shock axes is shown in the table at the end of this work. As can be seen from this table, ADD (long-range artillery), AR (destruction artillery), guards mortar and anti-aircraft army artillery groups were created, as well as anti-tank reserves.

In their turn, the following groups were created in the corps: a) a corps artillery group for the suppression of the most important strong points in the corps' breakthrough sector, for suppressing strong points along boundaries, for securing the corps' flanks, for preventing the arrival of the enemy's reserves, and for repelling enemy counterattacks, and b) a corps counter-mortar group for engaging the enemy's mortar batteries and rocket-firing installations.

The following were in the divisions: a) divisional artillery groups; b) regimental artillery groups in the regiments. Besides this, guns were detached for firing over open sights (not counting 45mm and 57mm guns). For example

- 113 guns in the 3rd Army, or 19 guns per kilometer of front;
- 216 guns in the 2nd Shock Army, or 36 guns per kilometer of front;
- 50 guns in the 70th Army, or 17 guns per kilometer of front.

In general, the presence of large artillery masses in the *front* made possible the combat organization of the artillery that was adopted, in which the army, corps and division commanders had in their hands sufficient artillery weapons to influence the course of the battle, while at the same time sufficient artillery was detached to the regimental artillery groups for direct infantry support.

The artillery density along the army breakthrough zones is shown in the following table.

Table III/3.10 Artillery Density within Army Breakthrough Zones of the Second Belorussian Front

Army	Breakthrough Sector (in km)	Mortars (82mm and 120mm)	Guns (76mm and higher)	Tubes	
				Total	Per Kilometer
3rd	6	735	1,052	1,787	298
48th	6	591	731	1,322	220
2nd Shock	6	715	945	1,660	276
65th	7	486	891	1,377	196
70th	3	144	392	536	179
Total	28	2,671	4,011	6,682	238

Thus an average artillery density of up to 238 guns and mortars per kilometer of front was created, with the greatest artillery density (298 tubes) in the 3rd Army and in the 2nd Shock Army (276 tubes per kilometer of front). Such a great massing of artillery along the shock axes fully guaranteed the breakthrough of the German defense.

The planning of the artillery offensive. The 48th, 2nd Shock, 65th, and 70th armies were to carry out an artillery preparation according to the following plan:

1. First, a 15-minute artillery onslaught by all our artillery, mortars and guards mortars against the enemy's artillery and mortars and throughout the entire tactical depth of his defense.
2. Then a period for destroying and suppressing targets was planned for 60 minutes, in which it was planned to carry out suppression throughout the entire tactical depth of the enemy's defense.
3. Following the destruction and suppression period, it was planned to conduct an artillery onslaught, from H-ten minutes before the attack up to the time of attack, with all the artillery and mortars against the enemy's first, second and, partially, third trenches, communications trenches and strong points. If by that time the first trench was occupied by our infantry, it was planned to conduct an artillery onslaught against the second and third trenches.
4. Along with this, the army artillery DD (long-range) groups and the counter-mortar groups were to conduct a second and third artillery onslaught against the enemy's artillery and mortar batteries:

the second onslaught would be from H-40 to H-35 minutes before the attack, and the third onslaught from H-ten minutes before the attack to H+five minutes after the attack.

It was planned to accompany the infantry and tank attack with a rolling barrage. A double rolling barrage was planned to a depth of 1.5-2 kilometers. The main boundaries of the rolling barrage were, as a rule, the trenches. Intermediate lines were planned every 100 meters.

Upon the completion of the rolling barrage, the accompaniment of the infantry and tanks was organized according to the method of the consecutive concentration of fire throughout the entire tactical depth of the enemy's defense.

The 3rd Army's plan for the artillery offensive was distinguished by certain features, because it was compiled with a consideration for other terrain conditions and the expected greater enemy resistance. The schedule for the artillery offensive was as follows:

> From H-15 minutes to H hour, a 15-minute fire onslaught was planned.
> From H hour to H+15 minutes the suppression and destruction of the enemy's firing points and personnel would continue in the depth of his defense and along the flanks of our attacking infantry.
> From H+15 to H+25 minutes a second fire onslaught was planned against the enemy's strong points facing the attack, and along the flanks.

The accompaniment of the infantry and tanks was to be carried out according to the method of successively concentrating fire.

In accordance with the *front* commander's instructions, the first-echelon divisions were to detach forward battalions. Following the first artillery's 15-minute fire onslaught, these battalions were to attack and seize the first, and then the second, trenches, if the enemy could not organize resistance. In connection with this, an order by the *front* command foresaw three variations to the artillery preparation schedule.

The first variation would kick in if the forward battalions failed to achieve a success. In this case, the artillery preparation would continue according to schedule.

The second variation would kick in if the forward battalions occupied the first enemy trench. The artillery preparation would then continue according to schedule, with the exception of the suppression of targets in the first trench.

The third variation would kick in if the forward battalions occupied the first and second trenches. The artillery preparation would cease and the artillery would switch to accompanying the infantry with a rolling barrage.

The employment of armored and mechanized troops. The distribution of tanks and self-propelled guns (SU) among the armies is shown in Table III/3.11 (below).

Thus the main mass of tanks and self-propelled artillery was employed in the attack sectors of the *front's* shock groups. It should be noted that among the direct infantry support (NPP) tank groups there was more self-propelled artillery (58 percent) than tanks (42 percent), which somewhat reduced the breakthrough strength of the NPP tank groups.

Assigning tasks to the tanks. Direct infantry support tanks (NPP) were to capture the indicated lines along with the infantry, hold them and support their consolidation by our infantry. In some cases, following the infantry's seizure of the enemy's first fortified zone, the tank brigades attached to the rifle corps were to race ahead in order to seize the enemy's rear line and hold it until the arrival of our infantry's main forces, preventing the enemy from organizing a defense here.

Table III/3.11 Distribution of Tanks & Self-Propelled Guns, Second Belorussian Front

Army and Formation	Tanks	Self-Propelled Guns	Total Tanks and Self-Propelled Guns
3rd Army	53	106	159
48th Army	127	83	210
2nd Shock Army	96	83	179
65th Army	71	84	155
70th Army	–	83	83
50th Army	–	25	25
49th Army	20	33	53
8th Mech Corps	211	42	253
8th Gds Tank Corps	210	42	252
1st Gds Tank Corps	60	175	235
5th Gds Tank Army	345	240	585
Total	1,193	996	2,189

Combat assignments for the mechanized and tank corps were assigned by the *front* commander.

The 8th Mechanized Corps received the following assignment: from the Makow area it was to move into the breach along the sector of the 48th Army's 53rd and 42rd rifle corps, prevent the enemy from occupying his intermediate lines, and by the close of the first day reach the Laguni (eight kilometers southwest of Przasnysz)—Dzbonie (eight kilometers northeast of Ciechanow) area, split the enemy's Przasnysz and Ciechanow groups of forces, and to be ready with part of its forces to assist the forces of the 2nd Shock Army in capturing Ciechanow. The army was to subsequently count on moving into the Grudusk area.

The 8th Guards Tank Corps received the following assignment: from the Grochy-Krupy area (12 kilometers northeast of Pultusk) it was to enter the breach in the general direction of Ciechanow and Szrensk (20 kilometers southwest of Mlawa) and Dlutowo (30 kilometers northwest of Mlawa). The immediate task was to capture Ciechanow from the march. In case of stubborn enemy resistance, a screen should be left there until the infantry's arrival, while the main forces would develop the offensive in the direction of Szrensk, outflanking Ciechanow from the south. The 108th and 98th rifle corps would support the corps' commitment into the breach. The line for passing the infantry was designated as Konarzewo (16 kilometers northwest of Pultusk)—Osiek (14 kilometers northwest of Pultusk).

The 1st Guards Tank Corps was to develop the offensive in the general direction of Plonsk, having the immediate task of taking Nowe-Miasto by the end of the day, and to subsequently force the Wkra River and reach the Plonsk area. The line for passing the infantry was designated as Kowalewice (18 kilometers southwest of Pultusk)—Nasielsk. The corps' movement to the jumping-off area of Rembkowo (18 kilometers northwest of Serock) and the beginning of the offensive would be indicated in a special order.

The 5th Guards Tank Army had the task of entering the breach along the Makow—Karniewo (eight kilometers southwest of Makow) sector in the general direction of Mlawa and Lidzbark. The immediate objective was to reach the Mlawa area by the morning of 18 January, and to subsequently capture Neidenburg and Dzialdowo by the morning of 19 January.

Accordingly, the mechanized corps and the tank corps were to be committed into the breach with the infantry's arrival at the enemy's second defensive zone (along the line Kadzidlo—Krasnosielc—west of Makow—Nasielsk). For its part, the 5th Guards Tank Army was to enter the breach upon our infantry's arrival at the enemy's third defensive zone. Thus the mobile groups would be committed into the breach in order to render assistance to the infantry in overcoming the enemy's next heavily fortified zone.

Besides this, it is necessary to note that alongside the assignment of tasks to the mechanized corps and tank corps, the *front* commander issued a number of orders in which it was stated that these corps were to be operationally subordinated as follows: the 8th Mechanized Corps to the commander of the 48th Army; the 8th Guards Tank Corps to the commander of the 2nd Shock Army, and; the 1st Guards Tank Corps to the commander of the 65th Army. At the same time, it was ordered that the corps be committed into the breach according to the army commanders' decision, although approximately from the line confirmed by the *front* commander. The army was to communicate to the *front* the time for the mobile group's commitment into the breach over high-frequency telephone.

It follows from this that the mechanized corps and the tank corps remained at the disposal of the *front*, while only the moment of committing these corps into the breach was determined by the corresponding army commanders.

The combat formation of the direct infantry support (NPP) tank groups. Given the presence of medium and heavy tanks in the NPP group, as well as self-propelled artillery, its combat formation was echeloned in depth. Medium tanks were to move ahead. Behind them, at a distance of 100-300 meters were to advance the heavy tanks, which would support the attack with their fire and cover the flanks of the medium tanks.

Finally, immediately behind the heavy tanks the infantry would advance, at a distance of 50-100 meters, with self-propelled artillery in its combat formations.

If the NPP tank group disposed of trawler tanks, then in order to clear a path through the minefields for the NPP tanks, they would move in pairs 100-150 meters ahead of the first tank echelon. After carrying out their assignment, the trawler tanks would head back to their shelters and remain there until summoned again.

Types of combat formations in the mechanized corps and the tank corps. At first the 8th Mechanized Corps organized its combat formation along three routes, with its main group along the left flank. However, as a result of the success achieved along the 48th Army's left flank, the 8th Mechanized Corps reformed itself along two routes.

The first echelon consisted of two mechanized brigades and self-propelled artillery; the second echelon consisted of a tank brigade; the corps reserve consisted of a heavy tank regiment.

The 8th Tank Corps was to enter the breach along a 6-kilometer sector in the 2nd Shock Army's zone.

The corps' first echelon consisted of two tank brigades and self-propelled artillery; the second echelon consisted of a motorized rifle brigade, while the corps reserve contained a tank brigade and a heavy tank regiment. The 8th Tank Corps' formation was conditioned by the width of the breakthrough, as well as by the necessity of first breaking through the enemy's tactical defense.

The 1st Guards Tank Corps was to be committed into the breach along the 65th Army's sector, bypassing the heavily fortified strong point of Powelin from the north. Besides this, the corps had to force the Wkra and Sona rivers. Self-propelled artillery (175 pieces) constituted the corps' main core; there were few tanks (60 vehicles).

In order to seize the crossings over the Wkra and Sona rivers, the first echelon deployed a motorized rifle brigade and two tank brigades, in which self-propelled artillery predominated. In the second echelon, which was located behind the right flank, one tank brigade was to advance for enveloping, if necessary, the enemy's Powelin group of forces from the north. Two self-propelled artillery regiments were in the corps' reserve.

The 5th Guards Tank Army's combat formation. The 5th Guards Tank Army was to be committed into the breach along four routes.

While being committed into the breach, the 5th Guards Tank Army was organized into two echelons, in which both tank corps were in the first echelon, with one mechanized brigade in the second echelon. For their part, each tank corps had two routes and was organized into two echelons. Such a combat formation would secure the seizure of the enemy's third defensive zone from the march.

Organizing cooperation. For an independent tank brigade and self-propelled artillery regiments, the main organizing instance was the rifle division, in which the cooperation between the combat arms was worked out and planned down to single tanks and self-propelled artillery pieces with the rifle platoons.

The employment of the independent heavy tank brigade was to be resolved at the corps level, while cooperation was to be worked out within the rifle division and down to the rifle company, on the one hand, and down to the heavy tank platoon, on the other.

The main questions of employing mechanized and tank corps (objectives, jumping-off lines, aviation support) were decided in the majority of cases by the *front* command. Questions of cooperation were worked out in detail in that combined-arms army, along the front of which the mechanized or tank corps was to be committed.

Aviation support. By 14 January 1945; that is by the beginning of the offensive, the 4th Air Army included the following units and formations.

Table III/3.12 4th Air Army Strength, 14 January 1945

Formation	Number of Air Regiments	Number of Aircraft
230th Assault Air Division	3	117
233rd Assault Air Division	3	123
260th Assault Air Division	3	87
332nd Assault Air Division	2	39
4th Assault Air Corps (196th and 199th assault air divisions)	6	268
325th Night Bomber Division	5	122
5th Bomber Corps (132nd and 327th bomber divisions	6	181
229th Fighter Division	3	125
269th Fighter Division	2	77
309th Fighter Division	2	73
329th Fighter Division	3	116
8th Fighter Corps (215th and 323rd fighter divisions)	6	289
164th Independent Reconnaissance Regiment	1	30
Total	45	1,647

Therefore, we disposed of 1,647 planes, which were distributed according to their combat designation in the following manner.

Table III/3.13 Distribution of Aircraft, 4th Air Army

Type of Aircraft	Total Aircraft	Percentage of Total
Assault Aircraft	634	39
Day Bombers	181	11
Night Bombers	122	7
Fighters	680	41
Reconnaissance	30	2
Total	1,647	100

By the start of the offensive, the presence of 350 enemy combat aircraft on 16 airfields had been established in the Second Belorussian Front's sector. Aside from this, the enemy could also bring in aviation against the Second Belorussian Front that was deployed against the Third and First Belorussian fronts, which was assumed to number up to 350 planes. In general, the German command could employ up to 700 aircraft against the Second Belorussian Front, of which 180 were bombers and 300-350 were fighters. The designation of the remaining planes was not established.

Thus if you count only the 350 enemy planes that were based in the Second Belorussian Front's offensive sector, then the 4th Air Army had almost a fivefold superiority over the enemy aviation. However, one could expect the concentration of up to 700 planes against the forces of the Second Belorussian Front, in which case the 4th Air Army would be superior to the German aviation, in the overall number of planes, only 2.4 times in assault aircraft, five times in bombers, and 2-2.3 times in fighters.

Planning the 4th Air Army's combat activities. During the night before the offensive, the 325th Night Bomber Division was to attempt to suppress through concentrated strikes the enemy's artillery, firing points, personnel, and headquarters, which were chiefly located in the tactical depth from 2-3 kilometers and up to 10-15 kilometers from the forward edge. Besides this, the 325th Air Division was to operate against the headquarters of the German XX Army Corps in Nowe Miasto (30 kilometers southwest of Pultusk).

Aside from the activities of Po-2 night bombers, it was also planned to conduct up to 100 sorties with "Boston"[7] aircraft from the 5th Bomber Corps for strikes against the headquarters of the German Second Army in Szrensk (20 kilometers southwest of Mlawa), against the headquarters of Army Group Center in Ortelsburg, and against the railroad stations and depots in Przasnysz, Ciechanow, Plonsk, and Mlawa, for the purpose of disrupting the enemy's troop control and the work of his army rear.

On the offensive's first day, our aviation was not supposed to take part in preparing the attack, while its daytime operations were supposed to begin with an aviation preparation simultaneously with the infantry attack.

Our aviation's main attack was to be launched in the 48th and 2nd Shock armies' zone with the forces of four assault air divisions (196th, 199th, 260th, and 233rd) against the enemy's entire defense to a depth of up to 16 kilometers, although the nearest targets were on an average of 1-2 kilometers from the forward edge.

It was planned to carry out the attack in eight consecutive echelons, consisting of the 44-56 Il-2[8] aircraft in each echelon. A repeat strike was to then follow by the same eight echelons. Thus along

---

7   Editor's note. This was the American-built A-20 "Havoc" light bomber.
8   Editor's note. The Il'2 ("Sturmovik") ground attack aircraft first appeared in 1941. It carried a crew of two and had a top speed of 414 kilometers per hour. Its armament consisted of two 23mm cannons, two 7.62mm machine guns, and one 12.7mm machine gun, and it could carry up to 600 kilograms of bombs.

the 48th and 2nd Shock armies' main attack axis the enemy was to be subjected to uninterrupted massive strikes during the course of five hours and 20 minutes. In all, it was planned to carry out 840 Il-2 sorties. Combat air operations were also planned along the flanks of the shock group: to the right, along the 3rd Army's sector, the 230th Assault Air Division was to carry out 328 Il-2 sorties, while on the left, along the 65th and 70th armies' sector, the 332nd Assault Air Division would operate.

From 1020 "Boston" bombers from the 5th Bomber Corps were to launch simultaneous strikes in groups of 18-27 planes and destroy depots and railroad stations in Przasnysz, Ciechanow and Plonsk, and to also carry out a strike against the enemy airfield in Ciechanow, to disrupt the work of the XX Army Corps' headquarters in Nowe Miasto, and to attack the enemy's reserves in Plonsk.

It was planned to cover the Second Belorussian Front's shock group in four areas; cover was to take the form of uninterrupted patrolling by an 8-plane flight of fighters in each area during the period from 0910 to 1740.

In all, the following number of sorties was planned for the first days:

Night bombers—1,400
Day bombers—316
Assault air—1,376
Fighters—1,031
Total—4,123

On the offensive's second and third day the 4th Air Army's combat plan called for the following:

1. The 325th Night Bomber Division (Po-2s) was to destroy the enemy's retreating units and attack his arriving reserves and rail shipments.
2. The assault air divisions were to continue to support the ground armies, and upon the commitment of the mobile groups they would be fully switched over to supporting them.
3. "Boston" bombers from the 5th Bomber Corps were to attack enemy reserves arriving from the depth and destroy the railroad junctions along the following lines: a) Ciechanow—Mlawa—Dzialdowo—Neidenburg; b) Plonsk—Sierpc; c) Myszyniec—Ortelsburg.
4. The fighter divisions were to continue covering the assault aircraft, while the 8th Fighter Corps was to cover the attacking forces' main group of forces.

Aside from carrying out combat assignments, it was also planned to carry out uninterrupted tactical reconnaissance throughout the entire operation with the forces of the 163rd Fighter Regiment, and long-range operational reconnaissance with the 164th Reconnaissance Regiment.

In all, it was planned to carry out the following number of sorties in the first three days of the offensive:

Night bombers—3,200
Day bombers—848
Assault air—3,074
Fighters—2,911
Total 10,033

2,883 tons of aviation fuel and 2,817 tons of bombs were required for supporting this amount of sorties.

The plan for the 4th Air Army's combat operations called for the aviation's very broad support for our forces' offensive. It is necessary to note that prolonged and uninterrupted pressure from the air, chiefly against the enemy's artillery, as well as against targets 1-2 kilometers from the front line, formed the basis of our aviation support for the attacking units. Powerful air strikes against the enemy's infantry and weapons along the forward edge were to be employed only rarely.

Aviation distribution. According to the 4th Air Army's combat operations plan, on the offensive's first day the 230th Assault Air Division would support the 3rd Army; the 233rd and 260th assault air divisions, as well as the 4th Assault Air Corps (196th and 199th assault air divisions) would operate in the 48th and 2nd Shock armies' sector; the 332nd Assault Air Division would assist the 65th and 70th armies' offensive.

The second day of the offensive called for the operational subordination of the following units: 230th Assault Air Division to the 3rd Army; 233rd Assault Air Division to the 48th Army; 260th Assault Air Division to the 2nd Shock Army, and; the 332nd Assault Air Division to the 65th Army. The 4th Assault Air Corps would continue to operate in the 48th and 2nd Shock armies' offensive sector.

Subsequently, upon the commitment of the mobile groups into the breach, the following would be transferred to their support: 230th Assault Air Division to the 3rd Guards Cavalry Corps; 233rd Assault Air Division to the 8th Mechanized Corps; 260th Assault Air Division to the 8th Guards Tank Corps; the 332nd Assault Air Division to the 1st Guards Tank Corps, and; the 4th Assault Air Corps to the 5th Guards Tank Army.

The cover of the troops' combat formations in their jumping-off positions and throughout the depth of the operation was to be entrusted to the 8th Fighter Corps (minus one regiment). Alongside this, the following fighter formations and units were to support the bombers and assault aircraft: 329th Fighter Division for the 5th Bomber Corps; 269th Fighter Division for the 4th Assault Air Corps; 229th Fighter Division for the 230th Assault Air Division; 309th Fighter Division for the 233rd and 260th assault air divisions, and; one air regiment from the 8th Fighter Corps for the 332nd Assault Air Division.

According to the instructions of the commander of the Second Belorussian Front, a special combat action plan for the 4th Air Army was drawn up against those enemy forces destroying roads and railroads.

Airfield basing. In all, by the start of the operation there were up to 95 airfields in the *front's* rear sector to a depth of 150 kilometers from the front line. However, in the center and along the *front's* left flank along the axis of the main attack, where all of our aviation was actually supposed to concentrate, we could use only 37 airfields, located within the following boundaries: from the right, Bialystok—Ostroleka, on the left Bielsk—Ciechanow—Jadow—Serock, and from the rear Bialystok—Bielsk. According to their size, these airfields could normally handle 37 air regiments. Only by overloading the available airfields were we able to deploy by the start of the offensive all our available aviation on them at a distance of no more than 150 kilometers from the front line, while supplies of ammunition for 8-10 regimental sorties were created at each airfield.

In general, the 4th Air Army's planes were brought up nearer to the front line and could fully support the troops' offensive to a depth of 80-100 kilometers, without rebasing.

Aviation command and control. Aviation command and control during the breakthrough period of the enemy's defense were to be centralized, and from the moment the mobile groups were committed into the breach it was to be partially decentralized, because the assault air divisions would be shifted over to supporting the mobile groups and control over them would be exercised by the air division commanders, who, with their radio sets, would move along with the commanders of the mobile groups.

The commander of the 4th Air Army would be located at a command post alongside the command post of the *front* commander and would control his planes through his own staff, which would remain in the area of the airfield network.

Requests for aviation would arrive from the land armies over high-frequency telephone to the commander of the 4th Air Army, who would issue assignments to the air formations through his staff. The role of the air division commanders came down to controlling groups of assault aircraft on the battlefield and guiding them to their target. Such a control plan was adopted because the air division commanders' command posts were so far removed from their headquarters that they lacked reliable radio communication with them.

Provision of ammunition and fuel. The overall provision of ammunition and fuel by the start of the offensive is shown in the next table.

Table III/3.14 Provision of Ammunition and Fuel, 4th Air Army

Storage Area	Ammunition (in Regimental Sorties)			Aviation Fuel in Refills
	Air Bombs	Shells	Bullets	
In airfield service battalions	15.3	8.3	28.0	5.3
In forward air depots	7.0	5.0	10.6	0.3
In army depots	4.6	9.7	23.4	1.1

At the same time, it is necessary to note that supplies for an air regiment were stored with the airfield service battalions; in forward air depots for aviation being serviced by the aviation basing for the given area, and; in army depots for all of the 4th Air Army's planes.

In general, by the start of the offensive, the 4th Air Army was supplied with ammunition to a sufficient degree. As concerns fuel, the supplies on hand were sufficient only for the operation's first days, as a result of which our aviation required the regular delivery of fuel and lubrication materials.

Engineering support. The tasks. As regards the engineering support for the forthcoming offensive operation, the *front's* forces had the following main tasks:

a) to prepare the Rozan and Serock bridgeheads for deploying forces and for their assumption of the offensive;
b) to carry out concealment maneuver in the Augustow and Lomza areas;
c) to continue to fortify our lines;
d) to reinforce the armies with engineering units during the preparation and conduct of the operation.

The *front* disposed of the following engineering formations and units for carrying out these tasks:

Type	Engineering Battalions
Three assault engineer-sapper brigades	17
Three motorized-engineering brigades	11
One pontoon-bridge brigade	4
Seven army engineering-sapper brigades	28
Pontoon battalions	12
Five military-field construction brigades	26
Corps sapper battalions	8
Division sapper battalions	61

In all, there were 167 engineering battalions of various specializations, of which 156 battalions were concentrated along the breakthrough sectors (28 kilometers), which worked out to an average of 5.5 battalions per kilometer of breakthrough front. In general, each of the armies of the *front's* shock groups disposed of 20-25 engineering and sapper battalions.

In committing the 5th Guards Tank Army into the breach, it was to be reinforced with the 21st Engineering-Sapper Brigade from the 2nd Shock Army.

The engineering preparation of the bridgeheads. As is known, the command of the Second Belorussian Front decided to widely employ the Rozan and Serock bridgeheads for going over to the offensive. The Rozan bridgehead was 40 kilometers broad and ranged in depth from four to 20 kilometers, while the Serock bridgehead was 35 kilometers wide and was 8-10 kilometers deep.

At the end of December 1944 work was carried out for the engineering outfitting of the bridgeheads. The overall volume of work is shown in the following table.

Table III/3.15 Engineering Preparation Within Bridgeheads, Second Belorussian Front

Type of Work	Units of Measurement	Completed	To Do	Work Force Needed (in Man Days)
Trenches and communications trenches	km	795	257	45,500
Deepening and widening existing trenches and communications trenches	km	–	397	19,900
Emplacements for machine guns and anti-tank rifles	units	7,370	2,230	8,060
Slit trenches	linear meters	–	52,000	8,800
Command and observation posts	units	614	304	15,940
Ramps for hiding combat equipment and auto transport	units	–	4,550	760
Concealment fences	linear meters	–	32,500	5,280
Overhead covers and dugouts	units	4,900	3,100	31,000
Wells	units	221	272	4,100
Total	–	–	–	139,340

Thus about 140,000 man days were required for the engineering outfitting of the bridgeheads.

Closing up to the enemy's forward trenches went on along the entire length of the bridgehead, by excavating "mustaches" (individual trenches) every 100-150 meters, which were then connected between themselves and created a jumping-off trench for the attack at a distance of 100-150 meters from the enemy. Excavating the communications trenches was carried out with a calculation of one communications trench for each first-line company. All the work for the engineering outfitting of the bridgeheads was completed in the beginning of January 1945.

Simultaneously, the engineering units carried out major and difficult work on clearing the bridgeheads of so-called "wild" minefields, that is, those minefields which had been laid by us and the enemy during the bitter fighting for the bridgeheads and for which there were no logs, or the logs had been lost. In all, 55,087 mines and unexploded shells were cleared or rendered harmless along the Rozan bridgehead, and 103,943 on the Serock bridgehead.

During the fighting for the expansion and retention of the Rozan and Serock bridgeheads along the Mlynarz (eight kilometers north of Rozan)—Serock sector, 18 bridges were built over the Narew River, or an average of one bridge per four kilometers. Subsequently, during the preparation period for the offensive, the number of bridges was raised to 25, with an average of one bridge per three kilometers of front. At the same time, the armies' provision with bridge crossings was as follows.

Table III/3.16 The Second Belorussian Front's Provision for Bridge Crossings

Army	Number of Bridges and Their Capacity			
	60 Tons	30 Tons	16 Tons	Total
49th	1	1	–	2
3rd	4	–	1	5
48th	4	–	–	4
2nd Shock	2	3	1	6
65th	4	–	–	4
70th	2	1	1	4
Total	17	5	3	25

Note: of 25 bridges, six were two-way. The bridges were 120-300 meters long.

In general, such a number of permanent bridge crossings completely supported the deployment of our forces along the Rozan and Serock bridgeheads, and the *front's* shock groups, which were occupying these bridgeheads, were by the start of the offensive securely linked to their rear organs.

Concealment maneuver. During the offensive preparation, we carried out concealment maneuver with the aim of revealing the concentration of major forces in the Augustow and Lomza areas, for the purpose of creating the impression with the enemy of our preparation for an attack along these axes.

An independent concealment company and *front* pontoon units, as well as the 49th Army's rifle units, artillery and tanks, were brought in to carry out concealment maneuver. 480 dummy guns and 220 tanks were prepared for establishing the false concentration of our artillery and tanks, while false artillery firing positions were also outfitted. Traces of tank tracks were laid down by real tanks leading to the location areas of the dummy tanks. False troop concentration areas and false artillery firing positions were carefully secured against the enemy's human intelligence, while individual guns were fired from the false artillery positions.

Besides this, the movement of small groups of troops and combat equipment was organized along those road sectors that could be viewed from the enemy's ground observation posts.

The enemy reacted weakly to all of these measures. 29 artillery bombardments of our false targets by the enemy were recorded, with an expenditure of 116 shells. Besides this, the enemy carried out 83 reconnaissance flights and strafed our false targets 11 times.

In general, our concealment maneuver did not yield major results and failed to have a great impact on the enemy's actions. The reasons for this should be searched for in the fact that concealment maneuver was carried out along axes unfavorable in the operational sense and that this maneuver was carried out with insufficient men and materiel.

Strengthening the occupied lines. Alongside the engineering preparation for the offensive, engineering work for strengthening our defensive lines was also carried out. This work was carried out not only along the troop line, but also along the intermediate line and compartments, along the army rear line and the *front* line. Here it should be noted that the following were constructed along all the defensive lines per kilometer of front: 17.4 kilometers of trenches and communications trenches, 119 machine gun emplacements, 10.8 command and observation posts, and 38 overhead covers and dugouts. Besides this, about 1.5 kilometers of barbed wire obstacles per kilometer of front was laid down along the troop and intermediate defensive lines.

In general, a great deal of attention was devoted to the engineering strengthening of our positions, while the troops and intermediate defensive lines were most heavily strengthened.

Troop and staff training. Simultaneous with the drawing up of an operational plan by the *front's* military council, a directive was also issued regarding troop training, including the forthcoming combat operations. This directive demanded that work proceed in all units, formations, headquarters and *front* establishments for systematic exercises in combat training, and a program to be drawn up embracing one month of training.

First-line defense units and formations studied and practically worked out the organization of the defensive battle and in particular questions of the combat arms' cooperation.

In the divisional, corps and *front* reserves our forces studied and practically worked out questions of attacking the enemy's heavily fortified defense and the forcing of a water barrier. Particular attention was devoted to the combat training of companies and battalions. Besides this, the infantry studied and trained for mine clearing in the offensive sector, as well as the laying of minefields.

The troops trained in terrain very similar to that which they were to attack along. At the same time, each division of the *front's* shock group outfitted training fields with fortified lines resembling the Germans' defense. The tactical training of companies, battalions and regiments was topped off by tactical exercises using live ammunition. Up to 30 percent of the exercises with units and formations were conducted at night.

Exercises were conducted with officers on organizing the supporting the offensive battle, as well as on controlling units in a dynamic battle, while breaking through the enemy's heavily fortified zone.

During 8-10 December 1944 the *front* headquarters conducted a war game around the theme of "The Offensive Operation for the Purpose of Defeating the Enemy's Przasnysz—Mlawa Group of Forces." Army commanders and chiefs of staff took part in this game, as well as the senior staff of the *front's* field directorate.

Then, on 15 December the *front* chief of staff conducted a separate war game with the army chiefs of staff on problems of organizing cooperation in the forthcoming operation. Finally, on 3-4 January 1945 a second war game was conducted at *front* headquarters on the theme of "The Operations of Mobile Formations and Aviation in the *Front* Offensive Operation." The commanders and chiefs of staff of the tank, mechanized and cavalry corps took part in this war game, as well as the commanders of air divisions. During the game problems of the ground forces' cooperation with aviation were worked out.

The significance of the war games was very great. First of all, all of the army commanders in the *front's* shock group were fully oriented in the plan for the forthcoming offensive operation throughout the entire depth of the operation. During the process of the games the army commanders made a number of suggestions on choosing the direction of the main attack by this or that army. Finally, playing out the battle in depth yielded a several instructive variants for the possible development of combat operations.

Political support for the operation. By the start of the operation, the forces of the Second Belorussian Front were distinguished by their diverse makeup. The *front* received the following reinforcements during the summer and fall of 1944: 53,000 men mobilized from the liberated areas; 10,254 men liberated from captivity, and; 5,290 men undergoing punishment. Aside from this, 20,000 men arrived from the rear and 39,066 from hospitals.

There were no more than 10-15 veteran soldiers in the rifle companies. The remainder was quite diverse. It was necessary to cohere all of this diverse mass and bring forth from it a high degree of offensive élan.

Alongside this, one could not speak openly of the forthcoming offensive. Therefore, in the beginning of January Red Army gatherings and meetings were conducted along the entire front on the theme "1945—the Year of the Final Defeat of the German Aggressors," in which Stalin's call, "We shall raise the banner of victory over Berlin" was widely discussed.

Alongside these gatherings, meetings were widely held on the theme of "Ruthlessly Wreaking Revenge on the German-Fascist Aggressors for their Criminal Deeds." The inculcation of hatred and revenge for the enemy was one of the most important tasks of our agitation and propaganda work while preparing the troops for the offensive. *Front* newspapers devoted serious attention to this question and leaflets were printed in the thousands.

A great deal of significance was attached to working with the new reinforcements. Solemn meetings with the new arrivals were organized in the units and formations. As a rule, the division commander and the chief of the division's political section would meet the new arrivals and conduct meetings with them. Group discussions were conducted for familiarizing them with the conditions of combat life and with the demands to be made on them. The equal distribution of the reinforcements among the companies was taken care of and the formation of groups of people from the same area was not allowed. Discussions were conducted with well-known people and with decorated soliders for the reinforcements. Weaponry, particularly which had belonged to fallen heroes, was presented in a solemn atmosphere. Discussions were conducted on various themes. The new arrivals were led to take the oath before the regiment's unfurled banner.

During the offensive, the political organs and party organizations carried out a great deal of work in strengthening the further development of the troops' offensive élan. The orders of Supreme Commander-in-Chief Stalin to the *front's* forces and reports from the *Sovinformburo*[9] were the main political documents, on the basis of which all of our party-political work was built. During this period meetings dedicated to comrade Stalin's orders, as well as meetings on the occasion of the Germans' atrocities and humiliations of the population and our Red Army prisoners of war, were widely practiced.

The political workers mobilized the troops to carry out their combat assignments not only in word, but by personal example, appearing where the most difficult combat situation arose.

The *front* disposed of a solid apparatus of 130 responsible workers, not counting technical personnel, for carrying out work to demoralize the enemy forces.

During the East Prussian operation ten million leaflets were dropped. In this operation the work on demoralizing the surrounded German garrisons (in Elbing and Graudenz) deserves special attention. In this regard, the most instructive is the work carried out for demoralizing the garrison of Graudenz. 442,000 leaflets were dropped on the garrison. 162 loudspeaker broadcasts were made to the garrison. More than 20 prisoners of war from among the anti-fascists were dispatched to the garrison, of which 14 returned. They brought with them 429 German soldiers.

The commandant of Graudenz, General Frienke, made the following statement on the effectiveness of our propaganda in his testimony: "Your propaganda lowered the morale of my soldiers. It undoubtedly played a major role in your victory over my garrison."

Our agitation among the enemy's troops weakened their resistance and made it easier for our forces to carry out their combat assignments. It is sufficient to say that during the East Prussian operation and the following offensive into eastern Pomerania, the *front's* forces took in 18,838 deserters.

Rear organization. The main features in the organization and work of the Second Belorussian Front's rear were as follows:

1. The large amount of forces and combat equipment that took part in the operation.
2. The wide expanse of the front, which reached up to 285 kilometers.
3. On the average, the operation's depth reached 250 kilometers.
4. The great length of the offensive (26 days, from 14 January through 8 February 1945).
5. The comparatively short preparation period of 35 days for the operation.

---

9   Editor's note. The *Sovinformburo* (Soviet Information Bureau) was the Soviet Union's official information organ during the war.

The rear's tasks. The chief task of organizing the rear consisted in securing the timely delivery of all types of supplies to the troops.

While carrying out this task, it was necessary to deliver to the troops and create the following reserves of the main types of supply.

Table III/3.17 Supply Reserves, Second Belorussian Front

	Tons	Train Cars and Tank Cars
Munitions	80,150	5,265
Weapons	5,576	448
Fuel	53,777	5,860
Food and Forage	97,000	7,000
Technical Equipment and Construction Materials	40,000	2,800
Total	276,503	21,373

An extremely important task was the construction and restoration of the railroads and dirt roads and supporting the operation in the medical and veterinarian sense, as well as the timely evacuation of wounded and sick people and horses.

Supply basing. By the start of the operation the *front* was based on the following railroads sections:

1. Grodno—Bialystok, 82 kilometers
2. Baranovichi—Volkovysk—Bialystok, 200 kilometers
3. Czeremcha—Bialystok, 75 kilometers
4. Bialystok—Osowiec, 58 kilometers
5. Bialystok—Lapy—Ostroleka, 110 kilometers
6. Lapy—Malkinia Gorna—Ostorleka, 50 kilometers
7. Malkinia Gorna—Tluszcz—Ostroleka, 76 kilometers
8. Tluszcz—Jablonna, 35 kilometers

The *front's* regulation station was located in Bialystok; its branches were in Baranovichi and Volkovysk, with an operational group in Ostrow Mazowiecka.

It was planned to shift the *front's* basing to the following railroad sectors during the offensive's development: 1) Ostroleka—Neidenburg—Dzialdowo—Deutsch Eylau—Marienwerder; 2) Tluszcz—Modlin—Sierpc—Torun; 3) Deutsch Eylau—Torun; 4) Modlin—Nasielsk—Dzialdowo.

Our troops' rapid advance, the presence of railroads with a different railroad gauge, and the resulting necessity of transferring freight from the Soviet gauge to a Western European one created a series of difficulties and made troop supply more difficult.

The main *front* depots were located as follows:

Artillery—Ostrow Mazowiecka, Gucin and Mostowka;
Fuels, oils and lubricants—Czarnowo Undy, Ostrow Mazowiecka, and an open-air branch in the Szawin woods (seven kilometers east of Rozan);
Food—Ostrow Mazowiecka, Wyszkow, Malkinia Gorna;
Engineering—Malkinia Gorna;
Chemical—Ostrow Mazowiecka

Therefore, all of the main *front* depots had been move close to the front line and were located within the bounds of the army rear area.

The remaining *front* depots (communications equipment, automobile and tank equipment, uniforms, medical and veterinary) were located in the Bialystok area. A food depot and a fuel, oils and lubricants depot were also located here.

The armies were based on the following railroad sections:

> 50th Army, Bialystok—Knyszyn—Osowiec, 58 kilometers;
> 48th Army, Wyszkow—Ostroleka, 58 kilometers;
> 65th Army, excluding Malkinia Gorna—excluding Tluszcz—Rybenko, 66 kilometers;
> 70th Army, Tluszcz—Jablonna, 35 kilometers.

The remaining armies did not have their own railroad basing sections. The Wyszkow—Ostroleka lateral railroad, besides the 48th Army, also serviced the 2nd Shock and 3rd armies.

The location of the army bases by the start of the operation is shown in Table 18.

Freight was delivered to the army bases exclusively by rail.

The *front's* rear area had the following boundaries:

a) right, excluding Dokudovo (16 kilometers southeast of Lida)—excluding Ostryna (65 kilometers north of Volkovysk)—Grodno—Augustow—excluding Stradaunnen—excluding Rhein.

b) left, Lyusino station (60 kilometers southeast of Baranovichi)—Pruzany—excluding Czeremcha—Jadow—Serock—Western Bug River as far as its mouth, then along the Vistula River to Torun.

c) rear, Krivichi (on the Neman River, 25 kilometers southeast of Lida)—Novogrudok—Gorodyshche (20 kilometers north of Baranovichi)—Baranovichi—Lyusino station.

Army boundaries:

a) right and left, the armies' operational boundary lines.

b) rear boundary, Grodno—Sokolka—Bialystok—Suraz—Bielsk—Bocki—Siemiatycze (all locales exclusively for the armies).

Thus the overall depth of the *front* rear (from the front line) was as follows: 200 kilometers along the right flank, and 330 kilometers along the left.

The average depth of the army rear area varied from 64 kilometers along the right flank, to 154 kilometers along the left.

During the operation the *front* and army bases and depots were shifted.

At the start of the offensive, it was planned to have up to 30 daily rations of food and forage in the army and *front* depots.

Table III/3.18 *Front* **and Army Base Depots, Second Belorussian Front**

Army	Army Base	Distance from Front (km)	Advance Section of Army Base	Distance from Front (km)	Final Delivery Locale	Distance from Front (km)
50th	Knyszyn	27	Czerwony Bor	10	Monki, Kamienna Nowa	16
49th	Sniadowo	15	Gucin	14	Korne	10
3rd	Paseki	13	–	–	Paseki	13
48th	Pszetycz	28	–	–	Pszetycz	28

Army	Army Base	Distance from Front (km)	Advance Section of Army Base	Distance from Front (km)	Final Delivery Locale	Distance from Front (km)
2nd Shock	Daleke	26	–	–	Daleke	26
65th	Lochow	46	Wyszkow	29	Lochow, Wyszkow	46
70th	Tluszcz	31	–	–	Weniaminow	7
5th Gds Tank	Sadowno	–	–	–	–	–

Actually, as can be seen from Table III/2.19, by the start of the offensive we had not managed to create a month's supplies of food and forage, as was called for by the supply plan. The reason for this must be searched for in the weakness of the rail and auto transport, which were not able to fully cope with delivering all the planned shipments. Alongside this, the accumulation of such large numbers of supplies proved to be excessive, because upon assuming the offensive the armies found such an amount of food and forage at hand that they stopped supplying themselves from the *front* depots and almost completely went over to supplying themselves through local resources and captured stores.

Table III/3.19 Food and Forage Provisioning (in Daily Rations), Second Belorussian Front

	Bread Products	Groats	Meat Products	Fats	Sugar	Grain Forage	Hay
1 January 1945							
In the armies	17.3	14.4	9.5	16.3	20.4	8.7	14.2
In *front* depots	4.1	1.4	1.0	1.8	2.9	3.9	0.1
Total	21.4	15.8	10.5	18.1	23.3	12.6	14.3
13 January 1945							
In the armies	19.7	16.8	9.8	23.6	19.4	13.9	10.2
In *front* depots	9.0	2.4	1.3	2.6	1.1	5.7	0.2
Total	28.7	19.2	11.1	26.2	20.5	19.6	10.4
20 January 1945							
In the armies	20.0	15.7	12.0	17.0	19.8	11.9	8.7
In *front* depots	14.1	5.6	6.6	13.2	6.9	4.3	–
Total	34.1	21.3	18.6	30.2	26.7	16.2	8.7
31 January 1945							
In the armies	19.2	14.0	20.4	16.2	15.1	11.6	11.9
In *Front* depots	16.2	10.8	11.0	18.2	24.1	10.3	0.3
Total	35.4	24.8	31.4	34.4	39.2	21.9	12.2

Besides this, large supplies of food, which remained until the end of the war, accumulated in the armies and *front* depots.

The provisioning of fuel. In the beginning and at the end of the operation, the supply of fuel in refills was as follows:

Table III/3.20 Supply of Fuel Refills, Second Belorussian Front

Type of Fuel	14 January 1945	10 February 1945
Aviation Fuel	5.3	4.5
Tank Fuel (KB-70)	4.4	1.8
Auto Fuel	4.0	3.5
Diesel Fuel	3.1	3.5

The planned expenditure of fuel for the entire operation and the actual expenditure are shown in the following table.

Table III/3.21 Planned Expenditure of Fuel, Second Belorussian Front

Types of Fuel	Planned		Actual		
	Daily Norm in Refills	For the Entire Operation (tons)	Average Refills per Day	For the Entire Operation (tons)	% of Planned Expenditure
Aviation Fuel	0.5	13,949	0.2	6,339	45.4
Auto Fuel	0.3	30,924	0.3	31,280	101.0
Diesel Fuel	0.23	6,174	0.17	4,655	75.4
Other Types	0.15	4,200	0.17	4,688	112.0

The expenditure of auto fuel exceeded its delivery, which is why during our offensive in January 6,581 tons of auto fuel was expended from our supplies. During January 28-29 only 300-500 tons of auto fuel was delivered to the unloading stations, given a daily expenditure of more than 1,000 tons.

There was no breakdown in the provisioning of the troops with fuel, oils and lubricants. However, during the 26-30 January time period our auto transport worked poorly and with major delays, due to the heavy snow cover, and the troops' provisioning with fuel fell to 0.4-1 refill.

The provisioning of ammunition (in combat loads) is shown in the following table.

Table III/3.22 Provision of Ammunition, Second Belorussian Front

Types of On Hand Ammunition	On Hand 13 January 1945	Expended During 14-31 January 1945	On Hand 1 February 1945
Rifle Rounds	2.1	0.5	1.7
TT Rounds	2.3	0.6	1.7
Hand Grenades	1.4	0.4	1.0
82mm Mortars	4.5	1.6	3.0
120mm Mortars	4.5	1.9	4.0
160mm Mortars	3.0	2.0	5.5
76mm Guns	3.5	1.3	2.2
100mm Guns	3.0	0.6	2.5
122mm Howitzers	3.5	2.0	2.0
122mm Guns	5.0	2.5	4.1
152mm Howitzers	5.0	2.5	5.5
152mm Guns	4.0	2.1	3.7

Types of On Hand Ammunition	On Hand 13 January 1945	Expended During 14-31 January 1945	On Hand 1 February 1945
203mm Howitzers	4.0	1.5	3.2
280mm Mortars	3.5	0.8	2.7

As can be seen from the table, the expenditure of rifle rounds and hand grenades was comparatively insignificant, because the infantry's offensive was supported by large masses of artillery. Besides this, the expenditure of howitzer and mortar rounds was greater than for the guns. It follows that our howitzer artillery was more widely employed than gun artillery. This may be explained by the presence of the enemy's developed system of fortified zones, his absence of major operational reserves, and his passive defense. Thus in the majority of cases, we chiefly had to employ our howitzer artillery for destroying and suppressing enemy forces in their trenches and shelters, and to a lesser degree employ our guns for repelling the enemy's infantry and tank counterattacks.

Automobile service. The overall presence of automobiles with the *front* is shown in the following table.

Table III/3.23 Availability of Automobiles, Second Belorussian Front

Automobiles	Total	Of These, in Working Order	
		Number	Percentage
Freight Automobiles	43,908	39,209	89
Specialized	9,275	8,714	95
Total	53,183	47,923	90

Of this number, the following numbers of motor vehicles were located in army and *front* auto transport units:

Table III/3.24 Number of Motor Vehicles Located in Army and *Front* Auto Transport Units, Second Belorussian Front

Units	Auto Units		Number of Vehicles	Lift Capability (in tons)
	Regiments	Independent Battalions		
Front	5	2	4,270	7,502
Army	–	20	2,353	5,065
Total	5	22	6,623	12,567

Auto transport's work during the development of our offensive proceeded in exceedingly difficult conditions. Black ice, frosts and snow drifts made the auto units' work more difficult and slowed down the movement and turnaround times for our motor vehicles. Our troops' rapid advance and the lengthening of our communications also significantly increased the auto transport's workload, because delivery by auto transport began to be carried out a distances from 110-240 kilometers.

Despite all of these difficulties, our auto transport coped with delivering supplies. The amount of freight delivered during the operation is shown in the following table.

Table III/3.25 Freight Delivered During the Operation Within the Second Belorussian Front's Zone

Type of Freight	In Thousands of Tons	Percentage
Munitions	128.4	32.2
Construction Materials for Restoring Railroads	122.4	30.7
Food and Forage	59.8	15.0
Engineering and Medical Supplies	27.9	7.0
Other Freight	52.3	13.1
Personnel and Wounded	7.9	2.0
Total	398.7	100.0

In all, 22,182.8 tons of freight per kilometer was transported. Of this number, 14,405.9 tons per kilometer (65 percent) weres carried out by *front* auto transport, and 7,776.9 tons per kilometer (35 percent) by army auto transport.

The condition of the railroads. The following railroad sections, which were on the USSR gauge, were employed during the preparatory period for the operation.

Table III/3.26 Railroads Within the Second Belorussian Front's Zone

Sections	Length (in km)	Capacity (in Pairs of Trains)
Bialystok—Malkinia Gorna—Tluszcz	137	10
Bialystok—Osowiec	58	8
Lapy—Ostroleka	68	10
Malkinia Gorna—Ostroleka	54	10
Tluszcz—Ostroleka	73	10

These rail lines, both due to their direction, as well as their carrying capacity, were able to fully support delivery to the *front's* forces. However, our exploitation of the railroads was made difficult due to the destruction carried out by the enemy, the shortage of operating units, rolling stock, and fuel, as well as the low restoration quality of the station routes and structures, particularly for communications and water supply.

Furthermore, the railroad stations were insufficiently developed and additional work was required for the location there of army bases and unloading stations. All of these shortcomings lowered the capacity of the railroad lines down to 3-4 pairs of trains per day.

As our forces advanced, the situation with railroad deliveries grew worse. It was not possible to convert even the main railroad lines to the USSR gauge, in light of a shortage of our locomotives and rail cars. Thus it was decided to convert only the Nasielsk—Dzialdowo line to the USSR gauge and to organize along this line a staging base for freight heading from the Soviet Union to the front.

Restoration of the railroads. Thanks to the high rates of our offensive, the enemy did not have time to completely destroy the railroads. Nonetheless, the volume of the destruction of railroad sites was, on the average, as follows: the main line—2.5 percent; station routes—1.6 percent; turn-outs—12.8 percent; water supply sites—41.2 percent; major bridges—30.4 percent, and; medium-sized bridges—24 percent.

The Military-Restoration Works Directorate No. 9 (UVVR-9) and three railroad brigades (4th, 8th and 23rd) worked on restoring the railroads in the Second Belorussian Front's offensive zone.

The restoration speed by the three railroad brigades is shown in the following table.

Table III/3.27 Restoration Work Undertaken by Railroad Brigades

Months	Restored in a Day				
	Main Line (in km)	Bridges (linear meters)		Communications (in km)	Water Supply (number of sites)
		Large	Medium		
January	50	120	6.2	18.6	0.6
February	43	15.6	9.2	16.8	1.5

As the table indicates, the restoration work was organized incorrectly. In chasing after kilometers, the restoration workers forgot about our exploitation demands. The restoration of station routes, communications lines, and water supply sites was conducted at significantly lower rates than work along the main line. As a result, the capacity of the railroads fell to 2-4 pairs of trains per day, instead of the possible 10-12 pairs. With the arrival of our forces at the shore of the Baltic Sea, movement had been restored only as far as the line Deutsch Eylau—Dzialdowo—Nasielsk.

The work of the directorate and organs of military communications (VOSO) during the operation's conduct unfolded in difficult conditions. During this period no one actually directed the railroads. Such control organs as the NKPS[10] and the Polish one were absent, and an attempt to unite the direction of the railroads in the hands of the *front* VOSO was not successful, in light of the shortage of technical and exploitation personnel and equipment.

The railroads worked with great delays, and thus by the close of the operation a great deal of attention was being paid to the organization of directing the railroads. By this time the *front's* rail network had increased from 390 to 1,215 kilometers.

The following were created to carry out directing functions: the 5th Military-Exploitation Directorate of the NKPS and a board of directors for the Polish railroads. Two exploitation regiments and two military-exploitation branches were assigned to exploit the railroads. The main stations were brought up to speed, and inter-station communications strengthened. As a result of these measures, the railroads' work improved and deliveries were made in a more systematic fashion.

Medical service. The work of the medical establishments throughout the operation unfolded in an intense situation, alongside a severe shortage of hospitals, which is obvious from the following table.

Table III/3.28 Availability of Hospitals & Beds, Second Belorussian Front

Type of Hospitals	Required		On-Hand		Shortage	
	Hospitals	Beds	Hospitals	Beds	Hospitals	Beds
Army	166	58,800	157	57,000	9	1,800
Front	106	64,000	58	31,700	48	32,300
Total	272	122,800	215	88,700	57	34,100

---

10 Editor's note. This stands for the People's Commissariat of Communications Lines (*Narodnyi Kommissariat Putei Soobshchenii*), which was responsible for, among other things, the country's railroads.

By the start of the offensive, the *front* disposed of 215 hospitals, with 88,700 authorized beds, which were already occupied by 31,912 wounded and sick, while up to 100,000 medical losses were expected in the first ten days of the offensive.

The bed shortage at the *front* base was to be covered by the increased deployment of hospitals, exceeding by 2-2.5 times the authorized number of beds.

Besides this, hospitals arrived from other fronts during the offensive, although with considerable delay.

By the start of the operation, the *front's* hospital bases were located in the following manner:

40th Field Evacuation Point, Wyszkow, Lochow;
77th *Front* Evacuation Point, Legionowo, Malkinia Gorna;
114th Medical Evacuation Point, Zambrow;
99th Medical Evacuation Point, Bialystok.

The armies' hospital bases were located in the area of the armies' bases.

The *front's* hospital bases, as a rule, were moved as close to the front as possible, insofar as the restoration of the railroads allowed. Thanks to this, the armies had the necessary number of hospitals ready to be moved forward.

The *front* had the following for evacuation:

- four auto medical companies (214 motor vehicles)
- one horse-drawn medical company (112 medical two-wheeled carts);
- 13 temporary military-medical trains (VVSP);
- 21 medical flying squads.

Besides this, returning empty vehicles were widely employed for evacuating the wounded and sick.

A medical transfer base was organized in Deutsch Eylau for transferring the wounded and sick from Western European-gauge flying medical squads to temporary military-medical trains using the USSR gauge.

The troops' regrouping and operational-combat formation by the start of the operation. By the close of 13 January the *front's* forces were supposed to fully complete their regrouping and occupy their jumping-off positions for the offensive, in accordance with the operational plan.

The *front's* first-echelon armies were deployed as follows:

The 50th Army occupied a broad front from Augustow to Nowogrod.

The 49th Army had its main forces along its left flank, ready to take exploit the breakthrough of the enemy's front along the 3rd Army's sector, in order to attack in the direction of Myszyniec.

The 3rd Army, in accordance with the assigned tasks, had deployed the 41st and 35th rifle corps for launching the main attack in the direction of Krasnosielc and had detached the 40th Rifle Corps for a supporting attack on Aleksandrowo.

The 48th Army's 29th Rifle Corps was deployed along the sector from the army's right boundary line as far as the Orzyc River, with both rifle divisions in the first echelon.

The 53rd and 42nd rifle corps occupied the sector from the Orzyc River to the army's left boundary line. Each of these corps had two rifle divisions in the first echelon, and one each in the second echelon.

Thus the army's combat formation fully corresponded to the decision to launch the main attack along the left flank.

The 2nd Shock Army's 108th and 98th rifle corps were located along the Rozan bridgehead, along the sector from the right boundary line to the Narew River. Each of these two corps had two rifle divisions in the first echelon and a rifle division apiece in the second echelon.

One of the 116th Rifle Corps' divisions (86th) occupied a sector along the left bank of the Narew River as far as the army's left boundary line, with another two rifle divisions in the second echelon. In its turn, the 86th Rifle Division had only one rifle regiment along this position, and was holding the other two rifle regiments in reserve in the woods behind its right flank.

Therefore, the 2nd Shock Army concentrated the main mass of its men and materiel along the Rozan bridgehead, along the axis of the main attack and, furthermore, planned to employ here another two rifle divisions (321st and 326th) from the 116th Rifle Corps.

The 65th Army's 18th Rifle Corps, was occupying the sector from the right boundary line to Pokrzywnica with two rifle divisions, with one rifle division in the second echelon.

The 46th and 105th rifle corps occupied their jumping-off positions along the Pokrzywnica—Ceppelin sector. Each of the corps had two rifle divisions in the first echelon, and one in the second.

Thus the army's combat formation fully corresponded to the decision to launch the main attack along the left flank.

The 70th Army's 96th Rifle Corps was deployed in a single echelon, with all three rifle divisions along the line Ceppelin—Guty.

One of the 47th Rifle Corps' divisions occupied the sector from Guty to the Western Bug River. Two divisions were in the second echelon.

The 114th Rifle Corps was in the army's second echelon, in the area northeast of Serock.

Therefore, the army's combat formation corresponded to the decision to launch the main attack along the center. Besides this, the deep echeloning of the left-flank 47th Rifle Corps made the corps' deployment toward the flank easier following the army's breakthrough of the enemy's defense.

The correlation of forces along the breakthrough front. As a result of the reinforcement of the Second Belorussian Front with men and combat materiel, as well as the arrival of new units and formations, the *front's* combat and numerical strength increased. The overall correlation of men and materiel along the *front's* sector by the start of operations is shown in the following table.

Table III/3.29 Correlation of Forces, the Second Belorussian Front's Zone

The Enemy Per km of Front	Men and Materiel		Our Forces		Correlation
	Total	(285-kilometer Front)	Total	Per km of Front	
One division per 13 kilometers	22	Rifle (infantry) divisions	63	One division per 4.5 kilometers	3:1
691	196,900	Men	527,033	1,849	3:1
37	10,583	Machine guns	19,959	70	2:1
5	1,507	Mortars	5,833	20	4:1
9	2,527	Guns (76mm and higher)	6,841	24	3:1
0.9	324	Tanks and self-propelled guns	2,205	8	7:1
–	700	Aircraft	1,647	–	2:1

A decisive superiority in forces over the Germans was achieved following the regrouping and the concentration of the main mass of troops along the shock axes.   We   had   the   following superiority over the enemy along the breakthrough sectors:

- six times in the number of divisions;
- five times in the number of men;
- 7-8 times in the number of guns;
- nine times in the number of tanks;
- five times in the number of planes.

Local fighting occurred along a broad front between the Neman and Vistula during the first ten days of January, while the troops improved their positions and trained for the forthcoming offensive. On 10 January the enemy carried out an attack along the sector of the First Baltic Front's 43rd Army in the Memel area, involving two regiments and 60 tanks, and made a dent in our position. On the following day the situation in this area was restored.

On the morning of 4 January 1945 the enemy's 170th and 367th infantry divisions, reinforced with more than 100 tanks, attacked along the 31st Army's sector, following a powerful artillery preparation, with the main blow in the direction of Czarne and Fillipow. As a result of stubborn fighting, the enemy managed to make a dent in our defense up to 2.5 kilometers deep along a 2-kilometer front.

By 5 January the situation along this sector of front had been had been restored by units of the 31st Army. During the fighting the enemy suffered heavy losses. Our forces killed up to 1,300 men and officers, and destroyed 20 guns, 44 machine guns and seven mortars, and knocked out up to 100 tanks and assault guns.

Typically, the enemy undertook this attack in just that area where disinformation measures had been conducted, according to the plan of the Third Belorussian Front's military council.

On the Third Belorussian Front's remaining sectors and in the Second Belorussian Front's sector, the usual crossfire and reconnaissance searches took place.

Thus the eve of the offensive, which was taken up with an enormous amount of organization work in preparing for the operation, included small combat actions.

The forces of the Second and Third Belorussian fronts occupied their jumping-off positions by the appointed time and were ready for the offensive.

4

The Beginning of the Third and Second Belorussian Fronts' Offensive. The Breakthrough of the German Defense North of Gumbinnen and along the Mlawa Axis

THE FIRST STAGE OF THE OPERATION, 13-18 JANUARY

The overall situation before the beginning of the Red Army's offensive in East Prussia unfolded as follows. Along the northern sector, the First Baltic Front's left wing occupied positions along the Neman River along the Tilsit axis (43rd Army), where local fighting broke out from time to time. The Third and Second Belorussian fronts were preparing to carry out crushing attacks. On 12 January along the sectors of the Third Belorussian Front's 2nd Guards and 31st armies; that is, where the main attack was to be made, reconnaissance detachments were operating, which in places broke into the Germans' first trenches and captured prisoners.

Our forces' offensive began on 13 January on the Third Belorussian Front, and on 14 January on the Second Belorussian Front. Despite the unfavorable weather (thick fog), the main forces of the Second and Third Belorussian fronts, following a powerful artillery preparation, advanced to storm the enemy's fortifications.

The combat actions of the Second and Third Belorussian fronts' forces in the first days were directed at carrying out the immediate combat tasks assigned to them: the breakthrough of the German defense, the commitment of the mobile formations, and the beginning of the development of the success. These operations were waged on the Third Belorussian Front during 13-18 January and along the Second Belorussian Front during 14-18 January. Taken together, they constitute the first stage of the East Prussian operation.

We will now successively examine the course of events by *front*.

THIRD BELORUSSIAN FRONT

The Beginning of the Offensive. Gnawing Through the Germans' Defense. The Maneuver by the Front's Second Echelon. The Breakthrough of the German Defense North of Gumbinnen

On the night of 12-13 January the *front's* forces were carrying out their final preparations for the offensive. Despite the careful masking and disinformation measures adopted by us, the enemy

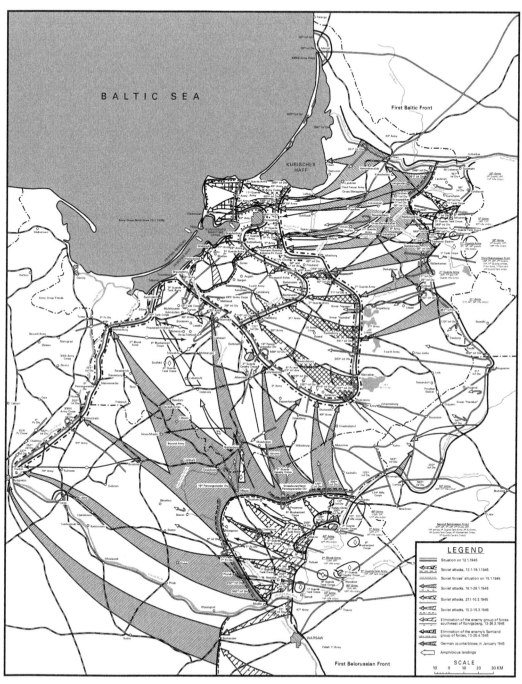

Map 6 Combat Activities in the East Prussian Operation (January 13-April 25, 1945).

nevertheless managed to establish the time of our attack. "We expected the Russian offensive as early as 7 January," testified the captured commander of the 1st squad/6th Company/1099th Infantry Regiment, "and at about 0200 on 13 January the company commander told me that at dawn the Russians would began an artillery preparation and then go over to the offensive."

Throughout the first half of the night the German artillery and mortars did not let up in their deliberate fire against our forces. At 0300 the firing became even stronger. The enemy's artillery, which numbered up to 40 batteries overall, subjected our first and then second trenches to a powerful barrage and carried out fire onslaughts against roads, individual heights, groves, and inhabited locales in the depth. The Dagutschen (southeast of Pilkallen)—Schilleningken—Kegsten—Bareischkemen (northwest of Stallupönen) and other areas were especially heavily subjected to fire. To a certain extent the enemy fire made it more difficult for our units to relieve and occupy their jumping-off positions for the attack, but the enemy could not interfere with this. Our artillery opened up a powerful answering fire. Simultaneously, the 1st Air Army's night bombers and our guards mortar units launched strikes against the enemy's batteries. The enemy's artillery and mortars suffered serious losses and were quickly forced into silence.

At 0600 on 13 January our forward battalions began to operate in the designated breakthrough zone. Energetically moving forward along many sectors, they overcame the enemy's engineering obstacles and broke into his forward edge. These detachments managed to establish in fighting that the first trench had been occupied only by an insignificant part of the defender's forces, while his main forces had been pulled back into the second and third trenches.

The information gained through reconnaissance made it possible to introduce some changes into the employment of fire by our artillery and mortars.

At 0900 the 39th, 5th and 28th armies began the artillery preparation. The main mass of our fire was directed at suppressing the enemy's personnel in the second and third trenches. The artillery worked at full strength during the fire onslaughts. Suffice it to point out that along the 5th Army's 9-kilometer front during the first five minutes of the fire onslaught about 6,870 shells were expended each minute. The army's artillery fired off 117,100 shells in 105 minutes.

The thick fog and low-lying clouds deprived us of the opportunity of employing our aviation and it was confined to its airfields throughout the entire day.

At 1100 the infantry, supported by direct infantry-support tanks and self-propelled artillery, attacked the enemy. From the offensive's first steps heavy fighting broke out along the entire breakthrough front.

Units of the 39th Army energetically attacked the enemy along the Wiltauten—excluding Schaaren front and, while moving forward, before long captured the second and third trenches. By 2100 they had penetrated into the enemy position to a depth of two kilometers and were engaged in stubborn fighting along the line of the western outskirts of Wiltauten—Pilkallen. Units of the enemy's 1st Infantry Division were resisting particularly fiercely and actively in the Pilkallen area, which had been transformed by them into a powerful strong point. Here the enemy launched up to 15 counterattacks in strength ranging from a company to a battalion, supported by 15-20 tanks.

Units of the 5th Army encountered no less stubborn resistance along the front Schaaren—Kischen. Taking advantage of the thick fog and the resulting lowered activity of our artillery, the Germans let our tanks and infantry approach close and, while widely employing *faustpatrones*,[1] anti-tank artillery and assault guns, and would fire on them from ambushes. Having determined the axis of our main attack, the German command began to bring up its immediate reserves to the

---

1   Editor's note. The *faustpatrone* was a popular hand-held anti-tank weapon, which appeared in the German army during the latter half of the Second World War. It was the forerunner of the larger and more effective *panzerfaust*.

area north of Gumbinnen. During the day the forces of the 5th Army were subjected to powerful counterattacks by units of the 349th and 549th infantry divisions, along with tanks. Only toward the close of the day did our forces manage to overcome the second and, in part, third trench lines, a large number of minefields, wire, post obstacles and other obstacles and, having advanced 2-3 kilometers into the Germans' defense, reached the line: Griben (1.5 kilometers southwest of Schaaren)—Juzdeggen (northern outskirst of Kattenau).

The offensive developed somewhat better along the 28th Army's offensive sector. Launching an attack with its right flank and center, the army broke through the enemy's defense along the Kischen—Grunhaus sector and, while energetically developing the offensive to the west, by the close of the day had penetrated up to seven kilometers into the enemy's position and reached the line: eastern outskirts of Kattenau—Alt Budupenen—Trakenen (two kilometers south of Grunhaus). Units of the enemy's 549th Infantry Division, being echeloned in depth and relying on previously prepared positions with a deeply developed system of engineering structures, put up powerful resistance.

During the day the army's units fought off 14 enemy counterattacks from the Kattau, Puspern and Zirgupenen areas. Up to a battalion of infantry, supported by 40-50 tanks and assault guns, took part simultaneously in these counterattacks.

According to preliminary data, our forces killed or destroyed in the day's fighting the following: up to 5,000 German soldiers and officers, 40 tanks, 71 guns, 52 mortars, and up to 150 machine guns. They captured 210 prisoners, belonging to the 1st, 349th, 549th, and 61st infantry divisions, as well as a large amount of weapons and ammunition.

Thus on the operation's first day, despite the noticeable success in the Kattenau area, as well as the serious losses inflicted on the enemy, not one of the *front's* armies was able to carry out the day's objective.

The *front* commander, General Chernyakhovskii, in calculating the results of the offensive for 13 January, pointed out, in particular, to the commander of the 5th Army:

> Despite the presence of a great deal of reinforcements and the expenditure of ammunition, the army did not achieve the day's objective.
>
> The reasons for this are:
> a) the coordination of the combat arms, infantry, tanks, and artillery, as well as the control of the battles was clearly organized unsatisfactorily at all levels;
> b) there were either no accompaniment guns in the companies, or there were extremely few;
> c) the clearing of the enemy's minefields was carried out slowly and without the necessary control or leadership.
>
> The commander of the 72nd Rifle Corps and his division commanders particularly poorly organized coordination and the control of battle.
>
> The direct infantry support tanks obviously operated in an unsatisfactory manner.

Further on, the following instructions were issued:

> In order to support our forces' offensive on 14.01.1945, I order the following:
> 1. The artillery is to be regrouped by dawn, creating a density of no less than 200 tubes along the axis of the main attack.
> 2. The battery and battalion observation posts are to be brought up to the line of the observation posts for the commanders of the first-echelon companies, securing reliable communications with the infantry.

3. Each first-echelon company is to be supported by an artillery battery, operating among the infantry as accompaniment artillery.
4. Ensure the fullest employment of mortars, particularly 82mm ones, which are to be attached to the companies for their more effective use.
5. With the onset of the dawn, you are to carry out the thorough reconnaissance of the position of the enemy's weapons and personnel for planning the artillery offensive.
6. The artillery preparation is to be conducted for 30-40 minutes using aimed fire, widely employing guns firing over open sights. The infantry attack is to be supported by the method of consecutively concentrating increasing fire.

General Chernyakhovskii issued similar instructions to the commander of the 28th Army.

In carrying out the *front* commander's order, our forces energetically prepared for the offensive throughout the night of 13-14 January, regrouped their forces, put the rank and file and weapons in order, and conducted reconnaissance. The artillery and mortars continuously fired on the enemy's position and launched concentrated blows against his concentration areas for infantry and tanks.

The German command, while attempting at all costs to delay the further development of the breakthrough by our forces, uninterruptedly brought up fresh reserves, chiefly tanks and assault guns, to the Kussen area throughout 13 January.

All types of intelligence established that more than 350 tanks and assault guns had arrived to reinforce units of the enemy's XXVI Army Corps by the close of the day.

At 0930 on 14 January the German forces unexpectedly counterattacked along several sectors of the front.

The enemy's counterattacks were beaten off with heavy losses for him along all the sectors of the front, and at 1230 on 14 January our forces themselves renewed the offensive, achieving their assigned objectives. However, on this day also our offensive developed very slowly. The German forces, relying on a thick network of trenches and communications trenches, put up stubborn resistance and threw in new reserves into the fighting. Enemy artillery, mortars and rocket-propelled weapons did not cease firing for a minute, while firing on our forces. Our infantry was often forced to hit the dirt under enemy fire and thus would fall behind the tanks. As before, the overcast weather limited visibility and made much more difficult the support for our infantry by our artillery, which by this time was operating jointly with the infantry to a significant extent. Only at 1400 did the improving meteorological conditions enable the air force to operate. Our planes rose into the air and subjected the enemy defense to an intensive bombardment opposite the 39th and 5th armies. For two hours the pilots of the 1st Air Army, taking advantage of the temporary clearing of the weather, carried out 490 sorties and destroyed up to 40 German tanks, 80 motor vehicles with infantry, suppressed 12 batteries, and shot down 25 enemy planes in air battles. However, even this support could not materially ease our infantry's situation and speed up its attack. The enemy delayed our forces' advance through heavy fire and fierce counterattacks, inflicting heavy losses. His aviation, in groups of 25-60 planes, repeatedly bombed our infantry and tanks in the Pilkallen—Griben (two kilometers southwest of Schaaren)—Kattenau area. Up to 250 enemy sorties were registered on this day along the axis of the main attack.

The 39th Army, while overcoming a deeply echeloned defense, repelled 15 enemy counterattacks that day in up to a battalion in strength, with 8-16 tanks apiece, and could only advance an insignificant distance along its left flank, where units of the 124th Rifle Division, which had been committed into the battle from behind the 358th Rifle Division's (94th Rifle Corps) right flank, broke into the powerfully fortified strong point of Pilkallen and seized the railroad station. The army's forces were not able to advance significantly along the other sectors of the front.

Units of the 5th Army, having resumed the offensive, broke through the enemy's fourth trench and, while accompanied by heavy artillery and tank fire, speeded up their advance to the west.

However, at 1400 the enemy in the army's sector unexpectedly launched a counterattack and launched powerful attacks from three axes: from the Jentkatkamen area with up to a battalion of infantry and 10-25 tanks and assault guns; from the Berzbruden area (two kilometers east of Tutschen) to the southeast, with up a regiment of infantry and 80 tanks, and; from the Tutschen area with up to two battalions of infantry and 40 tanks. The Germans were particularly stubborn in holding the strong point of Kattenau, along with the adjacent heights, which had important tactical significance for them. The German command employed units of the 5th Panzer Division to defend this strong point. Tanks and infantry repeatedly counterattacked the 65th Rifle Corps' 97th and 144th rifle divisions, which were attacking along this axis. However, the German units were not able to completely halt our offensive.

The 5th Army's forces, which were supported by artillery fire and massed air strikes, slowly but stubbornly advanced. By the close of the day they had penetrated into the enemy's position another two kilometers and captured the powerfully fortified strong points of Jentkatkamen and Berzbruden (two kilometers east of Tutschen).

No less fierce fighting took place on this day in the 28th Army's zone. The army's right-flank units repulsed 11 enemy counterattacks from a battalion to an infantry regiment in strength, supported each time by 12-20 tanks and assault guns. Some strong points and trenches in the Kattenau area changed hands several times. The Germans desperately launched counterattacks and fired heavily from ambushes and individual stone structures. While overcoming the enemy's stubborn resistance, the attacking units of the 3rd Guards Rifle Corps could only advance 1-1.5 kilometers along individual sectors and captured the Germans' powerful strong point of Kattenau.

In two days of fighting the Germans lost up to 10,000 men and officers killed and wounded, 126 guns, about 100 tanks, and a large amount of ammunition and equipment.

Thus on the offensive's second day the *front's* shock group was not able to break through the main zone of the enemy's defense. They were forced to wage heavy fighting in the tactical depth, while overcoming one defensive line after another.

The German command, having determined the axis of our main attack, began to remove its forces from the passive sectors of these armies and dispatch them to the Pilkallen—Gumbinnen area. The enemy moved the 5th Panzer Division, units of the 56th Infantry Division from the Schillenen area, and units of the 61st Infantry Division from the Gumbinnen area, to the breakthrough sector.

Brigades of assault guns, anti-tank artillery and other weapons were also being concentrated toward this zone for resisting our offensive. This may explain the slow advance by our armies on the operation's third day, as a result of which they penetrated only 3-4 kilometers into the enemy's position and by the close of 15 January had reached the line Pilkallen—Budzunen—Tutschen—Puspern, having once again encountered here a powerfully fortified defensive line (Gumbinnen).

In the developing situation it was necessary to activate the *front's* flanks in order to deprive the enemy of the opportunity of reinforcing the Gumbinnen axis, to disperse his reserves concentrating here and to thus ease and accelerate the development of the breakthrough. Alongside this, the slow development of the breakthrough was creating favorable conditions for the enemy's launching of counterblows from the flanks and the weakening of our forces that had penetrated into the Germans' defensive position.

Taking this into account, the *front* commander ordered the commander of the 2nd Guards Army to attack along his right flank on 16 January and, upon breaking through along the sector Zurguphen—Schoesteken, to develop the attack to the south of Gumbinnen.

The commitment of the 2nd Guards Tatsinskaya Tank Corps. During the night of 15-16 January the enemy, having been severely handled in the preceding fighting, was not particularly active. His artillery and mortars carried out deliberate fire against our forces' positions. His aircraft (Ju-88s) bombed the roads in our rear and the railroad stations, and launched mass strikes against the town of Stallupönen.

Having completed their preparations, at 1140 on 16 January our forces resumed the offensive, with the task of breaking through the Gumbinnen defensive line. However, even this time the enemy, despite heavy losses, put up stubborn resistance. The German command, under the cover of darkness, concentrated a large amount of field and assault artillery, catapult apparatuses and tanks at the breakthrough sector and sought with these weapons to retain control of the Gumbinnen defensive line at all costs. The Germans continually fired on our attacking infantry with powerful machine gun and mortar fire. Fierce fighting broke out for each building, each trench sector and strong point. Our forces' offensive unfolded slowly along all the sectors of the front. The infantry and tanks, deprived of the opportunity to undertake wide-ranging maneuver, were forced to carry out frontal fighting in conditions of a well developed system of trenches and switch positions. It was only at 1300 that the forces of the 5th Army captured the first trench of the Gumbinnen defensive line, but once again encountered stubborn enemy resistance in front of the second trench. The attacking infantry and tanks, having suffered heavy losses in the preceding fighting, began to give out; some subunits, while beating off continuous counterattacks, hugged the ground and barely moved forward. The threat that our offensive would sputter out and halt had arisen, despite the fact that the enemy's defense had already been deeply shaken. A new push was required, which would ensure the breakthrough of the enemy defense, which had been weakened but which still retained the capacity for resistance, and enable us to commit the *front* breakthrough development echelon (the 11th Guards Army and the 1st Tank Corps) into the fighting.

The *front* commander decided to use for this purpose the 2nd Guards Tatsinskaya Tank Corps, which had been concentrated by the close of 15 January northwest of Uzdeggen and to use it to launch an attack in the 5th Army's sector.

At 1245 on 16 January the tank corps received orders to begin moving into the breach along the front Budzunen—Wittkampen, with the objective of launching an attack in the general direction of Radschen.

At 1300 the 2nd Guards Tatsinskaya Tank Corps, organized into two echelons (the right group: the first combat echelon consisted of the 26th Guards Tank Brigade and the 4th Guards Tank Brigade the second combat echelon; the left group: the first combat echelon consisted of the 25th Guards Tank Brigade and the 4th Guards Motorized Rifle Brigade the second), passed through the infantry's formation and, accompanied by powerful artillery fire and aviation, attacked the enemy. However, the German units still maintained along this sector of front a sufficiently high combat capability and were trying to hold a continuous defensive front. The attacking tanks encountered heavy fire resistance from the enemy's assault guns, which were located in shelters, anti-tank guns and *faustpatrones*, which the Germans made great use of along this sector. The 25th Brigade, as well as in part the 26th, were before long involved in stubborn fighting with the enemy in the zone of the second and third trenches and were actually forced to finish breaking through the enemy defense, taking heavy losses as they did. The Germans began to more often throw their tanks and assault guns into the counterattacks and laid down heavy machine gun and mortar fire, striving to cut off the infantry following behind the tanks. Fw-189[2] aircraft, in groups of 18-50 planes, twice carried out massive strikes against our tanks. The tank corps' battle became prolonged. By the close of the day the tank brigades had advanced only 1-1.5 kilometers. The 26th Brigade threw the enemy out of the powerful strong point of Aimenischken and captured it; the

---

2   Editor's note. The Fw-189 was a twin-engine three-seat reconnaissance plane, which first appeared in 1941. It carried a crew of two and had a maximum speed of 560 kilometers per/hr. It was armed with two 20mm cannons and five 7.92mm machine guns.

25th Brigade captured Schokweten (two kilometers southwest of Aimenischken) and continued to advance slowly, while bypassing Radschen from the south. The corps commander, General Burdeinyi, decided to develop the success achieved with his tank brigades and at all costs break through the enemy's defense and achieve operational freedom. For this purpose, he committed the 4th Guards Tank Brigade (along the boundary between the 26th and 25th guards tank brigades) into the battle in the general direction of Radschen. However, this failed to accelerate the corps' movement. Throughout the entire day the 5th Army's main forces were involved in heavy fighting with the enemy and lagged behind the tanks.

With the onset of darkness, all the corps' tank brigades had reached the approaches to Radschen, a powerful German strong point, and outflanked it. The corps commander, striving to deprive the enemy of the opportunity of closing the breach that had opened here, decided to continue the corps' attack at night and in a night attack capture this locale. His plan proved to be correct. At 2330 the tank brigades attacked the enemy in Radschen, while the 26th Tank Brigade, having turned to the north with part of its forces, unexpectedly broke into Kussen. Stunned by the unexpected attack, the German soldiers ceased their resistance and began to fall back in panic to the west. At 0200 on 17 January the 25th and 4th guards tank brigades had cleaned the enemy out of Radschen. At 0300 the 26th Guards Tank Brigade, along with the 5th Army's forces, captured the important road junction of Kussen. While waging stubborn offensive battles, the tank corps continued to advance.

The 2nd Guards Army's goes over to the offensive. In carrying out the *front* commander's order, the 2nd Guards Army went over to the attack at 1430 on January 16. The attack was preceded by a 1 ½ hour artillery preparation and a powerful air strike. The enemy put up stubborn resistance from the very beginning. By the close of the day, the attacking divisions (the 13th Guards Rifle Corps' 24th Guards Rifle Division and the 11th Guards Rifle Corps' 32nd and 2nd Guards rifle divisions), having beaten off 12 enemy infantry and tank counterattacks, captured the first trench and in some sectors penetrated into the second trench. However, they were unable to advance further and were forced to consolidate along this line.

The 1st Tank Corps' commitment into the fighting. On 17 January our forces' offensive along the main axis sped up considerably. The 2nd Guards Tatsinskaya Tank Corps, without halting its active operations, repulsed four powerful enemy counterattacks along with units of the 5th Army and by 2100 hours had reached the line Kiggen—Jozden (three kilometers northwest of Radschen). The 5th Army's 72nd Rifle Corps, while closely cooperating with the 26th Guards Tank Brigade, occupied the inhabited locale of Kiggen with its right flank and with its left reached the inhabited locale of Abschrutten. To the left, the army's 45th and 65th rifle corps, having securely consolidated the strong point of Radschen, reached the line Mingschtimmen—Korellen (three kilometers east of Brakupenen). As a result of the stubborn fighting, the German forces were thrown out of the Gumbinnen defensive line's main positions and were conducting a slow fighting retreat to the west, while throwing their last reserves into the fighting. On this day the enemy west of Radschen carried out one of his powerful counterattacks along the boundary between the 72nd and 45th rifle corps, in which the newly arrived 10th Motorized Brigade, consisting of nine assault gun squadrons, took part, as well as the 56th Infantry Division's 234th Infantry Regiment, which had been transferred here from the Schillenen area.

On this day units of the 39th Army successfully developed the offensive. By a powerful attack in the center, in the 5th Guards Rifle Corps' zone, they broke through the Gumbinnen defensive line throughout its entire depth and, while decisively destroying the enemy retreating in disorder, by the close of 17 January reached the line Kurschelen—Gross Schorellen—Spullen, having turned its main forces to the northwest. On this day the enemy began to withdrawn in front of the army's right flank at dawn, evidently seeking to remove his 561st, 56th and 69th infantry divisions from the developing pocket in the Lazdenen area and to use them for occupying defensive positions along the Inster River. Units of the 152nd Fortified Area and the 113th Rifle Corps completely cleared the enemy out of Sudargas and reached Alt Lubenen, while another battalion of the same fortified area forced the Sesupa River northeast of Ladzenen and bypassed this inhabited locale from the north. The remaining battalions, along the 113th Rifle Corps' right-flank units, were fighting along the line Uzberdzen—excluding Kurschelen.

The commander of the 39th Army, while striving to destroy the enemy withdrawing along the southern bank of the Neman River, ordered his forces to speed up their attack and assigned them the following tasks: the 152nd Fortified Area was to capture Ladzenen on the night of 17-18 January and to continue to pursue the retreating enemy on the morning of 18 January and by the close of the day to reach the line Trappenen—Lebegalen; the 113th Rifle Corps was to reach the line Lebegalen—Brodlauken in night operations and to subsequently develop the attack toward Gross Skeisgirren (20 kilometers west of Zillen); the 5th Guards and 94th rifle corps were to decisively develop the attack without halting: the first, in the general direction of Neschtonweten, and the second toward Raudonatschen.

To the left, units of the 28th and 2nd Guards armies moved forward only slightly on this day. As before, the enemy was securely maintaining his positions along this axis, covering the important defensive center of Gumbinnen.

The offensive by the *front's* forces was actively supported by the 1st Air Army. During 16-17 January it carried out 3,468 sorties, of which about 1,500 were by bombers and assault aircraft.

The *front* commander, taking into account the developing situation, decided to immediately take advantage of the success achieved by the 39th Army along the northern axes and to vigorously develop it. For this he changed the tasks previously assigned to the 11th Guards Army and the 1st Tank Corps and hurriedly brought them up to the area of the breakthrough. On the night of 16-17 January the 11th Guards Army shifted to the north and on the morning of 17 January had concentrated in the Schilleningken—Kegsten—Zuggern area, while by this time the 1st Tank Corps had reached the Kussen area and here received an order from the *front* commander, instructing:

> By 0800 on 18.01.1945 the 1st Tank Corps is to occupy its jumping-off position in the Mingstimmen—Spullen—Henskischken area and by 1000 on 18.01.1945 be ready to enter the breach in the general direction Rautenburg—Neschtonweten—Zillen; by the close of 18.01.1945 the tank corps is to reach the Zillen area.
>
> The route of march is as follows: on the right—Mingstimmen—Rautenburg—Lengweten—Zillen; on the left—Spullen—Waldenau—Plauschinnen—Wittgirren. The movement is to begin upon my personal order.
>
> The commander of the 39th Army is to support the 1st Tank Corps' commitment into the breach, detaching for this purpose no less than three artillery regiments, and by 18.01.1945 its combined-arms formations are to reach the front Ikschen—Lengweten—Kraupischken at all costs.

At dawn on 18 January the tank corps had occupied its jumping-off position for the offensive. The enemy was not very active. The forward detachments operating ahead informed us that the severely worn-out units of the 1st Infantry Division did not have a solid defensive front and were putting up weak resistance with only small and scattered groups, mainly of infantry.

At 1030 on 18 January the tank corps, on orders of the *front* commander, went over to the offensive. Accompanied by powerful artillery fire and aviation, the tanks passed through the 39th Army's units along a broad front and surged forward. Destroying small enemy groups along its path, it headed to the northwest in two columns. The enemy, lacking reserves in depth along this axis, sought to delay the tank corps' advance with small detachments and threw his aviation and assault guns into the battle. However, they were already unable to halt the tank corps' vigorous advance. Destroying the remnants of the German forces retreating in confusion along their path to the west, by evening our tanks had reached the Inster River, forced it south of Heschtonweten, overcame here the Insterburg defensive line, and by 2100 reached the Lengweten—Marunen line.

Taking advantage of the 1st Tank Corps' success, the 39th Army also sped up its advance and, having made a fighting advance of up to 20 kilometers, its main forces at this time reached the Inster River, while the 5th Guards Rifle Corps captured Rautenburg and, upon forcing the river, continued to advance to the northwest. To the left, the 94th Rifle Corps reached the river along the Raudonatschen—Girrenen line.

Units of the army's right flank also advanced successfully on this day. By 2100 on 18 January the 152nd Fortified Area and the 113th Rifle Corps were fighting along the Trappenen—Gross Rudminnen—Waseninken line.

On this day the 1st Air Army energetically supported our forces' offensive from the air. In one day of fighting the air army carried out 690 sorties with bomber and assault aircraft and destroyed 45 enemy tanks, 300 motor vehicles, six armored transports, suppressed up to 70 artillery and mortar batteries, blew up six ammunition dumps, and scattered and partially destroyed up to 1 ½ regiments of infantry.

The German aviation was also very active. It bombed our formations in groups of 20-50 planes in the areas of Spullen, Radschen, Kussen, and Absprutten.

Thus on 18 January the forces of the Third Belorussian Front broke through the Germans' defense to the north of Gumbinnen. Advancing decisively, the 39th Army, along with the 1st Tank Corps, reached the Inster River and created the threat of encirclement of the Tilsit group of forces. The German command, wishing to preserve its forces operating to the south of Sudargas, began to pull them back, hoping to even out the front along the line Tilsit—Insterburg and, relying on the previously-prepared defense here, to once again offer organized resistance to our forces' offensive. Simultaneous with this, the German command sought to cover Insterburg from the north. Along the Zessliaken—Lindenberg line, hurriedly gathered units, chiefly construction battalions, engineering units and security subunits, were organizing a defense, strengthening the approaches to the town and creating continuous minefields between Grunheide and Aulowenen.

In the resulting situation the *front* commander decided to direct the *front's* main forces to the west, in order to reach the Deime River as quickly as possible, to completely split the Tilsit group of forces from the Insterburg group of forces and to destroy them in detail.

As early as the close of 16 January it had become obvious that that the breakthrough of the enemy's defense would be completed not in the 5th Army's sector, as had been called for by the plan, but further north, in the 39th Army's sector. The *front* commander decided to commit the 11th Guards Army and the 1st Tank Corps in the 39th Army's sector. He sought to develop the success that had arisen here and immediately committed into the fighting the 1st Tank Corps, which, while vigorously moving forward, reached the Inster River on the first day of the attack and forced it.

Bloody fighting continued along the main axis. The forces of the 5th and 28th armies, in overcoming the enemy's stubborn resistance, advanced slowly. The German units, relying on a thick network of trenches and strong points, carried out counterattacks and maintained a heavy mortar and artillery fire. General Chernyakhovskii, taking into account the fact that the problem of eliminating the Gumbinnen—Insterburg group of forces would not be resolved here, but further north, in the 39th Army's sector, directed his second echelons (11th Guards Army and 1st Tank Corps) there, so that, developing the success to the west, simultaneously with a decisive attack from the north, to outflank the Insterburg center of resistance and destroy the German forces operating there. This was the correct decision in the conditions of a strongly fortified and deeply echeloned enemy defense and would secure the successful fulfillment of the *front's* main task during the first stage of the East Prussian operation.

Along with the development of the offensive to the Inster River, the *front's* first-echelon forces were widening the breach through energetic attacks toward the flanks, thus supporting the commitment of the 11th Guards Army into the battle. By the close of 18 January the breakthrough front in the 39th Army's zone reached 35 kilometers. Simultaneous with this, units of the army's 113th Rifle Corps, advancing rapidly toward Tilsit, were seeking to encircle the retreating 548th, 561st and 56th infantry divisions.

Thus, in order to carry out the *front* commander's design, the commitment of fresh forces was required, along with the 2nd Guards Tatsinskaya Tank Corps operating northwest of Insterburg, to launch a vigorous attack toward Insterburg from the north and to cut off the route of retreat of the enemy's Insterburg—Gumbinnen group of forces to the west. Simultaneous with this, it was necessary to develop the success to the west as well, toward Königsberg, in order to deprive the enemy of the capability of employing his deep reserves and to use them to consolidate along the external defensive works of Königsberg.

Aside from the major operational success achieved by the forces of the Third Belorussian Front, the enemy suffered major losses in personnel and equipment. In six days of fighting 30,429 men and officers were killed, 290 tanks and assault guns destroyed, along with 244 motor vehicles, 305 guns, 1,124 machine guns, 195 mortars, and 40 catapult apparatuses, while 87 enemy planes were shot down in air battles and by our anti-aircraft artillery; 2,163 men were captured, as was a large amount of equipment, weapons and ammunition.

SECOND BELORUSSIAN FRONT

The Beginning of the Offensive. The Breakthrough of the Germans' Defense. The Commitment of the Mobile Formations

On 14 January 1945 the forces of the Second Belorussian Front, in accordance with directive No. 220274 of the *Stavka* of the Supreme High Command, began their offensive operation, with the task of defeating the enemy's Przasnysz—Mlawa group of forces and then attacking in the direction of Marienburg. On that morning a thick fog limited visibility to 150-200 meters.

At 1000 the artillery preparation for the offensive along the Rozan and Serock bridgeheads began with a 15-minute fire onslaught along the forward edge and tactical depth of the German defense. According to the unanimous statements of German prisoners, the artillery preparation was unexpected for them.

As a result of the worsening meteorological conditions, the results of the artillery and mortar fire were not visible. Fire was waged according to previously prepared data. We had to forego our aviation preparation for the attack.

Following the 15-minute artillery onslaught, the forward battalions, which had been specially detached from each first-echelon division and specially trained, advanced to the attack behind the explosions of the artillery shells. These battalions quickly overcame the enemy's minefields and barbed wire obstacles and broke into the Germans' first trench. Having cleared the first trench of small, individual enemy groups, the battalions continued to attack and by 1100 they had seized the second line of trenches and, in places, the third.

At 1125, following an 85-minute artillery preparation, the first-echelon rifle divisions of the 3rd, 48th and 2nd Shock armies, which were attacking from the Rozan bridgehead, and the 65th and 70th armies from the Serock bridgehead, began the general offensive, with the support of artillery and in conjunction with the tanks.

With the advance of our infantry into the depth of the enemy's tactical defense zone, his resistance began to increase. The Germans' resistance grew mainly by increasing the fire of machine guns and massive mortar fire from firing points, which, as a result of the poor visibility, our artillery was not able to suppress in time with aimed fire, while the actions of our guns firing over open sights were significantly limited for this reason as well. This circumstance told heavily on the pace of our infantry's advance.

One of the reasons for the slowing of the offensive pace by the close of the first day was the fact that the enemy, having recovered from the confusion of the attack's first hours, committed his immediate tactical reserves into the battle and undertook a series of counterattacks in groups of up to a company of infantry in strength, with 5-10 tanks and assault guns, while striving to delay our units' attack. However, all the Germans' counterattacks were successfully beaten off by our forces.

Besides this, one of the most important circumstances was the absence of our aviation over the battlefield. According to the aviation plan, a significant role in rendering assistance to the ground forces during the attack was set aside for the aviation. For example, according to the operational plan, we were supposed to carry out no less than 1,000 sorties along the breakthrough sector on the night before the attack, and during the day of 14 January no less than six assault air divisions were to systematically suppress enemy points of resistance.

The main burden of the fight to break through the Germans' defense lay upon the infantry, as well as the artillery, mortars, tanks, self-propelled artillery, and sappers immediately supporting it. Meanwhile, the experience of the first day showed that the tanks and self-propelled artillery from the immediate infantry support groups were not able to facilitate a high degree of offensive speed by the infantry.

The tanks and self-propelled artillery suffered heavy losses in the enemy minefields, and thus their advance was slowed down by the necessity of reconnoitering and clearing the attack sector of mines.

Finally, as was noted earlier, self-propelled artillery, moreover light models, predominated in the immediate infantry support groups and could not fully replace tanks.

However, despite the very difficult battlefield conditions, the Second Belorussian Front's forces broke through the forward edge of the enemy's defense on the first day and, overcoming his resistance and engineer obstacles in the depth, made a fighting advance of 4-8 kilometers along the Rozan and Serock bridgeheads.

The 3rd, 48th and 2nd Shock armies attacked along the Rozan bridgehead. The 3rd Army, having crushed the resistance by units of the Germans' 292nd and 129th infantry divisions, by the close of the first day had broken through the enemy's defense to a depth of five kilometers along a 10-kilometer front. The army's forces captured a number of major enemy strong points. The 3rd Guards Cavalry Corps, which was operationally subordinated to the army commander, carried out a march with the goal of concentrating in the Lipniki area (ten kilometers west of Rozan).

The 48th Army broke through the Germans' defense along a 6-kilometer front, and as a result of stubborn fighting advanced 3-6 kilometers, and by the close of the day was fighting along the approaches to Makow. The 8th Mechanized Corps, which had been operationally subordinated to the 48th Army, had concentrated in the Strachocin-Nowy area (12 kilometers southeast of Makow).

During 14 January the 2nd Shock Army, while outflanking the Germans' major Pultusk strong point along the Narew River from the north, advanced 3-6 kilometers and by the close of the day was stubbornly fighting with the German 7th Infantry Division on the approaches to Czarnostow (eight kilometers southwest of Makow). The army's left-flank 116th Rifle Corps was not involved in the fighting and remained in its previous position. The 8th Guards Tank Corps, which was operationally subordinated to the army, moved to the area ten kilometers north of Pultusk, with plans to enter the breach on 15 January for developing the 2nd Shock Army's success in the general direction of Ciechanow.

The 65th Army broke through the Germans' defense along its right wing along a 12-13 kilometer front. The army's units, while repelling enemy counterattacks, advanced in fighting 3-5 kilometers during the course of 14 January. The 1st Guards Tank Corps, which had been operationally subordinated to the army, crossed over to the western bank of the Narew River, and by the close of the day had concentrated in the area ten kilometers south of Pultusk.

During the course of 14 January the left-flank 70th Army advanced five kilometers along its right flank, and 2-3 kilometers in the center and along the left flank. At the same time, the army's forces captured the major strong points of Powelin and Dembe.

As a result of poor meteorological conditions, the 4th Air Army was not active on 14 January.

Throughout the night of 14-15 January the *front's* forces inflicted heavy losses on the Germans. For example, according to prisoner testimony, an anti-tank company from the 7th Anti-Tank Battalion (7th Infantry Division) lost on 14 January almost all of its equipment; the companies of the same division's 62nd Infantry Regiment lost up to 30 percent of their personnel in the battle's first hour, while the 1076th Infantry Regiment's (542nd Infantry Division) 2nd Company lost half of its personnel during the artillery preparation alone. During 14 January we captured 39 guns of various caliber, 41 mortars, 60 machine guns, 680 rifles and automatic rifles, 14 locomotives, and three depots. 859 enemy officers and men were captured. As for the armored and mechanized troops, we also captured 77 tanks and assault guns.

Prisoners and documents captured as a result of the attack's first day confirmed the presence of the 7th, 35th, 129th, 252nd, 292nd, and 542nd infantry divisions, the 104th Panzer Brigade, heavy mortars from the high command reserve and the 5th Light Infantry Division, facing the Second Belorussian Front. Prisoners from the 7th and 129th infantry and 5th Light Infantry divisions testified that the *Grossdeutschland* and 7th panzer divisions were expected to appear opposite the breakthrough front.

The offensive's first day showed that despite the poor visibility the results of the artillery preparation were quite effective. Our units' mortar fire quite accurately covered the enemy's minefields in front of the forward edge of his defense, which made it easier for the infantry to overcome these obstacles. Artillery and guards mortar fire, despite the fog, inflicted serious destruction on previously registered targets.

The reconnaissance in force by the forward battalions, which was conducted at the beginning of the artillery preparation, completely justified itself, enabling the troops on the day of the attack to pinpoint the enemy's forward edge, as well as the disposition of his weapons and their fire system.

As a result of the first day's fighting, it transpired that although the Germans expected our forces' offensive along the Rozan and Serock bridgeheads, on that day—14 January—our attack was a surprise, as the enemy did not expect that our forces would launch a major offensive under such unfavorable weather conditions.

The enemy put up his weakest resistance to our attacking units in the first 3-4 trenches. Subsequently, the Germans put up their greatest resistance in the fifth and sixth trenches and their strong points in the tactical defense zone, both in terms of fire and frequent counterattacks.

In general, the offensive developed slowly on the first day of the offensive; our forces advanced only 4-8 kilometers and they did not manage to fully disrupt the enemy's tactical defense system and develop a number of local breakthroughs into a single overall breakthrough of the enemy's front.

At 2255 on 14 January the *front* commander, Marshal of the Soviet Union Rokossovskii, ordered the armies of the *front's* shock groups to continue, from 0900 on 15 January, the offensive with the same objectives.

The second day of the breakthrough. On 15 January the weather conditions continued to be unfavorable—the heavy fog and limited visibility prevented our air operations and rendered artillery fire more difficult. Besides this, a heavy snowfall beginning at 1100, along with heavy fog, limited visibility even further.

The Germans, relying on their deeply echeloned defense and their previously prepared strong points, covered by barbed wire obstacles and minefields, continued to put up determined resistance to our attacking forces. During the night the enemy brought up to the front units of the *Grossdeutschland* and 7th panzer divisions. Besides this, the enemy put his tactical reserves in order. With these forces, the Germans carried out more than 70 counterattacks with infantry and tanks during 15 January, often throwing in groups of up to 50 tanks. The German counterattacks along the Rozan bridgehead and some other sectors began before our artillery fire onslaught, so that the fire from our artillery and mortars, which was called up for repelling the enemy counterattacks, essentially marked the beginning of our artillery preparation and the beginning of the troops' offensive on 15 January.

The troops of the *front's* shock groups, while overcoming growing resistance and counterattacks by the enemy, waged intense offensive battles on 15 January. Meanwhile, many strong points in the Germans' defense changed hands several times.

The forces of the Second Belorussian Front, while continuing the offensive from the Rozan and Serock bridgeheads and repelling counterattacks by German infantry and tanks, advanced 4-6 kilometers along several axes, and as a result of the 15 January fighting, occupied the Germans' major defensive strong point and paved road junction of Makow.

Despite the difficult offensive conditions, as a result of the poor weather conditions and the impossibility of employing our aviation, the *front's* forces insistently developed the offensive, overcoming the Germans' stubborn resistance. The infantry, while employing its own fire, operated boldly and decisively, outflanking and destroying the enemy's strong points and centers of resistance.

On 15 January the right-flank 50th Army continued to defend the line Augustow—Osowiec—Lomza—excluding Nowogrod.

The 49th Army, to which the 42nd Rifle Division had been returned from the 3rd Army and which had taken over the sector occupied by this division, committed into the fighting yet another rifle division from the same 121st Rifle Corps (380th Rifle Division), but encountered stubborn enemy resistance and advanced insignificantly on 15 January. The 70th Rifle Corps remained in the second echelon behind the army's left flank.

Throughout 15 January the 3rd Army was engaged in intense fighting. At first the army's units were successful and gradually advanced. However, the enemy committed into the fighting up to 130 tanks and assault guns from the *Grossdeutschland* Panzer Division and conducted more than 30 counterattacks, while the German infantry attacks were supported by10-50 tanks and assault guns. As a result, the enemy managed to push back our units a little.

The 48th Army continued to attack, launching its main blow along the left flank and, as a result of stubborn fighting throughout 15 January, advanced 4-6 kilometers. At the same time, the army's forces reached the Makow—Ciechanow paved road and captured the enemy's powerful Makow center of resistance. The army's forces, while repelling enemy infantry and tank counterattacks, had by the close of the day reached the line Makow—excluding Czarnostow. The 8th Mechanized Corps concentrated in the woods six kilometers southwest of Makow, in readiness to enter the breach in the 48th Army's offensive sector.

On 15 January the 2nd Shock Army encountered powerful resistance. The enemy, fearing the encirclement of his Pultusk group of forces, committed more than 100 tanks from the 7th Panzer Division into the fighting, and held up the attack by our forces through numerous counterattacks by the 7th Infantry and 5th Light Infantry divisions. As a result, by the close of the day the 108th and 98th rifle corps had not advanced far, only 1-2.5 kilometers. The 116th Rifle Corps remained in its previous position.

In order to crush the enemy's stubborn resistance, the 8th Guards Tank Corps was committed into the battle at 1145, along the Czarnostow sector and to the south. Throughout the day the corps completed the breakthrough of the enemy's defense and by the close of the day was fighting in the area six kilometers southwest of Czarnostow.

At 1000 on the offensive's second day, the 65th Army renewed its attacks following a 12-minute fire onslaught by all its artillery. Throughout the day the army's units repelled up to nine enemy counterattacks and, while overcoming the Germans' stubborn resistance, captured several major strong points and advanced 3-4 kilometers.

At 1300 the 1st Guards Tank Corps began its attack, passed through the infantry's combat formation, and by evening reached the area six kilometers northeast of Nasielsk, ready to develop the offensive on Nasielsk and Nowe Miasto on the morning of 16 January.

On 15 January the 70th Army's forces, following a 30-minute artillery preparation, continued their offensive from 1000. Crushing the Germans' stubborn resistance, by the end of the day the army's formations had advanced 3-4 kilometers and were fighting 3-4 kilometers southeast of Nasielsk.

On 15 January the 5th Guards Tank Army had finished concentrating in the woodes southeast of Ostrow Mazowiecka.

The *front's* aviation, as a result of the poor meteorological conditions on 15 January, was almost idle. Only 40 sorties were carried out that day, chiefly for reconnaissance purposes. On this day the enemy's aviation carried out only one sortie.

The enemy, as a result of the *front's* offensive operations, suffered heavy losses. During 15 January 272 men and officers were taken prisoner and the following equipment seized: two tanks, 25 armored transports, 39 guns of various calibers, 136 machine guns, six radio sets, and 1,236 rifles and automatic rifles.

To the left, the First Belorussian Front's 47th Army attacked on 15 January in the area between the Bug, Narew and Vistula rivers, threw back the enemy to the western bank of the Vistula and began forcing the river.

In general, as a result of the combat on 15 January, the enemy managed to slow down our offensive by committing two panzer divisions into the battle, as well as all his tactical reserves. Nonetheless, along with the 8th and 1st Guards tank corps, we managed to crush the enemy's resistance along the 2nd Shock and 31st armies' front, where we had planned to break through the entire depth of the Germans' tactical defense, and the enemy's Pultusk group of forces had been deeply outflanked along both flanks by our tank mobile groups. One could expect the enemy to withdraw.

On 15 January the *front* commander issued objectives to his armies regarding the subsequent development of the offensive, and it was pointed out that we could not allow the enemy to systematically withdraw and consolidate along intermediate lines, and that the offensive should be conducted both day and night.

The 3rd Army was ordered to reach the line of the Orzyc River with its main forces by the morning of 16 January.

The 48th Army was ordered to reach the line Szczuki (ten kilometers northwest of Makow)—Konarzewo (15 kilometers southwest of Makow).

At the same time the 2nd Shock Army was required to capture the line excluding Konarzewo—Gasiorowo (12 kilometers west of Pultusk) with its main forces. It was furthermore indicated in the order that despite its superiority of force, the 2nd Shock Army failed to carry out its assigned tasks over the last two days. The reasons for this were: a) the poor organization of the battle in the depth of the enemy's defense; b) the reserving and unskilled employment of tanks and self-propelled guns; c) the halting of the offensive as a result of the enemy's petty (platoon, company, battalion) counterattacks, and; d) the absence of initiative, decisiveness and maneuver on the battlefield.

The 65th Army was ordered to reach the line excluding Gasiorowo—Nasielsk with its main forces by the morning of 16 January, while the 70th Army was ordered to reach the line excluding Nasielsk and to the south with its main forces at the same time.

At 1615 on 15 January the *front* commander informed the commander of the 8th Guards Tank Corps that the enemy was undertaking counterattacks in order to cover the withdrawal of his forces and demanded a vigorous push forward in order to more quickly carry out his assignment.

The development of the breakthrough on 16 January. On the night of 15-16 January the forces of the Second Belorussian Front's shock group continued their offensive. The formations of the 2nd Shock and 65th armies, while attacking with battalions detached from each first-echelon division, and trained for night fighting and overcoming resistance by the enemy's rearguards, advanced up to ten kilometers along several sectors during the night and captured the town of Pultusk—a major German strong point along the right bank of the Narew River. Detachments from the *front's* other armies also waged night battles.

The enemy, while holding the offensive by units of the 3rd and 70th armies, carried out furious counterattacks against the flanks of the *front's* breakthrough. Simultaneously, in connection with the threat of complete encirclement of the Pultusk group of forces by units of the 2nd Shock and 65th armies, the Germans abandoned Pultusk under the pressure of our forces on the night of 15-16 January and began to withdraw from this area to the northwest and west.

During 16 January, as the result of night and day offensive activities along the Mlawa direction, the *front's* forces advanced 10-25 kilometers in fighting, captured the enemy's major strong points and rail and road junctions of Pultusk and Nasielsk and occupied more than 400 other inhabited locales. The *front's* forces cut the Mlawa—Modlin railroad.

The successful advance by the ground forces on 16 January was facilitated by assault air and bomber strikes by our aviation, which, thanks to the improvement in the weather, carried out more than 2,500 sorties on this day and dropped up to 1,800 tons of bombs on the enemy's combat formations.

The Germans, while putting up stubborn resistance to the *front's* offensive, carried out 45 counterattacks with infantry and tanks during 16 January. The most desperate fighting took place along the 3rd Army's front. Here, in the area southeast of Krasnosielc, prisoners confirmed the commitment of the *Grossdeutschland* Panzer Division into the battle. The presence of the Germans' 7th Panzer Division was confirmed along the Ciechanow axis.

Aerial reconnaissance confirmed the presence of up to 260 tanks and assault guns among the enemy's infantry along the breakthrough sector, with the largest group of tanks (up to 150 vehicles) discovered opposite the 3rd Army.

On 16 January the activities of the Germans' aviation increased somewhat. 120 enemy sorties were noted on this day. The enemy's aviation carried out reconnaissance and bombed our forces in groups of 9-20 planes.

On 16 January the right-flank 50th Army continued to defend its previous line. The 27th Anti-Tank Artillery Brigade was removed from the army and into the *front* reserve and was to concentrate by the morning of 17 January in the groves two kilometers south of Makow.

To the left, the 49th Army continued attacking along its left flank, but ran into stubborn enemy resistance and did not advance far (2-3 kilometers) during 16 January. The army's second-echelon 70th Rifle Corps was deployed by the close of the day in an area 5-10 kilometers northwest and northeast of Rozan. On 16 January the 1st Artillery Division, which was located within the 2nd Shock Army, was operationally subordinated to the 49th Army.

On 16 January the 3rd Army renewed its attack. The army's forces encountered the enemy's powerful fire resistance and counterattacks, and he committed up to 150 tanks and assault guns into the fighting along the army's front. Units of the 3rd Army, while overcoming the Germans' stubborn resistance, advanced only 1-3 kilometers that day, despite powerful artillery support.

On this day the 48th Army continued its attack and made a fighting advance of up to ten kilometers. Units of the army, while overcoming the enemy's fire resistance and repeated counterattacks, by the end of the day had reached the line of the woods five kilometers northeast of the line Makow—Konarzewo.

The successful advance by the army's left flank was facilitated by the commitment into the breach of the 8th Mechanized Corps, which by the end of the day was fighting ten kilometers east of Ciechanow.

On 16 January the 2nd Shock Army continued attacking. On the night of 15-16 January the enemy began to withdraw from the Pultusk area to the west, pulling out from under our attacks the 7th Infantry and 5th Light Infantry divisions, which had been defeated in the 14-15 January fighting, as well as the 7th Panzer Division. The 2nd Shock Army's forces captured Pultusk and, while pushing aside the enemy's covering units, advanced 20 kilometers. By the close of the day the army was fighting six kilometers southeast of Ciechanow along its right flank, and for Gonsocin station (16 kilometers northwest of Nasielsk) on its left.

The 8th Guards Tank Corps was advancing ahead of the 2nd Shock Army's right flank and by the evening of 16 January had reached in fighting the area eight kilometers southeast of Ciechanow.

The 65th Army, while developing the offensive to the northwest, advanced that day up to 20 kilometers. The army captured the Germans' strong point of Nasielsk and cut the Ciechanow—Modlin railroad. By 2000 the army's units were fighting along a line five kilometers northeast and southeast of Nowe Miasto.

By the close of the day the 1st Guards Tank Corps had reached the enemy's third defensive line and was fighting along the approaches to Nowe Miasto.

The 70th Army, in overcoming the enemy's stubborn resistance, was advancing echeloned to the rear, and by the close of 16 January had reached the line excluding Nasielsk and to the southwest.

On 16 January the 4th Air Army carried out 2,516 sorties, of which 775 were at night. 16 enemy planes were shot down in 18 air battles, while five enemy aircraft were destroyed at the Ciechanow airfield.

On 16 January the *front's* forces captured the following from the Germans: 26 tanks and assault guns, 14 armored transports and tows, 103 guns of various calibers, 41 mortars, 201 machine guns, 800 rifles and automatic rifles, and captured 315 men and officers.

The fighting of 16 January was decisive for the breakthrough of the enemy's main defensive zone.

As a result of three days of fighting, the *front's* forces broke through the enemy's defense. The mobile tank and mechanized formations, as well as the 2nd Shock and 65th armies, began to pursue the Germans withdrawing along the Mlawa direction. In three days the forces of the *front's* shock group advanced as much as 30 kilometers. A favorable situation was being created for the commitment of the tank army into the breach for the purpose of cutting off the Germans' East Prussian group of forces from the rest of Germany.

At 1415 on 16 January the commander of the Second Belorussian Front issued combat order no. 0034/op, ordering the 5th Guards Tank Army to concentrate by the morning of 17 January in the Makow—excluding Pultusk area. The army was to be ready to enter the breach from the Ciechanow line in the general direction of Mlawa and Lidzbark.

At 2000 on 16 January the 5th Guards Tank Army began moving to its jumping-off area, indicated by the *front* commander. The march unfolded in very difficult conditions. The night, the thick fog, the large number of minefields, and the crossings over the Narew and Orzyc rivers made the tanks' advance more difficult. But the army successfully completed its 40-kilometer march and by the morning of 17 January had concentrated to the west of Makow, having exactly carried out the *front* commander's order. Here the army received the following objective: "... at 1200 on 17 January to enter the breach along the Makow—Karnewo sector in the general direction of Grudusk, Mlawa and Lidzbark. The army's immediate objective is by the morning of 18 January to reach the line Mlawa, and by the morning of 19 January to capture Neidenburg and Dzialdowo."

The completion of the breakthrough. On the night of 16-17 January combat activities did not cease and specially detached units continued the offensive battles.

On the morning of 17 January the forces of the *front's* shock group continued the offensive along the Mlawa direction. The 5th Guards Tank Army was committed into the battle along the 48th Army's sector. Developing the success in the center of the breakthrough, our forces overcame the enemy's desperate resistance and counterattacks along the flanks.

During 17 January the *front's* formations advanced up to 15 kilometers along individual sectors and widened the breakthrough to 110 kilometers in width. As a result of the successful fighting, on that day the forces of the Second Belorussian Front captured the Germans' major strong points of Ciechanow and Nowe Miasto.

The enemy, relying on previously prepared intermediate defensive lines and strong points, undertook during the day more than 30 counterattacks, supported by tanks and assault guns. The Germans, covering themselves with mobile detachments from a company to a battalion in strength, supported by tanks and artillery, continued to pull back the remnants of their defeated units in the breakthrough sector to the northwest and west.

Prisoners testified that the remnants of the 252nd and 542nd infantry divisions had been amalgamated into combat groups, and that the 542nd Artillery Regiment (542nd Infantry Division) had knocked out the greater part of its weapons while withdrawing. Four enemy fortress and construction battalions, which had been hurriedly transferred from East Prussia for defending the approaches to Ciechanow from the southeast, suffered heavy losses of up to 60-70 percent. The "Moser" *Volkssturm*[3] Battalion, which had taken up defensive positions in the area 15 kilometers north of Nowe Miasto, scattered at our tanks' appearance, without putting up a fight. According to prisoner testimony, on the first day of our forces' offensive, 14 January, the entire male civilian population of the town of Mlawa had been mobilized into *volkssturm* detachments and transferred by rail to Przasnysz, while Mlawa's establishments, depots and population were evacuated. The Germans were hurriedly preparing the following centers of resistance for all-round defense: Zuromin, Biezun, Sierpc, and Rypin (all locales 30-70 kilometers west and southwest of Mlawa) and their garrisons reinforced with subunits retreating from the front.

On 17 January the right-flank 50th Army continued to defend its previous line.

The 49th Army's left-flank 121st Rifle Corps continued to attack, supported by artillery and aviation, and advanced that day 4-5 kilometers and reached in fighting the line Oleksy (12 kilometers north of Rozan)—Mamino (14 kilometers northwest of Rozan). Simultaneously, the 208th Rifle Division's right-flank regiment forced the Narew River in the area three kilometers southwest of Ostroleka, captured two enemy trenches and by the close of the day had created a bridgehead three kilometers wide and up to one kilometer deep. The 70th Rifle Corps, comprising the army's second echelon, remained in the area 5-10 kilometers northwest and northeast of Rozan.

The 3rd Army continued the offensive on the morning of 17 January and, while repelling counterattacks by units of the 129th and 292nd infantry divisions, as well as the *Grossdeutschland* Panzer Division, advanced 6-10 kilometers and by the close of the day was fighting for Krasnosielc.

On 17 January the 3rd Guards Cavalry Corps was removed from subordination to the commander of the 3rd Army and was given the task by the *front* commander to enter the breach in the general direction of Makow, Przasnysz and Muschaken (32 kilometers northeast of Mlawa).

---

3   Editor's note. The *volkssturm*, or people's militia, was organized in late 1944 as a last-ditch effort to stave off defeat. The *volkssturm* was made up of males between 16 and 60, who were not already serving in the armed forces. The highest *volkssturm* unit was the battalion. While organized by the Nazi Party, the *volkssturm* fought under armed forces command.

The 48th Army, while developing the offensive to the northwest, made a fighting advance of up to 16 kilometers and by 2000 on 17 January was fighting along the following line: its right flank was eight kilometers southeast of Przasnysz, and the left along the northern outskirts of Ciechanow.

The 8th Mechanized Corps captured the outer ring of the Mlawa fortified area and by 1900 was fighting for Grudusk (20 kilometers north of Ciechanow).

The 2nd Shock Army, while developing the offensive on 17 January, captured Ciechanow. The Germans continued to fall back to the west under the blows of the army's units. By the close of the day the 108th and 98th rifle corps had reached the line Ciechanow and to the south. The 116th Rifle Corps, comprising the army's second echelon, reached the area ten kilometers southeast of Ciechanow.

The 8th Guards Tank Corps was attacking in the direction of Szrensk (20 kilometers southwest of Mlawa), and by the close of 17 January was 3-4 kilometers in front of the 2nd Shock Army's center.

The 65th Army broke through the Germans' defense along the third defensive line, captured the major strong point of Nowe Miasto and made a fighting advance of up to 15 kilometers. The army's forces, having captured the enemy's defensive line along the west bank of the Sonia River, which consisted of four trench lines, and having repelled three counterattacks of up to a battalion of infantry, each supported by 10-20 tanks, was by 2000 on 17 January fighting along the line 10-15 kilometers northwest and southwest of Nowe Miasto.

By the close of the day the 1st Guards Tank Corps had made a fighting advance to the area six kilometers east of Plonsk.

On 17 January the left-flank 70th Army made a fighting advance of up to 14 kilometers, forced the Dzialdowka (Wkra) River and by the close of the day had begun fighting for the eastern and southeastern outskirts of the town and fortress of Modlin. On this day the 114th Rifle Corps was committed from behind the army's right flank. Two divisions remained in the second echelon—one each from the 114th and 47th rifle corps.

During 17 January the *front's* 4th Air Army carried out 2,512 sorties, of which 653 were at night. On 17 January one German plane was shot down in aerial combat.

The commitment of the 5th Guards Tank Army into the battle. On 17 January our aviation increased its activities in the sector for committing the tank army into the breach. In four hours the planes of the 4th Air Army carried out more than 1,000 sorties and dropped a large amount of bombs on the combat formations of the enemy, who was trying to organize resistance on the approaches to Mlawa. At 1200 the 5th Guards Tank Army, under the cover of a large number of fighters, deployed southwest of Makow and began to move forward along a broad front. Before long the tanks passed through the 53rd Rifle Corps' (48th Army) combat formations and from the march vigorously attacked the 299th and 7th infantry divisions, which had been reinforced by 20 tanks and assault guns. The Germans put up stubborn resistance. Widely employing fire from assault guns and anti-tank guns firing from ambush, as well as *faustpatrones*, they tried to defeat the attacking tanks and halt their further advance. The Germans put up the greatest resistance along the army's right flank, in the 10th Tank Corps' offensive sector. Here we discovered 12 assault guns, six tanks and four artillery batteries, which had been carefully disguised in the structures of inhabited locales. The Germans twice undertook powerful counterattacks and came down on our tanks from the flanks. The commander of the 10th Tank Corps was forced to deploy and commit both tank brigades into the battle. Following two hours of stubborn fighting, the attacking tanks completely defeated the enemy defending in the Krasne area (14 kilometers southeast of Przasnysz and began to quickly develop the offensive to the northwest. At 2100 on 17 January the 10th Tank Corps cut the Przasnysz—Ciechanow paved road and part of its forces broke into the southern outskirts of Przasnysz.

To the left, in the 29th Tank Corps' attack sector, the enemy put up less stubborn resistance. The lead tank brigades, without deploying their main forces, broke through the enemy's third defensive line from the march and, while moving forward, by the evening of 17 January reached the paved road northeast of Ciechanow. Following a brief halt, the corps' units resumed the offensive and at 0300 on 18 January reached the fortifications of the Mlawa defensive ring.

Combat operations on 18 January. The fighting for Mlawa. At dawn on 18 January the 5th Guards Tank Army continued its forward advance. The enemy's forces, relying on the powerful Mlawa fortified area, were widely employing maneuver with anti-tank mobile weapons, were organizing a large number of anti-tank ambushes, and unexpectedly counterattacking and throwing large groups of tanks and assault guns into the fighting. Before 0800 the tank corps had repelled 14 powerful enemy counterattacks, with up to 40 tanks participating in each of them, reinforced with infantry and anti-tank artillery. All of this slowed down our tanks' advance and they, despite the very favorable conditions for entering the breach, were unable to break free of the infantry following behind them. It was only during the latter half of 18 January, when units of the right-flank 10th Tank Corps broke through the third defensive line along a 5-kilometer sector southwest of Przasnysz, did the tanks' advance speed up significantly. Units of the 10th Tank Corps bypassed the Mlawa fortified area from the northeast.

At 0200 on 19 January the corps' lead brigades, having overcome the roadless, peat and swampy terrain, broke through north of Mlawa, captured Naperken (12 kilometers north of Mlawa) and cut the second very important Neidenburg—Mlawa paved road.

At the same time the 29th Tank Corps continued pursuing the enemy along the Ciechanow—Mlawa railroad, bypassing Mlawa from the south and southwest. The enemy was falling back in such a hurry that his sappers didn't have enough time to destroy the bridges over the Dzialdowka River that had been prepared for demolition. Our tanks broke into Dzialdowo on the heels of the retreating enemy, destroyed its garrison and by the morning of 19 January had captured the town. Among the large amount of captured equipment were four trains with ammunition, eight battle-ready tanks, 14 locomotives, more than 400 motor vehicles, 40 guns of various calibers, two depots with ammunition and fuel, and a large amount of ammunition. More than 15,000 prisoners of war and Soviet citizens driven into Germany were freed from the concentration camps located within the Dzialdowo area.

Thus by the close of 18 January the Mlawa fortified center had been completely blocked by our tank formations and the just-arrived motorized infantry.

Units of the 48th Army, taking advantage of the 5th Guards Tank Army's success, broke through several of the enemy's fortified lines girding Mlawa, and by the evening of 18 January had reached the town's outskirts. The German garrison, consisting of the remnants of the 7th and 299th infantry divisions, the 18th Panzergrenadier Division's 30th Panzergrenadier Regiment, and reinforcements, was occupying the major brick structures and a series of reinforced-concrete firing points, located chiefly at the intersections of streets, and were putting up stubborn resistance. Despite this, units of the 42nd Rifle Corps soon broke into the town. Bloody fighting went on here all night. By widely employing guns for firing over open sights, tanks and mortars, the 42nd Rifle Corps' elements won one block of the town after the other. On the morning of 19 January the enemy garrison had been completely destroyed and its remnants taken prisoner. A large amount of captured equipment fell into our hands. The right-flank 29th Rifle Corps took by storm the important road junction and major strong point of Przasnysz.

The *front* commander decided to take advantage of the success in the 48th Army's sector, particularly in the Przasnysz area, and to commit the 3rd Guards Cavalry Corps along this axis. From the Rozan area the corps, which had been preparing to be committed along the 3rd Army's sector, was shifted by a forced march through Makow to the Przasnysz area, where it was ordered to enter the breach in the general direction of Makow, Przasnysz and Muschaken (32 kilometers northeast of Mlawa). The cavalry corps' immediate objective was to reach the line Willenberg—Neidenburg by the close of 20 January, and to subsequently attack toward Allenstein.

In carrying out the *front* commander's order, by the close of 18 January the 3rd Guards Cavalry Corps had concentrated in the Przasnysz area and was preparing to attack.

The 2nd Shock Army captured Ciechanow and was successfully pursuing the enemy retreating in disorder. On 18 January the army advanced more than 30 kilometers and by the close of the day had cut the Mlawa—Biezun paved road.

On the right wing of the *front's* shock group, units of the Germans' 14th, 292nd and 129th infantry divisions, relying on the wooded and swampy areas, continued to resist stubbornly. The Germans, ceaselessly undertaking counterattacks with infantry and tanks, sought to prevent the widening of the breach toward the flanks and thus ease the situation of their forces operating in the Mlawa area.

The 49th Army, while continuing to attack along the western bank of the Narew River, by 2000 on 18 January was engaged in heavy fighting facing to the north along the line excluding Ostroleka—Zaniec (18 kilometers west of Ostroleka).

The 3rd Army, upon capturing the enemy's major strong point of Krasnosielc, forced the Orzyc River and, slowly advanced while fighting in wooded and swampy terrain.

On the *front's* left flank, the 65th Army, while pursuing the retreating enemy, by the close of 18 January had reached Glinojeck along its right flank, while on its left flank it had forced the Dzialdowka (Wkra) River and reached the area eight kilometers north of Plonsk. The 5th Light Infantry and the 35th Infantry divisions, covering themselves with rearguards, continued to fall back to the west and were waging delaying actions along the approaches to Plonsk.

Following stubborn fighting, the 70th Army captured the town and fortress of Modlin.

The unfavorable meteorological conditions limited our aviation's operations. On 18 January the 4th Air Army carried out only 192 sorties, mainly for reconnaissance purposes.

The First Belorussian Front's 47th Army, to the left, had by 1800 on 18 January reached the Bzura River along the sector excluding Wyszgrod—Sochaczew.

Results of the 14-18 January fighting. The forces of the Second Belorussian Front, having gone over to the offensive on 14 January from two bridgeheads along the western bank of the Narew River in the area of the towns of Rozan and Serock, broke through the enemy's powerful and deeply echeloned defense, supported by the massive blows of our artillery, tanks and aviation.

During the offensive our forces captured the powerful strong points of the Germans' defense— Makow, Pultusk, Ciechanow, Nowe Miasto, and Nasielsk, and also occupied in fighting more than 500 other inhabited locales.

The forces of the German Second Army's XXIII and XX army corps, having suffered a defeat, were thrown back from the Ciechanow—Nowe Miasto defensive line and, having been ejected from the important Ciechanow center of resistance, on 17 January were retreating to the north-west and west to their rear defensive lines.

On the breakthrough's right flank, units of the enemy's 292nd, 129th and 299th infantry divisions, the *Grossdeutschland* Panzer Division, and subunits of the 14th and 102nd infantry divisions, were putting up stubborn resistance to our forces' advance.

During the 14-17 January fighting the *front's* forces captured 1,859 men and seized 223 guns, 123 mortars, and 38 tanks and assault guns.

As a result of the 18 January fighting, the Mlawa fortified area was taken by our forces. The enemy's last organized resistance in this area was crushed. The Germans' defense had been pierced along the Przasnysz—Mlawa—Plonsk arc, stretching 110 kilometers and up to 60 kilometers deep. The *front's* forces attained operational freedom and were able to develop the subsequent offensive to the northwest or north, in order to reach the shore of the Baltic Sea for the purpose of isolating the enemy's East Prussian group of forces from the rest of Germany.

Conclusions

During the operation's first stage, the forces of the Second and Third Belorussian fronts achieved major operational results.

The Second Belorussian Front defeated the enemy in the sector of the *front's* main group of forces with a powerful blow and created a breach in the Germans' defense. Powerful mobile formations (5th Guards Tank Army, two tank corps, a mechanized corps, and a cavalry corps) were committed into the breach and, in conjunction with the attacking combined-arms armies, developed the success. In five days of stubborn fighting (14-18 January), the troops of the *front's* shock group, having begun the offensive from two bridgeheads, linked up and advanced up to 60 kilometers, expanding the breach up to 110 kilometers. The enemy, having been defeated in the *front's* main attack sector, began to fall back, pursued by our forces. The prospect of further great successes opened before the armies of the Second Belorussian Front, as well as the rapid accomplishment of the main operational assignment: the arrival at the sea and the cutting off of the East Prussian group of forces.

During 13-17 January the Third Belorussian Front was engaged in heavy fighting and gradually advanced, gnawing through the German defense. However, a breakthrough along the main axis was accomplished slowly and the first five days of the offensive did not yield decisive results. However, the advance by our forces along the main axis, first of all forced the enemy to bring up his reserves to the area and thus weaken his northern wing; secondly, it created a threat to the flank and rear of the German forces located in the front's northern salient (in the Sudargas—Schillenen area). The enemy began to fall back here.

The commander of the Third Belorussian decided to take advantage of the weak point in the enemy's defense and develop the success there where it had actually manifested itself. He began to carry out a maneuver with the *front's* second echelons (the tanks corps, and then the 11th Guards Army) to the north, in order to get into the flank of the enemy's Gumbinnen—Insterburg group of forces, divide it from the Tilsit group of forces and then defeat the enemy in detail. The operational results achieved during 18 January confirmed the correctness of this decision and also showed that on the Third Belorussian Front a turning point had been reached in our favor in the course of the intensive fighting.

To the right, the First Baltic Front was occupying a defensive position along its previous line. Its left-flank 43rd Army, which was located along the Tilsit direction, was transferred to the Third Belorussian Front in connection with the development of events along the northern sector.

On the left, the First Belorussian Front was developing a vigorous offensive in the general direction of Warsaw and Poznan. On 16 January the town of Radom was captured, on 17 January the capital of Poland, Warsaw, was liberated, and on 18 January our forces captured the town of Lowicz and began to vigorously attack toward Kutno and Lodz.

It was in this situation that the Red Army's forces entered into the second stage of the East Prussian operation.

5

The Development of the Soviet Forces' Offensive. The Second Belorussian Front's Arrival at the Baltic Coast and the Vistula River. The Cutting off of the Germans' East Prussian Group of Forces. The Third Belorussian Front's Capture of the Town of Insterburg. The Overcoming of the Fortified Lines Along the Deime and Alle Rivers

THE SECOND STAGE OF THE OPERATION, 19-26 JANUARY

In the stubborn offensive battles of the operation's first stage (13-18 January), the forces of the Second and Third Belorussian fronts broke through the German defense, committed their mobile formations and got the opportunity to develop the success, unfolding the breakthrough into the depth and toward the flanks.

The Second Belorussian Front, as a result of the successfully realized breakthrough and commitment of powerful mobile formations, could count on the rapid completion of the defeat of the Germans' Przasnysz—Mlawa group of forces, in order to vigorously attack further toward the Baltic coast (to the Frisches Haff) and, without losing a single day, cut off the Germans' paths of retreat from East Prussia.

The Third Belorussian Front had the objective of energetically developing the offensive in the gap between the Germans' Tilsit and Insterburg groups of forces and to defeat the enemy in detail, and to then force the fortified lines along the Deime and Alle rivers on the heels of the retreating enemy and to attack toward Königsberg.

The overall operational-strategic situation during the second stage of the East Prussian operation remained quite favorable for carrying out the tasks listed above. To the right, the First Baltic Front, while carrying out the necessary preparations, went over to the attack with two armies along the Libava axis. During 23 January our forces pierced the German defense to a depth of four kilometers, and on the following day advanced in places another 1-1.5 kilometers. Thus, although a decisive success against the German group of forces cut off in the Tukums—Libava area was not achieved, the enemy here had been pushed back, tied down and had suffered considerable losses.

To the left, the First Belorussian Front, having defeated the opposing German forces, continued to develop a vigorous offensive in the direction of Lodz and Poznan, pursuing the disjointed enemy groups. During 19-26 January the forces of the First Belorussian Front advanced at a daily rate of up to 35-40 kilometers. Lodz was captured on 19 January, Gnesen on 22 January, Bromberg (Bydgoszcz) and Kalisz on 23 January, while as early as 24-25 January we were already fighting for Poznan. Thus the First Belorussian Front's powerful shock group, having at its tip two tank armies and other mobile formations, was vigorously attacking and was echeloned ahead of the Second Belorussian Front.

THE SECOND BELORUSSIAN FRONT

The Pursuit of the Enemy and the Arrival of our Forces at the Coast of the Baltic Sea

Having lost such major centers of resistance as Mlawa, Przasnysz and Ciechanow, the German command could not, despite all its efforts, halt our forces' offensive. Large masses of tanks, supported by our aviation's renewed efforts, energetically advanced and were destroying all enemy centers of resistance in their path, and decisively suppressed his efforts to launch a counterblow or hang on to some line or another and organize a defense there. The German forces, having lost command and control, began a disorganized retreat along the entire front. Disjointed enemy groups, covering the retreat with small rearguards, sought to put up resistance, but were quickly destroyed. Special German commands mined the roads, destroyed them, blew up bridges, and set up obstacles.

On 19 January the *front's* forces in the center and along the left wing began their pursuit of the enemy. Major air assets from the 4th Air Army were committed into the battle. Throughout the day our planes launched strikes against the enemy's main routes of retreat. On 19 January the air army carried out 1,820 sorties with bombers and assault aircraft.

The 5th Guards Tank Army's tanks and motorized infantry, energetically advancing to the north, reached Neidenburg and began fighting here. The 3rd Guards Cavalry Corps, which had been committed into the breach, captured the Janowo strong point (16 kilometers northeast of Neidenburg) at 1700 on 19 January, crossed the East Prussian boundary and continued the offensive on Allenstein.

The 48th and 2nd Shock armies were particularly successful in pursuing the enemy. On that day the armies' main forces advanced as much as 30 kilometers and reached the line Dzialdowo—Biezun, which according to plan, they were to reach only on the operation's tenth-eleventh day. Our infantry here was quickly catching up to the 5th Guards Tank Army's tanks and the *front* commander was forced to order the commander of the tank army to speed up the army's offensive, without getting bogged down in fighting with the garrisons of the enemy's individual strong points, to bypass them and decisively advance.

A favorable situation had arisen for quickly accomplishing the cutting off of the Germans' East Prussian group of forces. By this time the forces of the Third Belorussian Front, while successfully developing the attack in the general direction of Königsberg, had defeated the Germans' Tilsit group of forces and created the threat to outflank and encircle their forces in the Insterburg area and were vigorously developing the success to the line of the Deime River. The enemy forces continued to stubbornly defend along the *fronts'* boundary along the Masurian axis. The German command evidently decided to continue the defense of East Prussia to the end, despite the fact that our breakthrough along the Mlawa direction constituted a serious threat to the land communications of the Germans' East Prussian group of forces with the rest of Germany.

Taking this into account, the *front* commander decided to turn the *front's* main forces to the north, in the general direction of Osterode and Elbing, with the idea of reaching the coast of the Baltic Sea by the shortest route and to tie down the German armies here, and with part of its forces reach the Vistula River along a broad front, in order to secure the main forces' offensive from the west. In connection with this, the *front* commander assigned his armies the following objectives at 1800 on 19 January.

The 49th Army was to continue the offensive in the direction of Myszyniec and Friedrichshof (ten kilometers north of Myszyniec). On 22 January the army was to capture the line Nowogrod—excluding Willenberg, and by the close of 23 January reach the line Nowogrod—Schwentainen (20 kilometers northwest of Myszyniec).

The 3rd Army was to continue its offensive further on Janowo. On 22 January it was to capture the line Willenberg—Muschaken (12 kilometers east of Neidenburg); then, attacking along its left flank, the army was to capture the line Ortelsburg—Allenstein on 25 January.

The 48th Army, along with the attached 8th Mechanized Corps, was to capture the line excluding Muschaken—Neidenburg—Dzialdowo on 20 January; then, attacking along its left flank, by the close of 25 January it was to capture the line Allenstein—Osterode. The army was to turn over the Dzialdowo—Lonzek (ten kilometers southwest of Dzialdowo) sector to the 2nd Shock Army.

The 2nd Shock Army, along with the attached 8th Guards Tank Corps, was to capture the line excluding Dzialdowo—Biezun on 20 January; then, while attacking in the direction of Lidzbark and Deutsch Eylau, on 25 January it was to capture the line Osterode—Deutsch Eylau.

The 65th Army, along with the attached 1st Guards Tank Corps, on 20 January was to capture the line excluding Biezun—Grombiec (eight kilometers southwest of Sierpc); then, while developing the attack in the general direction of Brodnica, on 25 January it was to capture the line Brodnica—Lysiny (16 kilometers southwest of Brodnica).

The 70th Army, while developing the success in the direction of Bielsk and Dobrzyn, on 21 January the army was to capture the line excluding Grombiec—Plock; then, on 25 January the army was to capture the line excluding Lysiny—Lipno—excluding Wloclawek.

On the morning of 20 January the 5th Guards Tank Army was to continue the offensive from the line Neidenburg—Dzialdowo in the direction of Osterode. The immediate objective was to occupy the Osterode—Deutsch Eylau area on 21 January. The army was to subsequently advance in the direction of Elbing.

The commander of the 50th Army was to pull the 369th and 330th rifle divisions into the *front* reserve. The 369th Division was to be concentrated by the morning of 22 January in the Makow area, and the 330th by the morning of 21 January in the Rozan area.

In carrying out this order, the *front's* left-wing forces advanced more than 40 kilometers on 20 January and captured the towns of Lidzbark, Sierpc and Wyszogrod. The 3rd Army crossed the East Prussian frontier along the Allenstein direction and penetrated 10-15 kilometers. The 5th Guards Tank Army, having captured the town and enemy strong point of Neidenburg at dawn on 20 January, continued to advance in the general direction of Osterode.

Our forces' offensive was supported by our aviation. On 20 January the planes of the 4th Air Army carried out 1,744 sorties. 14 enemy aircraft were destroyed in air battles and on their airfields.

The German forces, while putting up weak resistance, continued to fall back rapidly to the north and northwest. A part of these forces was falling back to the crossings over the Vistula, with the task of organizing a defense along its western bank.

In order to cut the enemy's path of retreat beyond the Vistula, the 8th Mechanized Corps was removed from the 48th Army's control and directed toward Marienburg, with the mission of continuing the offensive on Dzialdowo and Nowe Miasto (18 kilometers south of Deutsch Eylau, and to capture the Risenburg (30 kilometers northwest of Deutsch Eylau) area no later than 23 January.

Simultaneously, the *front* commander demanded that the 65th and 70th armies speed up their advance and prevent the enemy from conducting an organized withdrawal behind the Vistula. The commander of the 65th Army was ordered to reach the Vistula along the Marienwerder—Schwetz sector with the army's main forces by the close of 27 January and to seize a bridgehead on its western bank. Upon reaching the Brodnica area, the 1st Guards Tank Corps was to be pulled back into the army reserve to put itself in order.

By the close of 27 January the commander of the 70th Army was to reach the Vistula along the sector excluding Schwetz—Fordon and seize a bridgehead on its western bank.

Our forces' rapid advance along the Elbing axis, as well as the successful advance on Königsberg by the forces of the Third Belorussian Front, forced the German command, under the threat of complete encirclement, to begin withdrawing on the night of 21-22 January units of the Fourth Army, which were defending along the *fronts'* boundary in the area of the Masurian Lakes.

At the same time, the forces of the Second Belorussian Front were bending all efforts so as to reach the coast of the Baltic Sea as quickly as possible and thus accomplish the mission assigned by the Supreme High Command to the *front*. At 0325 on 22 January the 5th Guards Tank Army was ordered to capture the Osterode—Deutsch Eylau area, to continue the offensive to the north, and by the morning of 24 January to capture the Elbing area and cut the Germans' escape route to the west.

Simultaneously, the *front* commander ordered the 2nd Shock Army, along with the 8th Guards Tank Corps, to continue the offensive in the general direction of Marienburg, and no later than 26 January to capture the line Elbing—Marienburg—Marienwerder.

On the night of 21-22 January the Germans' 131st and 541st infantry and 286th Security divisions abandoned their positions and began to rapidly fall back to the northwest. Units of the 50th Army, discovered the enemy's withdrawal in time, while conducting a reinforced reconnaissance, and immediately began the pursuit. However, the German command along the Masurian axis still disposed of sufficient forces and was carrying out an organized withdrawal, taking broad advantage of the wooded and swampy terrain. The 50th Army's forces encountered stubborn resistance by the enemy' rearguards and continuous engineering obstacles and advanced slowly. By 1900 on 22 January our units reached Rajgrod (22 kilometers southwest of Augustow) and Graewo. In order to support the withdrawal of the Fourth Army's formations against attacks from the south, the German forces along the Myszyniec axis were putting up particularly stubborn resistance against the units of the 49th Army. Some inhabited locales changed hands several times in fierce fighting. In the Willenberg area the enemy committed the 24th Panzergrenadier Division and units of the 558th Infantry Division into the fighting. The enemy's resistance also increased in the 3rd Army's sector. On 22 January, the 3rd Guards Cavalry Corps, while developing the offensive, captured the important road and railroad junction of Allenstein, but in attempting to advance further to the north was counterattacked by up to two regiments of infantry, with tanks, and was forced to consolidate along the town's northern outskirts.

At 1200 on 22 January the 5th Guards Tank Army renewed its pursuit. The enemy, as before, resisted weakly and withdrew to the north and northwest in disorder. Our tanks pushed aside the German rearguards and quickly advanced. By evening the tank army had reached the following lines: 10th Tank Corps—Liebmuhl, and the 29th Tank Corps—Saalfeld (30 kilometers northwest of Osterode). On the following day the tank army advanced more than 20 kilometers and by the close of 23 January it had occupied Morungen and Freiwalde. Its forward subunits broke through toward Preussisch-Holland (18 kilometers southeast of Elbing).

Thus as early as 23 January the Second Belorussian Front's mobile formations, along with units of motorized infantry, which were advancing rapidly behind the tanks, had cut almost all the enemy's main paths of retreat beyond the Vistula. It was now necessary to cut the enemy's last avenue—the Königsberg—Elbing highway—as quickly as possible and reach the coast of the Frisches Haff. The commander of the 5th Guards Tank Army immediately threw the 29th Tank Corps toward Elbing, while continuing the offensive to the north with the remainder of his forces. The remnants of the defeated German forces (299th and 7th infantry divisions, the *Grossdeutschland* Panzer Division, the Mlawa training center for assault gun and anti-tank artillery, the 18th Panzergrenadier Division, and a large number of various other units and formations), while resisting weakly, were mostly withdrawing along two axes: toward Brandenburg, while attempting to consolidate along the eastern bank of the Passarge River, and toward Elbing. The enemy's resistance began to gradually increase along these axes.

Having defeated the enemy garrison in Preussisch-Holland, units of the 29th Tank Corps streamed toward Ebling. Throwing aside small enemy units, at 2100 on 23 January the 31st Tank Brigade's forward detachment reached the external fortifications of the town of Elbing. The tanks' advance had been so vigorous that the town's garrison, not expecting their rapid appearance, at first did not put up organized resistance. The commander of the forward detachment, Captain D'yachenko, decided to break into the town by a surprise attack and destroy its garrison. Having received their orders, the tanks moved forward at high speed and with illuminated headlights. Elbing was living the usual life of a rear-area town: lights burned in places, soldiers from the tank school were marching and singing songs, and trolley cars were working. The tanks, upon opening fire, attacked a troop column and also destroyed several motor vehicles. Panic broke out in the town and individual German weapons and machine guns opened a disorderly fire. By 2300 the 31st Tank Brigade's (29th Tank Corps) forward detachment, had passed through the entire town without losing a single tank and, rapidly advancing to the north, reached the shore of the bay north of Elbing. The 31st Tank Brigade's main forces had fallen a little behind their forward detachment and encountered the German garrison's organized resistance on the approaches to Elbing. Following a two-hour battle, the 31st Tank Brigade was forced to go over to the defense along the eastern outskirts of the town. Before long the entire 29th Tank Corps' main forces reached Elbing. The corps' powerful reconnaissance group, which was operating to the north of Elbing and meeting weak resistance, in conjunction with the tank army's 1st Motorcycle Regiment, broke through to the Baltic Sea and, while advancing along its shore, on the evening of 25 January reached the town of Tolkemit. On the following day, 26 January, the tank units, assisted by units of the 42nd Rifle Corps, captured Tolkemit following stubborn street fighting, finally cutting off the Germans' East Prussian group of forces' land communications.

The 10th Tank Corps, operating to the east, captured Mühlhausen, but encountered stubborn enemy resistance to the northeast of this inhabited locale and, while repelling multiple counterattacks by his tanks and infantry, went over to the defense.

Thus the 5th Guards Tank Army successfully carried out its assigned task. The army's main forces had reached the Frisches Haff along a 15-20 kilometer front and blockaded Elbing. The German troops' escape routes from East Prussia had been cut.

The armies of the *front's* right wing and center, taking advantage of the tank formations' success, continued to rapidly advance. The 50th Army, on the *front's* right wing, while pursuing the retreating enemy, occupied the strong points of Arys and Johannisburg, and on 26 January was fighting along a line eight kilometers southeast of Rhein, Rudczany, Nikolaiken and Kerwin Station. Units of the Germans' 131st, 541st, 203rd, and 547th infantry divisions were resisting weakly and, while waging holding actions, were withdrawing to the west.

The German forces facing the 49th Army, while supporting the withdrawal of their Augustow group of forces from the south, continued to resist stubbornly. Throughout 23 January there was stubborn fighting in the army's sector. The German command threw its aviation into this sector, which, operating in groups of 3-10 planes, repeatedly bombed our troops' combat formations. In a day of fighting the 49th Army advanced 3-6 kilometers and inflicted heavy losses on the enemy.

With the onset of darkness, the German forces' resistance was broken and they began a disorderly withdrawal to the north and northwest. On 24 January the 49th Army, while pushing aside the enemy's rearguards, advanced up to 20 kilometers along some axes, and on 26 January was already fighting along the line excluding Kerwin station—the heights six kilometers northeast of Ortelsburg.

To the left, the 3rd Army, having broken the resistance of the 299th and 129th infantry divisions, the 18th Panzergrenadier Division, and the *Grossdeutschland* Panzer Division, on 23 January captured the Germans' important defensive center of Willenberg, as well as the major strong points of Ortelsburg and Passenheim (25 kilometers southeast of Allenstein). The German forces, taking advantage of the wooded and swampy terrain, attempted to delay our forces' advance along the Allenstein axis and support the counterblow being prepared against the 48th Army from the Guttstadt—Wormditt area. In this area the German command was hurriedly creating a shock group numbering up to five infantry divisions and tanks, which were to break through our forces' combat formations and support the arrival of their forces to the Vistula.

On 24 January the 3rd Army's units repelled 11 counterattacks ranging in strength from a battalion to a regiment of infantry, with each attack supported by tanks. By 2000 the army's units were fighting along the line of the heights six kilometers north of Ortelsburg—the copses ten kilometers northeast of Allenstein. The enemy's resistance increased even further on the following day. The Germans, having brought up fresh forces, conducted a number of counterattacks. Many inhabited locales changed hands 2-3 times. The improving meteorological conditions enabled our aviation to assist our forces from the air. But even this could not decisively change the situation that had arisen here. During 25-26 January the 3rd Army's forces continued to fight intensively along the aforementioned line.

The 3rd Guards Cavalry Corps, having taken Allenstein, was conducting a fighting advance to the northeast, and by the close of 26 January had reached a line northeast and east of Allenstein.

The 48th Army, while developing the attack in the general direction of Morungen, was pursuing the enemy. The Germans (the 18th Panzergrenadier Division's 30th and 55th panzergrenadier regiments, the 11th Naval Battalion and the *Grossdeutschland* Panzer Division), while waging holding actions, were putting up stubborn resistance to the army's right-flank forces. The enemy counterattacked repeatedly. The 48th Army, while advancing, captured Morungen and Liebstadt and by the close of 26 January the 29th and 53rd rifle corps were fighting along the approaches to Guttstadt and had captured Wormditt. The left-flank 42nd Rifle Corps, as was already noted, supported the units of the 5th Guards Tank Army in the fighting for Mühlhausen and Tolkemit, and by the close of 26 January had reached the front Berchertsdorf (12 kilometers northeast of Mühlhausen)—Tolkemit.

Thus the 48th Army turned its front to the northeast and was in close communication with units of the 5th Guards Tank Army and had securely closed the escape route for the Germans' East Prussian group of forces to the west.

The 2nd Shock Army was also successfully developing the offensive during these days, with the objective of reaching the line Elbing—Marienburg. While pursuing the defeated units of the XXIII Army Corps to the north and northwest, the army advanced each day 20-25 kilometers.

On 25 January the 321st Rifle Division reached the southern outskirts of Elbing and began fighting the German garrison alongside units of the 29th Tank Corps. The 8th Mechanized Corps, which had been subordinated to the commander of the 2nd Shock Army, reached Marienburg in the latter half of 25 January. The army's remaining units reached the Nogat River along the sector between Elbing and Marienburg and forced the river in the area ten kilometers northeast of Marienburg.

To the south, the 2nd Shock Army's left-flank units were advancing to the west and by the close of 25 January were 8-15 kilometers east of the Vistula along the Marienburg—Marienwerder sector.

Throughout 26 January the 2nd Guards Army's units continued fighting along the southern outskirts of Elbing and also considerably expanded the bridgehead along the western bank of the Nogat River, northeast of Marienburg. On this day the army's units captured Marienburg, while to the south they reached the western bank of the Vistula along the sector Marienburg—eastern outskirts of Marienwerder.

The 8th Mechanized Corps took part in the capture of Marienburg and by the close of January 26 was fighting 3-4 kilometers northwest of the town.

The 8th Guards Tank Corps remained in the army's reserve on 26 January and was located in the copses 15-20 kilometers northwest of Osterode.

Simultaneous with the development of the offensive to the north, toward Elbing, the *front's* left-wing forces (65th and 70th armies) were advancing to the northwest and west toward the Vistula. Opposing them were the remnants of the enemy's defeated units, which were withdrawing in small groups; namely the 7th, 35th, 252nd, 337th, and 542nd infantry divisions and the 7th Panzer Division. The enemy was attempting to organize serious resistance along the fortified line along the line of the Drewenz River, but was thrown off this line and continued his disorderly withdrawal to the northwest. In their retreat the Germans threw away equipment along the roads, burned automobile columns, blew up industrial enterprises, mined inhabited locales, and killed off livestock.

Due to the complete loss of command and control, the German command was forced to resort to the open transmission of orders over the radio, as well as to the setting up of special indicators for the march routes and troop concentration areas. For example, in the area north of Lubawa (15 kilometers southeast of Deutsch Eylau) a sign was nailed to one of the houses, which read "The rallying point for the personnel of the 507th 'Tiger' Tank Battalion is in Bischdorf. Pass through the towns of Deutsch Eylau and Freistadt in the direction of Graudenz." According to prisoner testimony, disjointed groups of German troops received orders to break through to the western bank of the Vistula River.

As the 65th and 70th armies advanced toward the Vistula, the Germans' resistance increased. The German command was striving to ensure an organized withdrawal of its forces behind the Vistula and was forming individual detachments on the spot from scattered units, which seized road junctions and lake defiles and put up stubborn resistance, in order to delay our forces and win time. Besides this, our individual march columns were repeatedly subjected to enemy air attacks.

By the close of 26 January the 65th Army's units were fighting along the approaches to Marienwerder and Graudenz and to the south had reached the eastern bank of the Vistula in the area ten kilometers southwest of Graudenz.

To the left, the 70th Army was fighting along the right flank by the close of January 26 on the approaches to Kulm. In the center the 70th Army's units, taking advantage of the enemy's demoralization, forced the Vistula from the march along a broad front, captured Fordon and created a bridgehead 22 kilometers wide and up to six kilometers deep on the river's western bank. On the left flank the 70th Army's units reached the northern bank of the Vistula in the Scharnau area (six kilometers southeast of Fordon) and also blockaded the fortress of Torun from the east and north.

The 1st Guards Tank Corps was on the march from the Brodnica area to the area to the west of the Kulmsee (16 kilometers north of Torun), where it was to arrive on 27 January.

The 330th and 369th rifle divisions remained in the *front* reserve. The 330th Division left at 2000 on 26 January from Rozan, with the mission of moving to Zuromin by the morning of 30 January; the 369th Division left at 2000 on 26 January, with the mission of moving to Biezun by the morning of 29 January.

The meteorological conditions during 19-26 January were in general unfavorable for employing aviation. During this period the 4th Air Army carried out a total of 4,324 sorties, while much the greater number of sorties was carried out on 19-20 January (3,564 sorties).

The enemy's aviation was not particularly active and during this entire period only 272 sorties were noted.

To the left, the First Belorussian Front's 47th Army captured Bromberg and Nakel (24 kilometers west of Bromberg) and by the close of 26 January was fighting to the north of these towns

Thus during 19-26 January the forces of the Second Belorussian Front achieved major operational results. A final defeat was inflicted on the Germans' Przasnysz—Mlawa group of forces, along with the completion of combat operations to isolate the enemy's East Prussian group of forces from the rest of Germany. At the same time, the main mass of the Second Belorussian Front's forces were deployed along a broad front from the Masurian Lakes to the shore of the Baltic Sea.

At the same time, three of the Second Belorussian Front's left-flank armies had been turned to the west and were attacking toward the Vistula for the purpose of protecting the *front's* main group of forces against possible enemy counterblows from the west, as well as for the purpose of seizing bridgeheads along the Vistula's western bank. This had great significance for the subsequent offensive to the west for the purpose of protecting from the north the forces of the First Belorussian Front, which at this time were blockading the fortress of Poznan and were developing the offensive to the Oder River.

Such are the brief operational results of the Second Belorussian Front's operations.

The *front's* forces cleared the Germans out of territory of more than 34,000 square kilometers, including Polish territory of 20,000 square kilometers. During the offensive fighting of 14-24 January alone, the enemy suffered the following losses in men and materiel.

Destroyed were 38 planes, 490 tanks and assault guns, 830 guns, 470 mortars, 1,830 machine guns, 1,800 motor vehicles, and 44 armored transports. The enemy lost in killed alone more than 65,000 men and officers.

During this same time the *front's* forces captured the following equipment: 72 tanks and assault guns, 633 guns, 214 mortars, 1,042 machine guns, 729 motor vehicles, 38 locomotives, 1,800 railroad cars, and 161 depots with munitions, equipment and food.

5,530 German men and officers were captured.

Thus as a result of 11 days of offensive battles by the forces of the Second Belorussian Front, enemy losses in the main categories of military equipment and personnel amounted to: more than 70,000 captured and killed, 38 planes, 562 tanks and assault guns, 1,463 guns, 684 mortars, 2,872 machine guns, and 2,529 motor vehicles.

THE THIRD BELORUSSIAN FRONT

At the same time the Second Belorussian Front's shock group got the opportunity to develop a vigorous offensive to the northwest, the fighting continued with unremitting force in the offensive sector of the Third Belorussian Front's 5th Army.

The 2nd Guards Tatsinskaya Tank Corps, while closely cooperating with the infantry, was engaged in intense fighting throughout the day, beating off savage enemy tank and assault gun attacks during the day. The Germans, relying on the previously-prepared Suppinnen—Wittgirren defensive line, were putting up frenzied resistance. The 1st Tank Corps, which had been committed on the morning of 18 January in the 39th Army's sector, advanced up to 40 kilometers that day and by the close of the day was fighting in the Lengweten—Marunen area. Units of the 5th Army, while engaged in heavy fighting for each strong point and each trench advanced 6-7 kilometers and cut the Tilsit—Gumbinnen paved road west of Wittgirren. By the close of the day the army's main forces had reached the line Suppinnen—Antballen—Brakupenen.

Also throughout the day, the 28th Army was engaged in fierce fighting along the entire front. The attacking units of the 3rd Guards and 128th rifle corps beat off ten enemy counterattacks during the day, involving up to a battalion of infantry and 10-15 tanks each. Only along individual sectors did the army manage to push back the enemy units 1-2 kilometers and capture several of his strong points. Nor did the 2nd Guards Army achieve any material successes on 18 January.

The *front* commander decided to outflank the Insterburg fortified center from the north and to cut off the enemy's Insterburg—Gumbinnen group of forces. For this, employing the newly-made breach, he committed the 2nd Guards Tatsinskaya Tank Corps, which had been fighting southwest of Kussen, into the battle in the 39th Army's sector, while the corps commander was assigned the following task:

> By 0700 on 19.01.1945 the corps is to be moved to the Inster River in the Insterfelde area (one kilometer north of Raudonatschen) and to begin the attack in the direction of Marunen and Aulowenen. By 1800 on 19.01.1945 the corps is to reach the Aulowenen area. Its forward detachments are to seize the Lindiken, Zaken, Grunheide road junctions. I demand from you the most energetic and decisive actions; to vigorously advance, without getting involved in prolonged fighting and by bypassing enemy centers of resistance.

At the same time as this, General Chernyakhovskii was moving up to the Inster River his second echelon—the 11th Guards Army, which he planned on employing to develop the attack along the right bank of the Inster River in order to turn the Insterburg fortified area from the north. Along with this, the *front* commander issued an order to the 2nd Guards Army to attack to the west.

In carrying out the *front* commander's order, on the night of 18-19 January the 2nd Guards Tank Corps reached the Raudonatschen area and at 1000, having deployed here in two columns began its attack to the southwest. While destroying small enemy screens along its path, at 1930 the 4th Guards Tank Brigade reached the northern outskirts of Aulowenen. The German garrison, which had been taken by surprise by our tanks, was completely destroyed. Before long, the 4th Guards Motorized Rifle Brigade reached Aulowenen. The 26th Guards Tank Brigade, which was attacking to the left, by the close of the day had cut the paved road leading to Aulowenen from the east, while the 25th Brigade captured the inhabited locale of Grunheide.

The development of the 39th Army's success to the northwest and the capture of the town of Tilsit. The German group of forces (IX and XXVI army corps) continued to stubbornly resist within the confines of the Gumbinnen defensive line, while in the area to the north of Insterburg it began to withdraw, under pressure from our forces, to the northwest and west, covered by individual detachments, reinforced with tanks and assault guns. The 39th Army's forces, without halting their movement, pursued the retreating enemy at night as well. The 43rd Army's 54th Rifle Corps, energetically advancing along the southern bank of the Neman River, broke into Tilsit during the latter half of 19 January and, captured the town following a short battle. To the left, the 39th Army's 113th Rifle Corps, while developing the success toward Tilsit from the southeast, cut the Ragnit—Zillen paved road and by the close of the day reached the line Prewoizen—Kakscheiten. The 5th Guards and 94th rifle corps reached the Tilsit—Insterburg railroad and by 2300 were fighting along the line Argeningken—Zillen—Gaidzen.

The 1st Tank Corps, while developing its attack toward Gross Skeisgirren, captured the important road junction of Zillen, but to the west of the town unexpectedly encountered the enemy's organized resistance and throughout the entire second half of 19 January was engaged in fierce fighting along the line Padaggen—Anstipen.

The fighting in the Gumbinnen area. Despite the Tilsit group of forces' defeat and its retreat to the west, the enemy's Gumbinnen—Insterburg group of forces continued to hold on, putting up fierce resistance to the 5th and 28th armies' attacking units. Throughout 19 January heavy fighting continued within the confines of the Gumbinnen defensive line. The enemy repeatedly launched counterattacks, fired on our forces with artillery and mortars and threw groups of aircraft into the battle. The commander of the 5th Army, while taking advantage of the success by his neighbor to the right (39th Army), shifted part of the 72nd Rifle Corps' forces to the north and committed them into the fighting in the Girren area. However, this did not speed up the advance by the army's right flank. The 72nd and 45th rifle corps, in attempting to overcome the enemy's stubborn resistance, advanced slowly and by 2100 had captured the enemy's defensive line along the Tilsit—Gumbinnen paved road and were fighting along the line Kraupischken—Neudorf—Antballen. The 65th Rifle Corps, while trying to overcome the main zone of the Gumbinnen defensive line, captured its first trench and reached with its left flank the approaches to the enemy's strong point in Rudstannen.

The 28th Army advanced more successfully that day. The army commander concentrated the maximum amount of artillery in the 3rd Guards and 128th rifle corps' offensive sector. The enemy's personnel were quickly suppressed by massed fire along a narrow sector of front. The corps attacked and broke through three trenches, one after the other, and, energetically throwing back units of the Germans' 549th and 61st infantry divisions to the west, broke through to Gumbinnen with their main forces and began fighting in the northeastern outskirts of the town. Simultaneously, units of the 20th Rifle Corps arrived at Gumbinnen from the south. The German garrison put up organized resistance and the 28th Army's units were forced to temporarily consolidate.

The 2nd Guards Army was not able to advance on 19 January. Throughout the day its units repulsed uninterrupted attacks by large enemy infantry and tank forces along the entire front.

The commitment of the 11th Guards Army into the breach. Taking into account the favorable operational situation that had arisen to the north of Insterburg, the *front* commander made the decision to commit the 11th Guards Army into the breach and, developing its offensive in the general direction of Welau, to deeply envelop the enemy's Insterburg—Gumbinnen group of forces from the west and, together with the *front's* remaining forces, to encircle and destroy it. For this, he ordered the commander of the 11th Guards Army: moving along a 7-8 kilometer front (to the right, Schaaren—Meschkuppen—Marunen; to the left, Radschen—Draugupenen—Kraupischken), by 0600 on 19 January the army was to deploy west of the Inster River along the sector of the Marunen—Kaupischken paved road and go over to a decisive offensive in the general direction of Grunheide, Warkau and Gross Berschkallen. By the close of 20 January the army was to reach the line Aulowenen—Warkau—Neunischken. The army would subsequently develop the offensive toward Welau. The following boundary lines were to be established as of 1600 on 19 January: Marunen—Aulowenen with the 39th Army; Draugupenen—Kraupischken and then along the Inster River as far Insterburg with the 5th Army.

On 19 January, on the basis of a directive from the *Stavka* of the Supreme High Command, the First Baltic Front's 43rd Army (90th, 103rd and 54th rifle corps), which before this had been operating to the north of the Neman River, was subordinated to the Third Belorussian Front. The army was assigned the task of attacking on the morning of 20 January in the general direction of Heinrichswalde and Tawe (on the shore of the Kurisches Haff), launching its main attack along the left flank. By the close of the day the army was to reach the line Jagerischken—Tomaten—Schillkoen. Subsequently, developing a vigorous attack in the direction of the Kurisches Haff, on 22 January it was to completely clear the enemy from the shore of the Kurisches Haff and take up defensive positions along the front: mouths of the Neman and Deime rivers. From 20 January the boundary with the 39th Army was to be Ragnit—Argeningken—Schillkoen—the mouth of the Deime River.

On 20 January the 39th Army received orders to continue a vigorous offensive to the southwest and, while launching an attack in the general direction of Gross Skeisgirren, to seize the road junctions of Makonen and Smilginen with its forward detachments. Subsequently, while developing the offensive on Melauken and Goldbach, the army's main forces were to reach the Deime River by the close of 22 January.

The 5th Army, while continuing an energetic offensive on the morning of 20 January was to reach the Angerapp and Pissa rivers along the Insterburg—Florkemen sector with its main forces by the close of the day.

The 1st Tank Corps' task remained unchanged: it was to capture the road junction of Gross Skeisgirren on 20 January and seize the inhabited locales of Melauken and Popelken with forward detachments.

On the morning of 20 January the *front* commander ordered the 2nd Guards Tatsinskaya Tank Corps to continue its vigorous offensive in the general direction of Gross Berschkallen and Zaalau. By the close of the day it was to capture the Zaalau—Zimonen—Wirtkallen area, seize a crossing over the Pregel River in the Zimonen area and cut the Insterburg—Königsberg paved road with a strong detachment.

During the night of 19-20 January the 28th Army was to capture the town of Gumbinnen and, while continuing an energetic offensive to the west, by the close of the day it was to reach the Angerapp River along the Gross Gaudischkemen—Zuskemen sector. The boundary line on the right was Pakallnischken—Gross Gaudischkemen—Didlakken, and on the left Perkallen—Zuskemen—Kallnen.

On the morning of 20 January the 2nd Guards Army was also to continue to attack, with its immediate objective reaching the line Builin—Murgischken—Warkallen.

The 31st Army, while continuing to defend, was to regroup its forces and carry out a reconnaissance in force. The boundary line with the 2nd Guards Army was the southern bank of the Goldapgarsee—Ligetroken—Wenzken.

The 1st Air Army was to prepare on the morning of 20 January to support our forces' offensive and support the commitment of the 11th Guards Army into the breach.

The 11th Guards Army, in carrying out the *front* commander's order, left the Stallupönen area on the night of 18-19 January and in a forced march along two routes began to move toward the Inster River. However, there was insufficient darkness to carry out the 45-kilometer march, so the troops continued the movement during the day of 19 January. By 1800 on 19 January the army reached the Inster River and concentrated in the Marunen and Kraupischken areas.

The army's command post was deployed in Grunthal (three kilometers east of Kraupischken).

The enemy, despite the heavy losses suffered in the previous fighting, nevertheless maintained his combat capability and was in his previous formation. By 20 January the right-wing armies were opposed, as before, by the IX and XXVI army corps and the "Hermann Goring" Parachute-Panzer Corps. Attempting to delay the 39th Army's advance, the German command on 19 January committed into the fighting in the Ragnit area a newly formed group under Colonel Remer, which consisted of the 56th Infantry Division's 156th Field Reserve Battalion, the 25th *Volkssturm* Battalion, the Bartenstein sapper-screening group, the 809th Fortress Battalion, and the 23rd Artillery Regiment's 3rd Battalion from the high command reserve.

The German aviation, having lost more than half of its strength, sharply reduced its activity and only carried out episodic raids against the 5th Army in the Gumbinnen area.

It should be noted that the most powerful enemy group of forces was in the Insterburg area. Here formations of the XXVI Army Corps and the "Hermann Goring" Parachute-Panzer Corps were operating. The presence of major enemy forces in this area forced the *front* command to take measures to rapidly eliminate the enemy's Insterburg group of forces, on the defeat of which depended the successful development of the offensive along the Königsberg axis.

On the morning of 20 January the *front's* forces continued their offensive. The 11th Guards Army relieved units of the 39th and 5th armies with divisions from its first echelon along the line of deployment and immediately attacked to the west. Units of the enemy's 56th, 69th and 1st infantry divisions, which had been thrown back from the line of the Inster River by the 2nd Guards Tatsinskaya Tank Corps continued their retreat on Aulowenen, Grunheiden and

Zesslauken and were no longer putting up organized resistance in the army's attack zone. Despite the fact that some of the 11th Guards Army's divisions (31st, 18th and 16th Guards rifle) had been very late in reaching the line of deployment, which had been brought about by the difficulties of the march, the army's offensive on this day developed rapidly. The army's 26th Guards Rifle Division, having gone over to the offensive and not encountering the enemy's organized resistance, began to pursue the enemy, detaching a forward detachment consisting of a rifle battalion mounted on motor vehicles and reinforced by a battalion of self-propelled guns and a towed artillery battalion. The division's main forces were moving in column formation behind the forward detachment, with a rifle regiment in the vanguard. The army's remaining divisions, which went over to the attack a few hours later, also organized the energetic pursuit of the enemy on the spot, without deploying their main forces, having powerful forward detachments ahead of the main body. In a day of fighting the 11th Guards Army advanced 25 kilometers and, having captured more than 100 inhabited locales, by the close of the day had reached the line Lindenhausen—Molen—Gaidzen.

The German command adopted all measures in order to prevent the arrival of our forces before Insterburg. On 20 January it hurriedly organized a defense along the line Lindenburg—Zaken—Molen, employing for this purpose the remnants of the 1st, 56th and 69th infantry divisions, and the 13th Assault and 208th Sapper-Bridge battalions. However, the enemy was unable to delay our forces along this previously prepared intermediate defensive line. Having quickly regrouped their forces and brought up artillery, units of the 11th Guards Army, along with tanks from the 2nd Guards Tatsinskaya Tank Corps, broke through the Germans' defense organized along the Aulowenen—Insterburg paved road with a powerful attack at dawn on 21 January and, upon receiving the *front* commander's order to capture Insterburg, launched a vigorous offensive to the south. The enemy's defeated units, while putting up weak resistance, were falling back in disorder on Insterburg. At 1900 units of the 16th, 11th and 18th guards divisions reached the Gross Berschkallen—Horstenau railroad and their left flank became involved in fighting for Rossthal (eight kilometers north of Insterburg). The enemy put up resistance along this line. These divisions' attacks, carried out from the march, were beaten back. Nor were their tanks able to break through our defense. The Germans uninterruptedly threw their tanks, infantry and assault guns into the attack and made wide use of *faustpatrones*.

To the right, the 8th Guards Rifle Corps, attacking along the Gross Skeisgirren—Welau paved road, continued to successfully pursue the retreating enemy toward the Pregel River with units of the 26th Guards Rifle Division and the 1st Tank Corps. Decisively pushing aside covering detachments, the corps' infantry and tanks attacked the enemy's retreating columns and destroyed them. By 2100 on 21 January the 26th Guards Rifle Division, having completed a 40-kilometer march, reached Gross Schirrau. The 1st Tank Corps destroyed 11 enemy tanks and more than 100 motor vehicles and was rapidly approaching Welau, while at the same time its 159th Tank Brigade had reached Alt Ilchken, while its 117th and 89th tank and 4th Motorized Rifle brigades were fighting north of Ponnau.

Thus the 11th Guards Army, while carrying out its assigned task, advanced 45 kilometers in two days of fighting and reached the near approaches to Insterburg. At the same time, while developing the success along its right flank, the army reached the Pregel River northeast of Welau along with units of the 1st Tank Corps, deeply outflanking the enemy's Insterburg—Gumbinnen group of forces from the west.

To the right, the 43rd and 39th armies, while pursuing the retreating enemy, advanced up to 50 kilometers and by the close of 21 January were fighting along the following lines: the 43rd Army, Kurisches Haff—Nemonin—Lauknen; the 39th Army, having securely consolidated the important road junction of Gross Skeisgirren, was rapidly advancing to the west and, having captured Malaukon, reached the line Auerwalde—Abschruten—Neuwize along its right flank.

As before, the 5th and 28th armies were engaged in heavy fighting. Units of the XXVI Army Corps and the "Hermann Goring" Parachute-Panzer Corps, relying on a widely developed trench defense, continued to put up stubborn resistance. While striving to hold at all costs the Gumbinnen and Insterburg centers of resistance, the German command threw into the fighting against the 5th and 28th armies, aside from the previously cited troops, various special units, independent construction and pontoon battalions, communications battalions, and independent march companies, etc. In a day of fighting our units beat off 11-12 enemy counterattacks apiece along some sectors of the front. The 5th Army, attacking along the left bank of the Inster River, on 21 January completely cleared the enemy out of the large wooded area northeast of Insterburg and by the close of the day its main forces had reached the northern bank of the Pissa River. Over two days the 28th Army was engaged in stubborn fighting for Gumbinnen. Only during the second half of 21 January did units of the 128th Rifle Corps, in conjunction with units of the 20th Corps, manage to eliminate the German garrison in Gumbinnen and capture the town. However, even after this the resistance of the German forces defending along this axis did not decrease. While retreating to the Angerapp River, along which ran a powerful defensive line covering Insterburg from the east and southeast, the Germans sought to exhaust and bleed our attacking units in delaying actions. They waged powerful artillery and mortar fire, carried out numerous counterattacks, and threw tanks and assault guns into the battle. Despite this, the 28th Army overcame the Germans' resistance and by the close of the day its main forces reached the Angerapp River.

The 2nd Guards Army attacked successfully on this day. It broke through the enemy's defense with a powerful attack along its right flank and center and, vigorously advancing, penetrated more than 14 kilometers into his position, with units of the 3rd and 32nd guards rifle divisions reaching the approaches to the powerful center of resistance at Darkemen.

On 21 January the 1st Air Army, in view of the poor weather, did not take part in the fighting. Neither was any enemy air activity noted that day.

During 20-21 January our forces killed up to 6,000 German men and officers, destroyed 60 tanks and assault guns, 45 guns of various calibers, 155 machine guns, 209 motor vehicles, and six aircraft.

The fighting for Insterburg. In the developing situation, the *front* commander decided to employ the 11th Guards, 5th and 28th armies to encircle and eliminate the remnants of the enemy's Insterburg—Gumbinnen group of forces, for which purpose the *front's* right-wing forces were to continue their decisive pursuit of the enemy to the west, with the idea of breaking into Königsberg on the heels of the defeated enemy and to capture the fortified area and the city. In order to carry out this task, the commander detached both tank corps and the 43rd and 39th armies, assigning them the following tasks:

On the morning of 22 January the 1st Tank Corps was to continue its energetic offensive and by the close of the day capture the town of Tapiau; it was subsequently to advance on Königsberg;

The 2nd Guards Tatsinskaya Tank Corps was to force the Pregel River in the Norkitten area and by the close of 22 January was to reach the Klein Nur area; it was to subsequently attack toward Allenburg and seize crossings over the Alle River in the Leiszinen—Allenburg area, with an eye toward subsequently operating toward Königsberg;

The 43rd Army was to develop a vigorous offensive in the general direction of Labiau;

The 39th Army was to advance along the northern bank of the Pregel River toward the Deime River.

At the same time, the enemy's Insterburg—Gumbinnen group of forces, despite the rapid withdrawal of the IX Army Corps' units to the west, still retained its ability to resist and, even more so, represented a certain threat hanging over from the south the *front's* right wing, which had spread into East Prussia. It was necessary to deal with this group of forces as quickly as possible and thus speed up the advance to the west by the *front's* center and left wing. Taking this into account,

General Chernyakhovskii ordered the 11th Guards and 5th armies to break through the enemy's defensive line by means of a concentric attack from the north, east and south in the general direction of Insterburg and, upon encircling the Insterburg group of forces, to destroy it and capture the town on 22 January.

In carrying out the assigned task, the commander of the 11th Guards Army decided to attack Insterburg at night with the forces of the 36th Guards Rifle Corps, to break into the town from the north and destroy the German garrison along with units from the 5th Army. He assigned the 8th and 16th guards corps the task of developing the offensive—the first toward Tapiau, and the second toward Klein Nur and Ilmsdorf.

The commander of the 5th Army decided to launch his main attack with the 72nd Rifle Corps on Insterburg from the northeast and east and, upon entering here into close cooperation with units of the 36th Guards Corps, to capture the town. The 45th and 65th rifle corps, while supporting the 72nd Corps' operations from the south, were to attack toward Didlakken and Karlswalde. The time for the attack was set at 1100 on 22 January.

The corps designated for the storming of Insterburg had assigned to them these armies' direct infantry support tanks and their main artillery forces. Once again, due to the poor meteorological conditions, the 1st Air Army was unable to take part in supporting our forces' attack.

At 2300 on 21 January units of the 36th Guards Rifle Corps, having carried out the necessary regrouping of forces, attacked following a 20-minute artillery preparation. The remnants of the enemy's 349th, 1st and 56th infantry divisions, which overall numbered up to two regiments of infantry with tanks from the 5th Panzer Division, met the attacking troops with powerful machine gun and mortar fire and frenzied counterattacks. German units covering the road intersections north of Insterburg held on with particular stubbornness. Here units of the 16th Guards Rifle Division were counterattacked six times and forced to slow somewhat the pace of their advance. The corps commander, having assigned himself the objective of encircling the enemy garrison in Insterburg at any cost and isolating it from the main German forces, committed his second echelon—the 84th Guards Rifle Division—into the fighting with the task of launching an attack in the general direction of Gross Schunkern and Georgenthal and outflanking Insterburg from the west. At 0100 on 22 January the division's regiments broke through the defense with a decisive attack and, having outflanked Georgenthal from the west, pushed the Germans back toward the Pregel River. The 18th Guards Rifle Division's 51st Rifle Regiment, which was operating along with the 84th Division, forced the Pregel River southwest of Georgenthal and began to rapidly advance toward the western outskirts of the town. Fearful of being cut off, units of the 349th and 56th infantry divisions, which were being attacked from the front, began falling back to the south. The 18th and 16th guards divisions, which were in direct contact with the enemy, pursued him.

While destroying their covering detachments, our units pressed the Germans to the Inster River and following a short night battle completely cleared the north shore. Having suffered heavy losses, the small remnants of German troops, having failed to blow up the bridges after them, fell back in disorder behind the Inster River and sought shelter in Insterburg. Continuing their vigorous advance, units of the 18th and 16th guards divisions crossed the river and at 0200 reached the northern outskirts of the town. The German garrison, having organized a defense, once again put up stubborn resistance. The attacking units were subjected to powerful machine gun and mortar fire, were fired at from ambushes by flanking fire from assault guns and tanks camouflaged on the outskirts of the town, and repelled counterattacks by German automatic riflemen.

Despite this, at 0230 the 75th Tank Regiment, with a landing force of automatic riflemen, broke into Insterburg and, having destroyed a company of enemy infantry in the area of the town jail, seized a bridge over the Angerapp River. The tanks' success was immediately consolidated by the arriving infantry. Fierce street battles broke out along the entire northern outskirts of the town. Taking advantage of the illumination offered by the burning buildings, our subunits brought up guns and machine guns to pockets of enemy resistance and opened fire against windows in the upper stories, destroyed walls with armor-piercing shells and tore down attics. At the same time, mortars waged intensive fire against roofs and the approaches to buildings. Following a fire onslaught, the infantry would break into the buildings through windows, doors and holes in the walls and destroy their garrisons. Suffering heavy losses from our artillery and machine gun fire, the Germans started to abandon one building after another. Before long entire blocks along the northern outskirts of the town were cleared. Small groups of the enemy, having halted resistance, began to fall back to the center of town.

At 0230 the 5th Army's forces began to attack Insterburg from the east. Crushing the enemy's resistance, at 0400 they reached the town from the northeast and began street fighting along its outskirts. However, the enemy garrison was already so exhausted and demoralized by the previous fighting that by the morning of 22 January it was not able to offer organized resistance, despite the presence of large stone buildings in the center of Insterburg and engineering fortifications here. Units of the 36th Guards Rifle Corps, energetically advancing behind their tanks, broke into the center of town and, having destroyed the remaining small groups of automatic riflemen here, reached the railroad junction. At 0600 the 18th Guards Rifle Division's regiments captured the western part of the town and the 49th Regiment reached the area of the barracks along the eastern outskirts of Insterburg. By this time units of the 5th Army's 72nd Rifle Corps had entered the town from the east and assisted in eliminating individual pockets of enemy resistance.

At 0600 on 22 January the town of Insterburg was completely cleared of the enemy by units of the 11th Guards Army, assisted by the forces of the 5th Army.

The pursuit of the enemy and the arrival of the Third Belorussian Front's forces at the Alle and Deime rivers. At the same time that the 11th Guards, 5th and 28th armies were engaged in heavy fighting in the center to destroy the enemy's Insterburg—Gumbinnen group of forces, the right-wing armies continued to energetically pursue the remnants of the IX Army Corps, which was attempting to retreat behind the Alle and Deime rivers. The 43rd Army, which disposed of powerful forward detachments along a broad front, was vigorously advancing in the general direction of Labiau. The scattered units of the enemy's 548th, 551st and 56th infantry divisions were falling back before the army, putting up insignificant resistance. By the close of 22 January units of the 43rd Army, which had made a fighting advance of 23 kilometers, reached the following line: 90th Rifle Corps—the eastern shore of the Kurisches Haff as far as the Nemonin River; 103rd Rifle Corps—from the Nemonin River to Agilla; the 54th Rifle Corps' main force had reached Kelladen. The Germans were hurriedly fortifying the approaches to Labiau and were trying to organize a defense along the eastern bank of the Deime River.

To the left, the 39th Army, while pursuing the enemy with a single rifle corps (5th Guards) to the southwest, by the close of the day had overcome the wooded area to the west of Melauken and was approaching the Deime River along the front Permauern—Steindorf; the army's 94th Rifle Corps was on the march: its 124th Division had passed through Kirschnabek, the 358th Division Kukers, and the 221st Rifle Division's lead elements were near Schwentoie; the 113th Rifle Corps was advancing behind the 94th Rifle Corps and its lead elements had passed through Popelken. The army's units captured 200 prisoners, 16 guns, four tanks, 60 motor vehicles, and a large number of machine guns and rifles.

The tank corps were advancing no less successfully. The 1st Tank Corps, while fending off fierce enemy counterattacks with tanks and assault guns, which he had thrown into the defense of Tapiau, an important road junction on the approaches to Königsberg, broke through to the town from the northeast and, having destroyed 17 German tanks, five armored transports and a large number of enemy infantry, by 2000 on 22 January had reached the Deime River in the Friedrichsthal area. All of the corps' attempts to force the Deime River from the march were unsuccessful. The 2nd Guards Tatsinskaya Tank Corps, while pursuing the enemy to the south, by the close of the day reached the Zimonen area and, overcoming the heavy fire from assault guns and German anti-tank artillery, began crossing to the southern bank of the Pregel River with the onset of darkness. In the day's fighting the tank corps destroyed 14 enemy tanks, 11 armored transports, 47 motor vehicles, and killed more than 200 German soldiers and officers.

The 11th Guards Army's 8th Guards Rifle Corps, taking advantage of the 1st Tank Corps' success, was advancing rapidly and, having outflanked Welau from the northeast with its 5th Guards Rifle Division, had begun fighting along the town's outskirts. Throughout the day the 16th Guards Rifle Corps was involved in stubborn fighting with the enemy along his main defensive line of Wirbeln—Gross Berschkallen and by the close of 22 January had reached the Pregel River along the front Kuglaken—Zimonen. The corps' 83rd Division had concentrated in the Wilkendorf area.

To the south of Insterburg the enemy continued to put up stubborn resistance, relying on the defensive line along the Angerapp River. Throughout 22 January the 28th Army was engaged in fierce fighting to the west of Gumbinnen and, having broken through the enemy's defense along the Angerapp River, cut the Insterburg—Gumbinnen railroad.

The 2nd Guards Army while beating off fierce counterattacks along its right flank and in the center continued to wage heavy battles to break through the enemy's main defensive line and could only advance insignificantly with units from the 65th Rifle Corps (251st and 154th rifle divisions).

The 31st Army, which included the 152nd Fortified Area, began an attack on 21 January, on orders from the *front* commander, along its right flank and broke through the enemy's defense to the south of the Goldapgarsee and, developing the attack in the general direction of Angerburg, on 22 January captured the enemy's powerful strong point of Goldap.

Thus, simultaneous with the elimination of the enemy's powerful Insterburg—Gumbinnen group of forces, the *front's* right wing was energetically pursuing the remnants of the IX Army Corps, and by the close of 22 January the 43rd, 39th and 11th Guards armies had reached the Kurisches Haff—along the line of the Deime River—east of Welau and then along the Pregel River. As before, the shock group's center and left wing encountered stubborn enemy resistance and were echeloned back and were slowly advancing along the southern bank of the Pregel River.

The German command understood that the further splitting of its Tilsit—Insterburg group of forces' units would lead to their defeat in detail and enable our attacking units to get to Königsberg upon reaching the Deime River. For this reason, it threw all of its reserves to the Deime and Alle rivers, and even part of those forces slated for defending Königsberg, attempting at all costs to delay our troops' advance along this line. On 22 January units of the 286th Security Division, the 45th Security Regiment, the 78th Army Construction Battalion, a security company from the Königsberg garrison, an SS motorcycle battalion, and other units were identified in the Labiau area. However, the newly arrived German units did not represent a real force capable of delaying the offensive. The main German corps, which were defending the confines of the northeastern part of East Prussia, had been completely used up and disorganized and were retreating in disorder to the west.

At the same time, the commander of Army Group Center, fearing for the fate of the XXVI and XXVII army corps operating to the south of Gumbinnen, issued an order to begin an organized withdrawal to the Alle River on 23 January, while wearing out the enemy with delaying actions and halting him along this line.

The breakthrough of the Germans' defense along the Deime River and our forces' arrival at the approaches to Königsberg. On the night of 22-23 January combat operations along the entire front did not cease for a minute. While pursuing the retreating enemy, our units advanced rapidly to the west. At dawn the 43rd Army, following a short preparation, attacked the heavily fortified enemy strong point of Labiau. Units of the 551st and 548th infantry divisions, having taken up defensive positions to the east of this inhabited locale, put up a stubborn defense. Taking advantage of the favorable terrain conditions and employing heavy machine gun and mortar fire, they made it impossible for the units of the 103rd Rifle Corps to cross the Deime River and attack Labiau from the east. However, before long the corps' 115th Rifle Division and the 54th Rifle Corps' 263rd Rifle Division forced the river along the flanks and, decisively outflanking Labiau from the north and south, created the threat of completely encircling the garrison defending there. At the same time, units of the 319th Rifle Division broke into the town from the east. Finding itself in a hopeless situation, the German garrison ceased its resistance. Its remnants, which sought to escape from the town, were completely destroyed by arriving mobile units. By the close of 23 January the army had forced the Deime River and occupied Labiau.

In the fighting for Labiau the army's units captured more than 350 prisoners belonging to the 286th Security Division and the 561st and 551st infantry divisions, as well as a large amount of weapons and ammunition dumps.

On the evening of 23 January the *front* commander ordered the army's forces to continue a vigorous offensive to the west and reach the line Postnikken—Zelweten by the close of the day.

In the 39th Army's sector the enemy, taking advantage of a well prepared defensive line along the western bank of the Deime River, put up more stubborn resistance. Units of the 56th and 69th infantry divisions, which had fallen back here, carried out numerous counterattacks involving heavy machine gun and mortar fire. Fierce fighting raged throughout the day along the line of the Deime River. It was only by 1900 on 23 January that units of the 5th Guards Rifle Corps managed to force the river and secure a foothold on to the western bank. The 94th Rifle Corps also captured a series of enemy strong points on this bank. On the morning of 24 January the 39th Army received orders to continue the offensive along the northern bank of the Pregel River, to take Tapiau and by the close of 24 January reach the line excluding Zelweten—Heiligenwalde (ten kilometers northeast of Steinbeck).

As was noted earlier, the fortified line along the Deime River, which was linked with the overall defensive system located to the south (the Heilsberg fortified area), formed the external enclosure of the Königsberg fortified area. This defensive line, which consisted of field and permanent structures, played an important role in the Germans' defensive plans. Thus our forces' forcing of the Deime River was very important. Now the Soviet forces had the opportunity to advance to the approaches of Königsberg.

The 11th Guards Army, while vigorously developing the attack to the southwest, forced the Pregel River along its entire course from Tapiau to Staatshausen and captured the Germans' important strong point of Welau. The army was ordered to attack from the line of the Alle River along the southern bank of the Pregel River and by the close of 24 January to reach the front Steinbeck—Grunbaum (ten kilometers east of Uderwangen).

The 1st Tank Corps, following fierce fighting along the crossings over the Deime River near Tapiau, was pulled back to the Grunhein area and was to put itself in order. The 2nd Guards Tatsinskaya Tank Corps was operating along the 11th Guards Army's left flank and, while beating off fierce enemy tank and assault gun counterattacks, by 1900 had reached the Alle River in the Klein Nur area.

The 5th Army, while overcoming the enemy's stubborn resistance, advanced up to five kilometers on 22 January and captured a number of enemy strong points. The 72nd Rifle Corps, which was attacking in the army's first echelon, had by the close of the day captured the inhabited locales of Bubainen and Didlakken and was involved in a heavy fire fight along this line.

The enemy had begun a general withdrawal of his forces to the west opposite the *front's* left-wing armies. At 2300 on 23 January the enemy noticeably reduced his fire resistance opposite the 28th and 2nd Guards armies, and then facing the 31st Army. Reconnaissance elements, which had been uninterruptedly observing the enemy's behavior opposite the *front*, discovered his withdrawal before long.

Having gone over to a decisive pursuit, our units pushed aside the enemy covering forces left behind and rapidly surged forward. The mobile forward detachments, which had been detached beforehand and correspondingly trained for pursuit activities, energetically pushed aside the enemy's rearguards, bypassed the retreating German columns along the flanks and decisively attacked them. The Germans had heavily mined the roads, blown up the bridges and wrecked the roads. Taking advantage of the large number of inhabited locales and individual structures along their path of retreat, the German rearguards put up fierce resistance. However, the pace of the pursuit by our forces continually increased.

On 23 January the 28th Army advanced 12-15 kilometers and 18-20 kilometers on 24 January, arriving at the line Juganeuzas—Schoenwiese—Polleiken. The 2nd Guards Army, having captured the strong point of Darkemen, by the close of 24 January had reached the approaches to Nordenburg, having covered more than 45 kilometers. The 31st Army, while pursuing the retreating enemy, captured the important road junction of Benkheim with its 71st Rifle Corps and along the left flank the powerful strong point of Treuburg on the approaches to Lötzen. While vigorously developing the offensive toward Angerburg and Lötzen, the army penetrated more than 45 kilometers into the enemy position and by the close of 24 January stormed the Lötzen fortified area's heavily fortified strong point of Angerburg. In the succeeding days the pursuit of the enemy continued with unremitting force along the entire front.

On 25 January the enemy's resistance was finally crushed in the fortified positions along the Deime and Alle rivers as far as Friedland, and the *front's* forces, attacking with the forces of the 43rd and 39th armies north of the Pregel River and the forces of the 11th Guards and 5th armies south of the river, were rapidly approaching Königsberg. By the close of 26 January the armies had reached the following line: 43rd Army—Postnikken—Zelweten; 39th Army—Schoenwalde—Waldau; 11th Guards Army—Steinbeck—Uderwangen; 5th Army—Ober Blankenau—Allenburg; 28th Army—Kortmedin—Gerdauen; 2nd Guards Army—Birkenfeld—Drengfurt, and; the 31st Army—the western banks of the lakes near Lötzen.

Thus the forces of the Third Belorussian Front defeated the Germans' Tilsit—Insterburg group of forces in stubborn fighting over 14 days and captured such major centers of resistance as the towns of Tilsit, Insterburg, Gumbinnen, Darkemen, Angerburg, and Lötzen.

Decisively pursuing the enemy remnants to the west, they overcame fortifications, forced major water obstacles such as the Deime, Pregel and Alle rivers and energetically developed the offensive toward Königsberg.

By the close of 26 January the *front's* forces had penetrated up to 120 kilometers into the confines of East Prussia. The average daily rate of advance was 7-8 kilometers and along some axes the speed of our forces' advance during certain periods reached 20 kilometers per day and more.

The German forces, having lost their command and control, fell back rapidly to the west, putting up resistance along intermediary defensive lines.

The enemy suffered heavy losses: in only ten days, 13-23 January, our forces killed 60,570 German soldiers and officers, destroyed 790 tanks and assault guns, 719 guns of various calibers, up to 500 mortars, 1,940 machine guns, 2,560 motor vehicles, and 183 planes. 3,500 German soldiers and officers were captured, as were 38 tanks, 364 guns, 222 mortars, 2,500 machine guns, 118 planes, 522 motor vehicles, 73 ammunition dumps, 11 radio sets, and other prizes.

In the developing situation it was necessary, while maintaining high rates of pursuit, to break through to Königsberg and envelop the fortress from the north and south, to split up the German forces falling back to the shore of the Baltic Sea, to deprive them of the capability of organizing a defense and, while relying on the Königsberg fortifications, to destroy the enemy in detail.

Conclusions

Events unfolded very rapidly during the second stage of the East Prussian operation. In eight days of attack our forces achieved outstanding operational results and the entire situation in East Prussia radically changed in our favor.

The Second Belorussian Front rapidly completed the defeat of the Germans' Przasnysz—Mlawa group of forces and, while vigorously attacking to the north, northwest and west, arrived at the Frisches Haff and along the line of the Vistula River. An extremely important operational task had been fulfilled by the Second Belorussian Front: the land communications of the Germans' East Prussian group of forces had been cut and the powerful forces of the Red Army firmly stood astride their path of retreat, while all of East Prussia was cut off from the central areas of Germany.

The Third Belorussian Front also achieved great successes. The Germans' Tilsit—Insterburg group of forces was defeated; its remnants were retreating in disorder to the west. The *front's* armies forced the fortified lines along the Deime and Alle rivers and were now nearing the approaches to Königsberg—the Germans' final outpost along this axis.

The major successes achieved by our forces operating along the East Prussian strategic direction once again confirmed the outstanding role of the *Stavka* of the Supreme High Command in organizing and conducting operations.

Proceeding from an evaluation of the situation along the Soviet-German front, the *Stavka* of the Supreme High Command correctly determined the enemy's possible resistance along the East Prussian strategic direction. In accordance with this, the axes of the Second and Third Belorussian fronts' main attacks were selected and the necessary grouping of men and materiel created for achieving the assigned objectives.

The course of combat operations showed that the selected axes of the main attacks and assigned forces and means secured the defeat of the enemy's entire East Prussian group of forces.

Our forces' attacks along the Insterburg, Marienburg and Torun axes split of the enemy's entire group of forces located to the north of the Vistula River into isolated parts. In these conditions, the German command scattered his available operational reserves, employing them in detail along various axes. By the close of January 1945 the German command was feeding more and more new reserves into the battle.

New operational tasks now presented themselves to our forces in East Prussia: to prevent the encircled German forces from getting out of East Prussia and to complete the great success achieved by completely defeating and capturing the enemy.

6

The Battle with the Enemy's Isolated East Prussian Group of Forces. Combat Operations in the Königsberg Area and to the South. The Repulse of the German Forces' Attempts to Break Through to the Southwest

27 JANUARY-8 FEBRUARY

The two first stages of the East Prussian operation reviewed in the preceding chapters unfolded on a large scale and at increasing speed. Very major operational results were achieved in short time periods: the first stage, the operational breakthrough, lasted 5-6 days, while the second stage, the development of the offensive and the cutting off of the East Prussian group of forces, took 7-8 days. In the course of two weeks, from 13 to 26 January, the operational-strategic situation in East Prussia changed radically in our favor.

At the end of January began the third stage of this large operation, the chief objective of which was the complete elimination of the German forces cut off in East Prussia. The third stage embraces a lengthier period than the first two. The complete elimination of the major German forces in East Prussia, which were based on developed fortifications, required a significant amount of time and repeated efforts. Our forces were exhausted by the preceding battles, had suffered losses and, aside from this, the Second Belorussian Front had shifted to the west (beyond the Vistula and into Pomerania) for carrying out new strategic assignments, while subsequent unfavorable climatic and meteorological conditions had an effect. At this stage the entire weight of fighting to destroy the enemy's isolated East Prussian group of forces lay on the forces of the Third Belorussian Front.

Thus it is expedient to examine the third stage's most important events by period, taking into account the overall development of the situation and the character of the operational tasks being pursued.

The first period: 27 January-8 February. The continuation of the Third and Second Belorussian fronts' offensive. Operations on the Samland peninsula near Königsberg and in the area to the south.

The second period: 9 February-29 March. The complete defeat of the main forces of the Germans' East Prussian group of forces to the south of Königsberg.

Third period: 30 March-25 April: The conduct of the Königsberg operation and the elimination of the enemy group of forces on the Samland peninsula.

We will now examine the combat operations during the first period.

THIRD BELORUSSIAN FRONT

The Arrival of the *Front's* Right Wing at Königsberg and the Frisches Haff. The Battle Against the Isolated Enemy Group of Forces South of Königsberg

On 27 January the forces of the Third Belorussian Front continued their pursuit of the enemy. The right-wing armies, which were tasked with capturing Königsberg, on this day reached the near approaches to the fortress and became involved in stubborn fighting here. The German command took all measures in order to halt these armies' advance and to bleed them, thus giving the garrison the opportunity of organizing a solid defense. To the north of Königsberg the enemy's tank and infantry attacks increased significantly, while the Germans' aviation became more active. In the Schoenwalde area units of the 39th Army's 94th Rifle Corps were counterattacked twice. German artillery poured a heavy fire into the corps' infantry formation. The units attacking Königsberg from the east encountered the enemy's engineering obstacles more often and were forced into stubborn fighting for each defensive line and for each inhabited locale. The commander of the 39th Army, striving to block Königsberg as quickly as possible from the north, assigned his right-flank corps (5th Guards and 113th rifle) the task of energetically pursuing the enemy and, upon reaching the Frisches Haff, to prevent the German forces from withdrawing to the west. In order to carry out this task, the army commander regrouped his main artillery and mortar forces to the corps' sector. The *front* commander, in turn, dispatched two assault air divisions to the 39th Army's sector.

All day on 27 January, to the north and south of the Alter Pregel River, there was stubborn fighting. The 43rd Army, developing the attack along the seacoast, pursued the remnants of the 286th and 95th infantry divisions and by the close of the day had made a fighting advance to the line Stombeck—Norgenen. Units of the 54th Rifle Corps repelled four enemy infantry and tank attacks throughout the day and inflicted heavy losses on him.

Units of the 39th Army, while decisively destroying the retreating enemy, captured one defensive line after the other. By 2200 on 27 January the 5th Guards Rifle Corps reached the line Norgenen—Schugsten. The 113th Rifle Corps, which had been committed into the fighting by the commander of the 39th Army from behind the 5th Guards Rifle Corps' left flank, reached the front Zwehund (two kilometers south of Schugsten)—Truttenau. The 94th Rifle Corps, breaking through the fortified defenses north of the Alter Pregel River, captured the powerful enemy strong points of Gamsau and Praddau and on the following day reached the fortifications of the Königsberg fortress from the east and became involved in stubborn fighting.

The 11th Guards and 5th armies, tasked with reaching the shore of the Frisches Haff and outflanking with their main forces Königsberg from the south, on this day advanced rapidly. Scattered groups of the Germans' XXVI Army Corps, putting up weak resistance, strived to break free of our pursuing troops and take refuge in Königsberg, which the German command had prepared for stubborn perimeter defense.

On 27 January the 11th Guards Army, in conjunction with units of the 2nd Guards Tatsinskaya Tank Corps and supported by aviation, which resumed its activities on this day, captured the enemy strong points of Borchersdorf and Uderwangen.

In directing his attacks against Königsberg, General Chernyakhovskii was seeking to simultaneously isolate the Königsberg garrison from the main German forces operating to the south of the city. For this purpose, he moved up the 5th Army to Kreuzburg and the 28th Army to Preussisch Eylau.

The 5th Army, while closely cooperating with the forces of the 11th Guards Army, on 27 January was rapidly moving to the west. However, during the latter part of the day its position began to be more complicated. The enemy, having organized a solid defense along the Alle River to the south of Friedland, delayed that day the offensive by the 28th and 2nd Guards armies. All of the 28th Army's attempts to force the Alle River along its right flank were without result. Relying on the defense to the south of Friedland, the German units, whose combat orders were becoming denser as they withdrew, launched a counteroffensive during the second half of 27 January from the Preussisch Eylau area to the north and launched a powerful attack against the 5th Army's open flank. While repelling the attacks by German tanks and infantry, the 5th Army was forced to turn part of its forces to the south, where it became involved in heavy fighting along the line Abswangen—Bechschluss farm—Friedland. The 45th Rifle Corps, which was attacking along the army's right flank, had by the close of the day reached the Uderwangen area and, having turned to the southwest, attacked in the general direction of Preussisch Eylau. The 72nd Rifle Corps was advancing in the army's second echelon behind the 45th Rifle Corps, ready to develop the success achieved.

The 28th Army's main forces (3rd Guards and 128th rifle corps) captured the town and enemy strong point of Gerdauen on the night of 27-28 January. While developing the offensive to the west, at 1800 on 27 January the army's main forces reached the Alle River, where they were stopped by enemy fire from a previously prepared defensive line along the western bank of the Alle River. The army's right flank became involved in fighting alongside units of the 5th Army near Friedland, while the left was occupying Massaunen. During the day of 27 January the 2nd Guards Army, following a brief artillery preparation, broke through the enemy's defense along the intermediate line of the Masurian Canal (20 kilometers southeast of Gardauen), while its forward detachments pursued the enemy retreating to the west. Units of the 50th and 25th infantry divisions, while putting up resistance, were falling back in the general direction of Bartenstein, striving to occupy the previously prepared defensive zone along the western bank of the Alle River.

The 31st Army, having captured the fortress of Lötzen, on the morning of 27 January was pursuing the enemy to the west and southwest and by the close of the day its main forces had reached the line of the Zaine River. In a day of attacking the army captured more than 200 inhabited locales, including the towns of Drengfurt, Barten and Rastenburg.

Thus as early as 27 January the envelopment of Königsberg along the *front's* right flank was clearly outlined, and conditions for isolating it from the main body of the East Prussian group of forces operating south of Königsberg had also been created.

In the developing situation, the German command was adopting all measures so as to preserve the remnants of its forces and to deny our forces the capability of breaking them up. For this purpose, on 27 January they had completed the concentration of about a division of infantry and 100 tanks in the Brandenburg area (along the southeastern shore of the Frisches Haff). Our aerial reconnaissance discovered a concentration of infantry in the Fischausen area (Samland Peninsula). The garrison of the Königsberg fortress, the strength of which, counting the remnants of the Third Panzer and Fourth armies' units that had retreated there, exceeded 100,000 men and was hurriedly preparing for a prolonged and stubborn defense.

Despite all of these measures, the German command was no longer able to establish firm command and control over its forces and prevent our forces' further advance. The German forces continued to fall back to the west, searching for cover behind the walls of the fortress of Königsberg.

On 29 January units of the 39th Army's right wing, pursuing the remnants of the 69th Infantry Division, broke into the confines of the Samland Peninsula and cut the Granz—Königsberg and Fischausen—Königsberg paved roads and railroads, and on 31 January the army's 13th Guards Rifle Corps reached the Frisches Haff from the north along a 10-kilometer front, cutting off the path of retreat to the west out of Königsberg. In their turn, the 113th and 94th rifle corps invested Königsberg from the north and east and became involved in stubborn fighting along the outer ring of the fortress.

The 11th Guards Army continued to attack south of the Alter Pregel River, in the general direction of Königsberg. Overcoming the increasing resistance of the German units falling back toward the city, on 30 January the 16th Guards Rifle Corps captured the Brandenburg—Königsberg maritime paved road and its main forces reached the Frisches Haff as far as the mouth of the Frisching River, thus cutting off the Königsberg group of forces from the south. Units of the 36th and 8th guards rifle corps, upon turning their front to the north, attacked the enemy's Königsberg fortifications from the march and soon broke into his defensive zone and captured several permanent reinforced concrete structures.

The German command, in taking into account the serious situation that had arisen for the Königsberg garrison, sought to lift the blockade of the city and restore communications along the Brandenburg—Königsberg maritime paved road. The last reserves were moved up during the latter half of 30 January: the 562nd Infantry Division, reinforced with 110 tanks and assault guns from the remnants of the *Grossdeutschland* Panzer Division, launched a counterblow from the Brandenburg area against the flank of the 16th Guards Rifle Corps. As a result of the prolonged fighting, the enemy managed to push back our units, capture the maritime paved road and restore communications with Königsberg. In these battles the Germans lost in killed alone more than 2,500 men, 23 tanks, 10 assault guns, and a large number of guns and mortars.

To the left, the 5th Army continued to attack in the general direction of Zinten. On the morning of 28 January the 45th Rifle Corps was unexpectedly counterattacked from the south by units of the XXVI Army Corps. Up to 35 tanks and assault guns took part in the counterattack. However, all the attacks were beaten off with heavy losses for the enemy. Units of the 45th Rifle Corps, having repelled the enemy's push, threw the German units back to the south, forced the Frisching River and by the close of the day reached the line Mühlhausen—Abswangen. The commander of the 5th Army, while developing the success of the 45th Rifle Corps, committed the 72nd Rifle Corps from behind the right flank in the general direction of Kreuzburg, which by the close of 28 January was engaged in fighting for Schrombenen. On 29 January the army's 65th Rifle Corps turned over its sector to the north of the town of Friedland to the 28th Army and was shifted to the 45th Rifle Corps' left flank, from where it began an attack to the south. The German forces, relying on the fortifications of the Heilsberg fortified area here, were putting up fierce resistance. Launching one attack after another, they sought to halt our forces' advance to the southwest. During the succeeding days, units of the 5th Army advanced at an average rate of 2-5 kilometers per day and by the close of 31 January were involved in stubborn fighting along the line Kreuzburg—Romitten (eight kilometers southeast of Mühlhausen).

The 28th Army, as before, was involved in heavy fighting along the Alle River and by the close of 31 January had forced it and, having captured the town of Friedland, continued to attack toward Preussisch Eylau. The 2nd Guards and 31st armies' main forces, pursuing the retreating enemy, reached the Alle River along the line Schippenbeil—Bartenstein—Heilsberg and became involved in stubborn fighting here.

Thus on 31 January the forces of the Third Belorussian Front, while developing the success to the west, reached with their right wing the fortress of Königsberg and invested it, while the left wing reached the Heilsberg fortified area and continued in heavy fighting to eliminate the remnants of the Germans' Army Group Center, which had concentrated here. The fighting along the *front's* left wing became all the more stubborn.

The 5th Army, attacking along its center toward Kreuzburg, spent the next six days fighting for that strong point and it was only on 7 February that we captured it. The troops along the army's right flank continued as before to be involved in heavy fighting to the south of Kobbelbude. In developing the success to the west of Kreuzburg, the 5th Army's 72nd and 45th rifle corps, as well as the 36th Rifle Corps, which had been subordinated to the army, had by the close of 8 February reached the line Kobblebude—Schlautienen and continued to attack along the left flank toward Zinten.

The 28th Army, while engaged in stubborn fighting to the west of the Alle River, on 2 February captured the powerful enemy strong points of Domnau and Schoenbruch.

The 20th Rifle Corps, cooperating with the 5th Army's forces, on 8 February outflanked the inhabited locale of Preussisch Eylau from the north and began fighting along its outskirts.

On 2 February the 2nd Guards Army, having destroyed the German garrison in Schippenbeil, became involved in heavy fighting for the strong point of Bartenstein, outflanking it from the north and south. On the night of 3-4 February the army's units broke into this inhabited locale from the east and south and following stubborn street fighting captured it at 0700 on 4 February, destroying the defending garrison in almost its entirety. However, northwest of the town of Bartenstein, along the line Ziddau—Borken, our attacking forces once again encountered the enemy's defensive line, containing a large number of permanent reinforced concrete structures, wooden anti-tank post obstacles, ditches and wire obstacles. It was only on 8 February that we managed to break through the enemy's organized defense. Units of the Germans' 50th and 21st infantry divisions, having suffered heavy losses, began to fall back to the northwest. By the close of 8 February our forces reached the line Legden—Bandels and, bypassing Preussisch Eylau from the south, continued to attack in the general direction of Topprinen.

The 31st Army, having resumed the offensive, broke through the defense to the west of Helzberg and, advancing rapidly along its left flank to the northwest, on 2 February captured the enemy's major road junction of Landsberg. However, the army's subsequent advance was made more difficult. The German command, having regrouped the 129th and 558th infantry divisions to the Landsberg area, as well as units of the 24th Panzer Division, carried out powerful counterattacks, trying to encircle units of the 71st Rifle Corps in this area. Stubborn fighting went on here for several days, as a result of which the army's units beat off all the enemy's attacks and continued to slowly advance in the general direction of Kanditten.

Thus during the period under review—27 January-8 February—the forces of the Third Belorussian Front developed the offensive to the west and southwest. The right-wing armies reached the fortress of Königsberg and invested it from the landward side.

In the center, our forces also advanced, overcoming the enemy's resistance and seeking to isolate the main body of the East Prussian group of forces from the troops of the Königsberg group.

Along the left wing the Third Belorussian Front's armies, along with the Second Belorussian Front's armies, were involved in intense fighting with the Germans' East Prussian group of forces, which had been cut off from its land communications, in order to eliminate it. Our forces attacking here encountered the enemy's stubborn resistance. By the close of 8 February there was fighting along the line: Kobbelbude—Schlautienen—east of Preussisch Eylau—Landsberg—Workeim (12 kilometers northwest of Heilsberg).

SECOND BELORUSSIAN FRONT

The Battle Against the Germans' Isolated East Prussian Group of Forces. The Repulse of the Enemy's Attempts to Break out to the Southwest. The Fighting for Bridgeheads on the Vistula River

The elimination of the enemy's attempts to break through in the Gutstadt—Liebstadt area. Following the arrival of part of the shock group's forces at the coast of the Baltic Sea, the Second Belorussian Front's right-wing armies continued to attack to the northwest for the purpose of completely defeating the Germans' isolated East Prussian group of forces, alongside the forces of the Third Belorussian Front. The 50th Army attacked in the general direction of Sensburg, the 49th Army Bischofsburg, the 3rd Army on Gutstadt, and the 48th Army, operating along a very broad front, along with the 5th Guards Tank Army, was attacking along two axes: toward Landsberg (20 kilometers northwest of Heilsberg) along its right flank, and along the seacoast toward Braunsberg on the left.

By the close of 26 January the length of the front line had grown from an initial 285 kilometers to 430 kilometers, while the length of the individual armies' front had reached the sizes shown in the following table.

Table III/6.1 The Second Belorussian Front's Length, 26 January 1945

Army	Number of Divisions	Width of Front (km)	Kilometers per Division
50th	7	44	6
49th	9	24	3
3rd	9	56	6
48th	9	90	10
2nd Shock	9	72	8
65th	9	54	6
70th	9	90	10
Front reserve	2	–	–
TOTAL	63	430	7

As can be seen from the table, the 50th, 49th and 3rd armies, which were operating along a supporting direction, now had the greatest operational density. On the other hand, the 48th Army, which stood astride the German forces' path of retreat from East Prussia, now had the lengthiest front.

Meanwhile, the German command had made the decision to restore land communications between its East Prussian group of forces and the rest of Germany. For this purpose, units of the 131st, 170th and 299th infantry divisions, the 28th Light Infantry Division, the "Hermann Goring" Panzergrenadier Division, the 18th Panzergrenadier Division, the *Grossdeutschland* Panzer Division, and a brigade of assault guns, were hurriedly concentrated to the north of Gutstadt. All of these divisions were deployed along a front from Gutstadt to Wormditt.

At 2400 on 26 January German artillery and mortars unexpectedly opened fire on the 48th Army's right flank. Then German infantry and tanks went over to the offensive. The enemy attack struck the 53rd Rifle Corps. As a result of the fierce fighting on 27-28 January, the enemy managed to capture Liebstadt, while the 17th Rifle Division was surrounded one kilometer southwest of Wormditt and was fighting, while beating off persistent enemy attacks. On 29 January stubborn fighting continued in the area west of Liebstadt. The enemy undertook several attacks in forces of up to three divisions, each disposing of 70 tanks. Individual scattered enemy groups managed to break through to the wooded area 15-20 kilometers west of Liebstadt.

Throughout 27-29 January the weather was unfavorable and the 4th Air Army carried out during these three days only 189 sorties, primarily reconnaissance. As regards the enemy air force, up to 60 sorties were noted.

In connection with the situation that had arisen along the 48th Army's front, the army was reinforced with the 8th Guards Tank Corps. At the same time, the 42nd Rifle Corps (48th Army) was transferred to the 5th Guards Tank Army and the latter was ordered to turn its main forces to the east. At 1730 on 28 January an order was transmitted to the 3rd Guards Cavalry Corps through the 3rd Army's headquarters—to cover Allenstein with a single cavalry division, while the remaining forces were to strike the flank of those enemy units attacking along the 48th Army's sector; the choice of the axis of attack was to be made independently. On that same day the 3rd Guards Cavalry Corps set out for Morungen. Besides this, the 48th Army was to be reinforced with five anti-tank artillery brigades.

Finally, the 2nd Shock Army's 142nd Rifle Division occupied a position facing northeast along the left bank of the canal along the sector Freiwalde (12 kilometers west of Morungen)—the Draussensee (south of Elbing), for the purpose of cutting off the enemy's units in case they should break through the 48th Army's front.

At the same time heavy fighting was going on in the 48th Army's sector against major enemy units that were attempting to break through to the west and reestablish communications, the 50th, 49th and 3rd armies continued to develop their attack, and as their front moved forward it gradually contracted. Thus on 29 January the 49th Army was pulled into the *front* reserve and began moving to the west with the mission of concentrating by the morning of 4 February in the Freistadt (18 kilometers west of Deutsch Eylau)—Nowe Miasto—Lubawa area.

If one evaluates the situation only in the Second Belorussian Front's attack sector, then it is not quite clear why the *front* command did not transfer its reserve (330th and 369th rifle divisions) to the north to support the 48th Army and why the 49th Army was also directed to the west, to the Vistula River, instead of being turned in the direction of Liebstadt, where at that time a difficult situation had developed and where one could expect a breakthrough by major enemy forces out of East Prussia.

However, one should not lose sight of the fact that at the same time that the Second Belorussian Front's forces had reached the coast of the Baltic Sea, the First Belorussian Front's shock group was located 180-200 kilometers ahead of the Second Belorussian Front's left-flank units and was continuing the attack toward the Oder River. Meanwhile, the German command was concentrating major forces in Pomerania for an attack against the flank and rear of the First Belorussian Front's forces.

In order to secure the most important operation along the Berlin strategic direction, it was necessary to rapidly advance the Second Belorussian Front's left-flank armies to the west of the Vistula, for the purpose of securing the First Belorussian Front's right flank by defeating the enemy's Pomeranian group of forces. Thus the Second Belorussian Front command, on the basis of instructions from the *Stavka* of the Supreme High Command, persistently pushed its reserve divisions and the 49th Army to the west, to the Vistula River. Only the 49th Army's 124th Rifle Corps was directed to the Morungen area and transferred to the 48th Army.

Along with this, it should be noted that the correlation of forces along the Heilsberg axis was quite favorable for us and one could not expect the enemy's counteroffensive to have any great success.

On 30 January the Germans made their final attempt to break out of the encirclement. In the Liebstadt area the enemy committed a large number of infantry and 70 tanks into the fighting. All of the German attacks were beaten off and the enemy was forced to fall back to his jumping-off position. Thus thanks to the timely support of the 48th Army by units of the 5th Guards Tank Army, the 3rd Guards Cavalry Corps, the 8th Guards Tank Corps, and our anti-tank artillery, all of the Germans' attempts to break through our front and restore their communications with the rest of Germany were unsuccessful. The 5th Guards Tank and 48th armies not only beat off all the enemy's attacks, but in turn they resumed the offensive to the northeast. The 17th Rifle Division was relieved.

During 31 January-8 February the *front's* right-wing armies continued to develop the offensive and gradually, along with the Third Belorussian Front's forces, squeezed the enemy's East Prussian group of forces from three sides. By the close of 8 February the Second Belorussian Front's right-flank armies had reached the following lines:

The 50th Army captured Heilsberg, broke through the enemy's permanent fortified zone and was fighting to the west of Landsberg.

The 3rd Army also broke through the Germans' permanent fortified zone and, while outflanking the enemy's Wormditt group of forces from the east, was fighting along the line excluding Frauendorf (16 kilometers southwest of Heilsberg)—the heights four kilometers east of Wormditt.

The 48th Army, having been reinforced with the 124th Rifle Corps, captured Liebstadt and, while overcoming the enemy's stubborn resistance, reached the front of the heights four kilometers south of Wormditt—excluding Lauck (24 kilometers northwest of Liebstadt).

The 5th Guards Tank Army, having been reinforced with the 42nd Rifle Corps, was advancing slowly and along its right flank had reached the Passarge River in the Lauck area and in the center was fighting for Frauenburg (along the shore of the Frisches Haff), while along the left flank it continued to occupy Tolkemit. Our reconnaissance detachment crossed the Frisches Haff to the Frisches Nerung spit and mined the enemy's routes of retreat. However, the reconnaissance detachment was forced to fall back under enemy pressure.

The fighting for the bridgeheads on the Vistula River. The elimination of the enemy's Torun group of forces. At the same time the *front's* right-wing armies were repelling counterattacks by units of the enemy's East Prussian group of forces, which were trying to break through to the west, the *front's* left wing had reached the Vistula River, forced it and was involved in stubborn fighting to seize and maintain bridgeheads along its western bank.

During the 26-30 January time period the offensive developed successfully. The 2nd Shock Army relieved units of the 5th Guards Tank Army near Elbing and completely took over the blockade of and fighting against the enemy's Elbing garrison. Besides this, units of the 2nd Shock Army reached the Nogat River along a sector northeast of Marienburg.

The 65th Army captured Marinewerder and reached the Vistula along the entire Marienwerder—Graudenz sector. In the center the army was fighting along the eastern outskirts of Graudenz, while on the left flank the army's units had forced the Vistula along a broad front and were fighting to create and widen their bridgeheads.

The 70th Army was fighting to widen its bridgehead along the western bank of the Vistula along the Kulm—Fordon sector and in the center advanced up to 16 kilometers. Along the left wing the army's units were blockading the garrison of the fortress of Torun along the northern bank of the Vistula. In general, during 26-30 January the offensive by the left-flank armies was developing quite favorably. However, the situation subsequently changed drastically as a result of the attempt by the enemy's Torun garrison to break out to the northwest.

The blockading of the fortress of Torun along the northern bank of the Vistula was being carried out by the 136th Rifle Division and a regiment from the 71st Rifle Division. According to available data, there were a total of 3,000-4,000 men in the Torun garrison, and thus a single division, reinforced by a rifle regiment, was considered sufficient. In reality, the besieged fortress contained the following units: the newly-formed 340th Grenadier Division, units of the 73rd and 337th infantry divisions, the 488th Independent Infantry Regiment, the 9th Construction

Battalion, and the 384th Security Battalion. In all, there were 30,000 men. It follows that the enemy enjoyed a numerical advantage.

At the same time, the disposition of our forces facing the fortress did not correspond to the situation. It was most likely to expect a breakout by the Torun garrison to the northwest, while it was exactly the northwestern sector of the blockade that was occupied more weakly than the others, and besides, the division's second-echelon regiment was deployed behind the blockade's northeastern sector.

In turn, the Torun garrison believed that the fortress was being blockade by superior Russian forces. Thus the enemy made the decision to try to break through with all its forces along a narrow sector in the northwestern sector on the night of 30-31 January. As a result of his overwhelming superiority of forces along the attack sector, the enemy managed to break through our blockade. The Germans began moving in two columns to the northwest in the general direction of Unislaw (24 kilometers northwest of Torun), where the headquarters of the 70th Army was located. With the arrival of the enemy's units at Unislaw the army's headquarters was forced to move to the Kulmsee (16 kilometers north of Torun) and communications with the army's units were temporarily disrupted.

First of all, the 200th Rifle Division, which was in the army's second echelon and located on the western bank of the Vistula in the area 15-20 kilometers west of Kulm, was directed against the enemy's Torun group of forces. Then the 136th and 165th rifle divisions and part of the 1st Guards Tank Corps' tanks were drawn into the fighting against the German columns attempting to break out of Torun, as well as the 330th and 369th divisions from the *front* reserve, which were directed toward Unislaw and on 3 February transferred to the commander of the 70th Army.

Finally, the first-echelon corps detached special detachments, which were moved to the rear areas of their corps and deployed facing to the south for the immediate support of the troop rear.

Thanks to the measures adopted, the enemy columns were broken up and their advance to the north slowed. Several of the German groups trying to break through were destroyed on the march to the Vistula River. One group from the Torun garrison managed to cross the Vistula in the area 6-10 kilometers southwest of Kulm, but was surrounded here by our forces. Several small groups, after crossing the Vistula, even penetrated as far as the area 25-30 kilometers northwest of Unislaw, where they were encircled by the 330th Rifle Division. In the final analysis, all of these enemy groups were destroyed by our forces and the elimination of the Torun group of forces was essentially completed by the close of 8 February. Only an insignificant part managed to break through our front in the Schwetz area (six kilometers north of Kulm) and link up with its own forces, which at this time were waging insistent attacks against our units in order to make it easier for the Torun group of forces to get out of the encirclement.

By the close of 8 February our armies on the Nogat and Vistula rivers occupied the following positions.

On its left flank the 2nd Shock Army was continuing to fight to destroy the surrounded garrison of Elbing; along the remainder of the front the army's units occupied lines along the Nogat and Vistula rivers along the sector mouth of the Nogat River—the heights east of Neunberg. The 142nd Rifle Division was occupying is previous position along the Oberlandischer Canal, facing east. During 4-7 February the enemy carried out persistent attacks with large forces along the Elbing axis, for the purpose of relieving the Elbing garrison. Units of the new German 227th Infantry Division, which had been transferred from Libava, were noted in the area northwest of Marienwerder.

The 65th Army continued fighting along its right flank and in the center along the eastern outskirts of Graudenz and was holding a bridgehead on the western bank of the Vistula 5-15 kilometers southwest of Graudenz; units of the army's left wing were fighting along the western bank of the Vistula along the sector southern outskirts of Schwetz—Julienhof (ten kilometers northwest of Schwetz).

The 70th Army continued to fight to widen its bridgehead along the western bank of the Vistula, and by the close of 8 February had reached the front excluding Julienhof—Lubiewo (36 kilometers north of Bromberg), while the 1st Guards Tank Corps was in the reserve behind the boundary of the 65th and 70th armies.

The 3rd Guards Cavalry Corps had been transferred to the *front's* left flank and was located in an area 12-20 kilometers northeast of Bromberg.

The 49th Army (minus the 124th Rifle Corps) had begun to cross over to the western bank of the Vistula River along the 70th Army's sector and was getting ready to move up to the front line.

Duriing the 31 January-8 February time period the weather remained generally unfavorable for flying. During this period the 4th Air Army carried out a total of 3,450 sorties. 38 enemy planes were shot down or otherwise destroyed. The enemy air force, in its turn, carried out about 300 sorties.

During 31 January-8 February, of 30,000 men in the Torun group of forces, 15,025 were killed and 11,975 captured. Up to 200 guns were captured. Only 3,000 men managed to break out of the encirclement and link up with their forces in the Schwetz area. Thus the enemy's Torun group of forces was eliminated. None the less, it should be admitted that even the German forces' unsuccessful breakthrough had a serious influence on the course of military operations along the boundary between the First and Second Belorussian fronts. The fact of the matter is that the Second Belorussian Front's left-wing forces, tied down as they were in fighting the Torun group of forces, were unable to develop a decisive offensive to the west and deal with the enemy's group of forces that the German command was concentrating in Pomerania for an attack against the flank and rear of the First Belorussian Front, which was located at this time along the Oder River. It was only after the elimination of the Germans' Torun group of forces that the Second Belorussian Front's left-wing armies once again gained freedom of operational maneuver.

As early as the period of eliminating the Germans' Torun group of forces the commander of the Second Belorussian Front, while carrying out the *Stavka's* instructions, decided to concentrate his main forces along his left wing and renew the decisive offensive to the west in order, in conjunction with the forces of the First Belorussian Front, to defeat the enemy's Pomeranian group of forces. For this, the 70th Army's right-flank 114th Rifle Corps was transferred to the 65th Army, while the 49th Army was to be inserted in the front line between the 65th and 70th armies by the morning of 9 February.

This decision by the commander of the Second Belorussian Front was confirmed by *Stavka* directive No. 11021 of 8 February. In accordance with this directive, the Second Belorussian Front was to attack along its center and left wing (2nd Shock, 65th, 49th, and 70th armies, and the 1st Guards Tank, 8th Mechanized and 3rd Guards Cavalry corps, and no less than four artillery breakthrough divisions) to the west of the Vistula River and no later than 20 February reach the line of the mouth of the Vistula River—Dirschau—Berent—Rummelsburg—Neustettin (all locales to the west of the Vistula River). Later, upon the arrival of the 19th Army, the Second Belorussian Front was to develop the offensive in the general direction of Stettin, capture the Danzig—Gdynia area and clear the coastline of the enemy all the way to the Bay of Pomerania.

Then a second *Stavka* directive (No. 11022) was received on 9 February, in which the *front* was ordered to transfer to the Third Belorussian Front the 50th Army (six divisions), 3rd Army (nine divisions), the 48th Army (12 divisions), the 5th Guards Tank Army, the 29th Heavy Tank Brigade, 23rd Tank Brigade, and the 15th Artillery Breakthrough Division.

It should be noted that the armies and formations to be transferred from the Second Belorussian Front had been taking part in battles for about a month. They were significantly under strength in men and materiel. For example, the average strength of the 48th Army's rifle divisions did not exceed 3,500 men, while the army disposed of a total of 85 tanks and self-propelled guns.

The 5th Guards Tank Army had 155 tanks and self-propelled guns in line. Of this number, the overwhelming majority of vehicles had exhausted their motors' capabilities (by 10 February) or were close to it.

With these two *Stavka* directives the Second Belorussian Front's participation in the East Prussian operation, in conjunction with the Third Belorussian Front, was to come to an end. The elimination of the enemy's East Prussian group of forces was now to be fully entrusted to the Third Belorussian Front.

During the operation the forces of the Second Belorussian Front broke through the enemy's defense along a front up to 110 kilometers in width and up to 200 kilometers in depth, reached the Baltic Sea and cut off the enemy's East Prussian group of forces from the rest of Germany. The *front's* forces then beat off persistent counterattacks by an enemy trying to restore his communications, and created a favorable jumping-off position for the final defeat, in conjunction with the Third Belorussian Front, of the Germans' East Prussian group of forces.

At the same time, as a result of the German forces' defeat in East Prussia, the strategic securing of our offensive along the Berlin direction, where decisive events were unfolding, was secured.

Following our units' arrival at the Baltic Sea and the defeat of the German forces in the Liebstadt area, the combat tasks assigned to the Second Belorussian Front had been achieved, and the main mass of the *front's* forces were freed up and could be employed for new operations along new axes.

Finally, the seizure of bridgeheads along the western bank of the Vistula created a favorable jumping-off position for an offensive to the northwest and west.

During combat operations not only were the formations of the Second and Fourth German armies (in all, 24-25 divisions) defeated, but a serious defeat had been inflicted on another 9-10 enemy infantry and two panzer divisions, which had been transferred by the German command from other axes for the purpose of halting our offensive along the Mlawa—Elbing axis.

During 14-26 January the *front's* forces made a fighting advance of about 200 kilometers. From this it follows that the average rate of advance was 15 kilometers per day. Also, the breakthrough of the enemy's tactical defense was carried out at a pace of 6-8 kilometers per day. Subsequently, our force advanced 16-17 kilometers per day, and in some cases 30 kilometers per day.

The mobile formations' average daily rate of advance was as follows: 22 kilometers for the 1st Guards Tank Corps; 25 kilometers for the 8th Guards Tank Corps; 17 kilometers for the 8th Mechanized Corps; and; 36 kilometers for the 5th Guards Tank Army.

During the 14 January-8 February period of combat operations, we captured about 20,000 men and took the following equipment: 1,373 guns, 479 mortars, 248 tanks and assault guns, and 43 planes.

During January-February we shot down in air battles or destroyed on the ground 216 enemy aircraft. Our air losses during this period amounted to 168 planes, of which the major part was shot down by the enemy's anti-aircraft artillery.

Conclusions

During the course of the period under study (27 January-8 February), combat operations continued to develop favorably for us, while results were achieved having an important operational significance.

During the offensive along the Königsberg axis, a large part of the Samland peninsula was captured, and south of the Alte Pregel our forces also advanced, and in places reached the coast of the Frisches Haff. The Königsberg garrison was almost completely surrounded and the fortress of Königsberg was blockaded.

Further to the south, the Third Belorussian Front's left-wing armies, along with the Second Belorussian Front's right-wing armies, launched concentric attacks against the main forces of the enemy's East Prussian group of forces in the Kreuzburg—Preussisch Eylau—Heilsberg—Wormditt—Braunsberg area and were squeezing the encircling ring around them. The internal space occupied by the German troops was gradually contracting and by the end of this period amounted to about 40-50 kilometers across. This major German group of forces, cut off from its land communications and pressed against the sea, continued to put up stubborn resistance, although its situation became more and more hopeless with each passing day. At the same time, the German command undertook measures to restore communications with the group of forces operating in the Danzig area, and carried out a full-scale mobilization of the entire male population along the East Prussian territory not occupied by us.

At the end of the period under examination the Second Belorussian Front received a new operational-strategic assignment and was to leave for the Vistula and then further to the west to Pomerania, upon turning over its right-flank armies to the Third Belorussian Front.

The completion of the battle against the German forces in East Prussia was to be entrusted to the Third Belorussian Front.

Thus the main operational results achieved in the East Prussian operation during this period of time may be summed up as follows:

1. Our forces advanced further to the west, once again inflicted heavy losses on the enemy and pressed him to the sea, and blockaded the fortress of Königsberg.

2. The German forces in East Prussia had been split up into three groups:
    • on the Samland peninsula (four divisions);
    • the Königsberg group (about five divisions, fortress and other units);
    • the main forces of the East Prussian group of forces located south of Königsberg (about 20 divisions).

The subsequent tasks facing our forces in East Prussia consisted of eliminating these three German groups.

7

The Elimination of the German Forces Southwest of Königsberg

10 FEBRUARY-25 MARCH 1945

By the beginning of February, the German forces in East Prussia were located in three groups.

1. On the Samland peninsula a group of four infantry divisions, two independent regiments, five independent battalions, and newly created *volkssturm* battalions, was defending in the western part of the Samland peninsula.
2. In the Königsberg area the group consisted of about four infantry divisions, a panzer, regiment, three fortress regiments, and six independent *volkssturm* battalions defending in the area of the fortress of Königsberg, as well as a large number of independent units and subunits formed according to the instructions of the fortress commander, General Lausch, from the remnants of defeated divisions that had fallen back here from the Insterburg area.
3. A group of forces in the area south and southwest of Königsberg (Brandenburg—Preussisch Eylau—Braunsberg—Heiligenbeil) consisted of two panzer and 14 infantry divisions, a panz-ergrenadier division, two brigades, two division combat groups, two independent regiments, five independent battalions, and newly formed combat groups and *volkssturm* battalions.

According to intelligence data, the German command was aware of the entire danger of the situation for the three isolated groups. In order to win time necessary for the subsequent evacuation of its forces, the enemy sought to strengthen their resistance through rear units and subunits and the *volkssturm*, police, and reinforcements arriving by sea from the central regions of Germany. Transports with ammunition and other military equipment arrived to the Frisches Haff from Stettin. Along with this, the enemy began evacuating the civilian population from East Prussia, as well as some of the Fourth Army's rear organs.

The Soviet forces operating in East Prussia were faced with the task of destroying all of these enemy groups of forces and preventing their evacuation by sea. The Soviet command's operational plan called for the elimination of these three enemy groups of forces, beginning with the southern one, which was the strongest.

In accordance with this, the forces operating against the southern group of forces were united in the hands of the commander of the Third Belorussian Front; according to *Stavka* directive no. 11022 of 9 February 1945, the Second Belorussian Front's 50th, 3rd and 5th Guards Tank armies were transferred to the Third Belorussian Front, while the latter's 43rd, 39th and 11th Guards armies, which were operating in the Königsberg area, were transferred to the First Baltic Front, the headquarters of which by this time had been transferred to East Prussia.

At the end of January and the beginning of February, our forces were attacking the Heilsberg fortified area, which was the most powerful in the overall system of fortifications along the approaches to Königsberg. The length of the enemy's defensive front here reached 180 kilometers. The line of permanent fortifications ran from Tapiau south as far as Friedland, then along the western bank of the Alle River through the towns of Zippenbeil, Bartenstein, Heilsberg, and Wormditt, and then turned to the west and the northwest along the Passarge River to the coast. The construction of this zone had been started by the Germans as early as 1932. Since that time reinforced concrete pillboxes, post obstacles, anti-tank ditches, wire and other obstacles had been built. It was calculated that nine infantry divisions, with their corresponding reinforcements, could occupy defensive positions here, although, in fact, up to 20 German divisions, which had suffered heavy losses in the preceding fighting, fell back here. Divisional sectors consisted of strong points outfitted in inhabited locales, along individual hills and in wooded areas. The internal defensive line ran along the Frisching River and served as the rear boundary of the Heilsberg fortified area. A large military factory had been built in the woods west of Preussisch Eylau, which supplied the German forces with ammunition and some types of weaponry.

A shore defensive zone, which was based on the heavily fortified strong points of Brandenburg, Ludwigsort, Heiligenbeil, Braunsberg, and Frauenburg, ran along the Frisches Haff as far as the Frisching River. There were 911 reinforced concrete firing points (mainly machine gun ones) and a large number of wood and earthen defensive structures in the Heilsberg fortified area. The average size of a combat casemate was 200X300 centimeters, while the thickness of the walls reached 100 centimeters. There was an overall density of up to five reinforced concrete pillboxes per kilometer of front. There were wire fences in four layers in the wooded areas in front of the reinforced concrete pillboxes, as well as a wire network on the lower stakes; post obstacles, mining and other forms of obstacles were broadly employed.

As a result of our forces' offensive in January, the northern face of the Heilsberg fortified area had been pierced (along the Tapiau—Friedland sector) and the front line here had moved far to the west. Our offensive in the first ten days of February led to the elimination of the eastern face, which ran along the line of the Alle River, while the southern sector was overcome in subsequent fighting.

The *front* commander's decision. The commander of the Third Belorussian Front decided to first eliminate the enemy defending the salient in the Preussisch Eylau—Landsberg—Bartenstein area and subsequently continue the offensive in the general direction of Heiligenbeil. In accordance with this decision, the 28th Army was to launch an attack from the northeast toward Preussisch Eylau, with the task of capturing this strong point along with units of the 2nd Guards Army attacking from the east. The 31st Army would attack from the south in the general direction of Landsberg and was to capture this town and develop the attack toward Kanditten.

The 2nd Guards Army, attacking from the east, was supposed to split the enemy forces located in the salient and eliminate them together with the 28th and 31st armies and to then attack toward Augam.

The 5th Army, while supporting the *front's* main forces from the Brandenburg area, was to launch an attack in the general direction of Zinten.

Combat operations were conducted at the beginning of February on the basis of this decision and the troops gradually advanced.

The *front* commander ordered his new armies to continue the offensive on the morning of 11 February.

The 50th Army was to reach the line Finken—Plauten. It was to subsequently advance on Kildenen.

The 3rd Army was to attack in the general direction of Mehlsack and reach the line Lotterfeld—Zonnenfeld.

The 48th Army, while attacking along its right flank, was to capture Wormditt. It was to subsequently reach the line Mehlsack—Laungwalde.

The 5th Guards Tank Army was to continue the offensive in the general direction of Braunsberg, capture this strong point and reach the Passarge River.

Thus, General Chernyakhovskii, in eliminating the salient in the German defense in the Preussisch Eylau area, decided to launch an attack with his newly subordinated armies from the Second Belorussian Front's former right wing from the south along two axes: to Mehlsack and Braunsberg, with the idea of splitting up the encircled German forces, along with the armies attacking from the north and east, and destroying them in detail. The 5th Guards Tank Army, while developing the offensive along the shore of the Frisches Haff, was to cut the enemy off from the shore and prevent evacuations from the Frisches Nehrung spit.

The 1st Air Army was entrusted with the following tasks: to destroy the encircled forces' men and materiel through massive air strikes; to prevent evacuation and delivery from the Frisches Nehrung spit; while closely cooperating with the ground forces attacking in the direction of Zinten, Mehlsack and Braunsberg, support the capture of these strong points.

Upon completing a regrouping of forces, the *front's* forces renewed the offensive.

Despite the heavy fire by our artillery and mortars, which were supporting the offensive, the enemy put up stubborn resistance. Particularly fierce fighting broke out in the 5th Army's sector in the Zinten area. The enemy, having shifted a regiment from the 562nd Division and the 24th Panzer Division's 9th Panzergrenadier Regiment here, began to carry out powerful counterattacks, beginning in the morning, striving to cut off and destroy the army's left-flank units operating here and prevent their arrival at the Zinten—Königsberg railroad. Bloody fighting was going on to the east of Zinten. The army's units beat off five counterattacks involving up to a battalion of infantry and 12-15 tanks. At 1700 on 11 February the enemy once again undertook a powerful counterattack from the Poren area (ten kilometers north of Zinten) from three directions. As a result of the heavy fighting, units of the 5th Army advanced an insignificant distance along the right flank and in the center. The 36th Rifle Corps, which was operating near Zinten, did not advance.

By the close of 11 February the 28th Army, while overcoming the enemy's stubborn fire resistance and repelling numerous infantry and tank counterattacks, captured the inhabited locale of Dingort (15 kilometers northeast of Aichen). The enemy put up stubborn resistance to our troops' advance with units of the 1st, 56th, 50th, and 541st infantry divisions.

Neither did the forces of the 2nd Guards and 31st armies achieve material success. The Germans, widely employing previously outfitted positions, put up a powerful fire resistance to our attacking units and repeatedly carried out frenzied counterattacks.

Heavy fighting occurred on 11 February in the 50th, 3rd, 48th and 5th Guards Tank armies' sectors. Relying on the powerful Wormditt center of resistance, the enemy undertook several powerful counterattacks from the Lichtenau—Heinrichau area, forcing our units to halt their attack and consolidate. The 48th Army was unable to force the Passarge River along its center and advanced slightly along the right flank.

The *front's* aviation did not engage in combat operations due to the poor meteorological conditions. Our planes had been stuck at their airfields for several days in full combat readiness, finding it impossible to get into the air.

Thus on 11 February, despite the concentration of the main forces of artillery, mortars and tanks at the area of the encirclement, our troops could not carry out their assignment. This may be explained, first of all, by the fact that the resistance of the enemy, who had thickened his combat formation as a result of the retreat here of the main body of the East Prussian group of forces, had increased considerably. The Germans, disposing of a large amount of artillery and mortars, laid down heavy fire on our attacking units and inflicted heavy losses on them. Upon regrouping its force, the German command created reserves of infantry and tanks and carried out systematic counterattacks along the entire front. Finally, the area of military operations represented a system of old German fortifications, which had been strengthened by a highly developed system of field fortifications. The unfavorable meteorological conditions, in particularly the heavy fogs, made the employment of military equipment more difficult; our aviation had almost stopped working.

Heavy fighting to eliminate the southwestern group of forces continued in the subsequent days. All of our forces' attempts to split the enemy's encircled forces into parts were unsuccessful. The German command would immediately seal the resulting breach by committing fresh reserves and thus maintained a continuous defensive front. Upon breaking through one defensive line, our troops would encounter the next one and were forced to break through it all over again. The 5th Army's forces, while overcoming the enemy's stubborn resistance, advanced slowly. On 14 February its left flank reached the southeastern outskirts of Zinten and became involved in heavy fighting here. On 16 February, on orders from the *front* commander, the army turned over its sector along the front Nemritten—Zinten to the 28th Army and continued to attack along the southern shore of the Frisching River in the general direction of Ludwigsort. On 21 February the army's units cut the Zinten—Königsberg railroad and were fighting along the line Kobbelbude—Nemritten.

The 28th Army, having regrouped its forces to the north, continued to attack along the following sector: from the right, Moritten—Nemritten; from the left, Maggen—Zinten. The enemy had organized a solid defense here and was putting up stubborn resistance in the Zinten area. On 14 February the army's forces captured the strong point of Rositten and on 21 February, following several days of stubborn fighting, captured the Germans' major defensive center of Zinten.

In the 2nd Guards, 31st and 50th armies' sectors the enemy continued to defend just as stubbornly. These armies' forces were engaged in intensive fighting for each trench and were not able to advance significantly. However, on 16 February the enemy, while evidently trying to straighten out his front and avoid the encirclement of his forces located in a pocket to the south of Zinten, began to withdraw them to the line Zinten—Lichtenfeld—Mehlsack. Pushing aside the German rearguards, our units pursued the enemy. On 19 February the 31st Army captured the inhabited locale of Kanditten, and on 21 February reached Lichtenfeld. To the left, on 18 February the 50th Army was trying to reach the Landsberg—Mehlsack paved road, and by 21 February had begun fighting to the east of Peterswalde.

In the 3rd Army's sector the enemy's resistance increased as his troops advanced to the northwest to the shores of the Frisches Haff. The German command reinforced its Mehlsack group of forces. Here units of the 18th Panzergrenadier Division, the 75th, 1428th and 1438th fortress battalions, the 80th, 580th and 532nd construction battalions, and the 476th Anti-Tank Battalion were committed into the fighting. In order to defend the town and major road junction of Mehlsack, the enemy had carried out major defensive works, mined the roads and approaches to the town, and outfitted firing points in buildings and barricaded streets.

The army's formations suffered significant losses during the uninterrupted and stubborn fighting and were in need of men and materiel reinforcement. For this reason, during 12-13 February the troops put themselves in order so as to once again resume active operations on 14 February.

At 1200 on 14 February, following a 10-minute fire onslaught, units of the 41st and 35th rifle corps went over to a decisive offensive and, following a two-hour battle, broke through the enemy's defense and on that day advanced more than four kilometers. Without breaking off their attack, the army's forces on the night of 16-17 February began to storm the town of Mehlsack. The Germans, seeking to retain this important strong point in their hands, resisted fiercely, undertaking one counterattack after another. Before 0700 the 35th Rifle Corps had repelled several enemy counterattacks from a company to a battalion in strength each. However, the enemy garrison could not withstand the pressure from our troops and on the morning of 17 February was forced to abandon the town.

While pursuing the retreating enemy, the 3rd Army captured Peterswalde on 21 February.

The 48th Army, while closely cooperating with the 3rd Army's forces, defeated the Germans in the Bornitt area and reached the Plaswich area and captured it.

The 5th Guards Tank Army slowly advanced toward Braunsberg while engaged in heavy fighting.

By the close of 21 February the *front's* forces were fighting along the line Kobbelbude—Plessen—Zinten—Lichtenfeld—Peterswalde—Plaswich—Zagern.

The first period of the battle with the encircled enemy group of forces concluded along this line. Our forces had inflicted heavy losses on the enemy and pressed him against the Frisches Haff, squeezing the enemy forces into a limited area: along a front 50 kilometers wide and 15-25 kilometers deep. The German forces, employing their last capabilities, continued to put up stubborn resistance. It required concentrated attacks to split up the enemy group of forces into parts and destroy it, while preventing the evacuation of the remnants to the Frisches Nehrung spit.

On 18 February the valiant *front* commander, General Chernyakhovskii, died from a serious wound received on the battlefield in the Mehlsack area. The forces of the Third Belorussian Front lost in comrade Chernyakhovskii a loyal son of the Bolshevik party and one of the most talented young Stalinist commanders, who had arisen during the course of the Great Patriotic War.

Attaching great significance to the most rapid elimination of the Germans' East Prussian group of forces, the Supreme Commander-in-Chief comrade Stalin entrusted the command of the Third Belorussian Front to Marshal of the Soviet Union, comrade Vasilevskii, who on 21 February took up the command of the *front's* forces.

On that day the *Stavka* made the decision to carefully prepare a new attack for the final elimination of the enemy group of forces southwest of Königsberg.

In *Stavka* of the Supreme High Command directive no. 11032 of 21 February 1945, as of 24 February 1945 the First Baltic Front was to be renamed the Samland Group, which was subordinated to the commander of the Third Belorussian Front. The Samland Group (commander General Bagramyan[1] and chief of staff Colonel General Kurasov[2]) at that time consisted of the 43rd, 39th and 11th Guards armies and the 3rd Air Army.

In waging uninterrupted fighting during a month and a half, the forces of the Third Belorussian Front had suffered losses and by the beginning of March were seriously under strength, especially in personnel. For example, in the 5th Army the strength of the rifle divisions did not exceed 2,700 men, and in the 2nd Guards Army it did not exceed 2,500 men. In all, there were about 168,000 men in the armies operating southwest of Königsberg, which amounted to an average of 24,000-25,000 men in each army, 5,010 tubes, and 517 tanks and self-propelled guns. The enemy, according to data from the *front's* intelligence section, numbered up to 20 divisions (including two panzer and one panzergrenadier), 15 artillery regiments, 12 battalions of assault guns, two mortar brigades, and eight anti-aircraft regiments, for an overall strength of 110,000 men.

At the end of February and the first ten days of March the *front's* forces intensively prepared for a new offensive, received personnel and materiel reinforcements, brought up ammunition and carried out local combat operations, as a result of which our position was improved and we advanced somewhat.

The decision by the *front* commander, Marshal of the Soviet Union comrade Vasilevskii, for eliminating the encircled enemy came down to the following: while securely covering the

---

1   Editor's note. Ivan Khristoforovich Bagramyan (1897-1982) served as a junior officer in the Russian imperial army during the First World War. He joined the Red Army in 1920 and served in a number of command, staff and teaching posts during the interwar period. During the Great Patriotic War he served chiefly in staff positions at the *front* level, before making the jump to army commander. He later commanded the First Baltic Front and the Samland operational group in East Prussia at the end of the war. Following the war, Bagramyan commanded a military district and held a number of positions within the central military apparatus.

2   Editor's note. Vladimir Vasil'evich Kurasov (1897-1973) joined the Russian imperial army in 1915 and the Red Army three years later. His interwar service consisted mainly of teaching duties. During the Great Patriotic War he served primarily as chief of staff in a variety of *fronts* and ended the war as chief of staff of the Samland operational group. Following the war, Kurasov held a variety of administrative and staff positions.

Braunsberg axis and going over to the defensive here with the forces of the 48th Army, simultaneously launch attacks against the enemy from the east and southeast in the direction of Bladiau and Heiligenbeil; to split the enemy's front and destroy him in detail, preventing his evacuation to the Frisches Nehrung spit.

For this, the armies were given the following tasks.

The 11th Guards Army was to prepare an offensive operation with the task of breaking through the enemy's defense along the sector Wardinep—Zendern and to launch an attack in the direction of Brandenburg.

By the close of the operation's first day, it was to reach the line Wangitt—Kobbelbude. By the close of the second day it was to reach the Frisching River.

The commander of the 5th Army was to break through the enemy's defense along the sector Galgenberg (four kilometers south of Perwilten)—the Blindesee and launch an attack in the direction of Wolittnick. The army was to have its main strength along the left flank. By the close of the operation's first day, the army was to reach the line Perwilten—Lanck. In order to carry out its assignment, the army was to be reinforced with the 3rd Artillery Division, the 11th, 13th and 14th guards artillery brigades, the 120th Tank Brigade, the 81st Tank Regiment, and the 373rd Heavy Self-Propelled Artillery Regiment. In order to improve the jumping-off position for the offensive before the start of the operation, by operating in small detachments, the army was to capture the enemy strong point of Perwilten and clear the enemy out of the Gross Klingbeck woods (two kilometers southeast of Laukitten). The assigned task was to be carried out consecutively, predominantly in the dark and with a minimal expenditure of artillery shells. Tanks and self-propelled artillery were not to be employed.

During the period before 10 March 1945 the *front* commander demanded:

a) To put the army's forces in order, accumulate ammunition, absorb the reinforcements, knock the units and subunits together, bring up the rear services, and institute more precise command and control.

b) By employing all forms of military intelligence, mainly combat intelligence, amplify the enemy's dispositions opposite the army's front and discover his fire system, paying special attention to precisely determining his artillery and mortar firing positions. To carefully reconnoiter the enemy's system of engineering structures and obstacles.

c) To carry out a review of the latest combat activities with the officers and to point out to the unit and formation commanders' shortcomings in problems of organizing cooperation and troop command and control in battle.

The 28th Army was ordered to immediately begin preparations for a new operation, with the task of breaking through the enemy's defense along the Baumgarten (two kilometers south of Lanck)—Diedersdorf sector and to launch an attack in the direction of Bladiau. The main group of forces was to be on the right flank.

By the close of the operation's first day, the army was to capture: Lanck, the western edge of the Ripper-Wald Woods (two kilometers south of Lanck); by the close of the operation's second day, the army was to capture the road junction of Bladiau. The army was to subsequently develop the success in the direction of Rosenberg (on the eastern shore of the Frisches Haff) or Hailigenbeil.

In order to carry out its assigned task, the army was to be reinforced by the 1st Artillery Division, the 12th and 13th artillery brigades, the 16th Anti-Tank Artillery Brigade, the 213th Tank Brigade, the 77th Tank Battalion, and the 343rd and 395th heavy self-propelled artillery regiments.

The 2nd Guards Army was assigned the task of breaking through the enemy's defense along the Ritterhof—Bartlangen (two kilometers south of Ritterhof) sector and launching an attack in the direction of Lenhoeven. The army was to have its main group of forces on the right flank.

On the morning of 6 March the 31st Army was to begin preparing a new offensive operation. The army's task was to launch an attack in the direction of Hanswalde and Bielshoeven, break through the enemy's defense and by the close of the operation's first day reach the line Lauterback—Haswalde. By the close of the second day it was to reach the Omaza River south of Deutsche Tirau and be ready to be pulled back into the *front* reserve.

The 3rd Army was assigned the task of beginning to prepare a new offensive operation from the morning of 6 March, with the task of breaking through the enemy's defense and launching an attack in the direction of Heiligenbeil. The main group of forces was to be in the center. By the close of the operation's first day the army was to reach the line Keniglich (four kilometers southeast of Eisenberg)—Hohenwalde, and by the close of the second day reach the line Bielshoeven—Waltersdorf. The army was to subsequently develop the success in the direction of Heiligenbeil.

In order to carry out its assignment, the army was to be reinforced with the 8th Howitzer Brigade, 29th and 8th heavy mortar brigades, 18th Mortar Brigade, 85th Heavy Howitzer Brigade, the 56th Howitzer, 570th and 392nd corps artillery regiments, 23rd Guards Tank Brigade, 66th Heavy Tank Regiment, the 340th and 260th heavy self-propelled artillery regiments, and the 1050th and 1294th self-propelled artillery regiments.

By the morning of 5 March the 48th Army was to receive the 124th Rifle Corps from the 3rd Army and go over to a stubborn defense along the entire front and to immediately begin digging trenches and communications trenches. The main attention was to be devoted to the organization of an anti-tank defense in the direction of Braunsberg and along the auto highway to Elbing.

From 10 March the army was to be ready to operate with independent reinforced detachments in the direction of Lindenau, along the western bank of the Banau River.

The 5th Guards Tank Army was to concentrate by 0800 on 3 March in the Marienwerder area and be subordinated to the commander of the Second Belorussian Front.[3]

The 1st and 3rd air armies were ordered to support the offensive by the ground forces in breaking through the defense, concentrating their strikes mainly along the boundary between the 5th and 28th armies and in the 3rd Army's zone. The air force was to prevent the enemy's evacuation across the Frisches Haff and to prevent the enemy air force from operating, to blockade the port of Pillau and to neutralize the activities of the enemy's shore and ship artillery in the Frisches Haff.

Thus the *front* commander, while striving to destroy the enemy group of forces that had been cut off and pressed against the sea, decided to launch an attack in two main directions: along the joint flanks of the 5th and 28th armies in the general direction of Bolbitten, and with the forces of the 3rd Army in the general direction of Heiligenbeil, for the purpose of cutting up the enemy forces into three parts and then destroying them in detail.

The 48th Army was to securely close the exits for the isolated group of forces to the southwest and thus deprive it of the capability of breaking out of the encirclement and falling back behind the Vistula River. Along with this, the army (given the successful development of the offensive by the remainder of the *front's* forces) was to plan on eliminating the German forces along the western bank of the Banau River in cooperation with the 3rd Army.

The forces were to be ready for the attack at 2000 on 9 March.

The course of combat operations, 13-29 March 1945. At 1100 on 13 March the forces of the Third Belorussian Front, following a 40-minute artillery preparation, went over to the offensive. Poor weather (fog and sleet) heavily interfered with observation and our artillery was forced to resort to area fire. Our air force could not take part in the offensive. Despite this, the infantry, along with the tanks, while broadly employing fire from its own weapons, broke into the enemy's position. Stubborn fighting broke out in the trenches. The Germans disposed of a large amount of

---

3   Directive of the *Stavka* of the Supreme High Command of 1 March 1945.

weapons and put up fierce resistance. Striving to retain their positions at any cost, they uninterruptedly operated against our attacking forces with heavy fire from artillery, mortars and rocket-powered shells, while they undertook infantry and tank counterattacks along a number of sectors. The enemy put up particularly fierce resistance to units of the 11th Guards Army attacking in the direction of Brandenburg.

Spring had begun and the soil was highly permeated with water. Despite the good road net, the offensive along the shore unfolded in difficult conditions: the presence of mud, over which the tanks could not move off the roads, fog and extended sleet limited the employment of artillery and excluded our air forces' work. Significant losses in personnel and equipment also told.

Despite heavy enemy resistance and the unfavorable meteorological conditions, our forces broke through the Germans' defense along the main axes. Throwing the enemy to the southwest, the forces of the 11th Guards Army's left flank advanced 2-3 kilometers into the depth of the defense and seized more than 20 inhabited locales. The forces of the 5th, 28th, 2nd Guards, 31st, and 3rd armies advanced from two to four kilometers, while overcoming the enemy's stubborn resistance. On this day the German forces suffered heavy losses. They lost up to 5,000 men in killed alone, while up to 40 tanks and assault guns were destroyed, as were a large number of guns and mortars.

Nor did the *front's* forces cease their attacks at night. On the morning of 14 March the weather got even worse. Solid fog and uninterrupted sleet made orientation for the troops extremely difficult. However, the infantry and tanks continued to attack and gradually advanced. The Germans, employing local reserves, sought to restore the situation by counterattacking. At 1100 they launched an attack from the Pottliten area toward Lanck against the 28th Army's right flank in strength up to two battalions of infantry and tanks. The forces of the 2nd Guards and 28th armies repelled five powerful counterattacks from the Deutsche Tirau and Lenhoeven area. The enemy also launched counterattacks in the 3rd Army's attack zone. However, despite the enemy's stubborn resistance, our units, skillfully fighting in difficult conditions, again advanced and captured 15 inhabited locales.

On 15 March our forces captured Bladiau, Lauterbach and Eisenberg. Units of the 11th Guards Army's 36th Guards Rifle Corps on this day stormed and captured the inhabited locale of Wangitt on the shore of the Frisches Haff and thus finally isolated the Germans' southwestern group of forces from the fortress of Königsberg. On this day the *front's* forces advanced in places more than six kilometers.

In making its combat formations denser, the German command was moving up the necessary reserves and employing them to launch counterattacks. Suffice it to say, that on 15 March alone the Germans carried out more than 40 counterattacks involving infantry with tanks and self-propelled guns, supported by heavy artillery fire, six-barreled mortars and heavy firing apparatuses. The German units put up particularly heavy resistance in the Bladiau area, trying with all their might to retain a solid defensive front and prevent being split up into parts.

On 18 March the weather improved and for the first time in six days of attacking our aviation took part in the fighting. The 1st and 3rd air armies, launching heavy raids from the air throughout the day, operated against the enemy's combat formations while supporting our forces' offensive. The air force launched its main attack against the areas of Ludwigsort, Bladiau and Waltersdorf. More than 2,200 sorties were carried out that day; of which about 1,200 were bomber-assault air ones. The artillery was a great support to the infantry on this day. A significant amount of divisional artillery (as well as part of corps artillery) was advanced into the infantry's combat formations.

On 18 March the forces of the 11th Guards Army captured the major strong point of Ludwigsort, and on 19 March, in conjunction with the 5th Army's forces, completely eliminated the eastern part of the Germans' encircled group of forces and reached the Wolittnich area with is main forces.

The 28th Army, while overcoming the stubborn resistance by the enemy, who had hurriedly brought up reserves that had been thrown together from the remains of the 562nd and 50th infantry divisions and special elements, was engaged in heavy fighting to the west of Bladiau, having captured Jurkendorf along the left flank on 19 March. The 31st and 3rd armies were successfully advancing during these days. Having crushed the enemy's resistance along the line Lauterbach—Eisenberg, these armies' forces were pursuing units of the 14th, 21st, 299th, 61st, 131st, and 349th infantry divisions, which were slowly falling back on Heiligenbeil, captured the strong point of Waltersdorf, and by the close of 19 March had reached the line Jukendorf—Tormsdorf (four kilometers south of Heiligenbeil).

The German forces operating in the Braunsberg area, fearing encirclement as a result of the breakthrough by units of the 31st and 3rd armies in the Heiligenbeil area, began to fall back to the northeast on the night of 18-19 March. The 48th Army, having gone over from the defensive to the offensive, had reached the town of Braunsberg by the close of 19 March and had begun fighting along its southern outskirts.

As a result of our forces' attack, the internal space occupied by the enemy had shrunk significantly. On 19 March it comprised about 30 kilometers in width and 7-10 kilometers in depth. The German forces pressed against the sea were already under fire from our artillery and heavy mortars. They had been deprived of supply from the Frisches Nehrung spit. A large amount of German personnel and equipment was concentrated on a limited space. The swampy area also restricted maneuver by the enemy's units. The German forces, which were hoping to be evacuated, were defending stubbornly and, despite enormous losses and their already disrupted organization continued their desperate resistance.

Intense fighting continued on 20 March. On this day the *front's* forces advanced in places up to six kilometers and captured the major strong point of Braunsberg, as well as 40 other inhabited locales. Stubborn fighting broke out for each trench and each inhabited local and height. The Germans desperately threw themselves into counterattacks and were firing heavily from mortars and automatic rifles. The battlefield was covered with the corpses of German soldiers and officers, smashed equipment, and the corpses of animals.

By the close of 20 March the 31st Army had closed to the town of Heiligenbeil from the south, while on the following day the 3rd Army bypassed the town from the west. While engaged in heavy fighting along the outskirts, these armies' forces, supported by air power, crushed the enemy's resistance on 23 March and captured the last major strong point and road junction of Heiligenbeil, with its forward units reaching the Frisches Haff near the mouth of the Banau River.

Understanding the hopelessness of the situation, the German command on 24 March began to hurriedly evacuate the remnants of the rear units, special units and equipment from the shore of the Frisches Haff to the Frisches Nehrung spit and the port of Pillau.

While covering the feverish evacuation, the enemy continued with extreme stubbornness to hold a bridgehead 13 kilometers wide and 2-5 kilometers deep. Specially detached German commands were hurriedly destroying the remaining equipment, shooting all the livestock and burning the inhabited locales.

In the meantime, our forces continued their decisive offensive. On 25 March the 5th Army, following stubborn fighting, captured the inhabited locale of Wolittnich and a number of fortified heights northeast of Heiligenbeil, while left-flank units captured the strong point of Bregden and, developing the offensive, by the close of 25 March had begun fighting along the southeastern outskirts of Rosenberg; the 31st Army was attacking Rosenberg from the southwest; the 3rd Army, having defeated the enemy, forced the Banau River and captured Deutsche Banau; the 48th Army advanced up to six kilometers in the day's fighting and captured the major inhabited locales of Rossen and Runenberg.

The 1st and 3rd air armies, while supporting the offensive by the ground forces, systematically launched bomber-assault aircraft raids against the encircled enemy, destroying his personnel and equipment. On 25 March our air force carried out about 2,580 sorties.

During the night of 25-26 March the 28th Army's forces, supported by the 31st Army, stormed the town of Rosenberg and throughout the day advanced up to two kilometers in the direction of Balga and captured in this area 6,200 German soldiers and officers, 25 tanks, 220 guns of various calibers, and other prizes. The 3rd Army's main forces reached the shore of the gulf, having captured up to 12,000 prisoners, 82 tanks and assault guns, 237 guns of various calibers, 65 armored transports, 7,210 motor vehicles, 140 tractors, and other prizes. On this day the 31st Army supported units of the 28th and 3rd armies in taking Rosenberg, capturing up to 2,800 prisoners, five tanks, 4,685 motor vehicles, and 122 guns. Our aviation continued to launch strikes against the encircled enemy.

By the close of 26 March the remnants of the defeated and tangled German units had grouped in confusion in the area of Cape Kalholtz, pursued by units of the 5th and 28th armies. The *front's* remaining forces, having carried out their tasks, were putting themselves in order following the lengthy fighting and were clearing out the occupied areas of small enemy groups. As early as 22 March the 2nd Guards Army had been pulled into the reserve and had marched to the Samland peninsula.

Without ceasing their attacks, the forces of the 5th and 28th armies completely cleared the area of Cape Kalhotz during the succeeding days and thus completed the final elimination of the southwestern group of German forces.

Results of the operation. As a result of the fierce February-March fighting in the difficult conditions of the spring thaw, the forces of the Third Belorussian Front overcame the powerful defensive system of the Heilsberg fortified area and completely defeated the main East Prussian group of forces to the southwest of Königsberg (comprising up to 20 divisions, two independent brigades and up to 11 independent regiments and battalions).

During the 13-29 March fighting the Germans lost more than 50,000 in prisoners and 80,000 killed, while the *front's* forces captured 605 tanks and assault guns and more than 3,500 field guns. A large number of German soldiers drowned while trying to cross the Frisches Haff. The battlefield along the shoreline represented a shocking picture of the enemy's complete defeat and destruction.

Only a small part of the German forces managed to cross to the Frisches Haff spit, from where they were shifted to reinforce their Samland group. The elimination of the most powerful enemy group of forces enabled the *front* command to transfer the 50th, 2nd Guards and 5th armies to the Samland peninsula in order to take part in the forthcoming storming of Königsberg, while the 31st, 28th and 3rd armies were transferred to the *Stavka* of the Supreme High Command reserve.

The operation reviewed in this chapter on eliminating the German forces in the area southwest of Königsberg is very interesting and instructive in a number of areas. Of these, the following should be noted above all:

1)   the methods and means of eliminating a major enemy group of forces that has been pressed to the sea and is putting up stubborn resistance;
2)   the organization of the offensive in difficult meteorological and climatic conditions (the spring thaw, the troops' activities in poor visibility, with the weather changing several times during the day, and other factors;
3)   the regrouping of part of our forces to a new axis (Königsberg) and the preparation of a new operation during the destruction battle in the Balga—Hailegenbeil—Braunsberg area.

8

The Defeat of the Germans' Königsberg Group of Forces and the Capture of the Fortress of Königsberg

Simultaneously with the elimination of the enemy group of forces southwest of Königsberg, intensive preparation for the storming of the city was being conducted.

The concentration of forces for the forthcoming operation to capture Königsberg began as early as the beginning of March. In the first half of March the 50th and 2nd Guards armies were pulled back into the Third Belorussian Front's second echelon.

On 8 March the 50th Army was dispatched to a new concentration area: the 69th Rifle Corps along the route Kanditten—Preussisch Eylau—Gross Lindenau—Hohenrade, with the task of concentrating in the Trutenau—Praddau area; the 81st Rifle Corps along the route Landsberg—Schoenbruch—Schwenau—Tapiau—Stampelken, with the task of concentrating in the Botenen area. Army artillery (the 1321st Anti-Tank Artillery Regiment, 481st Artillery-Mortar Regiment, 144th Artillery Brigade) moved along the route Landsberg—Schoenbruch—Schwenau—Tapiau—Goldbach—Stampelken. Engineer troops and road units were employed in the areas of Tapiau and Podollen for outfitting crossings over the Pregel River. The army's forces carried out their march only at night, over shortened distances and with security measures. Formation and unit headquarters moved at the head of the main forces' columns. The rest areas had been previously reconnoitered and were scrupulously covered by anti-aircraft weapons. The routes of movement were supported by officer traffic posts, road signs and markers. By the close of 11 March this army had successfully carried out an 80-100 kilometer march and concentrated in the assigned area, becoming part of the Samland group of forces. On 14 March the 50th Army relieved units of the 39th and 11th Guards armies along the front Zudau—Pregel River and began preparing for the offensive.

The 39th Army, having turned over its sector to the 50th Army's units, was regrouped to the west and by 30 March occupied a front along the line Reessen—(excluding) Trankwitz (both locales northwest of Moditen).

In the second half of March the 2nd Guards Army was also regrouped to the Königsberg axis. The army's formations carried out a movement along the following routes: 60th Rifle Corps—Roditten—Preussisch Eylau—Domnau—Schwenau—Tapiau—Stampelken—Nikelsdorf—Granz.

The 11th Guards Rifle Corps moved along the route: Zinten—Frisching—Schwenau—Brasdorf—Grunhoff; army artillery units (150th Army Artillery Brigade and the 113th Anti-Tank Artillery Regiment) moved along the 60th Rifle Corps' route, and the 483rd Mortar Regiment along the 11th Guards Rifle Corps' route, while the 30th Engineer-Sapper Brigade was dispatched along both routes at a distance of five kilometers ahead of the rifle corps. The crossings in Tapiau were covered by an anti-aircraft artillery regiment. Having begun its march at 1900 on 21 March, the army covered 160 kilometers in four days and by 0700 on 25 March its main forces had concentrated in the area southwest of Granz. On the night of 27-28 March the army relieved units of the 43rd Army along the front from the shore of the gulf to Kumenen and took up defensive positions here.

The 43rd Army, having turned its defensive sector over to the 2nd Guards Army, reached the Königsberg area by 30 March and deployed along the line Trenk—Amalienhof.

Following the elimination of the Germans' group of forces southwest of Königsberg, the 5th Army was regrouped to the *front's* right flank along the route Kreuzburg—Poddolen—Nikelsdorf, and by 5 April had concentrated in the Kumenen—Wikau area and deployed between the 2nd Guards and 39th armies.

Thanks to the fact that the marches were well organized and carried out only at night, on 5 April the *front's* forces completely finished their regrouping of forces and were carrying out intensive preparations for the storming of Königsberg.

The fortress of Königsberg. Long before the Second World War the Germans had transformed Königsberg into a powerful fortress. At first the positions of the Heilsberg fortified area, the forward edge of which ran along the line of the Deime and Alle rivers to Bartenstein, Heilsberg, Wormditt, and Frauenburg, were to be included in the Königsberg defensive system.

At the end of 1944, when the Red Army's forces reached the borders of East Prussia and along the Gumbinnen axis had broken through the reinforced concrete belt along the state border and invaded the confines of the province, having captured the town of Stallupönen, the German high command issued an order to the commander of Army Group Center to reduce the defensive work along the Heilsberg fortified line and begin reinforcing Königsberg, considering the immediate perimeter of the city a fortress.

In carrying out this order, four defensive lines were built around Königsberg, the bases for which were field fortifications, which represented an augmentation and strengthening of the existing permanent structures. Each defensive line was built with an eye toward the perimeter defense of Königsberg.

The external defensive perimeter was located 8-15 kilometers from the city center and had the task of covering the Königsberg garrison's airfields and artillery positions, observation posts and industrial enterprises. The forward edge of this perimeter ran along the line Nautzwinkel, Zeerappen, north of Fuchsberg, Neuhausen—Zeligenfeld—Burgau—Hafstrom. From the east the external perimeter ran near the forts and had a well developed system of trenches, communications trenches, and a large number of minefields, barbed wire, and other engineering obstacles.

An internal defensive perimeter ran 6-8 kilometers from the city center and had as its task the covering of the paved ring road, preventing an enemy breakthrough into the city, and dragging the attacker into a prolonged struggle along its approaches and outskirts. The forward edge ran along the line Gross Holstein—Amalienhof—Neuhausen—Zeligenfeld—Hafstrom. The perimeter consisted of 2-3 trenches, connected among themselves by a large number of communications trenches. The number of trenches reached 6-7 along the northern and southern sectors. From the east, north and northwest the line was girded by an anti-tank ditch 6-10 meters wide and anti-tank post obstacles. There were a lot of wire obstacles and continuous minefields in front of the defensive front. The defensive system also counted a large number of earthen structures, reinforced concrete cupolas, and various structures configured for defense, etc.

The third defensive line (second position) ran directly along the city's outskirts. The basis of the defense here were the solid stone buildings, which had been configured for defense. The Germans had barricaded the streets, mined the outskirts, had built reinforced-concrete firing points along street intersections, and had set up a large number of anti-tank guns, tanks and assault guns.

The fourth defensive line (third position) ran in the center of the city—along the old town boundary. There were nine permanent structures—old fashioned forts.

The forts were in mutual fire support. Each of them represented a hexagon, extending across the front, stretching 360X180 meters, and housing a garrison of 250-300 men. A fort included the following basic structures: a wall and a moat, a caponier, a central structure (a three-story brick building), two-sided semi-caponiers, two internal courtyards, two barracks for the garrison, a gorge caponier, and firing points for protecting the entrance from the back side of the fort. The walls and coverings for the structures were built of brick, while the thickness of the walls was 1-3 meters. The caponiers and semi-caponiers were connected by underground corridors. There was a bridge from the back side over the ditch, which connected the fort with a road to the rear. For masking purposes, the forts had trees planted around them and were covered with an earth-colored mask. The approaches to the forts could be brought under artillery and machine gun fire from open positions. The caponiers were not configured for artillery fire. The fort's system of artillery and rifle-machine gun fire enabled the enemy to cover the far approaches to the fort in front of the fort and along the flanks, as well as to directly defend the fort while the attacker was trying to overcome the ditch.

The internal perimeter's permanent reinforced concrete and wooden and earth structures were the basis of the machine gun fire system and were in close fire connection with the other forts and with each other. There were frontal and multi-embrasure permanent reinforced concrete structures, with walls 70-100 centimeters thick and more, armed primarily with machine guns.

An anti-tank ditch, 6-10 meters wide and three meters deep, was filled with water and represented a serious obstacle for attacking tanks, all the more so that, while being within the system of trenches and other of the enemy's fortification structures, it could be covered by multi-layered fire. Such was the system of defensive structures around Königsberg. However, it should be borne in mind that as early as our winter operations around Königsberg the so-called external perimeter had been overcome and our forces had advanced to the first-line forts, while in the south they had even captured one of them—fort no. 9, "Dona" ("Ponart"). The fortress had been invested on three sides and actually the first line of forts, with adjacent field fortifications, were for us the external perimeter of the fortress of Königsberg, which we had to overcome first of all during a storming attack. In our reports and transmission this line was designated as the external defense perimeter, or the external belt of forts.

The enemy employed for the defense of the fortress of Königsberg four fully-outfitted infantry divisions (548th, 561st, 367th, and 69th), a fortress and a security regiments, a regiment from the 56th Infantry Division, as well as several independent regiments and battalions, newly formed from various units and subunits that had fallen back on Königsberg from the east. In all, the Königsberg garrison numbered more than 100,000 officers and men, 850 guns and up to 60 tanks an assault guns. The garrison disposed of a large amount of supplies of food, weapons and ammunition.

Thus Königsberg had been carefully prepared by the Germans for defense and represented a powerful fortress, despite the fact that the fortress forts were old fashioned. The strength of the defense lay in the presence of numerous field fortifications, in their combination with permanent defensive structures, in their skillful adaption to the terrain that had been well studied by the Germans, and, finally, in the large amount of men and materiel disposed of by the defender. However, one must take into account the fact that the combat capability of the large garrison of Königsberg had fallen as the result of the victories achieved by us.

In order to capture this fortress, it was necessary to concentrate large forces, powerful artillery and aviation in the Königsberg area, as well as to carry out the careful training of our forces for the forthcoming storming.

On 3 April 1945, in accordance with a directive by the *Stavka* of the Supreme High Command no. org/1/122, the Samland group of forces was disbanded. According to the same directive, the armies of the Samland group were directly subordinated to the Third Belorussian Front.

The situation at the beginning of April 1945. As a result of the regrouping of forces carried out, the sides' situation by the beginning of April was as follows: in the north, the area from the shore of the Baltic Sea to Spallwitten was being defended by the 2nd Guards Army, consisting of the 103rd, 60th and 11th Guards corps; to the left, as far as Reessen, was the 5th Army, consisting of the 65th, 72nd and 45th rifle corps. Facing these armies were the enemy's 551st, 931st, 95th, 93rd, and 58th infantry divisions, with the 5th Panzer Division located in reserve in the Kraam area.

To the northwest of Königsberg along the line excluding Reessen—Katzenblick the 39th Army, consisting of the 94th, 5th Guards and 113th rifle corps, was preparing to attack. The army was organized into a single echelon and the corps into two. To the left, as far as Amalienhof (three kilometers east of Katzenblick) the 43rd Army, consisting of the 90th, 13th Guards and 54th rifle corps, was preparing for the attack. The army was organized into a single echelon. From Amalienhof to the Pregel River the 50th Army was getting ready to attack, with its main group of forces (81st and 124th rifle corps) along its right flank. The army's 69th Rifle Corps was defending along a broad front, embracing the northeastern outskirts of Königsberg. To the south of the Pregel River the 11th Guards Army (8th, 16th and 36th guards rifle corps) was preparing to attack along the line Adel Neuendorf—Heide Waldburg, organized into a single echelon.

Opposite these armies the enemy's 548th and 561st infantry divisions, the 1st Fortress Regiment, the 75th Security Regiment, and three regiments from the 367th, 69th and 56th infantry divisions were defending in the first line.

Thus our forces outflanked the fortress of Königsberg in a semi-circle, and along the *front's* right wing the 2nd Guards and 5th armies, having penetrated deeply into the enemy's position on the Samland peninsula, were to support our operations in the Königsberg area. The Soviet forces' favorable operational situation in the area of the fortress enabled us to launch concentric attacks against the enemy occupying a limited space. Also favorable were the conditions for employing artillery and particularly aviation, which, as a result of our air superiority, was able to bomb the fortress in the daytime.

Planning and preparing the operation. During the preparatory period for the attack on Königsberg, special instructions were drawn up and distributed among the troops for preparing for the storming.

During this period the following were worked out:

- an operational plan;
- a calendar plan for the work of the *front* and army military councils and headquarters for preparing for the operation;
- a plan for regrouping the troops;
- a plan for deploying the armies;
- a plan for preparing for the storming;
- instructions on training the troops;
- plans for supporting the operation by special combat arms and services.

All of the operational preparation unfolded on the basis of these documents.

The operational plan. The most favorable axes for our troops' attacks were: a) from the northwest to the southeast, and b) from north to south, which met in the center of the city.

The plan of the commander of the Third Belorussian Front consisted of launching powerful concentric attacks from the south and north and defeating the garrison of Königsberg and capturing the city. Simultaneously, active operations would be conducted against the Samland group in order to secure our right flank.

In accordance with this, the *front* commander decided:

- to launch the main attack with the forces of four armies (39th and 43rd armies, the right flank of the 50th Army, and the 11th Guards Army);
- the forces of the 2nd Guards and 5th armies would launch supporting attacks on the Samland peninsula.

Such a decision called for a powerful attack against the fortress and the secure protection of the right flank of the armies attacking from the north against possible enemy counterblows from the Samland peninsula.

The *front's* forces received the following tasks:

The 39th Army, consisting of the 5th Guards, 113th and 94th rifle corps (nine rifle divisions), plus such reinforcements as the 28th Guards Tank Brigade, four self-propelled artillery regiments, the 15th Artillery Division (consisting of four artillery brigades and the 35th Anti-Tank Artillery Brigade), three howitzer regiments, and two guards mortar regiments, was to deploy six rifle divisions in its first echelon along an 8-kilometer front (the woods east of the line Wikau—Trenk) and prepare an attack in the general direction of Lendorf farm (four kilometers northwest of Metgeten)—Nautzwinkel, with the task of breaking through the enemy's defense in conjunction with the 5th and 43rd armies and by the close of the operation's first day reaching the shore of the Frisches Haff and the mouth of the Pregel River, thus cutting off Königsberg's communications with Pillau. The army was subsequently to have one rifle corps ready for an attack in the direction of Königsberg from the west and two rifle corps for an attack in the direction of Fischausen (to the west).

The 43rd Army, consisting of the 54th, 90th and 13th Guards rifle corps (nine rifle divisions) plus such reinforcements as the 153rd Tank Brigade, five self-propelled artillery regiments, the 3rd Artillery Division, which included six artillery brigades, the 4th Artillery Division's 1114th Artillery Brigade, the 8th Heavy Mortar Brigade, two independent heavy-caliber artillery battalions, the 37th Army Artillery Brigade, an army anti-tank artillery regiment, two guards mortar brigades, and two guards mortar regiments, was to deploy six rifle divisions in the first echelon along a 5-kilometer front (Trenk—Amalienhof) one kilometer southeast of height 35.0 and prepare an attack in the direction of Amalienau, with the task of breaking through the external perimeter of Königsberg's defense and by the close of the attack's first day reach the line Moditten—Lawsken—the courtyard (one kilometer west of Palfe). Subsequently, while developing the breakthrough to the southeast, by the close of the operation's third day it was to capture the city by storm, along with units of the 50th Army, as far as the Pregel River.

The 50th Army, consisting of the 81st, 124th and 69th rifle corps (the latter short one division), plus such reinforcements as the 159th Tank Brigade, three self-propelled artillery regiments, the 2nd Guards Artillery Division, which consisted of six artillery brigades, two heavy-caliber artillery battalions, the 144th Army Artillery Brigade, an anti-tank artillery regiment, a guards mortar brigade, and two guards mortar regiments, while securely defending with one corps along the front excluding Zudau—Neuhausen—Pregel River, was to launch a decisive attack with two rifle corps along the 5-kilometer front Amalienhof (one kilometer southeast of height 35.0)—Zudau in the general direction of Tragheimer and Kalthof. The main group of forces would have four rifle divisions in its first echelon. The army's task, in cooperation with the 43rd Army, was to break through the external defensive belt of Königsberg and by the close of the offensive's first day reach the line Tragheimer—Kwendau. Subsequently, while developing the breakthrough to the southeast, by the close of the operation's third day, the army was to take the city by storm as far as the Pregel River and completely clear its northeastern outskirts of the enemy.

The 11th Guards Army, consisting of the 8th, 16th and 36th Guards rifle corps (nine rifle divisions), plus such reinforcements as the 23rd Tank Brigade, three self-propelled artillery regiments, a guards tank regiment, the 10th Artillery Division, which consisted of six artillery brigades, the 4th Artillery Division's 12th Artillery Brigade, the 106th Heavy Caliber Howitzer Brigade, the 29th Heavy Mortar Brigade, two anti-tank artillery brigades, four corps artillery regiments, two independent high-powered artillery battalions, two army artillery brigades, an anti-tank artillery regiment, one guards mortar brigade, and three guards mortar regiments, was to deploy for the attack along an 8-kilometer front (Julienhof—Warten) eight divisions and, having up to six divisions in its first echelon, launch a powerful attack along the army's center in the direction of the park one kilometer west of Rosenau, with the task of breaking through the external defensive belt of Königsberg, and by the close of the offensive's first day capturing the line Schoenflis—Ponart—Kalgen. Subsequently, while developing the breakthrough to the northeast, to take by storm the entire southern part of Königsberg by the close of the operation's third day and reach the Pregel River, in readiness to force it and attack the enemy along the northern bank of the river.

Simultaneously, the armies located to the northwest of Königsberg were instructed to do the following:

The 2nd Guards Army was to defend the line west of Garbzaiden and Arissau. The army was to deploy two powerful rifle divisions along its left flank for an attack.

The 11th Guards Rifle Corps was to be withdrawn into the army reserve in the area of the Tannehein woods. The army's task was to support our attack on Königsberg through a stubborn defense and to prepare an attack by the army's left flank in the direction of Norgau.

The 5th Army was to prepare an offensive in the direction of Kragau and Bludau, with the following task: to break through the enemy's defense in conjunction with the 39th Army and by the close of the offensive's first day to reach the line Kompenen—Kondenen. Subsequently, while developing the success, by the close of the operation's second day, reach the line Damerau—Gross Heidekrug.

The Air Force

3rd Air Army:
a) to cover the concentration and deployment of the 5th and 39th armies' forces;
b) to firmly suppress the artillery and mortar batteries and destroy the fortification structures in the 5th and 39th armies' breakthrough sectors;
c) to consistently support the offensive by the 39th Army and then the 5th Army with all forces;
d) to prevent the arrival of the enemy's reserves from the west.

1st Air Army.
a) in conjunction with the 18th Air Army, to destroy the most important strong points and fortification structures of the fortress of Königsberg, up to the day of the attack;
b) to cover the concentration and deployment of the 43rd, 50th and 11th Guards armies' forces;
c) to firmly suppress the enemy's artillery and mortar batteries and destroy his fortification structures in the 43rd, 50th and 11th Guards armies' breakthrough sectors;
d) to paralyze the work of the harbor of Königsberg;
e) to support the troops while storming Königsberg.

In planning the aviation offensive, a great deal of attention was devoted to noting our troops' position during the course of the offensive. For this purpose, posts with signal rockets were specially detached in each rifle company (storm group).

The overall number of planes taking part in the operation is shown in Table III/8.1.

Table III/8.1 Aviation Involved in Reduction of the Königsberg Area, April 1945

Air Formation	Day Bombers	Assault Aircraft	Fighters	Torpedo Planes	Heavy Night Bombers	Light Night Bombers	Total
1st Air Army	199	310	510	–	–	88	1,107
3rd Air Army	59	100	240	–	–	104	503
18th Air Army	–	–	–	–	500	–	500
5th Guards Bomber Corps	–	–	–	–	–	–	–
15th Air Army	72	–	–	–	–	–	72
5th Bomber Corps (4th Air Army)	72	–	40	–	–	–	112
Baltic Fleet Aviation	30	60	40	20	–	–	150
Total	432	470	830	20	500	192	2,444
In percentages	17.7	19.3	34.1	0.8	20.5	7.6	100

On the whole, our aviation was 12-15 times superior to the enemy among all types of planes. The plan for aviation employment foresaw the following number of sorties:

- 5,316 sorties during the preparatory period, which were to drop 2,690 tons of bombs;
- 4,124 sorties on the attack's first day;
- according to operational needs during the following days.

Artillery support. The *front* commander confirmed the following disposition of artillery among the armies: each army was to create artillery breakthrough groups and long-range groups. It was decided to have the main artillery group along the breakthrough sectors in accordance with the assigned tasks.

The 39th Army was to have 1,169 tubes along its 8-kilometer breakthrough front, including 472 heavy ones, which would yield a density of 146 tubes per kilometer.

The 43rd Army was to have 1,289 tubes along its 5-kilometer breakthrough front, including 596 heavy ones, which would yield a density of 258 tubes per kilometer.

The 50th Army was to have 957 tubes along its 5-kilometer breakthrough front, including 471 heavy ones, which would yield a density of 191 tubes per kilometer.

The 11th Guards Army was to have 1,584 tubes along its 8-kilometer breakthrough front, including 819 heavy ones, which would yield a density of 198 tubes per kilometer.

Thus a high artillery density was created along the breakthrough sectors, including that of heavy systems.

Besides this, the shock group would dispose of about 300 RS-M-13[1] and M-31 guards mortar launchers.

The following measures were planned to better support the attack:

- to destroy with heavy-caliber and high-powered artillery over the course of four days preceding the operation the most important fortification structures (forts, permanent pillboxes, wooden and earth pillboxes, bunkers, and individual strong points);

---

1   Editor's note. The M-13 was an early, 132 caliber variant of the multiple rocket launcher system popularly known as "Katyusha."

- to unite the control of the counterbattery fight in the 43rd and 50th armies' attack sectors under the commander of the *front's* artillery;
- to attach regimental and divisional artillery to storm groups while storming the fortress; in certain cases 152mm and 203mm guns and 160mm mortars would be attached to the storm groups for destroying the most durable buildings;
- to create and detach to the commanders of the rifle divisions artillery-mortar groups of 122mm, 152mm and 203mm guns, and 120mm and 160mm mortars for battling the enemy's artillery and destroying and suppressing the most important targets, as well as guards mortar units (M-13);
- to create divisional artillery groups for fighting enemy tanks, consisting of 2-3 battalions of anti-tank artillery;
- to create corps or divisional destruction groups from high-powered artillery and guards mortar units (M-13) for destroying especially durable buildings, structures and engineering structures.

In accordance with the assigned tasks, the artillery's fire was planned as follows:

- one day for fire reconnaissance and unearthing concrete pillboxes and forts;
- three days to destroy concrete pillboxes and forts;
- two hours of destruction fire before the start of the attack;
- one hour of fire from guns firing over open sights and aimed fire against registered targets;
- accompanying the infantry-tank attack up to the seizure of the enemy's external defensive perimeter.

In all, it was planned to expend the following amounts on destructive fire and preparing the attack: 1.75 combat loads of 82mm mortar rounds; 1.24 combat loads of 120mm mortar rounds; one combat load of 160mm mortar rounds; 1.5 combat loads of 76mm regimental artillery shells; one combat load of 76mm divisional artillery shells; one combat load of 122mm howitzer shells; one combat load of 152mm cannon-howitzer shells; two combat loads of 203mm howitzer shells; three combat loads of 211mm mortar rounds; three combat loads of 280mm howitzer shells, and; three combat loads of 305mm howitzer shells.

Thus the heavy artillery calibers, having three combat loads, would be able to carry out their assigned tasks for destroying the main and most important targets in the enemy's defensive system.

Besides this, the schedule for the artillery offensive called for four onslaughts by counterbattery and countermortar groups.

Employment of tanks. By the start of the operation the *front's* troops disposed of five tank brigades, five heavy regiments of ISU-152[2] self-propelled artillery, four regiments of ISU-122[3] self-propelled artillery, a regiment of SU-100[4] self-propelled artillery, nine regiments of SU-76[5] self-propelled artillery, and nine independent battalions of SU-76 self-propelled artillery, which

---

2   Editor's note. The ISU-152 was a self-propelled gun that first appeared in 1943. Depending on the model, it carried a crew of four or five men and had a maximum weight of 47.3 tons. It was armed with a 152mm gun and two 12.7mm machine guns.

3   Editor's note. The ISU-122 was a self-propelled gun that first appeared in 1943. Depending on the model, it carried a crew of four or five men and had a maximum weight of 45.5 tons. It was armed with a 122mm gun and a 12.7mm machine gun.

4   Editor's note. The SU-100 was a self-propelled gun that first appeared in 1944. It contained a crew of four and had a maximum weight of 31.6 tons. It was armed with a 100mm gun.

5   Editor's note. The SU-76 was a self-propelled gun that first appeared in 1942. It contained a crew of four and had a maximum weight of slightly over 10.6 tons. It was armed with a 76mm gun.

amounted to: 120 T-34[6] tanks, 96 ISU-152s, 84 ISU-122s, 21 SU-85s,[7] and 223 SU-76s, for a total of 634 vehicles, which would guarantee an average density along the breakthrough sectors of more than 20 tanks and self-propelled artillery pieces per kilometer of breakthrough front.

Tanks and self-propelled artillery were to be primarily used as part of storm groups for supporting them with fire and for covering their movement.

Engineer support. By the start of the operation the *front's* engineer troops disposed of six engineer-sapper brigades, three storm engineer-sapper brigades, two motorized engineer brigades, one pontoon brigade, and corps and divisional sapper units and elements. The main part of the engineer troops was to be employed in the shock group's sector as storm detachments and groups. Road and bridge restoration detachments and obstacle removal detachments, which were to operate in front of the divisions' second-echelon rifle regiments, were created out of engineer units and subunits that did not go into making up the storm detachments and groups.

The obstacle removal detachments had as their main tasks the removal of mines from the areas over which the first-echelon troops had passed and the organization of headquarters commandant's service along passages in the engineer-mine obstacles.

By order of the army commanders, the complete removal of mines in the breakthrough sector was entrusted to road and bridge restoration detachments, which had army engineering and construction units subordinated to them.

Aside from these tasks, the engineer troops were entrusted with the following:

* the outfitting of the jumping-off point, trenches for the infantry attack, not more than 150-200 meters from the forward edge of the enemy's defense;
* the outfitting of trenches and individual foxholes with open areas for the second and subsequent echelons of infantry;
* the outfitting of command and observation posts and artillery firing positions, especially for storm guns and guns firing over open sights; the preparation of jumping-off positions for tanks and self-propelled artillery;
* the exact determination and careful masking (using vertical and horizontal masking) of communications trenches and the approaches to the forward trench.

Topographic support. 46 pages of 5,000:1 and 15,000:1 maps of Königsberg were issued before the beginning of the storming, on which were indicated the chief industrial targets and defensive structures (104,000 impressions); 83 pages of 15,000:1, 25,000:1 and 50,000:1 relief maps were issued.

Besides this, a 3,000:1 scale model of Königsberg was built, upon which the main defensive structures along the external and internal defensive perimeters of the Königsberg fortified area were indicated.

The maps and model made it significantly easier for the command element to study in detail the defensive targets and the entire city as a whole.

Aside from the enumerated work, the *front's* topographic section corrected and reissued 25,000:1 and 50,000:1 scale maps on 34 pages (137,550 impressions), while 15,000:1 and 25,000:1 scale reconnaissance maps were compiled and issued on 25 pages (51,000 impressions), along with various tables, charts, forms, and albums (27,275 impressions), plus maps with a coded grid on 16 pages (16,000 impressions).

---

6   Editor's note. The T-34 was the Red Army's premier medium tank of World War II. It first appeared in 1940 and weighed 26.5 tons. The early model carried a crew of four and was armed with a 76mm gun and two 7.62mm machine guns.

7   Editor's Note. The SU-85 was a self-propelled gun that first appeared in 1943. It carried a crew of four and had a maximum weight of 29.6 tons. It was armed with an 85-mm gun.

Chemical defense measures. By the start of the operation there were three independent chemical defense battalions among the *front's* forces, four independent motorized anti-tank flamethrower battalions, three independent flamethrower battalions, a flamethrower company, five independent portable flamethrower companies, three independent flamethrower battalions, and independent chemical defense companies in each division, which were to be employed mainly as part of the storm detachments and storm groups in attacking and consolidating captured lines.

Smoke equipment was employed for covering individual attack sectors and targets with smoke. The 43rd Army had a group of smoke operators numbering 65 men, with 57 in the 50th Army and 70 in the 2nd Guards Army.

The smoke groups in the chemical defense battalions were attached to the armies designated for storming the city.

Besides this, in order to increase the use of smoke directly by the infantry, each storm group had 50 smoke grenades. The obstacle removal groups had the same number of grenades. Groups for covering tanks and self-propelled guns, tank crews, and gun crews were also supplied with smoke grenades.

Flamethrower-incendiary equipment (portable flamethrowers, bottles with flammable liquid, thermite spheres, demolition blocks, and smoke equipment) were assigned to and widely used by the storm groups in street fighting.

Flamethrowers were employed for consolidating captured lines and targets, for building traps and for the fullest destruction of the target under attack.

During 6-9 April 1,200 rounds were fired from portable flamethrowers and flamethrowers, including 280 while breaking through the enemy's external defensive belt, 500 in breaking through the second belt, and 450 in street fighting.

Materiel supply. By the end of March the amount of ammunition had been raised to the following levels:

Mortars (all calibers)	3.4-3.8 combat loads
Shells (anti-tank and regimental artillery)	1.5-2.7 combat loads
Shells (divisional artillery)	1.0-1.3 combat loads
Shells (122mm guns)	1.7-2.2 combat loads
Shells (heavy calibers)	1.1-3.7

Food, forage and fuels and lubricants had also been delivered in sufficient quantities.

Occupying the jumping-off position. The preparation of the jumping-off positions had been carried out in complete accordance with the plan for the engineering support for the operation.

The movement of the troops to their jumping-off positions for the offensive was carried out over a period of three nights, in an order established by the plan for deploying the armies.

The first-echelon divisions and all the artillery were to be deployed in their sectors by the morning of 1 April 1945.

The relief and removal of troops was to be carried out in darkness to previously reconnoitered areas, zones and firing positions.

Relief was to be carried out under the cover of all our artillery, in complete readiness to repel possible enemy attacks during the relief.

The troops were deeply echeloned along the breakthrough sectors. A rifle corps, as a rule, had two divisions in the first echelon and one in the second; a rifle division had two regiments in the first echelon and one in the second, and; a rifle regiment had two battalions in the first echelon and one in the second.

While breaking through the fortified area, the rifle battalions (storm detachments) were to be assigned 200-250 meter wide sectors and organize their forces in two echelons.

By the start of the storming of Königsberg, the *front's* forces disposed of a significant amount of reinforcements, although, as before, there was still a great personnel shortage. The average number of men in a rifle division did not exceed 3,500 men.

The correlation of forces along the armies' front is shown in Table III/8.2.

Besides this, within the Königsberg garrison there were a large number of independent regiments, battalions, companies, and special units. The overall number of enemy soldiers and officers here was more than 100,000 men.

Thus the correlation of forces in personnel was almost equal, and it was only along the axis of the main attack that we outnumbered the enemy: 2.6:1 in personnel, 6:1 in artillery and mortars, and 9:1 in tanks and self-propelled artillery. We had an absolute superiority in the air over the enemy.

The storming of Königsberg. A period of destruction, lasting four days (one day was set aside for fire reconnaissance and unearthing pillboxes and forts, and three for destroying permanent engineering structures), immediately preceded the storming of Königsberg. During the preparatory period, as a result of poor meteorological conditions, we were not able to employ our aviation to the degree foreseen by the plan. In all, during 4-5 April our aviation, employing each possibility in the improvement of the weather, carried out 766 sorties, of which the majority were carried out at night by Po-2 aircraft.

Table III/8.2 Correlation of Forces – Storming of Königsberg, April 1945

Army	Soviet Forces Men (Only in Rifle Corps)	Tubes (Not Counting 45mm, 57mm)	Tanks and Self-propelled Guns	Enemy Men (Only in Infantry Divisions)	Tubes	Tanks and Assault Guns
39th						
Entire front	34,400	1,169	112	548th Infantry Div	1/3 of 561st Infantry Div	–
Active soldiers	9,907			6,100	111	
43rd						
Entire front	36,590	1,289	136	2/3 of 561st Infantry Div	2nd Fortress Rgt	8
Active soldiers	10,254			4,000	65	
50th						
Right flank	28,246	957	98	367th Infantry Div	75th Security Rgt	–
Active soldiers	7,200			6,500	125	
11th Guards						
Entire front	38,014	1,584	192	69th Infantry Div	124	8
Active soldiers	10,777			6,700		
Total	137,250	4,999	538	23,300*	425	16

* Taking into account independent infantry battalions, artillery battalions and also panzer companies operating along with the infantry divisions along the external defensive perimeter, the number of enemy effectives was 52,700 men, 849 tubes and 59 tanks.

At 1030 on 6 April the artillery preparation began along the external belt of the Königsberg fortifications. During an hour and a half the Germans' defensive position was covered with continuous explosions of mortar and artillery shells. Air operations, as was previously the case, were limited by the poor meteorological conditions. Up until 1400 only small groups of aircraft were able to take part in the artillery offensive and 274 sorties were carried out.

At 1200 the infantry and tanks, hugging the explosions of their artillery, moved to storm the fortress. The Germans, relying on a widely developed system of permanent and field fortifications and employing stone buildings, configured for defense, as strong points, put up stubborn resistance. More and more often hand to hand fighting broke out in the enemy trenches. By 1400 the forces of the 11th Guards Army broke through the forward edge of the defense in the area between the ninth and tenth forts and were developing the success along the paved road to Ponart. The 43rd Army managed to break through the defense of the external belt. Units of the 50th Army penetrated the enemy's defense and by this time were engaged in heavy fighting in the zone of the permanent fortifications.

Despite the difficult meteorological conditions, our aviation continued to strafe the enemy's pockets of resistance in small groups, paving the way for our infantry and tanks. A massed bomber strike, which was being prepared for this day, did not take place due to the poor weather.

Our artillery, waging intensive fire, supported the attacking troops, although it was not able to fully suppress the enemy's artillery and mortars, as well as a large number of his machine guns, located in buildings, and to destroy his strong points.

All day bloody fighting went on in the Königsberg area. Our forces, overcoming the German garrison's stubborn resistance, slowly but uninterruptedly advanced, taking over one strong point after another.

By the close of 6 April the 39th Army broke through the enemy's defense and, having advanced up to four kilometers, captured the strong points of Regitten and Rablauken and reached the Königsberg—Pillau railroad west of Metgeten.

In its attack zone, the 43rd Army attacked the fortifications of Königsberg's outer belt, which covered the city from the northwest, and advanced three kilometers as a result of the day's intensive fighting and cleaned the enemy out of 20 blocks.

The 50th Army, concentrating its efforts along the right flank, was engaged in fierce fighting throughout the day along the city's northern outskirts. The German forces, employing fire from fortifications, carried out powerful counterattacks. By the close of 6 April the army's units had advanced up to two kilometers, capturing a fort west of Baydritten and cleared the Germans out of 39 blocks.

The 11th Guards Army attacked the Königsberg fortifications from the south, concentrating its efforts in the center and along the left flank. Having broken through the enemy's defense, the army's units energetically advanced, penetrating four kilometers into the enemy position, blockading two forts (north of Julienhof and southeast of Kalgen) and, developing the offensive to the north, cleared the enemy out of 43 blocks, and had begun fighting for the railroad station.

Thus in the first day's fighting our forces, despite limited aviation support, broke through the outer perimeter of the Königsberg fortifications along all sectors and, developing the offensive, reached the city's outskirts.

The German command sought with all its might and main to delay our troops' advance. It hurriedly threw the 5th Panzer Division to the west and committed it into the fighting against the 39th Army. Individual infantry battalions and anti-tank artillery subunits were arriving here from the Samland peninsula.

Inside the city German soldiers were feverishly erecting fortifications, barricading the streets, outfitting firing points in buildings, blowing up bridges, and mining the roads.

At the end of the day on 6 April the *front* commander ordered the offensive to continue the following day, and the infantry's ranks be reinforced with guns for firing over open sights, as well as tanks, and that flammable weapons be more widely employed in the attack. The *front* commander demanded of the air army commanders that they launch concentric strikes against the northern and southern parts of Königsberg at dawn on 7 April.

On the morning of 7 April the weather improved significantly and at 0800 our aviation began its operations. Assault air aviation, in groups of 7-9 planes, attacked the enemy's anti-aircraft defense and suppressed it to a significant degree, simultaneously launching powerful strikes against the enemy's personnel. Simultaneously with the assault aircraft, our fighter-bombers operated against the enemy's airfields.

At 1000 Tu-2[8] and Pe-2 bombers rose in the air and in large groups launched three consecutive strikes against the enemy's centers of resistance. Subjected to bombardment were the firing points and fortifications in the northwestern and western parts of the city opposite the 39th and 43rd armies, where the enemy's resistance was particularly stubborn, as well as the southern part of the city's railroad junction, where the 11th Guards Army was engaged in intensive fighting. 102 Tu-2s and 144 Pe-2s took part in three strikes, dropping 338 tons of heavy bombs.

The ground forces were engaged in stubborn fighting in the city. The Germans continued to resist desperately. However, by 1300 the air strikes increased even more. The 18th Air Army's heavy bombers had arrived at the area of the fighting. For the first time during the Great Patriotic War, long-range bombers were employed during the day and in such large numbers. During 45 minutes flights of 516 bombers (330 Il-4s, 58 B-25s,[9] 18 Yer-2s,[10] and 110 Il-2s) flew over Königsberg and dropped on the city their heavy bombs in an uninterrupted stream. During this time 3,743 bombs were dropped, weighing 550 tons.

Almost simultaneously with the 18th Air Army's planes, planes from the Red Banner Baltic Fleet arrived at Königsberg and carried out two mass strikes against floating equipment and ships in the port of Pilllau, where by this time a concentration of up to 100 various ships had been observed, and dropped more than 75 tons of bombs. About 100 bombers from the 4th Air Army carried out a strike against the same port in the first half of the day and dropped 64 tons of bombs.

As a result of the massed artillery and air strikes, the Königsberg fortifications were seriously damaged. A large number of firing points were destroyed and enemy personnel perished due to bomb explosions and debris from buildings.

Taking advantage of aviation and artillery fire, the attacking infantry and tanks more and more squeezed the encirclement ring around the city, while advancing toward its center. Storm detachments, blocking individual blocks and buildings, destroyed the German garrisons holed up there. Tanks and individual guns, accompanying the infantry with their fire, shot up the enemy's firing points in buildings at point-blank range. During the second half of the day our forces captured 130 blocks in the northern and southern parts of the city, took three enemy forts, the "Ostwerk" artillery factory, a machine construction factory, a metal construction factory, the main railroad marshaling station and railroad repair shops. Despite the difficult conditions that had arisen in the area of the fortress as a result of the powerful bombardment from the air and the uninterrupted shelling of the city from several thousand guns, the German garrison continued to resist

---

8   Editor's note. The Tu-2 was a twin-engine bomber that first appeared in 1942. One version carried a crew of four and had a top speed of 521 km/hr. It was armed with two 20mm cannons and three 7.62mm machine guns. It could carry a bomb load of 1,500 kilograms internally and 2,270 kilograms externally.

9   Editor's note. The B-25 was a twin-engine bomber, which first appeared in 1941 and which was delivered to the Soviet Union as part of Lend-Lease. The bomber carried a crew of six and had a top speed of 438 km/hr. One version was armed with 12-18 12.7mm machine guns and could carry 1,300 kilograms of bombs.

10 Editor's note. The Yer-2 was a long-range medium bomber, which first appeared in 1941. It had a crew of four and a top speed of 420 km/hr. One version was armed with two 12.7mm machine guns, one 20mm cannon and could carry up to 5,000 kilograms of bombs.

stubbornly. On 7 April the Germans carried out more than 35 counterattacks, a significant part of which were directed at the forces of the 43rd and 39th armies. The German command undertook all measures to prevent the isolation of the Königsberg garrison from the troops along the Samland peninsula. In the 39th Army's sector the German forces counterattacked 18 times in strength up to a battalion, with tanks. As a result of the fierce fighting, parts of the army advanced a short distance along the right flank and captured the inhabited locale of Laserkeim.

The 43rd Army, while continuing to storm the fortifications in the northwestern part of the city, captured one fort and cleared the enemy out of more than 20 blocks.

A slightly better advance was made that day by the 50th Army, which, having penetrated 1.5-2 kilometers into the enemy's position, captured the courtyard of Ballit (three kilometers northwest of Palfe). The garrison of the fortress, having falling back opposite these armies to the second position, consolidated along it and once again put up stubborn resistance.

The 11th Guards Army continued to successfully storm the fortifications in the southern part of the city. By the close of 7 April its units had captured two forts and the suburbs of Zeligenfeld, Speihersdorf and Ponart and along the left flank had reached Nasser Garten.

On this day the *front's* right-wing forces, the 2nd Guards Army's 60th Rifle Corps, attacked and forced the Tierenberger River and reached the area north of Norgau.

The 5th Army, which was attacking in the general direction of Kragau, overcame two lines of trenches and captured the enemy's strong points.

While supporting our ground forces' offensive, our aviation on 7 April carried out 4,758 sorties and dropped 1,658 tons of bombs on the enemy's position, of which 1,248 tons fell on Königsberg. Of great help was the artillery, which pounded the enemy who had holed up in the fortifications and city's buildings.

Nor did the fighting in Königsberg cease at night. Taking advantage of the darkness, our units stormed buildings, penetrated through fortifications into the enemy's rear and unexpectedly fell upon his defense.

Night aviation began its activities as early as twilight. On the night of 7-8 April, the *front's* aviation carried out more than 1,800 sorties and dropped 569 tons of bombs.

At dawn on 8 April day our aviation resumed its activities and, alongside the artillery, subjected the enemy's forces and fortifications to a powerful bombardment in the course of two hours. The German garrison continued to put up fierce resistance against our attacking forces, while carrying out counterattacks. On this day the commanders of the 43rd and 11th Guards armies committed their second echelons into the fighting. During the second part of the day units of the 11th Guards Army, supported by powerful artillery fire, forced the Pregel River to the northwest of Ponart and linked up with units of the 43rd Army in the Amalienau area. The garrison of the fortress was completely cut off and isolated from the forces operating along the Samland peninsula. The Germans' main forces, which were operating in the city, fell back to its center and eastern part. The 50th Army, closely cooperating along its right flank with units of the 43rd Army, captured the Palfe area.

During the fighting on 8 April our forces completely captured the Königsberg port and railroad junction, as well as a number of important military-industrial targets, having cleared the Germans out of more than 300 blocks and capturing four forts. Simultaneously, the *front's* right-flank armies were engaged in intensive fighting along the Samland peninsula and advanced up to two kilometers on this day.

Throughout the day the *front's* aviation continued to launch powerful strikes against the enemy. During 8 April more than 6,000 sorties were carried out and 2,099 tons of bombs dropped on the enemy's forces in the Königsberg area and on the port of Pillau. A significant portion of our planes were employed for defeating the German forces concentrated to the west of Königsberg, which were trying to help the garrison to break out of the encirclement. The commandant of the fortress, General Lausch, testified on this account:

As early as the night of 7-8 April, I requested the commander of the Fourth Army, General Muller, to authorize a breakout of our remaining forces from the fortress. However, General Muller turned down my request. Later, he authorized a breakout for the purpose of linking up with the Fourth Army's other forces operating on the Samland peninsula, but this was already inopportune and the attempt failed. My main forces were thrown back to the city center with heavy losses, while the Fourth Army's concentrated reserves, which undertook a meeting attack from the west, were routed by aviation.

As early as the close of 8 April the enemy's Königsberg garrison had been squeezed by our forces into a small ring. The fire resistance of the Germans, who had suffered enormous losses during these days, declined significantly. Having fallen back toward the city center and its eastern part (Kalthof), they nevertheless continued the struggle.

The final day of the storm was also intense. On the morning of 9 April the fighting resumed with new force. However, the Germans did not withstand the massed strike from our artillery and mortars that had been moved up here, or the uninterrupted attacks by our infantry and tanks, and by the close of the day they capitulated.

On 10 April our forces were clearing Königsberg of the enemy's remaining scattered groups, escorting the soldiers and officers who had laid down their arms, and organizing the security of military-industrial targets. Simultaneously, our units were putting themselves in order, while the 2nd Guards, 5th and 39th armies were regrouping for subsequent operations in the western part of the Samland peninsula.

Results of the operation. The group of forces under the command of General of Infantry Lausch, which was to defend Königsberg, was cut off from the other forces of the Fourth Army operating on the Samland peninsula as a result of four days of fighting, was defeated and partially captured.

In all, defeated were four infantry divisions, 14 independent regiments, two artillery regiments from the high command reserve, four anti-aircraft regiments, four artillery battalions from the high command reserve, 13 anti-aircraft battalions, two searchlight battalions, nine infantry battalions, 11 machine gun fortress battalions, 19 sapper-construction battalions, 19 volkssturm battalions, and ten independent companies and batteries. 41,915 soldiers and officers were killed and 91,853 captured, including 1,819 officers and four generals. An enormous amount of weapons and other military hardware was captured: 2,023 guns, 1,652 mortars, and other equipment.

Besides this, among the prizes we uncovered was the heavy German cruiser *Seidlitz*, displacing 15,400 tons, which had been scuttled in the forest harbor of the Königsberg port.

The former commandant of the fortress of Königsberg, General of Infantry Lausch, testified:

> The German command considered Königsberg to be a powerful fortress, which would help us retain our beachhead in East Prussia. We were supposed to tie down significantly more Russian forces than we had ourselves.
>
> ... During the first two days the fortress's soldiers and officers held out stoutly, but the Russians outnumbered us and won. They were able to secretly concentrate a great amount of artillery and aviation, the massed employment of which destroyed the fortress's fortifications and demoralized the soldiers and officers ... One could not have believed earlier that such a fortress as Königsberg would fall so quickly. The Russian command skillfully worked out this operation and carried it out. We lost an entire 100,000-man army around Königsberg.

The successful completion of the storming of Königsberg enabled us to shift the main mass of our forces to a new axis—the Samland peninsula; although during the last two days the 2nd Guards and 5th armies had advanced insignificantly.

9

The Elimination of the German Group of Forces on the Samland Peninsula

The seizure of Königsberg by the forces of the Third Belorussian Front and the defeat and capture of the fortress's garrison had a decisive influence on the elimination of the remaining German forces defending the western part of the Samland peninsula.

The Hitlerite command, having lost Königsberg, was making its final attempts to hold off our forces' advance on the Samland peninsula.

The enemy's positions represented a network of non-continuous trenches running north to south, individual strong points and centers of resistance. The Germans, as a result of our forces' rapid arrival at the peninsula in January 1945, had not succeeded in building more powerful fortifications here, also hoping that they would succeed in holding on to Königsberg and tying down significant numbers of Soviet forces. The enemy's defense was more powerful along the Kumenen and Fischausen axis: its depth was equal to six kilometers from the forward edge to Kragau.

The defense of the peninsula's western part was entrusted to the 551st, 95th, 93rd, 58th, 1st, and 21st infantry, 28th Light Infantry, and 5th Panzer divisions, as well as various combat groups (for example, "Neukuren") and *volkssturm* battalions. Thus by the start of the operation there were up to 7-8 infantry divisions, one panzer division and a large number of independent battalions and special companies facing our forces.

In order to break through the defense and eliminate the enemy on the Samland peninsula, the *front* command decided to bring in five combined-arms armies, of which four would be in the first line and one in the second. For this reason, the 39th Army was additionally deployed along the front, which had earlier been occupied by the 2nd Guards and 5th armies, while the 43rd Army was dispatched to the southern shore of the Frisches Haff and the 11th Guards Army was pulled into the reserve.

Due to the losses suffered in the preceding fighting and the personnel shortages in the formations, the armies were assigned narrow sectors for the attack. The 2nd Guards Army was given a 20-kilometer front, and the 5th, 39th and 43rd armies were given fronts of 7-8 kilometers each.

The effective strength of the sides, as of 13 April 1945, is indicated by the figures shown in Table III/9.1.

Table III/9.1 Correlation of Forces, Samland Peninsula, 13 April 1945

Category	Third Belorussian Front	Enemy
Men	111,455	65,400
Field guns	3,022	1,204
Tanks and Self-Propelled Guns	324	166

Note. The number of men is based only on our rifle corps and the enemy's infantry divisions. The equipment covers everything, including the sides' reinforcements, but without counting the men in these units.

Given the overall correlation of forces, we enjoyed approximately a two to one superiority in men and nearly threefold in artillery, which would support the possibility of success in the given conditions.

The 2nd Guards Army was in more favorable circumstances, as it had occupied its positions during the course of a month, had studied the terrain and the character of the enemy's defense in detail, and had also trained its forces for the attack ahead of time. As regards the 5th and particularly the 39th and 43rd armies, they had been regrouped to this axis immediately upon the completion of the fighting for Königsberg and were forced to begin the offensive in conditions new to them.

The operational plan. According to the *front* commander's plan, the central armies—39th and 5th—were to launch the main attack in the general direction of Fischausen, so that, employing the shortest distance to this point, to split the enemy's Samland group into two parts, northern and southern, with a rapid attack and then destroy them in detail.

The 2nd Guards and 43rd armies were to support the central armies' activities, launching attacks along the northern and southern shores of the peninsula.

For this reason, it was ordered:

- the 2nd Guards Army, consisting of the 103rd, 11th Guards and 60th rifle corps was to launch an attack in the general direction of Gross Hubniken, with the task of reaching the line west of Schlaukalken and Rogenen by the close of the first day; a supporting attack would be launched in the direction of Germanu, with the troops arriving south of Tierenberg;
- the 5th Army, consisting of the 65th, 72nd and 45th rifle corps, received orders to launch its main attack along the right flank in the direction of Rotenen and to reach the line Norgau—Kompenen by the close of the first day and to subsequently reach the line southeast of Germau;
- the 39th Army, consisting of the 94th, 5th Guards and 113th rifle corps, was to attack in the general direction of Fischausen and to reach by the end of the day the Medenau–Schuntten line;
- the 43rd Army, consisting of the 54th, 90th and 13th Guards rifle corps was to attack in the direction of Nepleken and to subsequently capture the peninsula's salient.

The 11th Guards Army, in the *front* reserve, was ordered to advance behind the central armies in full readiness to enter the fighting.

The enemy's densest group of forces was located in the central and southern parts of the peninsula, where the 93rd, 58th, 1st, 21st, and 561st infantry divisions, and the 28th Light Infantry Division were defending, as well as the 5th Panzer Division.

Combat operations. Before the start of the operation, the forces of the 2nd Guards and 5th armies, which were defending, reconnoitered the enemy with reconnaissance detachments, which often encountered his counterattacks, supported by artillery fire.

Despite the Germans' high level of vigilance, the detachments managed to capture a significant number of prisoners from different formations. For example, on 12 April we captured seven men, belonging to the "Neukuren" group and the 551st, 95th and 93rd infantry divisions. The forces of the 39th and 43rd armies, which by this time had deployed in the first line, captured 38 prisoners from the 58th, 1st, 21st, and 561st infantry divisions, the 28th Light Infantry Division, and the 5th Panzer Division.

At 0800 on 13 April, following an hour-long artillery preparation, our forces attacked. Despite the enemy's resistance (powerful fire and counterattacks in strength up to a battalion, with 5-10 tanks and assault guns each), the attacking units advanced 3-5 kilometers along some sectors.

The 2nd Guards Army, attacking in the direction of Germau, broke through the enemy's defense in two places (south of Diwens and in the Arissau area) and advanced 2.5 kilometers. At the same time, the army's left flank forced the river to the east of Tierenberg. The army's forces captured 1,017 prisoners.

The 5th Army, launching an attacking along the right flank in the direction of Norgau and Rotenen, advanced five kilometers and captured more than 1,000 prisoners.

The 39th and 43rd armies attacking to the south advanced at the same speed: the first advanced three kilometers and captured 600 prisoners; the second advanced five kilometers and captured 1,500 prisoners.

The *front's* aviation actively supported the troops' attack on this day. The 1st Air Army carried out 4,019 sorties, of which 914 involved bomber-assault air actions at night and 1,930 during the day; the 3rd Air Army carried out 2,092 sorties, of which 617 involved bomber-assault air actions at night and 959 during the day. Thus the overall number of sorties was 6,111. 30 German planes were shot down in air battles in the day's fighting.

On 14 April the enemy began to fall back to the west opposite the 2nd Guards Army. The army's forces, without losing contact, continued to attack and in a day's fighting advanced up to 15 kilometers along the right flank, clearing the Germans out of the entire wooded area to the southeast of Gross Kuren and capturing 2,500 prisoners, 50 field guns, 32 mortars, 224 mortars, and other equipment.

The enemy put up more stubborn resistance along the 5th and 39th armies' front, the forces of which were able to advance three kilometers and take Medenau as a result of the day's fighting.

The 43rd Army attacked along the northern shore of the Frisches Haff. Its units captured the Germans' major strong point of Gross Heidekrug.

On 15 April the 2nd Guards Army reached the shore of the Baltic Sea, having cleared the enemy from the northwestern part of the Samland peninsula. The arrival of the 2nd Guards Army's forces at the Baltic Sea faced the enemy with the necessity of pulling back the remnants of his forces to the Fischausen area, due to the threat presented by our right flank overhanging him from the north. However, despite the rapid development of the offensive by this army along the shore of the Baltic Sea to the south, the enemy continued to put up stubborn resistance to the 39th and 43rd armies.

The 11th Guards Army moved behind the attacking troops and by the close of 16 April had concentrated in the Germau—Tierenberg area, ready to relieve or reinforce the first-echelon forces.

On this day our aviation carried out 4,577 sorties.

On 17 April the forces of the 39th Army, in conjunction with units of the 43rd Army, captured the town of Fischausen as a result of night fighting and attacks from the north and east, while the forces of the 2nd Guards Army, having broken through the enemy's defense along the line

Tenkitten—Rosenthal, advanced two kilometers to the south. Further advance was halted by the enemy's stubborn resistance.

Thus on the attack's fifth day the Samland peninsula had been completely cleared of the enemy.

The 11th Guards Army, which had been committed by the *front* commander into the first line on the night of 17-18 April, relieved the forces of the 2nd Guards Army to the east of Fischausen and on this day began a reconnaissance in force of the defense of the Pillau peninsula. As a result of this, the reconnaissance detachments captured a number of the enemy's fortified heights to the west of Lochstadt, capturing 130 prisoners from the 32nd, 58th and 558th infantry divisions. The reconnaissance continued on 19 April as well.

It was established that the enemy had heavily fortified in the woods west of Lochstadt, in order to cover Pillau.

At 1100 on 20 April the 11th Guards Army's 16th and 36th Guards rifle corps began their attack. It seemed as though the large amount of our artillery, which had been concentrated along the army's front, as well as the powerful air strikes, should have paralyzed the enemy's defense. However, the woods, which hid the enemy's troops, as well as the not completely favorable meteorological conditions and the narrow attack front, limited the success of the attacking troops. On this day their left flank advanced only one kilometer, captured a number of heights, 2-3 trench lines, and overcame an anti-tank ditch.

On 21 April units of the 16th and 36th Guards rifle corps repeatedly attacked the enemy's positions, but also achieved insignificant results. The enemy undertook nine fierce counterattacks in force up to a battalion of infantry, with 6-10 tanks and assault guns each.

The complete cloud cover, rain and fog once again prevented our aviation from supporting the ground forces. Only at night did Po-2 planes bomb the enemy in the Pillau area and in the northern part of the Frisches Nehrung.

Only on 22 April, the third day of the attack, with the commitment of the 3rd Guards Rifle Corps into the fighting, did units of the 11th Guards Army break through the enemy's defense and capture the strong point of Lochstadt, in the area of which four permanent pillboxes with armored cowls were uncovered. The subsequent attack unfolded in the form of fierce battles for the fortress and port of Pillau, which the army's forces managed to take on 25 April, thus eliminating the Germans' last beachhead on the southwestern part of the peninsula, after which the forces of the 11th Guards Army began to force the broad gulf from the march.

During the fighting it was discovered that the *front's* forces had overcome a system of field fortifications on the Samland peninsula, consisting of five positions of 2-3 trenches apiece, covered by anti-personnel and anti-tank obstacles.

With the defeat of the German forces on the Samland peninsula, the entire territory of East Prussia had been occupied by Soviet forces. Only in the area of the Frisches Nehrung spit and the mouth of the Vistula River did the remnants of the enemy's defeated East Prussian group of forces continue to put up stubborn resistance to the forces of the Third Belorussian Front.

10

Overall Conclusions

The military-political and strategic significance of the Red Army's victory in East Prussia is very great. The main forces of the central group of German armies were completely defeated and destroyed here. The Red Army occupied all of East Prussia, having for all time eliminated the seat and outpost of German imperialism in the east and the nest of Prussian militarism. The province's main city and powerful fortress of Königsberg, the Germans' strategically important stronghold on the Baltic Sea, was captured. The territory of the former East Prussia was partially turned over to the USSR and partially to Poland. East Prussia ceased to exist.

Such are the brief overall results of this historical victory.

1. The Soviet forces' offensive in East Prussia, which began in January 1945, was a component part of the Red Army's overall strategic offensive along a broad front between the Baltic Sea and the Carpathians. In order no. 5 of 23 February 1945, the supreme commander-in-chief, Marshal of the Soviet Union comrade Stalin, thus characterized this offensive:

> In January of this year the Red Army launched an unprecedentedly powerful blow against the enemy along the entire front from the Baltic to the Carpathians. The Red Army crushed along a 1,200-kilometer front the Germans' powerful defense, which they had been constructing over a period of years. During the offensive the Red Army's rapid and skillful operations threw the enemy far to the west.

In the Supreme High Command's overall strategic plan, the Second and Third Belorussian fronts were entrusted with the important task of cutting off East Prussia and the troops occupying it from the central areas of Germany, as well as the defeat and destruction of the entire northern strategic wing of the German front. The active securing of our troops' offensive along the most important Warsaw—Berlin direction would also be achieved through this.

The East Prussian operation, according to its plan and organization, was a typical major operation of the Great Patriotic War, conducted by the *Stavka* of the Supreme High Command in coordinating the men and materiel of two adjoining *fronts*. The *Stavka's* operational design called for the breakthrough of the enemy's heavily-fortified front, the cutting off of the East Prussian group of forces from the other German forces and the simultaneous launching of a deep frontal attack along the Königsberg axis, and the breaking up of the enemy forces and their destruction in detail. As is clear from the preceding narrative, this design was carried out in full. We see in the East Prussian operation, as in other offensive operations in 1945, the further growth in the power and might of the Red Army, and the further development of its military art, which corresponded to the concluding phase of the war. The Red Army's mighty offensive overturned the Germans' plans for active operations and holding East Prussia, which had been drawn up over decades, from Schlieffen to the Hitlerite command. Despite the fact that the Germans disposed of powerful forces in East Prussia, which were based on a developed and deeply echeloned defense, they were completely routed.

In passing, we should note the superiority of the operational-strategic leadership of the Red Army over the old Russian army. As is known, during the First World War the Russian command was not able in 1914 to unite two separate army operations (1st and 2nd Russian armies) into a single coordinated *front* operation. As a result of the poor and criminal leadership on the part of the high command of the czarist army, each of these armies operated in isolation in East Prussia and suffered a reverse. This circumstance was one of the main reasons for the Germans' success then (along with the interception of the Russian operational orders, and others).

In 1945 the task was more complex. It was necessary to unify and direct toward an overall goal the actions of two *fronts* and their numerous equipment—the defeat of the Germans in East Prussia. The scale of the operation was several times greater, and the operation itself much more complex. Despite this, the task was carried out brilliantly and the assigned objective was fully achieved. We saw how separate local operations, correctly and directly controlled by the *Stavka* of the Supreme High Command, flow into a single large operation of strategic significance.

The particulars of the task and the situation along each of the *fronts* were reflected in the operational decisions. The Third Belorussian Front was to carry out a breakthrough along a single overall sector. In adopting a deep formation, the *front* had in its second echelon not only mobile formations, but also an entire combined-arms army. The Second Belorussian Front was to launch its attacks along two sectors (with bridgeheads), having powerful mobile formations in its second echelon.

The Second Belorussian Front skillfully carried out a breakthrough, committed powerful mobile formations, which in conjunction with the combined-arms armies were the chief means of broad operational maneuver, and which had as their purpose the cutting off of the enemy's East Prussian group of forces. The Third Belorussian Front offered an interesting example of maneuver during the course of a breakthrough not only by mobile formations, but by an entire combined-arms army, in order to employ and develop the success there, where it actually took place.

The mutual connection, which exists at the present time between the activities of several adjoining *fronts* during the unfolding of major operations, should be noted. Thus during our January offensive the operations of the Second and Third Belorussian fronts were directed toward one overall goal: to the joint defeat of the Germans' East Prussian group of forces. Alongside this, the First Belorussian Front was forced, during its offensive through Poznan on Berlin, to detach major forces to secure itself from the north, because its neighbor on the right, the Second Belorussian Front, was making its main attack at the time to the north and was not able to cover the First Belorussian Front's right flank. On the other hand, despite the heavy fighting in the Liebstadt area and the threat of the German forces breaking out of East Prussia, the command of the Second Belorussian Front, in following the *Stavka's* instructions, directed its *front* reserves toward the Vistula River for an offensive to the west for the purpose of rendering assistance to the First Belorussian Front's forces. From these examples it is evident that modern large operations usually do not fit within the confines of a single *front*, but are conducted by an entire group of *fronts*, the operations of which are unified by the single design of the *Stavka* of the Supreme High Command.

The Second Belorussian Front's offensive unfolded (upon approaching the sea) along a 430-kilometer front and to a depth of up to 200 kilometers, and at an average rate of 16-17 kilometers per day. Thus the Second Belorussian Front's operation in 1945 confirms once again that the scope of modern operations, even within the confines of a single *front*, has increased significantly.

Following their arrival at the Baltic Sea and the encirclement of the enemy's East Prussian group of forces, the forces of the Second Belorussian Front forced the Vistula River and immediately began an offensive to the west into East Pomerania. It follows that the Second Belorussian Front's operation, which began in January 1945, grew directly into the *front's* East Pomeranian operation.

Thus one of the features of modern combat operations is their comparatively short pauses, or even the absence of pauses between consecutive offensive operations.

2. The preparation for the offensive operation in East Prussia was conducted in a timely manner and very scrupulously, and was one of the foundations for the outstanding success achieved. It included the training of troops and staffs for carrying out the tasks facing them, the organization of the artillery and aviation offensive, the employment of tank troops, and the engineering support for the operation, etc. Questions of outfitting the appropriate bridgehead for the offensive, the further study of the enemy, the organization of regroupings and the relief of the troops, and the support for reliable command and control also drew the command's attention. Finally, the organization of the rear and materiel-technical support required scrupulous planning, and the East Prussian operation is interesting and instructive on this score.

Thus problems of preparing for the offensive are given a significant place in this work.

Providing for the high political-morale condition of the troops was a very important and responsible task for the command and political organs. This work included: the propaganda and practical realization of comrade Stalin's instructions issued by him on the occasion of the 27th anniversary of the Great October Revolution; the inculcation of a high degree of offensive élan in the troops, a burning hatred for the enemy and confidence in our approaching victory; the ideological-political instruction of communists; the strengthening of the political-morale condition in our units, and troop discipline and the increase of vigilance. The content, form and particulars of this work in the Second and Third Belorussian fronts are listed in the corresponding sections. During the offensive the party organs and political organizations also carried out a great deal of work in strengthening and further developing the troops' offensive élan. This was one of the most important factors in our successes in the East Prussian operation.

Wonderful results were achieved in the East Prussian operation, despite the difficult climatic and meteorological conditions. At first there were frosts, blizzards and fog (January-February), followed in March by the addition to the fogs – freezing rain and impassable mud. People sometimes went for weeks without being able to dry off. Our aviation could only work for a few days. Our artillery fire was limited by poor visibility. And despite all this, the Soviet troops displayed miracles of heroism, bravery and hardihood, and in overcoming the enemy's stubborn resistance based on powerful fortifications.

The question of the correlation of forces (the overall correlation along the axis of the main attack) is one of the most important, and which is studied by the theory and practice of military art. The operations of 1945 developed upon a higher materiel-technical base than in the preceding years; the overall correlation of forces continued to grow in our favor. This enabled us to form powerful groups of forces along the breakthrough axes and to create a several-fold and overwhelming superiority in forces over the enemy. Such an overwhelming superiority in forces that we had in the decisive offensive operations of 1945 made it possible to quickly crush the enemy and vigorously attack to a great depth. At the same time the vigor of our offensive was the best means for completely defeating the enemy, because it prevented him from avoiding our attacks or carrying out a regrouping.

Prewar theory (based mainly on the combat experience from the first quarter of the 20th century) held, for example, that it was sufficient to have a threefold superiority in forces over the enemy along the axis of the main attack in order to successfully attack.

In the Second Belorussian Front's operation, as was the case in some other offensive operations, we outnumbered the enemy along the entire front: three times in infantry and artillery, four times in tanks and self-propelled guns, and four times in the number of planes. Such an overall superiority in forces enabled us to achieve a superiority over the enemy along the breakthrough sectors: sixfold in infantry, seven-eightfold in artillery and mortars, and ninefold in tanks and self-propelled guns. In the Third Belorussian Front's operations we had an overall superiority over the enemy: threefold in men and three-fourfold in equipment. This enabled us to achieve a superiority over the enemy along the main attack axis: fivefold in infantry and sevenfold in artillery and tanks. In some other operations in 1945 we managed to achieve an even greater superiority of force.

However, the experience of the Great Patriotic War shows that one can conduct successful operations with a smaller superiority of force than was the case in 1945. Much will depend on the situation (what kind of enemy, his degree of resilience, the quality of equipment, the level of troop training, the commanders' preparation, etc.).

3. The operational breakthrough had its peculiar features in the conditions of the 1945 winter offensive. The offensive was conducted along a broad front and attacks were launched simultaneously along several axes. Our forces had to break through the enemy's powerful and deeply-echeloned defense. It must nonetheless be noted that in all cases there was more than sufficient men and materiel to carry out the breakthrough and develop the success for decisive results. If a breakthrough was not achieved somewhere, or was not achieved immediately and additional attacks were required, then this usually happened not because there was a shortage of men and materiel, but because while preparing for and organizing the operation something was left out or a mistake was made, for example, in organizing cooperation among the troops, in employing artillery and tanks, in not taking into account conditions of poor visibility, etc. As experience shows, such a miscalculation, for the most part, should be looked for in the organization and conduct of the artillery preparation.

Prewar theory held that an army should break through along a 20-30 kilometer front. In this case, the breakthrough sector will not be exposed to enfilading fire and mobile formations can be committed to develop the success. The operations of the Great Patriotic War showed that the concrete conditions of the situation powerfully influence all norms and calculations, including the width of the break through front. The modern *front* can usually organize a breakthrough along 1-2 sectors with an overall width of 20-30 kilometers. An army disposing of average-strength divisions is capable of breaking through along a 10-12 kilometer sector. At the *front* level it is often sufficient to breakthrough along a 15-20 kilometer front: it is possible to commit *front* men and materiel and carry out a breakthrough to a great depth. However, we can and must employ narrower tactical breakthroughs. In this case (while committing formations into the breach along narrow sectors of the front) the decisive role is played by the following: the reliable securing of the breakthrough's flanks and its development along the flanks, the presence of the attacker's powerful reserves (especially anti-tank) and the reliable cover of troops against enemy air strikes.

We see in the 1945 operations that alongside the creation of powerful mobile formations for developing the success in depth that sufficient forces were allocated for simultaneously expanding the breaches in the direction of the flanks. This supported the rapid widening of the breach and eliminated enemy attempts to cut off our penetrating wedge by attacks from the flanks at the base. Troops from the shock group, which were allocated for the mission in question, expanded the breakthrough along the flanks, secured the firmness of our combat formation against the enemy's flank attacks, and in this way created favorable prospects for further developing the success.

Earlier the organization of the breakthrough on the Second and Third Belorussian fronts was analyzed in detail. We must remind the reader that the Second Belorussian Front was to carry out a breakthrough along a 28-kilometer front, while the armies received breakthrough fronts of 6-7 kilometers. The overall artillery density along the breakthrough front reached more than 230 tubes per kilometer of front, while on some armies' sectors this density reached almost 300 tubes. Such a high massing of artillery along the shock axes guaranteed the breakthrough of the German defense.

On the Third Belorussian Front it was planned to break through along a 24-kilometer front, while the armies received attack sectors of 7-9 kilometers. The artillery density along the breakthrough sectors reached 200-220 tubes per kilometer of front.

Tanks played a major role in the course of the East Prussian operation. In the majority of cases, powerful tank formations, committed into the breach, completed the enemy's defeat in the attack sector and then rapidly developed the success in conjunction with the ground forces and aviation. The conditions for the tanks' activities in the East Prussian operation were not easy: the Germans had a developed and deeply-echeloned defense; a large number of individual farms with sturdy stone buildings, which formed natural strong points for the enemy; a powerful anti-tank defense—all of this made our tanks' activities more difficult and complex. The fighting in East Prussia once again confirmed the great significance of direct infantry-support tanks (NPP), which were needed for overcoming the tactical defense, independent of the presence of tank corps or tank armies in the second operational echelon. Given an insufficient number of NPP tanks, we had to bring in tank formations to break through the tactical defense. Experience shows that in breaking through the enemy's powerfully fortified and deeply developed main defensive zone, we should have correspondingly more powerful direct infantry support tank groups. Given a low density of direct infantry-support tanks, the offensive will develop more slowly and it is possible that the second-echelon mobile formations may have to be brought in to finish breaking through the enemy's tactical defense, that is, to carry out the direct infantry-support tanks' task.

Forward battalions were widely employed in the Second Belorussian Front's operation. These battalions were employed in the Third Belorussian Front's operation, as well as in a number of other operations. These battalions were sometimes called storm battalions. The essence of their activities consisted on carrying out a reconnaissance in force against the enemy directly preceding the general attack, for the purpose of establishing whether or not the enemy has abandoned the first trench lines and to avoid the pointless expenditure of shells. For example, on 14 January, at the start of the Second Belorussian Front's attack, the forward battalions managed to easily capture the first 2-3 trench lines, which were weakly held by the enemy's infantry. Thus, in this case, the employment of forward battalions justified itself completely and enabled us to save about 40-50 percent of the shells designated for the artillery preparation. Alongside this, it is necessary to take into account the fact that the movement of the forward battalions ahead of the attacking divisions' combat formations makes somewhat more difficult the working out of plans for the artillery offensive and requires having several variations. This method, which yielded positive results in a number of cases, should not be transformed into a fixed routine.

In the East Prussian operation our forces accumulated important and valuable experience in overcoming powerfully-fortified and deeply-echeloned positions, which presented a unified system of field and permanent structures.

This experience develops and supplements our views on the attack and breakthrough of fortified positions, accumulated from the preceding war years. The breakthrough of fortified areas and powerful fortified positions usually requires scrupulous and prolonged preparation, the presence of powerful destruction and suppression weapons, and an action plan drawn up in detail, and centralized command and control. The offensive is carried out by destroying and blockading the most important defensive structures and the gradual overcoming of fortified zones by the methodical employment of powerful weapons of destruction and suppression.

However, the East Prussian operation offers instructive examples of other methods in attacking powerfully fortified positions and fortified areas. In those cases when the enemy did not have time to occupy beforehand and organize a defense along a fortified line, or when the combat capability of his forces was lowered, or in other cases favorable to the attacker, the method of sped-up attack may be successfully employed. In such cases an energetic attack, along with the employment of powerful aviation and tank formations, supported by powerful fire means concentrated along a narrow front, may lead to success. Upon seizing through a surprise attack a sector of the fortified zone from the march, or having broken through along a boundary between defensive centers, it is necessary to rapidly develop the success, to break through the main zone of the fortifications and captured the entire fortified area. We must remind the reader that important sectors of the fortified areas along the Deime River, the Heilsberg fortified area, the Mlawa fortified area, and others were captured by us from the march through a vigorous attack, and some reinforced concrete pillboxes were still locked up. The Germans, in panic, did not even have time to open them and install a garrison. The very powerful fortress of Königsberg required careful preparation and powerful suppression means, but it was nonetheless taken by storm.

4. We should note operational maneuver in the offensive operation. The forms of operational maneuver in the East Prussian operation are very interesting and instructive. The Second Belorussian Front quickly overcame the German defense, defeated the Germans' Przasnysz—Mlawa group of forces and, while developing a vigorous offensive to outflank the main forces of the East Prussian group of forces from the south, reached the sea. Thus by means of a powerful attack, which crushed the enemy front, and skillful flank maneuver, the cutting off of the German front was accomplished. The Third Belorussian Front was to launch a deep frontal attack along the Königsberg direction. This attack was to be an important component part of the overall operational plan for our forces' operations in East Prussia. As a result of our offensive along the Königsberg direction, the Germans' Tilsit—Insterburg group of forces was defeated and the entire East Prussian group of forces was split into three isolated parts: a) on the Samland peninsula; b) the Königsberg group, and; c) the main group (Heilsberg) of German forces south of Königsberg. Along with this, the Third Belorussian Front subsequently outflanked from the north the main core of the East Prussian group of forces, as if to form the northern part of those pincers in which it was trapped. The forces of the Third Belorussian Front also encircled the enemy's Königsberg group of forces.

Thus both *fronts*, depending upon the operational plan and the concrete conditions of its realization, employed different forms of operational maneuver and attack, while the frontal attack for carrying out a breakthrough and the flanking maneuver had great significance at the operational level. According to the conditions of the situation, the Second Belorussian Front was in a more favorable position for carrying out broad operational maneuver and brilliantly carried out the cutting off of the East Prussian group of forces from its land communications in conjunction with tank and combined-arms formations. Along the Third Belorussian Front the most important role was played by a deep frontal attack, which also led to major operational results. However, on the Third Belorussian Front, despite the limited opportunities for maneuver, operational maneuver played an important role, both in the breakthrough of the enemy front (the maneuver by the 11th Guards Army and the tank corps to the north, in order to take advantage of the success where it had been achieved) and in the subsequent development of the offensive to the west into the gap between the enemy's Tilsit and Insterburg groups of forces. On the whole, the coordinated actions of the Second and Third Belorussian fronts in January 1945 are an amazing example of the *Stavka* of the Supreme High Command's activities in organizing the coordination of two neighboring *fronts* for achieving the overall decisive goal of defeating the enemy's major forces.

During the course of the operation, not only mobile formations, but combined-arms ones as well, took part in carrying out operational maneuver over great distances. For example, during the Second Belorussian Front's operation, two rifle divisions (330th and 369th) were transferred from the *front's* right wing to the left, a distance of 300-350 kilometers, while the 49th Army carried out a march of 200 kilometers from the Bischofsburg area to the Kulm area.

In eliminating the main forces of the East Prussian group of forces in March 1945 in the area southwest of Königsberg, the freed-up armies (5th and 2nd Shock and 50th) were regrouped to the Samland peninsula for reinforcing our forces along this axis, covering 100-150 kilometers.

As for employing artillery, the widespread maneuver by transport for rapid artillery regroupings along the front should be noted. Such maneuver is necessary for the rapid massing of artillery along those sectors where the course of combat operations requires it.

In the coordinated actions of the Second and Third Belorussian fronts in January 1945 we also find the brilliant realization of one of the most important tenets of military art: to destroy the enemy in detail. As was already mentioned, the Second Belorussian Front's crushing attack and rapid flank maneuver cut off the East Prussian group of forces from the other German forces. The Third Belorussian Front's deep and energetic frontal offensive split the enemy front along the Königsberg axis. As a result of our forces' subsequent decisive actions in East Prussia, instead of a single group of German forces, there were three isolated groups: on the Samland peninsula, the Königsberg group, and a group south of Königsberg. This gave us the opportunity to eliminate them consecutively, concentrating our main forces first against the southern group, then against Königsberg, and finally against the group on the Samland peninsula.

5. Decisive air superiority over the enemy had great significance for the successful development of the offensive by our forces. However, if the air situation was easy for us in terms of combat, then there were serious difficulties in other areas. The poor meteorological conditions (fog, low clouds, etc.), which made it very difficult, and in many cases, even excluded the employment of aviation, have already been repeatedly pointed out. Thus we could by no means always fully take advantage of our superiority over the enemy in the air. Significant difficulties also arose in basing aviation (the limited number of airfields).

The methods of aviation employment were a continuation and development of the experience from the 1944 operations. A *front's* air army usually worked in its own operational zone. Long-range aviation was brought in along the most important directions, and sometimes neighboring air armies. The greatest concentration of aviation was achieved in the Königsberg operation, where parts of four air armies and naval aviation were active, and which played an important role in the enemy's rapid defeat.

Centralized command and control at the *front* level completely justified itself. At the same time, operational experience once again confirmed that the closest possible communications between the air commanders and with those ground armies and formations they support are necessary. As a rule, the aviation commanders should be quartered and move together with the corresponding ground force commanders.

6. The Second Belorussian Front's January offensive began from the Rozan and Serock bridgeheads, which had been seized by us as a result of the summer 1944 offensive. In turn, the Second Belorussian Front's operation was completed by the seizure of bridgeheads over the Vistula River.

It we turn to the experience of other operations in 1944-45, we will also see that in offensive operations involving the forcing of water barriers, an important role is played by bridgeheads seized on the opposite bank of the river. Many operations often began from bridgeheads and ended with the seizure of new bridgeheads. Both sides strived to maximally take advantage of these bridgeheads. Experience shows that in planning an offensive operation involving the forcing of water lines in the depth, it is necessary to strive to complete it with the seizure of bridgeheads on the opposite bank from the march. This is profitable in many ways:

- the very forcing of the river from the march is eased, less organic crossing equipment is required, and materials at hand are more widely used;

- given the presence of bridgeheads, it is easier to prepare for and conduct a new offensive operation, although many additional difficulties arise;
- a similar disposition is favorable in case of active defense.

The retention of bridgeheads often demands great efforts, because the enemy is striving to throw the crossed-over troops into the river, in connection with which there arises a prolonged and stubborn battle. The enemy creates powerful fortifications around the bridgeheads and brings up powerful groups of forces to them. The factor of surprise for our future offensive is lost to a significant extent, because the enemy is aware of the possible axes of our attacks from the bridgeheads. The deployment of large forces along limited bridgeheads is connected with major difficulties, etc. From the example of the Second Belorussian Front's operation in 1945 it can be seen how much more difficult the preparation and initial development of the operation is in those cases in which the troops deploy for an offensive from bridgeheads. All of this should be considered. In particular, it is often very favorable to force small rivers (no more than 50 meters wide) and then develop the offensive immediately from there, without the preliminary (timely) seizure of the bridgehead, that is, without operational pauses.

From the above one may conclude that it is necessary to carefully study the conduct of offensive operations involving the forcing of water obstacles. In particular, we should study in detail the preparation and conduct of the offensive from bridgeheads, as well as questions of seizing and retaining them.

7. The encirclement of major enemy groups of forces and their subsequent elimination was realized in peculiar conditions. Two powerful attacks, launched north and south of the Masurian Lakes and separated by a distance of 200 kilometers, came together on the coast of the Baltic Sea.

Two groups of German forces, dislodged along a limited space, were encircled: one near Königsberg and the other in the area to the south of the city. However, this was not a complete encirclement: the German forces had been flanked on three sides, their land communications had been cut, and they had been pressed against the sea, which although it protected them against our attacks from the rear, also created additional difficulties for them. Rear communications through the Frisches Haff were very poor and unreliable: it was impossible to use large ships in the shallow gulf, while movement along the Pillau—Königsberg maritime canal was limited, and our aviation had overwhelming air superiority.

Nonetheless, even in these conditions the encircled groups of forces put up prolonged resistance. Operational pauses, troop regroupings, the careful preparation of new attacks, and the consecutive elimination of both groups (the southern group in March and the Königsberg group in April) were required. Aside from the reasons already listed, the following circumstances also caused the elimination of encircled groups to drag out:

- the presence of large enemy forces in the encircled groups of forces and their stubborn resistance; the presence of powerful fortifications;
- our troops' exhaustion in the preceding battles and the rifle regiments' and divisions' small size;
- the unfavorable climatic and meteorological conditions: the spring thaw and large amounts of mud, fog and freezing rain made the employment of aviation and artillery more difficult and slowed down the pace of their attack.

The course of eliminating the encircled groups of forces and our forces' combat methods are obvious from the descriptions listed. In passing, we will make an additional note. The opinion is often expressed that the chief method for the speediest defeat of an encircled enemy is the gradual and consecutive closing of the encirclement ring around him, which is something the attacker should supposedly strive for. Such a method is possible, but it is by no means the most profitable for the attacker. First of all, large forces are needed in order to squeeze the enemy simultaneously from all sides. Secondly, in employing such a method, although the encircled enemy gradually loses ground, which is unfavorable for him, he nonetheless maintains his organized perimeter defense and makes his combat formations denser as the encirclement ring is squeezed.

In reality, the gradual squeezing of the encirclement ring, which we often saw in operations, is a consequence of two opposing reasons:

a) the attacker, in launching concentrated attacks along a narrow front, seeks to break up the encircled group of forces, to break up or split off from its larger or smaller parts, in order to destroy the enemy in detail;

b) the encircled party makes all efforts to resist his group of forces being broken up or split; he seeks to the last to maintain an organized and unbroken front and perimeter defense. He will more likely choose to abandon individual sectors and small areas that are in danger of being cut off rather than allow himself to be defeated in detail.

As a result, we have the gradual squeezing of the encirclement ring that we often saw in reality. For example, in eliminating the 20 German divisions south of Königsberg, we nonetheless did not manage to split up this group of forces into parts, although multiple attempts were made to do so. As soon as the threat of being split up or cut off arose, the enemy abandoned the threatened area, if he did not have any other opportunity to resist the breakup of his forces.

8. The preparation and storming of Königsberg are very interesting and instructive. As was already noted, multiple zones and permanent fortifications had been constructed along the far and near approaches to Königsberg, beginning from the line of the Deime and Alle rivers, which represented in total a broad fortified area, a distinctive and powerful reduit of which was the fortress of Königsberg. The strength of this fortress was in the combination of developed field and permanent defensive structures, in their good adaptation to terrain that had been well studied by the Germans and in the large garrison and large number of defensive weapons. The German command believed that Königsberg could hold out for a long time; on the eve of the fortress's capture the Hitlerite propaganda was still screaming about Königsberg's invulnerability.

Following careful study, the Red Army command adopted a successful operational plan: to cut off Königsberg from the outside world, and through concentric attacks defeat the German forces and take the fortress by storm. Large forces and powerful suppression weapons were concentrated, as well as a lot of artillery and aircraft.

The careful preparation for the storming is instructive in the tactical sense as well: the organization of coordination of the combat arms, the creation of storm detachments and groups for overcoming permanent fortifications, etc.

On the whole, the storming of Königsberg is a shining example of taking a large fortress in four days.

9. In the East Prussian operation, just as in other offensive operations of the Great Patriotic War, the command and control of troops was centralized.

This was conditioned by the growing strength of the armed forces, the growth of military equipment, the broad scope of modern operations, and the growing concentration of men and materiel along the axis of the main attack. Along with this, the centralization of command and control was also brought about by the circumstance that in the work of modern combat equipment (tanks and aviation), their fullest and rational employment does not fit within the confines of a single army, but becomes possible only with the scope of the *front*, and even several *fronts*.

Alongside this we see that in the East Prussian operation the centralization of command and control was combined with great independence and initiative at the subordinate levels. This, first of all, was achieved by the accepted method of drawing up plans for the forthcoming operation. For example, at first the *Stavka* assigned the Second and Third Belorussian front command a task and demanded that they submit their ideas for the operational plan. Upon reviewing the plan drawn up by the *front*, a *Stavka* directive followed for the offensive, which laid out concrete instructions and was simultaneously a confirmation of the *front's* plan. Work was carried out at the *front* level using this plan, and then in the armies and corps. Here, given time and opportunity, before issuing directives or orders, ideas were solicited from the subordinate commanders.

The greatest centralization of command and control was realized while preparing for and conducting the operational breakthrough (the regrouping of forces and their occupation of jumping-off positions for the offensive, the artillery and aviation preparation, the commitment of the mobile formations, etc.). In the subsequent course of operations, especially if the operation developed rapidly and there were no sharp changes in the plan, the subordinate commanders were given significant freedom of action and employed reasonable initiative within the bounds of the overall operational scheme.

Conversations over high-frequency radio and personnel interaction with subordinate commanders were broadly employed for exchanging opinions on the situation and for issuing preliminary instructions.

Given such methods of the higher command's work, the centralization of command and control was combined with the independence and initiative of its subordinates.

The command and control of troops in the East Prussian operation, particularly during operations in the coastal area, were complicated by the unfavorable climatic and meteorological situation. We often had to try to carry out an attack in conditions of poor visibility (heavy fog, freezing rain, darkness) and frequent changes in the weather. Thus it is necessary to adopt measures in a timely manner for:

* securing correct weather forecasts;
* serious attention to questions of weather and the correct consideration of the weather's influence on troop activities (artillery, aviation and tanks), in drawing up operational plans (different variants);
* the ability to profitably take advantage of conditions of poor visibility, that is, train and teach the troops so that they can successfully attack in fog and at night, employing massed artillery and aviation.

From this one can conclude for the future that it is necessary to carefully study and work out the conduct of an offensive in conditions of poor visibility, with the employment of powerful modern equipment.

10. In conclusion, we should note certain common features, which unite and link the East Prussian operation with other offensive operations during 1945.

Throughout the course of the Great Patriotic War of 1941-1945, the overall conditions for conducting operations changed. The Red Army's forces and might grew, it received more and more numerous and modern equipment and the correlation of forces changed in our favor. Our force's offensive élan increased, while the enemy's combat capabilities gradually decreased. The Red Army's military art grew in the course of the struggle as defensive and offensive forms changed and developed.

In the outstanding offensive operations of 1945 we see the further development of the Red Army's military art. Operations were conducted in different concrete situations and employing different forms of operational maneuver. However, alongside this there are a number of common traits. The overall political and military conditions that were characteristic of the war's concluding phase left their mark on the strategy and tactics of the belligerent sides. Thus one may speak with complete authority of several features of the Red Army's military art at the concluding stage of the war.

The Hitlerite command's plan for 1945 (in the broadest sense) consisted of prolonging the war, so that by employing all measures and means hold off the inevitable end. The German command sought to hold onto everything and allowed the dispersal of forces on the Eastern Front, and could not carry out a countermaneuver to oppose our offensive.

Our large winter offensive in 1945, along a broad front of 1,200 kilometers, led to the defeat of the German forces, broke them up into separate groups, pinned them to those axes along which they were located, and then they were eliminated in detail. By the beginning of 1945 more than 30 German divisions from Army Group North were located in the Baltic (in the Libava—Tukums area), cut off from their land communications. In East Prussia and the adjacent part of northern Poland lay the main core of the central group of German armies (35-40 divisions), which was also soon cut off from the remainder of Germany. The enemy group of forces to the south of the Carpathians was tied down by our active operations. The enemy group of forces along the very important Berlin direction was isolated and could not engage in broad strategic cooperation with the other groups of forces on the Germans' Eastern Front. Reserves arrived here in detail and were consecutively destroyed by our forces.

A marvelous expression of the Red Army's strategy in 1944 was Stalin's ten consecutive blows, through which during the course of the year the enemy's entire enormous front of 3,000 kilometers was crushed and decisive victories were achieved, which led to the clearing of Soviet territory of the German-Fascist aggressors. The results of these great victories, the further change of the correlation of forces in our favor and the reduction of the front's overall length by approximately half enabled us in 1945 to move from consecutive attacks to simultaneous attacks and the conduct of the offensive along the entire front occupied by Soviet forces. The simultaneous crushing attacks along a broad front were new and eloquent testimony to the Red Army's enormous offensive might and its increased superiority over the enemy in all categories.

The strategic results of the Red Army's winter offensive of 1945 are truly enormous. The enemy was defeated along a broad territory stretching from the Baltic Sea to the Carpathians. Our forces advanced 500 kilometers in 17 days in January and reached the Oder River along the very important Berlin direction. The East Prussian group of forces was cut off from the central areas and was subsequently completely eliminated.

Thus extremely important results were achieved. In order to better present the scale and possibilities of Stalin's strategy, let us make some comparisons with the past and turn to the experience of the First World War.

The line of the Red Army's deployment along the East Prussian and Berlin directions in 1945 was close to the Russian armies' deployment line along the same directions in 1914: the border with East Prussia—Warsaw—the middle Vistula. The overall strategic goals were also similar: in the final analysis, it was planned to attack toward Berlin. The strategic connection between these two directions was also approximately the same: East Prussia occupied a forward flanking position; the East Prussian direction exercised a pinning influence on the very important Warsaw—Berlin direction; to attack toward Berlin without having secured oneself against East Prussia was impossible, or in any event risky.

How were these strategic tasks resolved in 1914 and 1945?

In 1914 the czarist army's command planned an offensive on Berlin as its final strategic goal. However, the forces that it was able to initially concentrate along the East Prussian and Warsaw—Berlin directions were still insufficient for such a large and decisive offensive. Thus it was recognized as expedient to first carry out the East Prussian operation with the forces of the Northwestern

Front, while one army deployed in the Warsaw area for securing this direction and to maintain contact with the Southwestern Front, which was operating against Austria-Hungary. Subsequently, depending on the results of the first operations, following regroupings and the concentration of forces along the Berlin direction, the possibility was considered of carrying out the main offensive on the German capital. Thus the main goal was essentially put off for an undefined period of time, depending upon the outcome of the East Prussian and Galician operations, while a local goal was placed first: the occupation of East Prussia. However, in consecutively carrying out these tasks, the czarist army's strategy could not even cope with the first and immediate task in East Prussia. As is known, the Russian armies in 1914 suffered a defeat in East Prussia as a result of shortcomings in command and control on the part of the higher command. The plan for occupying East Prussia failed, and with it the entire strategic design for an offensive on Berlin collapsed.

The Red Army command in 1945 acted in an entirely different manner. It created enormous concentrations of forces and was highly skilled in the simultaneous conduct of the offensive along several strategic directions, as a result of which major successes were quickly achieved. Powerful forces deployed along the very important Berlin direction, which through a vigorous offensive crushed the enemy and raised the banner of victory over Berlin. Simultaneously, major forces were also operating along the East Prussian direction, which cut off the German forces there from the central parts of Germany and them completely eliminated them.

Thus the czarist strategy of 1914 could not even cope with the first task—the occupation of East Prussia. The Red Army in 1945 simultaneously and masterfully resolved both strategic tasks along the Berlin and East Prussian directions.

In the 1914-1918 war the organization of cooperation among the *fronts*, even neighboring ones, grew into a complex and often insoluble problem. It is sufficient to recall Brusilov's[1] efforts to achieve operational coordination between the Southwestern and Western fronts in 1916. Despite all of Brusilov's energy and military talent, the Southwestern Front's offensive was not supported by the other Russian *fronts*, as a result of resistance by these *fronts'* commanders, as well as the *Stavka's* softness and indecisiveness.

In 1945 we find in the Red Army's operations brilliant examples of the operational coordination of neighboring *fronts*, as for example the cooperation between the Second and Third Belorussian fronts in the East Prussian operation. At the same time, we see the organization of strategic coordination on a large scale in the entire theater of war: the operations along the East Prussian, Berlin and Budapest—Vienna directions develop in a coordinated manner and are guided by the unified plan of the *Stavka* of the Supreme High Command. In particular, our offensive to the south of the Carpathians attracted major enemy reserves and they could not be employed along the decisive Berlin direction.

Such are the strength, skill and scope of Stalin's strategy.

On the whole, the East Prussian operation is an outstanding example of Stalinist military art and one of the glorious pages of the history of the Great Patriotic War.

---

1   Editor's note. The reference is to the offensive by General Aleksei Alekseevich Brusilov's Southwestern Front against the German and Austro-Hungarian forces in the summer of 1916.

Annex 1

The Third Belorussian Front's Organizational Composition by the Start of the East Prussian Operation of 1945

Army, Commander, Chief of Staff	Corps	Divisions (Brigades)
39th	113th Rifle	262nd, 338th, 192nd rifle divisions
Colonel General Lyudnikov	94th Rifle	358th, 124th, 221st rifle divisions
Major General Siminovskii	5th Guards Rifle	17th, 19th, 94th guards rifle divisions, 152nd Fortified Area
5th	72nd Rifle	277th, 63rd, 215th rifle divisions
Colonel General Krylov	45th Rifle	159th, 157th, 184th rifle divisions
Major General Prikhid'ko	65th Rifle	144th, 371st, 97th rifle divisions
28th	3rd Guards Rifle	50th, 54th, 96th guards rifle divisions
Lieutenant General Luchinskii	20th Rifle	48th & 55th guards, 20th rifle divisions
Major General Rogachevskii	128th Rifle	61st, 130th, 152nd rifle divisions
2nd Guards	11th Guards Rifle	2nd, 32nd, 33rd guards rifle divisions
Lieutenant General Chanchibadze	13th Guards Rifle	24th, 87th, 3rd guards rifle divisions
Major General Levin	50th Rifle	154th, 251st, 334th rifle divisions
31st	36th Rifle	173rd, 174th, 352nd rifle divisions
Colonel General Glagolev (replaced by Lieutenant General Shafranov)	71st Rifle	88th, 220th, 331st rifle divisions
Major General Shchedrin	44th Rifle	54th, 62nd, 176th rifle divisions
11th Guards	8th Guards Rifle	1st, 5th, 26th guards rifle divisions
Colonel General Galitskii	16th Guards Rifle	83rd, 31st, 11th guards rifle divisions
Major General Semenov	36th Guards Rifle	16th, 18th, 84th guards rifle divisions

Army, Commander, Chief of Staff	Corps	Divisions (Brigades)
1st Air Colonel General Khryukin Lieutenant General Belov		129th, 130th, 240th, 330th, 303rd fighter divisions, 1st Independent "Normandy" Fighter Regiment 9th Guards Fighter Regiment, 6th Guards and 276th bomber divisions, 213th Night Bomber Division 1st Guards, 182nd, 277th, 311th assault air divisions 117th, 10th, 151st reconnaissance regiments, 151st Fire-Correction Reconnaissance Regiment
43rd (from 19.1.1945) Lieutenant General Beloborodov Major General Maslennikov	90th Rifle 103rd Rifle 54th Rifle	26th, 182nd rifle divisions 115th, 319th, 325th rifle divisions 126th, 235th, 263rd rifle divisions
3rd Air (from 24.2.1945) Colonel General Papivin Major General Dagaev		one fighter corps two bomber divisions one night bomber division two assault air divisions one fighter division one assault air regiment

	Reinforcements		
Army	Artillery and Mortar Units and Formations	Armored and Mechanized Formations and Units	Engineering Formations and Units
39th	139th Artillery Bde, 610th Anti-Tank Artillery Rgt, 555th Army Mortar Rgt, 621st Anti-Aircraft Rgt, 545th Mortar Rgt/11th Guards Army, 13th Artillery Bde, 20th Heavy Caliber Howitzer Bde, 1st Guards Anti-Tank Artillery Bde, 392nd, 570th corps artillery breakthrough rgts, 326th, 42nd guards mortar rgts, 20th Anti-Aircraft Division, four artillery rgts from the 11th Guards Army's rifle divisions (only for the artillery preparation)	28th Guards Tank Bde, 35th, 76th guards motorized rgts, 348th, 350th heavy self-propelled artillery rgts, 735th, 927th self-propelled artillery rgts, 1197th Self-Propelled Artillery Rgt, 517th Independent Flamethrower Tank Rgt	32nd Army Engineer-Sapper Bde, 9th Assault Engineer-Sapper Bde
5th	15th Army Artillery Bde, 696th Anti-Tank Artillery Rgt, 283rd Mortar Rgt, 726th Anti-Aircraft Rgt, 149th Artillery Bde/11th Guards Army; 3rd Guards Artillery Div (22nd Artillery Bde, 99th Heavy Howitzer Bde, 8th Howitzer 107th High-Powered Howitzer Bde, 37th Light Artillery Bde, 43rd Mortar Bde); 2nd Guards Artillery Div (8th Guards Artillery Bde, 114th Artillery Bde, 5th Howitzer Bde, 4th Light Artillery Bde, 33rd Mortar Bde); 11th, 14th artillery bdes, 29th Heavy Destruction Bde, 16th Guards Anti-Tank Artillery Bde, 226th Independent High- Powered Artillery Bn; 34th, 48th anti-aircraft divs, 7th Guards Mortar Div, 54th, 74th, 95th guards mortar rgts, five artillery rgts from the 11th Guards Army's rifle divisions (only for the artillery preparation)	28th Guards Tank Bde, 75th, 81st guards tank rgts, 253rd Tank Rgt, 373rd, 395th heavy self-propelled artillery rgts, 953rd, 954th, 958th self-propelled artillery rgts	63rd Army Engineer-Sapper Bde, 4th Assault Engineer-Sapper Bde

	Reinforcements		
Army	Artillery and Mortar Units and Formations	Armored and Mechanized Formations and Units	Engineering Formations and Units
28th	157th Army Artillery Bde, 530th Army Anti-Tank Artillery Bde, 133rd Army Mortar Rgt, 607th Anti-Aircraft Rgt 10th Artillery Div (154th Artillery Bde, 158th Heavy Howitzer Bde, 162nd Howitzer Bde, 117th Heavy Caliber Howitzer Bde, 33rd Light Artillery Bde, 44th Mortar Bde), 245th, 316th independent high-caliber artillery rgts 12th Artillery Bde, 8th Heavy Mortar Bde, 16th Anti-Tank Artillery Bde, 523rd, 1093rd, 1165th corps artillery breakthrough rgts; 307th, 317th guards mortar rgts; 33rd Anti-Aircraft Div	213th Tank Bde, 82nd, 77th guards tank rgts, 148th Tank Rgt, 345th, 343rd heavy self-propelled artillery rgts	36th Army Engineer-Sapper Bde, 2nd Guards Assault Engineer-Sapper Bde
2nd Guards	150th Army Artillery Bde, 113th Army Anti-Tank Artillery Rgt, 483rd Army Mortar Rgt; 1530th Anti-Aircraft Rgt; 47th Anti-Tank Artillery Rgt, 67th Guards Mortar Rgt; 1275th Anti-Aircraft Rgt	153rd Tank Bde 1402nd, 1490th self-propelled artillery rgts	30th Army Engineer-Sapper Bde
31st	140th Army Artillery Bde, 529th Anti-Tank Artillery Rgt, 549th Army Mortar Rgt, 1478th Anti-Aircraft Rgt, 21st, 46th, 23rd anti-tank artillery bdes	2nd Guards Motorcycle Rgt, 513th Independent Flamethrower Tank Rgt, 959th, 926th self- propelled artillery rgts, 337th Heavy Self-Propelled Artillery Rgt	31st Army Engineer-Sapper Bde
11th Guards	551st Army Anti-Tank Artillery Rgt, 1280th Anti-Aircraft Rgt, 66th Anti- Aircraft Div		66th Army Engineer-Sapper Bde
1st Air	–	–	–
43rd	2nd, 20th high-powered artillery rgts, 14th Anti-Tank Artillery Bde, 1281st, 1481st, 1480th anti-aircraft rgts; 64th, 324th, 500th, 525th, 16th, 17th, 18th, 31st independent anti-aircraft bns, 295th Anti-Aircraft Searchlight Co, 56th, 62nd searchlight cos	1st Guards Tank Corps (89th, 117th, 159th tank bdes, 44th Motorized Rifle Bde); 2nd Guards Tatsinskaya Tank Corps (4th, 25th, 26th guards tank bdes, 4th Motorized Rifle Bde), 120th Tank Bde, 43rd Guards Tank Bde	13th Motorized Engineer Bde, 8th Pontoon-Bridge Bde, 7th Independent Bridge Co, 17th Flamethrower Tank Co, 52nd Independent Military-Field Construction Directorate
3rd Air	–	–	–

Notes::
1. The basis for this document is the order of battle for the Third Belorussian Front's formations and units as of 13.1.1945
2. The composition of the 1st Air Army is as of 9.1.1945

Annex 2

The Second Belorussian Front's Organizational Composition by the Start of the East Prussian Operation of 1945

Army, Commander, Chief of Staff	Corps	Divisions (Brigades)
50th Colonel General Boldin (replaced by Lieutennt General Ozerov) Major General Garnich	69th Rifle 81st Rifle Army reserve	110th, 153rd rifle divisions 307th, 324th rifle divisions 343rd Rifle Division, 91st, 153rd, 161st fortified areas, 2nd, 191st rifle divisions
49th Lieutenant General Grishin Major General Kinosyan	124th Rifle 70th Rifle 121st Rifle	51st, 208th, 216th rifle divisions 139th, 238th, 385th rifle divisions 42nd, 199th, 380th rifle divisions
3rd Colonel General Gorbatov Lieutenant General Ivashechkin	40th Rifle 41st Rifle 35th Rifle 3rd Guards Cavalry	5th, 129th, 169th rifle divisions 120th Guards, 26th, 283rd rife divisions 250th, 290th, 348th rifle divisions 5th, 6th guards, 32nd cavalry divisions
48th Colonel General Gusev Lieutenant General Glebov	29th Rifle 53rd Rifle 42nd Rifle Army Reserve	73rd, 217th rifle divisions 17th, 96th, 194th rifle divisions 137th, 170th, 399th rifle divisions 102nd Rifle Division
2nd Shock Colonel General Fedyuninskii Lieutenant General Kokorev	108th Rifle 98th Rifle 116th Rifle	46th, 90th, 372nd rifle divisions 142nd, 81st, 381st rifle divisions 86th, 321st, 326th rifle divisions
65th Colonel General Batov Lieutenant General Bobkov	18th Rifle 46th Rifle 105th Rifle	37th Guards, 15th, 69th rifle divisions 108th, 186th, 413th rifle divisions 44th Guards, 193rd, 354th rifle divisions
70th Colonel General Popov Lieutenant General Lyapin	96th Rifle 47th Rifle 114th Rifle	38th Guards, 1st, 165th rifle divisions 71st, 136th, 162nd rifle divisions 76th Guards, 160th, 200th rifle divisions
Front Reserve		330th, 369th rifle divisions
5th Guards Tank Coloenl General of Tank Troops Vol'skii Major General of Tank Troops Sidorovich	10th Tank 29th Tank	47th Independent Mechanized Brigade, 1st Guards Motorcycle Regiment
4th Air Colonel General Vershinin Major General Alekseev	4th Assault Air 5th Bomber 8th Fighter independent air divisions	196th, 199th assault air divisions 132nd, 327th bomber divisions 269th, 323rd fighter divisions 32nd Assault Air Division, 215th, 323rd fighter divisions, 230th, 233rd, 260th assault air divisions, 229th, 309th fighter divisions, 325th Night Bomber Division, 164th Independent Reconnaissance Regiment

	Reinforcements		
Army	Artillery and Mortar Units and Formations	Armored and Mechanized Formations and Units	Engineering Formations and Units
50th	144th Artillery Bde, 27th Anti-Tank Artillery Bde, 1321st Anti-Tank Artillery Rgt, 181st Mortar Rgt, 1484th Anti-Aircraft Artillery Rgt	1444th Self-Propelled Artillery Rgt	50th Engineer-Sapper Bde, 8th Independent Heavy Exploitation Battalion (33rd Assault Engineer Bde
49th	143rd Artillery Rgt, 4th Anti-Tank Artillery Bde, 593rd Anti-Tank Artillery Rgt, 540th Independent Mortar Rgt, 1273rd Anti-Aircraft Artillery Rgt, 544th Independent Mortar Rgt, 43rd Anti-Aircraft Artillery Div	7th Guards Tank Rgt, 1819th Self-Propelled Artillery Rgt	11th Engineer-Sapper Bde, 48th, 122nd independent bridge-pontoon bns
3rd	44th Artillery Bde, 2nd Artillery Breakthrough Div, 2nd Corps Artillery Bde, 19th Mortar Bde, 44th Anti-Tank Artillery Bde, 584th Independent Anti-Tank Artillery Rgt, 475th Independent Mortar Rgt, 81st, 56th howitzer rgts, 517th Corps Artillery Rgt, 100th, 77th, 313th guards mortar rgts, 1284th Anti-Aircraft Artillery Rgt, 28th Anti-Aircraft Artillery Div Aside from this, the following were brought in from the 49th Army for the artillery preparation: five rifle division artillery rgts, 143rd Artillery Bde, 540th, 544th independent mortar rgts	66th Guards Heavy Tank Rgt, 260th Independent Tank Rgt, 1812th, 1888th, 1901st, 1294th self-propelled artillery rgts, 340th Guards Heavy Self-Propelled Artillery Rgt	10th Engineer-Sapper Bde, 41st Motorized Engineer Bde, 33rd Independent Exploitation Bn, 179th Independent Bridge Construction Co
48th	68th Artillery Bde, 15th Breakthrough Artillery Div (minus one battalion from the 106th Heavy Artillery Bde), 5th, 13th anti-tank artillery bdes, 31st Guards Mortar Bde, 479th Independent Mortar Rgt, 461st Anti-Aircraft Artillery Rgt, 220th Guards Anti-Tank Artillery Rgt, 41st Guards Corps Artillery Rgt, 16th Guards Howitzer Rgt, 557th Corps Artillery Rgt, 6th, 84th guards mortar rgts, 286th Mortar Rgt, 65th Anti-Aircraft Artillery Rgt	8th Mechanized Corps, 23rd Guards Tank Bde, 29th Guards Tank Bde, 342nd Guards Self-Propelled GuardsTank Heavy Artillery Rgt, 1902nd, 1199th, 881st self-propelled artillery rgts	57th Engineer-Sapper Bde, 1st Guards Assault Engineer-Sapper Bde, 34th Independent Flamethrower Company
2nd Shock	81st Artillery Bde, 8th Breakthrough Artillery Corps (23rd, 1st artillery divs) 4th, 7th guards mortar bdes, 138th, 1099th corps artillery rgts, 89th 43rd guards mortar regiments, 47th Anti-Aircraft Artillery Div, 760th Independent Anti-Tank Artillery Rgt, 230th Guards Mortar Rgt, 803rd Anti-Aircraft Artillery Rgt	8th Guards Tank Corps, 30th Guards Heavy Tank Bde, 46th Guards Heavy Tank Rgt, 1196th, 1294th, 1476th, 1434th self-propelled artillery rgts	21st Engineer-Sapper Bde, 3rd Assault Engineer-Sapper Bde

Reinforcements

Army	Artillery and Mortar Units and Formations	Armored and Mechanized Formations and Units	Engineering Formations and Units
65th	147th Artillery Bde, 3rd Breakthrough Artillery Corps (26th, 18th artillery divs), 1st Anti-Tank Artillery Bde, 5th Guards Mortar Bde, 143rd Guards Mortar Rgt 543rd Anti-Tank Artillery Rgt, 235th Anti-Aircraft Rgt, 49th Howitzer Rgt, 85th Guards Howitzer Rgt, 18th, 62nd guards mortar rgts, 12th Anti-Aircraft Div	1st Guards Tank Corps, 80th Guards Tank Rgt, 251st Independent Tank Rgt, 510th Independent Tank Flamethrower Rgt 40th Independent Engineer Tank Rgt, 985th, 922nd, 1495th, 999th self-propelled artillery rgts	14th Engineer-Sapper Bde, 1st Assault Engineer-Sapper Bde, 36th Independent Flamethrower Co
70th	148th Artillery Bde, 378th Anti-Tank Artillery Rgt, 136th Guards Mortar Rgt, 581st Anti-Aircraft Artillery Rgt 317th Heavy Caliber Bn, 325th Guards Mortar Rgt, 74th Anti-Aircraft Div (expected from the Leningrad Front)	1898th, 1890th self-propelled artillery rgts, 85th, 133rd, 259th independent self-propelled artillery bns	48th Engineer-Sapper Bde, 7th Pontoon-Bridge Rgt, 9th, 87th, 42nd, 89th independent motorized pontoon-bridge bns
Front Reserve	13th Guards Mortar Bde, 15th, 19th anti-tank artillery bdes, 1268th, 1270th, 1479th, 341st, 1709th, 1482nd, 225th, 739th independent anti-aircraft artillery rgts, 21st, 14th, 490th, 614th, 451st, 508th independent anti-aircraft bns (High Command Reserve)	3rd Guards Tank Corps, 233rd Independent Tank Rgt, 1023rd Self-Propelled Artillery Rgt	36th, 104th motorized pontoon-bridge bns, 8th Independent Exploitation Tank Bn, 49th Independent Exploitation Tank Co, 141st Independent Motorized Signals Co, 4th Pontoon-Bridge Bde, 5th Pontoon-Bridge Rgt, 72nd Guards Motorized-Engineer Bn, 33rd Motorized Engineer-Minesweeper Bridge Bde, 77th Independent Bridge Construction Bn, 3rd Independent Flamethrower Co, 11th Independent Engineer-Minesweeper Rgt
5th Guards Tank	201st Light Artillery Bde, 689th Independent Anti-Tank Artillery Rgt, 6th Anti-Tank Artillery Rgt	14th Guards Independent Tank Regiment, 376th Guards	21st Motorized Engineer Bde
4th Air		Heavy Self-Propelled Artillery Rgt	

Annex 3

Effective Strength of the Second Belorussian Front (15 January 1945)

Army	Divisions	Men	Light and Heavy Machine Guns	82mm and 120mm Mortars
50th	9	76,900	3,696	784
49th	8	62,600	2,279	555
3rd*	10	91,500	3,084	915
48th	9	81,800	3,751	925
2nd Shock	9	101,500	3,404	933
65th	9	87,100	2,243	673
70th	9	65,200	2,424	587
5th Guards Tank	–	35,600	421	171
Units and Formations Subordinated to the *Front*	–	82,700	1,787	524
TOTAL	63	684,900	23,089	6,067

* Note. The 42nd Rifle Division was operationally subordinated to the 3rd Army and is included in that army's total.

	Guns						
	122mm, 152mm, 203mm	76mm Divisional	76mm Regimental	Self-Propelled	Total Guns	Total Tubes	Tanks
50th	133	514	100	25	772	1,556	–
49th	134	289	93	33	549	1,104	20
3rd	431	410	114	106	1,061	1,976	53
48th	374	464	53	83	974	1,899	127
2nd Shock	481	389	107	83	1,060	1,993	96
65th	450	499	106	84	1,139	1,812	71
70th	147	243	87	83	560	1,147	–
5th Guards Tank	–	129	43	240	412	583	345
Units and Formations Subordinated to the *Front*	26	163	151	259	599	1,123	481
TOTAL	2,176	3,100	854	996	7,126	13,193	1,193

Annex 4

Artillery Distribution in the Armies Along the Second Belorussian Front's Shock Axes

| | Army Artillery Groups | | |
Army	Long-Range Artillery	Destruction Artillery	Guards Mortar Units
3rd Army	41st Rifle Corps subgroup-44th, 143rd artillery bdes (from the 49th Army), 2nd Corps Artillery Bde, 81st Howitzer Rgt, 517th Corps Artillery Rgt 35th Rifle Corps subgroup—16th Guards Artillery Bde, 48th Guards Heavy Howitzer Bde, 121st Howitzer Bde, (all units from the 2nd Artillery Div)		3rd, 100th guards mortar rgts, 77th Guards Mortar Rgt, (from 49th Army), 313th Guards Mortar Rgt
48th	29th Rifle Corps subgroup—557th Corps Artillery Rgt 53rd Rifle Corps subgroup—68th Artillery Bde 42nd Rifle Corps subgroup—31st Guards Howitzer Rgt from 15th Artillery Div), 41st Guards Corps Artillery Rgt	106th Heavy Howitzer Bde (from 15th Artillery Div)	31st Guards Mortar Bde, 6th, 84th guards mortar rgts
2nd Shock	108th Rifle Corps subgroup—87th Artillery Bde, 138th Corps Artillery Rgt 98th Rifle Corps subgroup—1099th Corps Artillery Rgt, and from the 1st Artillery Div—156th Heavy Howitzer Bde, 421st Howitzer Rgt (167th Howitzer Bde), 754th Howitzer Rgt (from 38th Howitzer Bde)	from 23rd Artillery Div—3rd, 96th heavy howitzer bdes, 21st Guards Heavy Howitzer Bde; from 1st Artillery Div—112th Heavy Howitzer Bde, 9th Mortar Bde	13th Mortar Bde (1st Artillery Div), 4th Guards Mortar Div, 43rd, 89th mortar rgts
65th	46th Rifle Corps subgroup—147th Artillery Bde, 2nd Heavy Howitzer Bde (18th Artillery Div) 105th Rifle Corps subgroup—56th Artillery Bde (26th Artillery Div), 80th Heavy Howitzer Bde (18th	120th Heavy Howitzer Bde 18th Artillery Div)	5th Guards Mortar Bde, 18th, 62nd guards mortar rgts
70th	148th Artillery Bde, 154th Artillery Rgt (76th Guards Rifle Div), 378th Anti-Tank Artillery Rgt	317th Heavy Caliber Artillery Bn	–

		Army Artillery Groups	
Army	Anti-Tank Guns	Anti-Aircraft Artillery	Artillery Reinforcement for the Rifle Corps
3rd	–	28th Anti-Aircraft Div, 1284th Artillery Rgt (National Air Defense)	41st Rifle Corps—19th Mortar Bde, 56th Guards Howitzer Rgt, 475th Mortar Rgt, 44th Anti-Tank Artillery Bde, 584th Anti-Tank Artillery Rgt; from the 49th Army—3rd, 4th, 500th, 693rd, 945th, 948th artillery rgts, 540th, 544th mortar rgts 35th Rifle Corps—(from the 2nd Artillery Div)— 20th Light Artillery Bade, 10th Guards Howitzer Bde, 5th Mortar Brigade, two artillery rgts from the 40th Rifle Corps' divisions
48th	5th, 13th anti-tank artillery bdes, 220th Guards Anti-Tank Artillery Rgt	65th Anti-Aircraft Div, 461st Artillery Rgt (National Air Defense)	53rd Rifle Corps—206th Light Artillery Bde (15th Artillery Div), 85th Heavy Howitzer Bde (15th Artillery Div), 479th Mortar Rgt; 42nd Rifle Corps—35th Howitzer Bde (15th Artillery Div), 16th Guards Howitzer Rgt, 18th Mortar Bde (15th Artillery Div), 286th Mortar Rgt
2nd Shock	79th Artillery Bde (23rd Artillery Div)	47th Anti-Aircraft Div, 803rd Artillery Rgt (National Air Defense)	108th Rifle Corps—38th Howitzer Bde, 23rd Artillery Div (minus 754th Howitzer Rgt), 248th, 888th artillery rgts (116th Rifle Corps), 28th Mortar Bde (23rd Artillery Div), 760th Anti-Tank Artillery Rgt, 230th Guards Mortar Rgt; 98th Rifle Corps—166th Light Artillery Bde (1st Artillery Div), 167th Howitzer Bde (1st Artillery Div, minus 421st Howitzer Rgt), 986th Artillery Rgt (116th Rifle Corps), 41st Mortar Bde (1st Artillery Div)
65th	1st Anti-Tank Artillery Bde	12th Anti-Aircraft Artillery Div, 235th Artillery Rgt (National Air Defense)	46th Rifle Corps—from the 18th Artillery Div 65th Light Artillery Bde, 58th Howitzer Bde, 42nd Mortar Bde 105th Rifle Corps—75th Light Artillery Bde (26th Artillery Div), 77th Howitzer Bde (26th Artillery Div), 85th Guards, 49th howitzer rgts, 143rd Guards Mortar Rgt, 543rd Anti-Tank Artillery Rgt
70th	–	581st Artillery Rgt (National Air Defense)	96th Rifle Corps—two artillery rgts from the 47th Rifle Corps, two artillery rgts from the 114th Rifle Corps, 136th Guards Mortar Rgt, 325th Guards Mortar Rgt

Annex 5

The Correlation of Forces Along the Breakthrough Sectors of the Second Belorussian Front's Shock Groups (14 January 1945)

Men and Materiel		3rd Army (6 km)			48th Army (6 km)		
		Soviet	Enemy	Correlation	Soviet	Enemy	Correlation
Divisions	Total	6	1	6:1	6	1	6:1
Men	Total	38,900	7,300	5:1	37,700	6,800	6:1
	per km	6,500	1,200	5:1	6,300	1,100	6:1
Light and Heavy Machine guns	Total	1,665	580	3:1	1,452	600	3:1
	per km	277	97	3:1	242	84	3:1
Mortars (82mm and 120mm)	Total	735	99	7:1	591	77	8:1
	per km	123	17	7:1	99	13	8:1
Guns (75mm and higher)	Total	1,052	133	8:1	731	125	6:1
	per km	175	22	8:1	122	21	6:1
Total tubes	Total	1,787	232	8:1	1,322	202	7:1
	per km	298	39	8:1	220	34	7:1
Tanks and Self-Propelled Guns	Total	131	24	6:1	150	12	3:1
	per km	22	4	6:1	25	2	3:1
Aircraft	Total	–	–	–	–	–	–

Men and Materiel		2nd Shock Army (6 km)			65th Army (7 km)		
Divisions	Total	6	1	6:1	6	1	6:1
Men	Total	43,400	7,000	6:1	37,900	8,000	5:1
	per km	7,200	1,200	6:1	5,400	1,100	5:1
Light and Heavy Machine guns	Total	2,007	491	4:1	1,293	408	3:1
	per km	335	82	4:1	185	58	3:1
Mortars (82mm and 120mm)	Total	715	77	9:1	486	68	7:1
	per km	119	13	9:1	69	10	7:1
Guns (75mm and higher)	Total	945	125	8:1	891	175	5:1
	per km	158	21	8:1	127	25	5:1
Total tubes	Total	1,660	202	8:1	1,377	243	6:1
	per km	276	34	8:1	196	35	6:1
Tanks and Self-Propelled Guns	Total	170	12	14:1	109	12	9:1
	per km	24	2	14:1	16	1.7	9:1
Aircraft	Total	–	–	–	–	–	–

Men and Materiel		70th Army (3 km)			Total Along Breakthrough Sectors (28 km)		
Divisions	Total	2	1/3	6:1	26	4 1/3	6:1
Men	Total	12,100	2,500	5:1	170,000	31,600	5:1
	per km	4,000	800	5:1	6,100	1,100	5:1
Light and Heavy Machine guns	Total	473	132	4:1	6,890	2,113	3:1
	per km	158	44	4:1	246	75	3:1
Mortars (82mm and 120mm)	Total	144	23	6:1	2,671	344	8:1
	per km	48	8	6:1	95	12	8:1
Guns (75mm and higher)	Total	392	57	7:1	4,011	615	7:1
	per km	131	19	7:1	143	22	7:1
Total tubes	Total	536	80	7:1	6,682	959	7:1
	per km	179	27	7:1	238	34	7:1
Tanks and Self-Propelled Guns	Total	68	12	6:1	631	72	9:1
	per km	23	4	6:1	23	2.5	9:1
Aircraft	Total	–	–	–	1,647	350	5:1

Notes:
1) In calculating the correlation of forces and densities for ourselves and the enemy, only first-echelon corps occupying the breakthrough zones, were counted, as well as the artillery and tanks supporting them.
2) The tank army, tank and mechanized corps, as well as the cavalry corps, were not included in this total.
3) The figures for the 3rd Army included artillery transferred to it from the 49th Army for the artillery preparation and breakthrough.

Part IV

The Second Belorussian Front's Combat Operations in the East Pomeranian Offensive Operation (February-March 1945)

Introduction

Among the Soviet army's operations of 1945 the Second and First Belorussian fronts' East Pomeranian operation occupies a prominent place.

Carried out according to the plan and under the leadership of the *Stavka* of the Supreme High Command, the operation concluded in the defeat of a major German group of forces along the Soviet forces' right strategic wing, as well as the clearing of the Germans from East Pomerania and the entire southern shore of the Baltic Sea as far as the mouth of the Oder. As a result of the defeat of the Germans' East Pomeranian group of forces, the threat of a flank attack against the Soviet forces operating along the Berlin direction was eliminated and favorable conditions for carrying out the Berlin operation were thereby created.

The East Pomeranian operation was conducted in the period between two major stages of the 1945 campaign: the January offensive by Soviet forces, which concluded with the encirclement of the Germans' East Prussian group of forces, the defeat of the German forces in Poland, and the arrival of the First Belorussian and First Ukrainian fronts' forces at the Oder, and the Second and First Belorussian and First Ukrainian fronts' Berlin operation.

The East Pomeranian operation was conducted under conditions of a distinct and complex situation.

In the first days of February 1945 there arose a gap of about 150 kilometers in length between the armies of the First Belorussian Front, which had arrived at the Oder, and the forces of the Second Belorussian Front, the main forces of which were fighting in East Prussia and had been turned facing north, where the forces of the First Belorussian Front's 3rd Shock Army were defending along a broad front.

By this time the Germans were concentrating a major group of forces in East Prussia for launching an attack against the First Belorussian Front's flank.

The overall military-political situation dictated the necessity of an all-round acceleration of the preparation for a final attack by Soviet forces along the Berlin direction. In these conditions the task of securely guarding the right wing of our forces' main group, which was designated to launch an attack along the Berlin direction, acquired particular importance. It was necessary to defeat the enemy's East Pomeranian group of forces and eliminate his encircled East Prussian group of forces and thus foil the German high command's intentions to interfere with our attack along the Berlin direction.

In order to resolve this task, the Supreme High Command, having transferred the Second Belorussian Front's right-wing forces to the Third Belorussian Front,[1] entrusted the task of destroying the Germans' East Prussian group of forces to the Third Belorussian Front. The Second Belorussian Front's forces were ordered to defeat the Germans' East Pomeranian group of forces, capture the Danzig and Gdynia area and clear the enemy from the shore of the Baltic Sea as far as the Bay of Pomerania (directives of the *Stavka* of the Supreme High Command No. 11021, of 8 February, and No. 11022 of 9 February 1945).

---

1 The Second Belorussian Front's 50th, 3rd and 48th armies and the 5th Guards Tank Army had been transferred to the Third Belorussian Front.

In accordance with the instructions of the *Stavka* of the Supreme High Command, the Second Belorussian Front's offensive in East Pomerania began on 10 February. However, because the *front's* forces had been attacking for a month before this time and had been weakened, the offensive that they began without a pause, in the difficult conditions of the lake and wooded terrain of East Pomerania, developed slowly.

As a result of the Second Belorussian Front's insignificant rate of attack in the first half of February, the High Command, proceeding from a consideration of the necessity of defeating the Germans in East Pomerania as soon as possible, decided to bring in the forces of the First Belorussian Front to carry out this task.

According to the new instructions by the *Stavka* of the Supreme High Command, the commander of the Second Belorussian Front was to organize an attack along the *front's* left wing on Koslin, using for this purpose the 19th Army, which had arrive from the *Stavka* reserve (directive of the *Stavka* of the Supreme High Command, No. 11026, 17 February, 1945). The offensive by the Second Belorussian Front's forces had the objective of, in conjunction with the forces of the First Belorussian Front, cutting off the main forces of the Germans' East Pomeranian group of forces and, having defeated it, to clear the enemy from the territory of East Pomerania to the east of the Koslin—Neustettin meridian and reach the shore of the Baltic Sea between Danzig and Kolberg.

The First Belorussian Front was to prepare an offensive operation along its right wing for the purpose of defeating, in conjunction with the Second Belorussian Front, the Germans' East Pomeranian group of forces and to clear the enemy from the eastern bank of the Oder as far as its mouth. During this period the Germans undertook fierce attempts to break through the defensive front of the First Belorussian Front's right-wing forces and sought to get into the rear of the group of Soviet forces operating along the Berlin direction. The forces of the *front's* shock group were to exhaust and bleed white the Germans' forces in defensive fighting, after which they were to launch an attack in the direction of Kolberg.

Thus the overall idea of the *Stavka* of the Supreme High Command's plan lay in cutting off the Germans' East Pomeranian group of forces from the German army's remaining forces, and to simultaneously split it up into isolated groups through a series of attacks and to destroy them.

The successful offensive by the troops of the Second Belorussian Front's left wing, which began on 24 February, joined in on 1 March with the attack by the First Belorussian Front's right wing. By 5 March both *fronts'* forces had reached the shore of the Baltic Sea in the Kolberg area and to the north of Koslin. As a result of these attacks, the main forces of the Germans' East Pomeranian group of forces were cut off from the German army's main forces and throughout March were defeated by the forces of the Second Belorussian Front. By the end of the first ten days of March the forces of the First Belorussian Front had cleared the eastern bank of the Oder of Germans and had immediately begun regrouping its forces for a new offensive operation along the Berlin direction.

This article primarily illuminates in this operation the military operations of the Second Belorussian Front, which following the cutting off of the main forces of the Germans' Pomeranian group of forces to the east of the Neustettin—Koslin line, independently resolved the task of defeating this group of forces and capturing the ports of Danzig and Gdynia along the Baltic Sea.

The activities of the First Belorussian Front's forces in the operation are illuminated only in general outline, enabling the reader to understand the operation's overall design as a whole and its final results.

The Second Belorussian Front's combat activities in the East Pomeranian offensive operation was be divided into four stages:

First Stage—the arrival of the *front's* forces at the line Mewe—Skurtz—Czersk—Chojnice—Preuss Friedland (10-19 February 1945);

Second Stage—an attack toward Koslin and the arrival of the *front's* left-wing forces at the Baltic Sea (24 February-5 March 1945);

Third Stage—a turn by the *front's* left-wing forces to the northeast and east and their arrival at the enemy's Danzig—Gdynia fortified area (6-13 March 1945);

Fourth Stage—the fighting along the approaches to Danzig and Gdynia and the storming of these towns (14-30 March 1945).

A Military-Geographical Description of the Area of Combat Operations and the Germans' Defensive Structures

The area of combat operations embraces East Pomerania in the following boundaries: in the north, the shore of the Baltic Sea from Bosniak at the mouth of the Vistula River, as far as the Diwenow Strait; in the east as far as the Vistula River from Bosniak to Bydgoszcz (Bromberg); in the south, the Bydgoszcz Canal and the Netze and Warta rivers as far as Küstrin, and; in the west the Oder River.

The Second Belorussian Front's area of combat operations included the eastern part of Pomerania to the east of the line Kolberg—Polzyn—Schneidemühl as far as the port of Danzig and the Vistula River.

The overall size of the area is 22,500 square kilometers.

A Description of the Area's Surface

The area under study is a hilly plain, covered 30-35 percent by coniferous and leafy woods.

The area is bordered from the south to the shore of the Baltic Sea by the area of the Baltic uplands, consisting of a large number of small hills and ridges, covered by boulders, sands and loamy soil.

The area of the Baltic uplands is distinguished by the Kaszub uplands, which stretch from the towns of Danzig and Gdynia to the west as far as the Stolp River, and the Pomeranian uplands, which stretch from the line of the Stolp River southwest to the Oder River.

The Kaszub uplands are the highest and most broken part of the entire zone of the Baltic uplands. The predominant absolute heights are 100-200 meters. The highest point in this area is Mount Tumberg, 331 meters above sea level. The area's relief is hilly; the relative height of the hilly ridges is 50-70 meters. The steepness of the slopes is 15-20 degrees and more. Between the hills is a multiplicity of lakes, predominantly of elongated form, with narrow defiles between the lakes. In a number of places chains of lakes stretching from north to south in several rows form a series of natural obstacles.

The Pomeranian uplands are a hilly plain, stretching 200 kilometers in length toward the southwest from the Kaszub uplands. The dominant heights are 150-200 meters.

The Pomeranian uplands are less broken and are distinguished by a softer relief, although the presence of a large number of lakes with narrow defiles between them impedes the maneuver by tank and mechanized forces.

The soils of the area of the eastern part of Pomerania along the coast are sandy and of clay in the middle and southern parts of the area. The presence of clay soil in the greater part of the area makes movement off the roads difficult in the spring and fall.

The Area's Hydrography

There are a large number of rivers and lakes in East Pomerania. The Vistula River flows along the area's eastern boundary. The Vistula River is navigable by ships along its entire course within the area's boundaries. The river's width along various sectors reaches 1,500-1,800 meters, while its depth varies from 1.5-6 meters, and there are no fords. The speed of the current is 0.5-1.5 meters per second.

The Vistula River is a powerful water line covering East Pomerania from the east.

Along the area's southern boundary, as if covering the approach to East Prussia from the south, are the Netze and Warta rivers, connected with the Vistula River by the Bydgoszcz Canal. The canal is 40 kilometers long, 15-20 meters wide and 1.5-3 meters deep.

The Netze River is 320 kilometers long, 20-50 meters wide, 1-3 meters deep, and has a speed of 0.5-0.7 meters per second. The Netze River has a broad flood plain, which in some sectors reaches 12-15 kilometers. This creates certain difficulties in overcoming it.

Along the sector from Santok to Küstrin, along the southern part of the area, flows the Warta River on its lower course. The width of the Warta River in this area is about 100 meters.

The Oder River flows along the area's western boundary.

The following major rivers, which flow into the Baltic Sea, in the northern part of East Pomerania are the Stolp, Wipper, Persante, and Rega rivers.

All the rivers, both in the north and the southern parts of East Pomerania, are not major water barriers and may be overcome at any time of the year by forces without special training. The exception is the February-March period, during the spring runoff, when the water rises 1-1.5 meters above its usual level.

To the north, East Pomerania is washed by the waters of the Baltic Sea. Along the entire territory of East Pomerania are a large number of large and small lakes. The southwestern part of East Pomerania is particularly rich in lakes. Up to 250 small and large lakes are scattered to the southwest of the line Schneidemühl—Polzyn.

There are also a significant number of lakes to the northeast of the line Schneidemühl—Polzyn.

Lakes, rivers and the canals connecting them restrict troop movements during an offensive and favor the creation of a solid defense.

Communications Lines

East Pomerania has a broadly developed road network.

The railroads are primarily two-tracked. The overall railroad density is sufficiently high and reaches 10.5 kilometers per 100 square kilometers of territory. The average density of the paved and dirt roads in the area is 30.5 kilometers per 100 square miles.

The majority of paved roads have a gravel and tar surface. The surface of all country and improved roads is covered by stones or bricks.

The Chojnice—Stettin highway passes through the area, with branches to Küstrin.

The main water arteries in the area are the Vistula, Netze, Warta, Oder and Brae rivers, and the Bydgoszcz Canal.

Seaports

From the north the shores of the eastern Pomeranian area are washed by the Baltic Sea for a distance of 250 kilometers. Here are located major seaports, which were bases for the Germans' surface and submarine fleets.

The port of Danzig was well outfitted as a commercial port and was of international significance. The port of Gdynia had been transformed into a major naval base for the German navy, where submarines and surfaces ships of all classes were based and repaired.

Besides this, there were a number of small ports along the coast of the Baltic Sea: Stolpmünde, Rugenwaldermunde and Kolberg. These ports were the best places for making naval landings.

Communications

The territory of East Pomerania was fitted out with a sufficiently dense communications network. All towns and the overwhelming majority of inhabited locales in rural areas were linked by a telephone-telegraph network, which made its easier to organize communications and troop control.

The presence of a network of underground communications lines and a large number of bypass lines, despite the Germans having destroyed a certain amount of them while retreating, enabled us to guarantee the Second Belorussian Front's attacking forces with reliable communications.

Climatic Conditions

East Pomerania has a moderate climate. The valley of the Oder River has the nicest climate.

Climatic conditions allow for operations by all the combat arms at any time of year, while somewhat restricting their maneuver during the spring.

Meteorological conditions during the period of the Second Belorussian Front's combat operations (February-March) were characterized by increased cyclonic activity. Masses of warm and moist sea air brought about increased winds, which led to sharp changes and unreliable weather. During February and March the weather in the *front's* area of combat operations was predominantly cloudy, with rain and fog.

The air temperature in February was from 0 to +3 degrees Celsius, and in March the temperature was from +7 to +10 degrees.

The weather was unfavorable for air operations during this period, as a result of the low cloud cover and fogs. There were only six (22-27 March) days of clear weather with good visibility, although even during this period visibility decreased in the mornings due to the fogs and smoke.

The onset of warmer weather and the large amount of precipitation made the operations of the ground forces more difficult and limited their maneuver. Due to the saturation of the soil, the troops' movement off the roads was almost impossible.

The Enemy's Defensive Structures

The Germans in East Pomerania had the so-called "Pomeranian fortress line" (the "Pomeranian wall"), which had been built in 1933 along the former Polish-German state boundary, facing east and southeast.

The Pomeranian fortifications ran along the line Stolp—Rummelsburg—Neustettin—Schneidemühl. The left flank of these fortifications was secured by the shore fortifications in the Stolpmünde area, while the right flank bordered on the fortifications along the Warta and Oder rivers.

The basis of the Pomeranian fortifications consisted of permanent fortification structures (reinforced concrete pillboxes, reinforced concrete caponiers and semi-caponiers), built to house garrisons ranging from a platoon to a company in strength. These permanent structures had been reinforced by field defensive fortifications. Field fortifications and the approaches to the permanent fortifications were covered by a developed network of anti-tank and anti-personnel obstacles. The towns of Stolp, Rummelsburg, Neustettin, Schneidemühl and Deutsch Krone were nodal strong points in the system of Pomeranian fortifications, around which there was a large number of permanent firing points, field structures, anti-tank and anti-personnel obstacles.

Along the shore, in the area of Danzig and Gdynia and the Putziger Nehrung spit in the Hel area, the Germans had shore fortified areas, and in the Leba, Stolpmünde, Rugenwaldemunde and Kolberg areas there were outfitted artillery positions for heavy shore artillery.

Besides this, the German defensive system in East Pomerania included the Gdynia and Danzig defensive areas, which had been built facing southwest.

The Danzig defensive area consisted of two defensive zones, outfitted with field engineer structures (trenches, open machine gun emplacements, and wood and earthen pillboxes).

The first defensive zone was 3-5 kilometers deep and its forward edge ran along the line Burgerwiesen—Ora—Praust—Unter Kalbude—excluding Zuchau—Oliwa and consisted of five lines of trenches.

The second defensive zone was outfitted 5-7 kilometers from the city of Danzig and its flanks rested on the shore of the bay. This zone consisted of three defensive positions. The first position, which ran along the line Straszin—Bankau—height 160—Glettkau, had 2-4 trench lines with an overall depth of 1.5-2.5 kilometers. The second position ran along the Ora—Emaus—Hochstriess—Bresen line and consisted of two lines of trenches. The third position was outfitted immediately along the city's outskirts.

The city of Danzig was covered from the southeast by terrain inaccessible to tanks and a canal, as well as a system of old forts.

The city of Danzig itself had been prepared for defense. Almost all the major stone buildings had been configured for waging battle. Embrasures had been built in the walls for firing; window and door openings had been built up with sandbags. Buildings and blocks were connected with each other by communications trenches and trenches. Barricades had been constructed on the streets and wooden and earthen pillboxes had been built along the intersections. Remote-controlled mines had been laid in buildings and on central streets.

The Gdynia defensive area consisted of two defensive zones. In organizing this defensive area, the Germans employed the available permanent structures, the artillery positions and observation posts that had been outfitted earlier, and had supplemented them with a system of trenches and obstacles, which enabled them to quickly gird the town of Gdynia with a solid ring of defensive structures in a radius of from 12-15 kilometers.

The first defensive zone, the forward edge of which ran along the line Zoppot—Kwaszyn—Kollecktzau—Reda—Rewa, consisted of two defensive positions, having five lines of trenches with an overall depth of 3-5 kilometers.

The second defensive zone was outfitted at a distance of 5-7 kilometers from the town of Gdynia, with its forward edge along the line Klein Katz—Weltzendorf—Janowo and had three lines of trenches, 4-5 reinforced concrete and wooden and earth pillboxes per kilometer of front. The town of Gdynia had also been well configured for defense and street fighting.

In case of a forced withdrawal from the Gdynia area to the north, the Germans had prepared a defensive area along the so-called Ochsheft bridgehead. The forward defense line on this bridgehead ran along the heights along the line Ochsheft, Oblusz, and Kazimierz.

In order to secure the boundary between the Danzig and Gdynia defensive areas, the Germans had built a defensive position along the line Zuchau—Echsau—Kable—Warschnau—Kelln—Kolletzkau, with a major strong point in the area of height 221. This defensive position had three broken trenches. Trenches had been built at a distance of 4-5 kilometers from this position: two along the line Ramkau—Tuchom—Kwaszyn; one trench along the line Bernewitz—Wittstock. A minefield had been laid along this trench.

In the Danzig and Gdynia areas the enemy had prepared anti-tank ditches, barriers, and barricades and reinforced steel beam posts. Near the anti-tank obstacles the Germans outfitted trenches for tank destroyers armed with *faustpatrones*.

During the January fighting and the retreat from Poland, the Germans built a defensive line along the left bank of the Vistula River and from its mouth to the city of Bydgoszcz, facing east, and then further along the Netze and Warta rivers as far as the Oder River, facing south. This defensive line was 3-5 kilometers deep and had from 2-5 lines of trenches, anti-tank and anti-personnel obstacles, and wooden and earth pillboxes on some sectors.

The Overall Situation along the Right Wing of the Soviet-German Front by the Beginning of February, 1945

At the beginning of February 1945 the forces of the Soviet army were continuing the offensive operations begun in the first half of January.

By this time the forces of the Third Belorussian Front were continuing to destroy the Germans' East Prussian group of forces (Fourth Army), which had been pressed to the Baltic Sea in the area of the fortress of Königsberg and to the southwest.

The forces of the Second Belorussian Front, following the encirclement of the Germans' East Prussian group of forces by land and the seizure of a bridgehead on the western bank of the Vistula River north of Bydgoszcz by its left-wing armies (65th and 70th armies), were waging offensive battles to expand the captured bridgehead.

The forces of the First Belorussian Front, while continuing the offensive begun on 14 January from the line of the Vistula River, were by this time fighting with their right-wing formations in the southern part of East Pomerania, while its center and left-wing formations were engaged in fierce battles to widen their captured bridgeheads on the western bank of the Oder River in the area north and south of Küstrin.

The enemy, having suffered a defeat in the January battles on the Vistula and to the west of the river, was putting up stubborn resistance with his isolated Courland and East Prussian groups of forces and was holding on to East Pomerania. Taking advantage of the favorable terrain conditions for defense and strengthening their East Pomeranian group of forces, the German command was taking all measures in order to halt the further offensive by the forces of the Second Belorussian Front and the First Belorussian Front's right wing.

The German command had the goal of tying down the Soviet forces operating in Courland, East Prussia and East Pomerania and to prevent their reinforcing the Soviet forces operating along the Berlin direction. Besides this, it planned, having halted the forces of the Soviet army, which were attacking toward East Pomerania, and having exhausted them in defensive battles, to launch a flank attack from the Pomeranian bridgehead against the First Belorussian Front's forces attacking along the Berlin direction.[2]

For the purpose of creating a powerful shock group in East Pomerania, the German command in the beginning of February reinforced Army Group Vistula, transferring from its reserve the Eleventh Army, consisting of the XXXIX Panzer Corps and the III SS Panzer Corps (the army group command also transferred the II Army and X SS corps from the Ninth Army). The East Prussian group of forces transferred to Army Group Vistula the headquarters of the Third Panzer Army, to which the XI Army, VII Panzer and XVI SS corps, which were in the army group reserve, were subordinated. Besides this, the German high command planned to concentrate in East Pomerania the Sixth Panzer Army, which was being transferred at this time from the Western Front, but as a result of the deteriorating situation in the south of the Soviet-German front the Sixth Panzer Army was transferred to the Budapest area.

By 10 February 1945 the Germans had in East Pomerania Army Group Vistula's Second and Eleventh armies. The army group command had in its reserve the Third Panzer Army, which at this time occupied defensive positions along the left bank of the Oder River, from Stettin to Schwedt.

---

2   "… in February-March 1945 it was planned to carry out a counteroperation against the forces attacking toward Berlin, employing for this purpose the Pomeranian bridgehead. It was planned having covered ourselves from the Graudenz area, that the forces of Army Group Vistula would break through the Russian front and, having arrived in the valley of the Netze and Warta rivers from the rear, that they would reach Küstrin." From the interrogation of the former chief of the German general staff, Keitel.

Thus by the beginning of February 1945, due to the Germans' retention of East Pomerania and their concentration in Pomerania of a powerful shock group, there had arisen the threat of a flank attack against the forces of the First Belorussian Front, which by this time had arrived at the Oder River along the Berlin direction.

The Decision and Instructions by the *Stavka* of the Supreme High Command on Conducting the East Pomeranian Operation

In connection with the situation that had arisen along the right wing of the Soviet-German front, the *Stavka* of the Supreme High Command made the decision to conduct the East Pomeranian offensive operation.

The operation had the goal of cutting off the Germans' East Pomeranian group of forces from the remainder of the German army's forces, breaking up this group of forces into parts and, having destroyed it, to occupy East Pomerania and clear the shore of the Baltic Sea of the enemy from the Bay of Danzig to the Bay of Stettin. The destruction of the enemy group of forces and the occupation of East Pomerania would eliminate the threat of the Germans' flank attack against the forces of the First Belorussian Front and would create favorable conditions for the Soviet forces to carry out an offensive operation along the Berlin direction.

On 8 February 1945 the Supreme High Command, in its directive no. 11021, ordered the forces of the Second Belorussian Front "to attack to the west of the Vistula River with its center and left-wing forces on 10 February and no later than 20 February capture the line: mouth of the Vistula River—Dirschau—Berent—Rummelsburg—Neustettin." Later, upon the arrival of the 19th Army,[3] the *Stavka* ordered the *front* "to develop the offensive in the general direction of Stettin, to capture the area of Danzig and Gdynia, and to clear the shore of the enemy as far as the Bay of Pomerania."

Thus this directive assigned the forces of the Second Belorussian Front the task of capturing all of East Pomerania from the Vistula to the Oder.

THE SITUATION OF THE SIDES BY 10 FEBRUARY, 1945

Soviet Forces

On 9 February 1945 *Stavka* of the Supreme High Command directive no. 11022 ordered the commander of the Second Belorussian Front to transfer his right-flank 50th, 3rd and 48th armies, and the 5th Guards Tank Army, along with the sectors occupied by them, to the Third Belorussian Front. From that moment the following boundary line was established between the Second and Third Belorussian fronts: Neidenburg—Osterode—Freiwalde—Elbing (all locales except Elbing were for the Third Belorussian Front).

Five combined-arms armies (2nd Shock, 65th, 49th, 70th, and 19th) and one air army (4th) remained with the *front*. In all, the *front* disposed of 45 rifle divisions, grouped into 14 rifle corps headquarters. Besides this, the *front* disposed of three fortified areas (153rd, 161st and 91st). The 4th Air Army had three air corps.

The *front's* armored and mechanized forces consisted of three tank corps (1st, 3rd and 8th tank corps) and a mechanized corps (8th). Besides this, the *front's* mobile troops included the 3rd Guards Cavalry Corps.

---

3   On 1 February 1945 the 19th Army was transferred to the Second Belorussian Front from the *Stavka* reserve.

By 10 February the Second Belorussian Front's forces, while waging battles along a 204-kilometer front, occupied the following position.

The 2nd Shock Army, consisting of the 98th, 116th and 108th rifle corps, occupied defensive positions along the right bank of the Nogat and Vistula rivers along the front Elbing—Zachrau. Part of the army's forces was engaged in street fighting in Elbing. The 91st, 153rd and 161st fortified areas were arriving to the army.

The 65th Army, consisting of the 18th, 105th, 46th and 114th rifle corps, having captured a bridgehead on the left bank of the Vistula River, was involved in offensive fighting along the line excluding Zachrau—excluding Graudenz—Gross Schwenten—Gross Ceppelin—Jungen—excluding Kulm.

The 49th Army, consisting of the 70th and 121st rifle corps, relieved the forces of the 70th Army on the left bank of the Vistula River along the line Kulm—Grodek—Sziroslaw—Liano—excluding Trutnowo.

The 70th Army, consisting of the 96th and 47th rifle corps was waging offensive battles on the left bank of the Vistula River along the line Trutnowo—Lubiewo—Prust station—Bagnitz—Dzidzinek.

The 19th Army, which was released from the high command reserve on 1 February and which consisted of the 40th Guards, 132nd and 134th rifle corps, was concentrating in the Dobrzyn—Lipno—Rypin area.

The 3rd Guards Cavalry Corps had concentrated behind the 70th Army's left flank in the Lutschmin—Wiesenthal area.

The 1st Guards Tank and 8th Mechanized corps, which were operationally subordinated to the 70th Army, had concentrated as follows: the first in the Buszkowo area and the second in the Krone area.

The 8th Guards Tank Corps, which was in the *front* reserve, had concentrated in the area Preuss-Holland (Preussisch Holland) (30 kilometers southeast of Elbing).

The 3rd Guards Tank Corps, which was in the *front* reserve, was completing its refitting and materiel reinforcement in the Mlawa area.

The Third Belorussian Front's forces were continuing to destroy the enemy's East Prussian group of forces.

The First Belorussian Front's right-flank forces were continuing to attack and were engaged in intensive fighting with the German Eleventh Army along the line excluding Dzidzinek—Zempelburg—Ratzebur—Markisch Friedland—Reetz—Arnswalde—Piritz—Zeden.

The Enemy

By the start of the East Pomeranian operation the Second Belorussian Front's forces were faced by the Army Group Vistula's Second Army, which by this time was occupying the following position:

Units of the "Rippard" corps group and the XX Army Corps were defending along the sector from the Frisches Haff to Mewe. From Mewe to Schwetz, units of the XXIII Army Corps were defending and holding the fortress of Graudenz on the right bank of the Vistula River.

Units of the XXVII Army Corps were defending from Schwetz to (excluding) Karlshorst, holding the Schwetz center of resistance on the left bank of the Vistula River. Units of the XLVI Panzer Corps were defending along the sector from Karlshorst to Bagnitz. Units of the XVIII Mountain Jaeger Corps were defending from Bagnitz to Linde.

The forces of the German Eleventh Army were operating opposite the First Belorussian Front's right flank.

The Decision by the Commander of the Second Belorussian Front and the Armies' Tasks

In accordance with *Stavka* directive no. 11021, *front* commander Marshal of the Soviet Union K.K. Rokossovskii issued orders to the forces of the 2nd Shock, 65th, 49th, and 70th armies. The order, in accordance with the directive from the *Stavka* of the Supreme High Command, called for the fulfillment by 10 February, as the troops' immediate task, the arrival of the *front's* forces at the line of the mouth of the Vistula River—Dirschau—Berent—Rummelsburg—Neustettin, while corresponding instructions were issued on preparing the troops for further operations for carrying out the *front's* subsequent task.

In order to avoid forcing the Vistula River, the 2nd Shock Army was ordered to prepare an attack from the 65th Army's bridgehead from behind the latter's right flank in the direction of Preussisch Stargard with no less than two rifle corps, with the immediate task of capturing the line Dirschau—excluding Hoch Stablau. The army's offensive was to begin approximately on 11 February.

The 65th Army had the task of continuing its offensive on 10 February from the line Gross Schwenten—Gross Zappeln—Jungen to the northwest and no later than 14 February reach the line Hoch Stablau—Czersk. It was subsequently planned to continue the offensive toward Butow.

The 49th Army was ordered to attack on the morning of 10 February from the line Sziroslaw—Liano—Trutnowo, and no later than 13 February capture the line excluding Czersk—excluding Chojnice; it was to subsequently continue attacking in the general direction of Baldenberg.

The 70th Army, along with the 8th Mechanized and 1st Guards Tank corps, was ordered to attack on the morning of 10 February from the line Lubiewo—Prust station—Bagnitz—Dzidzinek, with the task of reaching the line Waltersdorf—Schlochau—Steinborn—Preuss Friedland no later than 13 February; the army was to subsequently continue the offensive in the general direction of Tempelsburg.

The 3rd Guards Cavalry Corps, located in the *front* reserve, was ordered to reach the Waldau—Zempelburg area on 10 February and on the morning of 11 February attack in the direction of Kamin and Schlochau, with the task of capturing the Chojnice—Schlochau area. It was subsequently planned for the corps to reach the Rummelsburg—Baldenburg area.

The *front's* engineering chief was ordered to support the attacking armies with crossings over the Vistula River along the Neuenburg—Graudenz—Fordon sector.

1

The First Stage of the Second Belorussian Front's Combat Operations 10-23 February 1945

On the morning of 10 February the forces of the 65th, 49th and 70th armies renewed the offensive. While overcoming the resistance of the Germans, who were trying to hold our forces' advance through an active defense along the Graudenz—Zempelburg sector, the armies advanced 5-10 kilometers to the northwest in the day's fighting.

The 65th Army, while continuing the fight with the garrison of the fortress of Graudenz with part of its forces, at 1200 on 10 February attacked with its main forces from the bridgehead northeast of Schwetz and, as a result of stubborn fighting, by the end of the day had captured the Germans' centers of resistance on the western bank of the Vistula River—the towns of Schwetz and Schenau. The 49th Army's forces, having encountered the enemy's stubborn resistance and counterattacks, advanced 2-3 kilometers during the offensive's first day, capturing the enemy's major strong points of Bagnitz and Obendorf and advancing 5-10 kilometers on 10 February.

On 10 February the 2nd Shock Army's forces, having completed the defeat of the enemy blockaded in the town of Elbing with part of its forces, and having occupied the town, was regrouping its main forces and preparing to force the Vistula River.

Throughout the next five days the *front's* center and left-wing forces, while continuing the offensive, made a fighting advance of 15-40 kilometers.

During this period the forces of the left-flank 70th Army achieved the greatest success. While closely cooperating with the First Belorussian Front's 3rd Shock Army, the 70th Army's forces made a fighting advance of up to 40 kilometers in five days. On 14 February units of the 70th Army, in conjunction with units of the 8th Mechanized and 3rd Guards Cavalry corps, as a result of a turning maneuver and an attack from the southeast and west, captured the Germans' major strong point and railroad and road junction of Chojnice. The 65th and 49th armies' forces, which were operating in the difficult conditions of the lake and forest terrain, advanced 15-20 kilometers during this period. During this time the 2nd Shock Army was regrouping and did not take part in the offensive. As a result of the slow development of the 65th Army's offensive, the 2nd Shock Army's left-flank formations (108th Rifle Corps) were able to attack only on 16 February from the area west of Graudenz, while launching a blow along the left bank of the Vistula River to the north.

On this day the *front* commander ordered the forces of the 19th Army and 3rd Guards Tank Corps, which were located in the reserve, to begin moving to the left wing of the *front's* attacking forces.

The 19th Army was ordered to move from the Rypin—Dobrzyn—Lipno area and by the close of 21 February concentrate in the Chojnice—Zempelburg—Krone—Lubiewo—Tuchel area. The 3rd Guards Tank Corps was ordered to move from the Mlawa area and by the close of 23 February concentrate in the area Zempelburg—Fandsburg—Mrotschen—excluding Buszkowo.

While overcoming the enemy's resistance in the difficult wooded and lake areas, up to 16 February the *front's* forces advanced at a rate of 5-8 kilometers per day. However, during the following days, due to the Germans' increased resistance and the weakening of the *front's* formations, which had suffered heavy losses in the uninterrupted offensive fighting, which had been continuing for more than a month, the offensive pace began to slacken. From 19 February the Second Belorussian Front's offensive essentially stopped along the front Mewe—Czersk—Chojnice.

At this time along the First Belorussian Front's right wing intense battles were being waged with the Germans' Eleventh Army, which was putting up stubborn resistance. Throughout the first half of February the First Belorussian Front's right-wing forces hardly moved at all. On 17 February the German Eleventh Army launched a counterblow from the Stargard area to the south.

Thus the Second Belorussian Front's forces advanced 50-70 kilometers during the offensive's first ten days, but were unable to completely carry out their immediate task, as assigned by the *Stavka* of the Supreme High Command in its directive no. 11021. The *front's* forces, having encountered the Germans' increasing resistance, were not able to develop their preliminary success and, gradually reducing the pace of the advance, were forced to halt.

The First Belorussian Front's right-wing forces, having eliminated the Germans' group of forces blockaded in the towns of Schneidemühl, Deutsch Krone and Arnswalde, advanced only 5-10 kilometers along certain sectors during this time. The *front's* 47th Army, as a result of the counterblow by the Germans' Eleventh Army on 17 February from the Stargard area, was forced to abandon the towns of Piritz and Bahn and fall back 8-12 kilometers along the Delitz—Bahn sector.

2

The Second Stage of the *Front's* Combat Operations during 24 February-5 March 1945

The *Stavka* of the Supreme High Command's Instructions of 17 February 1945

Due to the increasing difficulty of the situation along the First Belorussian Front's right wing, the slowing down of the Second Belorussian Front's advance, and for the purpose of speeding up the resolution of the task of destroying the Germans' East Pomeranian group of forces, on 17 February 1945 the Supreme High Command assigned new tasks to the forces of the First and Second Belorussian fronts, proceeding from the situation that had arisen by this time.[1]

The Second Belorussian Front was assigned the task of launching its main attack along the left wing, having reinforced the latter with the 19th Army and 3rd Guards Tank Corps, in the direction of Koslin, to reach the shore of the Baltic Sea, to break up the Germans' East Pomeranian group of forces in conjunction with the First Belorussian Front, and destroy it. The First Belorussian Front, which was included in the East Pomeranian operation, was to attack with its right-wing forces in the direction of Falkenburg and Gollnow, and, in conjunction with the Second Belorussian Front's left-wing forces, break up the Germans' East Pomeranian group of forces and destroy the Germans' Eleventh Army, followed by its arrival at the Bay of Pomerania and the Oder River from its mouth to Zeden.

Thus the *front's* new tasks consisted of cutting off the enemy's East Pomeranian group of forces from the German army's main forces, and in breaking up and destroying it in detail through the forces of two *fronts*.

As of 2400 on 20 February the following new boundary line was to be established between the Second and First Belorussian fronts: Bydgoszcz—Flederborn—Neustettin—Kolberg, with all locales, except for Bydgoszcz, for the First Belorussian Front.

THE SIDES' SITUATION BY 20 FEBRUARY

The Soviet Forces

The Second Belorussian Front's forces, having arrived at the line excluding Halbstadt—Skurz—Mewe—Czersk—Chojnice—Ratzebur (an overall front length of 212 kilometers), consisted of five combined-arms armies (2nd Shock, 65th, 49th, 70th, and 19th) and one air army (4th). The combined-arms armies included 45 rifle divisions[2] and three fortified areas. The 4th Air Army had three air corps.

---

1   Directive of the *Stavka* of the Supreme High Command, No. 11026, of 17 February 1945.
2   Of these, 36 rifle divisions, which were part of the 2nd Shock, 65th, 70th, and 49th armies, as a result of

The armored and mechanized forces consisted of three tank corps (1st, 3rd and 8th guards tank), one mechanized corps (8th), one tank brigade, five tank regiments, 12 self-propelled artillery regiments, and three independent self-propelled artillery battalions.

Besides this, the *front's* mobile forces included the 3rd Guards Cavalry Corps.

Artillery subordinated to the *front* consisted of six artillery breakthrough divisions (1st, 2nd, 18th, 23rd, 26th, and 28th), four cannon and three howitzer (heavy caliber) artillery brigades, five anti-tank artillery brigades, three howitzer and five anti-tank artillery regiments, one mortar brigade, five mortar regiments, one guards mortar division (4th Guards Mortar Division), and seven guards mortar regiments.

The *front's* anti-aircraft weapons consisted of five anti-aircraft divisions (6th, 12th, 28th, 65th, and 74th), eight anti-aircraft regiments, and seven anti-aircraft battalions.

Engineer troops subordinated to the *front* included two assault destruction brigades, eight engineer brigades, two motorized engineer brigades, and one bridge-pontoon mechanized brigade.

The *front's* chemical troops consisted of one chemical defense brigade, three independent chemical defense battalions, and two independent flamethrower battalions.

The Enemy

According to the *front* staff's data, by the start of the second stage of the East Pomeranian operation the Second Belorussian Front's forces were faced by the Germans' Army Group Vistula, which included the German Second Army and part of the XVI SS Panzer Corps.

According to the *front's* data, at this time the forces of the Germans' Second Army occupied the following position.

Corps group "Rappard," consisting of four regiments and 15 independent battalions, occupied defensive positions along the Nogat River from its mouth to Pickel, and then along the left bank of the Vistula River to Mewe.

The XXIII Army Corps, consisting of the 337th, 35th and 252nd infantry divisions, elements of the 83rd Infantry Division,[3] and the 542nd *Volkssturm* Division, occupied defensive positions along the sector Mewe—Skurz—excluding Wda—Lubichowo.

The XXVII Army Corps, consisting of the 251st, 73rd and 227th infantry divisions occupied defensive positions along the line excluding Lubichowo—excluding Long—Karsin.

The VII Panzer Corps, consisting of the 4th and 7th panzer divisions and the 389th Infantry Division, was defending along the line excluding Karsin—excluding Rittel—Chojnice.

The XVIII Mountain Jaeger Corps, consisting of the 32nd Infantry Division, the 15th SS Infantry Division, the SS "Netherlands" Panzergrenadier Division's 48th Regiment, and the "Jutland" Infantry Regiment, was defending along the line excluding Chojnice—Richnau—Bucholz—Preuss Friedland—Landeck.

The XVI SS Corps, consisting of the 12th Panzer Division and units of the "Werwalde" Infantry Division was defending along the line excluding Landeck—Lottin—Krangen.

The commander of the German Second Army had in reserve a field reserve brigade, which had been concentrated in the area of Danzig. Besides this, according to the *front's* data, the German Second Army command had in reserve the 14th Panzer and 122nd Infantry divisions.

The *front* command assumed that the Germans were able to transfer up to five infantry divisions to the Second Belorussian Front's offensive sector from their Courland group of forces. By 20

---

the preceding uninterrupted offensive battles, which had continued more than a month, had a strength of 3-4,000 men apiece.

3   The 83rd Infantry Division's main forces were blockaded in the fortress of Graudenz.

February, according to the *front's* intelligence information, the Germans were already transferring the 93rd, 126th, 225th, and 290th infantry divisions from Group "Courland."

According to the *front's* data, the reinforcements that had been attached to the German Second Army by this time consisted of a brigade of assault guns, two high command special designation artillery regiments, six artillery battalions, two anti-tank battalions, and six anti-aircraft battalions.

The determination of the enemy's disposition and strength operating opposite the Second Belorussian Front by the start of the second stage of the East Pomeranian operation was arrived at by the *front* staff with insufficient accuracy. The corrections that were made later on the basis of captured German General Staff documents confirmed to a great extent the *front's* data as to the enemy's dispositions, but did not fully correspond to the actual presence of German forces operating at this time opposite the *front's* forces.

The 35th Infantry Division was missing from the XXIII Army Corps, and also included the "Lobach" Brigade and combat groups nos. 23 and 35. The XXVII Army Corps included, aside from the units already listed, units of the 31st Infantry Division and the 1st Screening Brigade. The XVIII Mountain Jaeger Corps included, aside from the "Netherlands" and "Jutland" regiments, the 1st SS Grenadier Brigade. No units of the XVI SS Corps were operating against the Second Belorussian Front, although there was the "Koslin" Infantry Division (*volkssturm*) from the "Tettau" corps group.

According to more precise data, the commander of the German Second Army had in his reserve the 14th Panzer and 122nd Infantry divisions by the start of the East Pomeranian operation,[4] although there was the headquarters of the XX Army Corps, which was in the city of Danzig and which included the 1st Field Reserve Brigade and individual elements from the garrisons of Danzig and Gdynia, with up to a division in each town.

Thus by the start of the second stage of the East Pomeranian operation, the Germans had the following units opposite the Second Belorussian Front:

> Panzer divisions—2
> Infantry divisions—14
> Infantry brigades—4
> Combat groups—2
> Independent infantry regiments—4
> Independent battalions—15

By the start of the second stage of the East Pomeranian operation, the Germans facing the Second Belorussian Front were occupying defensive positions built by them during the last 5-7 days and outfitted with field-type fortification structures. The Germans did not have defensive positions in the tactical depth, with the exception of anti-tank and anti-personnel obstacles covering individual sectors and defiles.

The Decision by the Commander of the Second Belorussian Front

The *front* commander, in carrying out the Supreme High Command's instructions of 17 February, had as his goal the splitting up of the enemy's East Pomeranian group of forces and decided to commit the 19th Army and 3rd Guards Tank Corps into the fighting along the *front's* left wing. This army, along with the 3rd Guards Tank Corps, was to attack on 24 February and, launching a

---

4   During this time the 14th Panzer Division was part of the Eighteenth Army, while the 122nd Infantry Division was part of the Sixteenth Army and were operating in Group "Courland."

blow toward Koslin, reach the shore of the Baltic Sea along the Jamundersee—Kolberg sector. The *front's* right-wing and center forces, which included the 2nd Shock, 65th, 49th, and 70th armies, while continuing the offensive, were to destroy the enemy group of forces being cut off by the 19th Army.

In accordance with this decision, the *front* commander on 19 February assigned the following tasks to his armies:

The 2nd Shock Army, was to hold the eastern bank of the Nogat River along the sector excluding Halbstadt—Zachrau with the forces of the 153rd, 161st and 91st fortified areas and two rifle divisions, while the main forces would continue the offensive in the direction of Preussisch Stargard and Danzig and by the close of 24 February they were to capture Danzig and reach the line Danzig—Zuchau—Karthaus.

The 65th Army was given the assignment of continuing the offensive in the direction of Alt Kischau and Berent, with the task of capturing the line Gorenschin—Borruschin—excluding Sullenschin by the close of 24 February.

The 49th Army was to continue attacking in the direction of Sommin and Butow, with the task of capturing the line Sommin—Kloden—the Liaskasee by the close of 24 February.

The 70th Army was ordered to resume the offensive on 22 February in the direction of Konarzyny, Reinwasser and Bartin.[5]

The 19th Army, reinforced by the 3rd Artillery Breakthrough Corps, was to relieve by 2400 on 20 February the 70th Army's units along the sector Deringsdorf—excluding Preuss Friedland, and then units of the First Belorussian Front's 3rd Shock Army as far as Ratzebur. On the morning of 24 February the army was to attack, launching its main blow from the front Bucholz—Babusch in the direction of Bischofswalde, Stegers and Baldenberg. The army's immediate objective was to capture the line Fleitenstein—Penkul—Neustettin by the close of 25 February and to subsequently develop the offensive in the direction of Baldenberg, Bublitz and Koslin. It was ordered to create an artillery and mortar density (76mm and more) along the army's breakthrough sector of no less than 150 guns and mortars per kilometer of breakthrough front.

In order to develop the offensive in the direction of Bublitz and Koslin, the army was to be reinforced on the morning of 25 February with the 3rd Guards Tank Corps.

On 20 February, due to the late concentration of the 19th Army's forces and the impossibility of occupying in time the combat sector along the line excluding Preuss Friedland—Ratzebur from the First Belorussian Front's forces, the *front* commander ordered the forces of the 3rd Guards Cavalry Corps to move to the Linde area (20 kilometers northwest of Zempelburg) by forced marches, and by 2400 on 20 February relieve the units of the First Belorussian Front's 3rd Shock Army, occupy the combat sector excluding Preuss Friedland—excluding Landeck—Ratzebur and securely defend this line.

The commander of the First Belorussian Front, having concentrated his shock group in the area excluding Merkisch Friedland—Arnswalde, decided to split the German Eleventh Army by an attack to the north and, upon destroying it in detail, reach the shore of the Baltic Sea and the Oder along the sector Kolberg—Kammin—Altdamm—Zeden. For this purpose, the Polish 1st Army was given the assignment of launching an attack in the direction of Falkenburg and Belgard. The 3rd Shock and 1st Guards Tank armies were to launch an attack in the direction of Daber, Regenwalde and Gross Estin, while the 61st and 2nd Guards Tank armies were to attack in the direction of Kammin and Gollnow, and the 47th Army had the task of attacking toward Altdamm. The 2nd Guards Cavalry Corps, which had been defending along the *front's* right wing,

---

5   On 21 February the 70th Army was to carry out a regrouping following the relief of its left-flank units by the forces of the 19th Army.

had the task of firmly holding the line excluding Ratzebur—Krangen—Rederitz. The deadline for the start of the First Belorussian Front's offensive was 1 March and was indicated in an additional order.

On 22 February *Stavka* of the Supreme High Command directive no. 11033) established the following boundary line between the Third and Second Belorussian fronts: Osterode—Saalfeld—Halbstadt (along the Nogat River)—Nickelswalde (all locales for the Third Belorussian Front). According to this directive, the commander of the Third Belorussian Front was ordered to relieve the Second Belorussian Front's forces inside the new boundary and to speed up the movement of its left flank to the shore of the Bay of Danzig and east of the Vistula River, for the purpose of closing off the Germans' path of retreat from the Frisches Nehrung spit.

The 19th Army's Plan for the Offensive Operation

By the start of the operation the 19th Army, which had relieved part of the 70th Army's forces and had been committed into the fighting along the line Deringsdorf—Preuss Friedland, consisted of nine rifle divisions organized into three rifle corps.[6] The army's artillery, including reinforcement artillery, included 1,098 guns and 1,210 mortars—in all, 2,308 guns and mortars of 76mm and higher. Besides this, the army had 473 anti-tank and anti-aircraft guns. The army's forces were supported by a single assault air division.

Facing the 19th Army along the front Gross Jenznig—Preuss Friedland, the enemy had the 32nd Infantry Division, reinforced by an SS school and three training and reserve battalions, the 15th SS Infantry Division, and the 1st SS Grenadier Brigade.

The Germans had in the first defensive line 19 infantry and two panzer battalions, and up to six infantry and two panzer battalions in the second line.

In all, facing the army along a 17-kilometer sector, the Germans had 29 infantry and panzer battalions, or 1.7 battalions per kilometer of front.

For the purpose of breaking through the enemy's defense and defeating his opposing group of forces, the commander of the 19th Army decided to launch his main attack along the sector Bucholz—Babusch in the general direction of Bischofswalde, Stegers, Baldenberg and to capture the line Fleitenstein—Penkul—Gross Kudde—Neustettin.

With the army's arrival at the line of the southern shore of the Gross Zitenersee—Elsenau—Rutenberg—Breitenfeld, it was planned to commit the 3rd Guards Tank Corps into the breach, having attached the 313th Rifle Division to it, and, while developing a vigorous offensive in the general direction of Baldenberg, Bublitz and Koslin, reach the shore of the Baltic Sea in the area north of Koslin and cut off the path of retreat of the Germans' Pomeranian group of forces to the west.

The army's combat formation was in two echelons. The 40th Guards and 134th rifle corps were to attack in the first echelon, with the 132nd Rifle Corps in the second. The 40th Guards Rifle Corps' combat formation consisted of two echelons, while that of the 134th Rifle Corps was in three echelons.

The width of the breakthrough sector of the enemy's front was ten kilometers. The average artillery density per kilometer of front along the breakthrough sector reached 152 guns and mortars (76mm and higher).

---

6   The 40th Guards Rifle Corps consisted of the 10th, 101st and 102nd guards rifle divisions; the 132nd Rifle Corps of the 310th, 272nd and 205th rifle divisions, and; the 134th Rifle Corps of the 27th, 18th and 313th rifle divisions. The average strength of the rifle divisions was about 8,000 men apiece.

The army's offensive operation was planned in two stages. The first stage included the breakthrough of the enemy's defense, the defeat of his opposing forces and the army's arrival at the line Fleitenstein—Penkul—Gross Kudde—Neustettin. The deadline for completing this stage was two days. The second stage included the defeat of the enemy's operational reserves and the army's arrival at the shore of the Baltic Sea north of Koslin. The depth of the operation would reach 114 kilometers.

Following a regrouping and the redistribution of the reinforcement weapons by the start of the operation's second stage, the Second Belorussian Front's forces occupied the following position.

The 2nd Shock Army, consisting of the 98th Rifle Corps (381st and 281st rifle divisions), 116th Rifle Corps (321st, 326th and 86th rifle divisions), 108th Rifle Corps (142nd, 90th, 46th, 372nd, and 37th Guards rifle divisions), the 8th Tank Corps, and the 153rd, 161st and 91st fortified areas, was fighting along the line of the Nogat and Vistula rivers from Halbstadt to Mewe and then to the west as far as a point excluding Skurz. The 37th Guards and 142nd rifle divisions and part of the 91st Fortified Area's forces were continuing to fight the enemy's group of forces blockaded in the town of Graudenz, while the 381st Rifle Division, having turned over its defensive sector to the Third Belorussian Front's forces, was moving from the Elbing area to the army's left flank.

The 65th Army, consisting of the 105th Rifle Corps (354th, 193rd and 44th Guards rifle divisions), 46th Rifle Corps (413th, 108th and 186th rifle divisions) and 18th Rifle Corps (69th and 15th rifle divisions) was fighting along the line excluding Skurz—Wda—Osowo—Schwartzwasser.

The 49th Army, consisting of the 70th Rifle Corps (139th, 238th and 191st rifle divisions), 121st Rifle Corps (199th, 380th and 42nd rifle divisions) and the 114th Rifle Corps (76th Guards, 160th and 385th rifle divisions) was occupying the line excluding Schwartzwasser—Osowo—Rittel.

The 70th Army, consisting of the 96th Rifle Corps (1st, 200th, 369th, and 38th Guards rifle divisions) and the 47th Rifle Corps (71st, 330th, 162nd, 136th, and 165th rifle divisions) was fighting along the line excluding Rittel—Muskendorf—Deringsdorf.

The 19th Army's 40th Guards Rifle Corps (10th, 101st and 102nd Guards rifle divisions) and 134th Rifle Corps (205th, 272nd and 310th rifle divisions) was preparing to attack from the line Deringsdorf—excluding Preuss Friedland, with the 132nd Rifle Corps (18th, 27th and 313th rifle divisions) in the second echelon in the area north of Zempelburg.

The 3rd Guards Cavalry Corps, consisting of the 6th and 5th guards and 32nd cavalry divisions, was defending along the line excluding Preuss Friedland—excluding Landeck—Ratzebur.

At this time the *front* had in reserve the 1st Guards Tank Corps, which had concentrated in the area of the town of Czersk; the 8th Mechanized Corps in the Chojnice area, and the 3rd Guards Tank Corps, which at this time had been concentrated in the Zempelburg area.

Units of the Third Belorussian Front (48th and 5th Guards Tank armies) were operating to the right, in the Elbing area; to the left the First Belorussian Front's forces were operating along the line excluding Ratzebur—Merkisch—Friedland—Reetz—Zeden, as far as the Oder River.

The Correlation of Forces

By the start of the East Pomeranian operation's second stage the correlation of forces according to the Second Belorussian Front's armies was as follows.

As may be seen from Table IV/2.1, along the Second Belorussian Front's 212-kilometer front our forces were a little more than 1 ½ times stronger than the enemy in rifle units and a little more than two times in artillery and mortars. As for tanks and self-propelled artillery, the two sides' forces were approximately equal.

Along the 19th Army's axis of the main attack, in particular the breakthrough sector of the enemy's defense, a significant superiority in infantry, artillery and tanks had been created. This superiority in favor of the Second Belorussian Front's forces along the axis of the main attack had been created by committing fresh forces from the 19th Army and the 3rd Guards Tank Corps, as well as by the transfer of artillery formations from other sectors of the front.

The 2nd Shock Army, which was to attack along the *front's* right wing in the direction of Danzig, had an insufficient superiority in infantry and tanks.

Along the sector of the 3rd Guards Cavalry Corps, which was defending at this time, the enemy enjoyed a superiority of forces.

As a result of the peculiarities of the operational-strategic situation, the saturation of the Second Belorussian Front's forces with combat equipment in this operation was significantly lower than in the preceding East Prussian and especially in the subsequent Berlin operations.

Nonetheless, as the course of the East Pomeranian operation showed, the saturation of the *front's* forces with combat equipment proved to be sufficient for the successful accomplishment of the tasks assigned to the *front's* forces by the Supreme High Command.

The Attack Toward Koslin and the Arrival at the Shore of the Baltic Sea (24 February-5 March 1945)

Table IV/2.1 The Correlation of Forces Facing the Second Belorussian Front by the Start of the Second Stage of the East Pomeranian Operation (24.2.1945)

		Soviet Forces		
Front (km)	Name	Forces	Total	Density per Km of Front
66	2nd Shock Army	Rifle Battalions	61	0.9
		Tanks and Self-Propelled Guns	127	11.9
		Mortars	1,094	16.6
		Guns	1,032	15.6
36	65th Army	Rifle Battalions	46	1.2
		Tanks and Self-Propelled Guns	77	2.0
		Mortars	512	14.2
		Guns	568	15.8
31	49th Army	Rifle Battalions	58	1.8
		Tanks and Self-Propelled Guns	50	1.6
		Mortars	472	15.2
		Guns	747	24.0
27	70th Army	Rifle Battalions	52	3.3
		Tanks and Self-Propelled Guns	198	7.3
		Mortars	541	20.0
		Guns	826	30.5
17	19th Army	Rifle Battalions	81	4.7
		Tanks and Self-Propelled Guns	293	17.3
		Mortars	1,210	71.8
		Guns	1,098	64.6
10	The Army's Breakthrough Front	Rifle Battalions	72	7.2
		Tanks and Self-Propelled Guns	208	20.3
		Mortars	745	74.5
		Guns	774	77.4

Soviet Forces

Front (km)	Name	Forces	Total	Density per Km of Front
33	3rd Guards Cavalry Corps	Rifle Battalions	12	0.3
		Tanks and Self-Propelled Guns	65	2.0
		Mortars	146	4.4
		Guns	110	3.3
–	The Reserve 1st Guards Tank Corps, 233rd Independent Tank Regiment, 342nd Heavy Self-Propelled Artillery Regiment	Rifle Battalions	6	–
		Tanks and Self-Propelled Guns	117	–
		Mortars	59	–
		Guns	60	–
212	The Entire Front	Rifle Battalions	316	1.4
		Tanks and Self-Propelled Guns	927	3.8
		Mortars	4,034	19.0
		Guns	4,441	20.8

The Enemy

Front (km)	Name	Forces	Total	Density per Km of Front	Correlation of Forces
66	Rappard's Group, XXIII Army Corps	Rifle Battalions	46	0.7	1.3:1
		Tanks and Assault Guns	70	1.0	1.8:1
		Mortars	301	4.5	3.6:1
		Guns	361	5.4	2.8:1
36	XXVII Army Corps, 251st and 73rd infantry divisions, one regiment from 227th Infantry Division	Rifle Battalions	21	0.6	2.0:1
		Tanks and Assault Guns	42	1.2	1.8:1
		Mortars	204	5.6	2.5:1
		Guns	272	7.5	2.0:1
31	Two regiments From 227th Infantry Division, 4th Panzer Division/VII Panzer Corps	Rifle Battalions	23	0.7	2.5:1
		Tanks and Assault Guns	139	4.5	1:2.7
		Mortars	218	7.0	2:1
		Guns	343	11.4	2.2:1
27	VII Panzer Corps (389th Infantry Division, 7th Panzer Division)	Rifle Battalions	15	0.6	2.4:1
		Tanks and Assault Guns	145	5.4	1.4:1
		Mortars	152	6.0	3.5:1
		Guns	288	10.7	2.8:1
17	XVIII Mountain Jaeger Corps (32nd and 15th infantry divisions, 1st Infantry Brigade, a regiment from the Koslin Infantry Division	Rifle Battalions	29	1.7	2.8:1
		Tanks and Assault Guns	140	8.0	2:1
		Mortars	262	15.4	4.4:1
		Guns	367	21.6	3:1

| | | The Enemy | | | |
Front (km)	Name	Forces	Total	Density per Km of Front	Correlation of Forces
10	15th Infantry Division, 1st Infantry Brigade, a regiment from the Koslin Infantry Division	Rifle Battalions	17	1.7	4:1
		Tanks and Assault Guns	84	8.4	2.4:1
		Mortars	176	17.6	4:1
		Guns	218	21.8	3.5:1
33	Koslin Infantry Division from Group Tettau (minus an infantry regiment)	Rifle Battalions	18	0.5	1:1.5
		Tanks and Assault Guns	86	2.6	1:1.3
		Mortars	172	5.1	1:1.1
		Guns	254	7.7	1:2.3
–	XX Army Corps, 1st Reserve Brigade, the garrisons of Gdynia and Danzig	Rifle Battalions	27	–	–
		Tanks and Assault Guns	119	–	–
		Mortars	258	–	–
		Guns	309	–	–
212	The Entire Front Second Army and units of Group Tettau and of the Eleventh Army	Rifle Battalions	179	0.8	1.6:1
		Tanks and Assault Guns	741	3.5	1.2:1
		Mortars	1,567	7.4	2.7:1
		Guns	2,194	10.3	2.1:1

Notes
1. Losses for the sides have been accounted for in determining these figures.
2. In calculating the cavalry corps' strength, one cavalry regiment corresponds to an infantry battalion.
3. Shore artillery is not counted here.

On the morning of 24 February, following a 40-minute artillery preparation, the 19th Army's forces went over to the attack, launching a blow in the general direction of Koslin. Having broken through the enemy's defense along the sector Firchau—Babusch (ten kilometers in width), the army's forces, while overcoming stubborn resistance and counterattacks by the enemy's tanks, advanced 10-12 kilometers throughout the day and widened the breakthrough sector to 20 kilometers. The Germans put up the greatest resistance in the Richnau area, and then in the Schlochau area, where up to 120 tanks and assault guns and up to two regiments of infantry took part in counterattacks. Left-flank units of the 134th Rifle Corps, in conjunction with units of the 3rd Guards Cavalry Corps, took the town of Preuss Friedland.

The 70th Army, which had attacked on the right, encountered the enemy's fierce defense and throughout the day advanced only 2-3 kilometers along its left flank.

The neighboring 3rd Guards Cavalry Corps on the left assisted the advance by the 19th Army's left wing with artillery fire. As the 19th Army's left wing advanced, the 3rd Guards Cavalry Corps was to contract its front and subsequently, while remaining in the *front's* reserve, concentrate in the Landeck—Ratzebur area.

The next day, 25 February, the 19th Army's forces continued to develop the attack to the northwest in conjunction with the 70th Army's left-flank formations and units of the 3rd Guards Cavalry Corps, and advanced another 10-12 kilometers, widening the breakthrough front to 30 kilometers. By the close of the day the army's forces were fighting along the line of the southeastern bank of the Grosser Amtsee—the southwestern outskirts of Schlochau—Kramsk—Berenhutte—Zenruten—Breitenfelde—Krummensee—Peterswalde—Prutzenwalde.

The 3rd Guards Tank Corps was committed into the breach from the line Kriegsfelde—Barkenfelde, which that day captured the inhabited locales of Elsenau and Loosen.

The 70th Army once again advanced three kilometers. The 4th Air Army assisted the advance by the *front's* left wing. Lacking the opportunity to support the ground forces on the operation's first day, due to the poor meteorological conditions, on 25 February units of the 4th Air Army took an active part in the fighting, closely cooperating with the attacking rifle and tank units. While launching bomber and assault air raids against the enemy's infantry and tank units, the 4th Air Army sought to destroy his men and materiel. On this day 915 sorties were carried out in the 19th Army's offensive sector.

The Second Belorussian Front's right-wing and center armies, having encountered stubborn resistance by the enemy, who was taking advantage of the favorable conditions of the wooded, and lake terrain and who had prepared a sufficiently outfitted field defensive line, had no success on 24-25 February and were fighting along their previous lines. The enemy launched his strongest counterattacks in the areas of Mewe, Skurz (Ossowo) and Czersk. As a result of the counterattacks along the Skurz—Ossowo line, on 25 February the enemy pushed back our forces and captured Ossowo. The Germans carried out a number of counterattacks along the Danzig axis in forces of 1-2 infantry regiments, supported by tanks and assault guns.

During 24-25 February the First Belorussian Fronts' right-wing forces regrouped, while preparing to attack and defending their lines and beating off German attacks in the area south of Piritz. On 26 February the commander of the Second Belorussian Front ordered the 2nd Guards Cavalry Corps to attack in the direction of Neustettin.

Due to the successful advance of the 19th Army's forces in the direction of Stegers and Fleitenstein, on 26 February the *front* commander ordered the 3rd Guards Cavalry Corps to attack on the morning of 26 February from the Landeck—Ratzebur line in the direction of Sparsee and Seckendorf, with the task of capturing the line Klein Kudde—Neustettin by the morning of 27 February. The commander of the 19th Army was ordered to attack with his left-flank formations in the direction of Hammerstein and Stepen. The remaining forces were to continue attacking along their previous axes.

On 26 February the *front's* left-wing units (19th and 70th armies and the 3rd Guards Cavalry Corps) were developing the offensive and had captured the towns of Schlochau, Stegers and Hammerstein, having advanced in fighting 8-22 kilometers and expanded the breakthrough front to 60 kilometers. The 19th Army's advance was assisted by the successful operations of the 3rd Guards Tank Corps, the forward units of which were fighting 30 kilometers ahead of the rifle formations and had reached the Sidow—Porst area.

Our troops' advance along the Koslin axis, particularly that of the 3rd Guards Tank Corps, forced the German Second Army's XVIII Mountain Jaeger and VII Panzer corps to begin falling back to the north, while at the same time putting up insignificant resistance. The enemy opposite the Second Belorussian Front's right wing and center continued to put up stubborn resistance.

The 19th Army's formations, taking advantage of the 3rd Guards Tank Corps' successful advance, continued to attack, putting part of their forces into columns. However, the pace of advance by the army's main forces was insufficient and the rifle formations began to lag behind the tank corps' units. The 3rd Guards Tank Corps' successful advance demanded a bold and organized forward movement by the army's main forces. However, at this time the army commander, Lieutenant General G.K. Kozlov,[7] and the army's headquarters lost communications with the

---

7   Editor's note. Georgii Kirillovich Kozlov (1902-70) joined the Red Army in 1918. During the Great Patriotic War he served as a division commander and army chief of staff, before being appointed commander of the 19th Army in 1943. He was removed from command in March 1945 and was later appointed a deputy army

troops, command and control began to be disrupted, and the threat arose of mixing up units and formations and the lagging behind of the artillery. Such a situation in the 19th Army led to a decrease in the army's offensive pace and to an increase in the gap between the tank and rifle formations.

The situation along the First Belorussian Front's right flank was also creating certain difficulties. The scheduled attack on 19 February by the First Belorussian Front's right-wing forces, as called for by the *Stavka* of the Supreme High Command's plan, and which was then switched to 26 February, was being delayed due to the incomplete conclusion of the regrouping.[8] As a result, the 3rd Guards Tank Corps, which had advanced far to the northwest and was located 30-40 kilometers from the 19th Army's forces, could end up in a very difficult situation and be open to a flank attack from the southwest, where the enemy had a powerful group of forces in the Eleventh Army, which was defending opposite the First Belorussian Front's forces.

The resulting situation forced the commander of the Second Belorussian Front to temporarily delay the 3rd Guards Tank Corps' further offensive and, before continuing the offensive, to put the 19th Army's forces in order.

On 27 February the *front* commander ordered the 19th Army's main forces to be moved to the line Fleitenstein—Penkul—Schenau—Sparsee. It was ordered to put the army in order along this line, bring up the artillery, organizing reliable communications in all units and formations, and to move the command posts nearer the troops. The army's forward detachments were to occupy Rummelsburg, Baldenberg and Worchow. The *front* commander ordered the army to capture the Prechlau area without fail by the morning of 27 February.

The *front* commander, due to the 19th Army's main forces' lagging behind the 3rd Guards Tank Corps', ordered the latter to consolidate in the Drawen—Bublitz area until the arrival of the 19th Army's main forces, after which it was to continue to carry out its previous assignment.

The *front's* forces continued to remain in place along the right wing and center.

On 27 February the 19th Army's forces, having halted along the lines reached on the previous evening, was putting itself in order. With part of its right-wing forces, the army, in conjunction with the 70th Army's forces, was attacking in the Prechlau area, while at the same time beating off counterattacks by the enemy, who undertook 24 counterattacks ranging from a battalion to a regiment of infantry in strength, supported by groups of 5-10 tanks. The 70th Army's forces, while overcoming the enemy's resistance, advanced 7-8 kilometers that day.

The 3rd Guards Tank Corps, having blockaded the town of Neustettin and having bypassed the Filmsee from the northeast, reached the line Sparsee—Streitsich—Hutten.

The 3rd Guards Tank Corps' main forces reached and consolidated in the area Drawen—Bublitz—Porst. The 313th Rifle Division, which had been attached to the tank corps, reached the Gross Karzenburg area. The corps' forward detachments reached the areas west of Rummelsburg, in which area up to 110 tanks and self-propelled guns were noted, as well as a concentration of infantry in the areas south of Pollnow and Kurow.

No changes in the situation occurred along the remaining sectors of the front.

On 27 February the First Belorussian Front's right-wing forces, while completing the regrouping of the 3rd Shock and 61st armies and the 1st and 2nd guards tank armies, occupied jumping-off positions for the offensive. Units of the 2nd Guards Cavalry Corps, which was cooperating with the 3rd Guards Cavalry Corps, were attacking southwest of Neustettin.

---

commander during the war with Japan. Following the war, Kozlov served as chief of staff of several military districts.

8   The offensive by the First Belorussian Front's right-wing forces, which was originally scheduled for 26 February, actually began only on 1 March.

On 27 February the commander of the Second Belorussian Front ordered the 19th Army to continue the offensive on 28 February and by the close of the day its main forces were to reach the line Rummelsburg—Gross Karzenburg—Porst—Worchow; the army's forward detachments were to occupy Gross Schwirsen, Sidow, Gerfin, Bublitz, and Seckendorf.

Due to the deep penetration by the 3rd Guards Tank Corps and the 19th Army into the depth of the enemy's defense along a narrow front and the enemy's concentration of major groups of forces along the flanks of the 19th Army in the areas of Rummelsburg and Berwalde, on 27 February the *front* commander ordered the following measures to be carried out:

a)   the 19th Army's 40th Guards Rifle Corps, which was attacking toward Gross Karzenburg, was to reach the front Rummelsburg—excluding Gross Karzenburg; in the Rummelsburg area, following its capture, the corps was to have not less than on rifle division with forward detachments along the line Georgendorf—Woknin; the corps was to be reinforced with artillery;
b)   the 134th Rifle Corps' main forces were to reach the line Gross Karzenburg—excluding the Wirchowsee; one rifle division was to be moved to the Worchow area;
c)   the army was to have a reserve (the 132nd Rifle Corps, minus one rifle division) in the Hammer—Penkul area.

The 3rd Guards Tank Corps was ordered to remain with its main forces in the Bublitz area until the 19th Army's arrival and to occupy Pollnow with a single tank brigade and to hold it. Upon the arrival of the 19th Army's main forces at the line Rummelsburg—Bublitz, the tank corps, having been reinforced with the 313th Rifle Division, was ordered to attack toward Koslin and to capture it.

The 3rd Guards Cavalry Corps was ordered to do the following: upon capturing the town of Neustettin, it was to continue the offensive and on 28 February capture the Buchwald—Kussow—Eschenrige—Eichen area, with its chief task being the securing of the *front's* left wing from the west and south. One cavalry division was to remain in the Neustettin area until the arrival of the First Belorussian Front's forces.

The *front* commander ordered that upon the arrival of the 70th Army's left wing at the line Konarzyny—Prechlau, the 8th Mechanized Corps[9] was to attack to the north with the task of reached the Smoldzin—Ostrowitt—Prondzona area and to then plan to move to the Butow area.

On the morning of 28 February the Second Belorussian Front's left-wing forces renewed their offensive.

The enemy, who was trying to delay the offensive by the *front's* left-wing forces, continued to strengthen his forces along the Rummelsburg—Sidow—Bublitz sector with infantry and tanks, and was launching frequent counterattacks east of Berwalde, attacking the flanks of our attacking troops. The Germans were putting up the fiercest resistance in the Rummelsburg area, where throughout the day they undertook a series of counterattacks of 1-2 infantry battalions in strength, supported by small groups of tanks.[10]

By the close of 28 February the 70th Army's forces reached the line of the Debzicksee—the Witochnosee—Neu Parschnitz—Popelewo—Junkenbruch, having advanced ten kilometers. The 8th Mechanized Corps, which had been committed that day into the fighting, reached Popelewo with its right column; while the left column's forward units had begun fighting in the Ferdinandshof area. By this time the 19th Army's forces reached the line

---

9   The 8th Mechanized Corps was in the *front* reserve and by this time had been concentrated in the Chojnice area.
10   The presence of the XLVI Panzer Corps, which had command over various units in the Rummelsburg area (4th SS Panzer Group, units of the 103rd Infantry Division, and the 549th *Volkssturm* Division), had been established in this area.

Eisenhammer—Fleitenstein—Alkenhagen—Helkewise—Gross Karzenburg—Porst—Worchow—Buchwalde—Eschenrige—Neustettin, advancing 18 kilometers. The 3rd Guards Cavalry Corps captured the town of Neustettin, having completely cleared it of the enemy. The corps' neighbor to the left, the First Belorussian Front's 2nd Guards Cavalry Corps was engaged in offensive fighting west of Neustettin. The 3rd Guards Tank Corps' main forces were located at this time in the Drawen—Bublitz area. Thus the tasks assigned by the *front* commander had been carried out.

On the next day the 19th Army's forces, with their main group of forces along the right flank and paying most of their attention to covering the left flank, were to, according to orders by the *front* commander, continue the offensive to the northwest and by the close of 1 March their main forces were to reach the line Gross Swirsen—Sidow—Gerfin—Goldowk—Grunewald, while forward detachments were to occupy Pollnow, Gross Woldechow, and Gross Tychow.

The 3rd Guards Tank Corps was ordered to continue the offensive on the morning of 1 March and no later than 2 March seize the Koslin area, throwing out powerful forward detachments to the northeast to the areas of Malchow and Pirostow (on the Grabow River), and to the west in the areas of Bast, Warchmin and Bitziker.

On 1 March the 70th Army's forces were to continue their offensive along the previous axis. During 1-3 March combat operations unfolded in the following manner. The 70th Army's forces, while holding the occupied lines along their right wing, continued the offensive with its center and left-wing formations and by the close of 2 March reached the line Modzel—Kedrau—Gura—Gross Peterkau—Starsen.

The 8th Mechanized Corps, the activities of which had been insufficiently decisive, could not break free of the 70th Army's infantry and was fighting in the Prondzona area.

On 2 March the *front* commander, in a special order, pointed out the indecisiveness of his actions to the commander of the 8th Mechanized Corps, as a result of which he had been unable to carry out his combat assignment, and demanded that the corps commander capture the Butow area by the close of 3 March. However, this task was not carried out. The corps was unable to break free of the infantry and on 3 March continued to operate in the latter's combat formations.

The 70th Army, while beating off with its right-flank units enemy counterattacks launched from the line Smoldzin—Tebowizna in the direction of Lonken, continued the offensive by its center and left-flank units to the northwest, having advanced six kilometers.

For the purpose of strengthening the forces of the *front's* shock wing, on 3 March the commander ordered that the 114th Rifle Corps (76th and 160th rifle divisions) be removed from the 49th Army's combat order and by the morning of 4 March be concentrated in the Swornigatz area (20 kilometers north of Chojnice), to be subordinated to the commander of the 70th Army. The 49th Army, consisting of seven rifle divisions, was ordered to go over to the defensive along its front from the morning of 3 March.

The 19th Army's forces, while enjoying the greatest success in the center, by the close of 2 March reached the line: southern outskirts of Rummelsburg—Sidow—Bruchenkrieg—Dargen—Atztum—Hopfenberg—Zeckendorf. The 3rd Guards Cavalry Corps, while occupying its former line, was fighting with one regiment along the eastern outskirts of Neu Walm. The 3rd Guards Tank Corps captured the town of Pollnow and its main forces reached the Pollnow—Alt Zowen—Kesternitz area, having seized Leikow, Nemitz and Schubben with its forward detachments.

By this time the situation along the 19th Army's front had grown more complex. The enemy, having reinforced his group of forces in the Rummelsburg area with the 4th SS Panzer Group, 203rd Infantry Division and 549th *Volkssturm* Division, was trying to hold the town of Rummelsburg and prevent Soviet troops from advancing to the north and northwest. The enemy's holding of the town of Rummelsburg, which was a major railroad and paved road junction and strong point in his defense, and the Germans' concentration of major forces in this area, created a threat to the 19th Army's right flank and the rear of the 3rd Guards Tank Corps.

Due to the developing situation, the *front* commander ordered the commander of the 3rd Guards Tank Corps to concentrate his main forces in the Pollnow area and hold it until the arrival of the 19th Army's right-flank forces. Simultaneously, the corps was ordered to uninterruptedly carry out reconnaissance along the eastern, northern, western and southwestern axes and be ready to attack toward Rummelsburg.

However, on 3 March the 19th Army's forces, while launching an attack along the right flank and center to the north, captured the town of Rummelsburg and, having advanced up to 20 kilometers that day, reached the area north of Pollnow. The 3rd Guards Tank Corps' forward detachments reached the shore of the Baltic Sea north of Koslin, in the Lase—Wusseken area. The corps' main forces, while occupying their previous areas, put out screens in the areas of Krangen, Leichow, Nemitz, and Zuchen, tasked with covering the right flank until the arrival of the 19th Army's main forces.

The 3rd Guards Cavalry Corps reached the line Glasenapp—Grunewald—Gramentz—Flackenheide.

Thus the Germans' East Pomeranian group of forces had already been split into two parts.

On 1 March the First Belorussian Front's right-wing forces attacked, launching their main blow in the direction of Kolberg and Kammin. On 2 March the 2nd Guards Cavalry Corps, which was operating along the First Belorussian Front's right flank and taking advantage of the success of the Second Belorussian Front's left-wing forces, reached the line excluding Neu Walm—Iuchow—Eulenburg—Krangen.

On 4 March the Second Belorussian Front's left-wing forces continued to develop the offensive to the northwest and advanced another 20 kilometers. The 3rd Guards Tank Corps, while launching an attack to the northwest and west, captured the town of Koslin, while its forward detachments reached the line Jamund—Gudenshagen—Alt Belz—Neu Klenz—Konikow.

On this day the *front's* right-wing and center armies, which had advanced along some sectors 6-15 kilometers, enjoyed some success.

By the end of 4 March the First Belorussian Front's forces, upon reaching the Sulchenhagen—Gross Poplow—the Gresinsee—Dramburg—Reptzin—Klutzkow—Schoenfeld—Regenwalde line with the formations of the 2nd Guards Cavalry Corps and the Polish 1st Army and 3rd Guards Army, had half-encircled in the area south of Poltzin a group of enemy forces up to four infantry divisions in strength. By this time the 1st Guards Tank Army's formations had reached the Belgard—Kerlin—Gross Estin—Darsow area. In order to cut the path of retreat of the enemy group of forces from the area west of Koslin, all of the bridges over the Persante River along the Belgard—Kolberg sector were blown up on orders of the commander of the First Belorussian Front and this sector was occupied by units of the 1st Guards Tank Army. The 2nd Guards Tank Army's formations, which were attacking to the northwest toward Kammin, arrived at the areas of Platte, Naugard, Schoenhagen, and Pflugrade with their forward detachments.

Due to the possible attempt by the semi-encircled enemy group in the Poltzin area to break out to the northeast and east, the commander of the Second Belorussian Front ordered the commander of the 3rd Guards Cavalry Corps by 1200 on 5 March to occupy the front facing south and hold the line Dubberow—Burzlaff—Gross Kressin and prevent the enemy from breaking through to the northeast.

On 5 March the 19th Army's forces, taking advantage of the success by the 3rd Guards Tank Corps, reached the shore of the Baltic Sea in the area north and northwest of Koslin along a 20-kilometer sector.

By this time the First Belorussian Front's right-wing forces had eliminated the enemy group of forces in the Poltzin area and, as a result of the vigorous attack by two tank armies, reached the line Damen—Redel—Belgard—excluding Kolberg—excluding Treptow—excluding Kammin—excluding Gollnow, having almost completely occupied the western part of East Pomerania.

Upon the Soviet forces' arrival at the Baltic Sea, the Germans' East Pomeranian group of forces was completely cut off by land from the German army's remaining forces. Thus the first task assigned by the Supreme High Command to the Second and First Belorussian fronts had been accomplished.

The Second Belorussian Front's left-wing forces, having overcome the enemy's resistance, while developing the offensive, during the 24 February-5 March period carried out a fighting advance of 130-150 kilometers, with an average pace of 15-20 kilometers per day.

During 24 February-5 March the *front's* right-wing and center forces advanced insignificantly. The 2nd Shock and 65th armies advanced only 8-10 kilometers. The 49th Army, which was operating along the *front's* center, advanced along its right wing 8-10 kilometers during this period, while its left wing advanced 35-40 kilometers.

The Germans, while trying to hold onto East Pomerania, were reinforcing the Second Army, moving troops from other sectors of the front. During 24 February-5 March the German command transferred by sea to the Second Army from Group "Courland" the 12th *Luftwaffe* Field Division and the 7th and 35th infantry divisions. The Germans transferred to the Second Army from the Königsberg area from Army Group North the LV Army Corps (61st Infantry Division and five independent infantry regiments). Aside from this, the headquarters of the XLVI Panzer Corps was transferred from the reserve of the commander of the Third Panzer Army (from the Stettin area) to the Second Army, and the 23rd Infantry Division was formed on the basis of one of these combat groups.

Despite their desperate attempts to delay the Soviet forces' offensive, the Germans failed to withstand our attack and, having suffered large losses in men and materiel, began to pull back the Second Army's right-flank formations along the coast of the Baltic Sea to the east, in the direction of Danzig and Gdynia.

On this note the second stage of the East Pomeranian operation ended, after which the Second Belorussian Front's left-wing forces turned to the northeast and continued the offensive, with the task of eliminating the enemy's isolated East Pomeranian group, while the First Belorussian Front's right-wing forces turned to the west, with the task of reaching the Pomeranian Bay and the Oder River.

During the fighting of the East Pomeranian operation's second stage, the Second Belorussian Front's forces inflicted major losses on the enemy (more than 32,000 men killed and 4,264 captured) and captured enormous amounts of equipment. During this period 436 various guns, 262 mortars, 216 tanks, 1,239 machine guns, and much other military property was either destroyed or captured.

3

The Operation's Third Stage. Offensive Operations by the *Front's* Left Wing to the East and Northwest, 6-13 March 1945

The successful completion of the second stage of the East Pomeranian operation and the arrival of the Second Belorussian Front's left-wing forces and the First Ukrainian Front's right-wing forces at the shore of the Baltic Sea enabled us to turn, without pause, the Second Belorussian Front's left-wing forces to the northeast and began to carry out the task set forth by the Supreme High Command to destroy the German Second Army, which had been cut off from the remaining German forces and pressed against the sea in the northeastern part of Pomerania.

By 6 March the German Second Army opposing the Second Belorussian Front consisted of the VII and XLVI panzer corps (4th SS Panzer Group, 4th and 7th panzer divisions, the 215th, 32nd, 289th, 227th, 73rd, and 251st infantry divisions, the XVIII Mountain Jaeger, XXIII and XXVII army corps (12th *Luftwaffe* Field Division and the 7th, 31st, 35th, 23rd, 83rd, 252nd, and 337th infantry divisions), the 549th *Volkssturm* Infantry Division, and two combat groups. The commander of the German Second Army had in reserve the LV Army Corps (61st Infantry Division and five independent infantry regiments) and the XX Army Corps (part of the 83rd Infantry Division, the "Hermann Goring" Reserve Panzer Brigade, and part of the Gdynia and Danzig garrisons).

In all, by the start of the operation's third stage, the Germans had facing the Second Belorussian Front two panzer and five army corps, consisting of one panzer group, two panzer divisions, one panzer brigade, 17 infantry divisions, two combat groups, and seven independent battalions.

Measures by the *Stavka* of the Supreme High Command

Following the arrival of the Second Belorussian Front's left-wing forces and the First Belorussian Front's right-wing forces at the shore of the Baltic Sea in the Koslin—Kolberg area, the Supreme Commander-in-Chief, in a 4 March high-frequency telephone conversation with the commander of the Second Belorussian Front, issued instructions for the defeat of the enemy group of forces in the Danzig—Stolp area, the capture of the cities of Danzig and Gdynia, and the *front's* arrival by no later than 20 March at the shore of the Baltic Sea along its entire sector.

In order to carry out this task, the *front's* forces were to continue attacking along their right wing along the western bank of the Vistula River toward Danzig, and along the left wing in the direction of Stolp, Lauenburg and Gdynia. As they cleared the shore of the Baltic Sea, the *front's* forces had the task of organizing its secure defense, employing for this purpose the 3rd Guards Cavalry Corps and units from the fortified areas.

In order to eliminate the Germans' Pomeranian group of forces as quickly as possible, the Supreme Commander-in-Chief instructed the commander of the First Belorussian Front to temporarily transfer, no later than 8 March, the 1st Guards Tank Army to the Second Belorussian Front, in order to develop the attack along the Second Belorussian Front's left wing. The commander of the Second Belorussian Front was ordered to bear in mind that the 1st Guards Tank Army must be returned to the First Belorussian Front no later than 24 March.[1]

The Decision by the Commander of the Second Belorussian Front and the Armies' Tasks

The commander of the Second Belorussian Front decided, upon turning the *front's* left-wing armies to the northeast, to launch his main attack along the shore of the Baltic Sea. A second attack would be launched by the right-wing's forces along the western bank of the Vistula toward Danzig and, along with a simultaneous attack by the center's forces, to defeat the German Second Army, completely clear the enemy from the eastern part of Pomerania and capture the ports of Danzig, Gdynia and Zoppot.

On 4 March the *front* commander assigned the following immediate tasks to his armies:

The 2nd Shock Army, along with the 8th Guards Tank Corps, was ordered to launch its main attack along the left wing in the direction of Preussisch Stargard, Schoeneck and Danzig and to capture the line Dirschau—Schoeneck.

The 65th Army, along with the 1st Guards Tank Corps,[2] was to continue the offensive in the general direction of Hoch Stablau, Gladau and Zuchau and capture the line excluding Schoeneck—Wischin—Nowa Karczma.

The 49th Army was assigned the task of continuing the offensive in the general direction of Berent, Miechucino and reaching the line Grabowko—Skorzewo—Schultzen.

The 70th Army, along with the 8th Mechanized Corps, was also to continue attacking in the direction of Butow, Wutzkow, Linde, Schoenwalde and to capture the line Sullenschin—Neuendorf—Wundichow—Muttrin.

The 19th Army, along with the 3rd Guards Tank Corps, had the task of continuing the offensive in the direction of Stolp and Putzing and capturing the line Sukers—Stolp—Stolpmünde.

The 3rd Guards Cavalry Corps was ordered to turn the corps' units as the First Belorussian Front's right wing advanced in the direction of Kolberg, and to subsequently defend the shore of the Baltic Sea along the sector Rugenwalde (35 kilometers northeast of Koslin)—Grossmelen—excluding Kolberg.

Thus the Second Belorussian Front's forces, without regrouping and without pause, were to continue the offensive with all their forces, launching their main attacks along converging axes: along the shore of the Baltic Sea to the east and along the western bank of the Vistula River to the north.

On 6 March the Second Belorussian Front's forces continued to attack along all axes and achieved the greatest successes along their flanks.

Units of the 2nd Shock Army's 98th Rifle Corps on this day completed the elimination of the Germans' group of forces encircled in the fortress of Graudenz, while units of the same army's 116th Rifle Corps, along with the 8th Guards Tank Corps, broke through the enemy's defense and, while developing the success, began waging street battles in the town of Preussisch Stargard.

---

1 These instructions were subsequently confirmed by directives nos. 11034 and 11035, of 5 March.
2 During the operation's first stage the 1st Guards Tank Corps was in the *front* reserve and located in the Czersk area.

The 65th Army, which on 5 March had been reinforced by the 1st Guards Tank Corps, in conjunction with the 2nd Shock Army's left-flank units and the 49th Army's right-flank units also broke through the enemy's defense and during the day advanced 18 kilometers to the north.

The 19th Army, which was attacking to the northeast with two rifle corps, crushed the enemy's resistance in conjunction with the 70th Army's left-flank units, and advanced 12 kilometers to the northeast along the army's entire sector, having reached the line of the Lantowersee—Schlawe—Pretz.

During 6 March the 19th Army's 134th Rifle Corps continued to operate west of Koslin, attacking to the southwest and west, and by the close of the day reached the line Altenhagen—Rutzow—Fritzow—Altlulfitz—Darkow.

During 6 March the 3rd Guards Tank Corps was in the Koslin area, clearing the area of enemy remnants. On this day, while the remnants of the garrison were being eliminated, the commander of the Koslin garrison, Lieutenant General von Zilow, and 16 other officers were taken prisoner eight kilometers southwest of Koslin.

At the end of the day the *front* commander ordered the 3rd Guards Tank Corps to attack on the morning of 7 March in the direction of Stolp and Lauenburg, with the task of capturing the town of Stolp on 8 March and reaching the line Unter Scharzow—Deutsch Plassow—Stolp, having secured in its rear the crossings over the Stolp River. The corps' forward detachments were ordered to capture the town and port of Stolpmünde. Should the town of Stolp prove to be fortified and impossible to take from the march, the *front* commander ordered the corps to bypass the town and avoid getting bogged down in fighting for it. The corps was ordered to subsequently keep in mind the development of the offensive toward Lauenburg.

Throughout 7 March the Second Belorussian Front's forces, while continuing to develop the success along the flanks, were attacking along the entire front and occupied more than 350 inhabited locales and 28 rail stations. During the day the right-wing forces captured the enemy's major communications centers of Mewe, Preussisch Stargard, Hoch Stablau, having advanced up to 25 kilometers, while the left-wing forces captured the towns of Schlawe and Rugenwalde, having advanced 20 kilometers. Units of the 19th Army's 134th Rifle Corps reached the eastern outskirts of Kolberg and linked up with the First Belorussian Front's forces.

The 3rd Guards Cavalry Corps reached the shore of the Baltic Sea and took up defensive positions along the line Rugenwaldermunde—Neuwasser—Grossmollen—Althagen—Neu Tram.

Under the pressure of our attacks, the enemy, while covering himself with powerful rearguards, began to fall back to the northeast for the purpose of occupying the previously prepared Danzig—Gdynia fortified area.

On 8 March the Second Belorussian Front's forces, while continuing to develop the offensive along the right, center and left, began to pursue the retreating enemy. The 8th and 1st guards tank corps, having established close cooperation between each other, were to boldly and decisive attack the enemy and in a daring raid capture the city of Danzig. The *front* commander ordered the 3rd Guards Tank Corps to vigorously move to the east and no later than 10-11 March capture the town of Gdynia. In the Lauenburg area the corps was to seize crossings over the Leba River with a specially assigned detachment and hold it until the arrival of the 19th Army's rifle formations. Simultaneously, the *front* commander ordered the commander of the 3rd Guards Tank Corps to establish reliable communications by radio with the commander of the 1st Guards Tank Corps and the commander of the 65th Army.

On 8 March the 1st Guards Tank Army, which by this time had concentrated in the Koslin area, was subordinated to the Second Belorussian Front. The *front* commander assigned the army the following task: it was to move out on the morning of 9 March toward the 19th Army's combat units and by the close of 9 March reach the Lupow Fliss River along the sector Lupow—Glowitz—Brenkenhof Canal, in the areas of Fingerkaten and Witzig (8-15 kilometers west and northwest of Lauenburg). On the morning of 10 March the army was to attack in the direction of Lauenburg and Neustadt and no later than 12 March reach the shore of the Bay of Danzig along the Gdynia—Putzig sector. The *front* commander emphasized to the commander of the 1st Guards Tank Army the necessity of rapidly capturing the area to the north of Lauenburg.

On 9 March the *front's* forces, while overcoming the Germans' stubborn resistance along the Danzig axis from the south, continued to pursue with their center and left-wing formations the enemy, who was retreating to the northeast. Having made a fighting advance of 10-50 kilometers during 8-9 March, the *front's* forces occupied more than 700 inhabited locales, including the towns of Pelplin, Schoeneck, Butow, Stolp, and 63 rail stations, reaching the line Gerdin, Dalwin, Postelau, Lappin, Kelpin, Kwiaty, Michrow, Schurow, Rowen, and Schmolzin.

By the close of 9 March the 1st Guards Tank Army, following a march, had concentrated its main forces in the Stolp—Schlawe area, while its forward units reached the line Lupow—Darsin—Glowitz.

By this time the 3rd Guards Tank Corps was fighting in the Hochwalde—Langbose (eight kilometers southwest of Lauenburg) area.

The 19th Army's 134th Rifle Corps, having completed in conjunction with units of the First Belorussian Front the defeat of the enemy's group of forces in the area east of Kolberg, was moving to link up with the army's main forces and by the close of 9 March, following a march, had concentrated in the Zirchow—Weddin—Klein Runow (ten kilometers southwest of Stolp) area.

On 9 March the *front* commander ordered the commander of the 65th Army and the commander of the 1st Guards Tank Corps, to attack toward Zoppot upon reaching the Kwaszyn area, to take the town and, having consolidated along the shore, split up the enemy group of forces putting up resistance in Danzig and Gdynia. The 3rd Guards Tank Corps was order to take the Neustadt—Luzin area by the close of 10 March and, continuing to attack toward Janowo and Gdynia on the morning of 11 March, by the close of the day to take Gdynia through a bold and decisive attack.

On 10 March the *front's* forces, while beating off enemy counterattacks along its right wing, with its center and left-wing forces continued to pursue the enemy retreating to the east. During the day the left wing's (49th, 70th and 19th armies) attacking forces, taking advantage of the 3rd and 1st guards tank corps' success, made a fighting advance of up to 30 kilometers and captured the towns of Karthaus, Lauenburg and Leba. The 1st Guards Tank Army crossed its main forces over the Leba River and the Brenkenhof Canal, while units of the 8th Guards Mechanized Corps bypassed the 19th Army's forces and reached the line Luzin—western outskirts of Neustadt.

Due to the movement of the 1st Tank Army's main forces into the Neustadt area, the *front* commander took personal control of the 3rd Guards Tank Corps and on 11 March ordered the corps to turn from the Luzin area to the south toward Schoenwalde and Kolletzkau and attack in the 70th Army's sector in the direction of Kolibken, with the task of reaching the shore and capturing Kolibken.

On this day the *front* commander, having established new boundary lines between the armies, changed the axes of the attacking armies. From 11 March the 2nd Shock Army was to attack toward Danzig from the south. The 65th Army was ordered to seize the northern part of Danzig and, as the 49th Army's forces advanced on Koln, it was ordered to remove its forces from the northern axis for use against Danzig. The 49th Army was given the task of reaching the line Koln—Lebno, after which it was to sharply turn to the east, with its main axis on Kwaszyn and Zoppot. The 1st Guards Tank Corps was to continue operations toward Zoppot. The 70th Army's main attack axis was set toward Schoenwalde and Kolibken.

During 11-12 March the Second Belorussian Front's right-wing forces, while overcoming the resistance of the enemy's Danzig group of forces, were moving slowly to the north and northeast. The *front's* left-wing forces were developing the offensive at a more vigorous pace and in two days advanced 45 kilometers.

The 2nd Shock Army, while attacking along the eastern and western banks of the Vistula River to the north, captured the towns of Neuteich and Dirschau and by the close of 12 March reached the line Ladekopp—Neukirch—Barendt—Zenslatz—Ostroschken. The 65th Army's forces reached the Danzig defensive line along the Unter Kalbude—Zuchau sector and, upon encountering the Germans' stubborn resistance and counterattacks, advanced very little. The 49th Army, along with the 1st Guards Tank Corps,[3] while developing the attack along its left wing, reached the line Julienthal—Kwaszyn. The 70th Army's forces, along with the 3rd Guards Tank and 8th Mechanized corps, while attacking in the direction of Zoppot and Kolibken and having advanced 30 kilometers over the past two days, reached the line Donasberg—Lenzits. The 19th Army, while developing the offensive in conjunction with the 1st Guards Tank Army's forces, advanced 35 kilometers and captured the towns of Neustadt and Reda, having reached the line excluding Lenzits—Pochlau—Putzig—Tupadel. The 1st Guards Tank Army captured the town of Putzig and was fighting for Janowo. The 3rd Guards Cavalry Corps was continuing to defend the shore of the Baltic Sea, having moved its right flank as far as Leba.

On 13 March the Second Belorussian Front's forces reached the defensive lines of the Danzig—Gdynia fortified area, along which the Germans had organized a stubborn defense. Throughout the day the *front's* left-wing forces cleared the enemy from the shore of the Putziger Wiek Gulf north and south of the town of Putzig. By the close of 13 March the Second Belorussian Front's armies were fighting along the line Fogtai—Schoensee—Barendt—Katzke—Ziegelei—Babenthal—Alte Muhle—excluding Zuchau—excluding Banin—Julienthal—Donasberg—Glodowken—excluding Janowo—Jakobsbruch—Rutzau and then to the north along the shore of the Baltic Sea. The Putzier Nehrung spit was held by forces of the German Second Army's LV Army Corps.

Upon the arrival of the Second Belorussian Front's forces at the Germans' Danzig—Gdynia defensive area, the third stage of the East Pomeranian operation, which had continued eight days (6-13 March), came to an end. During this time the *front's* right-wing forces carried out a fighting advance of 40-80 kilometers and those of the left wing 100-150 kilometers. The right-flank armies moved at a pace of 5-10 kilometers per day, and the left-flank armies at an average pace of 12-20 kilometers per day.

Of decisive significance for the development of events during this stage of the operation was the timely attack by all the *front's* forces along a new axis and the commitment into the battle of all the *front's* mobile formations (1st, 3rd and 8th guards tank corps and the 8th Mechanized Corps), as well as the 1st Guards Tank Army.

During this stage's fighting the enemy suffered heavy losses, but the *front's* forces were unable to destroy his group of forces and overcome from the march the defensive lines of the Danzig—Gdynia fortified area.

The completion of the German Second Army's defeat and the capture of the Danzig—Gdynia fortified area were accomplished during the course of the operation's fourth stage.

---

3   By this time the 1st Guards Tank Corps had been operationally resubordinated from the commander of the 65th Army to the commander of the 49th Army.

4

The Operation's Fourth Stage. The Defeat of the Germans' Danzig—Gdynia Group of Forces (14-30 March)

The fourth stage of the Second Belorussian Front's East Pomeranian operation had a number of features.

Upon their arrival at the Germans' Danzig—Gdynia fortified area, the Second Belorussian Front's forces encountered stubborn resistance by major enemy forces, supported from the sea by naval forces. Besides this, the German command, while striving to hold the Danzig—Gdynia beachhead, despite the catastrophic situation of its East Pomeranian group of forces, was reinforcing it, transferring reinforces by sea and air from Liepaja.

During the course of our forces' advance to the areas of Danzig and Gdynia, the Second Belorussian Front's operational sector was constantly narrowing, and by the moment they arrived at the Germans' Danzig—Gdynia defensive area, several of the *front's* armies were attacking along a 10-kilometer sector, which led to the excessive crowding of the offensive corridor with military equipment and rear services.[1]

The commander of the Second Belorussian Front decided to not allow any kind of pauses in combat operations for regrouping forces, and to continue the offensive with all the *front's* forces, in order to finally destroy the German Second Army, by depriving it of the capability of consolidating along a prepared defensive line immediately on the approaches to Danzig and Gdynia.

By the time the commander made this decision, the Germans opposite the Second Belorussian Front had the following forces. Along the southern face of the Danzig defensive area, from the Vistula to Leblau, were defending the XVIII Mountain Jaeger and XXIII Army corps, which included six infantry divisions (83rd, 23rd, 7th, 35th, and 37th infantry, and the 549th *Volkssturm* divisions), combat group "Gumpel," and units of the XXVII Army Corps' 31st Infantry Division. Further along the sector from Leblau to Leesen were defending the XXVII Army Corps' 251st Infantry Division and 12th *Luftwaffe* Field Division, which had been reinforced by two punishment battalions. The XLVI Panzer Corps, consisting of five infantry divisions (252nd, 73rd, 227th, 389th, and 215th), the 4th Panzer Division and one combat group was defending along the sector from Leesen to Janowo along the intermediary positions and in the second defensive zone. The garrison of Gdynia was subordinated to the corps commander. The VII Panzer Corps, consisting of the 7th Panzer Division, the 32nd Infantry Division and the 4th SS Panzer Group,

---

1   In the beginning of the operation's third stage, the width of the front was 200 kilometers, and at the beginning of the fourth stage the width of the offensive front was about 50 kilometers; the *front's* active operations developed along a 20-25-kilometer sector.

was defending along the Janowo—Rewa sector along the northern face of the Gdynia defensive area.

The LV Army Corps, consisting of the 61st Infantry Division, shore defense units and the remnants of various units that had fallen back, had been cut off from the army's main forces on the Putziger Nehrung spit.

The operations of the German Second Army's ground forces were supported by shore defense artillery, naval vessels[2] and aviation, having up to 100 combat aircraft, which were based on airfields in Danzig, Oliwa and Ramel.

The *front* commander came up with the following plan for defeating and destroying the enemy's group of forces. The main attack was to be launched in the direction of Zoppot, at the juncture of the Danzig and Gdynia defensive areas. For the purpose of separating the Danzig and Gdynia enemy groups of forces, it was decided to break through his defense and reach the shore of the Bay of Danzig in the Oliwa—Zoppot—Kolibken area; then to capture the towns of Danzig and Gdynia and complete the rout of the German Second Army.

On 13 March, in accordance with this plan, the armies were assigned their tasks.

The 65th Army, along with the 8th Mechanized Corps, with its main group of forces along the left flank, was to attack in the direction of Bissau and Mattern and no later than 15 March capture the line Emaus—Silberhammer—Pelonken. The army was ordered to be ready from the morning of 16 March to storm the northern part of the city of Danzig from the west.

The 49th Army, along with the 1st Guards Tank Corps, was to continue attacking with the task of capturing the Oliwa—Glettkau area and reach the shore by no later than 14 March. Immediately upon reaching the shore, the army was ordered to set up heavy artillery for destroying the enemy's ships and preventing them from approaching the ports of Gdynia and Danzig. Subsequently, the army was to storm the city of Danzig from the northwest.

The 70th Army, along with the 3rd Guards Tank Corps, was given the task of continuing the offensive with its main group of forces along the left wing, and no later than 14 March reaching the shore and capturing Zoppot; it subsequently was to attack along the shore to the south for the purpose of capturing Danzig from the north and northeast. Upon its arrival at the shore, the army was also to set up heavy artillery for destroying the enemy's ships.

The 19th Army, in conjunction with the 1st Guards Tank Army, was to reach the shore no later than 14 March and capture the town of Gdynia. The army was to make its main attack with the forces of two rifle corps and all its reinforcements along the front Witzlin—Janowo—Ramel. One corps was to remain defending along the sector excluding Rewa—Putzig—Grossendorf—Leba. It was also ordered to occupy the Putziger Nehrung spit with a reinforced detachment.

The 1st Tank Army's main forces, in conjunction with the 19th Army's right wing, were ordered to capture the town of Gdynia; part of these forces was to capture the Ochsheft—Mechlinken—Kasimierz area, while an independent detachment was to assist the 19th Army in capturing the Putziger Nehrugn spit.

The 2nd Shock Army, along with the 8th Guards Tank Corps, was ordered to temporarily go over to the defensive along the occupied line west of the Vistula River and to prepare an attack along the army's left wing in the direction of the southern outskirts of Danzig; along the eastern bank of the Vistula River, in conjunction with the Third Belorussian Front's left-wing forces, the army was to continue attacking with its right-wing formations.

By the start of the operation's fourth stage, the *front* commander detached the following artillery breakthrough weapons for strengthening the troops' artillery support.

---

2   At this time there were six cruisers, five destroyers, eight shore defense torpedo boats, 62 motor torpedo boats, and 35 submarines in the Bay of Danzig.

65th Army—the 23rd Artillery Breakthrough Division and the 5th Guards Mortar Brigade;

49th Army—the 2nd Artillery Breakthrough Division;

70th Army—the 26th Artillery Division and a guards mortar brigade;

19th Army—the 1st and 18th artillery breakthrough divisions and the 4th Guards Mortar Division.

The attacking forces would be supported by the 4th Air Army, which consisted of the 4th Assault Air, 8th Fighter and 5th Bomber corps. By this time the army had about 1,300 planes, of which about 500 were fighters, about 500 were assault aircraft, 260 bombers (including 110 Po-2 planes), and 40 reconnaissance planes. The army had the task of supporting the advance of the *front's* attacking forces through assault and bombing strikes against the defending enemy. Besides this, the army was fighting against the enemy's naval vessels.

The *front* commander demanded decisive and bold actions from the troops and the skillful employment of artillery and tanks, and to not by any means allow them to lag behind.

On the morning of 14 March the Second Belorussian Front's forces attacked the enemy's Danzig—Gdynia group of forces, launching their main attack in the direction of Zoppot.[3]

The shore of the Baltic Sea and the Putziger-Wiek Bay along the Beck—Jastszemba Gora sector were being defended by one of the 19th Army's rifle corps, and then along the sector as far as Kolberg, by units of the 3rd Cavalry Corps.

Up to 22 March the *front's* forces, while overcoming the Germans' stubborn resistance and beating off up to 20 counterattacks per day along some sectors, advanced no more than 1-1.5 kilometers per day. On some days the attacking forces did not advance at all, or the advance was measured in hundreds of meters. The *front's* forces attacking on Zoppot achieved the greatest successes.

The enemy, who had a powerful infantry group, with 200 tanks and assault guns, 180 batteries of artillery and mortars and more than 100 planes, supported by naval forces, put up fierce resistance and launched counterattacks, trying to prevent a breakthrough of his defense. The enemy aviation, based very close to the front lines in the Danzig and Zoppot areas, intensively attacked our attacking troops.

For the purpose of eliminating the German aviation based on the Danzig—Gdynia beachhead, the 4th Air Army launched a strike against the enemy's Danzig airfield. On 18 March units of the 4th Air Army's 8th Fighter Corps, despite the poor meteorological conditions, carried out a surprise attack against the enemy's airfields and launched an assault air strike in which 102 planes, organized into 13 groups, took part. As a result of this strike, 64 German planes were destroyed, burned or otherwise put out of action.

At the end of the preceding stage of the operation, the *front's* mobile formations, which were the first to reach the enemy's fortified positions and which were trying to break through the enemy's defense from the march, ended up in the infantry's combat formations. Due to the limited depth of operations (only eight kilometers remained to the shore), the tank formations subsequently operated essentially as direct infantry support tanks.

On 23 March the 70th Army's forces, in conjunction with the 49th Army's left-flank units and the 19th Army's right-flank units, having broken through the Germans' defense, captured the town of Zoppot. By the close of 23 March the *front's* forces had achieved the following results:

The 2nd Shock Army, together with the 8th Guards Tank Corps, while launching an attack along its left flank in the general direction of Danzig, from the south, reached the line: excluding

---

3 On the morning of 14 March the 2nd Shock Army attacked with its formations operating along the eastern bank of the Vistula River, and at 1200 on 16 March it attacked along the western bank of the Vistula River, with its main effort against Danzig from the south.

Stablau—excluding Kriefkohl—Rothof—Zipplau—excluding Praust—Straszyn—excluding Jenkau—Leblau. During this time particularly intensive fighting was waged along the Praust—Leblau sector, where the enemy was putting up stubborn resistance, and was frequently counterattacking along the main zone of the Danzig defensive area.

The 65th Army, along with the 8th Mechanized Corps,[4] which was operating among the 46th Rifle Corps' combat formation, broke through the main defensive zone of the Germans' Danzig defensive area along the Radaune River and reached the line excluding Leblau—the Ottominersee—Karzemken—Kokoschken—Leesen Station—Ellernitz—Pempau—excluding Banin.

The 49th Army, along with the 1st Guards Tank Corps, broke through the defense along the Germans' intermediate positions along the Barnewitz—Neue Welt sector and, while beating off the Germans' powerful counterattacks, was fighting along the main zone of the Danzig defensive area's northern face along the line Ramkau—excluding Hasenberg—Scheferai—Strauchmuhle—excluding Hochwasser—Schmirau. Fearing the complete encirclement of the XLVI Panzer Corps' units in the Bissau—Zappeln—Ramkau—Glauchau area, the Germans sought to prevent our troops' advance and launched counterattacks along the Hasenberg—Hochwasser sector.

The 70th Army, while operating with the 3rd Guards Tank Corps and having broken through the Germans' defense along the intermediate lines and the southern face of the Gdynia defensive area, captured the town of Zoppot and reached the shore of the Bay of Danzig. The army, having turned the 96th Rifle Corps' front to the north, continued to attack toward Kolibken, while the 114th Rifle and 3rd Guards Tank corps continued to attack to the south, in the direction of Oliwa. The 47th Corps had been pulled out of the fighting and concentrated in the woods south of Bernadowo and Gross Katz.

The 19th and 1st Guards Tank armies, which were attacking in the direction of Gdynia and not having achieved significant territorial results, were fighting by the close of 23 March and trying to break through the Gdynia defensive area's second defensive zone along the following line: Klein Katz—Weltzendorf—excluding Pustkowic—Zagorsz—Weisfluss—excluding Jakobsbruch—Bruch—Mechlinken. The 19th Army's 132nd Rifle Corps was defending the shore of the Putziger-Wiek Bay along the sector Beka—Grossensdorf and the shore of the Baltic Sea along the sector from Grossendorf to Jastszemba Gora. In the Grossendorf area the corps had one rifle regiment covering the exit from the Putziger Nehrung spit.

Thus as a result of the fierce fighting during 14-23 March and our troops' arrival at the shore of the Bay of Danzig, the German group of forces had been split into two parts—a Danzig and a Gdynia groups. Besides this, the enemy was holding the Putziger Nehrung spit, where there were also units of the German Second Army.

The Germans' Danzig group of forces consisted of the remnants of the XVIII Mountain Jaeger, XXIII, XXVII and XX army corps and part of the XLVI Panzer Corps' forces. By this time the enemy's Gdynia group of forces consisted of units of the VII Panzer Corps and part of the XLVI Panzer Corps' forces. Resistance by the enemy's forces continued to be stubborn, but the Germans' counterattacks became less and less organized with each day, and following each counterattack the German units, which were attacked by our forces in turn, were forced to abandoned their positions and fall back.

During 23-26 March the Second Belorussian Front's forces continued to push back the separated Danzig and Gdynia enemy groups of forces. The 2nd Shock, 65th, 49th, and 70th armies were operating against the Germans' Danzig group of forces, while the 19th Army and, a corps

---

4   By this time the 8th Mechanized Corps had been operationally subordinated to the 65th Army.

from the 70th Army and formations from the 1st Guards Tank Army fought against the Gdynia group of forces.

By the close of 26 March the enemy's Danzig group of forces, having suffered heavy casualties in the fighting along the near approaches to the city, had been squeezed back into Danzig, and our forces, having broken through the Danzig defensive area's second defensive zone, had begun fighting directly in the city's outskirts. By this time the 2nd Shock Army's left-flank formations had reached the line Kriefkohl—Muggenhal—Nobel—Albrecht—Matzkau—the western outskirts of Fogel Grief—excluding Altdorf—excluding Wonneberg. The 65th Army was fighting along the line Helle—Pitzkendorf—excluding Silberhammer. The 49th Army was engaged in street fighting in Hochstriess. The 70th Army, upon committing the 47th Rifle Corps into the fighting, had begun fighting along the northern outskirts of the Danzig suburbs—Hochstriess, Zaspe and Breussen.

At this time the *front's* left-wing forces, which were attacking the enemy's Gdynia group of forces, occupied the following position: the 19th Army and the 96th Rifle Corps (70th Army), along with the 1st Guards Tank Army's units, while launching an attack from the south and southwest, had broken through the second defensive zone of the Gdynia defensive area's southern face and were fighting along the southern and western outskirts of Gdynia. In the Grabau, Kilau, Puskowic, Janowo, Ramel, Bruch, and Mechlinken areas the attacking troops encountered the Germans' stubborn resistance and did not advance.

Recognizing that the Germans' Danzig group of forces was strongest and that its defeat depended upon speeding up the close of the operation, a large amount of forces was detached to the Danzig axis by the *front* commander.

In order to capture the fortress, city and port of Danzig as quickly as possible, on 26 March the *front* commander refined the axis of the attacks and the offensive sectors, and also established new boundary lines between the armies. The 2nd Shock Army was ordered to capture the southern part of Danzig; the 65th Army to capture the Zigankenberg suburb, the freight station and the center of Danzig; the 49th Army was to capture the northwestern part of Danzig and reach the Dead Vistula River; the 70th Army was to capture the Danzig, Lauenthal and Neufahrwasser areas and reach the Hafekanal Canal (along the southwestern outskirts of the Nesterplatte); if possible, it was to force the canal from the march and capture Weiselmunde and the Westerplatte. The *front* commander, having pointed out the peculiarities of street fighting, demanded from the army commanders the well-thought, thorough and precise organization of the fighting in Danzig, the full employment of all mortar and artillery weapons; the necessity was confirmed of attaching as many accompaniment weapons, tanks and self-propelled artillery as possible. The commander ordered that the remaining artillery be placed in firing positions and to precisely define its task for the entire period of the fighting to take Danzig. It was ordered to have forward artillery observers directly within the infantry's combat formations and to change the artillery's firing positions as rarely as possible. Ammunition for the troops was to be brought up by especially detached transportation, while the troop rear organs and transport were assigned special areas along the approaches to the city. Their arrival in the city was categorically forbidden.

The *front* commander entrusted the destruction of the Germans' Gdynia group of forces to the 19th Army's forces, while he ordered that the 1st Guards Tank Army be pulled out of the line on the night of 26-27 March and concentrated in the Lusin—Lebno—Schoenwalde area and on 27 March returned to the First Belorussian Front.

On 28 March the 19th Army's right-flank formations, following two days of street fighting, stormed and captured Gdynia and the suburbs of Grabau, Kielau and Zissau. The remnants of the enemy's Gdynia group of forces had been blockaded from the land along the Ochsheft beachhead. The army commander had been assigned the task of capturing the Ochsheft beachhead and no later than 31 March reaching the shore of the Putziger Wiek Bay, from Ochsheft to Rewa.

By the close of 28 March the *front's* right-wing forces had captured the central areas of Danzig. On this day the *front* commander ordered that the 1st and 3rd guards tank and 8th Mechanized corps be withdrawn from the army into the *front* reserve and concentrated in the Eggertshutte—Karthaus—Schoenwalde and Lebno areas. At the same time, he assigned the following tasks to the troops that were to storm Danzig:

- the 2nd Shock Army was to complete clearing the enemy from the fortress of Danzig, capture the Burgerwiesen area, and no later than 31 March to finish clearing the enemy from the area between the Vistula River and the Praust—Danzig railroad;
- the 65th Army was to capture the Treul and Heubude areas by no later than 30 March;
- the 49th Army was to clear of the enemy by no later than 30 March the area excluding Treul—excluding Heubude—the woods north of Heubude—excluding Weiselmunde.

The 70th Army was ordered to remain in its previous area with its main forces, to organize the defense of the shore along the Breussen—Kolibken area, and through artillery fire to prevent the approach of the enemy's ships to the shore, while part of its forces was to force the canal and capture the Weiselmunde and Westerplatte areas.

As a result of fierce street fighting, the *front's* right-wing forces on 30 March completely occupied the city and major maritime port on the Baltic Sea—Danzig.

With the capture of the city of Danzig the fourth stage of the East Pomeranian operation concluded successfully. As a result of 18 days of fighting, the Germans' Danzig—Gdynia group of forces had been defeated. The remnants of the German Second Army, which had been blockaded along the Ochsheft beachhead, were completely routed and captured by the 19th Army's forces on 4 April, while the army's remains, which had been blockaded on the Putziger Nehrung spit and the area of the Vistula River's delta southeast of Danzig, capitulated on 9 May.

The First Belorussian Front's right-wing forces defeated the German Eleventh Army and as early as 18 March completely occupied the western part of East Pomerania from the Neustettin—Kolberg line to the Bay of Stettin and the Oder River.

The East Pomeranian operation, which began on 10 February on the instructions of the Supreme Commander-in-Chief, Generalissimo of the Soviet Union Stalin, and conducted under his immediate leadership of the Second and First Belorussian fronts' forces, concluded on 30 March 1945 with the complete rout of the Germans' East Pomeranian group of forces.

A Short Summary and Conclusions on the Second Belorussian Front's Combat Operations During the East Pomeranian Operation

The Second Belorussian Front's East Pomeranian operation was a continuation of the Soviet army's winter offensive operations, which had begun in mid-January 1945, as a result of which the Second and Third Belorussian fronts' forces defeated the Germans' East Prussian group of forces, while the First Belorussian and First Ukrainian front's forces reached the Oder River on the approaches to Berlin and other vital areas of central Germany.

The Soviet forces' offensive in East Pomerania, which began without any kind of significant pause, foiled the flank attack, being prepared by the German command, against the Soviet forces operating along the Berlin direction, led to the defeat of the Germans' East Pomeranian group of forces and created favorable conditions for the subsequent offensive by Soviet forces on Berlin.

The defeat of the Germans' East Pomeranian group of forces, the capture of East Pomerania and the arrival of Soviet forces at the shore of the Baltic Sea along a sector from the Bay of Danzig to the Bay of Stettin securely covered the flank of Soviet forces operating along the Berlin direction and freed up the forces of two *fronts* (five of the First Belorussian Front's armies and five of the Second Belorussian Front's) for launching, together with the First Ukrainian Front, the concluding attack along the Berlin direction in April-May 1945.

During the time of the East Pomeranian operation—from 10 February to 30 March—the forces of the Second Belorussian Front occupied and completely cleared a significant part of East Pomerania, a territory of about 22,000 square kilometers, of the enemy. The *front's* right-wing forces covered a distance greater than 100 kilometers; the center's forces covered about 150 kilometers, and; the *front's* left-wing forces made a fighting advance of more than 300 kilometers. During the operation more than 4,500 inhabited locales were occupied, including 60 towns and 355 railroad stations, of which 34 were junctions. The occupied territory included a railroad network about 1,600 kilometers in length and a road network more than 4,600 kilometers in length.

During the East Pomeranian operation the Second Belorussian Front's forces defeated the German Second Army and completely eliminated the following number of units and formations in it:

Panzer divisions—2
SS panzer groups—1
Infantry divisions—15
Infantry brigades—10
Independent infantry regiments—22
Independent battalions—84
Military schools—2,

as well as many small subunits.

During the fighting the Second Belorussian Front's forces inflicted heavy losses on the Germans.

In the East Pomeranian operation the *front's* forces destroyed a large number of enemy military equipment and weapons and captured the following:

Tanks and self-propelled guns—680
Planes—430
Guns and mortars—3,450
Motor vehicles—24,000
Submarines (not combat-ready)—50
Various vessels—277
Various depots—610,

and a large amount of various military equipment.

Of greatest significance to the East Pomeranian operation's success was its timely beginning, which was defined by the high command on the basis of a profound evaluation of the operational-strategic situation and the enemy command's intentions.

Thanks to the *Stavka* of the Supreme Command's timely reinforcement of the troops attacking in East Pomerania, the non-stop nature of our attacks and their increasing power were secured.

The correct choice of both *front's* main attack axis facilitated the rapid defeat of the enemy's group of forces. The offensive by both *fronts'* shock groups to the north toward the Baltic Sea smashed the enemy's group of forces to pieces. The Second Belorussian Front's subsequent turn to the east, and that of the First Belorussian Front to the west, and the rapid development of the offensive along the shore of the Baltic Sea along diverging axes enabled the First Belorussian Front's forces to defeat the German Eleventh Army rapidly, and the Second Belorussian Front's forces to destroy the German Second Army.

A characteristic feature of the Second Belorussian Front's East Pomeranian operation was that the accumulation of forces for conducting and planning the operation was carried out during the course of an uninterrupted offensive. The offensive was begun without a pause and was essentially a continuation of the *front's* preceding offensive activities, but with new goals and tasks. The possibility of avoiding a break in the Second Belorussian Front's offensive activities was supported by the timely commitment of additional forces by the *Stavka* of the Supreme High Command.

As an instructive example from the Second Belorussian Front's activities, one may point to the rapid pace of the offensive along the main axes. Following their arrival at the seashore, our forces continued to carry out their operational tasks without halting or regrouping, having shifted their front 90 degrees. Despite the difficulty of such a maneuver, which demanded a great deal of troop mobility and precise command and control, the *front's* forces successfully coped with this task. The *front's* uninterrupted offensive won time and placed the enemy in even more difficult circumstances, depriving him of the capability of regrouping his forces.

The *front* commander exercised command and control from *front* command posts, which were located 60-100 kilometers from the troops and outfitted with reliable telegraph-telephone and radio communications, as well as through personal visits to the troops or by commandeering headquarters generals and officers to the most important sectors of the front. Such a method of command and control enabled him to uninterruptedly control the course of combat activities and made it possible to track the activities of subordinate commanders and their forces and, in case of necessity, to immediately take measures to eliminate shortcomings. An example of such intervention in an army commander's command and control was putting the 19th Army's forces in order during their offensive on Koslin.

A characteristic feature of the final stage of the Second Belorussian Front's East Pomeranian operation was the armies' offensive along narrow fronts. By the time of the forces' arrival at Germans' the Danzig—Gdynia defensive area, some armies were attacking along sectors up to ten kilometers in width, and while overcoming the enemy's defense along the approaches to Danzig and Gdynia, some armies' sectors fell to 5-6 kilometers. The armies' offensive along narrow fronts was due to the small strength of the attacking armies and the inadmissibility of the troops halting for any kind of regroupings. The armies attacked, having all their corps in the first echelon. Each corps, in its turn, had one division in its second echelon.

The methods for employing tank formations at various stages of the operation, depending on the situation, are a particularly interesting aspect of the Second Belorussian Front's activities.

At the start of the operation, the tank formations were employed as the *front* command's means for developing the breakthrough. The experience of the tank formation's activities during this period showed that during the tank formations' vigorous movement it is necessary to attach motorized infantry or supply attached infantry units with auto transport, which enables the tank formations to break free of the attacking armies' main forces to a great distance. In the opposite case, the tank formations that have broken clear of the infantry and not supplied with the necessary motorized infantry forces, may end up in a very difficult situation in the event of corresponding enemy countermeasures. For example, during the first two days following its commitment into the breach, the 3rd Guards Tank Corps made a fighting advance of 60 kilometers and leaped ahead of the 19th Army by 45-50 kilometers. The 313th Rifle Division, which was attached to the corps but not supplied with auto transport, fell behind the tank corps. Given such a separation from the infantry, the corps could have gotten into a difficult situation, which forced the *front* command to temporarily delay the corps in the Bublitz area and undertake measures to rapidly move rifle formations to this area.

During the fighting along the approaches to the towns of Danzig and Gdynia, a situation arose that excluded the possibility of employing a tank army and tank corps for independent operations apart from the combined-arms formations. Tank formations, by employing their tanks as direct infantry support tanks, operated with the rifle formations. Such an employment of the tank formations was dictated by the following conditions:

1) the tank formations, which had before this been pursuing the enemy, who was falling back on his previously prepared positions, were operating ahead of the infantry and, having arrived first at the enemy's Danzig—Gdynia defensive area, tried to break through the enemy's defense from the march, without infantry. With the arrival of our rifle units to the defensive line, the tank formations ended up in the infantry's combat formations and continued to attack along with it;
2) at the time of their arrival at the Danzig—Gdynia defensive line, our rifle formations were poorly supplied with direct infantry support tanks and needed additional reinforcement with tanks;
3) the limited operational depth (from the front line of the Germans' defense to the Bay of Danzig was a mere eight kilometers) did not allow us to employ tank formations for developing the success following the breakthrough of the enemy's defense;
4) the employment of tank formations for strengthening the rifle formations enabled us to more rapidly carry out the demand by the *Stavka* of the Supreme High Command to complete the rout of the Germans' East Pomeranian group of forces.

Soviet artillery played a major role in the East Pomeranian operation, just as it did in all the operations of the Great Patriotic War. Correctly employed and skillfully operating, it secured the breakthrough of all the defensive lines that the German command opposed to the *front's* offensive. It should be emphasized that the *front* command was able to carry out the augmentation of the artillery's forces immediately before the final attack around Danzig and Gdynia, in conditions of a rapid offensive. This, undoubtedly, facilitated the Second Belorussian Front's success.

Due to poor meteorological conditions, the air forces' participation in the East Pomeranian operation was limited. In all, there were no more than ten days during the operation which fully allowed us to employ our aviation. However, despite the extremely unfavorable conditions, the activities of the *front's* aviation (4th Air Army) were successful and fully facilitated the offensive by the combined-arms and tank formations. Most effective were its activities in defeating the Germans' Danzig—Gdynia group of forces and the fight against the enemy's naval forces.

Cavalry carried out two tasks in the course of the East Pomeranian operation. In the first stage, during the breakthrough of the Germans' defense and the arrival of the *front's* shock group at the shore of the Baltic Sea, units of the 3rd Guards Cavalry Corps covered the *front's* left wing. Subsequently, with the turn of the *front's* forces and their advance to the east, the cavalry guarded the shore of the Baltic Sea along a 160-kilometer sector.

The Second Belorussian Front's East Pomeranian operation had been successfully concluded. The tasks laid down by the supreme high command had been carried out.

Following the defeat of the German Second Army, the Second Belorussian Front's main forces, according to a decision by the *Stavka* of the Supreme High Command, were to be regrouped to the Stettin axis by 15 April 1945, in order to take part in the Berlin operation. The *front's* task consisted of launching an attack along the Stettin—Rostock axis, defeating the enemy's Stettin group of forces (the German Third Panzer Army) and securely protecting the right flank of the First Belorussian Front, which was to launch an attack directly on Berlin.

Part V

The First Ukrainian Front's Lower Silesian Offensive Operation (8-24 February 1945)

The article, 'The First Ukrainian Front's Lower Silesian Offensive Operation', was written by Colonel N.A. Fokin. Editor, Lieutenant General S.P. Platonov.

Introduction

The First Ukrainian Front's Lower Silesian offensive operation was carried out from 8-24 February 1945. It began immediately upon the completion of the *front's* January offensive and was conducted in complete accord with the *Stavka* of the Supreme High Command's overall design.

The 3rd Guards, 13th, 52nd, 6th, 5th Guards, and 21st combined-arms armies, the 4th and 3rd Guards tank armies, 2nd Air Army, the 25th, 4th Guards and 31st tank, and 7th Guards Mechanized corps took part in the Lower Silesian operation.

As a result of the operation, the *front's* right-wing forces, having defeated up to 27 enemy divisions and encircled in the Breslau area a group of German-Fascist forces numbering up to 40,000 men and officers, reached the Neisse River alongside the First Belorussian Front. The line that the *front's* forces occupied by the close of the operation offered them the opportunity in a subsequent operation of launching attacks to the west, on Leipzig and Dresden, and to the northwest—by outflanking Berlin, from the south and southwest—to the central areas of Czechoslovakia, where a large group of Hitlerite forces was located.

The Lower Silesian offensive operation was prepared during the course of the First Ukrainian Front's Sandomierz-Silesian operation and was conducted by the same forces.

The operation was prepared in an original situation. First of all, at the end of January the *front's* forces, which had been weakened by the preceding battles, were operating along a front of about 450 kilometers. At the same time, a significant part of the tank forces were located along the *front's* left wing, in the Silesian industrial area. Because, according to the conditions of the situation, the *front* was to launch its attack in a new operation along the right flank, the necessity arose of carrying out a major regrouping of our forces to the *front's* right flank. The organization and conduct of this regrouping in conditions of our ongoing offensive is very instructive.

Secondly, the operation was prepared while the *front's* communications were quite strained, which arose as a result of the vigorous pace of our forces' attack in the preceding Sandomierz-Silesian operation. In the present situation, given the increasing distance of the rear bases from the troops to hundreds of kilometers, the accumulation of supplies for a new operation was an extraordinarily difficult matter. The experience of resolving this complex and responsible task deserves intensive study.

Also instructive is the experience of conducting the operation. The *front's* forces attacked in wooded and swampy terrain during the spring thaw and in unfavorable meteorological conditions, which rendered the conditions for our offensive much more difficult, tied the troops to the roads and almost excluded our aviation's operations. But even in these conditions the *front's* forces showed a high degree of combat skill.

Characteristic of the operation were deep envelopments and the outflanking of major enemy groups of forces, which often culminated in their encirclement (Breslau, Glogau), and bold and decisive actions by the tank troops alongside the combined-arms armies and apart from them.

The operation was conducted in the absence of second echelons and reserves in the *front*, and thus the *front* commander's measures to create reserves during the operation for augmenting the efforts of the forces attacking along the axis of the *front's* main attack and for securing the main shock group's open left flank, are of enormous interest.

All of these characteristics of preparing and conducting the Lower Silesian offensive operation enable us to consider that the operation's experience may be employed both for elaborating the theory of a *front* offensive operation, as well as for training the Soviet army's staffs and troops.

The present work represents the first attempt to fill in the blanks in our military-historical literature in illuminating the First Ukrainian Front's combat operations along the Berlin direction in February 1945, that is, during the period between the Sandomierz-Silesian and Berlin operations.

This work examines only the general and most characteristic aspects of preparing for and conducting the operation. Thus we do not find questions of planning the operation fully illuminated here, nor are the army commanders' decisions cited, while the activities of the combat arms are examined in only a general way. All of these questions are touched upon only to that degree in which they help us to understand the general scheme and course of the operation.

Nor is the 6th Army's struggle to eliminate the enemy's encircled group of forces in the Breslau area examined, as well as the 3rd Guards Army's elimination of the encircled enemy in the Glogau area. The fighting in these areas lies outside the immediate boundaries of the First Ukrainian Front's February operation and continued in the Glogau area to 1 April 1945, and in the Breslau area to 6 May 1945.

An all-round illumination of this interesting and instructive operation must be the result of further research and the production of both a general monograph on the operation, as well as individual articles dedicated to generalizing the combat experience of employing the various combat arms.

1

The Operation's Preparation

A. THE SITUATION BY THE START OF THE OPERATION'S PREPARATION

The Overall Situation Along the Soviet-German Front by the End of January 1945

January 1945 was distinguished by the Soviet army's new and brilliant successes. Soviet troops, having unleashed offensive operations along the entire front from the Baltic Sea to the Carpathians inclusively, defeated the enemy's main forces, with which the German-Fascist command hoped to hold off the Soviet army along the approaches to the eastern borders of Germany.

As a result of the offensive by the forces of the Third and Second Belorussian fronts, the German-Fascist Army Group North was defeated, out of which about 30 divisions had been encircled in the Königsberg area. East Prussia—the nest of Prussian militarism and the springboard for Hitlerite aggression to the east—had been eliminated.

During the offensive by the forces of the First Belorussian and the First and Fourth Ukrainian fronts, about 50 divisions from Army Group Center were defeated. Soviet forces liberated allied Poland. Fascist Germany was deprived of the opportunity to exploit for war purposes the country's rich agricultural areas and the very important eastern coal and metallurgical area—the Silesian industrial area.

The Soviet forces, in developing the offensive along the Berlin direction, entered German territory. Upon reaching the Oder River at the end of January, they presented a real threat to Berlin, to which no more than 60-80 kilometers remained.

At the same time, in the Baltic area, Soviet forces continued to destroy a large group of German-Fascist forces, comprising 30 divisions pressed against the sea between Tukums and Liepaja.

The remains of the Hitlerite group of forces, surrounded in December 1944, were being destroyed in the western part of Budapest.

Thus by the end of January more than half of the German-Fascist ground forces along the Soviet-German front at the beginning of the month had been defeated by Soviet forces or were surrounded, while the remnants of Army Group Center, covering the Berlin direction, had been thrown beyond the Oder River by the attacks of the First Belorussian and First Ukrainian fronts.

The Soviet army's crushing attacks in January 1945 forced the German-Fascist command to pull its more combat-capable formations from the Western to the Soviet-German front, which foiled their successfully developing winter offensive in the Ardennes.[1] This saved the Anglo-American forces from a shameful defeat and enabled them by the end of January to restore the situation that they had occupied before the Germans' Ardennes attack.

The broad scope of our offensive and its results forced the Anglo-American command to speed up the preparation of its operations for overcoming the "Siegfried Line," in order to preempt the Soviet army in reaching the central regions of Germany.

---

1   Editor's note. This statement is patently false, as the crisis in the West occasioned by the German army's Ardennes offensive had already passed by the start of the Red Army's winter offensive, and the "bulge" in the Allied line was being rapidly eliminated.

However, during this period the Anglo-American command criminally delayed the conduct of major offensive operations. It was sure that the Soviet forces, following their gigantic offensive in January 1945, would not be in any condition to continue their offensive further without a break, and that they would have to halt for a prolonged period of time along the Oder in order to prepare for new operations.

At the same time, the Anglo-Americans clearly saw the catastrophic situation of the German-Fascist army on the Soviet-German front. It was for this reason that the Anglo-American command purposely avoided active military operations, which enabled the Germans to transfer, without consequences, not only individual formations, but entire armies (the Sixth SS Panzer Army, followed by the majority of the Fifth Panzer Army's formations) from the Western to the Eastern front.

Thus by freeing up the German-Fascist command's hands along the Western front through its lack of activity, the Anglo-American command hoped that the Germans, having strengthened their Eastern front, would be able to resist the Soviet army for an extended period of time. The Anglo-American command was waiting for all the German army's forces to be tied down along the Eastern front, and the Western front to be essentially open, in order to launch an unopposed offensive to the east. At the same time, it was planned the Anglo-American armies would be able to seize Berlin before the arrival of Soviet forces in the area.

The treacherous activities of the Anglo-American imperialists in relation to their Russian ally along the theaters of military activities were supplemented by their diplomacy's anti-Soviet actions.

The representatives of the US and English ruling circles continued behind the Soviet Union's back to intensively conduct behind-the-scenes negotiations with representatives of the German-Fascist government on concluding a secret separate peace, according to the terms of which Germany, with the all-round support of the USA and England, was to continue the war against the USSR.

The perfidious violation of their allied obligations to the USSR by the US and English governments, their disgusting desire to foil the Soviet army's successfully developing offensive against the German-Fascist forces, and their all-round assistance to the Hitlerite command in its struggle against the Soviet army unmasked the political aspirations of the Anglo-American imperialists, particularly the American imperialists' aggressive policy. As the end of the war drew nearer, their reactionary policy revealed itself more openly: untrammeled economic and political domination in Europe and Asia during the postwar period, the maintenance of fascism in Germany and militarism in Japan and their military potential, and the establishment of reactionary regimes in the European states, with a pro-American and pro-English orientation.

The chief goal of this policy was to knock together a bloc of imperialist states and unleash a new war against the Soviet Union. It was planned to employ the German-Fascist army as the main shock force in this war.

The sole force withstanding the neo-fascist aspirations of American imperialism and that of its English partner was the Soviet Union. It was for this reason that all the efforts of the American and English governments and their military command were directed at maximally weakening the economic and military might of the Soviet Union, to subordinate the USSR to the economic and military dictates of the USA and England and thus deprive the Soviet government of the ability to influence the postwar development of the world.

In order to foil these impudent and criminal schemes by the USA and England, the Soviet army had to launch new and powerful attacks against the German-Fascist army along the most important strategic directions.

In these conditions, the development of the Soviet forces' further offensive along the Berlin direction acquired enormous military-political significance.

In connection with this, the Soviet supreme high command undertook all necessary measures, alongside the organization of the offensive along the other sectors of the Soviet-German front, so as to prepare and launch a new attack as quickly as possible against the German-Fascist main group of forces covering the Berlin direction. This attack was to, independent of the position occupied by the American and English government, deprive Hitlerite Germany of the capability of putting up further resistance and force it to capitulate unconditionally.

The offensive by the forces of the First Ukrainian Front in February 1945 was one of those measures to support the preparation of conditions for launching the concluding attack against Hitlerite Germany.

The First Ukrainian Front's Operational Situation by 28 January 1945

In developing the offensive begun on 12 January 1945, the First Ukrainian Front (Marshal of the Soviet Union I.S. Konev, commander, Lieutenant General K.V. Krainyukov,[2] member of the military council, and General, now Marshal of the Soviet Union, V.D. Sokolovskii, chief of staff) reached the Oder River with its main forces along the sector from Keben to Ratiborhammer (15 kilometers north of Ratibor), about 250 kilometers in length. The overall length of the front along the entire sector of the *front's* attack zone upon reaching the Oder River was about 450 kilometers.

Having forced this major water line from the march along several individual sectors, the *front's* forces seized a number of bridgeheads along the river's left bank and were continuing to fight to expand them.

By this time the neighbor on the right—the First Belorussian Front, which was also developing the offensive toward the Oder, had advanced significantly further west of the First Ukrainian Front, while the neighbor to the left—the Fourth Ukrainian Front, had fallen behind and was echeloned to the rear.

The successful offensive by the First Belorussian Front and the absence of the enemy's serious enemy resistance against the First Ukrainian Front's right-wing armies during their approach to the Oder offered to the latter the opportunity to advance considerably further west than the *front's* left-wing armies. The lagging of the *front's* left-wing armies was conditioned by the stubborn fighting for the Silesian industrial area and the necessity of securing the *front's* left flank along the boundary with the Fourth Ukrainian Front.

By the end of January the *front's* right-wing armies occupied the following position.

The 3rd Guards Army, having deployed all of its corps in a single echelon during the course of pursuing the enemy, was attacking along a sector 70 kilometers wide. Its main forces (120th and 21st rifle corps), while overcoming the resistance of the German Ninth Army, which was falling back to the southwest under the blows of the First Belorussian Front, continued to approach the Oder. On 28 January its corps were on the line Gostyn—Bojanowo, 50-70 kilometers from the Oder. The 25th Tank Corps (commander, Major General Ye.I. Fominykh), which had been operationally subordinated to the army commander, had by this time advanced forward and was fighting west of Leszno (Lissa). The left-flank 76th Rifle Corps reached the Oder in the Keben area and, having forced the river here, captured a small bridgehead on its western bank.

The 13th Army (Colonel General N.P. Pukhov,[3] commander, Major General N.A. Kozlov, member of the military council, and Lieutenant General G.K. Malandin, chief of staff) had

---

2 Editor's note. Konstantin Vasil'evich Krainyukov (1902-75) joined the Red Army in 1919 and served throughout his career as a political officer. During the Great Patriotic War he served as a political commissar in several armies and finished the war as a member of the First Ukrainian Front's military council. Following the war, Krainyukov served as deputy chief of the armed forces' Main Political Directorate.

3 Editor's note. Nikolai Pavlovich Pukhov (1895-1958) was drafted into the imperial army in 1916 and he joined the Red Army two years later. During the Great Patriotic War he commanded a division and the 13th Army from 1942 until the end of the war. Following the war, Pukhov commanded a number of military districts.

reached the Oder along the entire front between Keben and Malcz. The army's forces forced the river and, with the support of the 4th Tank Army's forces, captured a bridgehead west of the towns of Keben and Steinau, up to 16 kilometers deep and up to 30 kilometers in width. On the army's left flank another small bridgehead, 2-3 kilometers deep and up to ten kilometers wide, was also seized.

The 102nd and 27th rifle corps, which were operating in the army's first echelon, occupied a front 86 kilometers wide and were engaged in heavy fighting to maintain and expand the captured bridgeheads. The 24th Rifle Corps—the army's second echelon—had not been committed into the fighting and was located on the eastern bank of the Oder, in the wooded area northeast of Wolau.

The 4th Tank Army (Colonel General D.D. Lelyushenko,[4] commander, Major General K.I. Upman, chief of staff), which was attacking in the 13th Army's sector, reached the right bank of the Oder with its main forces and began to cross its forced over to the captured bridgehead in the Steinau area.

The 52nd Army (Colonel General K.A. Koroteev,[5] commander, Major General I.P. Kabichkin, member of the military council, and Major General A.N. Kolominov, chief of staff), whose offensive front along the approaches to the Oder was 60 kilometers wide, reached the Oder with its flank formations in the areas of Auras (north of Breslau) and Ohlau (south of Breslau). At the same time, two small bridgeheads had been seized southeast of Breslau—one immediately to the south of Breslau, and the other to the north of Ohlau. In the center the army's forces were halted by the enemy's stubborn resistance along the outer ring of the Breslau fortified area.

While carrying out the offensive with its 73rd and 78th rifle corps, the army kept the 48th Rifle Corps in its second echelon during the approach to the Oder.

The 5th Guards Army (Colonel General A.S. Zhadov,[6] commander, Major General A.N. Krivulin, member of the military council, and Major General N.I. Lyamin, chief of staff) reached the Oder along a 70-kilometer front from Ohlau to Oppeln. All three of the army's corps (32nd, 33rd and 34th) were in the same echelon. By 28 January the army had seized three bridgeheads along the left bank of the Oder: one southeast of Ohlau, eight kilometers deep and ten kilometers wide, and two northwest of Oppeln, 3-4 kilometers deep and up to ten kilometers wide each.

The tasks assigned by the *front* commander for the right-wing armies—to reach the Oder and seize bridgeheads along its left bank—were accomplished. These armies' next assignments were to enlarge the bridgeheads in all directions, consolidate and to create favorable conditions for deploying their forces for a new offensive operation.

By 28 January the *front's* left-wing forces had accomplished their second major operational goal, assigned to the *front* in the Sandomierz-Silesian operation. Thanks to the combined efforts of the 3rd Guards Tank, and the 21st, 59th, and 60th combined-arms armies, as well as units of the 31st

---

4   Editor's note. Dmitrii Danilovich Lelyushenko (1901-87) joined the Red Army in 1919 and served in the cavalry. During the Great Patriotic War he commanded a mechanized and a rifle corps, as well as a number of combined-arms armies. In 1944 he was appointed commander of the 4th Tank Army (later 4th Guards Tank Army). Following the war, Lelyushenko held a number of command assignments.

5   Editor's note. Konstantin Apollonovich Koroteev (1903-53) joined the imperial army in 1916 and the Red Army in 1918. During the Great Patriotic War he commanded a corps and a number of armies and was appointed commander of the 52nd Army in 1953. Following the war, Koroteev commanded an army and a military district.

6   Editor's note. Aleksei Semyonovich Zhadov (before 1942, Zhidov) (1901-77) joined the Red Army in 1919 and fought in the civil war. During the Great Patriotic War he commanded an airborne and a cavalry corps, before being appointed commander of the 66th (later 5th Guards) Army in 1943. Following the war, Zhadov served in a variety of administrative posts.

and 4th Guards Tank and 1st Guards Cavalry corps, the Silesian industrial area was cleared of German-Fascist forces and the enemy group of forces defending the area was defeated.

On 28 January the 21st Army's (Colonel General D.N. Gusev,[7] commander, Lieutenant General V.P. Mzhavanadze, member of the military council, and Lieutenant General G.K. Bukhovets, chief of staff) 117th Rifle Corps was fighting for a bridgehead over the Oder (south of Oppeln) along a 30-kilometer front. The 55th and 118th rifle corps, following the completion of the fighting for the Silesian industrial area, were pulled back into the army's second echelon to the area northwest of Katowice and partially began to move toward the Oder.

The 59th Army (Lieutenant General I.T. Korovnikov,[8] commander, Major General P.S. Lebedev, member of the military council, and Major General N.P. Koval'chuk, chief of staff), having been freed up following the completion of the fighting in the center of the Dombrowo coal basin, began to move toward the Oder. The army was to relieve the 1st Guards Cavalry Corps (Lieutenant General V.K. Baranov, commander), which was defending the Oder's right bank along a 50-kilometer front from Krappitz to Ratiborhammer.

The 4th Guards Tank Corps (Lieutenant General P.P. Poluboyarov, commander), which had been operationally subordinated to the commander of the 59th Army, and the 31st Tank Corps (Major General G.G. Kuznetsov, commander), which had been operationally subordinated to the commander of the 21st Army, were concentrating in the Katowice area following the defeat of the enemy's Dombrowo group of forces and was putting itself themselves in order.

The 3rd Guards Tank Army (Colonel General P.S. Rybalko,[9] commander, Lieutenant General S.I. Mel'nikov, member of the military council, and Major General D.D. Bakhmet'ev, chief of staff), after clearing the German-Fascist forces out of the Silesian industrial area, had all of its corps drawn into fighting with the enemy, who was actively opposing our further offensive toward Rybnik and Zorau. Having deployed along a 40-kilometer front from Rybnik to Nikolai, and while repelling the Germans' numerous attacks, the army was moving slowly to the southwest, while simultaneously waging heavy battles for Rybnik.

The 60th Army (Colonel General P.A. Kurochkin,[10] commander, Major General V.M. Olenin, member of the military council, and Major General A.D. Goncharov, chief of staff), along with the attached 152nd Independent Tank Brigade, and in conjunction with the forces of the 3rd Guards Tank Army, was covering the *front's* left wing. Having deployed all three corps (15th, 106th and 28th) in a single echelon along a 34-kilometer front from Zulow to Wilamowice, the army was attacking in the direction of Zorau, Rybnik and Ratibor.

Aside from the forces freed up as a result of the completion of the fighting in the Silesian industrial area, the *front* commander also disposed of significant reserves: the 6th Army

---

7   Editor's note. Dmitrii Nikolaevich Gusev (1894-1957) joined the Russian imperial army in 1916 and the Red Army in 1918. During the Great Patriotic War he served in a number of staff positions until his appointment as commander of the 21st Army in 1944. Following the war, Gusev commanded a number of military districts.

8   Editor's note. Ivan Terent'evich Korovnikov (1902-76) joined the Red Army in 1919. During the Great Patriotic War he held a number of command positions and was appointed commander of the 59th Army in 1942. Following the war, Korovnikov commanded a military district and served in the central military apparatus.

9   Editor's note. Pavel Semyonovich Rybalko (1894-1948) joined the Russian imperial army in 1915 and the Red Army in 1919. During the Great Patriotic War he served in the General Staff apparatus and the tank troops, becoming commander of the 3rd Guards Tank Army in 1943. Following the war, Rybalko commanded the Red Army's armored forces.

10   Editor's note. Pavel Alekseevich Kurochkin (1900-89) joined the Red Guard in 1917 and the Red Army in 1918. During the Great Patriotic War he served as a military district, army and *front* commander, before being appointed commander of the 60th Army in 1944. Following the war, Kurochkin served as a military district commander and chief of the Frunze Military Academy.

(Lieutenant General V.A. Gluzdovskii,[11] commander, Major General V.Ya. Klokov, member of the military council, and Major General F.D. Kuleshov, chief of staff); the 7th Guards Mechanized Corps (Lieutenant General I.P. Korchagin, commander), and; the 150th Independent Tank Brigade. At the end of January these forces were concentrated in the Szczercow—Czestochowa—Krzepice area.

The Condition of the *Front's* Troops and Rear

During the January offensive the *front's* forces, while waging uninterrupted battles in difficult winter conditions, advanced 500 kilometers. As a result of the losses suffered during this period, the numerical strength of the formations and units fell significantly. The rifle divisions in the majority of armies numbered, on the average, 5,500 men. The rifle companies' composition was between 40-50 men. All of this led to a decline in the offensive capabilities of the *front's* forces.

Equipment losses, particularly among the armored and mechanized forces, also had a part in the reduction of the *front's* combat capabilities.

In all, the *front* numbered 2,215 tanks and self-propelled guns. Of these, the combined-arms armies had about 250-300 tanks and self-propelled guns, while the remainder formed part of the tank armies and independent tank and mechanized corps. There were a total of 414 tanks and self-propelled guns in the 4th Tank Army and 567 in the 3rd Guards Tank Army. Some independent tank corps had 150-200 tanks and self-propelled guns, while the 7th Guards Mechanized Corps had 241.

The quantitative reduction of the tank armies' combat strength was also exacerbated by the great wear and tear on the remaining tanks. For example, as of 1 February 1945 the engine life of 103 tanks in the 4th Tank Army was equivalent to zero, while it did not exceed 50 motor hours in the remaining 311 vehicles. The same picture existed in the 3rd Guards Tank Army.

At the end of January, in connection with the great extension of the rear organs, difficulties arose in the troops' materiel supply, particularly with munitions, fuels and lubricants.

The great amount of damage to the railroads, caused by the enemy while withdrawing along the *front's* attack sector, as well as the slow pace of their restoration, led to a situation in which the *front's* forces continued to be based on the rail stations located behind the Vistula in the Rozwadow—Mielec—Debica area. The gap between the *front* bases and the troops at this time exceeded 500 kilometers.

The entire burden of delivering supplies to the troops lay on auto transportation. Despite the extremely intensive work by the *front* automobile park, it failed to cope with the delivery of munitions and fuel. Besides this, a round trip by motor vehicles ate up a lot of fuel (approximately 15 percent of the fuel delivered).

Due to this, the provisioning of the troops with munitions and fuels and lubricants fell sharply, at the same time the supplies of all kinds of combat supply were more than sufficient at the *front* bases.

As of 28 January the supplies of munitions in the 3rd Guards Army's artillery units did not exceed 0.5 of a combat load. The supplies of automobile fuel amounted to 1.1 refill and 0.2 refills of diesel fuel. Taking into account the presence of fuel and lubricants at the army depots, these supplies did not exceed 1.4-1.7 refills.

---

11 Editor's note. Vladimir Alekseevich Gluzdovskii (1903-67) joined the Red Army in 1919. During the Great Patriotic War he served as an army chief of staff and army commander until his appointment as commander of the 6th Army in 1944. Following the war, Gluzdovskii served in a number of staff and teaching positions.

In the 13th Army the troops' provisioning as of 27 January was as follows. On the average, the artillery had 0.6 combat loads for medium guns and 0.9 combat loads for heavy guns. Taking into account the supplies available in the army depots, the artillery's supply of munitions reached 1.5-2 combat loads. The supply of automobile and diesel fuel with the troops was 0.4 refills. There was no gasoline in the army depots, while there were 0.9 refills of diesel fuel.

The situation was no better among the tank troops. For example, in the 4th Tank Army the troops had on the average 0.7 of a combat load of shells, 0.1 refills of gasoline, 1.4 refills of diesel fuel, and 1.1 refills of motor oil. If the supplies in the army depots are taken into account, this amount is slightly larger.

The significant remove of the *front* depots also had an influence on the repair and restoration of the tank troops' equipment. The employment of almost the entire auto transport for delivering munitions and fuel made the delivery of the necessary spare parts more difficult.

All of the circumstances listed above rendered the troops' combat activities much more difficult and reduced their capabilities.

A description of the situation along the *front's* offensive sector would be incomplete without the mention of the situation in the *front's* rear, within the territory liberated by our troops during the course of the January offensive.

The enormous political transformations that began in Poland immediately upon its liberation by the Soviet army from the German-Fascist occupiers brought about a great political uplift among the Polish people and a mass movement for the creation of a truly democratic Polish state. The Polish people expressed their feelings of profound thanks to the Soviet forces and the Soviet government for that inestimable aid that was rendered to Poland during these difficult days.

Thus in the political sense, our forces were assured of the moral and political support of the Polish people in their further struggle with the German-Fascist army.

However, the Polish people's democratic movement encountered the bitter resistance of Polish reactionary nationalist elements, which were directed by the Anglo-American imperialists. The underground armed organization of Mikolajczyk,[12] that traitor to the Polish people, having closed ranks with Ukrainian nationalists operating on Polish territory, embarked on a path of open armed conflict with the Soviet army. Terrorist and diversionary acts and open attacks by armed bands of the so-called "Home Army" on the Soviet army's forces and transport demanded increased vigilance of Soviet forces and a decisive struggle with these hostile elements.

Simultaneously, in our troops' rear the struggle continued against so-called wandering "pockets," which represented the remnants of the enemy's units and formations defeated in the January offensive, which in dispersed groups, often large ones, were attempting to break through to the west and southwest in order to link up with their forces that had retired behind the Oder. They attacked our transports, headquarters, depots, and airfields, seriously interfering with the normal work of the *front's* rear organs.

The *front* commander, in a special directive No. 0028/op of 27 January 1945, ordered the army commanders to clean out their rear areas of hostile bands and ensure normal conditions for the rear's work.

The presence of these bands and wandering "pockets" and the necessity of combating them, to a certain degree complicated the situation in the *front's* rear and distracted attention and forces from the resolution of the main combat tasks.

---

12 Editor's note. This is a reference to Stanislaw Mikolajczyk (1901-66), who was active in prewar Polish politics and was head of the Polish People's Party. From 1943 he headed the Polish National Council, which served as the government-in-exile in London. He returned to Poland after the war and became a deputy prime minister in the Soviet-dominated Provisional Government of National Unity. His party was defeated in the rigged elections of 1948 and he fled to Great Britain. He later immigrated to the US.

The Disposition and Condition of the Enemy's Forces by the End of January 1945

At the beginning of January the forces of the First Ukrainian Front were opposed by the German Fourth Panzer and Seventeenth armies, which were part of Army Group A. During the January offensive the Fourth Panzer and Seventeenth armies' main forces were routed. By the end of January the majority of these armies' formations had ceased to exist as combat entities. Their remnants had been combined into various combat groups, to which were attached either the numbers of the former divisions or the last names of the generals and officers commanding them.

Besides this, along the *front's* right flank, facing the 3rd Guards Army, there were several units and formations from the German Ninth Army, which in January was operating against the forces of the First Belorussian Front.

In the course of their disorganized retreat, the enemy's units and formations had become mixed up, while communications between them and command and control had become so disorganized that at the end of January the German-Fascist command was not in a position to fully account for which formations had survived and who and in what condition was withdrawing to the Oder's left bank. One thing was clear, and that was that an insignificant part of the formations had maintained any kind of combat capability. The majority of the formations and units were not combat-capable and were demoralized. In order to restore the remnants of the defeated formations as a combat force, it was necessary to withdraw them into the rear for reforming.

Thus the command of the reformed Army Group Center decided to entrust the defense of the Oder River line to those forces that had been moved up to the Oder from other sectors of the front at the end of January and which continued to arrive at the beginning of February, as well as those formations and units that had escaped complete defeat during the January fighting.

Captured German documents, data from all forms of intelligence, and prisoner testimony make it possible to establish the disposition of the German-Fascist forces facing the First Ukrainian Front on 1 February 1945. (See Table V/1.A.1).

The table shows that facing the armies of the *front's* right wing (3rd Guards, 13th and 52nd), which contained 27 rifle divisions (each numbering 5,500 men), the enemy had 8.5 divisions (taking into account different combat groups, independent units and subunits and transferred half-outfitted divisions numbering 5,000-5,500 men apiece) along a 216-kilometer front. It follows that each enemy division had a 25.5-kilometer front, while the First Ukrainian Front's right-wing forces had a front of eight kilometers per division. Thus the forces of the *front's* right wing enjoyed a threefold superiority in infantry. The enemy had (in terms of average outfitted division) four panzer divisions, while the *front* disposed of two tank and one mechanized corps.

Facing the center armies (5th Guards and 21st armies[13]), which had 18 rifle divisions along a 100-kilometer front, the enemy disposed of six divisions. Each enemy division had a 16.6-kilometer front, while the First Ukrainian Front's center forces had 6-kilometer front. Thus the *front's* forces along this sector outnumbered the enemy's infantry by a factor of three to one.

Facing the forces of the *front's* left wing (59th and 60th armies and the 1st Guards Cavalry Corps), which numbered 19 divisions along a 124-kilometer front; the enemy disposed of eight divisions. Each enemy division had an average front of 15.5 kilometers, while the First Ukrainian Front's left-wing forces had a front of six kilometers. The enemy had about 2 ½ panzer divisions, while we disposed along the *front's* left wing four tank and one mechanized corps. Thus along this sector the *front* had a significant superiority in infantry and tanks.

---

13 Counting the 55th and 118th rifle corps, which were moving up within their army's sector from the area north of Katowice.

Table V/1.A.1 The Strength and Disposition of the German-Fascist Forces Facing the First Ukrainian Front (as of 1 February 1945)

	3rd Guards Army	13th Army	52nd Army	5th Guards Army
Infantry Divisions	–	–	1	1
Infantry Divisions' Combat Groups	1	2	–	1
Independent Regiments	1	2	3	1
Independent Battalions	14	14	8	9
Independent Special Units and Subunits	–	–	–	3
Panzer Divisions	1	1	–	–
Panzergrenadier Divisions' Combat Groups	–	1	–	–
Independent Panzer Regiments	–	–	–	1
Independent Panzer Battalions	2	1	–	1
Motorized Divisions' Combat Groups	2	–	–	–
Anti-Aircraft Divisions' Combat Groups	1	–	–	–
Artillery Brigades	–	–	–	1
Artillery Brigades' Combat Groups	–	1	–	–
Assault Brigades	1	–	–	1
Artillery Regiments	1	1	–	1
Artillery Battalions	2	1	3	2
Independent Sapper Brigades	–	–	–	–

	21st Army	59th Army	60th Army	Total
Infantry Divisions	1	2	3	8
Infantry Divisions' Combat Groups	–	–	3	7
Independent Regiments	1	–	2	10
Independent Battalions	9	4	8	66
Independent Special Units and Subunits	–	–	1	4
Panzer Divisions	–	1	1	4
Panzer Divisions' Combat Groups	1	–	–	2
Independent Panzer Regiments	–	–	–	1
Independent Panzer Battalions	–	–	–	4
Panzergrenadier Divisions' Combat Groups	–	–	1	3
Anti-Aircraft Divisions' Combat Groups	–	1	–	2
Artillery Brigades	–	–	–	1
Artillery Brigades' Combat Groups	–	–	–	1
Assault Brigades	2	–	1	5
Artillery Regiments	–	–	–	3
Artillery Battalions	2	–	2	12
Independent Sapper Brigades	1	1	–	2

To all this must be added the fact that the German-Fascist supreme command, despite the measures taken to create operational reserves along the axis of the First Ukrainian Front's offensive, by the end of January Army Group Center had no such reserves.

The approximate correlation of forces and the description of the enemy's forces listed above show that the condition and situation of the German-Fascist forces facing the First Ukrainian Front was extremely unstable. In these conditions the uninterrupted offensive by Soviet forces and the launching of a new and powerful attack against the enemy should lead to the rapid breakthrough of the Germans' defensive line along the Oder River and the successful development of the breakthrough in the operational depth.

A Brief Description of the Condition of the Area of Combat Operations in February 1945

The First Ukrainian Front's offensive in February 1945 unfolded in Upper Silesia and the southern part of the province of Brandenburg.

The conventional boundary of the area of combat operations ran as follows: in the north, from the mouth of the Neisse River along the Oder River as far as the village of Odereck, and then to the east as far as the town of Smigiel; in the northeast and east, from the town of Smigiel, through Ostrow and Katowice as far as the town of Biala; in the south, from the town of Biala as far as Troppau (Opava); in the southwest, in the foothills of the Sudeten Mountains, from Troppau through Glatz as far as Gorlitz; in the west, from Gorlitz to the Neisse River as far as the Oder River.

The forces of the First Ukrainian Front, in attacking along the territory from the Oder to the west, could conduct combat operations along two main operational directions: in the northern part of the area—along the Berlin direction, and in the central part—along the Dresden direction. In the southern part of the area the main direction could be toward Prague, although an offensive here was linked to the necessity of overcoming the Sudeten Mountains.

The area of combat operations is not homogenous, both according to the character of the terrain and the opportunities for employing it for offensive and defensive operations.

To the north of the line Milicz—Glogau—Freistadt—Cottbus stretches the Barycz-Lauzitz "big valley" with its flat relief. Only in a few areas is the terrain cut by insignificant hills and ridges.

The southern part of the area of combat operations represents a hilly, foothill plain, which gradually rises from the Oder toward the Sudeten Mountains. The height of the uplands filling the valley varies. In places they reach up to 200-250 meters. The terrain's gradual rise toward the enemy in the southern and central parts of the area of combat operations offered the enemy a number of combat advantages, because he held the commanding heights and lines favorable for defense.

In the areas northwest of Liegnitz, especially between the Bober and Neisse rivers, and to the southwest of Oppeln, there lie large wooded areas, which exclude the possibility of massively employing mobile troops. Only insignificant copses are encountered along the rest of the area's territory.

The water barriers in the First Ukrainian Front's offensive zone were the Oder River and its left tributaries the Neisse, Bober, Kweis, and partially, the Neisse rivers. They all begin in the Sudeten Mountains or their foothills; during the spring thaw they fan out broadly and have a swift current.

The Oder River is a major water line, covering the Dresden and Berlin directions. Along the entire course from Ratibor to the mouth of the Neisse River (476 kilometers) the width of the Oder River varies from 120 to 200 meters. Along this sector the river has relatively low banks (up to two meters) and flows through a valley 5-10 kilometers wide. The surface of the Oder floodplain is uneven and occasional hills, ridges, flooded areas, and numerous old channels are encountered.

In February 1945 there was a major runoff, caused by the early spring (the rapid melting of the snow in the mountains and the heavy rains). The runoff began in the first days of February and continued about three weeks. During this time the water level in the river rose to two meters (during 7-8 February alone the water level along some of the river's sectors rose from 0.8 to one meter).

The wide and swampy and, for the most part, open floodplain of the Oder during the flood period created great difficulties for our forces in laying down crossings over the river and laying roads to the crossings along both banks. The presence of a large number of dikes, to a certain extent, limited the river's flooding, but in those places where there were dikes the river's width nevertheless grew to 1,000 meters.

The Bober River begins in the Rychory Mountains and flows through a mountainous area as far as the village of Len. Between Len and Bunzlau the river flows through a pre-mountainous and hilly area valley. From Bunzlau to its mouth, the river flows through a plain and a shallow valley, the width of which is about 1-2 kilometers. Along its upper course the river is 20-30 meters wide, and along the lower course 50-70 meters wide. The river's depth is 3-4 meters. The bottom is sandy and in places gravelly and rocky along its upper reaches. The banks reach about three meters in height. The river's floodplain is flat downstream from Bunzlau; the floodplain was under water during the February flooding, which created great difficulties in overcoming it.

The Kweis River, a tributary of the Bober River, is similar to the latter.

The Neisse River begins in the Iser Mountains. It can be divided into three sectors. Along the sector from the source as far as the inhabited locale of Ostritz the river flows through a mountainous area. Here the Neisse flows along a narrow valley with high and steep sides, overgrown with woods; its width in this area is 10-20 meters, it is 0.8-3 meters deep, its bottom rocky, and its banks high. From Ostritz to Penzig the river flows through hilly terrain and its valley reaches about one kilometer in width. The river's width along this sector is 20-40 meters, its depth 2.5-3.5 meters, and its banks are of clay and high. From Penzig until its confluence with the Oder, the Neisse flows through a plain. Its width along the lower course is 60-80 meters and its depth is 3-5 meters. The river's floodplain below the town of Forst is under water.

Aside from the enumerated rivers, there are a large number of less significant rivers and creeks with heavily flooded banks in the area of military operations.

Along the western banks of the rivers flowing from the south to the north, the enemy had prepared intermediate defensive lines, hanging on to which he tried to put up stubborn resistance to our forces. Along the banks of the rivers flowing to the east, the enemy had outfitted switch positions.

In the area north and northeast of there is a strip of swampy terrain, the length of which from north to south is up to 40 kilometers, and up to 20 kilometers from east to west. There are also similar swampy areas northeast of and north of Sommerfeld. In February these areas were almost impassable for military equipment and transport.

The road net in Silesia is well developed. On the average, there is one paved road for every 5-7 kilometers of front. The strategic roads connecting this area with Berlin are: the two-way highway from Oppeln through Breslau and Grunberg to Berlin, and the Breslau—Berlin highway.

The thickest network of paved roads is in the areas of the towns of Grunberg, Sagan, Sprottau, Glogau, Bunzlau, Liegnitz, Breslau, Hirschberg, Schweidnitz, Strelen, Munsterberg, Grottkau, Neisse, Neustadt, Leobschutz, Ratibor, and Troppau (Opava).

The paved roads were well built and capable of accommodating all kinds of transport. The majority of roads had been planted with trees. The network of paved roads is supplemented by the presence of a large number of dirt roads. However, the employment of the latter during the spring thaw was difficult. In February the dirt roads were passable for only three days. During the remaining days of the month they were either difficult of passage or completely impassable.

There are also a lot of railroads in the area under study. In Silesia along the overall length of the railroads is about 4,500 kilometers, which yields 12.5 kilometers of rail for every 100 square kilometers. The most important rail route linking Silesia with Berlin runs through Oppeln, Breslau, Sagan, and Frankfurt-on-Oder. Major rail junctions along this line are Breslau, Liegnitz, Sagan, and Frankfurt-on-Oder. Once the above-named rail junctions were put out of action, the rail lines' capacity fell sharply.

The rail line running from Breslau through Strelen to Troppau (Opava) was very important for the enemy during the operation. It was a lateral route, which connected Army Group Center with Army Group South.

The area of combat operations is heterogeneous in the economic sense. The heavy, textile and leather industries were developed in the towns of Silesia. Of particular importance for the enemy was the city of Breslau, in which were located and up to January 1945 were working the "Junkers" aircraft factory, machine building, mechanical, metallurgical, and aluminum factories, a large chemical factory, and many other enterprises. 12 kilometers from Breslau was the "Famo" factory, which produced motor vehicles, tractors and tanks. There were also weapons and tank factories in Gorlitz and Liegnitz. In the area's southern part there were a lot of large factories for producing synthetic fuel in the towns of Cosel and Ratibor.

Silesia's agriculture, which occupied up to 43 percent of the population, held a major place in the area's life and was, on the whole, very important for Germany. The main crops grown here were rye, oats, potatoes, and sugar beets. Animal husbandry also occupied a significant place in Silesia's agriculture.

Thus the area of combat operations was vitally important for Germany not only in the military-strategic, but in the military-economic sense as well. Thus the German-Fascist command undertook all measures to hold this area and prevent the Soviet forces from breaking through beyond the Oder.

The meteorological conditions during the First Ukrainian Front's offensive were unfavorable. Of the 28 days in February, 20 were bad, with only eight days without precipitation. For this reason, the dirt roads were very difficult of passage for auto transport and all types of combat equipment, while movement along the flooded areas was completely excluded. The porous soil, with a high degree of moisture, almost excluded the possibility of employing tanks off the roads, which made it easier for the enemy to conduct an anti-tank defense.

Our aviation's actions were conditioned by the limited flying weather. During the February operation there were only three flying days, ten days of limited flying, and eight days of no flying.

Thus if the area of Silesia by itself basically allowed the employment of all combat arms, then the spring thaw and unfavorable meteorological conditions limited these opportunities and made the conditions for conducting an operation more difficult.

An Overall Evaluation of the Situation by the Start of Preparing for the Operation

On the whole, in evaluating the situation that had arisen for the First Ukrainian Front at the end of January, one can make the following conclusion.

The necessity of foiling the perfidious plans of the American-English command and preventing the consolidation of the German-Fascist forces along the Oder, with the aid of reserves being transferred from the Western Front, demanded that the *front's* forces, without halting along the Oder, continue to develop the offensive into the depths of Germany. Alongside this, it was also necessary that a new operation be conducted without pause, or at least with a very short operational pause, following the completion of the Sandomierz-Silesian operation.

Aside from military-political considerations, this was caused by the necessity of maximally taking advantage of the enemy's extremely unstable situation, which had arisen as a result of his poor readiness to defend the Oder line with his available forces and his absence of reserves prepared beforehand along the Berlin and Dresden directions. We had to consider that each day missed would enable the enemy to strengthen his positions along the Oder, reinforce them with reserves from other parts of the Soviet-German front, and particularly with formations arriving from the Western front. Upon the completion of the above-named measures—and the German-Fascist command had already begun doing this at the end of January—the enemy's resistance could increase sharply and the *front's* forces would require greater efforts to break through the Oder line than in the first days following their arrival at the Oder.

The necessity of maximally speeding up the beginning of the offensive was also dictated by the early spring in the area of combat operations and by the expected opening of the rivers in the coming days. In these conditions, a delay of the offensive would have created significant difficulties in forcing the Oder and the organization of crossings over the river, as well as in the development of a subsequent offensive over wooded and swampy terrain.

It should be noted, however, that if the overall strategic situation was creating favorable conditions for the immediate launching of a subsequent offensive, then the operational situation of the *front's* forces did not completely favor the resolution of this task quickly.

The preparation of a new operation would have to be carried out during the completion of the broad and intensive Sandomierz-Silesian operation, as a result of which, aside from the major military-political results achieved, had brought about a considerable weakening of the *front's* forces, the unfavorable grouping of forces for conducting a new operation, and the great extension of the rear organs.

Aside from this, at the end of January the Soviet forces' active combat operations were unfolding along the entire Soviet-German front. Thus the possibility of supporting the First Ukrainian Front's offensive with reserves from the *Stavka* of the Supreme High Command was excluded for the immediate future. Thus the *front* commander had to rely only on his forces at hand in organizing an offensive.

All of this dictated the necessity of very scrupulously weighing the *front's* offensive capabilities, determining the possible scope of the forthcoming operation and the means for carrying it out, and the corresponding operational disposition of the *front's* forces.

What did the unfavorable situation of the *front's* forces at the end of January consist of?

According to the conditions of the situation and terrain, it was more expedient to launch the main attack in the new operation along the *front's* right wing along the Berlin and Dresden directions. However, at the concluding stage of the Sandomierz-Silesian operation, due to the necessity of eliminating the enemy in the Silesian industrial area, the center of the *front's* main efforts had shifted to the left wing. Thus a significant part of the *front's* forces, including a tank army and two tank corps, which had been brought in during the January operation for eliminating the enemy in the Silesian industrial area, were attacking along the *front's* left wing.

Thus in order to create a shock group along the right flank, it was necessary to carry out a major regrouping of forces, for which a certain amount of time was necessary.

Alongside this, in order to fully secure the offensive by the *front's* main group of forces along the Berlin and Dresden directions, it was necessary to eliminate as rapidly as possible the serious lagging of the *front's* left-wing forces and move them up to at least the foothills of the Sudeten Mountains. This would significantly reduce the overall length of the front, free up part of our forces and exclude the possibility of an enemy attack along the *front's* extended left wing. However, the speeding up of the offensive by the *front's* left wing required its reinforcement. Given the reduced strength of our forces, this would cause the weakening of the shock groups being created along the Berlin and Dresden directions.

No less of a difficulty, which faced the *front's* forces in preparing a new operation, was the enormous extension of the *front's* and armies' rear organs. As a result of the lagging behind of the *front's* bases by hundreds of kilometers, the threat of serious breakdowns in supplying the troops for the subsequent development of the offensive was growing. In connection with this, the problem of organizing the rear organs' work and the materiel supply of the troops arose as the chief and main task.

Thus despite a number of favorable conditions, serious obstacles were rising, which were threatening to extend the deadlines for preparing a new operation.

The overcoming of these difficulties and the successful resolution of the tasks facing the *front* required from commanders at all levels that they quickly carry out major organizational measures, and the enormous exertion of moral and physical strength from the *front's* rank and file.

B. THE OPERATION'S OVERALL IDEA AND THE *FRONT* COMMANDER'S DECISION

The Operation's Overall Idea

Having evaluated the situation that had arisen at the end of January along the Soviet-German front and immediately in the First Ukrainian Front's offensive zone, the *front* commander came to the conclusion that the *front's* forces were in a condition to overcome the difficulties linked to the rapid preparation of a new offensive operation and could, without halting the fighting for the expansion of the bridgeheads on the left bank of the Oder, prepare and launch a further offensive along the Berlin and Dresden directions.

The *front* commander made this conclusion the basis for his plan for the troops' further operations, and on 28 January reported his ideas on this matter to the *Stavka* of the Supreme High Command.

His report laid out the goal and idea of the proposed operation, the possible deadlines for its conduct, and the goals of the *front's* armies in the operation.

The new operation's goal, in accordance with the *front* commander's design, lay in defeating the Breslau—Dresden group of enemy forces, the arrival of the *front's* forces at the Elbe River and the capture of Berlin in conjunction with the First Belorussian Front.

It was proposed to achieve this goal through three simultaneous attacks—along the *front's* right wing, the center, and the left wing.

It was proposed to launch the main attack with the forces of the 3rd Guards, 13th and 6th combined-arms and the 4th and 3rd guards tank armies, and the 25th Tank and 7th Guards Mechanized corps, along the *front's* right wing from the bridgehead northwest of Breslau in the general direction of Sprottau, Cottbus and Juterbog., with the goal of defeating the enemy group of forces covering the southeastern approaches to Berlin and, in conjunction with the forces of the First Belorussian Front, to capture the capital of fascist Germany.

It was planned to launch a second attack with the forces of the 5th Guards and 21st combined-arms armies and the 4th Guards and 31st tank corps from the bridgehead southeast of Breslau in the general direction of Gorlitz and Leipzig, with the goal of defeating the enemy's Breslau—Dresden group of forces, reaching the Elbe River and capturing the Dresden industrial area.

It was planned to achieve the defeat of the enemy's Breslau group of forces by encircling and destroying it with those armies attacking along the internal flanks of the shock groups. At the same time, it was planned upon completing the defeat of the enemy in the Breslau area; the main shock group's left-flank army (6th) would be pulled into the *front's* second echelon and subsequently employed for developing the success along the Dresden axis.

The *front's* left-wing forces (59th and 60th combined-arms armies and the 1st Guards Cavalry Corps), while attacking from the bridgehead in the Cosel area in the general direction of Waldenburg and Zittau and, in conjunction with the forces of the Fourth Ukrainian Front, were to secure the *front's* main group of forces from the south and southwest.

This, in broad outline, was the basic content of the new operation's idea.

It was planned to begin the operation approximately on 5-6 February and conclude it on 25-28 February.

It was planned to use the time before the beginning of the operation for expanding and consolidating the bridgeheads along the left bank of the Oder and for bringing up supplies of munitions and fuel.

By relying mainly on its own forces, the *front* command asked the *Stavka* of the Supreme High Command only to reinforce the 6th Army, which had five divisions, with a single rifle corps, and to subordinate to the *front* the 5th Mechanized Corps, which it was planned to use to secure the *front's* left flank.

The *Stavka* of the Supreme High Command confirmed the *front* commander's plan for the *front's* subsequent operations, about which the chief of the General Staff informed the *front's* military council on 29 January. No additional forces were allotted to the *front*.

The *Front* Commander's Decision

The *front* commander laid out his decision and the troops' tasks in the forthcoming operation in his operational directive No. 0051/op, of 31 January 1945.

The overall task of the *front's* forces was defined in the following manner:

> On 6 February the *front's* armies are to go over to a decisive offensive, will launch their main attack in the general direction of Sprottau, Cottbus and Juterbog, with the task of defeating the enemy's Breslau group of forces and by 25 February reaching the Elbe River with their main forces. The *front's* right wing, in conjunction with the First Belorussian Front, is to take Berlin.

According to the operational plan, the *front*, upon deploying its combined-arms armies in the first echelon, was to launch its main attack along the right wing. In accordance with this, the *front* commander was to create along the *front's* right wing a powerful shock group, consisting of the 3rd Guards, 13th, 52nd, and 6th combined-arms and 4th and 3rd Guards tank armies, and the 25th Tank and 7th Guards Mechanized corps. The combined-arms armies of the *front's* main shock group, concentrated along a 66-kilometer front from Keben to Malcz, were to deploy their main forces along the bridgehead west of Steinau and from there attack in the general direction of Sprottau, Cottbus and Juterbog.

The 4th and 3rd Guards tank armies would be committed into the battle on the operation's first day, simultaneously with the combined-arms armies in the center of the main shock group. Following the breakthrough of the enemy's main defensive zone, they were to thrust forward and develop the success along the main axis: the 4th Tank Army in the 13th Army's attack zone, and the 3rd Guards Tank Army in the 52nd Army's attack zone.

The overall depth of the planned operation was to be 250 kilometers.

In accordance with the decision adopted, the armies of the *front's* main shock group received the following assignments.

The 3rd Guards Army, along with the 25th Tank Corps and the 17th Breakthrough Artillery Division, upon deploying its main forces along the bridgehead northwest of Keben, was to attack in the general direction of Freistadt, Gubben and Trebbin (the width of the breakthrough sector was eight kilometers).

The 13th Army, along with the 1st Breakthrough Artillery Division, was assigned the task of attacking with its main forces from the bridgehead west of Keben and Steinau (the width of the breakthrough sector was 18 kilometers) in the general direction of Sprottau, Cottbus and Juterbog.

The 52nd Army, along with the 10th Breakthrough Artillery Corps (4th and 31st breakthrough artillery divisions) was assigned the task of launching its main attack along the right flank from the bridgehead west of Steinau, along the Luben—Parchwitz sector[14] (the width of the breakthrough sector was 20 kilometers), and to develop the offensive in the general direction of Reisicht, Debern and Finsterwalde.

The 6th Army, for the deployment of which a 20-kilometer sector of front was allotted in the 52nd Army's sector along the bridgehead in the Malcz area, was to, along with the 7th Guards Mechanized Corps, having deployed from behind the left flank of the 52nd Army's shock group, launch a vigorous attack in the direction of Alt Bechern, Koischwitz, Neumarkt, and Breslau (into the rear of the enemy group of forces defending Breslau), and by the close of the operation's fourth day capture the capital of Lower Silesia, the city of Breslau. On the operation's first day the 7th Guards Mechanized Corps was to capture the area Pleswitz—Erschendorf—Panzkau, and then attack toward Kant, without getting bogged down in the fighting for Breslau.

Following the capture of Breslau, it was planned to pull the 6th Army into the *front* reserve, with the task of attacking behind the 5th Guards Army along the Dresden direction. The commander of the 7th Guards Mechanized Corps was warned that his corps would subsequently attack toward Dresden.

The 4th Tank Army was to be committed into the battle in the 13th Army's offensive zone on the operation's first day, with the task of attacking in the direction of Sagan, Cottbus and Wunsdorf.

The 3rd Guards Tank Army was to be committed into the battle in the 52nd Army's attack zone on the operation's first day, with the assignment of attacking in the direction of Heinau, Debern and Herzberg.

In carrying out the offensive within the zones of the boundary lines established by the directive, the combined-arms armies of the *front's* right wing were by the end of the operation's first day to capture the line Glogau—Kunzendorf—Heinau with their main forces (the depth of the advance for the first day was to be 20-25 kilometers). By this time the 25th Tank Corps was to capture the Klopschen area (27 kilometers); the 4th Tank Army the Gross Logisch—Primkenau—Kotzenau area (35 kilometers), and; the 3rd Guards Tank Army the Reisicht—Gremsdorf—Kreibau—Heinau area (35 kilometers).

By the close of the operation's third day, the combined-arms armies of the *front's* right wing were to reach the line Neusalz—Freistadt—Libichau—Eichberg—Neu Heidau (the depth of the advance for three days would be 50 kilometers), while the tank armies were to capture the following: 4th Tank Army—the Christianstadt—Sorau—Sagan area (80 kilometers), and the 3rd Guards Tank Army—the area Teichdorf—Burau—Rauscha—Lipschau (80 kilometers).

On the operation's fifth day the combined-arms armies were to reach the line Schloss Neetzow—Kreibau—Bertelsdorf—Kumelisch—Tiefenfurt (the depth of advance in five days would be 80-90 kilometers). By this time the 4th Tank Army was to occupy the area Taubendorf—Cottbus—Forst (140 kilometers), and the 3rd Guards Tank Army the area from Cottbus to the south as far as Spremberg, and to the east as far as Weisswasser (140 kilometers).

Further operations were planned only for the tank armies: the 4th Tank Army—to capture the Spremberg—Petkus—Zagelsdorf—Halbe area (the depth of advance from the deployment line was to be 230 kilometers), and the 3rd Guards Tank Army—the Damme—Schonwalde—Falkenberg—Finsterwalde area (240 kilometers).

The forces of the *front's* second shock group, which were to attack from the bridgehead southeast of Breslau along the Dresden direction, were assigned the following tasks.

The 5th Guards Army, along with the 4th Guards Tank Corps and the 3rd Breakthrough Artillery Division, was to attack from the bridgehead west of Ohlau a day before the *front's* right

---

14 It was planned that the bridgehead would be expanded as far as this locale by the start of the operation.

wing armies; that is, on 5 February. While launching the main attack along the left flank, the army was to attack in the general direction of Jauer, Goldberg, Naumburg, and Bautzen.

The 21st Army, along with the 31st Tank Corps and the 13th Breakthrough Artillery Division, was also to attack from the bridgehead west of Oppeln on 5 February. The army was assigned the task of initially launching its main attack along the right flank, and to then launch a general offensive in the direction of Strelen, Schweidnitz, Greiffenberg, and Ebersbach.

While attacking within the realm of the boundary lines established by the directive, the 5th Guards and 21st armies were, by the close of the operation's first day (6 February), to capture the line Klettendorf—Strelen—Schreibendorf (the depth of the advance from the position on 5 February was to be 15-25 kilometers); by the close of the third day they were to take the line Merschutz—Striegau—Reichenbach (60-70 kilometers), and by the close of the fifth day the line Kreibau—Scheinau—Merzdorf (110 kilometers).

The 59th and 60th armies, which comprised the *front's* third shock group, were assigned the task of attacking before the general directive was issued. According to the *front* commander's order, issued on 30 January, by the close of 2 February they were to expand their bridgehead on the left bank of the Oder as far as the line Neisse River—Neustadt—Troppau (Opava).

Based on the assumption that this task would be carried out by the forces of the 59th and 60th armies, the *front* commander, in his 31 January directive, ordered them to continue their decisive offensive from the morning of 5 February: the 59th Army—in the general direction of Besdorf, Munsterberg, Langenbielau, and Landeshut, and the 60th Army—Neustadt, Patschau, and Braunau, securing the *front's* left flank. In order to secure the 60th Army's left flank, the army commander was ordered to keep two rifle divisions and the 7th Anti-Tank Artillery Brigade echeloned behind the left flank of the army's first echelon.

While developing the offensive to expand the bridgehead, the 59th and 60th armies' forces were by the close of the operation's first day (6 February) to capture the line Boitmansdorf—Lentsch (the depth of the advance from the assumed jumping-off point was 10-20 kilometers); by the close of the third day of the operation, the line Reichenbach—Frankenstein—Weissbach (50-55 kilometers, and; by the close of the operation's fifth day, the line Merzdorf—Glatz (90-100 kilometers).

The commander of the 2nd Air Army was ordered, while organizing and conducting the aviation offensive, to concentrate his main forces in the attack zones of the 3rd Guards, 13th and 52nd armies, so as to securely support and cover the *front's* main forces from the air, including the 4th and 3rd Guards tank armies, as well as to cover the crossings over the Oder River created in the armies' attack zones.

For these purposes, it was recommended to the commander of the air army that he detach the 2nd Guards Assault Air and 2nd Fighter corps to support and cover the 3rd Guards and 13th armies. A division each from these corps was to be detached to support and cover the 4th Tank Army. The 1st Guards Assault Air, 6th Guards Fighter and 4th Bomber corps were to be detached for the 52nd Army. One division apiece was to be detached from the first two corps for supporting and covering the 3rd Guards Tank Army. A division from the 6th Guards Fighter Corps was to be detached for covering the 6th Army and 7th Guards Mechanized Corps. Aside from this, their activities would support the 4th Bomber Corps. The 3rd Assault Air and 5th Fighter corps would be detached for the 5th Guards and 21st armies; while during the armies' offensive on 5 February they would also be supported by the 2nd and 4th bomber corps.

The 2nd Air Army was assigned the following objectives: a) to destroy the enemy's personnel and artillery through massive strikes by assault aircraft and bombers, while supporting the forces of the 3rd Guards, 13th and 52nd armies in breaking through the enemy's defense; b) to prevent the arrival of the enemy's reserves along the Sprottau, Luben and Breslau axes; c) to upset the transport of the enemy's reserves and equipment through strikes against the Cottbus, Sagan and

Gorlitz railroad junctions and stages, and; d) to win air superiority, by launching strikes against the enemy's air assets in the air and on the ground.

The plan for the artillery offensive was drawn up only for the breakthrough period of the enemy's main defensive zone.

According to the plan, 55 minutes were allotted for the artillery preparation of the attack. A fire onslaught was planned for the first ten minutes by all the artillery against the enemy's artillery and mortar batteries, his headquarters, communications centers, observation posts, local reserves, and tank concentration areas. The following 30 minutes the artillery was to suppress and destroy targets in the strong points along the forward edge and in the depth of the enemy's main defensive zone. During this period the artillery was to continue to try and suppress the enemy's artillery batteries that had been discovered earlier and to attack newly-discovered ones as well. The final 15 minutes would be devoted to a repeat fire onslaught by all the artillery against the forward edge and the immediate depth of the defense; that is, against the objects of our attack.

It was planned to support the infantry and tank attack by the method of the consecutive concentration of fire during the course of an hour.

A combat load of munitions was to be set aside for carrying out the tasks of artillery preparation and supporting the attack.

The above-enumerated decision by the *front* commander shows that the main goal of the planned operation was the decisive defeat of the enemy throughout the entire sector of the First Ukrainian Front's offensive and the arrival of the *front's* main forces at the Elbe River. Simultaneously, the *front's* right-wing armies were to attack toward Berlin and capture the latter in conjunction with the forces of the First Belorussian Front.

This decisive goal fully met the demands of the situation, which had arisen along the Soviet-German front by the end of January 1945.

It was planned to achieve the assigned goal by launching a series of deep attacks, which would break up the enemy front, with the simultaneous encirclement and destruction of part of his forces in the Breslau area.

The elimination of the enemy's remaining groups of forces, pressed between the *front's* and armies' shock groups, as well as the defeat in detail of his arriving reserves, was to be carried out during the course of an uninterrupted pursuit of the enemy during the arrival of the *front's* forces at the operation's final objectives.

A rapid and vigorous offensive was to create favorable conditions for the seizure of a number of enemy intermediate defensive zones from the march in the operational depth before he could bring up the necessary reserves to the *front's* offensive sector.

These considerations lay at the heart of the *front* commander's plan.

The offensive was to unfold simultaneously along a front of more than 400 kilometers and develop during the course of 20 days to a depth of 250 kilometers.

In order to increase the strength of the initial attack, the *front* commander decided to deploy in a single echelon all the forces concentrated along the axis of the main attack. It was planned to commit the tank armies into the battle on the operation's first day.

A weak aspect of the adopted operational formation of the *front's* forces was the absence of a second echelon and reserve, necessary for augmenting the first-echelon troops' efforts in conducting the battle in the operational depth.

The operational plan foresaw that this shortcoming in the troops' operational formation would be corrected during the course of the offensive. Proceeding from the fact that at a high operational pace the offensive sector of the *front's* forces should contract to 200-250 kilometers by the fifth day, instead of the 450 kilometers occupied by the *front* at the end of January, the *front* commander figured that he could put at least one combined-arms army and one mechanized corps into the second echelon during the course of the offensive, which could be employed for augmenting the efforts of the *front's* main group of forces.

The exploitation of realistic opportunities, which were opening up before the *front* at the end of January, for achieving major operational results, depended to a significant degree on just how rapidly and successfully the *front* command and troops could carry out the planned preparatory measures, secure the vigorous development of the operation from the offensive's first days along all axes and during the operation create in a timely manner a sufficiently strong second echelon and a reserve.

The successful resolution of the tasks assigned to the troops by the *front* directive demanded that the following basic preparatory measures be carried out quickly: to expand the captured bridgeheads to a size called for by the operational plan and, in particular, to bring the *front's* left-wing armies to the line of the Neisse River—Neustadt—Troppau (Opava); to carry out a troop regrouping in accordance with the plan for employing them in the forthcoming operation; to resolve problems of the troops' materiel supply and to organize the work of the rear organs, and; finally, to mobilize the *front's* entire rank and file to carry out the forthcoming combat assignments.

The organization and realization of the above-enumerated measures, which would decide the success of the forthcoming operation, were in the center of attention of the command, the party-political apparatus, and the *front's* forces throughout the entire preparatory phase of the operation.

C. THE FIGHT TO HOLD AND EXPAND THE CAPTURED BRIDGEHEADS

The fight for the bridgeheads on the left bank of the Oder River comprised an entire stage in the development of the *front's* offensive activities in the winter of 1945 and occupied the period of time between the January offensive operation and the new offensive, which began on 8 February.

The seizure and expansion of the bridgeheads over the Oder was a component part of the plan for preparing for a new offensive operation and pursued the goal of reducing the length of the front, improving the position of the *front's* right-wing and center armies for attacking along the Berlin and Dresden directions and, finally, of eliminating the serious lagging behind of the *front's* left-wing armies.

Guided by these considerations, the *front* commander assigned his forces the following tasks.

The 3rd Guards Army was ordered, while developing the success achieved at the end of January, to reach by 5 February the line Eichewalde—Neusalz—the Oder River as far as Glogau and Raudten. The troops' arrival at this line was to significantly increase the bridgehead's operational capacity along the axis of the main attack, secure a more favorable jumping-off position for the offensive and shorten the front line along this sector from 104 to 75 kilometers.

The 5th Guards and 21st armies were assigned the task of reaching the line Breslau—Borau—Strelen—Friedewalde before the beginning of the general offensive, which would create a more favorable situation for outflanking and encircling the enemy's Breslau group of forces and unite in a single attack the efforts of the right wing and center forces. For this purpose, the start of the 5th Guards and 21st armies' offensive was planned for a day earlier than the general offensive. This decision pursued another objective—to distract the enemy's attention and forces from the axis of the main attack.

The 59th and 60th armies were to reach the line of the Neisse River—Neustadt—Troppau (Opava) before the start of the general offensive. The achievement of this task would enable us to significantly shorten the length of the front and securely protect the left flank of the *front's* main group of forces.

In connection with the adopted decision, three independent centers of conflict were delineated: on the right wing—on the approaches to Glogau in the area of the bridgehead west of Steinau; in the center—in the area of the bridgehead west of Ohlau and Brieg, and; on the left wing—on the Oder to the south of Oppeln.

The Fighting for the Bridgeheads along the First Ukrainian Front's Right Wing

The 3rd Guards Army, having reached with its left-flank 76th Rifle Corps the Oder River along the sector Wendstadt—Alt Heidau on 28 January, forced the river with one division in the Radschutz area and seized a small bridgehead on its left bank. The army's remaining corps on this day captured the major towns of Gostin, Kreben, Leszno (Lissa), and Bojanowo and continued to advance to the west, striving to reach the Oder.

At this time a major enemy group of forces (up to 27,000 men), consisting of the remnants of the Ninth Army's formations, which had been defeated and were being pursued by the forces of the First Belorussian Front, were falling back under their attack along the Leszno—Gurau road into the First Ukrainian Front's offensive zone, while striving to break through to the crossings over the Oder. Their arrival in the rear of the 76th Rifle Corps, the main forces of which on 29 January crossed over to the bridgehead and were engaged in heavy fighting against an enemy who uninterruptedly counterattacked, would have placed the corps in an extremely difficult situation.

For the purpose of the most rapid elimination of this group of forces, the 21st Rifle Corps was hurriedly dispatched to the Gurau area, and units of the 25th Tank Corps were moving here as well. Formations of the 120th Rifle Corps arrived in the Leszno area.

On 30-31 January major fighting broke out in the Leszno and Gurau areas, during which the Germans were dealt a heavy defeat.

The 15,000-man enemy group of forces in the Leszno area, along with 50 tanks and assault guns, was defeated and its remnants, now being pursued by our forces, were forced to turn to the west and break through to the crossings in the Glogau area.

The enemy group of forces in the Gurau area was also defeated. A significant part of it was cut off from the crossings and encircled in the woods south of Rutzen, while its remnants, having slipped out of the encirclement, streamed to the west toward the crossings that had not yet been seized by our forces. In the first days of February the enemy group of forces, which had been surrounded south of Rutzen, was completely eliminated through the efforts of the 3rd Guards Army's forces and units of the 4th Tank Army.

In all 13,000 men and officers were killed in the areas of Leszno and Gurau, while 50 tanks and assault guns, 81 armored transports, 109 guns and a large number of motor vehicles were knocked out and captured, as well as 2,800 men taken prisoner.

The fighting in the areas of Leszno and Gurau somewhat slowed the advance by the *front's* right-wing armies. The German-Fascist command took advantage of this. With the aid of those forces defending Glogau, and of those forces falling back to the crossings in this area, it organized a defense on the bridgehead fortifications and along the outer ring of the Glogau fortress area.

On 31 January the *front* commander ordered the 3rd Guards Army to continue an energetic offensive with the 120th Rifle and 25th Tank corps, and by the close of 2 February to reach the Oder along the sector Odereck—Glogau, where it was to establish tactical cooperation with units of the First Belorussian Front. Upon its arrival at the Oder, the 120th Rifle Corps was to force it and seize a bridgehead along the river's left bank. The army's main forces had the task of continuing the fight to expand the bridgehead that had been seized west of Keben, as far as the Glogau—Kreidelwitz line.

While carrying out the combat order, by 2 February the 120th Rifle Corps reached the Oder along the Kleinitz—Lippen sector, but was unable to force the river here. In the days preceding the start of the operation the corps' front stretched to 60 kilometers from Odereck to Hortingen. Held by uninterrupted enemy counterattacks along the approaches to Glogau, the corps was involved in unsuccessful offensive fighting along the line of the Gross Land Canal—Kutlau—Gulau until the start of the operation.

The 21st Rifle Corps, following the fighting in the Gurau area, quickly advanced to the Bark River. Here the enemy once again attempted to cover the crossings over the Oder north of Oderbelch with the remnants of his defeated units. Having crushed the enemy's resistance along this line, the corps' forces reached the Oder on 2 February along the sector Hortingen—Oderbelch. Here was completed the defeat of the enemy units that had withdrawn from Gurau to the west.

The fighting on the bridgehead west of Keben was quite intense. The enemy, in forces ranging from a battalion to a regiment of infantry, supported by tanks and aviation, undertook up to ten counterattacks per day, while striving to regain, at any cost, the positions lost along the left bank of the Oder. A particularly powerful attack was launched on 2 February, when the enemy threw up to a division of infantry, along with 80 tanks and armored transports, into the fighting and supporting the counterattack with aviation.

All the enemy's counterattacks were repulsed with great losses for him. However, the enemy's active operations prevented the army's forces, which had been fighting along the bridgehead, from advancing significantly. Thus by the start of the operation they occupied here basically those same positions which they had in the first days following the seizure of the bridgehead.

Thus as a result of ten days (28 January -7 February) of intensive fighting, the forces of the 3rd Guards Army, in conjunction with the forces of the 4th Tank Army, defeated a major German group of forces along the right bank of the Oder. The army's right-flank formations reached the Oder along a broad front and established tactical cooperation with the forces of the First Belorussian Front; the left-flank formations consolidated along the previously-seized bridgehead west of Keben.

However, the army did not carry out its main assignment for this period. The army did not manage to crush the enemy's resistance along the approaches to Glogau, to force the Oder along the entire offensive sector, and to expand the captured bridgehead to the size indicated by the *front* commander.

The army's failure can be chiefly explained by the fact that its main forces, having encountered along the approaches to the Oder stubborn resistance by enemy forces that were falling back under the blows of the First Belorussian Front, were not able to maintain the high offensive pace at which the operation was developing. This enabled the enemy to consolidate along the river's left bank and on the bridgehead fortifications north of Glogau before the arrival of the army's main forces at the Oder. Thus the 3rd Guards Army's attempt (following the arrival of its main forces at the Oder) to force the river from the march was not crowned with success. The army, whose front at this time reached 104 kilometers, was forced to launch a new attack against the enemy from the restricted bridgehead that had been seized in the first days following its arrival at the Oder.

During this period no major changes occurred in the 13th Army's offensive sector. Formations of the 102nd and 27th rifle corps, having encountered the enemy's fierce resistance, were not able to expand the bridgehead seized in the first days before the start of the operation.

The German-Fascist command, which clearly understood the significance of the major bridge-head seized by us on the left bank of the Oder, was bringing up troops here uninterruptedly from other sectors of the front and, while committing them into the fighting, sought to restore the front line along the Oder at any cost.

On 29 January, when the enemy group of forces, which had been concentrated in the Leszno area, began to try to break through to Gurau for the purpose of reaching the crossings in the Keben area, the Hitlerite command, with forces up to an infantry division and a panzer division in strength, tried to launch a counterblow from the Liegnitz area into the flank of the 13th Army's 27th Rifle Corps.

The 13th Army's forces successfully repulsed this counterblow. The immediate consolidation of the captured positions by our forces and the timely arrival of our artillery to the bridgehead had great significance for the successful repulse of the enemy counterblow. By the time the enemy launched his counterblow along the entire front occupied by the army's forces, trenches had been dug and anti-tank strong points had been outfitted, the approaches to which were covered by minefields and wire obstacles.

Despite the failure of the attempted counterblow, the Hitlerites, with no regard for the cost, did not cease their active operations in the bridgehead area up to the very start of our offensive.

The following figures speak to the intensity of the fighting during this period: during 1-7 February the enemy lost about 8,000 men killed and captured in the area of the bridgehead; we knocked out and captured in working condition about 200 tanks, assault guns and armored transports.

The 13th Army's battles to expand the bridgehead showed that the enemy had stopped retreating and had managed to consolidate along the lines occupied by him. His active operations to restore his positions along the left bank of the Oder, although they were unsuccessful, nonetheless forced our forces to temporarily go over to the defensive and consolidate the captured bridgehead.

The enemy's resistance could only be crushed and an offensive begun only following the creation of a new group of forces and the commitment of fresh forces into the fighting.

The Struggle for the Bridgeheads Along the First Ukrainian Front's Center

The 52nd Army conducted its fight for the bridgeheads in close cooperation with the forces of the 5th Guards Army.

On 28 January the 52nd Army's left-flank formations, which had seized a bridgehead north of Ohlau, were fighting along the line of the Jungfernsee—Jungwitz—excluding Stannowitz, while the forces of the 5th Guards Army, having seized a bridgehead south of Ohlau, that same day reached the line Oder-Steine—Gisdorf—Hennersdorf—Brizen.

These armies' forces, occupying a flanking position *vis a vis* the enemy group of forces defending the major town and railroad junction of Ohlau, directed all their efforts at encircling it. Attacking toward each other, the formations of the armies' adjoining flanks linked up on 29 January in the area southwest of Ohlau. On that day the town of Ohlau was occupied by the forces of the 5th Guards Army.

During 30-31 January the two armies' common bridgehead was expanded somewhat and by the end of January reached 25 kilometers in width and 16 in depth. The 52nd and 5th Guards armies' forward edge along the bridgehead ran along the line of the Jungfernsee—Saulwitz—Zottwitz—Krausenau—Mollwitz—Brizen.

On the 5th Guards Army's left flank the small bridgeheads, which had been captured on 23 January in the areas of Eichenried and Fischbach, had been expanded by the end of the month and had joined into one bridgehead from Ribing to Zakrau, with a width of 22 kilometers and a depth of five.

Beginning on 31 January the 21st Army was brought in to the fighting to expand the bridgeheads along the sector between Breslau and Oppeln. The *front* commander, in his 30 January order to the commander of the 21st Army for the relief of the 5th Guards Army's units along the bridgehead northwest of Oppeln, assigned the 21st Army the following task: to attack on the morning of 31 January for the purpose of expanding the bridgehead along the left bank of the Oder, and by the close of 1 February to reach the line Brieg—Neisse River as far as Bilitz.

The area to the west of Oppeln is very difficult for an offensive and an attack through the wooded area, followed by the forcing of the Neisse River, would have led to prolonged fighting and our forces' slow advance to the west. Thus the army commander decided to launch his main attack along his right flank through Lewin to Grottkau.

The successful realization of this idea would have enabled us, first of all, to clear the enemy out of the area to the west of Brieg through the joint efforts of the forces of the 21st and 5th Guards armies, and, secondly, to bypass from the north the enemy's natural defensive line and turn the flank of his main group of forces located in the Oppeln area. Subsequently, it would be possible to complete the defeat of the enemy's Oppeln group of forces through converging attacks from Grottkau and Oppeln and to clear him out of the entire area between the Oder and Neisse rivers.

On the night of 30-31 January the 21st Army's 55th Rifle Corps relieved the 5th Guards Army's 34th Guards Rifle Corps along the sector between Brieg and Oppeln, and during the latter half of 31 January its main forces attacked from the bridgehead in the Schurgast area in the direction of Losen.

Due to the shortage of time for organizing the attack, it was insufficiently prepared, particularly in the materiel sense, and developed slowly. On 31 January the corps' units advanced only 2-4 kilometers, and during 1-2 February even less. The shortage of munitions with the troops was telling. The enemy fought stubbornly for each inhabited locale and particularly for such major locales as Schurgast, Karbischau and Schenwitz. In connection with this, there was an increased demand for ammunition, the expenditure of which was limited by the slow pace of restoring their supply.

The 21st Army's failure to carry out its immediate task, which had been assigned on 30 January, would foil the plan for the army's subsequent operations according to the *front's* directive of 31 January.

The army commander drew up a new plan for an army operation, taking into account the situation that had arisen. According to this plan, on the morning of 3 February the army was to launch a decisive offensive in the general direction of Strelen and Schweidnitz, once again launching the main attack along its right flank.

The breakthrough of the enemy's defense and the forcing of the Neisse River were once again entrusted to the 55th Rifle Corps. However, with the corps' arrival at the line Rosenthal—Lewin, the 118th Rifle and 31st Tank corps were to be committed from behind its right flank for an attack in the direction of Kreisenwitz and Wansen. The 117th Rifle Corps, by employing the success of the right-flank corps, was to roll up the enemy's front with its right flank to the southwest and south.

By the close of 5 February the army's main forces were to reach the line Borau—Strelen—Detzdorf—Friedewalde.

The 31st Tank Corps, while attacking in the direction of Losen, Pogarell and Grottkau, was to capture Grottkau and the crossings over the Neisse River at Pilkendorf by the morning of 4 February.

The length of the attack's artillery preparation on 3 February was planned at 45 minutes. Of this, ten minutes was to be allotted for a fire onslaught by all our artillery against the enemy's weaponry and personnel in the first position, 30 minutes for suppressing and neutralizing his artillery and mortar batteries, and the last five minutes for a repeat fire onslaught against the enemy's weapons and personnel in the first position and the most important targets to a depth of 5-7 kilometers. Rocket-propelled artillery would launch a strike during the final 15 minutes of the artillery preparation.

It was planned to put in all the army's weapons, up to an including anti-aircraft artillery regiments, into the artillery preparation.

Support for the attack and the accompaniment of the troops during the battle in the depth of the enemy's defense were to be carried out through the method of the consecutive concentration of fire.

75 percent of a combat load was to be allotted for the artillery preparation, the support for the attack and the accompaniment of the attacking troops.

The 2nd Air Army's main task consisted of fighting the enemy's aviation, which was trying to hinder the activities of the Soviet forces to expand the captured bridgeheads with small groups of planes. However, due to the unfavorable weather, the activities of the 3rd Assault Air and 5th Fighter corps, which were supporting the 5th Guards and 21st armies, were limited during these days.

The offensive on 3 February began in accordance with the plan. Despite the fact that the offensive was organized much better than the first time, the army's success on this day was insignificant.

Great difficulties arose in forcing the Neisse River north of Schurgast. Due to the early spring, the river and its tributaries by this time were free of ice and the level of water in them rose very high. The rapid current carried away the crossings that were being erected. Only the decisiveness and great ingenuity of the Soviet soldiers and officers enabled us to cope with the difficult task of forcing the river in a complex situation.

The Neisse River was forced along its entire length from its mouth to Schurgast. However, the captured bridgehead was so insignificant that it was not possible to commit the 118th Rifle and 31st Tank corps into the battle on this day.

In order to take advantage of the success of the attack's first day and to speed up the fulfillment of the assigned task, the commander of the 21st Army ordered the commander of the 55th Rifle Corps to expand the bridgehead on the left bank of the Neisse River during the night. It was planned on the morning of 4 February from this bridgehead to commit along the right flank of the 55th Rifle Corps one division from the 118th Rifle Corps and the entire 31st Tank Corps, and then, given the successful development of combat operations, the remaining forces of the 118th Rifle Corps.

The 21st Army's offensive on 4 February was coordinated, in time and the direction of the attacks, with the attack prepared by the 5th Guards Army.

During 31 January-3 February, while the events described were occurring along the 21st Army's front, the forces of the 5th Guards Army, having relieved the 52nd Army's formations along the right flank, were engaged in constant fighting to improve their positions and to prepare for an offensive in accordance with the *front* commander's directive of 31 January 1945.

No major changes in the army's forces took place during this period.

As before, the enemy was stubbornly holding on to the Brieg area. By reinforcing the troops located here, the Hitlerite command was preparing an attack against the base of our bridgehead, in order to eliminate it and restore his position along the Oder.

In order to eliminate the growing threat and finish off the group of German-Fascist forces in the Brieg area, the *front* commander ordered the commander of the 5th Guards Army to launch on the morning of 4 February an attack, coordinated with the 21st Army, along the left flank to the south, towards the latter's forces.

According to the *front* commander's plan, the attacks by the 5th Guards and 21st armies, launched toward each other, were to lead to the destruction of the Germans in the Brieg—Schurgast—Grottkau area and to the formation of a large common bridgehead for the two armies.

In order to launch this attack, the commander of the 5th Guards Army selected the Tempelfeld—Mollwitz sector, where he concentrated the main forces of the 33rd Guards Rifle Corps and the 4th Guards Tank Corps. The beginning of both armies' attack was designated as 1030 on 4 February.

The coordinated activities of the forces attacking from the north and south led to favorable results. Upon going over to the offensive following a short artillery preparation, the forces of the 5th Guards and 21st armies broke through the heavily fortified German positions southwest of Brieg and along the Neisse River and, developing the success with the tank corps, by 1600 the forward units had linked up in the Schoenfeld area. The path of retreat for the enemy group of forces operating in the Brieg area was cut off.

The forward units of the 5th Guards Army's 33rd Rifle Corps and units of the 21st Army's 118th Rifle Corps, which had been committed from behind the 55th Rifle Corps' right flank, reached the Schoenfeld area by 2100 on 4 February.

By the close of the day the forces of the 5th Guards and 21st armies, having destroyed the opposing enemy units, established direct communications with each other along a front from Kreisewitz to Gross Enkwitz. By this time the 31st and 4th Guards tank corps had reached the Grottkau area and had begun fighting for the town.

As a result of the 4 February offensive a common bridgehead for both armies had been formed, up to 80 kilometers in breadth and up to 25 kilometers in depth. At the same time, the towns of Schurgast and Lewin had been captured and the enemy group of forces defending the town of Brieg, which numbered about 3,000 men, had been encircled.

During the following days up to the beginning of the general offensive, the enemy encircled in the Brieg area was destroyed. The 5th Guards Army, while overcoming the enemy's increasing resistance, advanced as far as Krentsch. The 21st Army's 55th Rifle Corps, having deployed during the attack with its front facing south, captured Grottkau along with the 31st Tank Corps and advanced along the western bank of the Neisse River as far as Friedewalde, occupying a favorable flanking position *vis a vis* the German-Fascist forces' Oppeln group of forces.

Thus as a result of intensive combat, which unfolded during 28 January-7 February, the forces of the 5th Guards and 21st armies, significantly expanded their bridgehead south of Breslau, captured more favorable jumping-off positions for the development of the subsequent offensive, attracted significant German-Fascist forces to their sector of the front, and to a certain extent distracted them from the axis of our main attack.

Having achieved major results in carrying out the tasks laid down by the *front* commander during the operations' preparatory period, the 5th Guards and 21st armies were nonetheless forced to commit all their corps into the fighting for the bridgeheads. Thus by the start of the operation they did not have the necessary reserves for augmenting their first-echelon forces' efforts in developing the offensive to a great depth. Moreover, the turn of significant forces from the 21st Army toward the left flank led to a situation in which the 55th Rifle and 31st Tank corps, which had been designated for employment along the army's main attack axis toward Strelen, had been drawn into the fighting along a secondary axis.

Due to the lagging behind of the 21st Army's left-flank corps and the armies of the *front's* left wing, as a whole, the 21st Army's main forces were now forced to try and cover not only their left flank, but the entire left wing of the *front's* main shock group.

There remained at the 21th Army commander's disposal only the 118th Rifle Corps for continuing the offensive, instead of the planned three rifle and one tank corps. The severe weakening of the 21st Army's shock group had a major influence on the character of its activities in the *front* operation's subsequent development and brought about serious changes to the army's overall offensive plan, which had been drawn up in accordance with the *front's* 31 January directive.

The Struggle for the Bridgeheads on the First Ukrainian Front's Left Wing

On 28 January, after the German-Fascist forces had been cleaned out of the Silesian industrial area, the 21st Army, 4th Guards Tank and 31st Tank corps, in accordance with the plan for regrouping, began to move out to the Breslau—Oppeln sector. The 3rd Guards Tank Army had been turned to the southwest, in order to capture, together with the 60th Army, the areas of Ratibor, Rybnik and Zorau, while the 59th Army, pursuing small and scattered groups of the defeated enemy, was advancing to the west toward the Oder.

The 1st Guards Cavalry Corps, which by this time had reached the Oder along a broad front from Oderthal to Wellendorf, on 28 January was given the following assignment: before the arrival of the 59th and 60th armies' forces at the Oder, to cover the front Oderthal—Ratiborhammer with part of its forces, while its main forces, in conjunction with the 3rd Guards Tank Army, were to attack in the direction of Eichendorf. The corps was to seize a bridgehead along the left bank of the Oder and to subsequently operate to outflank Ratibor from the northwest in the direction of Langenau, for the purpose of cutting the railroad and paved roads west of Ratibor.

In order to more closely coordinate the activities of the cavalry and tank formations, from 28 January the 1st Guards Cavalry Corps was operationally subordinated to the commander of the 3rd Guards Tank Army.

Because the advance by the 59th and 60th armies to the Oder was developing slowly, the *front* commander on the morning of 30 January ordered the commanders of these armies to organize a more energetic pursuit of the retreating enemy, to force the Oder from the march and, developing the offensive within the boundary lines: to the right—Krappitz—Friedewalde, to the left—Bogumin—Troppau (Opava), and by the close of 2 February reach the line Neisse River—Neustadt—Troppau (Opava). The 3rd Guards Tank Army and the 1st Guards Cavalry Corps, whose main forces were operating in the 60th Army's offensive sector, were to assist it in carrying out the assigned task.

In the following days combat operations along the *front's* left wing unfolded in the following manner.

By the close of 30 January the 59th Army reached the Oder along the Oderthal—Bachweiler sector and, having forced the river with its left-flank units in the area west of Bachweiler, captured a small bridgehead here.

By this time the 1st Guards Cavalry Corps had somewhat expanded the bridgehead west of Oderthal and west of Wellendorf, but was unable to break through into the rear of the enemy's Ratibor group of forces.

The 3rd Guards Tank Army's main forces continued to be involved in heavy fighting with the enemy along the approaches to Rybnik and Zorau.

The 60th Army reached the line Knizenitz—excluding Zorau—excluding Pszina.

The enemy's resistance along the Oder and the Ratibor—Rybnik—Zorau—Pszina line increased noticeably. Our forces more and more often had to repel enemy infantry attacks, which were supported by tanks.

The situation along the *front's* left wing was becoming more difficult because the neighbor to the left—the Fourth Ukrainian Front's 38th Army—which was attacking along the mountainous and wooded areas of the Carpathians, had fallen well behind and the 60th Army had to leave units behind to cover its left flank during the attack.

The advance by the 60th Army's right-flank formations to the Oder was accompanied by frequent brushes with enemy detachments of various strength, which were operating in the rear of the 3rd Guards Tank Army's forces and which were striving to break through beyond the Oder and link up with their forces, following their defeat in the center of the Silesian industrial area. Sometimes such detachments moved in large columns and fighting them slowed down the pace of the army's offensive.

The fighting that unfolded during the first days of February showed that the enemy had halted his withdrawal and with the aid of continuously arriving reserves sought with all his forces to consolidate along the lines occupied. The number of enemy counterattacks rose with each day.

Along the bridgeheads occupied by the 59th Army and the 1st Guards Cavalry Corps, stubborn fighting unfolded in the enemy defense's main zone. The situation remained almost unchanged along the front of the 3rd Guards Tank and 60th armies, if one does not consider that the 60th Army's right-flank formations, while advancing toward the tank troops' positions, stretched out the army's front more and more.

In accordance with its new operational designation, the 3rd Guards Tank Army, which was attacking in the 60th Army's offensive sector, according to the *front* commander's order, was by the close of 31 January to be completely pulled out of the fighting along the *front's* left flank and was to begin a regrouping to the *front's* right flank. In connection with this, the securing of the *front's* left wing from the Oder to Pszina was to be entrusted to the 60th Army. In order to carry out the assigned task, the 1st Guards Cavalry Corps was to be subordinated to the army commander.

Insofar as it was assumed that the enemy had not yet had time to create a solid defensive front opposite the 59th and 60th armies' bridgehead, the corps was given the assignment of attacking from the bridgehead toward Ratibor and to get in the rear of the enemy's Ratibor group of forces and in this manner assist the 60th Army in defeating this group of forces and seizing Ratibor.

The enemy's readiness to repel our attacks and the organization of his defense proved to be greater than had been assumed, and the cavalry corps was not able to carry out its assigned task.

Despite the sharp change in the situation along the *front's* left wing, the commanders of the 59th and 60th armies continued to press all their efforts toward this, in order to most fully take advantage of the January offensive and to achieve the maximum possible advance by our forces.

The commander of the 59th Army, assuming that the enemy had not yet managed to securely consolidate along the left bank of the Oder following his retreat, ordered his forces to break through the enemy's defense along the left bank of the Oder in the area of the bridgeheads and, while launching their main attack along the center in the direction of Ober-Glogau, to reach the Neisse River by the morning of 4 February.

However, the 1 February fighting showed that the army's forces were not in a condition to carry out their assigned task. The uninterrupted nearly month-long battles and the resulting significant losses; the shortage of ammunition and fuel caused by the lengthening of the rear organs; the unfavorable meteorological conditions, and; the growing resistance by an enemy who was relying on prepared defensive lines, with a system of permanent defensive structures—all of this influenced the course and results of the fighting. The army's forces did not only not manage to advance, but they had to repel multiple counterattacks by enemy infantry, supported by tanks, assault guns and aviation, and to consolidate their lines, in order to hold the bridgeheads along the left bank of the Oder.

The *front* commander, taking into account the situation that had arisen along the *front's* left wing, on the morning of 2 February ordered the commander of the 59th Army to temporarily consolidate with his right-flank 43rd Rifle Corps, while on the army's left flank three divisions were to expand the bridgehead throughout the day as far as the line Cosel—Gnadenfeld and assist the 60th Army in reaching the Oder River.

Simultaneously, the army was to prepare for a general offensive by the *front's* left wing, which was scheduled for 5 February. For this purpose, it was proposed to create along the army's left flank a shock group consisting of five divisions and the army's entire artillery reinforcements.

The offensive fighting along the army's left flank during 2-5 February was extremely bitter. Our forces' uninterrupted attacks alternated with the enemy's counterattacks. Thus despite all the efforts of the army's forces, there were no major changes in the latter's condition during this period.

Nor did the general offensive, which began in the latter half of 5 February, yield the expected results. Aside from the enemy's growing resistance, the hurried and insufficiently thought-through organization of the offensive, the lack of the troops' provision with ammunition, the insufficient reconnaissance of the enemy, as well as the weakening of the troops' strength, following an uninterrupted and prolonged offensive, influenced the lack of success. To all of this must be added that the recently-begun high water and the flooding of the Oder significantly complicated the offensive. The bridges and crossings over the Oder were washed away and, despite the sappers' intensive work, the restoration of the bridges progressed slowly, because the water often once again carried them away.

As a result of the poor preparation and the lack of foresight in organizing the offensive, the troops suffered heavy losses in personnel and the offensive was foiled.

The offensive was halted for the purpose of improving information about the enemy, improving the organization of the units' and formations' cooperation and the troops' materiel supply, and its resumption was set for 8 February. But on 8 February, and for the same reasons, the offensive once again proved barren of results.

On 9 February the *front* commander ordered the 59th Army to consolidate along the line reached and to go over to the defensive along its entire front.

The 60th Army, which had deployed in the early days of February along a 70-kilometer front from the Oder to Pszina, made repeated attempts to expand the bridgehead along the right flank, which had been seized by the 1st Guards Cavalry Corps, and in the center and along the left flank to capture the towns of Rybnik, Zorau and Pszina. However, all of these attempts did not lead to success in view of the altered correlation of forces.

Moreover, the enemy's growing counterattacks and information, arriving from all sorts of intelligence sources, of the uninterrupted arrival of forces from other axes to the Ratibor area, gave us reason to assume a possible counterattack by the Hitlerites along this sector. There was a growing threat of the enemy breaking through to the Silesian industrial area, because all of the 59th and 60th armies' forces had been drawn into the fighting along a broad front and both armies lacked reserves. Nor could the *front* remove a single division from the axis of the main attack in order to reinforce the left wing.

On 4 February the commander of the 60th Army, on the basis of an order by the *front* commander, ordered the army's left-wing forces to consolidate along the line reached and go over to an active defense.

On 6 February, following unsuccessful attempts to broaden the bridgehead along the left bank of the Oder, the 60th Army ceased its offensive activities along the entire front and set about consolidating the line achieved and the development of a defense in depth.

For the purpose of creating a stable situation along the *front's* left wing, the *front* commander on 5 February ordered the chief of the engineering troops to rapidly construct, with the forces of the 42nd Mine-Engineering Brigade, anti-tank and anti-personnel mine obstacles along the sector Rybnik—Zorau—Pszina—Goczalkowice. It was planned to carry out the mining not only immediately along the front, but in the depth of the defense, particularly along the tank-accessible axes: Ratibor—Gleiwitz, and Rybnik—Gleiwitz.

The commander of the 59th Army was ordered to pull the 92nd Rifle Division out of the fighting and put it into the defense along the boundary with the 60th Army along the sector Bergwalde—Sziglowice, facing to the south and southwest. The division was to outfit anti-tank strong points along the axes listed above and to maintain constant communication with the 60th Army command, so that it was always informed of the situation along the army's front and in constant readiness to repel the enemy's attack from the south and southwest.

On the night of 6-7 February the 1st Guards Cavalry Corps, which had been ordered to occupy and outfit a defensive zone from Brandkolonie along the Ruda River as far as Wielopole, and then to Starkowitz and Spendelmuhl, was pulled back into the 60th Army's second echelon.

Thus during the operation's preparatory period, the *front's* left-wing armies did not only not carry out their assigned tasks, but ended up unable to continue the further offensive in accordance with the *front* directive of 31 January.

The main reasons for the 59th and 60th armies going over to the defensive along the Oder were the major miscalculations in organizing and conducting the offensive, as well as the significant reduction in the armies' offensive capabilities, which had been brought about by the weakening of the troops' strength and the significant reduction of their operational density as a result of the lengthening of the offensive front. The halting of the offensive was also brought about by the rapid reinforcement of the enemy's group of forces opposite the *front's* left wing and the resulting danger that the enemy might launch a counterblow toward the Silesian industrial area.

The assumption by the *front's* left-wing armies of the defensive must have told, and did tell, not only in the character of the center armies' actions, but also on the right-flank armies, because the problem of securing the left flank of the *front's* main forces now had to be resolved by bringing in forces designated for the offensive along the Berlin and Dresden directions, that is, different that what had been called for by the *front's* 31 January operational directive.

Overall Results of the Struggle to Hold and Expand the Bridgeheads

The intensive combat activities by the *front's* forces to hold and expand the bridgeheads, which unfolded in the beginning of February along the *front's* entire offensive sector, concluded with the consolidation of a bridgehead seized earlier in the area northwest of Breslau and the formation of a second major bridgehead in the area southeast of Breslau. The operational significance of the results achieved consisted in the fact that the *front* command got the opportunity before the start of the operation to concentrate on the left bank of the Oder River the *front's* main forces, which had been designated for an offensive along the Berlin and Dresden directions, and to begin the operation without the forcing of a major water barrier, which in the conditions of the already-begun high water on the Oder, acquired special significance.

Besides this, the important significance of the bitter fighting for the bridgeheads south of Breslau consisted of the fact that they tied down significant enemy forces and attention and to a certain extent ensured the surprise of our troops' attack in the area north of Breslau. In this way the forces of the 5th Guards, 21st, 59th, and 60th armies rendered considerable assistance to the forces of the *front's* main shock group in resolving their assigned tasks.

Alongside this, changes took place in the operational situation that significantly worsened the conditions of conducting the forthcoming operation.

These changes were linked to, first of all, the fact that the enemy, following the defeat inflicted on him in January, was able to quickly put his forces in order, partially reinforce them with reserves transferred from other sectors of the front and, relying on the Oder fortified line, was in a state to organize a stubborn defense and hold off our forces' further advance. The results of the fighting along the *front's* left wing showed this particularly sharply.

Following the arrival of the *front's* left-wing forces to the Silesian industrial area, the enemy, fearing our breakthrough into the occupied industrial areas of Czechoslovakia, began to hurriedly bring up to the First Ukrainian Front's left wing his forces from the southern sectors of the Soviet-German front and from the interior of Czechoslovakia. At the end of January and beginning of February the 8th and 20th panzer, 1st Light Jaeger, 97th Mountain Infantry, 100th Light Infantry, and 208th Infantry divisions were transferred here from the Fourth and Second Ukrainian fronts' sectors. According to aerial and agent intelligence, as well as testimony from prisoners, the further transfer of enemy forces from Hungary and Slovakia were noted to the areas of Ratibor, Troppau (Opava) and Moravska Ostrava.

The enemy was able to consolidate along the Oder and along the approaches to Czech Silesia with his forces that had retreated from the Silesian industrial area and newly arrived reserves.

The forces of the 59th and 60th armies, which had deployed all their forces in a single echelon during the offensive along a 116-kilometers front from Krappitz to Goczalkowice, could not crush the enemy's growing resistance. Having exhausted their offensive capabilities, they were forced to go over to the defensive, having failed to carry out their assigned tasks.

The failure of the 59th and 60th armies' force, which negatively told on the operations of the 5th Guards and 21st armies, in turn was closely tied to the serious lagging by the Fourth Ukrainian Front's right-wing forces, which while fighting in the mountainous areas of the Carpathians, could not break through to the Ostrava valley, as had been called for in the Fourth Ukrainian Front command's operational plan. For this reason, the 60th Army was forced to deploy a large part of its forces toward the south in order to cover its flank and the entire left wing of the First Ukrainian Front.

From this it is obvious that the enemy's forces and resistance proved to be more significant than had been assumed while planning the operation. Our calculation of the enemy's weakness and his incapacity to stubbornly resist the *front's* forces along the Oder defensive line was not justified. As a result of this, the forces that had been allotted for an attack along the *front's* center and left wing proved insufficient for resolving their assigned tasks.

Alongside this, the limited results of the offensive in the center and along the *front's* left wing may be explained by a number of major miscalculations, committed by the armies' command and staffs in organizing and conducting combat operations on the left bank of the Oder, particularly the insufficient reconnaissance of the enemy, the poor training of the troops in forcing rivers, and the unsatisfactory organization of the artillery offensive.

The circumstances enumerated above explain to a significant degree the reasons that the *front's* forces failed to achieve their assigned tasks.

A serious reason, which made more difficult the *front's* forces' combat activities in the fight for the bridgeheads, was the unfolding spring wet season, the breakup of the ice and the rise in the water level on the Oder. These unfavorable conditions, which arose at the most intensive period of the fighting, extremely complicated the organization and crossing of troops and equipment to the bridgeheads, as well as the supply of the forces fighting on the bridgeheads with ammunition and all kinds of engineering-technical support and food.

It should be emphasized that the troops' insufficient materiel provisioning was one of the major circumstances that lowered the offensive capabilities of the *front's* forces during this period. The reason for this were not only the increasingly complicated meteorological conditions, but also the difficulties of bringing up ammunition and fuel to the *front's* forces, due to the great extension of the rear organs, as well as the necessity of accumulating materiel for the forthcoming operation. All of this forced the *front* command to limit the expenditure of ammunition and fuel during the operation's preparatory period. This led to a situation in which the forces fighting on the bridgeheads and disposing of sufficient artillery weapons were unable to create a significant fire superiority over the enemy. Our attacks, as a rule, were repelled by the enemy's organized artillery and mortar fire, which the attacking forces were not in a condition to suppress.

Nor could the First Ukrainian Front's aviation support and secure the offensive by the ground forces, because at this time it continued to be predominantly based on airfields behind the Vistula, while the poor flying weather limited opportunities for its employment.

Such are the chief reasons that conditioned the intensive character of the fighting for the bridgeheads and which forced the *front's* left-wing armies to go over to the defensive.

The stabilization of the front along the entire sector to the south of Oppeln materially altered the conditions for the offensive by the armies operating in the *front's* center. As early as the fighting for the bridgeheads, the 21st Army, while committing all of its corps into the battle, was forced to deploy its main forces facing south, in order to cover its flank. Only four divisions remained for an attack to the west. The 5th Guards Army, which also deployed all of its corps in a single echelon, directed its main efforts toward outflanking the Breslau group of forces from the southwest and was unable to dispatch sufficient forces for attacking to the west. The threat arose that these armies' offensive along the Dresden axis would be foiled at the very start of the operation.

Due to the situation that had arisen along the *front's* left wing and center, the problem of securing the left flank of the *front's* main group of forces was rapidly arising while developing the offensive toward Dresden and Berlin.

This problem could be resolved in two ways: either by extending the *front's* left-wing armies to the maximum or by bringing in forces designated for attacking along the Dresden direction.

The first way could be excluded in the conditions at hand, as the data possessed by the *front* indicated the preparation of a counterblow by the enemy against the *front's* left wing, for the purpose of seizing the Silesian industrial area. Fearing this counterblow, the *front* commander tried not to weaken his left wing, but to reinforce it in every way. For this purpose he even approached the *Stavka* of the Supreme High Command on 6 February with a request to attach a mechanized corps from its reserve.

The second way, given the absence of a second echelon and reserve within the *front*, would have inevitably led to a weakening of the *front's* efforts along the Berlin and Dresden directions, which given the noticeably increased enemy resistance could have resulted in the extinguishing of the operation at its very beginning.

Thus the situation that had arisen in the *front's* offensive sector by the start of the operation forced the *front* command to make significant amendments to its calculations. A new operation would have to be conducted in less favorable circumstances than had been imagined at the end of January, when the *front* directive for the operation was issued.

Such was the overall operational result for the fighting during this period.

D. THE ENEMY'S MEASURES FOR PREPARING TO REPEL THE OFFENSIVE BY THE FORCES OF THE FIRST UKRAINIAN FRONT

The Organization of the Enemy's Defense Along the Oder River

The German-Fascist command, in preparing to repel new attacks by the Soviet forces from the bridgeheads along the left bank of the Oder, adopted measures to strengthen its forces. It brought defeated formations back up to strength, qualitatively increased the group of forces facing the First Ukrainian Front and sought at any price to raise its forces' combat spirit. Alongside this, the Hitlerite command devoted a great deal of attention to the organization and strengthening of its defense.

All the German command's hopes in preparing to repel the Soviet forces' further offensive into the depth of Germany were linked with the Oder defensive line. The Oder was the final major obstacle for the Soviet forces, not only as a broad water barrier, but also as a fortified line that had been created in the course of many years.

The Germans began to raise their main defensive structures on the Oder well before the Second World War, during the 1932-37 time period. Following the perfidious attack on Poland and its occupation the German General Staff's attention to the development and maintenance of the Oder fortifications declined considerably.

At the end of 1944, when the Soviet forces reached the Vistula, the Oder once again acquired the significance of a strategic line to cover the capital and internal regions of fascist Germany. Hurried work on restoring and developing the fortifications on the Oder began.

The basis of the defensive line was the fortified fortress towns, such as Glogau, Breslau, Brieg, and Oppeln. Between them, along the left bank of the Oder, stretched a chain of permanent machine gun caponiers and semi-caponiers, located at a distance of 100-200 meters from each other. Each such structure could hold 8-25 men. The defensive structures were connected by a thick network of trenches and communications trenches. The communications trenches also connected the firing points with reinforced concrete observation points and shelters.

In the hurried conduct of defensive works, attention was mainly paid to strengthening the fortress towns, which were supposed to cement the entire defensive system along the Oder. In case of our forces' breakthrough of the Oder line, the garrisons of these fortress towns, even if they should be encircled, were to fight to the last man.

The great importance that the Hitlerite command attached to the defense of the fortress towns is evident, if only from the fact that their commandants were personally appointed by Hitler from among those generals enjoying his special trust.

The garrisons of the towns and the remaining population were provided with significant food supplies in case of fighting in a blockade situation.

The towns located on the Oder had, as a rule, two rings of fortifications—an external and an internal one. The defensive positions consisted of a system of trenches in conjunction with permanent firing structures, strong points and engineering obstacles. Particular attention was paid to the organization of anti-tank defense, particularly to the creation of deep anti-tank minefields and numerous anti-tank ditches.

As a typical example, one may cite the defensive organization of the city of Breslau. The city's outer ring, which had been broken through by our forces along individual sectors, was 15-20 kilometers from the center of town. It consisted of a continuous first trench and an intermittent second trench in conjunction with a system of strong points on heights in the inhabited locales. Behind the trenches, at a distance of 2-3 kilometers, a continuous anti-tank ditch had been dug. Along the ditch ran a line of fortress-type defensive structures in conjunction with reinforced concrete and wood and earth machine gun firing points.

The internal ring ran immediately along the city's outskirts. From north to south the defensive line ran along the Weide River, and from the west along the Los River. The banks of these rivers were made inaccessible to tanks along many sectors. Anti-tank ditches were dug along tank-accessible sectors, the overall length of which reached up to 15 kilometers.

All the railroads and paved roads leading to the center of town were blocked by barricades and mined along many sectors. The city had been broken up into defensive sectors.

The Soviet forces' rapid arrival at the Oder and the seizure from the march of several bridgeheads along the river's left bank prevented the Hitlerite command from fully realizing the planned defensive works along the Oder line. Moreover, it was not able to once again create defensive lines to the west of the Oder. For that the Germans lacked both time and forces.

In the developing situation the German-Fascist command, while planning defensive operations to the west of the Oder, had to rely on natural defensive lines and obstacles, of which there were more than enough in Army Group Center's area.

The large number of inhabited locales with stone structures, the abundance of wooded areas and rivers, which during the beginning period of high water represented a serious obstacle for the attacking troops, were creating favorable conditions for the organization of a defense.

For this reason, the Army Group Center command assigned the chief of the engineering troops in Lower Silesia the task of maximally configuring natural obstacles for defense, strengthening them with engineering structures and obstacles.

The defensive lines in the zone from the Oder to the Elbe were initially built along water lines or commanding heights, resembling a chain of individual emplacements, trenches and trench sectors covering the most important axes. It was planned to later improve these positions. However, the German-Fascist command did not have the forces to develop them. The able-bodied male population in the front-line area had been mobilized and sent to the front and a significant part of the remaining inhabitants had fled to the west. As a result, by the start of our offensive there were no continuous defensive lines in the depth of the enemy's defense. For example, structures resembling unimproved rifle and machine gun trenches had been built along the Bober River. The firing positions for guns and mortars had chiefly been prepared in the areas of inhabited locales, along road junctions and crossings.

The line along the Neisse River had been outfitted somewhat more strongly, in the engineering sense, although here the main defensive work was carried out only after the February fighting, by troops that had fallen back to this line during the course of the operation.

Defensive works were not being conducted in a timely manner along the northeastern slopes of the Sudeten Mountains. Defensive positions were being built by the troops that had fallen back here.

On the other hand, a great deal of attention was being devoted to preparations for defending the inhabited locales. Not only large towns, but also each small village had been transformed into strong points and resistance centers by the efforts of the local population under the leadership of sappers.

Roads and approaches to inhabited locales, to crossings and defiles were, as a rule, covered by various engineering obstacles and were under artillery and mortar fire. Aside from mining, the enemy built barricades and anti-tank fences or barriers in the form of one or several rows of reinforced concrete cylinders, two meters wide and filled with sand. Barricades and fences were also thrown together from materials at hand: logs, rock, wrecked vehicles, etc.

From this it is obvious that despite the hurried organization of the defense, the German-Fascist forces disposed of favorable conditions for waging defensive actions not only along the Oder line, but to the west of it.

Training the Enemy Forces for Defending Along the Oder

While striving to solidly consolidate along the Oder and to prevent the Soviet forces from further developing the offensive toward Berlin and Dresden, the German-Fascist command, along with the engineering preparation of the defense, devoted particular attention to restoring the combat capability of its troops that had fallen back behind the Oder. Simultaneously, the Hitlerites took emergency measures to strengthen their group of forces operating against the First Ukrainian Front by transferring troops from the neighboring sectors, chiefly from Czechoslovakia and Hungary, as well as from units taken from the Western Front.

Besides this, at the end of January and the beginning of February major troop regroupings within the German Fourth Panzer and Seventeenth armies were occurring, for the purpose of creating denser groups of forces along the threatened axes, mainly facing our bridgeheads.

During the 28 January-7 February time period intensive work was being carried out in the enemy rear. The defeated divisions were being put in order, brought up to strength and committed into the line.

In the last days of January a directive was issued, according to which the formations of the Ninth Field and Fourth Panzer armies, which had been defeated by Soviet forces, were to fall back behind the Oder in order to put themselves in order.

The reception of the retiring formations and the formation of combat-capable units and subunits from their remnants was entrusted to the headquarters of the XXIV Panzer Corps, which still retained some capacity for work.

On 28 January the commander of the XXIV Panzer Corps' order No. 261/45 defined the concentration areas and the points for fitting out the troop units, rear organs and supply trains.

According to this order, the points were as follows: for the formations of the XL Panzer Corps (25th and 19th panzer divisions)—Forst; for the formations of the XXIV Panzer and XLII Army corps (16th and 17th panzer, 20th Panzergrenadier, 72nd, 342nd, 391st, 168th, and 88th infantry divisions)—Zorau—Sagan; for the formations of the LVI Panzer Corps (17th and 214th infantry and 10th Panzergrenadier divisions)—Sprottau; for the formations of the VIII Army Corps (6th and 45th *volksgrenadier* divisions)—the area southwest of Friestadt; for the *Grossdeutschland* Panzer Corps (a parachute-landing division, the "Hermann Goring" Panzer Division, and the "Brandenburg" Panzergrenadier Division)—the areas of Muskau and Tribel.

The order also established the areas for concentrating the high command artillery reserve, of anti-tank units, sapper units, communications units, and other special units of the Ninth Field and Fourth Panzer armies.

Several screening detachments were allotted to the commander of the XXIV Panzer Corps for the collection of retreating units and elements, as well as for detaining soldiers who had fallen behind.

Insofar as at this time desertion in the German-Fascist army was particularly widespread, a special paragraph of the order foresaw the necessity of combing the entire area west of the Oder for the purpose of apprehending deserters and dispatching them to the collection points. Besides this, the screening detachments were entrusted with the task of confiscating from transport and rear units extra weapons, ammunition, transport, and equipment and dispatching all of this to the headquarters of the units undergoing formation.

Typically, during this period all the Germans' attempts to employ foreign soldiers in combat suffered a complete collapse. The absolute majority of them avoided battle and ran away at the slightest danger. The screening detachments were ordered to disarm the remnants of foreign formations and send them to the rear.

The decisiveness with which the Hitlerite command approached the restoration of the combat capability of its forces falling back in disorder across the Oder did not yield the expected results.

The German-Fascist command only managed to partially pull out of the fighting the remnants of its defeated divisions for reforming and bringing up to strength in the rear, because the commanders of the formations defending the Oder line would intercept the retreating, dispersed and unguided remnants of the defeated troops and used them for filling out their own units.

The shortage of forces in the formations and units located in the first line forced the Hitlerite command, not long after the issue of the order, to renounce the formation of entire units and formations in the rear. A new order was issued, according to which from among the soldiers and officers that were breaking through to the left bank of the Oder and just arriving at the collection points, companies and battalions would be formed and immediately dispatched to the forward positions. At the same time, it was recommended that companies and battalions be created from the soldiers and officers of the same division.

During this time *volkssturm* subunits were being formed at top speed. However, insofar as the combat capability of such subunits was extremely low, many of them were distributed among the units in the newly formed companies and battalions, with which they were sent to the front.

March companies, battalions, independent regiments, and groups, numbering from 100 to 3,000 men each, and which were arriving from the most far flung areas of Germany, served as a reserve for bringing the troops up to strength.

Combat subunits and units were hurriedly formed from the march reinforcements and arriving equipment and immediately dispatched to the forward positions, chiefly in the areas of our bridgeheads.

Simultaneous with this, entire enemy formations, which were being transferred from other sectors of the Soviet-German front, from the German rear areas, and also from the Western Front, continued to arrive opposite the First Ukrainian Front's attack sector.

During the 28 January-1 February time period the 208th and 254th infantry divisions arrived here from Czechoslovakia, the 8th Panzer Division from Hungary, and the 408th Infantry Division from the Reserve Army. A number of divisions being dispatched to the First Ukrainian Front's operational area were en route by the start of the operation (the 21st Panzer Division, which was being transferred from the Western Front and the 18th Panzergrenadier Division from the Second Army).

Simultaneous with the reforming, bringing up to strength and reinforcement of the enemy forces with reserves, a certain redistribution of forces by axes was also being carried out.

The regrouping of the enemy's forces involved a significant part of the formations of the German Fourth Panzer and Seventeenth armies and was chiefly linked to the creation of denser groups of forces facing our bridgeheads. By moving up everything possible to the area of the bridgeheads, the German-Fascist command was seeking to throw our forces back to the right bank of the Oder, or to at least halt their further advance and create conditions for the prolonged stabilization of the front along these axes.

The Composition and Disposition of the Enemy's Forces by 8 February in the First Ukrainian Front's Offensive Sector

By 8 February there were in the First Ukrainian Front's offensive sector in the first echelon and forming in the rear seven panzer, four panzergrenadier and 26 enemy infantry divisions, in all 37 divisions. Of this number six panzer, two panzergrenadier and 19 infantry divisions were in the first echelon, that is, 27 divisions.

A significant part of the first-echelon divisions were combat groups, which included beside the remnants of these divisions, which were often combined into 1-2 regiments, independent battalions, special units and numerous smaller combat groups.

The first-echelon divisions numbered from 2,000-7,000 men, while their average strength was 4,000 men.

The second-echelon divisions were still being brought up to strength. By the start of our offensive their numerical strength was even lower.

Besides this, the enemy had a large number of various combat groups, independent units and elements subordinated to corps.

Soviet intelligence established facing the First Ukrainian Front 13 various independent regiments, 115 independent battalions, 23 battalion combat groups, and a number of specialized subunits. It's possible that many of these subunits formed part of this or that division of divisional combat groups. However, the very presence of such a number of independent units and subunits testified to the fact that the Germans were very hurriedly reinforcing their troops and that their forces had increased considerably by the start of our offensive.

The disposition of Army Group Center's forces facing the First Ukrainian Front by the start of the operation is, in general, as follows.

Units of the XL Panzer Corps, consisting of the 608th Special Designation Division, the remnants of the 25th Panzer and 17th Anti-Aircraft divisions,[15] were defending, facing the 3rd Guards Army's right flank along the Oder River as far as Neusalz. The XXIV Panzer Corps, consisting of the 342nd and 72nd infantry and 16th Panzer divisions, was defending along the right bank of the Oder in the Glogau area.

The "Brandenburg" Panzergrenadier Division, "Hermann Goring" Panzer Division and the 20th Panzergrenadier Division, which were part of the *Grossdeutschland* Panzer Corps, were engaged in stubborn defensive fighting opposite the left flank of the 3rd Guards Army and the right-flank formations of the 13th Army.

The LVII Panzer Corps was defending opposite the southern part of the bridgeheads and then as far as the Breslau fortified area. By this time the corps consisted of the 103rd Independent Panzer Brigade (formed at the end of January from the remnants of panzer units and independent panzer battalions), the 19th Panzer and 408th Infantry divisions, the combat groups "Bohemia," "Moravia" and "Prague." These combat groups were covering the sector from Malcz to Auras.

The Breslau fortified area and the bridgehead fortifications on the right bank of the Oder were being defended by corps group "Breslau," consisting of a large number of different combat groups, regiments and battalions. The headquarters of the 609th Special Designation Division unified a part of these forces.

South of Breslau the XVII Army Corps, consisting of the 269th, 254th and 208th infantry divisions, was defending opposite the 5th Guards Army.

South of the XVII Army Corps the VIII Army Corps was engaged in defensive fighting. Of its units, the 45th *Volksgrenadier* (Infantry) and 20th Panzer divisions and combat groups from the

---

15 The 17th Anti-Aircraft Division had no equipment and operated as an infantry division.

168th, Estonian 20th and 304th infantry divisions were operating opposite the 21st Army. Part of the latter's forces was operating opposite the 59th Army's right flank. The 100th Light Infantry Division and part of the 8th Panzer divisions were defending opposite the 59th Army's center and left flank. The remaining forces of the 8th Panzer Division, the 344th Infantry Division's combat group, which also was part of the VIII Army Corps, and the entire XI Army Corps, which formed part of army group "Heinrici" (First Panzer Army) were defending opposite the 60th Army from the bridgehead north of Ratibor to the boundary with the Fourth Ukrainian Front. The XI Corps included combat groups from the 371st Infantry, 97th Light Infantry, 1st Jaeger Ski, and 68th Infantry divisions, as well as the 75th Infantry Division.

A combat group from the LIX Army Corps' 359th Infantry Division was operating along the boundary between the First and Fourth Ukrainian fronts.

On the basis of captured documents, prisoner testimony and other intelligence data, the *front* headquarters compiled a table showing the enemy's numerical strength and armaments facing the First Ukrainian Front on 1 February and 10. See Table V/1.D.1.

Taking as a base the data on the enemy presented in this table, and taking into account his regroupings during the 8-10 February time period, as well as the losses suffered by him during these days, one may conclude that the numerical composition and equipment of the German forces facing the First Ukrainian Front by 8 February was approximately equal to that as shown in Table V/1.D.2.

Table V/1.D.1 The Enemy's Disposition and Numerical Strength Facing the First Ukrainian Front on 1 and 10 February 1945 (According to Intelligence from the First Ukrainian Front's Intelligence Directorate)

Axis	Men (Not Counting Personnel from Rear Units and Establishments)			Machine Guns		
	1.2	10.2	Change	1.2	10.2	Change
Facing the *front's* right wing	50,100	43,450	−6,650	2,362	2,203	−159
Facing the *front's* center	35,350	34,300	−1,050	1,050	2,070	+1,020
Facing the *front's* left wing	41,700	55,800	+14,100	1,692	2,780	+1,088
TOTAL	127,150	133,550	+6,400	5,104	7,053	+1,949

Axis	Mortars			Guns			Tanks and Assault Guns		
	1.2	10.2	Change	1.2	10.2	Change	1.2	10.2	Change
Facing the *front's* right wing	196	228	+32	242	361	+119	237	190	-47
Facing the *front's* center	210	156	−54	307	300	-7	185	100	-85
Facing the *front's* left wing	543	726	+183	609	776	+167	141	227	+86
TOTAL	949	1,110	+161	1,158	1,437	+279	563	517	−46

Table V/1.D.2 The Enemy's Strength and Armament Facing the First Ukrainian Front (as of 8 February 1945)

Category	Opposite the *Front's* Right Wing	Opposite the *Front's* Center	Opposite the *Front's* Left Wing	Total
Men	56,485	44,590	72,540	173,615
Battalions	115	91	146	352
Machine Guns	2,864	2,691	3,614	9,169
Guns and Mortars	766	593	1,953	3,312
Tanks and Assault Guns	247	130	295	672

The Enemy Forces' Morale and Measures by the German-Fascist Command to Strengthen it

If the search for men and materiel to continue the war in 1945 was an enormously difficult problem for the Hitlerite command, then perhaps forcing the German soldiers to fight was no less difficult a task.

As early as soon after the start of the war the German workers and peasants began to understand that the unjust and aggressive character of this war, which had been unleashed by Hitler and his clique to please the German imperialists, contradicted the vital interests of the German people. For the progressive part of the German people, it was becoming all the more clear that the war, inspired by the Hitlerites, would be lost.

I.V. Stalin, in tallying the results of the first year of the war, noted in his 1 May 1942 order that "among the German people the realization of Germany's defeat is increasing more. For the German people it is becoming all the more clear that the single way out of the present situation is the liberation of Germany from the adventurist Hitler-Goring clique."

Under the influence of the Soviet army's victories and the unending defeats by the German forces on the Soviet-German front, with each year of the war defeatist sentiments more and more deeply penetrated into the German army, which was a blind tool in the hands of the fascist overlords, called upon to spill its own and others' blood and to cripple itself and others not for German interests, but for the sake of enriching the German bankers and plutocrats.

At the beginning of 1945 the situation along the fronts and the internal situation in Germany showed the German people and army that the war, unleashed by the fascists, had been lost, that the Hitlerite leadership was bankrupt and that all its attempts to win the war or achieve a peace acceptable to German imperialism were and would be doomed to a shameful failure. Wide swaths of the German people became more and more aware that the further continuation of the war would bring the German people only new heavy and vain losses and suffering.

Thus the notion of ending the war under any conditions was firmly implanted in the consciousness of the absolute majority of the German people, and despite the fierce fascist terror it more and more often broke to the surface. Thousands of letters, bypassing the censorship, from the rear to the front and from the front to the rear, and the testimony of an enormous number of prisoners and deserters clearly reflected this feeling in the army and people. Only a certain part of the soldiers that stilled believed its fascist officers and continued to hope in a favorable outcome to the war, although they could not coherently explain how this would come about. The majority of soldiers treated such people with distrust and often with hatred; they were feared and laughed at.

But why, nonetheless, despite the grave weakening of the German-Fascist army, the lowering of morale and the widespread dissemination of defeatist attitudes in the army and people, did the Germans continue to so stubbornly fight, and namely on the Soviet-German front? This may be explained by two basic reasons: Nazi propaganda's unbridled and unrestrained anti-Soviet slander and the ruthless terror in the country and army against everyone who in thought, word or deed expressed doubt as to the rightness of the fascists and their policies.

The cloudy streams of fascist slander against the Soviet people and the Soviet army literally washed over Germany, dulling the minds and hearts of people in the country and army, inspiring fear among the Germans.

The entire arsenal of Goebbels'[16] lying propaganda—press, radio, movies, thousands of posters, placards, leaflets, appeals, and orders—all screamed about death, about the insults and the shame which the Soviet forces were bringing to Germany. The soldier had been scared by fairy tales about the atrocities committed by Soviet forces against the peaceful population, about mass executions of prisoners, about exile to hard labor in Siberia, etc. On that score, in the minds of the German soldiers Siberia was associated with the idea of hell on earth. Many soldiers were ready to undergo the heaviest suffering under bullets and shells on the front, if only not to end up in Siberia.

All of this forced the main mass of German soldiers, who were cursing the war and those who were pushing them to a senseless death, to go into battle and fight without faith in the rightness of their cause, without inspiration, and without prospects for victory.

It was natural that such attitudes, in spite of harsh discipline, gave rise to desertion, sabotage, pillaging, and suicides. Following the Germans' defeat between the Vistula and Oder these phenomena became widespread.

Insofar as the influence of fascist propaganda on the awakening consciousness of the soldiers, and not only the soldiers, but the officers and state employees, fell sharply, the German command, which earlier had not hesitated to employ severe sanctions against insubordination, during the last months of the war went over to the wildest sort of terror in relation to all categories of people, at the front and in the rear, who doubted the possibility of victory.

At the end of January the fascist command's orders were announced in all units regarding the execution of all deserters and those seeking to surrender and the confinement of their families in concentration camps or their execution.

During the fighting along the Oder and later all the newspapers, posters, orders, and appeals abounded with announcements of the executions of deserters, marauders and of people who listened to foreign radio broadcasts and who expressed thoughts regarding the inevitability of defeat, or who sought to surrender, etc.

Such was the situation in the rear of the German army and its condition in February 1945, on the eve of our offensive.

Thus concerning the question of continuing the war, only an extremely small part of the soldiers consciously supported the officers who remained loyal to the fascist regime. The majority of frightened and stupefied German soldiers, who had lost faith in victory, fought under the threat of repressions at the front and in the rear. Terror and fascist propaganda still restrained these soldiers from an open rising against the senseless continuation of resistance and impelled them to fight desperately.

The overall conclusion as to the condition and readiness of the German-Fascist soldiers to resist in the First Ukrainian Front's offensive sector boils down to the following.

As a result of all the measures carried out by the enemy command for concentrating forces in the First Ukrainian Front's operational zone, in organizing a defense and outfitting the terrain for

---

16 Editor's note. This is a reference to Dr. Paul Joseph Goebbels (1897-1945), who served as Reich Minister of Propaganda from 1933 to 1945. Goebbels was an early and devoted follower of Hitler and remained a member of the Nazi leader's inner circle throughout his years in power. Goebbels and his wife committed suicide in the ruins of Berlin in May 1945.

defense, and also in connection with measures adopted to increase discipline among the troops and raising their combat spirit, the combat capability of Army Group Center's forces by the beginning of the Soviet forces' offensive had increased significantly compared to the end of January. The forces of the First Ukrainian Front were no longer faced with an enemy running away in panic, as had been the case in the latter half of January, but a more or less organized combat force. However, the short period in which the First Ukrainian Front prepared a new attack along the Oder prevented the Hitlerite command from fully realizing its planned measures for strengthening the Oder line and developing the defense in depth. Nor did it manage during this period to concentrate sufficient forces for creating a deeply echeloned defense. By the start of our offensive all the German forces on the Oder had been put into the first echelon. The Army Group Center command had no reserves, if one does not count the remnants of several defeated divisions undergoing reformation.

But the German-Fascist command attached great significance to the retention of the Oder defensive line, considering that the fate of Berlin, and along with it the fascist state, would be decided at that time on the Oder. Thus one could expect that despite the unfinished nature of the preparations of the Oder line for defense and the limited number of forces along this sector of the front, that the German-Fascist command would undertake all measures to strengthen it, and that the Hitlerite forces would put up fierce resistance in the fight to retain it.

E. THE REGROUPING OF THE FIRST UKRAINIAN FRONT'S FORCES AND THE DISPOSITION OF OUR FORCES BY THE START OF THE OPERATION

The Regrouping of Forces

During the Sandomierz-Silesian operation a significant part of the *front's* forces had been committed for defeating the enemy in the Silesian industrial area. That is why upon the completion of the January offensive the densest troop grouping arose along the *front's* left wing.

According to the plan for the new operation, the *front* was to launch its main attack along its right wing and a second attack in the center. In order to create powerful shock groups along these axes, a significant regrouping of forces was required, which to one extent or another had an effect on almost all of the *front's* forces.

In accordance with the decision by the *front* commander, the 3rd Guards Army was to be transferred in full from the left wing to the right. The 6th Army and 7th Guards Cavalry Corps were to be sent there as well from the *front* reserve. The 52nd Army's main forces were also to be brought up to the area north of Breslau. The main forces of the 21st Army and all of the 4th Guards and 31st tank corps were to be transferred from the Silesian industrial area to the area north of Oppeln.

Aside from this, due to the establishment of new offensive zones and the transfer of sectors to neighboring armies, we had to carry out significant regroupings within the armies.

From this it is clear that the scope of the forthcoming regroupings was significant, while the deadlines established for this measure were extremely tight.

The regrouping of the *front's* forces began immediately after the *Stavka* of the Supreme High Command's confirmation of the *front* commander's thoughts on a plan for further operations.

The complexity of the regrouping consisted of the fact that the relief and withdrawal of troops from the fighting was to be carried out in conditions of the continuing offensive by the *front's* forces and a high degree of enemy activity. Thus a high degree of exactitude was required of the command element at all levels in organizing the relief and withdrawal of troops from the fighting and conducting marches to new concentration areas, in order that the strict timetable for regrouping be carried out completely and in the required time. The smallest disruption of this schedule could upset the entire plan for regrouping the *front's* forces.

Front headquarters uninterruptedly followed the observance of the regrouping schedule, adopted emergency measures for ensuring that it was carried out by the troops and, should circumstances require, made corrections to the deadlines established for the armies, so that the overall regrouping plan was carried out on time.

On 29 January the 6th Army, which was located in the *front* reserve in the Szczerow area (180-200 kilometers east of the Oder), received orders to concentrate in the woods northeast of Trebnitz by the close of 2 February. While moving toward the front, the army's forces were at the same time to clear out the wooded areas along their advance sector of wandering remnants of defeated enemy units.

The 6th Army's forces, having begun their movement to the new area on 30 January, concentrated by the close of 2 February in the woods northwest of Obernigk, having covered 150-160 kilometers in four days. By the close of 3 February the army's forces, on the basis of an supplementary order by the *front* commander, were pulled into the area southwest of Wolau, into the salient that was formed here by the flow of the Oder River, in order to relieve the 52nd Army's forces on the bridgehead in the Malcz area, from where the 6th Army was to begin its attack.

The regroupings of those forces that were in combat contact with the enemy began on 30 January and were to be completed by the close of 5 February.

On the night of 29-30 January the commander of the 21st Army was ordered by the morning of 31 January to relieve the 5th Guards Army's formations on the bridgehead northwest of Oppeln, and for the latter to turn over to the 21st Army the bridgehead sector and army sector as far as Brieg (exclusively).

At the moment the order was received, the 21st Army's main forces were located in the Tarnowitz—Gleiwitz—Beuten area, that is, at a 90-kilometer remove from the planned operational area.

At 0500 on 31 January the *front* commander ordered the commander of the 5th Guards Army to begin on the night of 31 January-1 February the relief of the 52nd Army's formations along the Breslau—Ohlau sector.

The commander of the 52nd Army received orders to leave the 73rd Rifle Corps along the Auras—Breslau sector, while the second-echelon 48th Rifle Corps and the 78th Rifle Corps, which was to be relieved by the forces of the 5th Guards Army, were to be regrouped along with all their army reinforcements and concentrated in the Steinau—Leubsdorf—Wolau area. By the morning of 4 February they were to relieve the 13th Army's formations along the sector excluding Luben—Malcz.

It was ordered that the sector from the Oder River from Malcz to Auras was to be occupied by units of the 77th Fortified Area, which was to be transferred from the 6th Army to the 52nd Army on 2 February.

Due to the great distance which the 21st Army's forces had to travel during the regrouping and the inexact calculation of their rate of advance, they were late in arriving at their new concentration areas. The relief of the 5th Guards Army's forces was somewhat drawn out and was not completed by the morning of 31 January, but during the latter half of the day. For this reason the deadline for the relief of the 52nd Army's units by the forces of the 5th Guards Army was extended by a day.

The headquarters of the 5th Guards and 52nd armies and the corps' headquarters failed to organize the corresponding control for carrying out the *front* commander's order. As a result of this, even before the arrival of the 5th Guards Army's forces to the bridgehead, the 4th Artillery Division's artillery began to be removed from its firing positions when it was still daylight. A part of the 214th Rifle Division's rear establishments was also moved back to the right bank of the Oder River, while at the same time units of the 34th Guards Rifle Corps had not yet been moved up to their jumping-off areas for taking over the sectors.

The enemy, who was very active along this sector of the front, noticed the movement of our troops on the bridgehead during the daylight hours. Attacking the units of the 52nd Army's 78th

Rifle Corps, he threw them back several kilometers toward the Oder. As a result of this, the relief of the 78th Rifle Corps by units of the 5th Guards Army's 34th Guards Rifle Corps began well behind schedule on the night of 1-2 February and unfolded in an unorganized manner.

The 78th Rifle Corps, after turning over its sector, arrived at the east bank of the Oder and from here began its movement during the latter half of 2 February to the 13th Army's sector.

The regrouping of the 48th Rifle Corps began somewhat earlier. During the night of 3-4 February the corps had already relieved the right-flank formations of the 13th Army's 27th Rifle Corps along the sector from Luben to Jurtsch. The 27th Rifle Corps' left-flank formations along the sector from Jurtsch to the bridgehead in the Malcz area were relieved by the 78th Rifle Corps during 4-5 February.

During the night of 3-4 February units of the 6th Army arrived at the bridgehead in the Malcz area.

At the same time units of the 77th Fortified Area began their movement toward the Oder and the Malcz—Auras sector. On 4 February, following the repulse and defeat of the attacks by a German battalion that had crossed to the northern bank of the river in the Dichernfurt area, units of the fortified area occupied the entire assigned sector.

Simultaneous with the regrouping of the combined-arms armies, the tank troops were also regrouping.

Up to 30 January all of the 3rd Guards Tank Army's corps, along with the forces of the 60th Army, continued to fight in the Silesian industrial area along the line Ratiborhammer—Rybnik—Zorau. On the night of 29-30 January the 6th Guards Tank Corps was pulled out of the fighting. On the morning of 30 January the *front* ordered that the entire army be pulled out of the line by the close of the day and concentrated in the area northeast of Gross Strelitz. During 1-2 February the army's formations were pulled into the rear in order to put their equipment in order, and on the night of 2-3 February the army was to begin moving to a new concentration area—Wolau and the woods to the west. It was planned to complete the concentration by the morning of 5 February, while at the same time the march was to be carried out only at night.

On the night of 5-6 February the army was to have already crossed over to the bridgehead occupied by the 52nd Army's forces, for joint operations with the latter.

The distance between Gross Strelitz and Wolau along the route Rosenberg—Kreitzburg—Bernstadt—Els—Trebnitz—Prausnitz was equal to 180 kilometers. Two nights were allotted for the regrouping.

In carrying out the order, the commander of the 3rd Guards Tank Army pulled the 7th Guards Tank Corps out of the line on the night of 30-31 January, and by 1 February had concentrated it in the Gross Strelnitz area. The 9th Mechanized Corps, upon the request of the commander of the 60th Army and the approval of the *front* commander, remained temporarily along the *front's* left wing until the completion of the 60th Army's regrouping, which had been brought about by the departure of the tank formations.

The 3rd Guards Tank Army's tank corps began their movement on the night of 1-2 February from the Gross Strelnitz area to the new concentration area called for by the operational plan. On 3 February the army's main forces were bivouacked in the Namslau area, and by the morning of 5 February had completed their concentration in the Wolau area.

In connection with the failure to carry out the plan for accumulating ammunition and for the purpose of better preparing the *front's* right-wing armies for the attack, their commitment into the battle was shifted from 6-8 February. Thus the troops' occupation of their jumping-off positions for the attack was also delayed by two days. The transfer of the 3rd Guards Tank Army's tank corps to the bridgehead began only on the night of 6-7 February and was completed on the evening of 7 February. The 9th Mechanized Corps, which had been pulled out of the line along the *front's* left wing on the night of 4-5 February, moved by night marches on 6-7 February to the Wolau area, and during the night of 7-8 February its main forces had already crossed over to the Oder's left bank.

The 25th Tank Corps, which was operating together with the 3rd Guards Tank Army, was engaged in heavy fighting along the army's center up to the evening of 6 February, attacking Glogau from the north. During the night it was pulled out of the line along this sector and by the morning of 7 February had completed a march to the Gross Osten area. On the night of 7-8 February the corps was moved to the bridgehead, where the army's main forces were concentrating.

The 7th Guards Mechanized Corps, which was in the *front* reserve and slated for joint operations with the 6th Army, was operationally subordinated to the commander of the 6th Army and on 2 February had concentrated in the woods north of Els. Then, in accordance with a supplementary order, the corps was moved to the area southwest of Wolau. From here the corps moved out to the bridgehead in the Malcz area on the night of 7-8 February.

Up to 31 January the 4th Guards Tank Corps was subordinated to the commander of the 59th Army. Following the clearing of the Silesian industrial area, it was concentrated in the Kuferstedtel area. On 1 February the *front* commander resubordinated the corps to the commander of the 5th Guards Army and ordered the corps commander to concentrate his corps in the wooded area northeast of Brieg by the morning of 3 February, where he would be subordinated to the commander of the 5th Guards Army.

At 1700 on 1 February the corps' forward units left the Kuferstedtel area and on 3 February the corps finished its concentration in the new area, from where it was committed into the fighting on the following day.

The 31st Tank Corps, which was operating with the forces of the 21st Army during the January operation and which had been left under the latter's control during the new operation, had been concentrated north of Gleiwitz before the regrouping, in the Jasten area. On 2 February, after the 21st Army's rifle corps had been transferred to the bridgehead, the 31st Tank Corps began its movement to the new concentration area. On 3 February the corps concentrated in the woods northwest of Wolfsgrund and, following a short rest, was committed into the fighting on 4 February.

The 4th Tank Army was located in the 13th Army's sector, together with which it took part in the January offensive operation and was getting ready to carry out the February operation. In the first days of February the army's main forces were fighting to hold the bridgehead in the area west of Keben, helping the 3rd Guards and 13th armies' forces.

By 6 February the 4th Tank Army's tank and mechanized units had been pulled out of the line, concentrated behind the 13th Army's combined-arms formations, and until 8 February were putting their equipment in order, accumulating ammunition and fuel and carrying out other work, preparing for the new operation.

Thus by the close of 7 February the *front's* forces, having fully completed their regrouping called for by the operational plan, had concentrated within the boundary lines established by the *front* directive of 31 January, and had occupied their jumping-off positions for the offensive.

The Disposition of the First Ukrainian Front's Forces Along the Axis of the Main Attack

As a result of the regrouping conducted during 29 January-7 February along the *front's* right wing, four combined-arms and two tank armies had been concentrated (3rd Guards, 13th, 52nd, and 6th, and the 4th Tank and 3rd Guards Tank armies) along a 230-kilometer zone from Odereck to the bridgehead in the area southeast of Breslau, as well as one tank corps (25th) and one mechanized (7th Guards) corps.

Because the *front* was to launch its main attack from the bridgeheads in the areas west of Steinau and Malcz, the main forces of the troops that had been gathered for the offensive had been concentrated in the center of this sector along a 70-kilometer sector. In all, there were 26 rifle divisions, four tank and three mechanized corps here. The 96-kilometer sector from Odereck to the bridgehead northwest of Keben was covered by one rifle corps and one division from the 3rd Guards Army, while the 65-kilometer sector from the bridgehead in the Malcz area to the boundary with the 5th Guards Army was covered by a corps from the 52nd Army.

As a result of the regrouping, the operational density of the forces concentrated along the axis of the *front's* main attack increased sharply. If each rifle division occupied on the average a 7.2-kilometer front along the *front's* entire right wing, then within the group of forces created among the corps operating along the flanks of the main forces, each division had a 22-24 kilometer front, while it was 2.8 kilometers along the axis of the main attack. It should be taken into account here that all the tank troops and all reinforcements were also concentrated along the axis of the main attack.

The combined-arms armies that had been brought in for the attack along the *front's* right wing were deployed in a single echelon. The *front* did not have a second echelon and combined-arms reserve. The *front* commander held in reserve only the 150th Independent Tank Brigade and the 87th Guards Tank Regiment, which were located in the Schoenwald area and contained 64 tanks and three self-propelled guns. The 4th and 3rd Guards tank armies comprised the *front's* two mobile groups. They were designated for developing the success in the center of the shock group in the 13th and 52nd armies' attack sectors. The 25th Tank and 7th Guards Mechanized corps were operationally subordinated to the combined-arms armies attacking along the flanks of the shock group and, in conjunction with the latter, were to develop the success toward the flanks. The reasons conditioning such a formation and echeloning of the *front's* main forces were reviewed above in the analysis of the *front* commander's idea and decision.

The 3rd Guards Army, while operating on the *front's* right flank, between 29 January and 7 February expanded its attack sector from 70 to 104 kilometers. By 8 February the army's main forces (21st Rifle Corps, minus one division, the 76th Rifle Corps and the 25th Tank Corps), as well as all reinforcements, had been concentrated on the bridgehead west of Keben, along an 8-kilometer sector, from which the army was to launch its main attack. The remaining 96 kilometers of front was occupied by the 120th Rifle Corps, the 21st Rifle Corps' 127th Rifle Division, and an independent army battalion.

The army's operational formation was in a single echelon. All the rifle corps also had a single-echelon formation. Each rifle division had the following frontages: along the bridgehead—two kilometers, with 24 kilometers along the remainder of the front. The 76th Rifle Corps' 287th Rifle Division remained in the army commander's reserve. The 25th Tank Corps, which was the army mobile group, was located behind the left-flank rifle corps along the axis of the main attack, with one brigade among the 76th Rifle Corps' combat formation.

The 13th Army, whose front, following the regrouping, narrowed by nearly six times and by 8 February amounted to 18 kilometers, as opposed to the 86 kilometers of 28 January, was to operate in the center of the *front's* shock group. The army was to break through the enemy's front along the entire attack sector, and thus its forces were distributed comparatively evenly.

The army had a two-echelon operational formation. The 102nd and 24th rifle corps were in the first echelon. All six divisions of these two corps were deployed in the first echelon, having a regiment apiece in the second echelon. The division's sectors were the same, with each of them an average of three kilometers in width. The 27th Rifle Corps was in the army's second echelon. Its 287th Rifle Division was located along the boundary with the 3rd Guards Army, while the remaining divisions were on the left flank (including the 112th Division, attached to the 4th Tank Army for the duration of the operation).

The 4th Tank Army was located behind the first-echelon divisions in the 13th Army's attack sector. By the start of the operation the army had 38,405 men, 283 combat-ready tanks and 131 self-propelled guns (in all, 414 vehicles, which comprised 55 percent of its authorized strength).

While operating with two corps, the army was to attack in a single-echelon formation.

The army was desperately short of motorized infantry, the losses of which had not been made good after the January offensive. Upon the request of the army commander, the 27th Rifle Corps' (13th Army) 112th Rifle Division was subordinated to him.

By the start of the operation the 52nd Army occupied a 105-kilometer front.

The army was to make its main attack along the right flank along the Luben—Gross Kreidel sector. The army commander, in order to create the densest group of forces along the axis of the main attack, left the 73rd Rifle Corps along the army's left flank along a 65-kilometer sector from the bridgehead in the Malcz area to the boundary line with the 5th Guards Army. By decision of the *front* commander, a 20-kilometer sector of front along the bridgehead in the Malcz area was occupied by the forces of the 6th Army.

Thus the 52nd Army's main forces (48th and 78th rifle corps), along with army reinforcements, were concentrated along a comparatively narrow 20-kilometer stretch of front. The army's shock group was in a single echelon.

All of the 48th Rifle Corps' divisions were in the first echelon. The corps' divisions and regiments had a two-echelon combat formation; the 78th Rifle Corps had two divisions in the first echelon and one in the second. The first echelon's divisions and regiments also organized their combat formations in two echelons.

The greatest density of forces was in the right-flank 48th Rifle Corps' attack sector. Here the divisions occupied a 3-3.5 kilometer front. In the 78th Rifle Corps' sector each first-echelon division had a frontage of about five kilometers.

The 52nd Army's 73rd Rifle Corps, along with the units of the 77th Fortified Area subordinated to it, but without reinforcements, was to assist the 6th Army in capturing Breslau during the first stage of the operation. It was subsequently planned to pull the corps into the army reserve and employ it along the axis of the 52nd Army's main attack.

The significant remove of the 73rd Rifle Corps from the army's main forces undoubtedly made the army's command and control more difficult. However, it was thought that the elimination of the enemy in the Breslau area would be completed in the first days of the operation and that the 73rd Rifle Corps would be freed for operations in the sector of the army's main forces.

The 3rd Guards Tank Army, which was to attack in the sector of the 52nd Army's shock group, by 8 February, had 48,027 men (85.4 percent of authorized strength), 379 combat-ready tanks (56 percent of authorized strength) and 188 self-propelled guns (71.2 percent of authorized strength). In all, there were 567 combat-ready tanks and self-propelled guns (60.2 percent of authorized strength).

The army had a two-echelon operational formation. The 6th and 7th guards tank corps were to attack in the first echelon and the 9th Mechanized Corps in the second.

The 6th Army was to attack along the left flank of the *front's* shock group from the bridgehead in the Malcz area. The army was to launch an attack in the rear of the Breslau group of German-Fascist forces.

During the operation the 7th Guards Mechanized Corps was operationally subordinated to the army. During the operation the army was to be reinforced with the 37th Anti-Tank Artillery Brigade and the 31st Breakthrough Artillery Division from the 10th Breakthrough Artillery Corps.

By 8 February the army's attack sector was 20 kilometers. The army had a single-echelon operational formation. The 7th Guards Mechanized Corps was to serve as the army's mobile group.

The army was to launch its main attack along the right flank. In accordance with this, its main forces were concentrated along a narrow 5-kilometer sector of the front, from Alt Lest to Koitze.

The right-flank 22nd Rifle Corps was to break through the enemy's defense along a 1.5-kilometer sector, having a two-echelon combat formation; one division in the first echelon and one in the second. The first-echelon division was also in two echelons, with a rifle regiment in the second echelon. The army's right flank on the 3-kilometer sector from the Oder to Alt Lest was to be covered by individual elements of the 22nd Rifle Corps.

The 74th Rifle Corps, which occupied the remaining sector of the army's front, was also organized into two echelons. Along the axis of the corps' main attack, along a 1.5-kilometer sector, which was adjacent to the 22nd Rifle Corps' breakthrough sector, was the 359th Rifle Division, which was organized into two echelons. The 181st Rifle Division occupied the corps' remaining front of about 14 kilometers. Two of the division's regiments were concentrated along its right flank and occupied a front of two kilometers, while the third regiment occupied the remaining 12 kilometers. The 273rd Rifle Division, which was located in the corps' second echelon, had been temporarily subordinated to the army commander and comprised his reserve. The army commander planned on committing it into the battle along the axis of the main attack.

Thus along a 5-kilometer breakthrough sector there were concentrated 24 battalions out of 27 located in the first line, and if counting the second-echelon division—42 battalions out of 45.

By the start of the operation the 7th Guards Mechanized Corps had 178 tanks and 63 self-propelled guns. According to the operational plan, it was planned to employ the corps for developing the success along the axis of the 6th Army's main attack, followed by a turn to the east in order to attack the enemy's Breslau group of forces in the rear. Before the start of the operation the corps was located on the eastern bank of the Oder in the areas of Gross Kreidel and Klein Kreidel and was moved to the bridgehead on 8 February during the artillery preparation.

Such, in general, was the operational formation of the armies brought in for the offensive along the axis of the *front's* main attack. Below is Table V/1.E.1, which shows the tactical density of men and materiel in the armies of the *front's* main group of forces.

Table V/1.E.1 The Tactical Density of Men and Materiel Along the Axis of the *Front's* Main Attack by the Start of the Operation

Armies	Breakthrough Front (in km)	Men		Battalions	
		Total	Per Kilometer	Total	Per Kilometer
3rd Guards	8	27,754	3,469	45	5.6
13th	18	45,080	2,504	54	3
52nd	20	36,530	1,826	54	2.7
6th	20	34,678	1,734	45	2.25
TOTAL	66	144,042	2,182	198	3

Armies	Breakthrough Front (in km)	Light Machine Guns		Heavy Machine Guns	
		Total	Per Kilometer	Total	Per Kilometer
3rd Guards	8	816	102	273	34
13th	18	1,074	60	340	19
52nd	20	1,400	70	475	24
6th	20	1,178	59	402	20
TOTAL	66	4,468	68	1,490	23

Armies	Breakthrough Front (in km)	Guns (76mm and larger)		Mortars (82mm and larger)		Tanks and Self-Propelled Guns*	
		Total	Per Kilometer	Total	Per Kilometer	Total	Per Kilometer
3rd Guards	8	558	70	678	85	178	22
13th	18	1,090	65.6	705	39.2	525	29
52nd	20	701	35	506	25.2	604	30
6th	20	347	17.5	381	19	241	12
TOTAL	66	2,696	41	2,270	34	1,548	23.5

* Counting the tank armies' tanks and self-propelled guns and those of the independent tank and mechanized corps.

From the data reviewed above on the operational organization and tactical density of the forces brought in for the offensive along the axis of the *front's* main attack, one can come to the following conclusion.

The operational formation of the *front's* shock group guaranteed quite a high tactical density of forces, which was to create the prerequisites for the successful and quick breakthrough of the enemy's tactical defense zone. To be sure, the broad attack front and the launching of attacks along several axes prevented the *front* command from creating a high density of artillery and mortars. As Table V/1.E.1 indicates, this density amounted to an average of 75 guns and mortars per kilometer of front.

The saturation of troops with direct infantry support tanks also proved to be insufficient. However, given the low density of the enemy's combat formation and the limited saturation of his defense with artillery and tanks, the *front's* available forces guaranteed the successful realization of the breakthrough of the enemy's defense, which had been hurriedly occupied by him opposite our bridgeheads.

Absent were second echelons in the *front's* and armies' operational formation (with the exception of the 13th Army), which given the complex situation failed to guarantee the augmentation of the first echelon's efforts in developing the offensive in the operational depth.

The *front* command planned to make up for this deficiency during the operation by employing those forces which should be freed up following the defeat of the enemy's Breslau group of forces. But the second echelons could only form in the most favorable scenario of the operation's development. If this did not happen, then the reinforcing of the main group of forces with reserves was either altogether excluded, or would have to be carried out by weakening the *front's* center and left-wing armies.

The Disposition of the First Ukrainian Front's Forces in the Area South of Breslau

The 5th Guards and 21st armies, together with the operationally-subordinated 4th Guards and 31st tank corps, comprised the *front's* second shock group. By the start of the *front* operation these armies' forces, which were deployed in a single echelon, were engaged in heavy offensive battles along the approaches to Breslau and along the bridgehead west of Brieg. The 21st Army's left-flank formations occupied defensive positions along the sector from Oppeln to Krappitz.

The 5th Guards Army was to attack along a 38-kilometer front. Its forces were distributed comparatively equally. Each rifle division occupied an average of 4.2 kilometers of front.

The 21st Army operated along a 114-kilometer front. Its main forces were concentrated along the right flank, along a 44-kilometer sector, where the main attack would be launched. In accordance with this, given an average density of 13 kilometers per division along the army's entire front, the density along the axis of the main attack would rise to seven kilometers, while in the attack sector of the left-flank corps, which was deployed along a 70-kilometer sector, this decreased to 23 kilometers per division.

If one does not count the forces of the 21st Army's left-flank division and the sector it was defending to the south of Oppeln, then it works out that from Breslau to Oppeln, along a 102-kilometer front, the 5th Guards and 21st armies had 17 divisions, for an average frontage of six kilometers.

This density, given the sharply increased level of enemy resistance and the absence in the armies of second echelons and reserves, was obviously insufficient for developing the offensive to a great depth and at those speeds called for in the *front* directive.

Despite the fact that all the 5th Guards and 21st armies' forces were deployed in a single echelon, the troops' tactical density and their saturation with combat equipment also proved to be low, due to the broad attack front, particularly in the 21st Army. Suffice it to say that there were 2.1 battalions, 38 guns and mortars (76mm and higher) and 6.2 tanks and self-propelled guns for each kilometer of front in the 5th Army, counting the 4th Guards Tank Corps' artillery and guns. Along the axis of the 21st Army's main attack there were 1.2 battalions, 16.2 guns and mortars (76mm and higher) and 6.4 tanks and self-propelled guns, counting the 31st Tank Corps' artillery and guns.

All of this told negatively on the 5th Guards and 21st armies' fulfillment of the tasks assigned to them by the *front* directive.

The Disposition of Forces Along the First Ukrainian Front's Left Wing

By the start of the offensive by the *front's* right-wing armies the 59th and 60th armies and the 1st Guards Cavalry Corps had gone over to the defensive along the entire front from Krappitz to Goczalkowice.

The 59th Army, with two corps in its first echelon, occupied a 40-kilometer front from Krappitz to Unter Walden. The 92nd Rifle Division comprised the army's second echelon. According to the *front* commander's instructions, the division was to prepare a rear defensive zone along the sector Bergewalde—Sziglowice. The corps' combat formation was single-echelon. Each first-echelon division had an average frontage of seven kilometers.

The 60th Army occupied a 76-kilometer front from Schoenblick to Goczalkowice. The 1st Guards Cavalry Corps was operationally subordinated to the army. Besides this, it had been reinforced with the 152nd Independent Tank Brigade.

All of the army's rifle corps were defending in the first echelon. The second echelon consisted of the 1st Guards Cavalry Corps, which had been moved to the Bergewalde area, and the 152nd Independent Tank Brigade, which had been concentrated in the Leszczyny area.

The 15th and 106th rifle corps had a single-echelon combat formation. The 28th Rifle Corps had a two-echelon combat formation, with the 322nd Rifle Division in the second echelon. As a result of this formation, each first-echelon division had an average frontage of 9.5 kilometers.

In all, along the *front's* left wing 17 rifle (counting the 21st Army's left-flank division) and three cavalry divisions and a single tank brigade had been gathered to defend a 166-kilometer sector from Oppeln to Golczakowice. Of these, 15 rifle divisions were located in the first echelon, with an average frontage of 11 kilometers.

This, in general, was the distribution of the First Ukrainian Front's ground forces by axes.

By the start of the operation the following formations made up the 2nd Air Army: 2nd, 5th and 6th Guards fighter corps, 1st Guards, 2nd Guards and 3rd assault air corps, and the 2nd Guards and 4th bomber corps (the corps' combat strength is shown in Table V/1.E.2).

Besides these formations, the army included the 208th Night Bomber and 11th Guards Fighter divisions, and individual flying, reserve and training units.

By taking into account the independent formations and units, the 2nd Air Army on 1 February had 2,815 aircraft. Besides this, there were another 247 aircraft in those Air Force units directly attached to the combined-arms and tank armies and to *front* headquarters. Thus, in all, the *front's* air assets numbered 3,062 aircraft.

In accordance with *front* directive No. 0051/op of 31 January 1945, the 2nd Air Army's main efforts were to be directed at supporting the operations of the *front's* right-wing armies. The 1st and 2nd guards assault air corps, the 2nd and 6th guards fighter corps, and the 4th Bomber Corps—a total of 1,563 aircraft—were dispatched here. The armies attacking along the First Ukrainian Front's center from 8 February would be supported by the 3rd Assault Air and 5th Fighter corps, which included 592 aircraft.

The 2nd Guards Bomber Corps, which numbered 227 aircraft, remained in the *front* commander's reserve.

Such a distribution of the 2nd Air Army's air formations among the *front's* armies corresponded completely to the idea of the forthcoming operation. The concentration of the air army's main efforts in the operational sector of the *front's* main group of forces enabled us to securely cover the forces that formed that group and to support them during the operation.

The enemy's air assets in the First Ukrainian Front's offensive sector during this period were considerably inferior to the 2nd Air Army's forces. Besides this, the absence of the necessary fuel supplies limited their activities. Thus the 2nd Air Army had every opportunity to win and maintain air superiority for a prolonged period of time. However, as subsequent events showed, the poor meteorological conditions sharply limited the air activities of both sides and the capabilities that the 2nd Air Army disposed of were not fully employed.

Table V/1.E.2 The Combat Strength of the 2nd Air Army's Air Corps (as of 1.2 1945)

	Number of Aircraft with Corps Designation			
Aircraft Types	2nd Fighter Corps	5th Fighter Corps	6th Gds Fighter Corps	1st Gds Assault Air Corps
Fighters	300	212	360	–
Assault Air	–	–	–	403
Bombers	–	–	–	–
TOTAL	300	212	360	403

Aircraft Types	2nd Gds Assault Air Corps	3rd Assault Air Corps	2nd Gds Bomber Corps	4th Bomber Corps	Total
Fighters	–	–	–	–	872
Assault Air	264	380	–	–	1,047
Bombers	–	–	227	236	463
TOTAL	264	380	227	236	2,382

The Correlation of Forces by the Start of the Operation

During the short period of time in which the Lower Silesian operation offensive operation was being prepared, the First Ukrainian Front command successfully completed a major regrouping of forces to the right wing and in this way created a favorable correlation of forces for on along the axis of the main attack. The overall correlation of forces in the First Ukrainian Front's attack sector by the start of the operation and the correlation of forces along individual axes is show in Table V/1.E.3.

Table V/1.E.3 The Correlation of Forces in the First Ukrainian Front's Attack Sector (as of 8 February 1945)

Axes	Forces	Strength and Armament			
		Battalions*	Machine Guns	Guns and Mortars (76mm and higher)	Tanks and Self-Propelled Guns
First Ukrainian Front's entire sector	Soviet	597	14,516	9,328	2,274
	German	352	9,169	3,312	672
	Correlation	1.7:1	1.6:1	2.8:1	3.4:1
First Ukrainian Front's right wing	Soviet	260	6,665	5,066	1,548
	German	115	2,864	766	247
	Correlation	2.3:1	2.4:1	6.6:1	5.7:1
First Ukrainian Front's center	Soviet	167	4,030	1,966	521
	German	91	2,691	593	130
	Correlation	1.8:1	1.5:1	3.3:1	4:1
First Ukrainian Front's left wing	Soviet	171	3,920	2,296	205
	German	146	3,614	1,953	295
	Correlation	1.2:1	1.1:1	1.2:1	0.7:1

* The numerical strength of the Soviet rifle and German infantry battalions by the start of the operation was approximately the same and varied from 300-500 men.

From Table V/1.E.3 it is clear that the most favorable correlation of forces had been created along the axis of the main attack. Outnumbering the enemy by more than two to one in infantry, 6.6 times in artillery, and 5.7 times in tanks and self-propelled guns, the *front's* right-wing forces would have every opportunity of carrying out the rapid breakthrough of the enemy's defense.

Along the axis of the second attack—the *front's* center—the 5th Guards and 21st armies also enjoyed a numerical superiority over the enemy. However, as early as the fighting for the expansion of the bridgeheads, all of these armies' forces had been committed into the battle. By the start of the offensive by the *front's* main group of forces they had expended their reserves and were engaged in fierce and hardly successful fighting with a stubbornly defending enemy. In these conditions, while the enemy continued to bring up additional forces to the area south of Breslau, and all the attacking armies were already in action, the possibility that they could carry out the tasks called for in the operational plan, was almost excluded.

In this situation, the group of forces along the *front's* left wing was weak. However, by virtue of its active operations, it was capable of tying down the enemy forces here and, should they launch a counterblow, to repel it.

F. THE PREPARATION OF THE FRONT'S REAR FOR THE OPERATION AND THE TROOPS' MATERIEL-TECHNICAL SUPPLY

The organization of the rear organs' work and the materiel-technical provisioning of the troops comprised one of the most difficult facets of preparing for the forthcoming operation.

Due to the great damage to the railroads west of the Vistula as far as the line Kielce—Krakow and the slow pace of their restoration, by the end of January the First Ukrainian Front continued to be based on the railroad sector Przeworsk—Sandomierz—Debica, which was located on the eastern bank of the Vistula.

Thus during the period of fighting along the Oder ammunition and fuel were delivered to the troops from areas at a 350-400 kilometer remove from the front line.

If one takes into account that during the fighting for the bridgeheads on the Oder the enemy's resistance increased sharply, as a result of which the expenditure of munitions increased significantly, then the entire seriousness of the problem of accumulating supplies for the forthcoming operation becomes understandable.

The provisioning of the *front's* forces with munitions, as of 31 January, is shown in Table V/1.F.1.

The data presented in Table V/1.F.1 indicate that given an overall comparatively favorable supply situation at the *front*, the ammunition situation among the troops was difficult. But these figures do not fully reveal the true situation in provisioning the *front's* forces with ammunition.

The fact of the matter is that at the beginning of January; that is, by the start of the *front's* offensive from the Sandomierz bridgehead, between 1.5 and 2.5 combat loads of shells and mortar rounds were actually with the troops or stored on the ground. The expenditure of shells on the artillery preparation and the support for the attack proved to be less than planned. The *front's* forces quickly crushed the enemy's resistance in the enemy's main defensive zone and went over to an unrelenting pursuit. The *front's* combined-arms formations, having taken with them no more than 0.4-0.5 combat load, left stored on the ground a large amount of unused ammunition. For example, the 21st Army's rifle divisions left 154 motor vehicles with ammunition in their jumping-off position.

The army depots ended up in the same situation. By 1 February up to 9,700 tons of ammunition were located in the area of the former Sandomierz bridgehead in army artillery depots on the ground, which the armies could not deliver because of a shortage of auto transport. See V/1.F.2.

Table V/1.F.1 The Provisioning of the First Ukrainian Front's Forces with Ammunition and their Echelonment (as of 31.1.1945)

Types of Ammunition	With the Troops	At Army Depots	At *Front* Depots	Total
		In Combat Loads		
Small-Arms Ammunition	1.09	0.43	0.16	1.68
Mortar Ammunition	0.92	1.13	1.52	3.57
Artillery Ammunition (45mm, 76-mm regimental, 76mm divisional, 122mm)	0.86	0.76	0.48	2.10
Artillery Ammunition (152mm howitzer, 152mm 1937 howitzer-cannon)	1.45	0.96	3.45	5.86

Table V/1.F.2 The Availability of Ammunition Stored on the Ground in the Area of the Former Sandomierz Bridgehead (as of 1.2.1945)

Armies and Corps	3rd Gds Army	5th Gds Army	21st Army	52nd Army	59th Army	13th Army	4th Tank Army	31st Tank Corps
Ammunition (in tons)	2,310	1,620	580	1,190	390	2,000	950	660

Besides this, up to 5,000 tons of ammunition were located on the ground at *front* depot No. 3420, which was also located in the area of the former Sandomierz bridgehead.

Thus the actual provisioning of the troops with ammunition at the end of January was significantly lower than was shown in Table V/1.F.1.

The greatly extended delivery routes and the significant remove of the *front* and army depots from the troops led to a situation in which the *front* and army auto transport could not cope with the timely delivery of ammunition to the troops. Division depots were often empty. Division and regimental transport would stand idle for hours, and sometimes for days in expectation of deliveries from the army. This was namely at the time when the fighting on the bridgeheads was most fierce and the demand for ammunition was particularly acute.

All of this demanded that the *front* command adopt the most decisive measures, in order to maximally move the *front* and army depots closer to the troops and to ensure the rapid accumulation of materiel supply with the troops, which were necessary for conducting the forthcoming operation.

This problem could be resolved only upon the restoration of the railroads running from the rear to the front over Polish territory. The railroad in the center of the *front's* attack sector, which ran through Sandomierz, Kielce, Czestochowa, Lubliniec, and Kreitzburg, could be put into operation the most quickly. This rail line had been destroyed less than others along a significant length and could be restored comparatively easily. An exception was the Sandomierz—Kielce section, which actually required complete reconstruction.

The *front's* road reconstruction units, first of all, were brought in to restore this railroad.

During the second half of January the rail sector to the west of Kielce was restored. Simultaneously, the rail sector connecting Kielce and Jedrzejow was restored. Because of this, Jedrzejow station and Miasowa station (ten kilometers north of Jedrzejow) had been temporarily transformed into the *front's* staging base. *Front* auto transport was detailed for moving army freights from the bridgehead to Jedrzejow station. 250-300 3-ton motor vehicles worked daily along this sector. In Jedrzejow the *front* and army supplies of ammunition, which were brought up from the ground locations and main bases behind the Vistula, were transferred from auto transport to rail cars and moved to Rawicz, Els, Bernstadt, Namslau, Rosenberg, Lubliniec, and Gross Strelitz stations, from where they were delivered to the troops by army auto transport.

For the purpose of accumulating ammunition in the areas located closer to the troops, one of the *front* artillery depots was moved up to the Czestochowa area. Ammunition was delivered there from *front* depot No. 3420, which was located on the ground west of Osiek (in the area of the former Sandomierz bridgehead), through the staging base at Miasowa station.

During 1-3 February 40-50 train cars with ammunition departed daily by rail from Jedrzejow station, and during 4-7 February an average of 100 cars.

This route's coming on line did not exclude the necessity of forcing the restoration of the most heavily damaged section of the Sandomierz—Kielce railroad. The restoration of this section would make it possible to deliver freight by rail directly from the center's staging bases, which were located behind the Vistula, to the troops fighting on the Oder.

For the most rapid restoration of the Sandomierz—Kielce rail sector, aside from the *front* road restoration units, Polish railway workers, the local population and prisoners of war were brought in to the work. Work was carried out around the clock.

In the final days of January the restoration work was successfully completed and the Sandomierz—Kielce railroad sector, and along with it the entire indicated route from the Vistula to the Oder, began to operate.

From 28 January the center's staging base along the Rozwadow—Sandomierz sector began to work. Freight traveling from the center to the troops along broad-gauge track was transferred here to trains operating on the European gauge and dispatched along the route Sandomierz—Kielce—Czestochowa—Kreitzburg—Els—Krotoszyn—Rawicz. The restoration of rail communications along the sector from Sandomierz through Lubliniec as far as Krotoszyn enabled us to move the supply stations closer to the troops. From 2 February supply stations were opened for the majority of the armies along the Krotoszyn—Gross Strelitz lateral railroad. See Table V/1.F.3.

Table V/1.F.3 New Supply Stations and their Distance from the Troops (as of 2.2.1945)

Armies	Supply Station	Distance of the Supply Station from the Front Line (in km)
3rd Gds Army, 25th Tank Corps	Krotoszyn	80
13th Army	Frauenwaldau	85
4th Tank Army	Rawicz	40
52nd, 3rd Guards Tank armies, 10th Breakthrough Artillery Corps	Els	80
6th Army	Els (the northern part of the station, jointly with the 52nd Army)	60
5th Guards Army	Namslau	40
21st Army, 1st Guards Cavalry Corps, 31st Tank Corps	Wossowska	40
59th Army	Lubliniec	60
60th Army	Gross Strelitz	55

It was proposed that the army rear chiefs and the deputy corps commanders for the rear immediately deploy branches of the artillery depots, depots of fuels and lubricants and food at the above-listed stations.

The restored railroad's capacity in its first days of work was limited, due to the poor outfitting of the railroad and station equipment. Thus the railroad could not completely ensure the rapid accumulation of supplies for the forthcoming operation, before the start of which remained 2-3 days.

Because of this, all the transport that the *front* could get its hands on was thrown into the task of delivering ammunition in the final days before the start of the operation.

On 4 February the *front* commander pointed out to the army commanders that the delivery of ammunition in the armies for the operation had been allowed to slide. He ordered the creation in each army auto columns of 500 vehicles each, by using the assets of the divisions and rear establishments, under the command of efficient line officers, and to dispatch them to deliver ammunition from the army depots, deployed at the new supply stations. In case of a shortage of ammunition at the army artillery depots, they were ordered to direct the vehicles to the *front* artillery depot at Mielec. It was stressed in the order that the shells should be delivered, under any conditions, to the divisions by the close of 5 February.

The mobilization of troop transport, as well as the employment of the local population's horse-drawn transport, for delivering freight from the army and even the *front* depots to the troops lessened somewhat the acute ammunition situation and enabled us not only to meet the troops' daily needs (although in truncated form), but also to increase the ammunition reserve for the forthcoming operation.

An additional measure, which was supposed to ensure the accumulation of *front* ammunition stocks in those areas close to the troops, was the creation of a *front* artillery depot on the ground in the Wolau area. Ammunition was delivered to the depot by auto transport from the *front* depots located beyond the Vistula in the areas of Grembow, Mielec and Osiek. In order to resolve this task, 1,000 3-ton motor vehicles were brought in, which were to carry out three trips from the Vistula to the Oder and deliver to the depot in Wolau the most necessary shells for divisional and army artillery.

The allotted transport carried out two trips in the beginning of February. A third trip was cancelled, because by that time the work of the railroad had improved. Moreover, the shortage of fuel limited the employment of auto transport for long hauls.

The ammunition that arrived at the depot in Wolau was used for supporting the troops operating along the axis of the *front's* main attack; that is, the 3rd Guards, 13th, 52nd, and 6th armies and units subordinated to the *front*, which were suffering from a shortage of ammunition at this time.

Simultaneous with the resolution of the main task—the provisioning of the troops with ammunition—the *front* and army rear organs were dealing with the remaining problems of the troops' materiel provisioning. The mobilization of *front*, army and troop transport for delivering freight of all types helped us to blunt our desperate need for fuels and lubricants, engineering equipment, and spare parts for the repair of artillery equipment, tanks and auto-tractor equipment.

It should be emphasized that at a critical moment the troops widely employed, aside from centralized deliveries, local resources, captured materials, and fuel surrogates such as a mixture of gasoline, kerosene and alcohol. Equipment repair was carried out at the enemy's captured repair bases and at industrial enterprises located on captured territory. Captured auto transport was widely used.

As concerns food and forage, the troops went over almost completely to supplying themselves from captured stocks. This significantly eased the work of our transport for supplying the troops with combat supplies.

Simultaneous with the moving up of the *front* and army artillery depots closer to the troops, the medical and veterinary establishments were also brought up, which to a significant degree improved the conditions for the admission, treatment and evacuation of the sick and wounded.

By the start of the operation the *front* had managed to restore the Sandomierz—Czestochowa—Kreitzburg rail line along its entire length, as well as the lateral line along the front from Krotoszyn to Gross Strelitz. This considerably changed the conditions for basing the troops, because it enabled us to move the supply stations closer to the troops and to sharply reduce the delivery of supplies by auto transport. As a result, a significant amount of fuel was saved, which under the developing conditions had great significance.

Aside from this, the startup of the railroad created greater capabilities for restoring our supplies at the advance *front* and army depots during the operation.

However, despite all of these successes, the *front* command was not able to fully resolve the problem of materially provisioning the troops and, in particular, the task of accumulating the necessary amount of ammunition for the forthcoming operation.

The provisioning of the *front's* forces with ammunition and its echeloning as of 8 February is shown in Table V/1.F.4.

In comparing the provisioning indices for the troops on 31 January and 8 February, we see that by the start of the operation the *front's* supplies, both among the troops and in the army and *front* depots had hardly changed at all. Moreover, they had decreased, according to several indices. This testifies to the fact that all of the *front* and army command's measures, as well as the intensive work by the *front* and troop transport, enabled us only to restore the supplies expended during the fighting for the bridgeheads, but did not lead to the creation of supplies that would fully support the launching of a major offensive beyond the Oder.

Of course, if one takes into account the partial movement of supplies to the troops and the increased capabilities for delivering freight by rail transport, one may then maintain that the conditions for supplying the troops with materiel supplies, including ammunition, had undoubtedly improved. But this still does not mean that the problem of supplying the troops with the necessities had been resolved.

Not only ammunition was required for conducting an operation, although under the developing circumstances that was the most important, but fuel, engineering and military-technical equipment, forage, food, and much other besides. Under conditions when the main depots of the *front* and armies continued to remain behind the Vistula, the job of continually supplying the troops over an extended period was an extraordinarily difficult one. The recently restored railroad, with a low carrying capacity, could not, of course, full meet the requirements of the *front's* forces.

Table V/1.F.4 The Provisioning of the First Ukrainian Front's Forces with Ammunition and its Echeloning (as of 8.2.1945)

Types of Ammunition	With the Troops	At Army Depots	At Front Depots	Total
		In Combat Loads		
Small-Arms Ammunition	1.05	0.29	0.10	1.44
Mortar Ammunition	1.10	1.0	1.35	3.45
Artillery Ammunition (45mm, 76mm regimental, 76mm divisional, 122mm)	0.78	0.50	0.50	1.78
Artillery Ammunition (152mm howitzer, 152mm 1937 howitzer-cannon)	1.20	2.30	3.25	6.75

At best, the restoration of the Debica—Krakow—Katowice second rail line, which had begun in January, could only be completed by the end of the planned operation.

By taking into account the situation at hand, the *front* command and staff maintained unrelenting control over the rear area's work throughout the entire operation, strictly regulating the distribution of materiel and supplying, first of all, those axes where the operation's main goals were being resolved. All of these measures brought positive results. There were no serious snags in supplying the troops with ammunition and fuel during the operation. Nonetheless, the shortage of ammunition and fuel made itself known at every step and to a certain degree was reflected in the operation's final results.

G. POLITICAL SUPPORT FOR THE OPERATION

The Soviet forces' offensive in 1945 unfolded in conditions of the Soviet people's enormous political and labor uplift, which responded to the Soviet army's historic victories at the front with inspired labor feats in the rear. The heroic toilers in the Soviet rear, while relying on the highly developed military economy, guaranteed the front everything necessary for the victorious conclusion of the war.

The moral-political unity of the Soviet people and its rallying around the victorious Communist Party and the Soviet government, its heroic labor and all-round support for the front was a source of strength for the Soviet army and its high combat capability. The Soviet people and its army were united in their desire to carry out their great liberating goals. This unity was supported by the enormous political work by the Communist Party among the people and the army.

The foundation of the party-political work in the Soviet army was the guiding instructions of the Communist Party on the popular and just character of the Soviet people's war of liberation against the German-Fascist aggressors. As comrade I.V. Stalin noted in addressing the Soviet people, "The whole world looks upon you as a force capable of destroying the marauding hordes of the German aggressors. The enslaved peoples of Europe, who have fallen under the yoke of the German aggressors, look upon you as their liberators. A great liberating mission has fallen to your lot. Be worthy of this mission! The war that you are waging is a war of liberation, a just war."[17]

---

17 I. Stalin, *O Velikoi Otechestvennoi Voine Sovetskogo Soyuza*, 5th ed., pp. 39-40.

The Communist Party's guiding instructions served as a program for conducting party-political work among the troops. They lay at the basis of the political organs' and party organizations' activity throughout the entire period of preparing for and conducting the operation.

Insofar as the preparatory period for the new operation was, for the majority of the *front's* formations, filled with intensive fighting for the bridgeheads or in regrouping to new concentration areas, all of the party-political measures for readying the troops for the new operation were carried out during heavy fighting and troop movements.

The broad scope and effectiveness in propagandizing the Communist Party's instructions among the troops were supported by a great deal of party-organizational work, carried out by the political organs during this period.

A major organizational measure, which was carried out immediately upon the completion of the January operation, was the generalizing of the experience of party-political work in the preceding battles on German territory and the drawing up of concrete measures for the political support of the forthcoming operation.

As the experience of the January offensive showed, the conditions and content of party-political work among the troops, in connection with the transfer of combat operations onto German territory, had sharply changed. In the preceding operation, particularly in its first half, questions of defeating the enemy forces covering the approaches to the eastern boundaries of Germany, the liberation of the Polish people from the German-Fascist aggressors and the establishment of friendly relations with the fraternal Polish people, were at the center of attention. With the arrival of our forces on the territory of Hitlerite Germany, the task of supporting the concluding attacks against the enemy and the defeat of his armed forces in Germany itself—the lair of the fascist beast—arose. The necessity arose of taking into account the experience of the first days of combat on enemy territory and to make it the property of all the *front's* forces.

In connection with this, meetings and gatherings were conducted in all units, formations and headquarters, dedicated to exchanging experience and totaling up the results of the political support for the January offensive.

On the basis of these generalized materials, the *front's* military council and political directorate issued special directives that defined the concrete tasks for the commanders and political workers at all levels in the area of politically supporting the operation.

In the final days of January a conference of for the workers of the armies' political sections was conducted on questions of politically supporting the operation, after which they were dispatched to the troops for the conduct of organizational and agitation and propaganda work.

During this same period instructional exercises were conducted by battalion in all the *front's* armies, with agitators and propagandists from the lower subunits.

In this way the *front's* entire party-political apparatus was quickly armed with a concrete action program, ready for conducting broad explanatory work among the troops and mobilizing the soldiers to carry out new combat tasks.

Another important task was successfully resolved—the task of organizationally strengthening the company, battery and equivalent party organizations and the distribution of cadres of agitators and propagandists among the subunits.

Due to the significant personnel losses in the preceding operation, in some subunits not a single communist remained. Communists always were in the forefront of carrying out the most responsible and dangerous combat assignments, which is why the percentage of losses among them was greater than the average percentage of overall losses. The rapid and correct distribution of the party's forces among the subunits was eased by the fact that the *front's* political organs in the units and formations had already prepared a reserve of agitators, propagandists and party organizers.

Party-political work among the troops was conducted simultaneously with all service personnel and varied greatly.

Workers of the *front* and army political sections conducted exercises with unit commanders and their political deputies, put together officer gatherings, conducted party and Komsomol meetings, and organized soldiers' gatherings and meetings.

The theme for the conversations, lectures and reports varied. The chief themes in the exercises were "The USSR's International Situation," "On the Labor Victories of the USSR's Toilers," "Successes of the Soviet Armed Forces," "Tasks of the First Ukrainian Front's Forces in Defeating the German-Fascist Forces," "On Military Discipline," "The Behavior of the Soviet Soldier on Enemy Territory," "On the Military Oath," "On Revenge," "On Maintaining Socialist Property," and "On Vigilance," etc.

Platoon agitators and readers carried out a great deal of political-instruction work in the elements. Their main forms of work were individual and group discussions with the troops, the reading of specially selected materials or individual articles and notes from the central, army and division papers, the regular familiarization of the rank and file with reports from the Soviet Information Bureau. Particular attention in carrying out political work in the subunits was paid to bringing home to the consciousness of each soldier the forthcoming combat tasks and the mobilization of people for fulfilling them.

The chief combat task, around which revolved party-political work at the end of January and the beginning of February, was the struggle for the seizure, retention and expansion of the bridgeheads on the left bank of the Oder. This struggle, which had major operational significance, became very intense and required heroic efforts and combat mastery from the *front's* entire rank and file.

The high patriotic uplift among the troops was consolidated by widely conducted party-political work and led the *front's* forces to new and amazing victories. Despite the enemy's desperate resistance, several major bridgeheads of operational significance along the left bank of the Oder were occupied and consolidated through the heroic efforts of the *front's* forces. In the fighting for the bridgeheads the extremely high moral-political qualities of the Soviet soldiers once again manifested themselves. As always, communists and Komsomol members were in the first ranks of those fighting, mobilizing by word and deed their comrades to carry out their combat assignments.

Alongside the massive heroism of the troops, which comprises a characteristic and inalienable feature of the Soviet army, the fighting for the bridgeheads yielded a mass of examples of patriotic feats by individual soldiers and officers, who through their heroic deeds glorified for all time the army of the socialist state and the great Soviet people.

It is impossible to recount all the facts of the Soviet patriots' feats in the fighting during this period. One may only halt on a few more amazing and characteristic examples.

In the fighting along the approaches to Breslau the commander of a rifle section, Senior Sergeant Pavel Mikhailovich Zaitsev, displayed incredible heroism and self-sacrifice. His section was the first in his company to force the Oder. The entire company crossed to the left bank of the river behind it. The company's further advance was halted by enfilading fire from German machine guns, with one of them firing from a permanent structure.

The task of blocking and suppressing the permanent firing point was entrusted to Zaitsev's section. In carrying out the assignment, the section, headed by its commander, got nearer to the pillbox, under the enemy's flanking fire. The enemy's murderous fire pinned the soldiers to the ground. Senior Sergeant Zaitsev fearlessly crawled toward the pillbox and at a distance of several meters from it threw an anti-tank grenade into the embrasure. The enemy's machine gun was silent and the company rose to the attack.

However, after a few seconds the machine gun once again opened fire on the attackers. Not having at hand any weapons to silence the enemy machine gun, and seeing how his comrades were dying from its fire, Senior Sergeant Zaitsev decided to bring victory to his company over the enemy, at the cost of his own life. He threw himself on the pillbox's embrasure and covered it with his chest. As if by signal, the company rushed forward. The soldiers, avenging the death of their commander, destroyed the entire garrison of the enemy firing point.

The enemy was defeated along this sector and the captured bridgehead was significantly expanded. The enemy left behind the bodies of 38 of his men and officers near the pillbox.

This patriot of the Soviet Union, who repeated the immortal feat of Aleksandr Matrosov, was 21. He was born in the village of Vorochaevka, in the Bryansk Oblast's Vygonicheskii District.

The news about Pavel Zaitsev's feat spread like lightning through all the subunits of the regiment in which he served. Before long the details of the death of this loyal son of the Soviet people became known in all the units and formations of the First Ukrainian Front.

By order of the Presidium of the USSR Supreme Soviet, P.M. Zaitsev was posthumously awarded the title of Hero of the Soviet Union.

Pavel Zaitsev's feat brought about a new wave of patriotic enthusiasm and combat élan among the troops.

In the fighting along the approaches to Breslau, a heroic feat was carried out by machine gun operator and Komsomol member Andreitsev. The Germans, seeking to regain their lost positions, launched several counterattacks along the company's sector. Stubborn fighting broke out. Andreitsev destroyed four enemy firing points and, while severely wounded, continued to fire on the attacking Germans for two hours, helping his forces to prepare a counterblow. When the enemy's counterattack had been repulsed, our subunits rushed forward and captured the inhabited locale for which the fighting had been waged. However, the heroic Komsomol member did not see this happy moment. Andreitsev died by his machine gun, not letting this fearsome weapon out of his hands even after his death.

In the hero-patriot's Komsomol membership card there was the inscription: "Comrades! If I should be killed in this battle, let them know that I died honestly, carrying out comrade Stalin's order."

Soldier Andreitsev was posthumously awarded the title of Hero of the Soviet Union.

The deputy battalion commander for political affairs, Senior Lieutenant Spirin, accomplished a similar feat in the 13th Army. He, along with a group of brave men, was the first in his unit to force the Oder. Stubborn fighting broke out on the opposite bank. The enemy undertook several counterattacks, trying to throw the subunit back from the bank it had seized.

At the height of the fighting, the heavy machine gun crew was knocked out of action. The machine gun grew quiet and the Germans once again counterattacked. A critical situation arose. Then Senior Lieutenant Spirin took up the machine gun himself. Having helped to repulse the enemy's counterattacks and to hold the captured bridgehead, Senior Lieutenant Spirin died the death of the brave in this battle.

Similar examples of heroic behavior by Soviet soldiers and entire subunits in the fighting for the bridgeheads were not an exception, but a mass phenomenon characterizing the moral-political countenance of the Soviet soldiers.

Commanders, political workers and agitators did not let slip by a single case that could be employed to mobilize the attention and strength of the soldiers to carry out the command's assignments. The heroic and skillful actions of subunits, individual soldiers and officers were immediately popularized among the units' and subunits' entire rank and file.

Government decorations to soldiers who had particularly distinguished themselves in fighting for the Soviet Motherland were solemnly awarded in the subunits in which they served. Honoring the recipients raised the *front's* rank and file to new combat feats and solidified the soldiers even more closely around the party, the Soviet government and the beloved leader, I.V. Stalin.

Written thanks and congratulations to the hero soldiers and subunits from the unit and formation commands exerted a great mobilizing effect on the soldiers.

The political sections widely practiced the sending of letters about the heroes to their families, which also had an enormous mobilizing and instructional significance.

Each soldier knew that his feats to glorify the Motherland would become known to his comrades in arms, his relatives and acquaintances.

The commanders' and political workers' discussions with the soldiers about the shame and degradation to which the fascist swine subjected those Soviet citizens driven into Germany, had a great educational effect. Speeches at soldiers' meetings by Soviet people liberated from German-Fascist slavery, with tales of the hard-labor conditions in which they lived in Germany aroused among the Soviet soldiers anger and hatred for the enslavers and the desire to ruthlessly take revenge on the enemy for the sorrow, tears and blood of his brothers and sisters.

The soldiers expressed these sacred patriotic feelings not only in words at meetings, but through their heroic combat feats on the battlefield.

The great combat feats of the First Ukrainian Front's forces in the fighting for the bridgeheads were noted by the Supreme Commander-in-Chief in his order No. 270 of 6 February 1945.

At gatherings and meetings held in honor of this joyous event in the life of the *front*, the soldiers and officers took oaths to ruthlessly destroy the enemy in his own lair and to speed up the deadline for raising the victorious Soviet banner over Berlin.

The Komsomol organizations, guided by the party organizations, were the trend setters in these patriotic deeds. At their meetings, the Komsomol soldiers swore to their Communist Party and their Motherland to hold high the honor of the Soviet soldier and to not spare their lives in the name of victory over the enemy.

Here is an oath by the Komsomol members of the 657th Rifle Regiment's 1st Rifle Battalion, sworn to the regimental commander at a Komsomol gathering on the eve of the offensive:

> We, the Komsomol members of the 1st Rifle Battalion, in going into battle against the cursed enemy, are burning with desire to come to grips, face to face, with the enemy and fight him, while our hands hold our weapons and while our young hearts are beating. We will ruthlessly wreak vengeance on the German executioners for all the evil deeds that they committed in our country. We swear to carry out your order with honor and dignity, as befits members of the Leninist Komsomol and to multiply the regiment's combat glory.

The Komsomol members of the 749th Rifle Regiment's 1st Rifle Battalion swore the following:

> While our hands can hold our fearsome weapons, while our hearts beat in our breast and our eyes see the enemy before us, our lives belong to the Motherland. We will not spare them in the name of the complete destruction of the enemy. Not a single road will seem difficult to us, not a single obstacle will be insuperable. Let us finish off the fascist beast in his lair and raise the banner of victory over Berlin!

These and similar speeches by the Soviet soldier-patriots are testimony to their high level of moral-political consciousness and devotion to the Soviet Motherland and Communist Party.

A result of the enormous moral-political uplift among the troops and the political maturity was the thunderous growth of the *front's* party organizations. During the preparatory period for the February operation, several thousand glorious sons of the Soviet Motherland—the heroes of the forcing of the Oder—joined the ranks of the Communist Party, in order to be in its ranks, in order to even more strongly strike at the enemy and under its banners to complete the defeat of fascist Germany.

As a result of the party-educational work conducted among the troops, the *front's* political organs and party organizations solidified the rank and file even more closely around the beloved Communist Party and Soviet government. This enabled the troops and *front* command, despite the extremely difficult combat conditions, to achieve in February 1945 new major combat successes and to bring nearer the day of final victory over the enemy.

H. RESULTS OF THE OPERATION'S PREPARATION

As a result of the major regrouping of forces, which was carried out during the preparation for the operation, a shock group was created on the *front's* right flank that outnumbered the opposing enemy in men and equipment.

During the preparatory period for the operation the *front's* forces managed to significantly expand the bridgeheads they had seized on the left bank of the Oder and to firmly consolidate there. This enabled the *front* command to concentrate and deploy in a timely manner all the main shock group's forces on the left bank of the river, which played no small role in bringing about the breakthrough of the enemy's defense along the *front's* main axis of attack.

The large amount of work carried out by the *front* command in organizing the rear enabled us to restore the railroad on which the *front's* armies were based, to move the supply stations closer to the troops and thus sharply cut down the depth of the troop rear. All of this significantly improved the conditions of the troop's materiel supply.

Party-political work, which was directed at mobilizing the troops for resolving the combat tasks assigned to them, helped significantly to overcome those difficulties that arose during the preparation for the operation. It led to an increase in the combat capability of the *front's* forces and inspired them to heroic feats in the name of the Motherland.

The resolution of the above-enumerated tasks enabled the First Ukrainian Front command to begin the operation when the enemy had not yet fully completed preparing the Oder line for defense and had not completed the planned concentration already under way of men and materiel for repelling our offensive.

Thus the goal, which the *front* command had set for itself during the operation's preparatory period, was, on the whole, achieved. The necessary conditions for carrying out a subsequent offensive along the Berlin and Dresden directions had been created.

Alongside this, the short period of time set aside for the operation's preparation and the difficult conditions in which the offensive was prepared, kept us from fully resolving all the planned measures for the preparatory stage.

The problem of the troops' materiel-technical supply was not fully resolved, especially in the area of creating the necessary supplies of ammunition, which, as the course of the operation showed, was one of the material reasons for the offensive's low rate of advance.

The short preparation deadlines and our intelligence's insufficient activity prevented us from uncovering the disposition of the enemy's group of forces with sufficient accuracy, as well as his fire system in the main defensive zone. This led to major miscalculations in the organization of the artillery offensive and rendered more difficult the actions of our forces in carrying out the breakthrough of the enemy's defense along the Oder.

The underestimation of the enemy's forces and his capability for stubborn resistance along the Oder defensive line was one of the material reasons for the failure of the *front's* center and left-wing armies to carry out their assigned tasks and led to significant changes in the conditions for developing a general offensive beyond the Oder.

The transfer during the preparatory period of a large number of formations from the *front's* left wing to the right wing led, naturally, to a weakening of the left wing. Because of this, and also because of the strengthening of the enemy's group of forces along the Oppeln—Ratibor—Pszyna sector, our forces' offensive actions in the Oppeln area and to the south were unsuccessful. The *front* commander had to give up on the idea of a simultaneous offensive by all the *front's* armies and limit himself only to an offensive in the sector to the north of Oppeln during the first stage of the operation. The front's stable situation south of Oppeln led to a situation in which the 21st Army, which had begun its attack on 5 February north of Oppeln, by 8 February had committed into the fighting almost all its forces and turned its front to the south. As a result of this, the army's forces, which had been designated for attacking to the west, were sharply weakened.

The enemy, during the time when the *front* was preparing for a new operation, managed to consolidate along the Oder line, to put his forces in order, to organize command and control and, despite his significant losses in the attempts to drive us from the bridgeheads, to increase the number of forces facing the *front*, on the whole, and to create denser groups of forces facing the bridgeheads.

The switch over to the defense by the troops of the First Ukrainian Front's left wing enabled the enemy to employ that part of his forces operating south of Oppeln, in the Breslau area and to the north, which strengthened the enemy's group of forces along the axis of our main attack.

But there were other circumstances that complicated the situation in which the *front's* forces were to carry out their subsequent offensive.

The urgent task of eliminating the East Pomeranian group of German-Fascist forces, which had arisen in the beginning of February, distracted the First Belorussian Front's forces to the resolution of that task. As a result, the First Belorussian Front's forces were forced to temporarily set aside their further offensive along the Berlin direction and, consolidate along their achieved lines following their arrival on the Oder.

Thus the possibility of a simultaneous offensive by the two *fronts* along the Berlin direction, which seemed realistic at the end of January, by the beginning of February, due to the changed situation in the First Belorussian Front's offensive zone, began to fade.

The fact that the Fourth Ukrainian Front's forces were engaged in heavy fighting with a stubbornly resisting enemy along the Moravska Ostrava axis and had hardly advanced also told negatively on the First Ukrainian Front's situation. This, to a significant degree, determined the assumption of the defensive by the First Ukrainian Front's left-wing armies.

Thus the situation, in which the offensive was supposed to unfold, was sharply different from the situation at the end of January, in which the offensive was planned. It is natural that all of this would leave its imprint on the character of the troops' operations and to exert a material influence on the operation's final results.

It was obvious that in the conditions of the changed situation that the First Ukrainian Front, while conducting an offensive without the support of the neighboring *fronts*, could no longer during a single operation carry out all the tasks called for in the *front's* directive of 31 January 1945.

Proceeding from the available forces and capabilities that the *front* disposed of in the beginning of February, one could calculate that in the best case it would be able to eliminate the lagging behind of the left-wing armies and bring up its main forces abreast of the First Belorussian Front.

As concerns the final goals of the operation, which had been called for in the initial plan, the First Ukrainian Front could only achieve these as a result of a subsequent joint offensive with the forces of the First Belorussian Front, and that this must be in the form of a new operation.

2

The Conduct of the Operation

The First Ukrainian Front's Lower Silesian offensive operation may be divided into two stages, according to the character of the combat activities that unfolded.

The chief content of the first stage of the operation (8-15 February) was the breakthrough by the *front's* forces of the enemy's defense on the Oder River and the arrival of the 4th Tank Army at the Neisse River, and the right wing's combined-arms armies at the Bober and Kweis rivers. During the first stage, the troops of the *front's* main group of forces broke through the enemy's defense, which had been created facing the bridgehead north of Breslau, and, having crushed the enemy's resistance, began to pursue him. The pursuit was conducted as far as the line of the Bober and Kweis rivers, where the attacking forces, having seized bridgeheads, once again encountered the enemy's organized resistance along previously prepared positions along the left banks of these rivers.

At this time in the *front's* center, where as a result of a skillfully executed maneuver, the 6th Army's forces, in conjunction with the forces of the 5th Guards Army, encircled a major group of German-Fascist forces in the Breslau area.

The *front's* left-wing armies during this period, having failed to make territorial successes in the fighting to expand the bridgeheads on the left bank of the Oder to the south of Oppeln, halted their further offensive activities by order of the *front* commander and were consolidating on the lines reached.

The main content of the operation's second stage (16-24 February) was the breakthrough by the *front's* right-wing armies of the enemy's intermediate defensive line, which had been created along the Bober and Kweis rivers, and the arrival of the *front's* forces at the Neisse River from its mouth to Penzig. A major role in resolving this task belonged to the tank armies.

During this period the *front's* center forces continued to fight the enemy's surrounded Breslau group of forces with part of their forces, while the main forces deployed to the southwest, firmly covering the *front's* shock group from the southwest.

During the operation's second stage, the *front's* left-wing armies continued to improve their defensive lines, which were covering the Silesian industrial area from the west and south.

With the arrival of the *front's* forces at the Neisse River, the Lower Silesian operation was finished. The *front's* right-wing armies occupied a favorable line for launching subsequent attacks against the enemy along the Berlin and Dresden directions. Upon consolidating along the line reached, the *front* began to regroup its forces to the left wing for conducting a new operation to defeat the enemy's Upper Silesian group of forces.

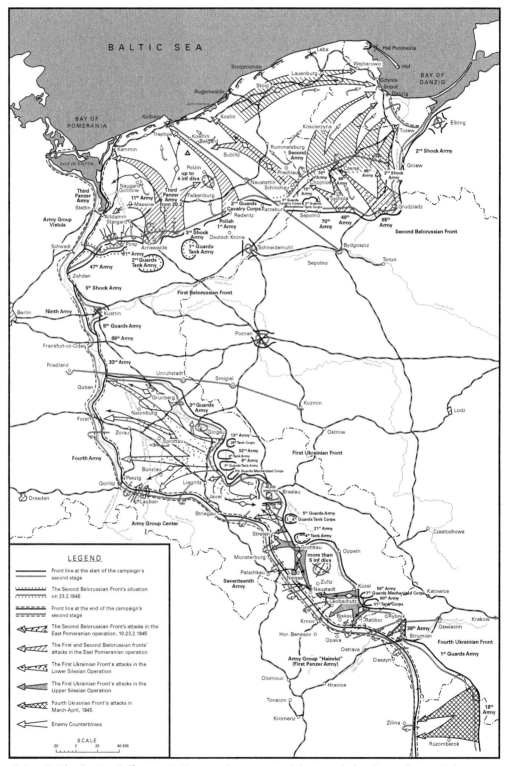

Map 7 The Soviet Offensive in Eastern Pomerania, Silesia and the Carpathians, February–March 1945.

A. THE BREAKTHROUGH OF THE ENEMY'S DEFENSE ALONG THE ODER RIVER AND THE ARRIVAL OF THE FIRST UKRAINIAN FRONT'S RIGHT-WING ARMIES AT THE BOBER AND KWEIS RIVERS. THE ENCIRCLEMENT OF BRESLAU (THE OPERATION'S FIRST STAGE: 8-15 FEBRUARY)

The Breakthrough of the Enemy's Tactical Defense Zone Along the Oder River Northwest of Breslau

The offensive by the *front's* right-wing armies began at 0930 on 8 February, following a 50-minute artillery preparation.

The attacking forces' insufficiently high artillery density, and in some cases an insufficient knowledge of the enemy's fire system, prevented us from reliably suppressing the defending enemy.

The poor flying weather hindered our aviation in taking an active part in suppressing the enemy's personnel and equipment, both during the period of the artillery preparation, and in the period of the attack and battle in depth.

Insofar as the enemy's personnel and equipment proved to have been insufficiently suppressed, the *front's* right-wing forces, which had gone over to the attack, were met with the enemy's organized infantry and artillery fire. The fighting immediately became intense. The enemy, taking advantage of terrain favorable to the defense, was very active throughout the day and repeatedly launched counterattacks. Particularly bitter fighting broke out in the areas of the inhabited locales that had been prepared by the enemy for defense. Many stone buildings, which had been configured as fortified firing points, were so sturdy that they could be destroyed only by employing 122mm shells and higher against them.

Despite all of these unfavorable circumstances, the *front's* right-wing armies achieved considerable results on the first day of the operation.

The 3rd Guards Army's shock group, which had been concentrated on the bridgehead west of Keben, attacked the enemy along the entire sector from the Oder to Klein Gafron. While crushing the enemy's resistance along his prepared defensive positions and repelling his unceasing counterattacks, the forces of the army's shock group had by the end of the day penetrated into the enemy's defense to a depth of up to seven kilometers. Thus as early as the operation's first day the main zone of the enemy's defense facing the 3rd Guards Army's bridgehead had been pierced. However, despite the success achieved, the army's offensive pace was twice as low as that planned and the day's assignment was not fulfilled.

The 13th Army's forces, supported by the 4th Tank Army's forward detachments, attacked along the army's entire front. The right-flank 102nd Rifle Corps, assisted by units of the 6th Mechanized Corps, quickly crushed the enemy in his first position and threw him out of the powerful strong point of Kreidelwitz. This immediately made the corps' subsequent progress significantly easier. By the close of the day the 102nd Rifle and 6th Mechanized corps occupied the village of Kummernick and Dornbusch, having penetrated into the enemy's defense to a depth of up to eight kilometers.

The situation developed somewhat differently in the 24th Rifle Corps' attack zone. Facing its right flank were two heavily fortified villages of Koslitz and Gulau, behind which began a large woods, stretching far to the west. All our attempts to throw the Germans out of these inhabited locales were unsuccessful. The 10th Tank Corps' forward detachment—the 61st Tank Brigade—which was committed into the fighting along this sector, also failed to achieve success. On this day only the 24th Rifle Corps' left-flank division, taking advantage of the success of the 52nd Army's 48th Rifle Corps, advanced four kilometers and reached Oberau.

As a result of the 8 February fighting, the forces of the 13th Army, which were attacking in close cooperation with the 4th Tank Army's forward detachments, broke through the enemy's main defensive zone along the right flank and from the north halfway outflanked units of the "Hermann Goring" Panzer Division, which were stubbornly defending in the woods northwest of Gulau. Besides this, the small success achieved along the 13th and 52nd armies' joint flanks, if developed subsequently, would enable us to outflank this enemy group of forces from the south.

Thus a situation had arisen that would enable us to encircle and destroy units of the "Hermann Goring" Panzer Division in the woods west of Koslitz and Gulau. In these conditions, the commander of the 4th Tank Army made the absolutely correct decision and decided against the initially planned commitment of the 10th Tank Corps into the battle along this axis, where its forward brigade was operating. He decided to bypass Luben with the 10th Tank Corps from the south and through an attack from Oberau, to reach the Oberglasersdorf area, into the rear of the German group of forces defending in the woods, in order that, in conjunction with units of the 6th Mechanized Corps and the forces of the 13th Army, to encircle and then destroy them. The correctness of this decision was confirmed by the entire subsequent course of combat operations.

Speaking of the successes achieved in the center of the *front's* main shock group, one should at the same time point out that the troops' offensive pace here was also considerably lower than what had been planned, as a result of which the tasks assigned to the 13th and 4th Tank armies for the first day of the operation were not achieved.

In the 52nd Army's offensive sector the greatest success on the first day of the operation was achieved along the right flank, where the 48th Rifle Corps was attacking. The 52nd Guards Tank Brigade—the forward detachment of the 3rd Guards Tank Army's 6th Guards Tank Corps—was attacking in the infantry's combat formation.

During the stubborn fighting, units of the 48th Rifle Corps threw the Germans out of Gross Krichen and Klein Krichen, captured Brauchitsdorf and by the close of the day had begun fighting for Braunau. The 52nd Guards Tank Brigade, having plunged ahead, had begun fighting for Kotzenau.

On the left flank of the 52nd Army's shock group, where its 78th Rifle and the 3rd Guards Tank Army's 7th Guards Tank Corps were attacking, the battles to break through the enemy's main defensive zone developed less successfully. Having comparatively quickly overcome the first defensive position, the attacking troops encountered the enemy's more organized resistance in the defensive depth, in the inhabited locales and the heights convenient for defense. The unfavorable meteorological conditions almost excluded the tank troops' maneuver off the roads. The fighting mainly unfolded along the roads and for the inhabited locales.

As a result of the heavy fighting during the day, the 78th Rifle Corps' formations, in close coordination with the 7th Guards Tank Corps, advanced six kilometers and threw the Germans out of the major strong points of Muhlredlitz and Merschwitz.

On that day units of the 7th Guards Tank Corps were unable to break away from the infantry and to the end of the day they operated with it. Only the 54th Guards Tank Brigade, which comprised the tank corps' forward detachment, plunged ahead six kilometers and by the close of the day had begun fighting for Schenborn.

By the close of the offensive's first day the 52nd Army's formations, in conjunction with the 3rd Guards Tank Army, broke through the enemy's defense along a 14-kilometer front and, having advanced into the depth 6-15 kilometers, captured 20 inhabited locales. The 3rd Guards Tank Army's forward detachments on that day advanced up to 25 kilometers along the right flank and up to 12 kilometers on the left. However, neither the 52nd Army nor the 3rd Guards Tank Army fully carried out the day's assignment, which had been established by the *front* commander's directive.

The 6th Army, which was attacking along the left flank of the *front's* main shock group from the bridgehead west of Malcz, captured with its right-flank formations on the operation's first day the major inhabited locale of Parchwitz, advanced 18 kilometers to the southwest and began fighting along the eastern and northeastern outskirts of Liegnitz. By the close of the day the army's remaining formations had reached the line Greibing—Roehn—Rausse, having, for the most part, carried out all the tasks called for by the operational plan.

Thus as a result of the first day of the offensive, the armies of the *front's* main shock group broke through the enemy's main defensive zone on the left bank of the Oder along three axes: on the right flank, along an 18-kilometer sector from Urschkau to Mlicz, having advanced up to ten kilometers west of Raudtena; in the center along a 24-kilometer sector from Gulau to Parchwitz, having advanced up to 15 kilometers in the area southwest of Luben, and; on the left flank in the 6th Army's offensive sector, along a 14-kilometer sector from Parchwitz to Rausse, having pierced the enemy's defense to a depth of up to 18 kilometers.

During the offensive the bridgeheads, which had been seized earlier in the areas west of Steinau and Malcz, were linked up into a single bridgehead 60 kilometers wide and up to 40 kilometers deep.

Despite the success achieved by the *front's* right-wing forces on the first day of the operation the offensive pace proved lower than planned and the assignment, as laid out in the 31 January *front* directive for the first day of the attack, was not completely carried out. The *front's* forces did not manage to break through the enemy's tactical defense zone along the entire attack front and gain freedom of maneuver for the development of the success in depth and toward the flanks.

The failure to accomplish the task of the day was linked mainly to miscalculations in preparing the attack, the poor intelligence on the enemy, and the insufficient fire against the enemy in his main defensive zone during the artillery preparation. The *front's* aviation took almost no part in suppressing the enemy's personnel and weapons, and the artillery alone, due to the low density and limited amount of ammunition, was not in a condition to carry out this task. The stubborn fighting that unfolded immediately following the beginning of our forces' attack showed that the effectiveness of our artillery preparation was insufficient. All of this told in the lowering of the troops' offensive pace. Of no little importance were the meteorological conditions. The beginning of the spring thaw limited our forces' maneuver capabilities and tied them to the roads, which made it easier for the enemy to organize a defense.

In the resulting situation the forces of the *front's* right wing were faced with the critical task of completing as quickly as possible the breakthrough of the enemy's tactical defensive zone along the entire offensive sector, ensuring the achievement of operational freedom by the tank armies and thus creating all the necessary conditions for the vigorous development of the operation in depth.

On the morning of 9 February, when the fighting along the *front's* right wing that had quieted somewhat during the night broke out again with new strength, the troops' main efforts were directed at resolving this task.

The 3rd Guards Army's shock group, while encountering stubborn enemy resistance and repelling his counterattacks, continued to attack against resistance to the northwest. While rolling up the enemy's defense along the left bank of the Oder, the formations of the 21st and 76th rifle corps, with the active support of the 25th Tank Corps, advanced six kilometers on 9 February.

On this day a success was registered in the army's attack sector north of Glogau, where formations of the 120th and 21st rifle corps, which were operating along the corps' common flanks, attacked the enemy and, having crushed the resistance by units of the 72nd Infantry Division and subunits of the 16th Panzer Division, reached the approaches to Glogau from the north. Retreating enemy units, with the assistance of arriving reinforcements from Glogau, managed to consolidate in the Zerbau area. The fighting along this line became protracted.

As before, the most stubborn fighting unfolded along the front's central sector in the 13th Army's attack sector. Units of the *Grossdeutschland* Panzer Corps, which were defending here, were better armed and proved to be more resilient than the remaining German formations. Thus our forces managed to advance only 5-6 kilometers.

A more significant success was achieved along the flanks of the 13th Army's breakthrough and the 4th Tank Army, which was attacking along with it.

The 6th Mechanized Corps' main forces, while developing the offensive, by the close of 9 February, reached the Primkenau area, while part of its forces, while bypassing the enemy group of forces that was fighting opposite the 13th Army's center, from the north, reached the Polkwitz area. Along the approaches to Primkenau the enemy, taking advantage of the favorable terrain for defense, bestrode the road leading to the town and, supported by up to a battalion of infantry, 10-12 tanks and a battalion of artillery, was putting up fierce resistance, holding up the further advance by the mechanized corps's forward detachments. The swamps and continuous woods, which were located along both sides of the road, prevented us from carrying out an outflanking maneuver. Thus the troops' attack along this axis was delayed somewhat.

On orders from the commander of the 4th Tank Army, the 10th Tank Corps bypassed Luben from the south and attacked in the direction of Oberglasersdorf. The 61st Tank Brigade was attacking along the corps' right flank. In the Oberau area the brigade encountered resistance from the enemy who had fortified himself in the village and fought him all day. The 62nd Tank and 29th Motorized Rifle brigades, having overcome the enemy's resistance in the Oberglasersdorf area, by the close of the day had seized Gross Heinzendorf. By this time the 63rd Tank Brigade had reached Herbersdorf. Having taken up a perimeter defense here, the brigade dispatched a small detachment to Polkwitz, in order to establish communications with the 6th Mechanized Corps.

On this day the 13th Army's rifle formations fought in close cooperation with the tank troops.

By the close of the day the 102nd Rifle Corps captured the paved road leading from Polkwitz to the north, along its entire attack area, while the 24th Rifle Corps, advancing up to 15 kilometers in fighting on that day, reached Kotzenau with part of its forces, while the remaining formations deployed facing north, blocking from the south the now-surrounded German tank group of forces in the woods east of Herbersdorf.

The 4th Tank Army's formations, having reached the Primkenau—Kotzenau—Polkwitz area, found themselves in an extremely difficult situation. There is a broad swamp in the middle of this area and to the north. Only two paved roads led to the west, which came together in Primkenau. Thus the army's further route lay only through Primkenau, where the enemy, according to intelligence data, had securely fortified himself and was getting ready for stubborn fighting.

While striving to seize the crossings over the Bober River as quickly as possible and foreseeing the possibility of prolonged fighting in the Primkenau area, the *front* commander as early as the day of 9 February ordered the commander of the 4th Tank Army to direct the 6th Mechanized Corps' 93rd Independent and 22nd Self-Propelled Artillery brigades to Neustedtel and Naumburg following the capture of Polkwitz, in order to capture crossings over the Bober River. At the same time, the *front* commander ordered that the brigades not get bogged down in fighting for the towns, but that they should bypass them.

During the latter half of 9 February the 93rd Independent Tank Brigade was relieved by units of the 112th Rifle Division in the Polkwitz area and began carrying out its assigned task.

The 22nd Self-Propelled Artillery Brigade, which was moving up from the rear to the Hoffnung area (13 kilometers northwest of Polkwitz) to link up with the 93rd Independent Tank Brigade, had by the close of the day reached Kreidelwitz and here was forced to halt for the night, due to the poor condition of the roads along the route of march.

As before, the right-flank formations advanced more successfully along the 52nd Army's attack zone. The enemy facing the army's right flank suffered heavy losses on the first day of the operation and now, lacking sufficient forces for the defense of this sector of the front, was conducting holding actions with small forces along terrain sectors favorable for defense.

While striving to preempt the enemy's forces in arriving at the crossings over the Bober River, units of the 6th Guards Tank Corps broke through Kotzenau in fighting and began to develop the attack through the woods along the paved road to Ruchenwaldau.

Along the Ruchenwaldau—Gremsdorf line the corps' units encountered the organized resistance of an enemy who was trying to close the route to Bunzlau.

The fighting along this line continued until late in the evening, but we were not able to crush the Germans' resistance on this day. On the other hand, the corps' right-flank brigade, having bypassed Ruchenwaldau from the north and not encountering the enemy along its path, reached the Bober River along the Cosel—Alt Els sector. The tank brigade's appearance in this area was completely unexpected for the enemy. Taking advantage of the surprise, the brigade forced the river from the march and seized the villages of Strans and Neu Els along its left bank.

The 48th Rifle Corps' formations, while attacking behind the tank units, advanced that day up to 15 kilometers and by evening had reached the area south of the line Kotzenau—Hintereck—Fuchsmuehle. It should be noted that the 6th Guards Tank Corps' success was not consolidated in time. Following the breakthrough of our tanks through Kotzenau, the Germans once again organized a defense of the town, and thus the 49th Rifle Corps' right-flank units had to become involved in the fighting for the town.

Along the army's left flank, in the 78th Rifle Corps' attack sector, the 7th Guards Tank Corps achieved a significant success during the first part of the day. The corps boldly pushed forward and reached the approaches to Genau, but four kilometers from the town it encountered the enemy's well organized anti-tank defense. Aside from the engineering obstacles, the advance was hindered by powerful artillery fire and numerous *faustpatrone* ambushes.

The 78th Rifle Corps' formations continued to attack behind the tank units. While overcoming the weak but nonetheless unremitting resistance by the retreating units of the enemy's 19th Panzer and 408th Infantry divisions and fighting for each inhabited locale, by the close of the day the rifle divisions had reached the line Neusorge—northern outskirts of Liegnitz.

Thus as a result of two days of fighting, the *front's* right-wing forces broke through the enemy's tactical defense zone along the entire attack front. By the close of 9 February the breakthrough front had been expanded up to 70 kilometers, while the combined-arms armies had penetrated into the enemy defense from ten to 25 kilometers, and the tank armies along some axes from 30 to 60 kilometers.

The combat operations during the second day of fighting showed that the German forces defending in the tactical zone had already been significantly weakened over two days. The absence of the enemy's operational reserves immediately in the zone of combat operations prevented him from influencing the course of the fighting through the commitment of fresh forces from the depth. Thus in order to economize forces and win time before the arrival of reserves from other sectors of the front, the main forces of the significantly depleted enemy units began to concentrate around major inhabited locales and towns, around road junctions and commanding heights, which controlled the approaches to the towns. The enemy calculated that by employing the meteorological conditions and lack of roads, which were unfavorable for the attacker, and by relying on favorable defensive lines, he could delay our forces' attack until the arrival of his fresh forces.

In order to foil the enemy's calculations and denying him the opportunity of occupying favorable defensive lines in the depth with his arriving reserves, it was necessary to develop the operation at a high speed, as this was called for by the operational plan. At the same time, despite the fact that the enemy's resistance in the tactical defensive zone had been crushed; the pace of advance of the *front's* forces on the operation's second day was considerably lower than had been planned. By the close of 9 February the tank armies had actually carried out only the first day's assignment, while the combined-arms armies had failed to do even that along the majority of the sectors. This may be chiefly explained by the fact that the troops, due to the onset of the bad roads, the difficulty of moving off the roads, and the low capacity of the dirt roads, were tied to the improved and paved roads, in the defense of which the enemy had the opportunity of holding significant attacking forces with limited strength.

Due to a certain lagging behind of our artillery behind the forward units and difficulties in delivering ammunition, as well as due to our aviation's limited activities, the fighting against small groups of Germans was often prolonged and the rate of our troops' advance fell sharply.

In the resulting situation, when the enemy's defeated units were no longer able to put up powerful and organized resistance along the entire front, and the enemy reserves moving up to the front had not yet arrived, it was necessary to speed up the arrival of our forces at the Bober River as quickly as possible, in order to capture crossings over the river and to prevent the enemy from consolidating along its left bank and to thus ensure the further development of the offensive and the defeat of the enemy's reserves in detail.

The Development of the Offensive by the Front's Right-Wing Armies to the Bober River and Toward the Flanks (10-11 February)

Having correctly evaluated the capabilities of the *front's* forces in the developing situation, the *front* commander and the army commanders demanded that their forces conduct the offensive in a more precise and thorough manner, to more decisively bring up their artillery to the forward units, to more boldly seek ways to go around enemy centers of resistance along road junctions and inhabited locales, to avoid getting drawn into fighting with small enemy groups, and to boldly advance, without paying attention to the fact that these groups remain in the spaces between and along the flanks of the attacking forces.

These instructions were perfectly timely and played a positive role.

The combat activities that unfolded on 10 February in the center of the *front's* main group of forces showed that the enemy, given our forces' daring and decisive actions, was not in a condition to wage a consecutive battle for each inhabited locale along the path of our attacking formations. The enemy, while reacting extremely sensitively to the bypassing and outflanking of his isolated positions, and putting up resistance by rearguards only in the areas of major towns and major road junctions, began to rapidly fall back behind the Bober River, where an intermediary defensive line was being hurriedly prepared.

The fighting unfolded somewhat differently along the breakthrough's flanks. In the Glogau and Liegnitz areas the enemy forces, while trying to prevent the development of the breakthrough toward the flanks and to hold the fortress areas of Glogau and Breslau, were putting up fierce resistance, often counterattacking and bringing up additional forces to the fighting area. Despite the stubbornness with which the enemy fought to retain a bridgehead along the right bank of the Oder north and northeast of Glogau, the formations of the 3rd Guards Army's 120th Rifle Corps, while developing the success achieved the previous evening, crushed the resistance by units of the 72nd Infantry Division along the Gross Land Canal, and by the close of 10 February had reached the Oder along a front from Aufhalt to Rabsen.

On the same day the forces of the 3rd Guards Army's shock group, while expanding the breakthrough along the front and in the depth, continued to roll up the enemy's defense with part of its forces along the left bank of the Oder, while the left-flank formations, together with the 25th Tank Corps, were bypassing the Glogau area from the south.

However, the offensive by the army's main forces along its left flank was developing significantly more slowly than the reigning situation demanded. The *front* commander pointed this out to the army commander. He pointed out that the army was carrying out the responsible task of securing the flank of the *front's* main forces and that in conditions when the *front's* main forces were successfully developing the offensive to the west, the rapid rolling up of the enemy's defense facing the army's front and its advance to the Bober River were particularly important. He thus demanded that the army commander undertake decisive measures to speed up the defeat of the enemy's group of forces defending in the Glogau area and to vigorously advance toward the Bober River.

Because the army's left-flank formations, upon encountering stubborn resistance, were not able to achieve a high offensive pace, the army commander decided to commit his reserve—the 287th Rifle Division—into the fighting along the army's left flank. As the subsequent fighting showed, this decision was correct and timely. The 287th Rifle Division, which had been committed into the fighting along the line to the west of Hochkirch, rapidly crushed the enemy's resistance and, while attacking in conjunction with the formations of the 76th Rifle Corps, by the end of the day had thrown back the opposing German units 17 kilometers.

The formations of the army's shock group, having reached the approaches to Glogau, once again ran into the enemy's organized defense. The commandant of Glogau, Colonel Schoen, who had been personally appointed to this post by Hitler, received instructions from the latter to defend the fortress to the last man. In accordance with these instructions, the fortress garrison continued to strengthen Glogau's defense, despite the looming threat of encirclement.

Because the enemy, even under the threat of Glogau's encirclement, did not slacken the fight for this powerful strong point along the line of the Oder River, the forces of the 3rd Guards Army received orders on 10 February to outflank it from the south and west and to cut all routes connecting Glogau with the remaining forces of the German Fourth Panzer Army, and as quickly as possible complete the encirclement of the enemy's group of forces concentrated in the Glogau area.

On the morning of 11 February the 3rd Guards Army's forces began carrying out this assignment.

As before, the 4th Tank Army's formations were operating ahead in the 13th Army's attack sector. Units of the 6th Mechanized Corps, having crushed the resistance of the German units along the approaches to Primkenau, arrived immediately before the town and, bypassing it from the north, attacked toward Hoenhofen. A part of the corps' forces was left behind in the Primkenau area for covering the corps' flank against enemy attacks from the south.

As before, the broad swamps, which ran north from Primkenau, and the solid wooded area to the south of town and to the west as far as the Bober River, hindered our broad maneuver. Therefore the tank troops' operations unfolded primarily along two paved roads, which diverged from Primkenau to the northwest and west.

By the close of the day the corps's main forces had occupied Hoehhof and Karpfreis, while its forward detachments had begun fighting for Waltersdorf and Rucherdorf.

The 10th Tank Corps' main forces, in conjunction with the 13th Army's combined-arms formations, fought until 1700 with the enemy group of forces encircled in the woods east of Herbersdorf. As a result of these battles, the main mass of the encircled troops and their equipment were destroyed or captured by our forces. Some of the enemy's infantry subunits and remnants of his tank units, employing the absence of a solid encirclement front, infiltrated along the country roads to the west, leaving behind a large amount of equipment in the mud.

During the second half of the day the 10th Tank Corps, having left some small tank detachments in this area to help the combined-arms formations complete the clearing of the area of enemy remnants, continued attacking to the west. By the close of the day the corps' main forces had concentrated in the Primkenau area.

By this time the 62nd Tank Brigade (the corps' forward detachment) had reached the approaches to the village of Sprottischwaldau, where it encountered organized resistance by the enemy, who was straddling the road. Following several unsuccessful attacks, the brigade consolidated along the occupied line, having sent forward a reconnaissance party to determine the enemy's strength and to find indirect routes.

The 93rd Independent Tank Brigade, which had been ordered the previous evening to break through through Neustedtel to the crossings over the Bober River near Christianstadt, attacked the enemy on the morning of 10 February near Neusorge and Wisau, pushed aside his screens and, attacking along roads intersecting at the village of Hoffnung, by 1400 arrived in this area. Along the approaches to the village of Klopschen, the brigade once again ran into the enemy's organized defense and was simultaneously attacked by German planes. By 1700 the 22nd Self-Propelled Artillery Brigade reached the village of Klopschen.

Due to the unsuccessful attempts to break through through Klopschen to Neustedtel, the commander of the 93rd Independent Tank Brigade requested permission from the commander of the 4th Tank Army to change the brigade's march route and to move toward Naumburg, not through Neustedtel, but through Waltersdorf and Ebersdorf; that is, without fighting along the route where the 4th Tank Army's main forces were successfully attacking. The army commander ordered the brigade commander, upon covering himself from the direction of Gustau, Meschkau and Neugabel with the 22nd Self-Propelled Artillery Brigade, to bypass this sector from the south, to capture the Metschlau area, and then to attack toward Neustedtel from the south. The brigade, having failed to manifest the necessary persistence in carrying out the assigned task, was by the close of the day fighting here along with units of the 13th Army's 102nd Rifle Corps, which had arrived in the area.

The 13th Army's formations, which were attacking behind the forces of the 4th Tank Army, were throughout the day clearing the enemy out of the swampy and wooded area to the west of Polkwitz. While fighting for individual inhabited locales, which were being defending by the enemy's rearguards, they advanced behind the tank units. By the close of the day the army's first-echelon rifle corps had reached the line Kwaritz—Hoenhofen—Neuforwerk, having covered up to 20 kilometers that day. Approximately the same route had been covered in fighting by the 4th Tank Army's units, and its forward units that day had advanced up to 40 kilometers to the west.

The commander of the 13th Army, calculating that the enemy might bring up fresh forces to the Bober River, demanded from his corps commanders still more decisive actions and assigned them the following task: by the close of 11 February to reach the line Ruchersdorf—Ionsdorf—Tschibsdorf, and to force the Bober River with their divisions' powerful mobile detachments, under the command of the deputy division commanders, between the towns of Naumburg and Sagan and ensure the crossing of the corps' main forces over the river.

Combat operations unfolded favorably this day along the 52nd Army's right flank. The 3rd Guards Tank Army's corps, which were attacking in the army's sector, achieved new successes this day: the 6th Guards Tank Corps' main forces reached the Bober River along the front Cosel—Waldforwerk, while the 7th Guards Tank Corps' main forces, having bypassed Genau from the north, advanced to the approaches to an important industrial center and major road and railroad junction of Lower Silesia—the town of Bunzlau.

The 52nd Army's 48th Rifle Corps, which was attacking behind the 6th Guards Tank Corps, while overcoming the resistance of the enemy's scattered units along the intermediary lines and in the inhabited locales, also advanced successfully. By the close of the day the corps' main forces reached the Bober River along the front Ober Leschen—Gross Gollnisch, having advanced about 25 kilometers in fighting that day.

The situation was developing quite differently along the 52nd Army's left flank.

Due to the fact that on the operation's first day the 6th Army deployed its main forces facing to the southeast for the offensive on Breslau from the west, while the 5th Guards and 21st armies, attacking south of Breslau and having encountered the enemy's stubborn resistance, were advancing very slowly, the 52nd Army's left flank was open. As the army moved to the west the army commander was forced to detach significant forces for securing the attacking forces from the south, all the more because the Germans were quite active here. These heavy two-day battles in the Liegnitz area and the stubborn fighting for Genau showed this.

The 78th Rifle Corps, which was attacking along the army's left flank, as early as the operation's second day, was forced to detach a part of its forces for covering its flank. Throughout 10 February it continued to deploy its divisions facing southwest and by the close of the day was operating along a 40-kilometer sector from Rosenthal to Liegnitz. In such conditions the corps not only lacked the opportunity to successfully continue a further attack, but should new enemy formations appear along this sector, it would not have been able to withstand them for long.

The *front* commander, taking into account the threat which was building not only for the 52nd Army, but for the flank of the *front's* entire shock group, on 10 February ordered the 3rd Guards Tank Army's 9th Mechanized Corps, which, following its transfer from the *front's* left wing was moving to the tank army's attack sector, to halt in the Genau area and direct it to capturing Goldberg.

On that day the 9th Mechanized Corps, which had entered the fighting for Genau, along with units of the 78th Rifle Corps, by evening had captured this important German strong point along the flank of the *front's* shock group. The arrival of the 9th Mechanized Corps in this area significantly strengthened the situation of the 52nd Army's extended left flank.

Simultaneously with the adoption of the decision to turn the 9th Mechanized Corps to the south, the *front* commander, in order to further strengthen the left flank of the *front's* main shock group, authorized the commander of the 52nd Army to remove a division from the 73rd Rifle Corps in the Breslau area and transfer it to the Liegnitz area to strengthen the 78th Rifle Corps.

Thus, as a result of the fighting on 10 February, the forces attacking in the center of the *front's* main shock group, had even more deeply penetrated into the enemy's defense. In the 52nd Army's offensive sector they had already reached the Bober River along a few sectors, while in the 13th Army's sector, having overcome the most impassable terrain sectors, they had created the prerequisites for a rapid advance to this water line.

However, by the close of 10 February, as a result of the slow development of the breakthrough toward the flanks and the lagging behind of the armies attacking along the *front's* center, the offensive front of the forces of the 3rd Guards, 13th and 52nd armies, which were operating along the left bank of the Oder, increased from 46 to 120-130 kilometers, while its width at the base of the breakthrough had hardly changed at all.

In this situation the *front* command had to, along with the development of the further offensive to the west, adopt measures to more energetically roll up the enemy's defense facing the 3rd Guards Army's right wing, which would enable us to shorten the length of the front and free up a part of our forces for the subsequent development of the operation. Simultaneous with this, it was necessary to strengthen the extended left flank of the shock group.

The efforts of the *front's* command and forces were directed toward resolving these tasks on 11 February.

On 11 February combat operations unfolded in conditions of growing enemy resistance along the entire attack sector of the *front's* shock group, and particularly along its flanks, because by this time the forward units of those troops, which were being hurriedly brought up by the enemy to the breakthrough area, were starting to appear opposite the *front*.

Along the right flank the fiercest fighting unfolded in the Glogau area. Despite the German forces' desperate efforts to hold off our advance to the town, the 3rd Guards Army's formations persistently threw the enemy out of one inhabited locale after another and by the close of the day units of the 21st Rifle Corps had outflanked the town from the north, east and south. A retreat route for the enemy group of forces remained open out of Glogau, but was already threatened with being cut by the army's left-flank formations, which by the close of the day had reached the line Buchenhang—Neugabel. It was clear that the garrison at Glogau was not preparing to abandon the town and was trying to distract to itself as many Soviet troops as possible.

Insofar as Glogau was a heavily fortified town, the battle for its capture in the developing situation might stretch out for a long time and tie down significant forces, which would have been reflected in carrying out the army's main task. Thus the decision was made to encircle the enemy in the Glogau area and to leave behind a single division from the 21st Rifle Corps to blockade the fortress, while the remaining forces of the army's shock group would continue the offensive along the Oder to the northwest. In accordance with this decision, the 21st Rifle Corps' main forces were assigned the task, along with the 25th Tank Corps, to continue a vigorous offensive along the Oder to the northwest, for the purpose of completely cutting off the path of retreat of the German group of forces from Glogau and as quickly as possible to roll up the entire front of the enemy's defense on the Oder.

The 76th Rifle Corps, which was attacking along the army's left flank, received orders to bypass the swampy area west of Wisau from the north and to develop a vigorous offensive through Freistadt to the Bober River. The resolution of this task, despite the stubborn resistance by German units covering the communications of the Glogau fortress, was made easier by the fact that the 4th Tank Army's 93rd Independent Tank and 22nd Self-Propelled Artillery brigades were continuing to operate in the corps' attack zone, and by the successfully developing offensive on 11 February by the 4th Tank and 13th armies.

In the center of the offensive by the *front's* main shock group, the troops' main efforts had been directed at arriving at the Bober River as quickly as possible and seizing bridgeheads along its left bank.

The 4th Tank Army's main forces and its forward detachments advanced significantly on this day.

The 6th Mechanized Corps, while encountering only small enemy screens and ambushes along its path, made a fighting advance throughout the day of up to 35 kilometers and by the close of the day had reached the Bober River along the front Neider Gorpe—Ober Gorpe.

As early as the corps' advance to the Bober River, the *front* commander ordered the army commander to force the river from the march and to seize a bridgehead along its left bank. Therefore the commander of the 4th Tank Army, upon the arrival of the corps at the river, demanded that the corps commander force it with his main forces and seize bridgeheads on the left bank and consolidate along them, while a forward detachment would seize Benau. As subsequent events showed, the skillful and timely fulfillment of the *front* commander's instructions by the 6th Mechanized Corps' forces played a decisive role in the army's achievement of a major operational success.

In the 10th Tank Corps' attack zone the enemy's resistance proved more significant. Along the sector west of Primkenau, units of the *Grossdeutschland* Panzer Corps, the "Liegnitz" Anti-Tank Battalion, and 5-6 different combat groups and companies, which had survived defeat, sought by fire and counterattacks to prevent a breakthrough by our tank troops to Sprottau. Nevertheless, the enemy was thrown out of a number of points covering Sprottau from the north and east, and by the close of the day's fighting was already going on along the town's outskirts.

The 13th Army's formations, while overcoming the resistance of scattered enemy groups, which remained in the rear of the tank troops, were persistently advancing behind the mobile units, and by the close of the day were fighting along the line Metschlau—Ruchersdorf—Ionsdorf, along the army's right flank and center. The 102nd Rifle Corps' left-flank division, in conjunction with units of the 10th Tank Corps, was fighting in Sprottau.

On the army's left flank, throughout the entire day the 24th Rifle Corps was fighting with enemy rear guards, which were covering the main forces' retreat to the Bober River.

By the close of the day the corps, despite the difficult fighting conditions along the forest roads, had reached the Bober River south of Sprottau and its left-flank division had forced the river from the march and seized a small bridgehead in the Boberwitz area.

On the 52nd Army's right flank, the 48th Rifle Corps, which had the evening before reached the Bober River along the sector Ober Leschen—Gross Gollnisch and forced the river on 11 February with all three of its divisions. Despite the enemy's heavy fire resistance, which was supported by his aviation, the corps' forces laid down several crossings over the river, pushed artillery and armored transports across the river, and following stubborn fighting threw the Germans out of all the inhabited locales along the river bank.

The corps' further offensive once again ran through a wooded area, which occupied the entire area between the Bober and Kweis rivers, and thus developed slowly. The enemy defending opposite the corps was not only putting up powerful fire resistance, but repeatedly launched counterattacks. The infantry attack was made more difficult by the fact that it unfolded without tank support. All of the 6th Guards Tank Corps' tanks remained on the river's right bank, because the previously constructed crossings had been destroyed by enemy aviation and had to be built again. Despite this, during a day of fighting the 48th Rifle Corps advanced six kilometers and had covered about half the distance separating the Bober and Kweis rivers.

On this day even more stubborn fighting unfolded along the 52nd Army's center and left flank. Throughout the day the 7th Guards Tank Corps was engaged in heavy fighting in Bunzlau, wresting block after block from the enemy. It was only by evening, when the 78th Rifle Corps' 31st Rifle Division arrived at the town, that it became possible to more successfully combat the enemy's anti-tank ambushes and to blockade his firing points. The fighting in the town continued all night, and by morning the town had been completely cleared of German forces. At dawn on 12 February the 31st Rifle Division reached the eastern bank of the Bober River along the entire course from the Eichberg to Bunzlau and, along with the tank units, began fighting for the crossings over the river to the west of Bunzlau.

The 78th Rifle Corps' remaining two divisions deployed facing the south and, while securing the army's flank and that of the *front's* entire shock group, was fighting along the line Tomaswaldau—Uberschar—Liegnitz.

By this time the 9th Mechanized Corps, which was attacking from the Genau area toward Jauer, had thrust 10-15 kilometers forward and was fighting in the Goldberg—Lasnig—Rotkirch area.

Thus by the close of the operation's fourth day, the forces of the *front's* main shock group, while developing the success achieved in the offensive's first days, had advanced up to 60 kilometers along the axis of the main attack and had expanded the width of the breakthrough to 160 kilometers.

Having suffered heavy losses, the German-Fascist forces operating opposite the center of the *front's* main shock group, were unable to put up organized resistance as early as the operation's third day and under the cover of rearguards had begun to fall back to the Bober River.

On the breakthrough's flanks, to which the troops defending opposite the center of the *front's* shock group had partially fallen back, the enemy continued to put up stubborn resistance, striving to prevent the further widening of the breakthrough front through its defense and to distract to the flanks the maximum possible number of our forces from the axis of the main attack.

Despite this, the tank and combined-arms formations that were attacking along the axis of the main attack, continued to pursue the retreating enemy forces and by the close of the offensive's fourth day had reached the Bober River along a number of sectors.

During these days the *front's* right-wing forces captured such important rail and road junctions and powerful defensive strong points on the left bank of the Oder as the towns of Liegnitz, Luben, Genau, and Bunzlau. By relying on these towns, the German forces counted on holding our offensive. In the fighting for these towns the Soviet soldiers once again covered themselves with undying glory. They multiplied the experience of fighting for towns, which had been accumulated by the Soviet army in the course of the Great Patriotic War, and at the same time manifested high examples of mass heroism peculiar only to Soviet people raised by the Communist Party.

During these days the *front's* party organizations accepted into their ranks hundreds of the best patriot-frontline soldiers, who had sworn to give all their strength and, if need be—their life—for the great goal of completely routing the hated enemy.

As the forces of the *front's* main shock group advanced to the west, the conditions for the further conduct of operations became more difficult. If on the eve of the offensive the length of the front occupied by the right-wing armies (not counting the 6th Army) was about 130 kilometers, then by the end of the operation's fourth day it had increased to 210-220 kilometers. By the end of the operation's fourth day the armies of the *front's* main shock group were actually operating along three diverging axes—to the northwest (3rd Guards Army), the west (4th Tank and 13th armies) and the southwest (3rd Guards Tank and 52nd armies).

Along with this, with each day the growing lag of the 5th Guards and 21st armies, which were attacking from the bridgehead south of Breslau, was diverting part of the forces of the *front's* main group of forces to cover its left flank, at the same time when signs had appeared that the enemy was trying to reinforce opposite the center of the main group of forces and delay our advance to the Bober and Kweis rivers.

The situation was unfolding a little more favorably along the right flank. Although intense fighting was going on along the approaches to Glogau and in the Neustedtel area by the close of 11 February, to the west and north of Neustedtel, along the entire bend of the Oder, the enemy's forces were quite limited. This circumstance was creating favorable prerequisites for developing the 3rd Guards Army's offensive to the northwest and for the vigorous arrival of the army's forces at the Bober River along its lower course.

The actions of the armies of the *front's* shock group from 12 February and to the end of the operation's first stage had taken on the appearance of a fan-shaped offensive along diverging axes.

The Arrival of the Forces of the Front's Shock Group to the Bober and Kweis Rivers and the Fighting for the Bridgeheads (12-15 February)

During 12-15 February the *front's* right-wing forces reached the Bober and Kweis rivers along their entire attack sector and, upon forcing them along a number of sectors, began fighting with the enemy's arriving reserves along the captured bridgeheads. The 4th Tank Army, having plunged ahead, had begun fighting for the crossings over the Neisse River. The 52nd Army's left-flank formations, which were operating along the left flank of the entire main group of forces, continued the stubborn fight along the front Bunzlau—Liegnitz.

The 3rd Guards Army's arrival at the Bober River. On 12 February the 25th Tank Corps' and the 21st Rifle Corps' left-flank formations launched a powerful attack against the enemy operating west of Glogau. Having crushed the resistance of the enemy units and developing the success in the direction of Nieder Herrndorf, the attacking forces completed the encirclement of the Germans in the Glogau area.

The 76th Rifle Corps, together with the 93rd Independent Tank and 22nd Self-Propelled Artillery brigades, crushed the resistance of the enemy who was stubbornly defending in the Kwaritz area, and began pursuing the enemy forces, while its main forces were bypassing Neustedtel from the west.

By the close of the day the 3rd Guards Army's main forces, having captured the inhabited locale of Reisen on the left flank, reached the approaches to the towns of Beiten and Neustedtel.

Following the defeat and encirclement of units of the German XXIV Panzer Corps in the Glogau area, the pace of the 3rd Guards Army's advance in the bend of the Oder began to increase rapidly, because the corps' remnants began to hurriedly fall back to the northwest and west, without hardly putting up any resistance.

By 15 February the entire bend of the Oder had been cleared of German forces, and the 3rd Guards Army's forces, having captured the towns of Grossen and Naumburg, had reached the Bober River from its mouth to Naumburg.

The successful movement of the 3rd Guards Army to the mouth of the Bober River enabled the forces of the First Belorussian Front's 33rd Army to eject on 15 February the German forces from the bridgehead north of Grossen and place in reserve the main forces of the 38th Rifle Corps, which had been defending along the right bank of the Oder from Grossen to the village of Odereck.

The arrival of the 3rd Guards Army at the Bober River significantly improved the situation along the right flank of the *front's* main shock group. The width of the 3rd Guards Army's attack front shrank from 104 to 36 kilometers. The 120th Rifle Corps had been pulled back to the army's second echelon. All of this created favorable prerequisites for the operation's further development on the left bank of the Bober River and for the launching of new attacks against the German-Fascist forces along the Cottbus axis.

The seizure by the 4th Tank and 13th armies' forces of a bridgehead on the left bank of the Bober River and the 4th Tank Army's breakthrough to the Neisse River. Our forces' offensive in the center of the *front's* main shock group during 12-15 February took place in a more complex situation than along the right flank.

The 4th Tank Army's forces, while pursuing the enemy, which had been defeated opposite the bridgeheads on the Oder River, advanced rapidly. On 11 February they reached the Bober River, having bypassed by 30-35 kilometers the formations of the 13th Army, in whose sector they were attacking.

The *front* commander, possessing information that the enemy was attempting to consolidate along the Bober and Kweis rivers, repeatedly and persistently demanded that the commanders of the 4th and 3rd Guards tank armies not disperse their armies' forces in fighting small enemy groups and not to look over one's shoulder at the enemy left behind in the rear and along the tank armies' flanks, but rather to vigorously advance forward, to force the Bober and Kweis rivers from the march and, without stopping, attack toward the Neisse River. On 11 February he ordered the commander of the 4th Tank Army to gather his entire army into a fist and to immediately force the Bober River with his main forces.

The correctness of the *front* commander's demands was confirmed by the fact that the enemy actually was determined to halt the Soviet forces' further advance along the line of the Bober River with formations that were being brought up here from the depth and from other sectors of the front, but at this time had not yet managed to occupy the sector from Christianstadt to Sagan with his arriving reserves. Thus the most favorable conditions had arisen for overcoming the Bober River without significant exertions. Individual enemy battalions, which were defending the river's left bank along a broad front, were not able to put up serious resistance to the tank army.

As was noted earlier, the commander of the 4th Tank Army, having correctly evaluated the situation, demanded that the commander of the 6th Mechanized Corps force the Bober River from the march in the Nieder Gorpe and Ober Gorpe area and to seize a bridgehead on the river's left bank. Now, in carrying out the *front* commander's instructions, he ordered the commander of the 10th Tank Corps to turn over the combat sector in the Sprottau area to the 13th Army's forces and to rapidly move the corps to the Sagan area, to force the Bober River here and to capture Zorau with a forward detachment.

By the evening of 12 February the corps had concentrated on the right bank of the Bober River in the area to the north of Sagan and immediately set about forcing the river. By this time the 6th Mechanized Corps had already crossed over a significant part of its forces to the left bank and had expanded the bridgehead seized the previous evening up to eight kilometers in width and four in depth. Units of the 13th Army's 102nd Rifle Corps, while exploiting the tank troops' success and advancing behind them, had by the close of the day reached the Bober River with their main forces.

Insofar as the combined-arms formations' arrival at the Bober River secured the 4th Tank Army's communications, the army commander decided to attack from the Bober River to the Neisse River, once again with all the army's forces in a single echelon. He left two tank and one self-propelled artillery brigades in reserve and counted on employing them in case of enemy counterattacks from the Naumburg and Sagan areas. For this purpose, he shifted the 22nd Self-Propelled Artillery Brigade to the area southeast of Naumburg, moved the 93rd Independent Tank Brigade to the Kalkreit area, and along the left flank, concentrated the 10th Tank Corps' 63rd Tank Brigade in the area north of Sagan.

On the morning of 13 February the 4th Tank Army's main forces, which had crossed over to the left bank of the Bober River, attacked in the direction of Sommerfeld and Zorau.

The offensive developed successfully. The 6th Mechanized Corps, which was attacking along the army's right flank, occupied the major railroad junction of Benau, and by 1900 had begun fighting for Sommerfeld with its main forces.

The enemy's weak and unorganized resistance along the path of our forces' advance to the Neisse River enabled the army's forward units to attack at night and throughout the entire next day.

On 14 February the 6th Mechanized Corps main forces, while attacking from Sommerfeld to the difficult wooded and swampy sector to the north, reached the right bank of the Neisse River in the Gross Gastrose area.

The 112th Rifle Division, which had been operationally subordinated to the 6th Mechanized Corps, had by the end of the day been brought up to the Pferten area.

The 10th Tank Corps, which was attacking along the army's left flank, occupied Zorau during the latter half of the day, and on the morning of 14 February its forward units broke into Teiplitz from the march. The enemy, numbering up to 200 men, who was covering this major railroad and road junction, was caught off guard, and was partially destroyed and partially captured in a short fight. While developing the attack, by 1000 the corps' units had reached the Neisse River in the Klein Bademeusel area and tried to force the river from the march. However, this attempt did not meet with success, as the enemy met the troops trying to cross over with organized artillery-mortar and infantry fire from the left bank of the river.

At that time, when the units of the 4th Tank Army that had lunged forward were fighting for bridgeheads over the Neisse River, stubborn fighting had broken out in the rear along the Bober River, with an enemy who was attempting to cut off the 4th Tank Army's forces from their crossings over the Bober River and restore the defense along its left bank.

As early as 13 February the 102nd Rifle Corps' forward formations, which had crossed over to the left bank of the Bober River, encountered resistance from German infantry and tanks along the southern approaches to Christianstadt and in the Reinswalde area. During the day the corps' units threw the enemy out of Reinswalde and captured the heavily fortified strong point of Benau along with the tank troops, but were not able to advance beyond this line.

The 16th Tank Brigade, which had been left in the town of Zorau to hold it until the infantry's arrival, on 13 February repulsed several of the enemy's panzer counterattacks along the southern approaches to the town.

The 24th Rifle Corps' formations which captured Sprottau after two days of fierce fighting, reached the Bober River in the Sagan area and to the south, while part of its forces forced the river north of Sagan. The corps' right-flank division encountered powerful resistance by the enemy's infantry and panzer subunits in the town's eastern part and along the northern approaches to it.

Thus as early as the close of 13 February the Germans had begun to create a solid defensive front opposite the 13th Army's forces, while trying to eliminate the breakthrough created by the 4th

Tank Army. Simultaneously, the enemy was continuing to stubbornly hold the firing points along the bridgehead's flanks in the areas of the towns of Christianstadt and Sagan.

On 14 February the fighting for the bridgehead became even fiercer.

The 102nd Rifle Corps, which had crossed all of its formations to the left bank of the river, attacked from the Benau area to the northwest.

During the first half of the day the corps' left-flank 121st Rifle Division crushed in the area west of Benau the resistance of a small detachment of infantry and tanks, which had been defending here, and, having thrown the enemy back to the north, attacked toward Sommerfeld. Not encountering resistance along its route, the division reached the Gassen area in the latter part of the day and occupied it.

At this time more than two regiments of German infantry, with 30-35 tanks and supported by assault guns, launched attacks from the areas of Christianstadt and the woods located to the southeast of Zorau, in the general direction of Benau.

Simultaneously, a powerful enemy tank group, supported by infantry, renewed the attacks on Zorau from the south and southeast. The ground forces' actions were accompanied by German air strikes against the crossings over the Bober River. Our aviation actively resisted the enemy's air attacks and launched strikes against his infantry and tank concentrations. However, both sides' air activities were, as before, restricted and ineffective, due to the poor weather. The 2nd Air Army carried out 763 sorties during the day in the *front's* sector. During the same time 174 enemy flights were noted.

The 102nd Rifle Corps' right-flank formations, which were holding the line occupied by them, repelled counterattacks by the enemy, who was attacking from the Christianstadt area, until evening. By 2000, on orders of the commander of the 4th Tank Army, the 6th Mechanized Corps' 17th Mechanized Brigade, which had been left prior to this on the right bank of the Bober River, arrived at the right flank. Somewhat later, the 93rd Independent Tank Brigade was moved up to this area from the 4th Tank Army commander's reserve. With the arrival of the tank units at the bridgehead, the situation along this sector of the front improved significantly, and all the enemy's subsequent counterattacks were without result.

The enemy's counterattacks on Zorau were repelled just as successfully on this day. The infantry units of the *Grossdeutschland* Panzer Corps, the remnants of which had fallen behind the Bober River, counterattacked from the south, supported by 20 tanks, against the 24th Rifle Corps' right-flank division. At 1600 in the Wellensdorf area they were met by the 10th Tank Corps' 63rd Tank Brigade, which was moving from Sagan area to the corps' main forces. The enemy's counterattack died out and the attacking German units went over to the defensive.

However, the German Fourth Panzer Army command did not limit itself to its first unsuccessful attempt to restore the defense along the Bober River. On the morning of 15 February an SS police brigade, reinforced with 20 tanks from the remnants of the XXIV Panzer Corps' tank units, was thrown into a counterattack from the Christianstadt area on armored transports, while from the south two infantry regiments and 20 tanks of the "Zimmerman" combat group, which had been formed from the remaining units of the *Grossdeutschland* Panzer Corps, attacked from the south toward Benau.

Upon encountering a powerful rebuff along the 102nd Rifle Corps' right flank, units of the police brigade bypassed this sector and attempted to counterattack Benau from the west. But their counterattacks were repulsed here as well.

The section of the bridgehead between Zorau and Sagan was somewhat more weakly defended, while the sector from the north of Zorau was open altogether. During the latter half of the day an enemy group of forces, which was attacking from the south, turned the 61st Tank Brigade's left flank east of Zorau. The threat of an enemy breakthrough to the Reinswalde area arose.

According to the decision by the commander of the 13th Army, the army's second echelon—the 27th Rifle Corps—was committed along the boundary between the 102nd and 24th rifle corps.

Two of this corps' divisions, which had deployed along the front excluding Benau—Waltersdorf—Wellersdorf and which had begun fighting the enemy group of forces, halted the enemy along this line.

During the fighting that unfolded on 15 February along the bridgehead northeast of Zorau, the Germans managed to close the breach created by the forces of the 4th Tank Army. Thus the 13th Army's forces were forced to try and overcome the enemy's solid defensive front.

By this time three groups of our forces were operating in the enemy rear: the 4th Tank Army's main forces were fighting for bridgeheads along the Neisse River; two regiments of the 121st Rifle Division occupied the areas of Sommerfeld and Gassen, and; the 61st Tank Brigade and a regiment from the 121st Rifle Division, having organized an all-round defense in Zorau, were fighting.

The situation that had arisen by 15 February in the 13th Army's attack sector, was testimony to the fact that the German-Fascist command, which had not been able to prevent the 4th Tank Army's breakthrough to the Neisse River, was now attempting to cut off the rifle formations from the mobile forces and to restore the defensive front along the Bober River, so that upon consolidating along this line, to destroy our forces that had broken through to the Neisse River.

In order to foil this plan, the 13th Army's forces, and units of the 4th Tank Army operating with them, had to quickly break through the defense that had grown up opposite the bridgehead and reach the 4th Tank Army's forces along the Neisse River with their main forces, before the German-Fascist command could undertake the necessary countermeasures.

The 52nd Army's arrival at the Kweis River and the 3rd Guards Tank Army's turn toward Breslau. The offensive by the 52nd and 3rd Guards armies' forces during 12-15 February unfolded in extremely unfavorable conditions. The stubborn fighting, which continued along the bridgehead south of Breslau and along the approaches to the city itself, tied down all of the 6th, 5th Guards and 21st armies' forces. Due to this, as the *front's* right-wing armies moved to the west, the gap between the forces of the *front's* main group and the forces attacking along the *front's* center continually grew. This gap was to have been covered by the 52nd Army, which was attacking along the left flank of the *front's* main shock group. This circumstance led to the significant expansion of the army's offensive sector, which by 12 February had reached 90 kilometers. At the same time, if the 52nd Army's right flank was securely protected all the time by the formations of the 4th Tank and 13th armies, advancing in echelon before it, then its left flank proved to be weakly defended. Two divisions of the 78th Rifle Corps, which had been turned to the south, were attacking along a 40-kilometer sector, which threatened us with major complications in conjunction with the enemy's hurried transfer of significant forces to the Breslau area and to the left wing of the *front's* shock group.

Only the decisive defeat of the enemy in the Breslau area and facing the 5th Guards and 21st armies' bridgehead could change the conditions of the 52nd Army's offensive and, as a whole, that of the *front's* entire shock group. The successful resolution of this task would have enabled us to rapidly bring up the center armies alongside that of the *front's* right wing and pull the 6th Army into the *front's* second echelon, which could fundamentally change the entire situation along the axis of the *front's* main attack.

At such critical moments in an operation the second echelons are usually committed, and if they are employed, the reserves. But since the *front* commander had neither a second echelon nor reserves, he was in an extremely difficult situation. The *front* commander could not decide on resolving the resulting task by bringing in forces from the *front's* left wing, where at that moment active operations were not being conducted, because as the *front's* main forces moved west he became more and more afraid for the stability of the left-wing forces, which were stretched out along a broad front. Their weakening, should the enemy launch a counterattack against the *front's* left wing, threatened the entire *front* with a great amount of unpleasantness. Not risking the weakening of his left wing, the *front* commander had to either forego the defeat of the enemy in the Breslau area, which was also extremely dangerous, because opposite the *front's* center was an enemy group of forces that was growing stronger each day and which could gather forces for an attack against the poorly covered left flank of the *front's* main group of forces, or to temporarily take part of the forces from the main group, so that later, upon defeating the enemy in the Breslau area, more significant forces could be freed up for employment along the axis of the main attack.

Having weighed all of the circumstances, the *front* commander chose the latter option. He decided to temporarily halt the 3rd Guards Tank Army's offensive along the Gorlitz axis and, leaving one tank corps with the 52nd Army, to turn the tank army's main forces to the east for an attack against the flank and rear of the enemy's Breslau group of forces. In the developing situation this was one of the most expedient decisions, although it must inevitably tell negatively on the success of the forces of the *front's* main group.

As a matter of fact, in carrying out the *front* commander's instructions, as early as 12 February the 3rd Guards Tank Army began resolving its assigned task. At this time the main forces of the 52nd Army's 78th Rifle Corps had been dispatched to cover the left flank of the *front's* entire main group of forces. It followed that there remained only three divisions from the 48th Rifle Corps, a division from the 78th Rifle Corps and the 3rd Guards Tank Army's 6th Guards Tank Corps to attack along the 52nd Army's main offensive axis. Naturally, this circumstance led to a noticeable reduction in the pace of the 52nd Army's offensive west of the Bober River.

The right-flank 48th Rifle Corps, while attacking in conjunction with the 13th Army, overcame comparatively easily the enemy's resistance between the Bober and Kweis rivers, but while forcing the Kweis River on 13 February the enemy put up increasingly strong resistance. Nevertheless, as a result of the day's fighting the 48th Rifle Corps occupied all of the nearby points on the left bank of the river in its attack zone.

On the following day the enemy, having brought up several infantry battalions, with tanks and assault artillery, became more active in the offensive zone and repeatedly counterattacked, with the intention of throwing the corps' units back across to the right bank of the Kweis River. Throughout the entire day the fighting continued along the line occupied the previous evening by our forces. The corps' formations, having repulsed all of the enemy's infantry and tank attacks, which supported by aviation, once more attacked and during 15 February they advanced another six kilometers to the west.

The offensive unfolded more slowly in the Bunzlau area. The enemy, having concentrated more significant forces here and relying on terrain sectors favorable to the defense, fought with particular stubbornness. In order to guarantee the more rapid development of the 52nd Army's offensive along the Gorlitz axis, the 3rd Guards Tank Army's 6th Guards Tank Corps, which had arrived at the left bank of the Bober River on 12 February in the Strans area and to the south, was turned to the south on the instructions of the *front* commander, with orders to attack toward Gorlitz and capture it by the morning of 13 February.

During 13-14 February the corps, while repelling enemy counterattacks, was engaged in heavy fighting along the approaches to Naumburg and the crossings over the Kweis River. The Germans fought for each inhabited locale with extreme stubbornness, holding up the tank units' advance toward Gorlitz. We were able to force the Kweis River only in the Neudorf area, but our units were not able to advance beyond this place. The enemy had already prepared a defensive line along the entire left bank of the Kweis River and, relying on it, through fire and counterattacks prevented us from either widening the bridgehead in the Neudorf area or forcing the river along other sectors. On 15 February the corps managed to capture Naumburg and Gissmandorf, but on this day was unable to break through over the Kweis River toward Gorlitz.

The 78th Rifle Corps' 31st Rifle Division, which had arrived with part of its strength at the Kweis River in the Neudorf area by the close of 15 February, was also halted on its right bank.

Thus due to the departure of the 3rd Guards Tank Army's main forces for Breslau and the resulting weakening of the left flank of the *front's* main group of forces, the pace of our forces' advance along the Gorlitz axis began to fall noticeably.

The offensive by the army's left-flank formations during these days had almost completely halted. On 12 February the 78th Rifle Corps' main forces, which were stretched out along a front from Thomaswaldau to Liegnitz and lacking the forces to attack along such an extended front, temporarily set about consolidating their line.

The further success of the offensive from this area to the south depended upon the considerable reinforcement of the shock group's left wing, or the successful advance by the armies of the *front's* central group of forces from the Breslau area. It was impossible to carry out one or the other until the completion of the defeat of the Germans' Breslau group of forces, the elimination of which was being drawn out and into which two of the 3rd Guards Tank Army's corps, aside from the 6th and 5th Guards armies, had been drawn. Thus the commander of the 52nd Army, with the permission of the *front* commander, made the decision to temporarily consolidate along the line reached and hold it until the arrival here of reserves from other sectors of the front.

One of the first measures adopted in this regard by the *front* commander was the transfer to the Liegnitz area of the 52nd Army's 73rd Rifle Corps from the Breslau area, where it had occupied defensive positions for some time along the right bank of the Oder. One of the corps' divisions (294th) was left in the Breslau area and operationally subordinated to the commander of the 6th Army.

The first stage of the *front's* right-flank armies' offensive activities concluded in battles for the seizure and expansion of bridgeheads on the Bober and Kweis rivers.

As a result of eight days of fighting (8-15 February), the forces of the *front's* main shock group overcame the enemy's Oder defensive line along a 150-kilometer front from the mouth of the Faule Obra River near Odereck, to Malcz, defeated the enemy's main forces defending along this line and, in pursuing their remnants, reached the Bober and Kweis rivers. Upon encountering the organized resistance of the newly-arrived enemy reserves, the *front's* right-wing armies pitched into battle against them and forced the Bober and Kweis rivers along a number of sectors and began fighting to expand the seized bridgeheads.

At this time the 4th Tank Army's forces, having thrust forward, reached the Neisse River along a number of sectors and, having been cut off by the enemy from the combined-arms armies, were fighting in the enemy's rear. The forces of the 3rd Guards Tank Army, which remained along the Gorlitz axis, could not cut loose from the infantry and were fighting in close coordination with the 52nd Army's formations.

In eight days of attacking through wooded and, in places, swampy, terrain in the difficult conditions of the spring thaw, the combined-arms armies of the *front's* right wing conducted a fighting advance of 60-100 kilometers, at an average pace of 8-12 kilometers per day.

The 4th Tank Army, which was attacking at an average pace of 15 kilometers per day, advanced 120 kilometers during this time.

The stubborn resistance by the enemy's Breslau group of forces delayed the western movement of the 5th Guards and 21st armies, which were attacking along the center of the front. Because of this, the left wing of the *front's* main group of forces proved to be weakly defended.

The 52nd Army, which by 15 February had deployed along a 120-kilometer front, was forced to go over to the defensive along the sector Bunzlau—Liegnitz.

The enemy, having brought up part of his reserves to the Bober and Kweis rivers, increased his degree of resistance, as a result of which the pace of advance of the *front's* main group of forces fell sharply. In order to eliminate the danger of the operation's dying out, it was necessary to commit fresh forces into the battle along the *front's* right wing. But because all the *front's* forces were engaged from the very beginning of the operation, the *front* command lacked available reserves at the moment of the fighting along the Bober and Kweis rivers. Under the circumstances, there was only one choice—to speed up the elimination of the enemy's Breslau group of forces in every way, to free up the 6th Army and bring up the 5th Guards and 21st armies to the forces along the *front's* right wing.

In assigning great significance to the resolution of these tasks, the *front* commander, as is known, decided on 12 February to forego employing the 3rd Guards Tank Army along the axis of the *front's* main attack and turn it toward Breslau to assist the forces of the 6th and 5th Guards armies.

The Fighting in the First Ukrainian Front's Center. The Encirclement of the German-Fascist Forces in the Breslau Area (8-15 February)

According to the operational plan, the defeat of the enemy's Breslau group of forces was entrusted to the 6th, 5th Guards and 21st armies.

The 6th Army, following the breakthrough of the enemy's main defensive zone in the Malcz area, was to deploy all of its forces facing east and, by means of an attack through Neumarkt, capture Breslau on the operation's fourth day. After this, it was planned to pull the army into the *front* reserve for its subsequent employment along the axis of the main attack.

The 5th Guards and 21st armies, having begun the offensive three days before the *front's* main shock group, were to reach the line Rosenich (east of Liegnitz)—Striegau—Schweidnitz—Reichenbach by the start of the 6th Army's offensive and thus secure with their activities not only the 6th Army's right flank, but also the left wing of the *front's* entire shock group.

During the operation our troops' offensive in the Breslau area unfolded significantly more slowly than what was called for by the plan, and the *front* command had to make major amendments to the plan during the operation and bring in additional forces for the fight against the enemy's Breslau group of forces.

The 6th Army's offensive (8-12 February). During the operation's first three days the 6th Army's offensive developed successfully. As early as the first half of 8 February the enemy's defense along the axis of the army's main attack was broken through. The army's forces, while pursuing the enemy's demoralized composite detachments and individual battalions, were rapidly developing the offensive to the southwest and south. By the close of the day the army's right-flank formations had reached the outskirts of Liegnitz, while the remaining formations reached the front Greibing—Rausse—Kamese.

On the operation's first day the 7th Guards Mechanized Corps was operating within the infantry's combat formation. On the morning of 9 February the corps, having concentrated all of its forces during the night in the area of Gross Tinza, pushed aside the enemy's small screens along its path and, while not getting drawn into fighting with the enemy's larger units, attacked toward the town of Kant. By the close of the day, as a result of a surprise attack against the Germans, the corps broke into the town and captured several inhabited locales around it. The corps' 24th Guards Mechanized Brigade, on orders of the commander of the 6th Army, moved to the line Grendorf—Damsdorf—Peicherwitz—Jerschendorf, in order to cover the army's flank.

Part of the 22nd Rifle Corps' forces, along with the 52nd Army's left-flank formations, was fighting in Liegnitz, while its remaining forces, while bypassing the town from the south, cut the Berlin—Breslau highway in the Neudorf area.

At the same time two of the 74th Rifle Corps' division had deployed facing east and, while overcoming the increasing resistance of the *volkssturm* detachements arriving from Breslau, and that of individual composite battalions, captured Neumarkt. By the close of the day the corps had reached the line Simsdorf—Neumarkt—Ober Stefansdorf—Breitenau.

Due to the fact that all of the 22nd Rifle Corps' formations were tied down in fighting in the Liegnitz area and that the 7th Guards Mechanized Corps was successfully attacking toward

Breslau, a 15-kilometer gap formed between the 22nd and 74th rifle corps. The enemy attempted to take advantage of this gap to launch an attack into the rear of the army's main forces. In order to cover the flank of those forces attacking toward Breslau and to secure the offensive's further development along this axis, the army commander committed his reserve—the 273rd Rifle Division—into the gap between the 22nd and 74th rifle corps, with the idea of subsequently pulling the 22nd Rifle Corps into the army's second echelon. Having thus secured the main group of forces against the enemy's flank attacks, the army commander ordered the commander of the 7th Guards Mechanized Corps to continue the offensive with his main forces in the direction of Rothsurben, with the task of linking up as quickly as possible with the 5th Guards Army. Simultaneously, the commander of the 74th Rifle Corps received orders to capture a crossing over the Striegauer Wasser River in the Deutsch Lissa area, in conjunction with the 7th Guards Mechanized Corps' 26th Guards Mechanized Brigade.

The offensive on 10 February unfolded in a more difficult situation than during the two preceding days.

The German-Fascist command, taking into account the threat hanging over Breslau, was hurriedly transferring here, at first individual combat groups and battalions from neighboring sectors of the front, where our offensive was unfolding slowly and was being conducted with small forces, and on 10 February committed into the fighting the 19th Panzer Division, which had been transferred to Breslau from near Ratibor. The Germans' 8th Panzer Division was already moving up to the Jauer—Striegau area.

When the 7th Guards Mechanized Corps began its offensive from the Kant area toward Rothsurben on 10 February, it had to overcome the already significant resistance of large groups of enemy infantry, supported by tanks from the 19th Panzer Division. By the close of the day the corps' forward brigades nevertheless broke into the Koberwitz area, but then the enemy cut them off from the 6th Army's main forces.

Simultaneous with the fighting along the southwestern approaches to Breslau, stubborn fighting with the Germans' tank units unfolded along the right flank of the 6th Army's main group of forces. The enemy's 19th Panzer Division, in groups of 50-60 tanks and assault guns, counterattacked twelve times during 10-11 February along different sectors of the front from Gross Wandris to Kostenblut, attempting to break through to Neumarkt and eliminate the army's success, which had been achieved during the preceding days. Each counterattack was undertaken by forces from approximately two battalions to a regiment of infantry, with tanks and assault guns. During these two days the enemy managed to push back our units somewhat. However, on 11 February the enemy was halted along the line Gross Baudiss—Kostenblut—Kant by the forces of two of the 7th Guards Mechanized Corps' mechanized brigades and the 309th Rifle Division, the latter of which had arrived from Liegnitz.

In the 74th Rifle Corps' offensive sector, an enemy group of forces, consisting of nine independent battalions with tank and artillery reinforcement, was putting up stubborn resistance, as a result of which our forces' advance along this axis was insignificant.

By the close of 11 February the army's forces broke through the enemy's defense to a depth of 35-40 kilometers, while the 7th Guards Mechanized Corps' forward units had advanced up to 50 kilometers. The overall length of the army's offensive front reached 100 kilometers by the close of 11 February. At the same time, up to half of all its formations had deployed on the army's right flank along a 60-kilometer sector from Liegnitz to Kant. Because of this, the forces for developing the offensive along the axis of the main attack were clearly insufficient and the pace of the troops' attack declined sharply. At the same time the enemy became more active opposite the extended flanks of the attacking forces, particularly opposite the right flank, where the enemy was launching continuous counterattacks, raising fears for the security of the successes achieved along the axis of the main attack. In order to consolidate these successes, gather the army into a fist and to secure a superiority of force along the axis of the main attack, it was necessary to free up the 22nd Rifle Corps, which was fighting in the Liegnitz area and to regroup it along the main axis.

On the orders of the *front* commander of 11 February, it was necessary to carry out the regrouping over the course of a single day. In order to better organize the regrouping, the concentration of forces along the axis of the main attack and to prepare the troops for resolving the latest tasks that had arisen during the course of the operation, the army commander, with the permission of the *front* commander, decided to temporarily halt the offensive along the entire front and, having consolidated along the lines reached, carry out during the course of a single day all of the necessary measures for launching new attacks against the enemy.

Order No. 273 of 11 February had enormous significance for the cause of mobilizing the army's rank and file of resolving the latest tasks that had arisen during the course of the operation. The order noted the successes that the 6th Army's forces had achieved during the operation's first days and expressed thanks to the troops for their heroism and courage manifested by them in seizing the towns of Neumarkt and Kant. The army's soldiers, officers and generals assured the Communist Party and the Soviet government, at numerous gatherings and meetings conducted in all units and formations, that they would justify the trust shown them and put all their efforts into resolving the tasks assigned to them by the command.

On 12 February and all night of 12-13 February the troops' regrouping and concentration in new areas were carried out.

The 22nd Rifle Corps, following its relief by units of the 52nd Army, was moved from the Liegnitz area and transferred to the Kant area. The corps' 309th Rifle Division, having relieved the 7th Guards Mechanized Corps' 24th and 26th guards mechanized brigades during the night of 11-12 February, occupied defensive positions along a broad 35-kilometer front: Gross Baudiss—Jerschendorf—Kostenblut—Kant—Puschwitz. The 218th Rifle Division and all the reinforcements attached to the corps had been concentrated by the morning of 13 February in the Kant area, from where the corps was to launch its main attack on Breslau.

The 74th Rifle Corps consolidated along the line Puschwitz—Schlaupe in readiness to continue attacking toward Breslau.

The 273rd Rifle Division was occupying its previous line along the army's extreme right flank and was ready to develop the offensive to the south.

The 7th Guards Mechanized Corps' 24th and 26th guards mechanized brigades, following their relief by units of the 22nd Rifle Corps, broke through the enemy's defense with a concentrated attack on 12 February and, while attacking to the southeast, by the close of the day had reached the Domslau area. Here they established communications with the remaining units of the 7th Guards Mechanized Corps, which at this time were located in the Wiltschau—Rothsurben area.

The 7th Guards Mechanized Corps, all the units of which had concentrated in the Domslau—Wiltschau—Rothsurben area, controlled the enemy's roads leading from Breslau to the southwest.

Elements of the 77th Fortified Area, which had been transferred to the 6th Army on 10 February, were covering the northern bank of the Oder from Praukau to the village of Kottwitz.

This was the 6th Army's situation by the morning of 13 February.

As can be seen from the above, the regrouping that was carried out enabled us to reduce the overall length of the army's attack front, to free up a significant part of its forces for employment along the axis of the main attack and to secure the right flank. However, actively operating enemy groups of forces continued to tie down up to half the army's formations along both flanks. Thus in order to secure the further development of the offensive toward Breslau and to free up additional forces for resolving the main task, it was necessary, simultaneous with the launching of an attack to the east, to defeat the enemy's flank groups of forces quickly and to expand the offensive front along the axis of the main attack.

The efforts of the army's main forces were directed toward resolving these tasks during 13-15 February.

The 5th Guards Army's offensive (8-12 February). The 5th Guards Army, during the fighting to expand the bridgehead it had seized, prepared and on 5 February began its attack according to the plan for the *front* operation.

The failure of the *front's* left-wing forces and the resulting turn of the 21st Army's main forces to the south made it necessary to expand the 5th Guards Army's offensive front by weakening its shock group. At the same time, the enemy, during the extended fighting in the area of our bridgehead, was continually strengthening his group of forces to the south of Breslau. By the start of the offensive the 269th Infantry Division, several combat groups, five independent battalions, including two panzer battalions, an NCO school, and several police companies were defending opposite the 5th Guards Army. During 2-9 February units of the 254th Infantry Division from army group "Heinrici" were transferred to the army's left flank in the Borau area.

Insofar as the offensive unfolded, for the most part, along the roads, along which was located an unbroken chain of inhabited locales, the enemy, relying on these locales, was able to put up stubborn resistance to our units with limited forces.

During the entire course of the fighting along the approaches to Breslau, the 5th Guards Army's forces had to literally take each inhabited locale from the enemy. Thus from the first day the army's offensive took on the character of a planned and methodical gnawing through the enemy's defense, with frequent regroupings of forces from one sector to another.

As was earlier noted, during the fighting for the bridgehead the 5th Guards Army deployed and committed three corps into the battle and by 8 February had reached the line excluding the Jungfernsee—Seifersdorf—Klein Peskerau—Kurcz—Grossburg—Lorzendorf. The width of the army's attack sector reached 40 kilometers. By this time the axis of the main attack had shifted from the left flank to the sector of the 32nd Guards Rifle Corps, which, upon deploying facing northwest, was attacking in the general direction of Rothsurben and Domslau.

During the army's offensive to the northwest, the enemy continued to throw new units and elements to this sector of the front, reinforcing them with tanks and assault guns. As early as 9 February the 32nd Guards Rifle Corps had to withstand a serious fight with the counterattacking units of the "Kurt" divisional combat group, which had been brought up the day before to the corps' offensive sector and which attacked toward Klein Peskerau on the morning of 9 February. The enemy's counterattacks were repeated several times during the offensive's subsequent days. Many inhabited locales changed hands several times.

The fighting for the inhabited locales demanded a large amount of artillery and ammunition, while the shortage of ammunition in the army was being felt very strongly by this time. In order to make up for this shortage, on the night of 10-11 February the *front* commander ordered the transfer of the 3rd Guards Mortar Division, which was supplied with ammunition, from the 21st Army to the 5th Guards Army. During the following days the rocket artillery rendered considerable aid to the combined-arms formations.

During 8-11 February the army's offensive developed very slowly. The army, while advancing in stubborn fighting 1-2 kilometers per day along some sectors, and even less in others, penetrated, on the whole, 3-5 kilometers during these days.

The successful advance of the 6th Army, which was trying to outflank Breslau from the northwest, forced the enemy on 11 February and the night of 11-12 February to transfer part of his forces from the 5th Guards Army's front against the 6th Army, which immediately told on the activities of the 5th Guards Army's forces. All of the army's formations, which up until then had been engaged in uninterrupted offensive fighting with little success, advanced to the northwest to a depth of four kilometers on 12 February and threw the enemy out of 12 inhabited locales.

The 4th Guards Tank Corps, which was attacking in close coordination with the 32nd Guards Rifle Corps' divisions, on that day leaped forward with part of its forces and began fighting along the southern approaches to Weigwitz and Rothsurben.

In order to speed up the encirclement of the Breslau group of forces, on 11 February the *front* commander ordered the operational subordination of the 31st Tank Corps from the 21st Army to the commander of the 5th Guards Army, in order to augment the efforts of the army's forces along the axis of its main attack. On 12 February the 31st Tank Corps was committed into the fighting along the 33rd Guards Rifle Corps' sector, with the immediate objective of capturing the Bogenau area.

By the close of 12 February the army had captured the line of the southern outskirts of the Jungfernsee—Rorau—Bismarcksfeld—Rorkwell—Libethal and was fighting for Rothsurben and Bogenau along the army's right flank and center, while it was holding its previous positions along the left flank.

As a result of the 5th Guards Army's advance to the northwest and the 6th Army's deep breakthrough toward the approaches to Breslau from the west, the very important railroad and road junction and major industrial center and capital of Lower Silesia, Breslau, which had been transformed by the Germans into a fortress on the Oder, was under threat of encirclement.

The completion of the encirclement of the German-Fascist forces in the Breslau area (13-15 February). So as to prevent the encirclement of Breslau, the German-Fascist command created the densest grouping of its forces here from the first days of fighting in this area. During the fighting the "Breslau" corps group was uninterruptedly strengthened with march reinforcements and individual units by weakening the neighboring sectors, and upon the start of the offensive by the *front's* shock group and the 6th Army's turn toward Breslau, the enemy's 19th and 8th panzer divisions were dispatched here.

The 19th Panzer Division's forward units began to arrive in the Breslau area as early as the evening of 8 February, and on 10 February its main forces attacked the 6th Army.

Almost simultaneous with the 19th Panzer Division, the transfer of the 8th Panzer Division to the Jauer—Striegau area began. Its forward units appeared in the Striegau area as early as 9 February and within a few days its main forces reached the area. By 12 February the entire 254th Infantry Division was fighting opposite the left flank of the 5th Guards Army.

The enemy's significant strengthening in the Breslau area sharply was sharply altering the correlation of forces and creating additional difficulties in carrying out the *front* command's plan for encircling and defeating the Germans' Breslau group of forces. In order to maintain a favorable correlation of forces for us and to successfully resolve the task of defeating the enemy's Breslau group of forces, it was necessary to immediately reinforce the forces of the 6th and 5th Guards armies with reserves. However, as is known, by this time it had also become vitally necessary to reinforce the *front's* main group of forces with reserves, while at the same time forces for strengthening the situation along the 52nd and 6th armies' extended joint flanks were needed. Thus it was not possible to carry out this task, without weakening the *front's* main group of forces.

Above we examined the conditions and reasons that led the *front* commander to the conclusion that the main task facing the *front* could be resolved only by defeating the enemy beforehand in the Breslau area. The resolution of this task would open the way for the 5th Guards and 21st armies' forces to quickly close to the *front's* right-flank armies and to free up the 6th Army, which could be employed for augmenting the efforts of the main shock group.

One of the chief measures for achieving this goal was the turning of the 3rd Guards Tank Army (minus one corps) from the Gorlitz axis to the Breslau axis. For this purpose, the 6th Army's 22nd Rifle Corps was relieved in the Liegnitz area by the 52nd Army's forces and moved to the Kant area for an attack toward the 5th Guards Army's forces, while the 5th Guards Army was reinforced with the 31st Tank Corps for developing the offensive toward the 6th Army's forces. In turn, by this time the commander of the 5th Guards Army had carried out an internal regrouping of the army's forces, having made the combat formations thicker along the axis of the main attack.

The realization of all these measures would create favorable prerequisites for the successful conclusion of the enemy's encirclement in the Breslau area and the strengthening of the situation along the left flank of the *front's* right-wing armies.

In accordance with the adopted decision, on the morning of 12 February the *front* commander assigned the commander of the 3rd Guards Tank Army the task of launching a vigorous attack in the general direction of Weidenwerder and Ossich with the forces of his 9th Mechanized and 7th Guards Tank corps and, in conjunction with the 6th and 5th Guards armies and particularly with the 7th Guards Mechanized and 31st Tank corps, that had been operationally subordinated to them, to defeat the enemy's Breslau group of forces.

The 9th Mechanized Corps, which had received orders to attack in the direction of Goldberg, Jauer and Striegau (15 kilometers southeast of Jauer), in order to destroy the enemy in these areas and consolidate there, began to carry them out on the morning of 12 February. Having carried out a vigorous rush in the indicated direction, by the close of the day the corps had captured the town of Jauer and reached the line Jauer—Guchdorf. By this time the 7th Guards Tank Corps, which was attacking in the direction of Kant, had reached the Damsdorf—Hertwigswaldau—Weidenwerder area with its main forces, while a forward battalion had arrived at the Ossich area. The 56th Guards Tank Brigade, along with the 16th Self-Propelled Artillery Brigade, was engaged in fighting on this day in the Goldberg area, which it captured on 13 February.

On 13 February the army's forces continued to develop the offensive to the east. The 9th Mechanized Corps captured Striegau from the march and by the close of the day had begun fighting on the crossings over the Striegauer Wasser River south of the town. The 7th Guards Tank Corps, which had been ordered to attack the flank of the Germans' 19th Panzer Division and reach the Kant—Schlantz—Yorckschwert area, had crushed the enemy's resistance with its forward units in the Neuhof area and, while developing the offensive, forced the Striegauer Wasser River with its main forces in the Ober Struse area. By the close of the day the corps' main forces had begun fighting for the crossing over the Weistritz River, a half kilometer south of Kant.

In order to consolidate the tank troops' success, the 6th Army commander moved into the Striegau area the 273rd Rifle Division, whose main forces deployed along the line Striegau—Laasan during the second half of the day, while part of its forces occupied Ossich. Simultaneously, the 22nd Rifle Corps, which had been concentrated along the axis of the 6th Army's main attack, having taken advantage of the distraction of the enemy's forces fighting the 3rd Guards Tank Army, attacked from the front Kant—Gross Golau to the east and southeast, with the idea of linking up with the 5th Guards Army's forces. As a result of these battles, which became quite intense in some areas, by the close of the day the corps' main forces had reached the line Domslau—Zweibrodt—Smolz. The 74th Corps, taking advantage of the 22nd Rifle Corps' success, advanced its right flank as far as Kriptau.

On 13 February the 5th Guards Army's offensive developed more successfully than in the preceding days. Although the enemy's resistance and his counterattacks not only did not cease, but increased even as the space dividing the 5th Guards Army's forces from those of the 6th Army shrank, the 4th Guards and 31st tank corps overcame the distance separating them from units of the 7th Guards Mechanized Corps, and, having advanced five kilometers to the north, established immediate contact with them in the Rothsurben area. Due to the linking up of the 6th and 5th Guards armies' mobile forces, the enemy's main withdrawal routes from the Breslau area to the west had been cut.

The 32nd Guards Rifle Corps, taking advantage of the tank formations' success, advanced behind them. The 34th Guards Rifle Corps' offensive was unfolding successfully.

On this day the Soviet troops' combat élan was in particular evidence. The moment of the two armies' meeting in the rear of the enemy's group of forces being surrounded by them was approaching.

A completely different picture could be observed in the enemy's camp. The German forces, as a result of enormous losses and the uninterrupted withdrawal, were in a depressed state. Seeing the pointlessness of further fighting, German soldiers voluntarily abandoned their combat sectors, deserted and gave themselves up. In order to force the soldiers to fight, punishment elements were located behind the combat formations, which would shoot down everyone who tried to avoid fighting. A large amount of motor vehicles and other vehicles, people and establishments that had not been able to evacuate in time piled up on the roads leading out of Breslau and to the southwest. Many people, having lost the hope of breaking through to the west, were returning to the city.

During the night of 13-14 February formations of the 32nd Guards Rifle Corps reached Rothsurben and occupied Gallen (three kilometers west of Rothsurben), having linked up here with units of the 7th Guards Mechanized Corps. The last road linking the enemy's Breslau group of forces with the German army's remaining forces had been finally cut. The Breslau area and the forces remaining there had been encircled.

The command of German Army Group Center ordered the commanders of those formations operating opposite the forces of the 5th Guards and 21st armies to gather all their forces located in the area to the southwest of Breslau and to break through the Soviet forces' encirclement front around Breslau with a concentrated attack. But it was already too late. As a result of the linkup by the forces of the 6th and 5th Guards armies, our forces' offensive front was shrinking and forces were being freed up for creating a sturdy outer encirclement ring.

On 14 February the 6th Army's 22nd Rifle Corps threw the enemy forces back to the outskirts of Breslau. The enemy's units defending opposite the 6th Army's left flank, fearing encirclement in the area to the northwest of Deutsch Lissa, began to fall back to Breslau under the cover of rearguards. The 74th Rifle Corps, which together with units of the 77th Fortified Area took up the pursuit, pushed aside the Germans' rearguards and by the end of the day had reached the line excluding Deutsch Lissa—Gross Breza—Brandschutz.

The forces of the 5th Guards Army, while continuing to attack toward Breslau from the south with its main forces, and with part of its forces operating along the external front, by the close of the day had reached the line Kraftborn—Reppline—Domslau—Magnitz—Wiltschau.

The successful conclusion of the enemy's encirclement in the Breslau area was the result of a skillfully executed maneuver by the 6th and 5th Guards armies and the 3rd Guards Tank Army's bold turn toward Breslau, as well as the result of these armies' close coordination, which was organized by the *front* commander and his staff, and the troops' skillful and decisive actions.

However, as the entire preceding experience of the Great Patriotic War showed, the rapid elimination of the encircled enemy was only possible in conditions when the measures for splitting up and destroying him are conducted simultaneously with the completion of the encirclement and comprise a single and uninterrupted process. The experience of Budapest[1] showed that if the enemy's encircled group of forces is not immediately broken up into parts and not eliminated in detail while the encirclement is being concluded or immediately upon the completion of the encirclement, then the fighting against this group of forces gets drawn out for a lengthy period of time and draws off significant forces.

Knowing and taking into account this experience, the *front* commander nevertheless made the decision to leave limited forces behind in the Breslau area. By consciously deciding to extend the

---

1   The encirclement of the German-Fascist forces in Budapest ended on 26 December 1944, while the elimination of the enemy's encircled group of forces concluded only on 13 February 1945.

fighting in the Breslau area, he dispatched the maximum amount of forces for operations along the external front, where the fate of the operation was being decided. The *front* commander entrusted the defeat of the encircled enemy group of forces in Breslau to the 6th Army, which consisted of two corps, while removing the 5th Guards Army's formations from the battle and directing them to the external front. Here part of the army's forces were to relieve the 3rd Guards Tank Army's formations and create a solid external front along the boundary with the 52nd Army, while its main forces were to defeat the remnants of corps group "Breslau" and units of the 19th Panzer Division, which had evaded encirclement which were operating opposite the army's front. It was decided to immediately turn the 3rd Guards Tank Army toward the Gorlitz axis.

If one takes into account the fact that the enemy along the external front still had significant forces and that he, while trying to relieve his surrounded group of forces, was continuing to reinforce his forces in the area southeast of Breslau, then it will become obvious that the turn of our forces to the external front for repelling the enemy's possible attempts to break through to the encircled group of forces was quite expedient. At the same time, it would enable us to free up the 3rd Guards Tank Army for operations along the axis of the main attack.

In accordance with the decision adopted, the *front* commander ordered the commander of the 5th Guards Army to transfer the 10th Anti-Tank Brigade, which was operating with the 5th Guards Army, to the area south of Liegnitz, with the task of taking up defensive positions by the morning of 15 February along the front Goldberg—Jauer. By the close of the same day the 32nd Guards Rifle Corps' 13th Guards Rifle Division was to reach the Wutende Noisse River. The division had the task of occupying the defensive line along the front Donau—Bremberg—Jauer and to securely hold it until the arrival of the 5th Guards Army's main forces.

The *front* commander ordered the 34th Guards Rifle Corps' 118th Rifle Division out of the line in the Breslau area and, together with one anti-tank artillery regiment, to transfer it by dawn on 15 February to the area south of Kant, with the task of preventing the enemy's breakthrough to that town.

The 5th Guards Army's main forces were ordered to make a decisive attack from the Magnitz area toward Koberwitz and then to the southwest and to defeat the German formations operating opposite the 32nd and 33rd guards rifle corps.

The 32nd Guards Rifle Corps was reinforced with the 14th Guards Rifle Division, which was taken from the 33rd Guards Rifle Corps' left flank. Its combat sector was occupied by forces of the 21st Army on orders from the *front* commander.

In carrying out this order, the commander of the 5th Guards Army assigned tasks to the above-listed formations and also determined the character of the tank corps' subsequent activities.

The 4th Guards Tank Corps was to develop the offensive in the general direction of Schlantz and Morschelwitz and Saarau, with the task of reaching the Saarau—Schweitnitz—Gross Merzdorf area on 15 February and here securely cover the operations of the army's main forces from the south and southwest.

The 31st Tank Corps received orders to continue the offensive toward Koberwitz and Jordansmuhl and on 15 February capture the area Naselwitz—Jordansmuhl—Stein. With the corps' arrival in the rear of the enemy group of forces operating opposite the 5th Guards Army and the 21st Army's right flank, it was to assist them in developing the offensive to the west.

In accordance with the adopted decision and the orders issued, the forces of the 3rd Guards Tank, 5th Guards and 6th armies began their subsequent combat operations.

As was already noted, the efforts of the 3rd Guards Tank Army's forces had been turned to resolving tasks along the axis of the *front's* main attack. In accordance with this, the army received orders to reach the Bober River for developing the offensive further toward Gorlitz. However, the fulfillment of these orders was somewhat delayed as a result of the sharply changed situation in the area where units of the 3rd Guards Tank Army were operating.

On the morning of 14 February the 7th Guards Tank Corps' main forces were located in the Kant area, where the troops were putting themselves in order, repairing their equipment and preparing to leave at 1500 for the Lewenberg area (on the Bober River). Part of the corps' forces was already en route to the Bober River.

The 9th Mechanized Corps, which before this day had been operating in the Jauer—Striegau—Guchdorf area, had already begun to regroup toward the Gorlitz axis. Thus the 3rd Guards Tank Army's regrouping to the 52nd Army's sector had begun even before the arrival in the latter's operational area of the 5th Guards Army's formations, which, in accordance with the *front* commander's order, were to begin relieving the tank troops from the morning of 15 February.

The tank troops' premature abandonment of their combat positions and the unsatisfactory conduct of reconnaissance in the army's operational area led to a situation in which by the middle of 14 February, when the 9th Mechanized Corps' main forces had already left their positions, they were unexpectedly attacked from the south by tanks of the Germans' 8th Panzer Division. The division, taking advantage of the hilly and wooded terrain, which was favorable for hidden movement, had concentrated in the areas of Waldenburg and Frieburg and, unexpectedly for the 3rd Guards Tank Army's forces, attacked toward Jauer for the purpose of landing a blow against the flank of the *front's* main group of forces.

The 9th Mechanized Corps' 69th Mechanized Brigade was forced to enter the fighting against superior enemy forces along the line Rosen—Guchdorf. An extremely difficult situation arose and the realistic threat of the 8th Panzer Division's breakthrough in the area of the town of Liegnitz. This danger was eliminated only thanks to the fact that the army commander managed to comparatively quickly gather the main forces of the 9th Mechanized and 7th Guards Tank corps into a fist. The battle against the counterattacking enemy continued throughout 14-15 February. It was only during the latter half of 15 February that it became clear that the German 8th Panzer Division, which had suffered significant losses during the two-day battle, no longer represented a serious force. Thus on 15 February the decision was made to begin regrouping the 7th Guards Tank Corps from the Striegau area to the 52nd Army's offensive sector.

In order to prevent repeating the mistakes made on 14 February, the *front* commander ordered the commander of the 3rd Guards Tank Army not to move the 9th Mechanized Corps from the Goldberg—Jauer—Striegau area until the arrival of the 5th Guards Army's formations to that area.

Throughout 15 February the forces of the 6th Army and the 5th Guards Army's 34th Guards Rifle Corps continued to battle the Germans' encircled group of forces in the Breslau area, while the 5th Guards Army's main forces, carrying out their assignments, reached by the end of the day the line Kammendorf—Yorckschwert—Jakschenau, increasing the gap between the encircled group of forces and the German army's main forces up to 13 kilometers.

In the following days, simultaneously with the development of the offensive to the southwest, the further transfer of the army's formations to the areas of Goldberg, Jauer and Striegau continued, for the creation of a solid front of our forces along the left flank of the *front's* main shock group.

The 21st Army's offensive in the area north of Strelen. At the same time as the events described above were unfolding in the Breslau area, the 21st Army, which was operating to the left of the 5th Guards Army, made an attempt to renew the offensive along its right flank and, in conjunction with the 5th Guards Army's left-flank formations, defeat the enemy who had consolidated along the approaches to Borau and Strelen. For this purpose, the *front* commander ordered the army to regroup its forces.

During the period from 8-12 February the 117th Rifle Corps, which had been relieved by the forces of the 59th Army along the sector from the south of Oppeln, was pulled out of the line and transferred to the army's right flank, where, upon relieving the 5th Guards Army's 14th Guards Rifle Division, it occupied a front four kilometers in length. The attack zone of the 118th

Rifle Corps, which was now located to the left of the 117th Rifle Corps, was reduced from 25 to eight kilometers. The 118th Rifle Corps' left-flank 291st Rifle Division, which was occupying a 17-kilometer sector, was transferred to the 55th Rifle Corps, which now occupied the army's entire remaining 80-kilometer front from Wansen to Oppeln. In place of the departed 291st Rifle Division, the 118th Rifle Corps received the 286th Rifle Division, which had been transferred to from the 59th Army by order of the *front* commander.

Thus by means of shortening the overall length of the front occupied by the army and the significant widening of the left-flank 55th Rifle Corps' front, a sufficiently strong shock group had been created along a 12-kilometer sector on the army's right flank. Both corps, which had been concentrated along the right flank, were organized into two echelons, having two divisions each in the first echelon, and one each in the second. Each of the 117th Rifle Corps' first-echelon divisions had a 2-kilometer front, and those of the 118th Rifle Corps a 4-kilometer front.

The regrouping and relief of the army's forces were conducted in conditions of the enemy's increasing activity. On 8 February the German 20th Panzer Division, which had begun intensive counterattacks against units of the 55th Rifle Corps, which was occupying the salient south of Grottkau, arrived in the Friedewalde area.

Under pressure by the enemy's significantly superior forces along this sector of the front, units of the 55th Rifle Corps had to abandon the salient. On 11 February the 20th Panzer Division's attack was halted along the line Klein Neudorf—Tiefensee.

On 13 February the offensive by the army's shock group began. Having crushed the resistance by units of the 254th and 208th infantry divisions along the line Borau—Wansen in three days, the attacking troops penetrated into the enemy's defense to a depth of 5-10 kilometers and by the close of 15 February had reached the line Borau—Mantze—Gregersdorf—Gurch—Wansen. However, in the succeeding days the offensive pace began to rapidly fall off. The enemy, who disposed of significant defensive forces in the area to the southwest of Breslau, held off the 21st Army's attack and the tactical results achieved did not grow into operational success.

The limited results of the battles can to a significant degree be explained by shortcomings in the artillery offensive, a shortage of ammunition, the absence of tank support, our aviation's limited effect on the enemy, and, finally, the overall weakening of the attacking troops during the course of the preceding battles. The 21st Army's combat operations showed that the army's offensive capabilities had been exhausted and that considerable time was required to restore them.

Review of the Combat Operations by the Front's Left-Wing Armies During 8-15 February

The regrouping of forces from the *front's* left wing to the right, which was carried out before the beginning of the operation, significantly weakened the shock power of the left-wing armies. The fighting for the bridgeheads up to 8 February showed that the *front's* left-wing armies were not in a state to overcome the enemy's main defensive zone and reach the lines indicated by the *front* commander.

One of the not unimportant reasons for the 59th and 60th armies' lack of success was the enemy's extremely stubborn resistance. The German command, while covering the important industrial areas of Czech Silesia and the path to the central areas of Czechoslovakia, created opposite the *front's* left wing quite a dense group of forces sufficient for stubbornly defending the occupied line against those forces disposed of by the 59th and 60th armies.

During 8-10 February along the 59th and 60th armies' front was most active, while at the same time lacking a result from the point of view of territorial gains, fighting took place in the area of our bridgehead north of Ratibor. The failure of the 59th and 60th armies in their attempts to break through the enemy's defense opposite their bridgehead showed the *front* commander the pointlessness of further offensive operations along the *front's* left wing, and he ordered the 59th and 60th armies to temporarily shut down the offensive and to consolidate on the lines reached.

In carrying out the *front* commander's orders, the left-wing armies consolidated along the occupied positions and immediately set about creating defensive lines in the defensive depth. Simultaneous with this, the 59th and 60th armies carried out a regrouping of part of their forces to the bridgehead north of Ratibor, having in mind conducting along this sector of front an offensive for the purpose of improving the occupied positions and simultaneously tying down the enemy's forces along this sector of the front.

During 10-16 February, due to a certain advance by the right-wing forces of the Fourth Ukrainian Front along the Moravska Ostrava axis, the 60th Army's left-flank corps, having gone over to the offensive, advanced several kilometers to the west on the first day. On 10 February the corps threw units of the Germans' 75th Infantry Division out of the town of Pszyna and occupied several inhabited locales west of the town. While continuing during the following days to develop the success of the offensive's first day, on 16 February the corps reached the line Kleszczowa—Pawlowice—Zbytkow, where it was halted by units of the Germans' 97th Light Infantry and 86th and 75th Infantry divisions.

Thus from the first days of the offensive the 59th and 60th armies dropped out of active participation in the operation and were to defend the southern sector of the front and secure the success of the armies attacking along the *front's* center and right wing.

Because of this, on 15 February the 1st Guards Cavalry Corps, which was located in the 60th Army's reserve, was removed from operational subordination to the army, by order of the *front* commander, and received orders to make a forced march and by the morning of 19 February concentrate in the Goldberg—Jauer—excluding Liegnitz area. It was ordered that the tank and mortar regiments on auto transport, which formed part of the corps, be moved to the Neudorf (south of Liegnitz) area by 16 February.

Brief Results of the Operation's First Stage

In eight days of attacking, 8-15 February, the *front's* forces reached the line Grossen—Christianstadt—Sadersdorf (on the Neisse River)—Tribel—Zorau—Sagan—Naumburg (on the Kweis River)—Goldberg—Jauer—Striegau—Kammendorf (five kilometers south of Kant)—Borau—Wansen—Grottkau—Oppeln—excluding Cosel—excluding Ratibor—Rybnik—Zorau—Strumen.

During this period the *front's* right-wing forces advanced in heavy fighting 110 kilometers to the west, reached the Bober River and captured bridgeheads on its left bank.

During the operation such important administrative and industrial centers of Lower Silesia and the province of Brandenburg were captured as Liegnitz, Bunzlau, Sprottau, Grunberg, Sagan, Zorau, Goldberg, and Genau, and tens of other towns and thousands of smaller inhabited locales. The enemy forces defending the main city of Lower Silesia—Breslau—and a major German strong point on the Oder—the town of Glogau—had been surrounded.

A strong fortified defensive line along the Oder River had been overcome along a 250-kilometer front from Odereck to Oppeln. Besides this, the forces of the First Ukrainian Front had cleared the left bank of the Oder of the enemy, who had been defending opposite the First Belorussian Front's left wing, along a 40-kilometer front from Odereck to Grossen.

The German Fourth Panzer Army, which had been defeated in the fighting along the Oder defensive line, withdrew only the remnants of its formations across the Bober and Kweis rivers. The XXIV Panzer Corps, which comprised the army's left wing, suffered enormous losses during the fighting between the Oder and Bober rivers. The corps' main forces had been defeated and partially surrounded by the forces of the 3rd Guards Army in the Glogau area. The corps' remaining formations had been defeated during their withdrawal to the Bober River. Only the remnants of combat groups, which here became part of the Ninth Army's XL Panzer Corps under the name of "Nehring," retreated behind the river north of Naumburg. The *Grossdeutschland* Panzer Corps, which was being pursued by the forces of the 4th Tank and 13th armies, although it had suffered major losses, nevertheless managed to pull back its main forces under the cover of rearguards to the left bank of the Bober and Kweis rivers to the Zorau—Sagan area. The LVII Panzer Corps, which had also suffered greatly, had been thrown back to the south by the forces of the 52nd and 6th armies to the line Bunzlau—Liegnitz—Kant.

The German Fourth Panzer Army, which had been split up into three parts during our offensive, was unable to create a solid defensive front along the Bober and Kweis rivers. Two large gaps formed, almost unguarded by German forces–the sector along the Bober River from Christianstadt to Sagan, and the sector along the Kweis River between Eisenberg and Borgsdorf. This enabled the *front's* forces to force the Bober and Kweis rivers from the march and to encounter the enemy's arriving reserves to the west of these rivers.

The significant results achieved by the *front's* forces during the first stage of the operation were achieved at the cost of enormous physical and moral efforts by the troops and the command at all levels. Only the *front* rank and file's unbending will to victory, mass heroism and high political consciousness, and the skillful and flexible leadership of the troops during the operation enabled us to achieve such results.

The combat activities of the *front's* forces during the first stage of the operation were suffused with the spirit of dynamic struggle. The prolongation of the fighting in the Breslau area, which prevented us from moving the 6th Army into the *front's* second echelon, as had been foreseen by the operational plan, the need for which was particularly felt in conditions of a rapidly changing and increasingly complex situation, required of the *front* commander and his staff a particularly thoughtful approach to the problem of the rational employment of all the forces of the *front* that had been drawn into the battle along its entire offensive sector. In this regard, the flexible maneuver of men and materiel during the operation is worthy of attention, as are the bold regroupings of forces from one axis to another, where at one moment or another tasks were being resolved which were determining the fate of the entire operation or the outcome of the fighting along one of the axes. In order to confirm this, it is sufficient to refer to the *front* commander's bold decision to turn the 3rd Guards Tank Army from the Gorlitz axis toward Breslau, to the *front* commander's instructions and the army commanders' decisions during the fighting for the bridgeheads along the Bober and Kweis rivers, to the maneuver by the 4th Tank Army during the encirclement of the enemy west of Gulau, and to the maneuver of the 6th and 5th Guards armies during the encirclement of Breslau.

Combat activities during this period were also characterized by skillful coordination, both between the armies and within them. Examples of this may be the coordination between the 4th Tank and 13th armies during the offensive toward the Bober River and during the fighting for the bridgeheads on the left bank of this river, that of the 3rd Guards Tank and 6th and 5th Guards armies during the encirclement of Breslau, and a large number of other facts testifying to the high skill of the command and troops. If one takes into account that offensive operations unfolded in conditions of the rivers' spring flooding, in wooded and, in places, swampy, terrain, the fact that the offensive was primarily conducted along paved roads and through inhabited locales, in which the enemy put up stubborn resistance throughout the entire period, maximally employing artificial and natural obstacles favorable to the defense—if one takes all of this into account, it would be difficult to overestimate the results achieved by the *front's* forces.

However, despite these successes, the pace of the operation's development and the deadlines for the *front's* forces fulfilling their tasks lagged significantly behind the deadlines called for by the operational plan. For example, by 15 February along the axis of the main attack, that is, on the operation's eighth day, the troops had approximately carried out the assignment for the fifth day.

It follows that the pace of the offensive along the axis of the main attack proved to be lower than planned and that during the final days indications of the operation's expiration appeared.

This difference between the planned and actual operational pace is even more clearly visible in the example of the 5th Guards and 21st armies. Instead of the planned offensive pace of five kilometers per day, the 5th Guards and 21st armies attacked at a pace of less than a kilometer per day. As for the left-wing armies, they did not advance at all.

The *front's* failure to carry out the tasks called for by the operational plan may be explained by a variety of reasons.

Due to the sharp lagging behind by the left-wing armies and the insignificant advance by our forces south of Breslau, the overall length of the front rose to 520 kilometers. This led to a significant decline in the troops' operational density.

Despite the fact that during the operation's preparatory period the *front's* and armies' advance depots had been partially brought closer to the troops, the main supply bases continued to lag behind at a distance of hundreds of kilometers from the front line. The pace of railroad restoration lagged badly behind the pace of the troops' advance. For this reason the delivery of all kinds of combat supplies to the troops was realized with enormous difficulty. The minimal norm of ammunition and fuel was delivered to the troops only with great exertions.

As a result of the continuous and intensive offensive battles from the moment of the breakthrough of the German defense along the Vistula to the arrival of the *front's* forces at the Bober River, the combat and numerical strength of the *front's* forces was significantly reduced. On 15 February the rifle divisions had an average of 4,600 men each. The tank and mechanized troops lost during this period up to 50 perecent of their equipment. All of this led to a weakening of the *front's* offensive capabilities.

The unfavorable meteorological conditions, the spring washing away of the roads and the wooded and swampy character of the terrain, particularly in the operational zone of the *front's* main group of forces, restricted maneuver by all the combat arms, and particularly that of the mobile formations, which made it necessary to undertake frontal attacks, which led to excessive losses. All of these conditions significantly limited the employment of aviation, because the airfields were out of action and the unfavorable flying weather allowed us to employ our air assets only to a limited degree. For example, the 2nd Air Army, which had 2,382 planes, carried out an average of only 546 sorties per day, that is, no more than 0.2 sorties for each plane.

As a result of the fact that the enemy continually threw his reserves into the attack sector as march reinforcements and entire formations, the correlation of forces in the *front's* offensive sector shifted each day in favor of the enemy. All of this made sharply more difficult the conditions of conducting the operation and made it necessary to tighten up the plans for the *front's* further activities.

B. THE BREAKTHROUGH OF THE GERMAN DEFENSE ALONG THE BOBER AND KWEIS RIVERS AND THE ARRIVAL OF THE FIRST UKRAINIAN FRONT'S RIGHT-WING ARMIES AT THE NEISSE RIVER (16-24 FEBRUARY)

The Situation Along the First Ukrainian Front's Right Wing by 16 February

By 16 February the line of the Bober and Kweis rivers was being defended by three corps of the German Fourth Panzer Army.

Facing the 3rd Guards Army along the sector from the mouth of the Bober River to Christianstadt was the 608th Special Designation Division, along with attached and subordinated reinforcement units, combat groups from the 342nd and 72nd infantry and 16th Panzer divisions, the "Nehring" combat group and, fighting immediately in the Christianstadt area along the boundary between the 3rd Guards and 13th armies were the "Wirt" Police Brigade and the 1st "Dirlewanger" SS Punishment Brigade, and a combat group from the 25th Panzer Division.

All of these formed part of the XL Panzer Corps, which by this time had been transferred from Army Group Vistula to Army Group Center and subordinated to the Fourth Panzer Army.

Facing the 13th Army and the bridgehead occupied by its forces, the above-named brigades were fighting, while along the left flank were fighting the *Grossdeutschland* Panzer Corps' main forces, which at this time consisted of the "Hermann Goring" Panzer Division, the "Brandenburg" Panzergrenadier Division, and the 20th Panzergrenadier Division.

Facing the 52nd Army's right flank were the 21st Panzer Division, which had arrived here from the Western Front, combat groups from the 17th Panzer and 6th *Volksgrenadier* divisions, and a number of small groups. All of these formations and units were united into corps group "Friedrich."

The remaining forces of the Fourth Panzer Army were defending opposite the 52nd Army's left flank, covering the front from Bunzlau to Liegnitz with the remains of the LVII Panzer Corps.

In the Jauer—Striegau area facing the 3rd Guards Tank Army's 9th Mechanized Corps was the Germans' 8th Panzer Division, which had been subordinated to the Seventeenth Army's XVII Panzer Corps since 10 February.

The German command, having committed into the fighting along the line of the Bober and Kweis rivers two SS brigades, the 21st Panzer Division, and having significantly reinforced the 17th Panzer and 6th *Volksgrenadier* divisions, by 15 February had created quite a dense group of men and materiel along this line.

The German Fourth Panzer Army's main forces had been concentrated opposite the center of the *front's* main group of forces along the sector from Christianstadt to Lipschau (on the Kweis River), and it was namely here that the most stubborn and prolonged fighting flared up during the operation's second stage.

The extreme stubbornness and activity with which the German forces fought to hold this sector of the front may be explained by two reasons.

During the war the Christianstadt area had been transformed by the Germans into a major center of military industry. In the town itself and in the woods to the west were located up to ten military factories, including underground ones producing the latest types of weapons. The German-Fascist command had not had time to evacuate these factories.

The threat which had arisen over this area due to the 4th Tank Army's breakthrough to the Neisse River and the capture by the 13th Army of a bridgehead on the western bank of the Bober River had evidently provoked those desperate attempts by the German command to throw our forces from the bridgehead to the right bank of the river, which had taken place during 11-15 February and which continued up to 19 February.

The stubborn defense by the enemy of the sector south of this area facing the 52nd Army's bridgehead over the Kweis River may be explained by the German command's desire to prevent our forces' breaking through to the Neisse River along the Breslau—Berlin highway. In the conditions of the spring washing away of the roads, this broad highway, which would lead our forces into the rear of the Fourth Panzer Army's main group of forces, represented an important defensive site for the German command and the 21st Panzer Division was moved up to cover it.

As can be seen from the above, the enemy, having brought up part of his reserves to the Bober and Kweis rivers, had the opportunity to put up stubborn resistance along the *front's* entire offensive sector. Thus significant efforts were required of the *front's* forces in order to develop the offensive to a depth called for by the operational plan. However, the disposition and condition of the *front's* forces did not correspond to the demands of the situation.

By the middle of February all of the First Ukrainian Front's forces had been deployed in a single echelon along a broad 520-kilometer front. Lacking reserves, the *front* command was not able to augment the efforts of the attacking troops from the depth. The low level of the attacking troops' strength, the significant equipment losses, the great extension of the rear organs, and the enormous difficulties in delivering materiel reduced the *front's* offensive capabilities even further.

Due to the switch of the First Belorussian Front's efforts to fighting the enemy's Pomeranian group of forces and the absence of success along the Fourth Ukrainian Front's offensive sector, these *fronts* could not take part in the offensive to the Elbe in conjunction with the forces of the First Ukrainian Front.

All of this, along with the reinforcement of the enemy in the First Ukrainian Front's offensive sector, forced the *front* command to conclude that under present conditions the *front* could not achieve the earlier planned goal in the near future. Having evaluated the capabilities possessed by the troops by the middle of February, the *front* commander on 16 February reported to the Supreme Commander-in-Chief his thoughts regarding the *front's* further activities. Having laid out the present situation in his report, the *front* commander proposed for the Supreme Commander-in-Chief's confirmation the following plan for the *front's* operations for the near future.

According to this plan, the *front's* main group of forces—3rd Guards, 13th, 4th Tank, and 52nd armies—were to reach the Neisse River, capture bridgeheads on its left bank and securely consolidate along the line reached. The 3rd Guards Tank Army was to capture the Gorlitz area, to bring up part of the 5th Guards Army's forces there, and to consolidate there as well. The left-wing armies (21st, 59th and 60th), along with the 4th Guards and 31st tank corps and supported by part of the 5th Guards Army's forces, were to continue the offensive for the purpose of throwing the enemy back into the Sudeten Mountains and to cover themselves along the axis of the Sudeten Mountains with the forces of the 59th and 60th armies.; the 6th Army was to capture Breslau.

Simultaneously with the resolution of these tasks, the *front* commander planned to restore the railroads in the *front's* rear, move the supply stations closer to the troops, deliver and accumulate supplies of ammunition and fuel, repair combat equipment, and prepare the rear for the unbroken supply of the troops.

The *Stavka* of the Supreme High Command, having examined the *front* commander's ideas, confirmed his proposals and authorized him to end the operation upon the troops' arrival at the line of the Neisse River. The *front's* further activities unfolded in accordance with these instructions and constituted the second stage of the Lower Silesian offensive operation.

The Breakthrough of the German Defense Along the Bober and Kweis Rivers and the Arrival of the Front's Right-Wing Armies at the Neisse River (16-24 February)

Combat operations along the 3rd Guards Army's front. The 3rd Guards Army's forces, having arrived at the Bober River on 15 February, encountered organized resistance from formations of the enemy's XL and remnants of the XXIV panzer corps along the entire front from the mouth of the river to Christianstadt. On this day the army's forces were unable to seize a single bridgehead on the left bank of the Bober River. While persistently striving to achieve the tasks assigned them, the forces of the 21st Rifle Corps, which were attacking along the army's right flank, broke through to the left bank of the Bober River on the night of 15-16 February along a bridge the enemy had not blown up in the area southwest of Grossen, and by the morning had seized a small bridgehead here.

On that day the corps' left-flank division forced the Bober River in the Bobersberg area and broke into the town from the march. Simultaneously with it, the 76th Rifle Corps' right-flank units forced the river. By the end of the day a single bridgehead, shallow but more than ten kilometers in width, had formed in the center of the army's attack sector.

Thus as a result of the 16 February fighting in the 3rd Guards Army's attack sector two bridge-heads had been seized, which would enable us to attack along two axes: to the Neisse River from the bridgehead southwest of Grossen, for the purpose of seizing Guben, a major industrial center and a powerful German strong point on the Neisse River, and toward Sommerfeld from the bridgehead west of Kunow, for the purpose of rolling up the enemy's defense on the Bober River and, together with the 13th Army, to encircle units of the German XL Panzer Corps west of Naumburg.

The enemy, fearing the development of our forces' offensive from the southern bridgehead in the direction of Sommerfeld, began to hurriedly bring up units of the XL Panzer Corps to this bridgehead, in order to eliminate the threat of a flank attack against its forces fighting opposite the 13th Army's bridgehead.

However, on orders by the *front* commander, the commander of the 3rd Guards Army made the decision to launch his attack not in the center, but along the army's right flank, along the Grossen—Guben paved road, for the purpose of capturing Guben and outflanking from the north the enemy's entire group of forces, which was defending between the Bober and Neisse rivers. In accordance with the decision taken, a regrouping of forces was carried out in the army. By the close of the day the 120th Rifle Corps had been brought up to the 21st Rifle Corps' attack sector, and during the night of 16-17 February the 25th Tank Corps was transferred here from the Naumburg area.

Having attacked on the morning of 17 February from the bridgehead southwest of Grossen along the paved road to Guben, the 25th Tank Corps, in conjunction with units of the 21st Rifle Corps, crushed the resistance by units of the "Matterstock" Special Designation Division and advanced 12 kilometers toward Guben during the day and on the following day seized the Forstadt suburb of Guben and had engaged with the enemy on the outskirts of the town.

During these two days the 21st Rifle Corps' right-flank formations were engaged in stubborn fighting for the inhabited locales, relying upon which the enemy was trying to hold the advance by our forces along the left bank of the Oder. Here by the close of 18 February the strong points of Neuendorf and Merzwise were occupied, while fighting continued for the last major strong point along the approaches to the Neisse River—Lindenheim.

As a result of the rapid offensive by the army's right-flank formations and the absence of an advance along the remainder of the front between the shock group's left flank and the army's units operating along the bridgehead west of Kunow, a gap developed. Formations of the 120th Rifle Corps were committed into this gap from the army's second echelon, with the task of reaching the Polo area and from there attacking toward Stargardt, so as to subsequently reach the Neisse River in the area of Gross Gastrose.

In carrying out their assigned task, the 120th Rifle Corps' formations reached the line Polo—Kanig—Grocho by the close of 19 February, while part of its forces had begun fighting along the eastern outskirts of Zaude.

On the night of 19-20 February the remnants of the units of the "Dirlewanger" 1st Punishment Brigade and the 16th Panzer Division's combat group, which numbered up to a regiment of infantry and 20 tanks and which was falling back from the Benau area toward Guben, tried to launch an attack against the flank of our forces that had broken through to Guben, but in the areas of Polo and Kanig ran into the 120th Rifle Corps's formations and got into a fight with them that continued throughout the night and the following day. At first the enemy managed to seize Polo and Kanig, but by the close of 20 February the German units had been thrown out of Kanig, while in the Polo area they were surrounded and then routed.

The arrival of the 120th Rifle Corps at the line Zaude—Polo—Kanig enabled the forces of the army's shock group to concentrate all their efforts toward fighting for Guben and arriving at the Neisse River north of the town.

On 20 February, following an intense two days of fighting for Lindenheim, units of the 120th Rifle Corps, which were attacking along the left bank of the Oder, finally crushed the enemy's resistance in this strong point and occupied it. In the latter half of the day the corps' formations overcame the wooded area northeast of Guben and reached the Neisse River from its mouth as far as Guben.

In the Guben area stubborn fighting broke out with a major German group of forces, which was covering this important German center of resistance on the Neisse River.

The "Matterstock" Special Designation Division, which was defending the town, had been reinforced with a significant amount of artillery and tanks and received an order from Hitler to hold the town to the last man. This order stated, by the way, that the struggle for Guben was the struggle for Berlin and that anyone who tried to retreat from the town would be shot.

The stubbornness with which the enemy defended the town attracted almost all the 3rd Guards Army's forces here over the subsequent days.

At the same time that the 3rd Guards Army's shock group was attacking along the Guben axis, the army's 76th Rifle Corps fought for three days to capture the Germans' powerful Christianstadt strong point on the Bober River. On 20 February this fighting ended with the complete defeat of the German group of forces defending Christianstadt and the capture of the town by Soviet forces.

Taking advantage of the success along the 3rd Guards Army's right flank and along the 13th Army's front, the corps began a pursuit along its entire attack front of the retreating units of the XXIV Panzer Corps' combat group (group "Nehring"), and by the close of 20 February had reached the line Ensdorf—Klein Altwasser.

Thus as a result of the 15-20 February fighting, the 3rd Guards Army, having crushed the enemy's resistance on the Bober River, reached the Neisse River with its right flank along a 10-kilometer front, while in the center and along the left flank it had begun pursuing the defeated enemy, with the immediate objective of reaching the Neisse River along the entire attack front.

Combat operations along the 13th Army's front. The main events during the operation's second stage unfolded in the center of the *front's* shock group in the 13th Army's offensive sector.

By 15 February the forces of the German XL Panzer Corps and the *Grossdeutschland* Panzer Corps had not only managed to cut the communications of the 4th Tank Army's main forces, which had reached the Neisse River, but also to cut off the 121st Rifle Division from the 13th Army's main forces in the Sommerfeld area, and the 61st Tank Brigade in the Zorau area. The enemy's main efforts after this were directed at eliminating our bridgeheads on the left bank of the Bober River north of Sagan.

On 16 February the "Dirlewanger" 1st SS Punishment Brigade was moved to the area north of Benau. Having entered the fighting from the march, this brigade, in conjunction with the 25th Panzer Division's combat group and the German units operating here earlier, attacked toward Benau.

The stubborn fighting that broke out in the area of this major railroad junction continued throughout the first half of 16 February, and only after noon did the units of the 102nd Rifle Corps, under pressure by significantly superior enemy forces, retreat to the eastern and southern outskirts of town.

At the same time, the 121st Rifle Division, on orders of the commander of the 13th Army, having abandoned Sommerfeld, consolidated with two corps in the Gassen area, while one regiment attacked toward Benau from the west. The German brigade, outflanked by our forces on three sides, halted all further attacks to the east and began to hurriedly consolidate in Benau, while simultaneously detaching part of its forces for repelling our attacks from the west. Taking advantage of this, units of the 102nd Rifle Corps, once again attacked, but they were not able to push the enemy out his positions on that day. Our forces' attacks and the enemy's counterattacks along the 13th Army's right flank did not halt until the onset of darkness.

In the army's center the 27th Rifle Corps' 6th Guards Rifle Division broke into the Zorau area on the morning of 16 February and with two regiments, along with the 61st Tank Brigade, consolidated along the western, southern and eastern outskirts of the town, while one regiment covered the corridor linking the division with the corps' main forces.

In order to create a firm anti-tank defense in Zorau, the 13th Army's artillery commander, on the army commander's orders, dispatched the 1st Artillery Division's light artillery brigade and the 1076th Anti-Tank Artillery Regiment to Zorau.

At the same time that the 6th Guards Rifle Division and its attached reinforcements were consolidating in the town, the Germans' *Grossdeutschland* Panzer Corps' main forces once again attacked the positions of the 27th Rifle Corps. The corps' "Hermann Goring" Panzer Division and the 20th Panzergrenadier Division, having bypassed Zorau from the west, counterattacked the 27th Rifle Corps' right flank. Part of the "Brandenburg" Panzergrenadier Division's forces attacked Goldbach from the south. Despite the extremely stout defense by the forces of the 27th Rifle Corps, by the end of the day they were forced to abandon Waltersdorf and Goldbach. The 6th Guards Rifle Division and the 61st Tank Brigade, which were in the town of Zorau, were once again cut off from the army's main forces.

On this day no less intensive fighting unfolded along the army's left flank, in the Sagan area.

Units of the 24th Rifle Corps, which had been trying to storm Sagan during the course of three days, forced the Bober River on this day in the center of town and by the close of the day had completely cleared this major rail and paved road junction and powerful strong point of the enemy. Simultaneously with this, the corps' left-flank units, which had crossed over to the left bank of the Kweis River, launched an attack into the flank and rear of the *Grossdeutschland* Panzer Corps' forces.

Our forces' capture of Sagan and the threat to outflank the *Grossdeutschland* Panzer Corps' main forces from the south forced the enemy to give up his counterattacks in the center of the 13th Army's offensive sector and to transfer part of his forces to his right flank. Units of the 27th Rifle Corps took advantage of this. On 17 February they once again threw the Germans out of Waltersdorf and Goldbach, thus eliminating the enemy's encirclement of our forces in the Zorau area.

The intensive fighting that unfolded on 16 February in the army's offensive sector continued throughout 17-19 February.

During these days, due to the improvement in the weather, both sides' aviation became more active. On 17 February the enemy's aviation, operating in groups of 30-35 planes, carried out 1,000 sorties. A significant part of the enemy's aviation was operating in the 4th Tank and 13th armies' offensive sector. Our aviation, while conducting active air battles and launching raids against the enemy's forces carried out 1,467 sorties on that day. Soviet pilots, together with anti-aircraft artillery, shot down 35 planes, while 17 planes were destroyed at enemy airfields. On 18 February 1,500 enemy sorties were noted, while our aviation carried out 1,777 sorties, having shot down or destroyed on their airfields 16 enemy planes.

On 19 February the 2nd Air Army put the maximum number of planes in the air during the operation. Launching massive raids against concentrations of the enemy's men and materiel, our aviation at the same time prevented the enemy's planes from appearing over the battlefield. Having carried out 2,016 sorties during the day, the *front's* aviation shot down 19 German planes. On this day the enemy carried out only 200 sorties.

The intensity of the fighting was just the same on the ground, where our attacks were succeeded by German counterattacks. Although the sides' territorial situation did not change markedly during these days, the enemy's forces, having suffered enormous losses in the fighting in front of the bridgeheads, had weakened noticeably, and their counterattacks were becoming rarer and weaker.

On 19 February the 13th Army's forces, following a regrouping carried out the night before, once again attacked toward Benau and Marsdorf.

In the Benau area the enemy's forces, which had been gathered into the "Dirlewanger" 1st Punishment Brigade, under threat of being shot should they fall back, were fighting with the stubbornness of those condemned to death, and the attacking forces of the 13th Army had to take each building in fighting. By the end of the day, having destroyed a significant part of the German forces in the Benau area, the 102nd Rifle Corps' formations, together with tank subunits, threw out the remnants of the German brigade from this inhabited locale and threw them back into the woods north of Benau.

No less intensive fighting flared up that day along the army's left flank in the Marsdorf area. The 27th Rifle Corps, along with subunits of the 61st Tank Brigade, throughout the day were fighting to eliminate the enemy's tank group defending here. Only the approaching darkness saved this group of forces from complete destruction.

With these major battles the 13th Army's week-long struggle for the purpose of breaking through the enemy's defense along the Bober River concluded. The remnants of the Germans' *Grossdeutschland* Panzer Corps and various "special designation" brigades once again suffered heavy losses and were now transformed into "combat groups," which under the 13th Army's blows were falling back to the Neisse River, trying to find salvation along its left bank. While pursuing the defeated German units, by the close of 20 February the 13th Army's main forces reached the line Leiten—Sommerfeld—Niwerle—Gurkau—Zibern.

Combat operations on the 52nd Army's front. The 52nd Army's combat operations after 15 February unfolded, as before, along a broad front.

By 15 February the right-flank 48th Rifle Corps had captured a significant bridgehead on the left bank of the Kweis River. Up to 20 February the corps, while repelling counterattacks, was engaged in difficult forest fighting with the enemy's 21st Panzer Division along the approaches to the Lauban—Zorau lateral railroad. Particularly heavy fighting unfolded along the corps' right flank, where its forces attacked along the highway. Here, during the course of four days, 16-19 February, the advance of the corps' units did not exceed 1-1.5 kilometers per day.

The offensive by the 78th Rifle Corps' main forces unfolded in similar circumstances. Only the corps' left-flank units advanced somewhat more successfully, and by 19 February had managed to reach the Neisse River north of Penzig.

The 78th Rifle Corps' breakthrough to the Neisse River led to the German 21st Panzer Division being cut off from the main forces of the "Friedrich" corps group. This circumstance, plus the serious losses suffered by the division in the fighting on the left bank of the Kweis River, forced it to begin a hurried retreat to the northwest, under the blows of the 52nd Army's right-flank formations. By the close of 20 February, the 48th Rifle Corps reached the line Leiten—Dobers, while pursuing the enemy forces. By this time the 78th Rifle Corps's main forces had reached the Neisse River along the entire sector from Senitz to Nieder Bilau.

Stubborn fighting along the same lines continued along the 52nd Army's left flank.

Thus by 20 February the enemy's resistance along the entire attack sector of the *front's* right-wing armies had been crushed along the line of the Bober and Kweis rivers. The formations attacking along the flanks of the *front's* main shock group broke through to the Neisse River, and in the center they had begun pursuing the enemy. The prerequisites had been created for the rapid clearing of the enemy from the entire territory along the right bank of the Neisse River, the forcing of the river and the seizure of bridgeheads on its left bank.

The arrival of the *front's* right-wing armies at the Neisse River. The defeat of the German Fourth Panzer Army's main group of forces in the Christianstadt—Sagan—Zorau area, the breakthrough by the 3rd Guards and 52nd armies' forces to the Neisse River, and the presence in the rear of the German forces of the 4th Tank Army's troops, which controlled the right bank of the Neisse River along a front from Gross Gastrose to Bucholz, forced the German command to begin a hurried withdrawal of its forces along the entire sector of the First Ukrainian Front's main shock group behind the Neisse River, so that there, they might halt the Soviet forces' further advance along a previously prepared defensive line.

Insofar as the sector of the Neisse River from Gross Gastrose to Bucholz was held by the forces of the First Ukrainian Front's 4th Tank Army, the German forces fell back to the sector's flanks—to the area south of Guben and to the crossings in the Muskau area.

While pursuing the enemy, the 3rd Guards Army's 76th Rifle Corps and the 13th Army's main forces on 21 February reached the Neisse River in the area controlled by the 4th Tank Army, while the forces of the 3rd Guards, 13th and 52nd armies had occupied by 24 February the entire right bank of the Neisse River from its mouth to the inhabited locale of Penzig. The exception was the town of Guben, in the eastern part of which intensive fighting was still going on, and the small town of Muskau, through which the main forces of Group "Zauchen" (the former *Grossdeutschland* Panzer Corps) and units of the 21st Panzer Division were retreating, under the cover of strong rearguards.

As soon as the *front's* forces reached the Neisse River, fighting immediately began to seize bridgeheads on its left bank. In view of the shortage of forces, the limited supply of ammunition and the enemy's organized resistance, this fighting was not crowned with success. To be sure, small bridgeheads were seized along individual sectors, but we were not able to expand them, while holding them led to excessive losses. Thus after several days of unsuccessful fighting, the bridgeheads were abandoned and the troops began to consolidate on the right bank of the Neisse River. The 4th Tank Army was withdrawn into the *front* reserve to put it in order and to refit it.

The 3rd Guards Tank Army's offensive along the Gorlitz and Lauban axes (16-24 February). Following the maneuver carried out by the 3rd Guards Tank Army toward Breslau and the repulse of the Germans' 8th Panzer Division's attack toward Striegau during 14-15 February, on 16 February the army's main forces were once again deployed for an attack along the Gorlitz axis.

In order to cover the Gorlitz and Lauban axes, the enemy moved up the combat groups of the 17th Panzer and 6th *Volksgrenadier* divisions, which before this had been located in the Gorlitz area for reforming. These groups were added to the "Friedrich" corps group for repelling our troops' successfully developing offensive to the southwest of Bunzlau.

In order to reach the Neisse River and seize Gorlitz, the commander of the 3rd Guards Tank Army decided to attack toward Gorlitz from the northeast with his 6th Guards Tank Corps, and to attack with his 7th Guards Tank Corps through Lauban toward Gorlitz from the east and defeat the enemy group of forces covering Gorlitz and reach the Neisse River.

Thus the army commander decided to defeat the enemy defending opposite the army along the approaches to Gorlitz by a two-sided envelopment and to throw his remnants across the Neisse River. Under the conditions at the time, this decision cannot be described as a happy one. Judging by the character of the intensive fight that the weakened 6th Guards Tank Corps was engaged in, the task assigned to it would be difficult to fulfill. As regards the 7th Guards Tank Corps, it had to force the Kweis River, along the left bank of which the enemy was defending, and then fight for Lauban, which of course would have devoured all of the corps' forces.

In order to achieve the rapid and decisive defeat of the enemy, it would have been better not to have dispersed the army's weakened forces, but rather to have gathered them along a single northern axis where the 6th Guards Tank Corps, which had already forced the Kweis River, was attacking, and here, upon launching a concentrated attack against the enemy, crush his resistance along the northeastern approaches to Gorlitz. This would probably have enabled us not only to clear the enemy from the right bank of the Neisse River as far as Gorlitz, but also to launch an attack in the rear of the German forces defending Lauban.

The mistaken nature of the decision adopted was realized by the army commander two days later, when he was forced to make the decision to regroup the 7th Guards Tank Corps' main forces to the 6th Guards Tank Corps' attack sector. However, by this time the situation in the Lauban area had already changed. The remaining units of the 7th Guards Tank Corps were forced to get involved in serious fighting with the enemy's newly-arrived tank reserves.

The 3rd Guards Tank Army's combat operations during this period developed in the following manner.

In accordance with the decision adopted, the 6th Guards Tank Corps launched an attack along the paved road from Neudorf to Gorlitz, but, upon encountering the enemy's organized resistance on the right bank of the Gross Chirne River, spent the entire day of 17 February in stubborn fighting against enemy tanks 4-5 kilometers to the west of the Kweis River.

The 7th Guards Tank Corps, in carrying out its assigned task, on this day arrived at the crossings over the Kweis River in the Lauban area, but also encountered powerful fire resistance from the left bank of the river. The corps did not manage to cross the river in this area. Then, according to the army commander's orders, two of the corps' tank brigades were dispatched to the 6th Guards Tank Corps' crossings in the Neudorf area, in order to attack from there toward Lauban along the left bank of the Kweis River, into the enemy rear. The 7th Guards Tank Corps' remaining forces began fighting the enemy along the approaches to the eastern outskirts of Lauban.

From 18 February the situation in the 3rd Guards Tank Army's offensive sector began to rapidly worsen.

The enemy, having failed to achieve success in the Jauer—Striegau area, gave up further active operations in this area and on the night of 17-18 February transferred his entire 8th Panzer Division to the Lauban—Lewenberg front. From here the division began its attack on Naumburg on the morning of 18 February, while simultaneously counterattacking from the east units of the 7th Guards Tank Corps, which were operating in the Lauban area. The Germans' individual tank detachments attacked the corps' subunits covering Lewenberg.

Due to the fact that two of the corps' tank brigades, having crossed to the left bank of the Kweis River in the Neudorf area, were unable to break through to Lauban from the west and were fighting alongside units of the 6th Guards Tank Corps in the area south of Rothwasser, the forces of the 7th Guards Tank Corps in the Lauban area proved to be insignificant and they were unable to prevent the arrival of enemy tanks at Seifersdorf. Having transferred part of its forces from the Lauban area to Seifersdorf, the corps, together with the newly-arrived subunits of the 9th Mechanized Corps, halted the enemy's further advance toward the north, but was unable to throw the Germans out of Seifersdorf on this day.

The attacks by German tanks on Lauban from the east were beaten back. In the Lewenberg area the attacks by units of the 8th Panzer Division were repelled by the 9th Mechanized Corps, the main forces of which on this day had been transferred from the Jauer—Striegau area to the Lewenberg—Zobten area, in order to cover the army's left flank.

On 19 February the situation in the 3rd Guards Tank Army's attack sector became even more complicated. The enemy threw against the army's left flank the 408th Infantry and 10th Panzergrenadier divisions, which increased the pressure on the 9th Mechanized Corps, while attempting to outflank the 3rd Guards Tank Army from the east. The 9th Mechanized Corps, having deployed its forces along a broad front from Lewenberg to Goldberg, was engaged in heavy fighting here to repel the German counterattacks.

The fighting by the 6th and 7th guards tank corps unfolded with the same intensity. At the cost of enormous efforts, the 6th Guards Tank Corps on 19 February managed to throw the enemy out of Chirne and the 7th Guards Tank Corps was able to capture Seifersdorf.

In order to reinforce the 3rd Guards Tank Army's left flank along the Siegersdorf—Naumburg—Lewenberg line, the 214th Rifle Division of the 52nd Army's 78th Rifle Corps was moved up. The division's arrival at the indicated line enabled us in turn to free up the 9th Mechanized Corps' main forces to assist the 7th Guards Tank Corps in defeating the Germans' tank group of forces, which had broken through to the north, east of Lauban.

On 20-22 February the 3rd Guards Army's formations, as a result of stubborn fighting, had advanced 4-5 kilometers along the Gorlitz axis, while in the area to the east of Lauban they repulsed the enemy's powerful tank counterattacks and pushed him back somewhat to the south.

By the close of 21 February the 214th Rifle Division, which was attacking in conjunction with units of the 7th Guards Tank and 9th Mechanized corps, had advanced its right flank as far as the line Waldau—Seifersdorf—Lewenberg, while along the left flank it continued to strengthen the line Lewenberg—Zobten.

On 22 February the 254th Rifle Division of the 52nd Army's 73rd Rifle Corps was moved up to the 6th Guards Tank Corps' offensive sector. By the close of the day the division, together with the tank units, was fighting for the inhabited locales of Nieder Langenau and Gruna.

By this time the 3rd Guards Tank Army's advance had almost halted. The army's strength during the prolonged offensive fighting had sharply decreased. On 21 February the army's tank brigades numbered 15-20 tanks each. The entire 7th Guards Tank Corps had only 55 combat-ready tanks, and the 9th Mechanized Corps 48 tanks. Moreover, the remaining tanks' motor life had been almost completely exhausted. The corps' motorized rifle brigades were also seriously under strength. For this reason, the tank army's shock power had fallen sharply and its attack against the Germans' powerful tank group of forces no longer yielded the necessary results.

During subsequent days the enemy continued to become more active and the fighting along the Gorlitz and Lauban axes took on the character of fierce meeting encounters. Individual heights and inhabited locales changed hands several times, although the overall front line did not change markedly.

Thus by 24 February the advance by the *front's* main shock group had ended along its entire offensive sector. The enemy reserves, which had arrived during our offensive, while they had suffered heavy losses, were nevertheless in a condition, covered by the major water barrier of the Neisse River, to consolidate on its left bank.

As a result of the altered correlation of forces, as well as considerations of an operational-strategic character linked with the preparation of the Upper Silesian operation, as well as preparing our forces for a new attack along the Berlin direction, the decision was made to temporarily halt our further offensive along the *front's* right flank and to consolidate the troops along the lines reached.

An Overview of Operations on the First Ukrainian Front's Center and Left Wing, 15-24 February

Following the encirclement of Breslau, it was necessary to resolve three major tasks along the center of the First Ukrainian Front's offensive sector, which had arisen during the course of the operation:

a)   to strengthen the situation along the left flank of the *front's* shock group;
b)   to crush the resistance by the enemy group of forces defending opposite the forces of the 5th Guards and 21st armies and to throw it back to the foothills of the Sudeten Mountains;
c)   to complete the defeat of the group of German forces surrounded in Breslau.

The resolution of the first of these tasks was accomplished in the following manner. As soon as the encirclement of Breslau had been completed, the 5th Guards Army's 32nd Guards Rifle Corps was dispatched to the Liegnitz area on orders from the *front* commander, in order to occupy the defensive line being held by the 3rd Guards Tank Army's 9th Mechanized Corps.

By the close of 17 February the 32nd Rifle Corps reached its designated area and with two divisions occupied the line Goldberg—Jauer—Striegau. The 9th Mechanized Corps, which had been relieved by the corps, reached the Bober River, during the course of a forced night march, in the

Lewenberg area and to the north of the town, and in the succeeding days, as we know, was engaged in intensive fighting there with a major enemy tank group.

On the same day (17 February) there arrived in the Liegnitz area the headquarters of the 52nd Army's 73rd Rifle Corps and its 50th Rifle Division, which had been transferred here, on the orders of the *front* commander, from the Breslau area. Thus by 17 February the entire 73rd Rifle Corps had been concentrated along the army's left flank.

As soon as the concentration had been completed, two of the corps' divisions occupied a defensive line along a front from the village of Paritz (along the Kweis River, west of Bunzlau) as far as the inhabited locale of Koischwitz (east of Liegnitz).

As a result of this, the 78th Rifle Corps' freed-up 373rd and 214th rifle divisions were employed for assisting the offensive by the 3rd Guards Tank Army, which was operating in the center of the 52nd Army's offensive sector.

The arrival of the 5th Guards Army's right-flank corps to the front Goldberg—Jauer—Striegau enabled the commander of the 52nd Army to employ on 22 February the 73rd Rifle Corps' 254th Rifle Division to fill in the gap along the army's front in the 6th Guards Tank Corps' attack sector, and on 24 February to dispatch the 50th Rifle Division to cover the unoccupied sector of the front from Zobten to Goldberg.

Thus as the result of the regroupings carried out along the central sector of the front, by 25 February a solid front of combined-arms formations had been formed along the *front's* left wing. The measures adopted significantly strengthened the situation along this sector and enabled us to eliminate the danger of an enemy breakthrough along the front Bunzlau—Liegnitz, which had arisen due to the concentration of his fresh forces opposite the left flank of the *front's* shock group.

Simultaneous with the movement of the 5th Guards Army to the front Goldberg—Striegau and the regrouping of our forces in the 52nd Army's offensive sector, regroupings by the 5th Guards and 6th armies' forces were taking place in the immediate area of Breslau.

During this period the 5th Guards Army took its 34th Guards Rifle Corps out of the line in the Breslau area.

By 24 February the corps' 118th Rifle Division had occupied the front from Raaben to Mettkau, while the 15th and 58th rifle divisions were located in the army's second echelon, in the Kostenblut area and south of Domslau.

The 6th Army's 273rd Rifle Division, which had been occupying a defensive sector east of Striegau, was relieved by the 5th Guards Army's units and withdrawn to the Breslau area.

By 24 February the 6th Army had completely relieved all of the other armies' units in the Breslau area. From this time the blockade of the city and the battle to destroy the troops defending it was waged only by the 6th Army's formations and units.

The weakness of the 6th Army made it extremely difficult to wage the subsequent battle with the encircled enemy. Moreover, the forces of the encircled enemy proved to be more substantial than had been supposed earlier. According to data disposed of by the *front's* intelligence organs, the encircled group had a strength of 17-20,000 men, while the Breslau garrison, together with the various *volksturm* units actually numbered more than 40,000 officers and men. For this reason, as well as due to a number of shortcomings in organizing combat operations on the part of the 6th Army command, the fighting in the Breslau area became protracted and concluded only in the beginning of May, when the Breslau garrison, having lost all hope of aid from the outside, capitulated unconditionally.

The offensive by the 5th Guards and 21st armies (16-24 February). Throughout the entire period of the offensive by the *front's* main shock group from the Bober River to the Neisse River and the deployment of forces for covering its left flank, the 5th Guards and 21st armies, having concentrated their main forces along adjoining flanks, continued to wage intensive offensive battles, trying to throw the opposing enemy back to the foothills of the Sudeten Mountains.

However, this task proved to be beyond both armies.

The command of Army Group Center, following the heavy defeat in the Breslau area, was trying not only to halt our further offensive in this area, but to liberate, through an attack toward Breslau, his forces encircled in the city. For this purpose, the 20th Panzer Division was transferred from the Grottkau area and the 100th Light Infantry Division from the area north of Ratibor, to aid the combat groups of the 269th Infantry, 19th Panzer and 254th Infantry divisions operating along the approaches to Breslau.

This sharply changed the correlation of forces in the 5th Guards and 21st armies' offensive sectors.

If on 16 February, before the arrival of new enemy formations, the 5th Guards and 21st armies had advanced along the entire offensive front at an average rate of 4-5 kilometers per day, then during the following eight days their maximum advance, and this was only along certain sectors, was no more than four kilometers per day.

The forces of the 5th Guards and 21st armies, exhausted by the prolonged previous fighting and having suffered serious losses in fighting for each inhabited locale and even the most insignificant tactical line, encountered the enemy's stubborn resistance. The German infantry, supported by tanks, counterattacked 10-15 times per day along various sectors of the front.

By 24 February the advance by the 5th Guards and 21st armies' forces had actually halted. During the subsequent days the armies' individual formations achieved only local tactical successes, while along individual sectors they even yielded previously occupied positions to the enemy.

During 17-24 February the *front* commander made an attempt with the forces of the 1st Guards Cavalry Corps, which had been transferred to the area west of Liegnitz from the *front's* left wing, to launch an attack from the Goldberg area toward Landeshut and Waldenburg in the rear of the enemy group of forces defending opposite the 5th Guards and 21st armies.

The 1st Guards Cavalry Corps, which had been committed into the fighting on the night of 21-22 February along the line Steinberg—Goldberg, by the evening of 22 February had advanced 5-7 kilometers. In the Konradswaldau area the corps got into a fight with the enemy's infantry and tanks. In the following days the area occupied by the cavalry corps was expanded somewhat toward the flanks, but it was unable to develop the offensive into the depth of the German defense.

The German-Fascist command reinforced its 408th Infantry Division operating here with the 10th Panzergrenadier Division's combat group and committed the fresh 31st SS Grenadier Division into the fighting.

These forces halted the 1st Guards Cavalry Corps' offensive and the front stabilized along the line Steinberg—excluding Konradswaldau—Seichau.

There was local fighting along the entire remaining front of the 5th Guards and 21st armies. The troops improved their tactical positions, repelled counterattacks and consolidated along their lines.

The situation along the *front's* left wing. During this period there were no significant changes in the troops' situation along the *front's* left wing.

As a result of the offensive that began on 16 February on the bridgehead north of Ratibor, the 59th and 60th armies managed during the first two days to somewhat expand the bridgehead in depth, although all subsequent attacks by the armies' forces ran into the enemy's Ratibor group of forces' stubborn defense, which had been reinforced by the 18th SS Panzergrenadier Division, which had been transferred from Czechoslovakia to the area of the bridgehead.

On 19 February the *front* commander ordered the commands of the 59th and 60th armies to cease the offensive and go over to the defensive along the entire front, in order to put their forces in order and accumulate ammunition.

The decision adopted testifies to the fact that the attempt to activate the 59th and 60th armies' combat operations during the operation's second stage had not yielded success, because the armies did not have the necessary forces for resolving the tasks assigned to them.

Thus by the end of February the *front's* forces along the First Ukrainian Front's offensive sector from the mouth of the Neisse River to the approaches to the Moravska Ostrava industrial region, having exhausted their offensive capabilities, went over to consolidating the lines reached. Fighting continued only along individual sectors for improving the troops' tactical position. However, these battles were only of local significance and could not materially change the *front's* operational situation as a whole. The operation, begun by the forces of the First Ukrainian Front on February 8, concluded with the arrival of the *front's* right-wing armies at the Neisse River.

The Results of the Operation's Second Stage

During the course of the operation's second stage the First Ukrainian Front's right-wing forces broke through the enemy's defense on the intermediate defensive lines along the Bober and Kweis rivers, defeated the reserves committed by the enemy into the battle and, having thrown their remnants beyond the Neisse River, captured all of Lower Silesia, and entered into the province of Brandenburg, having occupied a number of major towns and important military-industrial sites.

Having advanced as far as the Neisse River, the First Ukrainian Front's right-wing armies reached the same line as the forces of the First Belorussian Front. In this way, favorable prerequisites were created for these *fronts'* subsequent joint operations along the Berlin direction.

The offensive operations by the *front's* forces in the last days of February unfolded in conditions of the significant weakening of their offensive capabilities. Thus although they had inflicted a serious defeat on the German forces, they had not managed to organize the pursuit of the enemy at such a speed that they could force the Neisse River on the march on the enemy's heels and capture a bridgehead on the river's left bank. The *front* overcame the 45 kilometers that divide the Neisse River from the Bober and Kweis rivers in nine days, attacking at an average rate of five kilometers per day. As a result of the slow offensive pace, the enemy had time to pull back his surviving forces behind the Neisse River and, upon their occupying defensive positions along the left bank of the river, to prevent the *front's* forces from forcing it.

On the left flank of the *front's* shock group, where the 3rd Guards Tank and 52nd armies were attacking, the enemy delayed the attacking forces through a stubborn defense along the line Penzig—Lauban, as a result of which the arrival of these armies at the Neisse River in the Gorlitz area and to the south was not realized.

The offensive along the *front's* center and left wing unfolded even less successfully. Here the front actually stabilized. The attempts made to throw the enemy back into the Sudeten Mountains ended without result. The task of rapidly defeating the encircled enemy in Breslau was too much for the *front's* troops. The offensive against the German group of forces surrounded in Glogau was also conducted unsuccessfully.

As a result of the uninterrupted month-and-a-half offensive battles, the strength of the *front's* forces declined sharply, a large amount of combat equipment was put out of action, and all our reserves had been expended. Our weakened forces were deployed along a broad front of more than 500 kilometers and were forced to wage combat, in a grouping unfavorable for the offensive, against an enemy who had been reinforced throughout February with significant reserves. All of this forced the troops to wage an offensive with a maximum intensity of forces and led to the exhaustion of their offensive capabilities as early as the approaches to the Neisse River.

Of enormous influence on the weakening of the troops' offensive capabilities was the unsatisfactory work of the *front's* rear organs, which, as a result of the enormous extension of our communications, was not able to cope with the delivery of materiel necessary for conducting an operation.

All of this, alongside the unfavorable meteorological conditions, led to a situation in which, despite the maximum exertion of our forces, the troops were not able to achieve those results that had been foreseen by the operational plan. It is quite natural that a subsequent offensive in such conditions would have led to an even greater exhaustion of our forces, but did not promise a major success. Moreover, the advance of the *front's* right-wing armies toward the Neisse River, given the simultaneous lagging behind of the left-wing armies, which were continuing to fight along the line of the Oder River, led to such a large gap between them that any further advance by the *front's* right wing to the west, given the presence of significant enemy forces opposite the *front's* center, could have led to serious consequences.

Thus the resulting situation required the temporary halt of the offensive along the Berlin and Dresden directions for the purpose of consolidating the results achieved, putting the troops in order, reinforcing them, regrouping our forces, creating reserves, and bringing up the rear organs and accumulating materiel. Simultaneously with the resolution of all these tasks, the *front* command would have to immediately take measures to bring up the *front's* left-wing armies abreast of the right-wing armies, or at least defeat the enemy opposite the left wing and throw the remnants into the Sudeten Mountains. Only under these conditions could we count on success in the operation's further development along the Berlin and Dresden directions.

Such are the overall results of the second stage of the Lower Silesian offensive operation and the situation that arose at the end of February in the First Ukrainian Front's offensive sector.

No material changes occurred in the neighboring *front's* offensive sectors and along those sectors immediately adjacent to the First Ukrainian Front. The First Belorussian Front, having consolidated with its left-wing armies along the Oder River, with part of its forces continued fighting to expand the Küstrin bridgehead, while the main forces, which had been concentrated along the right wing, in conjunction with the forces of the Second Belorussian Front, were attacking in Eastern Pomerania for the purpose of defeating the enemy's Eastern Pomeranian group of forces and reaching the Oder along its lower course. In February the Fourth Ukrainian Front waged battles with little success in the Western Carpathians, trying to break out into the Moravska Ostrava valley.

Having evaluated the resulting situation and the capabilities of his troops, the commander of the First Ukrainian Front came to the conclusion that under current conditions the *front* would not be able to launch a further offensive along the Berlin and Dresden directions. Therefore, while not giving up in principle on the goals foreseen by the operation's initial plan, the *front* commander made the decision to temporarily halt the offensive by the right-wing armies, have them consolidate on the Neisse River and to organize the preparation of a new operation in conjunction with the First Belorussian Front.

In order to create the most favorable conditions for developing a subsequent offensive along the Berlin and Dresden directions, the *front* commander decided to carry out during the preparatory period for this offensive an operation with part of his forces along the *front's* left wing for the purpose of defeating the enemy opposing the *front's* center and left-wing forces and to throw them back into the Sudeten Mountains.

On 24 February Marshal of the Soviet Union Konev reported his thoughts on the plan for the *front's* subsequent operations to the Supreme Commander-in-Chief. These ideas were approved by the Supreme Commander-in-Chief and the *front*, while consolidating the results of the February offensive, began preparing for the new operation along the left wing.

3

The Results of the Lower Silesian Offensive Operation and Some Brief Conclusions

The Lower Silesian offensive operation lasted 17 days, from 8-24 February. During this time the First Ukrainian Front's forces broke through the enemy's defense along the Oder River along a 250-kilometer front and, while developing the offensive, overcame the intermediate defensive lines along the Bober and Kweis rivers from the march. By the close of the operation the *front's* right-wing forces had advanced more than 100 miles in intense fighting and reached the Neisse River along a sector from its mouth to Penzig.

As a result of the Lower Silesian operation the *front's* forces once again inflicted a serious defeat on the German's Fourth Panzer and Seventeenth armies, which had been reinforced following their defeat between the Vistula and the Oder. With the arrival of the First Ukrainian Front's forces at the Neisse River the enemy was deprived of important military-industrial regions in southeast Germany—Breslau, Glogau and Christianstadt, which supplied the German-Fascist army with military equipment, ammunition and synthetic fuel.

The successes achieved by the *front's* forces had important operational-strategic significance.

Having defeated the Germans' Fourth Panzer and Seventeenth armies' main forces, the First Ukrainian Front's forces came abreast along a 110-kilometer sector with the forces of the First Belorussian Front, which as early as the end of January 1945 had reached the lower reaches of the Oder River. Thus two of the Soviet army's *fronts* occupied favorable lines for carrying out the concluding attack against the enemy along the Berlin direction. At the same time, the First Ukrainian Front's forces had occupied an outflanking position *vis a vis* the enemy's Upper Silesian group of forces and simultaneously had the opportunity to prepare for a subsequent offensive to the west—in the direction of Dresden and Leipzig, as well as to the southwest—into the central regions of Czechoslovakia.

The conduct of the Lower Silesian operation foiled the plan of the German-Fascist command to securely consolidate on the Oder and realize its intention to launch counterblows.

The *front's* offensive attracted considerable enemy forces, which had been designated by the German-Fascist command for employment along other sectors of the Soviet-German front and thus aided the First Belorussian Front's forces in defeating the Eastern Pomeranian group of forces, and the forces of the Second and Third Ukrainian fronts in defeating the enemy's group of forces, which had broken through to the Danube in January.

In accordance with the available men and materiel that the *front* disposed of at the beginning of February, it managed to defeat 27 enemy divisions and reach the Neisse River, that is, abreast of the First Belorussian Front.

The Lower Silesian offensive operation is valuable and instructive in its experience of organizing and conducting a *front* offensive operation, prepared in a limited time, while in the course of concluding the preceding operation. It added many new shining examples to Soviet military art of the creative solution of complex operational tasks arising during the course of preparing for and conducting the operation.

The Lower Silesian operation was a consecutive *front* operation. During the Great Patriotic War such operations were broadly employed by the Soviet army in conducting an offensive to a great depth. As the experience of the war showed, the goals, forms and methods of preparing for and conducting consecutive *front* operations could be extremely varied. They depended upon the concrete conditions and demands of the situation. However, a general feature characteristic of all such operations is that they, as a rule, are prepared during the course of preceding operations and limited time is devoted to their preparation, and that they are realized without a break, or after a very short pause.

The Lower Silesian operation was prepared over a short time during the completion of the Sandomierz—Silesian operation.

Following the completion of the Sandomierz—Silesian operation it was very favorable to begin a new offensive operation so as to deny the enemy the opportunity of recovering from the defeat just inflicted on him, to prevent him from consolidating on the Oder and, by a vigorous offensive, to preempt the enemy's possible transfer of reserves from other sectors of the front and other theaters of military activities to the First Ukrainian Front's offensive sector.

The *front* commander made the correct decision to prepare in a short time a new offensive operation.

As was noted earlier, the decision by the *front* commander called for the simultaneous launching of attacks along three axes for the purpose of breaking up the enemy's defense and destroying the enemy's group of forces in detail. At the same time, the main group of forces was to attack along the *front's* right wing in the general direction of Sprottau, Cottbus and Juterbog.

In examining the *front* commander's decision to launch three deep and simultaneous attacks, it should be noted that it arose from a certain underestimation of the enemy's capabilities to organize resistance along the Oder defensive line. In reality, the stubborn fighting that unfolded for the bridgeheads on the Oder in the last days of January and the beginning of February showed that the enemy was capable of organizing the defense of the Oder line in a short time and to reinforce the remnants of the defeated forces with reinforcements and formations transferred from Czechoslovakia and Hungary.

The German forces' increased resistance led to a situation in which even before the start of the new offensive operation, all of the forces of the shock groups that had been created here for the offensive, had been drawn into the fighting to expand the bridgeheads in the center and along the left wing.

As a result of these battles, the armies that were attacking along the *front's* center formed a sizeable bridgehead in the area south of Breslau, but were unable to employ it for developing the offensive. As regards the *front's* left-wing armies, following prolonged and unsuccessful battles to expand their limited bridgehead, they had completely exhausted their offensive capabilities and were forced to go over to the defensive.

Thus the offensive could actually only be carried out by the shock group that had been created along the *front's* right wing. However, this group of forces' offensive capabilities was also limited, due to the absence of second echelons and reserves in the *front*.

According to the decision by the *front* commander, all of the armies comprising the *front's* main shock group, including the mobile groups, were to enter the fighting simultaneously on the first day of the operation. Only upon the 6th Army's capture of Breslau was it planned to pull the army into the *front* reserve. Should the 6th Army be delayed in the Breslau area, which is what actually happened, the offensive would have to develop without reserves, which would inevitably lead to various unforeseen complications during the offensive in the operational depth of the enemy's defense.

The absence of a second echelon and reserves in the *front* deprived the *front* commander of the capability of augmenting his efforts in a timely fashion along the main axis, to develop the offensive in depth toward the flanks and to adopt timely measures to repel the enemy's counterblows and to defeat his arriving reserves. Besides this, the complex and sharply changing situation forced the *front* commander to sometimes remove combined-arms and tank formations from important axes and move them to other axes, where a threat was arising, which severely disrupted the plan for the offensive operation as a whole and created additional difficulties for the troops' combat operations.

The experience of this operation once again confirms the extreme correctness of a basic tenet of Soviet military art to the effect that in modern operations, particularly in consecutive ones, during which the situation changes rapidly and sharply, it is necessary to have not only previously created second echelons and reserves, but to constantly be concerned with restoring them during the course of the offensive. Without this condition the successful conduct of a modern operation with a decisive goal is unthinkable.

In examining the problems of conducting the Lower Silesian operation, it is necessary to halt on the features of breaking through the enemy's defense and developing the offensive in the operational depth.

During the first two days of the offensive the *front's* shock group, which was operating along the right wing, managed to completely break through the enemy's tactical defense zone and transfer combat operations along the main axis to the operational depth. Bringing in the tank armies for the breakthrough of the enemy's main defensive zone, along with the combined-arms armies, was a forced measure and was conditioned by the combined-arms armies' weak saturation with immediate infantry support tanks. The weakened combined-arms armies would not have been able to overcome the enemy's defense along the Oder in the first two days of the operation without the support of the tank armies. The fighting in the tactical defense zone could have been prolonged.

The artillery played an important role in breaking through the German defense. Due to the unfavorable meteorological conditions, which limited our air activity, the entire burden of the fire preparation of the infantry and tank attack lay on the artillery. In breaking through the enemy's main defensive zone and in developing the offensive in depth, the regimental, and a significant part of the divisional artillery, as well as part of the larger-caliber artillery, which had been detached for firing over open sights, attacked alongside the infantry and tanks.

The combat activities of the engineering troops unfolded in close coordination with the remaining combat arms. The engineering troops rendered a great deal of help to the infantry, tanks and artillery in overcoming the numerous minefields created by the enemy on the roads and opposite inhabited locales in the depth of the tactical defense zone.

However, despite our superiority in force over the enemy and the persistence and stubbornness with which our soldiers fought while breaking through the enemy's tactical defensive zone, the offensive pace during the breakthrough was half as much as planned and failed to satisfy the demands of the actual situation. The slow pace of the breakthrough was caused mainly by shortcomings in preparing the offensive; first of all by the fact that sufficient attention was not paid to problems of reconnaissance on the whole, and particularly to reconnoitering the enemy's fire system. This shortcoming told on the first day of the operation. Our artillery, lacking sufficiently precise data about the enemy's fire system, fired on insufficiently reconnoitered targets during the artillery preparation, which failed to yield the proper results. The enemy's personnel and a significant part of his weapons remained unsuppressed.

The limited supply of ammunition forced the command to limit its expenditure while fighting in the depth, where due to the new situation the demand for it was particularly great. The shortage of ammunition limited the artillery's combat capabilities and worsened the offensive conditions.

The absence of the necessary support for the attacking troops by the *front's* air arm also influenced the fall in the pace of the breakthrough. The unfavorable meteorological conditions did not allow the 2nd Air Army to fully employ its capabilities for strikes against the enemy, as a result of which the latter could maneuver his tactical reserves with impunity and concentrate them along the most threatened axes, and at critical moments pull back his forces into the depth in order to occupy more favorable defensive lines.

The tank troops played a major role in developing the offensive. Despite the peculiar conditions in which the offensive unfolded, the tank troops, reinforced with artillery and engineer-sapper units, were in a condition to resolve tasks for overcoming the enemy's resistance in inhabited locales, to force rivers, to independently break through the enemy's hurriedly prepared defense in the operational depth, repel his counterattacks and counterblows, and to seize and to hold important operational lines in the face of high enemy activity.

The most instructive in this regard are the activities of the 4th Tank Army. Having carried out a successful maneuver that helped secure the encirclement and defeat of the enemy's main forces, which were defending opposite the 13th Army, the 4th Tank Army lunged forward and forced the Bober River from the march. While developing the offensive at a fast pace, the army preempted the enemy in occupying the defensive line prepared by him along the left bank of the river, overcame it and quickly arrived at the Neisse River with its main forces. After the enemy managed to cut off the 4th Tank Army off from the combined-arms armies with reserves newly arrived at the Bober River, for a week it fought in the enemy's rear to hold the line of the Neisse River along a 40-50 kilometer front, having manifested skill in waging independent operations apart from the infantry and with disrupted communications.

No less instructive are the actions of the 3rd Guards Tank Army at the concluding phase of the operation. The army waged an independent operation for a prolonged time to repel the enemy's counterblow in the Lauban area and, while defending along a 50-80 kilometer front, covered the movement and deployment of the combined-arms formations. This example highlights the tank army's capability, if necessary, to resolve tasks of waging an active defense along a broad front. To be sure, in these battles the tank army suffered from a severe shortage of infantry and was forced to commit all of its forces into the fighting, including a motorcycle regiment and special units. Such an employment of the tank army was a forced measure, due to the shortage of forces in the *front*. Artillery, particularly, anti-tank artillery, played a major role in the 3rd Guards Tank Army's repelling the enemy's attacks. Besides supporting the tank formations in their battle against the enemy's tanks, the artillery units sometimes occupied independent defensive sectors and supported the maneuver of the tank formations in the tank army's offensive sector.

When speaking of the offensive's development, one should note a number of unfavorable circumstances that exerted a material influence on the course of the operation and its final results.

The spring thaw and the uninterrupted precipitation, as a result of which throughout the entire operation the country and dirt roads were almost impassable for combat equipment and transport, forced the First Ukrainian Front's forces to attack mainly along the paved roads, which gave the enemy a number of advantages in conducting a defense with limited forces.

As was noted earlier, combat air activity in the operation under study also unfolded in unfavorable meteorological conditions.

There were only four days of good flying weather during the entire operation, while the remaining days either allowed limited flying or none at all. Besides this, the arriving thaw put almost completely out of action the unimproved airfields on which the *front's* aircraft were based. This, in turn, also limited the capabilities of the *front's* air force in carrying out an air offensive during the operation.

In the offensive's 17 days the 2nd Air Army, which at the beginning of the operation had 2,382 combat aircraft, carried out 13,113 sorties, which yields 5.5 sorties per plane. This data shows in just what a limited way the 2nd Air Army's capabilities were employed. If one takes into account that the figures cited above also embrace our aviation's reconnaissance activities, then it will be clear just how insignificant was the air force's help to the *front's* attacking ground forces. This complicated extremely the conditions of fighting the enemy and made it easier for him to bring up his reserves to the First Ukrainian Front's offensive sector.

The air forces' weak activity influenced the rapid exhaustion of the *front's* offensive capabilities.

The enemy's highly active and stubborn defense also influenced the character of combat operations during the development of the offensive.

The fascist command managed to force its forces to put up a stubborn defense against the First Ukrainian Front's units and formations throughout the operations by means of nationalist propaganda, repressions and activating screening detachments.

The Lower Silesian operation was characterized by the conduct of numerous operational regroupings.

During the conclusion of the Sandomierz-Silesian operation, as well as during the preparation of the Lower Silesian operation, large-scale and complex operational regroupings of forces were carried out in a limited amount of time. As is known, in order to create a shock group along the *front's* right flank, it was necessary to not only regroup units and formations from neighboring sectors to the armies' narrowed offensive sectors, but also to carry out the transfer of individual corps and entire armies from the *front's* left wing to the center and the right wing (21st and 3rd Guards Tank armies, 4th Guards and 31st tank corps).

The regrouping involved almost all the *front's* forces and was carried out in difficult conditions, when the troops were already engaged in intensive fighting to expand and hold the bridgeheads. The enemy was very active during this period, continuously counterattacked and tried to win back the territory won by our forces on the left bank of the Oder. Despite this, the *front's* forces successfully coped with the tasks assigned them.

Experience showed that the regrouping's successful conclusion was supported by precise planning and the regrouping's good organization.

During the operation the outflanking, envelopment and encirclement of large and small enemy groups of forces were skillfully organized and carried out, as well as the shifting of the troops' main efforts from one axis to another. The skillful organization of maneuver, both operational and tactical, and its successful realization by our forces testifies to the *front's* forces' high level of skill, persistence and decisiveness.

While noting this positive facet of the operation under study, one should also note that skillfully designed and conducted maneuvers were not always fully realized during the operation.

A glaring example of a skillfully conceived but unfinished maneuver was the actions of the 6th Army while encircling Breslau. The army, which at first was attacking to the west, sharply changed its axis of attack to the east and southeast and launched a surprise attack against the enemy in Breslau from the rear. Unfortunately, this attack was not driven to its conclusion. Disposing of two corps, the army, following the completion of its turn from the Liegnitz area toward Breslau, was forced to leave about half of its forces along its extended external front. As a result, there were not enough forces to quickly complete the encirclement and destroy the enemy in the Breslau area. The *front* commander, lacking reserves, was unable to help the 6th Army in time. The 6th Army's halt to regroup was used by the Germans to organize a defense, as a result of which the subsequent fighting along the approaches to Breslau was prolonged.

No less interesting is the 3rd Guards Tank Army's maneuver from the Bunzlau area to the east to assist the 6th and 5th Guards armies' forces in completing the encirclement of Breslau. At the most important moment of the offensive's development along the main axis, the *front* commander, in order to speed up the enemy's encirclement in the Breslau area, decided to remove the 3rd Guards Tank Army's main forces from there and direct them on Breslau. The 3rd Guards Tank Army, in carrying out the *front* commander's instructions, carried out a 180-degree turn from west to east and accomplished a vigorous 100-kilometer march to the Breslau area. Following the completion of the enemy's encirclement in Breslau, the *front* commander, while attempting to restore the 52nd Army's lost offensive pace along the Gorlitz axis, ordered the commander of the 3rd Guards Tank Army to return to the Bunzlau area in order to continue the offensive together with the 52nd Army.

Also of interest is the example of the 3rd Guards Army's maneuver, which was undertaken for the purpose of cutting off and then encircling the enemy group of forces in Glogau. Having encircled the German forces in the areas of Breslau and Glogau, the *front's* forces strongly secured the flanks of the breakthrough, broke up the enemy's forces into parts and deprived him of the opportunity, by relying on heavily fortified towns, of launching flank attacks against the base of the breakthrough.

The regrouping of the *front's* forces carried out toward the left flank of the main shock group, where the threat of an enemy attack against our forces' flank was arising, also testifies to the operation's maneuver character. In order to eliminate this threat and create the conditions for the subsequent development of the operation, the *front* commander transferred to the shock group's left wing near Breslau the 52nd Army's 73rd Rifle Corps, and then the 5th Guards Army's main forces, and then the 1st Guards Cavalry Corps from the *front's* left wing. The regrouping of forces to the main shock group's left wing completely justified itself.

The superior organizational capabilities of the *front's* command and political element played an extremely important role in achieving major operational successes and guaranteed the maintenance of the troops' high political-morale condition throughout the entire operation, the uninterrupted nature of troop control and the all-round organization of cooperation between the *front's* formations and major field forces, and between the combat arms. As the operation's experience showed, troop control and coordination among them was not disrupted, even in such difficult periods of combat as, for example, the fighting by the 4th Tank and 13th armies for the bridgehead on the Bober River, the 4th Tank Army's lengthy operations in the enemy rear apart from the combined-arms armies, during the 3rd Guards Tank Army's repulse of the enemy's counterblow in the Lauban area, and a number of other cases.

During the offensive, the *front* commander uninterruptedly followed the troops' combat activities and influenced the course of the operation in a timely manner. As a rule, the *front* commander amplified the armies' tasks.

Being constantly informed of all events along the *front's* operational sector, the commander carried out the maneuver of the *front's* forces to develop the success or to eliminate an impending threat.

Command and control was exercised from the *front* command post. In getting out among the troops, the *front* commander constantly informed his chief of staff about orders issued, which ensured the staff's solid control of their fulfillment.

Command and control in the combined-arms and tank armies was also conducted directly from the main command posts.

The difficulty of command and control within the armies during the Lower Silesian operation was due to the fact that even in their jumping-off position almost all the armies were deployed along a broad front, while some of them had their formations along various sectors of the front. The 52nd Army had two corps in the *front's* main shock group, with one corps in the Breslau area. Before the start of the offensive, the 3rd Guards Tank Army had two corps on the bridgehead north of Breslau and one corps along the *front's* left flank in the Rybnik area. Following the breakthrough of the Oder defensive line, the armies' offensive sectors expanded significantly, which made command and control even more difficult.

Headquarters at all levels transmitted assignments to the troops on time, exercised uninterrupted control over their fulfillment, and organized constant communications of all kinds, which, on the whole, guaranteed unbroken command and control during the operation.

However, it should be noted that insufficient attention was devoted to such an important type of combat and operational support as reconnaissance of the enemy. This shortcoming was highlighted in analyzing problems of preparing the operation and conducting the breakthrough of the enemy's defense on the Oder. In developing the operation, shortcomings in the organization of reconnaissance were noted in the combined-arms formations, which were attacking behind the tank troops. This led to instances of unexpected collisions with the enemy along lines and in inhabited locales through which the tank forces passed, made more difficult maneuver for the purpose of outflanking or enveloping enemy groups of forces and forced the troops to deploy for battle with them in unfavorable conditions. The example of the unexpected attack by the enemy's 8th Panzer Division against the flank of the 3rd Guards Tank Army speaks to the absence of insufficient attention paid to reconnaissance.

As for supporting uninterrupted command and control, uninterruptedly operating communications played a large role. At the same time, it should be noted that if at the army-*front* level the main means of communications was by wire, while radio communications and mobile communications equipment was employed for backup purposes, then at the corps-army level radio and mobile communications equipment played the decisive role.

Particularly great skill and persistence in organizing communications was required of the various headquarters while the troops were overcoming large wooded areas. Radio communications in these conditions proved to be an insufficiently reliable means of command and control, particularly at great distances, while the organization of wire communications was made more difficult by frequent enemy diversions. Communications officers played a major role in this situation. Thus the unbroken work of all kinds of communications at all levels of the *front* organism, despite the complex conditions of conducting the operation, and the bold and enterprising actions of the troops and their commanders were one of the decisive conditions in achieving successes.

The materiel-technical support of the troops during the offensive was carried out in extremely complex circumstances.

The through railroad movement from the Vistula to the Oder had been restored only by the very beginning of the operation. Thus the supplies of ammunition and particularly of fuel, which had been created among the troops with the help of auto transport, were limited and expended with a great deal of economy. Due to special conditions, the troops' demands for ammunition and fuel in the Lower Silesian operation proved to be significantly greater than in the preceding operation. During the offensive from the Oder to the Neisse the *front's* forces expended more ammunition than during the offensive from the Vistula to the Oder. If 4,324 tons of ammunition were expended in January, then their expenditure amounted to 4,827 tons in February.

Despite the enormous difficulties, the commanders at all levels, their staffs and the *front* rear-area workers carried out a great deal of work so as to maximally satisfy the troops' demands.

As regards tactical questions, the experience of the First Ukrainian Front's forces in fighting for towns and inhabited locales is deserving of special attention. The stubbornness with which the enemy fought to hold them demanded that the *front's* forces devote special attention to this type of combat activity.

Having pitted against the enemy's tactics against our tactics, which were based on the very rich experience of the preceding years of the Great Patriotic War, the *front's* forces, in difficult conditions, manifested a high degree of skill, flexibility of action, stubbornness and persistence in achieving their goal and achieved major results.

While conducting the offensive, the *front's* forces sought, first of all, to prevent the enemy from breaking free of our attacking units and organizing a defense. When the enemy would manage to break free from the attacking forces and organize a defense, our units and formations widely employed outflanking maneuvers and envelopments of the defending enemy, along with frontal attacks. As a rule, the enemy would hurriedly abandon the inhabited locales under threat of encirclement, trying to withdraw his forces to the next line or to the next inhabited locale.

If the enemy was defending this or that town with large forces that were putting up stubborn resistance, the *front's* forces would bypass these towns, leaving screens against them, which were significantly smaller than the enemy groups of forces that had been surrounded.

Surprise night storming of towns and inhabited locales were broadly employed, which, as a rule, led to their rapid seizure.

In cases when the attacking forces did not manage to outflank inhabited locales, due to special conditions, then the troops, following a short but powerful artillery preparation, undertook to storm them.

The attack within inhabited locales was conducted in close coordination by all combat arms. On orders from the *front* commander, small groups of tanks and accompaniment guns were attached to the rifle subunits. The storm groups also consisted of engineer and chemical subunits. Employing explosives, smoke and flamethrowers, they aided the attacking troops a great deal in eliminating the enemy's individual strong points.

We will not examine the experience of fighting for fortress towns such as Breslau and Glogau, because the fighting for these towns lies beyond the bounds of the operation and is deserving of separate study.

In noting the positive aspects in our forces' actions in fighting for towns and inhabited locales, it is necessary to mention that during the first stage of the operation the *front's* forces had not been sufficiently trained for this kind of fighting.

In organizing the pursuit of the enemy, the *front's* forces had not taken into account the changed conditions and underestimated that role which the enemy had consigned to the defense of towns and inhabited locales. For this reason, the proper attention had not been devoted to the troops' special training for this type of combat. By the way, the experience of the operation showed that in attacking in a theater of military activities with a thick network of towns and inhabited locales, which consisted solely of stone structures, not only must specially created storm groups be trained for fighting for towns and inhabited locales, but all the troops.

This shortcoming was corrected during the operation, when instructions and orders revealing the enemy's tactics were drawn up and transmitted to the troops, based on the tested experience in fighting for inhabited locales of the Great Patriotic War. Simultaneously with this, organizational measures were carried out, directed at strengthening the rifle subunits with tanks, accompaniment guns, and engineer and chemical subunits. All of this yielded positive results and the troops achieved significant successes, which were noted above.

Both the positive and negative experience of the fighting for inhabited locales, which had been accumulated by the *front's* forces in the Lower Silesian operation was, following its completion, generalized and successfully employed in planning for and conducting the *front's* succeeding operations—Upper Silesian and Berlin. This experience was a valuable contribution to the development of Soviet military art.

The broad scope and purposefulness of our political work during the preparatory period created a high morale-political feeling among the troops, which gathered them even closer around the Communist Party and our great leader, I.V. Stalin, ensured the troops' deep understanding of their combat tasks and mobilized them to overcome difficulties.

The actions of the *front's* forces during the operation and their conduct in the fighting showed that the political work carried out during the preparatory period was fruitful and was one of the decisive conditions guaranteeing the results achieved by the *front*.

The difficult conditions in which the offensive operations of the *front'* forces were waged, made it necessary to concentrate the commanders' and political workers' attention on questions of organizing and the methods of fighting for inhabited locales, the overcoming of water barriers in conditions of spring flooding, fighting the enemy's *faustpatrone* troops, carrying out maneuver on the battlefield, and other questions having practical significance in carrying out the combat assignment.

In this connection, the commanders and political workers paid particular attention to organizing the exchange of combat experience in new conditions and the rapid transmission of the leading elements' and soldiers' experience to the troops. *Front*, army and divisional papers, as well as leaflets, which were issued by the political sections, popularized this experience and made it the common property of all soldiers and officers. The party organizations were the inspirers and initiators of progressive experience in their subunits.

A significant place in our mass agitation work was devoted to explaining the enemy's tactics, which he employed on his own territory. The *front* headquarters drew up special instructions explaining the enemy's tactics and determining methods of fighting the enemy on his territory. The most important parts of these instructions, in the form of a soldier's notebook, were reproduced typographically and distributed among the troops.

All of these measures, and the explanatory work in the subunits connected with them, raised the troops' combat capabilities and directed them to better carrying out their combat assignments.

The personal example of communists and Komsomol members had a decisive significance in helping to carry out the command's orders. While occupying the vanguard role in battle, they carried along the remaining soldiers and by their selfless fulfillment of their combat duty they inspired the subunits and units to massive heroic feats in the name of the Motherland.

One of the forms for the political education of the troops and their mobilization to carry out their combat assignments was the systematic acquaintance of the entire rank and file with international events, with the situation along the fronts of the Great Patriotic War, and with the life of the Motherland and the heroic labor feats of the Soviet people. Along with political conversations and reports, which were conducted during breaks between battles, the political lecturers and readers read articles from newspapers during rest periods, information and releases from the Soviet Information Bureau, letters from home, and other materials. When for some reason or another the papers were delayed, Soviet Information Bureau reports were taken over the radio, copied and distributed among the subunits.

An important place in the troops' political education was occupied by the Supreme Commander-in-Chief's orders expressing thanks for the Soviet forces' new victories. They inspired the Soviet forces to new heroic feats. The skillful and timely transmission of these orders to the troops was one of the most important tasks of the commanders and political workers, and one with which they coped very successfully.

The entire multi-faceted activity of the *front's* military council and political directorate, army political sections, commanders, political workers, and all the *front's* party organizations, which was often conducted in extremely difficult conditions, led to amazing results. This activity was a very important factor and had a great influence on the final success of the *front's* February offensive.

During the Lower Silesian operation, the First Ukrainian Front's forces resolved a major operational-strategic task.

The enemy's important strategic line of defense on the Oder River, relying on which the German-Fascist command counted on securely covering the Berlin direction, was overcome by the *front's* forces in a short time. The enemy was thrown beyond the Neisse River, as a result of which the *front's* forces occupied a favorable jumping-off position for launching the final attack against fascist Germany.

The *front's* resolution of its assigned tasks in extremely complex conditions testifies to the generals' and officers' high level of military skill, to their great organizational capabilities, and to the greatness and wisdom of the Soviet military school, which raised and educated a galaxy of new commanders, armed with Soviet military science, the most progressive in the world.

The operation conducted once more showed the extremely high morale-combat qualities of the Soviet troops, raised by the Communist Party in a spirit of life-giving Soviet patriotism, a boundless devotion to one's Motherland and one's people.

The *front's* soldiers, from private to general, united around the Communist Party and the Soviet government, faced the enemy, firmly convinced of the right and majesty of the cause for which they fought, manifested mass heroism and through their feats multiplied the honor and glory of the Soviet socialist Motherland.

Part VI

The First Ukrainian Front's Upper Silesian Offensive Operation (15-31 March 1945)

The article, 'The First Ukrainian Front's Upper Silesian Offensive Operation', was written by Colonel I.P. Barabashin. The following took part in preparing the collection: major generals N.M. Zamyatin (deceased) and K.V Sychev, colonels V.V. Voznenko, A.N. Grylev and N.A. Fokin. The editor is Lieutenant General S.P. Platonov.

Introduction

The Soviet forces' January offensive, which unfolded along a 1,200-kilometer front from the Baltic Sea to the Carpathians, and which was conducted to a depth of up to 600 kilometers, comprised the first stage of the 1945 campaign in Europe. During this stage the Soviet forces defeated the enemy's main forces in East Prussia and Poland, encircled up to 30 German-Fascist divisions in the Königsberg area, and with their main forces, which were attacking along the central direction, reached the Oder along a broad front. In Hungary the Soviet forces, having repelled the enemy's counterblows, completed the defeat of the major enemy group of forces encircled in Budapest.

During the course of the second stage of the 1945 campaign in Europe, which lasted from February until the second half of April, the Soviet army defeated the enemy's East Prussian and East Pomeranian groups of forces, as well the enemy forces operating in Hungary, thus creating favorable conditions for the final rout of the German-Fascist armed forces.

The Upper Silesian offensive operation by the First Ukrainian Front's forces was conducted during 15-31 March, in accordance with the *Stavka* of the Supreme High Command's overall plan. The goal of the operation was the defeat of the enemy's Upper Silesian group of forces and the arrival of the First Ukrainian Front's left-wing forces at the foothills of the Sudeten Mountains and the creation of conditions for the *front's* subsequent offensive along the Berlin and Dresden directions. The Upper Silesian operation was conducted in operational and strategic cooperation with the Soviet army's other *fronts*, which at this time were resolving tasks to defeat the German-Fascist forces in the Königsberg area, in East Pomerania, the Carpathians, Hungary, and Austria.

The 5th Guards, 21st, 59th, and 60th combined-arms, 4th Tank, and 2nd Air armies took part in the Upper Silesian operation, as well as the 4th Guards and 31st tank and 7th Guards Mechanized corps. During the operation five German divisions were encircled and destroyed in the area southwest of Oppeln. With their arrival at the foothills of the Sudeten Mountains, the *front's* left-wing armies created conditions for the subsequent successful offensive by the *front's* forces along the Berlin and Dresden directions.

Despite its small scale, the Upper Silesian operation offers a number of instructive examples of an operational and tactical nature, which may be employed in the combat training of the Soviet army's troops and staffs.

Such instructive examples are:

—the encirclement and destruction of a large enemy group of forces by part of the forces of a single *front*;

—the skillful creation of a superiority in men and materiel, by weakening other sectors, along the axis of the armies' main attacks, given an insignificant overall superiority over the enemy along the entire offensive front;

—the maneuver to encircle the enemy's group of forces at a small depth, along with its simultaneous splitting up and destruction in detail;

—the skillful organization of flank security for the shock groups;

—the coordinated combat activities of the ground forces and aviation during the encirclement of the enemy group of forces southwest of Oppeln, and in destroying the encircled enemy;

—the massed employment of artillery in the fighting for towns;

—the employment of all calibers of guns for firing over open sights while breaking through the enemy's defense, and developing the offensive in the depth of his defense.

1

A Short Description of the Area of Military Operations

During the second half of March 1945, the First Ukrainian Front's forces were engaged in offensive battles along the territory bordered in the north along the line Schweidnitz—Brieg—Rosenberg; in the east, Rosenberg—Katowice—Biala; in the south, Biala—Troppau (Opava); in the west, in the foothills of the Sudeten Mountains, Troppau (Opava)—Schwiednitz. The overall territory of the area is equal to 25,000 kilometers.

The enemy's forces, which were defending in Upper Silesia, were covering the shortest route to Prague and into Czech Silesia—a coal basin and major military-industrial area.

The terrain in the area of combat operations is a plain of rolling foothills, which gradually rises from the Oder toward the Sudeten Mountains. The uplands filling the plain vary in height. Closer to the Oder the height of individual areas reaches 80-100 meters, 170-190 meters in the Grottkau area, and in the Neisse—Neustadt—Leobschutz area up to 220-225 meters. The gradual rise in elevation toward the enemy offered him a number of advantages. The commanding heights and favorable lines for defense were in his hands.

The soil around the Sudeten foothills is gravelly and loamy toward the northeast. The plentiful rains in March weakened the soil and made it difficult for all kinds of transport and military equipment, particularly during the 1-22 March time period.

A large wooded area stretches southwest of Oppeln, which excluded the possibility of the massed employment of mobile forces. Only insignificant copses are encountered along the area's remaining territory.

Water barriers along the offensive sector of the First Ukrainian Front's left wing included the Oder River and its left tributaries—the Neisse, Steinau and Hotzenplotz rivers, and a number of other small rivers and canals.

The valley of the Oder River in the area of military operations, from Ratibor to the mouth of the Neisse River, is up to 6-8.5 kilometers wide. The valley's slopes as far as Oppeln are high (15-25 meters) and steep, often precipitous, and from Oppeln they are gently sloping. Individual hills and ridges are encountered in the river's flood plain, as well as swampy sectors and numerous old river courses.

The Oder's width from Ratibor to the mouth of the Neisse River is 100-120 meters.

The plentiful rains and the melting of the snow in the mountains brought about flooding in the middle of March, while the water level rose one meter. The flooding coincided in time with the beginning of the Upper Silesian operation and created additional difficulties in supplying the troops.

The Neisse River from Ottmachauer Pond to its mouth has a winding course. The river's flood plain is 2-4 kilometers wide and swampy in some areas and is cut by a number of drainage canals. The river's width is 30-50 meters and is up to two meters deep, with a sandy bottom, as are the banks, which are steep and up to four meters in height. The significance of the river for the enemy as a water barrier was strengthened by the presence on enemy territory of the Ottmachauer Pond, located 14 kilometers west of the town of Neisse. The enemy could let water out of the reservoir in order to disrupt the crossings over the river and, should a large amount of water be let out, to flood the Neisse River's flood plain.

The Steinau River is 30-40 meters wide and up to 1.5 meters deep, having a sandy bottom and steep banks up to three meters high. The river's flood plain is swampy.

Aside from the rivers named, there are many small rivers in the area of combat operations, which flow to the east and north.

The enemy outfitted intermediate defensive lines along the left banks of the rivers flowing from south to north, by hanging on to which he could put up stubborn resistance to our forces. The enemy created switch positions along the banks of rivers flowing to the east.

The road network in Upper Silesia is well developed. There are many paved roads in the area. There is an average of one paved road per ten kilometers of front.

The densest network of paved roads is in the area of the towns of Strelen, Munsterberg, Grottkau, Neisse, Neustadt, Leobschutz, Ratibor, and Troppau (Opava).

The paved roads were in good condition and allowed for the passage of all types of transportation. The majority of the roads were bordered by trees. The network of paved roads was supplemented by a large number of dirt roads. However, it was very difficult to use them during the spring wet season and rainy weather. The dirt roads were impassable during the preparatory period for the operation, and were difficult of passage during the operation, from 15-23 March. Only during the operation's final days were the troops fully able to take advantage of the dirt road network.

An important railroad line, which ran through the area of combat operations from Breslau through Strelen, Neisse and Troppau (Opava) was a lateral one and connected the forces of Army Group Center with those of Army Group South. The seizure of this railroad by our forces would make it more difficult for the enemy to maneuver forces along the front.

In the economic sense, the area of combat operations was of great significance for Hitlerite Germany.

Many major synthetic fuel factories were located in the towns of Upper Silesia. For example, there were two factories in the Ratibor area and five in the Cosel area; there were two factories in Cosel itself, each of which produced up to 500,000 tons of fuel yearly.

The agriculture of Upper Silesia occupied a prominent place in the life of the area and was very important for Germany as a whole. Almost half the entire population of Upper Silesia was involved in agriculture, which was primarily in field crops.

Thus, in the military-economic sense, the area of combat operations was important to Germany.

The meteorological conditions during the Upper Silesian operation by the First Ukrainian Front's left-wing forces changed frequently. Of 17 days during which the operation was conducted, nine days were bad, as a result of which the dirt roads became difficult of passage for auto transportation and all types of military equipment. Tanks were often not able to operate off the roads. The enemy, taking advantage of this, was able to reinforce his anti-tank defense along those axes accessible to tanks.

The unfavorable meteorological conditions, especially during the first seven days of the operation, limited our aviation's activities. Only from 22 March did weather suitable for flying appear.

Thus, if the area of Upper Silesia itself basically allowed for the employment of all the combat arms in an operation, then the spring wet weather and unfavorable meteorological conditions rendered the troop's combat activities more difficult.

2

The Operational Situation of the First Ukrainian Front's Forces at the Beginning of March 1945

Following the completion of the Sandomierz-Silesian offensive operation in January 1945, the First Ukrainian Front (*front* commander, Marshal of the Soviet Union I.S. Konev, member of the military council, Lieutenant General Krainyukov, chief of staff, General, now Marshal of the Soviet Union, V.D. Sokolovskii) carried out an offensive operation in Lower Silesia in February. As a result of this operation, the *front's* right-wing forces reached the Neisse River and seized a bridgehead on its left bank, while the center armies reached the footholds of the Sudeten Mountains. The *front's* left-wing armies during this time were fighting to overcome the Oder defensive line to the south of Oppeln.

By the end of February the width of the First Ukrainian Front's sector reached up to 530 kilometers. The elongation of the front and the losses suffered by the *front's* forces during the course of the two preceding operations significantly reduced the attacking forces' operational density and curtailed their offensive capabilities. By this time the resistance of the enemy, who had been thrown back to the Neisse River, had increased. As a result, all our troops' attempts to transfer military activities from the march to the left bank of the river were unsuccessful. Our forces were forced to temporarily halt their offensive along the Berlin direction and consolidate along the lines reached.

The lagging behind of the *front's* left-wing forces was making the situation considerably more difficult. The enemy could launch a flank attack from the area southwest of Oppeln against the *front's* right-wing forces to the northwest, relieve his encircled forces in Breslau and restore the front line along the Oder.

As early as the First Ukrainian Front's offensive in Lower Silesia, comrade Stalin repeatedly pointed out to the *front* commander the lagging behind of the *front's* left-wing forces and emphasized that it would eventually make more difficult the preparation and conduct of an operation by the *front's* forces along the Berlin direction.

The following situation had arisen along the neighboring sectors in the beginning of March. The First Belorussian Front's forces, which were operating to the north of the First Ukrainian Front directly along the Berlin direction, were fighting for a bridgehead on the left bank of the Oder north and south of Küstrin. The *front's* right-wing forces, in conjunction with the Second Belorussian Front's forces, were successfully accomplishing the defeat of the enemy's East Pomeranian group of forces, were clearing the enemy from the shore of the Baltic Sea and from the mouth of the Vistula to the mouth of the Oder, and were fighting for the ports of Danzig and Gdynia, and to reach the Oder along its lower course.

In February the forces of the Fourth Ukrainian Front continued to attack in the Carpathians along the Moravska Ostrava axis, south of the First Ukrainian Front. This *front's* forces, being the connecting link between the Soviet army's two strategic groups of forces—the central and southern—had drawn to itself considerable German-Fascist forces and in this way was facilitating the successful resolution of the tasks assigned to the *fronts* operating along the main strategic directions.

By 1 March the First Ukrainian Front's forces occupied the following line: the *front's* right-wing armies had arrived at the right bank of the Neisse River from its mouth to Penzig; in the center the front line ran through Lewenberg—Jauer—Grottkau; the *front's* forces along the left wing were defending along the right bank of the Oder River, from Oppeln to Lenga, holding a bridgehead on the left bank of the Oder River north of Ratibor. Further on, the front line turned to the east and ran north of Rybnik and east of Zorau, where it once again turned to the south toward the town of Strumen.

All the combined-arms armies and the 3rd Guards Tank Army were operating in the first echelon and were engaged in defensive fighting. The 3rd Guards Army occupied defensive positions from Ratzdorf to Tribel along a 60-kilometer front, while part of its forces continued to fight to destroy the enemy forces in Glogau. The 13th Army had consolidated along the line Tribel—Penzig along a 70-kilometer front; the 52nd and 3rd Guards Tank armies were covering a 90-kilometer front from Penzig to Jauer; the 5th Guards Army was defending an 85-kilometer front from Jauer to Strelen; the 21st Army occupied a 75-kilometer defensive front Strelen to Oppeln; the 59th Army was defending along a 70-kilometer front from Oppeln to Polln and Gross Neukirch; the 60th Army was engaged in defensive fighting along a 70-kilometer front along the line Polln—Gross Neukrich—Strumen, and; the 6th Army was fighting to destroy the enemy blockaded in Breslau.

At this time the *front* commander had in reserve the 4th Tank Army in the Luben area, the 7th Guards Mechanized and 31st Tank corps in the area of the woods south of Gross Strelitz.

In all, as of 1 March the *front* disposed of 66 rifle divisions, 886 tanks and self-propelled artillery pieces (only combat-ready tanks are included), 6,139 artillery pieces of all types, 5,197 mortars of various calibers, and 1,737 planes.

During the preceding battles the *front's* forces suffered significant losses. Some rifle divisions had little more than 3,000 men. Such divisions usually consisted of six rifle battalions.

At this time the armies' provisioning with individual types of artillery munitions varied from 0.3 to two combat loads.

The great difficulties, which the troops would have to encounter in resolving the tasks assigned to them, did not weaken their will to victory. Despite the stubborn defense of the enemy, who fought for every favorable line with the desperation of the condemned, a high degree of morale was noted among the First Ukrainian Front's forces, and a desire to defeat the enemy. The soldiers and officers believed in the Soviet army's power and were filled with resolution to carry out their duty to the end. They knew that the hour of the enemy's final defeat and the final victory over fascist Germany was approaching.

3

The Disposition of the Enemy's Forcces and a Description of His Defense

In the beginning of March the First Ukrainian Front continued to be opposed by the forces of Army Group Center, which was composed of the Fourth Panzer and Seventeenth armies and army group "Heinrici." The Fourth Panzer Army was defending opposite the *front's* right wing along the Ratzdorf—Penzig sector, containing the XL Panzer Corps, the *Grossdeutschland* Panzer Corps and the XXXIX Panzer Corps. Defending opposite the *front's* center forces and covering the Dresden direction from Penzig to Waldau was the Seventeenth Army, which was comprised of the XXIV, LVII and XLVIII panzer corps and the XVII and VIII army corps. The Seventeenth Army also included the garrison encircled in Breslau. Defending opposite the *front's* left wing along the line from Waldau to Skoczow were the Seventeenth Army's VIII Army Corps and army group "Heinrici" (First Tank Army). The boundary line between these armies ran through Glatz, Ottmachau and Karlsmarkt.

The VIII Army Corps, consisting of the 254th Infantry and 100th Light Infantry divisions, the 45th Infantry Division's combat group, and about ten various independent battalions, was defending the line Jordansmuhl—Waldau.

Army group "Heinrici" was defending the line from Waldau to Skoczow and covering the axis to Prague. This group's forces occupied the following position: corps group "Silesia," consisting of the 20th SS Infantry Division's combat group, the 168th Infantry Division and 11 independent battalions was defending the line from Waldau to Mechnitz; the XI Army Corps, consisting of the 344th and 371st infantry and 1st Ski Destruction division's combat groups, the 97th Light Infantry Division, three independent regiments, and 17 independent battalions, was defending the sector from Mechnitz to Jeikowice; the LIX Army Corps, consisting of the 68th and 253rd infantry divisions and the 75th and 544th infantry divisions' combat groups, was defending the line Jeikowice—Skoczow.

In all, the enemy facing the First Ukrainian Front's forces had 43 divisions, 560 tanks and assault guns, 750 planes, more than 4,500 guns and mortars, and a large number of *faustpatrones*.

Army Group Center had in reserve four infantry, two panzer and one panzergrenadier divisions, and 60 battalions staffed by recovering troops, which were undergoing training in the Graetz-Kralewski area.

From this data on the enemy's dispositions, it is clear that the enemy had one division per each 12 kilometers of front and thus disposed of a sufficient amount of men and materiel for resisting our forces' offensive.

By the beginning of the planning for the March offensive, the overall correlation of forces was in favor of the First Ukrainian Front. The First Ukrainian Front outnumbered the enemy 1.5 times in men, 1.6 times in tanks and 2.3 times in planes.

Immediately opposite the First Ukrainian Front's left-wing armies, where units of the VIII, XI and LIX army corps and corps group "Silesia" were operating, the enemy disposed of 128 battalions, 1,420 guns and mortars and 94 tanks and assault guns,[1] taking into account all the independent regiments and subunits. This would enable the enemy to have, on the average, 0.67 battalions per kilometer of front, 7.5 guns and mortars, and 0.5 tanks and assault guns.

Army group "Heinrici" had in reserve the fully equipped 154th Infantry Division in the Glinsko area, the 18th SS Panzergrenadier Division in Steinau and Leobschutz, and the 320th Infantry Division's combat group in Ernau. Besides this, the group had in reserve two Hungarian divisions—the 16th Infantry and 2nd Reserve Infantry—which were located opposite the Fourth Ukrainian Front's right wing in the Prerau area (70 kilometers southwest of Moravska Ostrava). No more than a day would be required to transfer them to the area of combat operations.

The Seventeenth Army's VIII Army Corps and army group "Heinrici" could be reinforced during combat operations through the Army Group Center reserve from the Graetz-Kralweski area, where at this time there were 60 fully outfitted battalions.

Thus facing the *front's* left-wing armies along a 190-kilometer front, the enemy could concentrate about 230 battalions, or 25 divisions, which yielded an average of one division every eight kilometers.

The regroupings that were being carried out by the enemy along the First Ukrainian Front's sector in the first half of March were local in character, and thus by 15 March, that is, by the beginning of our offensive, no significant changes in the enemy forces' situation had occurred.

At the heart of the German-Fascist command's strategic plan in the east lay the idea of stubborn defense; however, the Army Group Center command nevertheless counted on carrying out an offensive in the area to the southeast of Breslau, for the purpose of relieving its forces encircled in Breslau and, should its offensive activities develop successfully, to restore the front line along the Oder. For this purpose, a local operation to eliminate our bridgehead on the left bank of the Oder north of Ratibor was planned.

All the German forces' attempts to carry out these designs during the last ten days of February and in the first days of March ended in failure. Our forces not only held their positions in active defensive battles, but having regrouped their forces, had prepared simultaneously for a new offensive.

The enemy, following his unsuccessful attempt to restore the front line along the Oder, was vigorously improving the defense along his lines, reinforcing his worn out divisions with men, materiel and munitions.

In the rear, the Hitlerites had prepared all the favorable lines, inhabited locales and road junctions for defense; the local population and prisoners of war were brought in to work on the defensive positions. Detachments of local residents, which were undergoing hurried military training, were being created in all more or less major inhabited areas.

The enemy had been preparing a defense for five weeks in the offensive sector of the *front's* left-wing forces. The majority of the enemy's defensive lines had field-type fortifications. The exception was the rear line on the Opava River. Here along the Jagerndorf—Troppau (Opava)—Darkovice sector, the Czechoslovak command had created a zone of permanent fortifications along the border with Germany even before 1938.

---

1   Intelligence on the enemy was compiled by the intelligence section of the First Ukrainian Front's staff and the German General Staff's operational directorate.

Strong points, echeloned in depth, formed the basis of the enemy's tactical defensive zone.

In the beginning of March the enemy was continuing to improve his defenses, deepening his trenches, building earth and wooden pillboxes, putting up wire obstacles, and minefields, particularly along axes favorable to tanks. In organizing their defense, the German troops were guided by a 25 February 1945 directive (No. 1182/45) from the Army Group Center command. In this directive particular attention was devoted to the creation of a deep first defensive zone and at transforming each inhabited locale into a powerful center of resistance.

By the start of our offensive the forward edge of the enemy's main defensive zone ran along a line three kilometers north of Strelen, four kilometers south of Grottkau, one kilometer south of Oppeln, and then along the left bank of the Oder River as far as Cosel. The front line opposite the bridgehead ran through Langlieben, Schneidenburg and Schoendorf. In the Lenga area the front line crossed over to the right bank of the Oder and then ran in the direction of Rybnik and Sohrau (Zory).

The first position of the main defensive line, for the most part, had one fully-outfitted continuous trench. Second and third trenches had been dug along some sectors, but they were noncontinuous and not fully outfitted. Along the axes of our likely attack, for example, along the Alt Grottkau—Schedlau sector and opposite the bridgehead along the western bank of the Oder River north or Ratibor, the first position had been reinforced with anti-tank minefields, wire obstacles, pillboxes and armored covers.

The strong points were echeloned in depth to the line Patschkau—Neisse—Zuckmantel—Jagerndorf—Troppau (Opava) and to the east. In order to create strong points, the enemy employed inhabited locales and heights. In the inhabited locales, homes, churches and other stone structures had been configured for firing from infantry weapons and artillery pieces. Houses located on the outskirts of the inhabited locales and along intersections were being configured most securely for defense.

The density of the inhabited locales enabled the enemy to establish fire communications between them with almost all kinds of infantry weapons.

In the spaces between the inhabited locales individual trenches and rifle trenches had been dug and firing positions fitted out.

It should be shown that towns and villages had been most securely prepared for defense to a depth of 20-25 kilometers.

The enemy's army defensive line ran along the line Patschkau—Neisse—Zigenhals—Zuckmantel—Jagerndorf—Troppau (Opava)—Darkovice. By the start of our offensive defensive works had been completed between 40-50 percent along the Patschkau—Jagerndorf sector.

Along the Jagerndorf—Troppau (Opava)—Darkovice sector there were 30 reinforced pillboxes built by the Czechoslovak government in 1936-37. Recently, the enemy had strengthened his permanent structures with field fortifications and dug continuous trenches in 1-2 lines. The trenches were linked together by communications trenches and outfitted with rifle and machine gun emplacements.

The enemy had also begun to build a defensive line along the approaches to Troppau (Opava), which ran through Lindau, Turkau, Piltsch, Oldrzichow and Steuberwitz. By the beginning of our offensive, only individual and unimproved trench sectors had been dug.

By creating a deep and developed engineering defense, the German-Fascist command was trying to make up for its shortage of ammunition.

By this time the provisioning of the enemy forces with ammunition for light and heavy field howitzers and for heavy infantry guns had declined. Thus the expenditure of ammunition for the listed types of guns was strictly limited among the troops. For example, the commander of the 18th SS Panzergrenadier Division, in his order of 6 March 1945 (No. 35/45) authorized his forces to fire from light and heavy field howitzers and from heavy infantry guns only in the following instances: for supporting an attack by forces up to a battalion and more in strength and, in exceptional cases, for repelling enemy attacks of more than a company in strength. In order to hide the true ammunition supply situation from Soviet forces, the division commander demanded that guns be employed using ammunition that did not present so many supply problems. An analogous situation with ammunition existed in all of Army Group Center's other formations. The enemy forces were better provisioned with anti-tank weapons. By this time the *faustpatrone* had been introduced into the German-Fascist army. By the start of our offensive the enemy had a tank-destroyer company, armed with *faustpatrones*, in each regiment.

The German food situation, which was worsening with each day, sharply told on the army's supply.

On 5 March 1945, on the orders of the commander of Army Group Center, Colonel General Schorner,[2] new reduced norms of food, tobacco and spirits were to be introduced. Schorner cynically stated that the German army had eaten very well throughout the war at the expense of the occupied countries, and now that these conditions no longer existed, the food situation had changed. The order declared to be wreckers and saboteurs all those who ate more than was authorized. The difficult ammunition and food situation testified to the fact that the German-Fascist rear could no longer supply the needs of the front in the required amounts.

The combat spirit of the German-Fascist army's soldiers and troop discipline had sharply declined under the influence of the latest major defeats on the Soviet-German front. In a top secret order of 6 March 1945 (No. 35/45), the commander of the 18th SS Panzergrenadier Division wrote:

> … after five years of war the quality of our infantryman and grenadier has sharply fallen in comparison with what we had when we had only begun to fight. This may be explained by the fact that the infantryman goes to take up his position not being as well trained as before and, on the other hand, what is most important to root out, is that the infantryman has completely lost faith in himself and his weaponry in connection with numerous defeats and related withdrawals. In the most recent fighting these shortcomings have revealed themselves with particular vividness.

The German-Fascist command, from division commander and higher, was forced in its orders to make note of the decline in troop discipline among the rank and file and NCOs, the manifestation of cowardice, looting, desertion, instances of subordinates failing to carry out orders, subordinates' failure to salute their seniors, etc. The Hitlerite army's discipline, which was based on crude force and blind obedience, was falling.

Hitlerite soldiers and officers, who had become used to thieving and looting, did not now spare their fellow countrymen.

The decline in the army's moral spirit and the presence of signs of its demoralization seriously worried the German-Fascist command. Keitel,[3] the Wehrmacht's chief of staff, issued a special decree, on the instructions of Hitler, "On the Conduct of Officers and the Rank and File in

---

2   Editor's note. Ferdinand Schorner (1892-1973) served in the German army during the First World War. During the Second World War he fought in Poland and the Balkans, before taking part in the Soviet campaign. Here he commanded a division, a corps and several army groups. He was later appointed field marshal and commander-in-chief of the German army. Schorner was later arrested by the Soviets and spent several years in prison for war crimes.

3   Editor's note. Wilhelm Keitel (1882-1946) joined the imperial German army in 1901 and fought in the First World War. He was appointed him chief of the Supreme Command of the Armed Forces (OKW) in 1938, from which post he proceeded to slavishly subordinate the country's military apparatus to Hitler. Keitel was arrested following the war and executed for war crimes.

the Critical Situation." The decree emphasized the necessity of severely dealing with all wavering elements that had lost faith in the victory of German-Fascist weaponry, pointed out the duty of commanders at all levels to employ weapons against such people, arrest them and turn them over to a military-field court. Particular attention was devoted to combating phenomena that contributed to the army's demoralization: against the manifestation of cowardice, failure to obey one's commander, withdrawing without orders, etc.

The harsh measures adopted by the German-Fascist command for restoring discipline in the army protected it from collapse to a certain extent and forced the German soldiers to continue fighting without hope for victory. The fascist forces' stubborn resistance can also be explained by the fact that fascist propaganda was spreading rumors about atrocities supposedly carried out by Russians against prisoners and the civilian population.

4

The Operation's Preparation

The Overall Scheme of the Upper-Silesian Offensive Operation and the Armies' Tasks

On 24 February; that is, following the completion of the Lower Silesian offensive operation, the *front* commander presented his plan for the *front's* subsequent activities to the *Stavka*.

According to this plan, the 3rd Guards and 13th armies, which were operating along the *front's* right wing, were to assume the defensive along the Neisse River from its mouth to Penzig (excluding the latter).

The 52nd and 3rd Guards Tank armies, while continuing to attack, were to reach the Neisse River in the Gorlitz area and to the south and consolidate along the line reached. Following its arrival at the indicated line, it was planned to pull the 3rd Guards Tank Army into the *front* reserve and concentrate it in the Bunzlau area.

It was planned to launch the main attack in the general direction of Schweidnitz, Frankenstein, Neisse, Neustadt, and Leobschutz, with the mission of defeating the enemy's group of forces opposite the *front's* center and left wing and throwing it back into the Sudeten Mountains. In order to carry out this assignment, a group of forces was to be employed comprising the 5th Guards, 21st and 4th Tank armies, the 7th Guards Mechanized and 4th Guards and 31st tank corps, and four artillery breakthrough divisions.

It was planned to employ the *front's* entire air army.

Upon the arrival of the main group of forces in the Neisse area, the 59th and 60th armies were to attack as well and develop the attack from the bridgehead north of Ratibor to the west and southwest.

The beginning of the operation was set for approximately 10-15 March.

The plan foresaw that prior to the beginning of the operation the 5th Guards and 21st armies would continue active operations for the purpose of improving their situation and to further wear out the enemy.

The 6th Army was to continue trying to destroy the enemy group of forces encircled in Breslau. Following the capture of Breslau, it was planned to concentrate the army in the Breslau—Liegnitz area, in the *front* reserve.

At the heart of the plan for the Upper Silesian offensive operation lay the Supreme Commander-in-Chief's instructions on the necessity of eliminating the lag of the *front's* left-wing forces as quickly as possible, in order to create favorable conditions for later launching a powerful attack against the enemy along the Berlin direction through the unified forces of the First Ukrainian and First Belorussian fronts.

The favorable flanking position of our forces in relation to the enemy group of forces defending in upper Silesia facilitated the successful conduct of an offensive operation along the *front's* left wing. The front occupied by the forces of the 5th Guards, 21st, 59th, and 60th armies following the February battles gave us the opportunity to realize an operation to encircle and destroy the enemy group of forces in the Oppeln salient without a complex regrouping.

The Supreme Commander-in-Chief, having approved in principle the idea of organizing an offensive operation to defeat the enemy in Upper Silesia, demanded that the *front* commander present a concrete plan for the operation. This plan was drawn up and on 27 February was presented to the *Stavka* of the Supreme High Command for confirmation. According to this plan, the *front's* center and left-wing forces were to "defeat the enemy opposite the *front's* center and left flank and throw him back into the Sudeten Mountains." It was planned to create two shock groups to conduct the operation: the first (northern) in the area southwest of Breslau, and a second (southern) north of Ratibor.

The northern group of forces, consisting of the 5th Guards, 21st and 4th Tank armies, the 7th Guards Mechanized, 4th Guards Tank, and 1st Guards Cavalry corps, four artillery breakthrough divisions, and a guards mortar division, was to break through the enemy's front along a 17-18 kilometer sector from Domantze to Wolfskirch and, while developing the offensive to the southeast, launch its main attack toward Reichenbach, Frankenstein, Patschkau, and Neustadt.

The southern group of forces, consisting of the 59th Army, reinforced with the 93rd Rifle Corps, the 60th Army and the 31st Tank Corps, was to attack along the armies' adjacent flanks from the bridgehead on the left bank of the Oder River north of Ratibor and break through the enemy's defense along an 8-kilometer front along the Langlieben—Polln—Gross Neukirch sector and, while attacking to the west and southwest, link up with the northern group of forces in the Neustadt area, and in joint actions defeat the enemy group of forces opposite the *front's* center and left wing and throw the remnants back into the Sudeten Mountains. The depth of the southern group's task was less than that of the northern one. It was planned to begin this group's offensive two days later than the start of the northern group's offensive.

The *front* command calculated that the northern group's offensive, beginning two days before that of the southern group, would draw the enemy's immediate reserves against itself and thus create favorable conditions for a successful offensive by the southern group's forces.

It was planned to commit 35 rifle divisions and about 700 tanks and self-propelled guns to carry out the operation. It was planned to raise the artillery density along the main attack's axis to 150 guns and mortars (not counting 82mm mortars) per kilometer of front.

It was planned to pull the 3rd Guards Tank Army into the *front* reserve in the Liegnitz—Bunzlau area.

It was planned to begin the operation between 10-15 March.

The Supreme Commander-in-Chief, taking into account the exhaustion of the *front's* rank and file following two months of offensive fighting, the strength of the units and the insufficient provisioning of the troops with ammunition, issued instructions to reduce the scope of the *front's* operation and limit it to eliminating the enemy only in the Oppeln salient, in order to move up the *front's* left-wing armies abreast of the center armies, thus creating favorable conditions for conducting the Berlin operation, which was already being planned and prepared for by the *Stavka* of the Supreme High Command.

On the basis of the *Stavka's* instructions, the First Ukrainian Front command drew up a new operational plan and on 28 February presented it to the *Stavka* for confirmation. According to this plan, the operation's goal was the encirclement and destruction of the enemy's group of forces southwest of Oppeln and the arrival of the *front's* left-wing forces at the line Strelen—Munsterberg—Patschkau—Troppau (Opava). It was planned to employ 31 rifle divisions and about 800 tanks and self-propelled guns to carry out the operation, creating from these forces two shock groups—Oppeln (in the salient northwest of Oppeln) and Ratibor (on the bridgehead north of Ratibor).

The Oppeln group of forces, consisting of the 21st Army (reinforced with the 5th Guards Army's 34th Guards Rifle Corps), 4th Tank Army, 4th Guards Tank Corps, two artillery breakthrough divisions, a guards mortar division, and an anti-tank artillery brigade, was to launch an attack in the general direction of Grottkau, Neisse and Neustadt, where it was to link up with the Ratibor group's forces and complete the encirclement of the enemy southwest of Oppeln. The operations of the 21st Army's shock group would be supported by an attack by the 5th Guards Army's 34th Guards Rifle and the 4th Guards Tank corps in the general direction of Priborn, with the task of reaching the line Strelen—Munsterberg by the close of the operation's second day.

According to the plan, the Ratibor group of forces included: the 59th Army (reinforced by the newly arrived 93rd Rifle Corps), 60th Army, 7th Guards Mechanized Corps, 31st Tank Corps, the 152nd Tank Brigade, an artillery breakthrough division, one guards mortar brigade, four anti-tank artillery brigades, and a mortar brigade. This group was to launch an attack from the bridge-head north of Ratibor to the west and southwest toward the 21st Army's forces and by the close of the third day of the operation link up with the latter in the Neustadt—Zultz area.

As before, it was planned to have the 3rd Guards Tank Army in the *front* reserve in the Liegnitz—Bunzlau area.

It was planned to create the following artillery densities: along the 21st Army's breakthrough sector—150 guns and mortars per kilometer of front (not counting 82mm mortars); along the 59th and 60th armies' breakthrough sector—170 guns and mortars per kilometer of front (not counting 82mm mortars). The difference in the artillery density of 20 guns and mortars per kilometer of breakthrough front is explained by the fact that the enemy's defense opposite the bridge-head on the left bank of the Oder River north of Ratibor, from which the 59th and 60th armies were to attack, was more powerful.

The start of the operation was set for approximately 15 March. Thus 15 days were set aside for preparing the operation.

On 1 March the Supreme Commander-in-Chief confirmed this variant of the plan and ordered that the operation begin two days earlier than the specified time.

In order to reinforce the Ratibor group of forces, the *Stavka* ordered the employment of the 25th Artillery Breakthrough Division, which was supposed to arrive at the *front* by the start of the operation.

It was ordered to immediately pull the 3rd Guards Tank Army into the *front* reserve in the Liegnitz—Bunzlau area and to bring it back up to strength.

The *Stavka* of the Supreme High Command ordered the commander of the Fourth Ukrainian Front to begin an offensive on 10 March, employing his right-wing forces, launching an attack in the direction of Moravska Ostrava, Hranice and Olomouc, for the purpose of destroying the enemy's Moravska Ostrava group of forces, capturing the Moravska Ostrava industrial area, and with its main forces reaching the line Beneschau (Benesov)—Beraun (Moravian Beroun)—Olomouc—Tovacov.

The offensive, planned by the *Stavka* of the Supreme High Command, of the Fourth Ukrainian Front's right-wing armies was to assist the First Ukrainian Front's left-wing armies in carrying out their assigned tasks. The attack by the Fourth Ukrainian Front's forces was supposed to deprive the enemy of the ability to maneuver his reserves and reinforce his group of forces operating opposite the First Ukrainian Front's left wing.

Following the *Stavka* of the Supreme High Command's confirmation of the plan for the offensive operation, the First Ukrainian Front's military council on 8 March issued operational directive no. 00128/op, in which it assigned tasks to the armies.

According to this directive, the *front's* left-wing armies were to break through the enemy's defense south of Grottkau and opposite the bridgehead on the left bank of the Oder River north of Ratibor; subsequently, while developing the attacks in the general direction of Neustadt, the armies were to encircle the enemy's group of forces southwest of Oppeln, destroy it and establish a front along the line Strelen—Munsterberg—Patschkau—Troppau (Opava). In accordance with the operation's overall scheme, the armies were assigned the following tasks.

5th Guards Army (commander, Colonel General A.S. Zhadov, member of the military council, Major General P.Ye. Sukharev, chief of staff, Major General N.I. Lyamin), while attacking along its left flank with the 34th Rifle and 4th Guards Tank corps, reinforced by army artillery and units of the 3rd Artillery Breakthrough Division, was to break through the enemy's defense along the following 3-kilometer sector: height 172.0—Voigtsdorf and, rolling up the enemy's defense in the direction of Priborn and Alt Heinrichau, by the close of the first day of the operation capture the line Lorentzberg—excluding Deutsch Jagel. By the close of the operation's third day the army was to reach the line Strelen—Munsterberg. The overall depth of the army's assignment was 30 kilometers.

The 4th Guards Tank Corps, which was to attack simultaneously with the rifle troops, was to launch an attack in the direction of Arnsdorf and Munsterberg, and capture Munsterberg on the operation's second day.

The army's center and right-wing formations received orders to tie down the opposing enemy forces through active operations and deprive him of the capability of maneuvering.

The 21st Army (commander, Colonel General D.N. Gusev, member of the military council, Lieutenant General V.P. Mzhavanadze, chief of staff, Lieutenant General G.K. Bukhovets), was to break through the enemy's defense with the forces of eight rifle divisions (of these, five would be in the first echelon), reinforced by two (13th and 31st) artillery breakthrough divisions and the 3rd Guards Mortar Division (RS M-31) along the following 10-kilometer sector: Voigtsdorf—Rogau and, while vigorously attacking in the general direction of Neisse and Neustadt, in conjunction with the 4th Tank and 59th armies, to encircle the enemy's group of forces southwest of Oppeln and destroy it. By the close of the operation's third day the army was to capture the line excluding Munsterberg—Ottmachauer Pond—Neustadt—Zultz—Wiesengrund.

The overall depth of the army's assignment was 60 kilometers. On the operation's first day the troops were to advance 12-14 kilometers, 15-20 kilometers on the second day, and 26 kilometers on the third day.

It was planned to commit the 4th Tank Army (commander, Colonel General D.D. Lelyushenko, chief of staff, Major General K.I. Upman) into the fighting on the operation's first day in the sector of the 21st Army's main attack, in the direction of Friedewalde, Neisse and Neustadt, so that by the close of the operation's second day it could capture the area Neustadt—Dittersdorf—Olbersdorf—Zultz. Here units of the army were to link up with the 7th Guards Mechanized Corps, which was to attack to meet it from the 59th Army's breakthrough sector. As a result of capturing this area and seizing Ziegenhals, by the close of the operation's second day the path of retreat of the enemy group of forces defending southwest of Oppeln would be cut; the enemy would be deprived of the capability of transferring reserves to reinforce his group of forces in the Oppeln area; the timely arrival of the 21st Army's forces to link up with the 59th Army's forces would be supported, and thus the encirclement and defeat of the enemy in the woods south and southwest of Oppeln would be achieved.

The 59th Army (commander, Lieutenant General I.T. Korovnikov, member of the military council, Major General P.S. Lebedev, chief of staff, Major General N.P. Koval'chuk, reinforced with the 7th Guards Mechanized Corps, three brigades from the 17th Artillery Breakthrough Division, the 1st Independent Guards Mortar Brigade, and the 18th and 11th anti-tank artillery brigades, with six rifle divisions (of these, three were in the first echelon) along the axis of the main attack, was to break through the enemy's defense along the 3-kilometer sector Langlieben—the unnamed height west of Rosengrund and launch an attack in the direction of Kostenthal and Zultz, toward the 21st Army. By the close of the operation's third day, the 59th Army's shock group was to capture the area Krappitz—Kuau—Altstadt—Neustadt, link up with units of the 21st and 4th Tank armies and then, in conjunction with the 21st Army's forces, destroy the enemy group of forces in the woods south and southwest of Oppeln. As the main group of forces advanced, three of the 59th Army's right-flank divisions were to roll up the enemy's defense to the northwest along the left bank of the Oder River.

The 7th Guards Mechanized Corps was to attack on the operation's first day and by the close of the second day capture the area Altstadt—Neustadt, where it was to link up with units of the 4th Tank Army.

The overall depth of the 59th Army's assignment was 40 kilometers.

The 60th Army (commander, Colonel General P.A. Kurochkin, member of the military council, Major General Olenin, chief of staff, Major General A.D. Goncharov), reinforced with the 31st Tank Corps, the 152nd Tank Brigade, three brigades from the 17th Artillery Breakthrough Division, the 1st Guards Mortar Brigade (RS M-31), the 35th Mortar Brigade, and the 7th and 48th anti-tank artillery brigades, with six rifle divisions (of these, three were in the first echelon) in its shock group, was to break through the enemy's defense along the 4-kilometer sector Pulau—the brick factory south of Polln—Gross Neukirch, and attack in the direction of Schneidenburg, Ernau and Biskau, with the task of defeating the enemy's Ratibor group of forces. By the close of the operation's third day, the army was ordered to capture the line Neustadt—Soppau—Biskau—Ratibor. The depth of the 60th Army's assignment was 40 kilometers.

With the army's arrival at the line Neustadt—Soppau—Biskau—Ratibor, the army's center and left-flank formations, in conjunction with the 4th Ukrainian Front's forces, were to attack in the direction of Troppau (Opava).

The 31st Tank Corps, which was to attack together with the infantry, was to capture the Lindau—Troppau (Opava)—Oldrzichow—Osterdorf area by the close of the second day of the operation and prevent the arrival of the enemy's reserves to reinforce his Ratibor group of forces.

The fulfillment by the 60th Army of its assignments to defeat the enemy's Ratibor group of forces was to secure the successful attack by the 59th Army's forces against the enemy's flank attacks from the south and would thus create favorable conditions for defeating the enemy's forces in the Oppeln salient.

According to the *front* commander's idea, during the operation it was planned to encircle six German divisions southwest of Oppeln. The plan foresaw carrying out the operation at a vigorous pace and to complete the encirclement on the third day.

The leading role in accomplishing the enemy's encirclement was to be given to the tank and mechanized forces, which as early as the close of the operation's second day, having linked up in the Neustadt—Zultz area, were to cut off the enemy's path of retreat from the salient southwest of Oppeln to the west and southwest and to support the combined-arms armies' activities in encircling and destroying the German-Fascist forces in the woods southwest of Oppeln.

The plan called for the reliable securing of the shock group's external flanks for the successful encirclement and destruction of the enemy group of forces southwest of Oppeln,. The activities of the 21st and 4th Tank armies were to be supported by an attack by units of the 5th Guards Army and 4th Guards Tank Corps in the direction of Priborn, and Alt Heinrichau. The 59th Army's attack was to be supported by an attack by the 60th Army's forces to the west and southwest toward Ernau and Biskau and their arrival at the line Neustadt—Soppau—Biskau—Ratibor. The arrival of the 60th Army's forces at this line would enable the 59th Army to fully employ its forces for destroying the enemy group of forces southwest of Oppeln.

The Decisions of the Army Commanders

21st Army. The commander of the 21st Army made the decision to launch his main attack along the right flank, with the forces of two corps, against the densest enemy group of forces, to break through his defense and, in conjunction with the 4th Tank Army's forces, to develop the success to the south and southeast toward Neustadt, before linking up with the 59th Army's forces, after which together they would destroy the enemy encircled in the woods south and southwest of Oppeln. It was planned to carry out the breakthrough of the enemy's defense with the internal flanks of the 118th and 117th rifle corps along a 6-kilometer sector from the Grottkau—Neisse railroad to Merzdorf. The 55th Rifle Corps, while launching a supporting attack with its right-flank division, was to break through the enemy's defense along the 2-kilometer sector from the Neisse River to Rogau, while the remaining forces would hold their defensive line and simultaneously tie down the opposing enemy through active operations.

In accordance with this decision, the rifle corps received the following assignments.

The 118th Rifle Corps (commander, Major General A.F. Naumov), having two rifle divisions (128th and 282nd) in the first echelon and the 286th Rifle Division in the second, and having concentrated its main forces along the left flank, was to break through the enemy's defense along a 3-kilometer sector from the Grottkau—Neisse rail line to Ulrichsdorf and, while attacking in the direction of Klein Neudorf, Bechau, Ottmachau, and Kalkau, in conjunction with the 4th Tank Army's 6th Mechanized Corps, by the close of the offensive's first day capture the line Deutsch Jagel—Seifersdorf—Nachkau—Breitenfeld. With the arrival of the 6th Mechanized Corps' units to the line Ottmachau—Neisse, it was planned to dispatch a forward detachment, consisting of a reinforced rifle battalion, to each of the indicated areas. Throughout the offensive's second day, the corps, while continuing to develop the offensive to the southwest, was to reach the line Schutzendorf—Ottmachau—Neisse, while the left-flank division's forces, in conjunction with the 117th Rifle Corps' right-flank units, were to capture the northwestern part of Neisse. The corps' task on the offensive's third day was to reach the line excluding Munsterberg—Alt Patschkau—Kalkau—Wiensdorf. Upon capturing this area, the corps was to securely consolidate there and organize anti-tank strong points along areas accessible to tanks, particularly along the Ottmachau and Neisse axes, in order to repel possible enemy attacks from the southwest and south. Along with consolidating along this line, the corps was assigned the task of being ready to develop the offensive to the west. The commander of the 21st Army made the commander of the 118th Rifle Corps responsible for securing the boundary with the 5th Guards Army's 34th Guards Rifle Corps.

The army commander ordered the 118th Rifle Corps' second-echelon 286th Rifle Division to be committed into the battle along the boundary between the first-echelon divisions from the line Klein Zindel—Kroschen; that is, following the accomplishment of the immediate task by the first-echelon divisions, in the direction of Patschkau for the purpose of seizing Ottmachau. Such a task was dictated by the expansion of the corps' offensive sector as it moved forward. For example, by the close of the operation's first day the breadth of the corps' offensive sector was supposed to reach 16 kilometers and 24 kilometers by the close of the second day.

The 117th Rifle Corps (commander, Major General V.A. Trubachev), having two rifle divisions (72nd and 125th) in the first echelon and the 120th Rifle Division in the second, and having concentrated its main efforts along the right flank, was to break through the enemy's defense along the 3-kilometer sector Ulrichsdorf—Merzdorf. Following the breakthrough of the enemy's main defensive zone, the corps was by the close of the first day of the offensive, while attacking in conjunction with the 4th Tank Army's 10th Tank Corps in the direction of Waldau, Geltendorf, Neisse and Neustadt, to capture the line Breitenfeld—Bilitz. With the arrival of the 10th Tank Corps' units at the line Neisse—Neustadt, the 117th Rifle Corps was to dispatch two forward detachments, each consisting of a reinforced rifle battalion, to the area of Neisse and Rothaus to seize and hold this area until the arrival of the corps' main forces. During the offensive's second day the corps' task would be to capture, in conjunction with units of the 118th Rifle Corps, Neisse and reach the line Neisse—Lindendorf—Mansdorf. In the course of the offensive, the corps was to conduct reconnaissance in the direction of Steinau. It was planned to commit the second-echelon division into the battle in the Gross Neudorf area to the southeast, that is, along the corps' left flank. Subsequently, by the close of the operation's third day the corps, in conjunction with the 10th Tank Corps' units and developing the offensive to the south and southeast, was to capture the area Deutsch Wette—Neustadt—Altstadt, in the area of which it was planned to establish communications with units of the 59th Army, attacking from the east and to complete the encirclement of the enemy group of forces in the woods west and southwest of Oppeln. Upon its arrival at the line Deutsch Wette—Neustadt—Altstadt, the corps was to consolidate there and outfit it for anti-tank defense, paying particular attention to the Zuchmantel—Neustadt and Jagerndorf—Neustadt axes as the most likely ones for enemy counterattacks. The corps had the task of destroying the encircled enemy with its left-flank rifle division, in conjunction with units of the 59th Army's 55th Rifle Corps.

The 55th Rifle Corps (commander, Lieutenant General Yu.V. Novosel'skii) received orders to break through the enemy's defense along the 2-kilometer sector from the Neisse River to Rogau with its 285th Rifle Division, reinforced with artillery and mortars, and in conjunction with the 4th Tank Army's 93rd Independent Tank Brigade, to attack to the south in the direction of Bilitz, followed by the commitment of the 229th Rifle Division along this axis. These formations were ordered, in conjunction with units of the 117th Rifle Corps, to capture the line Gross Malendorf—Falkenberg—Schedlau by the close of the operation's first day; on the operation's second day, while developing the attack to the southeast toward Friedland, the corps was to capture the line Mauschdorf—Annahof—Steinau River and by the close of the third day of the offensive link up with the 59th Army's forces along the line Schoenewitz—Moschen—Schelitz—Ringwitz. Following the completion of the enemy's encirclement in the woods south and southwest of Oppeln, all the corps' forces were to be directed at destroying the encircled enemy in conjunction with the 59th Army's forces.

The 225th Rifle Division, which was defending the 26-kilometer Gross Mangersdorf—Zachrau sector, was to pin down the enemy opposite it through active operations during the first days of the operation and, from the moment he began to withdraw, to begin an unrelenting pursuit.

Thus the 55th Rifle Corps, which at first had been directed at resolving a supporting task, was subsequently, along with the 59th Army, to take up the main role of destroying the encircled enemy.

The 291st Rifle Division, which was part of the 55th Rifle Corps, was ordered to securely defend the sector Spurwitz—excluding Grottkau, which comprised the offensive sector of the 5th Guards Army's 34th Guards Rifle Corps. Upon the 34th Guards Rifle Corps' arrival at the Krin River, it was planned to move the 291st Rifle Division from its position and by the morning of the offensive's third day concentrate it in the areas of Lehrhenhein, Klodebach and Seifersdorf, where it would enter the 21st Army's reserve.

The army commander decided to deploy all of the army's forces in a single operational echelon. The adoption of such a decision was conditioned by the insignificant depth of the planned operation and the related possibility of carrying out the army's assigned task in a single blow and in the troops' initial operational formation.

The depth of the army's troops' formation was to be arrived at by echeloning the corps' and divisions' combat formations, which were organized into two echelons. The second-echelon regiments and divisions were located behind the regiments and divisions of the first echelon, which were to launch the main attack.

According to the *front* directive, an attack by the forward battalions would precede the attack by the main forces. These battalions' task was to determine whether or not the enemy was occupying the first trench with his main forces, or whether was it occupied only by a combat screening force, and to simultaneously reconnoiter the enemy's fire system. The successful resolution of these tasks would enable us to avoid the useless expenditure of ammunition during the artillery preparation.

Guided by these instructions, the army commander ordered each first-echelon division to detach one rifle battalion, reinforcing it with 2-4 tanks or self-propelled guns and a sapper platoon, and to support the attack of each forward battalion with 6-8 battalions of artillery and mortars.

The army commander ordered the forward battalions to attack the forward edge of the enemy's defense and, following the successful seizure of the first trench, to attack along the following axes: the 128th Rifle Division's forward battalion toward Beatenhof; the 282nd Rifle Division's forward battalion toward height 165.5; the 72nd Rifle Division's forward battalion toward Waldau; the 125th Rifle Division's forward battalion toward Schwarzergrund, and; the 285th Rifle Division's forward battalion toward height 218.3. The forward battalions' attack was to begin at 0610 on 15 March, following a 10-minute artillery onslaught.

4th Tank Army. The army commander, in accordance with the *front* commander's instructions, made the decision to commit the army's forces into the battle following the capture of the first position of the enemy's main defensive zone by the 21st Army's infantry and, in conjunction with the 21st Army's shock group, to complete the breakthrough of the enemy's tactical defensive zone and to vigorously develop the offensive in the general direction of Friedewalde, Neisse and Neustadt. It was planned to capture the Neustadt—Dittersdorf—Olbersdorf—Zultz area by the close of the operation's first day and to link up there with units of the 7th Guards Mechanized Corps, which would be attacking to meet the army out of the 59th Army's breakthrough sector. The rapid arrival of the army's forces in this area would enable us to cut off the enemy's path of retreat from the Oppeln salient to the west and southwest and support the successful operations of the 21st and 59th armies to encircle and to subsequently destroy the enemy forces southwest of Oppeln.

In accordance with this decision, the army's forces were assigned the following tasks.

The 6th Mechanized Corps (commander, Guards Colonel V.F. Orlov) was to be committed into the battle along the front excluding Voigtsdorf—excluding Alt Grottkau, with the following task: to complete the breakthrough of the enemy's main defensive zone in conjunction with the 118th Rifle Corps and, while developing a vigorous offensive in the direction of Klein Zindel, Bechau and Ottmachau, by the close of the operation's first day the corps' main forces were to capture the line Ottmachau—Kalkau—Morau—Rosshof, while the forward detachment was to capture Zigenhals. On the second day, the corps had the task of seizing Neustadt, Dittersdorf and Buchelsdorf with its main forces, while the flank detachment would take Zuckmantel. The army commander ordered that a powerful detachment be left in Ottmachau in order to secure the corps' main forces against possible enemy counterattacks from the direction of Patschau.

With the corps' arrival in the Neustadt area, it was supposed to conduct reconnaissance in the directions of Sandhubel, Freiwaldau, Hermanstadt, Olbersdorf, and Leobschutz.

The 10th Tank Corps (commander, Guards Lieutenant General of Tank Troops Ye.Ye. Belov) received orders to enter the battle along the front Alt Grottkau—excluding Kirchberg and to complete the breakthrough of the enemy's main defensive zone with the 117th Rifle Corps and, while developing a vigorous offensive in the direction of Waldau, Geltendorf, Waltdorf, and Neisse, by the close of the operation's first day to capture the town of Neisse and the inhabited locales of Bilau and Oppersdorf with its main forces, while a forward detachment was to take Neustadt. On the operation's second day, the corps' main forces were ordered to take the inhabited locales of Zeiselwitz, Leuber, Olbersdorf, and Zultz, while a forward detachment was to link up with units of the 7th Guards Mechanized Corps in Ober Glogau and thus arrive at the path of retreat for the enemy group of forces southwest of Oppeln and create conditions for the complete encirclement and destruction of the latter.

A single tank brigade would remain in Neisse to secure the corps's operations from the rear until the arrival of the 21st Army's forces.

The 93rd Independent Tank Brigade received orders to break through the enemy's defense, in conjunction with the 285th Rifle Division, along the sector Kirchberg—Rogau, after which it was to vigorously attack along the eastern bank of the Neisse River in the direction of Gruben and Hermsdorf; in joint efforts with the 10th Tank Corps, the brigade was to capture crossings over the Neisse River in the Neizorge—Rothaus area; the brigade was to subsequently assist the 10th Tank Corps' units in taking the town of Neisse by an attack from the east and southeast. On the operation's second day, the brigade's main forces were to capture the town of Zultz, where it was to link up with units of the 7th Guards Mechanized Corps attacking to meet it.

The army commander left the 22nd Self-Propelled Artillery Brigade in his reserve, assigning it the task of following behind the 6th Mechanized Corps, as well as the 51st Independent Motorcycle Regiment, which was to follow behind the 10th Tank Corps.

Having defined each formation's tasks, the commander of the 4th Tank Army at the same time issued instructions to the troops regarding the order of their actions on the battlefield, while at the same time demanding from all unit and formation commanders, as well as the army's entire rank and file, decisive actions not only during the daytime, but at night as well.

59th Army. The army commander made the decision to launch his main attack along the left flank with the forces of the 115th and 93rd rifle and 7th Guards Mechanized corps in the general direction of Kostenthal and Zultz and, in conjunction with the 21st and 4th Tank armies' forces, encircle and destroy the enemy's group of forces in the woods south and southwest of Oppeln.

The 115th Rifle Corps (commander, Major General S.B. Kozachek), having the 92nd and 135th rifle divisions in the first echelon and the 245th Rifle Division in the second, was to launch its main attack along the left flank in the direction of Lenschutz, Ober Glogau, Repsch, and Wiesengrund and break through the enemy's defense along the following 3-kilometer sector: the individual buildings 0.5 kilometers southeast of the Froschweiler railroad station—the unnamed height one kilometer south of Langlieben, and in conjunction with the 7th Guards Mechanized Corps' units destroy the opposing enemy; by the close of the operation's first day the corps was to capture the line Nesselwitz—Groenweide; by the close of the offensive's second day, the line Schwarz—Ober Glogau, and; by the close of the offensive's third day the line Ringwitz—Wiesengrund—Elgut. It was here that the corps was to link up with the 21st Army's units, as a result of which the encirclement of the enemy in the woods south and southwest of Oppeln would be completed.

The 93rd Rifle Corps (commander, Major General Ya.S. Sharoburko), having the single 98th Rifle Division in the first echelon, was to break through the enemy's defense along the sector excluding the unnamed height one kilometer south of Langlieben—the creek near the unnamed height one kilometer north of Pulau, and then to develop the offensive in the direction of Neisedel, Deutsch Rasselwitz and Zeiselwitz, and by the close of the offensive's first day to capture the line Massdorf—Honfleur—Militsch. On the second day of the operation, with the 98th Rifle Division's arrival at the eastern bank of the Tiefenburg River, it was planned to commit the 391st Rifle Division into the fighting and by the close of the day to capture the line excluding Ober Glogau—Deutsch Rasselwitz—Stundorf. By the close of the offensive's third day, the corps was to capture the town of Neustadt and reach the line Zultz—Neustadt. The 239th Rifle Division (minus a rifle regiment) comprised the corps' third echelon and was designated for developing the offensive's success.

Thus according to the operational plan, with the troops' arrival at the line Zultz—Neustadt, a continuous external encirclement front would be created and the enemy's encircled troops would be separated from the Seventeenth Army's main forces by a 25-kilometer zone. Such an isolation of the enemy's encircled forces would create conditions for our forces to successfully and completely defeat them.

The 7th Guards Mechanized Corps (commander, Guards Lieutenant General of Tank Troops I.P. Korchagin) received orders to launch an attack in the direction of Kostenthal and Deutsch Rasselwitz and, while developing the rifle corps' breakthrough, by the close of the offensive's first day it was to capture the Ober Glogau—Deutsch Rasselwitz area; that is, to capture the area to which the 93rd Rifle Corps was to arrive in by the close of the offensive's second day. According to the plan for the offensive's second day, the 7th Guards Mechanized Corps had the task of reaching the Zultz—Zeiselwitz—Neustadt area and to link up here with the 4th Tank Army's forces.

It was planned to commit the 7th Guards Mechanized Corps into the battle following the infantry's capture of the enemy's first trench line.

The 7th Guards Mechanized Corps' operations were to support the vigorous maneuver to encircle the enemy's group of forces defending west, southwest and south of Oppeln, and the timely fulfillment of their tasks by the army's forces.

The organization of consolidating the lines achieved was entrusted to the commander of the army's artillery, for which it was planned to employ the 883rd Anti-Tank Artillery Regiment and the 11th Guards Anti-Tank Artillery Brigade.

The 43rd Rifle Corps (commander, Major General A.I. Andreev), which was defending along the Oppeln—Ritterfere sector, was to launch a supporting attack with the forces of its 314th Rifle Division and part of the 13th Rifle Division in the direction of Neumanske, Stoblau and Pechutte. While attacking, the corps was to roll up the enemy's defense along the left bank of the Oder River to the north. Upon capturing the line Mechnitz—excluding Hinterwald, the corps' left-flank formations were to be given the task of attacking toward Pechutte, in order to cut off the path of retreat of the enemy's group of forces to the southwest toward Zultz. Once the enemy began his withdrawal from the line Oppeln—Otmut, the corps was to attack along its right flank (units of the 80th and 13th rifle divisions) in the direction of Pechutte and in conjunction with the 314th Rifle Division encircle and destroy the enemy's units in the woods west of Krappitz.

From the tasks assigned, it is clear that the army commander was demanding that the 43rd Rifle Corps' units secure the right flank of the army's shock group against enemy activity from the northeast and north, and that it assist the army's forces in encircling the enemy group of forces in the Oppeln area, and in destroying part of the enemy's forces in the woods west of Krappitz.

The army's operational formation was conditioned by the same considerations that were mentioned in analyzing the 21st Army's operational formation. It was planned to deploy all of the 59th Army's men and materiel in a single echelon. A regiment from the 239th Rifle Division, and the 18th Anti-Tank Artillery Brigade were to be detached to the army commander's reserve. The creation of a powerful shock group along the axis of the main attack and its simultaneous commitment into the fighting would support the rapid breakthrough of the enemy's tactical defensive depth and the timely accomplishment of the task assigned by the *front* commander.

It was planned to carry out the augmentation of the attack's strength until the completion of the encirclement of the enemy's group of forces southwest of Oppeln by committing the divisions and corps of the second echelon into the battle. The 115th Rifle Corps was to organize its combat formation into two echelons and the 93rd Rifle Corps into three echelons. It was planned to carry out the commitment of the second-echelon divisions into the battle as the corps' and army's offensive sector broadened. The divisions' and regiments' combat formations were also organized into two echelons.

60th Army. The army commander decided, in conjunction with the 59th Army, to break through the enemy's defense along a 4-kilometer front with the forces of his 28th Rifle Corps. Then, while developing a vigorous offensive to the southwestern toward Troppau (Opava), units of the 28th and 15th rifle corps, in conjunction with the Fourth Ukrainian Front's 38th Army, were to encircle and destroy the enemy group of forces east and southeast of Ratibor. The left-flank 106th Rifle Corps was to securely hold its positions.

On the basis of this decision, the army commander assigned his forces the following tasks.

The 28th Rifle Corps (commander, Major General M.I. Ozimin), having three divisions in the first echelon, along with units of the 31st Tank Corps, received orders to break through the enemy's defense along a 4-kilometer front from Pulau to Polln and Gross Neukirch. Then, developing a vigorous offensive in the general direction of Leobschutz, by the close of the first day the corps was to capture the line excluding Militsch—Gross Grauden—Dittmerau and the heights three kilometers southeast of Dittmerau, and by the close of the offensive's second day reach the line Trenkau—Leobschutz—Wernesdorf—Hondorf—Schirinke.

The 15th Rifle Corps (commander, Major General P.N. Tertyshnyi) was to commit its 336th and 322nd rifle divisions into the battle through the 28th Rifle Corps' breakthrough sector, with the task of attacking in the general direction of Matzkirch, Rakau and Langenau and by the close of the first day of the offensive capture the line Machowaldau—Mosern—Eichendorf. Subsequently, the 15th Rifle Corps, while rolling up the enemy front in the direction of Proschwitz and Ratibor, by the close of the offensive's second day was to reach the front Knispel—Gross Peterwitz—Proschwitz.

The securing of the left flank of the attacking 28th and 15th rifle corps was to be entrusted to the 246th Rifle Division.

The 106th Rifle Corps (commander, Major General P.F. Il'inykh) had the task of securely defending the line Leng—Sumin—Welepole—Kleszcziwa—Zbytkow, up to 60 kilometers in length. In case of a successful advance by the Fourth Ukrainian Front's 38th Army and the enemy's possible retreat opposite the 60th Army's left flank, the 106th Rifle Corps was to launch a decisive pursuit of the enemy in the general direction of Ratibor.

The 31st Tank Corps (commander, Major General G.G. Kuznetsov), in conjunction with the 28th Rifle Corps, was to break through the enemy's main defensive zone and then rush vigorously forward, and by the close of the offensive's first day reach the line Leobschutz—Neudorf—Grebnig—Ernau. On the operation's second day the corps was to continue the offensive toward Troppau (Opava) and capture the area Lindau—Lodnitz—Jarkowice—Troppau (Opava)—Piltsch—Turkau.

At the heart of the decision adopted by the commander of the 60th Army lay the idea of encircling and destroying the enemy's Ratibor group of forces in conjunction with the Fourth Ukrainian Front's 38th Army. The defeat of this enemy group of forces would secure the 59th Army against the enemy's flank attacks from the south. However, the idea of encircling and destroying the enemy group of forces defending east and southeast of Ratibor was not fully reflected in the tasks assigned the army's forces and was not supported in terms of materiel.

In order to organize the successful breakthrough of the enemy's defense in the 28th Rifle Corps' offensive sector, almost all the army's artillery and the 31st Tank Corps' tanks were concentrated along a 4-kilometer front, which enabled us to create here a large density of artillery and tanks per kilometer of front.

The 15th Rifle Corps' commitment into the battle in the 28th Rifle Corps' offensive sector was supposed to significantly reduce the latter's possible losses in men and materiel and reduce the expenditure of ammunition. Alongside this, the launching of a surprise flank attack against the enemy defending along the line Polln—Gross Neukirch—Eichendorf would assist in carrying out the task of rolling up the enemy's defense and covering the 28th Rifle Corps' activities on the left against the enemy's flank attacks.

The 5th Guards Army was to carry out a supporting role in the operation and contribute the forces of one rifle and one tank corps. The commander of the 5th Guards Army, while planning the 34th Guards Rifle Corps' (commander, Guards Major General G.V. Baklanov) attack, reinforced it with the 116th Heavy Howitzer and 1st Howitzer brigades, the 7th Mortar Brigade, and the 1073rd Anti-Tank Artillery Regiment. The corps' combat formation was organized into two echelons. The first echelon consisted of the 58th and 15th guards rifle divisions, and the second echelon of the 112th Rifle Division. It was planned to commit the latter into the battle from the line Luisdorf—the circular grove (two kilometers southwest of Louisdorf) in the direction of Hussmitz, with the task of rolling up the enemy's front east and northeast of Strelen.

A forward detachment was to be detached from each first-echelon division, consisting of a reinforced rifle battalion. The forward detachments had the task of seizing Krummendorf, Priborn, Turpitz, and Haltauf by the close of the offensive's first day; by the close of the second day they were to seize Danschwitz, Schildberg and Heinrichau, and by the close of the offensive's third day Wonnwitz, Tarchwitz and Krelkau. Aside from the forward detachments, forward battalions were detached, which were to begin the offensive at 0600 on 15 March; that is, before the beginning of the offensive by the corps' main forces. The composition of these battalions was basically the same as in the 21st Army.

It was planned to commit the 4th Guards Tank Corps (commander, Guards Lieutenant General P.P. Poluboyarov) into the battle from the western outskirts of Grottkau simultaneously with units of the 34th Guards Rifle Corps.

The commander of the 32nd Guards Rifle Corps was ordered to attack on the morning of the operation's second day with a reinforced rifle regiment from the 97th Guards Rifle Division, in the direction of Gorkau and to assist the 34th Guards Rifle Corps in destroying the enemy in the Strelen area and to capture the town.

The troops were to occupy their jumping-off positions for the offensive on the night of 14-15 March. The movement of the 4th Guards Tank Corps from the holding area to the jumping-off area (the western outskirts of Grottkau) was planned for the period of the artillery preparation.

The Organization of the Artillery Offensive

The organization of the artillery offensive was carried out on the basis of the instructions by the *Stavka* of the Supreme High Command to create an artillery density of no less than 150-170 guns and mortars (not counting 82mm mortars) per kilometer of front along the breakthrough sector. The duration of the artillery preparation was set at 80 minutes.

On the basis of these instructions, it was planned to concentrate the following amount of artillery along the armies' breakthrough sectors: 1,419 guns and mortars along the 21st Army's breakthrough sector; 1,026 guns and mortars along the 59th Army's breakthrough sector, and; 475 guns and mortars along the 60th Army's breakthrough sector. In all, it was planned to concentrate 2,920 guns and mortars along the 21st, 59th and 60th armies' breakthrough sectors, which given an overall width of 17 kilometers for their breakthrough sectors, would yield an artillery density of 172 guns and mortars per kilometer of front. It was planned to create an artillery density of 177 guns and mortars along the 21st Army's breakthrough sector, 205 guns and mortars along the 59th Army's breakthrough sector, and 119 guns and mortars along the 60th Army's breakthrough sector, per kilometer of front. Taking into account 82mm mortars, the density per kilometer of front would increase up to 198 guns and mortars along the 21st Army's offensive sector, up to 235 guns and mortars in the 59th Army's sector, and up to 150 guns and mortars in the 60th Army's sector.

The main mass of artillery pieces was to be employed in regimental artillery groups. Aside from light howitzer artillery, heavy howitzer artillery, heavy mortars and heavy-caliber howitzer artillery was to be included. Such a makeup for the regimental artillery groups would enable us to quickly bring in heavy artillery pieces for destroying the enemy's stone structures during our troops' fight for the inhabited locales. A part of the heavy-caliber guns was slated for firing over open sights.

Aside from the regimental artillery groups, divisional groups, counter-mortar and long-range army groups were to be created. The latter were to be broken up into subgroups according to the number of corps.

The enemy's weak air activity, given our troops' significant saturation of anti-aircraft artillery, enabled us to order the troops to bring in anti-aircraft artillery units for firing on ground targets. For example, in the 59th Army's attack sector on the offensive's first day the 636th Regiment's small-caliber anti-aircraft artillery was assigned the task of destroying by direct fire an enemy anti-aircraft battalion, which was located on firing positions one kilometer southwest of Langlieben.

The plan-schedule for the artillery preparation included the following periods:

a) The first fire onslaught, lasting ten minutes, would be directed against the enemy's area targets, strong points and centers of resistance along the forward edge and in the immediate depth, inhabited locales, headquarters, communications centers, firing positions for the enemy's artillery and mortars, observation posts, both detected and supposed, against anti-tank artillery areas, and the edges of woods and heights. During this period long-range guns were to fire on headquarters areas and probable concentration areas for tanks and reserves.

   In order to more completely strike the enemy's gun crews, it was planned to begin the fire onslaught by the long-range army artillery groups against the enemy firing positions three minutes after the start of the general artillery preparation.

b) Deliberate fire, for the purpose of suppressing targets throughout the defense's entire tactical depth, was to last 50 minutes. Long-range guns, besides firing on the enemy's headquarters, reserves and tank concentration areas, were to continue to suppress and destroy newly-discovered and unsuppressed batteries, while part of the guns would be used to destroy centers of defense and stone structures along the forward edge of the defense, which had been configured as firing points.

c) A second fire onslaught would last five minutes, and include artillery from the divisional artillery groups and long-range artillery against the enemy's artillery and mortar batteries, their observation posts and most powerful strong points in the depth of the enemy's defense.

d) During the final 15 minutes of the artillery preparation a third fire onslaught was planned against the enemy's trenches and communications trenches, his strong points and defensive centers, and against inhabited locales to a depth of 3-4 kilometers. All types and calibers of artillery would be brought in to participate in the onslaught.

It was planned to support the infantry and tank attack by a rolling barrage, combined with a consecutive concentration of fire.

The intensity of fire against the first lines of the rolling barrage was to be the same as the intensity of fire by the final fire onslaught.

The fire support of the attacking infantry's and tanks' flanks was to be carried out through the consecutive concentration of artillery fire against the enemy's centers of resistance and strong points, groves, heights, and road junctions.

During the attack the suppression of newly-discovered enemy artillery and mortar batteries, as well as fire observation of suppressed batteries was to be entrusted to long-range artillery groups.

Accompaniment guns were to be detailed for accompanying the infantry during the battle in the depth.

During the fighting in the depth of the enemy's defense, it was planned to support the attack through the method of consecutively concentrating fire against the enemy's strong points and centers of resistance.

For the purpose of organizing a more scrupulous artillery reconnaissance during the fighting in the depth of the enemy's defense, the commanders of the artillery formations created reconnaissance groups, which while located in the infantry's combat formations, were to conduct reconnaissance, inform their commander of enemy activities and that of his detected targets, correct battery fire in necessary cases, and also to exercise control over the artillery battalions' reconnaissance.

It was planned to move the regimental artillery groups by leapfrogging from line to line, while for the majority of systems in these groups the distance of the leaps was about a third of the distance of their maximum effective range. It was planned to support the movement of one unit by the fire of another from the old firing positions.

At the heart of the artillery's cooperation with the infantry lay the decisions by the *front* and army commanders for the operation and the plan for employing the artillery. The artillery's cooperation with the infantry was to be achieved through the personal interaction of the artillery officers with the commanders of the rifle units and subunits being supported by means of joint reconnaissance, the coordination of fire assignments on the spot, and by organizing direct communications and mutual information.

Because the First Ukrainian Front's Upper Silesian operation was to be conducted by armies that had earlier been on the defensive along this axis and the artillery had not carried out major regroupings, then in this operation the question of concentrating artillery formations and units did not occupy such a large place as in the *front's* other offensive operations. The artillery units' and formation's positional areas had been prepared and outfitted prior to this.

The artillery that had been operating earlier along this axis had sufficient time to reconnoiter the enemy and by the start of the operation disposed of the necessary data for planning the artillery offensive. The exception was the 31st and 17th artillery breakthrough divisions, which had been brought in to participate in the operation from other sectors of the front. Their concentration along the breakthrough sectors was carried out according to a compressed timetable. In order to furnish the commanders of the newly-arrived artillery formations with the necessary information for training their crews, these formation's reconnaissance subunits had begun their work ahead of time, before the artillery's arrival at their designated areas.

For example, on 13 March the 31st Artillery Breakthrough Division was to lend fire support for the 6th Army's combat activities while storming the southern quarters of the city of Breslau and was reconnoitering the area north of Ratibor, where it was planned to employ the division in the forthcoming operation. In order to do this, up to 50 percent of the reconnaissance subunits, 40 percent of the communications equipment, and 60 percent of headquarters personnel at all levels, was transferred to the future combat area a few days before the start of the operation.

During 6-8 March the commanders of units and subunits, up to battery commanders, conducted a reconnaissance of the areas of the firing positions and observation posts. During 7-15 March the artillery headquarters of the rifle corps and divisions, artillery groups and battalions reconnoitered and conducted additional reconnaissance of enemy targets in the sectors of the forthcoming offensive.

During 9-12 March ammunition was brought up. The artillery's movement up to its positional areas was carried out during the night of 13-14 March.

The Organization of the Air Offensive

The 2nd Air Army was to support the March offensive by the First Ukrainian Front's left wing.

By 15 March the army included 1,737 planes, of which 369 were bombers, 430 assault aircraft and 861 fighters.

The 6th Guards Bomber, 1st and 2nd guards assault air and the 6th Guards Fighter corps were detached for cooperating with the forces of the 21st and 4th Tank armies, while the 4th Bomber, 3rd Assault Air and 5th Fighter corps were detached for cooperating with the 59th and 60th armies.

The following tasks were assigned to the 2nd Air Army.

During the preparatory period our aviation was to conduct uninterrupted reconnaissance of the enemy in the armies' offensive sector, in order to establish the direction and intensity of the enemy's movements along the paved and dirt roads and railroads, as well as to detect areas where the Germans' artillery and tanks were located and concentrated. It was ordered to pay particular attention while reconnoitering the enemy to the woods west and southwest of Grottkau, to the road from Neisse to Grottkau and Oppeln, to the woods southwest of Oppeln, the copses west of Cosel, as well as to the town of Ober Glogau. Simultaneously, our aviation was to determine in detail the presence and character of the defensive structures along the following lines: Deutsch Jagel—Schenheide—Friedewalde—Gross Malendorf; Kuau—Matzkirch; Ottmachauer Pond—Neisse—Friedland; Ober Glogau—Leobschutz—Ernau. The assault air and bombers' tasks consisted of suppressing the enemy's artillery and mortar batteries through mass strikes, to destroy his strong points and centers of resistance and his personnel and technical equipment in the areas of Strelen, Alt Grottkau, Friedewalde, Waldau, Stablau, Krappitz, Cosel, Ober Glogau, Langlieben, Schneidenburg, Gnadenfeld, Leinitz, Leobschutz, and Ernau. Fighter aviation's task during the preparatory period for the operation was to cover the *front's* troops while regrouping and in their jumping-off positions for the offensive, particularly in the areas of Lichtenberg, Lewin, Rogau, and Grottkau, and also on the bridgehead north of Ratibor. At this stage of the operation the 2nd Air Army was to be entrusted with the task of maintaining our previous air superiority and to disorganize the command and control and work of the enemy rear. For this purpose, our aviation was to launch bomber strikes against enemy airfield centers in the areas of Grieschberg, Schweidnitz, Neisse, Lamsdorf, Gradets-Kralewski, Troppau, Ratibor, and Krawarze, as well as against the enemy's army and corps headquarters and railroad junctions.

During the artillery preparation for the attack, the following tasks were to be entrusted to the 2nd Air Army. Fighter aviation, while covering the main group of ground forces in their jumping-off positions for the attack, was to continue the fight to maintain air superiority, as well as to escort bomber aviation during its combat sorties. Bomber and assault air aviation had the task of launching massed strikes against the areas of Priborn, Arnsdorf, Kroschen, Falkenberg, Fridewalde, Gnadenfeld, Proschwitz, Pirchwitz, Nesselwitz, Forzicht, and Matskirch, for the purpose of destroying the enemy's strong points, his headquarters, communications centers, suppressing his artillery, and destroying his men and materiel.

Upon the beginning of the infantry attack, bomber and assault air aviation were to launch echeloned strikes against the enemy's strong points, his headquarters, his troop concentration areas, and against concentrations of his infantry and tanks along the main road junctions, as well as against his artillery and mortar firing positions. Once the infantry had overcome the first position of the main defensive zone, it was planned to employ the 2nd Air Army's main forces to cover the 4th Tank Army and the 7th Guards Mechanized Corps during their commitment into the battle, and to subsequently cover the attacking armies' shock groups from the air.

During the fighting in the depth of the enemy's defense, our aviation was to prevent the arrival of the enemy's reserves to the battlefield from the areas of Strelen, Munsterberg, Neisse, Ottmachau, Ober Glogau, Leobschutz, Biskau, Langenau, Ratibor, and Ernau; to destroy the German units falling back under the blows of our forces and prevent them from organizing a defense along the Neisse River and along the Ober Glogau—Leobschutz line.

The combat activities of the *front's* aviation were planned for three days of the operation, while detailed tasks for the 2nd Air Army's corps and divisions had been drawn up only for the first day of the offensive.

It was planned to conduct 5,745 sorties in three days of the operation, of which 2,995 were to be on the first day. The planned number of sorties by axes, days of the operation and types of aviation is shown in Table VI/4.1.

Table VI/4.1 Planned Number of Sorties in the Upper Silesian Offensive Operation

Axis	Air Arm	1st Day	2nd Day	3rd Day	Total	Notes
21st and 4th Tank Army	Fighters	495	350	300	1,145	The number of fighter sorties
	Assault Air	710	300	250	1,260	could be increased or reduced,
	Bombers	580	160	150	890	depending on the air situation.
	Total	1,785	810	700	3,295	
59th and 60th Armies	Fighters	410	320	280	1,010	
	Assault Air	420	180	150	750	
	Bombers	380	160	150	690	
	Total	1,210	660	580	2,450	
Total	Fighters	905	670	580	2,155	
	Assault Air	1,130	480	400	2,010	
	Bombers	960	320	300	1,580	
	Total	2,995	1,470	1,280	5,745	

The commanders of the air corps were to carry out command and control of our aviation during the operation from the army commanders' observation posts, with their representatives at the tank and mechanized corps' command posts.

The headquarters of the combined-arms armies, along with the headquarters of the air corps, drew up detailed plans for the air formations' cooperation with the ground forces' units and formations for the preparatory stage and first day of the operation. In these plans the tasks for the infantry, tanks and aviation were distributed and coordinated by period of battle.

The air coordination plan with the 21st and 4th Tank armies is shown in Table VI/4.2.

Table VI/4.2 Plan for Coordinating the 1st Guards Assault Air, 6th Guards Bomber and 6th Guards Fighter Corps with the 21st and 4th Tank Armies During the Preparatory Stage and the Upper Silesian Operation's First Day

Period	Ground Forces' Tasks	Aviation Tasks
Preparatory	Move up to the jumping-off positions for the attack and occupy the attack line height 175.3—southern outskirts of Klein Neidorf—southern outskirts of Merzdorf—southern outskirts of Tiefensee—southern outskirts of Rogau and Gurau.	Conduct uninterrupted reconnaissance and photography in the army's offensive sector (from the right—Lorentzberg–Priborn—Munsterberg—Ottmachau; from the left—Oppeln–Wiesengrund—Zulz) as far as the line Ottmachauer Pond–Neisse—Zulz, with the following tasks: • to establish the direction and intensity of traffic along the railroads, paved and dirt roads; • to uncover the areas where the enemy's tanks and artillery are located, paying particular attention to the areas of the woods west and southwest of Grottkau and Schwarzengrund and the along the road from Neisse to Grottkau; • to establish the presence and character of the defensive structures along the lines Deutsch Jagel—Schoenheide–Friedewalde—Gross Malendorf—Gruben; the Neisse River, from the Ottmachauer Pond to Friedland. To cover the army's forces in their jumping-off positions and along the start line for the attack. Particular attention is to be paid to the Lichtenberg—Kreisewitz—Lewin—Hilbersdorf—Rogau—Grottkau area.

Time of Execution	Units and Formations	Intensity of Sorties
Several days before the beginning of the operation and on the day of the operation	1st Guards Assault Air Corps	10-20
	6th Guards Bomber Corps	8-10
	6th Guards Fighter Corps	15-20
On special orders	6th Guards Fighter Corps	Depending on the air situation.

Period	Ground Forces' Tasks	Aviation Tasks
Artillery preparation	1. 21st Army's forces at their jumping-off positions. 2. The 4th Tank Army's forces move up to their jumping-off area for the offensive: Komradswaldau–Lichtenberg—Grottkau—Gurau—Lewin—Pogarel.	Aviation continues to carry out reconnaissance as far as the line Ottmachauer Pond—Neisse—Friedland in the interests of the armies and units of the 1st Guards Assault Air and 6th Guards Bomber corps. Aviation launches a bomber raid against the enemy's strong points and artillery firing positions in the Alt Glogau, Waldau, Endersdorf, Kirchberg, Schwarzergrund areas, the woods east of Schwarzengrund, Rosdorf, the woods northeast of Rosdorf, Kroschen, and Koppendorf. Aviation covers the main group of forces located along the jumping-off line for the attack. Aviation covers the 6th Bomber Corps' sorties.
Attack	Breaks through the enemy's defense.	Launches echeloned strikes against the enemy's artillery and mortar firing positions in the Alt Grottkau, Waldau, Kirchberg, Schwarzergrund areas, the woods east of Schwarzengrund, Rosdorf, the woods east of Rosdorf and Kroschen. Prepares for a repeat sortie to strike targets in addition to those uncovered by reconnaissance. Continues to cover the armies' shock group during the breakthrough of the forward edge of the enemy's defense.

Time of Execution	Units and Formations	Intensity of Sorties
From dawn to H-hour.	1st Guards Assault Air Corps	8
H-hour—+15 minutes	6th Guards Bomber Corps	150
H-hour—+45 minutes	6th Guards Fighter Corps	Depending on the air situation
H-hour—+15 minutes	6th Guards Fighter Corps	90
H-hour—+1 hour	1st Guards Assault Air Corps	100
	6th Guards Bomber Corps	
	6th Guards Fighter Corps	Depending on the air situation

Period	Ground Forces' Tasks	Aviation Tasks
The battle in the tactical depth of the enemy's defense	The 21st Army, in conjunction with the 4th Tank Army, develops the offensive toward Neisse, with the task of reaching the line: a) 21st Army—Deutsch Jagel–Zeifersdorf—Breitenfeld—Falkenberg; b) 4th Tank Army—the Kalkau—Oppersdorf–Neisse area, and the forward detachments to the areas of Siegenhals, Neustadt and Zulz by the end of the day.	Have in readiness groups of assault aircraft (9-18 Il-2s each) for operating against the enemy's arriving reserves, by order of the army commanders. Maintains in readiness groups of 9 Pe-2 bombers for operating against arriving reserves and the uncovering by reconnaissance centers of resistance along the line of the Neisse River from Ottmachau to Rothaus. Covers the army's forces during the battle in the depth. Pays particular attention to covering the 4th Tank Army in the Ottmachau—Kalkau—Oppersdorf—Neisse area. Covers the 6th Guards Bomber Corps' operations.

Time of Execution	Units and Formations	Intensity of Sorties
To the end of the first day.	1st Guards Assault Air Corps	200
To the end of the first day.	6th Guards Bomber Corps	50
To the end of the first day.	6th Guards Fighter Corps	Depending on the situation
	6th Guards Fighter Corps	Depending on the air situation

Notes:

1. Immediate command and control of our aviation on the battlefield was exercised by the commanders of the air corps from the observation posts of the 21st and 4th Tank armies' commanders, having their representatives with the 6th Mechanized and 10th Tank corps.
2. The ground forces are to identify themselves by a series of white and green rockets fired toward the enemy, by smoke balls or smoke grenades.
3. Target designations for the assault aircraft are identified by tracer shells and red rockets fired toward the enemy. Assault aircraft identify strafing targets for the infantry and tanks by firing tracer shells and bullets.

An analogous plan for coordinating aviation with the ground forces was compiled in the 59th and 60th armies.

During the operation's preparatory period, the 2nd Air Army, while covering the *front's* ground forces from the air, launched bomber raids against military-industrial targets in Ratibor, Rybnik, Troppau, Neisse, and other towns, as well as against enemy airfields, disrupted railroad, automobile and air transport, suppressed the enemy's forces, and conducted uninterrupted reconnaissance throughout the entire operational depth of the enemy's defense in the interests of the ground forces.

During the 1-14 March period the 2nd Air Army carried out a total of 8,747 sorties. A significant part of the sorties was carried out against the enemy's airfield centers in the areas of Grischberg, Schweidnitz, Neisse, Lamsdorf, Gradets-Kralewski, and Krawarze.

Engineering Support for the Operation

In planning the engineering support for the operation, particular attention was devoted to engineer intelligence, the outfitting of the jumping-off area for the offensive, the outfitting of crossings over water obstacles and the preparation of crossing equipment, the maintenance of the roads in a usable condition for all kinds of transportation, and the consolidation of the lines seized. All the armies participating in the offensive were obligated to carry out engineering intelligence for the purpose of revealing the enemy's defense system and engineering obstacles; the creation of trenches along the jumping-off position for the attack at a distance of 150 meters from the forward edge of the enemy's defense; the creation of a developed network of trenches in the jumping-off areas for the offensive, communications trenches and disguised approach routes to the jumping-off positions, which would guarantee the complete cover of the troops slated for the offensive.

The following engineering measures were planned in the 21st Army.

Along the Leipusch—Klein Neudorf—Rogau—Gross Mangersdorf sector it was planned to remove all anti-tank mines, which had been laid in front of the forward edge of our defense and that of the enemy, and to remove all anti-personnel mines along the axes of the main attack. The removal of the mines was entrusted to the engineering troops that laid down the mines.

During the preparatory period for the operation, it was planned to build with engineering troops three bridges over the Neisse River, with a capacity of 60 tons each; one bridge east of Waldforwerk, the other south of Michelau, and; the third in the inhabited locale of Lewin.

In order to disencumber the roads and for the timely and disguised regrouping of forces for the offensive, as well as for the purpose of organizing the normal delivery of ammunition and other types of supply for the attacking units, it was planned to repair the road along the sector Stoberau—Koppen; to continue and outfit the road from Gross Enkwitz to Grottkau, through Niderseinffersdorf, and to prepare approaches for all types of transport and combat equipment to the bridge over the Neisse River east of Waldforwerk.

During the offensive the engineering troops were entrusted with the task of securing the troops' passage through our forward edge and the enemy's forward edge, removing mines from roads and maintaining them in usable condition. Particular attention was paid to the restoration of the Klein Neudorf—Kroschen—Ottmachau—Waldau—Friedewalde—Neisse—Schedlau and the Falkenberg—Gruben—Friedland roads. These roads were located in the attack sector of the army's main shock group and were to be restored first of all. Should the enemy damage the bridges over the Neisse River in the Neisse, Schwarzergrund and Rothaus areas, as well as over the Steinau River in the Falkenberg area, it was planned to either restore them or to build them anew.

The engineering consolidation of the lines achieved was to be carried out by the divisional sappers. It was planned to bring in men and materiel from the army engineering reserve for consolidating the most important lines.

The following engineering work was planned in the 59th Army.

It was planned to create two crossings over the Oder River, each with a capacity of 60 tons, for assisting the concentration of the 7th Guards Mechanized Corps and reinforcement artillery along the bridgehead.

The sappers had to make passages in the minefields, wire and other obstacles from the jumping-off position for the offensive to the forward edge of the enemy's defense, in order to support the infantry and tank attack, with two passages for each rifle and each tank company.

In order to support the battle in the depth of the enemy's defense and the crossing of tanks, artillery and infantry over water obstacles, particularly in forcing the Hotzenplotz River, the engineering troops were ordered to prepare bridge parts, light crossing equipment and other crossing materials ahead of time, and to also have in combat readiness a reserve of engineering men and materiel for consolidating lines, and to create obstacles for the purpose of securing the flanks of the attacking forces. Each rifle division was supposed to have a sapper platoon with 100 anti-tank mines in reserve, and each rifle corps and sapper company with 250 anti-tank mines.

Analogous measures for engineering support for the offensive were planned in the 60th Army as well.

During the operation's preparatory period the troops carried out a great deal of work in the engineering preparation of the jumping-off areas for the offensive.

The engineering preparation of the jumping-off areas for the offensive and the jumping-off positions for the attack was made easier by the fact that the troops had been in these areas for an extended period of time and had done a lot of work toward outfitting their positions.

By 10 March significant earthworks had been carried out in the jumping-off area for the offensive. The 21st Army's forces dug 54 kilometers of trenches and communications trenches, the 59th Army's forces 77.5 kilometers, and the 60th Army's forces 182.5 kilometers. The entire earth work was carried out by the forces of the rifle units and formations. The engineering troops were employed while preparing for the operation and for removing mines, bridge repair, and putting the destroyed roads into a usable state.

In the 21st Army the engineering troops removed mine obstacles, which had been laid along the forward edge of our defense, and also removed mines from eight bridges. In the Waldforwerk, Michelau and Lewin areas three new bridges were built, with a capacity of up to 60 tons and an overall length of 109 linear meters. Besides these, two bridges over the creek north of Tifensee were built, also with a capacity of up to 60 tons (23 linear meters in length). During this period 19.3 kilometers of roads were repaired and built anew.

By the start of the offensive the 59th Army's engineering troops had made the necessary number of passages in the minefields and wire obstacles, both ours and the enemy's. By this time crossings over the Oder River for tanks and artillery had been outfitted. Three bridges with an overall length of 146 linear meters had been built for light loads; one of them over the Oder River in Oppeln and two bridges over the Klodnica River in the area northeast of Cosel. A 30-ton capacity bridge was restored over this river after having been destroyed by the enemy.

During the first ten days of March the water level rose sharply due to the rapid melting of snow and the heavy rains along the headwaters of the Oder and its tributaries, which threatened to carry away the bridges built for low water. Thus the engineering troops undertook emergency measures to strengthen them. The bridges were braced with metal cables, while their surface, aside from the actual road, was weighted down with rock, sandbags and heavy metal objects. These measures for strengthening low-water bridges were also carried out in other armies' sectors. The measures adopted prevented the bridges from being washed away.

In this army's offensive sector roads underwent a complete overhaul, while bypasses and approaches to the bridges were outfitted.

By 15 March 61 passages had been made, each up to 50 meters wide, had been made in the 60th Army's minefields, including 32 passages along the bridgehead, and 21 passages up to 100 meters wide, including 16 along the bridgehead. The construction of two bridges was completed for crossing over the Oder River in the Wellen area. In case of the bridges' destruction by the enemy's air force, or as a result of flooding, piers were outfitted for laying down pontoon bridges, while construction materials were gathered for building a 60-ton capacity bridge 72 meters long.

All the roads, particularly those along the bridgehead, were made usable. The repair work was primarily carried out by filling in holes with gravel and crushed brick, and the construction of pole and plank flooring, grading and clearing the roadbed of mud.

Intelligence

It was demanded that all kinds of intelligence specify the enemy's disposition and combat strength in the offensive sector, the outline of the forward edge of the enemy's main defensive zone and its depth, the presence of succeeding defensive zones, and the degree to which they had been outfitted; revealing the system of anti-personnel and anti-tank obstacles in front of the forward edge and in the depth of the enemy's defense, and; revealing the enemy's fire system for all weapons and his command and observation posts.

The reconnoitering of the forward edge of the enemy's defense was carried out by reconnaissance raids and ambushes, in order to capture prisoners, as well as observation.

During the preparatory period, from 1 March to the beginning of the offensive, the 59th and 60th armies' forces alone organized and carried out about 150 reconnaissance raids and ambushes, as a result of which 83 prisoners were taken. Besides this, 179 prisoners were taken during the fighting for the bridgeheads.

As a rule, the reconnaissance groups included sappers, who simultaneously determined and studied the character of the Germans' defensive structures along the forward edge of their defense. Reconnaissance in force was carried out along a broad front by the rank and file of those units which had earlier occupied defensive positions along the given sector. The rank and file of the units and formations that had been regrouped from other sectors of the front was not involved in carrying out reconnaissance, which made it difficult for the enemy to establish our troops' actual dispositions and intentions. For example, in the 21st Army's sector reconnaissance raids and ambushes were conducted only by units of the 55th Rifle Corps along the army's entire 48-kilometer front. Particular attention was devoted to reconnoitering the axes along which the 117th and 118th rifle corps' main attacks were to be launched. Three reconnaissance raids each were conducted along each of these axes during the last four days of the preparatory stage.

Exceptionally great attention was devoted to observation reconnaissance, particularly along the axes of the armies' main attacks. Along the 21st, 59th and 60th armies' breakthrough sectors, 24-hour observation duty by officers was set up at the observation posts from regimental commander and higher, as well as in the observation posts of the combat arms commanders. The *front* commander demanded that the regimental, division and corps commanders exercise personal control of the reconnaissance of the enemy and, in particular, of the organization and work of the officer observation posts.

In the course of 13 days the *front's* reconnaissance aviation carried out 864 reconnaissance sorties, while at the same time it carried out observation reconnaissance along its indicated axes and lines and repeatedly photographed assumed locations of the enemy's reserves as far as the Sudeten Mountains.

The Troops' Combat Training

The troops' combat training was based on the experience that had been accumulated by the Soviet army in the preceding offensive operations, particularly of those operations conducted on enemy territory during January-February 1945.

Methods for attacking the enemy's fortified positions were scrupulously worked out in the companies and battalions, as well as fighting in an inhabited locale and in the woods. The 21st Army conducted a single company and one battalion exercises with tanks. The army's rifle divisions and regiments carried out short-term training for machine gunners, mortar layers, and the commanders of gun crews that had been detailed for firing over open sights, observers, air signalers, tank destruction and minesweeping groups. Special sections for firing captured *faustpatrones* were trained in all the companies taking part in the offensive. On orders of the corps commanders, the *faustpatrones* were distributed equally among the divisions.

The tank and mechanized corps commanders examined the positive and negative aspects of the tank troops' activities during the *front's* January-February fighting. Common tactical methods were established on the basis of studying this combat experience.

Questions of organizing the combat formations of the tank troops in the offensive and maneuvering subunits on the battlefield were worked out during exercises with the troops and studies with the officers. The officers' particular attention was directed at the necessity of rapidly deploying the tanks into their combat formation. During these exercises questions of organizing and conducting reconnaissance of the enemy and the terrain were also worked out, particularly of conducting reconnaissance by tank crews outside the tank and observing the flanks during battle.

Every day tank crews trained for two hours to destroy enemy tanks. The training concluded with practice firing, for which each crew received six rounds apiece. Alongside this, methods of combating the enemy's *faustpatrone* troops and defending tanks from being hit by *faustpatrone* rounds were worked out. For this purpose, 6-10mm boilerplate "screens" were set up on the tanks to defend their vital parts. A great deal of attention was devoted to training tank descents for fighting the enemy's *faustpatrone* troops.

As concerns the engineering troops' combat training, a great deal of time was devoted to the sappers' training classes for seizing crossings from the march. The sapper units' rank and file also trained to rapidly put together ferries, bridges and building piers.

In the officers' combat training a good deal of attention was devoted to questions of organizing coordination and its constant restoration during the offensive.

The Organization of Command, Control and Communications

As in the First Ukrainian Front's preceding operations, particular attention was devoted to continuous control over the troops' fulfillment of the directives and orders connected with preparing the operation, for which the *front* commander, his deputies, the army commanders, as well as headquarters generals and officers would visit the troops. In exercising control over the troops' training for the forthcoming operation, attention was chiefly paid to questions of planning the battle in the corps' and divisions' headquarters, to the combat knocking together of subunits and the staffing of rifle companies with the rank and file at the expense of combat-capable men from the rear organs, and to the delivery of supplies. Nor did such questions as the preparation of observation posts at the battalion-corps level, the preparation of the jumping-off area for the offensive, the working out of problems of coordination in the first-echelon units and divisions, and the organization of intelligence, remain beyond the view of commanders and staffs.

Command and observation posts for the armies, corps and divisions were moved closer to the troops. For the purpose of reliable command and control of the troops, it was categorically forbidden to locate observation posts in buildings. Thus the main observation posts were located on heights that guaranteed good observation of the enemy.

Central to the command were questions of organizing troop coordination. The fundamentals of organizing coordination were laid out in the *front* directive for the offensive. It showed the axes of the combined-arms armies' attacks, the order of the mobile forces' operations, the operational support for both shock groups, and the aviation's and artillery's tasks. However, the main work in planning and organizing the troops' coordination was done directly among the troops and the army headquarters.

All questions of coordination between the combined-arms formations, units and subunits, as well as the latter with tanks, attached artillery, sappers, and aviation, were worked out on site during reconnaissance.

Reconnaissance by the commanders of divisions and corps, along with the artillery and tank troops and, where necessary, with aviation representatives, was completed on 9 March. This work by the commanders of the rifle regiments, battalions and companies with the commanders of the reinforcement units and subunits, and the commanders of the supporting units and subunits was completed on 10 March in the 21st Army and on 11 March in the 59th and 60th armies.

During these reconnaissance efforts the artillery commanders sought to understand the task to be fulfilled by the artillery, infantry and tanks. The commanders of rifle units and subunits assigned the artillery additional tasks. A unified system of target identification and terrain reference points was established.

The commanders of the 5th Guards, 59th and 60th armies' rifle elements instructed the sappers where to make passages in the minefields on site and coordinated with them on the engineering support of the troops while fighting in the depth of the enemy's defense.

The *front* commander demanded that the commanders of the artillery groups and representatives of tank and air units be located at the same observation post along with the combined-arms commanders whose units they were supporting.

The aviation corps' commanders were to exercise air command and control on the battlefield from the army commanders' observation posts, while also having their representatives with the tank and mechanized corps.

In order to exclude the possibility of our aviation's attacking friendly troops, unified signals for recognizing one's own forces were established: ground forces—a series of white and green rockets fired toward the enemy; for indicating targets for assault aircraft from the ground—firing with tracer shells and red rockets toward the enemy; assault aircraft were to identify targets for the infantry and tanks by dive-bombing and firing tracer shells and bullets.

In the operational preparation by the *front's*, armies' and formations' headquarters a great deal of attention was devoted to problems of organizing communications.

Permanent communications lines, which had been destroyed by the enemy during his retreat, were completely restored along the attack sector of the *front's* left-wing forces. Work on restoring permanent communications lines was essentially completed by 10 March.

During the operation's preparatory period the communications troops of the tank army and combined-arms armies, which were to take part in the operation, were completely provided with wire and radio communications.

Wire communications in concentration areas and the jumping-off areas for the offensive were prepared ahead of time. This enabled the *front* headquarters and the armies' headquarters to establish wire communications with units immediately upon their arrival to their appointed areas and their occupation of their jumping-off position for the offensive.

The *front's* and armies' wire communications in the jumping-off position for the offensive had been broadly developed along the line of the command and observation posts, while at the same time a large number of bypass lines had been foreseen, which increased communications reliability as a whole. The armies' headquarters maintained telegraph-telephone communications with the headquarters of the corps and divisions operating along the axis of the main attack, both through command posts and through observation posts.

During the operation the plan called for securing uninterrupted wire communications while moving the command and observation posts at all levels.

Radio communications between the *front* headquarters and the armies' headquarters was organized along radio networks and lines. Cooperation radio networks were organized to facilitate coordination between the combined-arms armies and our air force and mobile forces.

Coordination communications between the combined-arms and tank formations with the air forces was secured through air representatives located, with their radio communications equipment, at the command or observation posts of the combined-arms and tank commanders.

Particular attention was devoted to the organization of radio communications with the mobile formations.

In organizing the communications of the *front's* headquarters with the armies, particular attention was devoted to strengthening communications with the 21st, 59th and 4th Tank armies, which were to carry out the main assignment in the operation to encircle the enemy group of forces in the area south and southeast of Oppeln. In accordance with this, the above-named armies were more significantly supplied with communications equipment.

The *front's* communications directorate commandeered its officers to the armies' headquarters during the operation's preparatory stage to render practical assistance in organizing communications in the armies and corps and for exercising control.

The radio control service was strengthened in order to prevent violations of the rules of radio exchange and the strict observation of the requirements for disguised command and control of the troops.

By the start of the operation the command's communications and coordination communications had been completely organized, while at the same time particular attention was devoted to radio communications. Only wire and mobile communications equipment was employed before the start of the attack. The employment of radio communications to transmit was authorized only with the start of the attack.

Materiel Support

The ammunition expenditure for the artillery and mortars for the entire operation was planned from 1.5 to two combat loads, of which it was planned to expend one combat load on the first day of the operation (0.7 of a combat load during the artillery preparation; 0.15 of a combat load for supporting the infantry and tank attack, and; 0.15 of a combat load for the battle in the depth).

By the start of the operation the amount of ammunition with the troops and at the army depots for battalion artillery ranged from 1.7 to 3.6 combat loads; for battalion and regimental mortars, 1.8 to 2.4 combat loads; for regimental artillery, 1.5 to 2.3 combat loads; for divisional artillery, 0.9 to 1.75 combat loads, and; for reinforcement artillery, 2.0 to 2.45 combat loads.

It is clear from the data presented above that ammunition stocks had been accumulated within the bounds of the planned expenditure for the operation for all artillery and mortar systems, with the exception of divisional artillery.

The presence of fuel and lubricating materials in the armies was raised to the following levels: 1.7-3.3 refills for auto fuel; 1.9-3.7 refills for motor oil; and2.0-3.6 refills for solidol. Taking into account the operation's insignificant depth and the planned arrival of fuels and lubricants, one could calculate that the existing supplies would be sufficient for conducting the operation.

The troops were fully supplied with all types of food.

By the start of the operation the armies' rear supply bases were located in the following areas: the 21st Army's supply base in the area of Bernstadt station; the 59th Army's supply base in the area of Gleiwitz station, and; the 60th Army's supply base in the area of Katowice station. It was not planned to shift the army supply bases during the operation, due to its insignificant depth.

The wounded and sick had been completely evacuated from the army hospitals by the start of the offensive. The hospitals could fully cope with the admitting and treating of wounded. The *front* hospital base, which was to service the *front's* left-wing armies, was located in Katowice.

Political Support

The basis for the entire work of politically supporting the operation during the operation's preparatory period and during its conduct was comrade Stalin's work *On the Great Patriotic War of the Soviet Union* and the Supreme Commander-in-Chief's order no. 5 of 23 February 1945.

Besides this, the commanders and political workers were guided in their work by the *front* military council's order no. 004 "On Measures for Establishing Order on German Territory Occupied by our Forces," and order no. 007 "On Increasing the Commanders' Responsibility for the State of the Rank and File's Discipline in Units and Elements Entrusted to Them."

At the beginning of March the *front's* political directorate conducted conferences for the chiefs of the political sections of armies, individual corps, artillery formations, engineer and sapper formations and units, and the *front's* rear and special units. During these conferences the results of work on the political support for the offensive operations in January and February were totaled up and tasks assigned relating to the troops' preparations to carry out their forthcoming combat assignment.

On 5 March the *front's* political directorate conducted a seminar of agitators and lecturers from the political sections of the armies and some corps. The particular attention of the seminar's participants was directed toward improving agitation and propaganda work, so that oral propaganda and print means assisted in the resolution of those tasks assigned to the troops, ideologically stiffened the soldiers and officers, gave them correct answers to questions that concerned them, and strengthened the troops' discipline and combat readiness.

During 5-7 March the armies' political sections conducted conferences with the political section heads of the corps, divisions and brigades. At these conferences they discussed the problem of shortcomings in party-political work among the troops and the tasks of the political organs, party and Komsomol organizations in preparing the troops to carry out their forthcoming combat task in the near future.

During 8-12 March meetings of the party activists took place in all the divisions and meetings of the primary party and Komsomol organizations in the units. On the agenda was the question:

"The Results of Party-Political Work in the Winter Offensive Battles and the Tasks of the Party and Komsomol Organizations Arising from Comrade Stalin's Order No. 5 of 23 February 1945."

Besides this, instructional conferences were conducted in the divisions' political sections on the tasks of subunit agitators in the offensive battles.

The conferences of the party activists and meetings of the primary party organizations that were carried out facilitated an increase in troop discipline, organization and the rise in communists' vigilance, and an improvement in the quality of party-political work directed at preparing the troops to carry out new tasks.

During the preparations for the operation, in connection with the study of comrade Stalin's order no. 5 of 23 February 1945, the soldiers, sergeants and officers had a large number of lectures and reports read to them. In the 60th Army's units and subunits alone more than 100 lectures and reports were read on the following themes: "Comrade Stalin's Order is the Combat Program for the Defeat of Hitlerite Germany," "Hold High the Honor of the Red Army Soldier," "The Red Army's New Historic Victories," "The Closer our Victory, the Greater Must be our Vigilance and the Stronger Must be our Attacks Against the Enemy," "Let's Finish off the Fascist Beast in his Lair and Raise the Banner of Victory over Berlin," "The Soviet Union's International Situation," "Rapacious German Imperialism," "The Enemy is Sly and Perfidious—be Vigilant," and "The Soviet Rear's Achievements in the Great Patriotic War."

Newspapers published by the *front's* political directorate in the Ukrainian, Kazakh, Uzbek and Tatar languages rendered great help in explaining comrade Stalin's order no. 5 of 23 February 1945 among the non-Russian rank and file.

In explaining the Supreme Commander-in-Chief's order of 23 February 1945 to the entire rank and file, particular attention was paid to comrade Stalin's instructions that

> Complete victory over the Germans is now near, but victory never comes on its own, but is achieved in heavy fighting and sustained labor. The doomed enemy is throwing his last forces into the battle and desperately resisting, in order to avoid harsh retribution. He is grasping and will grasp at the most extreme and low forms of battle. Thus we should remember that the closer our victory, the greater must be our vigilance, and the stronger must be our attacks against the enemy.[1]

Comrade Stalin's order no. 5 of 23 February 1945 further increased the morale-political condition and combat spirit of the *front's* forces.

Soldiers, sergeants and officers expressed their profound loyalty to their Motherland and our beloved leader, comrade Stalin, in their addresses at meetings and during conversations. For example, Guards Private Gunderin, 47th Rifle Regiment/15th Rifle Division/5th Guards Army, declared in his address at the meeting:

> During the war years I have become firmly convinced that what comrade Stalin writes in his order will surely come to pass. This order states that victory is near, which means that we will soon completely defeat Hitlerite Germany. For this, we must just try to fully carry out our dear Stalin's demands. Everything depends on how we will fight. The stronger and more intelligently we hit the enemy, the faster we'll finish him off.

A participant of three wars, holder of two St. George's crosses and the Order of Glory 3rd Class, Guards Sergeant Tikhomirov said at this meeting:

---

1   I. Stalin, *O Velikoi Otechestvennoi Voine Sovetskogo Soyuza*, 5th ed., p. 180.

I fought with the German aggressors in 1914-1918 and am fighting them now in their own lair. I well know the ways of these beasts and cannibals. Before dying they will employ the most perfidious and dirty means of fighting. Great Stalin warns us about this once again. Comrade Stalin's order has inspired and armed us for new combat feats for the glory of Russian arms, for the sake of complete victory over the enemy.

In their practical work, the commanders and political workers made use of the instructions of the Presidium of the USSR Supreme Soviet on awarding the *front's* units and formations with orders, Supreme Commander-in-Chief comrade Stalin's expressions of thanks to the *front's* forces for their brave feats in defeating the fascist aggressors.

Meetings were held in the units and elements on the occasion of the Presidium of the USSR Supreme Soviet's orders and the Supreme Commander-in-Chief's expressions of thanks.

On 1 March an order of the Presidium of the USSR Supreme Soviet awarded the 4th Guards Tank Corps the Order of Lenin. This news immediately made the rounds of the entire corps and brought a great increase in ardor among the corps' entire rank and file. Meetings took place in subunits and elements. Soldiers, sergeants and officers, speaking at these meetings, declared that this high government decoration obligated the corps' rank and file to carry out even more successfully combat operations toward completely defeating the fascist army.

In the same corps' 13th Guards Tank Brigade, Guards Junior Lieutenant Bereznoi declared at a meeting:

In accepting the title of Kantemirovka,[2] we swore to fight so that the corps was awarded with the Order of Lenin. Today is a happy and joyous day for us. We carried out our oath and the government has taken note of us with is highest decoration. In the name of the tank troops, I assure the party and government that in the forthcoming battles we will carry high the twice-decorated Kantemirovka guards banner. We will apply all our strength and skill to destroy the enemy in his own lair.

A mechanic-driver from the same brigade, Guards Senior Sergeant Kozlov, said:

I've been in the corps since its inception. I've traveled my entire combat path with it. I remember when the corps was awarded the guards and Kantemirovka designations, when they awarded the corps the Order of the Red Banner, and now I am limitlessly happy that our corps has been awarded the Order of Lenin. Our corps has covered itself in glory in battles, but each of our feats has not gone without a just evaluation. We tank troops are completely concerned and made happy by the Motherland's concern for us. How will we answer comrade Stalin for this high award? Only by new combat feats on the battle front with the Hitlerite aggressors. This is the reply of the guards Kantemirovka troops.

At meetings in the units and elements dedicated to the corps' being awarded the Order of Lenin, a resolution was adopted in which the following was stated:

Having listened to the news of the 4th Guards Kantemirovka Red Banner Corps being awarded the Order of Lenin, the soldiers, sergeants and officers greeted this news with great enthusiasm. This high government award obligates us to further strengthen military discipline, to double our vigilance and improve our combat skills. The great faith of the party and government inspires

---

2   Editor's note. A town in southern Russia, probably liberated by this unit.

us to new combat feats. We swear to attack the enemy even stronger. We assure the government, the party and comrade Stalin personally, that we are ready to double our corps' glory.

Combat community meetings took place in a number of artillery units and subunits on the eve of the operation's beginning. Appeals to the soldiers and officers of the rifle units and subunits were adopted at these meetings. For example, in the 245th Artillery Regiment's combat community meeting, the artillery troops adopted an appeal to the infantrymen to be supported by the elements. In their appeal, the artillery troops wrote:

> Comrade infantrymen! We, the soldiers, sergeants and officers of the 245th Artillery Regiment, burn with the desire to more quickly launch a crushing blow against the enemy. Having received orders to support you with artillery fire, we are full of resolve in any conditions, not knowing fear in battle, to crush the enemy with our terrible guns and mortars. Remember, comrade infantrymen, when you go into the attack, we will be there together with you. We assure you that the path of your advance will be secured.

In their reply letters, the soldiers and officers of the rifle subunits swore to strengthen their combat comradeship further and to more strongly launch joint attacks against the enemy.

The *front's* command, headquarters and political directorate and the armies' and divisions' political sections during the preparatory period devoted the necessary attention to questions of propagandizing the combat experience of the *front's* winter offensive operations. At the same time, particular attention was devoted to questions of organizing the breakthrough of the enemy's defense and supporting the cooperation of the combat arms in the battle.

The political organs put out leaflets and instructions on ways of battling the enemy's tank-destroyer subunits, armed with *faustpatrones*, as well as on using captured *faustpatrones*. Special discussions were conducted on this topic with the crews of tanks and self-propelled guns.

Front, army and division newspapers played a major role in popularizing combat experience among the troops. These newspapers published such articles as "Small Group Actions in Storming a Building," "Tanks in Fighting for a City," "How to Pass Through Gaps in Buildings with Artillery," "Self-Propelled Artillery in Street Fighting," "Gun Coordination in Street Fighting," "Descent Operations in a City Block," "Nighttime Sapper Combat Activities," "Using a Captured *Faustpatrone* in Street Fighting," "Fighting to Destroy the Surrounded Enemy in a Building," "A Cannon on the Second Floor," and others.

The reinforcements that had arrived at the *front* were, to a significant degree, made up of Soviet citizens who had lived for a considerable time on territory temporarily occupied by the enemy. Also among the reinforcements were Soviet citizens who had been repatriated from Germany. The greater part of these reinforcements lacked combat experience. Aside from this, the reinforcements had been divorced from Soviet reality for some time and had been subjected to hostile fascist propaganda.

The political organs and party organizations of the *front's* formations and units carried out a great deal of political-educational work with the new intake. At the basis of the political work with the new intake lay the propagandizing of the Soviet army's glorious victories, the formations' and units' combat traditions, the heroic deeds and self sacrifice of the troops and officers in fighting the enemy, and the Soviet people's great labor feat in the rear. The reinforcements were educated in the spirit of a profound recognition of the Soviet army's noble goals in the Great Patriotic War, hatred for the enemy, loyalty to one's Motherland, the Bolshevik Party and their leader, comrade Stalin.

Political-educational work with the soldiers of the new intake began as early as in the *front* and army reserve units, where they studied the text of the military oath and regularly conducted political discussions on the following topics: "The International Situation," "The Soviet People's

Great Feat in the Great Patriotic War," "Iron Discipline and a High Degree of Vigilance—the Key to a Quick Victory over Fascist Germany," "The Military Oath—the Sacred Promise of a Red Army Soldier," and "The Atrocities of the German-Fascist Aggressors."

On the way from the reserve regiments to the formations and units, discussions were conducted with the reinforcements about the Supreme Commander-in-Chief's orders in connection with the Soviet army's new victories, on communiqués from the Soviet Information Bureau, and on discipline and vigilance during on the march.

Receptions were organized for the arriving reinforcements in formations and units, in which division commanders, division political section chiefs, unit commanders and political workers, and staff officers were present. As a rule, in meeting the reinforcements in the divisions or regiments, meetings were conducted against a background of unfurled combat banners. At these meetings commanders, political workers, heroes of the Soviet Union, and decorated soldiers spoke, followed by a reply from the new intake. At these meetings people spoke of the division's or regiment's combat traditions, about their heroes and immediate combat tasks in light of the demands highlighted in comrade Stalin's order no. 5 of 23 February 1945.

The presentation of weapons to the new intake's soldiers was conducted in a solemn atmosphere by the subunit commanders and sometimes by the unit commanders. In presenting weapons it was sometimes mentioned to whom the weapon had once belonged and how he used it to fight the fascist aggressors.

Group discussions were conducted with the reinforcements in subunits, during which veteran soldiers—decorated ones and heroes of the Soviet Union—shared their combat experience and told how they should behave themselves in battle, about ways of fighting the enemy, about soldierly toughness, and how to hate the enemy in order to defeat him.

Having themselves experienced all the horrors of fascist captivity, the new intake's soldiers hated the fascist occupiers and burned with the desire to take armed revenge against them on the battlefield.

During the operation's preparatory period, the *front's* political directorate and the armies' and formations' political sections devoted a great deal of attention to questions of organizationally strengthening the primary and company party and Komsomol organizations. This measure was made necessary by the circumstance that as a result of the losses suffered in the *front's* winter offensive operations, the number of communists and Komsomol members had fallen and there were no party or Komsomol organizations in many subunits. In order to restore them, party and Komsomol forces in units were redistributed among the subunits. Besides this, party and Komsomol organizations were also filled out by newly-inducted members of the VKP(b) and candidate members of the VKP(b), and Komsomol members. Soldiers, sergeants and officers who had most manifested themselves in fighting the German-Fascist aggressors joined the party and Komsomol.

In those armies taking part in the Upper Silesian operation, 2,269 men were accepted into the VKP(b) in March, and 2,758 candidate members, for a total of 5,027 men.

The party organization's growth by armies is shown in Table VI/4.3.

Table VI/4.3 The Party Organization's Growth in March 1945

Army	Accepted		Total
	Party Members	Candidate Members	
5th Guards	587	628	1,215
21st	511	768	1,279
59th	364	319	683

60th	415	513	928
4th Guards Tank	392	530	922
TOTAL	2,269	2,758	5,027

The heightened desire of the rank and file and officers to join the ranks of the party of Lenin and Stalin was explained by the extremely high morale-political condition of the *front's* troops.

On the eve of the offensive party and Komsomol meetings were conducted in all the rifle, tank, artillery, mortar, and sapper subunits, where the question of the leading role of communists and Komsomol members in battle was discussed. Each communist and Komsomol member was assigned concrete tasks at these meetings.

Comrade Stalin's inspired words, calling on the troops to defeat the fascist beast as quickly as possible in his own lair, brought about a new combat renewal among the troops, imparting to them enormous offensive force.

Regrouping the Troops and Occupying the Jumping-Off Position

By the beginning of the regrouping, all of the *front's* left-wing armies located in the first echelon occupied the following defensive lines: 5th Guards Army: the Jauer—Strelen line; 21st Army: the Strelen—Oppeln line (both locales for the 21st Army); 59th Army: the Oppeln—Polln—Gross Neukirch line, and; 60th Army: the line excluding Polln—Gross Neukirch—Strumen. The remaining forces slated for participating in the March operation, following the First Ukrainian Front's February operation, were in the *front* reserve and stationed as follows: 4th Tank Army: in the Luben area; 7th Guards Mechanized and 31st Tank corps: in the area of the woods south of Gross Strelitz, and; the 93rd Rifle Corps: in the Tost area. In these areas the troops were restoring and receiving new equipment, were being reinforced with personnel, undergoing combat training, and absorbing the combat experience of the preceding operations.

The personnel strength of the 21st Army's divisions varied from 3,931 to 4,491 men. The divisions consisted of six battalions. The companies ranged from 48-76 men. The personnel strength of the 59th Army's divisions varied from 4,366 to 6,690 men. The personnel strength of the 60th Army's divisions, taking into account reinforcements, was increased to 4,500-5,000 men.

A complex operational regrouping of the *front's* forces was not required for the forthcoming operation, because the combined-arms armies were to mainly attack along the same sectors in which they had been previously operating. It was only the 4th Guards Tank Army that had to be regrouped from the Luben area to the sector of the forthcoming offensive.

It was necessary to carry out a more significant regrouping of units and formations within the armies, in order to create the planned density along the shock axes.

On 4 March the 4th Tank Army began its movement from the Luben area through Kant to its new concentration area of Olau, Laugwitz and Leibusch. The army's troops carried out a 150-kilometer march during darkness and by the morning of 11 March had concentrated in the indicated area, where over four days they continued to train, while studying the features of the enemy's defense and the terrain in the sector of the forthcoming offensive.[3] By the start of the offensive the 4th Tank Army's units and formations occupied the following jumping-off areas for the offensive: the 6th Mechanized Corps: Komradswaldau—northern outskirts of Grottkau; the 10th Tank

---

3   The 10th Tank Corps' 63rd Tank Brigade and the 6th Mechanized Corps' 49th Mechanized Brigade remained in the Luben area for personnel and equipment reinforcement and did not take part in the operation before 25 March.

Corps: Gross Enkwitz—Grottkau—Merzdorf—Deutsch Leippe; the 93rd Independent Tank Brigade: southeast of Dronfeld.

By the morning of 12 March the 7th Guards Mechanized Corps had concentrated in the woods northeast of Liebenbach and, on the night of 13-14 March, having crossed the Oder River, the corps' units had occupied their jumping-off positions for the offensive in the Erlen—Stoblau—Eichrode area.

By the morning of 14 March the 31st Tank Corps had moved to the Salzforst area and the woods to the south.

The 93rd Rifle Corps, which was subordinated to the 59th Army during the operation, carried out a march from the Tost area to the area of Rosengrund during 11-13 March and on 14 March occupied jumping-off positions for the attack.

The 21st Army began to regroup its forces during the night of 4-5 March. Units of the 117th and 118th rifle corps, after turning over their defensive sectors, marched to their new concentration area south of Brieg, where they concentrated on 7 March. Over five days the troops in this area engaged in combat and political training. The 55th Rifle Corps' formations and units conducted the defense of the army's entire sector from Strelen to Oppeln from 7 March until the troops' occupation of their jumping-off positions for the offensive.

On the night of 12-13 March the 59th Army's 115th Rifle Corps turned over its defensive sector from Rosengrund to Polln and Gross Neukirch to the 60th Army's 28th Rifle Corps.

By the morning of 15 March the regrouping of the units and formations of the *front's* left-wing armies had been completed and the troops of the armies scheduled to take part in the operation had occupied their jumping-off positions for the offensive.

In preparing for the offensive as a whole, and particularly while carrying out regroupings, all measures were taken to hide the operation's preparation from the enemy and to achieve offensive surprise. Troop regrouping and the delivery of ammunition were carried out only at night. Telephone conversations about the movement of units were categorically forbidden. Radio stations worked only to receive messages. Special radio sets were allotted in the armies' and corps' headquarters for enforcing this requirement.

As a result of the regrouping of forces, 31 rifle divisions (equal to 28 9-battalion divisions) were concentrated to take part in the operation along a 190-kilometer front, as well as 5,676 guns and mortars, and 800 tanks and self-propelled guns. 1,737 planes were to take part in the operation. Following the regrouping of forces, each rifle division had an average of 6.8 kilometers of front, with 30 guns and mortars and 4.2 tanks per kilometer of front. The enemy had the following forces in the offensive sector of the First Ukrainian Front's left-wing armies: 19 infantry divisions,[4] 2,305 guns and mortars, 340 tanks and assault guns, and 750 planes, meaning that each infantry division defended an average of ten kilometers of front, with each kilometer holding 12 guns and mortars and 1.8 tanks.

As a result of the regrouping of men and materiel for the offensive, our forces along the entire offensive sector outnumbered the enemy in infantry by 1.5 times, 2.5 times in artillery and mortars, and 2.3 times in tanks and planes. The superiority of the *front's* forces over the enemy along the projected breakthrough sectors was more significant. The *front's* forces outnumbered the enemy in men by five times, eight times in artillery and mortars, and nine times in tanks.

The tactical density along the armies' breakthrough sectors is shown in Table VI/4.5.

---

4   In calculating independent infantry units and elements, as well as sapper elements employed by the enemy as infantry, the latter have been counted as 9-battalion infantry divisions.

Table VI/4.5 The Concentration of Men and Materiel Along the Armies' Breakthrough Sectors

Army	Breakthrough Front (km)	Rifle Battalions	
		Total	Per Km of Front
21st and 4th Tank	8	31	3.9
59th	5	27	5.4
60th	4	27	6.7
TOTAL	17	85	5.0

Army	Guns and Mortars		Tanks and Self-Propelled Guns	
	Total	Per Km of Front	Total	Per Km of Front
21st and 4th Tank	1,587	198	515	64.4
59th	1,174	235	115	23.0
60th	600	150	101	25.0
TOTAL	3,361	583	731	43.0

Note. The table includes only the rifle battalions of the first-echelon divisions slated for breaking through the enemy's main defensive zone.

The correlation of men and materiel along the breakthrough sectors is shown in Table VI/4.6.

Table VI/4.6 The Correlation of Men and Materiel Along the Armies' Breakthrough Sectors (Overall Width of 17 kilometers)

Men and Materiel	Soviet Forces		Enemy Forces		Correlation
	Total	Per Km of Front	Total	Per Km of Front	
Rifle (infantry) battalions	85	5	17	1	5:1
Guns and Mortars (higher than 76mm)	3,361	198	396	23	9.8:1
Tanks and Self-Propelled Guns	731	43	82	5	9:1

Thanks to the correlation of men and material achieved along the breakthrough sectors and, on the whole, along the shock axes, favorable prerequisites were created for the successful resolution of their assigned tasks for the *front's* left-wing armies.

Despite the command's and troops' intensive work during the operation's preparatory period, the *front* was not able to fully cope according to the schedule, established by the Supreme Commander-in-Chief, with the preparation of the operation, particularly in the area of materiel supply. Taking this into account, the *Stavka* of the Supreme High Command authorized the *front* commander to put off the start of the operation by two days. This was sufficient to complete the preparation of the troops and rear for the offensive.

On 13 March the *front* command ordered that the 21st and 5th Guards armies' offensive begin at 0600 on 15 March with an attack by the forward battalions. The 21st, 5th Guards and 4th Tank armies' main forces were to attack on that day at 1020, while the 59th and 60th armies were ordered to begin their offensive at 0850. Forward battalions were not detached in these armies.

By the morning of 15 March all the preparations had been completed and the necessary materiel supplies had been created. By this time the artillery and mortars had been moved up to their firing positions and the troops had occupied their jumping-off positions for the offensive.

In toting up the brief results of the operation's preparation, it is necessary to note the following.

The operation's preparation was based upon the Soviet troops' rich combat experience, which had been acquired in the preceding years of the war, and particularly in the offensive operations on enemy territory in the winter of 1945.

The First Ukrainian Front's command, in carrying out the instructions of the *Stavka* of the Supreme High Command on rapidly eliminating the lagging behind of the *front's* left-wing forces and their arrival at the foothills of the Sudeten Mountains, successfully completed preparations for the operation in a short period of time.

57 percent of the infantry, 60 percent of the artillery and mortars and 91 percent of the tanks and self-propelled guns out of the overall amount of men and materiel designated to participate in the operation had been concentrated along the axes of the main attacks to resolve the tasks of encircling and destroying the enemy group of forces in the Oppeln salient. This enabled us to achieve a decisive superiority of men and materiel over the enemy along the axes of the main attacks. The *front's* forces outnumbered the enemy in men by 5:1, 8:1 in artillery and mortars, and 9:1 in tanks.

The organization of the Upper Silesian operation's material support unfolded in a difficult situation. Major offensive operations, conducted by the *front's* forces in January and February, preceded the beginning of this operation. Aside from this, one must take into account the wet spring weather, which made the delivery of ammunition and fuels and lubricants to the troops more difficult. Despite the indicated difficulties, the *front* command successfully resolved the task of accumulating materiel supplies for the forthcoming operation. All types of troop transport was brought in to deliver ammunition. By the start of the offensive the troops were fully supplied within the bounds of the expenditure norms for the operation.

The party-political work carried out during the operation's preparatory period inspired the *front's* forces to carry out the tasks laid out by comrade Stalin in his order no. 5 of 23 February 1945 and mobilized the entire rank and file to defeat the enemy at the concluding stage of the Great Patriotic War.

5

The Conduct of the Operation

The First Ukrainian Front's Upper Silesian offensive operation began during a period when major offensive operations, which tied down all of the German-Fascist command's reserves, were unfolding along the entire Soviet-German front.

In the middle of March along the right wing of the Soviet-German front, the Third Belorussian Front launched a successful offensive for the purpose of finally eliminating the major enemy group of forces encircled south of Königsberg; at the same time the Second Belorussian Front and the right wing of the First Belorussian Front were completing the elimination of the enemy's East Pomeranian group of forces, while the First Ukrainian Front had already cleared the enemy from the lower course of the Oder River. In the Carpathians, the Fourth Ukrainian Front continued its stubborn offensive fighting along the Moravska Ostrava axis.

In Hungary, along the left wing of the Soviet-German front, the Third Ukrainian Front, having repelled a major enemy counteroffensive in the area of Lake Balaton, launched a decisive offensive along the Vienna direction in conjunction with the Second Ukrainian Front's left wing.

The Soviet forces' attacks in East Prussia, East Pomerania, as well as along the Moravska Ostrava and Vienna axes, were tying down the enemy's forces and drawing upon themselves the reserves of the German-Fascist army, and limiting the fascist command's capabilities to reinforce his Upper Silesian group of forces. Thus quite a favorable situation had arisen for the First Ukrainian Front's forces in Upper Silesia.

The First Ukrainian Front's offensive in Upper Silesia ran from 15-31 March.

During 15-18 March the *front's* Oppeln and Ratibor groups of forces overcame the tactical depth of the Germans' defense and, having gone over to the pursuit of the retreating enemy, linked up in the Neustadt—Zulz area, having encircled more than five enemy divisions in the area southwest of Oppeln.

During 19-20 March the 21st, 59th and 4th Guards Tank armies' forces split up the encircled enemy group of forces and destroyed it in detail; at the same time, 15,000 soldiers and officers were taken prisoner.

During the last ten days of March the efforts of the First Ukrainian Front's forces were directed toward trying to reach the foothills of the Sudeten Mountains. At the same time, fighting had begun for the town of Strelen in the 5th Guards Army's offensive sector. The 21st and 4th Tank armies directed their efforts at seizing the town of Neisse. The 60th Army's main forces were fighting for the town of Ratibor. The operation concluded with the seizure of these towns and the arrival of the *front's* left-wing forces at the line Strelen—Neisse—Jagerndorf—Steuberwitz—Dolen, that is, at the foothills of the Sudeten Mountains.

The Breakthrough of Main Zone of the Enemy's Defense Northwest and South of Oppeln (15-16 March)

The *front's* offensive began with the actions of the 21st and 5th Guards armies' forward battalions northwest of Oppeln.

501

At 0600 on 15 March, following a 10-minute fire onslaught by our artillery, the forward battalions of the 21st and 5th Guards armies' first-echelon divisions attacked the enemy along the entire front of the armies' offensive. By pressing close to the artillery explosions, the attacking subunits broke into the enemy's trenches so vigorously that he was not able to prepare to repel the attack and, having been taken off guard, was forced to abandon his positions almost without a fight.

The forward elements' rapid and decisive actions yielded positive results. The 118th Rifle Corps' forward battalions seized Beatenhof and Ulrichshof. The 117th Rifle Corps' forward battalions broke into Waldau. The 285th Rifle Division's (55th Rifle Corps) forward battalion occupied height 218.3 The 34th Guards Rifle Corps' (5th Guards Army) forward battalion, which was attacking along the corps' left flank, captured the grove one kilometer north of Voigtsdorf. Only on the corps' right flank was the forward battalion unable to seize the enemy's first trench and carry out its assignment.

Having recovered from the first surprise blow, the enemy opened fire on our infantry with all his weapons. The forward battalions, upon encountering the enemy's organized resistance, could advance no further. During the course of the fighting they were able to establish that the enemy's main forces had not been withdrawn from the first position. Information about the enemy's artillery-mortar group of forces and his infantry fire system was also tightened up. Prisoners captured in the Beatenhof and Ulrichshof area fully confirmed the information held by our command regarding the enemy's dispositions along the 21st Army's breakthrough sector.

The capture of Beatenhof by the 118th Rifle Corps' forward battalion enabled us to delineate the forward edge of the enemy's main defensive zone, which ran not along the line Beatenhof—Ulrichshof, as had been earlier assumed, but a bit to the south, while only the enemy's combat security was located in these inhabited locales.

On the basis of amplified data on the outline of the forward edge of the enemy's defense, on the location of his artillery and mortar firing positions and the defenders' system of infantry fire, the necessary amendments and fine tunings were added to the plan for the artillery offensive. In particular, the commander of the 21st Army, considering that the forward battalions had overcome part of the enemy's defense, the suppression destruction of which had been called for by the plan for the artillery preparation of the attack, ordered that the artillery preparation be shortened from one hour and 20 minutes to 40 minutes. This decision was dictated by the desire of the army commander to economize on ammunition for the subsequent battle for the numerous strong points in the tactical depth of the enemy's defense. The 21st and 4th Tank armies' main forces, which were attacking toward Neisse, attacked at 1040, following a 40-minute working over of the main zone of the enemy's defense. While overcoming the enemy's stubborn fire resistance and repelling repeated counterattacks by his tactical reserves, the army's formations broke through two positions of the main zone of the enemy's defense by the end of the day along an 8-kilometer front and advanced eight kilometers into the depth of the enemy's defense.

The 5th Guards Army's 34th Guards Rifle Corps, along with the 4th Guards Tank Corps, began its attack at 1120, following an 80-minute artillery preparation. The corps' units, while overcoming powerful fire resistance, and subjected to enemy air action and repelling his infantry attacks ranging from a company to a battalion in size, along with tanks, insistently advanced. Having broken through the enemy's defense along a 3-kilometer front, by the close of the offensive's first day, the troops had widened the breakthrough to five kilometers and captured the second position of the enemy's main defensive zone along the left flank.

Although as a result of the attack on the first day of the operation, the 21st and 4th Tank armies' forces, which were attacking in the direction of Neisse, reached the line Endersdorf—Klein Zindel—Rosdorf—Klein Gurau—Schedlau, they nevertheless failed to carry out their first day's assignment. In order to carry out their assignment, they would still have to overcome the resistance of the enemy's defending troops to a depth of up to ten kilometers.

The 59th and 60th armies' forces, which were attacking from the bridgehead north of Ratibor in the direction of Neustadt, attacked at 0850, following an 80-minute artillery preparation. Having crushed the enemy's defense, they broke through the main zone of his defense along a 12-kilometer front and advanced 6-8 kilometers in a day of fighting. At the same time, they captured the Germans' strong points of Eichungen, Langlieben, Klein Nimsdorf, Ridgrund, and Schneidenburg. In the course of the fighting, the armies' forces had to repel ten enemy counterattacks, each with strength of a company to a battalion of infantry, supported by tanks and assault guns.

The troops' slow advance on the first day of the attack may be explained by a number of reasons. As a result of the fact that the artillery preparation in the 21st Army's offensive sector had been halved and that the enemy turned out to have more anti-tank weapons than had been revealed by our intelligence before the start of the operation, we were not able to completely suppress the enemy's anti-tank defense. Our tanks had to overcome it with heavy losses. The 62nd Tank Brigade alone lost 20 tanks knocked out or burned during the day. The 59th and 60th armies' intelligence also failed to fully reveal the enemy's anti-tank defensive system, as a result of which the 7th Guards Mechanized Corps lost a quarter of its tanks, and the 31st Tank Corps a third. The heavy tank losses may also be explained by the fact that our forces had not yet fully mastered the methods of fighting enemy elements armed with *faustpatrones*.

Besides this, before 1200 on 15 March, as the result of the poor meteorological conditions, our aviation did not carry out combat sorties. Only after 1200, as the weather improved, did our aviation begin to launch bomber and assault air strikes against the enemy's strong points, headquarters and communications centers.

Instead of the 2,995 sorties planned for the first day of the operation, our aviation carried out only 1,283. The 2nd Air Army's forced idleness during the artillery preparation and in the beginning of the infantry and tank attack unquestionably slowed the pace of our troops' advance.

The spring thaw limited our tanks' activities. The fighting was waged primarily for the roads, road junctions and inhabited locales, which had been transformed by the enemy into powerful strong points. While falling back under our troops' attacks, the enemy's units clung to each trench, all the tactically favorable heights and roads, and each inhabited locale, and was putting up stubborn resistance to our infantry and tanks. Covering units and subunits, and the artillery supporting them, were pulled back by the enemy only after his main forces had succeeded in occupying the defense along the latest intermediate position, along heights or in inhabited locales.

In order to deprive the enemy of the capability of employing the night for organizing his defense along new lines, the *front* commander demanded of the army commanders that they not halt the offensive at night. In order to accomplish the assignment for the operation's first day, he ordered that the regiments' and divisions' second echelons be committed into the fighting on the night of 15-16 March and to not halt the attack during the night.

In order to fight at night, it was ordered that in the morning of each day each rifle division was to detail a battalion each into the second echelon for rest and preparation for attacking at night.

It was ordered to move the artillery during the night to new firing positions, as close as possible to the attacking troops' combat formations. The tank troops were ordered to pull out all of their tanks that had become stuck in the mud, during the night.

Responsible officers were dispatched from the armies' and corps' headquarters to establish strict order along the roads.

The German-Fascist command, while trying to prevent a breakthrough by the 21st and 4th Tank armies to the town of Neisse, reinforced its group of forces that was operating southwest of Grottkau during 15-16 March, having transferred the main forces of the 10th Panzergrenadier Division and the entire 19th Panzer Division here from the Strelen area. Units of the 254th Infantry Division were being transferred to the 59th Army's attack sector from the central sector of Army Group Center's front. Independent units and subunits of these forces entered the fighting as early as 16 March. On this day units of the 5th Guards Army and the 21st and 4th Tank armies' right-flank formations had to repel numerous counterattacks by subunits of the enemy's 19th Panzer Division from the woods northwest of Hoen Giersdorf and subunits of the 10th Panzergrenadier Division from the Striegendorf—Kueschmalz area toward Klein Zindel. As a rule, up to a battalion of infantry and 12-20 tanks took part in each enemy counterattack.

During the fighting during the night of 15-16 March and during the day of 16 March, the 5th Guards Army's 34th Guards Rifle Corps and the 4th Guards Tank corps, and the 21st Army's right-flank 118th Rifle Corps, along with the 4th Tank Army's 6th Mechanized Corps, advanced three kilometers. Despite the insignificant advance, the corps carried out an important task, having secured the covering of the 21st and 4th Tank armies' main forces, which were attacking to the southwest in the direction of Neisse, against enemy flank attacks from the north.

At the same time that intense fighting was unfolding with the enemy's counterattacking infantry and tank units along the 5th Guards Army's front, the 118th Rifle Corps' left-flank units and, formations of the 117th and 55th rifle and 10th Tank corps, while overcoming the enemy's stubborn resistance, advanced ten kilometers by the close of 16 March and had reached the line Petersheide—Waltdorf—Jatzdorf.

Along the Neustadt axis, on 16 March the 59th and 60th armies also continued to attack, beating off numerous enemy infantry and tank attacks. During the day the forces of the 59th Army managed to advance 3-9 kilometers; units of the 43rd Rifle Corps' 314th Rifle Division reached the area north of Reinschdorf, while units of the 115th and 93rd rifle and 7th Guards Mechanized corps reached the line Rodemark—Kreitzlinden—Hoenfleur. Along the army's left turning flank units of the 93rd Rifle and 7th Guards Mechanized corps completely overcame the entire depth of the enemy's main defensive zone and thus set up the success of the attack on 17-18 March.

The 60th Army's 28th Rifle and 31st Tank corps advanced only four kilometers in a day of fighting.

It's necessary to note that guns of all calibers fired over open sights on 16 March and in the succeeding days of the offensive. This was conditioned by the peculiarities of the terrain, the presence of a large amount of inhabited locales with stone structures, which contained sturdy basements that had been configured for prolonged defense. Each firing point established in a building would cease firing only after it had been destroyed. Thus in order to suppress and destroy the enemy's firing points and personnel in sturdy cover, not only medium guns fired over open sights, but even large-caliber guns and even heavy artillery (203mm howitzers). In order to economize on ammunition, particularly large-caliber, we carried out "welded" fire by large-caliber guns (122mm and larger) with smaller-caliber guns (76mm and smaller). Firing from large-caliber guns was conducted against the walls of buildings and their foundations, and against windows and attics with smaller-caliber guns. Such a method of firing ensured the rapid suppression or the complete destruction of firing points in buildings, while at the same time economizing on shells.

During the fighting it was established that the enemy, in order to avoid heavy losses from massed strikes by our artillery and mortars, was seeking to disperse his personnel and combat equipment in strong points and centers of resistance. Thus while fighting to capture strong points, and particularly while fighting along intermediate lines, aside from massive fire against area targets, the *front* commander also ordered that aimed fire be conducted to destroy the enemy's protected personnel and combat equipment.

On 16 March our aviation carried out 1,697 sorties, including 750 sorties against enemy troops directly over the battlefield.

A characteristic feature of our aviation's activities on this day was its close cooperation with the ground forces in repelling the enemy's counterattacks. For example, during the second part of the day the enemy counterattacked the attacking forces of the 34th Guards Rifle Corps from the area north of Hoen Giersdorf with up to a battalion of infantry, supported by ten tanks and assault guns. The aviation representative located at the corps' command post summoned our aviation against the enemy's counterattacking infantry and tanks. At 1745 four assault aircraft and five fighters took off. On the approach to the target, the leader of the air group contacted the guidance station and amplified the assignment. At the same time, our infantry carried out target identification with rockets, and artillery through shell explosions. The assault aircraft and fighters scattered the enemy battalion, killed up to 50 infantrymen and set on fire two assault guns and a tank. The enemy's counterattack failed. Taking advantage of the air attack, units of the 34th Guards Rifle Corps attacked the enemy and captured the powerful strong point of Hoen Giersdorf.

The chief shortcoming of the second day's offensive was that along both axes the mobile forces, which were taking part in repelling the enemy's counterattacks with the infantry, had not succeeded in breaking clear of the infantry and had been forced to operate as immediate infantry support tanks.

The troops' adherence to the roads, which had been caused by the spring washing away of the roads, often caused traffic jams to form on them, which made the delivery of munitions, the need for which grew more and more as enemy resistance increased, more difficult. All of this made more difficult the troops' combat activities and led to a reduction in the pace of the offensive, particularly that of the mobile formations.

The *front* commander demanded that the commander of the 4th Tank Army and the commanders of independent tank and mechanized corps immediately establish order on the roads and, along with the infantry, crush the enemy's organized resistance and, having broken free of the infantry, by the close of 17 March reach the Neustadt—Zulz area, thus cutting off the enemy's route of retreat from the Oppeln salient.

The Development of the Breakthrough and the Encirclement of the Enemy Group of Forces in the Area Southwest of Oppeln (17-18 March)

On 17 March, as in the preceding days, the enemy put up strong resistance to our attacking forces, carrying out counterattacks with infantry and tanks. There were no changes in the enemy group of forces along the Neisse axis, while along the Neustadt axis the German-Fascist command committed into the battle units of the 100th Light Infantry Division and several battalions of *Volksturm*, trying to prevent our forces from capturing Ober Glogau.

Our troops' attack from the direction of Grottkau on the third day of the operation was developing more successfully than during the first two days. The attack by the forces of the 21st Army and 10th Tank Corps to the south and their comparatively successful advance along this axis during the course of 15-16 March forced the enemy to broaden his defensive front along the Neisse River. This significantly weakened the enemy's resistance. Units of the 118th Rifle and 6th Mechanized corps captured six inhabited locales in night fighting, while units of the 117th Rifle and 10th Tank corps reached the Neisse River, and the 117th Rifle Corps' 120th Rifle Division, which had been committed into the fighting on the night of 16-17 March, had forced the Neisse River in the Rothaus area by 0600 on 17 March. The enemy, while striving to prevent our forces from forcing the river and taking advantage of the Ottmachauer Reservoir, raised the water level in the Neisse River by 1.7-2 meters and also blew up the bridges in the areas of possible crossings. However, this did not halt the troops' crossing. The 120th Rifle Division's forward units and subunits forced the river from the march, using materials at hand, threw the enemy units out of the eastern half of Rothaus, occupied Mansdorf, and by 1300 on 17 March had created conditions for throwing crossings over the river and pushing units of the 10th Tank Corps and artillery across them.

With the arrival of the 120th Rifle Division and units of the 10th Tank Corps at the right bank of the Neisse River in the Rothaus—Mansdorf area, the tactical depth of the enemy's defense had been completely overcome. Our troops immediately took up the pursuit of the enemy to the southeast toward Neustadt. The pursuit was conducted by units of the 117th Rifle and 10th Tank corps not only during the daytime on 17 March, but throughout the night of 17-18 March.

Early on the morning of 18 March forces of the 4th Tank Army learned of order no. 050, by the USSR people's commissar of defense of 17 March 1945, of the army's designation as a guards force. The order read as follows:

> In battles for our Soviet Motherland against the German aggressors, the 4th Tank Army displayed examples of bravery and firmness, valor and intrepidity, discipline and a sense of organization.
>
> During the fighting along the front of the Great Patriotic War with the German aggressors, the 4th Tank Army has inflicted heavy losses on the fascist troops and by its crushing attacks has destroyed the enemy's men and materiel.
>
> For valor displayed in battles for the homeland against the German aggressors, for firmness, for bravery, for valor, discipline, organization, and the skillful fulfillment of its combat assignments, the 4th Tank Army is to be renamed the 4th Guards Tank Army.

News of the army's renaming as a guards unit raised the combat spirit of the army's entire rank and file. Enlisted men, sergeants and officers of the army, inspired by this news, with even greater zeal took on the fulfillment of the combat assignments facing them, striving to justify the high designation of a Soviet army's guards unit.

During the daytime of 18 March the 10th Guards Tank Corps' 61st Guards Tank Brigade captured Neustadt and Loiber. On that day units of the 21st Army's 117th and 55th rifle corps, having advanced 15 kilometers, captured 55 inhabited locales, including such important inhabited locales and road junctions as the towns of Zulz and Falkenberg, and the area northeast of Neustadt. Here on 18 March the 21st Army's forces linked up with the 59th Army's forces attacking toward Neustadt from the east.

To a great extent our aviation facilitated the success of the ground forces in pursuing and encircling the enemy on 18 March. Assault aircraft launched strikes against enemy forces on the roads southwest of Oppeln, interfering with their withdrawal in the directions of Steinau and Neustadt. Our aviation also launched strikes against concentrations of enemy units in Ober-Glogau and Kujau; through its actions it disorganized the enemy's retreating units and supported the 21st and 59th armies' forces in carrying out their tasks.

During 17-18 March the 5th Guards Army's left-flank formations and the 21st and 4th Guards Tank armies' right-flank formations beat off numerous counterattacks by small groups of enemy infantry and tanks. They made minor advances over two days.

On 17 March the enemy along the 59th Army's front, having reinforced his forces with units of the 254th Infantry and 100th Light Infantry divisions and several battalions of *volksturm*, tried to delay the advance by units of the 59th Army and the 7th Guards Mechanized Corps toward Ober Glogau and Neustadt. The enemy counterattacks from the area of Schenau were especially fierce. However, all of the enemy's counterattacks were beaten off by the army's forces.

By the end of the day on 17 March, as a result of three days of offensive fighting, the 59th Army's 93rd Rifle Corps and the 7th Guards Mechanized Corps, which was attacking along with it, had crushed the enemy's resistance along the army's left turning flank, had overcome the entire tactical depth of his defense and reached the line Tomas—Schenau—Kitteldorf. The army's right-flank forces, having deployed facing north, reached the immediate southern outskirts of Cosel, had broken into Nesselwitz and seized Frebel. In order to speed up the capture of the town of Cosel, the army commander ordered the commander of the 43rd Rifle Corps to commit the 13th Rifle Division into the fighting. Upon going over to the offensive, units of the 13th Rifle Division on that day captured Klodnitz and reached the approaches to Cosel from the east.

The turn by the 115th Rifle Corps' units north marked the beginning of the encirclement of the enemy group of forces in the area southwest of Oppeln from the south. Now the 115th Rifle Corps was covering units of the 93rd Rifle and 7th Guards Mechanized corps against enemy flank attacks from the north.

It should be noted that the slow advance of the 115th Rifle Corps during the latter half of 16 and 17 March was the fault of the corps commander, who, while not grasping the situation, exaggerated the strength of the enemy's resisting units and failed to make sufficient demands on his division, regimental and subunit commanders. The commanders of the corps' divisions, regiments and even some battalions and companies controlled the battle from inhabited locales and essentially did not know the course of the battle. The corps' and divisions' headquarters did not exercise control of combat activities. Artillery observation was not conducted within the infantry's combat formations. The artillery's combat formations became separated from the attacking troops by as much as ten kilometers. Few heavy guns for firing over open sights were detached, while those that were detached were positioned along firing positions at a great distance from the infantry's combat formations and rendered no practical assistance to the infantry. The corps commander himself failed to carry out the demand by the *front* and army commander on training battalions (one from each rifle division) for attacking at night and the 115th Rifle Corps basically engaged in no night fighting. Maneuver for the purpose of outflanking the stubbornly resisting enemy's strong points was poorly employed.

The 60th Army's right-flank formations, having repelled 13 enemy counterattacks by the close of 17 March and having advanced 13 kilometers, overcame the entire tactical depth of the enemy's defense, seized Konigsdorf and advanced right up to Leobschutz. The successes of the 60th Army's formations facilitated the rapid advance by the 59th Army's forces and deprived the enemy of the capability to counterattack their flank from the south.

The *Stavka* of the Supreme High Command, while attaching great significance to the successful conclusion of the Upper Silesian operation, demanded more decisive actions from the *front* commander and the vigorous advance by the *front's* left wing for the purpose of completing in a timely fashion the encirclement of the German-Fascist forces in the area southwest of Oppeln and arriving at the foothills of the Sudeten Mountains. At the same time, the *Stavka* paid special attention to the unacceptably slow advance by the 59th Army's forces. The untimely arrival of this army's forces at the Zulz—Neustadt line would enable the fascist command to pull its forces out of the Oppeln salient.

On 17 March the *front* commander personally traveled to the 59th and 60th armies' combat operations area. He instructed the commanders of the 59th and 60th armies that the main reason for the slow advance by the armies' forces, particularly those of the 59th Army, was the unsatisfactory development of the breakthrough along the flanks of these armies. The commander of the 59th Army was ordered to deploy the 115th Rifle Corps to the northwest, capture Ober Glogau and thus facilitate the vigorous advance by the 93rd Rifle and 7th Guards Mechanized corps. Simultaneously, the 43rd Rifle Corps was to go over to the attack. The *front* commander canceled the army commander's decision for the 7th Guards Mechanized Corps' attack toward Ober Glogau and demanded that he employ the corps for forcing the Hotzenplotz River along the line Dirschelwitz—Deutsch Rasselwitz, so as to subsequently develop the offensive to the west and by 1200 on 18 March link up with the 4th Tank Army along the line Zulz—Neustadt.

The *front* commander demanded that the commander of the 60th Army reinforce the left flank of the army's attacking troops with artillery, the 152nd Tank Brigade and independent self-propelled artillery regiments, and to commit its corps' second echelons into the fighting and to decisively develop the offensive toward Ernau and Biskau.

The commander of the 59th Army, while carrying out the *front* commander's order, ordered the commander of the 43rd Rifle Corps to leave a covering forces along the line Oppeln—Klodnitz and launch an attack in the direction of Proskau and Schelitz with the 80th Rifle Division's main forces from the bridgehead south of Oppeln and, having broken through the enemy's defense and having deployed in combat formation, to comb and clear the Germans out of the woods west of Krappitz. Two of the 13th Rifle Division's rifle regiments were to attack from the bridgehead southwest of Oppeln toward Kramelau and Kujau and destroy the enemy units defending the town of Krappitz.

The 115th Rifle Corps was ordered to commit its second echelon into the battle, to capture Ober Glogau, and by the close of 18 March to link up with the 21st Army's forces in the Elgut area.

The 93rd Rifle and 7th Guards Mechanized corps' tasks remained as before. They were to attack toward Neustadt. The 7th Guards Mechanized Corps was reinforced with the 39th Artillery Brigade and the 774th Howitzer Artillery Regiment from the 17th Artillery Breakthrough Division.

The measures adopted exerted a decisive influence on the successful course of the 59th Army's combat operations to encircle the enemy in the Oppeln salient.

The 59th Army's offensive on 18 March unfolded more successfully than during the preceding days. By 1200 units of the 7th Guards Mechanized Corps, along with units of the 93rd Rifle Corps, having crushed the resistance of the enemy's units, forced the Hotzenplotz River in the Dirschelwitz—Deutsch Rasselwitz area and began to pursue the remnants of the enemy's defeated subunits. The 26th Guards Mechanized and 57th Guards Tank brigades advanced particularly rapidly and advanced 12 kilometers in an hour and a half. At 1330 these brigades' subunits captured Loiber, where they linked up with subunits of the 10th Guards Tank Corps' 61st Tank Brigade (4th Guards Tank Army). During the latter half of the day part of the subunits of the 26th Guards Mechanized and 57th Guards Tank brigades occupied Altstadt and Zulz, to which the 21st Army's 120th Rifle Division had also arrived. Units of the 93rd Rifle Corps were successfully advancing behind the 7th Guards Mechanized Corps' brigades.

Upon the arrival of units of the 4th Guards Tank Army's 10th Guards Tank Corps and those of the 21st Army's 120th Rifle Division at the line Neustadt—Zulz—Elgut and their linkup along this line with units of the 59th Army's 7th Guards Mechanized and 93rd Rifle corps, the encirclement of the enemy's group of forces southwest of Oppeln was completed. The 21st, 4th Guards Tank and 59th armies, having completed the encirclement of the enemy on 18 March, continued to develop the offensive toward the west with part of their forces, as a result of which the encircled enemy was isolated from his main forces by up to 20 kilometers. This enabled the *front's* left-wing forces to immediately begin eliminating the encircled enemy.

Throughout 18 March units of the 59th Army's 115th Rifle Corps had to repel numerous counterattacks by small subunits of enemy infantry and tanks from the area of Ober Glogau and Friedersdorf, which were trying to break through the corps' combat ranks and get out of the encirclement to the south. The corps successfully repelled all the counterattacks and, pushing the enemy toward the north, threw him out of Walzen, seized the southern outskirts of Friedersdorf and reached the southern approaches to Ober Glogau.

As a result of intense fighting, units of the 43rd Rifle Corps' 314th and 13th rifle divisions captured the major river port and industrial center of Cosel. By 2100 on 18 March the corps was fighting along the Oppeln—Schoenkirch—Gross Schimmendorf—eastern outskirts of Krappitz—Tiefenburg—Neumanske line.

The 60th Army, having encountered the enemy's organized resistance along the previously prepared line Hoenplotz—Leobschutz—Ernau, which had been occupied by the enemy's retreating units, advanced only 2-7 kilometers that day.

In all, in four days of attacking the 60th Army's right flank units advanced 25 kilometers into the depth of the enemy's defense, having deployed their combat formations facing south and southwest. The army carried out only one of the tasks assigned to it by the *front* commander. It prevented the enemy from launching an attack against the flank of the 59th Army's attacking forces and facilitated the fulfillment of the task by its neighbor to the right of encircling the German-Fascist troops. However, the army failed to reach the line Neustadt—Zoppau—Biskau—Ratibor. This may be explained, first of all, by the fact that during the first three days of fighting the 31st Tank Corps lost 62 out of 118 tanks it possessed at the start of the operation. After the tactical defensive zone had been overcome, the corps no longer had the strength to develop the offensive in the operational depth and was forced to operate within the infantry's combat formations until the end of the operation. Secondly, the 4th Ukrainian Front's 38th Army, having begun its attack on 10 March in the direction of Moravska Ostrava, Granice and Olomouc, could not overcome the tactical depth of the enemy's defense in eight days of fighting. Thus the First Ukrainian Front's left wing was under threat of an enemy flank attack the entire time. The distraction of part of the 60th Army's forces to securing the *front's* left wing did not enable the army commander to reinforce his forces attacking along the main axis of the army's attack.

As a result of the four days of fighting, the *front's* left-wing armies carried out their assigned task of encircling the enemy group of forces. By the middle of the offensive's fourth day, the 21st Army's forces, which were attacking along with the forces of the 4th Guards Tank Army in the direction of Grottkau, Neisse and Neustadt, had reached the Neustadt—Loiber—Zulz—Elgut area and linked up with the 59th Army's forces attacking from the bridgehead north of Ratibor to the west toward Neustadt. This achieved the encirclement of the enemy in the area southwest of Oppeln. The 20th SS Infantry Division, the 168th and 344th infantry divisions, part of the 18th SS Panzergrenadier Division, and several independent regiments and battalions ended up in the encirclement.

A no less concrete result of the operation's first four days was the foiling of the German-Fascist command's intention to carry out a counterblow from the Zaarau—Schweitnitz—Zobten area to the northeast, for the purpose of helping the troops encircled in Breslau. The Army Group Center command was forced to transfer the greater part of its forces designated for resolving this task, to the First Ukrainian Front's left wing, so as to prevent our troops from advancing any further to the southwest and to help its group of forces that had just been encircled in the area southwest of Oppeln.

6

The Elimination of the Enemy's Encircled Group of Forces (19-20 March)

It was planned to destroy the encircled enemy group of forces by launching concentric attacks against the enemy, in order to split up the encircled troops along with their simultaneous destruction in detail.

Instructions on the elimination of the enemy formations in the Oppeln salient were issued by the *front* command on 18 March, while the encirclement was still being carried out.

In accordance with these instructions, the army commanders drew up detailed plans for their forces' actions in destroying the enemy group of forces encircled in the Oppeln salient.

The Army Commanders' Decisions on Destroying the Encircled Enemy

The commander of the 21st Army decided to carry out the task assigned to him in the following manner.

The 55th Rifle Corps was given the task of splitting and destroying the enemy's forces in the western part of the wooded area located between Oppeln and the Steinau River. For this purpose, the 225th Rifle Division was to attack with its right flank along the railroad in the direction of Falkenberg and Siefersdorf, and with its left flank toward Gumpertzdorf and Goldmor. The 229th Rifle Division was to launch an attack along its left flank along the Steinau River toward Elgut-Hammer and Brandewalde against the flank of the enemy group of forces trying to break out toward Friedland. The 285th Rifle Division received orders to securely defend the line Erlenburg—Friedland—Floste and prevent the enemy from breaking through to Neisse.

The 117th Rifle Corps was ordered to attack with part of its 120th Rifle Division in the direction of Schelitz toward the 59th Army's 80th Rifle Division and with part of its forces toward Ringwitz toward the 229th Rifle Division. the 125th and 72nd rifle divisions were to continue attacking toward Neisse from the line achieved by the close of 18 March.

The 118th Rifle Corps, which was attacking along with units of the 4th Guards Tank Army's 6th Guards Mechanized Corps, received orders to continue carrying out its assigned task to reach the line Munsterberg—Alt Patschkau—Kalkau.

The commander of the 59th Army assigned his corps the following tasks.

The 43rd Rifle Corps was ordered to attack with two rifle divisions to the southwest and west, to break up the encircled enemy and to destroy him in detail. The 80th Rifle Division's main forces were to attack in the direction of Rasselwitz toward units of the 21st Army's 120th Rifle Division and by the close of 19 March reach the line Schelitz—Rasselwitz—Schigau. The 13th Rifle Division, while attacking in the direction of Kramelau and Streibersdorf, was to capture the Kujau—Wiesengrund—Nassau area by the close of 19 March.

The 314th Rifle Division was pulled into the army commander's reserve in the Rodemark—Lenschutz—Pirchwitz area. It was planned to use it to parry possible enemy attacks.

The 115th Rifle Corps was ordered to securely defend the line Frebel—Poljacka with the 92nd Rifle Division, with the task of preventing the enemy from breaking out of the encirclement to the south, and attacking with the 135th and 245th rifle divisions from the Ober Glogau line, and by the close of the day to throw the enemy forces out of Ober Glogau and reach the line Kreenbusch—Rosenberg.

The 93rd Rifle Corps had the assignment of preventing the encircled enemy units from breaking through to the southwest. For this purpose, the 98th Rifle Division was to attack from the Deutsch Rasslewitz area toward Rosenberg, split up the opposing enemy and throw back the remnants of his defeated units to the north. The 391st Rifle Division and the 7th Guards Mechanized Corps' 26th Guards Mechanized Brigade received orders to securely hold the line Neustadt—Kunzendorf—Kreschendorf—excluding Hozenplotz, in order to prevent a breakthrough by enemy forces to the encircled group of forces from the south. The 239th Rifle Division was located along the line Glesen—Pommerswitz—Steubendorf, ready to repel possible enemy attempts to break out of the encirclement and render assistance to the encircled group of forces by an attack from without.

The 7th Guards Mechanized Corps (minus the 26th Guards Mechanized Brigade) received orders to attack, from the line achieved by the time the enemy was encircled, toward Rosenberg and, in conjunction with units of the 93rd and 115th rifle corps, to destroy the German-Fascist forces in the southwestern sector of the Oppeln salient.

The commander of the 4th Guards Tank Army made the following decision. The 6th Guards Mechanized Corps was to continue attacking to the west and, in conjunction with units of the 21st Army's 118th Rifle Corps, to capture the Ottmachau area. The 10th Guards Tank Corps was to, while attacking to the west, widen the corridor that had formed between the German-Fascist forces and their encircled group of forces and to prevent them from uniting; the 93rd Independent Tank Brigade was ordered to attack toward Ziegenhals and capture it.

The coordinated operations of the First Ukrainian Front's left-wing armies, which were to launch ten simultaneous attacks against the encircled group of forces from different axes, were supposed to deprive the enemy of his freedom of maneuver and to make it easier for our forces to destroy him.

The planned and scrupulously thought-through measures for creating and strengthening the external encirclement front were to facilitate the successful resolution of this task, as were measures adopted in case of attempts by the encircled enemy group of forces to break out of the encirclement or render assistance to the encircled group of forces by attacks from without.

The combat activities that unfolded during 19-20 March completely confirmed the correctness of the *front* commander's plan and that of the decisions adopted by the army commanders.

The course of combat operations to destroy the encircled enemy showed that the German-Fascist command was determined to pull its forces from out of the encirclement to the west. The encircled group of forces was ordered to throw our forces out of the Erlenburg—Lesthal—Elgut area, to bring in all its forces to this area and to break out of the encirclement by an attack in the general direction of Neisse. In order to render assistance to the encircled forces, it was planned to launch a simultaneous offensive from without with part of the forces of the 20th "Hermann Goring" Panzer Division, the 10th Panzergrenadier Division, and the 45th Infantry Division from the line Neisse—Riegersdorf in the general direction of Steinau.

The Course of Combat Operations for the Purpose of Eliminating the Encircled Enemy

Our troops' combat operations for the purpose of destroying the encircled enemy began on the morning of 19 March. On this day the enemy made a feint to break out of the encirclement in the Deutsch Rasselwitz area in order to disguise the actual axis along which it was planned to carry out a breakthrough and get out of the encirclement. In order to carry out his design, the enemy on the night of 18-19 March concentrated more than an infantry division with tanks and assault guns west of Ober Glogau, and at dawn on 19 March began his attack to the south toward Deutsch Rasselwitz, that is, against units of the 59th Army's 93rd Rifle Corps. Simultaneously, up to a battalion of enemy infantry, supported by tanks and assault guns, attacked the left flank of the 93rd Rifle Corps' 391st Rifle Division from the Hoenplotz area to the north, also toward Deutsch Rasselwitz. The enemy's demonstration activities were foiled by the start of our forces' offensive along the entire front. The enemy command's attempt to fool us concerning the location of his main group of forces was quickly seen through.

At 0830, following a 10-minute fire onslaught, units of the 59th Army's 43rd and 115th rifle corps attacked. While successfully splitting the enemy units and defeating his small groups, the 59th Army's right-flank formation captured the towns of Krappitz and Ober Glogau, cleared the enemy out of the Schelitz woods and the Proskau woods, and by 2000 had reached the line Schelitz—Klein Schelitz—Streibersdorf—Ober Glogau.

The 93rd Rifle Corps' 98th Rifle Division, supported by artillery and aviation, repelled an enemy attack from Ober Glogau toward Deutsch Rasselwitz and, having gone over to a vigorous offensive, threw back the enemy units into the woods east of Kreenbusch. By 2200 our forces were fighting along a line two kilometers south of Ober Glogau—Rosenberg—Radstein, facing to the north and northeast.

In the 21st Army's offensive sector the fighting unfolded in the following manner. On the night of 18-19 March the enemy concentrated in the Kreenbusch area and the woods to the east the greater part of the encircled subunits of the 20th SS "Estonia" Infantry Division, the 168th and 344th infantry divisions, and the 18th SS Panzergrenadier Division and, upon going over to the offensive on the morning of 19 March, pushed back somewhat the units of the 117th Rifle Corps' 120th Rifle Division, occupying the inhabited locales of Lesthal, Elgut and Erlenburg. Units of the 120th Rifle Division, while parrying the enemy's numerous attempts to break out of the encirclement in the direction of Steinau and Neisse, consolidated along the line four kilometers west of Erlenburg and Kohlsdorf. By 1000 the enemy had concentrated up to three infantry divisions, with tanks and assault guns, in the Lesthal—Elgut—Erlenburg area. It was from this area that he undertook attacks ranging up to two infantry regiments in strength, supported by tanks, in the directions of Elgut and Zulz; Lesthal and Steinau; Lesthal and Riegersdorf; and; Erlenburg and Prochendorf.

Units of the 120th Rifle Division, together with the 10th Tank Corps' 61st Guards Tank Brigade, beat off all the enemy's attacks and by 1800 had halted his advance.

The *front* commander, who was at the 21st Army's observation post, issued the following order at 1645 on 19 March:

> To the battalion, regimental and division commanders of the 225th, 285th, 229th, and 120th rifle divisions.
>
> The encircled enemy is trying to break out in the direction of Steinau. The enemy is demoralized and is trying to break out in small groups, without his equipment.
>
> I order:
> 1. To destroy and capture the escaping enemy forces before night. All sergeants and officers are to audaciously and bravely attack the enemy. Do not shame the

troops of the 21st and 4th Guards Tank armies and do not let the enemy out of the encirclement.

2. This order is to be relayed to all the rank and file, sergeants and officers from all the combat arms.

19.3.45—1645.

While fighting to destroy the encircled enemy, the rank and file of the 21st Army showed exceptional firmness and bravery. For example, the 2nd Battalion of the 120th Rifle Division's 543rd Rifle Regiment repulsed an enemy attempt to break out of the encirclement by a force four times its strength. During this attempt the enemy lost up to 500 men in killed alone, as well as many tanks and assault guns. In repelling the enemy's attacks the following particularly distinguished themselves: First Sergeant Lebedev, who was leading a group that was counterattacking the enemy in the flank; the commander of a 45mm gun, Senior Sergeant Plesenkov, who knocked out two tanks and an assault gun; the gunner for a 45mm gun, Private Kuralov Atakhan, who, being the only one left of his gun crew, knocked out a tank and an assault gun, and began firing on the enemy from an automatic rifle when all the shells had been fired. That same day the entire army learned of the heroism shown by Lebedev, Plesenkov and Kuralov Atakhan.

At 1600 the enemy launched a counterblow with part of a screening detachment and the "Hermann Goring" Panzer Division from the woods west of Prochendorf and from the area south of Prochendorf toward Steinau, toward his troops who were trying to break out of the encirclement. Units of the 10th Guards Tank Corps repelled the enemy attacks and foiled his counterblow. At the same time, one must note the exceptional heroism of the rank and file of the 29th Guards Motorized Rifle and 62nd Guards Tank brigades, which had to repel the pressure of the attacking enemy subunits, while disposing of a limited supply of ammunition.

At 1800 the 117th Rifle Corps' 120th Rifle Division and the 10th Guards Tank Corps' 61st Guards Tank Brigade, having repelled the attacks by the encircled enemy's main shock group, attacked and by 2300 had thrown him out of the inhabited locales of Elgut and Lesthal.

By 1400 on 19 March the 55th Rifle Corps' 225th and 229th rifle divisions had cleared the enemy out of the western part of the wooded area southwest of Oppeln and both banks of the Steinau River. By the night of 19-20 March both divisions had been transferred to the Steinau area for reinforcing the 4th Guards Tank Army's formations in case of an enemy counterblow from the Neisse area toward Steinau.

The 55th Rifle Corps' 285th Rifle Division, which was defending the line Friedland—Floste, attacked toward Erlenburg and by the close of the day had reached the line Erlenburg—Brandenwalde, with its front facing south and southwest. In the evening it received orders to continue the attack at night and, together with the 117th Rifle Corps' 120th Rifle Division, to destroy the encircled enemy forces in the area south of Erlenburg, north of Lesthal and Elgut.

As a result of the fighting on 19 March, the forces of the 21st, 59th and 4th Guards Tank armies occupied more than 100 inhabited locales, including the important road junctions of Ober Glogau and Krappitz, and also completely cleared the wooded area southwest of Oppeln of German-Fascist troops. In the fighting to destroy the encircled enemy forces, our forces captured more than 4,000 men and officers, and captured a large amount of arms and military equipment. Besides this, the enemy lost more than 11,000 men and officers killed. The remnants of the encircled enemy group of forces had been split into two parts. The smaller of these was in the woods east of Kreenbusch, while the larger was in the area south of Erlenburg, north of Lesthal and Elgut.

On 20 March the enemy tried to break out in the direction of Steinau, but was unsuccessful. By 1600 units of the 21st Army's 55th and 117th rifle corps had completely destroyed the enemy group of forces encircled in the Erlenburg—Lesthal—Elgut area. By this same time units of the

59th Army's 43rd and 115th rifle corps had destroyed the German-Fascist group of forces in the woods east of Kreenbusch.

Aviation played a large role in the elimination of the encircled enemy group of forces. During 19-20 March our aviation carried out 1,743 sorties. The greater part of the bomber and assault air strikes was launched against the Schelitz, Ringwitz, Erlenburg, Lesthal, and Radstein areas, and the woods east of Kreenbusch, that is, against those areas where the enemy tried to gather troops for organizing an attack to break out of the encirclement.

The attempts by the German-Fascist command to assist his encircled troops from without were also unsuccessful. The counterblow launched on 20 March by part of the forces of the 20th Panzer Division, the "Hermann Goring" Panzer Division, the 10th Panzergrenadier Division, and the 45th Infantry Division from the area north of Ottmachau to the east was successfully beaten off by the 21st Army's 118th Rifle Corps and units of the 4th Guards Tank Army's 6th Guards Mechanized Corps.

Beginning from the latter half of 20 March, the forces of the 21st, 59th and 4th Guards Tank armies began regrouping their forces for continuing the offensive for the purpose of reaching the line Munsterberg—Patschkau—Troppau.

At the same time that the forces of the 21st, 59th and 4th Guards Tank armies were fighting to destroy the encircled enemy southwest of Oppeln, the 5th Guards Army's 34th Guards Rifle Corps and the 4th Guards Tank Corps, operating alongside, continued to attack to the west. While overcoming the enemy's fire resistance and beating off his numerous counterattacks (up to a battalion of infantry, with 4-10 tanks each), the forces of the 5th Guards Army advanced somewhat and reached the east bank of the Krin River.

During 19-20 March the 60th Army consolidated along the line reached at the close of 18 March and was regrouping its forces for a continued offensive.

As a result of the fighting to encircle and destroy the enemy group of forces in the area southwest of Oppeln, our forces completely defeated three enemy infantry and one panzergrenadier divisions and several independent regiments and battalions. Up to 15,000 enemy men and officers were captured, along with the following amounts of equipment: 21 planes, 57 tanks and assault guns, 464 guns of various calibers, more than 1,000 machine guns, more than 13,000 rifles and automatic rifles, 3,000 motor vehicles, 27 locomotives, 1,520 rail cars, 5,000 horses, and 75 depots with ammunition, equipment and food. The enemy lost 30,000 men and officers in killed alone.

During the offensive of 15-20 March the *front's* left-wing forces captured in Upper Silesia the towns of Neustadt, Cosel, Steinau, Zulz, Krappitz, Ober Glogau, and Falkenberg, as also took more than 400 inhabited locales in fighting.

In his order no. 305 of 22 March 1945, the Supreme Commander-in-Chief, Marshal of the Soviet Union comrade Stalin, noted the outstanding combat actions of the troops that took part in the fighting during the breakthrough of the enemy defense and the defeat of his forces southwest of Oppeln, and expressed his thanks to them.

7

The Arrival of the First Ukrainian Front's Left-wing Armies at the Foothills of the Sudeten Mountains (22-31 March)

Following the elimination of the group of German-Fascist forces in the area southwest of Oppeln, all the efforts of the First Ukrainian Front's left wing were directed at battling to arrive at the line Strelen—Munsterberg—Patschkau—Troppau (Opava).

Combat operations for the purpose of arriving at the indicated line resumed on 22 March and ended on 31 March. During this period the ground forces were mainly fighting to capture the towns of Strelen, Neisse and Ratibor. The 2nd Air Army's formation concentrated all of their efforts to aid the forces of the 5th Guards, 21st, 59th, 60th, and 4th Guards Tank armies in carrying out their combat assignments. In ten days 10,962 sorties were carried out, of which 6,237 were against the enemy's forces on the battlefield.

Our aviation's dominance in the air limited the enemy's air activities, particularly during the daylight hours. During 22-31 March 1,138 enemy flights were noted. Of these, about a third were night flights by transport aircraft supplying the garrisons of Breslau and Glogau.

The enemy aviation's main efforts were directed at covering their forces, conducting reconnaissance and attacking our forces in the Strelen, Neisse and Leobschutz areas and especially on the approaches to the town of Ratibor.

During this time the *front's* left-wing armies, while resolving the overall task of reaching the foothills of the Sudeten Mountains, attacked along independent axes. As a result, the combat operations of the *front's* forces will be examined separately by army.

The 5th Guards Army's Capture of Strelen

The commander of the 5th Guards Army, while taking into account the fact that units of the 34th Guards Rifle and 4th Guards Tank corps had suffered significant losses in the preceding battles and could not capture the town of Strelen and reach the line Strelen—Munsterberg relying solely on their own forces, decided to commit into the fighting on the morning of 24 March the 32nd Guards Rifle Corps, which before this had been defending northwest of Strelen. The army commander's decision consisted in launching a surprise attack with the 32nd Guards Rifle Corps from the northwest and west and part of the 34th Rifle Corps' forces from the southeast and capturing the town of Strelen. Following the capture of Strelen, the army's left-wing forces were to develop the offensive in the general direction of Alt Heinrichau and reach the Ole River and consolidate.

The 32nd Guards Rifle Corps (Guards Lieutenant General A.I. Rodimtsev, commander), employing the forces of its 95th and 97th guards rifle divisions, reinforced by the 150th Tank Brigade and artillery, was to break through the enemy's defense along the sector point 168.8—Plomuhle and, while developing the offensive in the direction of Pench and Wammelwitz, capture Strelen by an attack from the northwest and west. Upon capturing the town of Strelen, the corps commander was to commit the 34th Guards Rifle Corps' 112th Rifle Division (operationally subordinated for the operation to the commander of the 32nd Guards Rifle Corps) into the fighting to develop the offensive's success in the direction of Alt Heinrichau and by the close of 24 March reach the line Praus—Stachau—Schildberg. The 34th Guards Rifle Corps, along with the 4th Guards Tank Corps, was to launch an attack along its center from the Arnsdorf area in the direction of Taschenberg, break through the enemy's defense and by the close of 24 March reach the line Wiesenthal—Heinrichau. Simultaneously, the corps had the assignment of attacking with part of its forces in the direction of Teppendorf and Strelen and to assist the 32nd Guards Rifle Corps in capturing Strelen.

By this time the provisioning of the army's forces with ammunition was as follows: 82mm mortars—1.6 combat loads; 120mm mortars—0.75 combat loads; 76mm divisional artillery—1.2 combat loads, and; 122mm howitzers—0.6 combat loads. Such an availability of shells and mortar rounds enabled us to plan the methodical suppression and destruction during the artillery preparation for the attack of planned targets for one hour and 15 minutes and two short fire onslaughts for a total of 15 minutes. It was planned to accompany the infantry and tank attack by means of the consecutive concentration of fire.

Because the 5th Guards Army had only a 2:1 superiority over the enemy in men and materiel in its offensive sector and a limited supply of ammunition, decisiveness and boldness in maneuver was required for capturing Strelen.

The town of Strelen was covered from the north and northwest by the Klein Loe Canal, which units of the 32nd Guards Rifle Corps would have to force. The small inhabited locales that girded the approaches to the town in a salient from the north, northwest and west had been transformed by the enemy into strong points, with fire coordination established between them. Thus the fight for the inhabited locales and the heights could be successful only under conditions of the skillful employment of flexible maneuver tactics: by outflanking and enveloping the enemy's strong points.

The 32nd Rifle Corps' combat formation was deeply echeloned, thanks to which fact there was the possibility of uninterruptedly augmenting the strength of the attack.

At 1020 on 24 March, following an artillery preparation, units of the 32nd and 34th guards rifle and 4th Guards Tank corps attacked.

The 32nd Guards Rifle Corps' 95th and 97th guards rifle divisions forced the Klein Loe Canal and by the close of the day captured several of the enemy's powerful strong points along the approaches to Strelen. During the fighting for the strong points, units of the 32nd Guards Rifle Corps had to repel several enemy counterattacks. In each of the counterattacks launched by the enemy, between a company and a battalion of infantry took part, supported by 4-10 tanks.

It's necessary to note that the forcing of the Klein Loe Canal (followed by the seizure of the strong points along the approaches to the town of Strelen) had been eased by the successful actions of the forward rifle companies, which had been detached from each of the division's rifle regiments that were attacking in the corps' first echelon. The forward elements pushed aside the enemy's combat security from the left bank of the canal with a decisive attack and on his heels forced the canal, captured the enemy's first trench line along the southern bank of the canal and, while repelling counterattacks by separate groups of enemy infantry and tanks, made it possible for the main forces of the corps' first echelon to force the canal and begin fighting to capture the strong points along the approaches to the town.

During 25-26 March the 32nd Guards Rifle Corps, covered by part of the 97th Guards Rifle Division's forces along the sector Karzen—Karschau, continued attacking with units of the 95th Guards Rifle and 112th Rifle divisions. The 95th Guards Rifle Division attacked the town of Strelen from the north, while the 112th Rifle Division attacked from the west and southwest. By the evening of 25 March units of the 95th Guards Rifle Division had seized the northern outskirts of the town. Units of the 112th Rifle Division managed only to blockade Strelen from the west. On 26 March units of the 95th Guards Rifle Division were engaged in fierce street fighting and in destroying the enemy's Strelen garrison. By the morning of 27 March the division's units managed to completely capture Strelen and a number of strong points south of Strelen. The corps' right-flank divisions, having encountered the enemy's powerful fire resistance, and uninterrupted counterattacks by his small groups of infantry and tanks, were not able to advance.

Units of the 34th Guards Rifle and 4th Guards Tank corps, having gone over to the offensive toward Wiesenthal from the area north of Arnsdorf, also encountered the enemy's strong resistance and were almost unable to advance to the west on this day and on subsequent days of the offensive. Only a small detachment, which was attacking to the northwest toward Strelen, managed to directly reach the southern part of the town of Strelen and thus make easier the 32nd Guards Rifle Corps' activities in taking the town of Strelen.

During the latter half of 27 March the enemy, having occupied a tactically favorable line and having committed into the battle several infantry battalions and police units from the neighboring sectors of the front, sharply increased his resistance. Due to this, all of the 5th Guards Army's attacks proved to be without result. On 28 March the *front* commander ordered the 5th Guards Army to halt its further offensive and consolidate along the line reached.

Thus while attacking along a secondary axis, the 5th Guards Army helped the 21st and 4th Guards Tank armies achieve their tasks through its actions and basically carried out its own task.

The Capture of the Town of Neisse by the Forces of the 21st and 4th Guards Tank Armies

The *front* command, as early as the fighting to eliminate the encircled enemy group of forces in the area southwest of Oppeln, ordered the 21st and 4th Guards Tank armies to continue their joint offensive to the west along the following sector: from the right, Grottkau—excluding Munsterberg; from the left, excluding Oppeln—Ringwitz—Steinau—Alt Wette, with the task of reaching within 24 hours the line excluding Munsterberg—Patschkau—Alt Wette, where it was to go over to the defensive. The depth of the assignment along various axes varied from 12 to 20 kilometers.

Guided by these instructions, the commanders of the 21st and 4th Tank armies had by the close of 22 March moved their forces from the Neustadt area to the area northwest of Steinau, reinforced them with ammunition and assigned tasks to their corps.

The 118th Rifle Corps was to, while attacking along a 20-kilometer front along the axis Altegel—Friedenthal—Gismansdorf, advance during the day 10-20 kilometers and reach the line excluding Munsterberg—Ottmachauer Pond—excluding Neisse. The corps' units were to securely consolidate along this line and be ready to repel possible enemy infantry and tank attacks.

Due to the fact that there was a shortage of ammunition, the 118th Rifle Corps was to attack following only a 10-minute fire onslaught. The 117th Rifle Corps, which was to attack with the forces of two rifle divisions along an 11-kilometer sector, was to capture the northern and eastern parts of the town of Neisse.

The 4th Guards Tank Army's 6th Guards Mechanized Corps was assigned the task of attacking in the direction of the western outskirts of the town of Neisse and, while cooperating with the 118th Rifle Corps' left-flank division and the 117th Rifle Corps' right-flank division, capture the left bank of the Neisse River from Ottmachauer Pond to the town of Neisse.

The 55th Rifle Corps, in conjunction with the 4th Guards Tank Army's 10th Guards Tank Corps, while attacking along an 8-kilometer front in the direction of Bilau, was to reach the Bila River by the close of the day and capture the town of Neisse from the south.

Upon reaching the Bila River, the 55th Rifle Corps' units, according to the operational plan, were to go over to the defensive.

65 minutes were to be devoted to the artillery preparation of the 117th and 55th rifle corps' attack, of which ten minutes would be a fire onslaught against enemy's headquarters, communications centers and reserve assembly areas, 45 minutes for suppressing and destroying targets along the forward edge of the enemy's defense, and ten minutes for a fire onslaught against the forward edge. Support for the infantry and tank attack would be conducted by the method of consecutively concentrating fire. The artillery offensive was severely limited by the number of shells. It was planned to expend on the offensive, on the average, 0.5 combat loads.

Along the 21st Army's offensive sector, our troops outnumbered the enemy 3.8:1 in men and 4.7:1 in artillery and mortars. However, there was an insufficient supply of ammunition for the artillery and mortars.

At 0810 on 23 March the forces of the 21st and 4th Guards Tank armies renewed their offensive.

Units of the 118th Rifle Corps, which attacked the enemy following a 10-minute fire onslaught, were unable before the close of the day to crush his resistance. During the following days they were engaged in a fire fight and repelled counterattacks by small groups of enemy infantry and tanks along their former line.

The 118th Rifle Corps' offensive was unsuccessful. This may be explained by the fact that the artillery preparation did not precede the infantry attack and that a single 10-minute fire onslaught was insufficient to suppress the enemy's fire means along the forward edge and in the immediate tactical depth of his defense. Thus the army commander's decision to begin the corps' offensive after a 10-minute fire onslaught was unfounded and led to unjustified losses in men and materiel.

Units of the 117th and 55th rifle corps, which were to attack along with the forces of the 4th Guards Tank Army, began their attack after a 65-minute artillery preparation and air softening up of the forward edge of the enemy's defense and its immediate depth.

Despite the limited amount of ammunition, the artillery preparation of the attack proved to be effective. The artillery managed to partially destroy the enemy's first trench, to completely destroy the enemy's wooden fences, which were two meters high and buttressed with rocks, and also to suppress his fire system.

By the start of our forces' offensive, the German 20th Panzer Division and the "Hermann Goring" Panzer Division, which were defending Neisse and the areas adjacent to the town from the northwest and southeast, were reinforced by the 2nd Anti-Tank Brigade, the "Kreizhofen" Police Regiment and the 273rd *Volksturm* Battalion.

During the fighting of 23 March the 117th and 55th rifle corps and the 4th Guards Tank Army's forces advanced ten kilometers and captured 19 inhabited locales. On the same day the 117th Rifle Corps seized the northwestern part of the town of Neisse, while units of the 55th Rifle Corps broke into the southern outskirts of the town.

The enemy put up strong fire resistance along the approaches to Neisse and carried out numerous counterattacks ranging in strength from a company to a battalion of infantry, supported by 4-10 tanks. The fighting for the town did not die down at night. The fighting raged for every block and for every building. The town's old fortress structures had been strengthened by new defensive ones. Barricades and anti-tank fences had been erected on the town's streets. Trenches ran along the stone fences. The cellars of buildings were employed by the enemy not only as machine guns nests, put also as cover for his artillery.

While overcoming all of these obstacles under enemy fire, on 24 March our forces continued to advance toward the center of town and by the close of the day had completely captured this powerful enemy strong point and railroad and road junction. The capture of the town of Neisse had been made easier by the fact that units of the 117th Rifle and 6th Guards Mechanized corps, which had been attacking toward the town from the north, prevented the enemy from blowing up the railroad bridge over the Neisse River. This bridge had been used by the corps during the latter half of 24 March for a vigorous breakthrough to the center of town.

The Supreme Commander-in-Chief, Marshal of the Soviet Union comrade Stalin noted in his order no. 307 of 24 March 1945 the exceptional actions of the 21st and 4th Guards Tank armies' forces and expressed his thanks to them.

On this day the *front* command, considering that the 21st and 4th Guards Tank armies' shock group had basically carried out its assigned task, ordered the commander of the 4th Guards Tank Army to pull his forces out of the fighting. The forces of the 4th Guards Tank Army received a new task: to defeat the enemy's Ratibor group of forces together with the 60th Army.

Following the withdrawal of the 4th Guards Tank Army's main forces, the 21st Army's forces continued to attack to the west, but were unable to achieved tangible results as a result of the absence of the necessary amount of ammunition for the artillery and mortars and increased resistance by the enemy, who had occupied a favorable defensive position along the left bank of the Bila River.

For this reason, on 27 March, by order of the *front* commander, the 21st Army ceased further offensive efforts and consolidated along the line Altegel—Seifersdorf—Stefensdorf—the eastern bank of the Bila River.

The Arrival of the 59th Army's Forces at the Foothills of the Sudeten Carpathians

On 21 March the commander of the 59th Army received the *front's* operational directive no. 00144/op. According to this directive, the army, along with the 7th Guards Mechanized Corps and its previous reinforcement units was to launch a decisive offensive on the morning of 22 March along the entire front along the sector: from the right, Oppeln—Ringwitz—Steinau—Alt Wette; from the left, excluding Cosel—Leinitz—Leobschutz—Zoppau—Jaegerndorf, with the task of defeating the remnants of the XI Army Corps and individual units of the 16th Panzer Division and the "Hermann Goring" Panzer Division, throw them back into the mountains and by the close of 23 March reach the front Alt Wette—Siegenhals—Zuchmantel—Albrechtiise—Jaegnerdorf.

The arrival of the 59th Army's forces at the indicated line and their seizure of the lateral railroad connecting Neisse and Troppau (Opava) would deprive the enemy of the capability of carrying out rapid maneuver with his reserves along the front.

According to the idea of the operation, the main attack would be launched by the army's left flank (by the forces of the 93rd Rifle and 7th Guards Mechanized corps) in the direction of Jaegerndorf. The 7th Guards Mechanized Corps received orders to capture the Jaegerndorf area by the close of 22 March, to link up here with the 5th Guards Mechanized Corps' left-flank units operating together with the 60th Army, and to complete the encirclement of the enemy's Leobschutz group of forces.

The commander of the 2nd Air Army was ordered to support the 59th Army's offensive with its bomber and assault air corps.

The attack was set for 1150 on 22 March.

Guided by the *front's* directive, the commander of the 59th Army on that day assigned his forces the following tasks.

The 115th Rifle Corps was ordered to launch a vigorous attack in the direction of Siegenhals and, having destroyed the opposing enemy, to capture the line Deutsch Wette—Siegenhals by the close of the day and securely consolidate it.

The 93rd Rifle Corps received orders to attack, in conjunction with the 7th Guards Mechanized Corps, in the direction of Jaegerndorf, to destroy the opposing enemy, and by the close of the operation's first day capture the line Heinzendorf—Pilgersdorf—Zoppau, and by the close of the offensive's second day the line Albrechtise—Jaegerndorf—Bleichwitz. The 7th Guards Mechanized Corps was to reach this line by the close of the offensive's first day.

The 314th Rifle Division, which was directly subordinated to the army commander, received orders to attack in the direction of Kroizendorf, to clear the enemy out of the woods northwest of Leobschutz and to reach the line Zoppau—Kreisewitz.

It was planned to conduct a 70-minute artillery preparation before the start of the offensive, of which 50 minutes would be devoted to suppressing and destroying targets. It was planned to support the infantry and tank attack through the consecutive concentration of fire.

In view of the insufficient supply of shells, a great deal of attention was devoted to firing over open sights.

By the morning of 22 March the army's units and formations had occupied their jumping-off positions for the offensive, in accordance with the tasks assigned by the army commander.

At 1040 on 22 March the artillery preparation began. As a result of poor target intelligence, the artillery preparation proved to be of little effect. The enemy's fire system was suppressed only along the forward edge of the defense. As soon as the army's forces attacked, the enemy opened an artillery and mortar fire from the depths of his defense and there, where our forces managed to advance a little bit, our forces had to beat off enemy counterattacks. In all, on 22 March the enemy launched 11 counterattacks. By the close of the operation's first day the army had been able to advance only five kilometers along some axes, while the right-flank 115th Rifle Corps did not advance at all. During the ensuing eight days of the offensive the pace of advance for the army's units remained the same as it had been on 22 March. The army's forces had to wage heavy fighting for each inhabited locale and for every height that had been transformed by the enemy into defensive strong points.

By 31 March the army's forces had advanced into the depth of the enemy's defense up to six kilometers along the right flank and up to 20 kilometers along the left and thus reached the line Altewalde—Maidelberg—Pilgersdorf—excluding Jaegerndorf. In view of the significant losses suffered by the army's formations and its poor provisioning with ammunition, its further offensive was not expedient. Thus the army was ordered to consolidate along the line reached.

The 60th Army's Capture of the Towns of Ratibor and Rybnik

During 19-20 March the 60th Army's forces, while supporting the 59th Army's efforts to destroy the encircled enemy southwest of Oppeln, were preparing to renew the offensive in accordance with the *front's* operational directive of 8 March.

In the *front* order of 20 March the 60th Army's tasks, which were assigned to it by operational directive no. 00128/op of 8 March, were amplified. The army was ordered to renew the offensive on the morning of 21 March, with the task of defeating the enemy's Ratibor group of forces and by the close of 23 March to reach the line of the Opava River from Jaegerndorf to Benesova. In order to carry out the assigned task, the 60th Army was reinforced with the 5th Guards Mechanized Corps and the 17th Artillery Breakthrough Division.

The army was to launch its main attack along its right flank along the front Grebnig—excluding Jaernau in the direction of Hoendorf, Biskau and Troppau (Opava). The shock group consisted of four rifle divisions, the 5th Guards Mechanized Corps, 31st Tank Corps, and the 17th Artillery Breakthrough Division. The 5th Guards Mechanized Corps received orders to attack from the Grebnig—Babitz area in the direction of Hoendorf, Bladen and Troppau (Opava), and the 31st Tank Corps from the area Babitz—excluding Jaernau in the direction of Langenau, Sauditz and Berendorf, bypassing the enemy's Ratibor group of forces from the west. On the second day of the operation the army's center and left-flank divisions were to begin their attack to the south and southwest.

Aviation support for the 60th Army's offensive was entrusted to two bomber corps, an assault air corps and a fighter corps from the 2nd Air Army.

In accordance with the *front* directive, the army commander assigned his forces the following tasks:

The 28th Rifle Corps, which was to launch the main attack, in conjunction with units of the 5th Guards Mechanized and 31st Tank corps, was to capture the towns of Leobschutz and Biskau by the close of the offensive's first day and to then attack in the direction of Kranowitz.

The 15th Rifle Corps was ordered on the offensive's first day to commit only a single right-flank division into the fighting and, in conjunction with units of the 28th Rifle and 31st Tank corps, reach the line Gross Peterwitz—Paulsgrund—Gammau, while the remaining divisions would attack on the second day and launch an attack to the south toward Ratibor. On the operation's second day it was planned that the 106th Rifle Corps would attack to the west on Ratibor.

The 5th Guards Mechanized Corps and the 31st Tank Corps were to operate jointly with the infantry on the first day of the offensive. On the operation's second day, having cut loose from the infantry, it was to vigorously develop the offensive toward the Troppau (Opava) area, while the 31st Tank Corps was to attack in the direction of Berendorf.

Thus it was planned to accomplish the destruction of the enemy's Ratibor group of forces with the forces of the 60th Army and the 31st Tank Corps. The 5th Guards Mechanized Corps had the task of capturing Troppau (Opava) and reaching the Opava River.

It was planned to conduct an artillery preparation lasting one hour and 40 minutes.

By the start of the offensive's renewal, the 60th Army, together with the 5th Guards Mechanized and 31st Tank corps, disposed of 61 rifle battalions and about 300 tanks and self-propelled guns.

At the same time the enemy disposed of four infantry divisions, a panzergrenadier division's combat group, nine independent infantry and reserve battalions, and an independent tank battalion opposite the 60th Army's offensive sector, for an overall total of about 40 infantry battalions and 130 tanks and assault guns.

Thus the 60th Army outnumbered the enemy in men 1.5:1 and 2.3:1 in tanks and self-propelled guns.

In accordance with the *front* command's instructions, the commander of the 60th Army concentrated the greater part of his men and materiel along the right flank, where the main attack was to be launched. Here, along a 20-kilometer sector, were concentrated four rifle divisions (31 rifle battalions) and all the tanks and self-propelled artillery. A supporting attack of five divisions was to be launched along the remaining 50 kilometers of front.

Simultaneously with the gathering offensive by the 60th Army's forces, the Fourth Ukrainian Front's 38th Army was to renew the offensive toward Moravska Ostrava and with part of its forces toward Troppau (Opava).

At 0850 on 22 March, following an artillery preparation, the army's right-flank forces began their offensive. The enemy put up stubborn resistance with fire and counterattacks by small groups of infantry and tanks. Thus on the offensive's first day our forces managed to penetrate into the depth of the enemy defense no more than eight kilometers. On the following day the enemy increased his resistance, having committed into the fighting units of the 8th and 17th panzer divisions, which had been transferred to the area of combat operations from other sectors of the front. This changed the correlation of forces in the sector of the 60th Army's shock group. Now our forces had a 1.5:1 superiority in tanks and self-propelled artillery. During a day of fighting the enemy counterattacked 11 times, each time committing up to a battalion of infantry and up to 15 tanks and assault guns. The attacking formations advanced very slowly, as they had to beat off enemy counterattacks the whole time.

On that day the entire 15th Rifle Corps attacked, but neither during the first or second days did it achieve any substantial success. The fighting on 24 March did not differ from the fighting during the offensive's first two days. As a result of the three days of fighting, the army over-came the enemy's defense to a depth of 5-15 kilometers and reached the line Zoppau—Bladen—Heinrichsdorf, having at the same time captured the towns of Leobschutz and Jaernau.

The low rate of advance by the army's forces may be explained, first of all, by the uninterrupted growth of resistance by the enemy, who committed into the fighting units which were being trans-ferred from other sectors of the front.

The terrain favorable for the defense and the high density of the inhabited locales in the area of combat operations placed the defending enemy in a more favorable position in relation to the attacking troops. Our artillery, due to a shortage of ammunition, was unable to reliably suppress at once the entire system of the main zone of the enemy's defense. Thus in fighting for every inhab-ited locale and for each height, we had to widely employ our artillery for firing over open sights at short ranges.

The broken character of the terrain, frequent rains and weak soil made it difficult for tanks to operate off the roads, limited their maneuverability and deprived them of the capability of rendering effective support to the attacking infantry.

The circumstance that the 5th Guards Mechanized Corps, which comprised the army's main shock force, consisted of a rank and file that lacked sufficient combat experience had a certain influence on the slow pace of the army's advance.

The *front* command, upon evaluating the situation in which the 60th Army was attacking and, seeing that it alone was not in a condition to carry out its assigned task of destroying the enemy's Ratibor group of forces, decided to resolve the problem by bringing in additionally the 4th Guards Tank Army, which at this time had basically carried out its tasks in the 21st Army's offensive sector.

On 24 March the *front* commander included the 5th Guards Mechanized Corps in the 4th Guards Tank Army (the 6th Guards Mechanized Corps would temporarily remain in the 21st Army's offensive sector) and assigned it the task of launching an attack with its main forces in the direction of Troppau (Opava), to defeat, in conjunction with the 60th Army, the enemy's Ratibor group of forces and capture the Jaegerndorf—Troppau (Opava)—Steuberwitz area.

With the commitment of the 4th Guards Tank Army into the 60th Army's offensive sector, a decisive superiority over the enemy was nevertheless not achieved. In reality, only the 10th Guards Tank Corps, which was heavily worn down, was actually committed into the fighting.

The joint offensive by the 60th and 4th Guards Tank armies, which began on 25 March, did not yield the desired result. The 4th Guards Tank Army and the 60th Army's 28th Rifle Corps did not manage to break through the enemy's defense along the Troppau (Opava)—Berendorf axis and gain operational freedom, in order to encircle and destroy the German-Fascist troops' Ratibor group of forces. During 25-31 March there was stubborn fighting to capture the numerous inhab-ited locales, road junctions and heights. Our forces suffered heavy losses in these battles.

On 27 March the enemy reinforced his forces opposite the 4th Guards Tank Army's front and that of the 60th Army's right flank with the "Fuehrer's Security" Panzer Division.

On 24 March, following a short pause, the Fourth Ukrainian Front's 38th Army renewed its offensive. While attacking in the general direction of Moravska Ostrava, by the close of 25 March the 38th Army's right flank had reached the line Marklowitz—Poloma. The 38th Army's successful offensive sharply changed the situation along the First Ukrainian Front's left flank. The real threat of encirclement in the Rybnik and Ratibor areas hung over the enemy. Along with this, favorable prerequisites for an attack by units of the 60th Army's 106th Rifle Corps had been created. The 106th Rifle Corps began its attack on 26 March. Through decisive attacks the corps managed to crush the enemy's resistance and capture the town of Rybnik, a major military-industrial center, a road and railroad junction and an important strong point in the enemy's defense. The capture of the town of Rybnik was made easier by the fact that our forces had managed to prevent the demolition of the bridge over the Ruda River. While developing the offensive toward Ratibor, the corps reached the left bank of the Oder River during the night of 30-31 March south of the town.

In preparing the storming of Ratibor, our aviation launched massed bomber strikes against the town during 29-30 March. In two days our aviation carried out about 2,000 sorties against the enemy's troops defending this center of resistance.

Besides this, in order to more rapidly capture Ratibor and avoid major losses in men and tanks, the *front* commander concentrated in this area by the close of 30 March the 25th Artillery Breakthrough Division, which had just arrived at the First Ukrainian Front, and the greater part of the 17th Artillery Breakthrough Division's guns.

Early on the morning of 31 March all of the artillery that had been concentrated in the Ratibor area opened fire on the enemy, who was defending the outskirts of the town. At the same time our aviation uninterruptedly bombed Ratibor and the enemy's artillery and mortar firing positions.

Following an hour-long artillery preparation, the 15th Rifle Corps and part of the 106th Rifle Corps' forces, together with tanks, began the decisive storming of Ratibor. The enemy could not withstand our units' pressure and began a hurried retreat through the town to the south. By 1000 Ratibor had been completely cleared of enemy forces.

Thus a major industrial town of Upper Silesia, an important railroad and road center, had passed into the Soviet army's hands. By 1 April the 60th and 4th Guards Tank armies' forces had reached the line Bleichwitz—Steuberwitz—Berendorf.

Further attack was halted and the army consolidated along the line reached.

As a result of the 60th Army's offensive in conjunction with the 4th Guards Tank Army, the tasks assigned to it were basically fulfilled. During the fighting the towns of Ratibor, Rybnik and Leobschutz were occupied and the enemy's Ratibor group of forces had been defeated and its remnants thrown back to the Opava River.

At the time when the events described above were unfolding along the *front's* left wing, the forces of the *front's* right wing and center were engaged in local fighting to improve their positions, were improving their defenses, were receiving reinforcements and military hardware, were undergoing combat training on the basis of the generalized experience of fighting on enemy territory, and were accumulating ammunition. All of the troops' activity was subordinated to the main task—the preparation for the Berlin operation, which began two weeks following the completion of the Upper Silesian operation.

8

Results of the Upper Silesian Operation and Brief Conclusions

The Upper Silesian operation by the First Ukrainian Front's left-wing armies continued for 16 days. During this time our forces advanced 60 kilometers into the depth of the enemy's territory, captured the southwestern part of Upper Silesia and carried out their assigned objectives by encircling and destroying the enemy's group of forces southwest of Oppeln and threw the enemy back into the foothills of the Sudeten Mountains. As a result the possibility of an enemy flank attack against the forces of the First Ukrainian Front from Upper Silesia was eliminated, the enemy's attempt at attacking from the Zobten—Schweidnitz area toward Breslau to assist the Breslau garrison in its attempt to break out of its encirclement was foiled and, finally, favorable conditions were created for carrying out the Berlin operation.

During the operation our forces occupied about 4,000 square kilometers of territory with an enormous amount of inhabited locales. The following towns and important road junctions were captured: Strelen, Neisse, Leobschutz, Ober Glogau, Neustadt, Cosel, Ratibor, Rybnik, and others, which covered the route to Dresden and Prague. The capture of the town of Neisse by our forces deprived the enemy of the capability of exploiting the lateral railroad linking Army Group Center with Army Group South.

In the 15-31 March fighting the *front's* attacking forces completely routed the 168th, 254th and 344th infantry divisions, the 20th SS Infantry Division and 18th SS Panzergrenadier Division, two independent police regiments, and more than ten independent battalions. The enemy lost about 60,000 men, including 18,518 men and officers captured.

The enemy suffered significant losses in combat equipment. Our forces captured the following equipment: 80 tanks and assault guns, 26 planes, 100 aircraft motors, 1,272 guns and mortars of all calibers, 1,253 machine guns, 13,000 rifles and automatic rifles, 243 depots with ammunition and food, 53 locomotives, 1,650 freight cars, and 13,250 motor vehicles. Besides this, a lot of combat equipment was destroyed during the fighting.

The operation's success was achieved primarily thanks to the leading role of the *Stavka* of the Supreme High Command.

In preparing the operation, the *Stavka* of the Supreme High Command, having correctly evaluated the developing situation and the correlation of forces along the *front's* operational sector, instructed the *front* command in a timely manner on the necessity of reducing the scope of the planned operation, because it was impossible to defeat the enemy along a broad front and reach the Sudeten Mountains with the men and materiel that the *front* disposed of.

These instructions by the *Stavka* of the Supreme High Command enabled the *front* command to draw up an operational plan, based on real capabilities and enabled us, given the skillful employment of the men and materiel allotted for participation in the operation, to successfully resolve such important tasks as defeating the enemy group of forces west, southwest and south of Oppeln, having the *front's* left-wing forces arrive at the foothills of the Sudeten Mountains and to create favorable conditions for conducting a follow-on offensive operation along the Berlin direction.

The *Stavka* of the Supreme High Command, while exercising operational control, insistently demanded a high offensive pace from the troops, as well as the rapid and complete elimination of the German-Fascist group of forces operating in the area southwest of Oppeln.

One of the decisive factors ensuring the operation's success was the enormous political work carried out by the command element, political organs and the party and Komsomol organizations among the troops during the preparation period and during the operation. This work ensured the morale-political uplift among the troops, a high degree of offensive zeal and mass heroism among the Soviet troops. At the base of our party-political work lay great Stalin's instructions to defeat Hitlerite Germany as quickly as possible and to victoriously complete the Great Patriotic War.

The *front* command, army commanders, staffs, and troops, following the high command's instructions, mobilized all their forces, knowledge and skill for resolving the tasks assigned to them and, despite the unfavorable conditions overcame all difficulties and successfully completed the operation.

The Soviet command's high degree of military skill was sharply manifested in the operation's skillful planning.

The First Ukrainian Front conducted the Upper Silesian operation with an insignificant overall superiority in men and materiel over the enemy. Despite this, the *front* command was able to create a decisive superiority in men and materiel along the axes of the main attacks, boldly choosing to weaken secondary sectors. The overall length of the attack front of the left-wing armies reached 190 kilometers. 31 rifle divisions, 5,676 guns and mortars of all calibers and 800 tanks and self-propelled guns operated along this front. The overall width of the 21st, 59th and 60th armies' breakthrough sectors was 17 kilometers, which accounted for 9 percent of the overall attack front. 16 rifle divisions, 3,361 guns and mortars and 731 tanks and self-propelled guns were concentrated along the breakthrough sectors, that is, 57 percent of the infantry, 60 percent of the artillery and mortars and 91 percent of the tanks and self-propelled guns. This yielded on an average one infantry division, 198 guns and mortars and 43 tanks per kilometer along the breakthrough front, while along these three armies' remaining sectors the ratio was an average of one division per approximately 15 kilometers. Our forces enjoyed along the axis of the main attack a fivefold superiority over the enemy in infantry, eightfold in artillery and ninefold in tanks and self-propelled guns. This, naturally, was one of the main prerequisites for successfully conducting the operation.

There was no routine in the organization of the of the *front's* and armies' forces. All of the *front's* forces brought in to take part in the operation were deployed in a single operational echelon. The formation of the shock groups of the *front's* armies was also in a single echelon. Depth was created by means of echeloning troops in corps and divisions that organized their combat formations in two and sometimes three echelons. Such a troop formation was conditioned by the *front's* insignificant forces, which did not allow us to create a deep operational formation for the troops. The employment of all men and materiel in a single operational echelon enabled us to create powerful groups of forces along the axis of the main attacks. This, in turn, ensured the rapid breakthrough of the tactical depth of the enemy's defense, which relied on a system of strong points, echeloned to a depth of up to 20-25 kilometers.

Also characteristic is the fact that the *front* and armies did not create mobile groups for developing the success. From the very beginning of the operation all of the mobile forces operated in close coordination with the infantry and only following the overcoming of the defense's tactical depth did the 4th Guards Tank Army's 10th Mechanized Corps and the 7th Guards Mechanized Corps break free of the infantry and pursue the enemy to a depth of 15-25 kilometers and, on 18 March, having linked up in the Neustadt area, did they complete the encirclement of the enemy. Such an employment of the mobile forces in the given operation was a forced measure and may be explained by the insufficient number of direct infantry support tanks. The overcoming of the defense's tactical depth by rifle troops alone, taking into account the character of the enemy's defense and his tactical conduct of the defensive battle during this period of the war, would have been very slow and accompanied by large personnel losses. Thus the *front* commander was forced to employ his mobile forces for breaking through the tactical depth of the enemy's defense.

The March offensive by the forces of the First Ukrainian Front in Upper Silesia was conducted for the purpose of encircling and destroying the major enemy group of forces in the area southwest of Oppeln.

The successful conduct of this operation became possible as a result of the fact that powerful shock groups had been created along the axes of the main attacks, particularly along the Neisse—Neustadt axis. As a result of including mobile field forces and formations in the shock groups, the rapid breakthrough of the enemy's defense was ensured. The average daily advance by the northern shock group's forces was 20 kilometers.

During the operation our troops boldly carried out maneuver to turn the enemy's flanks and get into the enemy's rear. Especially instructive were the combat activities of the northern shock group. The 21st and 4th Guards Tank armies, which were attacking along the Neisse axis to the south, on 17 March, that is, immediately following the overcoming of the tactical depth of the enemy's defense and the forcing of the Neisse River in the Rothaus area, turned sharply to the southeast toward Neustadt and outflanked the enemy group of forces from the southwest. The forces of the northern shock group, having linked up with the 59th Army's forces in the Neustadt area, later encircled more than five German divisions in the area southwest of Oppeln.

The northern shock group's offensive, which at first developed to the south toward Neisse, and that of the 5th Guards Army toward Strelen, fooled the German-Fascist command regarding the operation's plan and final goal. Judging by the prisoner testimony and the actions of the enemy's forces during the operation, the Hitlerite command believed that the First Ukrainian Front was trying to carry out a deep operation for the purpose of capturing the nearest and most convenient passes in the Sudeten Mountains in order to subsequently develop an offensive toward Prague. This is explained by the fact that the enemy's main forces during the operation's first days were directed at repelling our forces' attacks toward Strelen and Neisse.

The northern shock group's sharp turn from the Neisse axis toward Neustadt was completely unexpected for the German-Fascist command and it was not able to adopt timely measures for preventing the encirclement of its group of forces operating southwest of Oppeln.

The 5th Guards Army played an important role in this operation. Its forces, while attacking in the direction of Priborn and Alt Heinrichau for the purpose of capturing Strelen and Munsterberg, brought significant enemy forces upon themselves, secured the northern shock group against enemy flank attacks from the west and thus created all of the necessary conditions for the 21st and 4th Guards Tank armies to encircle the enemy group of forces in the Oppeln salient.

The enemy group of forces encircled in the area southwest of Oppeln was destroyed in the course of two days. Such a rapid destruction of a major group of encircled enemy forces was achieved thanks to the fact that the *front's* forces did not allow the enemy to organize a perimeter defense, but rather began to eliminate it even as the encirclement was being completed. The 21st and 59th armies' forces, while fighting the encircled enemy, broke him up into individual groups isolated from each other and destroyed them consecutively. The splitting up of the enemy through simultaneous attacks to the south, southeast, east, and west deprived the enemy of freedom to maneuver and hastened his defeat and capture.

The successful resolution of the task of eliminating the encircled enemy group of forces was facilitated by the scrupulously carried out measures for creating an external front, which had been foreseen by the plan. After the enemy group of forces southwest of Oppeln had been encircled, a part of the 21st and 59th armies' forces and the greater part of the 4th Guards Tank Army, while repelling enemy attacks from without, prevented the breakthrough of the enemy's units to link up with the encircled group of forces and thus facilitated its rapid defeat.

Characteristic of the operation under study was the employment of the attacking troops' major forces for night fighting. This was conducted for the purpose of developing the success achieved during the day and foiling the enemy's planned withdrawal. Night fighting played a very important role in the operation. For example, as a result of the fighting during the night of 16-17 March, the 21st Army's 120th Rifle Division forced the Neisse River in the Rothaus area. The forcing of the Neisse River in the Rothaus area completed the overcoming of the tactical depth of the enemy's defense and secured the pursuit of the enemy by units of the 10th Guards Tank Corps in the direction of Neustadt.

In the Upper Silesian operation the successes in night fighting for the inhabited locales were aided by flexible maneuver on the battlefield and by bold and unexpected actions of the part of small infantry subunits. The latter skillfully seeped in unnoticed into the depth of the enemy defense, caused a panic among the enemy's troops and destroyed the enemy through their decisive actions.

In issuing instructions on the organization of the artillery offensive, the *front* commander took into account the fact that in overcoming the tactical depth of the enemy's defense, the main fighting would unfold for the inhabited locales with a large number of stone structures configured for defense. In accordance with this, the main mass of artillery was concentrated in regimental artillery groups. Heavy artillery guns were included in these groups. The creation of powerful regimental artillery groups justified itself fully. They resolved the majority of tasks for infantry support independently and, what is particularly important, in a timely manner.

On the one hand, the character of the enemy's defense, and on the other, the amount of ammunition, conditioned the wide employment of artillery for firing over open sights throughout the entire operation. At first 200 guns were detached in the 21st Army for firing over open sights, while during the fighting this amount rose to 275 guns, while 35 percent of the detached guns were 122mm or higher. The massed employment of guns for firing over open sights yielded positive results in the fighting for the inhabited locales and reduced the expenditure of ammunition.

Artillery was massed during the operation and the fighting for major strong points. The most notable example of the massed employment of artillery was the fighting for the town of Ratibor. Over the course of several days, the 60th Army's forces unsuccessfully attempted to capture this powerful enemy center of resistance. The enemy was able to beat off all our attacks through the concentrated fire of artillery, mortars and infantry weapons. Then the *front* commander ordered the troops to hurriedly concentrate the 25th Artillery Breakthrough Division, which had just arrived at the *front*, in the Ratibor area. The enemy's resistance was quickly crushed through massed artillery fire and our forces captured the town on 31 March.

In the Upper Silesian operation the 2nd Air Army significantly assisted the ground forces in resolving their assigned tasks.

During the operation's preparatory period, the *front's* aviation destroyed and suppressed the enemy's forces throughout the entire depth of their position, destroyed military and industrial targets in the enemy rear, protected our forces in their concentration areas, in their jumping-off areas and jumping-off positions for the attack, disrupted the enemy's railroad, auto and air deliveries and, finally, carried out uninterrupted aerial reconnaissance.

During the operation, the *front's* aviation, while launching bombing and assault air strikes against the enemy's ground forces and while conducting an active struggle against the enemy's aviation, which attempted to hinder our forces' offensive through air strikes, carried out 15,408 sorties during 15-31 March. Our aviation and anti-aircraft artillery destroyed 138 enemy aircraft during this period. Our aviation played a particularly large role in breaking through the enemy's defense north of Oppeln and while eliminating the encircled enemy in the area southwest of Oppeln.

It is necessary to note that aviation control was centralized during the operation. Such control enabled us to purposefully employ all air arms in the interests of the ground forces. Air corps and divisions were distributed by axes for the purpose of more effectively supporting the ground forces' offensive operations and our aviation's cooperation with them. The location of the air commanders' command posts alongside those of the combined-arms commanders and the presence among the ground forces of a broad network of air controllers enabled our aviation to receive information about the ground situation in time, which facilitated the rapid suppression of those targets that were slowing down the infantry's and tanks' advance.

The method of centralized control and the distribution of air formations along axes in the First Ukrainian Front's Upper Silesian offensive operation justified itself completely.

The engineering troops in the operation carried out various tasks and played a not unimportant role in the operation's successful conduct.

During the operation's preparatory period the engineering troops chiefly carried out support tasks. They carried out successfully and on time the engineering reconnaissance of the enemy's defense, the preparation of the jumping-off area, the masking of the regrouping and concentration of troops in the jumping-off area for the offensive, and the clearing of anti-personnel and anti-tank minefields in front of the forward edge of their own forces and that of the enemy's defense. During this period the engineering troops instructed the rifle and artillery units' and subunits' rank and file how to overcome minefields and wire obstacles without the aid of sappers and to employ materials at hand for overcoming water barriers.

During the conduct of the operation the engineering troops carried out on time the engineering reconnaissance of terrain and routes, the removal of anti-tank obstacles, the overcoming of water barriers in the depth of the enemy's defense, and the consolidation of captured lines.

The presence of a deeply-echeloned defense and a large number of natural barriers and artificial obstacles conditioned the necessity of carrying out uninterrupted engineering reconnaissance not only in the defense's tactical zone, but in the operational depth. Corps routes, which mainly coincided with one of the divisional routes, were additionally cleared of mines by corps engineering units and those attached to the corps along a broader sector. Army routes, which coincided with one of the corps routes, were additionally reconnoitered and cleared of mines to an even greater width by army engineering units and those attached to the armies by the *front*.

While overcoming river barriers, the engineering troops quickly laid down crossings and assisted the troops in carrying out their tasks on time. For example, on 17 March our sappers quickly laid out a crossing over the Neisse River in the Rothaus area. This enabled the 4th Guards Tank Army's 10th Tank Corps to cross over to the right bank of the river and begin the pursuit of the enemy in a timely manner along the Neustadt axis.

In the fight for the town of Rybnik our sappers, operating as part of troop reconnaissance, infiltrated to the bridge over the Ruda River and cleared it of mines, which enabled our forces to cross the river from the march and capture the town.

The experience of the Upper Silesian operation, as well as that of many other operations, showed that all engineering support tasks for the troops' offensive operations cannot be fully carried out by the engineering troops alone. A significant part of the engineering tasks must be carried out and were carried out directly by the troops.

Troop command and control was firm and continuous throughout the entire operation. Commanders at all levels correctly understood the situation, foresaw changes in it, made decisions that corresponded to the situation in time, and stubbornly carried them out. The smooth work of the staffs and uninterruptedly-operating communications also had great significance.

In analyzing the developing situation, the *front* command correctly foresaw the operation's further development and adopted the necessary decisions in time and directed the army commanders toward carrying them out. For example, foreseeing that the German-Fascist forces would not have time to escape from the Oppeln "pocket" and that their encirclement was inevitable, the *front* command issued instructions on 18 March to the army commanders to eliminate the enemy formations in the Oppeln salient even before these formations could be completely encircled and isolated from the enemy's main forces. Another characteristic example is the decision to shift the 4th Guards Tank Army from the 21st Army's offensive sector to that of the 60th Army for the purpose of speeding up the defeat of the enemy's Ratibor group of forces. This decision arose from an objective evaluation of the 60th Army's offensive capabilities. The timely commitment of the 4th Guards Tank Army in the 60th Army's attack sector decided the outcome of combat operations to destroy the enemy's Ratibor group of forces.

During the operation particular attention was devoted to the personal interaction of commanders at all levels. In case of a sharp change in the situation along one or another axis, the *front* commander and the army commanders would immediately leave for the troops in the field and analyze the situation on the site and take the necessary measures for resolving as quickly as possible the tasks for defeating the enemy.

On 17 March, when the slow advance of the 59th and 60th armies' forces threatened to foil the operation to encircle the enemy forces in the area southwest of Oppeln, the *front* commander left for these armies' area of combat operations, determined the reason for the armies' slow advance and issued the corresponding instructions to the army commanders. The measures adopted had a decisive influence on the successful course of the combat operations to encircle the enemy in the Oppeln salient.

Throughout the entire operation troop command and control was eased by the presence of well organized and continually operating communications. Wire communications and radio communications worked steadily at all levels along the line of the command and observation posts. Radio equipment was widely employed for communications with the mobile forces and aviation, as well as for coordination.

Thus the First Ukrainian Front's Upper Silesia operation enriched Soviet military art, offering many examples of the creative resolution of the complex operational tasks that arose from the situation as it developed during the operation.

Part VII

Documents[1]

1   The documents cited in this section are taken from volumes 5(4) or 12(4) of the series *Velikaya Otechestven-naya*, V.A. Zolotarev, ed. (Moscow: "Terra," 1999, 2001). All entries are indicated by volume number and page.

1. Directive of the *Stavka* VGK No. 220250. To the *Stavka* Representative and the Commander of the First Ukrainian Front on the Relief of G.K. Zhukov from the Direction of the First Ukrainian Front's Operations[1]

26 October 1944, 1700 hrs

The *Stavka* of the Supreme High Command orders:

1. Marshal Zhukov is to retain the direction of the First and Second Belorussian fronts' operations, while relinquishing control of the First Ukrainian Front's operations.

2. To place the direct responsibility for the First Ukrainian Front's operations immediately upon the commander of the First Ukrainian Front, Marshal Konev.

Stavka of the Supreme High Command
I. Stalin
A. Antonov

---

1   *Velikaya Otechestvennaya*, 5(4):162-63.

2. Directive of the *Stavka* of the VGK No. 220257. To the Commander of the Third Belorussian Front, On Going Over to the Defensive[2]

5 November 1944, 0300 hrs

The *Stavka* of the Supreme High Command orders:

1. Upon receipt of this directive, the *front's* forces are to assume a static defense along the entire front.

2. The situation in the Goldap area is to be restored and this area securely held.

3. A deeply-echeloned defense should be created. No less than three defensive lines, with an overall depth of 30-40 kilometers should be prepared along the *front's* sector, with powerful corps, army and front reserves along the main axes.

4. Anti-tank defense should be constructed to a depth of 6-8 kilometers, with a density of 25-30 guns per kilometer of front along the most important tank-threatened axes, and broadly employing mine fields.

5. Particular attention should be paid to defense along the following axes: Pilkallen—Schirwindt; Kussen—Stallupönen; Gumbinnen—Walterkemen—Vistytis; Goldap—Przerosl; Treuburg—Suwalki.
    Major inhabited locales should be prepared for defense, regardless of their remove from the front line.

6. The responsibility for securing the boundaries with neighboring *fronts* is as before.

7. Simultaneously with the construction of defensive lines, begin scheduled exercises in all the *front's* formations and units in combat training and putting together units and elements, paying special attention to the offensive battle as applicable to the *front's* circumstances.

8. In all other matters be guided by *Stavka* directive on defense, no. 220194, of 29 August 1944.

9. Report on orders issued.

Stavka of the Supreme High Command
I. Stalin
A. Antonov

---

2   *Ibid*, 166.

3. Directive of the *Stavka* VGK No. 220258. To the Commander of the Second Belorussian Front, On Going Over to the Defensive[3]

5 November 1944, 0300 hrs

The *Stavka* of the Supreme High Command orders:

1. Upon receipt of this directive, the *front's* forces are to assume a static defense.

2. A deeply-echeloned defense should be created. No less than three defensive lines, with an overall depth of 30-40 kilometers should be prepared along the *front's* sector, and to the complete depth along the bridgeheads. Powerful corps, army and *front* reserves should be held along the main axes.

3. Anti-tank defense should be constructed to a depth of 6-8 kilometers, with a density of 25-30 guns per kilometer of front along the most important tank-threatened axes, and broadly employing mine fields.

4. Particular attentions should be paid to defending the bridgeheads in the area Rozan— excluding Pultusk, and in the Augustow area, as well as along the axes Osowiec—Bialystok; Lomza—Zambrow; Ostroleka—Ostrow Mazowiecka.
    Major inhabited locales should be prepared for defense, regardless of their remove from the front line.

5. The responsibility for securing the boundaries with neighboring *fronts* is as before.

6. Simultaneously with the construction of defensive lines, begin schedule exercises in all the *front's* formations and units in combat training and putting together units and elements, paying special attention to the offensive battle as applicable to the *front's* circumstances.

7. In all other matters be guided by *Stavka* directive on defense, no. 220194, of 29 August 1944.

8. Report on orders issued.

Stavka of the Supreme High Command
I. Stalin
A. Antonov

---

3   *Ibid*, 167.

4. Directive of the *Stavka* VGK No. 220259. To the *Stavka* Representative and the Commander of the Third Belorussian Front, on the Relief of A.M. Vasilevskii from Control of the *Front's* Operations[4]

8 November 1944, 0230 hrs

The *Stavka* of the Supreme High Command orders that Marshal of the Soviet Union Vasilevskii is to retain control of the First and Second Baltic fronts' operations, while relinquishing control of the Third Belorussian Front's operations.

Stavka of the Supreme High Command
I. Stalin
A. Antonov

---

4   *Ibid*, 168.

5. Directive of the *Stavka* VGK No. 220261. To the Commander of the First Belorussian Front, On Going Over to the Defensive[5]

12 November 1944, 0100 hrs

As a supplement to *Stavka* directive no. 220196 of 20.08.1944, the *Stavka* of the Supreme High Command orders:

1. Upon receipt of this directive, the *front's* right wing is to cease attacking and assume a static defense.

2. A deeply-echeloned defense should be created. No less than three defensive lines, with an overall depth of 30-40 kilometers should be prepared along the *front's* sector, and to the complete depth along the bridgeheads. Powerful corps, army and front reserves should be held along the main axes.

3. Special attention should be paid to the defense along the *front's* right wing along the axes: Pultusk—Wyszkow—Wegrow; Warsaw—Minsk Mazowiecki, and the retention of bridgeheads along the western bank of the Narew and Western Bug rivers.

4. In all other matters be guided by *Stavka* directive on defense, no. 220196, of 29 August 1944.

5. Report on orders issued. A detailed defensive plan is to be presented to the General Staff by 18 November 1944.

Stavka of the Supreme High Command
I. Stalin
A. Antonov

---

5   *Ibid*, 169.

6. Order of the *Stavka* VGK No. 220263. On Appointments and Shifts in the Command of the First and Second Belorussian Fronts[6]

12 November 1944

The *Stavka* of the Supreme High Command orders:

1. Appoint Marshal of the Soviet Union G.K. Zhukov commander of the First Belorussian Front.

2. Appoint Marshal of the Soviet Union K.K. Rokossovskii commander of the Second Belorussian Front, relieving him of the post of commander of the First Belorussian Front.

3. Appoint General G.F. Zakharov deputy commander of the First Belorussian Front, relieving him of the post of commander of the Second Belorussian Front.

4. Relieve Lieutenant General K.P. Trubnikov[7] of the post of deputy commander of the First Belorussian Front and appoint him deputy commander of the Second Belorussian Front.

5. Marshal of the Soviet Union G.K. Zhukov is to take up his duties as commander of the First Belorussian Front no later than 16.11.1944. Marshal of the Soviet Union K.K. Rokossovskii is to take up his duties as commander of the Second Belorussian Front no later than 18.11.1944.

6. In connection with the appointment of Marshal of the Soviet Union G.K. Zhukov as commander of the First Belorussian Front, he is relieved, as a *Stavka* representative, of the command of the First and Second Belorussian fronts' operations.

7. Report on execution.

Stavka of the Supreme High Command
I. Stalin
A. Antonov

---

6   *Ibid*, 170.
7   Editor's note. Kuz'ma Petrovich Trubnikov (1888-1974) joined the Russian imperial army in 1909 and the Red Army in 1918. During the Great Patriotic War he commanded a division and an army and served as deputy commander of several *fronts*. Following the war, Trubnikov served as deputy commander of the Northern Group of Forces.

7. Directive of the *Stavka* VGK No. 220271. To the Commander of the First Ukrainian Front on the Preparation of an Operation to Defeat the Enemy's Kielce—Radom Group of Forces[8]

25 November 1944, 2400 hrs

The *Stavka* of the Supreme High Command orders:

1. To prepare and conduct an offensive operation for the purpose of defeating, in conjunction with the First Belorussian Front, the Kielce—Radom enemy group of forces, and to reach the line Piotrkow—Radom—Czestochowa—Zawiercie—Miechow—Bochnia, no later than the 10-11th day of the offensive. The attack will subsequently be directed in the direction of Kalisz.

2. The main attack will be made with the forces of five combined-arms armies (45 rifle divisions), two tanks armies and four tank and mechanized corps from the Sandomierz bridgehead in the general direction of Chmielnik, Malogoszcz and Radomsko.
    The enemy defense is to be penetrated west of Staszow by the forces of three armies (13th, 52nd and 5th Guards) along a single sector 30 kilometers in width. Six artillery divisions are to be concentrated along the breakthrough sector to create an artillery and mortar (76mm and greater) density of no less than 220 tubes per kilometer along the breakthrough sector.

3. The *front's* second echelon will have two armies—3rd Guards and 21st—and will employ them after the breakthrough in the following manner: the 3rd Guards Army, along with one tank corps, is to be committed along the right flank of the breakthrough sector along the Skarzysko-Kamienna—Szydlowiec axis, with the mission of outflanking the enemy's Ostrowiec defensive system from the west and assist the forces of the First Belorussian Front in reaching the Radom area; following the breakthrough, the 21st Army is to follow behind the *front's* central group of forces and be employed for augmenting the attack along the main axis.

4. The main group of forces' operations are to be secured as follows: from the north, from Ostrowiec, by the 6th Army's (five rifle divisions and one fortified area) defense; from the south, from Krakow, by the 60th and 59th armies, for which purpose both armies (12 rifle divisions) and a tank corps are to be committed into the breach north of the Vistula River and to attack along the northern bank of the Vistula River in the general direction of Krakow and, under favorable conditions, to capture Krakow; the 60th Army's remaining four rifle divisions are to securely defend its left flank.

5. The tank armies are to be employed for developing the success following the breakthrough along the main direction.

6. The *front* will have in its reserve the 1st Guards Cavalry Corps and a tank or mechanized corps.

---

8   *Velikaya Otechestvennaya*, 5(4):174-75.

7. The 38th Army, consisting of nine rifle divisions and the Czechoslovak Corps, is to be transferred to the Fourth Ukrainian Front as of 2400 on 29.11.1944. The army is to be transferred with all its reinforcement equipment, rear units and establishments and on-hand supplies. 10,000 reinforcements are to be allotted to bring the army up to strength.

8. The following boundary lines are to be established:
    - with the First Belorussian Front from 2400 on 1.12.1944 as before as far as Jozefow, then Ilza—Opoczno—Pabianice—Miloslaw (all locales for the First Belorussian Front);
    - with the Fourth Ukrainian Front from 2400 on 29.11.1944, Przemysl—Jaslo—Bochnia—Nepolomice—Babice—Sosnowiec—Oppeln (all locales, except for Jaslo, Bochnia and Oppeln are for the Fourth Ukrainian Front).

9. The responsibility for securing the boundaries with neighboring *fronts* is as before.

10. The beginning of the offensive is to be in accordance with the instructions delivered to you personally.

11. All combat orders and instructions to the armies for the operation are to be presented to the General Staff.

Stavka of the Supreme High Command
I. Stalin
A. Antonov

8. To the Commanders of the First Ukrainian Front and the 6th Army. On the Transfer of the Army's Field Headquarters to the *Front*[9]

25 November 1944, 1600 hrs

Copies: to the chiefs of the General Staff's operational directorate and the directorate for operational-organizational measures.

The Supreme Commander-in-Chief has ordered the 6th Army's field headquarters in its entirety, plus all reinforcements, service establishments and army rear organs in the Rava-Russkaya area to be transferred at 2400 hrs on 25 November from the *Stavka* reserve to the First Ukrainian Front.

Report on execution.

Antonov
Karponosov[10]

---

9   *Velikaya Otechestvennaya*, 12(4):542.

10 Editor's note. Aron Gershevich Karponosov (1902-67) joined the Red Army in 1920. In 1942 he was appointed chief of the General Staff's main organizational directorate and simultaneously deputy chief of staff for organizational matters. Following the war, Karponosov served as deputy chief of staff of a military district.

9. To the Commanders of the First and Fourth Ukrainian Fronts. On the Resubordination of the 38th Army[11]

25 November 1944, 2400 hrs

In accordance with *Stavka* directive no. 220271 of 25.11.1944, the 38th Army, consisting of three rifle corps (nine rifle divisions), the Czechoslovak Corps, 135th Artillery Brigade, 491st Mortar Regiment, 1663rd Anti-Tank Artillery Regiment, 83rd Guards Mortar Regiment, 12th Tank Regiment, 39th Engineer-Sapper Brigade, 1954th Anti-Aircraft Artillery Regiment, and the 8th and 37th armored trains, is to be subordinated to the Fourth Ukrainian Front as of 2400 on 29.11.1944.

The army is to be transferred with all its rear units and establishments, a combat load of munitions and available supplies of fuel and food.

10,000 men are to be detached from the reinforcements slated for the First Ukrainian Front in order to bring the army up to strength.

From 2400 on 29.11.1944 the following boundary lines are to exist between the First and Fourth Ukrainian fronts: Przemysl'—Jaslo—Bochnia—Niepolomice—Bibice—Sosnowiec—Oppeln (all locales except for Jaslo, Bochnia and Oppeln are for the Fourth Ukrainian Front).

Report on the army's acceptance and transfer.

Antonov

---

11 *Velikaya Otechestvennaya*, 12(4):542-43.

10. To the Commander of the First Ukrainian Front. On the Transfer of the 59th Army and Two Rifle Divisions to the *Front*[12]

26 November 1944, 0300 hrs

Copies: To the chiefs of the General Staff's operational directorate and the directorate for operational-organizational measures.

By order of the Supreme Commander-in-Chief, the following units are being transferred to you by railroad:

a) the 59th Army, consisting of the 6th Guards Rifle Corps (13th, 80th and 327th rifle divisions) and the 115th Rifle Corps (92nd, 135th and 286th rifle divisions), with their reinforcements, service establishments and rear organs;

b) the 245th and 379th rifle divisions, which, upon their arrival are to be reformed into a single rifle division and included within the 59th Army. A directive on the reforming will be issued separately.

The army and divisions will arrive between 13-30 December of this year in the Lubaczow—Surochow area.

I request that you organize the reception and unloading of the arriving units and formations. Report daily on the arrival of the trains.

Antonov
Karponosov

---

12 *Ibid*, 543.

11. Directive of the *Stavka* VGK No. 220274. To the Commander of the Second Belorussian Front on the Defeat of the Enemy's Przasnysz—Mlawa Group of Forces[13]

28 November 1944, 2400 hrs

The *Stavka* of the Supreme High Command orders:

1. To prepare and conduct an offensive operation for the purpose of defeating the enemy's Przasnysz—Mlawa group of forces and reach the line Myszyniec—Willlenberg—Neidenburg—Dzialdowo—Biezun—Bielsk—Plock—excluding Piotrkow. The *front* will subsequently attack in the general direction of Nowe Miasto and Marienburg.

2. The main attack will be launched with the forces of four combined-arms armies, a tank army and a tank corps from the Rozan bridgehead in the general direction of Przasnysz, Mlawa and Lidzbark. The enemy's defense is to be broken through by the forces of three armies along a sector 16-18 kilometers wide. Three artillery divisions are to be concentrated along the breakthrough sector, in order to create a density of artillery and mortars (76mm and higher) of no less than 220 tubes per kilometer along the breakthrough sector.

   The *front* is to have one army in its second echelon and commit it after the breakthrough along the Rozan bridgehead in the general direction of Myszyniec, with the mission of rolling up the enemy's defense along the *front's* right wing and securing the main group of forces against the enemy's attack from the north.

3. The second attack will be launched with the forces of two combined-arms armies and one tank corps from the Serock bridgehead in the general direction of Nasielsk, Plonsk and Bielsk.

   In order to assist the First Belorussian Front's in defeating the enemy's Warsaw group of forces, part of the *front's* left-wing forces (no less than an army and a tank or mechanized corps) is to launch an attack to outflank Modlin from the west, in order to prevent the withdrawal of the enemy's Warsaw group of forces behind the Vistula River and be ready to force the Vistula River west of Modlin.

   The enemy's defense is to be penetrated along a 9-kilometer sector and two artillery divisions sent there for the breakthrough, in order to create an artillery and mortar (76mm and higher) of no less than 210 tubes per kilometer of breakthrough front.

4. The operations of the *front's* main forces, aside from the offensive by one army toward Myszyniec, are to be covered by the 50th Army's solid defense, along with two fortified areas, along the Narew River on the Augustow—Lomza—Ostroleka sector.

5. The *front* reserve will consist of a mechanized corps and a cavalry corps.

6. A large part of the tank formations is to be employed for developing the success after the breakthrough along the main direction.

---

13 *Velikaya Otechestvennaya,* 5(4):176-77.

7. Boundary lines: as before with the Third Belorussian Front; with the First Belorussian Front—as before as far as the mouth of the Bug River, and then along the Vistula as far as Torun.

8. The operation is to be supplied with the following: 4-6 combat loads of all calibers, 15 refuelings of air fuel and eight refuelings of auto fuel.

9. The beginning of the offensive is to be in accordance with the instructions delivered to you personally.

10. All combat orders and instructions to the armies for the operation are to be presented to the General Staff.

Stavka of the Supreme High Command
I. Stalin
A. Antonov

12. Directive of the *Stavka* VGK No. 220275. To the Commander of the First Belorussian Front on the Defeat of the Enemy's Warsaw—Radom Group of Forces[14]

28 November 1944

The *Stavka* of the Supreme High Command orders:

1. To prepare and conduct an offensive operation for the immediate task of defeating the enemy's Warsaw—Radom group of forces and to reach the line Piotrkow—Zychlin—Lodz. The *front* will subsequently develop the offensive in the general direction of Poznan.

2. The main attack will be launched with the forces of four combined-arms armies, two tank armies and a cavalry corps from the bridgehead along the Pilica River in the general direction of Bialobrzegi, Skierniewice and Kutno. With part of its forces, no less than one combined-arms army and one or two tank corps, the *front* is to attack to the northwest, in order to roll up the enemy's defense along the *front's* right wing and, assisted by the Second Belorussian Front, defeat the enemy's Warsaw group of forces and capture Warsaw.

    The enemy's defense is to be broken through by the forces of three armies along a sector 16 kilometers in width. Four artillery divisions are to be concentrated along the breakthrough sector, in order to create an artillery and mortar (76mm and higher) density of no less than 240 tubes per kilometer of breakthrough front.

3. A second attack is to be launched with the forces of two combined-arms armies, two tank corps and a cavalry corps from the bridgehead southwest of Pulawy in the general direction of Radom, Tomaszow and Lodz.

    A part of this force is to attack in the direction of Szydlowiec to meet up with the First Ukrainian Front's attack, for the purpose of defeating the enemy's Kielce—Radom group of forces in cooperation with the latter.

    The enemy's defense is to be pierced along a 12-kilometer front and two artillery divisions are to be concentrated here, in order to create an artillery and mortar (76mm and higher) density of no less than 215 tubes per kilometer of breakthrough front.

4. The *front* will have an army in its second echelon and employ it for developing the success after the breakthrough along the main direction.

5. Upon the beginning of the main forces' offensive, the 47th Army, in cooperation with the Second Belorussian Front's left-wing forces, is to clear the area between the Vistula and Bug rivers. The army will subsequently be used, depending upon the situation, for developing the success along the main direction, or for an attack to outflank Warsaw from the northwest.

6. The Polish 1st Army is to be employed initially for defending along the eastern bank of the Vistula River in the Warsaw area and, following the breakthrough, successively ferried across the Vistula River to be committed into the fighting for Warsaw.

---

14 *Ibid*, 177-78.

7. The tank armies are to be used for developing the success after the breakthrough along the main direction, while cutting off the enemy's Warsaw group of forces' path of retreat to the west.

8. Establish the following boundary lines: as before with the Second Belorussian Front as far as the mouth of the Bug River, then along the Vistula River as far as Torun; with the First Ukrainian Front from 2400 on 1.12.1944, as before as far as Jozefow, then Ilza—Opoczno—Pabianice—Jarocin (all locales for the First Belorussian Front).

9. The operation is to be supplied with the following: 4-6 combat loads of all calibers, 15 air refuelings and eight refuelings of auto fuel.

10. The beginning of the offensive is to be in accordance with the instructions delivered to you personally.

11. All combat orders and instructions to the armies for the operation are to be presented to the General Staff.

Stavka of the Supreme High Command
I. Stalin
A. Antonov

13. To the Commanders of the First Baltic and Third Belorussian Fronts and the 2nd Guards Army on the Army's Movement and Resubordination[15]

Copy: to the *Stavka* representative and the chiefs of the General Staff's operational directorate and the directorate for operational-organizational measures.

29 November 1944, 2330 hrs

The Supreme Commander-in-Chief has ordered:

1. The 2nd Guards Army, consisting of the 13th Guards Rifle Corps (3rd, 24th and 87th guards rifle divisions), 11th Guards Rifle Corps (2nd, 32nd and 33rd guards rifle divisions) and the 22nd Guards Rifle Corps (46th and 90th guards and 154th rifle divisions), along with army reinforcements, service establishments and rear services, is to move to concentrate in the Jurburgas area, where it is to be included in the Third Belorussian Front. The securing of its crossing of the Neman River is entrusted to the commander of the Third Belorussian Front.

    The army's movement is to begin with the onset of darkness on 3 December of this year, and its arrival in the Jurburgas area is to be completed by the morning of 13 December of this year.

2. In order to reconnoiter the army's new location area and the quartering of its units and formations, on 2 December of this year an operational group, headed by the deputy army commander is to be dispatched by automobile, with communications equipment.

3. The army is to be moved in its entirety, including all its personnel, horses, transport, weapons, and other property, removing nothing before its departure, and to supply it with 1.5 combat loads of ammunition, fuel and food along its route of march.

4. All measures are to be adopted to ensure the secrecy of the army's movement. The march is to be carried out in darkness, while observing masking measures. Correspondence and conversations relating to the army's movement are to be conducted only with the General Staff and the Third Belorussian Front's chief of staff.

5. By the morning of 1 December of this year the march plan is to be communicated to the General Staff and the commander of the Third Belorussian Front.

6. The commander of the Third Belorussian Front is to organize the reception and quartering of the army's arriving units.

The course of the march is to be communicated daily to the General Staff and the Third Belorussian Front's chief of staff.

Antonov
Karponosov

---

15 *Velikaya Otechestvennaya*, 12(4):545.

14. To the Commander of the Second Belorussian Front on the Dispatch of the 5th Guards Tank Army, the 19th Tank Corps and an Artillery Division to the *Front*[16]

Copy: to the *Stavka* representative and the chiefs of the General Staff's operational directorate and the directorate for operational-organizational measures.

29 November 1944, 2330 hrs

On orders from the Supreme Commander-in-Chief, you are being sent the following by rail:

a) the 5th Guards Tank Army, consisting of one tank corps and the 47th Mechanized Brigade, with army reinforcements and rear organs. Their arrival in the Ostrow Mazowiecka area will take place approximately from 25 December through 7 January.

b) the 19th Tank Corps. Its arrival in the Ostrow Mazowiecka area is approximately from 14 December through 24 December.

c) one artillery division. Its arrival in the Ostrow Mazowiecka area is approximately from 10 December through 21 December.

I request that you organize the reception and unloading of the arriving units and formations and report daily on the unloading of the trains.

Antonov
Karponosov

---

16 *Ibid*, 551.

15. To the Commander of the First Belorussian Front. On the Subordination of the 3rd Shock and 61st Armies to the *Front*[17]

29 November 1944, 2330 hrs

Copies: To the chiefs of the General Staff's operational directorate and the directorate for operational-organizational measures.

By order of the Supreme Commander-in-Chief, the following are being transferred to you by railroad:

a)   3rd Shock Army, consisting of:
7th Rifle Corps (146th, 265th and 364th rifle divisions);
12th Guards Rifle Corps (23rd and 52nd guards rifle and 33rd Rifle divisions);
79th Rifle Corps (150th, 171st and 207th rifle divisions), along with reinforcements, service establishments and rear organs. The army will arrive approximately between 11 December and 10 January at Lublin station;

b)   61st Army, consisting of:
9th Guards Rifle Corps (12th and 75th guards rifle and 415th Rifle divisions);
80th Rifle Corps (82nd, 212th and 356th rifle divisions);
89th Rifle Corps (23rd, 311th and 397th rifle divisions), along with reinforcements, service establishments and rear organs. The army will arrive approximately between 9 December and 1 January at the Lukow station.

I request that you organize the reception and unloading of the arriving units and formations and report daily on the unloading of the trains.

Antonov
Karponosov

---

17 *Ibid*, 554-55.

16. To the Commander of the Second Belorussian Front. On the Units and Formations Being Transferred to the *Front*[18]

29 November 1944

By a *Stavka* order of 28.11.1944, the following are being transferred to the front:

Cavalry:	From Third Belorussian Front	By march, by 15.12
3rd Guards Cavalry Corps	ten trains of heavy freight	By rail, by 27.12,
(5th, 6th Guards and 32nd cavalry divisions)	leaving 6.12	
Tank Troops		
5th Guards Tank Army	From First Baltic Front	By rail, by 7.01
a) a tank corps, headquarters of the 47th	From Second Baltic Front	By rail, by 15.12
Motorized Brigade	” ”	” ”
b) 10th Tank Corps	” ”	” ”
For the 5th Guards Tank Army		
332nd Guards Self-Propelled Artillery	From the reserve	By rail, by 23.12
Regiment (152mm)	” ”	” ”
365th Guards Self-Propelled Artillery	” ”	By rail, by 22.12
Regiment (152mm)	” ”	” ”
361st Guards Self-Propelled Artillery	” ”	By rail, by 23.12
Regiment (100mm)	” ”	” ”
1207th Self-Propelled Artillery Regiment	” ”	By rail, by 22.12
(100mm)	” ”	” ”
For the *Front*		
46th Guards Tank Regiment (KV[19] tanks)	From Leningrad Front	By rail, by 25.12
260th Tank Regiment (KV tanks)	From First Baltic Front	By rail, by 26.12
A regiment of 85mm self-	” ”	By rail, by 27.12
propelled artillery		
A regiment of 85mm self-propelled artillery	From Second Baltic Front	By rail, by 28.12
999th Self-Propelled Artillery Regiment	” ”	By rail, by 28.12
(76mm)	” ”	” ”
1199th Self-Propelled Artillery Regiment	” ”	By rail, by 29.12
(76mm)	” ”	” ”
90th Minesweeper Regiment	From the reserve	By rail, by 7.01
Artillery Units		
An artillery breakthrough division	From Second Baltic Front	By rail, in the first ten days of January

---

18 *Ibid*, 556.
19 Editor's note. This is a reference to the KV series of heavy tanks named after the former Soviet defense com-missar Kliment Yefremovich Voroshilov (1881-1969). These include the well-known KV-1 and KV-2 models, among others.

74th Anti-Aircraft Artillery Division	From the reserve	By rail, by 7.01
One anti-tank artillery brigade	From Third Belorussian Front	By march, by 20.12
One anti-tank artillery brigade	” ”	” ”
5th Guards Mortar Brigade	From Leningrad Front	By rail, by 18.12
24th Guards Mortar Regiment	” ”	By rail, by 15.12
317th Heavy Caliber Artillery Battalion	From the reserve	Transferred on site, By 1.12

Automobile Units		
Headquarters of the 2nd Automobile Brigade	From First Baltic Front	By march, by 12.12
One automobile regiment	” ”	” ”
16th Automobile Regiment	From Second Baltic Front	By march, by 15.12

Reinforcements (Men and auto transport)		
15,000 men	From various military districts	By rail, by 25.12
600 automobile tractors		
1,500 motor vehicles	Imported and domestic	By rail, 20-30.12

Antonov
Karponosov

17. Directive of the *Stavka* VGK No. 220227. To the Commander of the Third Belorussian Front on the Defeat of the Enemy's Tilsit—Insterburg Group of Forces[20]

3 December 1944

1. Prepare and conduct an offensive operation for the purpose of defeating the enemy's Tilsit—Insterburg group of forces, and no later than the operation's 10-12th day reach the line Nemonin—Zargillen—Norkitten—Darkemen—Goldap.

    To subsequently, while securing the *front's* main group of forces from the south, develop the offensive toward Königsberg along both banks of the Pregel River, with the main forces along the southern bank of the Pregel River.

2. The main attack is to be launched with the forces of four combined-arms armies and two tank corps from the area north of Stallupönen and Gumbinnen in the general direction of Mallwischken, Aulowenen and Welau.

    The enemy's defense is to be pierced with the forces of three armies (39th, 5th and 11th Guards) along a single 18-19 kilometer sector. Three artillery breakthrough divisions are to be stationed along the breakthrough sector, in order to create an artillery and mortar density (76mm and higher) of no less than 200 tubes per kilometer along the breakthrough front.

3. The *front's* second echelon is to contain one army (2nd Guards), with a tank corps, and it is to be employed following the breakthrough for augmenting the attack along the main axis.

4. The actions of the main group of forces are to be supported as follows: from the north, from the direction of the Neman River—by the defense of one of the 39th Army's corps and an attack by its main forces in the direction of Tilsit; from the south—by the 28th Army's defense south of Walterkemen and an attack by part of its forces from behind the left flank of the breakthrough sector in the general direction of Darkemen.

    Under all conditions, the 31st Army is to firmly defend its front to the south of Goldap.

5. The tank corps are to be employed for developing the success following the breakthrough along the main axis.

6. The boundary lines with the neighboring *fronts* are as before.

7. The beginning of the offensive is to be in accordance with the instructions delivered to you personally.

8. All combat orders and instructions to the armies for the operation are to be presented to the General Staff.

Stavka of the Supreme High Command
I. Stalin
A. Antonov

---

20 *Velikaya Otechestvennaya*, 5(4):179.

18. Directive of the *Stavka* VGK No. 220279. To the Commander of the First Baltic Front and the *Stavka* Representative on the Defeat of the Enemy's Tilsit Group of Forces[21]

6 December 1944, 2400 hrs

The *Stavka* of the Supreme High Command orders:

1. For the purposes of assisting the Third Belorussian Front in defeating the enemy's Tilsit group of forces, you are to concentrate no later than 28.12.1944 no less than 4-5 rifle divisions along the 43rd Army's left flank, in order that they be ready to develop the success of the Third Belorussian Front's right wing, employing these divisions for an attack along the southern bank of the Neman River for the purpose of rolling up the enemy's defense along the Neman River and bringing all of the 43rd Army's forces to the river's southern bank.

    The army's subsequent mission will be assigned later.

2. The start of operations will be according to special instructions.

Stavka of the Supreme High Command
I. Stalin
A. Antonov

---

21 *Ibid*, 180.

19. To the Commander of the First Belorussian Front and the Chiefs of the People's Commissariat of Defense's Main Directorates. On Reinforcing the 61st Army[22]

7 December 1944, 2355 hrs

Copies: To the commander of the 61st Army and the chief of the General Staff's operational directorate for operational-organizational measures.

The Supreme Commander-in-Chief has ordered:

1. The 61st Army, consisting of the 12th and 75th guards rifle, 23rd, 82nd, 212th, 311th, 356th, 397th, and 415th rifle divisions, upon arrival with the First Belorussian Front by 30 December of this year, is to be reinforced, by bringing the personnel strength of each rifle division to 6,500 men, up to 900 horses, and munitions and equipment to the norms stated in supplement no. 1.[23]

2. By 25.12 1944 the chiefs of the People's Commissariat of Defense's main directorates are to dispatch to the commander of the 61st Army at Lublin station, field postal address 15362, men, horses, munitions and other equipment for bringing the army's rifle divisions up to strength. The amount of dispatched material, complete with the numbers of the trains and transports, is to be communicated to the commander of the First Belorussian Front and the General Staff.

3. The chief of the *front* staff will report to the General Staff on the pace of the army's reinforcement:
   a) on the army's concentration—daily;
   b) on the numbers of the trains with reinforcements, horses, transports with munitions, and equipment arriving to reinforce the army—on the day of their arrival, and a copy to the corresponding chief of the People's Commissariat of Defense's main directorate.
   c) on the combat and overall strength of the rifle divisions—once every five days.

Antonov
Karponosov

---

22 *Velikaya Otechestvennaya*, 12(4):569.
23 Editor's note. The supplement was not published.

20. To the Commander of the First Belorussian Front and the Chiefs of the People's Commissariat of Defense's Main Directorates. On Reinforcing the 3rd Shock Army[24]

7 December 1944, 2355 hrs

Copies: To the commander of the 3rd Shock Army and the chief of the General Staff's operational directorate for operational-organizational measures.

The Supreme Commander-in-Chief has ordered:

1. The 3rd Shock Army, consisting of the 23rd and 52nd guards rifle, 146th, 265th, 364th, 33rd, 150th, 171st, and 207th rifle divisions, upon arriving with the First Belorussian Front by 10 January 1945, is to be reinforced, raising the strength of each rifle division to 6,500 men, up to 900 horses, munitions and equipment, according to the norms contained in supplement no. 1.[25]

2. By 5 January 1945 the chiefs of the People's Commissariat of Defense's main directorates are to dispatch to the commander of the 3rd Shock Army at Lukow station, field postal address 11065, men, horses, munitions and other equipment for bringing the army's rifle divisions up to strength. The amount of dispatched material, complete with the numbers of the trains and transports, is to be communicated to the commander of the First Belorussian Front and the General Staff.

3. The chief of the *front* staff will report to the General Staff on the pace of the army's reinforcement:
    a) on the army's concentration—daily;
    b) on the numbers of the trains with reinforcements, horses, transports with munitions, and equipment arriving to reinforce the army—on the day of their arrival, and a copy to the corresponding chief of the People's Commissariat of Defense's main directorate.
    c) on the combat and overall strength of the rifle divisions—once every five days.

Antonov
Karponosov

---

24 *Velikaya Otechestvennaya*, 12(4):569-70.
25 Editor's note. The supplement was not published.

21. To the Commander of the Second Belorussian Front. On the Dispatch of Military Equipment for Reinforcing the 5th Guards Tank Army[26]

8 December 1944, 2255 hrs

Copies: To the commander of the Red Army's armored and mechanized troops and the chief of the General Staff's operational directorate for operational-organizational measures.

By order of the Supreme Commander-in-Chief, the following will be sent through the *Stavka* reserve before 20 December, for bringing the 5th Guards Tank Army up to strength:

a)   145 tanks in small groups, of which 15 are IS,[27] 65 T-34s, and 65 Shermans;[28]

b)   85 self-propelled artillery vehicles in small groups, of which five are ISU-152s, 20 ISU-122s, 20 SU-85s, and 40 SU-76s;

c)   the 332nd and 365th Guards ISU-152 regiments, for a total of 42 ISU-152s;

d)   the 381st Guards and 1207th SU-100 regiments, for a total of 42 SU-100s.

In all, 314 combat vehicles will be sent from the *Stavka* reserve to bring the 5th Guards Tank Army up to strength, including 145 tanks and 169 self-propelled artillery vehicles. The arrival of the above-listed reinforcements to the *front* is approximately by 30 December of this year.

Along with the tanks and self-propelled artillery vehicles arriving to the army, upon reinforcement the army will have 305 tanks (219 T-34s, 21 ISs and 65 Shermans) and 210 self-propelled artillery vehicles (63 ISU-152s, 21 ISU-122s, 42 SU-100s, 42 SU-85s, and 42 SU-76s). In all, the army will contain 515 combat vehicles.

Instructions concerning the order of bringing the army's units and formations up to strength in tanks and self-propelled artillery vehicles will be issued by the commander of the Red Army's armored and mechanized troops.

Antonov

---

26 *Velikaya Otechestvennaya*, 12(4):571-72.
27 Editor's note. This refers to the Iosif Stalin heavy tank. This tank (IS-2) weighed 46 tons and had crew of four. Its armament consisted of a 122mm gun, three 7.62mm machine guns and a single 12.7mm anti-aircraft machine gun.
28 Editor's note. This refers to the M-26 "Sherman" tank, which was shipped by the US to the Soviet Union as part of the Lend-Lease program. The tank weighed 41.5 tons and had a crew of five. Its armament consisted of a 90mm gun, two 7.62mm machine guns and a single 12.7mm machine gun.

22. The Commander of the Second Belorussian Front's Report No. 00650/op. To the Supreme Commander-in-Chief on the Plan for the Defeat of the Enemy's Przasnysz—Mlawa Group of Forces[29]

17 December 1944, 1435 hrs

I submit for your confirmation my decision, according to directive no. 220274, of 28 November 1944.

I can report as follows:

First. Along the direction of the main attack, the gap between the left flank of comrade Colonel General Gorbatov's 3rd Army's shock group and the right flank of comrade Lieutenant General Gusev's 48th Army along the sector, excluding Dombrowka—Orzyc River, is explained by the unsuitability of the terrain for an offensive, the presence of the enemy's powerfully fortified defensive zone, and the necessity of forcing the Orcyz River.

Second. The gap between the 65th and 70th armies' shock groups is explained by the presence along this sector of the enemy's powerful center of resistance in the Powelin area.

Third. With the 70th Army's advance and its arrival north of Modlin, one of the 65th Army's tank corps will be subordinated to the 70th Army.

Fourth. The 50th Army, consisting of seven rifle divisions and three fortified areas, has been deployed along the sector Augustow—Osowiec—Lomza—Nowogrod, with the mission of defending statically. The stretching of the 50th Army's left flank as far as Ostroleka is not advantageous. It is expedient to keep the sector from Nowogrod to Ostroleka for the 49th Army, which, while attacking toward Myszyniec, will roll up the enemy's defense along the western bank of the Narew River and by the 10-11th day of the operation should reach the area west of Nowogrod with its right flank.

Fifth. It is planned to employ the *front* air army's main forces along the direction of the main attack (48th and 2nd Shock armies). Following the breakthrough of the enemy's defensive front, our aviation will support the mobile formations, based on a calculation of one assault air division per tank corps, or three assault air divisions; one assault air corps for the 5th Guards Tank Army, with one assault air division in the *front* reserve. Thus the *front* has no assault air formations for the 3rd Army, 3rd Cavalry Corps and 8th Mechanized Corps.

It is necessary to reinforce the *front's* aviation with an additional two assault air divisions.

Six. I have decided to commit the reserve designated by you—3rd Guards Cavalry Corps and 8th Guards Mechanized Corps—into the breach on the 2-3rd day of the operation along the 3rd Army's sector, for the purpose of seizing the Allenstein line and securing the *front's* shock group against an enemy attack from the north.

Only two rifle divisions and three anti-tank brigades remain in the *front* reserve.

Seven. The ammunition norm, which was confirmed by you for the operation at four combat loads for the main calibers, has been reduced to 3-3.5 combat loads. The reduction mainly affects the shells for 76mm regimental and divisional artillery and 122mm howitzers. This reduction puts the *front* in a difficult situation.

For the operation in question, based upon minimal calculations, it is necessary to have:

---

29 *Velikaya Otechestvennaya*, 5(4):310-11.

For the operation's first day—1.5 combat loads.
For the operation's second day—0.5 combat loads.
For the operation's third day—0.5 combat loads.
For the 4-10th day—0.75-1 combat load.
In all, 3.5 combat loads to fulfill the assignment.

Aside from this, it is necessary to have 0.5 combat loads of NZ fuel in the armies and 0.5 combat loads in the *front* reserve.

In total, the *front* should have 4.5-5 combat loads by the start of the operation.

Eight. The operational decision has been played out on maps with the commanders, and their suggestions have been taken into account.

Nine: I request the following:

a) to confirm my decision;
b) to release to the *front* the norm set by you—four combat loads for the main calibers—by the start of the operation;
c) in order to develop the offensive toward Marienburg and to secure the front's shock group from East Prussia, speed up the concentration of one combined-arms army in the Bialystok area.

Supplements:

1. The Second Belorussian Front's operational directive no. 00110/op, copy no. 1, 49 pages.
2. The Second Belorussian Front's combat order no. 00109/op, copy no. 2, four pages.
3. Instructions for the planning of the artillery offensive and the documentation for the operation's artillery support, 18 pages.
4. The plan for employing aviation, copy no. 1, 12 pages.
5. The engineering support plan, 13 pages.
6. The *front* commander's decision on 200,000, 100,000 and 500,000 maps; in all, three maps on 45 pages.

Commander of the Second Belorussian Front, Marshal of the Soviet Union Rokossovskii
Member of the Second Belorussian Front's Military Council, Lieutenant General Subbotin[30]
Chief of Staff of the Second Belorussian Front, Lieutenant General Bogolyubov[31]

---

30 Editor's note. Nikita Yegorovich Subbotin (1904-68) joined the Red Army in 1926. During the Great Patriotic War he served as a political commissar for a rifle division and an army and from 1944 was a member of the Second Belorussian Front's military council. Following the war, Subbotin was a member of the military council of the Northern Group of Forces and of a military district.
31 Editor's note. Aleksandr Nikolaevich Bogolyubov (1900-56) joined the Red Army in 1918. During the Great Patriotic War he served as chief of staff of an army and several *fronts*, including the Second Belorussian Front from 1944 to the end of the war. Following the war, Bogolyubov served as chief of staff of the Northern Group of Forces and assistant to the commander-in-chief of the Soviet Forces in the Far East.

23. The Second Belorussian Front's Operational Directive No. 00110/OP[32]

17 December 1944, 1430 hrs

1. Defending against the *front's* left wing are the forces of Army Group Center (units of the Second and Ninth armies), consisting of 11 (102nd, 14th, 292nd, 129th, 299th, 211th, 7th, 35th, 252nd, 542nd, and 5th) infantry divisions and four (6th, 3rd, 5th "Viking", and 3rd *Totenkopf*) panzer divisions, reinforced with artillery from the high command.

    The forward edge of the defensive zone runs along the western bank of the Narew River as far as Mlynarz, then along the line Mlynarz—Dlugoleka—Dombrowka—Chyliny—Glodowo—Pultusk—Powelin—Dembe.

    According to intelligence data, the enemy has up to three infantry divisions and a panzer-grenadier division in operational reserve as far as the line of the Vistula River in the areas of Plock, Rypin, Mlawa, and Brodnica. The arrival of enemy reserves from the area of Goldap and Königsberg is not excluded.

2. The *front's* forces will attack with the goal of defeating the enemy's Przasnysz—Mlawa group of forces and no later than the operation's 10-11th day reaching the line Myszyniec—Willlenberg—Neidenburg—Dzialdowo—Biezun—Bielsk—Plock—excluding Piotrkow.

    The *front* will subsequently attack in the general direction of Nowe Miasto and Marienburg.

    The main attack will be launched from the Rozan bridgehead by four combined-arms armies, reinforced with two tank corps, and a tank army in the general direction of Przasnysz, Mlawa and Lidzbark.

    The second attack from the Serock bridgehead will be launched by two combined-arms armies, reinforced by a single tank corps, in the general direction of Nasielsk, Plonsk and Bielsk.

    The operations by the *front's* main forces will be secured from the north with a solid defense by a single army along the line Augustow—Osowiec—Lomza—Nowogrod.

3. The forces of the Third Belorussian Front will be actively operating to the right. The boundary line with the *front* is: Sopockin—Augustow Canal—Augustow—Stradaunen—Rhein—Heilsberg (all locales, except for Sopockin and Augustow are exclusively within the Second Belorussian Front).

    To the left are the forces of the First Belorussian Front. The boundary with the *front* is Czeremcha—Jadow—Serock—the Western Bug River to its mouth, and then along the Vistula River as far as Torun.

4. The 3rd Army (the number of effectives is in the supplement) is to break through the enemy's defensive front along the sector excluding Ponikewka—Dombrowka (a breakthrough front of six kilometers) and launch its main attack along the army's left flank in the direction of Krasnosielc and Jednorozec, and a supporting attack with no less than a rifle corps in the direction of Aleksandrow.

    The army's immediate objective is to reach the line Rafaly-Glinki—Wlociane—Nowy Podos—excluding Jacionzek.

    By the close of the operation's third day the army is to reach the line Jednorozec—Przasnysz and, along the axis of the supporting attack, reach the Omulew River in the Aleksandrow area.

---

32 *Velikaya Otechestvennaya*, 5(4):311-16. This is the first supplement, mentioned in the conclusion of the previous document.

By subsequently developing the offensive along the Chorzele—Allenstein axis, by the close of the operation's tenth day the army is to reach the line Klein-Dankheim—Muschaken—Neidenburg.

Keep in mind that from approximately the Jednorozec—Przasnysz line the 3rd Guards Cavalry Corps and the 8th Mechanized Corps will be committed into the breach along the Neidenburg—Allenstein axis, with the objective of capturing the Allenstein area on the 5-6th day of the operation, cutting the enemy's most important communications, and preventing an attack by his reserves from the north.

The artillery and mortar (76mm and higher) density along the breakthrough sector is to be no less than 220 tubes per kilometer of front.

To the right, along the eastern bank of the Narew River as far as Chelstow, and along the Rozan bridgehead, units of the 49th Army are defending along the sector Mlynarz—Sendzenta. The boundary with the army is Czerwin—Kruszewo (both locales within the 3rd Army).

Upon the piercing of the front and the arrival of the 3rd Army at approximately the line Rafaly-Glinki—Wlociane—excluding Jacionzek, the 49th Army will attack in the general direction of Myszyniec. From this time the boundary line with the army will continue along the line Amelin—Chorzele—Allenstein (all locales inside the 3rd Army).

To the left is the 48th Army, the boundary with which runs along the line Przedswit—Dzbondz—Lipinki—Dombrowka—Nowe Goloniowo—Przasnysz—Dzierzgowo—Nowa Wies Elcka—Neidenburg—Osterode (all locales inside the 3rd Army).

With the commitment of the 49th Army into the fighting the army is to have no less than a rifle corps in reserve.

The army's headquarters as of 5.01.1945 is in the northwestern part of the Makow woods, with its axis of movement Zawady—Kuskow—Grabow (ten kilometers southwest of Chorzele)—Janow.

5. The 48th Army (the number of effectives is in the supplement) is to launch its main attack, in conjunction with the 2nd Shock Army along the left flank along the front Ciepielow—excluding Dzierzoniow (a 6-kilometer breakthrough front) along the axis Karniewo—Paluki—Dzbondz—Mlawa.

The immediate objective is to break through the enemy's defensive front, capture the Makow area, and by the close of the operation's first day reach the line Jacionzek—Zakrzewo—Karniewo.

By the close of the operation's third day the army is to reach the line Rostkowo—Wierzbowo—Pszonzewo.

Subsequently, no later than the operation's tenth day, the army is to reach the line excluding Neidenburg—Dzialdowo—Lonzek.

The artillery and mortar (76mm and higher) density along the breakthrough sector is to be no less than 220 tubes per kilometer.

No less than two rifle divisions should be held in the army reserve.

For developing the success along the Mlawa—Dzialdowo axis following the breakthrough of the enemy defense, the army is to be strengthened with the 1st Guards Tank Corps.

The 2nd Shock Army will attack to the left, with the boundary running along the line Przetycz—Golystok—Zambski Koscielne—Nowy Strachocin—Dzierzanowo—the Czarnystaw manor house—Ciechanow—Gluzek—Lidzbark (all locales, except for Przetycz, Golystok, Nowy Strachocin, and Lidzbark are inside the 48th Army).

The army's headquarters from 5.01.1945 is the woods north of Stary Strachocin, with the axis of movement Makow—Szweiki—Dzbondz—Mlawa—Dzialdowo.

6. The 2nd Shock Army (the army's effective strength is in the supplement) will launch its main attack, in conjunction with the 48th Army, along the right flank along the front Dzierzgowo—Przezmierowo (6-kilometer breakthrough front) along the axis Stary Golymin—Szrensk—Zielun.

The army's immediate objective is to break through the enemy's defensive front and by the close of the operation's first day reach the line Byszewo Vygoda—Konarzewo—Grochy Serwatki—Oldaki—Gasiorowo.

Part of the army's forces (no less than two rifle divisions), in cooperation with the 65th Army's right flank, is to eliminate the enemy in the Pultusk area during the first day of the operation.

By the close of the operation's third day the army is to capture Ciechanow and reach the line Chruszczewo—Gonski—Mlock.

Subsequently attacking along the axis Szrensk—Kuczbork—Zielun, the army is to reach the line Nowa Wies—Goscicino—Zelena—Zuromin—Biezun.

The artillery and mortar (76mm and higher) density along the breakthrough sector is to be no less than 220 tubes per kilometer of front.

There is to be no less than one rifle corps in the army reserve.

For developing the success along the axis Ciechanow—Szrensk—Zielun, following the breakthrough of the enemy's defensive front the army will be reinforced with the 8th Guards Tank Corps.

The 65th Army will attack to the left, with the boundary line Wyszkow—Stare Borsuki—Kokoszka—Gonsocin—Ojrzen—Glinojeck—Biezun—Skrwilno—Dlug (all locales, except for Wyszkow and Stare Borsuki are within the 2nd Shock Army).

From 5.01.1945 the army's command post will be in Sokolowo, with the axis of movement Dzierzoniow—Stary Golymin—Ciechanow—Szrensk.

7. The 65th Army (the number of effectives is in the supplement) will launch its main attack on the left flank along the front Obrenbek—Cepelin (a breakthrough front of seven kilometers) along the axis Jackowo—Nowe Miasto—Sochocin—Drobin.

The immediate objective is to break through the enemy's defense and by the close of the operation's first day reach the line Beliany—Kendzezawice—Nasielsk.

Part of the army's forces (no less than two rifle divisions) is to eliminate the enemy in the Pultusk area in conjunction with the 2nd Shock Army.

By the close of the operation's third day the army is to reach the line Luberadz—Sochocin—Plonsk.

Subsequently, in cooperation with the 70th Army and developing the offensive in the direction of Drobin, the army is to reach the line excluding Biezun—Grabowo—Bielsk by no later than the operation's tenth day.

Bear in mind that in the Raciaz—Drobin area part of the army's forces will turn toward Plock.

The artillery and mortar (76mm and higher) density along the breakthrough front is to be no less than 210 tubes per kilometer of front.

There is to be no less than two rifle divisions in the army reserve.

In order to develop the success along the axis Nowe Miasto—Plonsk—Plock following the breakthrough, the army will be reinforced with the 3rd Guards Tank Corps.

The 70th Army will attack on the left, with the boundary along the line Pludy—Kopaniec—Cepelin—Nasielsk—Plonsk (all locales in the 65th Army).

From 5.01.1945 the army's headquarters is in Zatory and its axis of movement is along the line Skorosze—Nowe Miasto—Sochocin—Raciaz.

8. The 70th Army (the number of effectives is in the supplement) will make its main attack along the center from the line Zablocie Borowe—Guty (southern) (a 3-kilometer breakthrough front) in the direction of Zabiczin and Nasielsk.

   The army's immediate objective is to break through the enemy's defensive front and by the close of the operation's first day reach the line excluding Nasielsk—Wongrodno—Psucin—Brody.

   Subsequently, while outflanking Modlin from the north and attacking to the west, the army is to prevent the withdrawal by the enemy's Warsaw group of forces behind the Vistula River and be ready to force it west of Modlin.

   The army will be reinforced with a single tank corps for operations west of Modlin.

   In breaking through the enemy's defense, the artillery and mortar (76mm and higher) density along the breakthrough sector is to be no less than 210 tubes per kilometer of front.

   There is to be no less than one rifle corps in the army reserve.

   From 5.01.1945 the army's headquarters will be in Dacha Popovo, with its axis of movement along the line Wongrodno—Lelewo—Szczytno.

9. The 49th Army (the number of effectives is in the supplement) is to firmly defend the line along the eastern bank of the Narew River from Nowogrod to Chelstow and the bridgehead along the sector Mylnarz—Sendzenta with one rifle corps; the army's main forces, taking advantage of the breakthrough of the enemy's defensive front along the 3rd Army's sector, will attack in the general direction of Myszyniec upon the latter army's reaching the line Rafaly-Glinki—Wlociane.

   The army's immediate objective, while rolling up the enemy's defense along the western bank of the Narew River, is to reach the line Kurpiewski Gury—Durlasy—Cerpenta—excluding Jednorozec.

   Subsequently, while solidly protecting the *front's* main group of forces against attacks from the north, the army is to reach the front Nowogrod—Klein-Dankheim no later than the operation's tenth day.

   To the right is the 50th Army, with the boundary along the line Sniadowo—Ptaki (all locales except for Ptaki are for the 49th Army).

   The army's headquarters is in Rososz, with its axis of movement along the line Slawkowo—Nowa Weis—Aleksandrowo—Myszyniec.

10. The 50th Army (the number of effectives is in the supplement) is to securely defend the line of the forward edge of the woods one kilometer northwest of Augustow—Nadawki—the southern edge of the woods two kilometers southeast of Nadawki, then along the eastern banks of the Netta River—Augustow Canal—Biebrza River as far as Gelczin—along the eastern and southern banks of the Narew River as far as Nowogrod. Special attention should be paid to defending the bridgehead west and southwest of Augustow, as well as the following axes: Augustow, Grodno, Wizna, Bialystok, Lomza, and Zambrow.

    The army is to have five rifle divisions and three fortified areas in the first line. The army reserve will consist of two rifle divisions, of which one will be in the Dombrowa area and the other in the Knyszyn—Tykocin area.

    The security of the boundary with the 49th Army is the responsibility of the commander of the 50th Army.

    Army headquarters from 25.12.1944 is in Choroszcz.

11. By the morning of 9.01.1945 the 5th Guards Tank Army is to concentrate in the Ostrow Mazowiecka area and be ready to be committed into the fighting approximately along the line Przasnysz—Ciechanow, in the general direction of Mlawa and Lidzbark.

12. By 9.01.1945 the 3rd Guards Cavalry Corps is to concentrate in the Goworowo—Dombrowka—Kaszewiec—Zaorze—Paseki area; by the morning of 9.01.1945 the 8th Mechanized Corps is to concentrate in the Wasewo—Jemeliste—Plewki—Grondy—Rynek—Kolonia Wasewo area.

The 3rd Guards Cavalry Corps and the 8th Mechanized Corps are to be ready for joint operations in the 3rd Army's sector in the general direction of Neidenburg and Allenstein, with the objective of capturing the Allenstein area by the 5-6th day of the operation, to cut the enemy's most important communications and prevent an attack by his reserves from the north.

13. The *front* reserve: 369th Rifle Division in the Zambrowo area and the 330th Rifle Division in the Sniadowo area; the 27th Anti-Tank Artillery Brigade in the woods 1.5 kilometers west of Ostrow Mazowiecka; the 35th Anti-Tank Artillery Brigade in the woods three kilometers southwest of Wasewo; the 15th Anti-Tank Artillery Brigade and the 33rd Independent Mortar Brigade in the woods north of Dzbondzbek

14. Artillery:
   a) an artillery group is to be created along the armies' shock axes with a density of no less than 210-220 tubes per kilometer of front (76mm and higher);
   b) the concentration and deployment of the artillery is to be carried out observing all masking measures;
   c) the artillery's main task is to support the breakthrough of the entire tactical zone of the enemy's defense and the subsequent accompaniment of the infantry and break-through development echelon throughout the entire depth of the operation;
   d) during the pursuit the heavy artillery should be in the armies' reserve, in readiness to be deployed for breaking through the enemy's intermediate defensive lines;
   e) the anti-aircraft plan should call for the reliable coverage of the troops in their jumping-off positions for the offensive and the constant accompaniment of the troops by anti-aircraft reinforcements;
   f) the planning of the artillery offensive is to be carried out according to the army commanders' plans, followed by my confirmation.

15. Air Force—4th Air Army:
   a) no less than 1,000 PO-2 sorties are to be carried out on the night before the offensive, for the purpose of exhausting the enemy's personnel, destroying his firing points along the forward edge, disrupting the work of his headquarters, and blocking the main dirt roads and railroads, bases and airfields;
   b) on the operation's first day the main air attack should be launched along the sectors of the 48th and 2nd Shock armies with a force of no less than four assault air divisions, assist the 65th and 70th armies with no less than an assault air division. Bomber aviation is to operate against the movements and concentrations of the enemy's troops, headquarters and junctions in the depth;
   c) the commander of the 4th Air Army is to have the commanders of those air formations supporting the armies at the command posts of those army commanders;
   d) plan for the operational transfer of one assault air division each to the 48th, 2nd Shock and 65th armies, and an assault air corps and a fighter corps to the 5th Guards Tank Army on the operation's second day. Upon the commitment of the mobile formations assault aviation is to be assigned to accompany these formations.
   e) fighter aviation will cover the troops in their jumping-off positions and throughout the entire depth of the operation;

16. Armored and mechanized forces:
    a) independent tank and self-propelled artillery regiments are to be employed for the immediate accompaniment of the infantry;
    b) upon the breakthrough of the enemy's defense by the *front's* army, the tank corps are to be committed into the breach for carrying out the *front's* assignment, and while carrying out these assignments they will be subordinated to the army commanders for developing the success throughout the entire depth;
    c) the commander of the *front's* armored and mechanized forces is to ensure the armored and mechanized forces' complete readiness by 5.01.1945, to organize their uninterrupted supply of munitions and fuel, and the evacuation and restoration of tanks and self-propelled artillery during the course of the operation.

17. Engineering troops:
    a) conduct uninterrupted engineering reconnaissance of the enemy's obstacles, for the purpose of informing the troops in a timely manner and rendering the discovered obstacles harmless;
    b) secure the passage in a timely manner of all the combat arms through the anti-personnel and anti-tank minefields in front of the forward edge and in the depth of the enemy's defense;
    c) secure the rapid passage of the troops and equipment through the difficult sectors by means of the timely forward dispatch of ready-made materials and parts for building bridges, corduroy roads and tread roads;
    d) secure the rapid consolidation of occupied lines with engineering obstacles;
    e) be ready to maneuver obstacle equipment (mobile obstacle detachments) to the axes of the enemy's counterattacks.

18. All preparatory measures should be carried out according to the *front's* combat order no. 00109/op of 14.12.1944.

    The reconnaissance of one's own attack sector with officers, down to regimental commanders inclusively, should be completed by 1.01.1945.

    No more than two days before the start of the offensive should be devoted to working out of the offensive tasks with the battalion commanders.

    Assignments should be passed down to company commanders inclusively a day before the offensive.

19. Army offensive plans should be presented for my confirmation on 1.01.1945.

20. The troops should be completely ready for the offensive, according to my instructions personally to the army commanders.

    Supplement: the *front's* effective strength.[33]

Commander of the Second Belorussian Front, Marshal of the Soviet Union Rokossovskii
Member of the Second Belorussian Front's Military Council, Lieutenant General Subbotin
Chief of Staff of the Second Belorussian Front, Lieutenant General Bogolyubov

---

33 Editor's note. The supplement is not included.

24. Directive of the *Stavka* VGK No. 220284. To the Commander of the Second Belorussian Front on the Confirmation of the Operational Plan for the Defeat of the Enemy's Przasnysz—Mlawa Group of Forces[34]

22 December 1944

The *Stavka* of the Supreme High Command confirms the operational plan presented by you[35] and orders:

1. The gap between the infantry and the cavalry and tank formations operating ahead of it should not be allowed to exceed 25-30 kilometers.

2. The employment of a mechanized corps or a tank corps alongside the cavalry is not required and should be allowed only in cases of particular necessity.

3. Keep in mind, that Popov's 8th Guards Tank Corps, Vol'skii's 5th Guards Tank Army, consisting of Sakhno's 10th Tank Corps and Malakhov's 29th Tank Corps, should be completely up to strength by the start of the offensive.
    Panov's 1st Guards Tank Corps will receive heavy tanks and heavy self-propelled guns up to 100 vehicles, which will make it more combat-capable.
    Panfilov's 3rd Guards Tank Corps is assigned to the *front*, in order to bring it up to strength during the second half of January. In connection with this, it is recommended to strengthen the *front's* left wing with Panov's 1st Guards Tank Corps.

4. Don't count on a *Stavka* reserve in the Bialystok area.

Stavka of the Supreme High Command
I. Stalin
A. Antonov

---

34 *Velikaya Otechestvennaya*, 5(4):184.
35 Editor's note. See document no. 22.

25. Directive of the Commander of the First Ukrainian Front No. 001472 (490)/op. To the Army Commanders on the Defeat of the Kielce—Radom Group of Enemy Forces[36]

23 December 1944, 1705 hrs

The First Ukrainian Front's forces are to break through the enemy's defense along the Rakow—Metel sector and launch their main attack along the axis Chmielnik—Malogoszcz—Radomsko, for the purpose of defeating, in conjunction with the First Belorussian Front, the enemy's Kielce—Radom group of forces and reach the line Piotrkow—Radomsko—Czestochowa—Zawiercie—Miechow—Bochnia; the *front* will subsequently develop the offensive in the general direction of Breslau.

I order:

1. To the commander of the 13th Army. To break through the enemy's defense along the Rakow—Szydlow sector. The main attack is to be launched in the general direction of Rudki, Pierczhnica, Checiny, Lopuszno, Czermno, and Rozprza.

    In conjunction with the 4th Tank Army, develop a vigorous offensive and prevent the enemy from organizing a defense along prepared lines along the Czarna, Nida and Pilica rivers. The main forces are to capture the following lines: Trzemeszno—Szczecno—Pierczhnica—excluding Suchowola by the close of the operation's first day; Czarnow—Zgorsko—Lukowo by the close of the second day, while part of the army's forces are to attack from the west to assist the 3rd Guards Army in taking Kielce; by the close of the operation's third day the army will reach the line Oblengor—Losenek-Vloscianskii—Malogoszca.

    Boundary lines: to the right, with the 3rd Guards Army—Selec—Gorne—Bogoria—Rakow—Smykow—Kielce—Ruda Maleniecka—Piotrkow (all locales except Bogoria are for the 13th Army); on the left, with the 52nd Army—Mechocin—Koprzywnica—Staszow—Szydlow—Lubania—Malogoszcz—Kluczewsko—Socerny (all locales except Staszow and Socerny are for the 13th Army).

2. To the commander of the 52nd Army. To break through the enemy's defense along the sector excluding Szydlow—excluding Dolna.

    The main attack will be launched in the general direction of Chmielnik, Korytnica, Wloszczowa, and Radomsko.

    The army is to develop a vigorous offensive and, in conjunction with the 3rd Guards Tank Army, prevent the enemy from organizing a defense along the prepared lines along the Nida and Pilica rivers.

    The army's main forces are to reach the following lines: Chmielnik—Mlyny by the close of the operation's first day; Michalinowka—Koprzywnica—excluding Sobowice by the end of the operation's second day, and; excluding Malogoszcz—Mniszek—Przonslaw by the close of the operation's third day.

    The boundary line on the left with the 5th Guards Army is Baranow—Osiek—Niziny—Dolna—Brzece—Koniecpol—Borowno (all locales except for Baranow, Dolna and Borowno are for the 52nd Army).

---

36 *Velikaya Otechestvennaya*, 5(4):316-20.

3. To the commander of the 5th Guards Army. To break through the enemy's defense along the Dolna—Metel sector.

   The main attack is to be launched in the general direction of Stopnica, Busko-Zdroj—Pinczow—Szczekociny—Czestochowa.

   The army is to commit on the operation's first day the 31st and 4th Guards tank corps, with the objective of vigorously developing the offensive and preventing the enemy from organizing a defense along the Nida River and, by the close of the operation's first day, to reach the area: 31st Tank Corps—Pinczow—Skrzipow—Zakrzow; 4th Guards Tank Corps—Neprowice—Zlota—Jurkow.

   The army's main forces are to reach the following lines: Wygoda—Busko-Zdroj—Chotel—Czerwony by the close of the operation's first day; Sobowice—Michalow—Sadsk by the close of the operation's second day; the 31st Tank Corps is to reach the area Niegoslawice—Brzezinki—Wolia Lubecka.

   By the close of the operation's third day the army's main forces are to reach the line Perszen—Wodzislaw—Maly Kszenz. On the morning of the operation's second day the 4th Guards Tank Corps is to be subordinated to the commander of the 59th Army.

   The boundary line on the left is the line Bugai—Pacanow—Chotel—Czerwony—Zarnowiece—Kamienica Polska (all locales within the 5th Guards Army).

4. To the commander of the 60th Army. In order to support the operation from the south, a group of forces, consisting of five divisions and, taking advantage of the breakthrough along the 5th Guards Army's left flank, is to develop the offensive with the immediate objective of destroying the enemy along the northern bank of the Vistula River; subsequently, while covering itself along the Vistula River with two divisions, three divisions are to continue the offensive in the direction of Kamimierz Welka, Proszowice and Krakow.

   By the close of the operation's first day the army is to reach the line excluding Chotel—Czerwony—Szczerbakow—Nowy Korczyn; by the close of the operation's second day Swoszowice—Zbeltowice—Przemykow, and; by the close of the operation's third day Winiary—Koscielec—Sieroslawice.

   The army is to subsequently, in conjunction with the 59th Army, take Krakow.

   The army is to solidly defend south of the Vistula River with four divisions.

   Boundary lines: on the right as far as the Nida, with the 5th Guards Army, Bugai—Pacanow—Chotel—Czerwony (all locales for the 60th Army); from the Nida River with the 59th Army, Wislica—Skalmierz—Slomniki (all locales except for Skalmierz are for the 60th Army); to the left, the boundary with the Fourth Ukrainian Front is Przemysl—Jaslo—Bochnia—Niepolomice (all locales except for Przemysl and Niepolomice are for the 60th Army).

5. To the commander of the 59th Army. The army is to be ready from the line of the Nida River to develop the offensive in the general direction of Dzialoszyce and Miechow, with the objective of supporting the *front's* main group of forces from the southwest.

   With one rifle corps and the 4th Guards Tank Corps outflanking Krakow from the north and northwest, the army, in conjunction with the 60th Army, is to take Krakow.

6. To the commander of the 3rd Guards Army. The army and the 25th Tank Corps are to be committed from behind the 13th Army's right-flank breakthrough.

   The army is to launch its attack with its main forces (six divisions and the 25th Tank Corps) in the direction of Rakow, Daleszyce, Skarzysko-Kamienna, and Sydlowiec, turning the enemy's Ostrowiec defensive system from the west. The objective is to surround and destroy the Kielce—Radom enemy group of forces in conjunction with units of the First Belorussian Front.

By the close of the operation's second day one of the army's rifle corps, in conjunction with units of the 13th Army, is to capture Kielce by a turning move from the north.

Part of the army's main group of forces is to launch a supporting attack in the rear of the enemy's Ostrowiec—Opatow group of forces.

The army is to reach the following lines: excluding Lagow—Widelki—Huta Szklana by the close of the operation's first day; Slupia—Jeziorko—Ciekoty—Kielce by the close of the operation's second day, and; Kunow—Wierzbnik—Suchedniow—Bobrza by the close of the operation's third day.

The boundary with the 6th Army is Sandomierz—Penchow—Iwaniska—Wszachow— Podlasie—Skaly (all locales except for Penchow and Iwaniska are for the 3rd Guards Army.

7. Artillery. The artillery's objective is to destroy and suppress the enemy's defense throughout his entire tactical depth; to destroy and suppress his artillery-mortar system, personnel and equipment and to destroy the enemy's defensive structures; to suppress his headquarters and communications centers.

The artillery preparation is to last one hour and 50 minutes.

The expenditure of artillery shells and mortar rounds on the operation's first day will be 2.0 combat loads.

The artillery offensive is to be carried out according to the attached schedule.[37]

During the breakthrough the breakthrough artillery is to be distributed as followed: the 1st and 13th artillery divisions for the 13th Army; the 4th and 31st artillery divisions for the 52nd Army, and; the 3rd and 17th artillery divisions and 3rd Guards Mortar Division for the 5th Guards Army.

8. To the commander of the 4th Tank Army. The army is to be committed into the breach along the 13th Army's sector. The army is to vigorously develop the offensive in the direction of Pierzchnica, Piekoszowie, Radoszyce, and Rozprza, with the task of destroying the retreating enemy and his arriving reserves, and reaching the path of retreat of the enemy's Kielce— Radom group of forces.

Bear in mind that the army is to be in combat cooperation with the forces of the First Belorussian Front in the Lodz area.

By the close of the operation's second day the army is to reach the line of the Czarna Nida River and reach the Bobrza—Rykoszin platform—Nepachlow area; to assist the 13th and 3rd Guards armies in taking Kielce by an attack from the northwest.

By the close of the operation's third day the army is to reach the Radoszyce—Czermno— Mnin area; its forward detachments are to capture the crossings over the Pilica River along the Sulejow—Przedbuz sector.

The army will subsequently reach the Piotrkow—Rozprza—Gorzkowice area.

Flanking and reconnaissance detachments are to capture the Wolow, Konskie and Zarnow road junctions.

During the offensive the army is to coordinate with the 3rd Guards Tank Army's right-flank units.

---

37 Editor's note. This schedule is not included.

9. To the commander of the 3rd Guards Tank Army. The army is to be committed into the breach along the 52nd Army's sector. The army is to vigorously develop the offensive in the direction of Duza, Jedrzejow, Wloszczowa, and Radomsko. One corps is to be moved into the army's second echelon, echeloned to the left.

    The army's task is to destroy the retreating enemy, defeat his arriving reserves, and to prevent the enemy from occupying his prepared defensive lines along the Nida and Pilica rivers.

    By the close of the operation's second day the army is to reach the area Zarczice Duze—Oksa—Naglowice—Jedrzejow.

    By the close of the operation's third day the army is to reach the area Krurzelew—Secemin—Modrzew; forward detachments are to seize crossings over the Pilica River in the Mosty—Koniecpol area.

    The Radomsko—Plawno—Cadow area is to be subsequently captured.

    From the line of the Pilica River a powerful flank guard is to be dispatched toward Czestochowa area.

    Reconnaissance is to be carried out toward Wodzislaw, Szczekociny and Lelow, establishing combat cooperation with the 5th Guards Army's 31st Tank Corps.

10. To the commander of the 6th Army. The army's main objective in the first part of the *front's* operation is a static defense, particularly along the sector of the Sandomierz bridgehead. The army is to subsequently be ready to pursue and destroy, together with the 3rd Guards Army, the enemy's Opatow—Ostrowiec group of forces.

11. To the commander of the 21st Army. Following the breakthrough, the army is to follow one march behind the center of the *front's* main group of forces. The army's main axis of movement is Baranow—Staszow—Chmielnik—Jedrzejow—Wloszczowa—Radomsko.

    The army will be employed subsequently for augmenting the attack along the main direction.

12. To the commander of the 2nd Air Army. To cover the concentration by the *front's* main group of forces along the Sandomierz bridgehead and the crossings over the Vistula River.

    To win air superiority and maintain it throughout the entire operation by fighting the enemy's aviation in the air and by blocking his airfields.

    The air army will support the *front's* forces in breaking through the enemy's defense through massed air strikes by bombers and assault aircraft against the enemy's artillery positions, communications centers and personnel.

    The air army will launch strikes against the enemy's arriving reserves and his retreating forces and prevent him from occupying defensive positions along the Nida and Pilica rivers.

    The air army will assist the *front's* right-wing forces with massed strikes to destroy the enemy's Kielce group of forces.

    The air army will support from the air the commitment of the tank armies into the breach and support their operations in the depth with assault and fighter aviation.

    The air army will destroy the enemy's crossings over the Vistula River along the Nowy Korczin—Krakow sector on the operation's first day.

    In order to support the troops in the offensive and support with the armies, the following units are designated:

    • 13th Army—an air division from the 2nd Guards Assault Air Corps and an air division from the 2nd Fighter Corps;

    • 52nd Army—the 1st Guards Assault Air Corps and a division from the 6th Guards Fighter Corps;

- 5th Guards Army—the 3rd Assault Air Corps and the 5th Fighter Corps.
- Upon the commitment of the tank armies into the breach, they are to be supported by:
- 4th Tank Army—an assault air division from the 2nd Guards Assault Air Corps and an air division from the 2nd Fighter Corps;
- 3rd Guards Tank Army—an assault air division from the 1st Guards Assault Air Corps and an air division from the 6th Guards Fighter Corps.

With the commitment of the 59th Army into the battle, it is to be supported by an assault air division from the 3rd Assault Air Corps and an air division from the 5th Fighter Corps.

Be prepared to support the 3rd Guards Army with two assault air corps and one fighter corps. My reserve consists of two fighter divisions from the 6th Guards Fighter Corps, the 2nd Guards Bomber and 4th Bomber corps, and the 208th Night Bomber Division.

13. The *front* reserve: 7th Guards Mechanized Corps in the area of the woods east of Maidan; 1st Guards Cavalry Corps—in the Rozwadow—Stale—Nisko area (all locales excluded).

14. The troops' readiness for the offensive is to be in accordance with personal instructions.
    The jumping-off position is to be occupied for the beginning of the offensive is to be carried out according to a special order.

15. Inform as to reception. Report on readiness by special messenger.

Commander of the First Ukrainian Front, Marshal of the Soviet Union Konev
Member of the First Ukrainian Front's Military Council, Lieutenant General Krainyukov
Chief of Staff of the First Ukrainian Front, General Sokolovskii

26. Report of the Commander of the First Belorussian Front No. 01223/op. To the Supreme Commander-in-Chief on the Plan for the Defeat of the Enemy's Warsaw—Radom Group of Forces[38]

25 December 1944

1. The *front's* immediate objective is to defeat the enemy's Warsaw and Radom groups of forces and, no later than the offensive's twelfth day, the combined-arms armies' main forces are to reach the front Piotrkow—Zychlin—Lodz. The front will subsequently develop the offensive in the general direction of Poznan.

2. Along the forward edge of the 235-kilometer front, the enemy has in the first line up to nine infantry divisions, a panzer division, an independent security regiment, and 11 independent battalions, reinforced with two high command artillery regiments, nine high command artillery battalions, five battalions of high command assault weapons, a high command panzer battalion, four high command anti-tank battalions, three high command mortar regiments, and two high command mortar battalions.

    In the second line the enemy has four panzer divisions, an independent infantry regiment, and ten independent battalions.

    There are more than seven divisions in reserve in the following areas:

- Blonie—presumably the 383rd Infantry Division, and in the Legonice (four kilometers west of Nowe-Miasto)—Tomaszow area an infantry division of unknown number.

- Radom—a "*volksgrenadier*" division of unknown number and, presumably, the 174th Reserve Division.

- Lodz—Pabianice—the 73rd "*Volksgrenadier*" Division and the 431st Reserve Division.

- Lask—Zdunska Wola—presumably the 620th "*Volksgrenadier*" Division.

- Piotrkow—the 604th Security Regiment and a panzer battalion of unknown number.

    Aside from this, the enemy may employ against the *front* his reserves located in the following areas: Plock—the 432nd Reserve Division; Wierzbnik—Lubien (east of Wierzbnik)—the 16th Panzer Division.

    The enemy's densest group of forces and most developed defense is opposite our bridgeheads along the western bank of the Vistula River.

    Opposite the bridgehead southeast of Warka the enemy has in the first line more than three infantry divisions, reinforced with a single high command artillery regiment, two high command artillery battalions, two high command brigades of assault guns, one anti-tank battalion, and one mortar regiment of unknown number. Facing the bridgehead southwest of Pulawy are more than two infantry divisions, reinforced with a high command artillery regiment, four high command artillery battalions, two brigades of high command assault guns, one high command anti-tank battalion, and a high command mortar battalion.

    In the second line there are in the following areas: Michalow (12 kilometers southwest of Warka)—Wysmierzyce—Czarnocin (20 kilometers west of Jedlinsk)—Stromiec—a panzer division of unknown number; Stanislawice (five kilometers west of Kozienice)—Stare Makosy

(13 kilometers east of Jedlinsk)—Pionki—presumably the 25th Panzer Division; Zwolen—19th Panzer Division.

3. The start of the operation is in accordance with your personal instructions.

4. The armies' objectives by day and line.

The 61st Army, consists of the 9th Guards Rifle Corps (12th, 75th Guards and 415th rifle divisions), 80th Rifle Corps (82nd, 212th and 356th rifle divisions), 89th Rifle Corps (23rd, 311th and 397th rifle divisions), the 119th Fortified Area, 4th Corps Artillery Brigade, 25th Anti-Tank Artillery Regiment, 59th and 41st guards mortar regiments, 88th Heavy Tank Regiment, 85th Tank Regiment, 5th Independent Motorized Pontoon-Bridge Battalion, 13th Independent Motorized Pontoon-Bridge Battalion, 2nd and 3rd motorized engineer battalions (1st Guards Motorized Engineer Brigade), the 81st and 82nd engineer battalions (17th Assault Engineer Sapper Brigade), and the 29th Independent Chemical Defense Battalion. Besides this, during the breakthrough of the enemy's main defensive zone, the 61st Army is to be reinforced with the 3rd Shock Army's artillery (nine artillery regiments from the rifle divisions, one artillery brigade, one anti-tank artillery regiment, and one army mortar regiment) and the Polish 1st Army's artillery (one artillery brigade and one howitzer brigade), and the 2nd Guards Cavalry Corps' artillery (one anti-tank artillery regiment, one mortar regiment, and one guards mortar regiment). The breakthrough front is four kilometers. The artillery density is 226 tubes per kilometer of front along the breakthrough sector.

The army's objective is to break through the enemy's defense along the Ostroleka—Pilica sector and with part of its forces attack along the left flank in conjunction with the 5th Shock Army and, while developing the attack in the general direction of Gonski, Drawlew and Tarczyn, reach the following lines:

a) on the operation's first day—Podguzice—Gonski—Laski—Grzegorzewice;
b) on the operation's fourth day—Wolka—Dworska (five kilometers north of Gora Kalwaria)—Dobesz—Los—Tarczyn—Bystrzanow—Karolew—Jozefow (14 kilometers southwest of Tarczyn).

Subsequently, part of the army's forces are to launch an attack along the Tarczyn—Grodzisk—Blonie axis for the purpose of, in conjunction with the Polish 1st Army and the 47th Army, destroying the enemy's Warsaw group of forces, while the army's main forces attack in the general direction of Grodzisk, Sochaczew and Kutno, and on the operation's twelfth day reach the line excluding Luszyn (30 kilometers northeast of Kutno)—Zychlin—Bedlno—Wieliszew—Orlow (18 kilometers southeast of Kutno).

The boundary lines are as follows:

a) to the right, Latowicz—Gora Kalwaria—Golkow (five kilometers southwest of Piaseczno)—Blonie—Sochaczew—Kiernozia—Luszyn (all locales except Blonie and Sochaczew are for the 61st Army);
b) to the left, Garwolin—Skurcze—Grabow Zalesny—Marynki—Gosnewice—Mszczonow—Lowicz—Sobota—Orlow (18 kilometers southeast of Kutno). All locales except for Garwolin and Lowicz are for the 61st Army.

The 5th Guards Army consists of the 9th Rifle Corps (230th, 248th and 301st rifle divisions), 26th Guards Rifle Corps (89th, 94th Guards and 226th rifle divisions), 32nd Rifle Corps (60th Guards, 295th and 416th rifle divisions), with the 6th and 22nd artillery divisions, 3rd and 40th anti-tank artillery brigades, 34th Heavy Caliber Artillery Battalion, 22nd and 23rd guards mortar brigades (5th Guards Mortar Division), 316th and 94th guards mortar regiments, 2nd Guard Anti-Aircraft Division, 220th Independent Tank Brigade, 89th Guards Heavy Tank Regiment, 396th Guards Self-Propelled Artillery Regiment, 91st Mine-Sweeper Tank Regiment, 63rd and 138th motorized pontoon-bridge battalions (7th Motorized Pontoon-Bridge Brigade), 4th and 7th motorized engineer battalions (7th Guards Motorized Engineer Brigade), 83rd, 84th and 85th battalions (17th Assault Engineer-Sapper Brigade), 25th Independent Chemical Defense Battalion, and the 10th Independent Flamethrower-Chemical Battalion.

Besides this, during the breakthrough of the enemy's main defensive zone, the army is to be reinforced with the 2nd Guards Tank Army's artillery (one light artillery brigade, two light artillery regiments, one army mortar regiment, and one guards mortar regiment).

The breakthrough front is six kilometers. The artillery density is 250 tubes per kilometer of breakthrough front.

The army's objective is to break through the enemy's defense along the Wybrowa—(excluding) Stszirzina sector and, while developing the attack in the general direction of Borze, Brankow, Goszczyn, and Bledow, reach the following lines:

a)   on the operation's first day—Opodrzew—Stare Biskunice—Paulin—Brankow—Pokrzwyna—Stromiec;

b)   on the operation's fourth day—Bronislawow—Wygnanka—Dankow—Biala Rawska.

Subsequently, while developing the attack in the general direction of Skierniewice and Piontek, by the operation's twelfth day the army's main forces are to reach the front excluding Orlow (18 kilometers southeast of Kutno)—Wlostowice—Piontek—Borowiec.

The boundary line on the left is Leokadia—Magnuszew—Tszeben—Cecylowka—Stary Ksawerow—Stromiec—Bialobrzegi—Pszybyszow—Kurzeszyn—Glowno—Leczyca   (all locales except Cecylowka are for the 5th Shock Army).

The 8th Guards Army consists of the 29th Guards Rifle Corps (27th, 74th and 82nd guards rifle divisions), 28th Guards Corps (39th, 79th and 88th guards rifle divisions), 4th Guards Rifle Corps (35th, 47th and 57th guards rifle divisions), with the 6th Artillery Corps, 41st and 38th anti-tank artillery brigades, 295th Artillery Brigade, 32nd Heavy Caliber Artillery Battalion, 1st Heavy Artillery Regiment, 16th Guards Mortar Brigade (5th Guards Mortar Division), 92nd and 311th guards mortar regiments, 3rd Guards Anti-Aircraft Division, 34th Heavy Tank Regiment, 259th Tank Regiment, 65th Tank Regiment, 394th and 351st heavy self-propelled artillery regiments, 371st, 694th and 1504th self-propelled artillery regiments, 61st and 136th motorized pontoon-bridge battalions (7th Motorized Pontoon-Bridge Brigade), 6th, 7th and 8th assault engineer-sapper brigades, 41st Flamethrower Battalion, 166th Minesweeper Tank Regiment, 516th Flamethrower Tank Regiment, (2nd Assault Engineer-Sapper Brigade), 71st and 72nd military construction detachments (27th Defense Construction Directorate), 19th Independent Flamethrower Chemical Battalion, and the 10th Independent Chemical Defense Battalion.

Besides this, during the breakthrough of the enemy's main defense zone the army is to be reinforced with the 1st Guards Tank Army's artillery (one light artillery brigade, one light artillery regiment, two army mortar regiments, and one guards mortar regiment).

The breakthrough front is seven kilometers. The artillery density is 250 tubes per kilometer of breakthrough front.

The army's objective is to break through the enemy's defense along the Matyldzin—Chmielnik sector and, developing the attack along the axis Lipa—Wychowanie, reach on the first day the line excluding Stromiec—Kalinowo—Franciszkow—Bartosy—Goryn.

Subsequently, it is to launch an attack toward Jadlinsk and Radom with a reinforced corps, for the purpose of, in conjunction with the 69th Army, defeating the enemy's Radom group of forces.

The army's main forces are to attack in the general direction of Nowe-Miasto, Rawa Mazowiecka, Jezow, Strykow, and Ozorkow and reach the following lines:

a) on the operation's fourth day—Slupce—Turobowice—Przyluski—Jankowice— Rozanna—Wysokin—Odrzwole;

b) on the operation's twelfth day—Borowiec—Astachowice—Dzerzonrzna—Zgierz.

The boundary line on the left is Jablonowiec—Opatkowice—Stanislawow—Lewaszowka— Radomka River, as far as Przytyk, Odrzwole, Zreczicy, Zrakowice, and Zgierz (all locales except for Lewaszowka are for the 8th Guards Army).

The 2nd Guards Tank Army consists of the 9th Guards Tank Corps, 12th Guards Tank Corps and the 1st Mechanized Corps, with the 3rd Anti-Tank Artillery Brigade, 316th Guards Mortar Regiment, 24th Anti-Aircraft Division, 4th Independent Motorized Pontoon-Bridge Regiment, and the 25th Independent Chemical Defense Battalion. Upon the 5th Shock Army's tanks and infantry reaching the line Gnewice—Zaborow—Goszczyn—Przybyszew, on the operation's third day, the tank army is to enter the breach along the sector Gnewice— Zaborow—Goszczyn and, while developing the attack in the general direction of Mszczonow, Sochaczew and Gombin into the rear of the enemy's Warsaw group of forces, is to cut off its path of retreat to the southwest and west from the Warsaw area and on the operation's fifth day reach the Gorki (five kilometers southwest of Plock)—Gostynin—Strzelce (ten kilometers north of Kutno)—Sanniki area.

Subsequently, the tank army is to develop the attack toward Kowal, Brzesc-Kujawski, Radziejow, and Inowroclaw.

The commander of the 5th Shock Army is responsible for the engineering support of the 2nd Guards Tank Army's commitment into the breach.

Air support is the responsibility of the commander of the 16th Air Army.

The 1st Guards Tank Army consists of the 11th Guards Tank Corps, 8th Guards Mechanized Corps, and the 64th Tank Brigade, with the 41st Anti-Tank Artillery Brigade, 92nd Guards Mortar Regiment, 1st Independent Motorized Pontoon-Bridge Regiment, and the 10th Independent Chemical Defense Battalion. Upon the 8th Guards Army's infantry and tanks reaching the line Bobrek—Romanow—Lisow on the operation's second day, the tank army is to enter the breach along the Urbanow—Lisow sector and, developing the attack in the general direction of Zdzar, Mlodynie Dolne, Nowe-Miasto, Rawa Mazowiecka, Skierniewice, Lowicz, and Kutno, reach the following areas:

a) on the second day following the commitment into the breach—Zelazna Nowa (six kilometers north of Nowe-Miasto)—Namglowy (17 kilometers northwest of Nowe-Miasto)—Bartoszowka—Nowe-Miasto;

b) on the third day following the commitment into the breach—Kompina—Lowicz— Lyszkowice—Belchow—Bolimow;

c) on the fourth day following the commitment into the breach—Kutno—Lenczica— Piontek.

The army is to subsequently develop the attack toward Klodawa, Kolo, Konin, and Poznan.

The commander of the 8th Guards Army is responsible for the artillery and engineering support of the 1st Guards Tank Army's commitment into the breach.

Aviation support is the responsibility of the commander of the 16th Air Army.

The 2nd Guards Cavalry Corps, consisting of the 3rd, 4th and 17th guards cavalry divisions, the 160th, 184th and 189th tank regiments, 1459th Self-Propelled Artillery Regiment, 2nd Guards Anti-Tank Artillery Battalion, 149th Guards Anti-Tank Artillery Regiment, 60th Independent Mortar Battalion, 10th Guards Mortar Regiment, and the 173rd Independent Anti-Aircraft Battalion, upon the arrival of the 5th Shock Army's infantry and tanks at the line Lewiczyn (seven kilometers south of Grojec)—Olszew—Sielec (12 kilometers northwest of Bialobrzegi) on the operation's third day, the cavalry corps is to be committed into the breach behind the 2nd Guards Tank Army along the sector Julianow—Olszew—Sielec and, while developing the success in the general direction of Biala Rawska, Skierniewice and Lowicz, the corps' main forces are to reach the following areas:

a)   on the first day of the commitment into the breach—Biala Rawska;
b)   on the second day of the commitment into the breach—Lowicz.

Subsequently, in conjunction with the 2nd Guards Tank Army, the corps will develop the success in the general direction of Kowal, Brzesc-Kujawski, Radzeow, and Inowroclaw.

Aviation support for the 2nd Guards Cavalry Corps' commitment into the breach and its operations in depth are the responsibility of the commander of the 16th Air Army.

The 69th Army consists of the 25th Rifle Corps (4th and 41st and the 77th Guards Rifle divisions), 61st Rifle Corps (134th, 247th and 274th rifle divisions), 91st Rifle Corps (117th, 312th and 370th rifle divisions), with the 12th Artillery Division, 4th and 8th anti-tank artillery brigades, 293rd Army Mortar Regiment, 2nd Guards Mortar Brigade, 37th and 303rd guards mortar regiments, 18th Anti-Aircraft Division, 11th Tank Corps, 68th Independent Tank Brigade, 33rd Heavy Tank Regiment, 12th Self-Propelled Artillery Brigade, 85th Independent Motorized Bridge-Pontoon Battalion, 21st, 25th and 220th military construction detachments (7th Front Defensive Construction Directorate), and the 40th Independent Chemical Defense Battalion.

Besides this, during the breakthrough the army is to be reinforced by the artillery of the 7th Guards Cavalry Corps (one anti-tank artillery regiment, one mortar battalion, on anti-tank artillery battalion, and one guards mortar regiment). The breakthrough front is seven kilometers. The artillery density is 220 tubes per kilometer of breakthrough front.

The army's objective is to break through the enemy's defense along the Kuroszow—Nowe Lawecko sector and, while developing the attack toward Zwolen, Radom and Glogow, reach the following lines:

a)   on the operation's first day—Gniewoszow—Sarnow—Czarnolas—Luczynow—Nowa Zelenka;
b)   on the operation's fourth day—Rdzow(18 kilometers southeast of Nowe Miasto)—Jamki—Dembiny—Kochanow—Jablonica.

The army is to subsequently attack in the general direction of Drziewica, Tomaszow and Lodz, and on the operation's twelfth day capture the city of Lodz and reach the line excluding Zgierz—Konstantynow—Pabianice.

The boundary line on the left is Wawolnica—Kazimierz—Obliasy Dwor—Zwolen—Makow—Augustow—Przysucha—Belowice—Celestynow—Pabianice (all locales except Wawolnica are for the 69th Army).

The 33rd Army consists of the 16th Rifle Corps (89th, 339th and 383rd rifle divisions), 38th Rifle Corps (64th, 95th and 323rd rifle divisions), 62nd Rifle Corps (49th, 222nd and 362nd rifle divisions), the 115th Fortified Area, 5th Artillery Division, 35th Mortar Brigade, 1091st Artillery Regiment, 20th Anti-Tank Artillery Division, 25th Guards Mortar Brigade, 305th and 56th guards mortar regiments, 64th Anti-Aircraft Division, 9th Tank Corps, 244th Tank

Regiment, 257th Tank Regiment, 360th and 361st self-propelled artillery regiments, and the 33rd Independent Chemical Defense Battalion.

The breakthrough front is six kilometers. The artillery density is 212 tubes per kilometer of breakthrough front.

The army's objective is to break through the enemy's defense along the Rudki—Lucimia River sector and, while developing the attack in the general direction of Sycina, Skaryszew and Dobrut, reach the following lines:

a) by the operation's first day—Stara Zelenka—eastern outskirts of Jasienica—Solecki—Sweselice—Bialobrzegi;

b) by the operation's fourth day—Korycyska—Kozice—Wysocko—Jastszomb—Mirowek—Osiny.

The army's main forces are to subsequently attack in the direction of Szydlowiec, for the purpose of, in conjunction with the First Ukrainian Front's forces, defeating the enemy's Szydlowiec group of forces. Part of the army's forces is to continue attacking toward Politow and Opoczno.

Following the breakthrough of the enemy's defense and the arrival of the mobile forces at the line Radom—Ilza, the 9th Tank Corps is to be removed from its operational subordination to the commander of the 33rd Army and employed, together with the 7th Guards Cavalry Corps, for developing the success in the direction of Tomaszow and Lodz.

The boundary line on the left is Krasnystaw—Jozefow—Ilza—Opoczno (all locales except Krasnystaw and Jozefow are for the 33rd Army).

The 7th Guards Cavalry Corps, consisting of the 14th, 15th and 16th Guards cavalry divisions, the 32nd, 57th and 114th tank regiments, 1816th Self-Propelled Artillery Regiment, 145th Anti-Tank Artillery Regiment, 57th Guards Mortar Battalion, 7th Guards Anti-Tank Artillery Battalion, 7th Guards Mortar Regiment, and the 1733rd Anti-Aircraft Regiment, upon the 33rd Army's infantry and tanks reaching the line Rawiec (14 kilometers southwest of Zwolen)—Zakszuwek—Kowalikow on the operation's third day, enter the breach behind the 9th Tank Corps along the Rawiec (southern)—Kowalikow sector and, while developing the success in the direction of Skaryszew, Pazrniece, Koryciska, Skszinno, Gelnow, Tomaszow, and Lodz, in conjunction with the 9th Tank Corps reach the following lines:

a) on the first day of the commitment into the breach—Mniszek (16 kilometers north of Szydlowiec)—Koryciska—Jankowice (five kilometers north of Szydlowiec)—Guzow (13 kilometers southwest of Radom)—Wolanow;

b) on the second day of the commitment into the breach—Inowlodz—Opoczno—Radzice;

c) on the third day of the commitment into the breach—capture Tomaszow and reach the Ujazd—Laznow—Biskupia Wola—Wolborz area;

d) on the fourth day of the commitment into the breach—to capture Lodz.

The artillery and engineering support for the commitment of the 7th Guards Cavalry Corps is the responsibility of the commander of the 33rd Army.

Aviation support during the commitment into the breach and in the corps' operations in depth is the responsibility of the commander of the 16th Air Army.

The 47th Army consists of the 77th Rifle Corps (234th, 328th and 185th rifle divisions), 125th Rifle Corps (76th, 60th and 175th rifle divisions), and the 129th Rifle Corps (132nd, 143rd and 260th rifle divisions), with the Polish 5th Artillery Brigade, Polish 2nd Howitzer Brigade, 75th Guards Mortar Regiment, 31st Anti-Aircraft Division, 70th Guards Tank Regiment, 334th Self-Propelled Artillery Division, 274th Independent Motorized Battalion,

20th Independent Flamethrower-Chemical Battalion, and the 77th Independent Chemical Defense Battalion.

The breakthrough front is four kilometers. The artillery density is 151 tubes per kilometer of the breakthrough front.

The army's objective on the operation's first day is to carry out a reconnaissance in force along the army's entire front with strong detachments, for the purpose of tying down the enemy.

On the operation's second day it is to break through the enemy's defense along the Koloszyn—excluding Chotomow sector and, while developing the attack toward Nowy Dwor, destroy the "Viking" Panzer Division in the area between the rivers, and on the operation's third day reach the Western Bug and Vistula rivers along the Topolina—Nowy Dwor—Jablonna sector.

The army is to subsequently force the Vistula River along the Nowy Dwor—Jablonna sector and, while developing the attack in the general direction of Lomna, Janowiec and Leszno and, in conjunction with the Polish 1st Army and the 61st Army, destroy the enemy's Warsaw group of forces, after which it is to attack along the Kampinos—Mlodzieszyn—Sanniki axis. On the operation's twelfth day the army is to reach the line Piotrkow—Sanniki—Luszyn (ten kilometers southwest of Sanniki).

The 47th Army cannot attack on the operation's first day because its jumping-off position is enfiladed by flanking fire from all sorts of weapons from the Dembe area. Therefore, in order to avoid excessive losses, the army will attack on the operation's second day, when the Second Belorussian Front's left-flank units capture the Dembe area.

The Polish 1st Army, consisting of the 1st, 2nd, 3rd, 4th, and 6th infantry divisions, the 1st Cavalry Brigade and the 1st Tank Brigade, upon the 61st Army's arrival at the line Gora Kalwaria—Tarczyn and taking advantage of the latter's success, will cross over to the western bank of the Vistula River with its main forces (no less than three infantry divisions) along the sector Gora Kalwaria—Czersk and attack in the direction of Gora Kalwaria, Piaseczno and Pruszkow, with the mission of rolling up the enemy's line along the western bank of the Vistula River and, in conjunction with the 47th and 61st armies, to destroy the enemy's Warsaw group of forces and capture the city and area of Warsaw.

The army is to defend its positions along the Jablonna—Praga—Karczew sector with no more than two infantry divisions.

As the army's main forces advance, the defending units are to cross over to the western bank of the Vistula River, from left to right, and attack toward Warsaw.

The 16th Air Army consists of the following: 6th Assault Air Corps—240 Il-2 aircraft; 9th Assault Air Corps—240 Il-2 aircraft; 2nd Guards Assault Air Division—120 Il-2 aircraft; 11th Guards Assault Air Division—120 Il-2 aircraft; 3rd Fighter Corps—240 Yak-1, Yak-3 and Yak-9 aircraft; 13th Fighter Corps—240 Yak-1, Yak-3 and Yak-9 aircraft; 6th Fighter Corps—240 Yak-3 "Airacobra"[39] aircraft; 1st Guards Fighter Division—120 "Airacobras"; 286th Fighter Division—120 La-5 and La-7 aircraft; 282nd Fighter Division—120 Yak-1 and Yak-9 aircraft; 176th Guards Independent Fighter Regiment—40 La-7 aircraft; 3rd Bomber Corps—192 Pe-2 aircraft; 183rd Bomber Division—96 Pe-2 aircraft; 221st Bomber Division—96 "Boston" aircraft; 9th Guards Night Bomber Division—120 Po-2 aircraft, and; the 242nd Night Bomber Division—120 Po-2 aircraft, for a total of 2,464 aircraft.

Of these, there are 720 assault aircraft, 1,120 fighters, 324 bombers, and 240 night bombers. Aviation employment.

---

39 Editor's note. This was the American-made P-39D fighter, which mounted a single 37mm cannon.

Upon the start of the infantry attack, all of the aviation will work in a centralized manner and on my orders. Within three hours after the beginning of the attack all of the assault aircraft and part of fighter aviation will be resubordinated to the following:

- To the commander of the 61st Army—2nd Guards Assault Air Division and the covering fighters of the 282nd Fighter Division;
- To the commander of the 5th Shock Army—6th Assault Air Corps and the covering fighters of the 6th Fighter Corps;
- To the commander of the 8th Guards Army—11th Guards Assault Air Division and the covering fighters of the 286th Fighter Division;
- To the commander of the 69th Army—3rd Guards Assault Air Division and the covering fighters of the 193rd Fighter Division (13th Fighter Corps);
- To the commander of the 33rd Army—300th Assault Air Division and the covering fighters of the 193rd Fighter Division (13th Fighter Corps).

The remaining aviation will continue to operate according to my orders. With the commitment of the mobile forces into the breach, all of the assault aviation and part of the fighters are once again resubordinated to:

- The commander of the 2nd Guards Tank Army—6th Assault Air Corps and the covering fighters of the 6th Fighter Corps;
- The commander of the 1st Guards Tank Army—2nd and 11th guards assault air divisions and the covering fighters of the 282nd and 286th fighter divisions;
- The commander of the 7th Guards Cavalry Corps—300th Assault Air Division and the covering fighters of the 193rd Fighter Division (13th Fighter Corps).

All remaining aviation will operate according to my orders.
Aviation objectives:
a) on the offensive's first day all of the assault and bomber aviation will assist the troops of the 5th Shock, 8th Guards, 69th, and 33rd armies to break through the enemy's defense through their operations on the battlefield. Moreover, the aviation's main forces will operate in the sectors of the 5th Shock and 8th Guards armies;
b) during the breakthrough all aviation will be in constant readiness to launch massive strikes against the enemy's immediate reserves, in order to prevent them from arriving at the breakthrough sectors;
c) from the beginning of the commitment of the mobile forces into the breach, the aviation's main forces will be concentrated on supporting the mobile forces' operations, mainly launching strikes against the enemy's operational reserves and his Warsaw group of forces.

The *front* reserve is the 3rd Shock Army, consisting of the 7th Rifle Corps (146th, 265th and 364th rifle divisions), 12th Guards Rifle Corps (23rd, 33rd and 52nd guards rifle divisions) and the 79th Rifle Corps (150th, 171st and 207th rifle divisions). By the start of the operation the army will be concentrated in the area excluding Pilawa—Stara Huta (five kilometers southwest of Pilawa)—Ewelin—Gorki—Kacpruwek (three kilometers northeast of Laskarzew) –Guzno—Zegrze (ten kilometers east of Garwolin)—Wilchta (eight kilometers northeast of Garwolin).

Following the completion of the crossing by the 1st Guards Tank and 2nd Guards Tank armies and the 7th Guards Cavalry Corps, the 3rd Shock Army will cross the Vistula

River on the operation's third day and reach the area Warka—Bialobrzegi—excluding Jedlinsk—Glowaczow.

From this area on the morning of the operation's fifth day the army will begin moving in the general direction of Nowe Miasto, Rawa Mazowiecka, Jezow, and Strykow, in readiness to develop the success in the general direction of Poznan.

5.   The necessary amount of the main types of materiel supply for conducting the *front* operation is as follows:
   a)   ammunition—4-6 combat loads;
   b)   aviation fuel—18 refills, eight refills of auto fuel, and eight refills of tank fuel;
   c)   food and forage—30 days' rations.

Of this amount, it is necessary to have by the start of the operation:
   a)   ammunition—3-4 combat loads;
   b)   aviation fuel—14 refills, six refills of auto fuel, and four refills of tank fuel;
   c)   food and forage—15 days' rations.

Supplements:[40]
   1.   A map of the First Belorussian Front's offensive on a 1:200,000 map.
   2.   A report on the preparation of the *front's* forces for the operation on six pages.

Commander of the First Belorussian Front, Marshal of the Soviet Union Zhukov
Member of the First Belorussian Front's Military Council, Lieutenant General Telegin[41]
Chief of Staff of the First Belorussian Front, Colonel General Malinin[42]

---

40 Editor's note. The supplements are not published.
41 Editor's note. Konstantin Fedorovich Telegin (1899-1981) joined the Red Army in 1919. During the Great Patriotic War he served as a member of the military council on a number of *fronts*, including the First Belorussian Front. Following the war, Telegin served as a member of the military council of the Group of Soviet Occupation Forces in Germany. He was arrested in 1948 in an attempt to gain compromising information on Marshal Zhukov, but was freed in 1953.
42 Editor's note. Mikhail Sergeevich Malinin (1899-1960) joined the Red Army in 1919. During the Great Patriotic War he served as chief of staff of a mechanized corps, an army, and a number of *fronts*, the last being the First Belorussian Front. Following the war, Malinin served as chief of staff of the Group of Soviet Occupation Forces in Germany and was later appointed first deputy chief of the General Staff of the Armed Forces.

27. Directive of the *Stavka* VGK No. 220290. To the Commander of the First Ukrainian Front on the Confirmation of the Operational Plan for Defeating the Enemy's Kielce—Radomsko Group of Forces[43]

29 December 1944, 0130 hrs

The *Stavka* of the Supreme High Command approves the operational plan you presented[44] and instructs you to do the following: it is not necessary to commit the tank armies into the breach on the first day of the operation, but after the tactical depth of the enemy's defense is pierced, having first received the *Stavka*'s permission for the commitment of the armies into the breach.

Stavka of the Supreme High Command
I. Stalin
A. Antonov

---

43 *Velikaya Otechestvennaya*, 5(4):185.
44 Editor's note. See document no. 25.

28. Directive of the *Stavka* VGK No. 11001. To the Commander of the First Belorussian Front on the Confirmation of the Operational Plan for the Defeat of the Enemy's Warsaw—Radom Group of Forces[45]

29 December 1944

The *Stavka* of the Supreme High Command confirms the operational plan presented by you.[46]

Stavka of the Supreme High Command
I. Stalin
A. Antonov

---

45 *Velikaya Otechestvennaya,* 5(4):187.
46 Editor's note. See document no. 26.

29. Directive of the *Stavka* VGK No. 11003. To the Commanders of the First and Second Belorussian and First Ukrainian Fronts on the Aviation Preparation of the Offensive[47]

4 January 1945, 1900 hrs

The *Stavka* of the Supreme High Command orders:

1. Cancel the air strike against the enemy airfields on 8.01.

2. Prepare an air strike by the movement day against the enemy's forces, simultaneous with the artillery offensive. Strikes against the enemy's airfield are to be subsequently carried out as suits the *front* commanders.

3. Manifest the maximum vigilance over our airfields, in order to counterattack possible enemy air strikes.

Stavka of the Supreme High Command
I. Stalin
A. Antonov

---

30. Directive of the *Stavka* VGK No. 11006. To the Commander of the First Ukrainian Front on the Development of the Offensive in Silesia and the Capture of Krakow[48]

17 January 1945, 2100 hrs

The *Stavka* of the Supreme High Command orders:

1. The *front's* main forces are to continue the offensive in the general direction of Wielun and Breslau, for the purpose of arriving no later than 30.01 at the Oder River to the south of Lissa (Leszno) and seizing bridgeheads along the river's western bank.

2. The *front's* left wing (59th and 60th armies) will capture the city of Krakow no later than 20-22.01, after which they are to continue the offensive toward the Dombrowo coal region, outflanking it from the north and, with part of their forces, from the south. The 21st Army and the 1st Guards Cavalry Corps are to be employed for outflanking the Dombrowo coal region from the north in the general direction of Tarnowiec and Cosel (on the Oder River).

3. From 2400 on 17.01.1945 establish the following boundary line between the First and Fourth Ukrainian fronts: as before as far as Niepolomice, then along the Vistula River as far as Strumenia and Bogumin (all locales for the Fourth Ukrainian Front).

4. Report on orders issued.

Stavka of the Supreme High Command
I. Stalin
A. Antonov

---

48 *Ibid*, 190-91.

31. To the Commanders of the Second Belorussian Front and the 19th Army. On the Army's Unloading Area[49]

17 January 1945, 2200 hrs

Copy: the chief of the General Staff's operational directorate for operational-organizational measures.

The Supreme Commander-in-Chief has ordered:

1. The 19th Army's unloading area is to be moved forward to the Ostrow Mazowiecka area, where it is to be concentrated according to the instructions of the commander of the Second Belorussian Front.

2. The units that have detrained in the Grodno—Czarna Wies area will be relocated to the Ostrow Mazowiecka area by order of the commander of the Second Belorussian Front.

3. Major General comrade Markushevich, along with an operational group, is to leave by motor vehicle to the headquarters of the Second Belorussian Front, in order to receive instructions for emplacing the army.

4. The army remains in the *Stavka* reserve.

Antonov

---

32. Directive of the *Stavka* VGK No. 11008. To the Commander of the First Belorussian Front on the Development of the Offensive on Poznan[50]

17 January 1945, 2300 hrs

The *Stavka* of the Supreme High Command orders:

1. The *front's* forces are to continue the offensive in the general direction of Poznan and are to no later than 2-4 February reach the line Bydgoszcz (Bromberg)—Poznan.

2. Establish the following boundary lines: as before with the Second Belorussian Front as far as Torun, and then along the Vistula River as far as Fordon; as before with the First Ukrainian Front as far as Jarocin, and then to Smigiel (for the First Belorussian Front).

3. Report on orders issued.

Stavka of the Supreme High Command
I. Stalin
A. Antonov

---

33. Directive of the *Stavka* VGK No. 11010 to the Commanders of the First Baltic and Third Belorussian Fronts and the *Stavka* Representative on the Resubordination of the 43rd Army[51]

19 January 1945, 1930

The *Stavka* of the Supreme High Command orders:

1. Beloborodov's[52] 43rd Army, consisting of two rifle corps (five rifle divisions in all), not counting the 54th Rifle Corps, which was dispatched earlier, is to be transferred to the Third Belorussian Front at 2400 on 19.01.

   The army is to be transferred with all existing army reinforcements, rear units and establishments, and available supplies, but no less than one combat load of munitions, two refills of fuel and 15 day's rations of food.

2. The commander of the Third Belorussian Front is to employ the 43rd Army for capturing the town of Tilsit and for subsequent operations along the Königsberg axis.

3. Report on orders issued.

Stavka of the Supreme High Command
I. Stalin
A. Antonov

---

51 *Ibid*, 192-93.
52 Editor's note. Afanasii Pavlant'evich Beloborodov (1903-90) joined the Red Army in 1919. During the Great Patriotic War he commanded a rifle division and a rifle corps, before being appointed commander of the 43rd Army in 1944. Following the war, Beloborodov commanded an army and a military district and served in the central military apparatus.

34. Directive of the *Stavka* VGK No. 11011. To the Commander of the Second Belorussian Front on the Development of the Offensive for the Purpose of Reaching the Vistula River[53]

21 January 1945, 0130 hrs

The *Stavka* of the Supreme High Command orders:

1. The *front's* forces are to continue their offensive in the general direction of Deutsch Eylau and Marienburg and no later than 2-4 February are to reach the line Elbing—Marienburg, and then to the south along the Vistula River as far as Torun, cutting off all the enemy's routes from East Prussia to central Germany.

    Upon reaching the Vistula River, bridgeheads are to be seized along its western bank to the north of Torun. Simultaneously, the *front's* right wing is to reach the line Johannisburg—Allenstein—Elbing.

2. Keep in mind the subsequent movement of a large part of the *front's* forces to the left bank of the Vistula River for operations in the area between Danzig and Stettin. The 19th Army, which is concentrating in the Ostrow Mazowiecka area, will on 1 February be transferred to the Second Belorussian Front.

3. Report on orders issued.

Stavka of the Supreme High Command
I. Stalin
A. Antonov

---

53 *Velikaya Otechestvennaya*, 5(4):193.

35. Report by the Commander of the First Belorussian Front No. 163/op. To the Supreme Commander-in-Chief on the Plan for Developing the Offensive and Forcing the Oder[54]

26 January 1945

I am reporting on the plan for further offensive operations by the First Belorussian Front.

The objectives I have set for the *front* up to 30.01.1945 are to reach the line Waldau—Preuss Friedland—Ratzebor—Zippnow—Freudenfeuer—Schoenlanke—Runau—Gulch—Scharfenort—Opalenica—Grec—Wielchowo—Kluczewo.

By this time the time armies are to reach the following areas: 2nd Guards Tank Army—Berlinchen—Landsberg—Friedeberg; 1st Guards Tank Army—Mesertiz—Schwiebus—Tirschtiegel.

Along this line we will bring up our forces (especially artillery) and rear organs, replenish our supplies, and put our combat equipment into order. Upon deploying the 3rd Shock and Polish 1st armies, on the morning of 1-2.02.1945 we will continue to attack with all the *front's* forces, with the immediate objective of forcing the Oder River from the march and subsequently developing a vigorous attack on Berlin, directing our main efforts to outflank Berlin from the northeast, north and northwest.

II. The armies' objectives by days and lines are as follows.

2nd Guards Tank Army—is to launch an attack from the Berlinchen—Landsberg line in the general direction of Neudamm, Ortwig, Heuchelberg, and Wiesenthal, force the Oder River from the march and outflank Berlin from the northwest and west.

1st Guards Tank Army—is to launch an attack in the general direction of Mezeritz, Silensieg—Drossen, Goeritz, Guzow, and Wernoheis and outflank Berlin from the north and northeast.

In the event of stubborn enemy defense along the approaches to the Oder River south of Küstrin, and in the event of successful operations by the armies north of Küstrin, I plan to turn the 1st Guards Tank Army in order to force the river north of Küstrin, parallel to the 2nd Guards Tank Army, which will be carrying out its previous task.

The Polish 1st Army, while securing its right flank against enemy counterblows from the north and northwest, will attack in the general direction of Ratzebor, Gross Zacharin, Brotzen, Nerenberg, Trampke, Kublank, and Rozow, and reach the following lines:

a) on the first day—Pilow—Muhle—Gross Zacharin—Turbruch—excluding Schenkelsieg;
b) on the third day—Dramburg—Samzow—Grassee—Flankensee;
c) on the sixth day—reach the line of the Oder River.

The Oder River is subsequently to be forced along the sector excluding Pommerensdorf—Harz and the offensive developed in the general direction of Penkun, Hassleben, Menz, and Wusterhausen.

The boundary line on the left is Osiek—Gross Welwitz—Illowo—Baumgarten—Flederborn—Sippnow—Wirchau—Jacobshagen—Stargard—Neumark—Garten—Harz—Kazekow—Gerswalde—Templin—Dannenwalde—Neuruppin (all locales except for Sippnow, Wirchau, Jacobshagen, Templin, Dannenwalde, and Neuruppin are for the Polish 1st Army).

---

54 *Ibid*, 326-28.

The 3rd Shock Army is to attack in the general direction of Hofstedt, Schoenfeld, Gross Spiegel, Jacobsdorf, Repplin, Leine, and Fiddichow, and reach the following lines:

a)   on the first day—Schoenhelzieg—Hofstedt—Georgstahl;
b)   on the third day—Zerten—Butow—Ziegenhagen—Altenwedel;
c)   on the sixth day—reach the line of the Oder River.
d)   subsequently force the Oder River along the sector excluding Harz—Schwedt and develop the attack in the direction of Fiddichow, Schoenermark, Greifenberg, Dargersdorf, Gransee, and Bechlin.

The boundary line on the left is Mrotschen—Flatow—Freudenfeuer—Markisch Friedland—Reetz—Piritz—Schwedt—Angermunde—Joachimsthal—Zedenik—Herzberg (all locales except for Mrotschen, Joachimsthal and Herzberg are for the 3rd Shock Army).

The 47th Army is to attack in the general direction of Deutsch Krone, Neuwedel, Arnswalde, Mellenthin, Tensdorf, and Hansenberg and reach the following lines:

a)   on the first day—Appelwerder—Marzdorf—Tutz;
b)   on the third day—Schlagentin—Ariswalde—Gottberg;
c)   on the sixth day—reach the line of the Oder River;
d)   subsequently force the Oder River along the sector excluding Schwedt—Zeden and develop the attack in the direction of Hirschsprung, Gross Schoenebeck, Lewenberg, and Ferbellin.

The boundary line on the left is Wirsitz—Schneidemühl—Tutz—Zatten—Gottberg—Lippene—Bad Schoenflies—Zeden—Oderberg—Finowfurt—Zommerseld (all locales except for Schneidemühl and Finowfurt are for the 47th Army).

The 61st Army is to attack in the general direction of Nikosken, Schloppe and Bernsee, Berlinchen, Solden, Morin, and Gabow, and reach the following lines:

a)   on the first day—excluding Tutz—Schloppe—Zelchau;
b)   on the third day—Buchol—Gross Ehrenberg—Herzlau—Bussow;
c)   on the sixth day—reach the line of the Oder River;
d)   the army is to subsequently force the Oder River along the sector excluding Zeden—Alt Blessin—Falkenberg—Prenden—Oranienburg—Deifoch.

The boundary line on the left is Kruszewo—Neudorf—Woldenberg—Falkenstein—Falnwerder—Berfelde—Alt Boessen—Alt Ranft—Biesenthal—Lehrbuch—Welenfanz (all locales for the 61st Army).

The 5th Shock Army is to attack in the general direction of Lukatz Kreutz, Alt Karbe, Baiersdorf, Neudamm, Gross Neuendorf, Lauenberg, Bernau, Birkenwerder, and Nauen and reach the following lines:

a)   on the first day—Nonnenbruch—Lukatz Kreutz—Schneidemulchen—Zirke;
b)   on the third day—Wildendower-Foreterei—Zansthal—Zantoch;
c)   on the sixth day—Zellin—Kinitz—Genschmar;
d)   the army's main forces are to subsequently force the Oder River along the sector excluding Alt Blessin—Alt Schaumburg, and develop the offensive along the axis Ortwig—Tiefensee—Bernau—Welten—Nauen.

The boundary line on the left is Oborniki—the Warta River as far as Küstrin—Zechin—Ilow—Werneihes—Hermsdorf (all locales for the 5th Shock Army).

The 8th Guards Army is to attack in the general direction of Ostrowo, Keme, Prittisch, and Goeritz and reach the following lines:

a) on the first day Gapoze—Kailch—Algir—Pawlowko;
b) on the third day—force the Obra River and reach the line Trebisch—Neuforwerk—Neudorf;
c) on the sixth day—force the Oder River along the sector excluding Küstrin—Wizen, and reach the line excluding Genschmar—Alt Tucheband—Werder—excluding Malnow.

The army is to subsequently develop the attack in the direction of Seelow, Alt Landsberg and Weisensee.

The boundary line to the left is the same as before as far as Poznan, then Duszniki—Neustadt—Betsche—Meseritz—Gleissen—Drossen—Geritz—Muncheberg—Petershagen—Lichtenberg (all locales except Duszniki, Neustadt and Meseritz are for the 8th Guards Army).

The 69th Army and the 11th Tank Corps are to attack in the general direction of Wonsowo, Bauchwitz, Hochwalde, Klauswalde, and Frankfurt, and reach the following lines:

a) on the first day—Neustadt—Bolewitz—Glinno—Kirchplatz—Borui;
b) on the third day—Tempel—Langenpfuhl—Schenow—Wutschdorf—Mestchen;
c) on the sixth day—force the Oder River along the sector Wizen—Schwetieg—Malnow—Schoenflies—Boossen—Sandgrund—excluding Lossow.

The army is to subsequently develop the attack in the direction of Boossen, Arensdorf, Herzfelde, and Friedrichsfeld.

The boundary line on the left is the same as before as far as Petzen Hauland, then Gretz—Stentsch—Schwiebus—Topper—Reipzig—Hechendorf—Wendenschloss—Mariendorf (all locales except Gretz and Schwiebus are for the 69th Army).

The 33rd Army and the 9th Tank Corps are to attack in the general direction of Rakwitz, Bomst, Dobersaul, Zibingen, and Ziltendorf and reach the following lines:

a) on the first day—Borui—Waldland—Tanheim—Kilpin—Lefelde—Obra;
b) on the third day—excluding Mestchen—Zelesgen—Schoenfeld—Mittewalde—Gross Blumberg;
c) on the sixth day—force the Oder River along the sector Lossow—Lindow—Politz—Dilo—Mebiskruge—Kumro—Welmitz.

The army is to subsequently develop the attack in the direction of Rissen, Goerzig, Storkow, Neumuhle, Didersdorf, and Potsdam.

The 2nd Guards Cavalry Corps is to attack with the mission of securing the *front's* right flank.

The 7th Guards Cavalry Corps is to attack with the mission of securing the *front's* left flank.

In reporting the above, I request the following:

1. To confirm my decision.
2. To establish the following boundary lines:
   a) between the Second and First Belorussian fronts as far as Besendorf—along the Vistula River, and then Neu Jaschinnitz—Prust—Pletzig—Preuss Friedland—Lumzow—Tempelberg—Dramburg—Freienwalde—Lenz—Munsterberg—

Pommerensdorf—Prenzlau—Krewitz—Furstenberg—Reinsberg (all locales except Prenzlau, Furstenberg and Reinsberg are for the First Belorussian Front).

b) between the First Belorussian and First Ukrainian fronts as before as far as Smigiel, then Unruhstadt—Faule Obra River—Oder River—Ratzdorf—Findland—Keris—Michendorf.

3. To order the delivery to the front of two combat loads of munitions, of which one is to be delivered by 5.02.1945 and the other by 15.02.1945.

Commander of the First Belorussian Front, Marshal of the Soviet Union Zhukov
Member of the First Belorussian Front's Military Council, Lieutenant General Telegin
Chief of Staff of the First Belorussian Front, Colonel General Malinin

36. Directive of the *Stavka* VGK No. 11016. To the Commander of the First Belorussian Front on the Confirmation of the Plan for Developing the Offensive and Forcing the Oder River[55]

27 January 1945, 1740 hrs

The *Stavka* of the Supreme High Command confirms the plan No. 163/op, which you presented[56] on 26.01.1945, and orders:

1. Establish the following boundary lines as of 2400 on 27.01:
   a) with the Second Belorussian Front as before as far as Fordon, then Krone—Zempelburg—Flederborn—Wirchow—Jacobshagen—Stargard—Greifenhagen (all locales for the Second Belorussian Front;
   b) with the First Ukrainian Front as before as far as Smigiel, then Unruhstadt—the Faule Obra River—Oder River—Ratzdorf—Friedland—Gross Keris—Michendorf (all locales for the First Belorussian Front).

2. Keep an army in reserve, reinforced by no less than a tank corps, behind the *front's* right wing, in order to reliably secure the right wing against the enemy's possible attacks from the north and northeast.

3. The responsibility for securing the boundary lines between the *fronts* is as before.

4. Report on orders issued.

Stavka of the Supreme High Command
I. Stalin
A. Antonov

---

55 *Ibid*, 195-96.
56 Editor's note. See document no.35.

37. To the Commanders of the 19th Army and Second Belorussian Front. On the Army's Concentration Area and its Inclusion in the *Front*[57]

28 January 1945, 1630 hrs

Copies: to the chiefs of the General Staff's operational directorate and the directorate for operational-organizational measures.

The Supreme Commander-in-Chief has ordered the 19th Army, consisting of the:

> 40th Guards Rifle Corps (10th, 101st and 102nd guards rifle divisions);
> 132nd Rifle Corps (18th, 27th and 313th rifle divisions);
> 134th Rifle Corps (205th, 272nd and 310th rifle divisions), which are concentrating in the Ostrow Mazowiecka area, is to be included in the Second Belorussian Front from 2400 on 28 January.

A list of the army's reinforcement units and rear organs is attached.[58]

Antonov
Karponosov

---

57 *Velikaya Otechestvennaya*, 12(4):612.
58 Editor's note. The supplement was not published.

38. Directive of the *Stavka* VGK No. 11021. To the Commander of the Second Belorussian Front on Shifting the *Front's* Main Efforts to East Pomerania[59]

8 February 1945, 1455 hrs

The *Stavka* of the Supreme High Command orders:

1. The *front's* center and left wing (2nd Shock Army, 65th, 49th and 70th armies, 1st Guards Tank Corps, 8th Mechanized Corps, 3rd Guards Cavalry Corps, and no less than four artillery breakthrough divisions) are to attack on 10 February to the west of the Vistula River and, no later than 20.02 are to reach the line mouth of the Vistula River—Dirschau—Berent—Rummelsberg—Neustettin.

2. Subsequently, upon the arrival of the 19th Army, these forces are to develop the offensive in the general direction of Stettin, capture the Danzig—Gdynia area, and clear the enemy from the shore as far as the Bay of Pomerania.

3. Report on orders issued.

Stavka of the Supreme High Command
I. Stalin
A. Antonov

39. To the Commander of the First Belorussian Front. On the Enemy's Intentions[60]

14 February 1945, 0225 hrs

I am relaying for your consideration a document, which I received from the English mission on 12.02.1945.

We have received from a very reliable source top secret information as to the movements of Germany units inside Germany. In this regard, I have been authorized to relay the following information to you:

On the intentions of the German command at the end of January.

The German command is striving to preserve its reserves, so that at the appropriate moment it can undertake a large-scale counteroffensive. For this purpose, troops are being concentrated in Pomerania and in the area northwest of Breslau.

The German command has in mind undertaking concentric attacks in the middle of February from the area northwest of Breslau and Pomerania against Marshal Zhukov's forces.

The troops concentrating northwest of Breslau include SS units.

The German command is determined to defend Berlin to the last.

Vasilevskii

---

60 *Velikaya Otechestvennaya*, 12(4):633.

40. To the Commanders of the First, Second and Third Belorussian, First, Second, Third, and Fourth Ukrainian Fronts. On Submitting Information on Our Allies' Liberated Prisoners of War[61]

16 February 1945, 0115 hrs

The Supreme Commander-in-Chief has ordered no later than 1300 on 16 February to submit to the General Staff information on the number of liberated military personnel and citizens of allied states (Englishmen, Americans, etc.) on occupied territory, by individual country, and the military personnel separately, according to category.

Vasilevskii

---

61 *Velikaya Otechestvennaya*, 12(4):634.

41. Report by the Commander of the Second Belorussian Front No. 3708. To the Chief of the General Staff on the Plan for Employing the 19th Army and the 3rd Guards Tank Corps[62]

15 February 1945

I report:

1. According to *Stavka* of the Supreme High Command directive No. 11021 of 8.02.1945,[63] the *front* has been entrusted with the objective of no later than 20.02.1945 of reaching the line mouth of the Vistula River—Dirschau—Berent—Rummelsberg—Neustettin. Subsequently, upon the arrival of the 19th Army, we are to develop the offensive in the general direction of Stettin, capturing the Danzig—Gdynia area, and clearing the coastline of the enemy as far as the Bay of Pomerania.

2. Taking into account the *front's* available forces, I believe that it is more expedient to employ the 19th Army and the 3rd Guards Tank Corps along the *front's* left wing, with the objective, deploying along the line Schlochau—Ratzebor, to attack in the general direction of Baldenburg, Bublitz and Kezlin, for the purpose of splitting up the enemy's Pomeranian group of forces and arriving at the shore of the Baltic Sea along the front of the Jamundersee—Kolberg.

    The elimination of the enemy east of the Konitz—Rugenwalde meridian will be entrusted to the *front's* right-flank forces, consisting of the 2nd Shock, 65th, 49th, and 70th armies.

3. The beginning of the commitment of the 19th Army and 3rd Guards Tank Corps into the fighting is possible only from 22-23 February, as it is necessary to carry out a 160-kilometer march to the deployment line. The beginning of the movement is from 17.02.1945.

4. In order to carry out the *Stavka* of the Supreme High Command's assignment on clearing the enemy out of Pomerania and reaching the Bay of Pomerania, the following are necessary:
    a) to reinforce the *front's* left wing with two combined-arms armies and two tank corps. Moreover, it is necessary to carry this out upon the arrival of the 19th Army and the 3rd Guards Tank Corps in the Neustettin area, for with the movement of these forces to the northeast it will be necessary to secure the Kezlin axis from the west;
    b) the *front's* right-wing armies, which have been involved in intensive fighting for the past month, have suffered heavy casualties and are now under strength, amounting to, on the average, 26 3,000-man and eight 4,000-man rifle divisions.

In order to bring these divisions at least up to 6,000 men, we need a centrally-trained reinforcement of up to 80,000 men, and up to 20,000 men for reinforcing the specialized combat arms.

Rokossovskii
Subbotin
Kotov[64]

---

62 *Velikaya Otechestvennaya*, 5(4):329-30.
63 See document no. 38.
64 Editor's note. Pavel Mikhailovich Kotov (1897-1962) served at this time as chief of the operational section of the Second Belorussian Front staff. Following the war, Kotov served as a military adviser in China.

42. Report by the Commander of the First Belorussian Front No. 00318/op. To the Supreme Commander-in-Chief on the Plan for Attacking Along the Stettin Direction[65]

16 February 1945, 2300 hrs

In fulfilling your personal instructions, I am reporting our ideas on conducting a separate offensive operation by the *front's* right-wing forces (map 1:200,000).

I. The purpose of the operation is to throw the enemy back to the north and for the *front's* right flank to reach the line Lubow—Tempelberg—Falkenberg—Dramburg—Wangerin—Massow—Gollnow—Stettin, cut the communications of the enemy's Pomeranian group of forces to the west, and help the Second Belorussian Front's left flank to more quickly reach the Stettin area.

II. I can begin the operation on the morning of 19 February of this year. The length of the operation is approximately 6-7 days.

III. I will make the main attack with all the forces of the 61st Army, and all the forces of the 2nd Guards Tank Army and the 7th Guards Cavalry Corps and the 9th Tank Corps, supported by two artillery divisions, from the line Reetz—Brallentin—Piritz, and then through Stargard in a northwesterly direction.

I am assigning this group of forces the objective of throwing back the enemy to the north and, upon arriving at the front Blankenhagen (six kilometers southwest of Wangerin)—Kannenberg (six kilometers northwest of Freienwalde)—Massow—Gollnow—Stettin, to cut the communications of the enemy's Pomeranian group of forces to the west.

I will launch a supporting attack with all the forces of the Polish 1st Army and two of the 3rd Shock Army's rifle corps from the line Rederitz—Markisch Friedland—Kallis—excluding Reetz.

This group's objective is, while directing its main efforts along the front Falkenberg—Dramburg and cooperating with the forces of the Second Belorussian Front, to throw the enemy back to the north and reach the line Lubow—Tempelberg—Falkenberg—Dramburg—Wangerin.

The 3rd Shock Army's 12th Guards Rifle Corps and the 2nd Guards Cavalry Corps are to continue to hold their positions along the line Battrow—Dobrin—Kelpin—Krumenflies—Lumzow—Gross Born—the eastern outskirts of Schacharin.

As the Second Belorussian Front's left flank advances, the 2nd Guards Cavalry Corps will successively, from right to left, go over from the defensive to the offensive in a westerly direction.

---

65 *Velikaya Otechestvennaya*, 5(4):328-29.

I plan to pull back the 12th Guards Rifle Corps into the 3rd Shock Army's reserve.

IV. The offensive by the *front's* main forces to the west is being moved to 1-2 March.
   In reporting the above, I request the following:
   1. To confirm my plans for conducting a separate offensive and the change in the beginning of the front's main forces' offensive to 1-2 March 1945.
   2. In order to make up losses in the tank units and self-propelled artillery, I request that you send to the front an additional 160 SU-76s, 40 SU-100s, 60 SU-122s, 40 SU-152s, and 100 T-34 tanks.

Zhukov
Telegin
Malinin

43. Directive of the *Stavka* VGK No. 11024. To the Commander of the First Belorussian Front on the Confirmation of the Plan for the Offensive Along the Stettin Direction[66]

17 February 1945, 1815 hrs

The *Stavka* of the Supreme High Command confirms the plan submitted by you in No. 00318/op of 15.02[67] on the conduct of an offensive operation by the *front's* right-wing forces, and orders:

1. The 47th Army and 1st Guards Tank Army are to be held in reserve closer to the *front's* right wing, so that, if necessary, they can be employed along the boundary with the Second Belorussian Front.

2. Establish from 2400 on 20.02 the following boundary line between the Second and First Belorussian fronts: Bromberg—Flederborn—Neustettin—Kolberg (all locales for the First Belorussian Front).

    The responsibility for securing the boundary between the Second and First Belorussian fronts remains with the commander of the First Belorussian Front.

3. Report on orders issued.

Stavka of the Supreme High Command
I. Stalin
A. Vasilevskii

---

66 *Velikaya Otechestvennaya*, 5(4):200.
67 Editor's note. See document no. 42.

44. Directive of the *Stavka* of the VGK No. 11025 to the Chief of the General Staff and the Commanders of the First Baltic and Third Belorussian Fronts on the Conferring on A.M. Vasilevskii the Duties of Controlling the *Fronts'* Combat Operations[68]

17 February 1945, 2000 hrs

The *Stavka* of the Supreme High Command orders that the control of the Third Belorussian and First Baltic fronts' combat operations be entrusted to Marshal of the Soviet Union Vasilevskii from 22 February of this year.

Stavka of the Supreme High Command
I. Stalin
A. Antonov

---

68 *Velikaya Otechestvennaya*, 5(4):200.

45. Directive of the *Stavka* of the VGK No. 11026. To the Commander of the Second Belorussian Front on the Confirmation of the Plan to Employ the 19th Army and the 3rd Guards Tank Corps[69]

17 February 1945, 2010 hrs

The *Stavka* of the Supreme High Command orders:

1.   The 19th Army and the 3rd Guards Tank Corps are to be employed in accordance with plan No. 3708, of 15.02,[70] which you presented.

2.   Establish from 2400 20.02.1945 the following boundary line between the Second and First Belorussian fronts: Bromberg—Flederborn—Neustettin—Kolberg (all locales for the First Belorussian Front).

3.   For your information, on 19.02.1945 the First Belorussian Front's right-wing forces will attack along the Falkenberg and Gollnow axes.

4.   Report on orders issued.

Stavka of the Supreme High Command
I. Stalin
A. Vasilevskii

---

69   *Ibid*, 201.
70   Editor's note. See document no. 41.

46. Directive of the *Stavka* VGK No. 11030. To the Commander of the First Baltic Front on the Defeat of the Enemy's Samland Group of Forces Along the Samland Peninsula[71]

17 February 1945, 2012

The *Stavka* of the Supreme High Command orders:

1.   The *front's* forces are to first clear the Samland peninsula of the enemy. In order to carry out this task, it will be necessary to bring in the *front's* main forces, leaving the necessary number of troops in the Königsberg area to securely blockade it. It is necessary to begin the operation to clear the Samland peninsula on 20 February and to finish it no later than 26-27 February.

2.   Upon accomplishing the indicated task, all of the *front's* forces are to be employed for capturing the city of Königsberg.

3.   Report on orders issued.

Stavka of the Supreme High Command
I. Stalin
A. Vasilevskii

---

71   *Velikaya Otechestvennaya*, 5(4):202.

47. Order of the *Stavka* VGK No. 11031 on the Appointment of A.M. Vasilevskii Commander of the Third Belorussian Front[72]

18 February 1945, 2000

In view of the death of the commander of the Third Belorussian Front, General I.D. Chernyakhovskii, which followed his serious wounding, Marshal of the Soviet Union A.M. Vasilevskii is to be appointed commander of the Third Belorussian Front.

1. Marshal Vasilevskii is to take up the command of the *front's* forces no later than 21 February of this year.

2. Prior to the arrival of Marshal Vasilevskii at the front, the duties of *front* commander are entrusted to the *front* chief of staff, Colonel General Pokrovskii.[73]

3. *Stavka* of the Supreme High Command order no. 11025 of 17.02, entrusting Marshal of the Soviet Union Vasilevskii with the control of the First Baltic and Third Belorussian fronts' operations is rescinded.[74]

Stavka of the Supreme High Command
I. Stalin
A. Antonov

---

72 *Ibid*, 204.
73 Editor's note. Aleksandr Petrovich Pokrovskii (1898-1979) joined the Russian imperial army in 1915 and the Red Army in 1919. During the Great Patriotic War he served as chief of staff in a number of armies and *fronts*, including the Third Belorussian from 1944 to the end of the war. Following the war, Pokrovskii was the chief of staff of a military district and also served in the central military apparatus.
74 Editor's note. See document no. 44.

48. To the Commander-in-Chief of the Polish Army and the Commander of the First Belorussian Front, on the Inclusion of the Polish 1st Army in the *Front*[75]

19 February 1945, 2330 hrs

The Supreme Commander-in-Chief has ordered:

The Polish 1st Army, consisting of the 7th, 5th, 9th, 10th, and 8th infantry divisions, the 9th and 14th anti-tank artillery brigades, 2nd Mortar Regiment, 16th Tank Brigade, 5th IS[76] Tank Regiment, and the 3rd Engineer-Sapper Brigade, along with all army reinforcement units and rear organs, is to be included in the First Belorussian Front.
   In accordance with this, I request the following:

1.   To concentrate the army during 7-13 March in the Schneidemühl—Kreutz—Czarnikow area in the First Belorussian Front's reserve.

2.   The army is to be concentrated by marching. Tanks, tracked vehicles and the 10th Infantry Division, without its auto transport, are to be transferred by railroad. A transport requisition is to be presented to the central directorate of military communications and the commander of the First Belorussian Front by 23 February of this year.

3.   The army is to be dispatched in full, with all its available supplies. The army is to be supplied with fuel along its route by order of the commander of the First Belorussian Front.

4.   The concentration plan is to be submitted to the commander of the First Belorussian Front, and a copy to the General Staff by 23 February 1945.

   Please report on execution.

Antonov

---

75   *Velikaya Otechestvennaya*, 12(4):637.
76   Editor's note. This is a reference to the IS series tanks, named after Stalin.

49. Directive of the *Stavka* VGK No. 11032. To the Commander of the Third Belorussian and First Baltic Fronts on the Transformation of the First Baltic Front into the Third Belorussian Front's Samland Group of Forces[77]

21 February 1945, 2000

In view of the fact that operations for eliminating the enemy's Königsberg and East Prussian groups of forces are closely interrelated and require unified leadership, the *Stavka* of the Supreme High Command orders:

1. The First Baltic Front is to be disbanded as of 2400 on 24.02.1945. The *front* headquarters is to be renamed the Samland group of forces and this group is to be absorbed into the Third Belorussian Front.

2. Gen. Bagramyan is appointed commander of the Third Belorussian Front's Samland group of forces and simultaneously deputy commander of the Third Belorussian Front.

3. The right boundary line of the expanded Third Belorussian Front is to be along the right boundary line of the former First Baltic Front.

4. Report on execution.

Stavka of the Supreme High Command
I. Stalin
A. Antonov

---

77 *Velikaya Otechestvennaya*, 5(4):204.

50. Directive of the *Stavka* VGK No. 11033. To the Commanders of the Third and Second Belorussian Fronts on the Elaboration of Their Objectives and the Change in Their Boundary Line[78]

21 February 1945, 2200 hrs

The *Stavka* of the Supreme High Command orders:

1. To establish from 2400 24.02 the following boundary line between the Second and Third Belorussian fronts: as far as Osterode as before, then Saalfeld—Christburg—Halbstadt (on the Nogat River)—Nickelswalde (all locales for the Third Belorussian Front).

    The commander of the Third Belorussian Front is to be ready by this date to relieve the forces of the Second Belorussian Front within the new boundary lines. The responsibility for securing the boundary between the *fronts* remains with the commander of the Third Belorussian Front.

2. The commander of the Second Belorussian Front is to employ the freed-up forces of the 2nd Shock Army to reinforce the army's left flank for an offensive along the western bank of the Vistula River, for the purpose of arriving as quickly as possible at the shore of the Bay of Danzig.

3. The commander of the Third Belorussian Front is to more quickly move his left wing to the shore of the Bay of Danzig east of the Vistula River, for the purpose of closing the exit from the Frische-Nehrung spit.

4. Report on orders issued.

Stavka of the Supreme High Command
I. Stalin
A. Antonov

---

78 *Ibid*, 205.

51. To the Commanders of the Third and Second Belorussian Fronts. On the Resubordination of the 5th Guards Tank Army[79]

28 February 1945, 0300 hrs

The Supreme Commander-in-Chief has ordered the transfer of the 5th Guards Tank Army, consisting of the 29th Tank Corps, the 47th Independent Mechanized Brigade and all army reinforcement units from the Third Belorussian Front to the Second Belorussian Front.

The army, with the exception of the 47th Independent Mechanized Brigade, is to be transferred at 2400 on 1 March, while the 47th Independent Mechanized Brigade is to be transferred to the Second Belorussian Front no later than 10 March.

The tanks and self-propelled guns of the 29th Tank Corps and 47th Independent Mechanized Brigade are not to be removed.

The commander of the Second Belorussian Front is to communicate the 5th Guards Tank Army's route of march and area of concentration to the Third Belorussian Front.

Report on execution.

Antonov

---

79 *Velikaya Otechestvennaya*, 12(4):644.

52. Directive of the *Stavka* VGK No. 11034. To the Commanders of the First and Second Belorussian Fronts on the Temporary Resubordination of the 1st Guards Tank Army[80]

5 March 1945, 2000 hrs

The *Stavka* of the Supreme High Command orders:

1. Following the elimination of the enemy in the Belgard—Kolberg area, but no later than 8 March, the First Belorussian Front's 1st Guards Tank Army will be temporarily subordinated to the Second Belorussian Front, with the inclusion of the Polish 1st Army's tank brigade.

2. The army is to be transferred intact, with all its reinforcement equipment, army rear units and establishments, with two refills of fuel and three refills of diesel fuel.

3. The commander of the Second Belorussian Front should keep in mind that the 1st Guards Tank Army, minus the Polish tank brigade, must be returned to the First Belorussian Front by no later than 24 March.

4. Report on fulfillment.

Stavka of the Supreme High Command
I. Stalin
A. Antonov

---

80 *Velikaya Otechestvennaya*, 5(4):206.

53. Directive of the *Stavka* VGK No. 11035. To the Commander of the Second Belorussian Front on the Development of the Operation in East Prussia[81]

5 March 1945, 2000

The *Stavka* of the Supreme High Command orders:

1. The forces of the Second Belorussian Front are to defeat the enemy group of forces in the Danzig—Stolp area and capture the cities of Danzig and Gdynia, and no later than 20 March reach the coast of the Baltic Sea.

2. In order to carry out this task, the *front's* forces are to continue the offensive by the right wing along the western bank of the Vistula River toward Danzig, and along the left wing toward Lauenburg and Gdynia. The 1st Guards Tank Army and the Polish 1st Army's tank brigade are to be employed for developing the attack along the *front's* left wing.

3. As the coastline is cleared, organize its solid defense, employing for this purpose the 3rd Guards Cavalry Corps, fortified areas and other units.

4. The boundary lines and the responsibility for securing the boundaries with neighboring *fronts* are as before.

5. Report on orders issued.

Stavka of the Supreme High Command
I. Stalin
A. Antonov

---

81 *Ibid*, 206.

54. To the Commander of the First Ukrainian Front. On a Report Regarding the Reasons for the Withdrawal by Units of the 52nd and 5th Guards Armies[82]

12 March 1945, 1915 hrs

The Supreme Commander-in-Chief is dissatisfied with the withdrawal by units of the 52nd Army from Lauban, and the abandonment by units of the 5th Guards Army of Striegau, given the presence of sufficient men and materiel enabling us to organize the secure defense of these lines.

Report to the Supreme Commander-in-Chief no later than 14 March the reasons for the abandonment by the 52nd and 5th Guards armies' forces of the above-mentioned defensive sectors, our losses, listing separately the losses for the Striegau garrison, and the measures taken by you for improving the defense of the *front's* right wing.

Antonov

---

55. Report by the Commander of the Third Belorussian Front No. 215/K. To the Supreme Commander-in-Chief on the Plan for Defeating the Enemy's Königsberg Group of Forces[83]

16 March 1945, 1717 hrs

I am reporting the decision to defeat the enemy's Königsberg group of forces and to capture the city and fortress of Königsberg.

1. The Königsberg fortified area is the basis of the Germans' defense along the Samland peninsula. With the loss of this area and the capital of East Prussia, the enemy's further stubborn defense on the Samland peninsula become nonsensical, or at least loses its significance.

    In all, the enemy has the following forces on the Samland peninsula: eight infantry divisions, one panzer division, six independent regiments, and 21 independent battalions.

    More than 1/3 of all these enemy forces have been deployed for defending the city of Königsberg along the outer perimeter of the fortified area, which is up to 50 kilometers in length. As opposed to other fortified areas, the Königsberg one has powerful defensive structures, forts, pillboxes, and bunkers. The old forts were redone before the war and improved during the recent operations. 2-3 continuous trenches and an anti-tank ditch have been dug along the outer perimeter of the city, up to 38 forts constructed, and up to 60 pillboxes. City blocks and streets with stone buildings have been configured for defense. In the center of the city-fortress there is a citadel with an inner belt of forts. The city's defense is considerably strengthened by the presence of the Pregel River, its flood plain, canals and ponds. Already within the bounds of the fortified areas up to 60 artillery and 300 mortar batteries have been identified.

2. Based upon this, I have decided:

    By means of a powerful and vigorous attack upon the city of Königsberg from the northwest and southwest, to block and defeat the enemy Königsberg group of forces and capture the city.

    Subsequently, without interrupting the operation, the offensive is to be developed to the northwest to completely defeat the enemy's group of forces occupying the Samland peninsula.

3. For this purpose, I consider it necessary, following the defeat of the enemy's East Prussian group of forces that the following grouping of forces is to be created:
    a) Lieutenant General Chanchibadze's[84] 2nd Guards Army, consisting of two rifle corps (six rifle divisions), reinforced with two anti-tank artillery brigades, upon relieving the 43rd Army's formations, is to deploy for defense along the front Klein Harbseiden (five kilometers southeast of Neukuren)—Pobeten—Kotzlauken—excluding Muhl-Trierenberg—Kumenen—excluding Dallwenen, having four rifle divisions in its first echelon.

        The army's task is to support our forces' offensive on Königsberg through a stubborn defense.

---

83 *Velikaya Otechestvennaya*, 5(4):333-36.
84 Editor's note. Porfirii Georgievich Chanchibadze (1901-50) joined the Red Army in 1921. During the Great Patriotic War he commanded a regiment, motorized rifle division and a rifle corps. In 1944 he was appointed commander of the 2nd Guards Army and served there until the end of the war. Following the war, Chanchibadze commanded a series of corps.

The boundary line on the left is Dallwenen—the Kompenen platform—Bonau (all locales for the 43rd Army);

b) Lieutenant General Beloborodov's 43rd Army, consisting of three rifle corps (nine rifle divisions), with six rifle divisions in the first echelon, is to deploy along the front excluding Dallwenen—excluding the Barseniken manor yard—(6.5 kilometers) for an attack in the direction of Medenau and Kobbelbude.

The army's task is to defeat the opposing enemy and reach the front Kompenen platform—Kobbelbude—Widitten—excluding Gross Heidekrug, supporting our forces' offensive on Königsberg.

The boundary line on the left is the grove (0.25 kilometers west of the Barseniken manor yard)—Gross Heidekrug (all locales exclusively for the 43rd Army). The Army is to be reinforced with artillery to ensure a density of 179 tubes per kilometer of front; 40 tanks and 20 122-mm self-propelled guns, and one assault engineer-sapper brigade.

c) Lieutenant General Lyudnikov's[85] 39th Army, consisting of three rifle corps (nine rifle divisions), is to launch an attack from the 6.5-kilometer front Barseniken manor yard—Katzenblick, with six rifle divisions in the first echelon, in the general direction of Nautzwinkel, with the task of defeating the opposing enemy, reaching the northern shore of the Frisches Haff, and securely blockading the city of Königsberg from the west.

The boundary line from the left is Katzenblick—Moditten—the mouth of the Laak River (both locales are exclusively for the 39th Army).

The army is to be reinforced with artillery to achieve a density of 193 tubes per kilometer of front; 40 tanks and 40 heavy self-propelled guns (IS-122 and IS-152); one assault engineer-sapper brigade;

d) Colonel General Krylov's[86] 5th Army, consisting of three rifle corps (nine rifle divisions), is to deploy along a five-kilometer front excluding Katzenblick—excluding Tannenwalde, having six rifle divisions in its first echelon, and launch an attack in the general direction of Amalienau, with the task of defeating the opposing enemy and capturing by storm the northwestern part of the city of Königsberg.

The boundary line on the left is the Tannenwalde manor yard—Piln (one kilometer north of Rosenau). Both locales are for the 5th Army.

The army is to be reinforced with artillery to guarantee a density of 209 tubes per kilometer of front; 65 tanks and 63 heavy self-propelled guns (IS-122, IS-152); one assault engineer-sapper brigade;

e) Lieutenant General Ozerov's[87] 50th Army, consisting of three rifle corps (nine rifle divisions), while securely defending with one rifle corps along the front

---

85 Editor's note. Ivan Il'ich Lyudnikov (1902-76) joined the Red Army in 1918. During the Great Patriotic War he commanded a brigade, division and corps. He was appointed commander of the 39th Army in 1944 and served until the end of the war and also commanded the army during the war with Japan. Following the war, Lyudnikov commanded a number of armies and a military district and was deputy commander-in-chief of the Group of Soviet Forces in Germany.

86 Editor's note. Nikolai Ivanovich Krylov (1903-72) joined the Red Army in 1919. During the Great Patriotic War he commanded a fortified area and was the chief of staff of several armies. He was appointed commander of the 5th Army in 1943 and served until the end of the war and the war with Japan. Following the war, Krylov commanded several military districts and was the commander-in-chief of the Strategic Rocket Forces.

87 Editor's note. Fedor Petrovich Ozerov (1899-1971) joined the Red Army in 1918. During the Great Patriotic War he commanded a division and served as chief of staff of an army and a *front*. He was appointed commander of the 50th Army in 1945. Following the war, Ozerov served as chief of staff of a military district and

Sudau—Neuhausen-Tiergarten—the eastern shore of the Lauterr Muhlenteich pond—the Nauer Pregel River, is to launch an attack with two rifle corps in the general direction of Tragheimer and Kalthof, with the task of defeating the opposing enemy and capturing the northeastern part of the city. Four rifle divisions are to deploy along a 4-kilometer front in the first echelon of the army's shock group.

The boundary line on the left is the Nauer Pregel River.

The army is to be reinforced with artillery guaranteeing a density of 188 tubes per kilometer of front; 65 tanks and 42 heavy self-propelled guns (IS-122 and IS-152); one assault engineer-sapper brigade;

f) Colonel General Galitskii's[88] 11th Guards Army, consisting of three rifle corps (nine rifle divisions), upon deploying along a 7.5-kilometer front Altenberg—excluding Warten and having five rifle divisions in its first echelon, is to attack in the general direction of Ponart and Nasser Garten, with the task of capturing the southern part of the city.

The army is to be reinforced with artillery, guaranteeing a density of 199 tubes per kilometer of front; 65 tanks and 40 heavy self-propelled guns (IS-122 and IS-152); two assault engineer-sapper brigades;

g) The Samland group's reserves consist of a single rifle corps, consisting of three rifle divisions, and a heavy self-propelled artillery regiment, consisting of 21 guns;

h) I am employing the entire strength of the 3rd and 1st air armies in the operation, as well as the 6th Bomber Corps.

4. I have planned to carry out the entire operation in the following three stages:
The first stage is preparatory.
The following measures are to be carried out during this stage:

a) to completely and fully discover the grouping of the enemy's forces and his defensive system, exactly defining his firing positions, fortifications and obstacles;

b) through frequent and active operations, to prepare and improve the troops' jumping-off positions for the forthcoming operation;

c) to prepare airfields for our planes;

d) to secretly move up and concentrate the forces of the 50th, 5th and 2nd Guards armies;

e) to reinforce the rifle divisions slated for the attack by bringing their strength up to 3,000-3,600 men;

f) to accumulate munitions and bring their number up to established norms'

g) to scrupulously and fully prepare the entire officer complement and the troops for carrying out their tasks in the forthcoming operation;

h) to carry out a number of measures to disorient the enemy;

i) during the final four days preceding the start of the operation, to carry out an air and artillery offensive, for the purpose of destroying beforehand the fortifications of the Königsberg fortified area. This is to be accomplished by bringing in an air corps of Tu-2s, the entire strength of the 3rd and 1st air armies, and heavy artillery;

---

in a number of academic postings.

88 Editor's note. Kuz'ma Nikitovich Galitskii (1897-1973) joined the Russian imperial army in 1917 and the Red Army in 1918. During the Great Patriotic War he commanded a division, corps and several armies and was the commander of the 11th Guards Army until the end of the war. Following the war, Galitskii commanded a number of military districts.

k) to have the troops in fully combat readiness for going over immediately to the offensive, in case the enemy begins to evacuate his forces from the Königsberg area during our preparation.

The second stage is the breakthrough of the enemy's defensive zone, his outer perimeter and the arrival of our forces at the following lines: the northern group-Poerstiten—Mossennen—Powaien Station—Klein Heidekrug—Nautzwinkel—Iuditten—Lawsken—Tragheimer—Rotenstein—Kwendau; the southern group (11th Guards Army)-Schoernflies—Speichersdorf—Ponart—Hawstrom.

This stage is to last one day.

The third stage entails the development of the breakthrough, the storming of the city of Königsberg, the capture of the city, and the arrival of our troops at the line Muhl-Trierenberg—the Kompenen platform—Kobbelbude—Gross Heidekrug, and then the northern bank of the Frisches Haff. This stage is to last four days.

5. I consider it possible to begin the operation within 8-10 days following the elimination of the enemy's East Prussian group of forces, if he does not begin the evacuation of his forces from the Königsberg area before the beginning of this time. In the latter case, the offensive will begin immediately with all available forces.

6. The entire disposition of our forces in the forthcoming operation along the Samland peninsula is to be created by the additional allocation of the Third Belorussian Front's forces and equipment: the 2nd Guards Army—six rifle divisions; 5th Army—12 rifle divisions; 50th Army—six rifle divisions, the 3rd, 10th and 15th artillery breakthrough divisions, the 4th Artillery Division, a single guards mortar division, an anti-aircraft division, eight guards mortar regiments, three tank brigades, five heavy self-propelled artillery regiments, and four assault engineer-sapper brigades.

However, in order to reconstitute several tank and self-propelled artillery units and raise them to the strength indicated in the text, as well as for creating the necessary supplies of munitions and fuels, oils and lubricants, the Third Belorussian Front is short of the following:

In tanks and self-propelled guns:
a) tanks—60 T-34s;
b) 60 SU-76s and 60 IS-122s and IS-152s.

In munitions by the start of the operation—above the March release—in thousands of units (combat loads):
a) 76mm regimental guns—up to 2.5 combat loads, 61,100 (one combat load; 76mm divisional artillery—271,000 (1.1 combat load);
b) 82mm mortars—up to three combat loads, 58,100 (0.25 combat loads); 120mm mortars—65,500 (0.6 combat loads); 122mm howitzers—141,900 (1.9 combat loads);
c) 152mm howitzers—up to 3.5 combat loads, 17,400, (three combat loads); 1937 152mm gun-howitzer—two combat loads, 480 (two combat loads); 280mm gun—540(one combat load);

d) 203mm gun—up to 4.5 combat loads, 14,900 (3.1 combat loads); 152mm from 2nd Factory "Barrikady"[89]—480 (two combat loads); 280mm gun—540 (one combat load);

e) up to ten M-13 salvoes—27,500 (seven salvoes); up to three M-31 salvoes—9,300 (two salvoes).

In fuels, oils and lubricants: 5,000 tons over the March order for B-78 aviation fuel.

I request that you confirm this decision and, if possible, to make up the *front's* shortages in equipment, munitions and fuels, oils and lubricants, with their arrival no later than 25-30 March of this year.

Vasilevskii
Makarov[90]
Pokrovskii

---

89 Editor's note. These guns were produced at the second "Barrikady" factory in Stalingrad, which was later evacuated to the east.

90 Editor's note. Vasilii Yemel'yanovich Makarov (1903-75) joined the VKP(b) in 1928 and was engaged in full-time party work since 1938. During the Great Patriotic War he served as a member of the military council on various *fronts* and on the Third Belorussian Front since 1944. Following the war, Makarov served as deputy chief of the Soviet army and navy's political directorate and deputy minister of state security.

56. Directive of the *Stavka* VGK No. 11042. To the Commander of the Third Belorussian Front on the Confirmation of the Plan to Defeat the Enemy's Königsberg Group of Forces[91]

17 March 1945, 1830

The *Stavka* of the Supreme High Command confirms the ideas presented by you in no. 215/K, of 16.03.1945[92] for the defeat of the enemy's Königsberg group of forces, and orders:

1. The defeat of the enemy's East Prussian group of forces southwest of Königsberg is to be completed by no later than 22.03.1945.

2. The operation to defeat the enemy's Königsberg group of forces is to be begun no later than 28.03.1945

Stavka of the Supreme High Command
I. Stalin
A. Antonov

---

91 *Velikaya Otechestvennaya*, 5(4):210.
92 Editor's note. See document 55.

57. To the Commander of the Second Belorussian Front. On the Report for Proposals for Eliminating the Enemy in the Areas of Danzig and Gdynia[93]

17 March 1945, 1900 hrs

For a report to the *Stavka*, I request that on March 18 you report your ideas on eliminating the enemy's group of forces in the areas of Danzig and Gdynia, indicating the stages and deadlines for conducting the operation.

Antonov

58. Directive of the *Stavka* of the VGK No. 112001. To the Commander of the First Belorussian Front on the Resubordination of the Polish 2nd Army[94]

19 March 1945, 1700 hrs

Copies: To the commander of the First Ukrainian Front and the commander-in-chief of the Polish Army

The *Stavka* of the Supreme High Command orders:

1. The transfer of the Polish 2nd Army to the First Ukrainian Front, directing it to the Breslau area;
    The army is to be transferred in the following composition: 5th, 7th, 8th, 9th, and 10th infantry divisions, 1st Tank Corps, 3rd Anti-Aircraft Division, 9th and 14th anti-tank artillery brigades, 16th Tank Brigade, 5th Heavy Tank Regiment, 28th Self-Propelled Artillery Regiment, 3rd Mortar Regiment, 4th Engineer-Sapper Brigade, and army rear units with all available supplies.

2. The Polish 2nd Army is to be moved on foot, with the exception of the tanks and artillery on mechanical traction. The march is to begin with the onset of darkness on 20 March.
    The army is to be subordinated to the First Ukrainian Front on 26 March along the line Leszno—Krotoszyn.
    The completion of the army's concentration in the Breslau is 30 March of this year.
    The march plan is to be presented to the General Staff on 20 March and in a copy to the commander of the First Ukrainian Front.

3. Tanks and artillery on mechanical traction and heavy freight are to be shipped by rail. These are to be loaded in the area of Kreutz station, beginning at 1800 on 21 March. Unloading will be in the area of Els Station.

4. The army is to be supplied with fuel, food and forage until it reaches its concentration area. Report to the General Staff daily on the course of the march and the loading onto the train cars.

Stavka of the Supreme High Command
I. Stalin
A. Antonov

---

94 *Velikaya Otechestvennaya*, 5(4):211.

Index

INDEX OF PEOPLE

INDEX OF PLACES

INDEX OF AXIS MILITARY UNITS

Miscellaneous

INDEX OF SOVIET MILITARY UNITS

Fronts

Armies

Divisions

Brigades

CPSIA information can be obtained at www.ICGtesting.com
Printed in the USA
BVOW10*0432100216

436124BV00004B/7/P